90 0398377 6

KW-406-836

INTERNATIONAL ORGANIZATIONS AND THE LAW OF THE SEA

**INTERNATIONAL ORGANIZATIONS AND THE LAW OF THE SEA -
DOCUMENTARY YEARBOOK** aims at improving access by scholars and practitioners to law of the sea related documents issued each year by international organizations.

THE NETHERLANDS INSTITUTE FOR THE LAW OF THE SEA (NILOS) is part
of the Faculty of Law of the University of Utrecht, The Netherlands. Its principle aim is
to conduct research on the international law of the sea and to provide expert assistance on
all matters relating to the law of the sea.

International Organizations and the Law of the Sea

Documentary Yearbook 1996

Barbara Kwiatkowska

Editor-in-Chief

Eric Molenaar
Alex Oude Elferink
Alfred Soons

Co-Editors

Issued by
The Netherlands Institute for the Law of the
Sea (NILOS)

Volume 12, 1996

MARTINUS NIJHOFF PUBLISHERS
THE HAGUE / LONDON / BOSTON

Library of Congress Catalog Card Number: 88-440074

British Library Cataloguing in Publication Data
International Organizations and the Law of the Sea : Documentary Yearbook. -Vol. 1 (1985)
   1.   International Law–Periodicals
   I.   Netherlands Institute for the Law of the Sea
341.4'5'05   JX4411

ISBN 90-411-1004-6
ISSN 0920-7767

Published by Kluwer Law International,
P.O. Box 85889, 2508 CN The Hague, The Netherlands.

Sold and distributed in North, Central and South America
by Kluwer Law International,
675 Massachusetts Avenue, Cambridge, MA 02139, U.S.A.

In all other countries, sold and distributed
by Kluwer Law International, Distribution Centre,
P.O. Box 322, 3300 AH Dordrecht, The Netherlands.

Printed on acid-free paper

Printed in the Netherlands

TABLE OF CONTENTS

ADDRESSES

United Nations Publications
Sales Section, 2 United Nations Plaza
Room DC2-853, Dept. 410
New York, N.Y. 10017, USA
Fax: 1-212-963 3489

United Nations Publications
Sales Office and Bookshop
CH-1211 Geneva 10, Switzerland
Fax: 41-22-740 0931

UN Sales publ US: http://www.un.org/Pubs/sales.htm
ICJ: http://www.icj-cij.org
ITLOS: http://www.un.org/Depts/los/_.htm

Division for Ocean Affairs
& the Law of the Sea (DOALOS)
Office of Legal Affairs
United Nations
New York, N.Y. 10017, USA
Fax: 1-212-963 5847

Oceans & Coastal Areas
Programme Activity Centre
UNEP
P.O. Box 30552
Nairobi, Kenya
Fax: 254-2-226 890/215 787

DOALOS: http://www.un.org/Depts/los/los_docs.htm

UNCTAD
United Nations Sales Section
Palais des Nations
CH-1211 Geneva 10, Switzerland
Fax: 41-22-907 0043

FAO
Via delle Termi di Caracalla
00100 Rome, Italy
Fax: 39-6-514 6172/579 73152

UNCTAD: http://www.unicc.org/unctad/en/pressref/bublead.htm
FAO: http://www.fao.org/CATALOG/GIPHOME.htm

IAEA
Wagramerstrasse 5
P.O. Box 100
A-1400 Vienna, Austria
Fax: 43-1-234 564

ILO
Publications Division
International Labour Office
CH-1211 Geneva 22, Switzerland
Fax: 41-22-798 8685

IAEA: http://www.iaea.or.at/worldatom/publications/
ILO: http://www.unicc.org/ilo/public/english/180publn/index.htm

IMO
4 Albert Embankment
London SE1 7SR, United Kingdom
Fax: 44-71-587 3210

IOC/UNESCO
7, Place de Fontenoy
75700 Paris, France
Fax: 33-1-405 69316

IMO: http://www.imo.org/imo/pubs/pubstart.htm
IOC/UNESCO: http://www.unesco.org/general/eng/publish/index.htm

WMO
Publications Unit
41, Giuseppe-Motta
Case postale No 2300
CH-1211 Geneva 2, Switzerland
Fax: 41-22-734 2326

http://www.wmo.ch/web/catalogue/NEW%20HTML/frame/frame.html

EDITORS' NOTE

This Volume 12 of *International Organizations and the Law of the Sea - Documentary Yearbook* was again prepared on the basis of experience gained in producing previous volumes and taking into account various comments and suggestions made by members of our Advisory Board and by reviewers.[1] The Volume covers the documents, both legal and non-legal, of the United Nations family of international organizations which are structured along two main categories. In particular, documents of the UN General Assembly (UNGA), Meeting of States Parties to the 1982 UN Convention on the Law of the Sea (LOS Convention), UN International Sea-Bed Authority (ISBA), International Tribunal for the Law of the Sea (ITLOS), Follow-up to the UN Conference on Straddling Fish Stocks and Highly Migratory Fish Stocks, Follow-Up to the UN Global Conference on the Sustainable Development of Small Island Developing States (SIDS), Universal Congress on the Panama Canal, UN ECOSOC, UNEP and UNCTAD are included first. They are followed by the documents of specialized agencies and other autonomous organizations within the UN system that include FAO, IAEA, IMO and UNES-CO/IOC. The numerous regional programmes and organizations, a number of which reports annually to the UNGA, are covered by documents of the respective global organizations.

The major General Assembly's documents remain the annual Law of the Sea Resolution (51/34) and the Report of the Secretary-General giving an excellent overview of all developments in the context of the new oceans regime. The 1996 Law of the Sea Report was prepared, as every year, by the Division for Ocean Affairs and the Law of the Sea (DOALOS) of the UN Office of Legal Affairs (OLA). In addition, the first Report of the Secretary-General Under Article 319 of the LOS Convention was prepared. The DOALOS operates (since 1 March 1992) in continuation of the UN Office for Ocean Affairs and the Law of the Sea (OALOS). It was headed in 1995 by its distinguished Director Dr. Jean-Pierre Lévy (France), who was succeeded since 1 February 1996 by Dr. Moritaka Hayashi (Japan), as followed since 20 October 1996 by Dr. Ismail Steiner (Tanzania). The DOALOS/OLA is charged with a general mandate to contribute to the better understanding and widespread acceptance of the LOS Convention at national, regional and international levels. The numerous DOALOS publications continue to be only listed in the *Yearbook*, but the reader will find (through the Index of Keywords) a detailed record of DOALOS activities in the relevant documents.

---

[1]   For reviews of Vol. 1 - 1985 (1987) of the *Yearbook*, see E. Decaux, 115 *Journal du Droit International* 282-283 (1988/1); M.I. Glassner, *Political Geography Quarterly* of 8 February 1989; L.A. Kimball, 12 *Marine Policy* 415-416 (1988/4); A.V. Lowe, 3 *International Journal of Estuarine & Coastal Law (IJECL)* (presently, *International Journal of Marine & Coastal Law [IJMCL]*) 280-281 (1988/3); Swan Sik Ko, 35 *Netherlands International Law Review* 100-101 (1988/1); R. Wolfrum, 30 *German Yearbook of International Law (GYIL)* 463-464 (1987); also noted in 33 *Annuaire Français de Droit International (AFDI)* 1077 (1987). For reviews of Vol. 2 - 1986 (1988) of the *Yearbook*, see D. Freestone, 4 *IJECL* 310-311 (1989/3); *Lloyd's Maritime Commercial Law Quarterly* (1989). For review of Vol. 3 - 1987 (1989) of the *Yearbook*, see D. Freestone, 6 IJECL 151-153 (1991/2). For joint reviews of Vols 1-5, see B. Boczek, "Basic Sources of Law of the Sea Documentation," 15 *Marine Policy* 455-459 (1991/6), and of Vols 5-6, see E.D. Brown, 17 *Marine Policy* 67 (1993/1), and D. Freestone, 10 *IJMCL* 143-144 (1995). For reviews of Vol.8 - 1992 (1994), see D. Köning, 38 *GYIL* 467 (1995); 40 *AFDI* 1208 (1994). For reviews of Vol.9 - 1993 (1995), see J. Thomas, 3 *OGLTR* 136-137 (1996), and J. Morris, 3 *Int.ML* 110-111 (1996). For review of Vol.10 - 1994 (1996), see U. Jenisch, 30 *Verfassung und Recht in Übersee* 280-281 (1997).

As a result of deposition of the 60th ratification (by Guyana) during the 48th session of the General Assembly in 1993, the LOS Convention entered into force on 16 November 1994. Prior thereto, further rounds of the UN Secretary-General's Informal Consultations led successfully to the adoption at the resumed 48th session of the General Assembly (by a vote of 121:0:7) of the Resolution 48/263 of 28 July 1994. The UNGA Resolution's Annex contains an Agreement Relating to the Implementation of Part XI of the United Nations Convention on the Law of the Sea, with the entry into force of the two instruments having been closely intertwined.[2]

The entry into force of the LOS Convention and the provisional application of the Part XI Agreement as followed by the Agreement's entry into force on 28 July 1996 marked, according to Dr. Moritaka Hayashi, the beginning of a new phase in the functions of the UN Secretary-General with regard to the two instruments.[3] A detailed set of (mostly long-term) mandates for the Secretary-General and, through him, particularly the DOALOS/OLA, include the increased reporting responsibilities, the unprecedented (and distinct from the usual depositary functions) responsibilities pertaining to deposit of charts and geographical coordinates concerning national maritime zones, as well as responsibilities relating to the Commission on the Limits of the Continental Shelf (CLCS), conducting special studies, dispute settlement (including in the context of the ITLOS' establishment), and provision of advice and assistance to states. Other mandates comprise functions relating to other agreements, normal depositary functions, and a number of short-term responsibilities of the UN Secretary-General. By mid-1996, the LOS Convention was in a crucial phase of its evolution because of the rapid move toward universalization of its States Parties; the building of the key institutions - ISBA,[4] ITLOS, CLCS - under the Convention;[5] the consolidation and further strengthening of its regime through the adoption of complementary instruments; and the emerging consensus on the role of the UNGA as the global ocean forum.[6]

The ITLOS was inaugurated in Hamburg on 18 October 1996, when the 21 Judges took their oath of office and signed solemn declarations in the presence of the UN Secretary-General, the Secretary-General of ISBA Assembly, Ambassador Satya N. Nandan, and other high dignitaries.[7] The

---

2 See *UN/DOALOS Law of the Sea Bulletin*, Special Issue IV, 16 November 1994, and for status of the Convention and the Part XI Agreement as at 1 April 1998, see *id*. No. 36 (1998). Cf. D.H. Anderson, "Legal Implications of the Entry Into Force of the UN Convention on the Law of the Sea," 44 *International & Comparative Law Quarterly (ICLQ)* 313-326 (1995); Anderson, "Resolution and Agreement Relating to the Implementation of Part XI of the UN Convention on the Law of the Sea: A General Assessment", 55 *ZaöRV* 275-289 (1995); J.P. Lévy, "Les Nations Unies et la Convention sur le droit de la mer," 28 *Revue belge de droit international* 11-35 (1995); M. Hayashi, "Prospects for Universal Acceptance of the Part XI Agreement," 7 *Georgetown International Environmental Law Review (GIELR)* 687-695 (1995); Hayashi, "The 1994 Agreement for the Universalization of the Law of the Sea Convention," 27 *Ocean Development & International Law (ODIL)* 31-39 (1996); B.H. Oxman, "Observations on the Agreement Relating to the Implementation of Part XI of the UN Convention on the Law of the Sea", in *Order for the Oceans at the Turn of the Century, Proceedings of the Fridtjof Nansen Conference, Oslo, Norway, 7-11 August 1998* (in press).

3 M. Hayashi, "The Role of the Secretary-General Under the LOS Convention and the Part XI Agreement," 10 *IJMCL* 157-164 (1995).

4 See Statements by H.E. Ambassador Satya N. Nandan, Secretary-General of the International Sea-Bed Authority, in B.H. Oxman ed., *Building New Regimes and Institutions for the Sea, 31st Law of the Sea Institute Proceedings, Miami, USA, 30-31 March 1998* (in press), and in *Order for the Oceans, supra* note 2.

5 See V. Golitsyn, "Interrelation of the Institutions Under the United Nations Law of the Sea Convention with Other International Institutions", in *Order for the Oceans, supra* note 2.

6 See M. Hayashi, "The Law of the Sea: The Year in Review," in *A Return to Abundant Seas: Management of Fisheries and the Ocean Environment, Proceedings of the 30th LSI Annual Conference, Al-Ain, Abu Dhabi, 19-22 May 1996* (in press).

7 See *ITLOS Press Release, ITLOS/Press/2*, 18 October 1996.

first ITLOS President became Dr. Thomas A. Mensah (Ghana) and Vice-President - Dr. Rüdiger Wolfrum (Germany), while the Tribunals Registrar is Mr. Kumar Chitty (Sri Lanka).[8] The ITLOS Rules and its Guidelines Concerning the Preparation and Presentation of Cases of 28 October 1997 and the ITLOS Resolution on Internal Judicial Practice of 31 October 1997, are all modelled on the respective instruments of the International Court of Justice (ICJ).[9] The first *Saint Vincent and the Grenadines v. Guinea M/V Saiga* Judgment delivered by the ITLOS on 4 December 1997 (Case No.1), was followed on 11 March 1998 by *M/V Saiga (Provisional Measures)* Order, which marked the phase of incidental proceedings of the *M/V Saiga (Merits)* case (Case No.2) presently pending before ITLOS.[10]

The General Assembly's Resolutions reflect the major - new and continuing - issues on the UN agenda, such as Declaring 1998 International Year of the Ocean, zones of peace (Indian Ocean, South Atlantic), biological diversity, climate change, naval armaments and disarmament, large-scale driftnet (gillnet) fishing, unauthorized fishing in zones of national jurisdiction and fisheries bycatch and discards, transit of land-locked countries, Universal Congress on the Panama Canal, international terrorism, UN Decade of International Law, question of Antarctica, ocean dumping, and actions in the follow-up to the United Nations Conference on Environment and Development (UNCED) that was held on 3-14 June 1992 in Rio de Janeiro, Brazil, and that was assessed by the 1997 Special Session of UNGA on the Overall Review and Appraisal of Agenda 21. These issues find further reflection in documents of relevant organizations, covered by this Volume, in the context of their respective mandates. In follow-up to Chapter 17 of the UNCED Agenda 21, the two major UN Conferences initiated in 1993 were those on the Sustainable Development of SIDS and on Straddling/Highly Migratory Fish Stocks which were meanwhile concluded in 1994 and 1995 respectively. At its 6th session, this Conference adopted (without a vote) on 4 August 1995 the text of the Agreement for the Implementation of the Provisions of the UN Convention on the Law of the Sea relating to the Conservation and Management of Straddling Fish

---

8   See *Id., ITLOS/Press/1*, 5 October 1996, and *ITLOS/Press/3*, 23 October 1996, respectively. Cf. "International Tribunal Starts Work", 27 *Environmental Policy and Law* 2-4 (1997).

9   Cf. Statement by H.E. Dr. Thomas A. Mensah, President of the ITLOS, in *Building New Regimes, supra* note 4; Mensah, "The International Tribunal for the Law of the Sea", 11 *Leiden Journal of International Law* (1998, in press); S. Rosenne, The ITLOS and the International Court of Justice: Some Points of Difference", in *The Baltic Sea: New Developments in National Policies and International Cooperation* 200-215 (1996); articles contributed by President Mensah, Vice-President Wolfrum, and Judges Eiriksson, Nelson, Treves, Yankov, Vukas, Akl and Laing, in 37 *Indian Journal of International Law* 347-477 (1997); B. Kwiatkowska, "The Future of the Law of the Sea Tribunal in Hamburg", in *The Hague, Legal Capital of the World, Proceedings of The Hague's 750th Anniversary International Law Conference, Kurhaus, 2-4 July 1998* (in press).

10   See E. Lauterpacht, "The First Decision of the ITLOS: The M/V *Saiga*, in G. Hafner et al. eds, *Liber Amicorum Professor Seidl-Hohenveldern* 395-418 (1998); B.H. Oxman, "The M/V 'Saiga'. ITLOS Case No.1", 92 *American Journal of International Law* 278-282 (1998); E.D. Brown, "The M/V 'Saiga' Case on Prompt Release of Detained Vessels: The First Judgment of the ITLOS", 22 *Marine Policy* 307-326 (1998); B. Kwiatkowska, "Inauguration of the ITLOS Jurisprudence: The *Saint Vincent and the Grenadines v. Guinea M/V Saiga* Cases, 29 ODIL (1998, in press).

Stocks and Highly Migratory Fish Stocks.[11] The Agreement has recently obtained a prominent attention in the written and oral proceedings in the *Spain v. Canada Fisheries Jurisdiction* case, which is presently pending (in the phase of jurisdiction) before the ICJ.[12]

The United Nations section contained in this Volume also covers various ocean-related documents submitted individually by states, by means of their Letters and Notes to the Secretary-General, on the navigational rights and freedoms (Russia and Turkey, Iraq, Republic of Korea), Iran's Marine Areas Act of 27 May 1993 (Saudi Arabia, Kuwait, UAE, Qatar, Bahrain), and the *Eritrea/Yemen* case which is pending before the five-Member Arbitral Tribunal presided over by the Former ICJ President, Sir Robert Jennings and also comprising the current Court's President Stephen M. Schwebel and Judge Rosalyn Higgins.[13] The Russian/Turkish[14], Georgian/Russian border (Sukhumi Port) and Iran/United Arab Emirates (Abu Musa Island) exchanges reflect three ongoing disputes which have been subjected to bilateral negotiations between the respective states. The Russian/Turkish controversy over the Turkish Straits (Strait of Istanbul, Strait of Canakkale and Sea of Marmara) has also been reflected in the debates of the respective IMO bodies which are covered by this Volume. Other reproduced documents of the General Assembly provide the reader with an access to important decisions taken in 1996 by the Meeting of States of the Zone of Peace and Cooperation of the South Atlantic, the Caspian Sea States and the South Pacific Forum. The reproduced ECOSOC document of 1996 is the Report of the Secretary-General on Protection of the Oceans and All Kinds of Seas.

Four of the individual organizations which are covered by our *Yearbook* are primarily responsible for implementation of the new oceans regime under the Law of the Sea Convention, i.e. UNEP - for environmental protection in general, UNESCO/IOC - for marine scientific research, FAO - for fisheries, and IMO - for shipping and marine pollution. Among their major documents reproduced in this Volume are the UNEP Report of the Intergovernmental Conference to Adopt a Global Programme of Action for the Protection of the Marine Environment from Land Based Activities, Held at Washington D.C. in 1995, and the 1996 FAO Report on Regional Bodies in the Fisheries Conservation and Management. The UNEP Governing Council, the FAO Committee on Fisheries and the IMO Assembly held all their regular biennial sessions in 1997, devoting special attention to their actions in

---

11   For Agreement's status as at 1 April 1998, see *UN/DOALOS Law of the Sea Bulletin* No. 36 (1998). Cf. M. Hayashi, "The 1995 Agreement on Straddling and Highly Migratory Fish Stocks," 8 *EC-ACP Bulletin* 4-7 (1995 No.4); D.H. Anderson, "The Straddling Stocks Agreement of 1995 - an Initial Assessment," 45 *ICLQ* 463-475 (1996); M. Hayashi, "The 1995 Agreement on Straddling Fish Stocks and Higly Migratory Fish Stocks: Significance for the Law of the Sea Convention," 29 *Ocean and Coastal Management* 51-69 (1996); Hayashi, "Enforcement by Non-Flag States on the High Seas Under the 1995 Agreement on Straddling and Highly Migratory Fish Stocks", 9 *GIELR* 1-36 (1996); A. Tahindro, "Conservation and Management of Straddling Fish Stocks and Highly Migratory Fish Stocks," 28 *ODIL* 1-58 (1997); B. Kwiatkowska, "Expansion of Protective Jurisdiction: Future Challenges", in *Lessons from the Past - Blueprints for the Future, Proceeedings of the 25th Anniversary Conference of the Canadian Council of International Law, Château Laurier, Ottawa, 16-18 October 1997* (in press); Hayashi, "The 1995 UN Fish Stocks Agreement and the Law of the Sea", in *Order for the Oceans, supra* note 2.

12   ICJ Reports 1995, 87, and 1996, 58; *ICJ Communiqué* No.96/18, 10 May 1996; No.97/17, 5 December 1997; No.98/20, 28 May 1998; and No.98/24, 17 June 1998. Cf. Kwiatkowska, *supra* note 11; and Kwiatkowska, "Commentary on the *Spain v. Canada Fisheries Jurisdiction (The Estai)* Case (ICJ General List No.96)", in *Order for the Oceans, supra* note 2.

13   Cf. *Report of the Secretary-General on the Work of the Organization* 108, para.766, UN Doc. A/51/1 (August 1996); and two essays by D.J. Dzurek, *Eritrea/Yemen* Dispute Over the Hanish Islands, 4 *IBRU Boundary and Security Bulletin* 70-77 (1996/1), and Commentary on the Hanish Islands Dispute, 1 *Eritrean Studies Review* 133-52 (1996).

14   See G. Plant, "Navigation Regime in the Turkish Straits for Merchant Ships in Peacetime", 20 *Marine Policy* 15-27 (1995); "New and Amended TSS and Routeing Systems", *IMO News* 19-22 (1997, Nos 2/3).

follow-up to the UNCED, as to be further reported upon at their sessions in 1999. The same applies to the IOC which in 1997 held its biennial session of the Assembly (alternating with sessions of the Executive Council). In May 1996, the first session of the Open-Ended Intersessional Working Group on IOC's Possible Role in Relation to the LOS Convention was also held.[15] Two additional UN organizations covered by the *Yearbook* have dealt continuously with other important aspects of ocean affairs within their broader mandates, i.e. IAEA - radioactive marine pollution, and UNCTAD - ports and shipping.

It is due to limited space that, as in the previous Volumes, the most important documents are reproduced in whole or in part, while other relevant documents are only listed. The listed documents include, as appropriate, the ocean-related conventions adopted under the auspices of international organizations which may be found in other accessible collections of legal documents, e.g., *International Legal Materials, Law of the Sea Bulletin* and other publications issued by the UN DOALOS/OLA, or *International Journal of Marine and Coastal Law*. For the convenience of readers who would wish to order documents only partly reproduced or listed in the *Yearbook*, the addresses of international organizations concerned are added after the Table of Contents. Moreover, an Index of Keywords is included with a view to facilitate access by the reader to the complex and often interrelated matters dealt with by various organizations as well as to the information concerning individual states, regions and international instruments.

Like previous volumes, this Volume 12 would not have been published without the kind, and in most cases continuous, assistance of number of individuals. The editors wish to express their gratitude to the following persons for their help in obtaining documents:

UN	-	Mrs. Alice ter Horst and other staff members of the United Nations Department, Netherlands Ministry of Foreign Affairs, The Hague;
UNEP	-	Ms. Elizabeth Mrema, Legal Officer, Environmental Law & Institutions Programme Activity Centre, Nairobi;
UNCTAD	-	Mr. R. Vogel, Deputy Director of the Shipping Division, Geneva;
FAO	-	Dr. William Edeson, Legal Adviser, Rome;
IAEA	-	the staff of the Division of Publications, Vienna;
IMO	-	Ms. Michele Fore of the Documents Section, London.

The editors remain grateful to the members of the Advisory Board for their continuing support and also to the reviewers for all valuable suggestions related to this *Yearbook*. Special thanks are due to Mrs. Annebeth Rosenboom and other staff members of Kluwer Law International (which presently incorporates Martinus Nijhoff Publishers), for their cooperation in the publication of the *Yearbook* in general and this Volume in particular.

Professor Barbara Kwiatkowska
Editor-in-Chief
NILOS, Achter Sint Pieter 200
3512 HT Utrecht - Netherlands
Fax: 31-30-2537 073
http://www.rgl.ruu.nl/english/isep/nilos-1a.asp

Utrecht, 6 October 1998

---

15   Cf. A.H.A. Soons, "Intergovernmental Oceanographic Commission", in *Building New Regimes, supra* note 4.

UNITED NATIONS
(UN)

DOCUMENTS REPRODUCED IN WHOLE OR IN PART:

GENERAL ASSEMBLY (UNGA)

Reports & Notes of the UN Secretary-General (see also under specific sections below)

Letters and Notes to the United Nations (UNGA & Security Council) Addressed to the Secretary-General

4

Marine Areas Act of 27 May 1993 of the Islamic Republic of Iran

Resolutions of the UNGA (see also under specific sections below)

MEETING OF STATES PARTIES TO THE 1982 UN CONVENTION ON THE LAW OF THE SEA (SPLOS) (see also ITLOS below)

Fourth Meeting – New York, 4-8 March 1996

Fifth Meeting – New York, 24 July-2 August 1996

INTERNATIONAL SEABED AUTHORITY (ISBA)

Resumed Second Session – Kingston, Jamaica, 5-16 August 1996

UN General Assembly

INTERNATIONAL TRIBUNAL FOR THE LAW OF THE SEA (ITLOS)

ITLOS Press Releases

Fifth Meeting of States Parties to the UN Convention on the Law of the Sea – New York, 24 July-2 August 1996

8

DOCUMENTS NOT REPRODUCED:

GENERAL ASSEMBLY (UNGA)

Reports & Notes of the UN Secretary-General

60.	Doc. no.:	A/51/230 and Add.1 & Corr.1
	Date:	25 July and 5 & 18 September 1996
	Title:	Strengthening of Security and Cooperation in the Mediterranean Region – Report of the UN Secretary-General

61.	Doc. no.:	A/51/390
	Date:	20 September 1996
	Title:	Question of Antarctica: State of the Environment in Antarctica – Report of the UN Secretary-General

62.	Doc. no.:	A/51/458
	Date:	7 October 1996
	Title:	Zone of Peace and Cooperation of the South Atlantic – Report of the UN Secretary-General

63.	Doc. no.:	A/51/484
	Date:	11 October 1996
	Title:	Environment and Development: Protection of Global Climate for Present and Future Generations of Mankind, Programme Budget for the Biennium 1996-1997 – Report of the UN Secretary-General

Letters and Notes to the United Nations (UNGA & Security Council) Addressed to the Secretary-General

64.	Doc. no.:	S/1996/427
	Date:	12 June 1996
	Title:	Letter of 10 June 1996 from the Permanent Representative of the Islamic Republic of Iran (Persian Gulf)

65.	Doc. no.:	A/51/210
	Date:	15 July 1996
	Title:	Letter of 28 May 1996 from the Chargé d'Affaires a.i. of the Permanent Mission of Turkey (Results of the 95th Conference of the Inter-Parliamentary Union and the 158th Session of the Inter-Parliamentary Council, Istanbul, 15-20 April 1996)

Resolutions of the UNGA

66.	Doc. no.:	A/Res.51/17
	Date:	12 November 1996
	Title:	Necessity of Ending the Economic, Commercial and Financial Embargo Imposed by the United States of America Against Cuba – UNGA Resolution

67.	Doc. no.:	A/Res.51/144
	Date:	13 December 1996
	Title:	Question of New Caledonia – UNGA Resolution

68.	Doc. no.:	A/Res.51/145
	Date:	13 December 1996
	Title:	Question of Tokelau – UNGA Resolution

MEETING OF STATES PARTIES TO THE 1982 UN CONVENTION ON THE LAW OF THE SEA (SPLOS)

Fifth Meeting – New York, 24 July-2 August 1996

69.   Doc. no.:   SPLOS/CLCS/INF/1
        Date: 10 June 1996
        Title: Commission on the Limits of the Continental Shelf: Its Functions and Scientific and Technical Needs in Assessing the Submission of a Coastal State – Study Prepared by the UN Secretariat

70.   Doc. no.:   SPLOS/CLCS/WP.1
        Date: 26 July 1996
        Title: Draft Rules of Procedure of the Commission on the Limits of the Continental Shelf

71.   Doc. no.:   SPLOS/12
        Date: 30 July 1996
        Title: Credentials of Representatives to the Fifth Meeting of States Parties to the UN Convention on the Law of the Sea – Report of the Credentials Committee

72.   Doc. no.:   SPLOS/13
        Date: 31 July 1996
        Title: Credentials of Representatives to the Fifth Meeting of States Parties to the UN Convention on the Law of the Sea – Second Report of the Credentials Committee

INTERNATIONAL SEABED AUTHORITY (ISBA)

Second Session – Kingston, Jamaica, 11-22 March 1996

73.   Doc. no.:   ISBA/A/L.9
        Date: 2 April 1996
        Title: Statement of the President on the Work of the ISBA Assembly During the First Part of the Second Session, Kingston, Jamaica, 11-22 March 1996

Resumed Second Session – Kingston, Jamaica, 5-16 August 1996

74.   Doc. no.:   ISBA/F/WP.1
        Date: 24 July 1996
        Title: Draft Rules of Procedure of the ISBA Finance Committee

75.   Doc. no.:   ISBA/A/13
        Date: 26 August 1996
        Title: Decision of the Assembly Concerning the Observer Status of the ISBA at the United Nations

76.   Doc. no.:   ISBA/A/14
        Date: 27 August 1996
        Title: Decision of the Assembly Relating to the Budget of the ISBA for 1997 (Adopted by Consensus on 16 August 1996)

77.   Doc. no.:   ISBA/C/9
        Date: 29 August 1996
        Title: Decision of the Council of the ISBA Relating to the Extension of the Membership, on a Provisional Basis, of the Authority of Bangladesh, Canada, Nepal, Poland and the USA

INTERNATIONAL TRIBUNAL FOR THE LAW OF THE SEA (ITLOS)

Fourth Meeting of States Parties to the UN Convention on the Law of the Sea – New York, 4-8 March 1996

78.   Doc. no.:   SPLOS/WP.2
        Date: 27 February 1996
        Title: Draft Agreement on the Privileges and Immunities of the ITLOS – Prepared by the UN Secretariat

79.   Doc. no.:   SPLOS/WP.3/Rev.1
        Date: 10 April 1996
        Title: Revised Budget Estimates for the ITLOS Covering the Period 1996-1997

Fifth Meeting of States Parties to the UN Convention on the Law of the Sea – New York, 24 July-2 August 1996

80.   Doc. no.:   SPLOS/9
        Date: 31 May 1996
        Title: Election of the Members of the ITLOS – Note by the UN Secretary-General

81.   Doc. no.:   SPLOS/10
        Date: 2 July 1996
        Title: Election of the Members of the ITLOS – Note by the UN Secretary-General

82.   Doc. no.:   SPLOS/L.3 & Rev.1
        Date: 30 & 31 July 1996
        Title: First Election of the Members of the ITLOS – Proposal by the President

UN General Assembly

83.   Doc. no.:   A/51/250/Add.3
        Date: 9 December 1996
        Title: Fourth Report of the UN General Committee (Observer Status for the ITLOS)

FOLLOW-UP TO UN GLOBAL CONFERENCE ON THE SUSTAINABLE DEVELOPMENT OF SMALL ISLAND DEVELOPING STATES

Report of the UN Secretary-General

84.   Doc. no.:   A/51/354
        Date: 18 September 1996
        Title: Action Taken at the International, Regional and National Levels to Implement the Programme of Action for the Sustainable Development of Small Island Developing States – Report of the UN Secretary-General

UNIVERSAL CONGRESS ON THE PANAMA CANAL – Panama City, 7-10 September 1997

85.   Doc. no.:   A/51/281
        Date: 8 August 1996
        Title: Universal Congress on the Panama Canal – Report of the UN Secretary-General

86.	Doc. no.:	A/51/477
	Date:	10 October 1996
	Title:	Universal Congress on the Panama Canal – Letter Dated 27 September 1996 from the Permanent Representative of Panama to the United Nations Addressed to the Secretary-General

ECONOMIC AND SOCIAL COUNCIL (ECOSOC)

87.	Doc. no.:	E/CN.17/1996/3/Add.1
	Date:	8 April 1996
	Title:	Protection of the Oceans, All Kinds of Seas, Including Enclosed and Semi-Enclosed Seas, and Coastal Areas and the Protection, Rational Use and Development of Their Living Resources – Report of the UN Secretary-General, Addendum

88.	Doc. no.:	E/CONF.89/L.1
	Date:	17 December 1996
	Title:	United Nations and Country Reports on the Implementation of the Resolutions of the 13th UN Regional Cartographic Conference for Asia and the Pacific: Status of Cartographic Activities in the United States of America – Paper Submitted by the USA (14th UN Regional Cartographic Conference for Asia and the Pacific, Bangkok, 3-7 February 1997)

DIVISION FOR OCEAN AFFAIRS AND THE LAW OF THE SEA, OFFICE OF LEGAL AFFAIRS (DOALOS/OLA)

89.	Doc. no.:	30
	Date:	1996
	Title:	Law of the Sea Bulletin

90.	Doc. no.:	31
	Date:	1996
	Title:	Law of the Sea Bulletin

91.	Doc. no.:	32
	Date:	1996
	Title:	Law of the Sea Bulletin

92.	Doc. no.:	Sales No.E.96.V.7
	Date:	1996
	Title:	The Law of the Sea – A Select Bibliography 1995

1. REPORT OF THE SECRETARY-GENERAL UNDER ARTICLE 319 OF THE UN CONVENTION ON THE LAW OF THE SEA

Doc. no.:SPLOS/6   11 April 1996

CONTENTS

		Paragraphs	Page

CONTENTS (continued)

I. INTRODUCTION

1.   The United Nations Convention on the Law of the Sea, in its article 319 (2) (a), requires the Secretary-General to report to all States Parties, the International Seabed Authority and competent international organizations on issues of a general nature that have arisen with respect to the Convention. In accordance with article 319 (3), such reports are to be transmitted also to those States which are listed in article 156 as observers of the Authority.

2.   Consequent upon the entry into force of the Convention, the General Assembly, at its forty-ninth session, requested the Secretary-General to fulfil this reporting function, and suggested that the comprehensive annual report of the Secretary-General on developments relating to the law of the sea, prepared for the General Assembly, could serve as a basis for such reports (resolution 49/28, para. 15 (a)). Attention is therefore drawn to the most recent report on the law of the sea, dated 1 November 1995. 1/

3.   The purpose of the present report is to provide a short summary of main current developments, including consideration of the item "Law of the sea" and related matters at the fiftieth session of the General Assembly and in other intergovernmental forums. The attention of States Parties, the Authority and competent international organizations is drawn, in accordance with article 319 (2) (a), to certain issues which have arisen and which warrant their consideration.

4.   For the convenience of Governments and international organizations, a list of the main current documentation of the United Nations relating to the law of the sea is contained in the annex to the present report.

II. LAW OF THE SEA ISSUES AT THE FIFTIETH SESSION OF THE GENERAL ASSEMBLY

A. The General Assembly debate

5.   It will be recalled that, at its forty-ninth session, following the entry into force of the Convention, the General Assembly first explicitly confirmed its role as the global forum competent to review overall developments relating to the law of the sea (resolution 49/28, preamble). Furthermore, at the fiftieth session, all issues relating to the effective implementation of the Convention on the Law of the Sea were for the first time considered together. This required reallocation of certain items dealing with marine fisheries, previously subsumed under the Second Committee item on "Environment and sustainable development", to be joined with the "Law of the sea" item in the plenary. In the future, these items and other such relevant issues are expected to form part of the General Assembly item "Law of the sea". The Secretary-General commends this development, convinced that a unified debate will promote the effective implementation of the Convention, as well as allow greater efficiency in the conduct of his responsibilities in this field. This

development also contributes to current efforts to rationalize the work of the Assembly.

6.   Documentation before the fiftieth session consisted of the comprehensive annual report of the Secretary-General on the law of the sea; 1/ his report on the outcome of the United Nations Conference on Straddling Fish Stocks and Highly Migratory Fish Stocks; 2/ and three reports on the issues of large-scale drift-net fishing, unauthorized fishing, and fisheries by-catch and discards respectively. 3/ A number of delegations also submitted documentation dealing with such important current concerns as passage through international straits (see annex).

7.   Discussions took place at the 80th and 81st plenary meetings, on 5 December; the main elements of these discussions are summarized below. Resolution 50/23 on the law of the sea was adopted by a vote of 132 to 1, with 3 abstaining. Resolution 50/24 on the 1995 Agreement for the Implementation of the Provisions of the United Nations Convention on the Law of the Sea of 10 December 1982 relating to the Conservation and Management of Straddling Fish Stocks and Highly Migratory Fish Stocks (1995 Agreement on fish stocks), and resolution 50/25 on drift-net fishing, unauthorized fishing and fisheries by-catch and discards, were both adopted without a vote.

8.   Important administrative elements of resolution 50/23 include: continued funding from the regular budget of the United Nations to cover the administrative expenses of the International Seabed Authority, 4/ and continuation of the existing interim secretariat until the Secretary-General of the Authority is able to assume effectively the responsibility of its secretariat. The provision of services to the Authority and to the Meetings of States Parties in 1996 was also approved, noting the intention to adopt an initial budget for the International Tribunal for the Law of the Sea and to provide for its efficient functioning, as well as to prepare for the establishment of the Commission on the Limits of the Continental Shelf. 5/

9.   In paragraph 10 of resolution 50/23 the General Assembly reaffirmed its basic policy objective - and therefore a fundamental component of planning and programming by the Organization in law of the sea and ocean affairs - namely, that of "ensuring the uniform and consistent application of the Convention and a coordinated approach to its effective implementation". The Secretary-General in his report to the fiftieth session had drawn particular attention to the need for Governments to monitor law of the sea issues as they arose in the deliberations of many intergovernmental bodies, and to support the harmonized development of international law and policy within the framework provided by the Convention.

10.   The debate in the General Assembly focused on the role of the Secretary-General's report to the Assembly; the status of the Convention and its implementation; the new Agreement on fish stocks; the other issues affecting the conservation and management of marine living resources, including regional cooperation; the setting up of institutions under the Convention; several special issues; and the work of the Division for Ocean Affairs and the Law of the Sea.

B.   Role of the Secretary-General's annual report
        to the General Assembly

11.   The annual report of the Secretary-General on the law of the sea covers all developments pertaining to the Convention, including the institutions established by the Convention, as well as other developments in the field of ocean affairs. It also serves as a report on the work of the Organization, and of the United Nations system as a whole, in the field of ocean affairs. The report thus provides the necessary basis for the "annual consideration and review of the overall developments relating to the law of the sea by the General Assembly, as the global institution having the competence to undertake such a review" (General Assembly resolution 49/28, preamble).

12.   The report for 1995 drew the particular attention of Member States to such significant developments as the increased acceptance of the Convention following upon the adoption of the Agreement relating to the implementation of Part XI of the United Nations Convention on the Law of the Sea of 10 December 1982 (1994 Agreement on Part XI), and to very important new advances in international law and policy, particularly in the fields of environmental protection and fisheries management and conservation, most particularly to the 1995 Agreement on fish stocks and to the Code of Conduct for Responsible Fisheries, which was subsequently adopted by the Conference of the Food and Agriculture Organization of the United Nations (FAO) in October 1995.

13.   The report also drew attention to the need for Governments to monitor law of the sea issues as they arose in the deliberations of many intergovernmental forums and to ensure that there was consistency in their conduct. 6/

14.   The General Assembly debate has become increasingly dependent on having an overview of developments as provided in the report of the Secretary-General. At the fiftieth session, various speakers emphasized that the report was an important vehicle for conveying to the world at large, and to the General Assembly in particular, the nature and extent of current developments. It should be a priority for the Secretary-General, therefore, to ensure that these reports continue to deal with all relevant developments in a comprehensive way. Considerable emphasis was placed on having the report available well before the debate, and on the inclusion of suggestions for possible actions, whether by States, the Organization, competent international organizations or indeed by the entire United Nations system.

C.   Status of the Convention and its implementation by States

15.   The more rapid rate of acceptance of the Convention is underlined. There are at present 87 States Parties (as of 1 April 1996), and in the light of the information provided by delegations during the debate and the indications at the subsequent Meeting of States Parties, 10 or more further ratifications/ accessions can be expected during 1996.

16.   During the debate in the General Assembly, a number of delegations also reported on their recent legislation, including new legislation on fisheries, shipping, marine scientific research, marine pollution and the establishment of contiguous zones. The Secretary-General notes that there is considerable value in Member States using the General Assembly item to announce any plans concerning acceptance of the Convention and related agreements, and to provide information on new or anticipated legislation and other relevant actions so that wide publicity can be given to the measures taken by States in the simplest and most direct manner.

D.   The 1995 Agreement on fish stocks

17.   The 1995 Agreement on fish stocks was opened for signature on 4 December 1995 and will remain open for 12 months thereafter. To date, it has received 31 signatures; no ratifications have been deposited as yet.

18.   During the General Assembly debate, delegations stressed particularly the role of the Agreement in strengthening regional organizations and the need for a major follow-up effort in this regard; the overall importance of the Agreement for greatly strengthening enforcement possibilities under international law; and the importance of continued consideration, within the framework of the General Assembly item on the law of the sea, of all matters related to the conservation and management of marine living resources. Attention is also drawn to the several comments made with regard to the Agreement's enforcement provisions relative to the basic rule of flag State jurisdiction on the high seas, as well as the comprehensive dispute settlement procedures based on the Convention on the Law of the Sea.

E.   Other issues in the conservation and management
     of marine living resources

19. Delegations reported on the adoption of new national legislation to promote observance of the global moratorium on large-scale pelagic drift-net fishing (General Assembly resolution 46/215) and, in one case, on steps taken to enable interception of fishing vessels on the high seas.

20. With respect to the issue of fisheries by-catch and discards, the view was expressed that FAO should deal with it because the problems involved were extremely technical and complex.

21. With respect to unauthorized fishing, several delegations attached considerable importance to the report to be prepared by the Secretary-General, under resolution 50/25, for the fifty-first session.

22. To underscore the need for follow-up action at the regional level to assure effective implementation of the 1995 Agreement on fish stocks, delegations reported on recent and upcoming developments in regions such as the Indian Ocean, the Atlantic and North Atlantic regions, and the South Pacific.

F.   Setting up institutions created by the Convention

23. Governments were aware that developments in the setting up of the institutions under the Convention had been slow to progress, particular reference being made to the election of the Council of the Authority. Some delegations commented that the projected expenditures for the establishment of the Authority were too high. Continued concerns, as a matter of general principle, were also expressed with regard to its expenditures being met from the United Nations budget instead of by the States Parties to the Convention. The subsequent action by the General Assembly in dealing with the regular budget of the United Nations reduced the proposed budget of the Authority.

24. With respect to the Tribunal it was noted that it could be called upon to perform functions which no other existing international court or tribunal could perform under its current constituent instrument. The projected initial budget had been substantially reduced. It had been adopted subsequently and apportioned by States Parties among themselves. The Secretary-General would encourage the fullest use of the expertise being made available to the Tribunal from within the United Nations.

25. With respect to the Commission on the Limits of the Continental Shelf, it was pointed out that the agreed deferment by 10 months of the election of its members should not unduly affect States in the application of article 4 of annex II of the Convention, which requires a State seeking to establish the outer limit of its continental shelf beyond 200 nautical miles to submit its information to the Commission within 10 years of the entry into force of the Convention for that State.

G.   Special issues

26. Attention was drawn to the references in the General Assembly resolution on the law of the sea linking the strategic importance of the Convention to chapter 17 on the oceans in Agenda 21 of the United Nations Conference on Environment and Development. This linkage is critical since it serves to strengthen international cooperation, especially in the area of marine environmental protection. It is important that States Parties continue to monitor closely developments within the purview of the Commission on Sustainable Development and their follow-up as regards its 1996 review of chapter 17 and , assessment of its implementation.

27.   Marine environmental issues continue to be of clear concern. During the
1995 General Assembly debate, particular attention was drawn once again to the
ecological situation in the Black Sea, as well as to the Sea of Azov. Attention
was drawn to the Washington Declaration and the Global Programme of Action
adopted by the Intergovernmental Conference to Adopt a Global Programme of
Action for the Protection of the Marine Environment from Land-based
Activities, 7/ and to the efforts made to ensure that the Programme was a
practical one. At its fifty-first session, the General Assembly will consider
the proposals to be made by the Commission on Sustainable Development on the
implementation of the Global Programme of Action, including the institutional
framework required at the global level. The United Nations Environment
Programme (UNEP) will be primarily responsible for secretariat support to the
Programme of Action.

28.   The debate on the law of the sea was also an occasion for many States to
call for the immediate cessation of all nuclear testing, and to enter their
concerns as to the effects of nuclear-related activities on the marine
environment generally. It was noted that at the regional level, States were
increasingly seeking to restrict the transit of nuclear wastes and other nuclear
materials by ship, particular reference being made to the recent Waigani
Convention. 8/

29.   Emphasis was placed in the debate on the clear need for even closer
coordination of the work of the United Nations and the various United Nations
agencies, especially on environment and development issues. Particular mention
was made of the need to make the work of the IMO/FAO/UNESCO-IOC/WMO/WHO/IAEA/
United Nations/UNEP Joint Group of Experts on the Scientific Aspects of Marine
Environmental Protection (GESAMP) and the Administrative Committee on
Coordination (ACC) Subcommittee on Oceans and Coastal Areas more effective.

30.   Important developments following upon the fiftieth session are referred to
below.

         H.   Work of the Division for Ocean Affairs and the Law of the Sea

31.   The Secretary-General is pleased to note that during the debate States
expressed their support for the work of the Division as fundamental to the
smooth development of activities related to the Convention. Indeed, many
delegations considered that the institutional capacity of the Organization
should be continuously enhanced in this area. In addition to the establishment
of the Commission on the Limits of the Continental Shelf, the continued role of
the Division to provide the necessary support to the Authority and the Tribunal
was noted. Besides the utility of its many work products, emphasis was placed
upon the need to strengthen the database with up-to-date information on national
legislation on law of the sea matters, to use the Internet for the rapid
dissemination of information and to strengthen the capacity to give technical
and legal support to developing States to help them implement the Convention at
the national level.

              III.   IMPORTANT DEVELOPMENTS AND EMERGING ISSUES

                    A.   Institutional questions

                1.   Regular and periodic review of ocean issues

32.   The impact of the entry into force of the Convention is perhaps most
evident in the actions that have been taken to implement chapter 17 of
Agenda 21.   The entry into force of the Convention made it possible to conclude
a binding legal agreement on the problems presented by straddling fish stocks
and migratory fish stocks, an outcome which could not have been predicted during
the negotiation of the relevant provisions of Agenda 21. It is also recognized
that the entry into force of the Convention has also provided a strong

foundation for the Global Programme of Action for the Protection of the Marine Environment from Land-based Activities.

33. The full impact of the Convention has yet to be felt, and the ability of the Organization to lend its fullest support to the ongoing implementation of chapter 17, as well as to the implementation of the Convention itself, has become a matter of considerable concern, seriously exacerbated by the further uncertainties caused by the current financial crisis of the United Nations and its effects on programme delivery.

34. It is important to note in this context also that many Governments attach considerable importance to the issue of regular comprehensive consideration of ocean issues to better serve the objective of ensuring effective implementation of the Convention or of chapter 17 of Agenda 21. The Secretary-General would recall that chapter 17 of Agenda 21 is based upon the Convention (para. 17.1) and that its call on the General Assembly to provide for regular consideration of "general marine and coastal issues, including environment and development matters" (para. 17.117, chapeau) reflects, inter alia, the long-standing recognition that all ocean issues are interrelated and need to be treated as a whole.

35. The need for periodic intergovernmental review of issues concerning marine environmental protection and resource conservation and management was discussed by the Commission on Sustainable Development at its fourth session (18 April-3 May 1996) in connection with the implementation of programme area F of chapter 17, which deals with institutional aspects. The Commission concluded that it should conduct a periodic overall review of all aspects of the marine environment, for which the overall legal framework is provided by the Convention, and that the General Assembly should consider the results of these reviews under an agenda item entitled "Oceans and law of the sea".

36. The Secretary-General is of the view that this decision of the Commission on Sustainable Development holds particular importance for States Parties to the Convention and for the competent international organizations under the Convention, since the results of an in-depth periodic review of a substantial portion of ocean issues - those dealing with environmental and resource matters - will greatly enhance the regular annual consideration of ocean issues by the General Assembly. The Secretary-General would note, however, that the current financial crisis may inhibit the ability of the Organization to provide the necessary support for the greatly enhanced monitoring, assessment and advisory functions that would be required.

2. Inter-agency cooperation

37. Both in the General Assembly debate on the law of the sea and in the Commission on Sustainable Development, considerable emphasis has been placed on the need to strengthen substantially existing inter-agency mechanisms, with particular reference to the ACC Subcommittee on Oceans and Coastal Areas and GESAMP. 10/

38. The outcome of the Washington Conference to Adopt a Global Programme of Action for the Protection of the Marine Environment from Land-based Activities has also contributed to the growing interest in having more effective inter-agency mechanisms and coherent intergovernmental arrangements for the consideration of ocean-related issues from cross-sectoral and multidisciplinary perspectives. The Secretary-General wishes to emphasize that a very important objective, in both contexts, is to strengthen the implementation of the Convention and promote the harmonized development of law and policy within its framework.

39. Considering the particular importance of the Washington Global Programme of Action for strengthening the implementation of the Convention and of agreements related to it, including in particular regional agreements and arrangements, the

Division for Ocean Affairs and the Law of the Sea will cooperate closely with UNEP and with the other international organizations concerned in the implementation of the Programme.

B. Emerging issues

1. Protection of the underwater cultural heritage

40. The 1995 report of the Secretary-General on the law of the sea 11/ had called attention to the work so far undertaken by UNESCO on the possible drafting of an international standard-setting instrument for the protection of the underwater cultural heritage. Subsequently, at its twenty-eighth session, the UNESCO General Conference adopted resolution 7.6 in which it recognized the need for a full discussion of not only the technical, but also the jurisdictional aspects of the subject. It called upon UNESCO to consult with the United Nations on law of the sea matters, as well as with IMO on such aspects as salvage, and to organize a meeting of experts. 12/ Comments will be invited on their findings, and a final report submitted to the General Conference at its twenty-ninth session in 1997, for it "to determine whether it is desirable for the matter to be dealt with on an international basis and on the method which should be adopted for this purpose".

2. Marine and coastal biodiversity

41. The 1995 report of the Secretary-General (paras. 203-204) had also drawn the attention of Member States to recent developments in the field of marine and coastal biodiversity and to the implications for the law of the sea.

42. Subsequently the Second Meeting of the Conference of Parties to the Convention on Biological Diversity (6-17 November 1995) declared a new global consensus on the importance of marine and coastal biological diversity, adopting decision II/10 on the "Conservation and sustainable use of marine and coastal biological diversity", and also urging parties, in its Jakarta Ministerial Statement on the Implementation of the Convention, to initiate immediate action to implement the decisions adopted on this issue. 13/

43. In decision II/10, in paragraph 12, the Conference of Parties requests the secretariat of the Convention on Biological Diversity, in consultation with the Division for Ocean Affairs and the Law of the Sea of the United Nations, "to undertake a study of the relationship between the Convention on Biological Diversity and the United Nations Convention on the Law of the Sea with regard to the conservation and sustainable use of genetic resources on the deep seabed, with a view to enabling the Subsidiary Body on Scientific, Technical and Technological Advice (SBSTTA) to address at future meetings, as appropriate, the scientific, technical and technological issues relating to bio-prospecting of genetic resources on the deep seabed".

44. Furthermore, in paragraph 13 of the decision, the Conference calls on "international and regional bodies responsible for legal instruments, agreements and programmes" which address relevant activities "to review their programmes with a view to improving existing measures and developing new actions which promote conservation and sustainable use of marine biological diversity", to report regularly to the Conference of Parties and to cooperate with SBSTTA in planning and implementing programmes. The Division is listed in this group along with a wide array of organizations, including the General Assembly itself. It is the intention of the Secretary-General to include in the scope of his report under paragraph 19 of General Assembly resolution 49/28 14/ a more comprehensive treatment of the subject of marine biodiversity and of the relationship between the Convention on the Law of the Sea and the Convention on Biological Diversity, going beyond the immediate issue of concern to the Conference of Parties to the latter Convention, namely, genetic resources of the deep seabed.

45. Attention is also drawn to decision II/14 of the Conference of Parties to the Biodiversity Convention, on the convening of an open-ended intergovernmental workshop on cooperation between the Convention and other international conventions on related issues, one purpose being to identify commonalities which would facilitate information exchange through the clearing-house mechanism and help the parties to prepare "appropriate and integrated national legislation on biodiversity matters".

46. It is important that States Parties be aware of these developments, in a timely way, considering also that the above-mentioned intergovernmental working group will meet in May 1996 along with the SBSTTA group working on marine and coastal biodiversity. The Secretary-General would urge States, particularly States Parties to the Law of the Sea Convention which are also parties to the Convention on Biological Diversity, to coordinate their activities particularly with respect to the conduct of reviews of the relationship between the two conventions, the identification of additional measures that may need to be taken, including the possible development of new or additional international rules, and to facilitating the adoption of appropriate national legislation relevant to the conservation of marine and coastal biodiversity, consistent with both conventions, as well as with relevant regional agreements.

3. Rules of origin

47. The entry into force of the Convention has brought new attention to all areas affected, or potentially affected, by the law of the sea. For example, new attention is now focused by the World Trade Organization (WTO) and the World Customs Organization on the possible need to formulate special provisions as to "rules of origin" to deal with products (both living and non-living) originating or derived from the various maritime zones. In addition to clarifying the concepts and the jurisdictional aspects of the territorial sea, the high seas, the continental shelf, the exclusive economic zone and the international seabed area, the Division for Ocean Affairs and the Law of the Sea has brought a broad range of issues to the attention of the Technical Committee of the World Customs Organization and the WTO Committee on Rules of Origin, which are charged with further legal development under the Agreement on Rules of Origin.

IV. CONCLUSIONS AND SUGGESTIONS

48. The present period is of particular significance for the future of international cooperation in ocean affairs. Efforts to quickly adjust, consolidate and strengthen international law and policy on ocean issues must be supported in a number of intergovernmental forums, including conferences of parties to conventions and such bodies as the Commission on Sustainable Development. Continuous attention is required by States Parties and the Secretary-General to ensure the pre-eminence of the Convention in all aspects of the law of the sea and its strategic role as "a framework for national, regional and global action in the marine sector" (General Assembly resolution 50/23, preamble).

49. As stressed in the introduction to the 1995 annual report, uncertainties or inconsistencies in the choice of the appropriate forum to deal with an issue can create problems for effective coordination between and among the United Nations and competent international organizations, and impede the harmonized development of international law relating to the oceans. As the Secretary-General concluded in the report, it is timely for Member States to consider further how best to fulfil the oversight role of the General Assembly, bearing in mind that that might entail frequent consideration of the implementation of important related conventions and instruments, as well as the Convention on the Law of the Sea. This conclusion has been further highlighted by the recent decision of the Commission on Sustainable Development to recommend periodic in-depth review of marine environmental and resource development issues (see paras. 34-36 above).

50.   Governments are urged to ensure that national delegations to the various intergovernmental forums where law of the sea issues arise adopt a consistent approach to Convention-related matters and take appropriate action, where necessary, to promote implementation of the General Assembly resolutions dealing with the law of the sea, and so facilitate the harmonious development of international ocean law and policy.   The Secretary-General will make every endeavour to facilitate this process as resources permit.

51.   Current examples of the issues which need coordinated and consistent approaches to international legal development relating to the Convention, concern, as discussed in paragraphs 40 to 47 above, the protection of the underwater cultural heritage, marine and coastal biodiversity, including access to deep-sea genetic resources, and the uniform rules of origin.   Particular issues will arise for States Parties to the Convention on the Law of the Sea which are also parties to conventions dealing with such matters or which are members of the bodies dealing with such issues.   It may be observed in this connection that a number of conventions on the environment, including particularly regional agreements, provide the channel through which States Parties implement their obligations under the Convention on the Law of the Sea.

52.   It is apparent that in the present period activities in the field of ocean affairs are increasing throughout the international system, many clearly strengthened by the entry into force of the Convention.   The Secretary-General anticipates that the results of the various reviews and assessments of the implications and impacts of the Convention, requested under General Assembly resolution 49/28 (paras. 18-20), 15/ will form a collective work of the United Nations system.   It should yield important guidance for States Parties to the Convention and the General Assembly and provide the basis for a new strategic plan for the effective implementation of the Convention across a broad range of issues.

53.   The comprehensiveness of the report to be prepared by the Secretary-General under paragraph 19 of resolution 49/28 will depend greatly on the timing and extent of the work done by international organizations in response to the call by the General Assembly.   Considering also that many organizations have experienced delays in conducting the kind of wide-ranging and in-depth reviews and assessments required, it may not be possible for the Secretary-General to present the report in complete form at the fifty-first session..

54.   With regard to the Secretary-General's annual report on the law of the sea to the General Assembly, the Assembly expressed a clear preference for having it available well in advance of the General Assembly session to allow proper consideration of the issues.   Emphasis was also placed on the need for the Secretary-General to offer suggestions for possible action by the Assembly, and in this respect attention is drawn to paragraph 15 (b) of resolution 49/28 whereby the Secretary-General is requested to formulate "recommendations for the consideration of, and for action by, the Assembly or other appropriate intergovernmental forums".   The Secretary-General wishes to note that while the comprehensive nature of his annual report requires him to submit it in the middle of the General Assembly session, the heavy demand on documentation relating to other priority items has often prevented it from being issued sufficiently in advance of the debate on the law of the sea item.   As a practical measure every effort will be made to circulate the report of the Secretary-General before the commencement of the session of the Assembly, and to issue addenda subsequently, updating its information as necessary.

55.   It is suggested that the future reports of the Secretary-General under article 319 focus on the identification and appropriate treatment of issues of particular importance to States Parties and competent international organizations, and so facilitate the subsequent consideration of these issues by the General Assembly.   It would not be the purpose of the article 319 report, however, to replace the Secretary-General's annual report to the General Assembly, which gives the comprehensive overview of all relevant developments.

Notes

1/ A/50/713 and Corr.1.

2/ A/50/550.

3/ A/50/553; A/50/549; A/50/552.

4/ This is in accordance with the 1994 Agreement relating to the implementation of Part XI of the United Nations Convention on the Law of the Sea of December 1982, annex, sect. 1, para. 14.

5/ As the General Assembly in resolution 50/23 specifically recalled resolution 49/28, adopted consequent upon the entry into force of the Convention on 16 November 1994, it did not need to reiterate the continuing mandate of the Division for Ocean Affairs and the Law of the Sea of the Office of Legal Affairs as set forth in the latter resolution.

6/ A similar recommendation on the coordination of national policy was made to the Commission on Sustainable Development in the report of the Secretary-General on chapter 17 of Agenda 21 (E/CN.17/1996/3, para. 24 (a)).

7/ See A/51/116.

8/ Convention to Ban the Importation into Forum Island Countries of Hazardous and Radioactive Wastes and to Control the Transboundary Movement and Management of Hazardous Wastes within the South Pacific Region, adopted at the twenty-sixth South Pacific Forum and opened for signature on 16 September 1995.

9/ Report of the United Nations Conference on Environment and Development, Rio de Janeiro, 3-14 June 1992, vol. I, Resolutions Adopted by the Conference (United Nations publication, Sales No. E.93.I.8 and corrigendum), resolution 1, annex II.

10/ GESAMP will begin this year to prepare a new report on the state of the marine environment.

11/ A/50/713 and Corr.1, paras. 228-231.

12/ The first meeting of experts is scheduled to be held in Paris from 22 to 24 May 1996.

13/ Report of the Second Meeting (UNEP/CBD/COP/2/19, annex II), 30 November 1995. In the decision the Conference Parties take note of the FAO Code of Conduct for Responsible Fisheries, the 1995 Agreement on fish stocks and the Washington Declaration and Global Programme of Action on Land-based Activities and support their implementation in ways that are consistent with the Convention on Biological Diversity. Decision II/10 based itself on recommendation I/8 adopted by the Subsidiary Body on Scientific, Technical and Technological Advice (SBSTTA) at its first meeting (UNEP/CBD/COP/2/5), which was reported on in the 1995 annual report of the Secretary-General. It carries also an annex I which presents "Additional conclusions" on recommendation I/8, and an annex II which presents a "Draft programme for further work on marine and coastal biological diversity".

14/ General Assembly resolution 49/28, paragraphs 18, 19 and 20, reads as follows:

"18. Invites the competent international organizations to assess the implications of the entry into force of the Convention in their respective fields of competence and to identify additional measures that may need to be taken as a consequence of its entry into force with a view to ensuring a uniform, consistent and coordinated approach to the implementation of the provisions of the Convention throughout the United Nations system;

"19. <u>Requests</u> the Secretary-General to prepare a comprehensive report on the impact of the entry into force of the Convention on related existing or proposed instruments and programmes throughout the United Nations system, and to submit the report to the Assembly at its fifty-first session;

"20. <u>Invites</u> the competent international organizations, as well as development and funding institutions, to take specific account in their programmes and activities of the impact of the entry into force of the Convention on the needs of States, especially developing States, for technical and financial assistance, and to support subregional or regional initiatives aimed at cooperation in the effective implementation of the Convention."

<u>15</u>/   Resolution 49/28, paras. 18-20 (see note 14 above).

Annex

LIST OF MAIN DOCUMENTS

I.   BASIC DOCUMENTS

The Law of the Sea: United Nations Convention on the Law of the Sea, with index and Final Act of the Third United Nations Conference on the Law of the Sea (United Nations publication, Sales No. E.83.V.5)*

1994 Agreement relating to the implementation of Part XI of the United Nations Convention on the Law of the Sea of 10 December 1982. <u>In</u>: Annex to General Assembly resolution 48/263, adopted on 28 July 1994. <u>In</u>: A/RES/48/263. <u>Also in</u>: <u>Law of the Sea Bulletin</u>, Special Issue IV (November 1994).*

General Assembly resolutions 49/28 and 50/23. Law of the Sea. Adopted on 6 December 1994 and 5 December 1995, respectively, <u>In</u>: A/RES/49/28 and A/RES/50/23.

1995 Agreement for the Implementation of the Provisions of the United Nations Convention on the Law of the Sea of 10 December 1982 relating to the Conservation and Management of Straddling Fish Stocks and Highly Migratory Fish Stocks. <u>In</u>: A/50/550, annex I, and <u>In</u>: A/CONF.164/37.

Resolutions adopted by the United Nations Conference on Straddling Fish Stocks and Highly Migratory Fish Stocks. <u>In</u>: A/50/550, annex II and <u>In</u>: A/CONF.164/38, annex.

II.   DOCUMENTS OF THE FIFTIETH SESSION OF THE GENERAL ASSEMBLY

<u>General Assembly debate</u>

A/50/PV.80   80th and 81st plenary meetings, 5 December 1995.
and 81   Agenda item 39, "Law of the sea": report of the Secretary-
               General (A/50/713 and Corr.1); draft resolution (A/50/L.34).
               Agenda item 96, "Environment and sustainable development:
               sustainable use and conservation of the marine living resources
               of the high seas" reports: of the Secretary-General (A/50/549,
               A/50/550, A/50/552, A/50/553); draft resolutions (A/50/L.35,
               A/50/L.36).

---

    *   The Convention will be reissued in due course in a single publication together with the 1994 Agreement on Part XI and an expanded Index.

Resolutions

A/RES/50/23   Law of the sea.   Adopted on 5 December 1995.

A/RES/50/24   Agreement for the implementation of the Provisions of the United Nations Convention on the Law of the Sea of 10 December 1982 relating to the Conservation and Management of Straddling Fish Stocks and Highly Migratory Fish Stocks.   Adopted on 5 December 1995.

A/RES/50/25   Large-scale pelagic drift-net fishing and its impact on the living marine resources of the world's oceans and seas; unauthorized fishing in zones of national jurisdiction and its impact on the living marine resources of the world's oceans and seas; and fisheries by-catch and discards and their impact on the sustainable use of the world's living marine resources.   Adopted on 5 December 1995.

Reports of the Secretary-General

A/50/713   Law of the sea.
and Corr.1

A/50/549   Environment and sustainable development: sustainable use and conservation of the marine living resources of the high seas: Unauthorized fishing in zones of national jurisdiction and its impact on the living marine resources of the world's oceans and seas.

A/50/550   Environment and sustainable development: sustainable use and conservation of the marine living resources of the high seas: United Nations Conference on Straddling Fish Stocks and Highly Migratory Fish Stocks.

   (Annex I contains the 1995 Agreement; annex II contains resolutions I and II of the Conference.)

A/50/552   Environment and sustainable development: sustainable use and conservation of the marine living resources of the high seas: fisheries by-catch and discards and their impact on the sustainable use of the world's living marine resources.

A/50/553   Environment and sustainable development: sustainable use and conservation of the marine living resources of the high seas: large-scale pelagic drift-net fishing and its impact on the living marine resources of the world's oceans and seas.

Submissions by Member States under agenda item 39 on the law of the sea

A/50/98   By Spain.
S/1995/252

A/50/216   By Greece.
S/1995/476

A/50/256   By Turkey.
S/1995/505

A/50/264   By Greece.
S/1995/526

A/50/279   By Turkey.
S/1995/568

A/50/303   By Greece.
S/1995/603

A/50/339   By Turkey.
S/1995/667

A/50/385   By Yugoslavia.

A/50/754   By the Russian Federation.

A/50/809   By Turkey.

Other documents relating, inter alia, to agenda item 39 on the law of the sea

A/50/425   Final Declaration of the Ninth Meeting of Heads of
S/1995/787   State and Government of the Rio Group (Quito Declaration), held
                in Quito on 4 and 5 September 1995. Submitted by Ecuador.

A/50/475   Communiqué of the Twenty-sixth South Pacific Forum, held at
                Madang, Papua New Guinea, from 3 to 15 September 1995. Submitted
                by Papua New Guinea.

A/50/518   Ministerial Declaration of the Group of 77, adopted on
                29 September 1995. Submitted by the Philippines.

A/50/673   Cooperation resulting from the summit meetings of the
                Ibero-American Conference. (Bariloche Declaration). Submitted
                by Argentina.

A/50/752   Eleventh Conference of Heads of State or Government of the
S/1995/1035   Movement of Non-Aligned Countries, held in Cartagena de Indias,
                Colombia, 18-20 October 1995. Submitted by Colombia.

Programme budget documents

A/C.5/50/28   Proposed programme budget for the biennium 1996-1997: Revised
                estimates for the International Seabed Authority for 1996.
                Report of the Secretary-General.

A/50/842   Proposed programme budget for the Biennium 1996-1997: Report of
                the Fifth Committee.

III. DOCUMENTS OF THE FIFTY-FIRST SESSION OF THE GENERAL ASSEMBLY

A/51/57   Submission by the Russian Federation under the agenda item on the
                law of the sea.

A/51/116   Note verbale dated 5 March 1996 from the United States Mission to
                the United Nations addressed to the Secretary-General.

IV. MAIN DOCUMENTS OF THE UNITED NATIONS CONFERENCE ON STRADDLING FISH STOCKS AND HIGHLY MIGRATORY FISH STOCKS

Basic documents

A/50/550	Report of the Secretary-General, containing the Agreement and the resolutions adopted by the Conference.
A/CONF.164/37	Final edited text of the Agreement.
A/CONF.164/38	Text of the Final Act of the Conference.

Reports of the sessions of the Conference

A/CONF.164/9	Report of the first (organizational) session of the Conference (19-23 April 1993).
A/CONF.164/16 and Corr.1	Report of the second session (12-30 July 1993).
A/CONF.164/20	Report of the third session (14-31 March 1994).
A/CONF.164/25	Report of the fourth session (15-26 August 1994).
A/CONF.164/29	Report of the fifth session (27 March-12 April 1995).
A/CONF.164/36	Report of the sixth session (24 July-4 August 1995).

Documents submitted by the Chairman of the Conference

A/CONF.164/7, 8, 11, 12, 15, 17, 19, 21, 24, 26, 28, 30 and 35	Statements by the Chairman.
A/CONF.164/10	A guide to the issues before the Conference.

Other documents

A/CONF.164/L.1 to L.50	Proposals and other communications submitted by delegations.
A/CONF.164/INF/2, 3, 4 and Corr.1, 5, 8 and 9	Reports and other studies submitted by the Secretariat, FAO and IOC.
A/CONF.164/INF/6, 10 and 13	Reports and comments submitted by intergovernmental organizations, regional and subregional fisheries organizations and arrangements.
A/CONF.164/INF/16 and Corr.1	List of documents of the Conference.

V. DOCUMENTS OF THE MEETING OF STATES PARTIES (SPLOS)

Basic documents

SPLOS/1/Rev.1	Agenda for the Meeting of States Parties.
SPLOS/2/Rev.3	Rules of Procedure for Meetings of States Parties.

<u>Reports of the meetings of States Parties</u>

SPLOS/3   Report of the first meeting of States Parties
                           (21-22 November 1994)

SPLOS/4 and   Report of the second meeting of States Parties
Corr.1   (15-19 May 1995).

SPLOS/5   Report of the third meeting of States Parties (27 November-
                           1 December 1995).

SPLOS/8   Report of the fourth meeting of States Parties (4-8 March
                           1996).

<u>Other documents</u>

SPLOS/WP.3/Rev.1   Revised budget estimates for the International Tribunal for
                           the Law of the Sea covering the period 1996-1997.

SPLOS/L.1   Decisions of the Meeting of States Parties on budgetary
                           matters (adopted on 8 March 1996).

SPLOS/L.2   Schedule for the nomination and election of the members of
                           the Commission on the Limits of the Continental Shelf.
                           Note by the Secretariat.

VI.   UNITED NATIONS SALES PUBLICATIONS ON THE LAW OF
      THE SEA (1994-1995)

The law of the sea: marine scientific research - legislative history
of article 246 of the United Nations Convention on the Law of the Sea (1994).
Sales No. E.94.V.9 (English, French, Spanish).

The law of the sea: a select bibliography - 1993 (1994). Sales No.
E.94.V.10 (English only).

The law of the sea: practice of States at the time of entry into force of
the United Nations Convention on the Law of the Sea (1994). Sales No. E.94.V.13
(English, French, Spanish).

The law of the sea: national legislation on the territorial sea, the right
of innocent passage and the contiguous zone (1995). Sales No. E.95.V.7
(English, French, Spanish).

The law of the sea: current developments in State practice (No. IV)
(1995). Sales No. E.95.V.10 (English, French, Spanish).

The law of the sea: a select bibliography - 1994 (1995). Sales
No. E.95.V.11 (English only).

The law of the sea: conservation and utilization of the living resources
of the exclusive economic zone - legislative history of articles 61 and 62 of
the United Nations Convention on the Law of the Sea (1995). Sales No. E.95.V.21
(English, French, Spanish).

VII.   LAW OF THE SEA INFORMATION CIRCULARS AND
       LAW OF THE SEA BULLETINS (1994-1995)

Law of the Sea Information Circulars (English, French and Spanish): No. 1
(June 1995); No. 2 (October 1995).

Law of the Sea Bulletins (English, French and Spanish)*: No. 25 (June 1994); No. 26 (October 1994); Special Issue IV (November 1994); No. 27 (June 1995); No. 28 (June 1995); No. 29 (October 1995).

VIII. PREPARATORY COMMISSION FOR THE INTERNATIONAL SEABED AUTHORITY AND FOR THE INTERNATIONAL TRIBUNAL FOR THE LAW OF THE SEA

Reports of the Plenary and the Special Commissions

LOS/PCN/152 (Vol. I)	Report of the Preparatory Commission under paragraph 10 of resolution I containing recommendations for submission to the Meeting of States Parties to be convened in accordance with annex VI, article 4, of the Convention regarding practical arrangements for the establishment of the International Tribunal for the Law of the Sea. [Report and addenda thereto]
LOS/PCN/152 (Vol. II)	Documents of Special Commission 4.
LOS/PCN/152 (Vol. III)	Documents of Special Commission 4.
LOS/PCN/152 (Vol. IV)	Plenary documents of particular relevance to Special Commission 4.
LOS/PCN/153	Report of the Preparatory Commission under paragraph 11 of resolution I of the Third United Nations Conference on the Law of the Sea, on all matters within its mandate, except as provided in paragraph 10, for presentation to the Assembly of the International Seabed Authority at its first session. (Index to LOS/PCN/153 (Vols. I-XIII).)
LOS/PCN/153 (Vol. I)	Provisional final report of the Plenary and documents relevant to the implementation of resolution II (Plenary).
LOS/PCN/153 (Vol. II)	Documents relevant to the implementation of resolution II (Plenary).
LOS/PCN/153 (Vol. III)	Documents relevant to the implementation of resolution II (General Committee) (except those relating to training).
LOS/PCN/153 (Vol. IV)	Documents relevant to the implementation of resolution II (General Committee). Documents relating to Training. (Part 1) Final report of the Training Panel to the General Committee of the Preparatory Commission (LOS/PCN/BUR/R.48 and Corr.1 (Russian only)). (Part 2) Documents issued after the twelfth session of the Preparatory Commission (up to March 1995).
LOS/PCN/153 (Vol. V)	Final draft rules of procedure for the organs of the Authority; final draft relationship agreements of the Authority; documents of the Finance Committee; on the administrative arrangements, structure and financial implications of the Authority and the draft budget for the first financial period of the International Seabed Authority.

---

*   As of 1995, the English version of the Law of the Sea Bulletin is available only on a subscription basis ($37.50 per year (three issues)). French and Spanish versions continue to be distributed free of charge, as in the past.

LOS/PCN/153   Provisional report of Special Commission 1 and statements to the
(Vol. VI)   Plenary by the Chairman of Special Commission 1 on the progress
                 of work in that Commission.

LOS/PCN/153   Working papers of Special Commission 1 (LOS/PCN/SCN.1/WP.1 to
(Vol. VII)   LOS/PCN/SCN.1/WP.2/Add.5).

LOS/PCN/153   Working papers of Special Commission 1 (LOS/PCN/SCN.1/WP.2/Add.6
(Vol. VIII)   to LOS/PCN/SCN.1/WP.15).

LOS/PCN/153   Conference room papers of Special Commission 1.
(Vol. IX)

LOS/PCN/153   Part One. Provisional final report of Special Commission 2.
(Vol. X)   Part Two. Statements to the Plenary by the Chairman of Special
                 Commission 2 on the progress of work in that Commission.
                 Part Three. Other documents relating to the work of Special
                 Commission 2.

LOS/PCN/153   Part One. Working papers of Special Commission 2.
(Vol. XI)   Part Two. Conference room papers of Special Commission 2.

LOS/PCN/153   Statements to the Plenary by the Chairman of Special Commission 3
(Vol. XII)   on the progress of work in that Commission in preparing draft
                 rules, regulations and procedures for the exploration and
                 exploitation of polymetallic nodules in the Area.

LOS/PCN/153   Part 1. Draft final report of Special Commission 3
(Vol. XIII)   (LOS/PCN/SCN.3/CRP.17 and LOS/PCN/SCN.3/CRP.17/Add.1) and
                 amendments and comments relating to the draft final report
                 (CRP.18, CRP.19, CRP.20 and CRP.21).
                 Part 2. Draft provisional final report of Special Commission 3
                 (chapter IV of LOS/PCN/130 - Consolidated provisional final
                 report of the Preparatory Commission, vol. I).

IX. MAIN DOCUMENTS OF THE INTERNATIONAL SEABED AUTHORITY

First session of the Assembly
(16-18 November 1994,
27 February-17 March 1995,
7-18 August 1995)

ISBA/A/4   Agenda of the Assembly, adopted on 28 February 1995.

ISBA/A/6   Rules of procedure of the Assembly, adopted on 17 March 1995.

ISBA/A/L.1/Rev.1 Statement of the President of the Assembly on the work of the
and Corr.1   Assembly.

ISBA/A/L.3   Statement of the President on the work of the Assembly.
and Corr.1

ISBA/A/L.5   Draft decision by the Assembly. Submitted by the President.

ISBA/A/L.6   Statement by the Rapporteur-General of the Preparatory
                  Commission for the International Seabed Authority and for the
                  International Tribunal for the Law of the Sea, presenting the
                  Final Report of the Preparatory Commission (LOS/PCN/153).

ISBA/A/L.7   Statement of the President on the work of the Assembly.

ISBA/C/1   Provisional agenda of the Council.

<u>First part of the second session of the Assembly</u>
(11-22 March 1996)

ISBA/A/L.8   Composition of the First Council of the International Seabed
and Corr.1   Authority.

ISBA/A/L.9   Statement of the President on the work of the Assembly during
the first part of the second session.

-----

2. LAW OF THE SEA - REPORT OF THE UN SECRETARY-GENERAL

Doc. no.: A/51/645 and Adds. 1 & 2   1 November 1996 and 30 December 1996 & 20 February 1997

CONTENTS

CONTENTS (continued)

CONTENTS (continued)

CONTENTS (continued)

I. INTRODUCTION

The law of the sea item at the fifty-first session

1.   The present report is submitted to the General Assembly in accordance with its resolution 49/28 of 6 December 1994, in which it requested the Secretary-General to report to it annually on developments pertaining to the implementation of the United Nations Convention on the Law of the Sea and on other developments relating to ocean affairs and the law of the sea.   Pursuant to resolution 50/23 of 5 December 1995, the present report also deals with the implementation of that resolution.

2.   At the current session, the General Assembly will also take up under the item on the law of the sea, developments in the field of the conservation and management of living marine resources concerning the Agreement for the Implementation of the Provisions of the United Nations Convention on the Law of the Sea of 10 December 1982 relating to the Conservation and Management of Straddling Fish Stocks and Highly Migratory Fish Stocks (pursuant to resolution 50/24 of 5 December 1995); and large-scale pelagic drift-net fishing and its impact on the living marine resources of the world's oceans and seas, unauthorized fishing in zones of national jurisdiction and its impact on the living marine resources of the world's oceans and seas, and fisheries by-catch and discards and their impact on the sustainable use of the world's living marine resources (pursuant to resolution 50/25).   The relevant reports of the Secretary-General have been issued under the symbols A/51/404 and A/51/383 respectively.   Attention is also drawn to the submission by the United States of America, the host Government of the Intergovernmental Conference to Adopt a Global Programme of Action for the Protection of the Marine Environment from Land-based Activities (23 October-3 November 1995) (A/51/116), which is presented under the agenda item on the law of the sea, and to the submission by a number of Member States on the question of the observer status of the International Seabed Authority at the General Assembly (A/51/231) and the Assembly's decision to take it up as a new agenda item.

The report to States Parties to the United Nations Convention on the Law of the Sea

3.   It will be recalled that the Assembly had suggested, in its resolution 49/28, that the annual report on the law of the sea should also serve as a basis for the reports on "issues of a general nature" which arise with respect to the Convention, which the Secretary-General is required to prepare under article 319, paragraph 2 (a), of the Convention.   Such reports are to be transmitted to all States Parties, the Authority and competent international organizations, in accordance with this provision of the Convention.

4.   The particular attention of the General Assembly is drawn, therefore, to the first "Report of the Secretary-General under article 319 of the United Nations Convention on the Law of the Sea" (SPLOS/6), which provides *inter alia* a

convenient summary of the law of the sea debate at the fiftieth session of the
General Assembly; identifies two important institutional questions, namely, the
question of regular and periodic review of ocean issues, and the strengthening
of inter-agency cooperation in respect of the implementation of the Convention;
and discusses several important emerging issues, including, in particular, the
protection of the underwater cultural heritage and marine and coastal
biodiversity. Important subsequent developments as to such institutional
questions and emerging issues are highlighted in the present report.

5.   The Secretary-General has also offered a number of conclusions and
suggestions in that report (ibid., paras. 48-55), in keeping also with the
General Assembly's request in paragraph 15 (b) of resolution 49/28 that he
formulate recommendations for the consideration of, and for action by, the
Assembly or other appropriate intergovernmental forums ... aimed at a better
understanding of the provisions of the Convention and facilitating their
effective implementation.

Important trends

6.   Since the entry into force of the Convention in late 1994, the
international community has devoted its main attention to the establishment of
the institutions it has created and to other institutional aspects, among them
the role of the General Assembly. This has also been a period of consolidation
as regards consistent implementation of the Convention, of harmonizing ongoing
international legal and policy development with the Convention in force, and
ensuring continued international cooperation within the framework of the
Convention to deal with emerging issues.

7.   The establishment of the new "treaty system of ocean institutions" is a
major feature of the Convention, and this process, which began in 1983, is now
almost complete. The new system of institutions consists of the International
Seabed Authority, the International Tribunal for the Law of the Sea, the
Commission on the Limits of the Continental Shelf and the United Nations
Secretariat, by virtue of the special responsibilities of the Secretary-General
under the Convention, and the central, ongoing role that the General Assembly is
required to play in keeping the implementation of the Convention as a whole
under review and monitoring important developments in law of the sea and ocean
affairs. In this respect, it should be noted that the Convention does not
provide for regular conferences of parties: rather, provision is made for
Meetings of States Parties to establish the Tribunal and the Commission, and for
subsequent Meetings as necessary, e.g., to conduct elections periodically and to
adopt the budget of the Tribunal. Thus, the Meeting of States Parties to the
Convention may also come to be regarded as an important component of this new
system of ocean institutions.

8.   While the Authority, the Tribunal, and also the Commission, will deal with
specific maritime zones and/or specific aspects of ocean affairs, the central
programme on oceans at the United Nations concentrates on matters of overall
implementation of the Convention. It focuses attention also on the monitoring
of State practice and provides information, advice and assistance on the uniform
and consistent application of the Convention in the different fields of interest
and concern for States and for international organizations, as well as
supporting efforts which help States to implement the Convention more
effectively and derive greater benefits from the new ocean order.

9.   The main landmarks in establishing the new ocean institutions have been the
successful conclusion in 1994 of the Agreement on Part XI, and its entry into
force in 1996; the entry into force of the Convention in 1994 in a favourable
environment for ensuring universal acceptance of the Convention; the adoption of
General Assembly resolution 49/28, whereby the Assembly affirmed its pre-eminent
role in respect of all matters relating to the Convention and to ocean affairs
more generally, as well as the role of the Secretary-General under the
Convention; the establishment and start-up of the organs of the Authority (the

Assembly and the Council, and two subsidiary bodies) and its secretariat; the election of the judges of the Tribunal by the Meeting of States Parties, and the commencement of their work, with secretariat support by its Registry, to which the United Nations Division for Ocean Affairs and Law of the Sea continues to render assistance. Furthermore, the lists of experts for the purpose of special arbitration under Annex VIII to the Convention have been drawn up by the Food and Agriculture Organization of the United Nations (FAO), the International Maritime Organization (IMO) and the Intergovernmental Oceanographic Commission (IOC) of the United Nations Educational, Scientific and Cultural Organization (UNESCO), and several Governments have nominated arbitrators and conciliators under Annexes VII and V to the Convention. Only the Commission on the Limits of the Continental Shelf remains to be established, and the Meeting of States Parties will be electing its members in March 1997.

10. The fundamental importance of the law of the sea institutions for international peace and security, the peaceful settlement of disputes, the sustainable development of marine resources and the protection of the environment has allowed them to evolve successfully, despite the increasing financial difficulties for Governments in providing for institutional development at the international level.

11. Ocean institutions, and in particular the institutions of the Convention, should continue to evolve along lines in keeping with the interrelationships among ocean issues and with the need to consider them as a whole, as emphasized in the preamble to the Convention. This is an ongoing task and the particular responsibility of the General Assembly. Being a comprehensive instrument also, the Convention holds considerable "strategic importance ... as a framework for national, regional and global action in the marine sector" (resolution 49/28, preamble), with further implications, in turn, for the manner in which the system of ocean institutions will evolve, in particular the core institutions established by the Convention.

12. The need for oversight of developments pertaining to the acceptance and implementation of the Convention, including the establishment of its institutions, was recognized early by the General Assembly, which retained a regular annual item on the law of the sea subsequent to the adoption of the Convention in 1982 and assigned all relevant responsibilities to an organizational unit within the Secretariat, now the Division for Ocean Affairs and the Law of the Sea; moreover, throughout the years from 1983 to 1994, prior to the entry into force of the Convention, the General Assembly played a crucial role as steward of the Convention, monitoring important related developments and nurturing the emergence of the institutions of the Convention.

13. The oversight role of the General Assembly, as stressed in resolution 49/28, may be expected to assume yet greater significance with universal acceptance of the Convention and be further consolidated by the addition of the new law of the sea institutions to the wider group of international organizations responsible in various specialized aspects of ocean affairs, whose competence therein is affirmed and further reinforced by the Convention.

14. It will also be noted that the adoption of a new instrument to further develop and facilitate the implementation of the Convention in respect of the conservation and management of living marine resources, namely the 1995 Agreement on fish stocks, also has significant institutional implications for the system of ocean institutions, in that the General Assembly is called upon to monitor the implementation of this instrument as a distinct component of its ongoing review of the implementation of the Convention itself. Since the Convention contains a great number of basic provisions of a general and framework nature, similar developments of the law in other aspects is likely to occur in the future when such a need arises.

15. The Secretary-General wishes, therefore, to emphasize the importance of the "law of the sea" debate in the General Assembly, in relation not only to the

development of the new treaty system of ocean institutions and the effective implementation of the Convention in all of its many aspects, but also for promoting international cooperation on important new issues in the field of law of the sea and ocean affairs. This role should also entail consideration as to the proper choice of intergovernmental forum for the discussion of issues of direct importance for the effective implementation of the Convention, as was emphasized also in the 1995 report of the Secretary-General on the law of the sea (A/50/713, paras. 7 and 8) and in his first report under article 319 of the Convention (SPLOS/6, paras. 32-36).

II.   THE CONVENTION AND THE IMPLEMENTING AGREEMENTS

A.   Status of the Convention

16.   The United Nations Convention on the Law of the Sea entered into force on 16 November 1994. Between 15 October 1995 and 31 August 1996, 25 more States deposited their instruments of ratification or accession to the Convention, bringing the total number of States Parties to 106.[1]

17.   In the short time since November 1994, the Convention has received 38 instruments of ratification, accession or succession. It is significant to compare this rate of acceptance with the 12 previous years, when 68 States consented to be bound by the Convention. Many recent acceptances are directly attributable to the adoption of the 1994 Agreement on Part XI and to the entry into force of the Convention. The goal of universal acceptance has almost been achieved and the Convention's important contributions to the steady development of the international law relating to the seas and oceans is everywhere apparent.

18.   The provisions of the Convention on the Law of the Sea[2] have been further developed in two implementing Agreements:

   (a)   The Agreement relating to the implementation of Part XI of the Convention,[3] adopted in 1994, which is to be interpreted and applied together with the Convention as a single instrument. In the event of any inconsistency between the Agreement and Part XI of the Convention, the provisions of the Agreement shall prevail. Furthermore, after the adoption of the Agreement, any ratification or accession to the Convention represents also consent to be bound by the Agreement, and no State or entity can establish its consent to be bound by the Agreement unless it has previously established or establishes at the same time its consent to be bound by the Convention. Following the entry into force of the Agreement (on 28 July 1996), States that were parties to the Convention prior to the adoption of the Agreement now have to establish their consent to be bound by the Agreement separately, by depositing an instrument of ratification or accession.

   (b)   The Agreement for the Implementation of the Provisions of the Convention Relating to the Conservation and Management of Straddling Fish Stocks and Highly Migratory Fish Stocks,[4] adopted in 1995, is a separate instrument of a different nature. It greatly elaborates upon the general provisions of the Convention relevant to these matters, but has to be interpreted and applied in the context of and in a manner consistent with the Convention. There is no linkage between the Agreement and the Convention in establishing a consent to be bound by these instruments.

B.   Status of the 1994 Agreement relating to the Implementation of Part XI of the Convention

19.   As of 31 August 1996, 67 States had consented to be bound by the 1994 Agreement.[5] Pursuant to its article 6, the Agreement entered into force on 28 July 1996. Article 6 states that the Agreement shall enter into force 30 days after the date on which 40 States have established their consent to be

bound, provided that this number includes at least seven of the States referred to in paragraph 1 (a) of resolution II of the Third United Nations Conference on the Law of the Sea[6] and that at least five of those States are developed States. With the ratification by the Netherlands, on 28 June 1996, those requirements were fulfilled.

20. A fundamental feature of the Agreement is its provisional application; this was done not only to facilitate universal acceptance of the Convention, but also to promote the viability of the International Seabed Authority by allowing for its provisional membership. States that are not parties to the Convention were also enabled to apply the Agreement provisionally. With the entry into force of the Agreement, this provisional application of the Agreement terminated.[7] However, States and entities that were applying it provisionally and for which it was not yet in force on the date of termination may continue to participate as members of the Authority on a provisional basis by sending a written notification to the depositary to this effect.[8] Eighteen States and the European Community notified the depositary of such intention.[9] It should be noted, however, that a number of States that had been applying the Agreement provisionally and which had not notified the depositary of their continued participation in the Authority, retain their membership in the Authority by virtue of being States Parties to the Convention.[10] Twenty-nine other States, not being States Parties to the Convention and not having notified the depositary regarding the continuation of provisional membership, have ceased to be members of the Authority on a provisional basis as of 28 July 1996.[11]

21. The Agreement further provides that membership on a provisional basis, if continued after the entry into force of the Agreement, would terminate either on 16 November 1996 or upon the entry into force of the Agreement and the Convention for the member concerned, whichever is earlier. Furthermore, it empowers the Council of the Authority to extend, upon the request of the State or entity concerned, such membership beyond 16 November 1996 for a further period or periods not exceeding a total of two years, provided that the Council is satisfied that the State or entity concerned has been making efforts in good faith to become a party to the Agreement and the Convention.

22. At the resumed second session of the International Seabed Authority (5-16 August 1996), the Council decided to extend the provisional membership of Bangladesh, Nepal, Poland and the United States of America for a period of two years as from 16 November 1996. It also decided to extend the provisional membership of Canada for a period of one year as from 16 November 1996, as requested.[12] With regard to such extensions beyond 16 November 1996 for the remaining 13 States and the European Community which had notified the depositary of their intention to continue their provisional membership, the Council decided that those States or entities which submit requests for an extension of such membership prior to the next session of the Council shall be deemed to be members of the Authority on a provisional basis until the end of that next session in March 1997.[13]

    C.   Status of the 1995 Agreement on the conservation and management of straddling fish stocks and highly migratory fish stocks

23. The 1995 Agreement on fish stocks was adopted on 4 August 1995 by the United Nations Conference on Straddling Fish Stocks and Highly Migratory Fish Stocks. The period of signature will end on 4 December 1996. As of 31 August 1996, the Agreement had received a total of 47 signatures.[14] The Agreement will enter into force 30 days after the date of deposit of the thirtieth instrument of ratification or accession. As of 31 August 1996, Saint Lucia, Tonga and the United States of America had ratified the Agreement.

III.   MEETINGS OF STATES PARTIES TO THE CONVENTION

24.   The Meetings of States Parties to the Convention, convened by the
Secretary-General in accordance with the relevant provisions of the Convention,[15]
have been dealing primarily with the elections for and the budget of the
International Tribunal on the Law of the Sea and with the establishment of the
Commission on the Limits of the Continental Shelf.[16]   The fourth and the fifth
Meetings were held in New York from 4 to 8 March and from 24 July to
2 August 1996 respectively.   The reports of those Meetings are contained in
documents SPLOS/8 and SPLOS/14.

25.   The sixth and seventh Meetings of States Parties to the Convention will be
held in New York from 10 to 14 March 1997, and from 19 to 23 May 1997.   The
sixth Meeting will be devoted primarily to the election of the 21 members of the
Commission on the Limits of the Continental Shelf, and the seventh Meeting to
the budget of the Tribunal.

IV.   ACTIONS TAKEN BY STATES

A.   Maritime limits

26.   According to the information available at the Secretariat as of
31 August 1996, the outer limits claimed by 146 coastal States to the various
maritime zones,[17] are as set out in the table below.   Of the total number of 151
coastal States, 5 have apparently no corresponding legislation (Bosnia and
Herzegovina, Eritrea, Georgia, Slovenia and Federal Republic of Yugoslavia).

	Number of States
Territorial sea	
12 miles[18]	122
Less than 12 miles	8
More than 12 miles	15
(200 miles)	10
(20-50 miles)	5
Contiguous zone	
24 miles	50
Less than 24 miles	6
More than 24 miles	1
Exclusive economic zone	
200 miles	90
Up to a line of delimitation, by determination of coordinates, or without limits	10

(13 States claim a fishery zone of 200 miles and 4 States
claim a fishery zone of less than 200 miles)

Continental shelf

200-metre isobath plus exploitability criterion   35

Outer edge of continental margin, or 200 miles   28

200 miles   7

Others   13

27.   In addition, a total of 17 States have claimed archipelagic status,
although not all have specified archipelagic baselines.[19] Most recently, the
Bahamas adopted legislation claiming such status and establishing baselines; and
Jamaica is in the process of enacting archipelagic legislation.

B.   Deposit of charts and lists of geographical coordinates
and compliance with the obligation of due publicity

28.   Under articles 16(2), 47(9), 75(2) and 84(2) of the Convention, "due
publicity" is to be given by the coastal State Party to the Convention to charts
or lists of geographical coordinates for baselines and outer limits of its
various zones, and a copy of each such chart or list is to be deposited with the
Secretary-General. Similarly, under article 76(9), the coastal State is to
deposit with the Secretary-General charts and relevant information, including
geodetic data, permanently describing the outer limits of its continental shelf,
to which the Secretary-General shall give "due publicity".

29.   In order to carry out the functions entrusted to the Secretary-General
under the Convention and to respond to the request made by the General Assembly
in resolution 49/28, paragraph 15, and resolution 50/23, paragraph 9, the
Division for Ocean Affairs and the Law of the Sea of the Office of Legal
Affairs, as the responsible substantive unit of the Secretariat, has established
facilities for the custody of charts and lists of geographical coordinates
deposited. The Division has also adopted a system for their recording and
publicity: an internal computerized "data record" summarizes the information
contained in the charts submitted, and to ensure publicity, the Division informs
States Parties of the deposit of charts and geographical coordinates through a
"Maritime Zone Notification". Such information is also included in the Law of
the Sea Information Circular (LOSIC). This is a new publication, issued
periodically, which provides relevant information on the implementation of the
Convention, bearing in mind also the particular needs of those States not yet
parties to it. A total of four LOSIC circulars have now been issued.

30.   As of 31 August 1996, the following States Parties have deposited charts
and lists of geographical coordinates with the Secretary-General: Argentina,
China, Cyprus, Finland, Germany, Italy and Norway.[20]

31.   The Division has sought to assist States also with other obligations of
"due publicity" established by the Convention, which relate to legislation as
well as charts. These concern navigation: all laws and regulations adopted by
the coastal State relating to innocent passage through the territorial sea; all
laws and regulations, adopted by States bordering straits relating to transit
passage through straits used for international navigation; and the designation
of sea lanes and prescription of traffic separation schemes, and their
substitution, in the territorial sea and such straits, as well as the
designation of sea lanes through and air routes over archipelagic waters and the
prescription of traffic separation schemes, and their substitution.

32.   In this regard, several communications have been issued by the Division:
note verbale MZ/SP/1 on the deposit of charts, lists of geographical coordinates
and geodetic data (articles 16(2), 47(9), 75(2), 76(9) and 84(2)); notes
verbales TS/IP/SP/1 and SIN/TP/SP/1 on laws and regulations in relation to the
territorial sea and straits (articles 21(3) and 42(3)); and note verbale
SLTSS/SP/1 on the designation, prescription and substitution of sea lanes,
traffic separation schemes and air routes (articles 22(4), 41(6) and 53(7)
and (10)).

33.   As at 31 August 1996, the following States Parties had submitted relevant
information: Argentina (laws and regulations in straits), Australia (a sea lane
and traffic separation scheme), Germany (a sea lane and traffic separation
scheme), Italy (laws and regulations in the territorial sea and straits),
Namibia (a sea lane and traffic separation scheme in the territorial sea),
Marshall Islands (a sea lane through and air route above archipelagic waters)
and Oman (a sea lane in a strait).[21]

C.   National legislation

1.   New legislation received by the Secretariat

34.   The Division for Ocean Affairs and the Law of the Sea has received new
legislation of Bahamas, China, Jamaica, New Zealand, South Africa and the
Russian Federation:[22]

(a)   Bahamas.   The 1993 Archipelagic Waters and Maritime Jurisdiction Act
of the Bahamas, which entered into force on 4 January 1996, covers archipelagic
waters, internal waters, the territorial sea, innocent passage and the exclusive
economic zone.   The Act provides for archipelagic and other baselines, extends
the outer limit of the territorial sea from 6 miles to 12 miles and establishes
an exclusive economic zone of 200 miles; for the use of the median line where
the territorial sea of the Bahamas meets with the territorial sea of another
State, pending negotiations; and for the designation of archipelagic sea lanes
and the prescription of traffic separation schemes.   The Act also includes a
definition of the right of innocent passage, along with the empowerment of law
enforcement officers to stop, board, search and seize foreign ships when
warranted;[23]

(b)   China.   On 15 May 1996, China issued a declaration regarding the
establishment of straight baselines from which the breadth of the territorial
sea is to be measured.[24]   The Declaration announces part of the baselines of
China's territorial sea adjacent to the mainland and those of the territorial
sea adjacent to the Xisha Islands.   Also to be noted is that, in its declaration
made upon ratification of the Convention, China claims sovereign rights and
jurisdiction over an exclusive economic zone of 200 miles and the continental
shelf.[25]   The Philippines and Viet Nam have protested the Declaration (see
para. 35 (a));

(c)   Jamaica.   The Exclusive Economic Zone Act (Baselines) Regulations of
Jamaica, promulgated on 12 October 1992, establishes charts with geographical
coordinates defining the basepoints to be joined by straight archipelagic
baselines around the mainland and the outlying islands of the Pedro and the
Morant Cays of Jamaica;[26]

(d)   New Zealand.   New Zealand has established a contiguous zone of
24 miles, consistent with the Convention.   This was done, on 26 July 1996, by an
Act amending the Territorial Sea and Exclusive Economic Zone Act, 1977.   This
legislation, which entered into force on 1 August 1996, also introduces new
circumstances for the drawing of straight baselines from which the breadth of
the territorial sea is to be measured;[27]

(e) <u>South Africa</u>. South Africa has enacted the Maritime Zones Act of 1994, which repealed the Territorial Waters Act of 1963, the Territorial Waters Act (Transkei) of 1978 and the Territorial Waters Act (Ciskei) of 1986.[28] This Act came into effect on 11 November 1994 and includes 16 sections and 3 schedules which, <u>inter alia</u>, give the coordinates for straight baselines (schedule 2) and the limits of the continental shelf (schedule 3). The Act also applies to the Prince Edward Islands, which are located about 700 nautical miles south-east of South Africa in the Indian Ocean. The Act establishes a contiguous zone wherein South Africa may exercise its powers in relation also to damage to the marine environment. Of particular note is the provision in the Act for a new maritime area, a "maritime cultural zone", extending from the outer limits of the territorial sea to the outer limits of the contiguous zone, with the specification that the "same rights and powers as it has in respect of its territorial waters" apply over archaeological and historical objects in that new zone. This new legislation is a significant development in relation to the implementation of the relevant provisions of the Convention (articles 33 and 303) and to recent consideration at the international level of the possible need for a more extensively elaborated legal regime to govern the protection of these objects (see also paras. 142-147);

(f) <u>Russian Federation</u>. On 25 October 1995, the Russian Federation adopted an important comprehensive law, the Federal Law on the Continental Shelf of the Russian Federation.[29] It defines the continental shelf and continental margin as the prolongation of the land mass of the Russian Federation, which consists of the seabed and subsoil of the shelf, the slope and the rise. The outer edge of the shelf extends up to 200 miles or, if beyond, up to a distance determined in accordance with the rules of international law. The legislation establishes exclusive jurisdiction over, and outlines procedures with respect to, the exploration and exploitation of the continental shelf, and the construction and operation of artificial islands, installations and structures, including safety zones. Jurisdiction is also established with respect to the laying and use of submarine cables and pipelines, the conduct of marine scientific research, the protection and conservation of minerals and living resources. The new Federal Law also deals with dumping at sea; harvesting licences, permits fees and payments; enforcement; and settlement of disputes.

2. Protests and responses

35. Communications have been recently received by the Secretary-General in respect of the following legislation:

(a) <u>China</u>. The Philippines and Viet Nam have issued statements of protest against China's recent Declaration described above. The Philippines, on 17 May 1996, stated that they were "gravely concerned" over China's proclamation of baselines around the Paracels as well as the baselines for the sea adjacent to China's mainland. Viet Nam, on 6 June 1996, stated that China's establishment of territorial baselines around the Hoang Sa archipelago (Paracel) was "a serious violation" of Vietnamese sovereignty over that archipelago. Viet Nam also reaffirmed its sovereignty over the Truong Sa (Spratly) archipelago. This protest underscored that the drawing of baselines as established by China was not in conformity with articles 7 and 38 of the Convention;

(b) <u>Iran (Islamic Republic of)</u>. A protest was filed by Germany, on behalf of the European Union, concerning the Act of 2 May 1993 on the Marine Areas of the Islamic Republic of Iran in the Persian Gulf and in the Sea of Oman.[30] The communication of 13 March 1996 of the Islamic Republic of Iran, made in response to this protest, stated, <u>inter alia</u>, that it did not consider all the provisions of the Convention to be customary in nature, and as contractual provisions, they were only binding on States parties.[31] Four other protests to the Iranian Act were filed by Saudi Arabia on 25 July 1996 (A/50/1028), the United Arab Emirates on 26 August 1996 (A/50/1033), Kuwait on 26 August 1996 (A/50/1029) and Qatar on

4 September 1996 (A/50/1034). Saudi Arabia stated that it neither recognized
nor acknowledged any jurisdiction, powers or practices that were assumed or
exercised pursuant to that Act, and objected to provisions which violated
international law and practice, particularly those concerning international
navigation. It did not recognize, therefore, any restrictions or impositions
that would affect international navigation in the Gulf and the Sea of Oman,
including passage through the Strait of Hormuz. Kuwait declared that it did not
feel obligated to respect rules contained in the Iranian Act which were
inconsistent with the international law of the sea and especially with the 1982
Convention on the Law of the Sea.

3. Regional review

36. Changes in the status of the Convention and main legislative developments
over the past year are briefly reviewed on a regional basis, as follows:

     (a) Africa. The situation has not changed very much since the last report
(A/50/713, para. 31). Only two African States, Algeria and Mauritania,[32] have
ratified the Convention compared to nine States from Asia[33] and 11 States from
Europe and North America.[34] With 32 States having ratified the Convention,
Africa still has the highest number of ratifications, as well as the highest
percentage of parties: 60.3 per cent. Algeria, in its second declaration made
at the time of ratification, repeated the requirements contained in its
legislation of 1963 and 1972 of prior authorization for the passage of warships
in its territorial sea.[35] It should be noted that the Convention states that all
ships, including warships, shall enjoy the right of innocent passage through the
territorial sea; it also calls on coastal States not to hamper the innocent
passage of foreign ships through the territorial sea except as provided for in
the Convention (article 24);

     (b) Asia and the Pacific. Three States Parties to the Convention - China,
Japan and New Zealand - have modified their legislation so as to bring it into
line with the Convention. In establishing its contiguous zone, redefining its
continental shelf and proclaiming an exclusive economic zone, Japan has
substantially modified its legislation to incorporate the relevant provisions of
the Convention. The Japanese Diet adopted eight pieces of legislation essential
for the implementation of both the Convention and the 1994 Agreement relating to
Part XI;

     (c) Latin America and the Caribbean. Three more States are now bound by
the Convention (Argentina, Haiti and Panama) bringing to 23 the total number of
States Parties for this region of 33 States. Among the 13 island States of the
Caribbean, only the Dominican Republic still claims a territorial sea of 3
miles. The Bahamas, which used to have a 6-mile territorial sea, has just
extended its seaward limits to 12 miles. Among the 18 States of Central and
South America, Panama and 4 other States not yet parties to the Convention,
namely Ecuador, El Salvador, Nicaragua and Peru, continue to claim a 200-mile
territorial sea. In its statement made upon ratification of the Convention,
Panama reaffirmed its exclusive sovereignty over the "historic Panamanian bay".[36]
The Convention does not expressly recognize "historic bays (or titles)" but
briefly mentions them in its article 10(6) in connection with straight baselines
and in article 298 (1)(a)(i) concerning exceptions to the application of
compulsory procedures which entail binding decisions. Other countries, such as
Argentina, Brazil and Chile, have already rolled back their territorial sea
claims to 12 miles. Uruguay, as a Party to the Convention, has set claims to
the extent permitted by the Convention;

     (d) Europe and North America. This region has seen the largest increase
in ratifications and accessions to the Convention. Eleven States, five of which
are members of the European Union, have deposited their instruments of
ratification of or accession to the Convention.[37] Finland and Sweden reaffirmed
in their declarations made upon ratification that the exceptions from the

transit passage regime in straits provided for in article 35(c) of the Convention is applicable to the strait between those two countries, since in that strait the passage is regulated in part by a long-standing international convention in force.[38]

4. Harmonization with the provisions of the Convention

37. It is worth recalling that about half of the relevant legislation was adopted by coastal States between 1974 and 1979, at a time when all the compromises had not been finalized by the Third United Nations Conference on the Law of the Sea. Much of that legislation does not conform with the Convention, as finally adopted. It is to be noted also that the rate at which States are introducing or modifying legislation has not matched the recent rapid increase in the number of parties to the Convention.

38. The General Assembly, in its resolutions on the law of the sea, has repeatedly called on States to harmonize their national legislation with the provisions of the Convention and ensure their consistent application (e.g. resolution 50/23, para. 2). One area in which there would appear to be a widening gap is legislation on the continental shelf: of the 35 States that continue to claim a shelf based on the criteria contained in the 1958 Convention on the Continental Shelf (200-metre depth and exploitability), 21 are Parties to the 1982 Convention on the Law of the Sea.[39] These continuing claims are contrary to article 76 of the Convention, and to article 1 which defines the international seabed area. Another persistent inconsistency with the Convention are the claims of 15 States[40] for a territorial sea extending beyond 12 miles.

39. Among areas requiring closer harmonization with the Convention is the nature of the "jurisdiction" provided in article 56 with respect to the exclusive economic zone, as concerns marine scientific research, protection and preservation of the marine environment, and offshore structures and installations. The provision does not allow for "exclusive jurisdiction" in these areas, and yet much legislation does, particularly with respect to marine scientific research.[41] All such legislation merits review and harmonization with the provisions of the Convention, particularly in the case of States which are parties to the Convention.

40. In order to maintain an accurate and current database on national legislation on the law of the sea and related matters, the Secretary-General, in compliance with General Assembly resolutions 49/28 and 50/23, has circulated to all States a note verbale requesting them to communicate to him their relevant national legislation. So far, replies have been received only from Australia, the Bahamas, Belgium, New Zealand, Thailand, Tunisia, the United Arab Emirates and the United Kingdom of Great Britain and Northern Ireland. It is essential that such information be communicated to the Division so it can continue its efforts to monitor closely the implementation of the Convention by States and identify current trends in State practice.

D. Access to and from the sea

41. With respect to the interpretation of Part X of the Convention, concerning the right of access of landlocked States to and from the sea and the freedom of transit, mention should be made of declarations made upon accession and ratification of the Convention by Germany and the Czech Republic on 14 October 1994 and 21 June 1996, respectively.[42] Germany in its declaration states that transit through the territory of transit States must not interfere with the sovereignty of those States and that the rights and facilities provided for in Part X must in no way infringe upon the sovereignty and legitimate interests of transit States. Further, the precise content of the freedom of transit has in each single case to be agreed upon by the transit State and the landlocked State concerned, and in the absence of agreement concerning the terms

and modalities for exercising the right of access of persons and goods, transit through the territory of the Federal Republic of Germany is regulated only by national law, in particular with regard to ways and means of transport and the use of traffic infrastructure. The Czech Republic, on the other hand, states that the declaration by Germany cannot be interpreted with regard to the Czech Republic in contradiction with the provisions of Part X of the Convention.

42. Also to be noted is the reaffirmation by the General Assembly, in its resolution 50/97 of 20 December 1995, of the right of access of landlocked (developing) countries to and from the sea and freedom of transit through the territory of transit States by all means of transport, in accordance with international law. In the same resolution the Assembly also specifically welcomed the entry into force of the Convention.

V.   ACTIONS TAKEN BY THE SECRETARY-GENERAL

A.   Development of information systems and databases

43. The Division for Ocean Affairs and the Law of the Sea has continued to update and improve a computer-generated information system on national legislation relating to the law of the sea. The system currently contains national legislative acts from 144 States, as made available over the years to the United Nations, and is being continuously updated on the basis of submissions by States. As an ever increasing number of States are becoming Parties to the Convention and undergoing the process of harmonizing their national legislation with its provisions, the system will further expand. Ongoing improvements in the system have further strengthened the Division's capacity in monitoring the practice of States. Outputs from the system already serve as a useful tool for assisting States, particularly at the preparatory stage of their legislative process. The system is fully operational and the Division is able to respond to various queries by interested Governments and international organizations.

44. Pursuant to the General Assembly's call in resolution 49/28 for the development of 'a centralized system with integrated databases for providing coordinated information and advice, inter alia, on legislation and marine policy', the Division has been consulting with the most concerned organizations of the United Nations system, beginning with FAO and IMO. The Division and FAO have already established an understanding as to the handling of computerized data and information obtained, through electronic transmission, from FAO databases on national fisheries legislation and agreements.

45. For wider and speedy dissemination of general information on the law of the sea, the Division has been using the United Nations Gopher, a part of the Internet, for more than 18 months. At its address, gopher://gopher.un.org:70/11/LOS, the menu "Law of the sea" provides Internet users with many documents, including the full texts of the Convention, the 1994 Agreement on Part XI and the 1995 Agreement on fish stocks, together with information on their current status. Information on the Meetings of States Parties, the International Tribunal for the Law of the Sea and the International Seabed Authority are also available, as well as many other selected documents and press releases. On the basis of access statistics (about 1,000 inquiries a week), it may be concluded that the Law of the Sea menu at the United Nations site has become a convenient and reliable resource for permanent missions to the United Nations, various government departments, universities, intergovernmental organizations, non-governmental organizations and the interested public.

46. The Division is about to launch its own home page within the United Nations Home Page. Located at

http://www.un.org/depts/los

it will have a content similar to that of the Gopher but will be more graphical and "interactive". This will provide a more attractive option for advanced users and will also allow for the use of the United Nations server search menu option in order to speed access to the specific information and provide customized outputs.

47. While the focus of its activities in this area is on marine policy and law, including national legislation, the Division continues to support, as a co-sponsoring partner, the maintenance and development of the Aquatic Sciences and Fisheries Abstracts (ASFA), an international bibliographical information service. As an ASFA input centre, the Division monitors documents and publications relating to the law of the sea and other marine-related activities, including ocean technology, policy and non-living resources from which abstracts, bibliographical data and index entries are prepared for inclusion in the ASFA computer-searchable database and CD-ROM and the corresponding ASFA monthly journals.

B.   Support for dispute settlement mechanisms

48. As part of its dispute settlement mechanisms, the Convention provides for the procedures of conciliation, arbitration and "special arbitration".

49. The arbitral tribunal consists of five members who may be chosen from a list of arbitrators drawn up and maintained by the Secretary-General of the United Nations in accordance with article 2 of annex VII. The following nominations have been received as at 31 August 1996 for the States Parties indicated: Renate Platzöder (Germany); M. S. Aziz, P. C., S. Sivarasan, P. C., C. F. Amerasinghe and A. R. Perera (Sri Lanka); Sayed Shawgi Hussain and Ahmed Elmufti (Sudan).

50. The conciliation commission consists of five conciliators chosen from a list of conciliators drawn up and maintained by the Secretary-General in accordance with article 2 of annex V. As at 31 August 1996, only one State Party, the Sudan, had submitted the nominations of Dr. Abd ElRahman Elkhalifa and Sayed Eltahir Hamdalla.

51. As regards special arbitration, in accordance with article 2 of annex VIII, the following international organizations are required to draw up lists of experts in their specialized field and to send a copy of the lists to the Secretary-General of the United Nations: in the field of fisheries, FAO; for protection and preservation of the marine environment, the United Nations Environment Programme (UNEP); for marine scientific research, IOC; for navigation, including pollution from vessels and by dumping, IMO; or in each case by the appropriate subsidiary body concerned to which such organization, programme or commission has delegated this function.

52. The Secretary-General has received lists from FAO and IMO, and an updated list from IOC. A list has not yet been received from UNEP. The lists maintained by IMO, FAO and IOC currently contain experts from the following countries:[43]

    (a) IMO list. Bahrain, Bolivia, Cameroon, Cook Islands, Egypt, Fiji, Greece, Guinea, Italy, Mexico, Nigeria, Samoa, Sierra Leone, Singapore, Slovenia, Togo and Uganda;

    (b) FAO list. Bahrain, Cyprus, Egypt, Iraq and Uruguay;

    (c) IOC list. Argentina, Brazil, Bulgaria, Cameroon, China, Cuba, Finland, Georgia, Italy, India, Iraq, Jordan, Kuwait, Lebanon, Mauritius, Nigeria, Senegal, Saint Lucia, Sudan, Tunisia and Ukraine.[44]

53. The names of the experts are available from the IMO, FAO and IOC
secretariats as well as from the Division for Ocean Affairs and the Law of the
Sea.

VI. DEVELOPMENTS CONCERNING THE INSTITUTIONS CREATED
BY THE CONVENTION

54. Member States may wish to recall that the Convention provides for specific
linkages among the institutions of the Convention: between the International
Seabed Authority and the International Tribunal for the Law of the Sea as
concerns seabed disputes; and between the Authority, the Secretary-General of
the United Nations and the Commission on the Limits of the Continental Shelf as
concerns the delimitation of the national and international areas of the seabed.
The linkages between these institutions, and the overarching role of the General
Assembly with respect to the implementation of the Convention, is further
demonstrated in the decision of the Assembly of the Authority to seek observer
status at the General Assembly, and in the consideration given by the Meeting of
States Parties to the need for the Tribunal to report to the General Assembly.
These linkages will need to be specifically addressed in the relationship
agreements yet to be concluded between the Authority and the United Nations and
the Tribunal and the United Nations.

55. Consistent with its programmed activities, the relevant General Assembly
resolutions and the decisions of the Meetings of States Parties, the Division
for Ocean Affairs and the Law of the Sea has continued to provide support to the
new institutions established under the Convention.

A. International Seabed Authority

56. The International Seabed Authority, established by the Convention, with its
seat at Kingston, Jamaica, is the organization through which its members shall
organize and conduct activities of exploration for, and exploitation of, the
resources of the seabed and ocean floor and subsoil thereof, beyond the limits
of national jurisdiction (the Area), particularly with a view to administering
the mineral resources. The membership comprises States Parties to the
Convention and States non-parties that have consented to apply the 1994
Agreement on Part XI of the Convention provisionally (see paras. 19-22).

57. The current period has been particularly important for this new
international organization: the principal organs of the Authority - the
Assembly, the 36-member Council and the Secretariat - have all been established,
together with the subsidiary expert bodies, and the organizational work required
to assume the substantive functions entrusted to the Authority by Part XI of the
Convention and by the 1994 Agreement has been initiated.

58. The Assembly of the Authority held its first session in three parts: from
16 to 18 November 1994, from 27 February to 17 March 1995, and from 7 to
18 August 1995. Its second session was held in two parts: from 11 to
22 March 1996 and from 5 to 16 August 1996. The Assembly, the Council and the
subsidiary bodies will meet from 17 to 28 March and from 18 to 29 August 1997.

59. The membership of the Council, elected by the Assembly at its second
session, comprises four groups representing four sets of special interests, as
well as a group reflecting the principle of equitable geographical distribution.
The four special interest groups are consumers/importers of the minerals that
could be supplied from deep seabed sources (4 seats); investors in deep seabed
mining (4 seats); producers/exporters of such minerals from land-based sources
(4 seats); and developing States representing special interests (6 seats); a
further 18 seats were allocated to meet the requirements of equitable
geographical balance in the representation of the five regional groups.[45]

60. This complex composition of the Council and the application of a multiplicity of previously agreed criteria had given rise to severe problems. Before a final solution could be found which would meet the requirements both with respect to the four special interest groups and the overall geographical balance, there were many highly contested elements to be accommodated. Many possible variants were proposed for the implementation of the criterion of "ensuring equitable geographical distribution of seats in the Council as a whole".[46] Up until the very last, the total of the seats demanded by the five regional groups continued to stand at 37, which was one seat too many for the composition decreed by the Convention. Finally, a unique scheme was devised consisting of a "floating seat", combined with "burden sharing", by which each region would in turn give up one seat every year, except for the Eastern European Group which had three seats. This arrangement will apply for the initial four-year period.

61. During the second session also, the Assembly elected Mr. Satya N. Nandan (Fiji) as the Secretary-General of the Authority. The Secretary-General has taken office, together with a nucleus of staff.

62. During the resumed second session, a 15-member Finance Committee and a 22-member Legal and Technical Commission were established. The Finance Committee reviewed the proposed budget of the Authority submitted by the Secretary-General of the Authority, and on the basis of its recommendations, which were endorsed by the Council, the Assembly adopted a budget of the Authority for 1997. It totals $4.1 million, including the costs of 30 posts - 15 posts at the Professional level and above, and 15 posts at the General Service level.[47] The budget for 1997 takes account of the need to initiate the substantive work programme of the Authority after the initial organizational matters are completed.[48]

63. It will be recalled that, pursuant to section 1, paragraph 14, of the annex to the 1994 Agreement on Part XI, the budgetary requirements of the Authority for 1997 shall be met through the regular budget of the United Nations. The Secretary-General of the Authority has accordingly submitted the budget of the Authority for 1997, as approved by its Assembly, to the United Nations.[49]

64. A number of organizational matters have also been addressed by the Assembly and the Council of the Authority, and decisions have been taken concerning the extension of the provisional membership of States that have yet to ratify or accede to the Convention and the Agreement; the finalization of the Headquarters Agreement with the Government of Jamaica and the relationship agreement with the United Nations; and application for observer status for the Authority at the United Nations.[50] On this last matter, a number of Member States have submitted a proposal to the General Assembly concerning the observer status of the Authority (A/51/231). Certain staff arrangements, e.g., participation in the United Nations Joint Staff Pension Fund, have also been addressed.[51]

B.   International Tribunal for the Law of the Sea

65. The International Tribunal for the Law of the Sea has now been constituted with the election of its 21 members, and its initial budget has been approved by the States Parties. The judges held their first, executive session from 1 to 30 October 1996, and were sworn in on 18 October at an inaugural session of the Tribunal at its seat at Hamburg, Germany.

66. In accordance with the decision of the Meeting of States Parties, the United Nations Legal Counsel has designated an officer from the Division for Ocean Affairs and Law of the Sea to be in charge of the Registry from 1 August 1996 until the Tribunal appoints its Registrar. Preparations have reached an advance stage: an interim office for the Registry has been opened; initial staff have been recruited; the temporary premises provided by the host country are being handed over to the Tribunal; and a library is being

established with the support of the Friends of the Tribunal, a non-governmental organization.[52]

67.   The Tribunal, as a matter of priority, will be proceeding with negotiations on relationship arrangements with the United Nations and the International Seabed Authority,[53] and on the Headquarters Agreement with Germany.

1.   Election of the judges

68.   The election of the judges took place on 1 August 1996 during the fifth Meeting of States Parties.[54] The election had been postponed until that time by the first Meeting of States Parties in 1994.[55]

69.   The Statute of the Tribunal (annex VI of the Convention), in article 3, paragraph 2, provides that there shall be no fewer than three judges from each geographical group as established by the General Assembly of the United Nations. There being five such regional groups, the Meeting had to find a fair and reasonable way to fill the six remaining seats. The problem was compounded by the fact that one of the candidates was a national of a country that was not a member of any such group. The solution was to distribute seats as follows: African Group (5); Asian Group (5); Latin American and Caribbean Group (4); Western European and Other States Group (4); and Eastern European Group (3). The decision also provided that the candidate who did not belong to any regional group would, if elected, come within the allocation of the Western European and Other States Group.

70.   The Meeting of States Parties elected the 21 judges of the Tribunal from the list of 33 candidates.[56] They will serve for periods of three, six or nine years,[57] as follows: for the three-year term, Joseph Akl (Lebanon), Paul Bamela Engo (Cameroon), Anatoly Kolodkin (Russian Federation), Vicente Marotta Rangel (Brazil), P. Chandrasekhara Rao (India), Joseph S. Warioba (United Republic of Tanzania) and Rüdiger Wolfrum (Germany); for the six-year term, Hugo Caminos (Argentina), Gudmundur Eiriksson (Iceland), Edward A. Laing (Belize), Tafsir Ndiaye (Senegal), Tullio Treves (Italy), Alexander Yankov (Bulgaria) and Lihai Zhao (China); for the nine-year term, David H. Anderson (United Kingdom), Mohamed Marsit (Tunisia), Thomas A. Mensah (Ghana), L. Dolliver Nelson (Grenada), Choon-Ho Park (Republic of Korea), Budislav Vukas (Croatia) and Soji Yamamoto (Japan).

71.   The judges may be re-elected in accordance with the Convention. They are also required to continue to discharge their duties after the expiry of their terms of office until their vacant places have been filled; and even after they are replaced, they shall finish any proceeding which they may have begun before the date of their replacement.[58]

2.   Budget of the Tribunal

72.   The budget of the Tribunal for the initial period (August 1996- December 1997) was adopted by the fourth Meeting of States Parties (4-8 March 1996).[59] It also takes account of start-up costs incurred from April to July 1996, which could not be met by the Office of Legal Affairs, as originally requested, in view of the reduction in United Nations budget appropriations. The Meeting adopted the budget and related matters by consensus.

73.   It was also decided that the States Parties should pay 15 per cent of their assessed contribution in advance to enable the Secretariat to undertake preparatory work in Hamburg for the setting up of the Tribunal. A provisional scale of assessments, including both the current States Parties and States likely to be parties by 1 August 1996, was drawn up by the fourth Meeting for this purpose[60] and was later revised to accord with actual participation in the

Convention on that date. States Parties were required to pay their assessed contribution for 1996 in full by 15 August, and for 1997, by 15 January 1997; adjustments to these assessments are made according to the increases in the numbers of States Parties.

74. The Tribunal has been authorized to establish its own financial rules and regulations, to be submitted to the Meeting of States Parties for its consideration and approval. In the meantime, the Financial Regulations of the United Nations will apply.[61]

3. Other matters

75. The Meeting of States Parties has not been able as yet to complete its consideration of the draft agreement on the privileges and immunities of the Tribunal[62] and will return to the matter at its next meeting in March 1997.

76. The fifth Meeting of States Parties agreed that, although the report of the Secretary-General under article 319 of the Convention and his annual comprehensive report prepared for the General Assembly under the agenda item on the law of the sea should cover the activities of the Tribunal to some extent, the Tribunal should also be encouraged to present a report on its work directly to the Meeting of States Parties. The Meeting also recognized that since the proceedings of the General Assembly were of interest to the Tribunal, it should be appropriately represented at its sessions and should apply for observer status.

C. Commission on the Limits of the Continental Shelf

77. The purpose of the Commission is to facilitate the implementation of the Convention in respect of the establishment of the outer limits of the continental shelf beyond 200 miles from the baselines from which the breadth of the territorial sea is measured; its recommendations and actions shall not prejudice matters relating to the delimitation of boundaries between States with opposite or adjacent coasts. The relevant provisions are those contained in article 76 and annex II of the Convention.

78. As set forth in article 3 of annex II, the functions of the Commission are:

(a) To consider the data and other material submitted by coastal States concerning the outer limits of the continental shelf extending beyond 200 nautical miles, and to make recommendations in accordance with article 76 and the Statement of Understanding adopted on 29 August 1980 by the Third United Nations Conference on the Law of the Sea;[63]

(b) To provide scientific and technical advice, if requested by the coastal State concerned during preparation of such data.

79. It should be recalled that the functions of the Preparatory Commission for the International Seabed Authority and the International Tribunal on the Law of the Sea (1983-1995) did not include preparations for the Commission on the Limits of the Continental Shelf. The Meetings of States Parties, therefore, provide the first concrete opportunity for States to consider the implementation of the Convention in this regard, including in particular its provision requiring a coastal State to make its submission to the Commission within 10 years of the entry into force of the Convention for that State.

80. In an effort to prepare the Commission for its work, and without prejudice to the decisions it may take, the Division for Ocean Affairs and the Law of the Sea has attempted to identify some of the issues that will need to be addressed by the Commission when it begins examination of the submissions of coastal States. The Division convened a meeting of a representative group of experts

from 11 to 14 September 1995 in order to discuss certain technical and scientific aspects of the work of the Commission. On the basis of those discussions, the Division prepared a study entitled "Commission on the Limits of the Continental Shelf: Its functions and scientific and technical needs in assessing the submission of a coastal State", which was submitted to the fifth Meeting of States Parties for its information.[64]

81. The Commission on the Limits of the Continental Shelf will be established at the sixth Meeting of States Parties, to be held at United Nations Headquarters from 10 to 14 March 1997. The Commission will consist of 21 members, serving in their personal capacities, who are experts in geology, geophysics or hydrography; they will be elected by States Parties from among their nationals, with due regard to the need to ensure equitable geographical representation.

82. The first election of the members of the Commission was to have been held within 18 months after the date of entry into force of the Convention (annex II, article 2(2)), i.e., before 16 May 1996. However, at the third Meeting of States Parties (27 November-1 December 1995), it was agreed that the election would be postponed until March 1997. In view of the 10-year time limit for submissions to the Commission (article 4 of annex II), the Meeting of States Parties also added the proviso that should any State that was already a Party to the Convention by 16 May 1996 be affected adversely in respect of its obligations under this provision as a consequence of the change in the date of the election, States Parties, at the request of such a State, would review the situation with a view to ameliorating the difficulty in respect of that obligation.[65]

83. The Secretariat has since suggested a revised schedule for nomination and election of the members of the Commission.[66] Candidates may be nominated from 11 November 1996 to 5 February 1997. A State in the process of becoming a party may also nominate a candidate, but this will remain provisional until its instrument of ratification or accession is deposited, which would need to be done on or before 5 February. The list of candidates will be circulated by the Secretary-General on 14 February 1997. The first election will commence on 13 March 1997. All other procedures relating to the election of the members of the Commission as provided for in annex II of the Convention will apply. States Parties, at their fifth Meeting, approved this schedule and also decided that no changes will be made to the schedule unless agreed to by consensus.

84. At the request of the fifth Meeting of States Parties, the Division also prepared the draft Rules of Procedure of the Commission, issued on 26 July 1996.[67]

> VII. LEGAL DEVELOPMENTS UNDER RELATED TREATIES AND INSTRUMENTS
>   AND RELATED ACTIONS OF INTERNATIONAL ORGANIZATIONS AND
>   BODIES

> A. IMO conventions and instruments

> 1. Main developments

85. Steady progress has been made by Governments in ratifying the various IMO conventions, on which the United Nations Convention on the Law of the Sea is greatly dependent for the implementation of its provisions concerning navigation and the prevention of pollution from ships and from dumping. There remain only 5 out of 36 IMO conventions which are not yet in force.[68]

86. The following instruments have recently entered into force:

(a) The 1989 International Convention on Salvage (on 14 July 1996);

(b)   The 1992 Protocols to the 1969 International Convention on Civil Liability for Oil Pollution Damage (CLC Convention) and the 1971 International Convention on Establishment of the International Fund for Compensation for Oil Pollution Damage (FUND Convention) (on 30 May 1996). They more than double the amount of compensation possible, extend the scope of application of the parent treaties to the exclusive economic zones of contracting States, and introduce a more expeditious system of amending the limitation amounts by the IMO Legal Committee;

(c)   The 1994 amendments to chapters VI and VII of the 1974 International Convention for the Safety of Life at Sea (SOLAS 74) (on 1 July 1996);[69]

(d)   The 1994 amendments to chapter V of SOLAS 74 (on 1 January 1996).[70] They include a new regulation 8-1 in chapter V on the procedures for the adoption of ship reporting systems;

(e)   The 1994 amendments to SOLAS 74 adopted by resolution I (annex I) of the 1994 Conference of Contracting Governments (on 1 January 1996). They include a new chapter X regulating safety measures for high-speed craft and a new chapter XI on special measures to enhance maritime safety, such as the obligation to insert an IMO ship identification number on the ship's certificates, and port State control of operational requirements. Resolution I (annex II) contains a new chapter IX on the management for safe operation of ships;

(f)   The 1994 amendments to the 1978 International Convention on Standards of Training, Certification and Watchkeeping for Seafarers (the STCW Convention), replacing the text of its chapter V on training (on 1 January 1996);[71]

(g)   The 1993 amendments to the 1972 Convention on the International Regulations for Preventing Collisions at Sea (COLREG) (on 4 November 1995);[72]

(h)   The 1994 amendments to the Protocol of 1978 relating to the 1973 International Convention for the Prevention of Pollution from Ships (MARPOL 73/78), relating to its annexes I, II, III and V (on 3 March 1996). The amendments extend port State control to operational requirements regarding the prevention of marine pollution from ships.

87.   The following recent amendments and new instruments have been adopted:

(a)   The 1996 International Convention on Liability and Compensation for Damage in connection with the Carriage of Hazardous and Noxious Substances by Sea and the 1996 Protocol to amend the Convention on Limitation of Liability for Maritime Claims;

(b)   The 1995 amendments to the SOLAS Convention aimed at enhancing the safety of ro-ro passenger ships (expected to enter into force on 1 July 1997);[73]

(c)   The 1996 amendments to SOLAS chapters II-1, III, VI and XI (expected to enter into force on 1 July 1998);

(d)   The 1996 amendments to annex V (garbage) of MARPOL 73/78, providing a basis for the enforcement of the requirements of annex V and adding new regulations (expected to enter into force on 1 July 1997).[74]

88.   A number of new instruments and amendments are also under consideration in the relevant IMO bodies. A draft new annex VI to MARPOL 73/78, concerning air pollution, is scheduled to be adopted at the end of 1997.[75] A draft convention on wreck removal is being considered by the Legal Committee; it is also looking at the feasibility of a new convention on offshore mobile craft based on the ongoing work of the Comité Maritime International (CMI). This has been given a low priority in the work programme, however, owing to other more urgent items and some concerns that such a comprehensive instrument on offshore structures

might exceed the competence of IMO.[76] The IMO/United Nations Conference on Trade
and Development (UNCTAD) Joint Intergovernmental Group of Experts on Maritime
Liens and Mortgages and Related Subjects has started to consider a new draft
convention on the arrest of seagoing ships, in the light of the 1993 Convention
on Maritime Liens and Mortgages. Finally, the Maritime Safety Committee (MSC)
has decided to review the International Convention on Maritime Search and Rescue
(SAR), 1979, with a view to updating its provisions and to facilitating its
wider acceptance by Governments.[77]

89. In response to the considerable concern about the safety of bulk carriers,
the IMO Assembly in 1995 adopted resolution A.797(19) on safety of ships
carrying solid bulk cargoes (see A/50/713, para. 218) and resolution A.798(19)
on guidelines for the selection, application and maintenance of corrosion-
prevention systems of dedicated seawater ballast tanks. Work in this area has
high priority for the MSC; amendments to SOLAS for the purpose of enhancing the
safety of bulk carriers are scheduled to be adopted next year.[78]

90. The Marine Environment Protection Committee (MEPC), as IMO's focal point
for follow-up actions for the United Nations Conference on Environment and
Development (UNCED), adopted by resolution MEPC.67(37) entitled 'Guidelines on
incorporation of the Precautionary Approach in the context of specific IMO
activities', on an interim basis until further experience with their application
has been gained. The guidelines will be applied to the work of MEPC in the
first instance. Based upon the experience gained, their application could be
extended to the work of other Committees. The guidelines set forth a decision-
making and management framework for incorporation of the precautionary approach
in the programmes and activities of IMO.[79]

Impact of the entry into force of the United Nations Convention on the Law of
the Sea

91. Specific steps have also been taken to review IMO conventions and
instruments in the light of the entry into force of the Convention and to ensure
that IMO can respond appropriately, particularly in its capacity as the sole
"competent international organization" under the Convention in respect of
maritime safety and the prevention of pollution from ships. The IMO Council had
agreed on the importance of ensuring a consistent and coordinated approach to
the implementation of the Convention, as requested by the General Assembly in
its resolution 49/28, and decided to update a study prepared in 1987 on the
implications of the Convention for IMO, as well as to keep the present
arrangements for communication and exchange of information with the United
Nations Division for Ocean Affairs and the Law of the Sea under review. The
decisions of the Council were conveyed to the IMO Assembly at its nineteenth
session.[80]

2. Issues of compliance, control and enforcement

92. Over the last two years, IMO has adopted numerous measures aimed at
enhancing maritime safety by improving ship design, construction, maintenance
and equipment, as well as ship operations and management. To address the
continuing problem of the ageing world fleet, the Maritime Safety Committee,
together with the Marine Environment Protection Committee, has approved interim
guidelines for the systematic application of the "grandfather clause" (an IMO
practice by which a rule applies only to ships built on or after the date of its
entry into force), thus providing a strategy for avoiding undue gaps in
standards between new and existing ships, and eventually producing equivalent
standards.[81] (The 1995 amendments to SOLAS had already accomplished this for
ro-ro passenger ships.)

93. Most accidents and incidents at sea are caused by human error and/or
mismanagement, rather than by inadequacies in the instruments concerned. The
series of major amendments adopted in 1994 and 1995 to the SOLAS Convention and

the STCW Convention (see paras. 87-88) represent a major attempt to overcome these problems. In a wider sense, these amendments also aim at strengthening flag State implementation, port State control and the role of management.

94. Particular attention is drawn to the amendments to SOLAS chapter XI on special measures to enhance maritime safety, now in force. They require flag States, which authorize recognized organizations acting on their behalf to carry out the surveys and inspections required of them under a number of IMO Conventions (SOLAS, 1966 Load Lines Convention, MARPOL 73/78, and 1969 Tonnage Convention), to comply with the guidelines adopted in 1993;[82] subject bulk carriers and oil tankers to the enhanced programme of inspection in accordance with the guidelines adopted in 1993;[83] require all ships of 100 gross tonnage and above and all cargo ships of 300 gross tonnage and above to be provided with an identification number conforming to the IMO ship identification number scheme, adopted in 1987;[84] and make it possible for port State control officers inspecting foreign ships to check operational requirements "when there are clear grounds for believing that the master or crew are not familiar with essential shipboard procedures relating to the safety of ships" (regulation 4).

Flag State implementation and compliance

95. Since the International Safety Management Code will become mandatory on 1 July 1998 by virtue of the entry into force of SOLAS chapter IX on management for the safe operation of ships, the IMO Assembly in 1995 adopted guidelines for its implementation by Administrations (resolution A.788(19)). A second resolution (A.789(19)) contains minimum specifications for organizations recognized as capable of performing statutory work on behalf of the flag State Administration, in terms of certification and survey functions connected with the issuance of international certificates. SOLAS was amended to make the specifications mandatory.[85]

96. Standards of vessel operation still vary considerably: some shipowners accept their responsibilities and conduct their operations with integrity at the highest level; others move their ships quite deliberately to different trading routes, when Governments introduce stricter inspections and control. The Organisation of Economic Cooperation and Development (OECD) has called particular attention to the fact that owners and operators of substandard ships are able to operate at an unfair competitive advantage, amounting to as much as a 13 to 15 per cent saving on the annual running cost.[86] IMO has also noted in the past that some Governments readily accept the fees for registering ships under their flag, but fail to ensure that safety and environmental standards are enforced.[87]

97. Some Governments have been unable to implement measures as rigorously as is necessary to achieve the level envisaged in the conventions and which the maritime world expects. The IMO Subcommittee on Flag State Implementation has been reviewing Assembly resolution A.740(18) containing interim guidelines to assist flag States in the implementation of IMO instruments, including guidance on the infrastructure, personnel and capabilities necessary.

98. Doubts have been expressed in the Subcommittee about the sufficiency of the present, non-mandatory resolution (A.740(18)) to ensure compliance by the flag State with safety and pollution prevention conventions, and thus discourage substandard shipping. A suggestion was to develop a new binding instrument to set out clearly the responsibilities of flag States and the criteria for assessing their operation, to focus technical cooperation activities on those States unable to comply with the agreed criteria made; and to identify measures, including sanctions, to ensure that States fulfil their responsibilities as flag States.[88]

99. Another suggestion was to examine the existing legal possibilities provided through the United Nations Convention on the Law of the Sea for strengthening flag State responsibilities and for responding to any shortcomings in the

performance of flag States.[89] It was proposed that IMO could adopt a set of measures for concrete and practical implementation of that aspect of the law of the sea rule on suspension of proceedings against the flag State, which allows the coastal State to pursue the proceedings in cases where the flag State has repeatedly disregarded its obligations (see article 228(1)). Criteria are suggested for assessing repeated violations by a flag State, e.g., an above-average record of deficiencies detected by port States, and disregard of its obligation under article 217(6). It would be important also, it was suggested, to take account of bareboat chartering, noting that the Convention distinguishes (e.g., in articles 211(2) and (3) and 217(1) to (3)) between a flag State and a State in whose registry a vessel may have been entered.[90]

Port State control

100. Increasing failures by some flag States to effectively implement and enforce international standards for safety and pollution prevention has greatly strengthened the role of port State control as a policing mechanism for the shipping industry and a "safety net" for the flag State.

101. With SOLAS chapter XI now in force, port States can not only monitor compliance with applicable maritime safety and pollution-prevention standards, but also assess the ability of ships' crews to perform essential shipboard procedures. In addition, in 1995, the IMO Assembly amalgamated all previous Assembly resolutions on port State control in a new resolution (A.787(19)), making it easier to apply the relevant procedures of SOLAS, the 1966 Load Line Convention, MARPOL 73/78, the 1978 STCW Convention and the 1969 Tonnage Measurement Convention. The resolution defines, inter alia, the terms "clear grounds", "detention" and "inspection" of ships, and "valid certificates". It further provides guidelines for the detention and inspection of ships, for discharge requirements under annexes I and II of MARPOL and for control of operational requirements.[91]

102. Port State control in Europe continues to be intensified. The 1995 European Council directive 95/21/EC on port State control (in force on 1 July 1996) requires each member State to carry out a total number of inspections corresponding to at least 25 per cent of the number of ships entering its ports during the year. Certain categories of ships, e.g., oil tankers within five years or less of being phased out, will be subject to an expanded inspection. Deficiencies which are clearly hazardous to safety, health or the environment will lead to detention or stoppage of an operation and will not be lifted until the hazard is removed or until the ship can proceed, having fulfilled any necessary conditions. Where an inspection gives rise to detention, the port State must notify the flag State of all the circumstances in which intervention was deemed necessary. All costs of inspecting a ship which warrant detention are to be borne by the owner or the operator.[92] The 1982 Paris Memorandum of Understanding will be extensively amended in order to align it with the provisions of this 1995 directive,[93] and the European Parliament has called for its rigorous enforcement in order to eliminate substandard vessels from European waters. The European Parliament has also called on the Council to accept the introduction of a European ship register, EUROS, for ships flying flags of the States members of the European Union, including financial incentives to use it.[94]

103. A new regional Memorandum of Understanding on port State control was concluded among the maritime authorities of 20 Caribbean States and Territories in Barbados on 9 February 1996. It is practically identical to the other Memorandum of Understandings (the Paris Memorandum of Understanding in Europe, the Tokyo Memorandum of Understanding in the Asia-Pacific region, and the Viña del Mar Agreement in Latin America, all of which are now in force), but also covers inspections on smaller ships which trade mainly within the region. Barbados will provide the regional secretariat. The needs in the region are more comprehensive than the institution of port State control, and concern also the lack of adequate maritime administrative infrastructure, of national

legislation to implement the requirements of international maritime conventions, and trained personnel at all levels. IMO efforts and those of donor Governments will continue.

104. Other such regional agreements on port State control are under preparation in the eastern and southern Mediterranean, the Persian Gulf area, West and Central Africa, and the East Africa and Indian Ocean region.[95] The Tokyo Memorandum of Understanding has now been accepted by 17 maritime authorities, and a 30 per cent annual rate has been achieved on the inspection of ships visiting ports in the Asia-Pacific region.

Enforcement by port and coastal States

105. The IMO ship identification numbering scheme, now mandatory, will support the effective enforcement of mandatory ship reporting systems, routing systems and pollution prevention measures. Easier identification of ships contravening mandatory systems, or discharge limits, will provide coastal States with better evidence to support legal actions against contraventions.[96]

106. There have been increasing calls to strengthen enforcement in respect of vessels which have violated internationally applicable discharge criteria. Recent reports by some port States suggest that violations of MARPOL 73/78 provisions referred to flag States have not been prosecuted effectively or to the satisfaction of the port State. Many of these port States have taken a more aggressive enforcement posture; some have extended their jurisdictional reach by prosecuting violations within their exclusive economic zone rather than just within the territorial sea and have increased the severity of sanctions against ships flying the flags of other countries.[97]

107. The mandatory annual reports on non-compliance with MARPOL 73/78 for 1994, submitted by 23 countries, show that there has been a dramatic increase in the number of ships boarded for port State control (from 27,040 in 1993 to 52,806 in 1994), and in the total number of ships detained in ports or denied entry (from 117 in 1993 to 468 in 1994).[98]

Regional developments

108. In 1995, the States bordering the North Sea agreed to develop common procedures, through a legal instrument and/or other cooperative arrangement, to harmonize the exercise of flag State, port State and coastal State powers of enforcement, taking into account the relevant provisions of the United Nations Convention on the Law of the Sea.[99] They also agreed to work within the Bonn Agreement (1969 Agreement for Cooperation in Dealing with Pollution of the North Sea by Oil and other Harmful Substances) to use aerial surveillance as a more effective deterrent against illegal discharges.[100] In their proposal to IMO to designate the North Sea and its western approaches as a special area under annex I of MARPOL 73/78, the North Sea States have reported on the impacts of continuous operational discharges, legal and illegal, in the region, e.g., illegal discharges of oil exceeding 50 parts per million have been detected in the major shipping corridor between the Strait of Dover and the German Bight.[101]

109. Similar action to substantially decrease operational discharges and to eliminate the illegal disposal of ships' wastes has been taken by the Baltic States. The recently adopted Baltic Strategy for Port Reception Facilities for Ship-generated Wastes and Associated Issues aims to improve implementation of MARPOL regulations and those of the 1974 and 1992 Helsinki Conventions. Recommendation 17/11, adopted by the Helsinki Commission in March 1996, forms part of the Strategy and recognizes the importance of applying an effective, harmonized penal system having a deterrent effect on illegal operational discharges, thereby encouraging the use of reception facilities.[102]

Air pollution from ships

110. Questions have been raised as to what enforcement regime, consistent with
the United Nations Convention on the Law of the Sea, would apply to the new
annex VI on air pollution to MARPOL 73/78, which will be adopted in 1997. It
may be noted that articles 194(3)(a), 212 and 222 of the Convention refer only
to the prevention of pollution of the marine environment from or through the
atmosphere, and do not address pollution of the atmosphere that does not cause
pollution of the marine environment. While the substances to be regulated by
annex VI are viewed as atmospheric pollutants, the new annex will also regulate
their discharge into the marine environment. It will be necessary to decide
what inspection and enforcement regime is desired for annex VI that is
consistent with the Convention.[103] It has also been suggested that the new
annex VI should generally be interpreted and applied consistent with
international law, including the relevant provisions of the Convention.[104]

B. Rules regarding navigation

111. The rules regarding navigation, as set forth in the Convention, have
particular importance in other contexts, also including in particular those
affecting peace and security. It is to be noted, therefore, that the Treaty on
the South-East Asia Nuclear-Weapon-Free Zone, adopted in December 1995,[105]
specifically provides that it shall not prejudice the rights or the exercise of
these rights by States under the provisions of the Convention on the Law of the
Sea, particularly with regard to the freedom of the high seas, rights of
innocent passage and archipelagic sea lanes passage or transit passage of ships
and aircraft (art. 2(2)).

112. In the current reporting period, IMO bodies have continued to consider
several issues of importance to the interpretation and application of the United
Nations Convention on the Law of the Sea, particularly those entailing
restrictions of navigational rights in the form of mandatory ship's routing and
mandatory reporting systems. These restrictions of rights, which had become
essential for the safety of maritime traffic, are of commensurate benefit to the
protection of the marine environment.

1. Routing systems and mandatory reporting systems

113. IMO has given increased recognition to the environmental protection aspects
of ships' routing and reporting, as well as maritime safety, and has gradually
moved towards the introduction of mandatory measures.

114. A ship's routing system, which comprises sea lanes and traffic separation
schemes, may be designated or prescribed by States Parties in accordance with
the Convention. Pursuant to article 22, such designation or prescription may be
done by coastal States in their territorial sea, taking into account the
recommendations of IMO. However, under articles 41(4) and 53(9) of the
Convention, States bordering straits and archipelagic States may designate sea
lanes and prescribe traffic separation schemes or substitute them only after
agreement with IMO.

115. Routing systems are also intended to ensure the protection of the marine
environment. The Convention provides in article 211 (1) for the establishment
by States, acting through the competent international organization (IMO), of
routing measures designed to minimize the threat of accidents which might cause
pollution of the marine environment. The coastal State may, pursuant to
article 211(6), under the conditions stipulated therein, adopt special mandatory
laws and regulations for the prevention, reduction and control of marine
pollution in a clearly defined area in its exclusive economic zone where such
special laws and regulations are required for recognized technical reasons in
relation to its oceanography, ecology, resource use and maritime traffic

conditions. The mandatory measures can include not only the regulation of navigational practices but also the limitation of operational discharges. Such laws and regulations, however, can only be adopted by the coastal State after a determination by the competent international organization (IMO) that the conditions in the area concerned correspond to the requirements set out in article 211(6).

116. New regulation V/8 of the International Convention on the Safety of Life at Sea, 1974 (SOLAS), which was adopted by the Maritime Safety Committee last year (MSC.46(65)) together with the adoption of amendments to the General Provisions on Ships' Routing by the IMO Assembly in November 1995 (resolution A.827(19)), will, as of 1 January 1997, enable a State to propose for adoption by IMO routing systems for mandatory use by ships in areas beyond the territorial sea for the purposes of environmental protection (see A/50/713, paras. 93-94). The amendments established, in particular, a new definition of "mandatory routing system" as well as procedures for adopting a routing system with a view to protecting an environmentally sensitive area.

117. In addition, with the entry into force in 1996 of SOLAS regulation V/8-1, together with the Guidelines and Criteria for Ship Reporting Systems (MSC.43(64)), it is now possible for States to introduce mandatory ship reporting systems in order to improve the safety of life at sea, the safety and efficiency of navigation and/or to increase the protection of the environment. Participation in ship reporting systems is free of charge to shipping. Once a system is adopted by IMO, ships entering areas covered by ship reporting systems are required to report in to the coastal authorities, giving details of their position and identity, as well as such supplementary information that has been justified in the proposal for adoption as being necessary to ensure the effective operation of the system. This may include, e.g., the intended movement of the ship through the area covered by the system, any operational defects or difficulties affecting the ship and the general categories of any hazardous cargoes on board. Nothing in the SOLAS regulation or the Guidelines and Criteria is to prejudice rights and duties under international law or the legal regime of international straits. Ship reporting systems may or may not be operated as part of a vessel traffic service.[106]

118. The initiation of mandatory ship reporting systems rests with the Government(s) concerned. The first mandatory ship reporting systems to be adopted on 30 May 1996, under the terms of new SOLAS regulation V/8-1 by the Maritime Safety Committee (MSC)[107] are those of Australia and Papua New Guinea for the Torres Strait region and the inner route of the Great Barrier Reef (an area which has been designated a particularly sensitive sea area) and of France (off Ushant).[108]

119. New mandatory ship reporting systems, one submitted by Denmark and two by Spain, were approved by the Subcommittee on Safety of Navigation in July, for adoption by the Maritime Safety Committee.[109] The first covers the Eastern Channel of the Great Belt in order to ensure that large ships do not by mistake use the Western Channel of the Great Belt across which a low-level bridge has been constructed.[110] Spain's submissions concern the Finisterre Traffic Separation Scheme area, and the Strait of Gibraltar traffic separation scheme area; Morocco later joined with Spain on the latter.[111] The Russian Federation has reserved its position on these new systems, pointing to the fact that they are set up within the framework of VTS, and IMO has yet to complete work on new SOLAS regulations and guidelines addressing, inter alia, the issue of VTS beyond the limits of the territorial sea.[112]

120. While the Convention provides a basis for enforcement powers for environmental purposes, it does not specifically address a coastal State's authority to enforce mandatory navigation measures in its exclusive economic zone. Similarly, it does not allow the port State to institute proceedings against a foreign vessel for violation of international rules or standards relating to navigational measures in another State's waters save in exceptional

circumstances. It was pointed out that such authority should be made clear if
the new rules regarding mandatory routing and reporting measures are to have any
effect.[113] The Second Meeting of Legal Experts on Particularly Sensitive Sea
Areas (1993) concluded that the Convention provided a precedent for coastal
State enforcement of environmental measures without specifically addressing the
issue. It was further concluded that it would not be inconsistent with the
Convention for a port State to take enforcement action against a vessel under
its jurisdiction for violation of another State's laws.[114]

Application to straits

121. IMO resolution A.827(19) amending the General Provisions on Ships' Routing
includes also the Rules and Recommendations on Navigation through the Strait of
Istanbul, the Strait of Çanakkale and the Marmara Sea. The approval by IMO of a
mandatory ship reporting system for the Strait of Bonifacio in 1989 and for the
Torres Strait this year, the decision to establish a new traffic separation
scheme through the Strait of Malacca, as well as the proposals currently before
IMO for mandatory ship reporting systems in the Eastern Channel of the Great
Belt and the Strait of Gibraltar, also demonstrate the mounting concerns of
States bordering straits regarding pollution prevention and navigational safety.

122. Some of the measures taken by States bordering straits have met with
protests by user States, e.g., Turkey's decision to impose its national maritime
traffic regulations in the Strait of Istanbul, the Strait of Çanakkale and the
Sea of Marmara met with protests, including a protest to the Secretary-General
of the United Nations by the Russian Federation (see A/49/631, para. 121).[115]

123. Not only have some strait States sought more effective measures to ensure
safety of navigation in straits, but some also have called for consideration of
the sharing of the cost of such measures by all States which use the strait.
Indonesia, Malaysia and Singapore raised this issue when the IMO Subcommittee on
Safety of Navigation invited them to resubmit their proposal for the extension
and joining of the existing traffic separation scheme in the Malacca Strait to
the scheme in the Singapore Strait; the three States pointed out that
implementation of the proposed schemes required further hydrographic survey,
which would take up to three years to complete, as well as the provision and
upgrading of aids to navigation.[116] A joint survey of critical areas and
investigation of dangerous or unconfirmed shoals and wrecks in the straits of
Malacca and Singapore has now been agreed on among the three States and Japan
and is scheduled to begin at the end of 1996.[117]

124. As part of its follow-up action to UNCED, IMO will be considering potential
mechanisms by which user States and States bordering straits used for
international navigation could facilitate the development of appropriate
financial mechanisms, consistent with article 43 of the United Nations
Convention on the Law of the Sea, so as to provide for the establishment and
maintenance of necessary navigational aids and other safety aids to navigation
as well as the prevention, reduction and control of pollution from ships. Such
financial mechanisms are to be designed to achieve an equitable sharing of this
burden.[118] Some delegations expressed their opposition to the imposition of a
tax on shipping as a means of obtaining funds.[119]

Application to particularly sensitive sea areas

125. IMO mandatory ship reporting and routing systems can assist in the
protection of an area identified as a particularly sensitive sea area in
accordance with the 1991 IMO Guidelines for the Designation of Special Areas and
the Identification of Particularly Sensitive Sea Areas and thus may prompt more
States to submit proposals to IMO for the identification of such areas. It may
however also result in the continuation of the current practice of establishing
"areas to be avoided" without formally identifying an area as a particularly
sensitive one. A proposal was submitted by Cuba in 1996 to the Marine
Environment Protection Committee for the designation of the Sabana-Camguey
archipelago as a particularly sensitive sea area.[120]

126. The European Parliament, in its resolution of 27 March 1996 on the <u>Sea Empress</u> maritime disaster,[121] expressed the belief that member States should, in close cooperation with the Commission, establish the areas in their territory which are considered very sensitive or difficult for shipping and set rules under which such areas must be navigated, the type and size of vessels allowed to navigate in those areas and the weather conditions under which they can be open to shipping.

127. In the Ministerial Declaration of the Fourth International Conference on the Protection of the North Sea (8-9 June 1995), the Ministers, recognizing the need for adequate measures to protect environmentally sensitive areas which are also at risk from shipping, agreed to cooperate in order to make use of the range of routing measures available through IMO, including "areas to be avoided" and "deep-water routes". They also agreed to actively support the work of the European Union on establishing criteria for the identification of such areas and to monitor sites where routing measures are established in order to assess ships' compliance with such measures.[122]

128. There is substantial evidence, therefore, that IMO's work to develop criteria for the designation of particularly sensitive sea areas is an ongoing exercise. Moreover it has been suggested that there should be criteria for restricting or excluding ships carrying irradiated nuclear fuel (INF) from particularly sensitive sea areas (see also para. 225).

2. Sea lanes in archipelagic waters

129. Indonesia is the first archipelagic State to submit a proposal to IMO for the designation of archipelagic sea lanes in accordance with article 53 of the Convention.[123] Pursuant to article 53, paragraph 1, an archipelagic State may designate sea lanes and air routes suitable for the continuous and expeditious passage of foreign ships and aircraft through or over its archipelagic waters and the adjacent territorial sea.[124] Paragraph 9 requires an archipelagic State to refer proposals for the designation or substitution of sea lanes, or for the prescription or substitution of traffic separation schemes, to the competent international organization for adoption. IMO is the competent international organization; it may adopt only such sea lanes and traffic separation schemes as may be agreed upon with the archipelagic State.

130. Indonesia has proposed for adoption by IMO, if possible before the end of 1997, three archipelagic sea lanes running in a north-south direction. They are defined, in accordance with paragraph 5 of article 53, by a series of continuous axis lines. Indonesia has informed IMO in its submission that the coordinates and maps were submitted to the International Hydrographic Organization (IHO) for review. According to Indonesia, the proposed axis lines are the result of years of careful study of various factors, such as: the need of international transportation and aviation in transiting Indonesian waters; the hydrographic and natural marine conditions in and near the relevant axis lines; the intensity of coastal and inter-island navigation and overflight; the intensity of fishing activities, particularly of local artisanal fishermen; the existence of oil and gas exploration and exploitation; the presence of maritime installations and structures, as well as underwater cables and pipelines; the need to protect the marine environment and marine parks as well as the marine ecosystem; the development of coastal and marine tourism; the peace, stability and security of Indonesia, particularly the heavily populated coastal zones; the capacity of law-enforcement agencies to monitor navigation and overflight in relevant areas so that law and order can be safeguarded.

131. The proposal notes that, pending the designation of other sea lanes through other parts of the archipelagic waters, the right of sea lanes passage may be exercised in the relevant archipelagic waters in accordance with the Convention. For the purposes of safety of navigation and the safety of Indonesia, foreign tankers, vessels using nuclear energy, foreign vessels carrying nuclear

substances and other dangerous goods, foreign fishing vessels, as well as
foreign warships transiting through the Indonesian waters from one part of the
exclusive economic zone or the high seas to another part of the exclusive
economic zone or the high seas are recommended to transit through the sea lanes
in accordance with the Convention and other applicable rules of international
law.

132. The Indonesian proposal will be considered by the Maritime Safety Committee
at its session in December 1996. Since this will be the first time that IMO is
asked to consider a proposal for the designation of archipelagic sea lanes, it
has been proposed that IMO should first agree on and establish appropriate
procedures for adopting such sea lanes, which, it is suggested, must take into
account the legitimate rights and concerns of the archipelagic State and those
of the States whose ships and aircraft transit archipelagic waters.[125]

133. When Indonesia held a series of talks earlier this year with some of the
major users to solicit their views on the proposed three archipelagic sea lanes,
it was reported that the major users wanted Indonesia also to designate east-
west sea lanes which would then connect directly with the Strait of Malacca.[126]

C.   Offshore installations and structures

1.   Removal and disposal

134. Fifty-three countries in the world have offshore platforms; about 1,000 out
of 7,000 have been removed so far. Since most are in relatively shallow waters,
it has been estimated that 90 per cent of the platforms would need to be
completely removed following their decommissioning, in order to ensure safety of
navigation.[127]

135. States, when removing a platform (installation or structure), are required
under article 60(3) of the Convention to take into account the 1989 IMO
Guidelines and Standards for the Removal of Offshore Installations and
Structures on the Continental Shelf and in the Exclusive Economic Zone. They
provide that after 1 January 1998, no installation or structure should be placed
on any continental shelf or in any exclusive economic zone unless the design and
construction of the installation or structure is such that entire removal upon
abandonment or permanent disuse would be feasible.

136. While some regional conventions include provisions on the removal of
offshore installations and structures and have established guidelines and
standards relating thereto, for example in the Baltic Sea, North Sea, the
Mediterranean Sea and in the region covered by the Kuwait Regional Convention
for the Protection of the Marine Environment from Pollution, other regions have
no regime in place to regulate this activity. At a 1995 Economic and Social
Commission for Asia and the Pacific (ESCAP) training seminar on the removal and
disposal of obsolete offshore installations and structures in the exclusive
economic zone and on the continental shelf, participants recommended that the
contracting parties to the London Convention be informed of their concerns that
possible requirements for the total removal or a ban on disposal at sea of
offshore platforms would impose harmful consequences on the oil and gas industry
in the ESCAP region.[128] The 1992 Convention on the Protection of the Marine
Environment of the Baltic Sea requires complete removal and disposal on land.
In the North Sea/North-east Atlantic there is a moratorium on disposal at sea of
decommissioned offshore installations. A recent draft resolution of the
Assembly of the Council of Europe calls for the promotion of the complete
removal of discarded oil and gas installations through international
cooperation.[129]

137. The question of whether disposal at sea of decommissioned offshore
platforms should remain an option under the London Convention is awaiting the
final decisions on the amendment of the 1972 London Convention (see also

paras. 207-212 below). There are two amendment proposals: (a) to include within the definition of dumping "any abandonment or any toppling at site of platforms or other man-made structures at sea, for no other purpose than disposal"; and (b) to include among the wastes that may be considered for dumping, "vessels and platforms or other man-made structures at sea", with the following footnote: "Provided that material capable of creating floating debris or otherwise contributing to pollution of the marine environment has been removed to the maximum extent and provided that material dumped poses no serious obstacles to fishing or navigation".[130] The contracting parties had earlier concluded, pending the final decision in this area, that the parties should apply the London Convention and the IMO Guidelines and Standards in their national practice on a case-by-case basis.

2. Pollution from offshore activities

138. The Convention imposes the basic obligation on States to prevent, reduce and control pollution of the marine environment arising from or in connection with seabed activities subject to their jurisdiction and from artificial islands, installations and structures under their jurisdiction, which must be no less effective than international rules, standards and recommended practices and procedures (art. 208).

139. A proposal has been made to consider at the special meeting to amend the London Convention the possible development of future regulatory activities concerning offshore oil and gas exploration and exploitation under the Protocol, pending the outcome of the discussion on this matter in the Commission on Sustainable Development.[131]

140. The Commission on Sustainable Development has taken note of the report submitted by IMO on the implementation of Agenda 21, including its paragraph 17.30 (see A/50/713, paras. 235-237) and has agreed with IMO's conclusion that there was no compelling need at the time to further develop globally applicable environmental regulations in respect of the exploitation and exploration aspects of offshore oil and gas activities. The Commission encouraged States to continue relevant national and regional reviews of the need for additional measures to address the issue of degradation of the marine environment from offshore oil and gas platforms, as called for in paragraph 17.30, taking into account the relevant expertise of IMO, UNEP and the Division for Ocean Affairs and the Law of the Sea. To this end, the Commission called for partnership, within specific regions, between Governments and the private sector. The Commission encouraged relevant and competent international and regional bodies to make available appropriate inputs to expert meetings to be held in the Netherlands on offshore oil and gas activities.[132]

D. Archaeological and historical objects found at sea

141. As noted in the previous report (A/50/713, paras. 228-231), growing attention is being paid to the legal issues relating to the protection of the underwater cultural heritage, at both the international and the national levels. The Convention deals in general terms with these issues: for objects found beyond the limits of national jurisdiction, in article 149; and, within national jurisdiction, in article 303, which also refers to article 33 dealing with the contiguous zone.

142. Developments at the international level have centred on UNESCO. More recently, the International Law Commission (ILC) has also indicated its intention to study the question (see para. 146). In 1993, the Executive Board of UNESCO adopted a resolution by which it requested the Director-General to undertake a preliminary study on the advisability of preparing an international instrument for the protection of the underwater cultural heritage. That study (March 1995) concluded that "it would be feasible to elaborate a legal

instrument for this seriously threatened part of humanity's heritage".[133] Having examined the study, the General Conference of UNESCO, by resolution 28C(3.13) of 15 November 1995, considered that the technical and, in particular, the jurisdictional aspects should be discussed in full and invited the Director-General to organize, in consultation with the Division for Ocean Affairs and the Law of the Sea and with IMO, a meeting of experts on the underwater cultural heritage. Interested States were also invited to participate as observers in the meeting, which took place from 22 to 25 May 1996.

143. The expert meeting agreed that there was a need for a legally binding instrument for the protection of the underwater cultural heritage and that UNESCO was the appropriate forum for its adoption. Furthermore, there was general agreement that the incentives regarding commercial value, contained in some national salvage law, should not be included in the future instrument; that warships should be excluded from the scope of application of the instrument; that an approach based on flag State jurisdiction, and port State jurisdiction, supplemented by existing coastal State jurisdiction, was the more acceptable solution for enforcement; and that the establishment of a new zone under coastal State jurisdiction was not a realistic approach since it would affect the delicate balance achieved in the Convention on the Law of the Sea regarding the different maritime zones. The creation of protected underwater reserves or sanctuaries was favoured by some experts who were concerned with the protection of memorial sites. The need was also expressed for an international body charged with the promotion and monitoring of international cooperation regarding underwater cultural heritage.

144. The experts recommended also the adoption of a resolution by the UNESCO General Conference (October 1997) which would urge States to take provisional measures within the areas of their jurisdiction and through international cooperation to protect the underwater cultural heritage pending the adoption and entry into force of a convention, should the General Conference decide to draft such a convention.

145. At the request of the expert meeting, UNESCO is drafting a "reference document", taking into account the draft conventions prepared by the International Law Association[134] and the Council of Europe as well as the discussions of the expert meeting.[135] This will be submitted with the report of the expert meeting to the UNESCO General Conference in 1997.[136]

146. With respect to archaeological and historical objects beyond national jurisdiction, note should also be taken of possible future work by the International Law Commission on the topic "Ownership and protection of wrecks beyond the limits of national jurisdiction". The Working Group for the long-term programme of work of the ILC has identified this topic as one of three such future topics, noting also that the question had never been studied before and had practical value. The suggested provisional outline for future work includes such elements as the definition of "wreck", and the disposal of recovered vessels or objects;[137] a number of the elements suggested address issues also raised by the UNESCO expert meeting on the underwater cultural heritage. The ILC Working Group has stated, however, that it has no intention of overlapping with the competence of other institutions concerned. Should the Commission decide to take up the topic, therefore, there will be a need to clearly define the scope of its work, taking into account work in progress in other forums.

147. Further developments in this area are indicated by reference to the growing debate on protected marine areas, the adoption of new national legislation, as in the case of the above-mentioned South African law (see para. 34 (e) above) and statements such as that made by the Netherlands in its declaration on ratification of the Convention, which pointed out that while jurisdiction over these objects is limited to that allowed in articles 149 and 303 of the Convention, further development in international law on the matter might be needed.

E. Removal of wrecks

148. The subject of the removal of wrecks has long been inscribed on the long-term work programme of the IMO Legal Committee, and has now been upgraded to a second-level priority.[138]

149. Wrecks can constitute a danger to navigation, to the marine environment or to its coastline and related interests, particularly in the heavily trafficked waters of many enclosed and semi-enclosed seas and straits used for international navigation. They also raise such other practical problems as refunding or recovering the costs of removal. No specific instrument exists concerning removal of wrecks; nor does the Convention specifically refer to wrecks, although there are a number of relevant provisions conferring certain powers on coastal States whether with respect to ensuring the safety of navigation or the protection and preservation of the marine environment.

150. To address the practical problems of removing wrecks located beyond the territorial sea, Germany, the Netherlands and the United Kingdom submitted a draft International Convention on Wreck Removal to the IMO Legal Committee (October 1995). The draft is aimed at establishing uniform rules for wreck removal operations beyond the territorial sea and to achieve consistency with coastal State powers under the Convention. It recalls that article 221 of the Convention and the International Convention relating to Intervention on the High Seas in Cases of Oil Pollution Casualties 1969, as amended by the Protocol of 1973 thereto, provide for action by coastal States on the high seas following a maritime casualty, in order to protect their interests against pollution. As to scope, the draft leaves open the question of whether, and to what extent, it should apply to offshore oil and gas installations; State-owned ships would be excluded. It provides that the State whose interests are the most directly affected by the wreck would be responsible for determining whether a hazard exists. One of the criteria which can be taken into account by a State when determining whether a hazard exists, is whether the area is identified as a particularly sensitive sea area "according to guidelines adopted by the Organization, or established in accordance with article 211, paragraph 6, of the United Nations Convention on the Law of the Sea, 1982".[139]

151. The draft Convention on wreck removal has invited various comments concerning, most notably, the lack of a proper role for the coastal State and the introduction of an obligation of removal to the detriment of other options.[140] Also commented upon is the exclusion of State-owned ships, since decommissioned warships lost while under tow present serious problems; they also clearly fall outside the definition of warships in the Convention (art. 29).[141] The Subcommittee established on the subject by the Comité Maritime International has concluded that while there may be divergencies in State practice on the matter, the Convention on the Law of the Sea provides the necessary rights to coastal States to remove or require the removal of wrecks in the territorial sea. With regard to wreck removal beyond the territorial sea, this group of experts has concluded that there is no bar to concluding a new convention to confer on coastal States the right of wreck removal, as long as it is compatible with the Convention.[142]

F. Conservation and management of living marine resources

152. Several important milestones in the field of marine fisheries have been established at the global level in the past several years: the establishment of important commitments concerning high seas fisheries and fisheries within areas under national jurisdiction in chapter 17 of Agenda 21, adopted in 1992; the 1995 Agreement for the Implementation of the Provisions of the United Nations Convention on the Law of the Sea of 10 December 1982 relating to the Conservation and Management of Straddling Fish Stocks and Highly Migratory Fish Stocks (the 1995 Agreement on fish stocks); the 1993 Agreement to Promote Compliance with International Conservation and Management Measures by Fishing

Vessels on the High Seas (Agreement on flagging on fishing vessels); and the 1995 FAO Code of Conduct for Responsible Fisheries. It should be stressed, for the purposes of a comprehensive review of ocean affairs and the law of the sea, that the 1995 Agreement on fish stocks is an important component of the law of the sea, serving to strengthen dramatically certain general provisions in Part IX on the high seas, including in particular the strengthening of compliance, control and enforcement. Developments with respect to its implementation are contained in the Secretary-General's report of 4 October 1996 (A/51/383). Attention is also drawn to the Secretary-General's report of 25 September 1996 (A/51/404) concerning other special issues related to the conservation and sustainable use of marine living resources.

153. The Commission on Sustainable Development has specifically welcomed these major accomplishments in its first review of the implementation of chapter 17. It also recognized the significance of the Rome Consensus on World Fisheries of the FAO Ministerial Meeting on Fisheries (March 1995); decision II/10 of the Conference of Parties to the Convention on Biological Diversity (see para. 230 below); General Assembly resolutions 50/23, 50/24 and 50/25 on the law of the sea and sustainable use and conservation of marine living resources; and the Kyoto Declaration and Plan of Action on the Sustainable Contribution of Fisheries to Food Security (Kyoto, December 1995). In its first review of the implementation of chapter 17, the Commission dealt with its programme areas C and D, under the heading "Implementation of international fishery instruments".[132]

1. Regional fisheries bodies and arrangements

Atlantic Ocean

154. The International Commission for the Conservation of Atlantic Tunas (ICCAT), at its fourteenth regular meeting (10-17 November 1995), adopted various recommendations, including: supplemental management measures for Eastern Atlantic bluefin tuna; quota exemption for small-scale domestic bluefin tuna fisheries in the western Atlantic; establishment of percentage shares of total allowable catch; over-age and under-age provisions for States fishing for North Atlantic swordfish; and implementation of an alternative option for the conservation of undersized Atlantic swordfish and the reduction of fishing mortality. The Commission also expressed continuing concern over the increase in tuna fishing activities by fishing vessels of non-contracting parties in the ICCAT convention area, particularly those that failed to comply with the conservation and management recommendations adopted by the Commission. It urged non-contracting parties to take the necessary measures to comply with these internationally agreed regulatory measures for the conservation of the living marine resources and to submit statistical information on their catches of tuna and tuna-like fish in the ICCAT regulatory area.[143]

Eastern Central Atlantic

155. The Fishery Committee for the Eastern Central Atlantic (CECAF), at its thirteenth session (18-20 December 1995),[144] endorsed the conclusions of the CECAF Subcommittee on Management of Resources within the Limits of National Jurisdiction, recommending that fishing effort for several stocks within the national jurisdiction of several coastal States should be stabilized at current levels and that fishing effort should be reduced for demersal fish in the Gambia. CECAF also approved the recommendation of the Subcommittee that ICCAT's regulatory measures should be considered for adoption in the region, since a large quantity of tunas were caught there.

156. The Committee emphasized the need for fisheries to be integrated into the overall framework of coastal area management and to study issues of by-catch discarded at sea, including management measures and selective gear to reduce such discards. It was also agreed that management of stocks of high value

should be improved given their excessive exploitation in most areas of the region.

157. The Committee also discussed the relevance of the 1995 Agreement on fish stocks to East Atlantic fisheries. Although few straddling fish stocks occur in the region and highly migratory species are already covered by ICCAT, the Committee noted that many principles contained in the Agreement were applicable to all fisheries. Pointing particularly to the shared stocks occurring throughout the CECAF region, the Committee urged its members to consider becoming parties to the Agreement, to ensure that its provisions on highly migratory species were implemented by ICCAT and to implement the relevant provisions for the management of shared resources.

158. CECAF expressed its full support for the FAO Code of Conduct and emphasized its importance for management and development work in the region, highlighting the need for the Code and subsequent guidelines for its practical implementation to be widely disseminated in the appropriate languages.

Western Central Atlantic

159. The Committee for the Development and Management of Fisheries in the Lesser Antilles of the Western Central Atlantic Commission (WECAFC), at its fifth session (14-16 November 1995), adopted various recommendations including those concerning the specific problems of small island States and integration of fisheries into coastal area management.[145]

160. Following on the report of the WECAFC secretariat on the status of fishery resources in the region which indicated the need for resources assessment for most species, the Committee agreed that the States of the Lesser Antilles should collate the data on catches of demersal or reef resources, expressed as catches per unit area on individual island shelves and enhanced by rough indices on the fishing effort, to enable production modelling on an areal basis. This could provide useful information on potential production and the state of exploitation of the resource of individual island shelves.

161. The Committee agreed that, given the current trends in demand for fish and fish products and the absence of adequate management mechanisms and practices in the region, there was a growing risk of over-exploitation and eventual depletion of fishery resources. Social as well as economic forces were considered to play a substantial role in determining the attitude of Governments to fisheries management.

North-east Atlantic

162. The North-East Atlantic Fisheries Commission (NEAFC) held an extraordinary session (19-21 March 1996) on oceanic-type redfish and Norwegian spring spawning herring, and agreement was reached that appropriate management measures were needed for these stocks. A 1996 total allowable catch of 153,000 tonnes was recommended for the redfish, for allocation among NEAFC members, and the introduction of a monthly catch reporting system for the herring. NEAFC also called on non-contracting parties to cooperate with it to ensure respect of the management measures.[146]

North-west Atlantic

163. The Fisheries Commission of the Northwest Atlantic Fisheries Organization (NAFO), at its seventeenth annual meeting (11-15 September 1995), adopted recommendations concerning control and enforcement measures as well as conservation of fish stocks.[147] It agreed on amendments which would introduce the following: objectivity in the distribution of inspections; transmission of information from inspections to provide advance notification of apparent infringements; reporting of catch on board fishing vessels entering and exiting the regulatory area; establishment of minimum mesh size for capelin fishery;

amended provisions on dockside inspections; follow-up of apparent infringements; pilot project for observer and satellite tracking; effort plans and catch reporting; minimum fish size of 30 cm for Greenland halibut; and adoption of processed length equivalents for Atlantic cod, American plaice and yellowtail flounder.

164. On the recommendation of its Standing Committee on Fishing Activity of Non-Contracting Parties in the regulatory area, the NAFO General Council agreed to undertake diplomatic démarches to Belize, Honduras, Sierra Leone and New Zealand asking them to withdraw their vessels from the NAFO regulatory area. The General Council also emphasized that any such fishing activity would be contrary to the letter and spirit of the then draft Agreement on fish stocks and the objectives of NAFO.[148]

South-west Atlantic

165. The South Atlantic Fisheries Commission, composed of Argentina and the United Kingdom, adopted a joint statement on 21 November 1995 whereby a commitment was made to reach an understanding in 1996 on the conservation of fish stocks in the region in which priority would be given to the conservation, principally of illex squid and southern blue whiting, on the basis of the best scientific advice available. It was agreed that fishing activity for illex stock ought to be tightly controlled throughout the south-west Atlantic, with no increase in the level of fishing in the relevant areas. The statement expressed concern over the high level of fishing activity directed at the illex stock on the high seas, which could undermine the conservation goals of the Commission, and consequently recommended to Governments that appropriate measures be taken to monitor and exchange relevant information.[149] The implications of the 1995 Agreement on fish stocks for the work of the Commission would be considered at a future time.

166. The States members of the Zone of Peace and Cooperation of the South Atlantic, at their fourth meeting, in April 1996, in a decision on illegal fishing activities in the Zone, decided to examine at their fifth meeting the possibility of establishing cooperative ways and means in support of the surveillance of illegal fishing activities and to prepare a report thereon.[150]

Inter-American region

167. The Inter-American Convention for the Protection and Conservation of Sea Turtles, adopted on 5 September 1996, will be opened for signature on 1 December 1996; Venezuela will be the depository country. The area of implementation of the Convention will include the waters of the Atlantic Ocean, the Gulf of Mexico, the Caribbean and the Pacific Ocean, where the parties exercise sovereignty or sovereign rights over living marine resources. The Convention provides, in its article III, that these rights are in accordance with international law, in particular as it is reflected in the United Nations Convention on the Law of the Sea. The Latin American Fisheries Development Association (OLDEPESCA) will serve as the temporary secretariat to the Convention.

Antarctica

168. At its fourteenth annual meeting (24 October-3 November 1995), the Commission for the Conservation of Antarctic Marine Living Resources (CCAMLR) adopted various decisions for the 1995/96 season, including precautionary catch limits for several fish stocks, and for the development of a new survey of krill in area 48 to take specific account of the need to derive precautionary catch limits. With regard to the status of dependent species, including incidental mortality of marine animals during fishing operations, the Commission endorsed the advice of its Scientific Committee aimed at reducing seabird mortality and improving fishing efficiency. It also endorsed a number of specific recommendations by its Standing Committee on Observation and Inspection

supplementing relevant provisions of the system of inspection, including the extent to which the new regulations would not apply to certain types of fisheries. As to the operation of the scheme of international scientific observation, the Committee recognized that it was the only means to obtain reliable data and information from fisheries and to educate ships' crews in the use of measures aimed at mitigating the incidental mortality of seabirds.[151]

Indian Ocean

169. The Agreement for the establishment of the Indian Ocean Tuna Commission (A/49/631, para. 167) entered into force on 27 March 1996 following the deposit of the tenth instrument of acceptance by the Republic of Korea. The future role of this Commission, dealing with highly migratory species, would be affected by the 1995 Agreement on fish stocks, particularly its article 10 which details the functions of subregional and regional fisheries management organizations and arrangements.[152]

South Pacific

170. The twenty-sixth South Pacific Forum (13-15 September 1995) urged all interested States to become parties as soon as possible to the 1995 Agreement on fish stocks. The Forum considered that comprehensive regional fisheries management arrangements, and a structure consistent with the Agreement to administer them, should be developed as a matter of urgency. Such management arrangements must be based on a precautionary approach to ensure the sustainable exploitation of the region's valuable tuna resources.

171. The Forum also noted significant progress over 1994 in the implementation of regional fisheries commitments, including the conclusion of the Arrangement for Regional Fisheries Access; the significant contribution of the region to the preparation of the 1995 Agreement; the work to develop comprehensive regional fisheries management arrangements; progress in the development of the regional vessel monitoring system; and progress in the pursuit of multilateral fisheries access arrangements. Continued efforts will be made to conclude additional multilateral fishing agreements with distant water fishing States under which no member country would be made worse off than under its existing bilateral fishing agreements.[153]

2. Other developments

172. Continuing concern with overcapacity in fishing fleets and overfishing of fish stocks, as well as the lack of employment alternatives for European fishermen in the fishing industry, have led the Committee on Agriculture and Rural Development of the Parliamentary Assembly of the Council of Europe to produce a comprehensive report on fisheries management policies, including a draft resolution and draft order for approval by the Assembly.[154]

173. The Committee stressed the importance of prudent long-term management policies and their basis in detailed knowledge and understanding of the marine ecosystem concerned and the interrelationships between species, as well as a sound understanding of the interdependence between technical, biological and economic factors. It stressed the need to greatly improve multispecies fisheries management policies in areas of major importance for Europe, European fishermen and related industries. Important objectives for further development of global and regional legal regimes and management policies would be the re-establishment of a balance between fishing efforts and fishing yields, proper enforcement of agreed conservation measures, the regulation and control of all catches (including those from the high seas) and the offsetting of all catches (including discards) against the determined quotas for each stock. Emphasis was also placed on the importance of fully involving fishermen and other groups concerned in the development and implementation of fisheries management policies, and on the maintenance of a varied and differentiated fishing fleet -

with coastal fisheries at the core and with a capacity in keeping with the objective of sustainable development. The Committee also called attention to the need to foster research and development on fisheries, and their marine ecosystems, in European waters, taking into account the links with other uses, and proposed that a study be made of the many relevant institutional arrangements and activities. Furthermore, it urged the creation of a European programme or marine agency, as recommended earlier by the Assembly in its resolution 1012 (1993), to coordinate research into marine ecosystems, formulate and monitor conservation and exploitation policies, and provide information for the public and for all policy makers concerned with issues of the sustainable development of living marine resources.

174. The continued viability and economic stability of fishing around the world has also invited the attention of international bodies with more general mandates. The Inter-Parliamentary Union has called on States to ratify the 1982 Convention on the Law of the Sea and the 1995 Agreement on fish stocks. In the relevant resolution, adopted on 19 April 1996, it called for legislation and other measures to ensure responsible fisheries management, including application of the precautionary principle and provision of appropriate enforcement mechanisms and dispute resolution. It acknowledged the need to restructure fishing fleets and eliminate government subsidization of the fishing industry to overcome the problems of excessive fishing capacity and promote a fishing industry that operates on a commercial basis. Of importance also for the implementation of the 1995 Agreement on fish stocks is the resolution's call for more active participation in international and regional bodies dealing with the conservation and sustainable use of marine and coastal biodiversity and for the review of their programmes with a view to improving existing measures and developing new actions.[155]

3. Conservation, management and study of marine mammals

175. Marine mammals worldwide continue to suffer from heavy pressure from incidental catches in coastal small-scale artisanal fisheries and high seas driftnet fisheries. Other detrimental factors of particular concern are mass mortality events, pollution and habitat loss and degradation, especially in coastal areas. Articles 65 and 120 of the Convention refer to marine mammals as follows: "... States shall cooperate with a view to the conservation of marine mammals and in the case of cetaceans shall in particular work through the appropriate international organizations for their conservation, management and study".

(a) UNEP-FAO Global Plan of Action

176. The Global Plan of Action for the Conservation, Protection and Utilization of Marine Mammals (MMAP) is currently undergoing revision by the Planning and Coordinating Committee (PCC), which is composed of both inter-governmental (UNEP, FAO, IOC/UNESCO and Inter-American Tropical Tuna Commission (IATTC)) and non-governmental organizations (World Conservation Union (IUCN), World Wildlife Fund (WWF), Greenpeace and International Fund for Animal Welfare (IFAW)).[156]

177. A scientific advisory committee provides advice both to the PCC and the UNEP secretariat on such key elements of the Action Plan as enhancing understanding of large-scale mortalities of marine mammals, investigating and evaluating such events and providing technical assistance in non-emergency situations. An emergency response team is intended to intervene and carry out quick investigations of marine mammal stranding and die-off events which otherwise might go uninvestigated. A fund has been established to cover basic requirements for the work of a task force once it is deployed.[157] The PCC, at its most recent meeting (May 1996), discussed the work of the emergency response team, including a report on the sperm whale mortalities in the North Atlantic. The team has had other consultations in the past on die-offs around the world, but there has been no deployment of the task force.

178. The PCC has decided to conduct a comprehensive review of the legal aspects of the conservation of aquatic mammals, including the legal framework provided by the United Nations Convention on the Law of the Sea; the provisions of new related conventions and other principles; and new approaches to the enforcement of legal measures. Account will also be taken of threats to aquatic mammals and their habitat (e.g., effects of fisheries and degradation of habitats). The review is expected to be published by the end of 1996.

(b) International Whaling Commission

179. At its forty-eighth annual meeting (24-28 June 1996), the International Whaling Commission (IWC) adopted several decisions regarding the management of marine mammals and small cetaceans.[158]

180. With respect to catch limits for commercial whaling, the Commission did not adopt a proposal by Japan for an interim relief allocation of 50 minke whales to be taken by coastal community-based whaling, but agreed to hold a workshop to consider such whaling in four small coastal communities in Japan. Norway has lodged objections to the relevant items in the schedule and has exercised its right to set national catch limits for its coastal whaling operations for minke whales. The Commission passed a resolution calling on Norway to cease all whaling activities under its jurisdiction.

181. Although the Commission has accepted and endorsed the revised management procedure for commercial whaling, it has noted that work on a number of issues, including specification of an inspection and observer system, must be completed before the Commission would consider establishing catch limits other than zero.

182. The Commission agreed on various catch limits for aboriginal subsistence whaling in accordance with its 1994 decision to undertake a major review of stocks subject to such whaling and their associated catch limits.

183. The Commission also considered other issues, such as whale killing methods, the legal competence of IWC to manage small cetaceans, the environment and whale stocks, and whale watching and the research programme under a newly designated IWC-SOWER (Southern Ocean Whale and Ecosystem Research) programme. It adopted a resolution calling on Japan to refrain from issuing permits for scientific catches.

(c) Regional developments

184. The Council of the North Atlantic Marine Mammal Commission (NAMMCO), at its sixth meeting in Tromso, Norway (27 and 28 March 1996),[159] adopted the Joint NAMMCO Control Scheme for Hunting of Marine Mammals, which provides both national inspection of coastal whaling and an international observation scheme. Its purpose is to ensure a common standard in the control systems of member countries, as well as to provide NAMMCO with the opportunity of monitoring the extent to which national regulations for the management of marine mammals are upheld.

185. An agreement for the conservation of cetaceans of the Black and Mediterranean seas was drafted within the framework of the Bonn Convention on the Conservation of Migratory Species of Wild Animals, at a negotiating meeting in September 1995.[160] Since the draft is considered to affect fisheries regulations, the European Commission and the States members of the European Community have pointed to the need to reconcile its provisions with the Common Fisheries Policy. Similar concerns as to the impacts of conservation measures for small cetaceans on fisheries have been expressed by the Black Sea States, which are developing a common fisheries policy under the auspices of the Convention on fisheries and conservation of the living resources of the Black Sea and the future Black Sea Fisheries Commission. The geographic scope of the draft agreement will be determined largely by the results of negotiations between the Russian Federation and Ukraine.[161]

186. UNEP activities under the Global Action Plan include support for the development of a marine mammal component within the Black Sea Environment Programme, funded by the Global Environment Facility (GEF) and managed by the World Bank. Priorities for regional cooperation were discussed at a meeting of six Black Sea countries (December 1995), including coordination of a population census and assessments of incidental mortality. Training workshops are planned, which will likely also count on assistance from the biodiversity component of the programme.

G.   Developments in international environmental law and policy

187. The Convention provides the overall legal framework for marine environmental protection and resource conservation. It expressly recognizes, and indeed mandates, the need for further elaboration of international rules, standards and recommended practices and procedures for marine environmental protection at the global and regional levels, but at the same time ensures that these more specialized processes are guided by its basic structure.

188. The relationship between the obligations that States have under Part XII and other relevant parts of the Convention to protect and preserve the marine environment, and the obligations that they have assumed under the wide range of global and regional instruments, which either directly or indirectly seek to protect the marine environment, is dealt with in article 237. Paragraph 2 provides that specific obligations assumed by States under special conventions, with respect to the protection and preservation of the marine environment, should be carried out in a manner consistent with the general principles and objectives of the Convention.

189. Such developments as the draft Protocol amending the London Dumping Convention and the decision by the Conference of Parties to the Convention on Biological Diversity to study the relationship between that Convention and the United Nations Convention on the Law of the Sea demonstrate the increasing attention that States are giving to the need to ensure uniformity and compatibility between the Convention and subsequent legal developments. Moreover, recent proposals to and discussions at IMO meetings indicate that States are increasingly looking to the provisions of the Convention to effectively enforce other conventions in the maritime field.

190. At the regional level also, States emphasize the importance of the Convention as a framework for all legal measures contributing to the protection and preservation of the marine environment. For example, the States members of the Zone of Peace and Cooperation of the South Atlantic, at their fourth meeting in April 1996, stressed regional cooperation in accordance with the Convention. In a Decision on the Protection of the Marine Environment, Member States that had not done so were encouraged to ratify or adhere to multilateral conventions and protocols dealing with the protection and preservation of the marine environment, including the Convention, the 1995 Agreement on fish stocks; the London Convention on dumping; and MARPOL 73/78.[162]

191. The Convention is increasingly recognized as making an important contribution to the new and emerging field of international law dealing with sustainable development. Attention is therefore drawn to the work of the Commission on Sustainable Development in respect of international legal instruments and mechanisms, in which it is assisted by the Expert Group on the identification of Principles of International Law for Sustainable Development. It brings together experts from organizations of the United Nations system, multilateral financing institutions, universities and secretariats of relevant conventions, including the United Nations Division for Ocean Affairs and the Law of the Sea. The Commission has emphasized the importance of compliance and monitoring mechanisms of international agreements, including reporting requirements, and the need for capacity-building to improve compliance, monitoring, inspection and enforcement of international obligations.

Furthermore, the Commission specifically recognized the need for consolidation and integration of procedures and cooperation among the secretariats of different conventions to this end.[163] It should be noted that the system of law of the sea focal points, developed by the Division to ensure coordination on all matters pertaining to the implementation of the Convention, continues to be expanded to include, inter alia, the secretariat of the Convention on Biological Diversity.

1. Review of the implementation of chapter 17 of Agenda 21

192. The Commission on Sustainable Development, at its fourth session (18 April-3 May 1996), reviewed chapter 17 of Agenda 21, thus completing its review of all the chapters. Chapter 17 consists of 7 programme areas, the last of which deals with small island developing States, a subject which is dealt with separately by the Commission.[164] The review of chapter 17 was based on the report of the Secretary-General,[165] which was prepared by the Administrative Committee on Coordination (ACC) Subcommittee on Oceans and Coastal Areas, established in 1993 by the Inter-Agency Committee for Sustainable Development (IACSD), inter alia, for the purpose of preparing the necessary reports for the Commission.

193. The Commission welcomed the very important advances made in this area since 1992. In addition to the entry into force of the Convention, explicitly recognized as being fundamental to the implementation of chapter 17, the Commission welcomed also the 1994 Agreement on Part XI, as well as the 1995 Agreement on fish stocks, the 1993 Agreement on fishing vessels, the FAO Code of Conduct for Responsible Fisheries and the Global Programme of Action for the Protection of the Marine Environment from Land-based Activities (see paras. 198-205). It also recognized such other important international policy statements as the Kyoto Declaration and Plan of Action, and the Jakarta Mandate (decision II/10 of the Parties to the Convention on Biological Diversity). In its decision 4/15 concerning, inter alia, chapter 17 issues, it addressed primarily the implementation of international fishery instruments and international cooperation and coordination.[166]

194. The main recommendations of the Commission, submitted to the General Assembly by the Economic and Social Council, concern the following:

(a) The establishment of institutional arrangements for the implementation of the Global Programme of Action for the Protection of the Marine Environment from Land-based Activities and for periodic intergovernmental review (a draft resolution for adoption by the General Assembly at its fifty-first session);[167]

(b) The introduction of periodic, intergovernmental review of "all aspects of the marine environment and its related issues" (by the Commission, on the basis, inter alia, of a report by the ACC Subcommittee) (see also paras. 238-242 below);

(c) Reporting to the Secretary-General on the implementation of international fishery instruments and on "progress made in improving the sustainability of fisheries" (by FAO);

(d) A review of the ACC Subcommittee with a view to improving its status and effectiveness, including the need for closer inter-agency links (by the Secretary-General);

(e) A review of the Joint Group of Experts on the Scientific Aspects of Marine Pollution (GESAMP) with a view to improving its effectiveness and comprehensiveness while maintaining its status as a source of agreed, independent scientific advice (by GESAMP sponsoring organizations);

(f) Ongoing review of the need for additional measures to address the issue of degradation of the marine environment from offshore oil and gas development (by IMO, UNEP and the Division) (see para. 140 above).

Final decisions on important aspects of these recommendations will await the special session of the General Assembly on sustainable development, to be held in June 1997.

ACC Subcommittee on Oceans and Coastal Areas

195. In preparation for the special session of the General Assembly, the Commission for Sustainable Development at its fifth session, in April 1997, will consider a report of the Secretary-General giving an overall assessment of the progress achieved in the implementation of Agenda 21 and recommending future actions and priorities, including recommendations on the future role of the Commission.[168] Those elements of the report which relate directly to chapter 17 issues will again be prepared by the ACC Subcommittee.

196. The ACC Subcommittee on Oceans and Coastal Areas has initiated follow-up action to decisions of the Commission of relevance to chapter 17. Among other actions, the Subcommittee agreed that the Global Programme of Action for the Protection of the Marine Environment from Land-based Activities would be considered as the cooperative programme framework for programme areas A (integrated management and sustainable development of coastal areas, including exclusive economic zones) and B (i) (marine environmental protection: land-based sources).

197. The Subcommittee also discussed at its fourth session (May 1996) procedures for strengthening inter-agency cooperation in project planning, particularly ways in which an agency originating a project should ascertain the possibilities for participation by other member organizations, as well as any potential overlaps identified. The United Nations and the United Nations Development Programme (UNDP) have volunteered to test the new procedures with the proposed TRAIN-SEA-COAST project document entitled "Training support to GEF international waters operational programmes" (see also paras. 304-308 below).

2. Global Programme of Action on Protection of the Marine Environment from Land-based Activities

198. The Washington Declaration and the Global Programme of Action for the Protection of the Marine Environment from Land-based Activities, adopted by the Intergovernmental Conference (October/November 1995), have been submitted to the General Assembly (A/51/116) under the item on the law of the sea by the United States, as host Government of the Conference. The Conference was convened by UNEP, pursuant to the request made in chapter 17 of Agenda 21, and UNEP will be responsible for facilitating the implementation of the Global Programme of Action.

199. While this new instrument has no binding character, it rests on a firm international legal basis, most particularly on the United Nations Convention on the Law of the Sea,[169] and also on the 1972 London Convention, particularly in the light of its forthcoming amendment, and on the numerous regional instruments for the protection of the marine environment against land-based activities, including most recently the revised Protocol on Protection of the Mediterranean Sea from Pollution by Land-based Sources and Activities (March 1996). Also important are the requirements of the United Nations Framework Convention on Climate Change, the Convention on Biological Diversity and the Basel Convention on the Control of Transboundary Movements of Hazardous Wastes and their Disposal and related regional instruments.

200. The Global Programme of Action is expected to contribute substantially to the progressive development of international law, including the law of the sea;

in particular, it calls for the development of "a global, legally binding instrument for the reduction and/or elimination of emissions, discharges and, where appropriate, the elimination of the manufacture and use of the persistent organic pollutants identified in decision 18/32 of the Governing Council" of UNEP.[170]

201. The recommendations of the Commission on Sustainable Development, currently before the General Assembly in a draft resolution for its adoption (A/C.2/51/L.2), are particularly notable for the emphasis placed on the need for States to take direct action in all the relevant governing bodies of the United Nations system to ensure the effective implementation of the Global Programme,[171] and also to ensure that such action is coordinated, particularly for the efficient development of a clearing-house mechanism for the main source categories.[172]

202. The approach taken by UNEP to the implementation of the Global Programme of Action has involved extensive consultation with its regional seas programmes, with organizations of the United Nations system, particularly those assigned responsibilities to develop the clearing-house mechanism,[173] and with Governments and non-governmental organizations. The final form of the institutional arrangement, including particularly the role of the UNEP Water Unit and the Regional Seas Programme, will be approved by the UNEP Governing Council at its nineteenth session in 1997. It should be noted that UNEP has subsumed the previous Oceans and Coastal Areas Activity Centre in the new Water Unit, set up to deal in an integrated fashion with all water problems; the World Bank has also adopted a similar approach.

203. Considerable concern has been expressed that, although the Global Programme of Action has widespread support on a conceptual basis,[174] there has been no evidence that it would be given high priority in the current activities of the organizations of the United Nations system. Inter-agency consultations convened by UNEP (May 1996) have underscored that some organizations do not currently have a clear mandate or the resources for implementing the Global Programme, nor is there additional funding with respect to new activities. Moreover, there has not as yet been any clear indication as to what assistance might come through the avenue of the Global Environmental Facility.

204. As a result of inter-agency consultations, a closer look is being given to strengthening support given by the system at the regional level; however, more specific regional requirements will need to be articulated before the international agencies can render effective assistance. It was generally concluded also that the clearing house system could only evolve slowly.

205. The inputs from UNEP's partner agencies will be described in greater detail in annexes to the final implementation plan. For example, FAO will contribute on the problems of pesticides, nutrients and sediment mobilization, as well as on the management of forests and aquaculture in coastal areas. It is important to note that the Global Programme of Action now provides an umbrella for the specific inclusion of mangrove ecosystems and aquaculture in the integrated resource management of coastal watersheds. Also of direct relevance, is the new agreement for a joint programme among UNEP, UNESCO-IOC and the International Atomic Energy Agency (IAEA) Marine Environment Laboratory (Monaco), to assist States to conduct comparable assessments of pollution in coastal and ocean environments and to develop and implement strategies for marine environmental protection.

    3.   <u>Amendment of the 1972 Convention for the Prevention</u>
       <u>of Marine Pollution by Dumping of Wastes and Other</u>
       <u>Matter at Sea (London Convention)</u>

206. The rules and standards contained in, or adopted under, the 1992 London Convention have been recognized as global rules on dumping as referred to in

article 210 of the United Nations Convention. The Parties to the Law of the Sea Convention are accordingly obliged to enact laws and regulations which are no less effective than those contained in, or adopted under, the London Convention and to enforce such rules and regulations in accordance with article 216, even if they are not parties to the latter Convention. The proposed amendments to the London Convention, which are to be adopted in the form of a protocol at a Special Meeting of Contracting Parties at the end of 1996, are thus of particular importance to Parties to the United Nations Convention on the Law of the Sea.

207. The draft 1996 Protocol to the London Convention, which extensively revises its provisions, incorporates the work of the Amendment Group, the discussions of the 16th, 17th and 18th Consultative Meetings of Contracting Parties, and the review by the Jurists' and Linguistic Group. The draft includes both the text of amendments agreed to in principle by the Consultative Meeting and the text of amendments, the consideration of which has not yet been completed.[175]

208. The Consultative Meeting has agreed in principle to amend the existing definition of dumping, which is also the definition used in article 1 of the 1982 Law of the Sea Convention, to include "any storage of wastes or other matter in the seabed and the subsoil thereof from vessels, aircraft, platforms or other man-made structures at sea"; and to exclude from that definition "abandonment in the seabed and the subsoil thereof of matter (e.g., cables, pipelines and marine research devices) placed for a purpose other than the mere disposal thereof". The definition of "sea" will be amended accordingly to include "the seabed and the subsoil thereof". Following intense negotiations at the 18th Consultative Meeting, it was agreed to continue to exclude internal waters from the definition.[176] However, a new article on internal waters would require each contracting party at its discretion either to apply the provisions of the Protocol or to adopt other effective measures to control deliberate dumping or incineration. Information on legislation and institutional mechanisms regarding implementation, compliance and enforcement would have to be provided to IMO. There is also agreement in principle to add a definition of "pollution", which is based on article 1 of the United Nations Convention on the Law of the Sea.

209. Also agreed to in principle is a new article on general obligations, paragraph 3 of which is based on article 195 of the 1982 Convention. The development of this new article, which introduces both the precautionary approach and the polluter pays principle, is connected with proposals to include "reverse lists" - i.e., instead of "black and grey lists", which means that all dumping would be strictly prohibited with the exception of clearly identified waste categories - and the Waste Assessment Framework.

210. The amendments requiring further consideration by the Special Meeting include the questions of whether to accept the reverse list or to retain the existing prohibition list; whether to permit or completely prohibit incineration at sea, and if the latter, whether to include "fish waste, or material resulting from industrial fish processing operations" in the list of wastes that can be incinerated; whether to include new articles dealing with export of wastes or other matter, compliance control, scientific and technical research and provisional application; and whether to extend the application of the Convention to vessels, etc., entitled to sovereign immunity.

211. The Special Meeting will also have to consider an amended article on settlement of disputes, which proposes that where the parties fail after 12 months to resolve their dispute by negotiation, mediation or conciliation, the dispute must be settled by means of the arbitral procedure set forth in the annex, unless the parties agree to use one of the procedures listed in article 287 (1) of the United Nations Convention on the Law of the Sea.

4. Liability and compensation for damage: new instruments

212. Article 235, paragraph 3, of the Convention calls on States to cooperate in the further development of international law relating to responsibility and liability for environmental damage, including the development of criteria and procedures for payment of compensation, and the settlement of related disputes.

The 1996 HNS Convention

213. Developments at IMO have considerably advanced the implementation of article 235 of the Convention. The International Conference on Hazardous and Noxious Substances and Limitation of Liability (15 April-3 May 1996) adopted the International Convention on Liability and Compensation for Damage in Connection with the Carriage of Hazardous and Noxious Substances, 1996 (the HNS Convention)[177] and the Protocol of 1996 to amend the Convention on Limitation of Liability for Maritime Claims, 1976 (the LLMC Protocol).

214. The HNS Convention introduces strict liability for the shipowner, higher limits of liability than the present general limitation regimes and a system of compulsory insurance and insurance certificates. It covers not only pollution but also other risks such as fire and explosion caused by HNS substances. Compensation is accordingly provided not only for pollution damage in the territory, including the territorial sea and exclusive economic zone of a State party, but also for loss of life or personal injury on board and outside the ship and damage to property outside the ship.

215. The HNS Convention establishes a regime of liability and compensation based on a two-tier system. The shipowner's liability, which creates the first tier, is supplemented by a second tier, the HNS Fund, financed by cargo interests. Contributions to the second tier are to be levied on persons who receive a certain minimum quantity of HNS cargo during the year.

216. The Convention defines the hazardous and noxious substances to which it applies by reference to existing lists such as the International Maritime Dangerous Goods Code and annex II of MARPOL 73/78, and thus contributes to the clarification of the relevant provisions of the Convention on the Law of the Sea, which are concerned with these kinds of substances. The Conference decided to exclude from the scope of the Convention radioactive materials on the one hand, and coal and other low-hazard bulk cargoes on the other. A resolution adopted by the Conference recommends that IMO and IAEA work together in defining and considering issues of liability and compensation for damage occurring during the transport of radioactive materials.

217. Limits of Compensation regulated in the Convention are calculated using the special drawing right (SDR) of the International Monetary Fund as unit of account. The aggregate upper limit of compensation regulated by the Convention is 250 million SDRs (approximately US$ 362 million).

218. The 1996 Protocol to the Convention on Limitation of Liability for Maritime Claims deals with claims for loss of life or personal injury and property claims. The new Protocol substantially increases the original limits of compensation regulated in the parent Convention of 1976 and introduces a simplified system for adopting amendments to these limits, thus allowing the possibility of their periodic updating to preserve real values of compensation.

Pollution caused by ships' bunkers

219. The 1992 Protocols to the CLC and FUND Conventions (see para. 86 (b) above), now in force, cover also pollution damage caused by the bunkers of oil tankers, whether laden or unladen; however, pollution caused by the bunkers of other types of ships is not covered, and the victims of such pollution cannot benefit from the protection of strict shipowner liability and compulsory insurance. The IMO Legal Committee decided to give this matter high priority at

its meeting in October 1996,[178] and a proposal has been submitted by a number of delegations favouring the development of a free-standing convention.[179]

5. Carriage of radioactive materials

Developments at IMO

220. In 1995, the IMO Assembly adopted resolution A.790(19) on the review of the Code for the Safe Carriage of Irradiated Nuclear Fuel, Plutonium and High-level Radioactive Wastes in Flasks on Board Ships (INF Code). It endorsed the Secretary-General's initiative to convene a Special Consultative Meeting of entities involved with the carriage of materials subject to the 1993 INF Code and the coastal States concerned for the purpose of sharing information, concerns and ideas and to gain a better understanding of the safety and environmental aspects involved. The Assembly also noted the importance of an effective liability and compensation regime for damage in connection with the carriage of radioactive material by sea.

221. At a meeting of the Marine Environment Protection Committee in March 1996,[180] 13 of the 34 member States participating specifically requested in a declaration that the INF Code be made mandatory.[181] Both the Maritime Safety Committee and the Marine Environment Protection Committee had earlier noted that the mandatory application of the Code might be problematic and that there was a difference of opinion as to what a mandatory INF Code should contain; both committees have requested further submissions on the matter.

222. The Maritime Safety Committee, taking into account the issues listed in the above Assembly resolution and the outcome of the special meeting, has identified a number of issues requiring action or monitoring by IMO. These include mandatory application of the INF Code; route planning, notification to coastal States, and availability of information on the type of cargo being carried, including its hazards; tracking of ships carrying INF materials throughout the voyage by a shore-based authority; restriction or exclusion of INF-carrying ships from particularly sensitive sea areas; adequacy of existing emergency response arrangements; measures to locate, identify and salvage a sunken ship or lost flasks; adequacy of existing liability regimes covering accidents with INF materials; and environmental impact of accidents involving INF materials.[182]

223. The Committee decided that it was not necessary to consider the notification of coastal States in the event of an accident, as had been suggested in the Assembly resolution, since this was regulated by existing reporting requirements under both the SOLAS and the MARPOL Conventions and, therefore, no further action was required currently in this regard.[183]

224. The issues of route planning, notification to coastal States and availability of information on the type of cargo being carried raise questions of interpretation and application of the Convention on the Law of the Sea as regards the extent of the rights of the coastal State to control activities off its coast and the interests of the flag States in preserving their freedom of navigation. There is a need for guidance as to which States would qualify to be considered as "concerned coastal States" with respect to these issues.[184] The Subcommittee on the Safety of Navigation has recommended that provisions be developed for voyage planning for all ships; however, most delegations have opposed prior notification to coastal States for voyages of ships carrying INF materials.[185]

225. As regards the issue of restriction or exclusion of INF-carrying ships from particularly sensitive sea areas, the Marine Environment Protection Committee has noted that while the 1989 IMO Guidelines for the Designation of Special Areas and the Identification of Particularly Sensitive Sea Areas make no reference to INF material, the issue could be addressed in any proposal submitted by a Government seeking designation of an area as a particularly sensitive sea area.[186]

Regional developments

226. The States members of the South Atlantic Zone of Peace and Cooperation have decided to examine the question of establishing a monitoring system to control and prevent the dumping of hazardous and other harmful material into the Zone. At their fourth meeting, they also expressed their concern regarding the safe and secure transportation of INF materials through the region.[187] They called on all States to maintain cooperation and exchange information on the transportation of nuclear material and radioactive waste and to continue working through IMO and IAEA in the development of additional measures which would complement the 1993 INF Code. They affirmed their conviction that effective international liability mechanisms were essential.

227. The Caribbean Community (CARICOM) has called on nations currently engaged in the shipment of hazardous substances through the Caribbean Sea to respect the wishes of the Community by immediately halting such operations. The 1992 Declaration of the Special Meeting of the Conference of Heads of Government of CARICOM stated that shipments of plutonium and other radioactive or hazardous materials should not traverse the Caribbean Sea.[188]

228. The Commonwealth Ministerial Group on Small States, at its second meeting in November 1995, emphasized the possible dangers of the transboundary shipment of nuclear and hazardous waste through busy sea lanes in small States and welcomed the statement on the matter issued by the CARICOM Heads of Government in February 1995 and the Waigani Convention on hazardous and radioactive wastes adopted by the South Pacific Forum in September 1995, as useful instruments for addressing this critical issue.[189] The South Pacific Forum reiterated the need for full consultations on shipments transiting the region and expressed its appreciation to Japan for its provision of information on and consultation about its shipments.[190]

6. Marine and coastal biodiversity

229. In the previous report the Secretary-General drew attention to the scientific and commercial value of deep seabed genetic resources and noted that questions had been raised regarding the legal status of these resources and activities involving them (A/50/713, paras. 143-244).

230. In view of their special importance for States Parties to the Convention, the Secretary-General included in his first report under article 319 of the Convention (SPLOS/6, paras. 41-46) a discussion of developments concerning the implementation of the Convention on Biological Diversity, most particularly decision II/10 of the Parties to that Convention, adopted in November 1995. In paragraph 12 the parties called for a study of "the relationship between the Convention on Biological Diversity and the United Nations Convention on the Law of the Sea with regard to the conservation and sustainable use of genetic resources on the deep seabed, with a view to enabling the Subsidiary Body on Scientific, Technical and Technological Advice (SBSTTA) to address at future meetings, as appropriate, the scientific, technical and technological issues relating to bio prospecting of genetic resources on the deep seabed".[191] Since, in accordance with the above decision, the study is to be prepared in consultation with the Division for Ocean Affairs and the Law of the Sea, communication has recently been established between the two secretariats. Pending the submission of the study, SBSTTA refrained from discussing the issues at its last meeting (Montreal, 2-6 September 1996).

231. The general subject of marine and coastal biodiversity, as well as the specific issue of access to the genetic resources of the deep seabed, raise important questions. The topic touches not only on the protection and preservation of the marine environment, including that of the international seabed area, but also on such other matters as the application of the consent regime for marine scientific research, the regime for protected areas in the

exclusive economic zone, the duties of conservation and management of the living resources of the high seas, and the sustainable development of living marine resources generally. The specific issue of access points to the need for the rational and orderly development of activities relating to the utilization of genetic resources derived from the deep seabed area beyond the limits of national jurisdiction. The study to be prepared for Parties to the Biodiversity Convention will be of equal, or possibly greater importance to States Parties to the United Nations Convention on the Law of the Sea, as well as to Member States in the General Assembly reviewing the overall implementation of the Convention and the implications of current trends and developments for the law of the sea.

232. In addition to the questions that may be raised concerning applicable or relevant international law and the possible development of generally accepted international rules and regulations, a number of concerns exist as to the appropriate intergovernmental forum for consideration of the issues now raised, as well as other institutional issues, including coordination among treaty bodies and the competent international organizations. Some of these elements have been touched upon in documentation for the Third Conference of Parties to the Convention on Biological Diversity.[192]

233. The group of experts on marine and coastal biodiversity, established pursuant to decision II/10 of the Second Conference of Parties, has not been able to meet as planned; however, the first step has been achieved in drawing up a roster of nominated experts from which the group will be composed. SBSTTA has recommended that this expert group should concentrate on determining the following areas where the Biodiversity Convention can have the greatest effect: integrated marine and coastal area management, marine and coastal protected areas, sustainable use of coastal and marine living resources, mariculture and alien species.[193] Other items of particular note discussed by SBSTTA included the economic valuation of biological diversity and its components, in particular in relation to access to genetic resources (art. 15 of the Convention).

234. Attention is also drawn to the new prominence given to the subject of marine and coastal biodiversity at the fourth session of the Commission on Sustainable Development, particularly in connection with chapter 17 of Agenda 21. The Commission devoted particular attention to coral reefs and other special ecosystems (mangroves, estuaries and seagrass beds), welcoming the 1997 International Year of the Reefs and emphasizing the need for integrated coastal and marine area management plans to protect biodiversity.[194]

7. Protected areas

235. The subject of protected areas is of wide interest, and their establishment is provided for in an increasing number of instruments, including the Convention. They serve the purpose of preventing pollution from ships (art. 211 (6)) and protecting "rare or fragile ecosystems as well as the habitat of depleted, threatened or endangered species and other forms of marine life" (art. 194 (5)). The relationship between article 211 (6) of the Convention and the concepts of a particularly sensitive sea area and a special area under MARPOL 73/78 has yet to be clarified fully. In this regard, note should be taken of the recent draft for a convention on wreck removal submitted to IMO (see paras. 150-151 above).

236. There is a need to harmonize the increasing number of differing terms used to describe areas in need of special protection from maritime activities and to coordinate the measures that can be taken to protect and preserve them, e.g., "special area" under MARPOL 73/78; "special areas" in article 211(6) of the 1982 Convention; "particularly sensitive sea areas" in the 1991 IMO Guidelines; "environmentally sensitive areas" used in IMO General Provisions on Ships' Routeing; and "marine and coastal environmentally sensitive areas" proposed by the European Commission.

237. There is also a need to coordinate the measures which are required under the various instruments dealing with the protection of ecosystems and habitats of "depleted, threatened or endangered species and other forms of marine life" (art. 194 (5) of the Convention); biological diversity (art. 8 (a) of the 1992 Convention on Biological Diversity);[195] rare or fragile ecosystems (Agenda 21, para. 17.31 (a) (v)); particularly sensitive sea areas (identified in accordance with the IMO Guidelines and referred to in Agenda 21, para. 17.31 (a) (iv)); and environmentally sensitive sea areas (General Provisions on Ships' Routeing). There are also provisions in a number of regional conventions, as well as protocols dealing with marine protected areas and their designation. For example, the "Waters between Corsica, Liguria and Provence" have recently been designated as a "specially protected area of Mediterranean importance" in accordance with articles 8 and 9 of the 1995 Protocol to the Barcelona Convention Concerning Specially Protected Areas and Biological Diversity in the Mediterranean.[196] Specific mention is made therein of the framework provided by the United Nations Convention on the Law of the Sea.

H. Role of the General Assembly on ocean and law of the sea issues

238. Following the entry into force of the Convention, the General Assembly emphasized the principle stated in the preamble to the Convention that the problems of ocean space were closely interrelated and needed to be considered as a whole; pointed to the strategic importance of the Convention as a framework for national, regional and global action in the marine sector; stressed the importance of the annual consideration and review of the overall developments relating to the law of the sea; and decided, being the global institution having the competence to undertake such a review, "to undertake an annual review and evaluation of the implementation of the Convention and other developments relating to ocean affairs and the law of the sea" (resolution 49/28, preamble and para. 12).

239. The Secretary-General, in his first report under article 319 of the Convention (SPLOS/6, paras. 32-36), has drawn the attention of States Parties, the International Seabed Authority and the competent international organizations to section C.2 of decision 4/15 of the Commission on Sustainable Development dealing with section F of Chapter 17 of Agenda 21.[197] The Commission conducted its first review of the implementation of Chapter 17 at its fourth session (18 April-3 May 1996) (see also paras. 192-194 above).

240. The Commission recommended that there should be "a periodic overall review by the Commission of all aspects of the marine environment and its related issues, as described in chapter 17 of Agenda 21, and for which the overall legal framework is provided by the United Nations Convention on the Law of the Sea." The recommendation was based on the following needs: "(a) to better identify priorities for action at the global level to promote conservation and sustainable use of the marine environment; (b) for better coordination among the relevant United Nations organizations and intergovernmental financial institutions; (c) to ensure sound scientific, environmental, economic and social advice on these issues."

241. It is important to note also that the recommended review would cover other relevant elements of Agenda 21, in addition to chapter 17; preparation of the report would be coordinated by the Administrative Committee on Coordination (ACC) Subcommittee on Oceans and Coastal Areas; and that the results of such reviews by the Commission would be considered by the General Assembly under an item entitled "Oceans and the law of the sea". The Commission also recommended, with respect to the implementation of international fishery instruments, that FAO report to the United Nations, as well as to its Committee on Fisheries, noting that such a report "would be relevant to the review of ocean issues recommended by the Commission".[198] These recommendations (see para. 195) are to be considered at the Special Session of the General Assembly in June 1997.

242. While there is an ever increasing need for comprehensive or wide-ranging reviews which bring together developments in various sectors and examine them from a multidisciplinary perspective, addressing also the interrelationships among issues and among legal and policy instruments,[199] there is an ever increasing problem as to potential duplication in reporting responsibilities and in consequential decision-making. This problem appears to be particularly marked in the marine sector, given the relatively large number of organizations and bodies with competence in one or more aspects.

VIII.   MARITIME DISPUTES AND CONFLICTS

A.   Settlement of disputes

Guinea-Bissau - Senegal

243. In 1991, Guinea-Bissau had filed with the International Court of Justice an application for the delimitation of "the whole of the maritime territories" of Guinea-Bissau and Senegal. On its first application, made in 1989, concerning the validity of the Arbitral Award of 31 July 1989, the Court had found the Award to be both valid and binding; the fact that the Award had not dealt with the boundaries of the exclusive economic zone and had not therefore delivered a complete delimitation of the maritime areas involved, was attributed to the wording of the 1985 Arbitration Agreement. On the second application in 1991, the Court held that it would be highly desirable that the elements of the dispute not settled by the 1989 Award should be resolved. Negotiations between the two Governments culminated in the Management and Cooperation Agreement between the Government of the Republic of Guinea-Bissau and the Government of the Republic of Senegal,[200] done at Dakar on 14 October 1993 and signed by the two Heads of State.

244. The 1993 Agreement provides, inter alia, for the joint exploitation, by the two parties, of a "maritime zone situated between the 268° and 220° azimuths drawn from Cape Roxo" (art. 1) and the establishment of an "International Agency for the exploitation of the zone" (art. 4). It will enter into force upon the conclusion of an agreement concerning its establishment and functioning (art.7). Such an agreement was concluded at Bissau on 12 June 1995,[201] and entered into force in December 1995.

245. In November 1995, both parties agreed to discontinue the proceedings at the Court, and in accordance with the terms of the Rules of Court, and with the consent of the parties, the President of the Court issued an Order (8 November 1995) discontinuing the proceedings and ordering that the case be removed from the list.

Qatar - Bahrain

246. In 1991, Qatar had filed an application with the Court instituting proceedings against Bahrain "in respect of certain existing disputes between them relating to sovereignty over the Hawar islands, sovereign rights over the shoals of Dibal and Qit'at Jaradah, and the delimitation of the maritime areas of the two States" (see A/50/713, paras. 119-124). The original time limit (29 February 1996) fixed by the Court for each Memorial on the merits has been extended, at the request of Bahrain, to 30 September 1996. This Order of 1 February 1996 also reserved the subsequent procedure for further decision.

Cameroon - Nigeria

247. In 1994, Cameroon had filed an application instituting proceedings against Nigeria in a Case concerning the Land and Maritime Boundary between Cameroon and Nigeria, referring to the occupation of several localities on the Bakassi peninsula by Nigerian troops and requesting the Court to affirm its sovereignty over the peninsula and determine the course of the maritime frontier between the

two States insofar as that frontier had not already been established in 1975. More precisely, Cameroon had requested the Court to "prolong the course of its maritime boundary with Nigeria up to the limit of the maritime zones which international law places under their respective jurisdiction". Both Cameroon and Nigeria have made declarations accepting the compulsory jurisdiction of the Court.

248. The Court had fixed the time limits for the submission of the Memorial of Cameroon and the Counter-Memorial of Nigeria. However, since Nigeria had filed certain preliminary objections to the jurisdiction of the Court and the admissibility of the claims of Cameroon, the Court suspended the proceedings on the merits of the case (by Order of 10 January 1996) and fixed 15 May 1996 as the time limit for Cameroon to file its written observations on the preliminary objections. Cameroon did so on 1 May 1996.

249. The Court received communications from both parties expressing concerns over incidents in the Bakassi peninsula, with Cameroon requesting the Court to indicate provisional measures on 12 February 1996. The Court held several hearings and then issued an Order on 15 March 1996 so indicating. The parties were to ensure that no action of any kind, and particularly no action by their armed forces, was taken which might prejudice the rights of the other in respect of whatever judgment the Court might render in the case, or which might aggravate or extend the dispute before it; that armed forces currently in the Bakassi peninsula did not go beyond the positions held prior to 3 February 1996; and that all relevant evidence within the disputed area was conserved. The Order also called on the parties to lend every assistance to the fact-finding mission which the Secretary-General sent to the Bakassi peninsula.

Eritrea - Yemen

250. The dispute between Yemen and Eritrea concerning sovereignty over the Greater and Lesser Hanish islands chain in the Red Sea near its entrance continued to be the subject of occasional armed confrontations between the two countries, although they have agreed in principle to submit the dispute to arbitration.

251. France, which had been mediating between the disputants, announced on 21 May 1996 that the Governments of Eritrea and Yemen had agreed to settle peacefully through arbitration their dispute and have approved the terms of an accord on the principles of that arbitration.[202]

252. In July 1996, in a letter addressed to the Secretary-General (A/51/260, annex), Yemen objected to the publication by Eritrea of a map showing oil exploitation zones that included parts of the Red Sea, including parts referred to as "the Hanish-Zuqur quadrangle". In its letter, Yemen rejected any Eritrean claim that infringed upon Yemeni sovereignty and regarded the map's implications as a clear violation of the Agreement on Principles signed in Paris on 21 May 1996. It also indicated that it would ask France, which had undertaken to monitor the area in dispute, to take appropriate measures with regard to "this clear breach of the Agreement on Principles". Subsequently, the parties concluded an agreement setting out the procedures for arbitration, and ratified it on 3 October 1996.

B. Other developments

Russian Federation - Ukraine

253. The status of the Sea of Azov and Kerch Strait, and the demarcation of the Black Sea continental shelf, are now under discussion in the subcommission of the Russian-Ukrainian Commission on border delimitation, which held its first meeting in August 1996.[203]

Israel - Jordan

254. In accordance with the 1994 Treaty of Peace between Jordan and Israel,[204] the two sides have concluded an agreement on the delimitation of their maritime boundary in the Gulf of Aqaba.[205] In essence, the two agreed that the maritime boundary would follow the median line of the Gulf southward until the last point of the maritime boundary of the two countries.

Islamic Republic of Iran - United States of America

255. In a letter to the Secretary-General, the Islamic Republic of Iran has protested actions of the United States in "creating nuisances" and violating its airspace and territorial sea. Among the actions referred to was that of 8 February 1996, when an Iranian helicopter, in flight from an oil platform to Bushehr, was forced to return to the platform owing to the frequent warnings and preventive measures of United States warships. The Islamic Republic of Iran stated its belief that, while respecting and complying with Security Council resolutions, the proper implementation of those resolutions could not hinder its legitimate measures in its exclusive economic zone.[206]

Israel - Lebanon

256. The IMO Maritime Safety Committee has taken note of the statement by Lebanon that, since April 1996, the Israeli Navy had violated Lebanese territorial waters and committed acts of aggression and forcibly prevented commercial vessels from entering the port of Beirut and other commercial ports on the coast of southern Lebanon by imposing a maritime blockade. In its report, note is also taken of the position of several delegations that the Committee is not the proper forum for the consideration of security issues, but only of the technical aspects of maritime issues.[207]

The dispute over Persian Gulf Islands

257. The dispute between the Islamic Republic of Iran and the United Arab Emirates concerning sovereignty over the islands of Abu Musa, Greater Tunb and Lesser Tunb has continued to create tensions in the region. In a letter to the Secretary-General, the Islamic Republic protested overflight by United States aircraft over Iranian territory, including the Abu Musa[208] island; in response, the United Arab Emirates, in a letter to the Secretary-General, protested the allegation that the airspace over Abu Musa island belonged to the Islamic Republic, categorically rejecting any infringement of its sovereignty over Abu Musa island and reaffirming its willingness to settle the question of the three islands "through peaceful means, including recourse to the International Court of Justice."[209]

Japan - Republic of Korea

258. The establishment of exclusive economic zones by both Japan and the Republic of Korea has revived a dispute concerning sovereignty over two small islets, which lie some 150 miles offshore, halfway between the two States. The two islets - variously known as Takeshima (in Japan), and Tok To or Tok Do (in the Republic of Korea) - lie some 150 miles offshore. The islets have a land area of just 300 square yards, but are surrounded by rich fishing grounds.

China - Viet Nam

259. Viet Nam reported in August 1996 that useful talks had been held with China on demarcation of the Gulf of Tonkin, which the two countries share. The reported progress was made during a meeting of the joint working group on overlapping maritime zones off northern Viet Nam and south-east China which was held in Hanoi during August. The meeting was the seventh of the group since the two sides agreed to start negotiations on disputed areas in the gulf almost three years ago. The area has been a source of disputes over fishing rights and oil exploration.[210]

China - Japan

260. Since the 1970s, China and Japan have continued to dispute sovereignty over a group of five islets and barren rocks, known in Japan as Senkaku and in China as the Diaoyu, located about 200 miles east of the Chinese coast, and under the effective control of Japan. In July 1996, a group of Japanese nationalists built a lighthouse on the islands and flew a Japanese flag; in a strong protest, China maintained that the islands had been Chinese territory since ancient times.

261. It has been reported that a main reason the islands have become the focus of such attention is that surveys have suggested there may be large oil reserves nearby. Two Chinese marine survey vessels have conducted exploration activities in what Japan regards as Japanese waters around the islands.[211]

IX.   CRIMES AT SEA

262. The United Nations Commission on Crime Prevention and Criminal Justice, at its fifth session, in May 1996, adopted an 11-article draft declaration on crime and public security for transmission to the General Assembly (A/C.3/51/L.11, annex), by which States would pledge a wide range of crime control measures. Provisions include commitments by States to combat serious transnational crimes, including illicit trafficking in narcotic drugs to prevent those who engage in such crimes from finding a safe haven on their territories.[212]

263. There are important maritime aspects to transnational crimes. Maritime vessels, including fishing and pleasure craft, as well as ports are being used extensively by crime syndicates for the smuggling of drugs, human beings, endangered species, arms and mercenaries.[213] Concerns extend also to illicit trafficking in nuclear materials and other radioactive substances, so that the European Community has asked the IMO Working Group on Ship/Port Interface to include in its work programme the question of the installation of systematic border controls at seaports in the region.[214]

A.   Illicit traffic in narcotic drugs and psychotropic substances

264. The 1982 Convention on the Law of the Sea and the 1988 United Nations Convention against Illicit Traffic in Narcotic Drugs and Psychotropic Substances are closely linked. Article 108 of the 1982 Convention requires States to cooperate in the suppression of illicit traffic in narcotic drugs "contrary to international conventions", while the 1988 Convention refers in its article 17, paragraphs 1 and 11, to the "international law of the sea" and in paragraph 3 to "freedom of navigation in accordance with international law". As of 31 August 1996, 82 States were parties to both Conventions.

265. Given the worldwide increase in drug trafficking by sea, particular attention has been given to strengthening on a global basis the implementation of article 17 of the 1988 Convention. The valuable recommendations and report of the Working Group on Maritime Cooperation of the Commission on Narcotic Drugs, which met in 1994 and 1995 (see A/50/713, paras. 156-160), have been followed up by an expert group meeting (Vienna, 27-29 February 1996)[215] to develop training and technical assistance programmes in maritime law enforcement in the context of article 17. The meeting also examined the boarding and searching of different kinds of vessels and the seizure of illicit drugs, identifying areas which should be included in training curricula, such as enforcement strategies, the use of intelligence profiles, surveillance, controlled delivery, boarding, search and seizure, as well as post-seizure procedures.

266. The Commission on Narcotic Drugs considered that the work done in this area has contributed to the development of a cooperative framework for countering drug trafficking by sea and has urged the United Nations International Drug Control Programme (UNDCP) to prepare training guides, as well as other forms of technical cooperation, and to convene a regional training seminar for maritime law-enforcement personnel.[216]

267. Regional cooperation in this field is being strengthened generally. As part of their Plan of Action for Drug Control Coordination and Cooperation in the Caribbean, the States and Territories of the region have recently decided to consolidate the numerous bilateral cooperation agreements into a regional agreement that would include all Caribbean States, as well as France, Netherlands, the United Kingdom and the United States; and to develop a system to maximize and coordinate all maritime and aerial resources available in the region. The Regional Security System of the seven Eastern Caribbean countries has been requested to plan a framework to oversee all maritime aspects of drug operations in the Caribbean, with particular attention to the development of subregional coast guards.[217]

268. It is important for Governments to work with the shipping industry to ensure that its ships are not used to transport illicit drugs and that the crews are not involved in drug trafficking. The World Customs Organization is thus cooperating with industry bodies under Memoranda of Understanding, and the IMO Facilitation Committee is developing guidelines for the prevention of drug smuggling on ships engaged in international trade for submission to the IMO Assembly in 1997.[218]

B. Smuggling of aliens

269. The smuggling of aliens is continuing unabated, and with no laws in place in some countries to punish the offenders, the business is said to be booming. There are several established networks stretching from the Balkans to the Baltic: Central Asians travel through the Russian Federation to the Baltic States and on to the Scandinavian countries; the Balkan route, favoured by Africans and East Asians, runs from Turkey to Hungary, with Northern Europe as its destination.[219] But the web also extends beyond Western Europe to the United States and Canada.[220] According to a recent report, Western Europe, West Africa, Zaire, the United Republic of Tanzania, South Africa, Peru and Colombia are currently the world's hot spots for stowaways. In many instances around the world, stowaways often have the assistance of criminal organizations in getting on board, and containers are by far the most common hiding place.[221]

270. The IMO Assembly, at its last session, noted with concern the considerable risk not only to the stowaways themselves but also to seafarers who, owing to the large scale on which some of these operations are being carried out, may be overwhelmed by the number of stowaways on board.[222] The Facilitation Committee subsequently approved a circular on "Guidelines on the allocation of responsibilities to seek the successful resolution of stowaways cases",[223] and pending their adoption by the IMO Assembly in 1997, recommended their immediate use by all parties concerned.[224] The guidelines offer practical guidance as to the procedures to be followed to ensure that the return and repatriation of a stowaway is done in an acceptable and humane manner.

271. In determining what further action could be taken, the United Nations Commission on Crime Prevention and Criminal Justice was invited to explore "the important issue of the law of the sea"; maritime control is of special importance given the known volumes of illegal population movements that occur by sea and the fact that maritime and coastal border controls are central to preventing and detecting a good deal of the illegal global trafficking.[225] A draft resolution calling for action to combat the smuggling, including streamlined procedures for international inspection in the territorial sea of

vessels suspected of such activities, was tabled at the May session of the Commission but was later withdrawn to allow for extended discussion of other items.[226]

C. Piracy and armed robbery at sea

272. The number of incidents of piracy and armed robbery against ships reported to IMO continues to rise. A regional analysis by IMO of reported incidents during 1995 shows that out of 132 incidents worldwide, 68 took place in the China Sea; 20 in South America; 15 in the Indian Ocean; 12 in the Strait of Malacca; 11 in East Africa; 4 in West Africa; and 2 in the Mediterranean Sea. The majority of these incidents took place at sea: 66 in territorial seas, and 44 beyond.[227]

273. Two recent incidents of hijacking have been reported to IMO, one off the Thai/Cambodian border,[228] and the other in the Turkish territorial sea.[229] It was possible to recover the vessels in both incidents. However, in the case of the former incident, where the vessel and its cargo with the pirates on board were found three weeks later in a port of southern China, the International Maritime Bureau (of the International Chamber of Commerce) informed IMO that it had taken more than six months for the shipping industry to resolve the situation with the authorities, in spite of the existence of indisputable evidence giving the true identity of the ship and the ownership of the cargo. The Bureau suggested that the Maritime Safety Committee consider whether any recommendations could be made for dealing with such situations, suggesting that the 1988 International Convention on the Suppression of Unlawful Acts against the Safety of Navigation was insufficient for this purpose.[230]

X. DEVELOPMENT OF NON-LIVING MARINE RESOURCES

274. The past year witnessed important developments relating to non-living marine resources, both fuel and non-fuel minerals. After years of sluggish activity, there are signs of a marked revival of the offshore oil and gas industry worldwide: 1996 is expected to see the highest expenditure for exploration and production in more than five years, and the high growth period for the offshore industry may last till 2002, experts believe.[231] The move into deeper waters is a clear trend in almost every country worldwide. For example, 40 per cent of the leases bid in the lease sale in the United States for the Gulf of Mexico in April 1996 were at water depths below 2,700 feet, the deepest at 9,280 feet; and Nigeria has just opened for bidding six newly created leases for tracts lying at depths of 3,900 to 8,200 feet.[232] At present, the deepest waters at which exploration drilling has been carried out are about 7,000 feet, but drilling at depths of up to 10,000 feet is expected in the near future. Currently, the world's deepest oil well is in offshore Brazil, at a depth of about 3,300 feet.

275. With respect to coal, the other fossil fuel mineral extracted from marine sources, offshore coal mining commenced more than 400 years ago and is still being carried out through undersea extensions of mine shafts sunk on land or shafts sunk from artificial islands. Possibilities of exploiting coal energy by in situ gasification are being considered.[233]

276. Research interest is being shown also in the recovery of gas hydrates, frozen compounds of methane. Vast deposits are held at high pressure 600 to 1,500 feet under the ocean floor on continental shelves around the world. Scientists have estimated that the organic carbon bound up in ocean floor hydrates is twice that found in all recoverable and non-recoverable oil, gas and coal deposits on earth.[234] Scientists are researching how to mine these deposits without causing an environmental disaster, particularly since an accident could cause ocean floor avalanches, in turn possibly leading to a sudden release of methane, which has a greenhouse effect many times that of carbon dioxide.[235]

277. Research and development activities with respect to the non-conventional and renewable energy sources - waves, tides, currents, offshore wind and ocean thermal gradients - are still at experimental stages. While their huge potential is widely recognized (e.g., the world's total exploitable wave energy resource is conservatively estimated at 400 gigawatts),[236] economical exploitation at a large scale has yet to be achieved. While a British company in 1995 installed a wave-powered generator anticipated to produce enough electricity to supply 2,000 homes, the United States National Oceanic and Atmospheric Administration (NOAA) this year abandoned the 15-year-old ocean thermal energy conversion (OTEC) licensing programme because no applications had been received.[237]

278. Compared to the offshore fuel industry, the size of the offshore non-fuel industry, currently limited to shallower waters, is relatively small, but it is growing rapidly in many parts of the world.

279. Sand and gravel are perhaps the most important such offshore mineral resources currently exploited. Commercial exploitation of these construction materials is taking place in Western Europe and Asia and off the eastern United States. Coastal quarries are an important new feature in some areas, for example, Norway.

280. Dredging of placer deposits is taking place in many countries, for example: tin, in Indonesia, Thailand and Malaysia; and gold in the Philippines and Alaska. Beach and near-shore deposits of mineral sands (ilmenite, rutile, zircon, monazite) are mined in Australia, Malaysia, India, China, Sri Lanka, South Africa and the United States. Offshore diamond exploration has been taking place off southern Africa for many years and is under way off north-western Australia. Phosphate, used for fertilizer, is also derived from offshore sources, and although most of the world supply of phosphate currently comes from land-based deposits, the very rapid increase in demand (500 per cent growth in world production in 40 years) may lead to an increasing reliance on marine sources.[238]

281. Marine mineral resources attracting commercial interest in deeper waters, both within and outside zones under national jurisdiction, are polymetallic nodules on the ocean floor, cobalt-rich manganese oxide crusts on bedrock, polymetallic sulphides along ocean floor spreading centres and metalliferous red clay. None are commercially exploited at this time, but considerable research and/or development activity has been devoted to these resources.

282. With respect to polymetallic nodules, research and development initiated in the 1970s is continuing currently at a slow pace, concentrating on four critical areas: exploration, design and development of a pilot mining system, extraction of the metals of interest (copper, nickel, cobalt and manganese), and environmental baseline studies. Japan is planning a pilot system test of the mining technology in 1997. India projects a semi-industrialized phase of metal extraction in 1997. The Republics of Korea and China are also active in research and development and exploration activities. The mining entities involved were registered as "pioneer investors" by the international community, under the regime created with the adoption of the 1982 Convention on the Law of the Sea.[239] Though the initial research and development was carried out by Western countries, research on deep ocean mining in the United States and in many of the European countries practically ceased in the late 1980s and 1990s. It is expected that for the next 10 years, the Pacific Rim countries will be most active in research and development, mainly because of their late start.[240]

283. The cobalt-rich manganese oxide crusts can be found at depths of 2,500 to 8,000 feet, distributed in various forms and sizes on the ocean floor above the substrates as well as buried beneath the sediment. A recent survey reveals that the crusts are also located below the ocean floor, buried beneath the calcareous sediment layer. Confirmation of the existence of the crust deposits beneath the sediments has raised the resource estimates three to five times above previous evaluations.[241]

284. Survey and research work on polymetallic sulphides has been going on for nearly 15 years. Recent studies have considerably advanced the knowledge of ore deposit geology, which in turn contributes to the discovery of these types of deposit on land. Recently, research funding was guaranteed for at least the next decade for the most active programme, a multinational programme linking scientists from 15 countries.[242]

285. Finally, there has been a new interest in desalination of sea water in view of water shortages in many countries. The General Conference of IAEA has requested the Director-General to assign appropriate priority to the nuclear desalination of sea water in preparing the Agency's programme and budget and has also called for the establishment of an advisory body on nuclear desalination to develop appropriate measures to assist member States in developing demonstration projects.[243]

XI. MARINE SCIENCE AND TECHNOLOGY

A. Marine scientific research

1. Climate change and the oceans

286. The Intergovernmental Panel on Climate Change (IPCC) completed its second assessment report in December 1995.[244] The report deals with the degree of climate change projected to occur as a result of human activities and, inter alia, discusses the vulnerabilities of ecosystems to a possible rise in the sea level.

287. The global sea level has risen by between 10 and 25 centimetres over the past 100 years, and much of the rise may be related to an increase in global mean temperature. Models project a further increase in sea level of approximately 50 centimetres by 2100 as a result of thermal expansion of the oceans and melting of glaciers and ice sheets. This estimate is approximately 25 per cent lower than the comparable estimate in 1990, owing to the lower temperature projection, but also reflecting improvements in the climate and ice-melt models. The range in the projections of sea-level rise by 2100, reflecting the high and low scenarios of emission rates and climate and ice-melt sensitivities, varies from about 15 to 95 centimetres. IPCC agreed that even if concentrations of greenhouse gases are stabilized by 2100, the sea level would continue to rise at a similar rate for some centuries beyond that time. The Panel also notes that confidence in regional projections remains low; regional sea-level changes may differ from the global mean value owing to land movement and ocean current change.[245]

288. In general, coastal systems are expected to vary widely in their response to climate and sea level changes. The coastal ecosystems particularly at risk are saltwater marshes, mangrove ecosystems, coastal wetlands, sandy beaches, coral reefs and atolls and river deltas. The kinds and the severity of changes that would most likely occur in the salinity of estuaries and freshwater aquifers, altered tidal ranges in rivers and bays, changes in sediment and nutrient transport and in the pattern of chemical and microbiological contamination would have major impacts on fisheries, biodiversity, freshwater supplies and tourism, all important factors necessary for sustainable development. These impacts would be coupled with modifications in the coastal oceans and inland waters that have already resulted from pollution, physical modification and material inputs from human activities.

289. Besides the projected increase in the sea level, climate change could also lead to altered ocean circulation, vertical mixing, wave climate and reductions in the sea-ice cover. Nutrient availability, biological productivity, the structure and function of marine ecosystems, and heat and carbon storage capacity may be affected, which would in itself have an impact on the climate system, with obvious implications for coastal regions, fisheries, tourism and recreation, transport, offshore structures and communication.

290. It should be noted that the Commission on Sustainable Development specifically noted the interrelationships between chapters 9 (Protection of the atmosphere) and 17 (Protection of the oceans) in view of the exchange of matter and energy between atmosphere and ocean and their combined influence on marine and terrestrial ecosystems. The Commission therefore called for a more integrated approach to the adoption of protective measures.

2. Marine environmental assessments

291. The Joint Group of Experts on the Scientific Aspects of Marine Pollution (GESAMP), which prepared the highly influential 1990 "State of the marine environment" report, has now created a standing Working Group on Marine Environmental Assessments. It will embark on a new global assessment, to be completed by 2002, and the first step towards the next assessment will be the preparation of a report on land-based sources and activities affecting the quality and uses of the marine, coastal and associated freshwater environment, due in 1998, as part of UNEP's responsibilities under the Global Programme of Action on land-based activities and its new integrated water programme.[246] GESAMP's decision to concentrate efforts on the preparation of periodic assessments also came in response to the recommendation of the Commission on Sustainable Development concerning GESAMP's basic purposes (see para. 194 (e) above).

292. This is a major undertaking by the sponsoring organizations (IMO/FAO/UNESCO-IOC/WMO/WHO/IAEA/UNEP/United Nations), GESAMP members, the members of the new Working Group, as well as by the many other experts around the world who contribute their time and knowledge to the work of GESAMP. Concerns have consequently been expressed as to the availability of adequate financial resources, particularly in the relatively short time allowed.

293. GESAMP will continue to keep under continuous review the condition of the marine environment, reporting regularly on apparent trends and emerging issues. At its twenty-sixth session (25-29 March 1996),[247] it drew particular attention to such issues as the effects of fishing, which in some localities may outweigh the environmental effects of contaminant discharges in terms of their ecological significance; to the increase in phytotoxin occurrences and human exposures, particularly chronic exposures; and, given the proliferation of coastal management programmes and projects, to the urgent need for an accepted evaluation methodology for assessing their impacts and efficacy.[248] GESAMP also expressed its concerns that much of the focus on marine biodiversity is directed at the deep sea, while the most urgent threats concerning marine biodiversity losses are in coastal areas, so that the priorities for action should be research on and assessment of key coastal habitats; the development of strategies for their conservation as parts of integrated coastal management programmes; studies of effects of fishing on biodiversity; and development of methods for rapid assessment of coastal biodiversity.

294. Attention is drawn to the statement made by GESAMP in 1995 expressing its concern as to recent data on the effects of a wide variety of different chemicals (including DDT, PCB, dioxins, PAH) which are found to mimic natural oestrogens (hormones). GESAMP called for new efforts to study the impacts of "oestrogen mimic" chemicals (also known as "endocrine disruptors") on the marine environment.[249] Concerns continue to mount, and action is being taken to improve knowledge in this area: OECD is reviewing chemical testing to take account of the potential for endocrine disruption; and the subject has been added to the agenda of the Intergovernmental Forum on Chemical Safety. It may be noted that not all endocrine disruptors are persistent organic pollutants (see para. 200), so that arguments are being made for additional specific action on this category of chemicals.

B. Marine technology

295. As a post-cold war dividend, marine science benefited immensely from the release of vast amounts of oceanographic data and access to new oceanographic equipment. The data from systematic surveys by the United States Navy of most of the world oceans over several decades, are now in the public domain, yielding new information on ocean depth, sediment composition, marine gravity, seabed magnetism, water temperature, salinity, sea-surface height, ice depth, ice shape, light transmissibility and bioluminescence. Moreover, data collected by various methods (e.g., towed sensors, submarines, fixed and floating buoys, remote sensing and satellites) were combined to produce yet newer data with potential dramatic benefits in many fields: environmental studies, geology, climatology, weather forecasting, pollution studies, marine engineering, commercial fisheries management and deep sea oil and mineral exploration. It is estimated that so far about 10 to 20 per cent of United States Navy data has been declassified; eventually about 95 per cent of the data would be made public.[250]

296. The oceans were not considered to be as well mapped as Venus, until the release this year of the first global map of the ocean floor by the United States National Oceanic and Atmospheric Administration (NOAA).[251] It was based on recently declassified satellite data acquired by the United States Navy, combined with recent readings from a European satellite. Besides being of great scientific importance for studies of active geological processes in deep ocean basins, including plate tectonics, as well as climate studies, the map has proved of commercial value: already, fishermen use it to locate seamounts that produce upwellings of deep, nutrient-rich water that in turn supports abundant living resources; industries use it to find the kinds of rocks that overlay oilfields and the kinds of volcanic eruptions that form undersea deposits of copper, iron, silver and gold.

297. There is now a global network of hundreds of undersea microphones (or hydrophones), known as Sosus (sound surveillance system), originally deployed by the United States Navy in the early 1990s. During the past year, many more institutions and private companies have gained access to the system, which can "hear" noises over distances of hundreds, even thousands of miles. Expectations of the system are high, e.g., to study seaquakes and volcanic activities, monitor distant nuclear blasts, track ships involved in drift-net fishing, as well as movements of marine mammals, and to avoid maritime collisions.[252] An early benefit for science came when a research ship could be quickly deployed to collect data and samples of hot water resulting from the hundreds of seaquakes which were detected off the west coast of the United States. It was only the second time, the first being in 1993, that seismic disturbances below the sea could be studied so directly.[253]

298. Three-dimensional seismic data acquisition, modelling and interpretation represent a recent technological innovation, coming as a direct consequence of the growth in computer technology, particularly parallel processing. The offshore industry has also begun to benefit from three-dimensional seismic data, greatly reducing the number of drilling operations and increasing the success rate, so that "no other factor has been more influential in the growth of (offshore oil and gas) production internationally."[254] Deeper water, deeper geological targets and complex stratigraphy of frontier areas present more problems for accurate acquisition of three-dimensional seismic data than do normal depths. Technology has now been developed to address these problems.

299. The move of the offshore oil and gas industry to deeper waters (see also para. 274) entails major technological development. Floating drilling operations are under new investigation,[255] as is production technology, where one concept is to automate most of the production technology and locate it on the ocean floor, linking up a number of these semi-autonomous wells to a central hub, and passing the combined output on to a conventional offshore platform, where the oil and gas would be separated. One platform would then suffice for

dozens of wells over hundreds of square miles.[256] Another approach under
development would have application as an independent production platform on
deep-sea fields having smaller reserves or as a utility, satellite or early
production platform for larger deep-water discoveries. In yet another approach,
a multi-purpose tanker would be designed to serve as production vessel and
shuttle tanker.[257]

300. Deep-water development faces substantial capital costs and lead time before
initial production can occur. In addition, uncertainties about ultimate
production rates and total reserves increase risks. There is thus considerable
interest in combined, multifunctional systems. A key concept in reducing the
costs of deep-water operations is the light drilling rig, so that technological
development focuses on combining a lighter drilling rig with a vessel used for
sub-sea completion of a production well, having the deck-load capacity of a
monohull and motion characteristics of a semi-submersible. Another development
has been the design of a single mobile unit capable of drilling, early
production, testing, storage and offloading.[258]

301. The development of hard minerals in near-shore areas is expected to be
greatly facilitated by a new technology that can cover a wider area at much less
cost and time than current technology: a Dutch company has developed a system
for screening and bulk sampling of ocean floor minerals to depths of 400 feet,
which is currently being used off southern Africa to sample and recover
diamond-bearing sediments.[259]

XII.   TECHNICAL COOPERATION AND CAPACITY-BUILDING
IN THE LAW OF THE SEA AND OCEAN AFFAIRS

A.   The Hamilton Shirley Amerasinghe Fellowship Programme

302. Under this fellowship programme, Hamilton Shirley Amerasinghe fellows
pursue postgraduate-level research and training in the field of the law of the
sea, its implementation and related marine affairs at a participating university
of their choice. They also have the opportunity to work as interns in the
Division for Ocean Affairs and the Law of the Sea for up to three months. Ten
awards and one special award have been made under this programme since 1986.[260]
The Advisory Panel recommended Ms. Alisi-Numia Tamoepeau, Acting
Solicitor-General for the Kingdom of Tonga, for the tenth annual award.[261]

303. The United Kingdom again made a special contribution to fund a fellowship
under the programme.[262] The Advisory Board welcomed this contribution to the
1996/97 school year and once again expressed the hope that this could become an
ongoing commitment. It also urged other countries to consider making similar
contributions.

304. The Panel has again called attention to the very high calibre of the
candidates under the programme, appealing for additional funding to support the
programme and encouraging universities to award fellowships to all finalists.
It also decided to designate selected candidates as "finalists", encouraging
them to include this information when applying directly to universities for
fellowships. As a consequence, 14 finalists for the 1995 award have been
invited to apply for scholarships by the newly inaugurated Rhodes Academy of
Ocean Law and Policy, which has expressed an interest in participating in the
fellowship programme. Other new participating institutions, both located in the
United Kingdom, are the Oxford University Faculty of Law and the Southampton
University Faculty of Law. The Institute of International Studies of the
University of Chile has also expressed an interest in an association with the
programme.

B. The TRAIN-SEA-COAST Programme

305. The TRAIN-SEA-COAST Programme was started in 1995 (see A/50/713, paras. 251-256), with the Division for Ocean Affairs and the Law of the Sea providing the Central Support Unit. The programme has seen good progress, particularly in the production of the first standardized training package by the Course Development Unit located in the Philippines at the International Centre for Living Aquatic Resources Management.

306. This new "National course on integrated coastal zone management" (ICZM), designed for middle-level managers and supported by various government departments and institutions, is also part of a broader project (supported by the Rockefeller Brothers Fund) to develop a pool of coastal management practitioners who will work together on an integrated coastal plan for each of the 14 regions in the Philippines and develop an informal network of institutions involved in ICZM in South-east Asia.

307. Despite the financial constraints in most course development units and the shortage of course developers, it is anticipated that by early 1997 four more training packages will be available for sharing among the network. The Division is pursuing further funding sources for the programme as a whole and is assisting the different units in obtaining additional resources.

308. Also of note is the workshop held by the Unit in Brazil (at the Foundacao Universidade do Rio Grande) to identify national priorities for marine and coastal management, and consequently, the training needs. This was the first time that a thorough training needs analysis was undertaken at the national level using the TRAIN-SEA-COAST methodology; it will be of considerable importance for other units.[263]

309. In keeping with the need to promote integrated management of marine and coastal areas, the TRAIN-SEA-COAST Programme cooperates closely with its sister programmes: TRAINFORTRADE in the field of tourism; and CC:TRAIN in the field of climate change and ICZM. The Division also works closely on the development of the programme with UNEP, particularly in respect of its Strategic Initiative on Ocean and Coastal Area Management. This initiative will focus on the development of training courses through the programme and will encourage the exchange of knowledge and experience among UNDP projects.[264]

Notes

[1] These States are: Algeria, Angola, Antigua and Barbuda, Argentina, Australia, Austria, Bahamas, Bahrain, Barbados, Belize, Bolivia, Bosnia and Herzegovina, Botswana, Brazil, Bulgaria, Cameroon, Cape Verde, China, Comoros, Cook Islands, Costa Rica, Côte d'Ivoire, Croatia, Cuba, Cyprus, Czech Republic, Djibouti, Dominica, Egypt, Fiji, Finland, France, Gambia, Georgia, Germany, Ghana, Greece, Grenada, Guinea, Guinea-Bissau, Guyana, Haiti, Honduras, Iceland, India, Indonesia, Iraq, Ireland, Italy, Jamaica, Japan, Jordan, Kenya, Kuwait, Lebanon, Mali, Malta, Marshall Islands, Mauritania, Mauritius, Mexico, Micronesia (Federated States of), Monaco, Mongolia, Myanmar, Namibia, Nauru, Netherlands, New Zealand, Nigeria, Norway, Oman, Panama, Paraguay, Philippines, Republic of Korea, Saint Kitts and Nevis, Saint Vincent and the Grenadines, Saint Lucia, Samoa, Sao Tome and Principe, Saudi Arabia, Senegal, Seychelles, Sierra Leone, Singapore, Slovakia, Slovenia, Somalia, Sri Lanka, Sudan, Sweden, The former Yugoslav Republic of Macedonia, Togo, Tonga, Trinidad and Tobago, Tunisia, Uganda, United Republic of Tanzania, Uruguay, Viet Nam, Yemen, Yugoslavia, Zaire, Zambia and Zimbabwe.

[2] Official Records of the Third United Nations Conference on the Law of the Sea, vol. XVII (United Nations publication, Sales No. E.84.V.3), document A/CONF.62/122.

[3] General Assembly resolution 48/263, annex.

[4] A/CONF.164/37.

[5] The 67 States are: Algeria, Argentina, Australia, Austria, Bahamas, Barbados, Belize, Bolivia, Bulgaria, China, Cook Islands, Côte d'Ivoire, Croatia, Cyprus, Czech Republic, Fiji, Finland, France, Georgia, Germany, Greece, Grenada, Guinea, Haiti, Iceland, India, Ireland, Italy, Jamaica, Japan, Jordan, Kenya, Lebanon, Malta, Mauritania, Mauritius, Micronesia (Federated States of), Monaco, Mongolia, Myanmar, Namibia, Nauru, Netherlands, New Zealand, Nigeria, Norway, Panama, Paraguay, Republic of Korea, Samoa, Saudi Arabia, Senegal, Seychelles, Sierra Leone, Singapore, Slovakia, Slovenia, Sri Lanka, Sweden, The former Yugoslav Republic of Macedonia, Togo, Tonga, Trinidad and Tobago, Uganda, Yugoslavia, Zambia and Zimbabwe.

[6] Official Records of the Third United Nations Conference on the Law of the Sea, vol. XVII (United Nations publication, Sales No. E.84.V.3), document A/CONF.62/121, annex I.

[7] In accordance with its article 7, paragraph 3.

[8] Section 1, para. 12 (a), of the Annex to the Agreement.

[9] Bangladesh, Belgium, Cambodia, Canada, Chile, European Community, Gabon, Luxembourg, Malaysia, Nepal, New Zealand, Poland, Russian Federation, South Africa, Suriname, Switzerland, Ukraine, United Kingdom of Great Britain and Northern Ireland and United States of America.

[10] They are: Bahrain, Botswana, Cameroon, Cape Verde, Cuba, Egypt, Ghana, Guyana, Honduras, Indonesia, Iraq, Kuwait, Marshall Islands, Oman, Philippines, Sudan, Tunisia, United Republic of Tanzania and Viet Nam.

[11] These States are: Afghanistan, Albania, Andorra, Armenia, Belarus, Benin, Bhutan, Brunei Darussalam, Burkina Faso, Burundi, Congo, Eritrea, Estonia, Ethiopia, Hungary, Lao People's Democratic Republic, Libyan Arab Jamahiriya, Liechtenstein, Madagascar, Maldives, Mozambique, Pakistan, Papua New Guinea, Qatar, Republic of Moldova, Solomon Islands, Swaziland, United Arab Emirates and Vanuatu.

[12] See ISBA/C/9.

[13] See press release SEA/1532 of 19 August 1996.

[14] Argentina, Austria, Australia, Bangladesh, Belize, Brazil, Canada, Côte d'Ivoire, Denmark, Egypt, European Community, Fiji, Finland, Germany, Greece, Guinea-Bissau, Iceland, Indonesia, Israel, Italy, Jamaica, Luxembourg, Marshall Islands, Mauritania, Micronesia (Federated States of), Morocco, Namibia, Netherlands, New Zealand, Niue, Norway, Pakistan, Papua New Guinea, Philippines, Portugal, Russian Federation, Saint Lucia, Samoa, Senegal, Sweden, Tonga, Ukraine, United Kingdom of Great Britain and Northern Ireland (signed on 4 December 1995 on behalf of its territories and on 27 June 1996 on behalf of the United Kingdom), United States of America, Uruguay and Vanuatu.

[15] Article 319(2)(e); Annex II, article 2(3); and Annex VI, article 4(4) and article 19(1).

[16] For the agenda and organization of work of the Meetings of States Parties to date, see documents SPLOS/1/Rev.1 and SPLOS/CRP.1, 2, 3, 4 and 7.

[17] Each maritime zone is measured from the same baselines.

[18] "Miles" throughout this document refers to nautical miles.

[19] The 17 States are: Antigua and Barbuda, Bahamas, Cape Verde, Comoros, Fiji, Indonesia, Jamaica, Kiribati, Mauritius, Papua New Guinea, Philippines, Saint Vincent and the Grenadines, Sao Tome and Principe, Solomon Islands, Trinidad and Tobago, Tuvalu and Vanuatu.

[20] See Law of the Sea Information Circular, Nos. 3 and 4.

[21] Ibid.

[22] Japan, upon becoming a State Party on 20 July 1996 has amended its existing laws and adopted new legislation relating in particular, to the contiguous zone, the exclusive economic zone and the continental shelf. The texts of legislation are not yet available to the Division.

[23] For the text of the Act, see Law of the Sea Bulletin, No. 31 (1996).

[24] For the text of the declaration, see ibid., No. 32 (1996).

[25] China deposited its instrument of ratification on 7 June 1996 and made a declaration contained in ibid., No. 31 (1996).

[26] Text to be reproduced in ibid., No. 32 (1996) (in press).

[27] Ibid.

[28] Ibid.

[29] Ibid.

[30] See Law of the Sea Bulletin, No. 31 (1996). The 1993 Iranian Act is contained in ibid., No. 24 (1993).

[31] Ibid., No. 24 (1993).

[32] Algeria deposited its instrument of ratification on 11 June 1996 and Mauritania, on 17 July 1996.

[33] China, Japan, Jordan, Mongolia, Myanmar, Nauru, New Zealand, Republic of Korea and Saudi Arabia.

[34] Bulgaria, Czech Republic, Finland, France, Georgia, Ireland, Monaco, Netherlands, Norway, Slovakia and Sweden.

[35] See Decree No. 63-403 of 12 October 1963 establishing the breadth of territorial waters and Decree No. 72-194 of 5 October 1972 for the peacetime regulation of the passage of foreign warships through the territorial waters and of their port calls, reproduced in The Law of the Sea: National Legislation on the territorial sea and the right of innocent passage and the contiguous zone (United Nations publication, Sales No. E.95.V.7), pp. 11-18. In addition to Algeria, 16 other States require a prior authorization or consent for a warship to exercise the right of innocent passage in the territorial sea. These States are: Antigua and Barbuda, Bangladesh, Barbados, China, Grenada, Islamic Republic of Iran, Maldives, Myanmar, Pakistan, Romania, Saint Vincent and the Grenadines, Somalia, Sri Lanka, Syrian Arab Republic, United Arab Emirates and Yemen. Other States require prior notification, such as Denmark, Estonia, Guyana, India, Malta, Mauritius, Republic of Korea, Seychelles and Sweden.

[36] Text of the statement to be reproduced in Law of the Sea Bulletin, No. 32 (1996) (in press).

[37] See note 34 above.

[38] Law of the Sea Bulletin, No. 32 (1996) (in press).

[39] Costa Rica, Egypt, Fiji, Finland, France, Germany, Greece, Honduras, Italy, Jamaica, Kenya, Malaysia, Malta, Netherlands, Nigeria, Sierra Leone, Sudan, Sweden, Tonga, Trinidad and Tobago and Yugoslavia.

[40] Angola, Benin, Cameroon, Congo, Ecuador, El Salvador, Liberia, Nicaragua, Nigeria, Panama, Peru, Sierra Leone, Somalia, Syrian Arab Republic and Togo.

[41] Namely, the legislation of Brazil, Cape Verde, Colombia, Djibouti, Equatorial Guinea, Guatemala, Guyana, India, Kenya, Maldives, Mauritius, Morocco, Myanmar, Pakistan, the Philippines, Saint Kitts and Nevis, Saint Lucia, Seychelles, Sri Lanka, Turkey, Vanuatu, Viet Nam and Yemen.

The 1995 Federal Law of the Russian Federation provides for the exercise of its jurisdiction over marine scientific research on the continental shelf, but without any reference to the Convention, which would limit the rights provided for therein, in particular to accord with article 246 of the Convention.

[42] The German declaration is reproduced in Law of the Sea Bulletin, No. 27 (1995), p. 6. The Czech declaration will be reproduced in ibid., No. 32 (1996) (in press).

[43] A State Party is entitled to nominate two experts in each field. Their competence may be legal, scientific or technical. See article 2(3) of Annex VIII of the Convention.

[44] IOC has received nominations also from the following countries, not yet parties to the Convention: Chile, Colombia, Gabon, Malaysia, Mozambique, Pakistan, Romania, Russian Federation and Ukraine.

[45] See article 161(1) of the Convention and sect. 3, para. 15, of the annex to the Agreement.

[46] For details, see United Nations press release SEA/KIN/9/Rev.1 of 9 March 1995.

[47] For the revised budget proposal, see ISBA/14.

[48] ISBA/A/9 and ISBA/C/5, sect. A.

[49] A/C.5/51/21.

[50] The decision of the Assembly of the Authority concerning its observer status at the United Nations (ISBA/A/13) also emphasizes "the importance of the annual consideration and review by the General Assembly of overall developments pertaining to the implementation of the Convention, as well as of other developments relating to the law of the sea and ocean affairs".

[51] For the various decisions of the Assembly and the Authority, see ISBA/A/13, ISBA/A/15, ISBA/A/L.10, ISBA/C/3, ISBA/C/8 and ISBA/C/9.

[52] This organization was granted observer status at the fifth Meeting of States Parties.

[53] A draft relationship Agreement between the Tribunal and the United Nations was recommended by the Preparatory Commission for the International Seabed Authority and the International Tribunal for the Law of the Sea; see LOS/PCN/152 (vol. I), p. 132. The Preparatory Commission reviewed the issue of relationship arrangements between the Tribunal and the Authority and approved the application of certain principles; see ibid., p. 142.

[54] See SPLOS/14.

[55] SPLOS/3.

[56] SPLOS/10.

[57] The Statute of the Tribunal provides that in the first election, the Secretary-General will draw lots to determine the terms of office of the judges (Annex VI, article 5(2)).

[58] In accordance with article 5(3) of the Statute of the Tribunal.

[59] The budget, adopted by decision SPLOS/L.1, is set out in SPLOS/WP.3/Rev.1.

[60] SPLOS/L.1.

[61] United Nations staff regulations will also apply. The Tribunal was also requested to apply to the United Nations Joint Staff Pension Fund, with the understanding that such request would need the sponsorship of States Members of the United Nations in the General Assembly.

[62] SPLOS/WP.2 and Add.1. The next meeting will also consider a proposal by Germany concerning taxes and customs duties.

[63] The Statement of Understanding is reproduced in the Final Act of the Third United Nations Conference on the Law of the Sea; Official Records of the Third United Nations Conference on the Law of the Sea, vol. XVII (United Nations publication, Sales No. E.84.V.3), document A/CONF.62/121, annex II.

[64] SPLOS/CLCS/INF/1.

[65] SPLOS/5, para. 20.

[66] SPLOS/L.2.

[67] SPLOS/CLCS/WP.1.

[68] See IMO document C 76/4.

[69] Adopted by resolution MSC.42(64). The amendments incorporate as mandatory for parties to SOLAS 74, the Code of Safe Practice for Cargo Stowage and Securing.

[70] Set out in annex 1 to resolution MSC.31(63). Annex 2 to the resolution includes amendments that are expected to enter into force on 1 January 1998.

[71] Resolution MSC.33(63).

[72] Resolution A.736(18).

[73] At its nineteenth session the IMO Assembly subsequently adopted resolutions on particular safety aspects of ro-ro passenger ships and ferry operations.

[74] See IMO documents MEPC 37/22, paras. 11.4-11.11, and annex 13 of MEPC 37/22, containing resolution MEPC 65(37) concerning amendments to regulation 2 and new regulation 9 of MARPOL annex V.

[75] See IMO documents MEPC 37/22, para. 13.6, MEPC 37/WP.9/Add.1, para. 17.9, and MEPC 38/WP.17, which contains the text of the draft annex. There continue to be divergent views as to the figure of the global cap to be placed on the sulphur content in oil (MEPC 37/22, para. 13.43).

[76] IMO document, LEG 73/14, paras. 14-18.

[77] IMO document MSC 66/24, paras. 10.14 and 10.20-10.26. The Committee also made progress towards the completion of the international SAR plan.

78 IMO document MSC 67/2/1, para. 2.2.

79 IMO document MEPC 37/22/Add.1, annex 10.

80 IMO documents C 74/22(b)/1; C 74/SR.4; C 74/27(c), paras. 225-228; C/ES.18/10, paras. 270-273; and A 19/27, paras. 9-11.

81 Report of the sixty-sixth session, IMO document MSC 66/24, annex 26.   The MEPC has endorsed these interim guidelines.

82 IMO Assembly resolution A.739(18).

83 Assembly resolution A.744(18).

84 Assembly resolution A.600(15).

85 Resolution MSC.47(66).   See IMO document MSC 66/24, annex 2.

86 See the OECD report, circulated as IMO document MSC 66/12/1, and extensively quoted by IMO in its statement on World Maritime Day 1996, "IMO: seeking excellence through cooperation".

87 A message from the Secretary-General of IMO on the World Maritime Day 1995.

88 Proposal submitted by the United Kingdom and Australia; IMO document FSI 4/3/3.

89 Proposal by Canada; IMO document FSI 4/3/1.

90 Proposal submitted by Germany; IMO document FSI 4/3/4.

91 The 1994 amendments to annexes I, II, III and V of MARPOL 73/78 provide the legal basis for port State control of operational requirements; they entered into force on 3 March 1996.

92 Official Journal of the European Communities, vol. 38, No. L157 (7 July 1995).

93 IMO document FSI 4/7/2, para. 3.

94 European Parliament resolution on safety at sea, adopted on 1 February 1996; and resolution on the Sea Empress disaster, adopted on 27 March 1996; IMO documents MSC 66/20/1 and MEPC 38/INF.14.

95 IMO document FSI 4/18, paras. 7.9 and 7.10.   A comparative table of port State control agreements is contained in IMO News, No. 2 (1996).

96 Note by the United Kingdom; IMO document MSC 66/7/5.

97 "MARPOL - How to enforce it.   Manual on compliance assurance programme for the effective enforcement of the Convention", submitted by the IMO secretariat to the Subcommittee on Flag State Implementation; IMO document FSI 4/3/2, para. 9.4.

98 IMO document FSI 4/4/2.

99 Ministerial Declaration of the Fourth International Conference on the Protection of the North Sea (June 1995); IMO document MEPC 37/INF.14, annex 3, sect. 6.

[100] Parties to the Bonn Agreement have decided to examine the possible consequences of the entry into force of the Convention and the possible establishment of new exclusive economic zones, e.g., on the delimitation of zones of responsibility under the Agreement; see IMO document MEPC 37/INF.33.

[101] The States bordering the North Sea have confirmed that the necessary waste oil reception facilities are available; IMO documents MEPC 38/8/5 and MEPC 38/8/3.

[102] It also provides for the establishment of a harmonized fee system for the use of reception facilities; see IMO document MEPC 38/INF.4.

[103] IMO document MEPC 38/9/9.

[104] See IMO document MEPC 37/22, para. 13.10.

[105] Signed by Brunei Darussalam, Cambodia, Indonesia, the Lao People's Democratic Republic, Malaysia, Myanmar, the Philippines, Singapore, Thailand, and Viet Nam.

[106] The Subcommittee on Safety of Navigation is currently working on a revision of the 1985 Guidelines for VTS and on a draft SOLAS regulation on VTS for inclusion in the proposed revision of SOLAS chapter V.

[107] In accordance with IMO Assembly resolution A.826(19), MSC will now adopt traffic separation schemes (TSSs), routing measures other than TSSs and ship reporting systems, as well as amendments thereto, i.e., they no longer require Assembly confirmation.

[108] Resolution MSC.52(66); IMO document MSC 66/24, annex 10.

[109] Report of the forty-second session of the Subcommittee; IMO document NAV 42/23, paras. 5.4-5.7, and annexes 8-10.

[110] IMO document NAV 42/5. The regime governing navigation in the Danish straits has been developed on the basis of the Copenhagen Convention on the Sound and the Belts, 1857. Another fixed link is currently under construction across the Sound. Denmark and Sweden have informed IMO of the measures both Governments are taking to ensure safety of navigation.

[111] IMO documents NAV 42/5/1 and NAV 42/5/2.

[112] IMO document NAV 42/23, para. 5.8.

[113] Submission of World Wildlife Fund and International Union for the Conservation of Nature, IMO document MEPC 38/7/2.

[114] IMO document MEPC 35/INF.17.

[115] In a letter dated 13 November 1995 addressed to the Secretary-General (A/50/754), the Russian Federation complained that Turkey had not taken steps to align its national maritime regulations to the IMO Rules and Recommendations. Turkey, in a letter dated 7 December 1995 (A/50/809), maintained that its national regulations were in full conformity with the IMO Rules and Regulations.

[116] See IMO document NAV 41/23, paras 4.1-4.4.

[117] IMO document NAV 42/23, para. 4.4.

[118] IMO's Strategy for Extrabudgetary Activities Relating to Environmentally Sustainable Development, adopted by MEPC at its thirty-seventh session; IMO document MEPC 37/22/Add.1/Corr.1, annex 11.

[119] IMO document NAV 41/23, paras. 4.1-4.4.

[120] IMO document MEPC 38/19.

[121] Paras. 4 and 7; circulated as document MEPC 38/INF.14.

[122] Annex 3 on "Follow-up actions related to the Strategy for the Protection of Pollution from Ships" to the Ministerial Declaration; IMO document MEPC 37/INF.14.

[123] IMO document MSC 67/7/2. The proposed sea lanes are as follows: (a) from the South China Sea to the Natuna Sea then through the Karimata Strait to the Java Sea and through the Sunda Strait to the Indian Ocean; (b) from the Sulawesi Sea through the Makassar and Lombok Straits to the Indian Ocean; (c) from the Pacific Ocean to the Maluku Sea, Seram Sea and Banda Sea either (i) through the Ombai Strait to the Sawu Sea, or (ii) through the Leti Strait to the Timor Sea, or (iii) through the archipelagic waters between the islands of Aru and Tanimbar to the Arafuru Sea.

[124] The right of innocent passage applies outside the sea lanes in archipelagic waters, in accordance with article 52, paragraph 1, of the Convention.

[125] Submission by Australia; IMO document MSC 67/7/3.

[126] International Herald Tribune, 16 May 1996.

[127] Note by the Oil Industry International Exploration and Production Forum (E & P Forum) to the Scientific Group of the London Convention, IMO document LC/SG 19/3/4, para. 4.1.1.

[128] Report of the ESCAP training seminar (19-22 September 1995).

[129] Council of Europe document ADOC 7514 of 12 April 1996.

[130] Article 1, and annex I, para. 2.4, of the draft Protocol; IMO document LC/SM/1/4.

[131] IMO document LC 18/11, paras. 5.34-5.35.

[132] See Official Records of the Economic and Social Council, 1996, Supplement No. 8 (E/1996/28), chap. I.C, decision 4/15.

[133] UNESCO document 146 EX/27, para. 38.

[134] The Buenos Aires Draft Convention on the Protection of the Underwater Cultural Heritage of the International Law Association has been transmitted to the UNESCO secretariat. For the text, see Marine Policy, vol. 20 (1996), pp. 305-307.

[135] Draft European Convention on the Protection of the Underwater Cultural Heritage (1985); Council of Europe document CAHAQ(85)5.

[136] A draft Charter on the protection and management of underwater cultural heritage has also been prepared for archaeologists; it will be attached to the Draft Convention prepared by the International Law Association.

[137] Official Records of the General Assembly, Fifty-first Session, Supplement No. 10 and corrigendum (A/51/10 and Corr.1), annex II, addendum 2.

[138] IMO document LEG 73/14, paras. 45-50.

[139] IMO document LEG 73/11, article V.

[140] See note by France, IMO document LEG 74/5/1.

[141] Comment by the Comité Maritime International, which has established an International Subcommittee to study the law of wreck removal; see IMO document LEG 74/5/2, p. 7.

[142] IMO document LEG 74/5/2/Add.1.

[143] Communication from the Executive Secretary of ICCAT, 21 December 1995.

[144] FAO Fisheries Report No. 534 (FIPL/R534 (Bi)).

[145] FAO Fisheries Report No. 539 (FIPL/R539(TRI).

[146] Communication from the Secretary of NEAFC dated 25 March 1996.

[147] Meeting Proceedings of NAFO for 1995, sect. V, part I, pp. 186-197.

[148] Ibid., sect. IV, annex 6, pp. 151-152.

[149] United Nations Secretariat working paper on the Falkland Islands (Malvinas), prepared for the Special Committee on the Situation with regard to the Implementation of the Granting of Independence to Colonial Countries and Peoples, A/AC.109/2048, para. 18.

[150] See A/51/183, annex II.

[151] Report of the fourteenth CCAMLR Meeting, document CCAMLR-XIV.

[152] "Process for the establishment of the Indian Ocean Tuna Commission", FAO Fisheries Circular No. 913 (FIPL/C 913), 1996.

[153] Communiqué of the twenty-sixth South Pacific Forum Meeting.

[154] Council of Europe, Parliamentary Assembly, document 7514, 12 April 1996.

[155] See A/51/210, annex IV.

[156] All are signatories to a Memorandum of Understanding with UNEP on cooperation in the implementation of the MMAP concluded in December 1991. The International Whaling Commission and the Whale and Dolphin Conservation Society have also participated as observers.

[157] The Fund is managed by the Dutch Institute for Forestry and Nature Research, at Den Burg.

[158] Final press release on the annual meeting of IWC, 28 June 1996.

[159] Communication from the Secretary of NAMMCO, 13 June 1996.

[160] Reported in ICCOPS Newsletter, No. 6, January 1996. International Centre for Coastal and Ocean Policy Studies, Genoa, Italy.

[161] Draft article 1(1) presently defines the scope, inter alia, as "the maritime waters of the Mediterranean Sea and the Black Sea, including its gulfs and seas".

[162] See A/51/183, annex I, para. 35, and annex II.

[163] Official Records of the Economic and Social Council, 1996, Supplement No. 8 (E/1996/28), chap. I.C, decision 4/6.

[164] The programme areas are: (a) integrated management and sustainable (b) development of coastal and marine areas, including exclusive economic zones; marine environmental protection; (c) sustainable use and conservation of marine living resources of the high seas; (d) sustainable use and conservation of marine living resources under national jurisdiction; (e) addressing critical uncertainties for the management of the marine environment and climate change; (f) strengthening international, including regional cooperation and coordination; (g) sustainable development of small islands. The report of the Secretary-General on programme area G is contained in E/CN.17/1996/20 and Add.1-5.

[165] E/CN.17/1996/3 and Add.1.

[166] Official Records of the Economic and Social Council, 1996, Supplement No. 8 (E/1996/28), chap. I.C, decision 4/15, sect. C.1-2.

[167] Ibid., chap. I.A.

[168] In accordance with General Assembly resolution 50/113, para. 13.

[169] As noted, for example, in UNEP decision 18/31 of 25 May 1995. See Official Records of the General Assembly, Fiftieth Session, Supplement No. 25 (A/50/25), annex.

[170] A/51/116, appendix II, para. 17. UNEP decision 18/32 lists 11 persistent organic pollutants belonging on the short list under discussion by the Economic Commission for Europe in the context of the 1979 Convention on Long-range Transboundary Air Pollution.

[171] Ibid., paras. 3 and 4.

[172] These are sewage, persistent organic pollutants, heavy metals, radioactive substances, nutrients and sediment mobilization, oils (hydrocarbons), litter and physical alterations, including habitat modification and destruction of areas of concern.

[173] WHO, IAEA, FAO, IMO Inter-organizational Programme for the Sound Management of Chemicals, the International Programme on Chemical Safety and the Intergovernmental Forum on Chemical Safety.

[174] Many global and regional bodies have already specifically endorsed the Global Programme e.g., the Meeting of States Members of the South Atlantic Zone of Peace and Cooperation.

[175] IMO document LC/SM 1/4.

[176] IMO document LC 18/11/Rev.1, paras. 5.25-5.29.

[177] IMO document LEG/CONF.10/8/2.

[178] IMO documents LEG 73/14, paras. 51-54, and LEG 73/12.

[179] IMO document LEG 74/4/1; see also LEG 74/4/2, in which the Comité Maritime International summarizes a number of the issues it considers relevant to the subject.

[180] IMO document MEPC 38/6/5.

[181] The request was made by Argentina, Australia, Brazil, Chile, Colombia, Cuba, Indonesia, Ireland, Mexico, New Zealand, Solomon Islands, Spain and Venezuela.

[182] IMO documents MSC 66/24, para. 21.17, and MSC 67/15.

[183] IMO document MSC 66/24, para. 21.18.

[184] Submission by Solomon Islands, IMO document MSC 67/15/1.

[185] IMO document NAV 42/23, paras. 6.6-6.17. Ships carrying INF materials are generally tracked throughout their voyage, by either the shipowner or a shore-based authority of one of the countries involved in the transport activity.

[186] IMO document MSC 67/15, para. 6.

[187] See A/51/183, annex II. See also the proposal submitted by Argentina to IMO, document LEG 74/12/1: it suggests, *inter alia*, that ships carrying INF materials should navigate exclusively by a high-seas route; and if this does not prove possible, alternative routes can only be established in consultation with the coastal State.

[188] CARICOM secretariat press release 50/1996.

[189] The Auckland Communiqué, 10-13 November 1995.

[190] See A/51/357, annex.

[191] UNEP/CBD/COP/2/19, annex II.

[192] See note by the Executive Secretary, UNEP/CBD/COP/3/35.

[193] UNEP/CBD/COP/3/3, recommendation II/10.

[194] Official Records of the Economic and Social Council, 1996, Supplement No. 8 (E/1996/28), chap. I.C, decision 4/15, para. 24.

[195] The second Conference of Parties to the Biodiversity Convention, in paragraph 13 of decision II/10, called on relevant organizations to review their programmes with a view to improving existing measures and developing new actions which promote the conservation and sustainable use of marine biological diversity (UNEP/CBD/COP/2/19).

[196] Reported in International Centre for Coastal and Ocean Policy Studies newsletter, No. 6, January 1996.

[197] Official Records of the Economic and Social Council, 1996, Supplement No. 8 (E/1996/28), chap. I.C, decision 4/15, paras. 44-45.

[198] Ibid., para. 43.

[199] E.g., the Third Conference of Parties to the Convention on Biological Diversity will be examining, *inter alia*, a suggestion by the Executive Secretary to have "a regular overview report on activities under other institutions and/or conventions relevant to the implementation of the Convention (along the lines of the report submitted by the Secretary-General of the United Nations to the General Assembly in relation to the law of the sea)" (UNEP/CBD/COP/3/35, para. 80).

[200] Text reproduced in Law of the Sea Bulletin, No. 31 (1996), p. 40.

[201] Ibid., p. 42.

[202] See the "Agreement on Principles", done at Paris on 21 May 1996 (S/1996/447, annex); also reproduced in Law of the Sea Bulletin, No. 32 (1996), p. 94 (in press).

[203] Itar-Tass, 14 August 1996.

[204] A/50/73-S/1995/83. The 1994 Treaty was also brought to the attention of the International Maritime Organization by Israel in view of its provisions on maritime matters; IMO document MSC 66/24.

[205] Done at Aqaba on 18 January 1996; reproduced in Law of the Sea Bulletin, No. 32 (1996), p. 97 (in press).

[206] S/1996/427.

[207] IMO document MSC 66/24, paras. 23.16 to 23.20, and annex 29 containing the full statement of Lebanon.

[208] S/1996/627.

[209] S/1996/692.

[210] Reuters, 8 August 1996.

[211] The New York Times, 16 September 1996.

[212] Official Records of the Economic and Social Council, 1996, Supplement No. 10 (E/1996/30), chap. I.A, draft resolution II.

[213] The European Community has requested inclusion in the work programme of the IMO Working Group on Ship/Port Interface of the installation of systematic border controls at seaports in European Union countries against illicit trafficking of radioactive materials; IMO document FAL 25/12, para. 15.3.

[214] A serious criminal situation has emerged in the Caucasus region, aggravated by the infiltration of mercenaries, arms, narcotics and contraband into the territory of Abkhazia, Georgia. By the Decree of 31 January 1996, Georgia has closed the seaport of Sukhumi and ports and the marine area between Georgia and the Russian Federation within the territory of Abkhazia to international shipments (S/1996/240, annex I).

[215] Convened pursuant to recommendation 9 of the Working Group and resolution 8 (XXXVIII) adopted by the Commission on Narcotic Drugs in 1995 (see Official Records of the Economic and Social Council, 1996, Supplement No. 9 (E/1996/29, chap. 12).

[216] A/51/437.

[217] Report of the Regional Meeting on Drug Control Cooperation in the Caribbean, Bridgetown, Barbados, 15-17 May 1996.

[218] IMO document FAL 24/19, paras. 7.17-7.26.

[219] Bulletin of the Baltic and International Maritime Council, vol. 90, No. 5.

[220] Canada has noted that most of the aliens coming to it are in fact asylum seekers. An agreement between Canada and the United States on the return and readmittance of refugees aimed at subjecting them to a full and fair refugee determination procedure was expected to be signed in February 1996; IMO document FAL 24/19, para. 18.4.

[221] Report by the West England P & I Club (September 1995), in the Bulletin of the Baltic and International Maritime Council, vol. 90, No. 5.

[222] IMO document FAL 24/2/5, para. 6.

[223] IMO circular FAL.2/Circ.43.

[224] IMO document FAL 24/19, paras. 10.1-10.5.

[225] E/CN.15/1996/4, para. 45.

[226] The draft resolution was advanced by the United States; press release SOC/CP/192/Rev.1.

[227] IMO document MSC 66/16/Add.1.

[228] Submission to IMO by the International Maritime Bureau of the International Chamber of Commerce; IMO document MSC 66/16/2.

[229] Note by the Government of Turkey; IMO document MSC 67/INF.2.

[230] IMO document MSC 66/24, para. 16.11.

[231] Offshore, vol. 56, No. 5 (May 1996).

[232] Offshore, vol. 56, No. 6 (June 1996); and vol. 56, No. 8 (August 1996).

[233] Cook, P. J., Social trends and their impact on the coastal zone and adjacent seas, British Geological Survey Technical report WQ/96/3, 1996.

[234] Offshore, vol. 56, No. 4 (April 1996).

[235] The New York Times, 27 February 1995.

[236] The Christian Science Monitor, 15 August 1995.

[237] Ocean Science News, 29 February 1996.

[238] Cook, op. cit.

[239] For current information on "pioneer investors", see document ISBA/A/10.

[240] Offshore, vol. 56, No. 1 (January 1996).

[241] Ibid.

[242] Mining magazine, June 1996.

[243] Press release, IAEA/1309, dated 24 September 1996.

[244] IPCC second assessment: Climate Change 1995. Report of the UNEP/WMO IPCC.

[245] Ibid., p. 23.

[246] The Working Group, which is supported also by the Division for Ocean Affairs and Law of the Sea, held its first meeting, at Geneva on 17 and 18 May 1996.

[247] Report of the twenty-sixth session, GESAMP Rep. Stud. 60 (1996).

[248] See also "The contribution of science to integrated coastal management", GESAMP Rep. Stud. 61 (1996).

[249] Report of the twenty-fifth session, GESAMP Rep. Stud. No. 56, para. 8.2.

[250] The New York Times, 28 November 1995, p. C1.

[251] Ibid., 24 October 1995, p. C7.

[252] Ibid., 2 July 1996.

[253] Ibid., 19 March 1996, p. C1.

[254] Offshore, vol. 56, No. 5 (May 1996), p. 33.

[255] Ibid., vol. 56, No. 5 (May 1996).

[256] Business Week, 30 October 1995.

[257] Offshore, vol. 56, No. 6 (June 1996), and vol. 56, No. 8 (August 1996).

[258] Ibid., vol. 56, No. 5 (May 1996), and vol. 56, No. 8 (August 1996).

[259] Mining journal, 5 January 1996.

[260] The fellowship is given by the United Nations Legal Counsel, on the recommendation of the Advisory Panel of prominent personalities in law of the sea and international affairs under the chairmanship of Professor John Norton Moore, Director of the Center for Oceans Law and Policy, University of Virginia School of Law.

[261] Ms. Tamoepeau is expected to carry out her fellowship and research and study at the Oxford University Faculty of Law.

[262] The United Kingdom has requested that the candidate be chosen from a developing country and pursue a one-year LL.M. programme or carry out advanced study and research, at the graduate level, at a university in the United Kingdom.

[263] A report of the meeting will be published.

[264] Currently UNDP has a portfolio of over $70 million in ocean/coastal projects and plays an active role in developing the international waters and marine biodiversity components of the Global Environment Facility.

<u>Addendum</u>

LETTER DATED 27 DECEMBER 1996 FROM THE PERMANENT REPRESENTATIVE OF
THE PEOPLE'S REPUBLIC OF CHINA TO THE UNITED NATIONS ADDRESSED TO
THE SECRETARY-GENERAL

[Original: Chinese]

Upon instructions of my Government, I have the honour to bring to your
attention the following errors appearing in paragraphs 260 and 261 of the
Secretary-General's report on the law of the sea (A/51/645), and urge that
immediate and effective measures be taken to correct them:

1.   The Diaoyu Island and all the islands appertaining thereto have been
part of China's territory since ancient times, which has been justified by
historical facts and international law.   In the aforementioned report, however,
the Diaoyu Islands are erroneously described as under Japan's "effective
control", which term carries a specific meaning under international law.

2.   The Diaoyu Island and all the islands appertaining thereto are located
about 92 miles north-east of Jilong City of China's Taiwan Province.   In the
report, nevertheless, they are said to be "located about 200 miles east of the
Chinese coast", which could be understood as excluding China's Taiwan Province
from the Chinese territory.

3.   It is presumed in the report "that a main reason the islands have
become the focus of such attention is that surveys have suggested there may be
large oil reserves nearby", while what actually brings the issue of the Diaoyu
Islands to the focus of attention once again is the provocative actions by a
group of Japanese right-wingers who set up a lighthouse and a Japanese flag on
the islands in July of this year.

I further have the honour to request that Your Excellency respond with a
letter and have my letter officially circulated as an addendum to the
Secretary-General's report on the law of the sea (A/51/645).

(Signed)   QIN Huasun

*   *   *

LETTER DATED 30 DECEMBER 1996 FROM THE SECRETARY-GENERAL ADDRESSED
TO THE PERMANENT REPRESENTATIVE OF THE PEOPLE'S REPUBLIC OF CHINA
TO THE UNITED NATIONS

[Original: English]

In response to your letter of 27 December 1996, I have the honour to inform
you as follows:

With respect to the location of the Diaoyu Islands, I wish to assure you
that the formulation used in the report to which your letter refers should in no
way be understood as derogating from the official position of the United Nations
with respect to the lawful rights of the People's Republic of China as set out
in General Assembly resolution 2758 (XXVI) of 25 October 1971.

As concerns the other matters dealt with in your letter, I take note of the
position of your Government.   I should in this context like to emphasize that
the purpose of the report, which contains references to eight different maritime
disputes, is simply to inform about the existence of the disputes, and that it
should not be interpreted as taking a position in the disputes referred to.

I have decided to issue your letter and my response as an addendum to the
report.

(Signed)   Boutros BOUTROS-GHALI

<u>Addendum</u>

LETTER DATED 10 FEBRUARY 1997 FROM THE PERMANENT REPRESENTATIVE
OF JAPAN TO THE UNITED NATIONS ADDRESSED TO THE SECRETARY-GENERAL

Upon instructions from my Government, I have the honour to refer to your
report on the law of the sea (A/51/645) and state the following regarding
paragraphs 260 and 261 of the said report.

The report on the law of the sea (A/51/645) was prepared and submitted to
the General Assembly by the Secretary-General, who bears sole responsibility for
it. As such, Member States of the United Nations are not in a position to grant
recognition of or support for its content. Nor does the content of the report
affect the position of Japan.

In view, however, of the fact that a letter from the Permanent
Representative of the People's Republic of China stating the position of his
Government concerning the said paragraphs has been made a part of this report in
the form of an addendum to it, I am obliged to state the following position of
my Government in this regard:

"In view of the history of the Senkaku Islands and in the light of the
relevant principles of international law, there is no question that the
islands are an integral part of the territory of Japan, and that Japan has
always been exercising effective control over them. It is thus the
position of the Government of Japan that no question of territorial title
should arise with respect to those islands."

I further have the honour to request that the present letter be circulated
as an addendum to the above-mentioned report.

                                                   (<u>Signed</u>) Hisashi OWADA

                                * * *

LETTER DATED 14 FEBRUARY 1997 FROM THE SECRETARY-GENERAL ADDRESSED
TO THE PERMANENT REPRESENTATIVE OF JAPAN TO THE UNITED NATIONS

In response to your letter of 10 February 1997, I have the honour to inform
you as follows:

I have taken note of the position of your Government. I should in this
context like to emphasize that the purpose of the report, which contains
references to eight different maritime disputes, is simply to inform about the
existence of the disputes, and that it should not be interpreted as taking a
position in the disputes referred to.

I have decided to issue your letter and my response as an addendum to the
report.

                                                   (<u>Signed</u>) Kofi A. ANNAN

                                -----

3. LAW OF THE SEA: LARGE-SCALE PELAGIC DRIFTNET FISHING AND ITS IMPACT ON THE LIVING MARINE RESOURCES OF THE WORLD'S OCEANS AND SEAS; UNAUTHORIZED FISHING IN ZONES OF NATIONAL JURISDICTION AND ITS IMPACT ON THE LIVING MARINE RESOURCES OF THE WORLD'S OCEANS AND SEAS; AND FISHERIES BY-CATCH AND DISCARDS AND THEIR IMPACT ON THE SUSTAINABLE USE OF THE WORLD'S LIVING MARINE RESOURCES - REPORT OF THE UN SECRETARY-GENERAL

Doc. no.: A/51/404   25 September 1996

CONTENTS

CONTENTS (continued)

I. INTRODUCTION

1.   The General Assembly, at its fiftieth session, in resolution 50/25 of 5 December 1995, took note of the reports of the Secretary-General on large-scale pelagic drift-net fishing and its impact on the living marine resources of the world's oceans and seas (A/50/553) and on unauthorized fishing in zones of national jurisdiction and its impact on the living marine resources of the world's oceans and seas (A/50/549), as well as the report of the Food and Agriculture Organization of the United Nations (FAO) on fisheries by-catch and discards and their impact on the sustainable use of the world's living marine resources (A/50/552, annex).

2.   In the same resolution, the General Assembly, expressing deep concern about continuing reports of activities inconsistent with the terms of Assembly resolution 46/215 1/ of 20 December 1991 and unauthorized fishing inconsistent with the terms of its resolution 49/116 of 19 December 1994, and, while recognizing the efforts that international organizations and members of the international community had made to reduce by-catch and discards in fishing operations, urged all authorities of members of the international community to take greater enforcement responsibility to ensure full compliance with resolution 46/215 and to impose appropriate sanctions against acts contrary to the terms of that resolution. The Assembly also called upon States to take the responsibility to adopt measures to ensure that no fishing vessels entitled to fly their national flags fished in areas under the national jurisdiction of other States unless duly authorized by the competent authorities of the coastal State or States concerned and that such authorized fishing operations should be carried out in accordance with the conditions set out in the authorization.

3.   The General Assembly further urged States, relevant international organizations and regional and subregional fisheries management organizations and arrangements to take action to adopt policies, apply measures, collect and exchange data and develop techniques to reduce by-catch, fish discards and post-harvest losses consistent with international law and relevant international instruments, and called upon development assistance organizations to make it a high priority to support efforts of developing coastal States, in particular the least developed countries and the small island developing States, to improve the monitoring and control of fishing activities and the enforcement of fishing

regulations. In addition, the Assembly requested the Secretary-General to bring the resolution to the attention of all members of the international community, relevant intergovernmental organizations, the organizations and bodies of the United Nations system, regional and subregional fisheries management organizations, and relevant non-governmental organizations with a view to providing him with information relevant to the implementation of the resolution, and to submit to it at its fifty-first session a report on further developments relating to the implementation of resolutions 46/215, 49/116 and resolution 49/118 of 19 December 1994, taking into account the information thus provided.

4.   Accordingly, the Secretary-General sent a note verbale to all members of the international community, drawing their attention to the relevant provisions of resolution 50/25. Letters were also addressed to relevant intergovernmental organizations, specialized agencies of the United Nations, organizations and bodies of the United Nations system, as well as regional and subregional fisheries management organizations and arrangements, and relevant non-governmental organizations. In response, the Secretary-General has received a number of submissions and comments. He wishes to express his appreciation for all the contributions.

5.   The present report, which takes into account such contributions, is submitted to the General Assembly in response to the request contained in resolution 50/25.

II.   LARGE-SCALE PELAGIC DRIFT-NET FISHING AND ITS IMPACT ON THE
      LIVING MARINE RESOURCES OF THE WORLD'S OCEANS AND SEAS

A.   General

1.   Information provided by States

6.   In its reply of 10 June 1996 to the Secretary-General, Colombia 2/ stated that it did not conduct large-scale pelagic drift-net fishing, emphasizing that the Government of Colombia supported the moratorium on large-scale drift-net fishing because it was in the common interest of the conservation of over-exploited fish stocks, birds and marine mammals caught incidentally by those practices.

7.   In its submission to the Secretary-General dated 10 June 1996, Qatar 3/ informed him that there were no vessels belonging to Qatar that currently used large-scale pelagic drift-nets.

8.   In its reply to the Secretary-General dated 18 June 1996, Maldives 4/ stated that it was opposed to any form of large-scale pelagic drift-net fishing on the high seas. It further indicated that the use of such nets was prohibited in the waters under the national jurisdiction in the Maldives.

9.   In its response of 21 June 1996 to the Secretary-General, Saudi Arabia 5/ indicated that although Saudi fishing agencies did not use large-scale pelagic drift-nets, assurances had already been given that such nets were not used in fishing on the high seas or in the Kingdom's territorial sea or its economic zone.

10.   In its reply to the Secretary-General dated 28 June 1996, Italy 6/ informed him that in circular 60707 of 16 April 1996, it had reiterated the ban on keeping on board or conducting fishing activities with drift-nets greater than 2,500 metres in length. The ban had been introduced by Ministerial Decree of 22 May 1991, modified by the Ministerial Decree of 6 August 1991 and extended by Court of Cassation sentence No. 12310 of 1995. It further indicated that inspection measures, along with legislative measures for more severe penalties, were under consideration by the Italian authorities.

11.   In its response of 28 June 1996 to the Secretary-General, New Zealand 7/
stated that it remained opposed to large-scale pelagic drift-net fishing and
attached great importance to the full implementation of the global moratorium in
accordance with resolution 46/215. New Zealand also indicated that it was aware
of reports of continued drift-net fishing in other areas and wished to express
its deep concern about such reports, and to urge all countries to direct their
fishing industries to comply fully with the global moratorium. It therefore
welcomed the decision taken by the General Assembly at its fiftieth session to
urge authorities of members of the international community to take greater
enforcement responsibility to ensure full compliance with resolution 46/215 and
to impose appropriate sanctions, consistent with international law, against acts
contrary to the terms of the resolution.

12.   In its submission to the Secretary-General dated 2 July 1996, Mauritius 8/
indicated that it did not allow pelagic drift-net fishing in its waters and had
banned the landing or trans-shipment of fish caught by drift-nets in its
harbours pursuant to its Drift-net Act of 1992.

13.   In its reply of 2 July 1996 to the Secretary-General, Norway 9/ informed
him that a ban had been put in place by its authorities in respect of
large-scale pelagic drift-net fishing on the high seas.

14.   In its response of 10 July 1996 to the Secretary-General, Morocco 10/
indicated that it had established since 1992 rules regulating the use of
large-scale drift-nets, including the number of nets allowed aboard fishing
vessels as well as the length of such nets.

15.   In its submission to the Secretary-General dated 10 July 1996, Spain 11/
stated that since 1990 it had prevented its vessels from engaging in large-scale
pelagic drift-net fishing in any area of the seas, thereby strongly enforcing
the prohibition and encouraging the use of selective fishing gear. In addition,
it had supported in international forums the banning of the use of that kind of
gear because of its effect on non-target species, cetaceans and marine mammals.

16.   In its reply of 22 June 1996 to the Secretary-General, Kuwait 12/ informed
him that it supported an end to all indiscriminate and environmentally damaging
fishing, whether carried out within or beyond its territorial sea. Kuwait
further indicated that it did not have a national fleet operating on the high
seas, and it worked through competent governmental agencies for the protection
and development of local fish stocks, focusing its attention on the types of
fishing nets used in zones under its national jurisdiction, in order to stop
environmental pollution and ensure better management of its fishing grounds. In
addition, it had adopted several measures aimed at ending the use of nylon
drift-nets which, despite the existence of laws forbidding the use of such nets,
continued to aggravate the depletion of fish stocks and impede their development
by becoming lost at sea. Consequently, work was being done to develop an
alternative type of net made of fibres that would be less damaging to the marine
environment.

17.   In its response to the Secretary-General dated 25 July 1996, Tunisia 13/
stated that it had recently adopted an executive order which prohibited the use
of large-scale pelagic drift-nets greater than 2.5 kilometres in length.

18.   In its response to the Secretary-General dated 29 July 1996, South
Africa 14/ informed him that regulations banning the use of drift-nets in South
African waters, prohibiting vessels visiting South African ports from carrying
such nets and banning their use on the high seas by South African citizens had
become law in 1988. It added that South Africa was therefore committed to
continuing its efforts to actively enforce the global moratorium on all
large-scale pelagic drift-net fishing on the high seas.

19.   In its submission of 7 August 1996 to the Secretary-General, the United
States of America 15/ provided the following information:

"...

"As a principal sponsor of General Assembly resolution 46/215, as well as resolutions 44/225 (1989) and 45/197 (1990), and supporter of decisions 47/443 (1992), 48/445 (1993), 49/436 (1994) and resolution 50/25 (1995), the United States takes a particular interest in the effective and full implementation of a global moratorium on large-scale pelagic drift-net fishing on the high seas in the light of the adverse impacts such fishing has upon the world's living marine resources.

"The United States firmly believes that the best available scientific evidence demonstrates the wastefulness and potential ecosystem-scale negative impacts of large-scale pelagic drift-net fishing on the high seas. The United States believes that it was appropriate that the General Assembly, in recognition of the unacceptable impacts of large-scale pelagic drift-net fishing on the high seas, called upon all members of the international community to ensure that a global moratorium on all large-scale pelagic drift-net fishing on the high seas be fully implemented by 31 December 1992 in resolution 46/215.

"The United States attaches great importance to compliance with resolution 46/215 and has taken measures individually and collectively to prevent large-scale pelagic drift-net fishing on the high seas. It has called upon all members of the international community to implement and comply with the resolution. In addition, the United States has urged all members of the international community, intergovernmental organizations, non-governmental organizations and scientific institutions with expertise in living marine resources to report to the Secretary-General any activity or conduct inconsistent with the terms of resolution 46/215.

"Since 1990, it is unlawful under the Magnuson Fishery Conservation and Management Act (the Magnuson Act) for any United States national or fishing vessel to engage in large-scale drift-net fishing in any area under the fisheries jurisdiction of the United States or beyond the exclusive economic zone of any nation.

"The Drift-net Act Amendments of 1990, and more recently the High Seas Drift-net Fisheries Enforcement Act, enacted in November 1992, made it the stated policy of the United States, among other things, to implement resolution 46/215, and secure a permanent ban on the use of destructive fishing practices, in particular large-scale drift-nets, by persons or vessels fishing beyond the exclusive economic zone of any nation. Additionally, the Act provides for the denial of port privileges for any large-scale drift-net fishing vessel and for a prohibition on the importation of certain products from any nation whose nationals or vessels conduct large-scale drift-net fishing beyond the exclusive economic zone of any nation.

"On 8 March 1993, the United States announced plans to promote observance of the global moratorium on large-scale pelagic drift-net fishing on the high seas, including steps the United States intends to take in the event United States enforcement authorities have reasonable grounds to believe that any foreign flag vessel encountered on the high seas is conducting, or has conducted, large-scale pelagic drift-net fishing operations inconsistent with resolution 46/215. United States enforcement officials will follow established procedures for determining flag-State identity or registration and will take law-enforcement actions in conjunction with the flag State and consistent with the 1982 United Nations Convention on the Law of the Sea. Under customary international law and United States law, a vessel considered stateless and found to be conducting large-scale pelagic drift-net fishing operations on the high seas is subject to penalty in the United States.

'Since submission of its reports to the Secretary-General in
June 1995, the United States has taken a number of steps to implement the
General Assembly's resolutions and decisions on large-scale pelagic
drift-net fishing on the high seas.

'...

'Under a Memorandum of Understanding between the United States
departments of Transportation, Commerce and Defense, signed
11 October 1993, the United States will utilize the surveillance
capabilities of the Department of Defense to locate and identify vessels
suspected of violating resolution 46/215. Formal procedures for
communicating vessel positions to the Department of Commerce, the Coast
Guard and concerned Governments have been established.

'The United States continues to attach extreme importance to
compliance with resolution 46/215 and encourages all members of the
international community to take measures to prohibit their nationals and
vessels from undertaking any activity contrary to the terms of
resolution 46/215 and to impose appropriate penalties against any that may
undertake such activities.'

2.   Information provided by international organizations

(a)   Specialized agencies of the United Nations

20.   In its reply to the Secretary-General dated 19 July 1996, FAO 16/ submitted
the following report:

'...

'FAO members do not report specifically to the Organization whether
their nationals are engaged directly in large-scale drift-net fishing.
Although information is sought, by means of questionnaires, on the
composition of members' fishing fleets, there is a low response rate.

'Status of large-scale pelagic drift-net fleets

'There have been no reports of flag-vessels from Asian States and
entities using large-scale pelagic drift-net fishing gear in the 1995/96
period. Policies put in place in the early 1990s by the Asian
distant-water fishing nations and entities to decommission vessels with
large-scale pelagic drift-net fishing gear have been successful. These
distant water fishing nations and entities are to be commended for their
efforts in addressing this issue.

'France has enforced European Community Council
regulation 345/92, which limits the length of drift-nets to 2.5 km per
vessel, thereby abiding by the European Community law and the United
Nations international moratorium. However, Greenpeace International
has reported that a Spanish fleet of vessels, with large-scale pelagic
drift-nets of about 7 km in length, has been operating in the Alboran
sea in the Mediterranean.

'Italy's fleet of large-scale pelagic drift-net vessels, totalling
about 650 vessels, remains in existence and has commenced fishing for the
1996 season. The fleet targets swordfish in the Mediterranean sea on a
seasonal basis. The Italian fishermen maintain that operating in this
fishery is not viable unless they can utilize large-scale pelagic
drift-nets of at least 9 km in length. The fishermen have therefore
requested the Government to authorize the use of such nets or to compensate
fishermen if they are required to abandon the fishery.

"The Italian General Directorate of Fisheries has submitted a compensation plan to the Government involving a compensation package for fishermen of 100 billion lire. No decision has been reached on whether the plan will be implemented by the Government. The plan would eliminate the Italian large-scale pelagic drift-net fishery.

"In the United States, non-governmental organizations have brought a case against the Department of State for not taking appropriate action against Italy, under the 1992 High Seas Drift-net Fisheries Enforcement Act, for the continued use of large-scale pelagic drift-nets. The United States Government has initiated action in line with the provision of the 1992 Act. The consequences for Italy, if it fails to implement the required measures to terminate fishing with large-scale pelagic drift-nets by the Italian fleet before 28 July 1996, include a possible embargo on the import of seafood of Italian origin into the United States. Currently, this trade is valued at approximately US$ 1.2 billion per year.

"If the Italian compensation plan for the large-scale pelagic drift-net fleet is implemented, action must be taken by the Government to prevent the movement of this gear from Italy to countries in the southern Mediterranean Sea. According to Greenpeace International, there is a real risk that this could happen if Italy opts to abide by General Assembly resolution 46/215 and European Community Council regulation 345/92.

"...

"Conclusion

"On the basis of information available to FAO, the incidence of large-scale pelagic drift-net fishing in contravention of General Assembly resolution 46/215 and subsequent resolutions declined marginally in the 1995/96 period. Currently, the major area for large-scale pelagic drift-net fishing is the Mediterranean Sea, with vessels being predominantly of Italian flag or origin."

(b)   Organs, organizations and programmes
      of the United Nations

21.   In its response of 6 May 1996 to the Secretary-General, the United Nations Conference on Trade and Development indicated that it had no comments on resolution 50/25.

3.   Information provided by non-governmental organizations

22.   In its reply to the Secretary-General dated 28 June 1996, the Federation of Japan Tuna Fisheries Cooperative Associations 17/ stated that, while it understood that the United Nations had a number of important roles to play in international forums, its most active role should be the establishment of the framework and the coordination of opposing interests where there was no mechanism to reconcile such interests and when conflicts of those interests occurred. Fortunately, the United Nations had established several agencies and entities under its competence to cope with the ever diversifying problems of the world. The Federation was of the view that such agencies had competence, expertise and human resources to manage and solve specific issues effectively. In the field of fisheries, it was FAO that had such expertise and resources. Moreover, regional organizations and arrangements had been established to manage particular fishing activities. Those organizations had been established in order to avoid a heavy concentration of roles in the United Nations and to pursue more efficient problem-solving mechanisms. Therefore, specific issues such as those considered in resolution 50/25 were better dealt with by more appropriate entities in the United Nations system and the role of the United

Nations should be limited to establishing a broader framework to utilize the system in a more effective manner.

23. As to the relationship between drift-net fishing and General Assembly resolution 50/24 of 5 December 1995 on the Agreement for the Implementation of the Law of the Sea Convention, provisions relating to straddling and highly migratory fish stock conservation and management, the Federation believed that the validity of resolution 50/25 banning drift-net fishing on the high seas should only be questioned from the viewpoint of the compatibility of conservation and management measures, both within areas of national jurisdiction and beyond, which had been established as a principle in the 1995 Agreement on straddling fish stocks and highly migratory fish stocks. Therefore, it hoped that the United Nations would this year approach that issue from such a perspective.

B. Review by region

1. Atlantic Ocean

(a) Information provided by States

24. No States have reported any activities involving large-scale pelagic drift-net fishing in any high seas areas of the Atlantic Ocean.

(b) Information provided by specialized agencies of the United Nations

25. In its submission to the Secretary-General, FAO reported that the FAO Fishery Committee for the Eastern Central Atlantic (CECAF) had indicated that there had been no reports of large-scale pelagic drift-net fishing in the CECAF area during 1995/96.

(c) Information provided by regional and subregional fisheries organizations and arrangements

26. In its report to the Secretary-General dated 24 April 1996, the International Commission for the Conservation of Atlantic Tunas (ICCAT) 18/ provided the sections of the Proceedings of the Fourteenth Regular Meeting of ICCAT held in Madrid in November 1995 relevant to large-scale drift-net fishing and its effects on tuna stocks. The proceedings indicate that, although member States subscribed to the General Assembly resolutions banning drift-net fishing on the high seas, there was no agreement regarding the actual effects of drift-nets on the environment or the size of drift-nets that could be harmful to the ecosystem.

27. In its reply of 11 June 1996 to the Secretary-General, the North-East Atlantic Fisheries Commission (NEAFC) 19/ stated that no use of large-scale pelagic drifts was made in the areas of high seas within the NEAFC Convention area for fish species to which the Convention related.

28. In its response of 18 June 1996 to the Secretary-General, the Northwest Atlantic Fisheries Organization (NAFO) 20/ informed him that there was no large-scale pelagic drift-net fishing in the NAFO Regulatory Area.

29. In its submission to the Secretary-General dated 22 July 1996, the North Atlantic Salmon Conservation Organization (NASCO) 21/ indicated that it was not aware of any activities within the area covered by its establishing Convention which would be inconsistent with resolution 46/215.

(d)   Information provided by non-governmental organizations

30.   In its reply of 1 July 1996 to the Secretary-General, Greenpeace
International 22/ informed him that, in response to the violent conflicts in
which traditional albacore fishermen were opposed to drift-netters in the North-
east Atlantic, fishery had been subject to stricter control by the European
Commission and the European Union member States concerned. The European
Commission "Report on the Enforcement of Community Legislation concerning the
Use of Drift-nets in 1995 in the North-east Atlantic and the Mediterranean"
concluded that the "costs incurred by member States throughout the season were
both considerable and disproportionate given the level of participation by
fishing vessels using drift-nets and the economic value of the quantities
landed", thus raising the question as to how long the European Union would
sustain such levels of control and enforcement in order to ensure the respect of
Union legislation.

2.   Baltic Sea

(a)   Information provided by States

31.   In its response to the Secretary-General dated 3 July and 18 September
1996, Finland 23/ considered it important that the European Union Council
regulations on the matter be reformed, given the fact that long drift-nets
caught varying quantities of protected undersized species as by-catches, such as
dolphins and other marine mammals and turtles. It nevertheless was of the view
that there was no need for a drift-net ban in the closed Baltic brackish water
basin because studies had shown that undersized species were not caught in
salmon drift-nets in the Baltic, and in addition, such a ban would put an almost
complete end to fishing of salmon beyond coastal waters.

3.   Indian Ocean and Asia-Pacific region

(a)   Information provided by regional and subregional
       fisheries organizations

32.   In its reply of 24 June 1996 to the Secretary-General, the Asia-Pacific
Fishery Commission (APFIC) 24/ informed him that there was no more large-scale
pelagic drift-net fishing in the Asia-Pacific region, as recommended by the
General Assembly in its resolution 46/215.

4.   Mediterranean Sea

(a)   Information provided by States

33.   The United States informed the Secretary-General that it had held
consultations with Italy and the European Union concerning reports of drift-net
activity in the Mediterranean Sea by Italian nationals and vessels. As a result
of those consultations, an agreement was reached under which Italy had committed
itself to take a variety of measures to effectively end large-scale high seas
drift-net fishing by Italian nationals. The United States had worked
extensively with Italy on this issue and was confident that the measures to be
undertaken by Italy would accomplish the goals of the United Nations moratorium
on high seas drift-net fishing. It added that central to the steps Italy
planned to take was a fishing vessel conversion programme, to be funded jointly
by Italy and the European Union. Through that programme, Italian drift-net
fishing vessels would either be retired from fishing activity or converted to
operate in other fisheries. The conversion plan would be scheduled to start
before the beginning of the 1997 fishing season.

34.   In its submission to the Secretary-General dated 10 July 1996, Morocco 25/
stated that, with respect to the implementation of the global moratorium on

large-scale pelagic drift-net fishing on the high seas, it had established since 1992 provisions governing the use of this type of gear, including the number and length of nets authorized on board fishing vessels.

(b)   Information provided by specialized agencies of the United Nations

35.   FAO indicated that there had been reports of fishing with large-scale pelagic drift-nets in the Mediterranean Sea, although the General Fisheries Council for the Mediterranean (GFCM) had advised it that there had been no complaints from members concerning fishing with such nets in the 1995/96 period.

(c)   Information provided by non-governmental organizations

36.   Greenpeace International reported that large-scale pelagic drift-nets continued to be used in the Mediterranean Sea. The biggest fleet was still the Italian one, with more than 600 licensed boats. Other Mediterranean countries might be developing their fleets and/or buying nets from Italy. Despite some efforts by the European Commission to ensure effective enforcement by European Union member States of the legislation on drift-nets, Italian drift-netters had continued to operate with large-scale nets, longer than the legal maximum length of 2.5 km, established by EU Council Regulation (EEC) No. 345/92 amending Council Regulation (EEC) No. 3094/86.

37.   According to the Greenpeace submission, in its 1995 report on inspections in the Mediterranean Sea, the European Commission noted that there were problems with respect to compliance with European Union legislation in the Mediterranean and that the level of enforcement undertaken by Italian authorities was far from sufficient. Despite this, Italian authorities had not substantially increased enforcement measures and only a few of the vessels operating illegally had been arrested. The first sightings of Italian vessels using large-scale high seas drift-nets in the western Mediterranean were reported by Spanish fishing boats from Cartagena, Carboneras and Xabia, as early as in March 1996. Since then, more vessels had been sighted periodically. At the end of May 1996, the European Commission patrol vessel Northern Desire spent a few days controlling the Balearic Sea zone and, according to Greenpeace information, it found illegal Italian drift-netters. At the same time, illegal drift-netters fishing in international waters off Milos island in the Aegean Sea were reported by Greek authorities to the European Commission. Between 16 May and 25 June 1996, the Northern Desire inspected 16 Italian drift-net vessels on the high seas. Of these, 15 vessels were found using illegal nets. During a control at sea by the Italian Coast Guard, 44 vessels were sent back to the harbour of Lipari (Sicily) for further investigation. It was found that 33 of them had been using illegal nets.

38.   Greenpeace further noted that its observers had also documented drift-net activities in Italian harbours, inter alia, in Sardinia and Sicily. All the vessels sighted had on board nets far longer than 2.5 km. According to Greenpeace observers, some vessels had even more nets on board than last year, as evidenced by available photo documentation. On 28 and 30 June and 1 July, five sperm whales were found entangled in drift-nets 20 to 24 miles off the coast of Mallorca. That type of incident had been repeated for years. On 1 July 1996, the European Commission disclosed results of its inspection trip in the Mediterranean this year. According to the Commission, inspections only confirmed continued widespread illegal drift-net fishing by Italian fleets and the Commission suggested that those operations were in contravention of General Assembly resolution 46/215 and subsequent decisions with respect to drift-net fishing. According to artisanal Italian longliners, illegal drift-net operations occurred in the central Mediterranean. Other local Mediterranean fishermen had reported large-scale high seas drift-nets in both the eastern and the western Mediterranean.

39. Greenpeace further stated that, considering the lack of control in international waters of the Mediterranean, it was very likely that fleets from other countries used illegal large-scale drift-nets. According to an Italian Government report, vessels from Japan, the Republic of Korea, Morocco, Tunisia, Turkey, Algeria, Malta and Albania were currently using high seas drift-nets in the Mediterranean Sea. A parliamentary written question to the European Commission from the Liberal Group of the European Parliament on 6 June 1996 referred to Italian drift-net vessels having been reflagged to Croatia, Albania and Cyprus. Greenpeace thus concluded that, despite the few steps taken by the European Commission to ensure enforcement of European Union legislation, the situation of drift-net fishery in the Mediterranean Sea remained similar to previous years. European Union drift-net fleets and in particular the Italian fleet continued to violate resolution 46/215.

5. Pacific Ocean

(a) Information provided by States

40. Canada 26/ reported that during 1995 it had conducted several surveillance overflights in the North Pacific as part of its cooperative enforcement programme with other members of the North Pacific Anadromous Fish Commission. The cooperation of Canada, Japan, the Russian Federation and the United States in implementing that moratorium on large-scale high seas drift-net fishing and the provisions of the North Pacific Anadromous Stocks Convention had clearly contributed to the virtual elimination of drift-net fishing in the North Pacific Ocean.

41. The United States informed the Secretary-General that the United States Coast Guard and the National Marine Fisheries Service had continued to carry out enforcement and surveillance activities in 1995 in the North Pacific Ocean in areas of former large-scale drift-net fishing to monitor compliance with the drift-nets moratorium. Coast Guard cutters logged 93 vessel-days at sea and Coast Guard aircraft flew 294 hours in conjunction with the 1995 drift-net monitoring programme. In addition, 212 vessel-days were available for response to specific incidents.

42. On 10 July 1995, according to the United States, in response to information received from United States fishermen, a Coast Guard aircraft had located and filmed a stateless vessel conducting high seas drift-net fishing operations in the North Pacific Ocean. Following a five-day pursuit by a Coast Guard cutter, the fishing vessel was boarded, seized and taken under tow to Guam. In Guam the vessel's master, a citizen of Taiwan Province of China, was charged under the Magnuson Act for refusing to allow authorized officers to board his vessel for inspection; he was sentenced to six months in jail, received an $8,000 fine, and forfeiture action was brought against the vessel. Furthermore, since the master, the first mate and the engineer of the stateless vessel were citizens of Taiwan Province of China, the latter's fisheries authorities and Ministry of Justice Investigation Bureau undertook an investigation of the incident. The United States also cooperated with Taiwanese authorities in July 1996, when a Taiwanese flag fishing vessel was observed conducting high seas drift-net operations by a United States Coast Guard cutter in the North Pacific Ocean. The fishing vessel was monitored by the cutter until Taiwanese enforcement vessels arrived. After a joint boarding, Taiwanese authorities took custody of the fishing vessel and accepted an evidence package from the United States. Taiwan Province of China had indicated that it planned to investigate the matter and, if the evidence warranted, to prosecute fully those responsible.

43. The United States further reported that under the terms of a Memorandum of Understanding dated 3 December 1993, the United States and China were working together to ensure effective cooperation and implementation of resolution 46/215 in the North Pacific; the agreement remained in effect until December 1996. It allowed enforcement officials of either country to board and inspect vessels

flying the flag of the other country in the North Pacific Ocean which were found using or equipped to use large-scale high seas pelagic drift-nets. The agreement also provided for enforcement officials of either country to ride on high seas drift-net fishery enforcement vessels of the other country. During 1996, the United States Coast Guard would have on board Chinese officials on three high seas fishery enforcement patrols. One of those patrols would also be conducted jointly with an enforcement vessel from the Russian Federal Border Service. A similar operation was conducted with Japan in June 1996. The Coast Guard's high seas enforcement plan for 1996 would allocate resources at levels consistent with 1995. Coast Guard air patrols would be coordinated with similar enforcement efforts by Canada to provide maximum patrol-area coverage.

44. New Zealand stated that there had been no drift-net activity within areas under its jurisdiction over the past 12 months. It also noted that the Forum Fisheries Agency had confirmed that it had received no reports of large-scale pelagic drift-net fishing in the South Pacific over the past year. It also reiterated its call for all countries eligible to do so to support fully the Convention for the prohibition of fishing with long drift-nets in the South Pacific and its two protocols.

(b)   Information provided by specialized agencies of the United Nations

45. FAO reported that the Inter-American Tropical Tuna Commission (I-ATTC) and the South Pacific Forum Fisheries Agency (FFA) had informed it that there had been no reports of fishing with large-scale pelagic drift-nets in their respective areas of competence in 1995/96.

(c)   Information provided by subregional and regional fisheries organizations and arrangements

46. The South Pacific Commission (SPC) 27/ stated that it had no information indicating that large-scale pelagic drift-net fishing had occurred in the South Pacific since the adoption of resolution 46/215.

6.   Antarctica

Information provided by specialized agencies of the United Nations

47. FAO reported that the Commission for the Conservation of Antarctic Marine Living Resources (CCAMLR) had informed it that the Commission had agreed in its resolution 7/IX that there would be no expansion of large-scale pelagic drift-net fishing into the high seas areas of the Convention area. Since its adoption in 1990, no cases of activities or conduct inconsistent with the terms of that resolution had been reported to the Commission within the CCAMLR area.

III.   UNAUTHORIZED FISHING IN ZONES OF NATIONAL JURISDICTION AND ITS IMPACT ON THE LIVING MARINE RESOURCES OF THE WORLD'S OCEANS AND SEAS

A.   Information provided by States

48. Canada stated that since May 1994 all fishing activities undertaken by its vessels outside zones under its national jurisdiction, including high seas and zones under the national jurisdiction of other States, ought to be authorized by it. The regulations were introduced, *inter alia*, to allow Canada to become party to the FAO Agreement to Promote Compliance with International Conservation and Management Measures by Fishing Vessels on the High Seas. It also pointed out that Canadian regulations went further than the FAO Agreement, which required States to authorize all high seas fishing but was silent as to fishing

activities being conducted in zones under the national jurisdiction of other States. Those regulations therefore allowed Canada to ensure compliance by Canadian fishing vessels with applicable conservation and management measures wherever they operated, including areas subject to the fisheries jurisdiction of other States.

49. Colombia stated that it granted authorization and fishing permits to vessels flying its flag when they intended to carry out fishing activities only in zones under the national jurisdiction of Colombia or on the high seas.

50. Qatar informed the Secretary-General that, in accordance with its legislation, it granted fishing licences only to masters of vessels that were owned by nationals of Qatar and, under the terms of such licences, they were permitted to fish in zones under national jurisdiction. In addition, foreign fishing vessels were permitted to engage in fishing activities in zones under national jurisdiction only after obtaining a licence from the Qatar authorities.

51. Maldives indicated that it did not have any vessels fishing in any areas other than those that were under its national jurisdiction.

52. Saudi Arabia stated that vessels flying its flag were allowed to fish on the high seas or in zones under the national jurisdiction of other States only after obtaining authorization to do so from the competent authorities of the Kingdom or from the State in whose zones they would intend to fish. It further indicated that foreign fishing activities in zones under its national jurisdiction without proper authorization were subject to fines and penalties.

53. Italy reported that it had reiterated to its port authorities and professional organizations the requirement to respect domestic legislation on fishing or boating limits, with specific reference to the Italian law on the ratification of the United Nations Convention on the Law of the Sea.

54. Norway stated that access to fishery zones of foreign countries by vessels flying the flag of Norway was regulated by international agreements with such countries. Norwegian vessels could thus only fish in such areas upon the express consent of and under such terms as were laid down by host Governments. In the event of fishing activities by a Norwegian vessel contrary to those terms, Norwegian authorities were empowered to take action against such a vessel upon its return to port.

55. Finland said that Finnish vessels fished only in the Baltic Sea. Exploitation of fish resources in the Baltic Sea was based on precisely regulated fish stocks, quota exchanges, technical fishing regulations and fishing monitoring measures, which were governed by regulations issued by the European Union and by fishing agreements between Baltic States and the Union.

56. Spain reported that legislation in force since 1982 required Spanish vessels fishing on the high seas and in zones under the national jurisdiction of other States to carry a special permit. Fishing activities on the high seas without the authorization of Spanish authorities, as well as fishing activities in zones under the national jurisdiction of other States without a permit, constituted an infringement of Spanish law. In addition, as a member of the European Community, Spain was bound to abide by European Community regulation 3317/94, which required fishing vessels operating in zones under the national jurisdiction of other States to have a "fishing permit/agreement" (permis de pêche - accord de pêche). 28/ It therefore concluded that it had sufficient control measures to prevent a vessel flying its flag to engage in unauthorized fishing in zones under the national jurisdiction of other States.

57. Kuwait stated that, in compliance with General Assembly resolution 49/116, it had adopted legislation that prohibited vessels flying its flag to fish in areas under the national jurisdiction of other States unless duly authorized by the competent authorities of those States.

58. Tunisia indicated that the majority of its fleets fished in its internal
waters, territorial sea and protected areas. Those which were engaged in
fishery beyond those areas operated in zones situated within the limits of its
continental shelf, and few units fished in other areas of the high seas beyond
those limits.

59. The United States stressed the view that States had an obligation under
international law, as reflected in the United Nations Convention on the Law of
the Sea, to take measures to prevent fishing vessels entitled to fly their
national flag from fishing in zones under the national jurisdiction of other
States unless duly authorized to do so, and to ensure that such fishing was in
accordance with applicable laws and regulations. Article 56(1) of the
Convention provided that coastal States had sovereign rights for the purpose of
exploring and exploiting, conserving and managing the natural resources, whether
living or non-living, within their respective zones of national jurisdiction.
Furthermore, article 62(4) of the Convention provided that nationals of other
States fishing in the exclusive economic zone should comply with the
conservation measures and with the terms and conditions established in the laws
and regulations of the coastal State.

60. The United States had long acted to prevent unauthorized fishing in zones
under the national jurisdiction of other States by vessels entitled to fly its
flag. The oldest and broadest instrument available to the United States to
implement this objective was the Lacey Act amendments of 1981. Originally
enacted in 1900, a violation of the Lacey Act was dependent upon a separate
violation of an underlying state, foreign, federal or Indian tribal law. It was
one of the United States' primary laws directly targeting illicit interstate or
foreign commerce in illegally taken fish, wildlife and plant species. Under the
Lacey Act, it was unlawful for any person or other entity subject to the
jurisdiction of the United States to import, export, transport, sell, receive,
acquire or purchase (or attempt to commit any of these acts) in interstate or
foreign commerce, any fish or wildlife taken, possessed, transported, or sold in
violation of any law or regulation of any state of the United States or in
violation of any foreign law. In addition, the Lacey Act provided that within
the special maritime and territorial jurisdiction of the United States, it was
unlawful for any person to possess any fish taken, possessed, transported or
sold (or attempt to commit any of these acts) in violation of any law or
regulation of any state of the United States or in violation of any foreign law.
Enforcement of the Lacey Act was supported by both civil and criminal penalties.

61. Furthermore, the United States was party to a variety of international
agreements that further prohibited its nationals and vessels from engaging in
unauthorized fishing in certain areas under the fisheries jurisdiction of other
States. Several such agreements had been concluded with the Governments of
Colombia, the United Kingdom of Great Britain and Northern Ireland, the Russian
Federation, Canada and numerous Governments in the South Pacific Ocean. The
Lacey Act and the treaties and agreements mentioned above had worked well to
promote bilateral and multilateral cooperation. Those measures had contributed
significantly to supporting the conservation of fisheries resources within zones
under national jurisdiction. Ensuring full implementation of resolution 50/25
by the United States, however, was limited by several problems. Firstly,
detection of any alleged illegal fishing activity within zones of national
jurisdiction depended largely on the enforcement capability of the coastal
State. The fishery enforcement capability of many coastal States, however (and
especially among developing States with large national zones), was frequently
limited because of inadequate resources. Secondly, prosecution under the Lacey
Act was dependent upon a separate violation of an underlying foreign or federal
law. Such prosecutions could involve difficult evidentiary issues, for example
proving that a United States flag fishing vessel had violated a law or a
regulation of a foreign country. Thirdly, effective prosecutions under the
Lacey Act and in accordance with other international agreements and treaties
required strong cooperation between United States and foreign officials. Such
cooperation might not always be forthcoming. Fourthly, prosecuting violations

of unauthorized fishing activities which occurred within the jurisdiction of a foreign country was expensive, involving, for example, the expense of providing transportation to witnesses. The United States had defrayed the costs of litigating violations of its fisheries law and regulations through a fund which consisted of monies collected through fines, penalties and forfeitures. Despite those difficulties, it was committed to fulfilling its responsibilities as a flag State and believed it had achieved much to prevent unauthorized fishing in zones under the national jurisdiction of other States by fishing vessels flying its flag.

62. In addition to the above, the United States indicated that it had prohibited unauthorized fishing by fishing vessels from foreign countries within its own zone of national jurisdiction. The Magnuson Act stated that no foreign fishing was authorized within the exclusive economic zone of the United States unless authorized and conducted under and in accordance with a valid and applicable permit. Such permits could only be issued if the relevant foreign country had concluded an international fishing agreement with the United States. Such agreements acknowledged the exclusive fishery management authority of the United States, required foreign nations and the owner or operator of any foreign fishing vessel to abide by all its regulations and provided for enforcement of its fisheries law and regulations. Foreign fishing activities within its exclusive economic zone were monitored and enforced by the Coast Guard and the National Marine Fisheries Service. The United States attached extreme importance to compliance with resolutions 49/116 and 50/25 and encouraged all flag States of the international community to take measures to prevent fishing vessels entitled to fly their national flag from fishing in zones under the national jurisdiction of other States unless duly authorized and to ensure that such fishing operations were conducted in accordance with the conditions set out in such authorizations.

B. Information provided by specialized agencies of the United Nations

63. FAO reported that its Fisheries Department did not maintain specific records concerning the incidence of unauthorized fishing in zones of national jurisdiction. At meetings and consultations convened by FAO, the matter was often commented upon by members in their statements. However, in the current reporting period there had been no FAO meetings or consultations at which such reports had been made. Nonetheless FFA had reported that in the South Pacific, there had been a number of incidents of unauthorized fishing in zones of national jurisdiction in the 1995/96 period. One Japanese vessel was reported to have been fishing without a licence in the exclusive economic zone of Papua New Guinea; three vessels of the Republic of Korea were reported to be fishing without licences in the exclusive economic zone of Papua New Guinea, the Federated States of Micronesia and Solomon Islands; and two vessels from Taiwan, Province of China, were fishing without a licence in the exclusive economic zones of Papua New Guinea and the Federated States of Micronesia. FFA had reported that some of those violations had been settled with the owners of the vessels concerned.

64. In addition, FAO's Regional Fishery Office for the Near East had reported that unauthorized fishing in the zones of national jurisdiction had taken place in the reporting period in the Red Sea area, and in particular involving Egyptian flag trawlers fishing unauthorized in waters of Yemen. Action to address the situation had been taken by the Governments concerned. Egyptian flag trawlers had also made incursions into Eritrean waters and Governments were negotiating arrangements to solve the problem. In the case of Somalia, owing to the political situation in that country it was believed that a significant amount of unauthorized fishing had taken place. However, factions in Somalia had agreed to issue fishing licences in their respective areas of control to foreign fleets in return for commissions based on catch.

C.   Information provided by regional and subregional
fisheries organizations and arrangements

65.   APFIC indicated that there was still some unauthorized fishing in the
exclusive economic zones of coastal States in Asia. The situation was being
improved through bilateral arrangements for joint ventures and monitoring,
control and surveillance among the countries concerned.

IV.   FISHERIES BY-CATCH AND DISCARDS AND THEIR IMPACT ON THE
SUSTAINABLE USE OF THE WORLD'S LIVING MARINE RESOURCES

A.   Information provided by States

66.   In its reply to the Secretary-General, Canada provided the following
information:

"(a) Pacific groundfish fishery

'Trawl fishing in Canada's Pacific groundfish fishery is generally
non-selective and by-catches can be significant. The three principal
types of by-catches are: (a) species which the fisher is not licensed
to catch; (b) species which are protected because of low abundance;
and (c) species that are unwanted in the market place.

'Starting in 1996, most vessels in the Canadian trawl fleet were
required to carry observers certified by the Department of Fisheries
and Oceans while fishing. Fishing logbooks and all landings continue
to be fully monitored. These measures are providing reliable
estimates of the catches and their disposition.

'On-vessel observers also make it practical to manage the fishery by
allocating catch and by-catch quotas to each vessel. Managing the
fishery with individual vessel quotas helps ensure that the overall
harvests remain within the total allowable catches (TAC) set for the
various species. The quotas are set, by species, for two or more
fishing periods in the year (known as 'period limits'). Fishers are
permitted to average their catches over the fishing periods, thereby
reducing the need to discard fish caught in excess of a fishing-period
quota. Any landings that cannot be averaged within allotted quotas
are relinquished by the fisher. Vessels exceeding by-catch quotas not
only relinquish the excess by-catch but also have their fishing
privileges restricted or withdrawn.

'In addition, there are halibut by-catch limits established for major
groundfish fishing areas. The areas are closed to trawl fishing when
an area halibut by-catch limit is reached.

"(b) Halibut by-catch

'In 1989, the Pacific halibut by-catches occurring in the
Canadian and the United States groundfish trawl fisheries became a
focus for action by fishery managers and fishers of both countries.
(The halibut resource is a single stock extending from the Bering Sea
southward to the states of Washington and Oregon in the United States,
and supports valuable fisheries.)

'In 1991, the Governments of both countries undertook to reduce
the by-catch mortalities significantly. Canada is committed to
reducing the by-catch in the Canadian groundfish trawl fishery by
50 per cent by the end of 1997.

"(c) <u>Atlantic groundfish fishery</u>

"Canada has a mandatory landing requirement and discarding is not permitted. Minimum mesh sizes are sufficiently large to reduce the amount of undersized fish caught. As Canada does not have a market for small fish and fisheries can be closed should excessive amounts of small fish be caught, fishers ensure that the gear is used properly in order to reduce or eliminate catches of unwanted fish. For other fisheries, such as shrimp, where groundfish by-catches are common and unwanted, fishers must install grates (i.e. Nordmore grate) to reduce or eliminate by-catches of groundfish."

67. Colombia reported that it took part in a programme implemented by the United States Fishing and Wildlife Service for the prevention of by-catches of turtles during industrial shrimp fisheries by trawling, and had therefore made compulsory the use of turtle-excluding devices aboard vessels fishing for shrimp in the Caribbean and the Pacific.

68. Qatar stated that in order to reduce by-catches, fish discards and post-harvest losses, it had required the implementation of its laws and regulations regarding the conservation of fish stocks and the protection of the marine environment. These included the prohibition of the dredging practised by large fishing vessels; prohibition of fishing with nets made of nylon and three-walled trammel nets and a ban on the importation of such nets in view of the damage they caused to fish stocks; and control of fishing gear in use that had to meet legal specifications and sound fishing practices.

69. Maldives indicated that, as a traditional tuna fishing State, it had a highly developed and selective live bait and live tuna fishery that excluded the discard of by-catches.

70. Saudi Arabia reported that it had elaborated rules and regulations to reduce by-catches, fish discards and post-harvest losses and protect fish stocks from abusive fishing practices. It had also undertaken studies and was being kept informed of recent international research on selective types of trawl nets that did not capture young fish. In addition, Saudi Arabia has established rules and specifications for fishing gear allowed to be used in areas under its jurisdiction in order to reduce by-catches, fish discards and post-harvest losses.

71. Italy informed the Secretary-General that a draft regulation of the European Union was being prepared on the use of appropriate equipment according to the type of fish. Once approved, the regulation would enter into force in the internal legal system of Italy.

72. Mauritius indicated that no discards were obtained from its artisanal and bank fisheries. It added that for tuna fishery, the volume of by-catches was very small and that fish caught as by-catches were used for the production of pet foods and fish meal.

73. Norway stated that a comprehensive ban was in place against the discarding of fish in waters under its fisheries jurisdiction. Strict by-catch regulations were in force, stipulating maximum legal by-catch levels in different fisheries and a requirement for vessels to leave a given fishing area when permissible by-catch levels were being exceeded.

74. Finland indicated that it had complied with the regulations of the European Union on the issue, which were themselves based on the recommendations of the International Baltic Fisheries Commission. It also said that the quantities of by-catches and fish discards and other fishing drawbacks in the Baltic area were minor because fisheries were quite selective and affected very few species. Furthermore, fishing technology was specialized and highly advanced.

75.   Morocco stated that, in accordance with Royal Decree No. 1-73-255 of 23 November 1973 regulating marine fisheries activities, it was mandatory for fishermen to return immediately at sea any fish that had not reached commercial size.   In addition, an executive order dated 3 October 1988 had established a minimal commercial size for various fish species caught in areas under the national jurisdiction of Morocco.

76.   Spain said that, as a member of the European Community, it had complied with conservation and management measures of marine living resources established by the Community.   It also expressed the view that the use of selective fishing gear was the appropriate way to avoid the capture of non-target species.   It further indicated that Spanish vessels were largely equipped with traditional fishing gear that kept incidental catches at the lowest level.   It added that there were proposals within the Common Fisheries Policy of the Community to improve the selectivity of authorized gear.

77.   Kuwait informed the Secretary-General that it had adopted important fisheries policies that were aimed at developing its fish stocks and reducing fish discards and by-catches.   Measures included the prohibition of dragnets used to catch cetaceans and the restriction of dragnets used for shrimp fishing; ongoing evaluation of nets used to catch shrimp and cetaceans with a view to preventing by-catches and discards; technical improvement of nets; and the prohibition of unauthorized fishing by any vessel as well as the placing of appropriate markers on all authorized vessels that would indicate the types of fisheries they could undertake.

78.   Tunisia stated that it had recently adopted technical provisions aimed at reducing undersized catches, including provisions regulating the technical characteristics of nets and fishing gear, sizes of catches, areas of fishing activities and fishing seasons.

79.   South Africa expressed its concern about the heavy wastage of fisheries resources resulting from the discarding of unwanted catches at sea.   It was of the view that those practices had a direct and negative impact on the resource, on the environment and on the availability of fish for consumption.   South Africa indicated that it was participating in an FAO review of the estimates of wastage in the South-East Atlantic region as part of the organization's revision of estimates on wastage.   It further indicated that discarding unwanted catch was illegal under the terms of South African fisheries legislation.

80.   The United States stated that it had undertaken important steps to reduce fish discards and by-catch in domestic and international fisheries.   The National Marine Fisheries Service had established a by-catch team to develop a long-term strategic plan that prioritized by-catch research, management and education needs.   The by-catch plan was expected to be implemented in spring 1997, and included both straddling and highly migratory fish stocks, and organisms subject to capture in pelagic nets, as well as all other fisheries stocks subject to federal management.   A major component of the plan was a comprehensive description of the status of information on by-catch for each United States fishery resource.   In addition, the Service was incorporating measures to reduce by-catch associated with fisheries for Atlantic highly migratory species into the fisheries management plan for those species.   The fishery management plan was expected to be ready in late 1997.

81.   It further indicated that it was actively involved in efforts to reduce by-catch and fish discards in international fisheries through international treaties and domestic legislation.   Those efforts included measures to reduce dolphin mortality in the Eastern Pacific tuna fishery, the incidental mortality of sea turtles in commercial shrimp fisheries throughout the world and efforts to enforce the worldwide ban on drift-nets.   It was also party to several international agreements that contained provisions on by-catch and discards, including the Convention on the Conservation and Management of Pollock in the Central Bering Sea, the Convention for the Conservation of Anadromous Stocks in

the North Pacific Ocean and the Convention for the Preservation of the Halibut Fishery of the Northern Pacific Ocean and the Bering Sea.

82. It added that the United States interpreted the term post-harvest losses, as defined in the FAO Code of Conduct for Responsible Fisheries, to mean waste, unutilized or underutilized catch or losses from protected resources (marine mammals, sea turtles and such fishes as salmon and sturgeon) resulting from interactions with fishing operations. Post-harvest losses, including issues of required by-catch utilization and other management measures to reduce wastage (e.g., closed seasons/closed areas and incentive programmes), constituted areas currently under policy review. It was not anticipated that national policies to address post-harvest losses would be proposed until certain social and economic information was collected and analysed. As data increasingly demonstrated, fish losses from the above sources were significant and could undermine conservation efforts. The United States Congress was currently considering amendments to the Magnuson Act which would include measures to address by-catch, discards and post-harvest loss. Reauthorization of the Act would form the basis for additional efforts in these areas.

B. Information provided by specialized agencies of the United Nations

83. In its reply to the Secretary-General, FAO provided the following report:

"The need to minimize by-catch and discards in industrial fisheries has become a major issue since the combined effect of these practices could threaten the long-term sustainability of fisheries and the maintenance of biodiversity. Moreover, the international focus on by-catch and discards reflects the concern that fisheries resources are not being utilized efficiently and production is not supporting food security to the extent possible.

"As a follow-up to work already supported by FAO on the by-catch and discard issue, the Fisheries Department is collecting additional data from different parts of the world and from different types of fisheries. The matter will be further discussed at an Expert Consultation on the subject organized by the Government of Japan, in close consultation with FAO, in October 1996. The outcome of the Expert Consultation will be reported to the twenty-second session of the Committee of Fisheries in March 1997.

"Other initiatives on by-catch and discards are being initiated at the national and regional levels. Some States, including Iceland, New Zealand and Norway, for example, already have policies in place to prohibit or limit discarding the unwanted part of the catch at sea. Other countries are expected to enact similar policies. In addition, several subregional and regional fisheries organizations have commenced or strengthened programmes aimed at securing enhanced information concerning the scope and extent of by-catch and discards, and of refining assessments relating to their impact.

"APFIC is actively encouraging its members, through appropriate national institutes, to initiate assessments on the by-catch and discards issue. Thailand has already completed such a study. A regional review of by-catch and discard is being undertaken, on behalf of FAO and APFIC, by the Fisheries Research Institute, in Penang, Malaysia. APFIC anticipates being able to compile a series of studies and a statement so that an up-to-date evaluation of the issue in the APFIC area can be made.

"I-ATTC has a comprehensive observer programme, in place since 1972, which has sampled tuna purse seiners operating in the eastern tropical Pacific Ocean. The programme is designed to make observations on incidental capture and mortality of dolphins in the fishery. Since 1988,

observers have collected information on the by-catch of other living marine
resources on an ad hoc basis and, in 1993, the I-ATTC members and other
cooperating countries whose vessels exploit the fishery instituted a
regular programme which records all by-catch species taken by large purse
seiners in the eastern Pacific. The Commission's 1995 annual report will
provide data showing discards by species and methods of capture for the
years 1992 to 1995.

        "The South Pacific Commission (SPC) is currently involved in the
collection by its observers of by-catch and discard information from
vessels operating in the South Pacific region. It is also involved in the
coordination of national observer programmes and the sampling of vessels in
ports. Information relating to by-catch and discards in the South Pacific
is published in the Commission's tuna technical reports.

        "CCAMLR has adopted Conservation Measure 29/XIV concerning
Minimization of the Incidental Mortality of Seabirds in the Course of
Longline Fishing or Longline Fishing Research in the Convention area, which
has been in force (with several amendments) since the 1993/94 fishing
season. In 1995, CCAMLR initiated an exchange of information with a number
of international organizations, including the United Nations and FAO, in
relation to incidental mortality of seabirds caused by fishing activities.
This was to make known CCAMLR's experience in applying mitigating
techniques and in formulating conservation measures, and to be informed of
the steps other organizations had taken, or were studying, to address the
issue of incidental mortality of seabirds associated with fisheries,
especially longline fisheries. This is a matter of continuing concern to
CCAMLR and is an ongoing subject for discussion and review at CCAMLR
meetings."

C.   Information provided by regional and subregional fisheries organizations and arrangements

84.   I-ATTC informed the Secretary-General that it had an observer programme
which had sampled tuna purse seiners fishing in the eastern Pacific Ocean to
make observations on incidental capture and mortality of dolphins in the fishery
since 1972. Observers had collected information on the by-catch of other marine
resources since 1988 on an ad hoc basis, and in 1993, I-ATTC members and other
cooperating countries whose vessels exploited the fishery had instituted a
regular programme which recorded all by-catch species taken by large tuna purse
seiners in the eastern Pacific. In addition, in the Declaration of Panama, the
members of I-ATTC and other countries whose vessels were involved in the
fishery, expressed their commitment "to the assessment of the catch and by-catch
of small yellowfin tuna and other stocks of living marine resources related to
the tuna fishery in the eastern Pacific Ocean and the establishment of measures
to, inter alia, avoid, reduce and minimize the by-catch of juvenile yellowfin
tuna and the by-catch of non-target species, in order to ensure the long-term
sustainability of all these species, taking into account consideration of the
interrelationship among species in the ecosystem."

85.   The South Pacific Commission indicated that it was currently involved in
the collection of by-catch and discards information from vessels fishing in the
region through the South Pacific Regional Tuna Resource Assessment and
Monitoring Project which was funded by the European Union and implemented by
SPC's Oceanic Fisheries Programme. The programme was also involved in the
coordination of national observer programmes and the sampling of vessels in
port. SPC was of the view that those activities were consistent with actions
called for in paragraph 4 of resolution 50/25.

86.   NEAFC expressed the view that the issues of by-catch, discards and
post-harvest losses fell more to individual contracting parties than to NEAFC,
which, given its management responsibilities, had not so far had to address
those problems.

87. NAFO indicated that it had taken measures to reduce by-catch in the regulatory area and in particular redfish by-catch in the Flemish Cap shrimp fishery. It added that the NAFO Fisheries Commission and scientists would hold a workshop on fish discards in September 1996.

88. APFIC informed the Secretary-General that it encouraged studies on by-catch and discards by national institutes of member States. It also indicated that a regional review of the issue in South-East Asia was being conducted by FAO.

D. Information provided by non-governmental organizations

89. The World Wide Fund for Nature (WWF) 29/ expressed deep concern about the last-minute weakening of the text of article 5 (f) of the 1995 Agreement for the conservation and management of straddling fish stocks and highly migratory fish stocks at the final session of the United Nations Conference on Straddling Fish Stocks and Highly Migratory Fish Stocks. It also said that destructive fishing techniques used in many regions of the world included bottom trawling, long-lining, poison and explosives. It indicated that a recent WWF Australia study had found that longliners fishing for tuna in the Southern Ocean were responsible for killing 44,000 albatrosses and other seabirds annually. WWF believed that Governments ought to demonstrate their commitment to sustainable fisheries conservation and management by making full and unreserved implementation of article 5 (f) of the 1995 Agreement a priority. It also indicated that effective by-catch reduction devices should be used more widely and that incentives such as by-catch quotas should be put in place to encourage the use of the least destructive fishing gear and practices. It stressed that when implementing programmes to reduce waste by allowing landing of by-catch, extreme caution should be used to ensure that such programmes did not impede by-catch reduction efforts. It added that reduction of waste should go hand-in-hand with the elimination of by-catch.

90. WWF finally believed that the General Assembly should seriously consider the enormous destruction and waste of marine life by commercial fishing and how best to ensure rapid progress towards reduction of by-catch and waste in commercial fisheries worldwide, using the framework provided by the 1995 Agreement.

Notes

1/ In resolution 46/215, the General Assembly called, *inter alia*, for full implementation of a global moratorium on all large-scale pelagic drift-net fishing on the high seas.

2/ All the comments and views expressed by Colombia summarized in this document are contained in two notes verbales from the Permanent Mission of Colombia to the United Nations dated 10 June and 9 July 1996, respectively.

3/ All the comments and views expressed by Qatar summarized in this document are contained in an information note attached to a note verbale from the Permanent Mission of the State of Qatar to the United Nations dated 10 June 1996.

4/ All the comments and views expressed by Maldives summarized in this document are contained in a note verbale from the Permanent Mission of the Republic of Maldives to the United Nations dated 18 June 1996.

5/ All the comments and views expressed by Saudi Arabia summarized in this document are contained in a note verbale from the Permanent Mission of Saudi Arabia to the United Nations dated 21 June 1996.

<u>6</u>/   All the comments and views expressed by Italy summarized in this document are contained in a note verbale from the Permanent Mission of Italy to the United Nations dated 28 June 1996.

<u>7</u>/   All the comments and views expressed by New Zealand summarized in this document are contained in a note verbale from the Permanent Mission of New Zealand to the United Nations dated 28 June 1996.

<u>8</u>/   All the comments and views expressed by Mauritius summarized in this document are contained in a note verbale from the Permanent Mission of Mauritius to the United Nations dated 2 July 1996.

<u>9</u>/   All the comments and views expressed by Norway summarized in this document are contained in an annex to a note verbale from the Permanent Mission of Norway to the United Nations dated 2 July 1996.

<u>10</u>/   All the comments and views expressed by Morocco summarized in this document are contained in a note verbale from the Permanent Mission of the Kingdom of Morocco to the United Nations dated 10 July 1996.

<u>11</u>/   All the comments and views expressed by Spain summarized in this document are contained in an annex to a note verbale from the Permanent Mission of Spain to the United Nations dated 10 July 1996.

<u>12</u>/   All the comments and views expressed by Kuwait summarized in this document are contained in an annex to a note verbale from the Permanent Mission of the State of Kuwait to the United Nations dated 22 July 1996.

<u>13</u>/   All the comments and views expressed by Tunisia summarized in this document are contained in a note verbale from the Permanent Mission of Tunisia to the United Nations dated 25 July 1996.

<u>14</u>/   All the comments and views expressed by South Africa summarized in this document are contained in an annex to a note verbale from the Permanent Mission of South Africa to the United Nations dated 29 July 1996.

<u>15</u>/   All the comments and views expressed by the United States summarized in this document are contained in a report attached to a letter from the Permanent Representative of the United States of America to the United Nations dated 7 August 1996.

<u>16</u>/   All the comments and views expressed by FAO reproduced in this document are contained in a report attached to a letter from the Fisheries Department of FAO dated 19 July 1996.

<u>17</u>/   All the comments and views expressed by the Federation of Japan Tuna Fisheries Cooperative Associations summarized in this document are contained in a letter from its Managing Director dated 28 June 1996.

<u>18</u>/   Proceedings of the Fourteenth Regular Meeting of ICCAT, Madrid, Spain, 10-17 November 1995, Item 11, large-scale drift-net fishing and its effects on tuna stocks, paras. 11.2-11.6.

<u>19</u>/   All the comments and views expressed by the North-East Atlantic Fisheries Commission summarized in this document are contained in a letter from the NEAFC Secretary dated 11 June 1996.

<u>20</u>/   All the comments and views expressed by the Northwest Atlantic Fisheries Organization summarized in this document are contained in an information paper annexed to a letter from the NAFO Executive Secretary dated 18 June 1996.

21/ All the comments and views expressed by the North Atlantic Salmon Conservation Organization summarized in this document are contained in a letter from the NASCO Secretary dated 22 July 1996.

22/ All the comments and views expressed by Greenpeace International summarized in this document are contained in a letter from Greenpeace Fisheries campaign dated 1 July 1996.

23/ All the comments and views expressed by Finland summarized in this document are contained in a note attached to notes verbales from the Permanent Mission of Finland to the United Nations dated 3 July and 18 September 1996, respectively.

24/ All the comments and views expressed by the Asia-Pacific Fishery Commission summarized in this document are contained in a letter from the APFIC Regional Office for Asia and the Pacific dated 24 June 1996.

25/ All the comments and views expressed by Morocco summarized in this document are contained in a note verbale from the Permanent Mission of the Kingdom of Morocco to the United Nations dated 10 July 1996.

26/ All the comments and views expressed by Canada summarized in this document are contained in a report attached to a note verbale from the Permanent Mission of Canada to the United Nations dated 28 June 1996.

27/ All the comments and views expressed by South Pacific Commission summarized in this document are contained in a letter from the SPC Secretary-General dated 28 June 1996

28/ A "fishing permit/agreement" means an authorization to fish, in any form, issued to a fishing vessel from the Community by the flag State member, within the framework of a fishing agreement between the Community and a third State in addition to the fishing licence issued by the third State concerned (Regulation 3317/94, art. 2 (b)).

29/ All the comments and views expressed by the World Wide Fund for Nature summarized in this document are contained in a letter from the WWF International Treaties Coordinator dated 5 July 1996.

-----

4. ENVIRONMENT AND SUSTAINABLE DEVELOPMENT: SPECIAL UNGA SESSION FOR THE PURPOSE OF AN OVERALL REVIEW AND APPRAISAL OF THE IMPLEMENTATION OF AGENDA 21 - REPORT OF THE UN SECRETARY-GENERAL

Doc. no.: A/51/420

1 October 1996

CONTENTS

I. INTRODUCTION

1.   The convening of a special session of the General Assembly for the purpose
of an overall review and appraisal of the implementation of Agenda 21 was
envisaged in paragraph 38.9 of Agenda 21 adopted by the United Nations
Conference on Environment and Development, held at Rio de Janeiro, Brazil, in
June 1992. That recommendation of the Conference was endorsed by the General
Assembly in its resolution 47/190 on the report of the United Nations Conference
on Environment and Development.

2.   At its fiftieth session, the General Assembly considered a report of the
Secretary-General containing proposals on the format, scope and organizational
aspects of such a special session (A/50/453) and decided to convene that special
session for a duration of one week during the month of June 1997 at the highest
possible level of participation (resolution 50/113). The Assembly also
determined organizational modalities for the preparations for the special
session, including the relevant role of the Commission on Sustainable
Development and of other relevant organizations and bodies of the United Nations
system. Furthermore, the Assembly recognized the important role played by major
groups, including non-governmental organizations, in the implementation of
Conference recommendations and the need for their active involvement in the
preparations for the special session, as well as the need to ensure appropriate
arrangements for their contribution during the special session. The Assembly
requested the Secretary-General to prepare a number of reports for the
consideration of the Commission containing an overall assessment of progress
achieved since the Conference, together with recommendations for future actions
and priorities; and to mount a public information programme to raise global
awareness of both the special session and work undertaken by the United Nations
in the follow-up to the Conference. Finally, the Assembly requested the
Secretary-General to submit to it at its fifty-first session a progress report
on the state of preparations for the special session.

II. PREPARATIONS FOR THE SPECIAL SESSION

A. Commission on Sustainable Development and its Bureau

3.   The General Assembly in its resolution 50/113 decided that the Commission
on Sustainable Development would act as a central intergovernmental forum for
the preparations for the special session. In particular the Assembly encouraged
the participants in the fourth session of the Commission (18 April-3 May 1996)
to address matters related to the special session; invited the Commission to
devote its Ad Hoc Open-ended Inter-sessional Working Group meeting, to be held
in February 1997, to assisting the Commission in undertaking the review for the
special session; welcomed the decision of the Commission to devote its fifth
session, in 1997, to preparations for the special session; and decided that that
session of the Commission would be open-ended in its deliberations, allowing for
the full participation of all States.

1. Fourth session of the Commission on Sustainable Development

4.   The high-level segment of the fourth session of the Commission on
Sustainable Development, held from 1 to 3 May 1996, was attended by almost
50 ministers and policy makers from all the regions of the world. The thrust of
the discussion on matters related to the preparations for the special session
was reflected in the Chairman's summary of the high-level segment that was
included in the report of the Commission on its fourth session. 1/ The
participants in the high-level segment stressed the vital importance of the
special session, when the General Assembly will review the overall progress
achieved in implementing the Rio commitments and discuss appropriate strategies
for implementation in the coming years. It was stressed that participation in

the special session at the highest possible level would be essential for its success.

5.   The discussion showed that there was a broad consensus that the special session should not attempt to renegotiate Agenda 21, or other intergovernmental agreements in the field of sustainable development, but should concentrate on their further implementation. In this context, participants highlighted a number of objectives:

(a)   To revitalize and energize commitment to the concept of sustainable development, to ensure it a central place on the political agenda and to reinforce momentum for its implementation at the international, national and local levels. Participants recognized the need to strengthen the Commission's public visibility and improve its outreach;

(b)   To frankly recognize failures to meet certain goals and identify reasons for failure;

(c)   To boost implementation of the Rio commitments through such means as the identification of innovative approaches to cooperation and financial assistance, and through concrete proposals for action;

(d)   To define priorities for the period beyond 1997. A number of participants felt that the Commission should focus on a limited number of key issues rather than reviewing every chapter of Agenda 21, in particular those issues where it is felt that real progress could be made;

(e)   To raise the profile of issues that had not been sufficiently addressed by the Conference or where significant developments had taken place since the Conference. Such issues might include changing consumption and production patterns, energy (including renewables) and transport, urban issues, enterprises, fresh water, and management of risks.

6.   Participants in the high-level segment recognized that, in future work, more attention should be paid to addressing the driving forces that impacted on the sustainable management of natural resources while at the same time giving more attention to the economic and social dimensions of sustainable development, including combating poverty. The crucial link between the driving forces - economic growth and trade, consumption and production patterns and population growth - and resource management were the economic sectors that often defined the way that policy-making and implementation were organized. To be truly effective, the Commission's consideration of resource management issues had to be combined with an equal emphasis on sectoral policy development. Many sectors, such as agriculture, forestry, fisheries, industry, human settlements and social services, were already dealt with in existing forums in the United Nations system. The impact of the Conference and Agenda 21 on the work in those forums had helped to inject considerations of sustainability into their discussions. However, there were some gaps and, from the perspective of sustainability, the most obvious gap related to transport and energy.

7.   Participants reflected on the implementation of Agenda 21 objectives since the Conference and noted the continuing need to strengthen mechanisms within the United Nations system which helped to integrate environmental concerns more fully into regular decision-making processes. Participants encouraged other intergovernmental bodies, especially the Bretton Woods institutions, the World Trade Organization (WTO) and the Organisation for Economic Cooperation and Development, to ensure that sustainable development issues were taken into consideration in a systemic and consistent manner. A number of participants stressed the link between international and national follow-up and encouraged the Commission to promote the integration of conclusions from major international conferences, including those held at Cairo, Copenhagen and Beijing and the then forthcoming Habitat II conference in Istanbul.

8.   Particular stress was laid on the importance of devolving implementing actions from global to regional level, and decentralizing responsibilities from national to local level where appropriate. In highlighting the value and effectiveness of local empowerment, it was suggested that the United Nations might sponsor an award that would recognize globally significant examples of sustainable development undertaken at the local or micro-level.

9.   Participants in the high-level segment stressed the importance of developing a broad-based consensus involving major groups for achieving sustainable development. The development of new partnerships between stakeholders, such as educators, scientists, Governments, non-governmental organizations, business and industry, trade unions, youth and the media, among others, was encouraged as a means to foster better communication and to get across the key issues of sustainable development. It was noted that closer involvement of the private sector was essential for achieving sustainable development, but that appropriate mechanisms of interaction still needed to be developed in that area.

10. Participants emphasized the importance of the involvement of major groups in the preparations for the 1997 special session and in the session itself, in accordance with the appropriate rules of procedure. They also welcomed initiatives for self-reporting by major groups in 1997.

2.   Bureau of the Commission on Sustainable Development

11. The Bureau of the Commission on Sustainable Development met in New York on 15 July 1996. Preparations for the special session were in the focus of the discussion. The Bureau was informed about the process of preparation and format of documentation for the 1997 review to meet the requests for reporting related to the review contained in General Assembly resolution 50/113, decisions of the Commission and other intergovernmental mandates.

12. The Bureau welcomed the fact that the United Nations system, through the system of task managers of the Inter-Agency Committee on Sustainable Development, demonstrated its continuing commitment to and support for the Commission's work programme and would actively contribute to the preparations for the 1997 review. In particular, the Bureau expressed its satisfaction with the intention of the Secretariat to finalize most of the documentation early in 1997 so that it would be available prior to the 1997 meeting of the Commission's Ad Hoc Inter-sessional Working Group when formal intergovernmental preparations for the special sessions would commence.

13. Bearing in mind the discussions held during the high-level segment of the fourth session of the Commission, members of the Bureau considered that the special session should focus on the implementation of Agenda 21 and result in the adoption of an agreed statement or a declaration which would be action-oriented, and that the special session should have a high political profile. As for the process leading to the preparation of the final document of the special session, the Bureau, taking into account the provisions of General Assembly resolution 50/113, felt that it could be organized along the following lines:

     (a) The Ad Hoc Inter-sessional Working Group of the Commission (24 February-7 March 1997), taking into account reports of the Secretary-General and other documentation, outcomes of various inter-sessional activities organized by Governments and organizations and other relevant inputs, would strive to agree on the format and structure of a final document and the main elements to be included in it. The outcome of the Working Group meeting would be a detailed outline of the final document;

     (b) Such an outline would form the basis for negotiations during the fifth session of the Commission (7-25 April 1997), when the Commission should attempt to agree on the draft final document of the special session;

(c)   The special session in June 1997 would resolve all outstanding issues
that might remain bracketed after the fifth session of the Commission, and also
reflect in the document any new developments, or proposals made, in the period
between the fifth session of the Commission and the special session.

14.   The Bureau agreed on the need for involvement of the Chairman and/or its
members in the main inter-sessional activities and relevant intergovernmental
meetings expected to make an input to the preparations for the special session.

15.   The Bureau stressed the need for effective arrangements to allow major
groups, including non-governmental organizations, to contribute to the
preparations for and the deliberations during the special session. While the
Bureau agreed that the rules of procedure needed to be fully respected and that
specific decisions on the participation of major groups in the session would be
taken by the General Assembly, it also agreed that a number of activities could
be organized during the special session with a view to ensuring effective input
of major groups and their active inter-action with government representatives.
The Bureau considered that it would be useful to assess and build upon the
experience gained during previous special sessions of the General Assembly, and
sessions of the Commission, as well as Habitat II and other recent meetings and
intergovernmental processes, such as hearings in the context of the elaboration
of the Agenda for Development.

B.   Relevant activities carried out by the Inter-Agency Committee
on Sustainable Development and by organizations and bodies of
the United Nations system

16.   The General Assembly in its resolution 50/113 invited all relevant
organizations and bodies of the United Nations system, including the United
Nations Conference on Trade and Development (UNCTAD), the specialized agencies
and other multilateral organizations, including multilateral financial
institutions and WTO, to contribute to the special session, and requested the
Inter-Agency Committee on Sustainable Development, in close coordination with
the Commission on Sustainable Development, to ensure an effective and
coordinated system-wide response to the preparation of the special session. The
Assembly also welcomed the decisions of the Governing Council of the United
Nations Environment Programme (UNEP), in which the Council emphasized the need
for the Programme, in accordance with its mandate in the implementation of
Agenda 21, to continue to provide effective support to the work of the
Commission, and in which the Council decided to hold its nineteenth session
early in 1997 with a view of making a contribution to the special session.

17.   The Inter-Agency Committee on Sustainable Development at its eighth session
(10-12 July 1996) stressed the political importance of the preparations for the
1997 special session. The Committee agreed that the United Nations system,
including the Bretton Woods institutions and other relevant bodies, should
actively contribute to making the special session a highly visible international
event that would energize global commitment to the implementation of Agenda 21
and advance international dialogue and action for sustainable development.

18.   The Committee agreed that it would be essential for the 1997 review to go
beyond assessment of progress achieved in the Commission and in the United
Nations system and to make a frank and analytical appraisal of the overall
progress made and problems encountered at the international, national and local
levels.

19.   During the session of the Committee it was suggested that, in addition to
their active involvement through the Committee's system of task managers in the
preparation of the reports of the Secretary-General for the 1997 review, the
organizations of the United Nations system would consider making their own
contributions to the review process with a view to enriching the preparations
for the fifth session of the Commission and the special session itself. In this
context the Committee welcomed work carried out in UNCTAD in accordance with

General Assembly resolution 50/95 to prepare a comprehensive assessment on trade and environment and the work carried out by the World Health Organization to prepare a world health and environment report as important inputs to the special session. Preparatory work for the special session would also benefit from a mid-term review of the achievements in reaching the goals set out by the World Summit for Children, whose outcome had been fully incorporated in Agenda 21. The Committee considered that other important contributions could be received from regional commissions and the regulatory bodies of relevant conventions. Furthermore, there were high expectations that the final report of the Ad Hoc Intergovernmental Panel on Forests of the Commission would provide a significant contribution to the 1997 review and to forest-related work in general in the period after the special session. Another important expectation was connected with the ongoing global freshwater assessment.

20. Furthermore, it was considered that it would be essential to engage in this process, as far as possible, relevant governing bodies and intergovernmental meetings held under their auspices. An important input to the 1997 review would come from the World Food Summit which would address the issue of sustainability, and from the nineteenth session of the UNEP Governing Council, which would specifically consider the UNEP contribution to the special session.

21. The Committee underlined the significance of various country-driven initiatives, which would build up a political momentum leading to the special session. The Committee also noted with satisfaction a proposal made during the high-level segment of the fourth session of the Commission to organize a joint meeting of Ministers of Environment and Ministers of Finance as part of the preparatory process for the special session, and expressed the hope that interested countries would follow up on this promising initiative. Important contributions were also expected from non-governmental organizations and major groups.

22. The Administrative Committee on Coordination decided to submit a statement to the General Assembly at its special session, in which it would analyse the effectiveness of inter-agency arrangements established to follow up the Rio Conference and, on the basis of experience gained after the Conference, suggest ways of promoting more effective and efficient United Nations system-wide support in the area of sustainable development for the period after 1997.

C. High-level Advisory Board on Sustainable Development

23. The High-level Advisory Board on Sustainable Development, at its fifth session (29-31 January 1996), agreed that it should contribute to the 1997 review of progress achieved in the implementation of the Rio commitments by means of a concise report focusing on a few critical areas. The Board decided that it would examine the impediments to sustainable development in those areas and make independent recommendations as to how the impediments might be overcome. It proposed that the report be made available to the Commission on Sustainable Development at its fifth session in April 1997. The Board also agreed that its members would consider initiatives to generate debate on the review in their own constituencies.

24. At its sixth session (4-6 September 1996), the Board agreed that its report would focus on three critical areas of sustainable development, namely, energy, transport and water resources. Within each of those areas, the report would examine policy measures for improving sustainable use, with an emphasis on economic factors, and make recommendations concerning policy packages that Governments might use, individually or collectively, to overcome the impediments to sustainable development. In addition to the policy analysis and recommendations, the report would include a number of brief descriptions of successful sustainable development policies in various countries, including rural wind energy programmes, energy taxes, tradeable emissions permits, urban transportation management, and river basin management. The Board also agreed

that members would disseminate the report within their constituencies and organize meetings to consider how their recommendations might be implemented. The Board will complete its work on the report at its seventh session, in January 1997.

D. Information from Governments on progress achieved at the national level

25.   The General Assembly, in its resolution 50/113, requested the Secretary-General to prepare for the consideration of the Commission on Sustainable Development at its fifth session country profiles providing a concise presentation of progress made and constraints encountered in implementing Agenda 21 at the national level, compiled on the basis of national information received and in close cooperation with the Governments concerned.   At its fourth session, the Commission welcomed and supported the preparation of those country profiles.

26.   In response to those requests, the Secretariat prepared a common format for the profiles and circulated it to all Governments.   For those 74 countries that have submitted national reports to the Commission, the Secretariat is preparing the draft profiles on the basis of the information contained in the national reports.   As they are completed in draft form, the profiles are sent to the appropriate national focal points for comments, updating and approval by the Governments as necessary.   Countries that have not yet been able to provide the Secretariat with a national report to the Commission have also been requested to complete a national profile in the common format.

27.   The national profiles will support the analysis and assessment required for the documentation for the fifth session of the Commission, as envisaged in General Assembly resolution 50/113.   In addition, all national profiles will be made available on the Internet following their approval by the Governments concerned.   The Secretary-General would like to encourage all countries to continue providing the Commission with information on progress made and constraints encountered in implementing Agenda 21 at the national level, which will be of great value for the 1997 review.

E. National, regional and subregional activities to support the preparatory process

28.   The General Assembly in its resolution 50/113 invited Governments as well as relevant regional and subregional organizations to consider undertaking reviews of progress achieved since the Rio Conference at the national, subregional, regional and interregional levels with a view to contributing to the preparations for the special session.   The Assembly welcomed the preparation of hemispheric, regional and subregional conferences on sustainable development and invited Governments concerned to contribute to the special session the outcomes of such conferences.

29.   A number of Governments are undertaking or are considering undertaking inter-sessional meetings and initiatives with a view to contributing to the 1997 review.   The outcomes of such initiatives are expected to be presented to the Commission on Sustainable Development and/or the General Assembly at its special session directly by the Governments concerned.   However, if such meetings or initiatives conclude by the end of November 1996, the Secretary-General would appreciate being informed of their outcomes so that they can be reflected, as appropriate, in the documentation prepared by the Secretariat.

30.   With regard to the regional commissions and other regional organizations, various activities are being conducted as a contribution to the preparations for the special session of the General Assembly:

(a)   In Africa, the first Conference of African Ministers Responsible for Sustainable Development and Environment was held in March 1996 at the initiative of the Economic Commission for Africa. It adopted the guidelines for monitoring the progress made in building critical management capacities for sustainable development in Africa as a framework instrument for harmonizing relevant activities in the region.

(b)   In the Asian and Pacific region, the Committee on Environment and Sustainable Development of the Economic and Social Commission for Asia and the Pacific, which will hold its third session in October 1996, will conduct a regional review of progress achieved in the implementation of the outcome of the Rio Conference as an input to the fifth session of the Commission and the special session.

(c)   In the region of the Economic Commission for Europe (ECE), a special session of the Committee on Environmental Policy was held in January 1996, which considered the outcome of the Ministerial Conference on Environment for Europe, held at Sofia in October 1995. The Environmental Programme for Europe adopted at the Sofia Conference represented a first attempt to set out a common direction to make Agenda 21 more operational in the ECE region.

(d)   In the Latin American and Caribbean region, the contribution to the special session will be considered at the Tenth Meeting of Ministers of the Environment of Latin America and the Caribbean, to be held on 11 and 12 November 1996 at Buenos Aires, and the Hemispheric Summit on Sustainable Development, to be held on 7 and 8 December 1996 at Santa Cruz de la Sierra, Bolivia, under the auspices of the Organization of American States.

(e)   Upon the suggestion of the Economic and Social Commission for Western Asia (ESCWA), the Council of Arab Ministers Responsible for Environment, in May 1996, called upon all Arab countries to participate actively in the 1997 review, by such means as setting up national committees to prepare national reports on the implementation of Agenda 21. A synthesis of those reports will be considered at the next Council meeting in November 1996 and then forwarded to the special session. Furthermore, the ESCWA Committees on Energy and Water Resources are holding meetings early in 1997 to review ongoing and planned activities, thus providing regional perspectives on these issues to the 1997 review.

(f)   Belarus announced at the fourth session of the Commission on Sustainable Development that it is organizing at Minsk a conference on sustainable development of countries with economies in transition.

31.   Furthermore, the regional commissions, in cooperation with the regional offices of UNEP, are preparing inventories of regional initiatives in the area of sustainable development undertaken since the Rio Conference, or conducting regional reviews. The results of those exercises will be available at the special session.

F. Rio Conventions

32.   The General Assembly, in its resolution 50/113, invited the conferences of parties or other regulatory bodies of the United Nations Framework Convention on Climate Change, the Convention on Biological Diversity and the United Nations Convention to Combat Desertification in Those Countries Experiencing Serious Drought and/or Desertification, Particularly in Africa, as well as the regulatory bodies of other relevant instruments, as appropriate, and the Global Environment Facility, to provide their inputs to the special session.

33.   The Conference of the Parties to the United Nations Framework Convention on Climate Change agreed to make a special input, through its Subsidiary Body on Implementation, to the special session. The secretariat of the Convention has

been requested by the Conference of the Parties, at its second session, to prepare a relevant submission for consideration by the Subsidiary Body on Implementation at its fifth session in February 1997.

34. In the case of the United Nations Convention to Combat Desertification, its interim secretariat will prepare, after the January 1997 session of the Intergovernmental Negotiating Committee, an input summarizing the key provisions of the Convention, action taken prior to the Convention's entry into force and the outlook for the first session of the Conference of the Parties.

35. Pursuant to decision II/18 (annex), adopted by the Conference of the Parties to the Convention on Biological Diversity at its second session, a report will be submitted to the General Assembly at its special session from the perspective of the Convention's three objectives: the conservation of biodiversity, the sustainable use of its components and the fair and equitable sharing of the benefits arising out of the utilization of genetic resources. The report will be considered by the Conference of the Parties at its third session (Buenos Aires, 4-14 November 1996).

36. The Global Environment Facility will also make an input to the special session.

G.   Initiatives by major groups

37. The General Assembly in its resolution 50/113 recognized the important role played by major groups, including non-governmental organizations, at the Rio Conference and in the implementation of its recommendations, and recognized the need for their active involvement in preparations for the special session, as well as the need to ensure appropriate arrangements for their contribution during the special session.

38. The secretariat of the Commission on Sustainable Development prepared and distributed a set of guidelines (1997 Guidelines for Major Groups' Input) to all major group contacts currently in the database. These guidelines provide information on how major groups can contribute to the 1997 review process, the fifth session of the Commission and the special session of the General Assembly.

39. Major group organizations are also organizing various meetings independently or jointly with international organizations, non-governmental partners and Governments. These events aim to review and assess the Rio follow-up process as well as raise awareness about the 1997 review and follow-up activities in the period after 1997. Such initiatives include:

   (a) Rio+5. A global assessment of sustainable development progress led by the Earth Council, in collaboration with numerous network non-governmental organizations and major group organizations, and in consultation with the secretariat of the Commission. In addition to organizations from each of the nine major group categories, the event involves the national councils for sustainable development, the media, and the religious and education communities, as well as various United Nations and non-United Nations international organizations. The culminating event is a week-long meeting at Rio de Janeiro (13 to 19 March 1997).

   (b) Sustainable Development Indicators for Youth Project, Phase II. The project, led by Rescue Mission and other youth organizations around the world, is a follow-up to the youth panel/exhibition prepared for the fourth session of the Commission. The Children's State of the Planet Television Report, also led by Rescue Mission, is a major media campaign by youth on sustainable development and the 1997 review process.

   (c) Survey of local Agenda 21 initiatives. This comprehensive survey of local efforts is led by the International Council for Local Environmental

Initiatives and the Division for Sustainable Development of the Department for Policy Coordination and Sustainable Development. This survey is the first comprehensive stocktaking exercise on the fast-growing local Agenda 21 movement around the world. It is estimated that more than 2,000 local governments and authorities have developed projects and frameworks for achieving local sustainable development. The results of the survey will be presented to the Commission on Sustainable Development at its fifth session and to the General Assembly at the special session.

(d) Survey on the future of the Commission on Sustainable Development, led by the World Federalist Movement and INTGLIM. 2/ This is based on a short survey and a series of interviews with United Nations staff members, as well as governmental and non-governmental experts. The leading organizations will submit the final report to the Ad Hoc Inter-sessional Working Group of the Commission, and to the Commission at its fifth session.

(e) The World Business Council for Sustainable Development is preparing a report and various events on the business perspective on sustainable development.

(f) Earth Summit II: A Business Input. A national level meeting organized by the United Nations Environment and Development (United Kingdom) and the International Chamber of Commerce (United Kingdom) to review business responses to sustainable development in the United Kingdom of Great Britain and Northern Ireland.

(g) The Inter-Parliamentary Union will emphasize changing consumption and production patterns in its input to the 1997 review process, and it will follow up on its declaration on financing and transfer of technology, which was submitted to the Commission at its fourth session.

(h) Global Cities 21: Local Agenda 21 for Sustainable Communities. A meeting organized jointly by the International Council for Local Environmental Initiatives, the Global Action Plan and the Earth Council to review contributions of local authorities, which will be held at Lisbon on 8 and 9 October 1996.

(i) A meeting of indigenous people will be held in Colombia in 1996 to prepare an input to the fifth session of the Commission and the special session, with special emphasis on forests.

H. Public information activities

40. The General Assembly in its resolution 50/113 requested the Secretary-General to mount a public information programme to raise global awareness of both the special session and the work undertaken by the United Nations in the follow-up to the Conference.

41. In response to that request, the Department for Policy Coordination and Sustainable Development and the Department of Public Information are joining their efforts with a view to designing and implementing the media/public information strategy that will ensure broad outreach of the preparatory activities and of the special session, build awareness of sustainable development issues, promote further the goals and objectives of the Rio Conference and of the 1997 review, and, as follow-up to the special session, ensure dissemination of its results.

42. In implementing the strategy, the Secretariat intends to prepare various information materials and radio and television programmes and organize special media/public outreach activities. It will also strive to ensure the broadest possible dissemination, *inter alia*, through electronic means, of the official reports and documents prepared in connection with the 1997 review, including the

outcomes of the fifth session of the Commission on Sustainable Development and
of the special session itself. One of the challenges will be to ensure
effective outreach in the developing countries.

I. Status of contributions to the Trust Fund

43. The General Assembly in its resolution 50/113 invited Governments to assist
the developing countries, in particular the least developed among them, in
participating fully and effectively in the special session and its preparatory
process, and in that regard invited them to make appropriate contributions to
the Trust Fund to Support the Work of the Commission on Sustainable Development.

44. Pursuant to that resolution, a note verbale soliciting contributions for
the above-mentioned purposes has been circulated by the Secretary-General to all
Member States and Observers. The Secretary-General would like to reiterate his
appeal to all interested countries for relevant contributions to the Trust Fund,
earmarked for assisting the participation of developing countries in the special
session of the General Assembly.

III. SOME PROPOSALS FOR ORGANIZATIONAL MODALITIES DURING THE FIFTH SESSION OF THE COMMISSION ON SUSTAINABLE DEVELOPMENT AND THE SPECIAL SESSION

45. A number of general proposals for the organization of the 1997 special
session and its preparatory process were brought to the attention of the General
Assembly at its fiftieth session (see A/50/453). While specific decisions about
the organization of work during the fifth session of the Commission on
Sustainable Development and the special session itself will be taken by the
Commission upon the recommendation of its Bureau and by the General Assembly,
the Secretary-General would like to make some additional suggestions on this
matter for the consideration of Member States.

46. Concerning the formal intergovernmental part of the 1997 review, bearing in
mind previous practice, the provisions of General Assembly resolution 50/113 and
current discussions in the Commission and its Bureau, it is likely that the main
work on the text of the final document of the special session will be done
during the fifth session of the Commission, which will largely be a negotiating
meeting. During the special session itself, in parallel to the plenary meetings
of the Assembly where a high-level debate will take place, an ad hoc committee
of the whole, reporting to the plenary, could be established. The role of the
committee will be to reach agreement on all outstanding matters in the final
document.

47. Bearing in mind the provisions of General Assembly resolution 50/113 and
the recommendations of the Commission at its fourth session, an important
challenge will be to ensure appropriate arrangements that will allow major
groups, including non-governmental organizations, to make their contribution to
the meetings with due respect to the existing rules of procedure.

48. It is likely that during the fifth session of the Commission and the
special session of the General Assembly a number of Governments, international
organizations and major groups will organize, individually and jointly, various
informal side events, presentations and briefings with a view to contributing to
a more formal intergovernmental process. It would be useful to ensure that
contributions from major groups to such events will be organized in a systematic
way. Some suggestions in this regard are made in the following paragraphs.

49. During the fifth session of the Commission, one possibility would be to
organize, in parallel with the drafting groups that will work on the text of the
final document of the special session, hearings involving representatives of
Governments, major groups and eminent persons, devoted to an assessment of the

existing and potential role, and contribution to its implementation, of each of the major groups identified in Agenda 21. Summaries of such hearings could either be included in the report of the Commission on its fifth session or made orally by the Commission at the special session.

50. During the special session itself, the formal debate in plenary meeting could be interspersed with panels and/or dialogue sessions with world leaders or other eminent persons covering a wide spectrum.

51. While the organizational recommendations relating to the fifth session of the Commission could appropriately be made by the Bureau of the Commission, the views and recommendations of the General Assembly will be important for the organization of the special session and parallel events envisaged at that time.

52. As to the dates for the special session, the Secretary-General, bearing in mind the calendar of other United Nations meetings and conferences and the provisions of General Assembly resolution 50/113, recommends that it be held from 7 to 13 June 1997.

Notes

1/ Official Records of the Economic and Social Council, 1996, Supplement No. 8 (E/1996/28).

2/ International non-governmental organization working group on legal and institutional matters.

-----

5. IMPLEMENTATION OF THE UN CONVENTION AGAINST ILLICIT TRAFFIC IN NARCOTIC DRUGS AND PSYCHOTROPIC SUBSTANCES OF 1988 - REPORT OF THE UN SECRETARY-GENERAL

Doc. no.: A/51/437   30 September 1996

CONTENTS

CONTENTS *(continued)*

INTRODUCTION

1.   The General Assembly, in its resolution 49/168, section VI, of 23 December 1994, on international action to combat drug abuse and illicit production and trafficking, requested the Secretary-General to submit to the Assembly at its fifty-first session an updated report on the status of the implementation of the United Nations Convention against Illicit Traffic in Narcotic Drugs and Psychotropic Substances of 1988.[1]

2.   The present report, prepared pursuant to General Assembly resolution 49/168, reviews the implementation of the 1988 Convention over a two-year period, from 1 July 1994 to 30 June 1996.

I. STATUS OF ADHERENCE TO AND IMPLEMENTATION OF THE 1988 CONVENTION

3.   The General Assembly, in its resolution 49/168, section II, urged States to ratify or accede to the 1988 Convention, as well as to the other main international drug control treaties, namely, the Single Convention on Narcotic Drugs of 1961 as amended by the 1972 Protocol[2] and the Convention on Psychotropic Substances of 1971.[3]

4.   As at 30 June 1996, 156 States were parties to the Single Convention on Narcotic Drugs of 1961[4] or to that Convention as amended by the 1972 Protocol (of those 156 States, 17 were parties to the 1961 Convention only), 144 States were parties to the 1971 Convention and 132 were parties to the 1988 Convention (see annex I for the status of adherence). During the reporting period, ratification or accession to the international drug control treaties evolved as follows: 13 States[*] became parties to the 1961 Convention as amended by the 1972 Protocol (either by directly becoming parties to the 1961 Convention as amended by the 1972 Protocol or, for those that had been parties to the 1961 Convention only, by becoming parties to the 1972 Protocol); 13 States[**] became parties to the 1971 Convention; and 31 States[***] became parties to the 1988 Convention.

---

[*] Ethiopia, Gambia, Guinea-Bissau, Kyrgyzstan, Mali, Mauritius, Republic of Moldova, Russian Federation, Swaziland, Switzerland, Turkmenistan, Uzbekistan and Yemen.

[**] Chad, Belgium, Gambia, Guinea-Bissau, Kyrgyzstan, Lebanon, Mali, Republic of Moldova, Swaziland, Switzerland, Turkmenistan, Uzbekistan and Yemen.

[***] Algeria, Belgium, Cape Verde, Chad, Cuba, Ethiopia, Gambia, Guinea-Bissau, Haiti, Jamaica, Kyrgyzstan, Lebanon, Lesotho, Malawi, Mali, Malta, Norway, Philippines, Republic of Moldova, Saint Kitts and Nevis, Saint Lucia, Swaziland, Tajikistan, Tonga, Trinidad and Tobago, Turkey, Turkmenistan, United Republic of Tanzania, Uruguay, Uzbekistan and Yemen.

5.   The General Assembly, in its resolution 49/168, section II, called upon all States to adopt adequate national laws and regulations, to strengthen national judicial systems and to carry out effective drug control activities in cooperation with other States in accordance with international instruments. Texts of drug control laws and regulations provided by States to the Secretary-General are published by the United Nations International Drug Control Programme (UNDCP) in the E/NL.. series of documents. Legislation adopted and published during the reporting period includes the following: amendments in lists of controlled substances, usually to bring the domestic scope of control into line with treaty provisions; comprehensive drug control acts dealing with the organization of licit drug-related activities, the prohibition and repression of illicit operation, and the treatment and rehabilitation of drug abusers; and amendments to penal codes providing for more severe penalties for drug trafficking or establishing new forms of criminal offences. There has been intensive legislative activity in the following three areas covered by the 1988 Convention: the control of illicit drug proceeds, with the adoption of numerous laws providing for the detection and repression of money-laundering activities and the confiscation of proceeds;[****] the provision of mutual legal assistance in criminal matters, including drug-related offences; and the establishment of precursor control mechanisms.

II. IMPLEMENTATION OF ARTICLE 5, PARAGRAPH 4, AND ARTICLES 6 AND 7 OF THE 1988 CONVENTION

6.   In response to an increasing number of enquiries addressed to UNDCP concerning three articles of the 1988 Convention, the Programme sent a special questionnaire to States in 1995 on the implementation of article 5, paragraph 4, concerning requests for confiscation of proceeds, property, instrumentalities or any other things used in or intended for use in any manner in offences established in accordance with article 3, paragraph 1, of the Convention; the implementation of article 6, concerning extradition for drug-related offences; and the implementation of article 7, concerning mutual legal assistance in investigations, prosecutions and judicial proceedings related to drug offences.

A. Article 5, paragraph 4: request for confiscation or related investigations

.7.   Most of the States that returned the questionnaire reported that they had neither made nor received requests for confiscation. Six States reported having made requests for confiscation of narcotic drugs and psychotropic substances. One State reported having received funds following a request for confiscation of proceeds of drug trafficking.

B. Article 6: request for extradition

8.   Nine States made or received requests for extradition pursuant to the provisions of article 6 of the 1988 Convention during 1995. Some States reported, however, that they could not furnish statistics for extradition for drug-related offences as their legal systems made no such distinctions.

C. Article 7: request for mutual legal assistance

9.   Of the three fields for which data were requested, mutual legal assistance was by far the most frequently resorted to. The majority of States that returned the questionnaire reported having made and/or received a considerable number of requests for mutual legal assistance. Some reported having received and/or made requests for tracing property derived from drug trafficking, locating witnesses, taking evidence and, in some instances, providing evidence before courts of requesting countries, while others reported making or receiving requests for service of judicial documents. One State party to the 1988 Convention reported that in four instances the Convention was used as the basis for mutual legal assistance in the absence of treaties on mutual legal assistance in criminal matters.

[****] Of the laws providing for the confiscation of proceeds, a few provide for the enforcement of foreign confiscation orders, while others provide for the sharing of forfeited proceeds of drug trafficking and of amounts paid on account of fines among authorities that cooperated in the investigations leading to confiscation.

III. ACTIVITIES UNDERTAKEN BY THE UNITED NATIONS INTERNATIONAL DRUG CONTROL PROGRAMME FOR THE IMPLEMENTATION OF THE 1988 CONVENTION

A. Provision of legal assistance to Member States

10.   The General Assembly, in its resolution 49/168, section II, requested UNDCP to continue to provide legal assistance to Member States, upon request, in the adjustment of their national laws, policies and infrastructure to implement the international drug control conventions, as well as assistance in training personnel responsible for applying the new laws.

11.   During the reporting period, legislative assistance was provided by UNDCP to requesting States (see annex II) using the following four-step methodology:

(a)   Holding of evaluation missions, where the need for new or revised legislation was assessed and supported at both the political and executive levels;

(b)   Preparation of new or revised legislation, once political and executive commitments had been made;

(c)   Advisory support to Governments during the legislative approval and ratification process;

(d)   Transfer of technical expertise to ensure the implementation of the conventions and domestic legislation, through training and the holding of legal workshops to resolve national, subregional and regional implementation problems.

Many States that had received legal assistance and had ratified the international drug control conventions either enacted new drug control legislation or had a draft law ready for submission to parliament.

12.   Model legislation has been developed by UNDCP to promote more uniform implementation of the international drug control treaties and to facilitate international cooperation. A package of model laws on the regulation of licit activities, the repression of illicit activities, extradition and mutual legal assistance, money-laundering and confiscation of proceeds, as well as on the creation of required drug control bodies and coordination mechanisms, is available in Arabic, English, French, Portuguese, Russian and Spanish, for use in the main legal systems. Model laws are updated and upgraded periodically, in line with significant trends and developments and are reviewed by informal meetings of international experts.

B. Commentary on the 1988 Convention

13.   The Economic and Social Council, in its resolution 1993/42 of 27 July 1993, requested the Secretary-General to prepare a commentary on the 1988 Convention. The Commentary is expected to be ready by December 1996.

14.   Like the commentaries on the 1961 Convention,[5] on the 1972 Protocol amending that Convention[6] and on the 1971 Convention,[7] the Commentary on the 1988 Convention will be aimed at guiding Governments in framing legislative and administrative measures for effective implementation and uniform interpretation of the Convention. In addition, the Commentary on the 1988 Convention will, for the first time, contain practical guidelines for the implementation of the Convention. This innovation, requested by the Commission on Narcotic Drugs, is expected to be of particular interest to Governments.

IV. ACTIVITIES UNDERTAKEN BY THE DEPARTMENT OF PUBLIC INFORMATION TO DISSEMINATE INFORMATION ABOUT THE 1988 CONVENTION

15.   The Department of Public Information of the Secretariat continues to promote the 1988 Convention, as requested by the General Assembly in its resolution 47/97 of 16 December 1992 and within the inter-agency efforts requested by the Assembly in its resolution 49/168 of 23 December 1994. The Department has provided substantial follow-up to earlier campaigns. The 1988 Convention and the role of the United Nations in combating drug trafficking and money-laundering were highlighted by the Department in two of its "UN in Action" television programmes, two television interviews for "World Chronicle", two articles in its publication Development Update, four articles in the UN Chronicle and more than 100 United Nations radio programmes during the past two years.

16.   The Department produced press kits for each of the two annual reports released by the International Narcotics Control Board, which make prominent mention of the 1988 Convention. In conjunction with the release of the annual reports, the Department organized press conferences at Headquarters in New York as well as in scores of cities around the world, with the assistance of the United Nations information centres and services. The Department also produced press kits for the observance on 26 June of the "International Day against Drug Abuse and Illicit Trafficking", in 1995 and 1996. The Department has carried out extensive media outreach both at Headquarters and at Vienna, successfully arranging broadcast and print interviews for the reports of the International Narcotics Control Board and the International Day.

17.   The United Nations International Drug Control Programme, assisted by the Department, prepared a major exhibition on "Sports against drugs", that was inaugurated at Vienna. The exhibit moved to Headquarters to coincide with the high-level segment of the Economic and Social Council on drug abuse and drug trafficking, before moving to the Olympics at Atlanta, Georgia, where it was the only United Nations exhibit. Prominent athletes and personages attended the opening of the exhibit in all three cities. In addition, wide press coverage was given to the Economic and Social Council high-level segment, with radio interviews on the report of the Secretary-General and the work of the United Nations International Drug Control Programme.

V. RECOMMENDATIONS BY THE COMMISSION ON NARCOTIC DRUGS FOR FURTHER IMPLEMENTATION OF THE 1988 CONVENTION

18.   In accordance with a request of the Commission on Narcotic Drugs at its thirty-seventh session, the Secretariat submitted a note to the Commission at its thirty-eighth session on the adequacy of existing national drug control legislation (E/CN.7/1995/12), for consideration under item 6 of its agenda, entitled "Implementation of the international drug control treaties". It also submitted a thematic list of its collection of texts of legislation on money-laundering, confiscation of proceeds, extradition, mutual legal assistance, controlled delivery and the control of precursors, prepared as a background document to the note on the adequacy of national legislation. The note dealt with whether States parties to international drug control treaties translated into their domestic national legislation their obligations under those treaties. While stressing the fundamental importance of national legislation for treaty implementation and for an efficient drug control system, it was noted that certain factors, such as administrative policies, strategies used by the control authorities and the human and financial resources available for drug control, were decisive in the effective implementation of legislative provisions on drug control.

19.   Cumulative indexes for 1994 and for the period 1991-1995,[8] listing drug control legislation adopted by States parties and non-parties to international drug control treaties were presented by the Secretariat to the Commission at its thirty-eighth and thirty-ninth sessions, respectively.

A. Adherence to and implementation of the international drug control treaties

20.   In its resolution 3 (XXXIX) of 25 April 1996, the Commission urged all States to accede to the international drug control treaties before the end of the United Nations Decade against Drug Abuse, covering the years from 1991 to 2000. In the same resolution, it invited Member States to monitor the conformity of national legislation with the existing international drug control treaties and to adopt the measures necessary to strengthen the effectiveness of action involving prevention and cooperation of the judiciary and law enforcement agencies. As regards regional and international cooperation, the Commission requested Member States to strengthen joint strategies designed to control various forms of crime linked to drug trafficking, for instance by adopting and intensifying the use of the technique of controlled delivery, which had proved effective in dealing with the increasingly complex activities of organized crime.

B. Recommendations of the Working Group on Maritime Cooperation

21.   The Commission, in its resolution 8 (XXXVIII) of 23 March 1995, endorsed the report, including the recommendations, of the meeting of the Working Group on Maritime Cooperation, which met at Vienna from 19 to 23 September 1994 and from 20 to 24 February 1995. The Working Group had been entrusted with the mandate to develop a set of comprehensive principles and specific recommendations to enhance on a global basis the implementation of article 17 of the 1988 Convention.

22.   In the same resolution, the Commission urged Governments to consider closely the recommendations of the Working Group in implementing article 17 of the 1988 Convention. In order to achieve broad-based cooperation against drug trafficking by sea, the Commission recommended that Governments should encourage commercial carriers and professional groups active in maritime transport to become involved in the fight against

the illicit drug traffic, on the basis of voluntary cooperation and through memoranda of understanding at the national and international levels, as well as through training to increase the awareness of maritime transport personnel with regard to illicit drug trafficking.

23. Pursuant to the recommendations contained in the report of the Working Group (E/CN.7/1995/13, para. 9), the Commission, in its resolution 8 (XXXVIII), requested UNDCP to convene an expert group meeting to develop training and technical assistance programmes in maritime drug law enforcement. Accordingly, an Expert Group on Maritime Drug Law Enforcement met at Vienna from 27 to 29 February 1996. It considered the development of a training programme for minimum standards and safeguards in the conduct of stopping and boarding vessels and carrying out searches at sea, in accordance with the international law of the sea; the formation of multinational mobile training teams to carry out such training programmes in States at their request; and the development of training materials on techniques and methods for inspecting vessels and establishing timetables for their dissemination. Its recommendations were submitted to the Commission at its thirty-ninth session.

24. In its recommendation, the Expert Group identified a need for common standard training curricula designed to promote a consistent international approach to maritime law enforcement. Such an approach would foster closer cooperation and greater uniformity in the implementation of article 17 of the 1988 Convention. The Expert Group also recommended that UNDCP should undertake missions to requesting States in order to conduct a thorough needs assessment, to identify the assistance and training required, particularly in the establishment of or upgrading of ship registries, and to enable States to provide timely and reliable information.

25. In the light of the recommendations of both the Working Group on Maritime Cooperation and the Expert Group on Maritime Drug Law Enforcement, the Commission urged UNDCP to prepare training guides as well as other forms of technical cooperation. It stressed that holding a regional seminar on operational training for maritime law enforcement would be useful. In that connection, the Commission endorsed the proposal of the Government of Japan to convene a UNDCP regional seminar on maritime drug law enforcement in Asia and the Pacific and to make a voluntary financial contribution to the holding of such a seminar.

C. Role of Governments and the International Narcotics Control Board in furthering the implementation of article 12 of the 1988 Convention

26. In considering the report of the International Narcotics Control Board for 1995 on the implementation of article 12 of the 1988 Convention,[10] the Commission noted the emphasis placed by the Board on the application of a minimum set of controls by Governments to prevent diversions of precursor chemicals. It also noted that all Governments that had not already done so should take immediate action in establishing practical systems to monitor the movement of precursors, adding that such systems could be established with or without having relevant or comprehensive legislation in place. To assist in that endeavour, the Commission concluded that all Governments should re-examine the recommendations made in the report of the Board for 1994 on the implementation of article 12,[11] as endorsed by the Economic and Social Council in its resolution 1995/20 of 24 July 1995, and should take the steps described in the report of the Board for 1995 on the implementation of article 12.

27. While welcoming the continuing cooperation between Governments, the Commission endorsed the view of the Board that controls could be made more effective if there was a greater exchange of information on a regular and routine basis, either through the Board or directly between national authorities. It agreed that timely sharing of information, on a global basis, was essential if diversions were to be prevented and that Governments should continue to develop appropriate systems for sharing information so that they could identify and investigate suspicious transactions. Governments with such systems already in place were urged to use them to alert other Governments, as appropriate, through the Board, as soon as suspicious transactions had been identified and stopped.

28. Noting that free ports and free export processing zones had been frequently used as points of diversion, the Commission recalled that it was a treaty obligation to monitor closely the movements of precursors in such trading centres. It noted that Governments should provide for a mechanism to seize consignments of precursors when adequate grounds for suspicion had been established.

D. Action that States should take to broaden measures against money-laundering

29. In its resolution 5 (XXXIX) of 24 April 1996, the Commission expressed its awareness that the proceeds generated by drug trafficking and other illicit activities were being placed into banks and other legitimate financial institutions and that the ability of banks and other financial institutions to screen potentially criminal

customers was a potent weapon in the fight against money-laundering. In the same resolution, the Commission specified measures that States and banks and other financial institutions should take to combat money-laundering.

E. Cooperation between the United Nations International Drug Control Programme, together with the Crime Prevention and Criminal Justice Division of the Secretariat, and the Financial Action Task Force

30.   In its resolution 5 (XXXIX), the Commission noted that the 40 recommendations of the Financial Action Task Force established by the heads of State or Government of the Group of Seven major industrialized countries and the President of the Commission of the European Communities remained the standard by which measures against money-laundering adopted by the States concerned should be judged. In the same resolution, the Commission urged UNDCP, together with the Crime Prevention and Criminal Justice Division of the Secretariat, to continue to work with the Financial Action Task Force and other relevant multilateral and regional institutions, in the fight against money-laundering and drug trafficking, with a view to strengthening international efforts in this field, and to review progress made by States in implementing the provisions of the 1988 Convention against money-laundering.

Notes

[1] *Official Records of the United Nations Conference for the Adoption of a Convention against Illicit Traffic in Narcotic Drugs and Psychotropic Substances*, vol. I (United Nations publication, Sales No. E.94.XI.5).

[2] United Nations, *Treaty Series*, vol. 976, No. 14152.

[3] Ibid., vol. 1019, No. 14956.

[4] Ibid., vol. 520, No. 7515.

[5] *Commentary on the Single Convention on Narcotic Drugs, 1961* (United Nations publication, Sales No. E.73.XI.1).

[6] *Commentary on the 1972 Protocol Amending the Single Convention on Narcotic Drugs, 1961* (United Nations publication, Sales No. E.76.XI.6)

[7] *Commentary on the Convention on Psychotropic Substances* (United Nations publication, Sales No. E.76.XI.5).

[8] *Cumulative Index 1994: National Laws and Regulations Relating to the Control of Narcotic Drugs and Psychotropic Substances* (United Nations publication, Sales No. E.96.XI).

[9] *Cumulative Index 1991-1995: National Laws and Regulations Relating to the Control of Narcotic Drugs and Psychotropic Substances* (United Nations publication, Sales No. E.96.XI.5).

[10] *Precursors and Chemicals Frequently Used in the Illicit Manufacture of Narcotic Drugs and Psychotropic Substances: Report of the International Narcotics Control Board for 1995 on the Implementation of Article 12 of the United Nations Convention against Illicit Traffic in Narcotic Drugs and Psychotropic Substances of 1988* (United Nations publication, Sales No. E.96.XI.4).

[11] *Precursors and Chemicals Frequently Used in the Illicit Manufacture of Narcotic Drugs and Psychotropic Substances: Report of the International Narcotics Control Board for 1994 on the Implementation of Article 12 of the United Nations Convention against Illicit Traffic in Narcotic Drugs and Psychotropic Substances of 1988* (United Nations publication, Sales No. E.95.XI.1).

Annex I

STATUS OF ADHERENCE TO THE INTERNATIONAL DRUG CONTROL TREATIES
AS AT 30 JUNE 1996

A. **Single Convention on Narcotic Drugs of 1961 and that Convention
as amended by the 1972 Protocol**

1.   The following 156 States are parties to the Single Convention on Narcotic Drugs of 1961[a] (underlined) or are parties to that Convention as amended by the 1972 Protocol:[b]

Afghanistan, Algeria, Antigua and Barbuda, Argentina, Armenia, Australia, Austria, Bahamas, Bahrain, Bangladesh, Barbados, Belarus, Belgium, Benin, Bolivia, Bosnia and Herzegovina, Botswana, Brazil, Brunei Darussalam, Bulgaria, Burkina Faso, Burundi, Cameroon, Canada, Cape Verde, Chad, Chile, China, Colombia, Costa Rica, Côte d'Ivoire, Croatia, Cuba, Cyprus, Czech Republic, Denmark, Dominica, Dominican Republic, Ecuador, Egypt, Ethiopia, Fiji, Finland, France, Gabon, Gambia, Germany, Ghana, Greece, Guatemala, Guinea, Guinea-Bissau, Haiti, Holy See, Honduras, Hungary, Iceland, India, Indonesia, Iran (Islamic Republic of), Iraq, Ireland, Israel, Italy, Jamaica, Japan, Jordan, Kenya, Kuwait, Kyrgyzstan, Lao People's Democratic Republic, Latvia, Lebanon, Lesotho, Liberia, Libyan Arab Jamahiriya, Liechtenstein, Lithuania, Luxembourg, Madagascar, Malawi, Malaysia, Mali, Malta, Marshall Islands, Mauritania, Mauritius, Mexico, Micronesia (Federated States of), Monaco, Mongolia, Morocco, Myanmar, Nepal, Netherlands, New Zealand, Nicaragua, Niger, Nigeria, Norway, Oman, Pakistan, Panama, Papua New Guinea, Paraguay, Peru, Philippines, Poland, Portugal, Qatar, Republic of Korea, Republic of Moldova, Romania, Russian Federation, Rwanda, Saint Kitts and Nevis, Saint Lucia, Saudi Arabia, Senegal, Seychelles, Sierra Leone, Singapore, Slovakia, Slovenia, Solomon Islands, Somalia, South Africa, Spain, Sri Lanka, Sudan, Suriname, Swaziland, Sweden, Switzerland, Syrian Arab Republic, Thailand, the former Yugoslav Republic of Macedonia, Togo, Tonga, Trinidad and Tobago, Tunisia, Turkey, Turkmenistan, Uganda, Ukraine, United Arab Emirates, United Kingdom of Great Britain and Northern Ireland, United States of America, Uruguay, Uzbekistan, Venezuela, Yemen, Yugoslavia, Zaire, Zambia and Zimbabwe.

B. **Convention on Psychotropic Substances of 1971**

2.   The following 144 States are parties to the Convention on Psychotropic Substances of 1971:[c]

Afghanistan, Algeria, Antigua and Barbuda, Argentina, Armenia, Australia, Bahamas, Bahrain, Bangladesh, Barbados, Belarus, Belgium, Benin, Bolivia, Bosnia and Herzegovina, Botswana, Brazil, Brunei Darussalam, Bulgaria, Burkina Faso, Burundi, Cameroon, Canada, Cape Verde, Chad, Chile, China, Colombia, Costa Rica, Côte d'Ivoire, Croatia, Cuba, Cyprus, Czech Republic, Denmark, Dominica, Dominican Republic, Ecuador, Egypt, Ethiopia, Fiji, Finland, France, Gabon, Gambia, Germany, Ghana, Greece, Grenada, Guatemala, Guinea, Guinea-Bissau, Guyana, Holy See, Hungary, Iceland, India, Iraq, Ireland, Israel, Italy, Jamaica, Japan, Jordan, Kuwait, Kyrgyzstan, Latvia, Lebanon, Lesotho, Libyan Arab Jamahiriya, Lithuania, Luxembourg, Madagascar, Malawi, Malaysia, Mali, Malta, Marshall Islands, Mauritania, Mauritius, Mexico, Micronesia (Federated States of), Monaco, Morocco, Myanmar, Netherlands, New Zealand, Nicaragua, Niger, Nigeria, Norway, Pakistan, Panama, Papua New Guinea, Paraguay, Peru, Philippines, Poland, Portugal, Qatar, Republic of Korea, Republic of Moldova, Romania, Russian Federation, Rwanda, Saint Kitts and Nevis, Saudi Arabia, Senegal, Seychelles, Sierra Leone, Singapore, Slovakia, Slovenia, Somalia, South Africa, Spain, Sri Lanka, Sudan, Suriname, Swaziland, Sweden, Switzerland, Syrian Arab Republic, Thailand, the former Yugoslav Republic of Macedonia, Togo, Tonga, Trinidad and Tobago, Tunisia, Turkey, Turkmenistan, Uganda, Ukraine, United Arab Emirates, United Kingdom of Great Britain and Northern Ireland, United States of America, Uruguay, Uzbekistan, Venezuela, Yemen, Yugoslavia, Zaire, Zambia and Zimbabwe.

C. **United Nations Convention against Illicit Traffic in Narcotic Drugs and
Psychotropic Substances of 1988**

3.   The following 132 States are parties to the United Nations Convention against Illicit Traffic in Narcotic Drugs and Psychotropic Substances of 1988:[d]

Afghanistan, Algeria, Antigua and Barbuda, Argentina, Armenia, Australia, Azerbaijan, Bahamas, Bahrain, Bangladesh, Barbados, Belarus, Belgium, Bhutan, Bolivia, Bosnia and Herzegovina, Brazil, Brunei

Darussalam, Bulgaria, Burkina Faso, Burundi, Cameroon, Canada, Cape Verde, Chad, Chile, China, Colombia, Costa Rica, Côte d'Ivoire, Croatia, Cuba, Cyprus, Czech Republic, Denmark, Dominica, Dominican Republic, Ecuador, Egypt, El Salvador, Ethiopia, Fiji, Finland, France, Gambia, Germany, Ghana, Greece, Grenada, Guatemala, Guinea, Guinea-Bissau, Guyana, Haiti, Honduras, India, Iran (Islamic Republic of), Italy, Jamaica, Japan, Jordan, Kenya, Kyrgyzstan, Latvia, Lebanon, Lesotho, Luxembourg, Madagascar, Malawi, Malaysia, Mali, Malta, Mauritania, Mexico, Monaco, Morocco, Myanmar, Nepal, Netherlands, Nicaragua, Niger, Nigeria, Norway, Oman, Pakistan, Panama, Paraguay, Peru, Philippines, Poland, Portugal, Qatar, Republic of Moldova, Romania, Russian Federation, Saint Kitts and Nevis, Saint Lucia, Saint Vincent and the Grenadines, Saudi Arabia, Senegal, Seychelles, Sierra Leone, Slovakia, Slovenia, Spain, Sri Lanka, Sudan, Suriname, Swaziland, Sweden, Syrian Arab Republic, Tajikistan, the former Yugoslav Republic of Macedonia, Togo, Tonga, Trinidad and Tobago, Tunisia, Turkey, Turkmenistan, Uganda, Ukraine, United Arab Emirates, United Kingdom of Great Britain and Northern Ireland, United Republic of Tanzania, United States of America, Uruguay, Uzbekistan, Venezuela, Yemen, Yugoslavia, Zambia and Zimbabwe.

4.   On 31 December 1990 the European Community deposited its instrument of formal confirmation of the 1988 Convention (extent of competence: article 12).

Notes

ᵃ Entry into force: 13 December 1964.
ᵇ Entry into force: 8 August 1975.
ᶜ Entry into force: 16 August 1976.
ᵈ Entry into force: 11 November 1990.

Annex II

**LEGAL ASSISTANCE PROVIDED TO GOVERNMENTS BY UNDCP
BETWEEN 1 JULY 1994 AND 30 JUNE 1996**

A. Legal assistance missions

1.   Between 1 July 1994 and 30 June 1996, legal assistance missions were carried out in the following countries or territories:

Albania, Angola, Anguilla, Antigua and Barbuda, Bahamas, Barbados, Belize, Bolivia, Brazil, Cambodia, Cameroon, Cape Verde, Colombia, Congo, Cook Islands, Costa Rica, Croatia, Dominican Republic, El Salvador, Estonia, Fiji, Ghana, Grenada, Guatemala, Guyana, Honduras, Jamaica, Kiribati, Lao People's Democratic Republic, Latvia, Lebanon, Lithuania, Mauritius, Namibia, Nauru, Nicaragua, Nigeria, Niue, Pakistan, Panama, Papua New Guinea, Republic of Moldova, Romania, Russian Federation, Saint Kitts and Nevis, Saint Lucia, Saint Vincent and the Grenadines, Solomon Islands, Slovakia, Slovenia, Tajikistan, United Republic of Tanzania, Tonga, Trinidad and Tobago, Tuvalu, Vanuatu, Viet Nam and Zambia.

B. Regional legal workshops

2.   Regional legal workshops were held in which the following countries or territories participated:

Albania, Anguilla, Antigua and Barbuda, Bahamas, Barbados, Belize, Botswana, Brunei Darussalam, Cambodia, Cyprus, Comoros, Costa Rica, Dominican Republic, El Salvador, Estonia, Gambia, Ghana, Grenada, Guatemala, Guyana, Honduras, India, Indonesia, Jamaica, Kazakstan, Kenya, Kyrgyzstan, Kiribati, Lao People's Democratic Republic, Latvia, Lesotho, Lithuania, Madagascar, Malaysia, Malawi, Mauritius, Mozambique, Myanmar, Namibia, Nicaragua, Nigeria, Panama, Philippines, Saint Kitts and Nevis, Saint Lucia, Saint Vincent and the Grenadines, Solomon Islands, Seychelles, Singapore, South Africa, Swaziland, Tajikistan, United Republic of Tanzania, Thailand, Trinidad and Tobago, Turkmenistan, Uganda, Uzbekistan, Viet Nam, Zambia and Zimbabwe.

C. Legal training workshops

3. Legal training workshops were held in which the following countries or territories participated:

Anguilla, Antigua and Barbuda, Bahamas, Barbados, Belize, Bolivia, Burkina Faso, Cape Verde, Costa Rica, Côte d'Ivoire, El Salvador, Gambia, Ghana, Grenada, Guatemala, Guinea, Guyana, Honduras, Jamaica, Lao People's Democratic Republic, Lebanon, Liberia, Mali, Mauritania, Namibia, Nicaragua, Niger, Nigeria, Panama, Saint Kitts and Nevis, Saint Lucia, Saint Vincent and the Grenadines, Senegal, Sierra Leone, Togo, Trinidad and Tobago and Yemen.

-----

6. LETTER OF 9 JANUARY 1996 FROM THE PERMANENT REPRESENTATIVE OF THE RUSSIAN FEDERATION (NAVIGATION IN THE BLACK SEA STRAITS)

Doc. no.: A/51/57   15 January 1996

I have the honour to submit the text of a document related to the issue of navigation in the Black Sea Straits (see annex).

I should be grateful if you would have this letter and its annex circulated as a document of the General Assembly under the agenda item entitled "Law of the sea".

(Signed)   S. LAVROV

ANNEX

The Russian side has drawn attention to the appearance of General Assembly document A/50/809 of 8 December 1995, which explains the position of the Turkish Government regarding navigation in the Black Sea Straits and the action taken in that respect by the Turkish authorities. In this connection, the Russian side confirms that its views on this issue, as set forth in document A/50/754 of 14 November 1995, remain unchanged. Accordingly, the detailed arguments adduced in that document need not be repeated, and the response can at this stage be confined to the following points.

Document A/50/809 sets out in great detail considerations relating to the need to ensure safety of navigation in the Black Sea Straits. The Russian side also proceeds on the assumption that such safety of navigation must be ensured. This is indeed an important problem, and precisely for this reason it is being dealt with in detail by the International Maritime Organization (IMO) (in particular the IMO Maritime Safety Committee), which exercises the relevant competence with regard to ensuring the safety of navigation. Thus, on 23 November 1995, at its nineteenth session, the IMO Assembly adopted without a vote a resolution on the question of navigation in the Black Sea Straits. The resolution _inter alia_ confirms the Rules and Recommendations on Navigation through the Straits drawn up by IMO and previously adopted by it. At the same time, it emphasizes that national regulations for navigation in Straits should be in total conformity with the IMO rules and recommendations.

The essence of the issue raised in the Russian document of 14 November 1995 (A/50/754) is something different. The document emphasizes that a State must discharge its obligations under international treaties and abide by the universally recognized principles and norms of international law, which are embodied in particular in the 1982 United Nations Convention on the Law of the Sea.

The Turkish document, A/50/809, is apparently designed to dispel all the existing doubts in this respect. It indicates in paragraph 18 that "the Turkish Regulations [which have been enacted in the form of a law] are fully in line with applicable international law and freedom of navigation. The Regulations uphold the 1936 Montreux Convention and in no way infringe upon its provisions. They are not aimed at restricting or impairing the right of navigation."

However, this statement does not reflect the true state of affairs. Article 2 of the Montreux Convention provides that "... merchant vessels shall enjoy complete freedom of transit and navigation in the Straits, by day and by night, under any flag and with any kind of cargo". The Regulations adopted by Turkey, however, provide for what are in essence procedures for regulating passage through the Straits by certain categories of merchant vessels. Furthermore, under the terms of the Turkish Regulations, the Straits may be completely closed to navigation for an unspecified period on various grounds which are for the most part artificial and unjustified in nature.

The Russian side wishes to emphasize once again that, in drawing the attention of the United Nations to this issue, it is guided solely by the desire to prevent a situation arising which could lead to tension in the region. We have no doubt that Turkey, like the Russian Federation and the other countries of the region, endeavours to build its relations on a basis of good-neighbourliness and cooperation. However, the difficulties that have arisen can be overcome not by unilateral action, but through constructive dialogue, for which the Russian side is always ready.

The Russian side notes Turkey's reluctance to acknowledge the fact that the problem which has arisen in connection with the regime for navigation through the Black Sea Straits has its origin not in a "purely technical issue", as is stated in paragraph 39 of document A/50/809, but in a point of principle relating to the discharge by a State of its obligations under international treaties. In this context, the Russian Federation considers that the General Assembly is an entirely appropriate forum for dealing with this issue.

-----

7. LETTER OF 28 JUNE 1996 FROM THE PERMANENT REPRESENTATIVE OF SOUTH AFRICA (FINAL DECLARATION OF THE 4TH MEETING OF THE STATES OF THE ZONE OF PEACE AND COOPERATION OF THE SOUTH ATLANTIC, SOMERSET WEST, SOUTH AFRICA, 1-2 APRIL 1996)*

Doc. no.: A/51/183   8 July 1996

I have the honour to transmit herewith the documents adopted by the Fourth Meeting of the States of the Zone of Peace and Cooperation of the South Atlantic, held in South Africa on 1 and 2 April 1996.

I should be grateful if you would have the present letter and its annexes distributed as a document of the General Assembly, under item 32 of the preliminary list.

(<u>Signed</u>) **Khiphusizi J. JELE**
Ambassador
Permanent Representative

Annex I

FINAL DECLARATION OF THE FOURTH MEETING OF THE STATES OF THE
ZONE OF PEACE AND COOPERATION OF THE SOUTH ATLANTIC

The representatives of the Member States of the Zone of Peace and Cooperation of the South Atlantic (ZPCSA - hereafter referred to as "the Zone"), meeting in Somerset West, South Africa, on 1 and 2 April 1996 and recalling the conclusions of the Third High-Level Meeting, which took place in Brasilia, on 21 and 22 September 1994:

---

*   A/51/50.

1. Congratulate the Chair and the Bureau of the Permanent Committee of the Zone for their valuable work as Coordinators since the Brasilia meeting;

2. Reaffirm the validity of the Zone as an instrument for promoting understanding and cooperation among South Atlantic countries, as well as for contributing to international peace and security; and agree on the need to strengthen its role as a regional instrument of coordination and dialogue;

3. Decide that cooperation among the countries of the Zone must be pursued in all areas with a potential for joint action and benefit, especially in the economic, technological, environmental, cultural and sporting fields;

4. Reaffirm also that the cooperation in the forum of the Zone is based on the principles of the respect for sovereignty and territorial integrity of States and other relevant principles of international law, and the right of all peoples to freely determine their economic and political systems;

5. Reiterate the commitment of the members of the Zone to encourage democracy and political pluralism, to promote and defend all human rights and fundamental freedoms and to cooperate towards the achievement of these goals;

6. Agree that the Zone has a valuable role to play as a forum for dialogue in multilateral issues, including those relating to the maintenance of international peace and security, the promotion of international cooperation for economic and social development, the protection of the environment and the strengthening of the role of the United Nations;

7. Reiterate their commitment to the non-proliferation of weapons of mass destruction in all its aspects, with a view to the complete elimination of such weapons, and to the non-introduction of such weapons into the Zone, and in this regard reiterate the validity of the Declaration on the Denuclearisation of the South Atlantic, adopted at the Third Meeting of the Member-States of the Zone, and encourage the Conference on Disarmament to conclude a Comprehensive Test Ban Treaty as soon as possible;

8. Emphasize the importance of the understanding and close cooperation of the countries of the Zone in nuclear matters, which is making possible the progress towards the full entry into force of the Treaty on the Prohibition of Nuclear Weapons in Latin America, the Treaty of Tlatelolco, and the conclusion of the Treaty on an African Nuclear-Weapon-Free Zone, the Pelindaba Treaty;

9. Welcome the adoption of the final text of the Pelindaba Treaty and call upon all African States and others concerned to sign and ratify the Treaty and its Protocols, in order to expedite its entry into force;

10. Urge the countries possessing weapons of mass
destruction to fully respect the status of the Zone as
a region free of such weapons;

11. Express their conviction that the Tlatelolco and
Pelindaba Treaties, together with the Antarctic Treaty,
the Rarotonga Treaty and the recently concluded
Southeast Asia Nuclear Weapon Free Zone Treaty,
contribute to make the Southern Hemisphere and adjacent
areas covered by those treaties free of nuclear
weapons;

12. Support efforts by the countries of the Zone in finding
negotiated solutions for conflicts and in promoting the
principle of settling disputes by peaceful means;

13. Urge all Member States of the Zone to support current
peace processes in the region and call upon them to
contribute to United Nations peace-keeping operations
taking place in different parts of the Zone;

14. Acknowledge with appreciation the sustained sacrifice
and support of the member states of ECOWAS,
particularly its Chairman and the other leaders of the
sub-region, for their untiring efforts to bring peace
to Liberia, and reiterate the call on the
international community to honour their commitments
towards the implementation of the Abuja Agreement and
for the reconstruction of Liberia;

15. Warmly welcome the holding of democratic elections in
the Republic of Benin and in the Republic of Sierra
Leone and express the hope that the establishment of
new freely elected governments in both countries would
enhance peace, security and stability in the sub-region
for the socio-economic development of their peoples, as
well as reinforce the objectives of the ZPCSA;

16. Call on the parties to the conflict in Sierra Leone to
pursue the goals of the Yamoussoukro Peace Process;

17. Welcome the positive steps taken by the Government of
Angola in implementing its commitments towards the
peace process in Angola; express deep concern at the
numerous delays in the implementation of the Lusaka
Protocol; and urge UNITA to proceed immediately with
the orderly, large-scale and verifiable movement of its
troops to quartering areas;

18. Express their appreciation for the support of the
international community and the United Nations, in
particular the efforts of the Secretary-General and his
special representative, to the peace process in Angola
and to UNAVEM III, and exhort them to continue to
provide their support in the future;

19. Express their willingness to contribute by all means at
their disposal to an effective and lasting peace in
Angola and once again invite the international
community to provide on a predictable and timely basis
the pledged funds for the rehabilitation and economic
reconstruction of Angola;

20. **Reaffirm** the importance of preventive diplomacy, **peace-making**, peace-keeping and peace-building as suitable means for the maintenance of peace and security, while stressing that eradication of poverty and promotion of economic and social development are essential for long-lasting peace and security;

21. **Express** their conviction of the need for restructuring and revitalisation of the United Nations system and their support for actions intended to strengthen the United Nations in all its aspects, and in this regard encourage ongoing deliberations of the Open-ended Working Group on the question of equitable representation on and increase in the membership of the Security Council and other matters related to the Security Council; they also express the need to improve coordination with the institutions created in Bretton Woods and prepare the UN system to meet the needs of the international community in the 21st century;

22. **Affirm** the increasing importance of greater cooperation in economic and financial matters and the relevance of the "Agenda for Development";

23. **Reiterate** their conviction that the Uruguay Round agreements should result in greater market access, the expansion of world trade and an increase in income and employment opportunities throughout the world, particularly in developing countries;

24. **Express** their confidence that, with the functioning of the World Trade Organisation, rapid progress will be made towards abolishing unfair trade practices and unilateral protectionist measures, while taking appropriate steps to protect the legitimate interests of least developed countries;

25. **Emphasize** the role of regional and subregional integration in improving international competitiveness of national economies and in contributing to the development process;

26. **Invite** the Academic, Scientific, and Technological communities of the member states to participate in discussions on fostering cooperation in the Zone and pledge their support to the organisation of seminars and other means to improve mutual knowledge;

27. **Note** with satisfaction progress in the establishment of the Community of Portuguese Speaking Countries, whose aims coincide with and strengthen the major goals of peace and cooperation in the Zone;

28. **Encourage** Member States to further investigate and implement means to facilitate business initiative in exploring and expanding regional economic cooperation and commercial links across the South Atlantic, among member states of the Zone;

29. **Likewise** encourage Member States to facilitate the establishment of sea, air and telecommunications links

across the South Atlantic, among member states of the
Zone;

30. Urge Member States, within the context of enhancing
South-South Cooperation, to pursue regional
collaboration in the development of new technologies at
both private and public sector levels, sharing of
natural resources and international communication
systems in both science and technology, and developing
human resources in these fields;

31. Express their concern regarding the question of the
safe and secure transportation through the South
Atlantic of irradiated nuclear fuel, plutonium and
high level nuclear radioactive waste in flasks on board
ships, which should meet the standards set out by the
1983 International Maritime Organisation Code on the
subject;

32. Call on all States to maintain cooperation and exchange
of information on the transportation of nuclear
material and radioactive waste and to continue working
through the International Maritime Organisation and the
International Atomic Energy Agency in the development
of additional measures which would complement the Code;

33. Affirm their conviction that effective international
liability mechanisms are essential to provide
compensation for nuclear related damage which may occur
during transportation of irradiated nuclear fuel,
plutonium and high-level nuclear waste;

34 Reiterate the importance, for the Zone, of the
fulfilment of international environmental agreements,
specially those related to climate change; combatting
desertification in countries experiencing serious
drought and/or desertification, especially in Africa;
the protection of the ozone layer; the conservation and
sustainable use of the biodiversity, and transboundary
movement of hazardous waste;

35. Reaffirm the importance of the Declaration on the
Marine Environment, adopted at the Third Meeting and
once again express their support for regional
cooperation amongst Member States of the Zone in
accordance with the United Nations Convention on the
Law of the Sea of 10 December 1982;

36. Emphasize the importance, for the Zone, of the
Agreement for the implementation of the provisions of
the United Nations Convention on the Law of the Sea of
10 December 1982, related to the conservation and
management of straddling fish and highly migratory fish
stocks of 4 August 1995, whose provisions complement
and reinforce the Declaration on the Marine Environment
adopted at the III Meeting of Member States of the
Zone;

37. Encourage Member States to effectively implement,
nationally and regionally, the Global Programme of
Action for the Protection of the Marine Environment

from Land-based Activities, adopted at the Intergovernmental Conference in Washington DC in November 1995, under the auspices of the United Nations Environment Programme (UNEP);

38. Express their concern at the increase of the illegal drug trafficking in or through countries of the Zone, and affirm their commitment to develop a programme of cooperation with a view to assisting one another in the effort to monitor and eliminate the existing drug trafficking routes affecting the security of the countries of the Zone. In this context they agreed to cooperate in the exchange of information on drug traffickers and their illegal activities in the countries of the Zone in order to stem the tide of drug-related crimes and violence;

39. Urge Member States which have not acceded to or ratified the three main United Nations Drug Conventions, to do so as soon as possible. Member States are also called upon to promulgate and adopt domestic legislation which should satisfy the provisions of the United Nations Drug Conventions. Member States should further consider possible measures for dealing with the proceeds of illicit drug trafficking;

40. Urge Member States to support the efforts of specialised institutions on Aids, Research and Education with a view to halting the spread of the Aids pandemic;

41. Express their conviction that the Zone will continue to be an active instrument for enhancing intra regional and inter-regional cooperation and, in this respect, commit themselves to promoting the objectives of the Zone;

42. Express their gratitude to the people of South Africa for their hospitality and to the Government for hosting the IV Meeting of the Member States of the Zone;

43. Congratulate the Government of South Africa for the strong support provided to the objectives of the Zone and its vitality.

44. Welcome the offer made by the Government of Argentina, to host the Fifth Ministerial Meeting of the ZPCSA.

<u>Annex II</u>

DECISIONS OF THE FOURTH MEETING OF THE STATES OF THE ZONE OF
PEACE AND COOPERATION OF THE SOUTH ATLANTIC

DECISION ON DRUG TRAFFICKING

The representatives of the Member States of the Zone of
Peace and Co-operation of the South Atlantic (ZPCSA), gathered in
Somerset West on the 1st and 2nd of April, 1996;

Evaluating the new aspects of the international scene,
important among which is the illicit production of and
trafficking in narcotic drugs as a threat to the health and
well-being of their peoples and to the democratic stability of
their Governments;

Conscious of the need to take joint action, of a regional
scope, with the objective of curbing the perverse effect of the
dynamics of drug traffic and of ensuring better standards of
living for their peoples;

Noting the convening of a joint SADC/EU Regional Conference
on Illicit Cross-border Drug Trafficking, held in Mmabatho, South
Africa, between 30 October - 2 November 1995;

1.   Reaffirm their desire to co-operate closely in the
      control of demand, production and illicit traffic of
      narcotics in the ZPCSA and to contribute to the
      completion of the objective of the proposed anti-drug
      initiative.

2.   Welcome the adoption of an anti-drug initiative for
      cooperation in the field of narcotic control, to be
      developed and implemented within the framework of the
      Zone of Peace and Co-operation of the South Atlantic.

3.   Request the United Nations Drug Control Program
      to examine forms of assistance to be granted in the
      framework of the proposed anti-drug initiative.

4.   Emphasize the need for strengthening co-operation among
      member states of the ZPCSA and their law enforcement
      agencies and within international and regional
      organisations, in the fight against illicit
      trafficking in narcotic drugs, and psychotropic
      substances.

DECISION ON THE PROTECTION OF THE MARINE ENVIRONMENT

The representatives of the Member States of the Zone of
Peace and Cooperation of the South Atlantic ("the Zone"), meeting
in Somerset West on 1 and 2 April 1996;

Reaffirming the principles and purposes set forth in the Declaration on the Marine Environment adopted at the III Meeting of the Member States of the Zone (Brasilia, 1994);

RECOGNIZE that in order to adopt effective measures to preserve the marine environment of the Zone, information on any fact or activity that may have an impact on the marine environment of the Zone should be exchanged and disseminated among the Member States through the Chair. To that effect Member States of the Zone will indicate within the next six months national focal points to which such information will be conveyed by the Chair;

DECIDE that, on the basis of the information received, Member States may request the Chair to convene a meeting of the ZPCSA Permanent Committee to examine the case and submit specific proposals;

ENCOURAGE Member States that have not done so, to ratify or adhere to multilateral conventions and protocols dealing with the protection and preservation of marine environment, including the United Nations Convention on the Law of the Sea, the Agreement for the Implementation of the Provisions of the UNCLOS relating to the Conservation and Management of Straddling Fish Stocks and Highly Migratory Fish Stocks; the London Convention on the Prevention of Marine Pollution by Dumping of Wastes and Other Matter; and the International Convention for the Prevention of Pollution from Ships as modified by the Protocol of 1978 (MARPOL);

RECOMMEND that Member States of the Zone carry out consultations among themselves with the view to coordinating their positions in international conferences and other international fora, on matters relevant to the Zone, in particular the protection and preservation of the marine environment;

DECIDE to examine at the Fifth meeting of the Member States the need and possibility to establish a monitoring system to control and prevent the dumping of hazardous and other harmful materials into the Zone. To that effect Member States are requested to submit to the Chair written views for their consideration at the Fifth Meeting.

DECISION ON ILLEGAL FISHING ACTIVITIES IN THE ZONE

The representatives of the Member States of the Zone of Peace and Cooperation of the South Atlantic (the Zone), meeting in Somerset West on 1 and 2 April 1996;

DECIDE to examine at its V Meeting the possibility of establishing cooperative ways and means in support of the surveillance of illegal fishing activities, and invite the current Chair to prepare a report thereon.

-----

8. LETTER OF 3 APRIL 1996 FROM THE PERMANENT REPRESENTATIVE OF GEORGIA (DECREE NO.140 OF 31 JANUARY AND STATEMENT OF 25 MARCH 1996)

Doc. no.: S/1996/24   3 April 1996

I have the honour to transmit herewith the text of a decree issued on 31 January 1996 by the President of Georgia concerning border and customs control on the sector of the State border between the Russian Federation and Georgia within the territory of Abkhazia, Georgia, in the seaport of Sukhumi, port sites and the marine area (see annex I), as well as a statement on this subject issued by the Ministry of Foreign Affairs of Georgia on 25 March 1996 (see annex II).

I should be grateful if you would have the text of this letter and its annexes circulated as a document of the Security Council.

(Signed) Peter ĆHKHEIDZE
Permanent Representative

ANNEX I

[Original: Russian]

<u>Decree issued on 31 January 1996 by the President of Georgia concerning border and customs control on the sector of the State border between the Russian Federation and Georgia within the territory of Abkhazia, Georgia, and in the seaport of Sukhumi, port sites and the marine area</u>

In the light of the conflict in Abkhazia, Georgia, and the serious criminal situation that has emerged in the Caucasus region in general - a situation aggravated by the infiltration into the territory of Abkhazia, Georgia, of mercenaries, arms, narcotics and contraband - which poses a threat to the State security of Georgia, its vital interests and its good-neighbourly relations with adjacent States, and also considering that it is impossible to guarantee the safety of transport facilities of foreign countries in the Abkhaz part of Georgia's territory, and with a view to implementing the decision adopted on 19 January 1996 by the Council of Heads of State of the Commonwealth of Independent States, entitled "On measures to settle the conflict in Abkhazia, Georgia":

1.   The seaport of Sukhumi, port sites and the marine area and the sector of the State border between Georgia and the Russian Federation within the territory of Abkhazia, Georgia, shall be closed to all forms of international shipments, with the exception of consignments of humanitarian aid shipped in accordance with this Decree;

2.   The import of consignments of humanitarian aid into the territory of Abkhazia shall be allowed only on the basis of single-entry permits issued by the competent authorities of Georgia, following a preliminary customs inspection by the Customs Department of Georgia;

3.   A special working group of the Government of Georgia shall be instructed to inform applicants, through the diplomatic channel, of the decision to issue single-entry permits for the import of humanitarian goods into the territory of Abkhazia, Georgia;

4.   The Ministry of Foreign Affairs of Georgia shall be instructed:

-    to receive, through the diplomatic channel, applications for permission to import humanitarian goods into the territory of Abkhazia, Georgia;

-    to inform the border troops of the Russian Federation through the Georgian embassy that permission has been granted for the entry of transport facilities conveying humanitarian goods into the territory of Abkhazia, Georgia;

-    to inform the appropriate international organizations, including the Mutual Insurance Club, that the sector of the State border between Georgia and the Russian Federation within the territory of Abkhazia, and the seaport of Sukhumi, port sites and the marine area are closed to international shipments;

5.   The State Border Protection Department and the Customs Department of Georgia shall be instructed to inform immediately the appropriate agencies of Georgia of the results of the customs inspection of consignments of humanitarian goods being shipped to Abkhazia, Georgia;

6.   The State Border Protection Department and the Customs Department of Georgia shall be instructed to develop a mechanism for implementing this Decree and, together with the appropriate services of the Russian Federation, hold talks on the joint implementation of border control;

7.   The decision of 24 May 1995 of the Cabinet of Ministers of the Republic of Georgia on the seaport of Sukhumi and port sites in the territory of Abkhazia, Georgia, shall be considered null and void.

E. SHEVARDNADZE

Tbilisi

ANNEX II

[Original: Russian]

Statement issued on 25 March 1996 by the Ministry of
Foreign Affairs of Georgia

In conformity with the decision adopted on 19 January 1996 by the Council
of Heads of State of the Commonwealth of Independent States, entitled "On
measures to settle the conflict in Abkhazia, Georgia", and in the light of the
difficult situation in Abkhazia and the Caucasus region as a whole, and the
recent exacerbation of the situation in the port of Sukhumi and port sites in
the territory of Abkhazia, Georgia, which poses a threat to the State security
of Georgia and its vital interests, and pursuant to Decree No. 140 issued on
31 January 1996 by the President of Georgia [see annex I], the seaport of
Sukhumi and port sites of Abkhazia, Georgia, are closed to all forms of
international shipments, with the exception of consignments of humanitarian aid.

Consignments of humanitarian aid may be imported into the territory of
Abkhazia only if the supplier submits a prior request to the Government of
Georgia in respect of each individual shipment, and on the basis of single-entry
permits issued by the competent authorities of Georgia, following customs
inspection in the port of Poti by agencies of the Customs Department of Georgia.

Georgia calls upon States sending their vessels to Georgian ports, and the
relevant departments, organizations and private companies, to bear in mind the
above circumstances and refrain from sending their vessels to the port of
Sukhumi and port sites in Abkhazia, Georgia.

Tbilisi

-----

9. NOTE VERBALE OF 9 JULY 1996 FROM THE PERMANENT REPRESENTATIVE OF BRAZIL (DECLARATION ON THE MALVINAS OF 25 JUNE 1996)*

Doc. no.: A/51/205

10 July 1996

The Permanent Representative of Brazil to the United Nations presents his compliments to the Secretary-General and requests that the attached declaration be circulated among the States Members as an official document.

ANNEX

[Original: Spanish]

Declaration on the Malvinas

The Presidents of the States members of the Southern Common Market (MERCOSUR) and the Presidents of the Republic of Bolivia and the Republic of Chile reaffirm their support for the legitimate rights of the Argentine Republic in the sovereignty dispute on the question of the Malvinas Islands and recall the desire of the countries of the hemisphere that an early solution be found to the long-standing sovereignty dispute between the Argentine Republic and the United Kingdom of Great Britain and Northern Ireland with respect to the said territory, in accordance with the resolutions of the United Nations and the Organization of American States.

DONE on 25 June 1996 at Potrero de los Funes, San Luis province, Argentine Republic, on the occasion of the Tenth Meeting of the Presidents of MERCOSUR.

---

* A/51/50.

10. LETTER OF 25 JULY 1996 FROM THE PERMANENT REPRESENTATIVE OF YEMEN (ERITREA/YEMEN ARBITRATION)*

Doc. no.: A/51/260   29 July 1996

I have the honour to transmit to you herewith a letter from Mr. Abdulkarim Al-Eryani, Deputy Prime Minister and Minister for Foreign Affairs of the Republic of Yemen, protesting against the publication by the Eritrean Government of a map showing oil exploitation zones in the Red Sea that include areas subject to Yemeni sovereignty, among them what the map refers to as "the Hanish-Zuqur quadrangle".

I should be grateful if you would have the present letter and its annex circulated as a United Nations document.

(**Signed**)   Abdalla Saleh AL-ASHTAL
Ambassador
Permanent Representative

ANNEX

Letter dated 23 July 1996 from the Deputy Prime Minister
and Minister for Foreign Affairs of Yemen addressed to
the Secretary-General

I should like to inform you that the Republic of Yemen recently noted the fact that the Eritrean Government has published a map showing oil exploitation zones that include parts of the Red Sea. These zones include areas that are subject to Yemeni sovereignty, among them what the map refers to as "the Hanish-Zuqur quadrangle".

The Government of the Republic of Yemen rejects any Eritrean claim that infringes upon Yemeni sovereignty, and it regards the map's implications as a clear violation of the Agreement on Principles signed in Paris on 21 May 1996 (S/1996/447, annex).

---

*   A/51/150.

In view of the fact that the two parties have entrusted the Government of France with the task of monitoring the area in dispute, the Yemeni Government will request France to take appropriate measures with regard to this clear breach of the Agreement on Principles.

We request you to have this protest circulated as a United Nations document.

(<u>Signed</u>)   Abdulkarim AL-ERYANI
Deputy Prime Minister
and Minister for Foreign Affairs

-----

11. LETTER OF 5 AUGUST 1996 FROM THE PERMANENT REPRESENTATIVE OF THE ISLAMIC REPUBLIC OF IRAN (ABU MUSA ISLAND)

Doc. no.: S/1996/627*   13 August 1996

Upon instructions from my Government and pursuant to the letter of 3 August 1996 addressed to you by H.E. Mr. Ali Akbar Velayati, Minister for Foreign Affairs of the Islamic Republic of Iran (S/1996/632), I have the honour to inform you of a series of violations of the airspace of the Islamic Republic of Iran and provocative acts by the forces of the United States of America in the Persian Gulf.

1.   On 3 August 1996, at 1745 hours, an American fighter violated the airspace of the Islamic Republic of Iran in Bushehr and broke the sound barrier.

2.   On 3 August 1996, at 2300 hours, an American fighter flying from west to east violated the airspace of the Islamic Republic of Iran over Abu Musa island.

3.   On 3 August 1996, at 2330 hours, more than 20 American F-14 and F-15 fighters were observed flying 30 miles south of Bushehr.

It would be appreciated if the text of the present letter could be circulated as a document of the Security Council.

(Signed)   Kamal KHARRAZI
Ambassador
Permanent Representative

---

*   Reissued for technical reasons.

12.   LETTER OF 26 AUGUST 1996 FROM THE PERMANENT REPRESENTATIVE OF THE UNITED ARAB EMIRATES (ABU MUSA ISLAND)

Doc. no.: S/1996/692   26 August 1996

On instructions from my Government, and with reference to paragraph 2 of the letter dated 5 August 1996 addressed to you by the Permanent Representative of the Islamic Republic of Iran to the United Nations (S/1996/627), I have the honour to inform you of the following.

The United Arab Emirates protests against the allegation in the above paragraph according to which the airspace over Abu Musa island belongs to the Islamic Republic of Iran.

My Government rejects this allegation, which it considers a flagrant violation of the sovereignty of the United Arab Emirates over Abu Musa island, as one of the persistent measures which the Islamic Republic of Iran has taken and continues to take with respect to the island, in violation of the memorandum of agreement concluded in November 1971, with a view to dominating the island and annexing it by force.

The United Arab Emirates categorically rejects any infringement of its sovereignty over Abu Musa island and reaffirms that it is fully disposed to settle the question of the three islands (the Greater Tunb, the Lesser Tunb and Abu Musa) through peaceful means, including recourse to the International Court of Justice.

I should be grateful if you would have the text of this letter circulated as a document of the Security Council.

(Signed)   Mohammad J. SAMHAN
Ambassador
Permanent Representative

-----

13. LETTER OF 12 SEPTEMBER 1996 FROM THE PERMANENT REPRESENTATIVE OF THE MARSHALL ISLANDS (COMMUNIQUÉ OF THE 27TH SOUTH PACIFIC FORUM, MAJURO, MARSHALL ISLANDS, 3-5 SEPTEMBER 1996)*

Doc. no.: A/51/357

13 September 1996

REPORT OF THE INTERNATIONAL COURT OF JUSTICE

REPORT OF THE INTERNATIONAL ATOMIC ENERGY AGENCY

ELECTIONS TO FILL VACANCIES IN PRINCIPAL ORGANS

IMPLEMENTATION OF THE DECLARATION ON THE GRANTING OF INDEPENDENCE TO COLONIAL COUNTRIES AND PEOPLES

LAW OF THE SEA

IMPLEMENTATION OF THE COMPREHENSIVE NUCLEAR-TEST-BAN TREATY

GENERAL AND COMPLETE DISARMAMENT

REVIEW OF THE IMPLEMENTATION OF THE RECOMMENDATIONS AND DECISIONS ADOPTED BY THE GENERAL ASSEMBLY AT ITS TENTH SPECIAL SESSION

EFFECTS OF ATOMIC RADIATION

INFORMATION FROM NON-SELF-GOVERNING TERRITORIES TRANSMITTED UNDER ARTICLE 73 e OF THE CHARTER OF THE UNITED NATIONS

---

* A/51/150.

IMPLEMENTATION OF THE DECLARATION ON THE GRANTING
OF INDEPENDENCE TO COLONIAL COUNTRIES AND PEOPLES
BY THE SPECIALIZED AGENCIES AND THE INTERNATIONAL
INSTITUTIONS ASSOCIATED WITH THE UNITED NATIONS

MACROECONOMIC POLICY QUESTIONS

SUSTAINABLE DEVELOPMENT AND INTERNATIONAL
ECONOMIC COOPERATION

ENVIRONMENT AND SUSTAINABLE DEVELOPMENT

OPERATIONAL ACTIVITIES FOR DEVELOPMENT

CRIME PREVENTION AND CRIMINAL JUSTICE

I have the honour to transmit to you the final text of the
Forum Communiqué, adopted by the twenty-seventh South Pacific Forum,
held at Majuro, Marshall Islands, from 3 to 5 September 1996
(see annex).

I should be grateful if you could arrange to have the text of
the present letter and its annex circulated as a document of the
General Assembly under items 13, 14, 15, 19, 24, 66, 71, 73, 82, 88,
90, 96, 98, 99, 100 and 103 of the provisional agenda.

(Signed)   Laurence N. EDWARDS
Ambassador
Permanent Representative

ANNEX

Forum communiqué adopted by the twenty-seventh
South Pacific Forum

Majuro, Marshall Islands, from 3 to 5 September 1996

The Twenty-Seventh South Pacific Forum was held in Majuro from 3 to 5
September 1996 and was attended by Heads of State and Government, or their
representatives of Australia, the Cook Islands, Federated States of Micronesia, Fiji,
Kiribati, Nauru, New Zealand, Niue, Palau, Papua New Guinea, the Republic of
Marshall Islands, Solomon Islands, Tonga, Tuvalu, Vanuatu and Western Samoa.

2.   The Forum thanked the people and the Government of the Republic of Marshall Islands for the generous hospitality provided to all delegations to the Forum and the arrangements made for its meeting. It expressed its deep appreciation to the outgoing Chairman for his excellent leadership during the year.

PACIFIC SOLIDARITY FOR THE COMMON GOOD

3.   Leaders held an intensive discussion on the Forum Theme of "**Pacific Solidarity for the Common Good**" and agreed on a range of measures to achieve more progress in economic reform and development. The measures are outlined in the separate statement adopted by the Forum and attached as appendix I.

4.   The Chair thanked the Prime Minister of Papua New Guinea, Western Samoa, and New Zealand, and the Beretitenti of Kiribati, for their comprehensive presentations they had made on the sub-themes. He expressed his appreciation also to the University of the South Pacific for provision of discussion papers on the sub-themes.

DEVELOPMENT

Fisheries

5.   Regional fish stocks are an internationally significant resource, and regional fisheries must be developed sustainably and in a way that maximises the benefit to Forum members. The Forum called upon the Forum Fisheries Committee to continue with urgency its development of comprehensive arrangements for the sustainable management of the region's fisheries across the full geographical range of the stocks, including the high seas. It endorsed the initiative of the Republic of Marshall Islands to convene a ministerial meeting to help advance this process. It also endorsed a second High Level Multilateral Consultation on the Conservation and Management of Fisheries Resources of the Central Western Pacific in early 1997, and noted the offer by the Republic of Marshall Islands to host the meeting.

Forestry

6.   Recognising the economic and ecological importance of forest resources, the Forum endorsed action to date by member countries to implement the South Pacific Code of Conduct for Logging of Indigenous Forests in Selected South Pacific Countries, and called for continuing efforts by all Forum members to manage their forests sustainably.

ECONOMIC POLICY ISSUES

Forum Economic Ministers' Meeting

7.   The Forum noted the progress made by Forum Finance Ministers during their meetings in 1995 towards defining a practical, regionally-focussed, economic reform agenda. It agreed that, in order to allow the Ministers' agenda to cover the breadth of economic issues, Forum Ministers with appropriate economic portfolios should meet annually, prior to the Forum and report to the Forum.

Tariff Reform

8   Leaders recognised that tariff reform was often critical to achieving sustainable economic development and thanked Australia and New Zealand for assisting the Forum Secretariat to produce a very useful assessment of the contribution tariffs make to national revenues and policy. They agreed that tariff policies should be reviewed in the light of the need to liberalise trade in the region, consistent with the global liberalisation focus, and supported measures that countries can undertake without compromising other national policy objectives. Each member country undertook to consider in detail the Secretariat study, in the light of their national circumstances, and report to the next Economic Ministers' Meeting. Leaders welcomed the offers by Australia and New Zealand to expand the scope of the review to other countries in the region.

Investment Transparency

9.   The Forum acknowledged the importance of attracting quality investment if members were to achieve sustainable economic development, and noted the report

prepared by the Secretariat outlining national investment policies. The next Forum Economic Ministers' Meeting will report to the 1997 Forum on the progress of Forum Island Countries (FICs) in developing their national investment policies, and advise on efforts to bring these into line with APEC investment principles by the end of 1998. Leaders noted that the Secretariat is to publish in 1997 a handbook on FICs' investment policies.

Trade Representation

10.   The Forum warmly welcomed the imminent opening in Tokyo of the South Pacific Economic Exchange Support Centre (SPEESC), to be known operationally as the Pacific Islands Centre. Leaders expressed their appreciation to the Government and people of Japan for their generous support for this important Forum initiative. The Forum reaffirmed its on-going commitment to the SPEESC, including member island countries' financial contributions, and the further development of trade, investment and tourism linkages between the FICs and Japan.

11.   Leaders also directed the Secretariat to proceed with work to develop and broaden trade representation in other markets which offered FICs export and investment sourcing opportunities. They noted progress made towards the establishment of the proposed trade office in the People's Republic of China, and the options which had been developed for the establishment of a trade office in Taipei. The Secretariat will continue discussions to these ends. However, the Forum noted that such work should not divert resources from other priority issues facing the Forum, and should take into account evaluations of existing trade offices.

Relations with APEC

12.   The Forum reiterated the need for further strengthening of APEC/Forum links. It discussed Papua New Guinea's initiative for the establishment of the proposed APEC Centre and invited Papua New Guinea to develop its proposals further.

ENVIRONMENTAL ISSUES

Climate Change

13.   The Forum highlighted its concern that climate change had become a crucial issue within the region. It called for urgent action, particularly in view of the Second Assessment Report of the Intergovernmental Panel on Climate Change (IPCC) which stated that the balance of scientific evidence suggested a discernible human influence on the global climate. The Forum welcomed the outcomes of the Second Conference of the Parties to the Framework Convention on Climate Change (FCCC) in endorsing the second assessment report; advancing the national communications reporting process in implementing commitments; and giving impetus to the Berlin mandate negotiations. It called for acceleration of negotiations on the text of a legally binding protocol or another legal instrument to be completed in time for adoption at the Third Session of the Conference of the Parties in order to achieve significant progress towards the goal of lower greenhouse gas emissions.

14.   The Forum called upon all countries to support the activities of the Ad-Hoc Group on the Berlin Mandate (AGBM) and reaffirmed its support for the inclusion for the Alliance of Small Island States' Draft Protocol for consideration in the negotiating process.

Biological Diversity

15.   The Forum called upon the United Nations Development Programme and the Global Environment Facility for the extension of the funding period for the South Pacific Biodiversity Conservation Programme (SPBCP) to provide adequate time for the community-based conservation activities to build effective community management groups, and to establish effective relationships between Government and non-Government agencies and communities.

Sea Turtles

16.   The Forum noted the successful outcomes of the Year of the Sea Turtle campaign and acknowledged the importance of building on existing regional awareness and goodwill. Forum members resolved to continue their support for the Regional Marine Turtle Conservation Programme and to examine further ways of working together to enhance conservation efforts.

International Coral Reefs Initiative (ICRI)

17.   The Forum noted the inextricable link between healthy coral reefs and successful coastal zone management. It called on all Forum countries and development partners to recognise the Pacific region's 1997 "Year of the Coral Reef", and to encourage participation in its development and implementation. The Forum welcomed Australia's hosting of the ICRI Secretariat for the two years from June 1996.

Barbados Programme of Action

18.   The Forum welcomed progress achieved in the region in implementing the Barbados Programme of Action from the 1994 Global Conference on the Sustainable Development of Small Island Developing States and noted with appreciation the report submitted to the 1996 meeting of United Nations Commission on Sustainable Development jointly by the South Pacific Regional Environment Programme (SPREP) and the ESCAP Pacific Operations Centre (EPOC). The Forum expressed appreciation for the work undertaken by SPREP and EPOC through the regional consultative mechanism established by the Forum in 1994 to implement the Barbados Conference outcomes.

UNGA Special Session on Environment and Development

19.   The Forum noted the importance of the 1997 UN General Assembly Special Session to review progress since the UNCED, and asked that the Advisory Committee to

the regional consultative mechanism convene before the end of 1996 to consider the specific issues and concrete proposals for action to be submitted for consideration at the Special Session. It called on all Forum countries, development partners, and regional organisations to support the region's effort in preparation for the Special Session.

SPREP Action Plan

20.   The Forum noted that the five yearly ministerial meeting of SPREP would be held on 28 November 1996. The Meeting will consider and adopt an Action Plan for regional cooperation in environmental management over the next five years. The Forum noted that the draft 1996-2000 Action Plan gave particular attention to building national capacity in environmental and resource management through support to government agencies, NGOs and the private sector. Forum members resolved to support SPREP in adopting and effectively implementing the Action Plan.

Global Environment Facility (GEF)

21.   The Forum noted the considerable progress in the implementation of the Pacific Strategy for the GEF and that Pacific Island Countries have fared reasonably well in accessing GEF funding. It supported the proposal that SPREP should coordinate a Strategic Action Programme for the Pacific under the GEF's International Waters portfolio and called upon relevant regional organisations to undertake the preliminary reviews outlined in the draft proposal.

Coastal Protection Action Plan

22.   Forum Leaders called upon Development Partners to support regional concerns and efforts to address coastal protection in Forum countries.

Hazardous and Radioactive Wastes

23.   The Forum reiterated the importance of the Waigani Convention on Hazardous Wastes which it had adopted in 1995. It urged all members which had not yet done so to

ratify or accede to the Convention expeditiously, in order to bring it into effect as soon
as possible.

24.   The Forum agreed that shipments of plutonium and radioactive wastes through
the region posed a continuing concern. It reiterated the expectation that such shipments
should be carried out in accordance with the highest international safety and security
standards, in a manner which satisfactorily addressed all possible contingencies, and in
full consultation with Forum countries. In this regard, it appreciated the cooperation of
Japan in responding to Forum concerns by provision of information on, and consultation
about, its shipments.

25.   The Forum noted with concern that, despite the long-standing regional
opposition to the use of the Pacific as a dumping ground for others' wastes, and the
adoption of the Waigani Convention, new proposals for creating storage sites for nuclear
wastes in the region were emerging. It was particularly concerned at the recent revival
of a proposal to create such a site on Palmyra Atoll, although encouraged that the US
administration had opposed the proposal.

26.   The Forum recalled that in 1979, when a proposal to develop a storage site for
spent nuclear fuel on Palmyra had first been made, it had expressed its strong
opposition. The Forum reiterated its 1979 position, strongly opposing any move to use
the Pacific as a dumping ground for nuclear waste. In that regard it will seek to ensure a
firm commitment by the United States that the proposal for Palmyra Atoll will not be
implemented.

27.   The Forum again reaffirmed the existence of a special responsibility toward
those peoples of the former United Nations Trust Territory administered by the United
States, the Marshall Islands, who had been adversely affected as a result of nuclear
weapon tests conducted during the period of the Trusteeship. This responsibility included
safe resettlement of displaced human populations and the restoration to economic
productivity of affected areas.

28.   The Forum again expressed the region's continuing concerns about the Johnston Atoll Chemical Agent Destruction System (JACADS). It noted the commencement of operations of a major chemical agent disposal facility in Tooele, Utah, and reiterated its position that JACADS should be permanently closed when the current programme of chemical weapons and agent destruction was completed.

POLITICAL AND SECURITY ISSUES

Nuclear Testing and Nuclear Free Zones

29.   Forum Leaders expressed satisfaction at the permanent cessation of French nuclear testing in the South Pacific. This marked the end of all nuclear testing in a region which had been subjected to both atmospheric and underground testing for five decades. China's recent announcement of a moratorium on nuclear testing meant that all five nuclear weapon states were now observing testing moratoria, as long urged by the Forum.

30.   Forum Leaders also warmly welcomed the signature and ratification by Vanuatu of the South Pacific Nuclear Free Zone Treaty, the signature of Tonga, and the signing of the Protocols to the Treaty by France, the United Kingdom and the United States of America. As a result of these developments, all states within the Treaty area had now given their support to the Treaty, and all five nuclear weapons states had undertaken to respect its provisions. The Forum urged early ratification of the Protocols by France, the United Kingdom and the United States of America.

31.   Forum Leaders were encouraged by the establishment since their last meeting of two nuclear weapon-free-zones - in South East Asia (Treaty of Bangkok) and Africa (Treaty of Pelindaba). Leaders noted with satisfaction that these developments represented progress with respect to the decisions accompanying the indefinite extension in 1995 of the Treaty on the Non-Proliferation of Nuclear Weapons. In this context, Forum Leaders expressed support for an appropriate resolution at the forthcoming 51[a] session of the United Nations General Assembly whereby signatory states of southern hemisphere nuclear weapons free zone treaties and other members of the international

community could affirm their support for these zones and cooperate in furtherance of the goals of these zones and of nuclear non-proliferation and disarmament.

32.   Forum Leaders welcomed the completion of the report of the Canberra Commission on the Elimination of Nuclear Weapons. The Forum viewed the report as a constructive contribution to the important international debate on nuclear disarmament and non-proliferation. The Forum looked forward to the transmission of the report to the UN General Assembly and the Conference on Disarmament.

33.   The Forum noted the advisory opinion of the International Court of Justice on the legality of nuclear weapons as a further impetus towards nuclear disarmament. It urged all states concerned, particularly the nuclear weapon states, to continue meaningful negotiations with a view to early further significant reductions of nuclear stockpiles as a step towards the ultimate elimination of nuclear weapons.

Environmental Monitoring of French Test Sites

34.   The Forum noted France's invitation to the International Atomic Energy Agency (IAEA) to conduct a radiological study of French nuclear testing sites in the Pacific and expressed its appreciation for the cooperation given so far to the project by the French authorities. The Forum noted that France's invitation to the IAEA to conduct the study was consistent with the desire of Forum countries expressed in the declaration of the August 1995 meeting of South Pacific Environment Ministers for France to provide access by the international community to all French scientific data and to the testing sites themselves, to enable an independent and comprehensive assessment of the effects of nuclear testing.

Comprehensive Test Ban Treaty (CTBT)

35.   Forum Leaders regretted that the Conference on Disarmament had been unable to agree by consensus on the draft CTBT text, and considered that this historic opportunity must not be lost to bring finally the nuclear testing era to an end. By

permanently banning nuclear testing, the CTBT would secure invaluable nuclear non-proliferation and disarmament benefits, and enhance international security. Forum Leaders gave their full support to the adoption of the CTBT by the current session of the UN General Assembly, and called on all other members of the international community to do likewise. They expected Forum members to take the lead in the United Nations by early co-sponsorship of the CTBT resolution. Forum Leaders urged all nations to join with them in signing and ratifying the CTBT as soon as possible, to facilitate the treaty's earliest implementation.

Civil Liability Regime for Nuclear Damage

36.   The Forum recalled the ongoing negotiations of the Standing Committee on Nuclear Liability (SCNL) under the auspices of the International Atomic Energy Agency to establish a comprehensive international legal regime covering civil liability for nuclear damage, and expressed the hope that negotiations would be brought to a conclusion in the near future. The Forum expressed its support for the establishment of a credible civil nuclear liability regime, including a dedicated transboundary fund of sufficient size and adequate compensation for the victims of transboundary damage. The Forum believed that a regime must be capable of attracting widespread adherence from both nuclear and non nuclear generating states around the world. The Forum noted that, consistent with the Convention for the Protection of the Natural Resources and Environment of the South Pacific Region (SPREP), it was important that a civil nuclear liability regime incorporate environmental damage within its scope.

Implementation of Honiara Declaration

37.   The Forum expressed concern over the continuing threats to the region from criminal activities, noted that some criminal elements had sought to take advantage of rapid developments in technology, and recognised the importance of effective regional cooperation in the law enforcement field to combat these threats. The Forum reiterated its commitment to the principles contained in the Honiara Declaration on Law Enforcement Cooperation, and agreed to give high priority to enhancing cooperation, and by supporting the more effective use of existing liaison and coordination networks.

They agreed on the need for an early meeting of the Regional Security Committee to examine ways to take forward the objectives of the Honiara Declaration more effectively.

Common Approach to Weapons Control

38.   The Forum recognised the potential seriousness of any increased movement of weapons throughout the region and called on Forum members to work together to control such weapons movements. The Regional Security Committee has been directed to study and report on how this might be implemented.

Regional Support Arrangements

39.   The Forum noted progress in developing the concept of Regional Support Arrangements which Leaders had discussed at their meeting in Madang. It expected that the proposed Regional Support Arrangements would be complementary to and strengthen existing security cooperation through the Regional Security Committee. It directed the Forum Officials Committee to set up a sub-Committee to develop the proposal further, including possible implementation mechanisms.

Post-Forum Dialogue

40.   The Forum appreciated Malaysia's interest in the development of the Pacific region and would welcome Malaysia as a post-Forum Dialogue Partner.

41.   The Forum agreed also that consideration should be given to restructuring the Dialogue, to reduce the time taken by its meetings and allow more focussed discussion. It directed the Forum Officials Committee to develop some proposals in this regard for consideration at the 1997 Forum. Leaders agreed that decisions on other expressions of interest in Dialogue Partner status should be deferred pending this examination.

42.   The Forum agreed on the lifting of the suspension of France as a dialogue partner, with immediate effect. It adopted a separate statement on this issue attached as Annex 2.

New Caledonia

43.   The Forum endorsed the recommendations of a report presented by its Ministerial Committee on New Caledonia. It expressed its appreciation to the members of the Committee, and to the Government of France and the authorities in New Caledonia for facilitating the Ministers' visit to the territory.

44.   Leaders were pleased that all parties to the Matignon Accords appeared generally satisfied with the progress being made in implementing the provisions of the Accords.   They encouraged all parties to maintain their commitment to the Accords process and to the promotion of economic, social and political development in New Caledonia. They likewise encouraged all parties to continue dialogue in the search for a durable political solution to the question of the territory's long term future.

45.   The Forum reaffirmed its support for continuing contact with New Caledonia as a constructive contribution towards the Matignon process, and agreed that the Ministerial Committee should continue its work in monitoring the situation. It expressed its disappointment at France's decision not to welcome Nauru's participation in the Ministerial visit to New Caledonia in 1996.

UN Security Council Candidatures

46.   The Forum reaffirmed its strong and unanimous support for Australia's candidature for the UN Security Council for the two year term 1997-98. It looked forward to Australia's term on the Security Council. In recognising the importance of Japan as a constructive partner for the region, the Forum also expressed its strong and unanimous support for the candidature of Japan for the UN Security Council for the same two year term.

DATE AND VENUE OF NEXT MEETING

47.   The Forum reaffirmed its appreciation and acceptance of the kind offer of the Cook Islands to host the 28th South Pacific Forum. The date for the Forum would be finalised by the Cook Islands in consultation with the Secretariat.

APPENDIX I

FORUM LEADERS TACKLE ECONOMIC ISSUES

Forum Leaders have today agreed on a range of measures to achieve more progress in both economic reform and development, which is so important for the future benefit of their peoples. This follows up the Forum's decisions in Brisbane on resources and transport issues, and of Madang on Securing Development Beyond 2000.

In line with the 27th Forum's theme - Regional Solidarity for the Common Good', Leaders agreed to jointly pursue the following goals:

- Support national economic development strategies through regional and sub-regional cooperation by means of regular meetings of Forum Economic Ministers and the strengthening of the policy role of the Forum Secretariat. Leaders accepted Australia's offer to host the first meeting next year.

- Enhance the region's ability according to each nation's circumstance, to respond to global economic changes (eg. WTO and APEC developments) and in particular increasing trade liberalisation, which will progressively make preferential trading arrangements (including SPARTECA and the Lomé Convention) less relevant

    - Economic Ministers to consider the appropriate next steps to maintain the momentum of tariff reforms;

    - Member countries wishing to attract foreign direct investment, to quickly develop and publish investment policy statements which are comprehensive and clear;

    - Member countries to pursue domestic policies which facilitate the development of the private sector, including reducing public sector costs as necessary.

- Aid donors to ensure their assistance supports our key reform objectives, including a recognition that the manner in which Forum Island Countries respond to global changes will vary according to size, geography and relative economic strength.

Leaders considered that the establishment of clearly defined goals would generate a renewed spirit of commitment to Pacific solidarity. At the same time they agreed that the process should be reinforced by effective assessment at both regional and national levels.

APPENDIX II

RELATIONS BETWEEN FRANCE AND THE SOUTH PACIFIC FORUM

The Forum agreed that the suspension of France's Post-Forum Dialogue Partner status had been a significant and effective part of the region's campaign against nuclear testing. In light of France's permanent cessation of testing, and other welcome measures, including independent environmental monitoring of the test sites, to comply with the Forum's position on testing, Forum Leaders have decided to lift the suspension with immediate effect.

A dialogue meeting with France will be arranged separately as soon as it is convenient for both sides.

Leaders looked forward to the resumption and further development of a constructive relationship at regional level with France.

-----

14. LETTER OF 18 OCTOBER 1996 FROM THE PERMANENT REPRESENTATIVE OF AZERBAIJAN AND KAZAKSTAN (BAKU JOINT STATEMENT ON CASPIAN SEA OF 16 SEPTEMBER 1996)

Doc. no.: A/51/529   21 October 1996

We have the honour to transmit herewith the text of the joint statement on Caspian Sea questions adopted by the Presidents of the Azerbaijani Republic and the Republic of Kazakstan in Baku on 16 September 1996 (see annex).

We should be grateful if the text of this letter and its annex could be circulated as a document of the General Assembly under agenda items 24, 64, 96, 97 and 98.

<table>
<tr>
<td>

(Signed) E. KOULIEV
Ambassador
Permanent Representative of the
Azerbaijani Republic to the
United Nations

</td>
<td>

(Signed) A. ARYSTANBEKOVA
Ambassador
Permanent Representative of the
Republic of Kazakstan to the
United Nations

</td>
</tr>
</table>

ANNEX

Joint statement on Caspian Sea questions adopted
by the Presidents of Azerbaijan and Kazakstan in
Baku on 16 September 1996

The President of the Republic of Azerbaijan, Mr. G. A. Aliyev, and the President of the Republic of Kazakstan, Mr. N. A. Nazarbaev, following their discussion in Baku on 16 September 1996 of questions relating to the legal status of the Caspian Sea and cooperation among the littoral States in the exploration, development and use of the Caspian's mineral and biological resources and protection of its natural environment, reached the following mutual understanding.

1.   The Parties consider that the immediate and urgent task of the littoral States is to elaborate and conclude, on the basis of consensus, a convention on the legal status of the Caspian Sea. The legal status of the Caspian Sea must be based on the generally recognized rules and principles of international law and the international treaty practice of States situated on the shores of similar bodies of water and include the regulation of questions of navigation, the use of biological and mineral resources, the ecology, including changes in the sea level, etc., and the definition of the jurisdictional limits of the littoral States on the basis of respect for their sovereign rights over their respective parts and sectors of the Caspian Sea.

Agreements on specific types of activity on the Caspian may be concluded on the basis of a convention on the legal status of the Caspian Sea.

2.   The Parties agree that the activities of the littoral States on the Caspian Sea must be conducted in keeping with the following principles:

- Compliance with the principles of the Charter of the United Nations providing for respect for sovereignty, territorial integrity, political independence, the sovereign equality of States and the non-use of force or threat of force;

- The demilitarization of the Caspian and its use exclusively for peaceful purposes;

- The maintenance of the Caspian Sea as a zone of peace, good-neighbourliness, friendship and cooperation, and the peaceful settlement of all questions concerning the Caspian Sea;

- The protection of the environment and the prevention of the pollution of the Caspian Sea;

- The conservation, reproduction and rational use of the biological resources of the Caspian Sea;

- The responsibility of the States bordering the Caspian Sea for any damage to the environment or each other as a result of their use of the Caspian Sea and exploitation of its resources;

- The freedom and safety of the commercial shipping of the States bordering the Caspian Sea;

- And compliance with any other principles that may be agreed upon among the littoral States.

3.   The Parties agree that only vessels belonging to the States bordering the Caspian Sea may sail on the Caspian Sea.

The procedure and conditions for navigation on the Caspian may be defined in separate agreements.

4.   The Parties consider that the delimitation of the Caspian Sea between the littoral States in one form or another is fully consistent with international practice and the principles and rules of international law and will facilitate their cooperation on the basis of equal rights and mutual advantage and help to attract investments and modern technology for the purpose of the effective, rational and safe use of the natural resources of the Caspian.

5.   The Parties recognize each other's rights and the rights of each of the littoral States to carry out activities connected with the exploitation of the mineral and biological resources in their respective parts and sectors of the Caspian Sea, and they will exchange concrete proposals on the development of mutually advantageous cooperation, including geophysical and geological survey activities and the exploitation of hydrocarbon deposits, bearing in mind the experience and capabilities of the Parties.

6.   The Parties are in favour of intensifying and raising the level of negotiations between the littoral States with respect to the legal status of the Caspian Sea and to this end endorse the proposal to hold a meeting of the Ministers for Foreign Affairs of the five States bordering the Caspian Sea to conclude a mutually acceptable agreement on its legal status.

DONE in Baku on 16 September 1996 in two copies, each in the Azerbaijani, Kazak and Russian languages.

(<u>Signed</u>) Heydar ALIYEV   (<u>Signed</u>) Nursultan NAZARBAEV
     President of the   President of the Republic
    Azerbaijani Republic   of Kazakstan

------

15.   LAW OF THE SEA: LARGE-SCALE PELAGIC DRIFTNET FISHING AND ITS IMPACT ON THE LIVING MARINE RESOURCES OF THE WORLD'S OCEANS AND SEAS; UNAUTHORIZED FISHING IN ZONES OF NATIONAL JURISDICTION AND ITS IMPACT ON THE LIVING MARINE RESOURCES OF THE WORLD'S OCEANS AND SEAS; AND FISHERIES BY-CATCH AND DISCARDS AND THEIR IMPACT ON THE SUSTAINABLE USE OF THE WORLD'S LIVING MARINE RESOURCES - LETTER OF 18 NOVEMBER 1996 FROM THE PERMANENT REPRESENTATIVE OF THE REPUBLIC OF KOREA

Doc. no.: A/51/694   16 November 1996

I have the honour to draw your attention to an unfounded allegation made by Greenpeace that Korean vessels are engaged in draft-net fishing in the Mediterranean Sea contained in your report on "Law of the sea: large-scale pelagic drift-net fishing and its impact on the living marine resources of the world's oceans and seas; unauthorized fishing in zones of national jurisdiction and its impact on the living marine resources of the world's oceans and seas; and fisheries by-catch and discards and their impact on the sustainable use of the world's living marine resources" (A/51/404).

In paragraph 39 of the report, reference is made to a Greenpeace report which refers to an Italian Government report alleging that Korean vessels are "currently using high seas drift-nets in the Mediterranean Sea".

The Government of the Republic of Korea has taken all necessary measures to suspend drift-net fishing operations by Korean vessels on the high seas since 1 January 1993, including the revocation of fishing licences, in compliance with General Assembly resolutions 44/225 of 22 December 1989, 45/197 of 21 December 1990 and 46/215 of 20 December 1991. At considerable financial and social cost, the Korean Government has taken measures to scrap all remaining 139 drift-net fishing vessels and to retrain fishermen for alternative employment.

In the light of the fact that the Government of the Republic of Korea has faithfully implemented all General Assembly resolutions relevant to drift-net fishing, the inclusion of this unsubstantiated information in the above-mentioned report is regrettable.

I would like to take this opportunity to confirm to you that no vessels of the Republic of Korea are currently engaged in drift-net fishing operations on the high seas.

I should be grateful if you could circulate the text of the present letter as a document of the fifty-first session of the General Assembly, under agenda item 24 (c).

                                   (Signed) PARK Soo Gil
                                   Permanent Representative

-----

16. LETTER OF 26 NOVEMBER 1996 FROM THE PERMANENT REPRESENTATIVE OF IRAQ

Doc. no.:S/1996/980

26 November 1996

On instructions from my Government, I have the honour to inform you that at 1230 hours on 19 November 1996 an Iraqi patrol boat came under fire from four Kuwaiti patrol boats while it was heading, in performance of its regular duties, from Umm Qasr towards the Mathabah area near buoy 3. The Iraqi boat was hit by a burst of fire that damaged the left side of the bridge.

I request your intervention with Kuwait with a view to halting the repeated and unwarranted acts of aggression carried out by Kuwaiti gunboats against Iraqi vessels. Such acts are in flagrant violation of the Charter of the United Nations and the provisions of public international law, and they create a situation of instability and unrest in this part of the region. I also affirm the legally established right of the Republic of Iraq to seek compensation for the damage caused to its property by this act of aggression, in accordance with the principle of international responsibility.

I should be grateful if you would have this letter circulated as a document of the Security Council.

(Signed) Nizar HAMDOON
Ambassador
Permanent Representative

-----

17. LETTER OF 28 NOVEMBER 1996 FROM THE PERMANENT REPRESENTATIVE OF IRAQ (*SHATT AL-ARAB* INCIDENT)

Doc. no.: S/1996/992   29 November 1996

On instructions from my Government, I have the honour to inform you of an incident that took place on 23 November 1996. At 0530 hours the Iraqi fishing vessel <u>Shatt al-Arab</u> was fishing five nautical miles south of Mina' al-Bakr when the United States frigate bearing hull number 33 demanded that the master should allow his vessel to be searched. At 0730 hours a number of men from the frigate boarded the Iraqi vessel, and they left at 0850 hours after completing their search.

I request your intervention with the United States of America with a view to halting and preventing any repetition of acts of aggression and provocation by United States warships against Iraqi civilian vessels, given that such acts are in violation of the Charter of the United Nations and the provisions of public international law.

I also affirm the legally established right of the Republic of Iraq to seek compensation for the damage caused to its property by this act of aggression, in accordance with the principle of international responsibility.

I should be grateful if you would have this letter circulated as a document of the Security Council.

(Signed) Nizar HAMDOON
Ambassador
Permanent Representative

-----

18. LETTER OF 4 DECEMBER 1996 FROM THE PERMANENT REPRESENTATIVE OF IRAQ (*AL-TAIF* INCIDENT)

Doc. no.: S/1996/1008   5 December 1996

On instructions from my Government, I have the honour to inform you that, at 1230 hours on 19 November 1996, the vessel <u>Al-Taif</u>, registered in the United Arab Emirates, was the subject of an attack by armed Kuwaiti patrols aboard four fibreglass gunboats near buoy No. 13 in the Khawr Abd Allah channel within Iraqi territorial waters, after which the Kuwaitis escorted the vessel in the direction of Kuwait. Still nothing is known about the fate of the vessel, which was heading for Khawr al-Zubayr port with a cargo of rice.

I request your intervention with the Government of Kuwait with a view to halting and preventing any repetition of such acts of aggression and provocation by Kuwaiti gunboats against civilian vessels within Iraqi territorial waters, given that such acts are in violation of the Charter of the United Nations and the provisions of public international law. I also affirm the established right of the Republic of Iraq to seek compensation for the damage caused to it by this act of aggression, in accordance with the principle of international responsibility.

I should be grateful if you would have this letter circulated as a document of the Security Council.

(<u>Signed</u>)   Nizar HAMDOON
Ambassador
Permanent Representative

-----

19. LETTER OF 27 AUGUST 1996 FROM THE ACTING PERMANENT REPRESENTATIVE OF SAUDI ARABIA

Doc. no.: A/50/1028

28 August 1996

NOTIFICATION BY THE SECRETARY-GENERAL UNDER ARTICLE 12,
PARAGRAPH 2, OF THE CHARTER OF THE UNITED NATIONS

REPORT OF THE SECRETARY-GENERAL ON THE WORK
OF THE ORGANIZATION

LAW OF THE SEA

IMPLEMENTATION OF THE DECLARATION OF THE INDIAN OCEAN
AS A ZONE OF PEACE

MAINTENANCE OF INTERNATIONAL SECURITY

With reference to our letter dated 21 August 1996 and our note verbale dated 25 July 1996 transmitting the position of the Kingdom of Saudi Arabia on the so-called "Act on the Marine Areas of the Islamic Republic of Iran in the Persian Gulf and the Oman Sea", I have the pleasure to request you to circulate the above-mentioned note verbale as a document of the General Assembly, under items 7, 10, 39, 76 and 81.

(Signed) Gaafar M. ALLAGANY
Ambassador Extraordinary
and Plenipotentiary

ANNEX

Note verbale dated 25 July 1996 from the Permanent Mission of Saudi Arabia to the United Nations addressed to the Secretariat

The Permanent Mission of Saudi Arabia to the United Nations presents its compliments to the United Nations Secretariat.

The Mission refers to the law entitled "Act on the Marine Areas of the Islamic Republic of Iran in the Persian Gulf and the Oman Sea", which was promulgated on 20 April 1993 and has been communicated to the United Nations Secretariat.

The Government of Saudi Arabia wishes to place on record that it objects to and does not recognize those provisions of the aforesaid Iranian Act on Marine Areas that purport to give the Islamic Republic of Iran powers and jurisdiction that violate or conflict with the consensus of international law and international practice with regard to the legal regime governing seas and straits used in international navigation.

Accordingly, Saudi Arabia declares that it does not recognize or acknowledge any jurisdiction, powers or practices that are assumed or exercised pursuant to the aforesaid Act on the Marine Areas of the Islamic Republic of Iran in such a way as to violate the provisions of international law and international practice and that it does not recognize any restrictions or impositions that may be placed on international navigation in the Gulf and in the Sea of Oman, including passage through the Strait of Hormuz, pursuant to the Iranian law in question.

The Government of Saudi Arabia affirms its legitimate rights vis-à-vis the application of those provisions of the Iranian law in question that are in conflict with or violate the international law of the sea and international practice.

The Permanent Mission of Saudi Arabia takes this opportunity to convey to the Secretariat of the United Nations the assurances of its highest consideration.

-----

20. LETTER OF 26 AUGUST 1996 FROM THE PERMANENT REPRESENTATIVE OF KUWAIT

Doc. no.: A/50/1029

29 August 1996

NOTIFICATION BY THE SECRETARY-GENERAL UNDER ARTICLE 12,
PARAGRAPH 2, OF THE CHARTER OF THE UNITED NATIONS

REPORT OF THE SECRETARY-GENERAL ON THE
WORK OF THE ORGANIZATION

LAW OF THE SEA

On instructions from my Government, I have the honour to transmit herewith the text of the statement issued by the Government of the State of Kuwait on the act promulgated by the Islamic Republic of Iran on 27 May 1993 concerning the delimitation of its marine areas:

"On 27 May 1993 the Islamic Republic of Iran promulgated an act concerning the delimitation of its marine areas. The State of Kuwait does not contest in any way the right of the Islamic Republic of Iran to delimit its marine areas, but;

"Considering that the law contains provisions which run counter to the principles of international maritime law, in particular the 1982 United Nations Convention on the Law of the Sea, which requires States to fulfil in good faith the obligations assumed under the Convention and to exercise the rights, jurisdiction and freedoms recognized in the Convention in a manner which will not constitute an abuse of right; and

"Considering further that the principles of international law require any State signatory to an international convention or bound by it to refrain from any act running counter to the object or purpose of the Convention;

"The State of Kuwait does not consider itself bound by any law running counter to the provisions of the 1982 United Nations Convention on the Law of the Sea."

I should be grateful if you would have the text of this letter circulated as a document of the General Assembly under agenda items 7, 10 and 39.

(Signed)   Mohammad A. ABULHASAN
                Permanent Representative

-----

21. LETTER OF 26 AUGUST 1996 FROM THE PERMANENT REPRESENTATIVE OF THE UNITED ARAB EMIRATES

Doc. no.: A/50/1033

3 September 1996

NOTIFICATION BY THE SECRETARY-GENERAL UNDER ARTICLE 12,
PARAGRAPH 2, OF THE CHARTER OF THE UNITED NATIONS

REPORT OF THE SECRETARY-GENERAL ON THE
WORK OF THE ORGANIZATION

LAW OF THE SEA

IMPLEMENTATION OF THE DECLARATION OF THE INDIAN
OCEAN AS A ZONE OF PEACE

MAINTENANCE OF INTERNATIONAL SECURITY

On instructions from my Government, I have the honour to inform you that the United Arab Emirates wishes to register its objections to certain provisions of the Islamic Republic of Iran's Act on the Marine Areas of 1993, inasmuch as the provisions in question are inconsistent with international law and would impede navigation in the Gulf, including transit through the Strait of Hormuz.

The United Arab Emirates also declines to recognize any provisions of the above-mentioned Act that call into question its sovereignty over the three islands of Greater Tunb, Lesser Tunb and Abu Musa and their territorial waters.

I should be grateful if you would have this letter circulated as an official document of the General Assembly under agenda items 39, 76 and 81.

Accept, Sir, the assurances of my highest consideration.

(Signed) Mohammad J. SAMHAN
Ambassador
Permanent Representative

-----

22. LETTER OF 4 SEPTEMBER 1996 FROM THE PERMANENT REPRESENTATIVE OF QATAR

Doc. no.: A/50/1034　　　　　　　　　　　　　　　　5 September 1996

NOTIFICATION BY THE SECRETARY-GENERAL UNDER ARTICLE 12,
PARAGRAPH 2, OF THE CHARTER OF THE UNITED NATIONS

REPORT OF THE SECRETARY-GENERAL ON THE WORK OF THE ORGANIZATION

LAW OF THE SEA

IMPLEMENTATION OF THE DECLARATION OF THE INDIAN OCEAN
AS A ZONE OF PEACE

MAINTENANCE OF INTERNATIONAL SECURITY

I have the honour to transmit to you herewith a note verbale dated
20 August 1996 outlining the position of Qatar with regard to the promulgation
by the Islamic Republic of Iran of the act entitled "Act on the Marine Areas of
the Islamic Republic of Iran in the Persian Gulf and the Oman Sea, 1993".

I should be grateful if you would have the text of the present letter and
its annex circulated as a document of the fiftieth session of the General
Assembly under agenda items 7, 10, 39, 76 and 81.

　　　　　　　　　　　　　　　(Signed)　Hassan Ali Hussain AL-NI'MAH
　　　　　　　　　　　　　　　　　　　　　Permanent Representative

Annex

Note verbale dated 20 August 1996 from the Permanent Mission
of Qatar to the United Nations addressed to the Secretariat

The Permanent Mission of the State of Qatar to the United Nations presents
its compliments to the Secretariat of the United Nations and has the honour to
inform it that Qatar, after careful consideration of the Act on the Marine Areas
of the Islamic Republic of Iran in the Persian Gulf and the Oman Sea, 1993, is
of the opinion that some articles of the aforementioned Act are inconsistent

with the provisions of international law. Qatar therefore reserves its rights and the rights of its citizens in this regard.

Qatar would like to draw attention to the fact that the use by the Islamic Republic of Iran of the baseline to measure its territorial sea, in accordance with the above-mentioned Act, contravenes the customary law enshrined in international law and the 1982 United Nations Convention on the Law of the Sea. This is because there are no geographical phenomena other than natural ones on the Iranian coast to justify using such lines.

Further, the above-mentioned Act states that the waters between islands belonging to the Islamic Republic of Iran, where the distance of such islands does not exceed 24 nautical miles, form part of the internal waters of the Islamic Republic of Iran. This clearly contravenes the provisions of the law of the sea: the waters between the islands cannot be considered internal waters of the Islamic Republic of Iran except under certain conditions, which do not obtain on the Iranian coastline.

Qatar would also like to refer to article 19, paragraph 2 (h), of the 1982 United Nations Convention on the Law of the Sea, which states that "any act of wilful and serious pollution" is considered contrary to the provisions of the Convention. The provisions of article 6 (g) of the Iranian Act are therefore in clear contravention of the Convention with regard to activities prejudicial to the peace and security of the coastal State.

Similarly, it is necessary to refer to article 21, paragraph 4, of the 1982 United Nations Convention on the Law of the Sea, which provides for compliance with the laws and regulations adopted by a coastal State inasmuch as such laws and regulations conform to generally accepted international regulations. Here, Qatar would like to note that article 7 of the Iranian Act, which states that the Government of the Islamic Republic of Iran "shall adopt such other regulations as are necessary for the protection of its national interests", gives Iran no more rights than those provided for by the law of the sea.

Article 9 of the Iranian Act states that the passage of warships and nuclear-powered ships and vessels through the Iranian territorial sea is subject to the prior authorization of the relevant authorities of the Islamic Republic of Iran. The same article also requires that submarines exercising the right of innocent passage should navigate on the surface, and show their flag. There is no basis for these demands in the 1982 Convention, and Qatar will continue to reject outright such restrictions on the right of innocent passage.

Attention should be paid to the scope of the coastal State's jurisdiction in the contiguous zone, that is, the area adjacent to its territorial sea. It should be confined to the right of the coastal State to exercise the necessary authority in order to prevent contravention of its laws and regulations governing customs, taxes, immigration and health inside its territory or territorial sea. The authority of the coastal State to apply its environmental rules outside its territorial waters was provided for by article 220 of the Convention. The provisions in article 13 of the aforementioned Act regarding measures to be taken in the contiguous zone to prevent the infringement of the environmental and security regulations of the Islamic Republic of Iran go well beyond what is permitted by international law.

Similarly, article 14, subparagraph (a), of the Act gives the Islamic Republic of Iran the right to demand greater authority in order to control the laying of marine cables and pipelines on the part of the continental shelf belonging to the Islamic Republic of Iran than is permitted by international law and laid down in article 79 of the Convention.

Furthermore, international law permits the coastal State to conduct only marine scientific research in its exclusive economic zone, not "any kind of research", as stated in article 14, subparagraph (b) (ii), of the aforementioned

Iranian Act. Specifically, hydrographical research outside territorial waters
is not considered marine scientific research as it is understood in the
Convention, and therefore does not come under the jurisdiction of the coastal
State.

Qatar would also like to note that article 16 of the Iranian Act, which
seeks to prohibit the military aircraft and shipping of other States from
exercising the right of innocent passage in the Iranian exclusive economic zone,
contravenes the provisions and principles of international law regarding the
high seas.

Qatar would like to emphasize that these objections are not intended as
criticism of the Islamic Republic of Iran, but merely to clarify the position of
the State with respect to the international provisions and principles of the law
of the sea as laid down in international customary law, treaties and practices.

-----

23. LETTER OF 18 OCTOBER 1996 FROM THE PERMANENT REPRESENTATIVE OF THE ISLAMIC REPUBLIC OF IRAN (REPLY TO KUWAIT, A/50/1029)

Doc. no.: A/51/544

23 October 1996

NOTIFICATION BY THE SECRETARY-GENERAL UNDER ARTICLE 12,
PARAGRAPH 1, OF THE CHARTER OF THE UNITED NATIONS

REPORT OF THE SECRETARY-GENERAL ON THE WORK OF
THE ORGANIZATION

LAW OF THE SEA

I wish to refer to the letter dated 26 August 1996 from the Permanent Representative of Kuwait to the United Nations (A/50/1029), containing the statement of the Government of Kuwait relating to certain provisions of the Act on the Marine Areas of the Islamic Republic of Iran in the Persian Gulf and the Sea of Oman, 1993 ("Marine Areas Act"), and make the following clarifications:

1. Even before the enactment of the said Act, there existed a few acts and decrees pertaining to the Islamic Republic of Iran's rights and jurisdiction over its maritime areas, each of which dealt with one or more issues involving the law of the sea. The Marine Areas Act was drafted to consolidate and supplement all previous relevant legislative provisions into a single statutory instrument, taking into account the progressive development of the law of the sea, including the extension of the jurisdiction of coastal States.

2. It should be noted that the Islamic Republic of Iran has not as yet ratified the United Nations Convention on the Law of the Sea. Nevertheless, as a signatory State, the Islamic Republic has not defeated the object and purpose of the Convention.

I should be grateful if you would have the text of the present letter circulated as an official document of the General Assembly, under agenda items 7, 10 and 24.

(Signed)   Kamal KHARRAZI
Ambassador
Permanent Representative

-----

24. LETTER OF 18 OCTOBER 1996 FROM THE PERMANENT REPRESENTATIVE OF THE ISLAMIC REPUBLIC OF IRAN (REPLY TO SAUDI ARABIA, A/50/1028)

Doc. no.: A/51/545

23 October 1996

NOTIFICATION BY THE SECRETARY-GENERAL UNDER ARTICLE 12,
PARAGRAPH 2, OF THE CHARTER OF THE UNITED NATIONS

REPORT OF THE SECRETARY-GENERAL ON THE WORK OF THE ORGANIZATION

LAW OF THE SEA

I wish to refer to the note verbale dated 25 July 1996 from the Permanent Mission of Saudi Arabia to the United Nations addressed to the Secretariat (A/50/1028, annex), regarding objections of Saudi Arabia to certain provisions of the Act on the Marine Areas of the Islamic Republic of Iran in the Persian Gulf and the Sea of Oman, 1993 ("Marine Areas Act"), and make the following clarifications:

1.   Even before the enactment of the said Act, there existed a few acts and decrees pertaining to the Islamic Republic of Iran's rights and jurisdiction over its maritime areas, each of which dealt with one or more issues involving the law of the sea.   The Marine Areas Act was drafted to consolidate and supplement all previous relevant legislative provisions into a single statutory instrument, taking into account the progressive development of the law of the sea, including the extension of the jurisdiction of coastal States.

2.   It should be noted that the international law of the sea comprises various rules and provisions that were codified and/or developed in the 1958 and 1982 Conventions on the Law of the Sea.   Therefore, it is hard to believe that there is an international consensus on various rules and practices pertaining to this body of law.

3.   There is no provision in the Marine Areas Act to impede navigation in the Persian Gulf and the Sea of Oman.   The Islamic Republic of Iran does not object to the freedom of navigation, provided that such freedom is not prejudicial to the peace, good order or security of the coastal States, in conformity with international law.

I should be grateful if you would have the text of the present letter circulated as an official document of the General Assembly, under agenda items 7, 10 and 24.

(<u>Signed</u>) Kamal KHARRAZI
Ambassador
Permanent Representative

-----

25. LETTER OF 18 OCTOBER 1996 FROM THE PERMANENT REPRESENTATIVE OF THE ISLAMIC REPUBLIC OF IRAN (REPLY TO QATAR, A/50/1034)

Doc. no.: A/51/546   23 October 1996

I wish to refer to the note verbale dated 20 August 1996 from the Permanent Mission of Qatar to the United Nations addressed to the Secretariat (A/50/1034, annex) regarding objections of the State of Qatar to certain provisions of the Act on the Marine Areas of the Islamic Republic of Iran in the Persian Gulf and the Sea of Oman, 1993 ("Marine Areas Act") and make the following clarifications:

1.   Even before the enactment of the said Act, there existed a few acts and decrees pertaining to the Islamic Republic of Iran's rights and jurisdiction over its maritime areas, each of which dealt with one or more issues involving the law of the sea. The Marine Areas Act was drafted to consolidate and supplement all previous relevant legislative provisions into a single statutory instrument, taking into account the progressive development of the law of the sea, including the extension of the jurisdiction of coastal States.

2.   The Islamic Republic of Iran does not consider that the United Nations Convention on the Law of the Sea (the "Convention") has merely codified customary rules of international law of the sea, as the President of the Third United Nations Conference on the Law of the Sea stated on 10 December 1982:

> "The argument that, except for Part XI, the Convention codifies customary law or reflects existing international practice is factually incorrect and legally insupportable. The regime of transit passage through straits used for international navigation and the regime of archipelagic sea lane's passage are only two examples of the many new concepts in the Convention." 1/

The recent adoption by various States of laws and regulations similar to the Marine Areas Act concerning their rights and jurisdiction in maritime areas that are not fully compatible with the Convention is further evidence that supports this argument.

3.   It should be noted that the Islamic Republic of Iran has not as yet ratified the Convention. Nevertheless, as a signatory State, it has not defeated the object and purpose of the Convention.

4.   The drawing of straight baselines by the Islamic Republic of Iran should not be considered unusual, as the same method has been used by other States under similar circumstances. Moreover, it was based on several recognized criteria, among them the drawing of a baseline in a way not to depart to any

appreciable extent, from the direction of the coast, and also the coastal State's right to consider the economic interests peculiar to the region concerned, the reality and importance of which are clearly evidenced by long usage. Decree No. 2/250-67 dated 31 Tir 1352 (22 July 1973) was approved and entered into force nearly 25 years ago, and was circulated in the United Nations Legislative Series 2/ but so far no objections have been raised by Qatar to the said Decree.

5. As regards waters between islands within a distance of less than 24 nautical miles, we note that there is no rule in international law prohibiting use of that method. Furthermore, the same method was used in the Act on the Territorial Waters and the Contiguous Zone of Iran dated 24 Tir 1313 (15 July 1934) 3/ and the Act amending the Act on the Territorial Waters and the Contiguous Zone of Iran dated 22 Farvardin 1338 (12 April 1959). 4/ In the Marine Areas Act the same method has been employed, while taking into account the extension of the breadth of the territorial sea.

6. With respect to the laying of marine cables and pipelines on the part of the continental shelf belonging to the Islamic Republic of Iran, it should be clarified that there is no customary rule limiting the right of coastal States in this respect. Furthermore, it needs to be emphasized that, in accordance with article 79 (3) of the Convention, the consent of the coastal State is essential for the delineation of the course for the laying of such pipelines on the continental shelf.

7. As for article 16 of the Marine Areas Act, it should be mentioned that it is almost certain that foreign military exercises and manoeuvres impede and/or cause harm to economic activities of coastal States, for which they enjoy sovereign rights. Accordingly, those exercises and manoeuvres that affect the economic activities in the exclusive economic zone and the continental shelf are prohibited.

8. With regard to marine scientific research in the exclusive economic zone, it should be mentioned that any research conducted in that area would be directly linked to the rights of coastal States concerning the exploration and exploitation of living and non-living resources. Therefore, the Islamic Republic of Iran has reserved its right for the adoption and enforcement of appropriate laws and regulations in this respect.

9. As regards article 9 of the Marine Areas Act, the attention of the Permanent Mission of Qatar is drawn to the statement by the Islamic Republic of Iran on signing the Convention, which provides, inter alia:

> "In the light of customary international law, the provisions of article 21, read in association with article 19 (on the Meaning of Innocent Passage) and article 25 (on the Rights of Protection of the Coastal States) recognize (though implicitly) the rights of the Coastal States to take measures to safeguard their security interests including the adoption of laws and regulations regarding, inter alia, the requirements of prior authorization for warships willing to exercise the right of innocent passage through the territorial sea." 5/

I wish to take this opportunity to remind the esteemed Permanent Mission of Qatar that, in accordance with article 20 of the Convention, the "submarines and other underwater vehicles are required to navigate on the surface and to show their flag".

10. Finally, I wish to draw the attention of the Permanent Mission of Qatar to the unique ecological situation of the Persian Gulf. Considering the small area of this enclosed sea, its shallow water and the intensity of the economic activities that take place within that region, especially fishing and hydrocarbon extraction, it is a highly vulnerable zone which has been designated as a "special zone" in 1973/78 International Convention for the Prevention of Pollution from Ships (MARPOL Convention). For these reasons, the requirement of obtaining prior authorization for the passage of some categories of foreign

vessels, especially for ships carrying hazardous substances, was incorporated in the Marine Areas Act to employ more supervision over the traffic of such vessels and to protect the marine environment of the region.

I should be grateful if you would have the text of the present letter circulated as an official document of the General Assembly, under agenda items 24 and 77.

(Signed) Kamal KHARRAZI
Ambassador
Permanent Representative

Notes

1/   Official Records of the Third United Nations Conference on the Law of the Sea, vol. XVII, (United Nations publication, Sales No. E.84.V.3), Verbatim records of meetings, 193rd meeting, para. 48.

2/   ST/LEG/SER.B/19, pp. 55-56.

3/   ST/LEG/SER.B/6, p. 24.

4/   ST/LEG/SER.B/15, p. 88.

5/   Law of the Sea Bulletin, No. 5 (July 1985), p. 14.

-----

26. LETTER OF 18 OCTOBER 1996 FROM THE PERMANENT REPRESENTATIVE OF THE ISLAMIC REPUBLIC OF IRAN (REPLY TO THE UNITED ARAB EMIRATES, A/50/1033)

Doc. no.: A/51/547   23 October 1996

I wish to refer to the letter dated 26 August 1996 from the Permanent Representative of the United Arab Emirates to the United Nations, which has been circulated as document addressed to you (A/50/1033), regarding objections of the United Arab Emirates to certain provisions of the Act on the Marine Areas of the Islamic Republic of Iran in the Persian Gulf and the Sea of Oman, 1993 ("Marine Areas Act"), and make the following clarifications:

1.   Even before the enactment of the said Act, there existed a few acts and decrees pertaining to the Islamic Republic of Iran's rights and jurisdiction over its maritime areas, each of which dealt with one or more issues involving the law of the sea. The Marine Areas Act was drafted to consolidate and supplement all previous relevant legislative provisions into a single statutory instrument, taking into account the progressive development of the law of the sea, including the extension of the jurisdiction of coastal States.

2.   There is no provision in the Marine Areas Act to impede navigation in the Persian Gulf and the Sea of Oman. The Islamic Republic of Iran does not object to the freedom of navigation, provided that such freedom is not prejudicial to the peace, good order or security of the coastal States, in conformity with international law.

3.   Although paragraph 2 of the letter from the United Arab Emirates is irrelevant to the subject matter in question, I wish to refer to my previous letter dated 1 October 1996 addressed to you in this regard (S/1996/818).

4.   The Islamic Republic of Iran reserves its right to make comments as regards certain provisions of the Federal Law No. 19 of 1993 in respect of the delimitation of the maritime zones of the United Arab Emirates of 17 October 1993 that contravene the relevant rules and provisions of the international law of the sea.

I should be grateful if you would have the text of the present letter circulated as an official document of the General Assembly, under agenda items 24 and 77.

(Signed)   Kamal KHARRAZI
Ambassador
Permanent Representative

-----

27. LETTER OF 4 NOVEMBER 1996 FROM THE PERMANENT REPRESENTATIVE OF BAHRAIN

Doc. no.: A/51/659

8 November 1996

NOTIFICATION BY THE SECRETARY-GENERAL UNDER ARTICLE 12, PARAGRAPH 2, OF THE CHARTER OF THE UNITED NATIONS

REPORT OF THE SECRETARY-GENERAL ON THE WORK OF THE ORGANIZATION

LAW OF THE SEA

REVIEW OF THE IMPLEMENTATION OF THE DECLARATION ON THE STRENGTHENING OF INTERNATIONAL SECURITY

On instructions from my Government, I have the honour to inform you of the concern of the Government of the State of Bahrain regarding the act promulgated by the Islamic Republic of Iran on 27 May 1993 delimiting the marine areas of the Islamic Republic of Iran.

The Government of the State of Bahrain does not dispute the right of the Islamic Republic of Iran to delimit its marine areas but wishes to place on record its objection to those parts of the act of 1993 that are not in accordance with international law and practice. In particular, the State of Bahrain wishes to place on record its objection to those parts of the 1993 act that are not in accordance with the requirements of the 1982 United Nations Convention on the Law of the Sea which made it incumbent on States to exercise their rights, jurisdiction and freedoms established in the Convention in a manner that does not constitute an abuse of right. Accordingly, the State of Bahrain does not recognize those parts of the act that are not in accordance with international law and practice, in particular the 1982 United Nations Convention on the Law of the Sea.

I should be grateful if you would have the text of this letter circulated as an official document of the General Assembly under agenda items 7, 10, 24 and 81.

(Signed) Jassim BUALLAY
Permanent Representative

-----

28. LAW OF THE SEA - UNGA RESOLUTION

Doc. no.: A/Res.51/34   9 December 1996

The General Assembly,

Emphasizing the universal character of the United Nations Convention on the Law of the Sea 78/ and its fundamental importance for the maintenance and strengthening of international peace and security, as well as for the sustainable use and development of the seas and oceans and their resources,

Considering that, in its resolution 2749 (XXV) of 17 December 1970, it proclaimed that the seabed and ocean floor, and the subsoil thereof, beyond the limits of national jurisdiction ("the Area"), as well as the resources of the Area, are the common heritage of mankind, and considering also that the Convention, together with the Agreement relating to the implementation of Part XI of the United Nations Convention on the Law of the Sea of 10 December 1982 79/ ("the Agreement"), provides the regime to be applied to the Area and its resources,

Noting the entry into force of the Agreement on 28 July 1996,

Noting with satisfaction the increase in the number of States parties to the Convention,

Recalling its resolution 49/28 of 6 December 1994 on the law of the sea, adopted consequent to the entry into force of the Convention on 16 November 1994,

Aware of the importance of the effective implementation of the Convention and its uniform and consistent application, as well as of the growing need to promote and facilitate international cooperation on the law of the sea and ocean affairs at the global, regional and subregional levels,

Recognizing the impact on States of the entry into force of the Convention and the increasing need, particularly of developing States, for advice and assistance in its implementation in order to benefit thereunder,

Welcoming the establishment of the International Tribunal for the Law of the Sea ("the Tribunal"), 80/ the Council of the International Seabed Authority, its Legal and Technical Commission and Finance Committee, and the election of their respective members as well as the election of the Secretary-General of the International Seabed Authority ("the Authority"), 81/

78/   Official Records of the Third United Nations Conference on the Law of the Sea, vol. XVII (United Nations publication, Sales No. E.84.V.3), document A/CONF.62/122.

79/   Resolution 48/263, annex.

80/   SPLOS/14, paras. 13-31.

81/   See ISBA/A/...

Noting the decisions taken by States parties to the Convention facilitating the organization of the Tribunal 82/ and those by the Assembly 83/ and the Council 84/ of the Authority facilitating the organization of the Authority,

Noting also the decisions taken by States parties to the Convention to elect the members of the Commission on the Limits of the Continental Shelf in March 1997, 85/

Recalling article 287 of the Convention regarding the choice of means for the settlement of disputes concerning the interpretation or application of the Convention,

Recalling also that the Agreement provides that the institutions established by the Convention shall be cost-effective, 86/ and recalling further that the meeting of States parties to the Convention decided that this principle would apply to all aspects of the work of the Tribunal, 87/

Emphasizing the importance of making adequate provisions for the efficient functioning of the institutions established by the Convention,

Reiterating its appreciation to the Secretary-General for his efforts in support of the Convention and in the effective implementation of the Convention, including providing assistance in the establishment of the institutions created by the Convention,

Noting the responsibilities of the Secretary-General and competent international organizations under the Convention, in particular pursuant to its entry into force and as required by resolution 49/28,

Noting with appreciation the development, as part of the Organization's Home Page on the Internet, of the sites of the Division for Ocean Affairs and the Law of the Sea of the Office of Legal Affairs of the Secretariat (Gopher/World Wide Web), which provide users with convenient means for obtaining timely, well-organized and cross-referenced materials and information dealing with various aspects of the oceans, marine affairs and the law of the sea,

Conscious that the problems of ocean space are closely interrelated and need to be considered as a whole,

Conscious also of the strategic importance of the Convention as a framework for national, regional and global action in the marine sector, as recognized also by the United Nations Conference on Environment and Development in chapter 17 of Agenda 21, 88/

Noting the recommendation of the Commission on Sustainable Development, 89/ endorsed by the Economic and Social Council, 90/ concerning international cooperation and coordination in the implementation of chapter 17 of Agenda 21,

---

82/   SPLOS/14, paras. 32-36.

83/   ISBA/A/14.

84/   ISBA/C/10 and 11.

85/   SPLOS/14, para. 41.

86/   Resolution 48/263, annex: Annex to the Agreement, sect. 1, para. 2.

87/   SPLOS/4, para. 25 (e).

88/   Report of the United Nations Conference on Environment and Development, Rio de Janeiro, 3-14 June 1992 (A/CONF.151/26/Rev.1 (Vol. I and Vol. I/Corr.1, Vol. II, Vol. III and Vol. III/Corr.1)) (United Nations publication, Sales No. E.93.I.8 and corrigenda), vol. I: Resolutions Adopted by the Conference, resolution 1, annex II.

89/   See Official Records of the Economic and Social Council, 1996, Supplement No. 8 (E/1996/28), chap. I.A, para. 1

90/   See Official Records of the General Assembly, Fifty-first Session, Supplement No. 3, chap. V.B.1, para. 119, resolution 1996/1.

Noting also the Washington Declaration and the Global Programme of Action for the Protection of the Marine Environment from Land-based Activities, 91/

Conscious of the need to promote and facilitate international cooperation, especially at the subregional and regional levels, in order to ensure the orderly and sustainable development of the uses and resources of the seas and oceans,

Reaffirming the importance of the annual consideration and review by the General Assembly of the overall developments pertaining to the implementation of the Convention, as well as of other developments relating to the law of the sea and ocean affairs,

1.   Calls upon all States that have not done so to become parties to the United Nations Convention on the Law of the Sea and to ratify, confirm formally or accede to the Agreement relating to the implementation of Part XI of the United Nations Convention on the Law of the Sea of 10 December 1982 in order to achieve the goal of universal participation;

2.   Calls upon States to harmonize their national legislation with the provisions of the Convention, to ensure the consistent application of those provisions and to ensure also that any declarations or statements that they have made or make when signing, ratifying or acceding are in conformity with the Convention;

3.   Reaffirms the unified character of the Convention;

4.   Recalls its decision to fund the budget for the administrative expenses of the International Seabed Authority initially from the regular budget of the United Nations, in accordance with the provisions of the Agreement; 92/

5.   Approves the provision by the Secretary-General of such services as may be required for the two meetings of the Authority to be held in 1997, from 17 to 28 March and from 18 to 29 August;

6.   Requests the Secretary-General to convene the meetings of States parties to the Convention from 10 to 14 March and from 19 to 23 May 1997;

7.   Notes with appreciation the progress made in the establishment of the institutions created by the Convention, requests the Secretary-General to continue to provide assistance to those institutions, and invites the Secretary-General to take steps to conclude relationship agreements between the United Nations and the Authority, and between the United Nations and the Tribunal, to be applied provisionally pending the approval of the General Assembly, and as appropriate by the Assembly of the Authority or the States parties to the Convention;

8.   Encourages States parties to the Convention to consider making a written declaration choosing from the means set out in article 287 of the Convention for the settlement of disputes concerning the interpretation or application of the Convention;

9.   Expresses its appreciation to the Secretary-General for the annual comprehensive report on the law of the sea 93/ and the activities of the Division for Ocean Affairs and the Law of the Sea, in accordance with the provisions of the Convention and the mandate set forth in resolution 49/28;

10.   Reaffirms the importance of ensuring the uniform and consistent application of the Convention and a coordinated approach to its overall implementation, and of strengthening technical cooperation and financial assistance for this purpose, stresses once again the continuing importance of the Secretary-General's efforts to these ends, and reiterates its invitation to the competent international organizations and other international bodies to support these objectives;

11.   Requests the Secretary-General to ensure that the institutional capacity of the Organization adequately responds to the needs of States, the newly established institutions and other competent international organizations by providing advice and assistance, taking into account the special needs of developing countries;

91/   A/51/116, annex I, appendix II, and annex II.

92/   See resolution 48/263, para. 8; and ibid., annex: Annex to the Agreement, sect. 1, para. 14.

93/   A/51/645.

12.   Invites Member States and others in a position to do so to contribute to the further development of the fellowship programme on the law of the sea and training and educational activities on the law of the sea and ocean affairs established by the General Assembly in its resolution 35/116 of 10 December 1980, as well as advisory services and assistance in support of effective implementation of the Convention;

13.   Requests the Secretary-General to continue his efforts to further strengthen the existing system for the collection, compilation and dissemination of information on the law of the sea and related matters and to further develop, in cooperation with relevant international organizations, a centralized system for providing coordinated information and advice;

14.   Reaffirms its decision to undertake an annual review and evaluation of the implementation of the Convention and other developments relating to ocean affairs and the law of the sea;

15.   Reiterates its request to the Secretary-General to prepare a comprehensive report on the impact of the entry into force of the Convention on related existing and proposed instruments and programmes throughout the United Nations system, for submission to the Assembly at its fifty-second session, and calls upon competent international organizations and other international bodies to cooperate in the preparation of the report;

16.   Requests the Secretary-General to report to the Assembly at its fifty-second session on the implementation of the present resolution, including other developments and issues relating to ocean affairs and the law of the sea, in connection with his annual comprehensive report on oceans and the law of the sea;

17.   Decides to include in the provisional agenda of its fifty-second session an item entitled "Oceans and the law of the sea".

RECORDED   VOTE ON RESOLUTION 51/34:

In favour: Algeria, Andorra, Antigua and Barbuda, Argentina, Armenia, Australia, Austria, Bahamas, Bahrain, Bangladesh, Belarus, Belgium, Belize, Benin, Bhutan, Bolivia, Botswana, Brazil, Brunei Darussalam, Bulgaria, Burkina Faso, Cambodia, Cameroon, Canada, Cape Verde, Chad, Chile, China, Costa Rica, Côte d'Ivoire, Croatia, Cuba, Cyprus, Czech Republic, Denmark, Dominica, Egypt, El Salvador, Estonia, Ethiopia, Federated States of Micronesia, Fiji, Finland, France, Gambia, Germany, Ghana, Grenada, Guatemala, Guinea-Bissau, Guyana, Haiti, Honduras, Hungary, Iceland, India, Indonesia, Ireland, Israel, Italy, Jamaica, Japan, Kazakstan, Kenya, Kuwait, Lao People's Democratic Republic, Latvia, Lebanon, Liberia, Libya, Liechtenstein, Lithuania, Luxembourg, Madagascar, Malawi, Malaysia, Maldives, Mali, Malta, Marshall Islands, Mauritania, Mauritius, Mexico, Monaco, Mongolia, Morocco, Mozambique, Myanmar, Namibia, Nepal, Netherlands, New Zealand, Niger, Nigeria, Norway, Oman, Pakistan, Panama, Philippines, Poland, Portugal, Qatar, Republic of Korea, Russian Federation, Rwanda, Saint Kitts and Nevis, Saint Lucia, Samoa, San Marino, Saudi Arabia, Senegal, Seychelles, Sierra Leone, Singapore, Slovak Republic, Solomon Islands, South Africa, Spain, Sri Lanka, Sudan, Suriname, Sweden, The former Yugoslav Republic of Macedonia, Togo, Trinidad and Tobago, Tunisia, Uganda, Ukraine, United Arab Emirates, United Kingdom, United Republic of Tanzania, United States, Uruguay, Vanuatu, Viet Nam, Yemen, Zambia, Zimbabwe.

Against: Turkey.

Abstaining: Ecuador, Peru, Tajikistan*, Venezuela.

Absent: Afghanistan, Albania, Angola, Azerbaijan, Barbados, Bosnia and Herzegovina, Burundi, Colombia, Comoros, Congo, Democratic People's Republic of Korea, Djibouti, Dominican Republic, Equatorial Guinea, Eritrea, Gabon, Georgia*, Greece, Guinea, Iran, Jordan, Kyrgyz Republic, Lesotho, Nicaragua, Palau, Papua New Guinea, Paraguay, Republic of Moldova, Romania, Saint Vincent and the Grenadines, Sao Tome and Principe, Slovenia, Swaziland, Syria, Thailand, Turkmenistan, Uzbekistan, Zaire.

---

*   Later advised the Secretariat that it had intened to vote in favour.

29. ZONE OF PEACE AND COOPERATION OF THE SOUTH ATLANTIC - UNGA RESOLUTION

Doc. no.: A/Res.51/19   14 November 1996

The General Assembly,

Recalling its resolution 41/11 of 27 October 1986, in which it solemnly declared the Atlantic Ocean, in the region between Africa and South America, the "Zone of peace and cooperation of the South Atlantic",

Recalling also its subsequent resolutions on the matter, including resolution 45/36 of 27 November 1990, in which it reaffirmed the determination of the States of the zone to enhance and accelerate their cooperation in the political, economic, scientific, cultural and other spheres,

Reaffirming that the questions of peace and security and those of development are interrelated and inseparable, and that cooperation for peace and development among States of the region will promote the objectives of the zone of peace and cooperation of the South Atlantic,

Aware of the importance that the States of the zone attach to the region's environment, and recognizing the treat that pollution from any source poses to the marine and coastal environment, its ecological balance and its resources,

1.   Reaffirms the importance of the purposes and objectives of the zone of peace and cooperation of the South Atlantic as a basis for the promotion of cooperation among the countries of the region;

2.   Calls upon all States to cooperate in the promotion of the objectives established in the declaration of the zone of peace and cooperation of the South Atlantic and to refrain from any action inconsistent with those objectives and with the Charter of the United Nations and relevant resolutions of the Organization, particularly action which may create or aggravate situations of tension and potential conflict in the region;

3.   Takes note of the report of the Secretary-General of 7 October 1996, 26/ submitted in accordance with its resolution 50/18 of 27 November 1995;

4.   Recalls the agreement reached at the third meeting of the States members of the zone, held at Brasilia in 1994, to encourage democracy and political pluralism and, in accordance with the Vienna Declaration and Programme of Action adopted by the World Conference on Human rights on 25 June 1993, 27/ to promote and defend all human rights and fundamental freedoms and to cooperate towards the achievement of those goals;

26/   A/51/458.

27/   A/CONF.157/24 (Part I), chap. III.

5.   Welcomes with satisfaction the holding of the fourth meeting of the States members of the zone of peace and cooperation of the South Atlantic at Somerset West, South Africa, on 1 and 2 April 1996, and takes note of the Final Declaration, the decision on drug trafficking, the decision on the protection of the marine environment and the decision on illegal fishing activities in the zone, adopted at the meeting;

6.   Welcomes the progress towards the full entry into force of the Treaty for the Prohibition of Nuclear Weapons in Latin America and the Caribbean (Treaty of Tlatelolco), and the conclusion of the "African Nuclear-Weapon-Free Zone Treaty" (Treaty of Pelindaba);

7.   Welcomes the efforts of the Government of Angola to implement the Lusaka Protocol, expresses its deep concern at the delay in fully implementing the Lusaka protocol and calls upon the National Union for the Total Independence of Angola to fulfil immediately the tasks enumerated in the "Mediation Document" formulated by the Special Representative of the Secretary-General in consultation with the three observer States, as contained in Security Council resolution 1075 (1996) of 11 October 1996;

8.   Reaffirms its willingness to contribute by all means at its disposal to an effective and lasting peace in Angola;

9.   Urges the international community to fulfil expeditiously its pledges to provide assistance to facilitate the rehabilitation of the Angolan national economy and the resettlement of displaced persons, and stresses the importance of such assistance at this time in order to consolidate the gains in the peace process;

10.   Welcomes the outcome of the summit meeting of the Economic Community of West African States Committee of Nine on Liberia, which revalidated the Abuja Agreement and, inter alia, foresees the holding of democratic elections in Liberia by 30 May 1997;

11.   Commends and encourages Nigeria in its capacity as chair of the Committee of Nine, as well as all the members of the ECOWAS, to pursue positive efforts towards peace in Liberia, and requests the international community to support the endeavours of the new chairperson of the Council of States of the Liberian National Transitional Government and to provide the necessary assistance to the Economic Community of West African States Monitoring Group to enable it to carry out its mandate;

12.   Commends the efforts of Member States and humanitarian organizations to render humanitarian assistance to Angola and Liberia, and urges them to continue to provide and to increase such assistance;

13.   Affirms the importance of the South Atlantic to global maritime and commercial transactions and its determination to preserve the region for all peaceful purposes and activities protected by international law, in particular the United Nations Convention on the Law of the Sea;

14.   Welcomes the offer by Argentina to host the fifth meeting of the States members of the zone;

15.   Requests the relevant organizations, organs and bodies of the United Nations system to render all appropriate assistance which States of the zone may seek in their joint efforts to implement the declaration of the zone of peace and cooperation of the South Atlantic;

16.   Requests the Secretary-General to keep the implementation of resolution 41/11 and subsequent resolutions on the matter under review and to submit a report to the General Assembly at its fifty-second session, taking into account, inter alia, the views expressed by Member States;

17.   Decides to include in the provisional agenda of its fifty-second session the item entitled "Zone of peace and cooperation of the South Atlantic".

RECORDED VOTE ON RESOLUTION 51/19

In favour: Albania, Algeria, Angola, Argentina, Armenia, Australia, Austria, Bahamas, Bahrain, Bangladesh, Belarus, Belgium, Benin, Bolivia, Bosnia and Herzegovina, Botswana, Brazil, Brunei Darussalam, Bulgaria, Canada, Cape Verde, Chile, China, Colombia, Congo, Côte d'Ivoire, Croatia, Cuba, Cyprus, Czech Republic, Democratic People's Republic of Korea, Denmark, Dominican Republic, Egypt, Ethiopia, Federated States of Micronesia, Fiji, Finland, France, Gambia, Germany, Ghana, Greece, Guatemala, Guinea, Guinea-Bissau, Guyana, Honduras, India, Iran, Ireland, Italy, Jamaica, Japan, Kazakstan, Kenya, Kuwait, Lebanon, Libya, Liechtenstein, Luxembourg, Madagascar, Malawi, Malaysia, Maldives, Marshall Islands, Mauritania, Mexico, Monaco, Mongolia, Mozambique, Myanmar, Namibia, Nepal, Netherlands, New Zealand, Nigeria, Norway, Oman, Pakistan, Panama, Peru, Philippines, Poland, Portugal, Qatar, Republic of Korea, Romania, Russian

Federation, Saint Kitts and Nevis, Saint Lucia, Samoa, Saudi Arabia, Senegal, Seychelles, Sierra Leone, Singapore, South Africa, Spain, Sri Lanka, Sudan, Suriname, Sweden, Syria, The former Yugoslav Republic of Macedonia, Togo, Tunisia, Uganda, Ukraine, United Arab Emirates, United Kingdom, United Republic of Tanzania, Uruguay, Venezuela, Viet Nam, Yemen, Zambia.

<u>Against</u>: None.

<u>Abstaining</u>: United States.

<u>Absent</u>: Afghanistan, Andorra, Antigua and Barbuda, Azerbaijan, Barbados, Belize, Bhutan, Burkina Faso, Burundi, Cambodia, Cameroon, Chad, Comoros, Costa Rica, Djibouti, Dominica, Ecuador, El Salvador, Equatorial Guinea, Eritrea, Estonia*, Gabon, Georgia, Grenada, Haiti, Hungary, Iceland, Indonesia, Israel, Jordan, Kyrgyz Republic, Lao People's Democratic Republic*, Latvia, Lesotho, Liberia*, Lithuania, Mali, Malta, Mauritius*, Morocco, Nicaragua*, Niger*, Palau, Papua New Guinea, Paraguay, Republic of Moldova, Rwanda, Saint Vincent and the Grenadines, San Marino, Sao Tome and Principe, Slovakia, Slovenia, Solomon Islands, Swaziland, Tajikistan*, Thailand, Trinidad and Tobago, Turkey, Turkmenistan, Uzbekistan, Vanuatu, Zaire, Zimbabwe.

---

*   Later advised the Secretariat that it had intended to vote in favour.

30. LARGE-SCALE PELAGIC DRIFTNET FISHING; UNAUTHORIZED FISHING IN ZONES OF NATIONAL JURISDICTION; AND FISHERIES BY-CATCH AND DISCARDS - UNGA RESOLUTION

Doc. no.: A/Res.51/36   9 December 1996

The General Assembly,

Reaffirming its resolutions 46/215 of 20 December 1991, 49/116 and 49/118 of 19 December 1994 as well as other relevant resolutions,

Reaffirming also its resolution 50/25 of 5 December 1995 on large-scale pelagic drift-net fishing and its impact on the living marine resources of the world's oceans and seas; unauthorized fishing in zones of national jurisdiction and its impact on the living marine resources of the world's oceans and seas; and fisheries by-catch and discards and their impact on the sustainable use of the world's living marine resources,

Conscious of the need to promote and facilitate international cooperation, especially at the regional and subregional levels, in order to ensure the sustainable development and use of the living marine resources of the world's oceans and seas, consistent with the present resolution,

Mindful that the Agreement for the Implementation of the Provisions of the United Nations Convention on the Law of the Sea of 10 December 1982 relating to the Conservation and Management of Straddling Fish Stocks and Highly Migratory Fish Stocks 96/ provides in its general principles that States shall minimize pollution, waste, discards, catch by lost or abandoned gear, catch of non-target species, both fish and non-fish species, and impacts on associated or dependent species, in particular endangered species, through measures including, to the extent practicable, the development and use of selective, environmentally safe and cost-effective fishing gear and techniques, and further provides that States shall take measures, including the establishment of regulations, to ensure that vessels flying their flags do not conduct unauthorized fishing within areas under the national jurisdiction of other States,

Noting that the Code of Conduct for Responsible Fisheries sets out principles and global standards of behaviour for responsible practices to conserve, manage and develop fisheries, including guidelines for fishing on the high seas and in areas under the national jurisdiction of other States, and on fishing gear selectivity and practices, with the aim of reducing by-catch and discards,

Expressing deep concern at the detrimental impact of unauthorized fishing in areas under national jurisdiction, where the overwhelming proportion of the global fish catch is harvested, on the sustainable development of the world's fishery resources and on the food security and economies of many States, particularly developing States,

---

96/   A/CONF.164/37; see also A/50/550, annex I.

Reaffirming once again the rights and duties of coastal States to ensure proper conservation and management measures with respect to the living resources in areas under their national jurisdiction, in accordance with international law as reflected in the United Nations Convention on the Law of the Sea, 97/

Taking note of the report of the Secretary-General on large-scale pelagic drift-net fishing and its impact on the living marine resources of the world's oceans and seas; unauthorized fishing in zones of national jurisdiction and its impact on the living marine resources of the world's oceans and seas; and fisheries by-catch and discards and their impact on the sustainable use of the world's living marine resources, 98/

Acknowledging with appreciation the measures taken and the progress made by members of the international community, international organizations and regional economic integration organizations to implement and support the objectives of resolution 46/215,

Recognizing the efforts that international organizations and members of the international community have made to reduce by-catch and discards in fishing operations,

Once again expressing deep concern that there are continuing reports of activities inconsistent with the terms of resolution 46/215 and unauthorized fishing inconsistent with the terms of resolution 49/116,

1. Reaffirms the importance it attaches to compliance with its resolution 46/215, in particular to those provisions of the resolution calling for full implementation of a global moratorium on all large-scale pelagic drift-net fishing on the high seas of the world's oceans and seas, including enclosed seas and semi-enclosed seas;

2. Notes that a growing number of States and other entities as well as relevant regional and subregional fisheries management organizations and arrangements have adopted legislation, established regulations or applied other measures to ensure compliance with resolutions 46/215 and 49/116, and urges them to enforce fully such measures;

3. Urges all authorities of members of the international community that have not done so to take greater enforcement responsibility to ensure full compliance with resolution 46/215 and to impose appropriate sanctions, consistent with their obligations under international law, against acts contrary to the terms of that resolution;

4. Calls upon States to take the responsibility, consistent with their obligations under international law as reflected in the United Nations Convention on the Law of the Sea and resolution 49/116, to take measures to ensure that no fishing vessels entitled to fly their national flags fish in areas under the national jurisdiction of other States unless duly authorized by the competent authorities of the coastal State or States concerned; such authorized fishing operations should be carried out in accordance with the conditions set out in the authorization;

5. Urges States, relevant international organizations and regional and subregional fisheries management organizations and arrangements to take action to adopt policies, apply measures, including through assistance to developing countries, collect and exchange data and develop techniques to reduce by-catches, fish discards and post-harvest losses consistent with international law and relevant international instruments, including the Code of Conduct for Responsible Fisheries;

6. Reiterates its call on development assistance organizations to make it a high priority to support, including through financial and/or technical assistance, efforts of developing coastal States, in particular the least developed countries and the small island developing States, to improve the monitoring and control of fishing activities and the enforcement of fishing regulations, including through financial and technical support for regional and subregional meetings for this purpose;

7. Requests the Secretary-General to bring the present resolution to the attention of all members of the international community, relevant intergovernmental organizations, the organizations and bodies of the United Nations system, regional and subregional fisheries management organizations, and relevant non-governmental organizations, and invites them to provide the Secretary-General with information relevant to the implementation of the present resolution;

97/ Official Records of the Third United Nations Conference on the Law of the Sea, vol. XVII (United Nations publication, Sales No. E.84.V.3), document A/CONF.62/122.

98/ A/51/404:

8.   Also requests the Secretary-General to ensure that reporting on all major fisheries-related activities and instruments is effectively coordinated and duplication of activities and reporting minimized and that relevant scientific and technical studies are disseminated to the international community, and invites the relevant specialized agencies, including the Food and Agriculture Organization of the United Nations, as well as regional and subregional fisheries organizations and arrangements, to cooperate with the Secretary-General to that end;

9.   Further requests the Secretary-General to submit to the General Assembly at its fifty-second session and biennially thereafter a report on further developments relating to the implementation of resolutions 46/215, 49/116 and 49/118, taking into account the information provided by States, relevant specialized agencies, in particular the Food and Agriculture Organization of the United Nations, and other appropriate organs, organizations and programmes of the United Nations system, regional and subregional organizations and arrangements and other relevant intergovernmental and non-governmental organizations;

10.   Decides to include in the provisional agenda of its fifty-second session, under the item entitled "Oceans and law of the sea", a sub-item entitled "Large-scale pelagic drift-net fishing; unauthorized fishing in zones of national jurisdiction; and fisheries by-catch and discards".

Doc. no.: A/Res.51/45   10 December 1996

Votes: A - 167-0-2   K - 170-0-1
        B - 129-3-38   L - Adopted without a vote
        C - 163-2-5   M - 115-22-32
        D - Adopted without a vote   N - Adopted without a vote
        E - 137-4-27   O - 110-39-20
        F - Adopted without a vote   P - 165-0-7
        G - 159-0-11   Q - 164-1-2
        H - 154-0-15   R - 160-0-11
        I - 107-37-24   S - 155-0-10
        J - Adopted without a vote   T - Adopted without a vote

[...]

J

Prohibition of the dumping of radioactive wastes

The General Assembly,

Bearing in mind resolutions CM/Res.1153 (XLVIII) of 1988 56/ and CM/Res.1225 (L) of 1989 57/ adopted by the Council of Ministers of the Organization of African Unity, concerning the dumping of nuclear and industrial wastes in Africa,

Welcoming resolution GC(XXXIV)/RES/530 establishing a Code of Practice on the International Transboundary Movement of Radioactive Waste, adopted on 21 September 1990 by the General Conference of the International Atomic Energy Agency at its thirty-fourth regular session,58/

56/   See A/43/398, annex I.

57/   See A/44/603, annex I.

58/   See International Atomic Energy Agency, Resolutions and Other Decisions of the General Conference, Thirty-fourth Regular Session, 17-21 September 1990 (GC(XXXIV)/RESOLUTIONS (1990)). ·

Welcoming also resolution GC(XXXVIII)/RES/6, adopted on 23 September 1994 by the General Conference of the International Atomic Energy Agency at its thirty-eighth regular session,59/ inviting the Board of Governors and the Director General of the Agency to commence preparations for a convention on the safety of radioactive waste management, and noting the progress that has been made in that regard,

Taking note of the commitment by the participants at the Moscow Summit on Nuclear Safety and Security to ban the dumping at sea of radioactive wastes,60/

Considering its resolution 2602 C (XXIV) of 16 December 1969, in which it requested the Conference of the Committee on Disarmament, 61/ inter alia, to consider effective methods of control against the use of radiological methods of warfare,

Recalling resolution CM/Res.1356 (LIV) of 1991, adopted by the Council of Ministers of the Organization of African Unity,62/ on the Bamako Convention on the Ban on the Import of Hazardous Wastes into Africa and on the Control of Their Transboundary Movements within Africa,

Aware of the potential hazards underlying any use of radioactive wastes that would constitute radiological warfare and its implications for regional and international security, in particular for the security of developing countries,

Recalling all its resolutions on the matter since the thirty-third session of the General Assembly in 1988, including Assembly resolution 50/70 E of 12 December 1995,

Desirous of promoting the implementation of paragraph 76 of the Final Document of the Tenth Special Session of the General Assembly,63/ the first special session devoted to disarmament,

1. Takes note of the part of the report of the Conference on Disarmament relating to a future convention on the prohibition of radiological weapons;64/

2. Expresses grave concern regarding any use of nuclear wastes that would constitute radiological warfare and have grave implications for the national security of all States;

3. Calls upon all States to take appropriate measures with a view to preventing any dumping of nuclear or radioactive wastes that would infringe upon the sovereignty of States;

4. Requests the Conference on Disarmament to take into account, in the negotiations for a convention on the prohibition of radiological weapons, radioactive wastes as part of the scope of such a convention;

5. Also requests the Conference on Disarmament to intensify efforts towards an early conclusion of such a convention and to include in its report to the General Assembly at its fifty-second session the progress recorded in the negotiations on this subject;

6. Takes note of resolution CM/Res.1356 (LIV) of 1991, adopted by the Council of Ministers of the Organization of African Unity, on the Bamako Convention on the Ban on the Import of Hazardous Wastes into Africa and on the Control of Their Transboundary Movements within Africa;

7. Expresses the hope that the effective implementation of the International Atomic Energy Agency Code of Practice on the International Transboundary Movement of Radioactive Waste will enhance the protection of all States from the dumping of radioactive wastes on their territories;

59/   Ibid., Thirty-eighth Regular Session, 19-23 September 1994 (GC(XXXVIII)/RES/DEC   (1994)).

60/   A/51/131, annex I, para. 20.

61/   The Conference of the Committee on Disarmament became the Committee on Disarmament as from the tenth special session of the General Assembly. The Committee on Disarmament was redesignated the Conference on Disarmament as from 7 February 1984.

62/   See A/46/390, annex I.

63/   Resolution S-10/2.

64/   See Official Records of the General Assembly, Fifty-first Session, Supplement No. 27 (A/51/27), sect. III.F.

8. *Welcomes* the current efforts of the International Atomic Energy Agency in the preparation of a draft convention on the safe management of radioactive wastes and the appropriate recommendations made by the participants at the Moscow summit on nuclear safety and security, in particular their call on all States generating nuclear wastes with nuclear installations to participate actively in the preparation of this convention under the auspices of the International Atomic Energy Agency and to encourage its effective finalization and prompt adoption;

9. *Decides* to include in the provisional agenda of its fifty-second session the item entitled "Prohibition of the dumping of radioactive wastes".

[...]

M

Advisory opinion of the International Court of Justice on the legality of the threat or use of nuclear weapons

The General Assembly,

Recalling its resolution 49/75 K of 15 December 1994, in which it requested the International Court of Justice to render an advisory opinion on whether the threat or use of nuclear weapons is permitted in any circumstance under international law,

Mindful of the solemn obligations of States parties, undertaken in article VI of the Treaty on the Non-Proliferation of Nuclear Weapons,67/ particularly to pursue negotiations in good faith on effective measures relating to cessation of the nuclear arms race at an early date and to nuclear disarmament,

Recalling its resolution 50/70 P of 12 December 1995, in which it called upon the Conference on Disarmament to establish an ad hoc committee on nuclear disarmament to commence negotiations on a phased programme of nuclear disarmament and for the eventual elimination of nuclear weapons within a time-bound framework,

Recalling also the Principles and Objectives for Nuclear Non-Proliferation and Disarmament adopted at the 1995 Review and Extension Conference of the Parties to the Treaty on the Non-Proliferation of Nuclear Weapons,68/ and in particular the objective of determined pursuit by the nuclear-weapon States of systematic and progressive efforts to reduce nuclear weapons globally, with the ultimate goal of eliminating those weapons,

Recognizing that the only defence against a nuclear catastrophe is the total elimination of nuclear weapons and the certainty that they will never be produced again,

Desiring to achieve the objective of a legally binding prohibition of the development, production, testing, deployment, stockpiling, threat or use of nuclear weapons and their destruction under effective international control,

Reaffirming the commitment of the international community to the goal of the total elimination of nuclear weapons, and welcoming every effort towards this end,

Reaffirming the central role of the Conference on Disarmament as the single multilateral disarmament negotiating forum,

[...]

67/   United Nations, Treaty Series, vol. 729, No. 10485.

68/   See 1995 Review and Extension Conference of the Parties to the Treaty on the Non-Proliferation of Nuclear Weapons, Final Document, Part I (NPT/CONF.1995/32 (Part I)).

Noting the adoption of the Comprehensive Nuclear-Test-Ban Treaty by the General Assembly in its resolution 50/245 of 10 September 1996,

Regretting the absence of multilaterally negotiated and legally binding security assurances against the threat or use of nuclear weapons against non-nuclear-weapon States,

Convinced that the continuing existence of nuclear weapons poses a threat to all humanity and that their use would have catastrophic consequences for all life on Earth,

1. Expresses its appreciation to the International Court of Justice for responding to the request made by the General Assembly at its forty-ninth session;

2. Takes note of the advisory opinion of the International Court of Justice on the Legality of the Threat or Use of Nuclear Weapons, issued on 8 July 1996; 69/

3. Underlines the unanimous conclusion of the Court that there exists an obligation to pursue in good faith and bring to a conclusion negotiations leading to nuclear disarmament in all its aspects under strict and effective international control;

4. Calls upon all States to fulfil that obligation immediately by commencing multilateral negotiations in 1997 leading to an early conclusion of a nuclear-weapons convention prohibiting the development, production, testing, deployment, stockpiling, transfer, threat or use of nuclear weapons and providing for their elimination;

5. Requests the Secretary-General to provide the necessary assistance to support the implementation of the present resolution;

6. Decides to include in the provisional agenda of its fifty-second session an item entitled "Follow-up to the Advisory Opinion of the International Court of Justice on the Legality of the Threat or Use of Nuclear Weapons".

[...]

RECORDED VOTE ON RESOLUTION 51/45 I:

In favour: Afghanistan, Algeria, Angola, Antigua and Barbuda, Bahamas, Bahrain, Bangladesh, Barbados, Belize, Benin, Bhutan, Bolivia, Botswana, Brazil, Brunei Darussalam, Burkina Faso, Burundi, Cameroon, Cape Verde, Chad, Chile, China, Colombia, Congo, Costa Rica, Côte d'Ivoire, Cuba, Democratic People's Republic of Korea, Djibouti, Dominica, Ecuador, Egypt, El Salvador, Equatorial Guinea, Eritrea, Ethiopia, Fiji, Gabon, Gambia, Ghana, Guatemala, Guinea, Guinea-Bissau, Guyana, Haiti, Honduras, India, Indonesia, Iran, Jamaica, Jordan, Kenya, Kuwait, Lao People's Democratic Republic, Lebanon, Lesotho, Liberia, Libya, Madagascar, Malawi, Malaysia, Maldives, Mauritius, Mexico, Mongolia, Morocco, Mozambique, Myanmar, Namibia, Nepal, Nicaragua, Niger, Nigeria, Oman, Pakistan, Panama, Peru, Philippines, Qatar, Saint Kitts and Nevis, Saint Lucia, Saint Vincent and the Grenadines, Samoa, Saudi Arabia, Senegal, Sierra Leone, Singapore, South Africa, Sri Lanka, Sudan, Suriname, Swaziland, Syria, Thailand, Togo, Trinidad and Tobago, Tunisia, Uganda, United Arab Emirates, United Republic of Tanzania, Uruguay, Vanuatu, Venezuela, Viet Nam, Yemen, Zambia, Zimbabwe.

Against: Albania, Andorra, Armenia, Belgium, Bulgaria, Canada, Czech Republic, Denmark, Estonia, Federated States of Micronesia, Finland, France, Georgia, Germany, Hungary, Iceland, Israel, Italy, Latvia, Lithuania, Luxembourg, Marshall Islands, Monaco, Netherlands, Norway, Poland, Portugal, Republic of Moldova, Romania, Russian Federation, Slovak Republic, Slovenia, Spain, The former Yugoslav Republic of Macedonia, Turkey, United Kingdom, United States.

Abstaining: Argentina, Australia, Austria, Azerbaijan, Belarus, Bosnia and Herzegovina, Cambodia, Croatia, Cyprus, Ireland, Japan, Kazakstan, Kyrgyz Republic, Liechtenstein, Malta, New Zealand, Paraguay, Republic of Korea, San Marino, Solomon Islands, Sweden, Tajikistan, Ukraine, Uzbekistan.

69/   Legality of the Threat or Use of Nuclear Weapons, Advisory Opinion, A/51/218, annex; see also Official Records of the General Assembly, Fifty-first Session, Supplement No. 4 (A/51/4), paras. 176-183.

Absent: Comoros, Dominican Republic, Greece, Grenada, Mali, Mauritania, Palau, Papua New Guinea, Rwanda, Sao Tome and Principe, Seychelles, Turkmenistan, Zaire.

RECORDED VOTE ON RESOLUTION 51/45 K:

In favour: Afghanistan, Albania, Algeria, Andorra, Angola, Antigua and Barbuda, Argentina, Armenia, Australia, Austria, Azerbaijan, Bahamas, Bahrain, Bangladesh, Barbados, Belarus, Belgium, Belize, Benin, Bhutan, Bolivia, Bosnia and Herzegovina, Botswana, Brazil, Brunei Darussalam, Bulgaria, Burkina Faso, Burundi, Cambodia, Cameroon, Canada, Cape Verde, Chad, Chile, China, Colombia, Congo, Costa Rica, Cote d'Ivoire, Croatia, Cuba, Cyprus, Czech Republic, Democratic People's Republic of Korea, Denmark, Djibouti, Dominica, Ecuador, Egypt, El Salvador, Equatorial Guinea, Eritrea, Estonia, Ethiopia, Federated States of Micronesia, Fiji, Finland, France, Gabon, Gambia, Georgia, Germany, Ghana, Grenada, Guatemala, Guinea, Guinea-Bissau, Guyana, Haiti, Honduras, Hungary, Iceland, Indonesia, Iran, Ireland, Israel, Italy, Jamaica, Japan, Jordan, Kazakstan, Kenya, Kuwait, Kyrgyzstan, Lao People's Democratic Republic, Latvia, Lebanon, Lesotho, Liberia, Libya, Liechtenstein, Lithuania, Luxembourg, Madagascar, Malawi, Malaysia, Maldives, Mali, Malta, Marshall Islands, Mauritius, Mexico, Monaco, Mongolia, Morocco, Mozambique, Myanmar, Namibia, Nepal, Netherlands, New Zealand, Nicaragua, Niger, Nigeria, Norway, Oman, Pakistan, Panama, Paraguay, Peru, Philippines, Poland, Portugal, Qatar, Republic of Korea, Republic of Moldova, Romania, Russian Federation, Saint Kitts and Nevis, Saint Lucia, Saint Vincent and the Grenadines, Samoa, San Marino, Saudi Arabia, Senegal, Seychelles, Sierra Leone, Singapore, Slovak Republic, Slovenia, Solomon Islands, South Africa, Spain, Sri Lanka, Sudan, Suriname, Swaziland, Sweden, Syria, Tajikistan, Thailand, The former Yugoslav Republic of Macedonia, Togo, Trinidad and Tobago, Tunisia, Turkey, Uganda, Ukraine, United Arab Emirates, United Kingdom, United Republic of Tanzania, United States, Uruguay, Uzbekistan, Vanuatu, Venezuela, Viet Nam, Yemen, Zambia, Zimbabwe.

Against: None.

Abstaining: India.

Absent: Comoros, Dominican Republic, Greece, Mauritania, Palau, Papua New Guinea, Rwanda, Sao Tome and Principe, Turkmenistan, Zaire.

RECORDED VOTE ON RESOLUTION 51/45 M:

In favour: Afghanistan, Algeria, Angola, Antigua and Barbuda, Bahamas, Bahrain, Bangladesh, Barbados, Belize, Bhutan, Bolivia, Bosnia and Herzegovina, Botswana, Brazil, Brunei Darussalam, Burkina Faso, Burundi, Cambodia, Cameroon, Cape Verde, Chad, Chile, China, Colombia, Congo, Costa Rica, Côte d'Ivoire, Cuba, Democratic People's Republic of Korea, Dominica, Ecuador, Egypt, El Salvador, Eritrea, Ethiopia, Federated States of Micronesia, Fiji, Gabon, Gambia, Ghana, Grenada, Guatemala, Guinea, Guinea-Bissau, Guyana, Haiti, Honduras, India, Indonesia, Iran, Ireland, Jamaica, Jordan, Kenya, Kuwait, Lao People's Democratic Republic, Lebanon, Lesotho, Liberia, Libya, Madagascar, Malawi, Malaysia, Maldives, Mali, Malta, Marshall Islands, Mauritius, Mexico, Mongolia, Morocco, Mozambique, Myanmar, Namibia, Nepal, New Zealand, Nicaragua, Niger, Nigeria, Oman, Pakistan, Panama, Paraguay, Peru, Philippines, Qatar, Saint Kitts and nevis, Saint Lucia, Saint Vincent and the Grenadines, Samoa, San Marino, Saudi Arabia, Sierra Leone, Singapore, Solomon Islands, South Africa, Sri Lanka, Sudan, Suriname, Swaziland, Sweden, Syria, Thailand, Trinidad and Tobago, Tunisia, Uganda, United Arab Emirates, United Republic of Tanzania, Uruguay, Vanuatu, Venezuela, Viet Nam, Yemen, Zambia, Zimbabwe.

Against: Albania, Belgium, Canada, Czech Republic, France, Germany, Hungary, Italy, Luxembourg, Monaco, Netherlands, Poland, Portugal, Romania, Russian Federation, Slovakia, Slovenia, Spain, The former Yugoslav Republic of Macedonia, Turkey, United Kingdom, United States.

Abstaining: Andorra, Argentina, Armenia, Australia, Austria, Azerbaijan, Belarus, Benin, Bulgaria, Croatia, Cyprus, Denmark, Equatorial Guinea, Estonia, Finland, Georgia, Iceland, Israel, Japan, Kazakstan, Kyrgyz Republic, Latvia, Liechtenstein, Lithuania, Norway, Republic of Korea, Republic of Moldova, Senegal, Tajikistan, Togo, Ukraine, Uzbekistan.

Absent: Comoros, Djibouti, Dominican Republic, Greece, Mauritania, Palau, Papua New Guinea, Rwanda, Sao Tome and Principe, Seychelles, Turkmenistan, Zaire.

32. STRENGTHENING OF SECURITY AND COOPERATION IN THE MEDITERRANEAN REGION - UNGA RESOLUTION

Doc. no.: A/Res.51/50   10 December 1996

The General Assembly

Recalling its previous resolutions on the subject, including resolution 50/75 of 12 December 1995,

Reaffirming the primary role of the Mediterranean countries in strengthening and promoting peace, security and cooperation in the Mediterranean region,

Bearing in mind all the previous declarations and commitments, as well as all the initiatives taken by the riparian countries at the recent summits, ministerial meetings and various forums concerning the question of the Mediterranean region,

Recognizing the efforts made so far and the determination of the Mediterranean countries to intensify the process of dialogue and consultations with a view to resolving the problems existing in the Mediterranean region and to eliminate the causes of tension and the consequent threat to peace and security,

Recognizing also the indivisible character of security in the Mediterranean and that the enhancement of cooperation among Mediterranean countries with a view to promoting the economic and social development of all peoples of the region will contribute significantly to stability, peace and security in the region,

Recognizing further that prospects for closer Euro-Mediterranean cooperation in all spheres can be enhanced by positive developments worldwide, in particular in Europe, in the Maghreb and in the Middle East,

Noting the developments in the Middle East peace process that will lead to achieving a comprehensive, just and lasting peace in the region and therefore to promoting confidence-building measures and a good-neighbourly spirit among the countries of the area,

Expressing satisfaction at the growing awareness of the need for more joint efforts by all Mediterranean countries so as to strengthen economic, social, cultural and environmental cooperation in the region,

Reaffirming the responsibility of all States to contribute to the stability and prosperity of the Mediterranean region and their commitment to respect the purposes and principles of the Charter of the United Nations, as well as the provisions of the Declaration on Principles of International Law concerning Friendly Relations and Cooperation among States in accordance with the Charter of the United Nations, 135/

135/   Resolution 2625 (XXV), annex.

Expressing its concern at the persistent tension and continuing military activities in parts of the Mediterranean that hinder efforts to strengthen security and cooperation in the region,

Taking note of the report of the Secretary-General on this item,136/

1. Reaffirms that security in the Mediterranean is closely linked to European security as well as to international peace and security;

2. Expresses its satisfaction at the continuing efforts by Mediterranean countries to contribute actively to the elimination of all causes of tension in the region and to the promotion of just and lasting solutions to the persistent problems of the region through peaceful means, thus ensuring the withdrawal of foreign forces of occupation and respecting the sovereignty, independence and territorial integrity of all countries of the Mediterranean and the right of peoples to self-determination, and therefore calls for full adherence to the principles of non-interference, non-intervention, non-use of force or threat of use of force and the inadmissibility of the acquisition of territory by force, in accordance with the Charter and the relevant resolutions of the United Nations;

3. Commends the efforts by the Mediterranean countries in meeting common challenges through coordinated overall responses, based on a spirit of multilateral partnership, towards the general objective of turning the Mediterranean basin into an area of dialogue, exchanges and cooperation, guaranteeing peace, stability and prosperity;

4. Encourages Mediterranean countries to strengthen such efforts through, inter alia, a lasting, multilateral and action-oriented cooperative dialogue among States of the region;

5. Recognizes that the elimination of the economic and social disparities in levels of development as well as other obstacles in the Mediterranean area will contribute to enhancing peace, security and cooperation among Mediterranean countries through the existing forums;

6. Recognizes also that respect and greater understanding among cultures will contribute to enhancing peace, security and cooperation among Mediterranean countries;

7. Calls upon all States of the Mediterranean region that have not yet done so to adhere to all the multilaterally negotiated legal instruments related to the field of disarmament, thus creating the necessary conditions for strengthening peace and cooperation in the region;

8. Encourages all States of the region to favour the necessary conditions for strengthening the confidence-building measures among them by promoting genuine openness and transparency on all military matters, by participating, inter alia, in the United Nations system for the standardized reporting of military expenditures as well by providing accurate data and information to the United Nations Register of Conventional Arms;

9. Encourages the Mediterranean countries to strengthen further their cooperation in combating terrorism, in all its forms and manifestations, which poses a serious threat to peace, security and stability in the region and therefore to the improvement of the current political, economic and social situation;

10. Invites all States of the region to address, through various forms of cooperation, problems and threats posed to the region, such as terrorism, international crime and illicit arms transfers, as well as illicit drug production, consumption and trafficking, which jeopardize the friendly relations among States, hinder the development of international cooperation and result in the destruction of human rights, fundamental freedoms and the democratic basis of pluralistic society;

11. Encourages the continued widespread support among the Mediterranean countries for the convening of a conference on security and cooperation in the Mediterranean, as well as the ongoing consultations to create the appropriate conditions for its convening;

136/   A/51/230 and Corr.1 and Add.1.

12. <u>Requests</u> the Secretary-General to submit a report on means to strengthen security and cooperation in the Mediterranean region;

13. <u>Decides</u> to include in the provisional agenda of its fifty-second session the item entitled "Strengthening of security and cooperation in the Mediterranean region".

33. IMPLEMENTATION OF THE DECLARATION OF THE INDIAN OCEAN AS A ZONE OF PEACE - UNGA RESOLUTION

Doc. no.: A/Res.51/51   10 December 1996

The General Assembly,

Recalling the Declaration of the Indian Ocean as a Zone of Peace, contained in its resolution 2832 (XXVI) of 16 December 1971, and recalling also its resolution 50/76 of 12 December 1995 and other relevant resolutions,

Recalling also the report of the Meeting of the Littoral and Hinterland States of the Indian Ocean held in July 1979, 137/

Emphasizing the need to foster consensual approaches, in particular given the prevailing international climate, which is conducive to the pursuit of such endeavours,

Noting the initiatives taken by countries in the region to promote cooperation, in particular economic cooperation, in the Indian Ocean area and the possible contribution of such initiatives to overall objectives of a zone of peace,

Convinced that the participation of all the permanent members of the Security Council and the major maritime users of the Indian Ocean in the work of the Ad Hoc Committee on the Indian Ocean is important and would assist the progress of mutually beneficial dialogue to develop conditions of peace, security and stability in the Indian Ocean region,

Having considered the report of the Ad Hoc Committee, 138/ including the statement by its Chairman on 8 July 1996, as contained in paragraph 8 of the report,

1. Takes note of the report of the Ad Hoc Committee on the Indian Ocean; 139/

2. Reiterates its conviction that the participation of all the permanent members of the Security Council and the major maritime users of the Indian Ocean in the work of the Ad Hoc Committee is important and

---

137/   Official Records of the General Assembly, Thirty-fourth Session, Supplement No. 45 and corrigendum (A/34/45 and Corr.1).

138/   Ibid., Fifty-first Session, Supplement No. 29 (A/51/29).

139/   Ibid.

would greatly facilitate the development of a mutually beneficial dialogue to advance peace, security and stability in the Indian Ocean region;

3. Requests the Ad Hoc Committee to examine its future work, taking into account, inter alia, the statement made by the Chairman on 8 July 1996, and to make recommendations for consideration by the General Assembly at its fifty-second session;

4. Also requests the Ad Hoc Committee to hold a session during 1997, of a duration of not more than three working days;

5. Further requests the Ad Hoc Committee to submit to the General Assembly at its fifty-second session a report on the implementation of the present resolution;

6. Requests the Secretary-General to continue to render all necessary assistance to the Ad Hoc Committee, including the provision of summary records;

7. Decides to include in the provisional agenda of its fifty-second session the item entitled "Implementation of the Declaration of the Indian Ocean as a Zone of Peace".

RECORDED VOTE ON RESOLUTION 51/51:

In favour: Afghanistan, Algeria, Angola, Antigua and Barbuda, Argentina, Australia, Azerbaijan, Bahamas, Bahrain, Bangladesh, Barbados, Belarus, Belize, Benin, Bhutan, Bolivia, Bosnia and Herzegovina, Botswana, Brazil, Brunei Darussalam, Burkina Faso, Burundi, Cambodia, Cameroon, Cape Verde, Chad, Chile, China, Colombia, Congo, Costa Rica, Côte d'Ivoire, Cuba, Democratic People's Republic of Korea, Djibouti, Dominica, Ecuador, Egypt, El Salvador, Eritrea, Ethiopia, Federated States of Micronesia, Fiji, Gabon, Gambia, Ghana, Grenada, Guatemala, Guinea, Guinea-Bissau, Guyana, Haiti, Honduras, India, Indonesia, Iran, Jamaica, Jordan, Kazakstan, Kenya, Kuwait, Kyrgyz Republic, Lao People's Democratic Republic, Lebanon, Lesotho, Liberia, Libya, Madagascar, Malawi, Malaysia, Maldives, Mali, Malta, Marshall Islands, Mauritius, Mexico, Mongolia, Morocco, Mozambique, Myanmar, Namibia, Nepal, New Zealand, Nicaragua, Niger, Nigeria, Oman, Pakistan, Panama, Papua New Guinea, Paraguay, Peru, Philippines, Qatar, Republic of Korea, Russian Federation, Saint Kitts and Nevis, Saint Lucia, Saint Vincent and the Grenadines, Samoa, San Marino, Saudi Arabia, Senegal, Seychelles, Sierra Leone, Singapore, Solomon Islands, South Africa, Sri Lanka, Sudan, Suriname, Swaziland, Syria, Tajikistan, Thailand, Togo, Trinidad and Tobago, Tunisia, Uganda, Ukraine, United Arab Emirates, United Republic of Tanzania, Uruguay, Uzbekistan, Vanuatu, Venezuela, Viet Nam, Yemen, Zambia, Zimbabwe.

Against: France, United Kingdom, United States.

Abstaining: Albania, Andorra, Armenia, Austria, Belgium, Bulgaria, Canada, Croatia, Cyprus, Czech Republic, Denmark, Equatorial Guinea, Estonia, Finland, Germany, Hungary, Iceland, Ireland, Israel, Italy, Japan, Latvia, Liechtenstein, Lithuania, Luxembourg, Netherlands, Norway, Poland, Portugal, Republic of Moldova, Romania, Slovak Republic, Slovenia, Spain, Sweden, The former Yugoslav Republic of Macedonia, Turkey.

Absent: Comoros, Dominican Republic, Greece, Mauritania, Monaco, Palau, Rwanda, Sao Tome and Principe, Turkmenistan, Zaire.

34. QUESTION OF ANTARCTICA - UNGA RESOLUTION

Doc. no.: A/Res.51/56

10 December 1996

The General Assembly,

Recalling its resolution 49/80 of 15 December 1994, in which it requested the Secretary-General to submit information provided by the Antarctic Treaty Consultative Parties on their consultative meetings and on their activities, and on developments in relation to Antarctica,

Taking into account the debates on the question of Antarctica held since its thirty-eighth session,

Conscious of the particular significance of Antarctica to the international community, including for international peace and security, the global and regional environment, its effects on global and regional climate conditions, and scientific research,

Reaffirming that the management and use of Antarctica should be conducted in accordance with the purposes and principles of the Charter of the United Nations and in the interest of maintaining international peace and security and of promoting international cooperation for the benefit of mankind as a whole,

Recognizing that the Antarctic Treaty, 149/ which provides, inter alia, for the demilitarization of the continent, the prohibition of nuclear explosions and the disposal of nuclear wastes, the freedom of scientific research and the free exchange of scientific information, is in furtherance of the purposes and principles of the Charter,

Recognizing also the designation, in the Protocol on Environmental Protection to the Antarctic Treaty, of Antarctica as a natural reserve devoted to peace and science and the provisions contained in the Protocol regarding the protection of the Antarctic environment and dependent and associated ecosystems, including for environmental assessment, in the planning and conduct of all activities in Antarctica,

Welcoming the continuing cooperation among countries undertaking scientific research activities in Antarctica, which may help to minimize human impacts on the Antarctic environment,

Welcoming also the increasing awareness of an interest in Antarctica shown by the international community, and convinced of the advantages to the whole of mankind of a better knowledge of Antarctica,

---

149/ United Nations, Treaty Series, vol. 402, No. 5778.

Reaffirming its conviction that, in the interest of all mankind, Antarctica should continue forever to be used exclusively for peaceful purposes and that it should not become the scene or object of international discord,

1. *Takes note* of the report of the Secretary-General on the question of Antarctica 150/ and the role accorded by the Secretary-General to the United Nations Environment Programme in preparing his report and also of the Nineteenth and Twentieth Antarctic Treaty Consultative Meetings, which took place at Seoul on 8 and 9 May 1995 and at Utrecht, the Netherlands, from 29 April to 10 May 1996, respectively;

2. *Recalls* the statement under chapter 17 of Agenda 21, 151/ adopted by the United Nations Conference on Environment and Development, that States carrying out research activities in Antarctica should, as provided for in article III of the Antarctic Treaty, continue:

(a) To ensure that data and information resulting from such research are freely available to the international community;

(b) To enhance the access of the international scientific community and specialized agencies of the United Nations system to such data and information, including the encouragement of periodic seminars and symposia;

3. *Welcomes* the invitations to the Executive Director of the United Nations Environment Programme to attend Antarctic Treaty Consultative Meetings in order to assist such meetings in their substantive work, and urges the parties to continue to extend such invitations for future consultative meetings;

4. *Welcomes also* the practice whereby the Antarctic Treaty Consultative Parties regularly provide the Secretary-General with information on their consultative meetings and on their activities in Antarctica and encourages the Parties to continue to provide the Secretary-General and other interested States with information on developments in relation to Antarctica, and requests the Secretary-General to submit a report which shall consist of that information to the General Assembly at its fifty-fourth session;

5. *Decides* to include in the provisional agenda of its fifty-fourth session the item entitled "Question of Antarctica".

150/   A/51/390.

151/   See Report of the United Nations Conference on Environment and Development, Rio de Janeiro, 3-14 June 1992 (A/CONF.151/26/Rev.1 (Vol. I and Vol. I/Corr.1, Vol. II, Vol. III and Vol. III/Corr.1)) (United Nations publication, Sales No. E.93.I.8 and corrigenda), vol. I: Resolutions Adopted by the Conference, resolution I, annex II, chap. 17, para. 17.105.

35. UNITED NATIONS DECADE OF INTERNATIONAL LAW - UNGA RESOLUTION

Doc. no.: A/Res.51/157   16 December 1996

The General Assembly,

Recalling its resolution 44/23 of 17 November 1989, by which it declared the period 1990-1999 the United Nations Decade of International Law,

Recalling also that the main purposes of the Decade, according to resolution 44/23, should be, inter alia:

(a) To promote acceptance of and respect for the principles of international law;

(b) To promote means and methods for the peaceful settlement of disputes between States, including resort to and full respect for the International Court of Justice;

(c) To encourage the progressive development of international law and its codification;

(d) To encourage the teaching, study, dissemination and wider appreciation of international law,

Recalling further its resolution 49/50 of 9 December 1994, to which was annexed the programme for the activities for the third term (1995-1996) of the Decade,

Expressing its appreciation to the Secretary-General for his report 6/ submitted pursuant to resolution 50/44 of 11 December 1995,

Having considered the above-mentioned report,

Recalling that at the forty-fifth session of the General Assembly the Sixth Committee established the Working Group on the United Nations Decade of International Law with a view to preparing generally acceptable recommendations on the programme of activities for the Decade,

Noting that at the fifty-first session the Sixth Committee reconvened the Working Group to continue its work in accordance with resolution 50/44 and all previous resolutions on the item,

Having considered the oral report of the Chairman of the Working Group submitted to the Sixth Committee, 7/

6/   A/51/278 and Add.1.

7/   See A/C.3/51/SR.48.

1. Expresses its appreciation to the Sixth Committee for the elaboration, within the framework of its Working Group on the United Nations Decade of International Law, of the programme of activities for the final term (1997-1999) of the Decade, and requests the Working Group to continue its work at the fifty-second session in accordance with its mandate and methods of work;

2. Also expresses its appreciation to States and international organizations and institutions that have undertaken activities in implementation of the programme for the third term (1995-1996) of the Decade, including sponsoring conferences on various subjects of international law;

3. Adopts the programme of activities for the final term (1997-1999) of the Decade contained in the annex to the present resolution;

4. Recalls, with appreciation to the Secretary-General, the successful organization of the United Nations Congress on Public International Law, held from 13 to 17 March 1995, which focused on the four main purposes of the Decade, as well as on new challenges and expectations for the twenty-first century, and welcomes the publication of the proceedings of the Congress;

5. Welcomes the establishment of the International Tribunal for the Law of the Sea under the United Nations Convention on the Law of the Sea 8/ as a new means of settlement of disputes;

6. Encourages the Office of Legal Affairs of the Secretariat to continue in its efforts to bring up to date the publication of the United Nations Juridical Yearbook ;

7. Invites all States and international organizations and institutions referred to in the programme to undertake the relevant activities outlined therein and to provide information in this respect to the Secretary-General for transmission to the General Assembly at its fifty-fourth session;

8. Requests the Secretary-General to submit, on the basis of such information and of new information on the activities of the United Nations relevant to the progressive development of international law and its codification a final report to the General Assembly at Its fifty-fourth session on the implementation of the programme;

9. Encourages States to disseminate at the national level, as appropriate, information contained in the report of the Secretary-General;

10. Appeals to States, international organizations and non-governmental organizations working in the field of international law and to the private sector to make financial contributions or contributions in kind for the purpose of facilitating the implementation of the programme;

11. Once again requests the Secretary-General to bring to the attention of States and international organizations and institutions working in the field of international law the programme annexed to the present resolution;

12. Takes note with appreciation of the activities undertaken by the International Committee of the Red Cross in the field of international humanitarian law, including with regard to the protection of the environment in times of armed conflict;

13. Decides to include in the provisional agenda of its fifty-second session the item entitled "United Nations Decade of International Law".

8/   Official Records of the Third United Nations Conference on the Law of the Sea, vol. XVII (United Nations publication, Sales No. E.84.V.3), document A/CONF.62/122.

ANNEX

<u>Programme for the activities for the final term (1997-1999)</u>
<u>of the United Nations Decade of International Law</u>

I. PROMOTION OF THE ACCEPTANCE OF AND RESPECT
FOR THE PRINCIPLES OF INTERNATIONAL LAW

1. The General Assembly, bearing in mind that maintenance of international peace and security is the underlying condition for the success of the implementation of the programme for the United Nations Decade of International Law, calls upon States to act in accordance with international law, and in particular the Charter of the United Nations, and encourages States and international organizations to promote the acceptance of and respect for the principles of international law.

2. States are invited to consider, if they have not yet done so, becoming parties to existing multilateral treaties, in particular those relevant to the progressive development of international law and its codification. International organizations under whose auspices such treaties are concluded are invited to indicate whether they publish periodic reports on the status of ratifications of and accessions to multilateral treaties and, if they do not, to indicate whether in their view such a process would be useful. Consideration should be given to the question of treaties that have not achieved wider participation or entered into force after a considerable lapse of time and the circumstances causing the situation.

3. States and international organizations are encouraged to provide assistance and technical advice to States, in particular to developing countries, to facilitate their participation in the process of multilateral treaty-making, including their adherence to and implementation of multilateral treaties, in accordance with their national legal systems.

4. States are encouraged to report to the Secretary-General on ways and means provided for in the multilateral treaties to which they are parties, regarding the implementation of such treaties. International organizations are similarly encouraged to report to the Secretary-General on ways and means provided for by the multilateral treaties concluded under their auspices regarding the implementation of such treaties. The Secretary-General is requested to prepare a report on the basis of this information and to submit it to the General Assembly.

5. The General Assembly, recognizing the importance of the protection of cultural property in the event of armed conflict, takes note of the efforts under way to facilitate the implementation of existing international instruments in this field.

II. PROMOTION OF MEANS AND METHODS FOR THE PEACEFUL SETTLEMENT
OF DISPUTES BETWEEN STATES, INCLUDING RESORT TO AND FULL
RESPECT FOR THE INTERNATIONAL COURT OF JUSTICE

6. States, the United Nations system of organizations and regional organizations, including the Asian-African Legal Consultative Committee, as well as the International Law Association, the Institute of International Law, the Hispano-Luso-American Institute of International Law and other international institutions working in the field of international law, and national societies of international law, are invited to study the means and methods for the peaceful settlement of disputes between States, including resort to and full respect for the International Court of Justice, and to present suggestions for the promotion thereof to the Sixth Committee.

7. Noting the establishment of the International Tribunal for the Law of the Sea in October 1996 in accordance with the United Nations Convention on the Law of the Sea, 9/ States and other entities referred to in article 20 of annex VI of the Convention are encouraged to consider making use of the Tribunal for the peaceful settlement of disputes in accordance with article 21 of annex VI of the Convention.

8. Taking into account the suggestions mentioned in paragraph 1 of the present section and with due regard to the recommendations contained in the report of the Secretary-General entitled "An Agenda for

---

9/   <u>Official Records of the Third United Nations Conference on the Law of the Sea</u>, vol. XVII (United Nations publication, Sales No. E.84.V.3),document A/CONF.62/122.

Peace", 10/ the Sixth Committee should consider, where appropriate, on the basis of a report of the Special Committee on the Charter of the United Nations and on the Strengthening of the Role of the Organization, or of the Working Group on the United Nations Decade of International Law, the following questions:

(a) Strengthening the use of means and methods for the peaceful settlement of disputes, with particular attention to the role to be played by the United Nations, as well as methods for early identification and prevention of disputes and their containment;

(b) Procedures for the peaceful settlement of disputes arising in specific areas of international law;

(c) Ways and means of encouraging greater recognition of the role of the International Court of Justice and its wider use in the peaceful settlement of disputes;

(d) Enhancement of cooperation of regional organizations with the United Nations system of organizations in respect of the peaceful settlement of disputes;

(e) Wider use of the Permanent Court of Arbitration.

III. ENCOURAGEMENT OF THE PROGRESSIVE DEVELOPMENT OF INTERNATIONAL LAW AND ITS CODIFICATION

9. International organizations, including the United Nations system of organizations and regional organizations, are invited to submit to the Secretary-General of the United Nations summary information regarding the programme and results of their work relevant to the progressive development of international law and its codification, including their suggestions for future work in their specialized field, with an indication of the appropriate forum to undertake such work. Similarly, the Secretary-General is requested to prepare a report on the relevant activities of the United Nations, including those of the International Law Commission. Such information should be presented in a final report by the Secretary-General to the Sixth Committee.

10. On the basis of the information mentioned in paragraph 9 above, States are invited to submit suggestions for consideration by the Sixth Committee and, as appropriate, recommendations. In particular, efforts should be made to identify areas of international law that might be ripe for progressive development or codification.

11. The Sixth Committee should study, taking into account General Assembly resolution 684 (VII) of 6 November 1952, 11/ its coordinating role with respect, inter alia, to the drafting of provisions of a legal nature and the consistent use of legal terminology in international instruments adopted by the General Assembly. States are invited to present proposals in this regard to the Sixth Committee.

12. The Special Committee on the Charter of the United Nations and on the Strengthening of the Role of the Organization should continue to study possible measures to strengthen the United Nations system for the maintenance of international peace and security. In that context, the Special Committee should bear in mind the debate within the United Nations, in particular in the General Assembly, of the Secretary-General's report entitled "An Agenda for Peace".

IV. ENCOURAGEMENT OF THE TEACHING, STUDY, DISSEMINATION AND WIDER APPRECIATION OF INTERNATIONAL LAW

13. Within the context of considering appropriate activities to mark the final term of the Decade's programme, States, the United Nations system of organizations and regional organizations and institutions referred to in the programme should encourage:

(a) The publication of essays on subjects of international law written by legal advisers of States and international organizations, scholars and other legal practitioners providing a useful perspective on international law as viewed from their standpoint;

10/   A/47/277-S/24111.

11/   See annex II to the rules of procedure of the General Assembly (A/520/Rev.15).

(b) The organization at the national, regional and international level of symposia, conferences, seminars, lectures and meetings on selected topics or themes of international law during the remaining years of the Decade to celebrate the end of it. Suggested topics for consideration could include, without limiting other suggestions, the contribution of the United Nations to international law; more effective means of implementing the rules of international law; merits or otherwise of treaties and other forms of instruments such as resolutions, declarations and so on; future topics for the International Law Commission; and the role of the International Court of Justice in the settlement of disputes and advisory opinions.

14. The Advisory Committee on the United Nations Programme of Assistance in the Teaching, Study, Dissemination and Wider Appreciation of International Law should, in the context of the Decade, continue to formulate, as appropriate and in a timely manner, relevant guidelines for the Programme's activities and report to the Sixth Committee on the activities carried out under the Programme in accordance with such guidelines. Special emphasis should be given to supporting academic and professional institutions already carrying out research and education in international law, as well as to encouraging the establishment of such institutions where they might not exist, in particular in the developing countries. States and other public or private bodies are encouraged to contribute to the strengthening of the Programme.

15. States and law faculties of higher educational institutions are encouraged to include international law as a core subject in their curricula. They are also encouraged to introduce courses in international law for students studying law, political science, social sciences and other relevant disciplines; they should study the possibility of introducing topics of international law in the curricula of schools at the primary and secondary levels. They should also consider introducing public international law courses geared towards career training and the establishment of clinical programmes in various areas of international law. Cooperation between institutions at the university level among developing countries, on the one hand, and their cooperation with those of developed countries, on the other, should be encouraged.

16. States should consider convening conferences of experts at the national and regional levels in order to study the question of preparing model curricula and materials for courses in international law, training of teachers in international law, preparation of textbooks on international law and the use of modern technology to facilitate the teaching of and research in international law.

17. States, international organizations and professional and academic institutions should consider making available materials to the United Nations audio-visual library on international law proposed by the Advisory Committee on the United Nations Programme of Assistance in the Teaching, Study, Dissemination and Wider Appreciation of International Law.

18. States are encouraged to organize special training in international law for legal professionals, including judges, and personnel of ministries of foreign affairs and other relevant ministries as well as military personnel. The United Nations Institute for Training and Research, the United Nations Educational, Scientific and Cultural Organization, the Hague Academy of International Law, the International Institute of Humanitarian Law, regional organizations and the International Committee of the Red Cross are invited to continue cooperating with States in this respect.

19. In connection with training of military personnel, States are encouraged to foster the teaching and dissemination of the principles governing the protection of the environment in times of armed conflict and should consider the possibility of making use of the guidelines for military manuals and instructions prepared by the International Committee of the Red Cross. 12/

20. Cooperation among developing countries, as well as between developed and developing countries, in particular among those persons who are involved in the practice of international law, for exchanging experience and for mutual assistance in the field of international law, including assistance in providing textbooks and manuals of international law, is encouraged.

21. In order to make better known the practice of international law, States and international and regional organizations should endeavour to publish, if they have not done so, summaries, repertories or yearbooks of their practice. They should also endeavour to place this material on computer networks for wider and instant distribution. The Office of Legal Affairs of the Secretariat is encouraged to continue its efforts in this regard, including through its participation in the Global Legal Information Network project.

12/   A/49/323, annex.

22. The Secretary-General, in cooperation with the Registry of the International Court of Justice, is encouraged to publish, to the extent feasible and in a timely manner, the publication updating the <u>Summaries of the Judgments, Advisory Opinions and Orders of the International Court of Justice (1949-1991)</u>, <u>13</u>/ at present under preparation, in all official languages of the Organization.

23. Other international courts and tribunals, including the European Court of Human Rights and the Inter-American Court of Human Rights, are invited to disseminate more widely their judgements and advisory opinions, and to consider preparing thematic or analytical summaries thereof.

24. International organizations are encouraged to publish treaties concluded under their auspices, if they have not yet done so. Timely publication of the <u>United Nations Juridical Yearbook</u> is also encouraged.

V. PROCEDURES AND ORGANIZATIONAL ASPECTS

25. The Sixth Committee, working primarily through its Working Group on the United Nations Decade of International Law and with the assistance of the Secretariat, will be the coordinating body of the programme for the Decade. The question of the use of an intra-sessional, inter-sessional or existing body to carry out specific activities of the programme may be considered by the General Assembly.

26. States are encouraged to establish, as necessary, national, subregional and regional committees, which may assist in the implementation of the programme for the Decade. Non-governmental organizations are encouraged to promote the purposes of the Decade within the fields of their activities, as appropriate.

27. Voluntary contributions from Governments, international organizations and other sources, including the private sector, would be useful and are strongly encouraged in order to implement the programme for the Decade. To that end, the establishment of a trust fund to be administered by the Secretary-General might be considered by the General Assembly.

<u>13</u>/   ST/LEG/SER.F/1   (United Nations publication, Sales No. E.92.V.5).

36. TRANSIT ENVIRONMENT IN THE LANDLOCKED STATES IN CENTRAL ASIA AND THEIR TRANSIT DEVELOPING NEIGHBOURS - UNGA RESOLUTION

Doc. no.: A/Res.51/168   16 December 1996

The General Assembly,

Recalling its resolutions 48/169 and 48/170 of 21 December 1993 and its resolution 49/102 of 19 December 1994,

Recalling also the agreed conclusions and recommendations of the First 13/ and the Second 14/ Meeting of Governmental Experts from Landlocked and Transit Developing Countries and Representatives of Dónor Countries and Financial and Development Institutions, held in New York from 17 to 19 May 1993 and from 19 to 22 June 1995, respectively, and in particular the conclusions and recommendations of those meetings pertaining to the newly independent and developing landlocked States in Central Asia and their transit developing neighbours,

Recognizing that the overall socio-economic development efforts of newly independent and developing landlocked States, seeking to enter world markets through the establishment of a multicountry transit system, are impeded by a lack of territorial access to the sea as well as by remoteness and isolation from world markets,

Supporting the current efforts being undertaken by the newly independent and developing landlocked States in Central Asia and their transit developing neighbours through relevant multilateral, bilateral and regional arrangements to address the issues regarding the development of a viable transit infrastructure in the region,

Considering that the outcome of the Symposium for Landlocked and Transit Developing Countries, held at United Nations Headquarters from 14 to 16 June 1995, in particular the document entitled "Global framework for transit transport cooperation between landlocked and transit developing countries and the donor community", 15/ is a practical contribution to the development objectives and efforts of the United Nations,

Taking note of the progress report of the Secretary-General of the United Nations Conference on Trade and Development on measures designed to improve the transit transport environment in Central Asia, 16/ and considering that the problems of transit transport facing the Central Asian region need to be seen against the backdrop of economic changes and the accompanying challenges, including especially the impact of those changes on the international and intraregional trade of the countries concerned,

---

13/   TD/B/40(1)/2-TD/B/LDC/AC.1/4.

14/   TD/B/42(1)/11-TD/B/LDC/AC.1/7.

15/   TD/B/42(1)/11.

16/   A/51/288, annex.

Recognizing that, to be effective, a transit transport strategy for the newly independent and developing landlocked States in Central Asia and their transit developing neighbours should incorporate actions that address both the problems inhering in the use of existing transit routes and the early development and smooth functioning of new, alternative routes,

Emphasizing the importance of strengthening international support measures to address further the problems of the newly independent and developing landlocked States in Central Asia and their transit developing neighbours,

1. Takes note of the results of the Technical Meeting on Central Asia's Transit Transport Links with World Markets, 17/ held at Ankara from 7 to 9 November 1995, under the auspices of the United Nations Development Programme and the United Nations Conference on Trade and Development;

2. Invites the Secretary-General of the United Nations Conference on Trade and Development and the Governments concerned, in cooperation with the United Nations Development Programme, the Economic and Social Commission for Asia and the Pacific, the Economic Commission for Europe and relevant regional and international organizations and in accordance with approved programme priorities and within existing financial resources, to continue elaborating a programme for improving the efficiency of the current transit environment in the newly independent and developing landlocked States in Central Asia and their transit developing neighbours;

3. Invites donor countries and multilateral financial and development institutions, within their mandates, to provide newly independent and developing landlocked States in Central Asia and their transit developing neighbours with appropriate financial and technical assistance for the improvement of the transit environment for those countries;

4. Calls upon the United Nations system to continue studying, within the scope of the implementation of the present resolution, possible ways of promoting more effective cooperative arrangements between landlocked States in Central Asia and their transit neighbours and to encourage a more active supportive role on the part of the donor community;

5. Requests the Secretary-General of the United Nations Conference on Trade and Development to prepare a report on the implementation of the present resolution, to be submitted to the General Assembly at its fifty-third session.

17/   See UNCTAD/LLDC/MISC.4,1996.

37. SPECIAL SESSION FOR THE PURPOSE OF AN OVERALL REVIEW AND APPRAISAL OF THE IMPLEMENTATION OF AGENDA 21 - UNGA RESOLUTION

Doc. no.: A/Res.51/181   16 December 1996

The General Assembly,

Recalling its resolution 47/190 of 22 December 1992, in which it decided to convene, not later than 1997, a special session for the purpose of an overall review and appraisal of the implementation of Agenda 21 58/

Reaffirming its resolution 50/113 of 22 December 1995, as the agreed basis that determines the modalities for the preparations for the special session, including the relevant role of the Commission on Sustainable Development, as the functional commission of the Economic and Social Council mandated to follow up the United Nations Conference on Environment and Development, as well as the role of other relevant organizations and bodies of the United Nations system,

Strongly reaffirming that the special session for the overall review and appraisal of the implementation of Agenda 21 will be undertaken on the basis of and in full respect of the Rio Declaration on Environment and Development, 59/

Taking note of the progress report of the Secretary-General on the state of preparations for the 1997 special session, 60/ and taking into account the views and concerns expressed by delegations to the Commission on Sustainable Development at its fourth session, the Economic and Social Council at its substantive session and the Second Committee of the General Assembly at its fifty-first session,

1. Decides to convene the special session envisaged in its resolution 47/190 for a duration of one week, from 23 to 27 June 1997, at the highest political level of participation;

2. Decides also that the Commission on Sustainable Development will devote the forthcoming meeting of its ad hoc open-ended inter-sessional working group, to be held from 24 February to 7 March 1997, to preparing for the special session, and that the Commission will devote its fifth session, to be held from 7 to

---

58/   Report of the United Nations Conference on Environment and Development, Rio de Janeiro, 3-14 June 1992, vol. I, Resolutions Adopted by the Conference (United Nations publication, Sales No. E.93.I.8 and corrigendum), resolution 1, annex II.

59/   Report of the United Nations Conference on Environment and Development, Rio de Janeiro, 3-14 June 1992, vol. I, Resolutions Adopted by the Conference, (United Nations publication (Sales No. E.93.I.8 and corrigendum), resolution 1, annex I.

60/   A/51/420.

25 April 1997 as a negotiating meeting, to final preparations for the special session for the overall review and appraisal of the implementation of Agenda 21;

3. Recognizes the important contributions made by major groups, including non-governmental organizations, at the United Nations Conference on Environment and Development and in the implementation of its recommendations, and the need for their effective participation in preparations for the special session, as well as the need to ensure appropriate arrangements, taking into account the practice and experience gained at the United Nations Conference on Environment and Development, for their substantive contributions to and active involvement in the preparatory meetings and the special session, and in that context invites the President of the General Assembly, in consultation with Member States, to propose to Member States appropriate modalities for the effective involvement of major groups in the special session;

4. Decides to invite States members of the specialized agencies which are not members of the United Nations to participate in the work of the special session in the capacity of observers;

5. Stresses that there should be no attempt to renegotiate Agenda 21, the Rio Declaration on Environment and Development, the Non-Legally Binding Authoritative Statement of Principles for a Global Consensus on the Management, Conservation and Sustainable Development of All Types of Forests 61/ or other internationally recognized intergovernmental agreements in the field of environment and sustainable development, and that discussions at both the preparatory meetings and the special session should focus on the fulfilment of commitments and the further implementation of Agenda 21 and related post-Conference outcomes;

6. Requests the Secretariat to provide all relevant reports called for in General Assembly resolution 50/113, including all other reports related to the outcome of the United Nations Conference on Environment and Development, for consideration by the ad hoc open-ended inter-sessional working group of the Commission on Sustainable Development and by the Commission at its fifth session, in accordance with the six-week rule and preferably not later than 15 January 1997;

7. Also requests the Secretary-General to ensure that preparations for the comprehensive report are conducted in accordance with paragraph 13 (a), (b), (c) and (d) of Assembly resolution 50/113;

8. Invites the Secretary-General to include in the reports requested in Assembly resolution 50/113 for the preparation of the special session information on the application of the principles contained in the Rio Declaration, and invites the Governing Council of the United Nations Environment Programme to include in its report to the General Assembly at its special session information and views on ways to address, in a forward-looking manner, national, regional and international application of these principles and the implementation of Agenda 21 in the interrelated issues of environment and development;

9. Decides to consider at its special session, inter alia, the application of the principles of the Rio Declaration at all levels - national, regional and international - and to make relevant recommendations thereon;

10. Also requests that other contributions to the special session, in addition to those identified in its resolution 50/113, include submissions from relevant bodies and organizations of the United Nations, including the Ad Hoc Intergovernmental Panel on Forests of the Commission on Sustainable Development and the Global Environmental Facility, information on the outcomes of United Nations conferences held since the United Nations Conference on Environment and Development, such as the Programme of Action for the Sustainable Development of Small Island Developing States, 62/ regional and subregional conferences, summits and other inter-sessional meetings on sustainable development organized by countries, and information on the activities of relevant United Nations conventions on the environment and development and the global freshwater assessment, and that account be taken of the activities organized by major groups, including business and industry and non-governmental organizations;

61/   Report of the United Nations Conference on Environment and Development, Rio de Janeiro, 3-14 June 1992, vol. I, Resolutions Adopted by the Conference (United Nations publication, Sales No. E.93.I.8 and corrigendum), resolution 1, annex III.

62/   Report of the Global Conference on the Sustainable Development of Small Island Developing States, Bridgetown, Barbados, 25 April-6 May 1994 (United Nations publication, Sales No. 94.I.18 and corrigendum), chap. I, resolution 1, annex II.

11. Further requests the Secretary-General, in the report on cross-sectoral issues of Agenda 21 for the special session, to give special consideration, without prejudice to other priority issues that may be identified in the preparatory process, to combating poverty and to health, financial resources and mechanisms, education, science, transfer of technology, consumption and production patterns, trade, environment and sustainable development, major groups, demographic dynamics, capacity-building and decision-making;

12. Requests the Secretary-General, in the reports for the special session, to give consideration, where appropriate and without prejudice to other priority issues that may be identified in the preparatory process, to linkages between the cross-sectoral issues of Agenda 21 and relevant sectoral issues;

13. Welcomes the outcome of the United Nations Conference on Human Settlements (Habitat II), held at Istanbul from 3 to 14 June 1996, and its relevance to the field of sustainable development, calls for effective interaction and exchange of information on work carried out by the Commission on Sustainable Development and the Commission on Human Settlements, and invites the Commission on Human Settlements to make a contribution to the special session in connection with the implementation of the Habitat Agenda 63/ adopted in Istanbul;

14. Invites Governments and regional organizations to cooperate with the Secretary-General in preparing country profiles for review at the fifth session of the Commission on Sustainable Development, as envisaged in paragraph 13 of General Assembly resolution 50/113;

15. Invites Governments to assist developing countries, particularly the least developed among them, in participating fully in the special session and its preparatory process, and to make timely contributions to the Trust Fund for Support of the Work of the Commission on Sustainable Development;

16. Requests the Secretary-General to enhance the public information programme of the United Nations so as to raise global awareness in a balanced manner, in all countries, of both the special session and the work undertaken by the United Nations in the follow-up to the Conference, and invites all Governments to promote widespread dissemination at all levels of the Rio Declaration on Environment and Development, and to make voluntary contributions to support the public outreach activities of the United Nations for the special session;

17. Decides to include in the provisional agenda of its fifty-second session the sub-item entitled "Special session for the purpose of an overall review and appraisal of the implementation of Agenda 21", and requests the Secretary-General to submit to it at that session a report on the special session.

63/   A/CONF.165/14, chap. I, resolution 1, annex II.

38. PROTECTION OF GLOBAL CLIMATE FOR PRESENT AND FUTURE GENERATIONS OF MANKIND - UNGA RESOLUTION

Doc. no.: A/Res.51/184   16 December 1996

The General Assembly,

Recalling its resolutions 45/212 of 21 December 1990, 46/169 of 19 December 1991, 47/195 of 22 December 1992, 48/189 of 21 December 1993, 49/120 of 19 December 1994 and 50/115 of 20 December 1995,

Noting with satisfaction that most States and one regional economic integration organization have ratified or acceded to the United Nations Framework Convention on Climate Change, 76/ and inviting States that are not Parties to take appropriate action to that end,

Welcoming the achievements of the second session of the Conference of the Parties to the United Nations Framework Convention on Climate Change, which was convened at Geneva from 8 to 19 July 1996, and noting that the Conference of the Parties at its second session adopted by consensus a series of substantive decisions, 77/

Recalling that at its second session the Conference of the Parties took note, without formal adoption, of the Geneva Ministerial Declaration which received majority support among ministers and other heads of delegations attending the Conference, which, inter alia, called for acceleration of negotiations on the text of a legally binding protocol or another legal instrument to be completed in due time for adoption at the third session of the Conference of the Parties, as mentioned in the Geneva Declaration,

Taking note with appreciation of the scientific contribution to the convention process of the Intergovernmental Panel on Climate Change of the World Meteorological Organization/United Nations Environment Programme, and also taking note of its second assessment report as the most comprehensive assessment available to date of the issues related to global climate change,

Concerned that changes in climate may result in significant and often adverse impacts on many ecological systems and socio-economic sectors, including food supply and water resources, and on human health, and noting that in some cases the impacts are potentially irreversible, and that developing countries and small island developing States are typically more vulnerable to climate change,

Looking forward to the continued efforts of the Conference of the Parties and its subsidiary bodies in addressing climate change and, in particular, to the successful conclusion of the Berlin Mandate 78/ process at the third session of the Conference of the Parties,

---

76/   A/AC.237/18 (Part II)/Add.1 and Corr.1, annex I).

77/   See FCCC/CP/1996/15/Add.1.

78/   FCCC/CP/1995/7/Add.1, decision 1/CP.1.

Reiterating that a comprehensive approach should be adopted by the Conference of the Parties and its subsidiary bodies in the implementation of the Convention, including the full consideration of the particular situation of the developing countries as recognized by the Convention,

Taking note with appreciation of the generous offer of the Government of Japan to host the third session of the Conference of the Parties at Kyoto from 1 to 12 December 1997, 79/

Noting that the relocation of the Convention secretariat to Bonn, Germany is well under way, and expressing its appreciation to the Government of Germany and the city of Bonn for the facilities and support they are providing to the secretariat,

Recalling its request to the Secretary-General, as put forth in General Assembly resolution 50/115, paragraph 9, to make the necessary arrangements to include in the calendar of conferences and meetings for the biennium 1998-1999 those sessions of the Conference of the Parties and its subsidiary bodies that the Conference may need to convene in that period, and noting that those arrangements should be made without prejudice to the outcome of the review referred to in paragraph 3 of the present resolution,

Having considered the report of the Secretary-General on the implementation of General Assembly resolution 50/115, 80/

1. *Notes* the administrative arrangements regarding personnel and financial matters that have been established in the context of the transitional arrangement for administrative support to the secretariat of the United Nations Framework Convention on Climate Change for the biennium 1996-1997; 81/

2. *Also notes* the arrangements made for the provision of conference services to the Conference of the Parties to the Convention and its subsidiary bodies for the biennium 1996-1997; 82/

3. *Reiterates* its request to the Secretary-General, as set forth in General Assembly resolution 50/115, paragraph 10, to review the arrangements mentioned in paragraphs 1 and 2 above towards the end of the biennium 1996-1997 and to report on the results of that review to the Assembly at its fifty-second session, taking into account evolving needs arising from the relocation to Bonn of the Convention secretariat;

4. *Notes with appreciation* contributions made to the extrabudgetary funds established under paragraphs 10 and 20 of General Assembly resolution 45/212, and maintained in accordance with Assembly resolution 47/195, and calls upon Member States that are Parties to the Convention to also contribute generously to the trust fund for participation in the Convention process envisaged in paragraph 15 of its financial procedures, and to the trust funds envisaged for supplementary activities under the Convention; 83/

5. *Calls upon* Member States that are Parties to the Convention to pay in full and in a timely manner for each of the years 1996 and 1997, in accordance with the indicative scale adopted by consensus by the Conference of the Parties, 84/ the contributions required for the trust fund for the core budget of the Convention, envisaged in paragraph 13 of its financial procedures, so as to ensure continuity in the cash flow required to finance the ongoing work of the Conference of the Parties, the subsidiary bodies and the Convention secretariat;

6. *Invites* the Executive Secretary of the United Nations Framework Convention on Climate Change to report to the General Assembly at its fifty-second session and, pending the outcome of the special session of the General Assembly in 1997, to report on the results of future meetings of the Conference of the Parties to the Convention;

7. *Decides* to include in the provisional agenda of its fifty-second session the item entitled "Protection of global climate for present and future generations of mankind" and to consider at that session the reviews requested in paragraph 10 of General Assembly resolution 50/115.

79/ FCCC/CP/1996/15/Add.1, decision 1/CP.2.

80/ A/51/484.

81/ Ibid., paras. 14-18.

82/ Ibid., para. 9.

83/ FCCC/CP/1995/7/Add.1, decision 15/CP.1, annex I, and decision 18/CP.1.

84/ Ibid., decision 15/CP.1, annex II.

39. MEASURES TO ELIMINATE INTERNATIONAL TERRORISM - UNGA RESOLUTION

Doc. no.: A/Res.51/210   17 December 1996

The General Assembly,

Recalling its resolution 49/60 of 9 December 1994, by which it adopted the Declaration on Measures to Eliminate International Terrorism, and its resolution 50/53 of 11 December 1995,

Recalling also the Declaration on the Occasion of the Fiftieth Anniversary of the United Nations,76/

Guided by the purposes and principles of the Charter of the United Nations,

Deeply disturbed by the persistence of terrorist acts, which have taken place worldwide,

Stressing the need further to strengthen international cooperation between States and between international organizations and agencies, regional organizations and arrangements and the United Nations in order to prevent, combat and eliminate terrorism in all its forms and manifestations, wherever and by whomsoever committed,

Mindful of the need to enhance the role of the United Nations and the relevant specialized agencies in combating international terrorism,

Noting in this context all regional and international efforts to combat international terrorism, including those of the Organization of African Unity, the Organization of American States, the Organization of the Islamic Conference, the South Asian Association for Regional Cooperation, the European Union, the Council of Europe, the Movement of Non-Aligned Countries and the countries of the group of seven major industrialized countries and the Russian Federation,

Taking note of the report of the Director-General of the United Nations Educational, Scientific and Cultural Organization on educational activities under the project entitled "Towards a culture of peace",77/

Recalling that in the Declaration on Measures to Eliminate International Terrorism the General Assembly encouraged States to review urgently the scope of the existing international legal provisions on the prevention, repression and elimination of terrorism in all its forms and manifestations, with the aim of ensuring that there was a comprehensive legal framework covering all aspects of the matter,

---

76/   Resolution 50/6.

77/   A/51/395, annex.

Bearing in mind the possibility of considering in the future the elaboration of a comprehensive convention on international terrorism,

Noting that terrorist attacks by means of bombs, explosives or other incendiary or lethal devices have become increasingly widespread, and stressing the need to supplement the existing legal instruments in order to address specifically the problem of terrorist attacks carried out by such means,

Recognizing the need to enhance international cooperation to prevent the use of nuclear materials for terrorist purposes and to develop an appropriate legal instrument,

Recognizing also the need to strengthen international cooperation to prevent the use of chemical and biological materials for terrorist purposes,

Convinced of the need to implement effectively and supplement the provisions of the Declaration on Measures to Eliminate International Terrorism,

Having examined the report of the Secretary-General, 78/

I

1. *Strongly condemns* all acts, methods and practices of terrorism as criminal and unjustifiable, wherever and by whomsoever committed;

2. *Reiterates* that criminal acts intended or calculated to provoke a state of terror in the general public, a group of persons or particular persons for political purposes are in any circumstance unjustifiable, whatever the considerations of a political, philosophical, ideological, racial, ethnic, religious or any other nature that may be invoked to justify them;

3. *Calls upon* all States to adopt further measures in accordance with the relevant provisions of international law, including international standards of human rights, to prevent terrorism and to strengthen international cooperation in combating terrorism and, to that end, to consider the adoption of measures such as those contained in the official document adopted by the group of seven major industrialized countries and the Russian Federation at the Ministerial Conference on Terrorism, held in Paris on 30 July 1996 79/ and the plan of action adopted by the Inter-American Specialized Conference on Terrorism held at Lima from 23 to 26 April 1996 under the auspices of the Organization of American States, 80/ and, in particular, calls upon all States:

(a) To recommend that relevant security officials undertake consultations to improve the capability of Governments to prevent, investigate and respond to terrorist attacks on public facilities, in particular means of public transport, and to cooperate with other Governments in this respect;

(b) To accelerate research and development regarding methods of detection of explosives and other harmful substances that can cause death or injury, undertake consultations on the development of standards for marking explosives in order to identify their origin in post-blast investigations, and promote cooperation and transfer of technology, equipment and related materials, where appropriate;

(c) To note the risk of terrorists' using electronic or wire communications systems and networks to carry out criminal acts and the need to find means, consistent with national law, to prevent such criminality and to promote cooperation where appropriate;

(d) To investigate, when sufficient justification exists according to national laws, and acting within their jurisdiction and through appropriate channels of international cooperation, the abuse of organizations, groups or associations, including those with charitable, social or cultural goals, by terrorists using them as a cover for their own activities;

78/   A/51/336 and Add.1.

79/   A/51/261, annex.

80/   A/51/336, para. 57.

(e) To develop, if necessary, especially by entering into bilateral and multilateral agreements and arrangements, mutual legal assistance procedures aimed at facilitating and speeding investigations and collecting evidence, as well as cooperation between law enforcement agencies in order to detect and prevent terrorist acts;

(f) To take steps to prevent and counteract, through appropriate domestic measures, the financing of terrorists and terrorist organizations, whether such financing is direct or indirect through organizations which also have or claim to have charitable, social or cultural goals, or which are also engaged in unlawful activities such as illicit arms trafficking, drug dealing and racketeering, including the exploitation of persons for purposes of funding terrorist activities, and in particular to consider, where appropriate, adopting regulatory measures to prevent and counteract movements of funds suspected to be intended for terrorist purposes without impeding in any way the freedom of legitimate capital movements and to intensify the exchange of information concerning international movements of such funds;

4. *Also calls upon* all States, with the aim of enhancing the efficient implementation of relevant legal instruments, to intensify, as and where appropriate, the exchange of information on facts related to terrorism and, in so doing, to avoid the dissemination of inaccurate or unverified information;

5. *Reiterates* its call upon States to refrain from financing, encouraging, training for or otherwise supporting terrorist activities;

6. *Urges* all States that have not yet done so to consider, as a matter of priority, becoming parties to the Convention on Offences and Certain Other Acts Committed on Board Aircraft, 81/ signed at Tokyo on 14 September 1963, the Convention for the Suppression of Unlawful Seizure of Aircraft, 82/ signed at The Hague on 16 December 1970, the Convention for the Suppression of Unlawful Acts against the Safety of Civil Aviation, 83/ concluded at Montreal on 23 September 1971, the Convention on the Prevention and Punishment of Crimes against Internationally Protected Persons, including Diplomatic Agents, 84/ adopted in New York on 14 December 1973, the International Convention against the Taking of Hostages, 85/ adopted in New York on 17 December 1979, the Convention on the Physical Protection of Nuclear Material, 86/ signed at Vienna on 3 March 1980, the Protocol for the Suppression of Unlawful Acts of Violence at Airports Serving International Civil Aviation, supplementary to the Convention for the Suppression of Unlawful Acts against the Safety of Civil Aviation. 87/ signed at Montreal on 24 February 1988, the Convention for the Suppression of Unlawful Acts against the Safety of Maritime Navigation, 88/ done at Rome on 10 March 1988, the Protocol for the Suppression of Unlawful Acts against the Safety of Fixed Platforms located on the Continental Shelf, 89/ done at Rome on 10 March 1988, and the Convention on the Marking of Plastic Explosives for the Purpose of Detection, 90/ done at Montreal on 1 March 1991, and calls upon all States to enact, as appropriate, domestic legislation necessary to implement the provisions of those Conventions and Protocols, to ensure that the jurisdiction of their courts enables them to bring to trial the perpetrators of terrorist acts and to provide support and assistance to other Governments for those purposes;

81/   United Nations, Treaty Series, vol. 704, No. 10106.

82/   Ibid., vol. 860, No. 12325.

83/   Ibid., vol. 974, No. 14118.

84/   Ibid., vol. 1035, No. 15410.

85/   Resolution 34/146, annex.

86/   United Nations Treaty Series, vol. 1456, No. 24631.

87/   International Civil Aviation Organization document DOC 9518.

88/   International Maritime Organization, document SUA/CONF/15/Rev.1.

89/   Ibid., document SUA/CONF/15/Rev.1.

90/   S/22393, annex I; see Official Records of the Security Council, Forty-sixth year, Supplement for January, February and March 1991.

II

7. Reaffirms the Declaration on Measures to Eliminate International Terrorism, contained in the annex to resolution 49/60;

8. Approves the Declaration to Supplement the 1994 Declaration on Measures to Eliminate International Terrorism, the text of which is annexed to the present resolution;

III

9. Decides to establish an ad hoc committee, open to all States Members of the United Nations or members of specialized agencies or of the International Atomic Energy Agency, to elaborate an international convention for the suppression of terrorist bombings and, subsequently, an international convention for the suppression of acts of nuclear terrorism, to supplement related existing international instruments, and thereafter to address means of further developing a comprehensive legal framework of conventions dealing with international terrorism;

10. Decides also that the Ad Hoc Committee will meet from 24 February to 7 March 1997 to prepare the text of a draft international convention for the suppression of terrorist bombings, and recommends that work continue during the fifty-second session of the General Assembly from 22 September to 3 October 1997 in the framework of a working group of the Sixth Committee;

11. Requests the Secretary-General to provide the Ad Hoc Committee with the necessary facilities for the performance of its work;

12. Requests the Ad Hoc Committee to report to the General Assembly at its fifty-second session on progress made towards the elaboration of the draft convention;

13. Recommends that the Ad Hoc Committee be convened in 1998 to continue its work as referred to in paragraph 9 above;

IV

14. Decides to include in the provisional agenda of its fifty-second session the item entitled "Measures to eliminate international terrorism".

ANNEX

Declaration to Supplement the 1994 Declaration on Measures to Eliminate International Terrorism

The General Assembly,

Guided by the purposes and principles of the Charter of the United Nations.

Recalling the Declaration on Measures to Eliminate International Terrorism adopted by the General Assembly in its resolution 49/60 of 9 December 1994,

Recalling also the Declaration on the Occasion of the Fiftieth Anniversary of the United Nations, 91/

Deeply disturbed by the worldwide persistence of acts of international terrorism in all its forms and manifestations, including those in which States are directly or indirectly involved, which endanger or take innocent lives, have a deleterious effect on international relations and may jeopardize the security of States,

Underlining the importance of States developing extradition agreements or arrangements as necessary in order to ensure that those responsible for terrorist acts are brought to justice,

---

91/   Resolution 50/6.

Noting that the Convention relating to the Status of Refugees, 92/ done at Geneva on 28 July 1951, does not provide a basis for the protection of perpetrators of terrorist acts, also noting in this context articles 1, 2, 32 and 33 of the Convention, and emphasizing in this regard the need for States parties to ensure the proper application of the Convention,

Stressing the importance of full compliance by States with their obligations under the provisions of the 1951 Convention and the 1967 Protocol 93/ relating to the Status of Refugees, including the principle of non-refoulement of refugees to places where their life or freedom would be threatened on account of their race, religion, nationality, membership in a particular social group or political opinion, and affirming that the present Declaration does not affect the protection afforded under the terms of the Convention and Protocol and other provisions of international law,

Recalling article 4 of the Declaration on Territorial Asylum adopted by the General Assembly in its resolution 2312 (XXII) of 14 December 1967,

Stressing the need further to strengthen international cooperation between States in order to prevent, combat and eliminate terrorism in all its forms and manifestations,

Solemnly declares the following:

1. The States Members of the United Nations solemnly reaffirm their unequivocal condemnation of all acts, methods and practices of terrorism as criminal and unjustifiable, wherever and by whomsoever committed, including those which jeopardize friendly relations among States and peoples and threaten the territorial integrity and security of States;

2. The States Members of the United Nations reaffirm that acts, methods and practices of terrorism are contrary to the purposes and principles of the United Nations; they declare that knowingly financing, planning and inciting terrorist acts are also contrary to the purposes and principles of the United Nations;

3. The States Members of the United Nations reaffirm that States should take appropriate measures in conformity with the relevant provisions of national and international law, including international standards of human rights, before granting refugee status, for the purpose of ensuring that the asylum-seeker has not participated in terrorist acts, considering in this regard relevant information as to whether the asylum-seeker is subject to investigation for or is charged with or has been convicted of offences connected with terrorism and, after granting refugee status, for the purpose of ensuring that that status is not used for the purpose of preparing or organizing terrorist acts intended to be committed against other States or their citizens;

4. The States Members of the United Nations emphasize that asylum-seekers who are awaiting the processing of their asylum applications may not thereby avoid prosecution for terrorist acts;

5. The States Members of the United Nations reaffirm the importance of ensuring effective cooperation between Member States so that those who have participated in terrorist acts, including their financing, planning or incitement, are brought to justice; they stress their commitment, in conformity with the relevant provisions of international law, including international standards of human rights, to work together to prevent, combat and eliminate terrorism and to take all appropriate steps under their domestic laws either to extradite terrorists or to submit the cases to their competent authorities for the purpose of prosecution;

6. In this context, and while recognizing the sovereign rights of States in extradition matters, States are encouraged, when concluding or applying extradition agreements, not to regard as political offences excluded from the scope of those agreements offences connected with terrorism which endanger or represent a physical threat to the safety and security of persons, whatever the motives which may be invoked to justify them;

7. States are also encouraged, even in the absence of a treaty, to consider facilitating the extradition of persons suspected of having committed terrorist acts, insofar as their national laws permit;

92/   United Nations, Treaty Series, vol. 189, No. 2545.

93/   Ibid., vol. 606, No. 8791.

8. The States Members of the United Nations emphasize the importance of taking steps to share expertise and information about terrorists, their movements, their support and their weapons, and to share information regarding the investigation and prosecution of terrorist acts.

* **** *

40. CREDENTIALS OF REPRESENTATIVES TO THE FOURTH MEETING OF STATES PARTIES TO THE UN CONVENTION ON THE LAW OF THE SEA - REPORT OF THE CREDENTIALS COMMITTEE

Doc. no.: SPLOS/7

7 March 1996

Chairman: Mr. Gilberto B. ASUQUE (Philippines)

1.   The Second Meeting of States Parties to the United Nations Convention on the Law of the Sea held in New York from 15 to 19 May 1995, appointed a Credentials Committee consisting of the following nine members: Cameroon, Croatia, Germany, Malta, Marshall Islands, Philippines, Senegal, Trinidad and Tobago and Uruguay.

2.   The Credentials Committee held two meetings, on 6 and 7 March 1996 respectively.

3.   At the first meeting of the Committee, on 6 March, Mr. Gilberto B. Asuque (Philippines) was elected Chairman of the Committee by acclamation.

4.   The Committee had before it a memorandum by the Secretariat dated 6 March 1996, as well as the additional information provided by the Secretariat during the two meetings, on the status of credentials of representatives to the first four Meetings of States Parties to the United Nations Convention on the Law of the Sea.

5.   As noted in paragraph 1 of the memorandum by the Secretariat, for the first three Meetings held in New York - on 21 and 22 November 1994 and from 15 to 19 May, and 27 November to 1 December 1995 respectively - formal credentials issued by the Head of State or Government or by the Minister for Foreign Affairs or by another competent authority had been received by the Secretariat for the representatives of the following States Parties: Australia, Austria, Barbados, Belize, Cameroon, Cape Verde, Costa Rica, Croatia, Cyprus, Fiji, Germany, Grenada, Iceland, Indonesia, Jamaica, Kenya, Kuwait, Lebanon, Malta, Marshall Islands, Mauritius, Mexico, Micronesia (Federated States of), Namibia, Oman, Paraguay, Philippines, Samoa, Senegal, Singapore, Slovenia, Sri Lanka, Sudan, the former Yugoslav Republic of Macedonia, Togo, Trinidad and Tobago, Uganda, Viet Nam and Zimbabwe.

6.   As noted in paragraph 2 of the memorandum by the Secretariat, for the first three Meetings of States Parties, information concerning the appointment of representatives participating in those Meetings has been communicated by means of facsimile or in the form of letters or notes verbales from ministries, embassies, permanent missions to the United Nations or other government offices or authorities, or through local United Nations offices, by the following States

participating in those Meetings: Angola, Antigua and Barbuda, Bahamas, Bahrain, Bolivia, Botswana, Brazil, Cuba, Djibouti, Egypt, Gambia, Ghana, Greece, Guinea, Guyana, Honduras, Italy, Mali, Nigeria, Saint Kitts and Nevis, Saint Lucia, Sierra Leone, Tunisia, United Republic of Tanzania, Uruguay, Yemen and Zambia.

7.   As noted in paragraph 3 of the memorandum by the Secretariat and as supplemented by the additional information obtained as of 7 March 1996, formal credentials issued by the Head of State or Government or by the Minister for Foreign Affairs or by another competent authority have been submitted for the representatives of the following States participating in the fourth Meeting of States Parties: Argentina, Australia, Austria, Barbados, Belize, Cameroon, Croatia, Cyprus, Fiji, Germany, Greece, Iceland, India, Indonesia, Malta, Marshall Islands, Mauritius, Mexico, Micronesia (Federated States of), Philippines, Republic of Korea, Samoa, Senegal and Slovenia.

8.   As noted in paragraph 4 of the memorandum by the Secretariat and as supplemented by the additional information obtained as of 7 March 1996, information concerning the appointment of representatives participating in the fourth Meeting of States Parties has been communicated by means of facsimile or in the form of letters or notes verbales from ministries, embassies, permanent missions to the United Nations or other government offices or authorities, or through local United Nations offices, by the following States participating in that Meeting: Antigua and Barbuda, Bosnia and Herzegovina, Cape Verde, Costa Rica, Ghana, Grenada, Guinea, Guinea-Bissau, Guyana, Iraq, Italy, Jamaica, Lebanon, Namibia, Nigeria, Oman, Sierra Leone, Singapore, Sri Lanka, Sudan, Tunisia, Uganda, United Republic of Tanzania, Uruguay, Yemen, Zaire and Zimbabwe.

9.   The Chairman proposed that the Committee accept the credentials of all representatives mentioned in the memorandum of the Secretariat, supplemented by the additional information, on the understanding that formal credentials of representatives referred to in paragraph 4 of the Secretariat's memorandum would be communicated to the Secretariat as soon as possible. The following draft resolution was proposed by the Chairman for adoption by the Committee:

>   "<u>The Credentials Committee</u>,

>   "<u>Having examined</u> the credentials of the representatives to the first four Meetings of States Parties to the United Nations Convention on the Law of the Sea referred to in paragraphs 1 to 4 of the memorandum of the Secretariat dated 6 March 1996, supplemented by the additional information provided by the Secretariat during the two meetings of the Committee,

>   "<u>Accepts</u> the credentials of the representatives concerned."

10.   The draft resolution was adopted by the Committee without a vote.

11.   Subsequently, the Chairman proposed that the Committee recommend to the Meeting of States Parties the adoption of the following draft resolution:

>   "<u>Credentials of representatives to the first four</u>
>   <u>Meetings of States Parties to the United Nations</u>
>   <u>Convention on the Law of the Sea</u>

>   "<u>The Fourth Meeting of States Parties to the United Nations Convention</u>
>   <u>on the Law of the Sea</u>

>   "<u>Approves</u> the report of the Credentials Committee."

12.   In the light of the foregoing, the present report is submitted to the Fourth Meeting of States Parties to the United Nations Convention on the Law of the Sea.

RECOMMENDATION OF THE CREDENTIALS COMMITTEE

13.   The Credentials Committee recommends to the Fourth Meeting of States
Parties to the United Nations Convention on the Law of the Sea the adoption of
the following draft resolution:

"Credentials of representatives to the first four
Meetings of States Parties to the United Nations
Convention on the Law of the Sea

"The Fourth Meeting of States Parties to the United Nations Convention
on the Law of the Sea

"Approves the report of the Credentials Committee."

-----

41. DECISIONS OF THE FOURTH MEETING OF STATES PARTIES TO THE UN CONVENTION ON THE LAW OF THE SEA ON BUDGETARY MATTERS (ADOPTED ON 8 MARCH 1996)

Doc. no.: SPLOS/L.1   10 April 1996

1.   The Meeting of States Parties approved the budget of the International Tribunal for the Law of the Sea covering the initial period from 1 August 1996 to 31 December 1997, amounting to $6,170,900, as set out in annex III to document SPLOS/WP.3; 2/ together with the staffing table for the Registry during the start-up period of the Tribunal as contained in annexes I and II thereto. In adopting the budget the Meeting also approved the administrative arrangements to be carried out by the Secretary-General and by the officer in charge of the Registry pending the election of the Registrar described in paragraphs 27-29 of document SPLOS/WP.3. 3/

2.   Without prejudice to the application of the provisions of article 19 of annex VI of the Convention on the Law of the Sea in respect of future budgets regarding the contribution by the International Seabed Authority, the budget of the Tribunal for the initial period will be financed by all States that are Parties to the Convention as at 1 August 1996. States that become Parties to the Convention thereafter and during the period of the budget will contribute pro rata for the remainder of the initial budget period.

3.   The contributions to be made by States Parties shall be based upon the scale of assessments for the regular budget of the United Nations applicable at the time of the adoption of the budget of the Tribunal for the corresponding financial year, adjusted to take account of participation in the Convention. This shall be applied provisionally pending the adoption of a scale by the Meeting of States Parties.

4.   The Secretary-General of the United Nations will, on the basis of a list of States Parties and States likely to be States Parties by 1 August 1996, determine the assessed contributions and advise all such States, not later than 15 March 1996, of their contribution payable to the initial budget in accordance with the provisional scale of assessments referred to in paragraph 3. The indicative scale of assessed contributions to the budget of the Tribunal as at 8 March 1996 applicable to States Parties and States likely to be Parties by 1 August 1996 appears in the annex to the present document. States Parties will be requested to pay at least 15 per cent of their contribution within 30 days in order to meet the start-up costs, the balance to be paid in accordance with paragraphs 5 and 6 below.

5.   The provisional scale of assessments will be revised on 1 July 1996 on the basis of participation in the Convention as at 1 August 1996. 4/ The

Secretary-General will notify States of their revised assessed contributions by
15 July 1996.

6.   The notification will specify the details of the assessed contribution of
each State Party that is attributed to each calendar year of the biennium
1996-1997. Contributions paid earlier to meet the start-up costs will be
credited towards contributions due. The notification will call upon States to
pay promptly and in full the assessed contribution for 1996 by 15 August 1996
and for 1997 by 15 January 1997.

7.   Adjustments will be made to the scale referred to in paragraph 5 to take
into account any increase in the number of States Parties. The contribution
paid by a State that is a Party as at 1 August 1996 which is in excess of its
assessed contribution as a result of adjustments to the scale will be credited
to the assessment of the State Party concerned for the next financial period.

8.   All contributions will be paid into a separate bank account, and in a
convertible currency, to be designated by the Secretary-General of the United
Nations, and subsequently into a bank account, and in a convertible currency, as
may be designated by the Registrar of the Tribunal. States Parties will be
periodically notified of the status of contributions.

9.   The collection and management of all contributions shall be undertaken by
the Registry, except such services that the Secretary-General of the United
Nations will provide from within existing resources, in accordance with General
Assembly resolutions 49/28 of 6 December 1994 and 50/23 of 5 December 1995. The
Meeting also approved the utilization of the contingency funds as set out in
annex III, item D, of document SPLOS/WP.3, 5/ in the event that the officer in
charge of the Registry considers it essential before the President of the
Tribunal is elected.

10.   The draft financial regulations and staff regulations which will govern the
management of the resources of the Tribunal shall be prepared and submitted for
the approval of the Meeting of States Parties in accordance with rule 72 of the
rules of procedure of the Meeting of States Parties. Until such regulations
have been approved the Financial Regulations and the Staff Regulations of the
United Nations will apply mutatis mutandis.

11.   The Meeting requests the Secretary-General of the United Nations, in
accordance with General Assembly resolutions 49/28 and 50/23 and the programmed
activities of the Division for Ocean Affairs and the Law of the Sea of the
Office of Legal Affairs, to continue assistance in establishing the Tribunal and
to cooperate with and lend support to the Tribunal in the fulfilment of its
functions.

Adopted by consensus
8 March 1996

Notes

    1/   The present document together with its annex is the revision of
document SPLOS/CRP.6 dated 7 March 1996 and annex thereto as adopted by the
Meeting of States Parties on 8 March 1996.

    2/   As revised by the Meeting and issued as document SPLOS/WP.3/Rev.1.

    3/   See SPLOS/WP.3/Rev.1, paras. 25-27.

    4/   States that are Parties to the Convention as of 1 August 1996 would
have deposited their instrument of ratification or acceptance no later than
1 July 1996 (see art. 308, para. 2, of the Convention).

    5/   Annex III as revised by the Meeting and issued as SPLOS/WP.3/Rev.1,
annex III.

Annex

Indicative scale of assessments and contributions to the budget of the International Tribunal for the Law of the Sea a/ b/

Date of UNCLOS ratification/ accession/ succession	State/entity	Scale of assessment for United Nations budget	Indicative scale of assessment for Tribunal	Proposed contribution to budget of $6,170,900
14 October 1994	Germany	8.94	22.84	1 409 434
--	[France] c/	6.32	16.15	996 600
--	[United Kingdom] c/	5.27	13.46	830 603
13 January 1995	Italy	4.79	12.24	755 318
--	[Netherlands] c/	1.58	4.04	249 304
22 December 1988	Brazil	1.62	4.14	255 475
5 October 1994	Australia	1.46	3.73	230 175
	[Sweden] c/	1.22	3.12	192 532
--	[China] c/	0.72	1.84	113 545
14 July 1995	Austria	0.85	2.17	133 909
29 January 1996	Republic of Korea	0.80	2.04	125 886
18 March 1983	Mexico	0.78	1.99	122 801
--	[Finland] c/	0.61	1.56	96 266
--	[Norway] c/	0.55	1.41	87 010
1 December 1995	Argentina	0.48	1.23	75 902
21 July 1995	Greece	0.37	0.95	58 624
29 June 1995	India	0.31	0.79	48 750
--	[New Zealand] c/	0.24	0.61	37 642
2 May 1986	Kuwait	0.20	0.51	31 472
--	[Georgia] c/	0.16	0.41	25 301
14 August 1986	Nigeria	0.16	0.41	25 301
30 July 1985	Iraq	0.14	0.36	22 215
3 February 1986	Indonesia	0.14	0.36	22 215
17 November 1994	Singapore	0.14	0.36	22 215
5 May 1986	Yugoslavia	0.11	0.28	17 279
5 April 1995	Croatia	0.10	0.26	16 044
15 August 1984	Cuba	0.07	0.18	11 108
16 June 1995	Slovenia	0.07	0.18	11 108
26 August 1983	Egypt	0.07	0.18	11 108
8 May 1984	Philippines	0.06	0.15	9 256
17 August 1989	Oman	0.04	0.10	6 171
25 April 1986	Trinidad and Tobago	0.04	0.10	6 171
10 December 1992	Uruguay	0.04	0.10	6 171
21 June 1985	Iceland	0.03	0.08	4 937
24 April 1985	Tunisia	0.03	0.08	4 937
29 July 1983	Bahamas	0.02	0.05	3 085

Date of UNCLOS ratification/ accession/ succession	State/entity	Scale of assessment for United Nations budget	Indicative scale of assessment for Tribunal	Proposed contribution to budget of $6,170,900
30 May 1985	Bahrain	0.02	0.05	3 085
12 January 1994	Bosnia and Herzegovina	0.02	0.05	3 085
12 December 1988	Cyprus	0.02	0.05	3 085
5 December 1990	Angola	0.01	0.03	1 851
2 February 1989	Antigua and Barbuda	0.01	0.03	1 851
12 October 1993	Barbados	0.01	0.03	1 851
13 August 1983	Belize	0.01	0.03	1 851
28 April 1995	Bolivia	0.01	0.03	1 851
2 May 1990	Botswana	0.01	0.03	1 851
19 November 1985	Cameroon	0.01	0.03	1 851
10 August 1987	Cape Verde	0.01	0.03	1 851
21 June 1994	Comoros	0.01	0.03	1 851
15 February 1995	Cook Islands d/	0.01	0.03	1 851
21 September 1992	Costa Rica	0.01	0.03	1 851
26 March 1984	Côte d'Ivoire	0.01	0.03	1 851
8 October 1991	Djibouti	0.01	0.03	1 851
24 October 1991	Dominica	0.01	0.03	1 851
10 December 1982	Fiji	0.01	0.03	1 851
22 May 1984	Gambia	0.01	0.03	1 851
7 June 1983	Ghana	0.01	0.03	1 851
25 April 1991	Grenada	0.01	0.03	1 851
6 September 1985	Guinea	0.01	0.03	1 851
25 August 1986	Guinea-Bissau	0.01	0.03	1 851
16 November 1993	Guyana	0.01	0.03	1 851
5 October 1993	Honduras	0.01	0.03	1 851
21 March 1983	Jamaica	0.01	0.03	1 851
27 November 1995	Jordan	0.01	0.03	1 851
2 March 1989	Kenya	0.01	0.03	1 851
5 January 1995	Lebanon	0.01	0.03	1 851
16 July 1985	Mali	0.01	0.03	1 851
20 May 1993	Malta	0.01	0.03	1 851
9 August 1991	Marshall Islands	0.01	0.03	1 851
4 November 1994	Mauritius	0.01	0.03	1 851
29 April 1991	Micronesia (Federated States of)	0.01	0.03	1 851
18 April 1983	Namibia	0.01	0.03	1 851
23 January 1996	Nauru d/	0.01	0.03	1 851
26 September 1986	Paraguay	0.01	0.03	1 851
1 October 1993	Saint Vincent and the Grenadines	0.01	0.03	1 851

Date of UNCLOS ratification/ accession/ succession	State/entity	Scale of assessment for United Nations budget	Indicative scale of assessment for Tribunal	Proposed contribution to budget of $6,170,900
27 March 1985	Saint Lucia	0.01	0.03	1 851
7 January 1993	Saint Kitts and Nevis	0.01	0.03	1 851
14 August 1995	Samoa	0.01	0.03	1 851
3 November 1987	Sao Tome and Principe	0.01	0.03	1 851
25 October 1984	Senegal	0.01	0.03	1 851
16 September 1991	Seychelles	0.01	0.03	1 851
12 December 1994	Sierra Leone	0.01	0.03	1 851
24 July 1989	Somalia	0.01	0.03	1 851
19 July 1994	Sri Lanka	0.01	0.03	1 851
23 January 1985	Sudan	0.01	0.03	1 851
19 August 1994	The former Yugoslav Republic of Macedonia	0.01	0.03	1 851
16 April 1985	Togo	0.01	0.03	1 851
2 August 1995	Tonga	0.01 _d_/	0.03	1 851
9 November 1990	Uganda	0.01	0.03	1 851
30 September 1985	United Republic of Tanzania	0.01	0.03	1 851
25 July 1994	Viet Nam	0.01	0.03	1 851
21 July 1987	Yemen	0.01	0.03	1 851
17 February 1989	Zaire	0.01	0.03	1 851
7 March 1983	Zambia	0.01	0.03	1 851
24 February 1993	Zimbabwe	0.01	0.03	1 851
TOTAL OF 85 STATES PARTIES PLUS 9 PROSPECTIVE STATES PARTIES		39.14 _e_/	100.26 _e_/	6 186 930 _e_/

85 States Parties and 9 prospective States Parties as at 8 March 1996.

Notes

_a_/ Percentages representing indicative scale of assessments to the Tribunal's budget assuming that the States/entities would account for 100 per cent of the Tribunal's budget.

_b_/ The United Nations scale of assessment was derived from document ST/ADM/SER.B/479, annex II.

_c_/ Anticipates that it will be a Party by 1 August 1996.

_d_/ For the purposes of this analysis, non-members of the United Nations were given a "scale of assessment for United Nations budget" of 0.01 per cent.

_e_/ The figures for the totals in this row are at minor variance, as a result of rounding.

-----

42. SCHEDULE FOR THE NOMINATION AND ELECTION OF THE MEMBERS OF THE COMMISSION ON THE LIMITS OF THE CONTINENTAL SHELF - NOTE BY THE UN SECRETARIAT

Doc. no.: SPLOS/L.2   25 April 1996

1.   In accordance with article 76 of the United Nations Convention on the Law of the Sea, the Commission on the Limits of the Continental Shelf shall be established in conformity with Annex II of the Convention. The Commission consists of 21 members, serving in their personal capacities, who shall be experts in the field of geology, geophysics or hydrography, elected by States Parties to the Convention from among their nationals, having due regard to the need to ensure geographical representation. 1/ The functions of the Commission shall be:

(a)   To consider the data and other material submitted by coastal States concerning the outer limits of the continental shelf in areas where those limits extend beyond 200 nautical miles, and to make recommendations in accordance with article 76 and the Statement of Understanding 2/ adopted on 29 August 1980 by the Third United Nations Convention on the Law of the Sea;

(b)   To provide scientific and technical advice, if requested by the coastal State concerned during the preparation of such data. 3/

2.   The members of the Commission are to be elected at the Meeting of States Parties convened by the Secretary-General at United Nations Headquarters. According to article 2 (2) of Annex II of the Convention, the first election was to be held within 18 months after the date of its entry into force, i.e., before 16 May 1996, and the Secretariat had proposed a schedule for nomination and election on that basis. 4/

3.   However, at the Third Meeting of the States Parties, held in New York from 27 November to 1 December 1995, it was agreed that the election of the members of the Commission would be postponed until March 1997. 5/

4.   In view of the above, the Secretary-General suggests the revised schedule for nomination and election of the members of the Commission as follows:

(a)   The first election of the 21 members of the Commission would be held at the Meeting of States Parties which is scheduled to be convened in March 1997. Since no decision has been taken concerning the precise date of election, it is proposed that Monday, 3 March 1997, the earliest possible date for election within the planned meeting, be used for purposes of computing the timing for notifications inviting submission of nominations;

(b) The nomination of candidates would open on 3 November 1996. A State in the process of becoming a Party to the Convention may also nominate a candidate. The nomination by such a State would remain provisional and would not be included in the list mentioned in (d) below unless the State concerned had deposited its instrument of ratification or accession before 3 February 1997;

(c) The nominations would close on 3 February 1997;

(d) The list of all persons thus nominated would be circulated to all the States Parties by the Secretary-General on 14 February 1997.

5.   It should be noted that the submission of nominations should be made after appropriate regional consultations, and not less than three members shall be elected from each geographical region. 6/

6.   Finally, the State Party which submitted the nomination of a member of the Commission shall defray the expenses of that member while in the performance of duties of the Commission. However, the coastal State concerned shall defray the expenses incurred in respect of the advice referred to in paragraph 1 (b) above. The secretariat of the Commission shall be provided by the Secretary-General of the United Nations. 7/

<u>Notes</u>

1/   United Nations Convention on the Law of the Sea, Annex II, article 2 (1).

2/   Final Act of the Third United Nations Conference on the Law of the Sea, annex II (United Nations publication, Sales No. E.83.V.5).

3/   Convention, Annex II, article 3 (1).

4/   See SPLOS/CRP.2.

5/   SPLOS/5, para. 20.

6/   Convention, Annex II, article 2 (3).

7/   Ibid., article 2 (5).

-----

43. REPORT OF THE FIFTH MEETING OF STATES PARTIES TO THE UN CONVENTION ON THE LAW OF THE SEA, NEW YORK, 24 JULY-2 AUGUST 1996 - PREPARED BY THE UN SECRETARIAT

Doc. no.: SPLOS/14

20 September 1996

CONTENTS

I. INTRODUCTION

1.   The fifth Meeting 1/ of States Parties to the United Nations Convention on the Law of the Sea was convened from 24 July to 2 August 1996 in accordance with article 319, paragraph 2 (e), of the Convention and the decision taken at the . fourth Meeting. 2/ Pursuant to that decision, and in accordance with rule 5 of the rules of procedure adopted by the Meeting of States Parties, 3/ invitations to participate in the Meeting were addressed by the Secretary-General of the United Nations to all States Parties to the Convention, and also to the observers referred to in rule 18 of the rules of procedure.

2.   The Meeting was held primarily to prepare for and conduct the first election of the 21 Members of the International Tribunal for the Law of the Sea in accordance with the Convention and its Annex VI. It was also to complete the review of the draft Agreement on Privileges and Immunities of the Tribunal with a view to its adoption.

3.   The Meeting was opened by the President, Mr. Satya N. Nandan (Fiji).

4.   In addition to the documentation available at previous Meetings, the following documents were before the current Meeting:

- Report of the Secretary-General under article 319 of the United Nations Convention on the Law of the Sea (SPLOS/6 and Corr.1);

- Report of the fourth Meeting of States Parties, 4 to 8 March 1996 (SPLOS/8);

- Election of the Members of the International Tribunal for the Law of the Sea: note by the Secretary-General (SPLOS/9);

- Election of the Members of the International Tribunal for the Law of the Sea: List of candidates submitted by Governments: note by the Secretary-General (SPLOS/10);

- Curricula vitae of candidates nominated by States Parties for election to the International Tribunal for the Law of the Sea: note by the Secretary-General (SPLOS/11);

- First election of the Members of the International Tribunal for the Law of the Sea: proposal by the President (SPLOS/L.3 and Rev.1);

- Credentials of representatives to the fifth Meeting of States Parties to the United Nations Convention on the Law of the Sea: reports of the Credentials Committee (SPLOS/12 and SPLOS/13);

- Informal proposals for the organization of work for the session: note by the President (SPLOS/CRP.7);

- Draft Agreement on Privileges and Immunities of the International Tribunal for the Law of the Sea (SPLOS/WP.2 and Add.1);

- Germany: Proposals relating to the draft Agreement on the Privileges and Immunities of the International Tribunal for the Law of the Sea (SPLOS/CRP.8);

- Revised budget estimates for the International Tribunal for the Law of the Sea covering the period 1996-1997 (SPLOS/WP.3/Rev.1);

- Schedule for the nomination and election of the members of the Commission on the Limits of the Continental Shelf: note by the Secretariat (SPLOS/L.2);

-   Schedule for the nomination and first election of the Members of the
    Commission on the Limits of the Continental Shelf: draft decision
    (SPLOS/CRP.9);

-   Draft rules of procedure of the Commission on the Limits of the
    Continental Shelf (SPLOS/CLCS/WP.1);

-   Commission on the Limits of the Continental Shelf: its functions and
    scientific and technical needs in assessing the submission of a
    coastal State: study prepared by the Secretariat (SPLOS/CLCS/INF/1).

II. ORGANIZATION OF WORK

A. Introductory statement by the President

5.   In his opening statement, the President stated that, as delegations were
aware, he was personally in a state of transition, 4/ and his intention had been
to open the meeting and then take his leave. However, a large number of
delegations had prevailed on him to provide continuity and to complete the
current phase of work, which had begun in November 1994. He invited the States
Parties to elect a new President and a new Bureau at the next meeting, which
would take place in March 1997.

6.   The President stated that the current session was of historic significance
for a number of very important reasons. Firstly, the Agreement to implement the
provisions of Part XI of the Convention would enter into force during the
current meeting. He noted that by a remarkable coincidence the Agreement, which
had been adopted by the General Assembly two years before, would also enter into
force on 28 July. For the first time, the Convention and the Agreement, which
by its terms is an integral part of the Convention, would be in force together.

7.   The second matter of significance was that the Convention had reached an
important milestone since the last meeting, as the number of States Parties had
now grown to more than 100. Given the momentum it had generated already, in the
not too distant future the Convention would achieve the highest number of States
parties for a treaty of such significance in international law. The
international community had striven to make the Convention a universal
instrument, and the growing numbers of States Parties attested to the fact that
it was achieving that goal. When the Convention had entered into force, there
were only two industrialized countries out of the 60 States Parties. Now, among
the 100 States Parties, there was a significant representation from all regions
and all interest groups.

8.   The President concluded that the third historic event consisted in the
first election of the Members of the International Tribunal for the Law of the
Sea. The election would be the culmination of the work done by the Meeting of
States Parties since 1994 and indeed going back to the Third United Nations
Conference on the Law of the Sea. He pointed out that the success of the
Tribunal would depend on two factors: firstly, how wisely the Meeting would
choose its Members to ensure its quality and to reflect its universal character,
and secondly how the Tribunal would organize itself to ensure that its
procedures were user-friendly and cost-effective and conduct itself in order to
inspire confidence.

9.   He recognized that the Meeting was very fortunate because the nominations
had produced excellent candidates from all regions and all the principal legal
systems, and represented all the various interests in the law of the sea. There
were 33 candidates from which the Meeting had to elect 21 judges. All
candidates were highly qualified, able and distinguished. Most if not all had
long associations with the law of the sea. The President was of the view that
the Tribunal and the international community would be well served by any 21 of
the 33 candidates.

B.   Organization of work

10. With respect to the work programme, the President referred delegations to the note prepared by him on the organization of work of the session (SPLOS/CRP.7). The election of the Members of the Tribunal was identified as being of the highest priority for the Meeting. The completion of the review of the draft Agreement on Privileges and Immunities of the Tribunal constituted the other matter of urgency.

11. On the understanding that the above matters would be given priority, the Meeting decided also to examine the other issues referred to in the note by the President.

C.   Election of officers

12. On the nomination of the Eastern European Group of States, the Meeting elected Slovakia as a Vice-President by acclamation.

III.   ESTABLISHMENT OF THE INTERNATIONAL TRIBUNAL FOR THE
       LAW OF THE SEA

A.   Election of the 21 Members of the Tribunal

13. The President explained that out of 21 seats on the Tribunal, 15 seats had already been committed in accordance with article 3, paragraph 2, of Annex VI to the Convention, which provides that there shall be no fewer than three members from each of the five geographical groups as established by the General Assembly of the United Nations. He pointed out that one candidate was a national of a country that was not a member of any such group. He urged the Meeting to adopt a fair and reasonable solution to the question of how to deal with the six remaining seats. He further urged that all candidates must be given an equal opportunity to contest the election. The President proposed, and it was agreed by the Meeting, that he would hold informal consultations on the question.

14. On the basis of his consultations and various suggestions made, the President put forward a proposal (SPLOS/L.3). After further consultations, the President issued a revised proposal (SPLOS/L.3/Rev.1), which contained the procedures for the election of the Members of Tribunal. That proposal was adopted by consensus on 31 July 1996.

15. In adopting the proposal contained in SPLOS/L.3/Rev.1 the Meeting, *inter alia*, decided that the 21 Members of the Tribunal shall be elected as follows: 5/

    (i)   Five judges from the African Group;

    (ii)   Five judges from the Asian Group;

    (iii) Four judges from the Latin American and Caribbean Group;

    (iv)   Four judges from the Western European and Other States Group;

    (v)   Three judges from the Eastern European Group;

The decision also provided that in case there was a candidate who did not belong to any regional group, that candidate would be grouped with any of the regional groups mentioned above according to the principles contained in the Convention. For the purpose of the current election, the candidate who was a national of a State which did not belong to any regional group, if elected, would be within the allocation in (iv) above.

16.   On 1 August, the Meeting proceeded to the election.   Ireland, the Federated States of Micronesia, Slovenia, Uruguay and Zambia were appointed Tellers for the election.

17.   Eight rounds of balloting were conducted.

18.   At the first round, 100 valid ballots were cast.   There were no invalid ballots and no abstentions.   The following candidates were elected with the required majority of 67 votes: 6/   Mr. Caminos (Argentina) (78), Mr. Kolodkin (Russian Federation) (79), Mr. Laing (Belize) (88), Mr. Marotta Rangel (Brazil) (74), Mr. Marsit (Tunisia) (74), Mr. Nelson (Grenada) (84), Mr. Park (Republic of Korea) (69), Mr. Rao (India) (68), Mr. Vukas (Croatia) (80), Mr. Warioba (United Republic of Tanzania) (68), Mr. Wolfrum (Germany) (76), Mr. Yamamoto (Japan) (82) and Mr. Yankov (Bulgaria) (85).

19.   After the second round of balloting, with 100 ballots cast, one invalid ballot and no abstention, Mr. Treves (Italy) was elected with 67 votes, against the required majority of 66.

20.   At the third round of balloting, 99 ballots were cast with 1 invalid ballot and no abstentions.   No candidate received the required majority of 66 votes.

21.   Following the third round, the representatives of Austria, Côte d'Ivoire, Finland and Zaire withdrew the candidatures of Mr. Rosenne, Mr. Degni-Segui, Mr. Hakapää and Mr. Bula-Bula, respectively, whom their Governments had nominated.

22.   A fourth round was then carried out, with 100 ballots cast.   There were no invalid ballots and no abstentions.   The following candidates were elected with the required majority of 67 votes: Mr. Mensah (Ghana) (81) and Mr. Ndiaye (Senegal) (82).

23.   Thereafter, in accordance with the agreed procedure, the President suspended the meeting briefly in order to allow some time for reflection.   When the meeting was reconvened, the representatives of the Sudan, Mali and Sri Lanka respectively withdrew the candidatures of Mr. El-Hussein, Mr. Fomba and Mr. Pinto.

24.   A fifth round of balloting was carried out for the remaining seats.   There were 99 ballots cast with no invalid ballots and no abstentions.   The required majority was 66 votes and Mr. Akl (Lebanon) (80) and Mr. Eiriksson (Iceland) (74) were elected.

25.   Thereafter, the representative of Uganda withdrew the candidature of Mr. Ochan.

26.   At the sixth round of balloting, 98 ballots were cast with no invalid ballots and no abstentions.   The required majority was 66 votes and Mr. Engo (Cameroon) (81) and Mr. Zhao (China) (69) were elected.

27.   Thereafter, the representative of Australia withdrew the candidature of Mr. Shearer.

28.   At the seventh round of balloting, 97 ballots were cast, with no invalid ballots and two abstentions.   No candidate obtained the required majority of 64 votes.

29.   An eighth round of balloting was then carried out.   Ninety-seven ballots were cast, with 1 invalid ballot and 2 abstentions.   The required majority was 63 and Mr. Anderson (United Kingdom of Great Britain and Northern Ireland) (63) was elected.

30.   On 2 August, in accordance with article 5, paragraph 2, of Annex VI to the Convention and the agreed procedure, the Director of the Office of the Legal

Counsel, Office of Legal Affairs, in his capacity as representative of the Secretary-General, drew lots on the terms of office of the 21 Members of the Tribunal, with the following results:

(a) Seven Members to serve a 3-year term: two from the African Group: Mr. Engo and Mr. Warioba; two from the Asian Group: Mr. Akl and Mr. Rao; one from the Eastern European Group: Mr. Kolodkin; one from the Latin America and Caribbean States Group: Mr. Marotta Rangel; and one from the Western European and Other States Group: Mr. Wolfrum;

(b) Seven Members to serve a 6-year term: one from the African Group: Mr. Ndiaye; one from the Asian Group: Mr. Zhao; one from the Eastern European Group: Mr. Yankov; two from the Latin America and Caribbean States Group: Mr. Caminos and Mr. Laing; and two from the Western European and Other States Group: Mr. Eiriksson and Mr. Treves;

(c) The remaining seven Members would serve for the full nine-year term: Mr. Marsit, Mr. Mensah, Mr. Park, Mr. Yamamoto, Mr. Vukas, Mr. Nelson and Mr. Anderson.

31. The President on behalf of the States Parties congratulated those elected to the Tribunal. He stated that the States Parties had selected an outstanding set of individuals to compose the Tribunal. The President believed that the opinions and pronouncements of the Tribunal, which was of equal efficacy to any other existing tribunal, would be carefully watched and in time achieve a status second to none. The President further stated that the election of the complete set of 21 Members of the Tribunal was a rare and historical opportunity to introduce a new "breed" and large number of international lawyers in the international judicial ranks. The President repeated his opening remarks that the success of the Tribunal would depend on how user-friendly and how innovative it would be. He concluded that the international community had revolutionized the international law of the sea, and since the Tribunal was the product of that revolution, it was to be hoped that it would continue that process of reform and reflect the new realities in international relations.

B. <u>Other matters relating to the establishment of the Tribunal</u>

32. The President recalled that the initial budget of the Tribunal had been approved at the fourth Meeting. 7/ The Secretariat had advised States Parties on their advance contribution in order that preparatory work could be undertaken by the Secretariat. The responses received by the end of July had been very limited in number: out of 85 States Parties, only 13 States had paid their advance contributions, totalling approximately US$ 289,000. In the meantime, preparations for the Tribunal by the host city of Hamburg and the German Federal Government, including for the ceremonial inauguration to be held on 18 October 1996, were well under way, for which he expressed appreciation on behalf of the Meeting of States Parties.

33. On 25 July, the Meeting decided to authorize the Tribunal, as a matter of priority, to undertake negotiations with the United Nations on relationship arrangements and with Germany on a headquarters agreement. 8/ At the same meeting, the States Parties also decided to authorize the Tribunal to enter into negotiations with the International Seabed Authority on relationship arrangements.

34. The Meeting was informed by the representative of Germany on matters relating to the convening of the first meeting of the Members of the Tribunal, the ceremonial inauguration of the Tribunal and the practical arrangements with regard to its seat in Hamburg.

35. It also considered certain administrative matters to facilitate the establishment of the Tribunal. Thus, the Meeting decided to authorize the

Tribunal to establish its own financial and staff rules and regulations to be submitted to the Meeting for consideration. It also decided to request the Tribunal to apply for membership in the United Nations Joint Staff Pension Fund with the understanding that such a request would require the sponsorship of States Members of the United Nations in the General Assembly.

36. On the issue of a report on the Tribunal's activities, the Meeting agreed that although the Secretary-General's report under article 319 of the Convention and his annual report under the item "Law of the Sea" at the General Assembly should cover those activities to a certain extent the Tribunal should also be encouraged to present a report on its work directly to the Meeting of States Parties. It also recognized that since the proceedings of the General Assembly were of interest to the Tribunal, the Tribunal should be appropriately represented at the meetings of the Assembly and should apply for observer status.

IV.   CONSIDERATION OF THE DRAFT AGREEMENT ON THE PRIVILEGES AND IMMUNITIES OF THE TRIBUNAL

37. The Meeting of States Parties decided to create a working group of the whole to discuss the draft Agreement on the Privileges and Immunities of the Tribunal (SPLOS/WP.2 and Add.1). Mr. P. Tomka of Slovakia, one of the Vice-Chairmen of the Meeting, was appointed Chairman of the Working Group.

38. The Working Group held three meetings, but owing to lack of time it was not able to complete its review of the draft Agreement.

39. The President suggested that in order to have sufficient time to consider the proposals put forward by the German delegation on the question of taxes and customs duties, a discussion of the proposal should be postponed until the next session. He stated that the matter was important and would affect the Tribunal and set a precedent for the negotiations of the Headquarters Agreement between the Tribunal and the host country. Since the Tribunal was to convene in October 1996, it would have the opportunity to look at the proposals and perhaps give its views so that they could be taken into account at the next Meeting of States Parties. He stated that while he could agree with the suggestion of the representative of Germany that experts on fiscal and customs matters be included in the delegations of States Parties for the deliberations on the issues at the next Meeting, he felt that the issues under consideration were not merely tax and customs issues but also those of privileges and immunities and therefore were of a legal and political nature and should also be seen in that light. The President further stated that if a country submitted itself as a host country for an international body, it also assumed certain obligations in respect of that body, unless those obligations were expressly excluded at the time the decision was taken to select the host country concerned. In that regard the host country was required to provide the same level and standard of privileges and immunities for the Tribunal and its functionaries as was well established in international practice. No attempt whatsoever should be made to undermine such practice. A change in circumstances should not result in a change in the terms of the acceptance of a particular host country; otherwise the terms of such an acceptance would have to be looked at very carefully. He expressed the hope that the States Parties would conclude discussions of the agreement at its next Meetings, adopt it and seek accession thereto.

40. The States Parties decided to hold further meetings on the draft Agreement and finalize it at the next Meeting of States Parties in March 1997.

V.   PREPARATIONS FOR THE ESTABLISHMENT OF THE COMMISSION ON THE LIMITS OF THE CONTINENTAL SHELF

A.   Dates for the nomination and election of the members of the Commission

41.   The Meeting decided that the first election of all 21 members of the Commission would commence on 13 March 1997 at the sixth Meeting of States Parties, to be held from 10 to 14 March 1997.

42.   Furthermore, it was decided that:

(a)   The nominations of candidates would open on 11 November 1996 for any State Party.   States in the process of becoming a party to the Convention could also nominate candidates.   The nominations by the latter States would remain provisional and would not be included in the list to be circulated by the Secretary-General of the United Nations in accordance with article 2, paragraph 2, of Annex II to the Convention, unless the States concerned had deposited the instrument of their ratification or accession on or before 5 February 1997;

(b)   The nominations would close on 5 February 1997;

(c)   The list of candidates would be circulated by the Secretary-General on 14 February 1997;

(d)   Subject to the above, all procedures relating to the election of the members of the Commission as provided by the Convention shall apply;

(e)   No changes might be made to the above schedule unless the States Parties agreed by consensus.

B.   Documentation prepared by the Secretariat

43.   The Meeting took note of the study by the Secretariat entitled "Commission on the Limits of the Continental Shelf: Its functions and scientific and technical needs in assessing the submission of a Coastal State" (SPLOS/CLCS/INF/1).

44.   The Secretariat circulated draft rules of procedure of the Commission, which it had prepared at the request of the Meeting (SPLOS/CLCS/WP.1).

VI.   OTHER MATTERS

A.   Reports of the Credentials Committee

45.   On 25 July 1996, the Meeting of States Parties appointed a Credentials Committee consisting of the following members: Cameroon, Croatia, Germany, Malta, Marshall Islands, Philippines, Senegal, Trinidad and Tobago and Uruguay.

46.   The Credentials Committee held its first meeting on 30 July and elected Mr. Gilberto B. Asuque (Philippines) as its Chairman.   At that meeting, it examined the credentials of representatives to the fifth Meeting of States Parties.

47.   On 31 July, the Committee presented its first report (SPLOS/12 and Corr.1) to the Meeting, which approved the report.

48.   On the same day, the Committee held its second meeting to examine additional credentials.   A second report (SPLOS/13) of the Credentials Committee was presented to and approved by the Meeting of States Parties later on the same day.

49. At its two meetings held during the fifth Meeting, the Credentials Committee examined and approved credentials submitted by representatives of 100 States Parties to the Convention.

B. Dates and programme of work for the sixth and seventh Meetings

50. The Meeting decided to hold its sixth Meeting from 10 to 14 March 1997.

51. The following programme of work was adopted for the sixth Meeting:

(a) Election of the President of the Meeting of States Parties;

(b) Election of the 21 members of the Commission on the Limits of the Continental Shelf;

(c) Consideration of the draft Agreement on Privileges and Immunities of the International Tribunal for the Law of the Sea.

52. The Meeting of States Parties decided also to hold its seventh Meeting in New York from 19 to 23 May 1997. That session would be convened to deal in particular with the budget of the Tribunal.

C. Concluding statement by the President

53. In his closing statement, the President stated that the current Meeting of States Parties was the last that he would be chairing, and thanked delegations for their guidance and cooperation. His preoccupation throughout his long involvement with the law of the sea had been to keep all parties together in spite of different views that had previously prevailed on parts of the Convention and to promote convergence. In that regard, the Agreement on the implementation of Part XI constituted a success and one of the most critical achievements since it had opened the door for universal participation. He felt confident that with the important milestone of over 100 States becoming parties to the Convention, still more ratifications would be forthcoming. The President stated that he felt great satisfaction in having guided the work at the formative stage of establishing the institutions under the Convention. He said that the Convention had established norms for the conduct of relations among States on maritime issues. Although there were conflicts in the oceans, they were not based on what the law was, but rather related to its interpretation and its application in particular situations. The Convention had also provided peaceful means for the settlement of disputes relating to areas covering some 70 per cent of the Earth's surface. Tremendous progress had thus been achieved, with a very important and significant contribution to peace and security of the world.

Notes

1/   The previous four Meetings of States Parties were held on 21 and 22 November 1994, from 15 to 19 May 1995, from 27 November to 1 December 1995 and from 4 to 8 March 1996.

2/   SPLOS/8, para. 16.

3/   SPLOS/2/Rev.3.

4/   Mr. Satya Nandan was elected in March 1996 Secretary-General of the International Seabed Authority.

5/   SPLOS/L.3/Rev.1, para. 2.

6/   Figures in parentheses indicate votes obtained.

7/   SPLOS/WP.3/Rev.1.

8/   See LOS/PCN/152, Vol. I (LOS/PCN/SCN.4/WP.16/Add.2), p. 91.

-----

44. FUNCTIONS OF THE ISBA IN THE FIRST YEAR OF ITS FULL FUNCTIONAL PHASE, INCLUDING MATTERS PENDING FROM THE WORK OF THE PREPCOM FOR THE ISBA/ITLOS - REPORT OF THE UN SECRETARY-GENERAL

Doc. no.: ISBA/A/10   26 July 1996

EXECUTIVE SUMMARY

1.   The present report describes the functions of the International Seabed Authority and the matters that it has to attend to during the early stages of its operations. An attempt has been made in the paper to review these functions, in order to establish a programme of work for the Secretariat.

2.   The functions of the Secretariat of the Authority derive from the responsibilities of the Secretary-General under the United Nations Convention on the Law of the Sea and the Agreement relating to the Implementation of Part XI of the Convention (hereinafter referred to as the Implementing Agreement), and from the functions to be undertaken by the Assembly, the Council, the Legal and Technical Commission, the Finance Committee and any subsidiary bodies to be established by the Assembly.

3.   The functions of the Secretariat outlined below are based on the early functions of the Authority as indicated in the Implementing Agreement as well as the matters that have been transmitted to the Authority by the Preparatory Commission for the International Seabed Authority and for the International Tribunal for the Law of the Sea (hereinafter referred to as the Preparatory Commission) and include, inter alia, the matters arising from the implementation of resolution II, and the review and completion of the draft seabed mining code, taking into account the provisions of the Implementation Agreement in relation thereto, and the review and completion of other agreements.

4.   In addition to the substantive functions identified in this report, there are a number of internal and external administrative functions that are to be undertaken by the Secretariat on behalf of the Authority, which arise from the Authority's status as an autonomous international organization whose ultimate objective is to administer the Area for commercial purposes and to benefit mankind from the eventual exploitation of the mineral resources of the Area.

5.   As a result of the review of the substantive functions of the Secretariat of the Authority, it became apparent that while a considerable amount of work has been undertaken in respect of the rules and regulations for the protection and preservation of the marine environment from activities in the Area, this work has not been completed and requires further review in the light of new information. In addition, the review reveals that a considerable amount of

research work on this subject-matter had, and continues to take place by national bodies, research institutions, pioneer investors and potential applicants. In order to complete this aspect of the draft seabed mining code, it will be useful to come to a common understanding in a number of areas, such as the establishment of acceptance criteria (a kind of basic standard for protecting the environment against harmful effects) and the linkages between, *inter alia*, the Authority's monitoring programme, the programme for oceanographic and baseline environmental studies and the assessment of the potential environmental impacts of proposed activities in a plan of work.

6.   With regard to the non-environment parameters of the content of a plan of work for exploration, the review also reveals that, based on considerations such as annual periodic reports of the registered pioneer investors, it would be very useful to come to a common understanding on their achievements and to establish reasonable performance targets during the 15-year period of an approved plan of work for exploration.

7.   It is important to note that, in addition to the substantive functions described in the present report, the Secretariat is responsible for providing the services that facilitate the deliberations of the representatives of Member States in the Assembly, the Council, the Legal and Technical Commission and the Finance Committee and that part of the work programme that they assign to it. These services include, *inter alia*, producing reports and other documents that facilitate their deliberations; secretariat services to the organs and subsidiary bodies, including the provision of secretaries; meeting services (interpretation, verbatim reporting and précis-writing services); providing editorial, translation and documents reproduction services for the issuance of the documents of the Authority in the different working languages; organizing conferences, expert group meetings, seminars and workshops on topics of concern; and providing the programme planning, financial, personnel, legal, administrative, management and general services essential for the rational selection of work items and allocation of resources for the effective, economic and efficient performance of the functions of the Authority.

8.   Finally, in relation to the protocol functions of the Secretariat and the status of the Authority as an autonomous international organization, the varied responsibilities of the Secretariat as contained in the draft Headquarters Agreement must be pointed out.

CONTENTS

CONTENTS (continued)

I. INTRODUCTION

1.   The functions reviewed below are reproduced from paragraph 5 of section I of the Annex to the Agreement Relating to the Implementation of Part XI of the United Nations Convention on the Law of the Sea of 10 December 1982 (hereinafter referred to as the Implementing Agreement). Paragraph 16 of section I of the Annex to that Agreement states that

> "The draft rules, regulations and procedures and any recommendations relating to the provisions of Part XI, as contained in the reports and recommendations of the Preparatory Commission, shall be taken into account by the Authority in the adoption of rules, regulations and procedures in accordance with Part XI and this Agreement".

As a result, the review undertaken is to establish the point of departure for the Authority in discharging each function based on Part XI, the Implementing Agreement and the reports and recommendations of the Preparatory Commission as appropriate.

2.   In this regard, for each function, an effort is made to:

(a) Identify the extent to which there was agreement on the modalities for discharging the function as reflected in the relevant reports of the Preparatory Commission;

(b) Establish the effect of relevant provisions of the Implementing Agreement on the outcome of the deliberations of the Preparatory Commission as contained in its reports and recommendations;

(c) Identify the priority tasks that are required to be undertaken by the Authority in discharging those functions that have to be completed in the first year of its full functional phase in accordance with paragraphs 2 and 3 of section 1 of the annex to the Implementing Agreement.

3. The list of functions that the Authority is required to concentrate on until the approval of the first plan of work for exploitation is reproduced below. It will also be recalled that in accordance with paragraph 1 of section 2 of the Annex to the Agreement, the Secretariat of the Authority is also expected to provide services to facilitate the performance of the functions of the Enterprise until it begins to operate independently of the Secretariat.

(a) <u>Functions of the Authority</u>

(i) Processing of applications for approval of plans of work for exploration in accordance with Part XI and the Implementing Agreement;

(ii) Implementation of decisions of the Preparatory Commission for the International Seabed Authority and for the International Tribunal for the Law of the Sea (hereinafter referred to as the Preparatory Commission) relating to the registered pioneer investors and their certifying States, including their rights and obligations, in accordance with article 308, paragraph 5, of the Convention and resolution II, paragraph 13;

(iii) Monitoring of compliance with plans of work for exploration approved in the form of contracts;

(iv) Monitoring and review of trends and developments relating to deep seabed mining activities including regular analysis of world metal market conditions and metal prices, trends and prospects;

(v) Study of the potential impact of mineral production from the Area on the economies of developing land-based producers of those minerals which are likely to be most seriously affected, with a view to minimizing their difficulties and assisting them in their economic adjustment, taking into account the work done in this regard by the Preparatory Commission;

(vi) Adoption of rules, regulations and procedures necessary for the conduct of activities in the Area as they progress. Notwithstanding the provisions of annex III, article 17, paragraph 2 (b) and (c), of the Convention, such rules, regulations and procedures shall take into account the terms of the Interim Agreement, the prolonged delay in commercial deep seabed mining and the likely pace of activities in the Area;

(vii) Adoption of rules, regulations and procedures incorporating applicable standards for the protection and preservation of the marine environment;

(viii) Promotion and encouragement of the conduct of marine scientific research with respect to activities in the Area and the collection and dissemination of the results of such research and analysis, when available, with particular emphasis on research related to the environmental impact of activities in the Area;

(ix) Acquisition of scientific knowledge and monitoring of the development of marine technology relevant to activities in the Area, in particular technology relating to the protection and preservation of the marine environment;

(x)   Assessment of available data relating to prospecting and exploration;

(xi) Timely elaboration of rules, regulations and procedures for exploitation, including those relating to the protection and preservation of the marine environment.

(b)   Functions of the Enterprise

(i)   Monitoring and review of trends and developments relating to deep seabed mining activities including regular analysis of world metal market conditions and metal prices, trends and prospects;

(ii) Assessment of the results of the conduct of marine scientific research with respect to activities in the Area, with particular emphasis on research related to the environmental impact of activities in the Area;

(iii) Assessment of available data relating to prospecting and exploration, including the criteria for such activities;

(iv) Assessment of technological developments relevant to activities in the Area, in particular technology relating to the protection and preservation of the marine environment;

(v)   Evaluation of information and data relating to areas reserved for the Authority;

(vi) Assessment of approaches to joint-venture operations;

(vii) Collection of information on the availability of trained manpower;

(viii) Study of managerial policy options for the administration of the Enterprise at different stages of its operation.

4.   It is apparent from the above lists that the functions contained in items (b), (i) to (iv) to be performed by the Authority on behalf of the Enterprise are already incorporated in the functions of the Authority in respect of data gathering for decision-making.

II. SUBSTANTIVE FUNCTIONS OF THE AUTHORITY DURING ITS EARLY FUNCTIONAL PHASE

A.   Rules, regulations and procedures relating to the conduct of activities in the Area

5.   During 1997, the first year of the full functional phase of the Authority, not all the functions listed in the Implementing Agreement will be initiated by the Authority. In keeping with paragraph 2 of section 1 of the Annex to the Implementing Agreement, it is necessary to identify those functions that are most likely to be initiated and for which the Secretariat must be in a position to provide the services that will facilitate the deliberations of the representatives of Member States in the Assembly, the Council, the Finance Committee and the Legal and Technical Commission as required. With respect to the conduct of activities in the Area, the Implementing Agreement, *inter alia*, establishes when registered pioneer investors may submit applications for approval of plans of work for exploration and provides guidelines on the content of applications for the approval of a plan of work for exploration and the procedures relating thereto, the internal procedures for the Council and the Legal and Technical Commission regarding the consideration of such applications and decision-making, and the terms of contract.

6.   In accordance with paragraph 6 (ii) of section 1 of the Annex to the Implementing Agreement, registered pioneer investors may request approval of

their plans of work for exploration within 36 months of the entry into force of the Convention (i.e., by 15 November 1997). In accordance with the same provision, for registered pioneer investors,

> "The plan of work for exploration shall consist of documents, reports and other data submitted to the Preparatory Commission both before and after registration and shall be accompanied by a certificate of compliance, consisting of a factual report describing the status of fulfilment of obligations under the pioneer investor regime, issued by the Preparatory Commission in accordance with resolution II, paragraph 11 (a)".

7.   Paragraphs 6 (a) (i) of section 1 of the Annex to the Implementing Agreement establishes the financial and technical qualifications necessary for the approval of a plan of work submitted on behalf of a State or entity, or any component thereof referred to in resolution II, paragraph 1 (a) (ii) or (iii), other than a registered pioneer investor, which had already undertaken substantial activities in the Area prior to the entry into force of the Convention.   In keeping with the principle of non-discrimination, paragraph 6 (a) (iii) establishes that such applicants shall obtain similar treatment to that received by registered pioneer investors.

8.   Paragraph 7 of section 1 of the Annex to the Implementing Agreement also requires that any application for approval of a plan of work for exploration shall be accompanied by an assessment of the potential environmental impacts of the proposed activities and by a description of a programme for oceanographic and baseline environmental studies in accordance with the rules, regulations and procedures adopted by the Authority.

9.   Other than these references to the content of an application for approval of a plan of work for exploration and the content of a plan of work, the only documentation available for the consideration of the Legal and Technical Commission in the formulation of rules, regulations and procedures for the approval of applications for plans of work for exploration are the reports and recommendations of the Preparatory Commission.

10.   Indeed, a similar analysis of the framework and guidelines provided by the Implementing Agreement in relation to the complete set of regulations and procedures until the Council approves a recommendation by the Legal and Technical Commission points once again to the reports and recommendations of the Preparatory Commission.

11.   These considerations require that a thorough review of the draft regulations relating to prospecting and exploration as well as the content of applications for the approval of plans of work for exploration considered by the Preparatory Commission be conducted together with an assessment of existing knowledge of the environmental impacts of activities in the Area, with a view to reformulating them in accordance with the Agreement and its Annex.   To meet the deadline prescribed by the Agreement would require the adoption of the rules, regulations and procedures for the matters discussed in paragraph 5 above by the second part of the third session of the Assembly of the Authority in 1997, in order to provide the applicants time to submit their applications in accordance with the rules, regulations and procedures of the Authority.

B.   Regulations on the protection and preservation
        of the marine environment

12.   Special Commission 3 of the Preparatory Commission was charged with the mandate to prepare rules, regulations and procedures for the exploration and exploitation of the polymetallic nodules in the Area.   Document LOS/PCN/SCN.3/WP.6 (Draft regulations on prospecting, exploration and exploitation of polymetallic nodules in the Area) was issued in 1985 and accepted by Special Commission 3 of the Preparatory Commission as the basis for discussion of its mandate to prepare rules, regulations and procedures for the

exploration and exploitation of the polymetallic nodules in the Area, i.e., the seabed mining code. 1/ As pointed out in the explanatory note to that document, the set of articles contained therein begins with scope and use of terms, and goes on in sequential order to deal with prospecting and applications for approval of plans of work for activities in the Area, i.e., draft regulations on the content of applications for approval of plans of work, procedures relating thereto and terms of the contract. While the draft regulations did not contain provisions of the Convention dealing with general principles and objectives of Part XI which are constitutional in character and not of a regulatory nature, a set of addenda were issued to it, some of which contain provisions that are relevant to processing of applications for approval of plans of work for exploration in accordance with Part XI and the Implementing Agreement.

13. With regard to specific provisions dealing with the processing of applications for approval of plans of work for exploration, Parts III and IV of LOS/PCN/SCN.3/WP.6 provide a sequential order to deal with the application. Part III - Applications for Approval of Plans of Work is divided into four sections dealing with general provisions, content of the application, Plans of Work and Fees respectively. Part IV - Processing of Applications is divided into two sections dealing with Recording and transmittal of applications, and consideration of applications, approval of plans of work and execution of contracts. Within each section of both parts of the document are contained the specific provisions of relevance to that section. For example, under section 3, (Plans of Work) of Part III are provisions dealing with the contents of a proposed plan of work for exploration, the contents of a proposed plan of work for exploitation and Preference and priority among applicants.

14. Although the Implementing Agreement renders the provisions contained in some of the addenda that were issued for clarity and certainty to document LOS/PCN/SCN.3/WP.6 inapplicable, a number of them contain provisions of relevance to the content of applications for approval of a plan of work for exploration, procedures relating thereto and terms of contract. These are:

    (a) LOS/PCN/SCN.3/WP.6/Add.5 - Protection and preservation of the marine environment from activities in the Area;

    (b) LOS/PCN/SCN.3/WP.6/Add.6 - Accommodation of activities in the Area and in the marine environment;

    (c) LOS/PCN/SCN.3/WP.6/Add.8 - Labour, health and safety standards.

15. Document LOS/PCN/SCN.3/WP.6 was discussed at 31 formal and informal meetings of Special Commission 3 in 1985 and 1986. In 1988, the Chairman of Special Commission 3, Mr. Jaap Walkate (Netherlands), after taking into account discussions on the document, revised it and issued it as document LOS/PCN/SCN.3/WP.6/Rev.1. 2/

16. The views expressed by delegations during the consideration of LOS/PCN/SCN.3/WP.6 and WP.6/Rev.1 are contained in the statements to the Plenary by the Chairman of Special Commission 3 (LOS/PCN/L.16, LOS/PCN/L.26 and LOS/PCN/L.32). 3/

17. Document LOS/PCN/SCN.3/WP.6/Add.5, "Protection and preservation of the marine environment from activities in the Area", was discussed at 25 meetings of the Special Commission in 1990 and 1991. The working paper was revised by the Chairman following several sessions of informal consultations and was issued on 27 August 1991 under a new title, "Protection and preservation of the marine environment from unacceptable changes resulting from activities in the Area" (LOS/PCN/SCN.3/WP.6/Add.5/Rev.1). 4/

18. For details on the issues of substance addressed during the consideration of LOS/PCN/SCN.3/WP.6/Add.5, see the statements to the Plenary by the Chairman of Special Commission 3 (LOS/PCN/L.79, LOS/PCN/L.84 and LOS/PCN/L.89). 5/

19. Document LOS/PCN/SCN.3/WP.6/Add.8, "Labour, health and safety standards" was discussed at six meetings of the Special Commission during the spring of 1992. During those discussions, a representative of the International Labour Organization (ILO) made a statement relating to the working paper and the role of the ILO in establishing labour standards. 6/

20. Of the three addenda to LOS/PCN/SCN.3/WP.6, document LOS/PCN/SCN.3/WP.6/Add.5 and its revision (LOS/PCN/WP.6/Add.5/Rev.1) as well as the documents containing the issues of substance addressed during their consideration are the main documents that along with the Implementing Agreement significantly add to the draft regulations on the content of applications for approval of plans of work, procedures relating thereto and terms of contract.

21. With regard to the regulations contained in documents LOS/PCN/SCN.3/WP.6/Add.5 and WP.6/Add.5/Rev.1, it will be recalled that in accordance with paragraph 12 of document LOS/PCN/L.87 (annex) relating to the Understanding on the Fulfilment of Obligations by the Registered Pioneer Investors and their certifying States, the Group of Technical Experts established in accordance with paragraph 6 of document LOS/PCN/L.41/Rev.1, annex, was mandated to review the state of deep seabed mining and to make an assessment of the time when commercial production might be expected to commence, within three months of the deposit of the sixtieth instrument of ratification or accession to the Convention. In paragraph 29 of document LOS/PCN/BUR/R.32 which contains the report by the Group of Technical Experts, it is stated:

> "The Group wishes to draw the attention of the Preparatory Commission to the importance of the environmental protection provisions of modern regulatory regimes. In the case of land-based mining, the approach to integrating environmental and economic objectives in a regulatory regime is cited by the mining industry as a significant factor that influences their investment decisions.

> "This part of the deep seabed mining regime has yet to mature and there are many details and procedures to be worked out. There remains the potential for the regime to be developed in a manner that will promote investment or discourage it." 7/

22. Within this context, account must be taken of four other functions that the Authority is required to concentrate on under the terms of the Agreement which are directly related to the processing of applications for approval of plans of work for exploration. These are:

    (a) Adoption of rules, regulations and procedures incorporating applicable standards for the protection and preservation of the marine environment;

    (b) Monitoring of compliance with plans of work for exploration approved in the form of contracts;

    (c) Promotion and encouragement of the conduct of marine scientific research with respect to activities in the Area and the collection and dissemination of the results of such research and analysis, when available, with particular emphasis on research related to the environmental impact of activities in the Area;

    (d) Acquisition of scientific knowledge and monitoring of the development of marine technology relevant to activities in the Area, in particular technology relating to the protection and preservation of the marine environment.

23. Taken together with the provision that "the duration of a plan of work for exploration shall be 15 years", 8/ and the requirement of paragraph 7 of section 1 of the Annex to the Agreement which requires that

"An application for approval of a plan of work shall be accompanied by an assessment of the potential environmental impacts of the proposed activities and by a description of a programme for oceanographic and baseline studies in accordance with the rules, regulations and procedures adopted by the Authority",

the four additional functions noted above provide a long-term basis for the Authority to adopt regulations that take advantage of current knowledge of the environmental impact of activities in the Area, and through the approved plans of work for exploration and other mechanisms such as the promotion and encouragement of the conduct of marine scientific research with respect to the environmental impact of activities in the Area, to establish measures to protect the environment and monitor the effectiveness of these safeguards, in particular for subsequent exploitation activities in the Area. In any event, rules, regulations and procedures incorporating applicable standards for the protection and preservation of the marine environment in consonance with the scope and means of verification by the Authority of compliance with measures to protect the environment will be required in some form before plans of work for exploration can be approved.

24. Prior to the commencement of commercial exploitation and during the exploration phase for mining polymetallic nodules, it is important to continue national and international cooperative research efforts that have been conducted to determine the significance of the impacts that could arise from collecting, washing and lifting nodules from the seabed to the sea surface on the ability of the organisms that inhabit these environments to reproduce and repopulate the said areas.

25. The results of these research efforts will be invaluable in the formulation of acceptance criteria that will form the material content of standards for protecting the environment against harmful effects caused by certain activities.

26. At the present time knowledge is limited with regard to the environmental effects of commercial exploitation of deep seabed polymetallic nodules on the deep seabed itself. It has been suggested that the acquisition of the detailed knowledge of the environmental effects will necessarily involve comprehensive and large-scale activities over a prolonged period of time. In this context it is important to note the number of cooperative arrangements that were entered into by pioneer investors with other pioneer investors and potential applicants and reported upon in their periodic reports to the Preparatory Commission. 9/

27. It will be recalled that the Legal and Technical Commission is expected to make recommendations to the Council on, inter alia,

(a) The protection of the marine environment, taking into account the views of recognized experts in that field (article 165, para. 2 (e));

(b) The establishment of a monitoring programme to observe, measure, evaluate and analyse, by recognized scientific methods, on a regular basis, the risks or effects of pollution of the marine environment resulting from activities in the Area and to ensure that existing regulations are adequate and complied with (article 165, para. 2 (h));

(c) The implementation of the monitoring programme approved by the Council (article 165, para. 2 (h));

(d) The establishment of appropriate mechanisms for directing and supervising a staff of inspectors who shall inspect activities in the Area to determine whether the provisions of Part XI, the rules, regulations and procedures of the Authority and terms and conditions of any contract with the Authority, are being complied with (article 162, para. 2 (m)).

The Commission will also, *inter alia*:

(e) Formulate and submit to the Council the rules, regulations and procedures referred to in article 162, paragraph 2 (o), taking into account all relevant factors including assessment of the environmental implications of activities in the Area.

28. To facilitate this work, a need appears to exist to convene a group of experts meeting/workshop to assess the current state of knowledge on the environmental consequences of deep seabed mining. Such a workshop will have multiple objectives including recommendations on the most appropriate acceptance criteria for formulating standards for the protection of the environment against harmful effects and modifying them as more information becomes available, the status of national and international environmental impact study programmes and recommendations for additional work resulting from completed studies, a framework within which future work can be undertaken, whether as part of scientific research or as a component of the plan of work for exploration, approved in the form of a contract incorporating the major elements of the monitoring programme of the Authority.

C. Regulations on the non-environment related elements
of a plan of work for exploration

1. Administering the resources of the Area 10/

29. The area of the world's oceans totals approximately 361.1 million square kilometres (sq km), which represents 71 per cent of the Earth's surface. If all coastal States were to claim a 200-nm exclusive economic zone limit, the extent of ocean areas under national jurisdiction would be approximately 109.4 million sq km, making the size of the area beyond the limits of national jurisdiction (the Area) approximately 251.7 million sq km or 49 per cent of the Earth's surface. 11/

30. Article 157, paragraph 1, of the Convention states that:

"The Authority is the organization through which States Parties shall, in accordance with this Part, organize and control activities in the Area, particularly with a view to administering the resources of the Area."

31. In view of the interest of States Parties in conservation and rational management in the development of the resources of the Area, 12/ the Authority needs an effective and sustained effort to collect, manage and distribute information on the Area in order, *inter alia*, to provide an adequate understanding of the environmental impacts likely to be caused by deep seabed mining, to estimate the magnitude of the polymetallic nodule resources in the world's oceans, in particular the potentially recoverable resources in various ocean areas, and, in accordance with paragraph 2 of article 143 of the Convention, to promote and encourage marine scientific research to foster the objective of States Parties to increase the global reserves of the metals available in polymetallic nodules.

32. The interests of the Enterprise, which is to conduct its initial operations through joint ventures, are best served, in accordance with paragraph 1 of article 170 of the Convention, by its participation in activities in the Area through the reserved areas. Indeed, the area reserved for the Authority in the central region of the north-east Pacific Ocean is the only mine site for which the Authority already has a comprehensive plan for exploration that provides an assessment of the geological and related data available to formulate the plan and that sets out the objectives, estimated costs, nature and form of information required at various stages, and the duration of the plan. As such it is the area for which the Authority has the most resource assessment data.

33. The same reserved area also has been the site where collaborative efforts among pioneer investors have demonstrated the possibilities that exist in that regard. 13/

2. Polymetallic nodule resource data for the Area

34. Recent years have seen considerable activity to generate survey data as well as detailed information concerning deep seabed areas expected to contain mineral deposits. In addition to polymetallic nodule resources that the Convention identifies as the priority mineral resources for which rules, regulations and procedures are to be adopted and approved by the Assembly, 14/ other known mineral resources drawing considerable interest are cobalt-rich manganese oxide on bedrock, polymetallic sulphide deposits along ocean-floor spreading centres and red clay deposits. With respect to these and other minerals to be found in the Area, the Convention stipulates that rules, regulations and procedures for the exploration and exploitation of such resources shall be adopted within three years from the date of a request to the Authority by any of its members for the adoption of such rules in respect of such resources. 15/ With regard to polymetallic nodule resources, prospecting and pioneer activities have resulted in basic information that has made it possible to indicate the resource potential in future mining areas. The characteristics of these selected areas are also important for the design of mining equipment and for concept selection. The deep seabed area is vast and to date only a very small portion of it has been explored and charted. Three ocean areas in the Area are considered as primary areas:

(a) The Clarion-Clipperton area between the west coast of the continental United States and Hawaii, whose size is approximately 2.5 million sq km. Hitherto, the largest nodule resources have been found in this area between the two fracture zones, Clarion and Clipperton, in the Pacific Ocean. Several nations and consortia have been carrying out prospecting and surveying work in order to register the precise location, scope and accessibility of these resources. Indeed six of the areas registered to the pioneer investors can be found in this area; 16/

(b) The second area lies in the south-western Pacific basin. This area is about 1 million sq km;

(c) The third area, in the central Indian Ocean basin, is about 500,000 sq km. The pioneer site awarded to India is in this area.

35. These three areas account for about 2 per cent of the Area. Analyses of stations in the Scripps Institution of Oceanography's sediment data bank reveal, however, that several other areas appear to contain sufficiently metal-rich nodules to justify exploration for sites suitable for first-generation mining. These include, *inter alia*, the Peru basin (between latitude 8° and 5° S and longitude 90° and 92° W), the South Atlantic Ocean (between latitude 23° and 45° S and longitude 5° W and 30° E) and the central south equatorial Indian Ocean.

36. Assessments prior to the establishment of the Authority and based on public data took the form of compilations of chemical data from the literature and were presented as tables and maps. 17/ As sampling increased, the development of computerized data banks, nodule chemical data and computerized mapping became a necessity. 18/ Worldwide, as the results of various prospecting expeditions became available, various regions of the world ocean in the Area were assessed for their resource potential. These included utilizing, *inter alia*, the work of the R.V. Valdiva and the R.V. Gaveshani in the Indian Ocean, the results obtained by CNEXO from 13 cruises in the South Pacific and CCOP/SOPAC also in the South Pacific, and cruises conducted by the Geological Survey of Japan in the north central Pacific as well as United States-based consortia and registered pioneer investors.

3. Resource assessments after the registration of pioneer investors

37. It will be recalled that after the registration of France, Japan and the Russian Federation, the Group of Technical Experts of the Preparatory Commission was convened to prepare a comprehensive plan for the early stages of exploration of one mine site in the area reserved for the Authority in the central region of the north-east Pacific, indicating the nature of activities to be undertaken, the data and information to be obtained and the costs involved.

38. In the report of the Group of Technical Experts to the General Committee (LOS/PCN/BUR/R.5), the Group of Experts suggested that the exploration plan should be broken down into two stages:

(a) Stage I would be designed to provide additional information on the total area and to establish a uniform database to allow identification of prime areas;

(b) Stage II would be designed, through evaluation of the results of stage I, to undertake detailed survey activities to identify possible mine sites and the reserves that could be mined. 19/

39. The Group considered that the exploration plan as developed in its report would be completed at the same time that mining and processing technology were tested and considered appropriate, adequate mine sites identified, the market environment proved attractive for investment, and when a decision to proceed to a feasibility study would have to be taken.

40. In chapter IV of the report prepared by IFREMER/AFERNOD, DORD and Yuzhmorgeologiya in fulfilment of the obligations to undertake this work in respect of their contributed areas, titled "Preparatory work in the International Seabed Authority reserved area - August 1991", they make the following statement with regard to some of the technological problems that will have to be overcome to facilitate stage I exploration and its impact on the assessment of polymetallic nodule resources in the reserved area.

"The multi-frequency exploration system (MFES) and seismo-acoustic methods yield valuable information on the continuity of manganese nodules coverage on the sea floor in broad areas. However, the density of the information is not adequate to estimate the resources of each mineable field in the area reserved for the Authority. This is confirmed by geostatistical calculations using data from neighbouring areas. Only a global estimation can be made of the in situ resources of polymetallic nodules, which is equal to 565 million wet tonnes.

"From the available information, it is also difficult to identify the best areas for future detailed exploration, because:

- The density of station data information is not regular over the area reserved for the Authority;

- The bathymetric methods used were not sufficiently reliable for specific mapping of the bottom relief.

"The best objective of exploration during stage I would be to delineate the best areas for detailed exploration, leaving aside some parts of lesser economic interest.

"From the present knowledge acquired by the three pioneer investors, the following recommendations can be made:

- A complete survey of the area reserved for the Authority by multi-beam echosounder;

-     Additional survey using multi-frequency acoustic systems to
      complete the grid on the whole area reserved for the Authority;

-     Additional sampling stations to complete the grid of information
      on the whole area reserved for the Authority.

"All those surveys must be done using the best navigation systems
presently available."

41.   The preparatory work was subsequently reviewed by the Group of Technical
Experts, which made, *inter alia*, the following observations on the report with
respect to the information provided on the bathymetry of the area, the
concentration of the information for estimating the resources in mineable areas
and the systems used for surveying the area: 20/

"Bathymetry

"This limitation of bathymetric maps in providing detailed local
topography is exemplified when a comparison is made among the
interpretations obtained by each pioneer investor of the same part of the
area reserved for the Authority. While main features of the relief are
present in the three maps prepared by the three pioneer investors
respectively, such as a small seamount culminating at 4,500 metres in one
instance, some details were missed by one pioneer investor or another.
(This is a common problem because, *inter alia*, the sea floor tracks covered
by different investigators can vary.)

"Concentration of information for estimating the
resources in mineable areas

"However, the concentration of the information is not adequate to
estimate the resources of each mineable field within the area reserved for
the Authority. This is confirmed by geostatistical calculations using data
from neighbouring areas. Thus, only a 'global estimation' could be made of
the *in situ* resources of the whole of the area reserved for the Authority.
(In 'global estimation' (global in the sense that the whole of the relevant
area is covered), the total amount of polymetallic nodules in the whole of
the area reserved for the Authority is computed by multiplying the average
abundance for the whole of the area reserved for the Authority by the total
surface, i.e., 71,750 square kilometres; this method contrasts with the
method of estimating the resources of specific parts of the whole area and
adding those estimates to arrive at the total for the whole. The
application of the latter method was not possible owing to the inadequacy
of the concentration of information.)

"Survey systems

"As the report of the three pioneer investors explained, measurements
obtained from equipment held at the sea surface lack the necessary accuracy
and resolution to display bottom features of less than a few tens of metres
in width. Detailed exploration to assess the location of all possible
obstacles to mining as well as the distribution and content of nodule
fields must rely upon more sophisticated systems. However, with most
sophisticated systems currently available, the time needed to survey large
areas is tremendously long and the cost very high, because (a) the width of
the area surveyed along the track is very limited, and (b) the along-track
speed of the system is very slow."

4. Activities undertaken by the registered pioneer investors in their pioneer areas

42. It is important to note that since their registration, each of the six registered pioneer investors has undertaken some work in the area allocated to them in respect of up to four critical areas; exploration, environmental baseline studies, design and development of a test deep seabed mining system and extraction of the metals of interest from polymetallic nodules. Of direct relevance to the Authority until the approval of the first plan of work for exploitation are those activities connected to:

(a) Exploration (stage I of the comprehensive plan);

(b) Environmental baseline studies;

(c) Design and development of a test deep seabed mining system (end of stage II of the comprehensive plan for exploration).

43. As part of its mandate to review the state of deep seabed mining and to assess the time when commercial production might be expected to commence, the Group of Technical Experts, drawing upon information notes provided to it by the registered pioneer investors as well as their annual periodic reports, made the following summary of the activities of the six registered pioneer investors since their registration. 21/

"India

"After the registration of India as a pioneer investor, exploration activities have continued with the use of improved technologies. These have included sea floor mapping of the entire area (150,000 sq km) using a multi-beam swath bathymetric mapping system called Hydrosweep, sampling of polymetallic nodules at closer grids, geotechnical studies and collection of baseline environmental data in addition to gravity and magnetic data.

"As a first step towards the development of various components of deep seabed mining technology, a design and development programme has been initiated. The first phase of the programme, aimed at the development of a polymetallic nodule collector system for testing on land and in a shallow basin, has been completed. The second phase of the programme covers the design of a collector unit, studies of hydraulic and airlift systems, development of a remotely operated vehicle for pipelines inspection, waterproofing, development of an electrical/hydraulic component for underwater use, a hydraulic nodule pick-up system and an instrumentation and control system, etc.

"In the field of extractive metallurgy, 3 of the 15 processing routes for extraction of metals have been selected for upscaling. The campaigns at the upscaled levels are in progress.

"Deep Ocean Resources Development Co., Ltd. (DORD) - Japan

"Exploration work has been carried out by collecting polymetallic nodules, conducting chemical analyses of the nodules and compiling detailed topographic data. Exploration work will be continued. The research and development project of the mining system has been carried out since 1981 and a comprehensive ocean test is planned to take place in 1996 for obtaining efficient and sufficient data and information for future commercial deep seabed mining. 22/

"The project entailing metal recovery from polymetallic nodules has been carried out since 1989.

"Baseline environmental investigations were begun in 1991. Using the
data from these investigations, a model will be elaborated which will
enable the estimation of the environmental impact on the ocean, including
its ecosystem.

"IFREMER/AFERNOD - France

"Following the result of the pre-feasibility study carried out from
1984 to 1989, IFREMER/AFERNOD took the decision to reduce its activities
and limit them only to the fulfilment of its obligations under
resolution II and a general monitoring of the situation.

"This monitoring included the revision and compilation of all acquired
data, the reorganization of the databases and a continuous survey of the
evolution of the metals market and the world economy.

"Yuzhmorgeologiya - Russian Federation

"Since August 1990 Yuzhmorgeologiya has not conducted regular
geological and geophysical research aimed at further enhancing the study of
polymetallic nodules in the sector allocated to it because it was concluded
that there was a high degree of probability that industrial extraction of
nodules in the Clarion-Clipperton zone could not commence before the year
2010.

"Research efforts have concentrated on correlation and statistical
analysis of the information already obtained: verification of certain
general trends throughout the Clarion-Clipperton zone, technical and
economic studies ot the feasibility of industrial extraction of nodules and
selection and study of the monitoring zones required for the conduct of
environmental experiments.

"China Ocean Mineral Resources Research and Development Association (COMRA) - China

"COMRA is in the process of implementing a long-term programme
focusing on exploration, design and development of a deep seabed mining
system and of processing techniques. Other investigations are being
conducted to compare planning options and to develop market projections for
future supply and demand of metals as well as to establish an economic
model for the exploitation of polymetallic nodules.

"Priority is being given to exploring the remaining part of the
pioneer area with a view to reducing the intervals between sampling
stations as well as the grids used in order to identify the deep seabed
mining area. Efforts include developing the technical criteria for both
exploration at sea and laboratory analyses and testing, preparing standard
samples and establishing a database. Survey work includes geological
sampling, bottom photography and geophysical surveys.

"Research is being carried out on ore collection and lifting,
including a remote operational system. The current work in extractive
metallurgy is devoted to carrying out comparative studies on several
processes in the laboratory and studies on ore dressing techniques, such as
the technique for special processing of polymetallic nodules and the study
on high-efficiency flotation agents.

"Interoceanmetal Joint Organization (IOM) - Poland

"Activities of IOM have focused on the following areas: correlation
of the results of regional geological and geophysical studies of the site

reserved for IOM; research into the development of technologies for deep seabed mining and the metallurgical processing of polymetallic nodules; and preparation of a computerized database on the site reserved for the Authority."

5. Status of exploration

44. On the basis of the exploration effort reported upon since registration along with the results of the preliminary work done by IFREMER/AFERNOD, DORD and Yuhzmorgeologiya in the Authority's reserved area as a precursor to stage I of the comprehensive exploration plan, it is very difficult to assess the results of the pioneer work undertaken since registration in relation to exploration. While it is clear that a fundamental consideration in the resource assessment work that has to be conducted during stage I of exploration will require improvements in the survey systems (reduction in the length of time for surveys and associated costs) and methods for bathymetric mapping of the bottom relief (reliability), the progress made in these areas since registration is unknown to the Authority. The reports submitted by the pioneer investors are for the most part inadequate to obtain a clear picture of their progress, pointing to a need for a more precise format. 23/

45. With regard to the progress that has been made since registration in relation to exploration, it is proposed that a workshop/seminar be convened to assess the current state of deep seabed mineral exploration with a view to determining if there are any outstanding technical issues to be overcome as well as to provide the Authority with a clear set of guidelines for work that may be expected of a contractor in a plan of work for exploration approved in the form of a contract (stage I of the exploration plan).

46. The considerations given above together with the progress achieved by the registered pioneer investors in their efforts to convert polymetallic nodule resources to reserves provide part of the basis for the work that the Authority has to fulfil to, _inter alia_, administer the polymetallic nodule resources of the Area.

47. In addition, with respect to the Area, the Authority will need to initiate its own resource assessment work taking into account its mandate to administer the resources of the Area and to facilitate the conversion of resources to reserves of metal as follows:

   (a) <u>Global estimates</u>. Recovering data in the public domain on resources of the Area, in particular, polymetallic nodules, with a view to estimating their economic potential;

   (b) <u>Regional estimates</u>: Recovering data available on polymetallic nodule resources in the primary areas (Clarion-Clipperton, South Pacific Ocean and central Indian Ocean basin) with a view to monitoring trends in the development of technologies for mining nodule resources as well as encouraging marine scientific research and the work of contractors in the conversion of potential ore bodies located in these areas to reserves;

   (c) <u>Site-specific information</u>, developed from its reserved areas and allocated areas on the conversion process. This would include the results of measures taken during the exploration phase to protect the environment and to monitor the effectiveness of environmental safeguards during the subsequent exploitation phase, and resource conservation issues in connection with mining (pattern mining as opposed to mining of the richest zones of a mine site first) and the issue of the retention of manganese tailings in a three-metal operation.

48. The effectiveness of the Authority's work in resource assessment of polymetallic nodules in the Area will be greatly facilitated by its ability to take advantage of advantage in computer technology and software designed for

this purpose. A fundamental consideration in this regard is for the Authority
to obtain the bathymetry of the relevant parts of the Area and to acquire the
capability to zoom in and out of various parts of the Area. Bathymetric charts
showing the contour of the sea floor are, like topographic maps on land, the
basis on which many other types of information are plotted. It is essential
that good bathymetric charts be available if other information, such as the
distribution of geologic formations and structures and delineation of mineral
deposits are to be analysed and interpreted in a meaningful way. Mineral
resource data are also best portrayed by means of graphical representations.
Mapping (bathymetric charts) and graphical representations of mineral resource
data can both be achieved at the present time through computer applications. As
a result, the Authority will require this capability (personnel as well as
software and hardware) to effectively discharge its functions.

6.   Design and development of a test deep seabed mining system

49.   In respect of the work undertaken by the registered pioneer investors in
this regard, the Group of Technical Experts reported that India, Japan and to a
limited extent China and Poland had been active during the period. France had
taken the decision to reduce its activities and to monitor the situation while
the Russian Federation had reported no activities in this regard. It was stated
that India had completed "the first phase of a design and development programme
aimed at the development of a polymetallic nodule collector system for testing
on land and in a shallow basin" and that Japan, which had been carrying out a
research and development effort since 1981, was planning a comprehensive ocean
test in 1996 "to obtain efficient and sufficient data and information for future
commercial deep seabed mining." 24/

50.   In the same report, the Group of Technical Experts stated:

> "In the field of deep seabed mining, two of the three basic design
> concepts have been abandoned or shelved: the continuous line-bucket dredge
> and the shuttle system. The system envisaged and developed in parts
> included the collection of polymetallic nodules by either a towed or a
> self-propelled collector, and the lifting of nodules through a 5-km-long
> vertical riser pipe utilizing a centrifugal pump or an air lift. However,
> an integrated mining system, even on a pilot scale of long duration, has
> not yet been demonstrated. The collector system, to be operational in a
> high-pressure and low-temperature environment while operating on soil of
> poor strength, demands special equipment components and material which need
> to be tested in the actual deep seabed environment. The development of an
> integrated mining system that would be operational in an actual deep seabed
> environment on a sustained basis is demanding both in terms of time and
> effort and requires substantial financial inputs." 25/

51.   It will be recalled also that in two consecutive annual reports presented
by IOM and its certifying States, they call for cooperation in the development
of technologies for deep seabed mining "with a view to reducing costs while
simultaneously enhancing the effectiveness of research." 26/

52.   In view of the above, a need appears to exist to convene a seminar/workshop
to help to identify the most effective and cost-efficient system, and to explore
possible areas of cooperation in the development of deep seabed mining
technology, bringing together registered pioneer investors, potential applicants
for approval of plans of work for exploration and concerned organizations,
institutions and potential suppliers of such technology.

7.   Functions of the Authority during 1997

53.   In the light of the priority issues and functions identified for the
Authority during the early stages of its full functional phase and the need to

adopt an evolutionary approach in the setting up and the functioning of the organs and subsidiary bodies of the Authority, it may be said that during 1997, the Authority shall begin to implement the functions specified below, which form a part of the functions specified by the Implementing Agreement in paragraph 5 of section 1 of the Annex:

(a) Processing of applications for approval of plans of work for exploration in accordance with Part XI and the Implementing Agreement;

(b) Implementation of decisions of the Preparatory Commission relating to the registered pioneer investors and their certifying States, including their rights and obligations, in accordance with article 308, paragraph 5, of the Convention and resolution II, paragraph 13;

(c) Monitoring of compliance with plans of work for exploration approved in the form of contracts;

(d) Adoption of rules, regulations and procedures necessary for the conduct of activities in the Area as they progress. Notwithstanding the provisions of annex III, article 17, paragraph 2 (b) and (c), of the Convention, such rules, regulations and procedures shall take into account the terms of the Implementing Agreement, the prolonged delay in commercial deep seabed mining and the likely pace of activities in the Area;

(e) Adoption of rules, regulations and procedures incorporating applicable standards for the protection and preservation of the marine environment;

(f) Promotion and encouragement of the conduct of marine scientific research with respect to activities in the Area and the collection and dissemination of the results of such research and analysis, when available, with particular emphasis on research related to the environmental impact of activities in the Area;

(g) Acquisition of scientific knowledge and monitoring of the development of marine technology relevant to activities in the Area, in particular technology relating to the protection and preservation of the marine environment;

(h) Assessment of available data relating to prospecting and exploration.

Functions of the Enterprise. On behalf of the Enterprise, these functions are:

(a) Evaluation of information and data relating to areas reserved for the Authority;

(b) Collection of information on the availability of trained manpower;

(c) Assessment of approaches to joint-venture operations.

III. MATTERS PENDING FROM THE WORK OF THE PREPARATORY COMMISSION

54. The statement of the Chairman of the Preparatory Commission at the end of its resumed twelfth session (1994, New York) provided an updated report on the status of the implementation of the obligations of the registered pioneer investors under resolution II and the related understandings (LOS/PCN/L.115/Rev.1). In that statement, in relation to the certificate of compliance that the General Committee of the Preparatory Commission had agreed to provide each registered pioneer investor, it is indicated that:

"There will be annexed to each certificate a revised version of the report on the status of implementation of the obligations of the registered pioneer investors under resolution II and the related understandings

(LOS/PCN/BUR/INF/R.12), supplemented by documents LOS/PCN/BUR/R.43,
LOS/PCN/BUR/R.44, LOS/PCN/BUR/R.45, LOS/PCN/BUR/R.46 and other relevant
documents. This document will be issued under the symbol LOS/PCN/145."

55. By the final session of the Preparatory Commission, seven pioneer investors
had been registered by the General Committee (the executive body of the
Preparatory Commission for the implementation of resolution II). These were
India on 17 August 1987, IFREMER/AFERNOD (France), DORD (Japan) and
Yuzhmorgeologiya (Union of Soviet Socialist Republics) all on 17 December 1987,
COMRA (China) on 5 March 1991, Interoceanmetal Joint Organization (Bulgaria,
Cuba, Czech and Slovak Federal Republic, Poland and Union of Soviet Socialist
Republics) on 21 August 1991 and the Republic of Korea on 2 August 1994.

56. Pursuant to the decisions of the General Committee to register the pioneer
investors, a series of understandings on the fulfilment of obligations by the
registered pioneer investors and their certifying States was subsequently
adopted. The understandings created several new obligations as a quid pro quo
for the waiver of certain conditions for registration required under
resolution II, and the granting of certain concessions to the first group of
pioneer investors such as self-selection of substantial parts of the areas
allocated to them.

57. The obligations of the registered pioneer investors are considered under
the following headings: (a) periodic expenditures; (b) reporting by the
certifying State; (c) provision of data; (d) relinquishment; (e) exploration
plan for reserved areas in the central region of the north-east Pacific; and
(f) training.

A. Periodic expenditures by registered pioneer investors

58. Resolution II, paragraph 7 (c), calls for periodic expenditures by pioneer
investors in the pioneer areas of an amount to be determined by the Preparatory
Commission. For India, France, Japan and the Russian Federation, paragraph 4 of
LOS/PCN/L.87, annex, states that periodic expenditures incurred in respect of
the development of their respective pioneer areas shall be determined by the
Preparatory Commission in consultation with and with the cooperation of each
registered pioneer investor within 12 months of the adoption of the
Understanding. The Understanding was adopted on 30 August 1990.

59. By paragraph 4 of LOS/PCN/L.102, annex, the same obligation applies to
COMRA, and by paragraph 4 of LOS/PCN/L.108, annex, to IOM. By paragraph 4 of
LOS/PCN/L.115/Rev.1, annex, the same obligation also applies to the Government
of the Republic of Korea.

Status

60. The Preparatory Commission did not determine the amount of the periodic
expenditures. The Commission recognized that it was difficult during its period
of existence to provide annual amounts of expenditure (LOS/PCN/L.113/Rev.1,
para. 13). The Russian Federation reported a total expenditure for 1990-1991 of
US$ 850,000 (LOS/PCN/BUR/R.14). No other pioneer investor provided the
Preparatory Commission with annual expenditure amounts.

B. Reporting by the certifying State

61. Resolution II, paragraph 12 (b) (ii), requires the certifying State to
report on activities carried out by it, its entities or natural or juridical
persons. Paragraph 5 of LOS/PCN/L.87, annex, provides that reports to the
Commission on pioneer activities as defined in resolution II, paragraph 1 (b),
carried out in the areas by the registered pioneer investors would be provided
annually by the concerned certifying States (India, France, Japan and the
Russian Federation). Paragraph 5 of LOS/PCN/L.102, annex, paragraph 5 of

LOS/PCN/L.108, annex, and paragraph 5 of LOS/PCN/L.115/Rev.1, annex, contain the same obligation for the certifying States: China, Bulgaria, Cuba, Czech and Slovak Federal Republic, Poland and the Russian Federation, and the Republic of Korea respectively.

Status

62. The following periodic reports on the activities of the registered pioneer investors were submitted to the Preparatory Commission by the certifying States:

Certifying State	Documents	Period covered
India 1991	LOS/PCN/BUR/R.11 (27 February 1992)	1 September 1990-31 December 1991
	LOS/PCN/BUR/R.24 (27 March 1993)	1 January-31 December 1992
	LOS/PCN/BUR/R.34 (7 February 1994)	1 January-31 December 1993
Japan 1991	LOS/PCN/BUR/R.12 and Corr.1 (28 February 1992)	1 September 1990-31 December 1991
	LOS/PCN/BUR/R.23 (25 March 1993)	1 January-31 December 1992
	LOS/PCN/BUR/R.35 (31 January 1994)	1 January-31 December 1993
France 1991	LOS/PCN/BUR/R.13 (2 March 1992)	1 September 1990-31 December 1991
	LOS/PCN/BUR/R.22 (23 March 1993)	1 January-31 December 1992
	LOS/PCN/BUR/R.31 (31 January 1994)	1 January-31 December 1993
Russian Federation	LOS/PCN/BUR/R.14 (6 March 1992)	16 August 1990-1 January 1992
	LOS/PCN/BUR/R.25 (26 March 1993)	1 January-31 December 1992
	LOS/PCN/BUR/R.43 (2 August 1994)	1 January 1993-1 August 1994
China	LOS/PCN/BUR/R.20 (2 March 1993)	1 January-31 December 1992
	LOS/PCN/BUR/R.33 (1 February 1994)	1 January-31 December 1993
Bulgaria, Cuba, Czech and Slovak Federal Republic, Poland and Russian Federation	LOS/PCN/BUR/R.30 (2 September 1993)	20 August 1992-30 June 1993
Republic of Korea		

Other than the Russian Federation, which submitted a periodic report through 1 August 1994, India, Japan, France and China submitted periodic reports through 31 December 1993. Poland submitted a periodic report on behalf of the certifying States of IOM through 30 June 1993.

63. It will be recalled that paragraph 5 of document LOS/PCN/L.114/Rev.1 states that

"During the discussion of this item in the General Committee certain delegations stated that it was difficult to understand the scientific terms used in the reports. It was also suggested that a more systematic format should be used for these periodic reports. In addition, the view was expressed that these reports should indicate the impact of the activities of the registered pioneer investors on the marine environment."

The Authority may wish to address this matter.

C. Provision of data

64. The three registered pioneer investors IFREMER/AFERNOD (France), DORD
(Japan) and Yuzhmorgeologiya (Russian Federation) were required as part of their
preparatory work to compile and illustrate all the existing data in the areas
reserved for the Authority (LOS/PCN/L.87, annex, para. 7 (a)).

65. By paragraph 8 of LOS/PCN/L.102, annex, LOS/PCN/L.108, annex, and
paragraph 7 of LOS/PCN/L.115/Rev.1, annex, COMRA (China), IOM (Bulgaria, Cuba,
Czech and Slovak Federal Republic, Poland and Russian Federation) and the
Republic of Korea respectively were required to provide computer diskettes
containing data collected by them on stations, grade and abundance of nodules in
the areas reserved for the Authority resulting from their registration.

Status

66. IFREMER/AFERNOD, DORD and Yuzhmorgeologiya submitted a joint report
entitled "Preparatory work in the International Seabed Authority reserved
area - August 1991" to the Preparatory Commission. That report was considered
by the Group of Technical Experts from 18 to 20 February 1992. The Group found
that the objective of the preparatory work had been fully met.

67. China submitted a diskette containing the required data to the Preparatory
Commission (LOS/PCN/BUR/R.21).

68. The delegation of Poland, on behalf of IOM, submitted a preliminary report
containing the required data (LOS/PCN/BUR/R.46).

69. The Government of the Republic of Korea was only registered by the General
Committee as a pioneer investor on 2 August 1994; it is now to submit the
required data to the Authority.

D. Relinquishment

70. Under resolution II, paragraph 1 (e), the pioneer investor shall relinquish
portions of the pioneer area to revert to the Area, in accordance with the
following schedule:

    (a) 20 per cent of the area allocated by the end of the third-year from
the date of the allocation;

    (b) An additional 10 per cent of the area allocated by the end of the
fifth year from the date of the allocation;

    (c) An additional 20 per cent of the area allocated or such larger amount
as would exceed the exploitation area decided upon by the Authority in its
rules, regulations and procedures, after eight years from the date of allocation
of the area or the date of the award of a production authorization, whichever is
earlier.

Status

71. In document LOS/PCN/L.41/Rev.1, annex, it is stated that applicants which
had relinquished in advance portions of the application areas simultaneously
with the application would be deemed to have complied with resolution II,
paragraph 1 (e). This applies to France, Japan and the Russian Federation.

72. LOS/PCN/L.41/Rev.1, annex, paragraph 13 (3), requires India to conform to
the provisions on relinquishment of resolution II. Under those provisions,
India, which became a registered pioneer investor on 17 August 1987, was due to
relinquish 20 per cent of its allocated area by 17 August 1990, a further
10 per cent of the area allocated by 17 August 1992 and an additional
20 per cent by 17 August 1995.

73. India notified the General Committee that, in accordance with resolution II, 20 per cent of its pioneer area (30,000 sq km) had been relinquished. The area relinquished was that bounded by the lines joining the turning-points and the geographical coordinates indicated in the schedule annexed to document LOS/PCN/BUR/R.44. The date 17 August 1992 marked the fifth year of India's allocation and 17 August 1995 the eighth. India is therefore still to relinquish the remaining 30 per cent of its pioneer area.

74. The Interoceanmetal Joint Organization, registered on 21 August 1991, was due to relinquish 20 per cent of its allocated area by 21 August 1994 and a further 10 per cent of the area allocated by 21 August 1996.

75. The delegation of Poland, on behalf of the registered pioneer investor, IOM, and its certifying States, notified the General Committee that, in accordance with the schedule established in paragraph 1 (e) (i) of resolution II, IOM had relinquished 20 per cent of the pioneer area that was situated in the southern part of the pioneer area and adjoined the area reserved for the Authority. The relinquished area measured 30,672 sq km or 20.45 per cent of the pioneer area (LOS/PCN/BUR/R.45).

76. COMRA (China), which became a registered pioneer investor on 5 March 1991, was due to relinquish 20 per cent of its allocated area by 5 March 1994 and a further 10 per cent of the allocated area by 5 March 1996.

77. At the twelfth session of the Preparatory Commission, held at Kingston from 7 to 11 February 1994, China had reported the sinking of its research vessel R.V. <u>Xiangyanghong 16</u>. As a consequence China had to postpone its arrangements to comply with the prescribed schedule for the relinquishment of areas (LOS/PCN/L.114/Rev.1, para. 14). China reiterated its intention to relinquish 30 per cent of its allocated area at the end of the fifth year, in accordance with resolution II, paragraph 1 (e). As 5 March 1996 marked the end of the fifth year, China is still to relinquish 30 per cent of its allocated area.

78. The Republic of Korea, registered on 2 August 1994, is due to relinquish 20 per cent of its allocated area by 2 August 1997 and a further 10 per cent of the allocated area by 2 August 1999.

79. The General Committee recommended to the International Seabed Authority that the Council should continue monitoring the relinquishment of areas by the registered pioneer investors. 27/

E. <u>Exploration plan for reserved areas in the central region of the north-east Pacific</u>

General plan

80. A comprehensive plan for the early stages of exploration of one mine site in the area reserved for the Authority in the central zone of the north-east Pacific is contained in a report of the Group of Technical Experts to the General Committee (LOS/PCN/BUR/R.5).

Preparatory work

81. Three registered pioneer investors, IFREMER/AFERNOD (France), DORD (Japan) and Yuzhmorgeologiya (Russian Federation), had to prepare jointly the preparatory work which consisted of compiling and illustrating all the existing data on the areas reserved for the Authority in the central region in order to facilitate detailed planning and implementation of the first stage of the exploration plan.

Status

82.   The list of data and information gathered by France, Japan and the Russian
Federation on the Authority's reserved areas was submitted in August 1991.   The
report, entitled "Preparatory work in the International Seabed reserved
area - August 1991", was submitted to the Preparatory Commission and considered
by the Group of Technical Experts from 18 to 20 February 1992.   The Group found
that the objective of the preparatory work had been fully met and recommended
that the implementation of stage I of the exploration plan could then be
undertaken.   It also recommended that a detailed plan of work and operational
schedule for stage I could be developed jointly by the three pioneer investors
(LOS/PCN/BUR/R.10).

83.   The General Committee approved the recommendations of the Group of
Technical Experts on 12 March 1992 (LOS/PCN/L.102).

Stage I of the plan for exploration

84.   The basis of the obligation for the first group of applicants (France,
Japan and the Russian Federation) to assist the Preparatory Commission in the
exploration of a mine site and in the preparation of a plan of work with respect
to the mine site is to be found in document LOS/PCN/L.41/Rev.1, annex,
paragraph 14, which states:

> "Notwithstanding the provisions of paragraph 12 (a) (i) of
> resolution II, the first group of applicants will assist the Preparatory
> Commission and the Authority in the exploration of a mine site for the
> first operation of the Enterprise and in preparing a plan of work in
> respect of such a mine site.   The conditions and extent of this assistance
> will be discussed and agreed following registration, applying
> mutatis mutandis the provisions of paragraph 7 (c) of resolution II."

85.   In the Understanding on the Fulfilment of Obligations of the Pioneer
Investors and their Certifying States of 30 August 1990 (LOS/PCN/L.87,
annex), the three registered pioneer investors (France, Japan and the then
Soviet Union) undertook to carry out stage I of the plan of work for the
exploration in accordance with paragraphs 25 to 35 of LOS/PCN/BUR/R.5.   The work
for stage I of the plan for exploration had to be implemented no later than the
end of the second fiscal year after the completion of the review of the results
of the preparatory work by the Group of Technical Experts, in accordance with
paragraph 17 of LOS/PCN/BUR/R.5.

86.   The cost of stage I work was estimated to be in the range of US$ 7 million
to US$ 9 million, to be shared among the three pioneer investors.

87.   As the report of the preparatory work was approved on 12 March 1992, work
on stage I was to begin no later than the end of 1994 (LOS/PCN/BUR/INF/R.12,
para. 25).

88.   With respect to the annual fixed fee payable under paragraph 7 (b) of
resolution II, the Understanding stated that:

> "Provided that the obligations under paragraphs 2, 7 and 8 above have
> been satisfactorily complied with, the obligations of the three registered
> pioneer investors, France, Japan and the Soviet Union, under resolution II,
> paragraph 7 (b), to pay US$ 1 million per annum shall upon the completion
> of stage I of the exploration plan be waived as of the date of their
> registration." (LOS/PCN/L.87, annex, para. 10).

89.   At the resumed twelfth session (New York, 1-12 August 1994), the General
Committee took up the issues of the annual fixed fee and the obligation of the
three registered pioneer investors, France, Japan and the Russian Federation,
and of their certifying States to carry out stage I of the exploration work.
The General Committee considered the issues relating to the waiver of the annual

fixed fee payable under annex III, article 13, paragraph 3, in the light of the conclusions of the Group of Technical Experts contained in paragraph 57 of its report (LOS/PCN/BUR/R.32) and the decision of the Preparatory Commission embodied in document LOS/PCN/L.87, annex, paragraph 12, and decided to recommend to the Authority that the annual fixed fee by the registered pioneer investors upon the entry into force of the Convention should be waived in a manner consistent with section 8, paragraph 2, of the annex to the Implementing Agreement (LOS/PCN/L.115/Rev.1, para. 16).

90. The General Committee also decided to waive the annual fixed fee of US$ 1 million provided for in resolution II, paragraph 7 (b), as of the date of registration, as also referred to in document LOS/PCN/L.87, annex, paragraph 10.

91. The General Committee considered the obligation of the three registered pioneer investors, IFREMER/AFERNOD, DORD and Yuzhmorgeologiya, and of their certifying States, France, Japan and the Russian Federation, to carry out stage I of the exploration work referred to in LOS/PCN/L.87, annex, paragraphs 7 and 8, and decided, without prejudice to the understanding on stage II contained in LOS/PCN/L.87, annex, paragraph 9, that the performance of this obligation should be deferred until the Legal and Technical Commission determined that substantial exploration work was being carried out by a contractor, unless the Council decided, at the request of any registered pioneer investor, to make adjustments in accordance with paragraph 40 (a) of LOS/PCN/L.87 and section 1, paragraph 6 (a) (iii), of the annex to the Implementing Agreement (LOS/PCN/L.115/Rev.1, para. 17).

F. Training

92. Resolution II, paragraph 12 (a) (ii), requires every registered pioneer investor to provide training at all levels for personnel designated by the Commission. The Special Commission for the Enterprise, Special Commission 2, was established in accordance with paragraph 8 of resolution I of the Third United Nations Conference on the Law of the Sea and was entrusted with the functions referred to in paragraph 12 of resolution II.

93. By paragraph 2 of LOS/PCN/L.87, annex, France, India, Japan and the then Soviet Union were required to provide training pursuant to paragraph 12 (a) (ii) of resolution II in conformity with the specific programme for training approved by the Preparatory Commission in accordance with the principles, policies and guidelines contained in document LOS/PCN/SCN.2/L.6/Rev.1 and LOS/PCN/SCN.2/L.7, taking into account the report contained in document LOS/PCN/BUR/R.6. It was agreed that the cost of such training would be borne by the four registered pioneer investors and would be free of cost to the Preparatory Commission. The precise number of trainees, the duration and the fields of training were to be agreed upon between the Preparatory Commission and each registered pioneer investor according to its capabilities. It was further agreed that the first group of trainees would consist of no fewer than 12 individuals.

94. By paragraphs 2 of LOS/PCN/L.102, annex, LOS/PCN/L.108, annex, and LOS/PCN/L.115/Rev.1, annex, the same obligation as had been agreed upon with respect to the first group of registered pioneer investors, with the exception of the number of individuals to be trained, which it was agreed "shall consist of no less than four individuals", applied to COMRA, IOM and the Government of the Republic of Korea respectively.

Status

95. The Training Panel approved all the training programmes of the registered pioneer investors, i.e., France, Japan, the Russian Federation, India, China and the Interoceanmetal Joint Organization, and selected candidates for the traineeships offered under those programmes. It also received progress reports on the implementation of some of those programmes.

96.   In its final report to the Preparatory Commission, the Training Panel made a number of recommendations to the General Committee on those issues which would be outstanding on 16 November 1994 and thus required the consideration of the Authority.   These recommendations, contained in document LOS/PCN/BUR/R.48, are reproduced below.

G.   Outstanding issues (training)

Monitoring of the implementation of the training programme of the registered pioneer investors

97.   Since the Panel would not be in a position to monitor, on the basis of the progress reports of the registered pioneer investors, the implementation of those training programmes which would not have been completed by the first week of August 1994, the Panel recommended that its monitoring function be continued by the Authority.

Evaluation of the training received

98.   While the Panel was able to evaluate the training received by the three trainees under the training programme of Japan and the training received by one trainee under the training programme of France, it was unable to evaluate the training received by the other trainees.   In this connection, the Panel underlined the necessity for trainees to submit a report on the training they had received.   Evaluations could only be carried out on the basis of both the report of the trainee on the training he or she had received and the report of the registered pioneer investor on the trainee.   A satisfactory outcome of the evaluation process was the prerequisite for a recommendation to the Preparatory Commission to issue a training certificate.

99.   The Panel recommends that the Authority ensure that this evaluation function is continued.

Issuance of training certificates

100. The majority of the trainees were still undergoing training when the final report of the Training Panel was submitted.   The Panel was therefore not in a position to evaluate the training they had received and recommend to the Preparatory Commission the issuance of training certificates to all those who might be eligible.

101. The Training Panel therefore recommended that the Authority issue those training certificates.

Training programmes of new registered pioneer investors

102. Following the approval of the application submitted by the Government of the Republic of Korea as a pioneer investor under resolution II of the Third United Nations Conference on the Law of the Sea at the summer meeting of the Preparatory Commission in August 1994, a training programme was to have been submitted by the Republic of Korea as soon as an understanding on the fulfilment of obligations by that registered pioneer investor was adopted.

103. The Training Panel drew the attention of the Authority to the procedures it had established with respect to the review and approval of training programmes of registered pioneer investors, the elements to be included in the note verbale and the selection of candidates.

Other training programmes

104. It has already been pointed out that the Panel could not pursue the offer of training provided by the Government of Finland.

105. The Training Panel recommended that the offer of training by Finland and any other future offers by other technologically advanced States be pursued by the Authority. It also drew the attention of the Authority to the procedures established by the Panel for the training programmes of non-registered pioneer investors.

106. The Training Panel also drew the attention of the Authority to the offer of training that was made by the Intergovernmental Oceanographic Commission.

IV.   FUNCTIONS OF THE SECRETARIAT OF THE INTERNATIONAL
      SEABED AUTHORITY

107. The Secretariat is one of the three principal organs of the International Seabed Authority, the others being the Assembly and the Council. The Secretariat is to provide services to the Assembly and Council as well as the Legal and Technical Commission and the Finance Committee. In accordance with article 160, paragraph 1, of the Convention, the Assembly has the power to establish general policies in conformity with the relevant provisions contained in Part XI of the Convention and the Implementing Agreement on any questions or matters, within the competence of the Authority. As the executive organ of the Authority and in accordance with article 162, paragraph 1, of the Convention, the Council has the power to establish, in conformity with the Convention, the Implementing Agreement and the general policies established by the Assembly, the specific policies to be pursued by the Authority on any question or matter within the competence of the Authority. The Council supervises and coordinates the implementation of the provisions of Part XI of the Convention and the Implementing Agreement.

108. To assist the Council on matters relating to the exploration for, exploitation and processing of polymetallic nodules, as well as on matters relating to oceanology, protection of the marine environment or economic or legal matters relating to ocean mining and related fields, the Legal and Technical Commission, *inter alia*, makes recommendations on a variety of matters to the Council for its consideration, approval or adoption. These recommendations include those relating to the approval of plans of work for activities in the Area, the protection of the marine environment, the establishment of an environmental monitoring programme for the Authority and that proceedings on behalf of the Authority be instituted before the Seabed Disputes Chamber. The Legal and Technical Commission is also required to assist the Council through the formulation of rules, regulations and procedures on prospecting, exploration and exploitation in the Area.

109. To assist the Assembly or Council on all matters having a financial and budgetary implication, the Finance Committee has to make a recommendation. The Finance Committee also has to make recommendations on, *inter alia*, draft financial rules, regulations and procedures of the organs of the Authority, the financial management and internal financial administration of the Authority, the proposed annual budget prepared by the Secretary-General, the financial aspects of the implementation of the programme of work of the Secretariat and the financial obligations of States Parties to the Convention and the Implementing Agreement.

110. The Secretariat provides the services that facilitate the deliberations of the representatives of States Parties in the Assembly, the Council, the Legal and Technical Commission and the Finance Committee and carries out the work programme they assign to it. The work of the Secretariat is carried out by the staff of the Authority who are appointed by the Secretary-General.

111. With regard to the functions of the Authority as identified in the Implementing Agreement and reproduced below, the broad responsibilities of the Secretariat are as follows:

(a)   Producing reports and other documents containing information, analysis, historical background, research findings, policy suggestions, etc. that facilitate the deliberations and decision-making by the organs and subsidiary bodies of the Authority;

(b)   Providing secretariat services to the organs (e.g., providing secretaries, assisting in planning the work of the sessions and in conducting the proceedings and in drafting reports) and other documents;

(c)   Providing meeting services (interpretation, verbatim reporting and précis-writing services) to the organs, in accordance with the policies adopted by the Assembly;

(d)   Providing editorial, translation and documents reproduction services for the issuance of International Seabed Authority documents in the different working languages, in accordance with the policies adopted by the Authority;

(e)   Conducting studies and providing information that answer to the priority needs of States Parties;

(f)   Producing publications, information bulletins and analytical work which the Assembly has decided should be issued by the Authority in the field concerned;

(g)   Organizing conferences, expert group meetings, seminars and workshops on topics of interest to the Authority;

(h)   Arranging for dissemination to the public of information on the Authority's activities and decisions;

(i)   Providing the programme planning, financial, personnel, legal, management and general services that are essential for the rational selection of work items and allocating resources among them and for the effective, economical and efficient performance of the services and functions of the Secretariat, within the legal framework of regulations, rules and policies adopted by the Assembly.

V.   PROGRAMME OF WORK OF THE SECRETARIAT IN 1997

112. In order to facilitate the processing of applications for the approval of plans of work for exploration in accordance with Part XI of the Convention and the Implementing Agreement within 36 months of the entry into force of the Convention (15 November 1997), rules and regulations on the content of the application and the procedures relating thereto, the internal procedures for the Council and the Legal and Technical Commission regarding the consideration of such applications, the scope and means of verification by the Authority on compliance by contractors and the terms of contract need to have been adopted for provisional application by the Council, pending approval by the Authority, soon enough to provide registered pioneer investors with enough time to submit their applications by the date specified above.

113. While clarity has been provided by the Implementing Agreement in respect of some of the issues raised during discussions in the Preparatory Commission on the protection and preservation of the marine environment from activities in the Area, in a number of areas, such as the incorporation of appropriate acceptance criteria for the protection of the marine environment and subsequent modification of such criteria as more information becomes available, questions remain. The monitoring programme of the Authority, the assessment of the potential environmental impacts of the proposed activities in a plan of work and the programme for oceanographic and baseline environmental studies, while all linked, require further precision through the introduction of scientific indicators.

114. With regard to other non-environmental activities to be included in the plan of work for exploration, activities during the pioneer regime have been varied and the results unknown. In order to ensure that proposed activities and expenditures by contractors reflect the intention to bring mine sites into commercial production within the 15-year time period provided for by the Implementing Agreement, some clarification must be sought from experts on the current status of activities and impediments to the timely conclusion of activities in exploration. Again, this clarification resulting in the general acceptance of certain types of activities as priority tasks would be useful for elaboration of the contents of a plan of work for exploration.

115. To achieve these results it is proposed that, in respect of the adoption and application on a provisional basis of the regulations relevant to the processing of applications for approval of plans of work for exploration by the Council at the resumed third session in 1997, taking into account the fact that the regulations must be formulated and submitted to the Council by the Legal and Technical Commission, the following schedule of activities, which dovetail the requirements of Part XI of the Convention and the Implementing Agreement, be undertaken on behalf of the organs of the Authority by the Secretariat during 1997:

(a) **Protection and preservation of the marine environment**. As a result of the review of the substantive functions of the Secretariat of the Authority, it became apparent that while a considerable amount of work had been undertaken in respect of the rules and regulations for the protection and preservation of the marine environment from activities in the Area, this work has not been completed and requires further review in the light of new information. In addition, the review revealed that a considerable amount of research work on this subject-matter had, and continues to take place by national bodies, research institutions, pioneer investors and potential applicants. In order to complete this aspect of the draft seabed mining code, it will be useful to come to a common understanding in a number of areas such as the establishment of acceptance criteria (a kind of basic standard for protecting the environment against harmful effects) and the linkages between, *inter alia*, the Authority's monitoring programme, the programme for oceanographic and baseline environmental studies and the assessment of the potential environmental impacts of proposed activities in a plan of work;

(b) **Non-environmental related activities in plans of work for exploration**. With regard to the non-environment parameters of the contents of a plan of work for exploration, the review also revealed that, based on considerations such as annual periodic reports of the registered pioneer investors, it would be very useful to come to a common understanding on their achievements and to establish reasonable performance targets during the 15-year period of an approved plan of work for exploration.

116. In addition to the reports and other documents that may be requested of the Secretary-General for the third session of the Assembly in 1997, and the services to be provided the organs of the Authority during that session (secretaries, assisting in planning the work of the session and drafting reports), the Secretariat of the Authority will therefore be responsible for organizing two workshops in 1997, providing secretariat and meeting services for them (interpretation, verbatim reporting and précis-writing services) and also editorial, translation and documents reproduction services.

117. In relation to the resource assessment work to be performed by the Authority, it is suggested that resources be made available to the Secretary-General to, *inter alia*: (a) recruit as core technical staff, specialists in the various disciplines that are required in the exploration/exploitation phase of deep seabed mining; 28/ (b) obtain the services of a systems analyst with demonstrated expertise in mapping; and (c) acquire the necessary computer hardware and software for mapping and providing graphical representations of polymetallic nodule resource data of the various areas and data on baseline environmental conditions that the Authority obtains from the public domain or

otherwise. The facility which such a core group of specialists with such a
computing capability can bring the Authority is noteworthy. In addition to
helping the Authority keep track and continually update resource and
environmental information on the Area as they become available, such a
capability will help the Authority to establish a central data repository of
polymetallic nodule resources of the Area.

<u>Notes</u>

<u>1</u>/   LOS/PCN/SCN.3/1992/CRP.17, para. 6; contained in document LOS/PCN/153
(Vol. XIII) - Report of the Preparatory Commission, under paragraph 11 of
resolution I of the Third United Nations Conference on the Law of the Sea, on
all matters within its mandate, except as provided in paragraph 10, for
presentation to the Assembly of the International Seabed Authority at its first
session; dated 30 June 1995.

<u>2</u>/   Ibid.

<u>3</u>/   See LOS/PCN/153 (Vol. XII).

<u>4</u>/   See LOS/PCN/153 (Vol. XIII).

<u>5</u>/   See LOS/PCN/153 (Vol. XII).

<u>6</u>/   See LOS/PCN/L.99; see also LOS/PCN/153 (Vol. XII).

<u>7</u>/   See LOS/PCN/153 (Vol. III).

<u>8</u>/   Paragraph 9 of section 1 of the Annex to the Implementing Agreement.

<u>9</u>/   Examples include the Benthic Impact Experiment (BIE) international
experiment initiated between the National Oceanographic and Atmospheric
Administration (NOAA) of the United States of America and the Geology Committee
of the Russian Federation. This experiment was later joined by the Metal Mining
Agency of Japan and the Eastern European Consortium Interoceanmetal (IOM). It
was also reported in document LOS/PCN/BUR/R.43 of 2 August 1994, "Periodic
report on the Activities of Yuzhmorgeologiya in the Pioneer Area over the period
1 January 1993 to 1 August 1994", that scientific exchanges were under way with
groups from the Republic of Korea, China and Western Europe. Another example is
provided in document LOS/PCN/BUR/R.30 of 2 September 1993, "Periodic report on
the activities of the Interoceanmetal Joint Organization (IOM) and its
certifying States in the pioneer area from August 1992 to July 1993". In
section IV of that report "Negotiations with other Pioneer Investors and
Potential Applicants to identify possibilities and conditions for cooperation in
exploring and developing specific sites in the Clarion-Clipperton Zone", it is
stated: "This cooperation arises from the need to join forces in exploring and
developing polymetallic nodules with a view to reducing costs while
simultaneously enhancing the effectiveness of research." IOM and COMRA
concluded talks in May 1993 on a cooperative effort in the development of
technologies for deep seabed mining which resulted in the transfer of data and a
commercial quantity of nodules from IOM to COMRA for, <u>inter alia</u>, assessing the
level of environmental pollution from mining them.

<u>10</u>/   Article 133 of the Convention defines the resources of the Area as
follows: "'Resources' means all solid, liquid or gaseous mineral resources
<u>in situ</u> in the Area at or beneath the seabed, including polymetallic nodules."
It will be recalled that in discussions on document LOS/PCN/SCN/WP.6, article 1,
on the question of whether the mining code should apply only to polymetallic
nodules or to other resources, it was decided to concentrate on polymetallic
nodules at the present time in accordance with article 162 (2) (o) (ii) of the
Convention (see LOS/PCN/L.16).

<u>11</u>/   Office of the Geographer, United States Department of States, based on
<u>Limits in the Seas</u>.

12/ Article 150, para. (b).

13/ LOS/PCN/BUR/R.10 and Add.1.

14/ Article 162, para. 2 (o) (ii).

15/ Ibid.

16/ McKelvey, V. E., "Subsea Mineral Resources", U.S. Geological Survey Bulletin 1689-A.

17/ This work was supported by the United States National Science Foundation as part of the International Decade of Ocean Exploration.

18/ The Scripps Institution of Oceanography's World Ocean Sediment Data Bank served as the main compilation and source of chemical data for almost every researcher in the field of manganese nodule resource assessment.

19/ LOS/PCN/153 (Vol. III), document LOS/PCN/BUR/R.10.

20/ Ibid., document LOS/PCN/BUR/R.10/Add.1.

21/ Ibid., document LOS/PCN/BUR/R.32.

22/ It is believed that there has been slippage from the target date of 1996.

23/ LOS/PCN/L.114/Rev.1.

24/ LOS/PCN/153 (Vol. III), document LOS/PCN/BUR/R.32.

25/ Ibid.

26/ Ibid., LOS/PCN/BUR/R.30 and LOS/PCN/BUR/R.39.

27/ LOS/PCN/L.115/Rev.1, para. 7.

28/ The Group of Experts to the Preparatory Commission identified the following priority disciplines for seabed mining: marine geology/geophysics, oceanography, mining engineering, marine ecology and data processing (LOS/PCN/BUR/R.6).

-----

45. STATEMENT OF THE PRESIDENT ON THE WORK OF THE ISBA ASSEMBLY DURING THE RESUMED SECOND SESSION, KINGSTON, JAMAICA, 5-16 AUGUST 1996

Doc. no.: ISBA/A/L.13   11 November 1996

1.   The second part of the second session of the Assembly of the International Seabed Authority was held at Kingston, Jamaica, from 5 to 16 August 1996.

2.   At the opening meeting (the 32nd meeting of the Plenary), I recalled the statement I had made on the work of the Assembly at the conclusion of the first part of the second session of the Assembly, in which I enumerated the most important issues that remained pending before the Assembly and the Council. These issues included the election of the Finance Committee, the election of the next President of the Assembly, the adoption of the rules of procedure of the Council and the election of the Chairman of the Council.   In addition, I noted that the Council had still to elect the members of the Legal and Technical Commission.

3.   It was agreed that the most important issue to be resolved was the election of the members of the Finance Committee since, unless a Finance Committee was formed, there would be difficulty in approving a budget for the Authority.

Status of provisional membership

4.   At the first meeting of this part of the second session I reported to the Assembly on certain technical difficulties that had arisen with regard to the status of the provisional membership of a number of States. Following discussions with the Chairmen of the regional groups on this issue, the Assembly agreed that, in order to facilitate participation in the current meetings of the Authority by those States which have communicated in various forms their intention to continue implementation of the Agreement on a provisional basis but which have not yet, following the entry into force of the Agreement, notified the depositary in the required form, such States should continue to participate in the current meetings of the Authority on a provisional basis.   The decision of the Assembly in this regard is contained in document ISBA/A/L.10.

Election of a President of the Assembly

5.   At the end of the first part of the second session, it was agreed that a new President of the Assembly would be elected at the beginning of the second part of the second session.   Nevertheless, at the first meeting of this part of the second session, there being at that time no candidate for the position of President of the Assembly, the Assembly decided to request me to continue to preside over the work of the Assembly until a new President is elected.

Election of the members of the Finance Committee

6. Noting that several candidates had been nominated for election to the
Finance Committee, I proposed, with the approval of the Assembly, to hold
informal consultations regarding the composition of the Finance Committee with
the Chairmen of the regional groups and the Chairman of the Group of 77. I also
invited to those consultations the coordinators of the interest groups. It was
noted that the criteria for membership of the Finance Committee were set out in
paragraph 3 of section 9 of the Annex to the Implementing Agreement and
included, inter alia, the criterion that due account should be given to
equitable geographical distribution and the representation of special interests.
Following my suggestion, and with the approval of the Assembly, the major part
of the first week of this part of the second session was devoted to intensive
consultations within and among regional groups as to the balance of
representation on the Finance Committee between the regional groups and the
special interest groups mentioned in the Annex to the Implementing Agreement.

7. At the 36th meeting of the Plenary, I reported that, despite intensive
consultations, no consensus had been reached as to the composition of the
Finance Committee. I therefore urged the regional groups to persevere in their
efforts to achieve a consensus, while noting that the need to establish a
Finance Committee was becoming increasingly urgent.

8. At the 37th meeting of the Plenary, I was able to report that substantial
progress had been made, although there was still a need for one regional group
to get instructions. I therefore agreed to postpone the election of the Finance
Committee for one more day in order to enable further consultations to take
place. I also offered, with the approval of the Assembly, to meet with the
Chairmen of each of the regional groups on an individual basis if that would
assist them in reaching a consensus.

9. After further protracted and difficult consultations within and among the
regional groups, and consultations I held, both individually and collectively,
with the Chairmen of the regional groups and the Chairman of the Group of 77, I
was able to announce, at the 38th meeting of the Plenary, that, on the basis of
a proposal for the distribution of seats between the regional groups, it had
been possible for the regional groups to find an accommodation in order that we
could advance our work and proceed to elect a Finance Committee.

10. I informed the Assembly that, in order to enable agreement to be reached on
the proposal so as to accommodate some regional interests, it had been agreed
that:

(a) The Latin American and Caribbean Group will relinquish one of its
seats on the Finance Committee at the expiration of the first two years
(1997-1998) in favour of a candidate of the Asian Group for the remainder of the
five-year term;

(b) The Western European and Others Group will relinquish one of its seats
on the Finance Committee at the expiration of the first two and one half years
of the five-year term commencing in 1997 in favour of a candidate from the
Eastern European Group for the remainder of the term;

(c) In the light of the special circumstances of this election, the term
of office of the members of the Finance Committee for the period preceding
1 January 1997 shall not be counted against the five-year term.

11. I further advised the Assembly that this agreement on the first composition
of the Finance Committee is without prejudice to the overall composition of the
Finance Committee for future elections and in particular to the claims of the
regional groups; nor will this agreement prejudice elections to other bodies.
It is understood that this situation may need to be reviewed in view of the
circumstances prevailing after 16 November 1998 when provisional membership of
the Authority terminates.

12. On the basis of the above agreement, I proposed the election of the
following candidates to the Finance Committee: Ernesto Belo Rosa (Uruguay),
Craig John Daniell (South Africa), Domenico da Empoli (Italy), David Etuket
(Uganda), Jobst Holborn (Germany), Lou Hong (China), Tadanori Inomata (Japan),
Serguey Ivanov (Russian Federation), Samia Ladgham (Tunisia), Jean-Pierre Levy
(France), Isaac Klipstein Margulis (Mexico), S. Rama Rao (India), Coy Roache
(Jamaica), Michael C. Wood (United Kingdom of Great Britain and Northern
Ireland) and M. Deborah Wynes (United States of America). The Assembly
proceeded to elect these candidates by acclamation.

13. With regard to the draft protocol on the privileges and immunities of the
Authority, the Assembly established a working group, under the chairmanship of
Mr. Wael Aboulmagd (Egypt), to undertake a review of the draft document
submitted by the Preparatory Commission (LOS/PCN/153, vol. V) and report to the
Assembly.

14. Taking into account the painstaking experience in composing the Council,
and the Finance Committee and in electing the President of the Assembly, I
proposed for the consideration of the Assembly a system of rotation in the
chairmanship of the Assembly, the Council, the Finance Committee and the Legal
and Technical Commission.

15. As a result of circumstances which required me to leave Kingston before the
end of the session, H.E. Mr. José Luis Vallarta, Ambassador of Mexico to Jamaica
and Vice-President of the Assembly, presided over the meetings of the Assembly
as from 14 August 1996. The following items were therefore considered under his
presidency:

Budget of the Authority for 1997

16. The Assembly considered a proposed revised budget for the Authority for
1997 submitted to it by the Council (ISBA/A/9/Add.1-ISBA/C/5/Add.1). In
reviewing the proposed revised budget, the Assembly took into account the
recommendations of the Finance Committee in its report of 14 August 1996
(ISBA/A/12-ISBA/C/7) and the recommendation of the Council to approve those
recommendations.

17. The Assembly adopted the revised budget of the Authority for 1997 in the
sum of US$ 4,150,500, subject to the points raised by the Finance Committee in
paragraphs 4, 5 and 6 of its report (ISBA/A/12-ISBA/C/7), and endorsed the
evolutionary approach. The Assembly also requested the Secretary-General to
submit the revised budget to the United Nations. It noted the reservations
expressed in the Council in respect of certain aspects of this budget by the
Russian Federation, members of the Council from the Eastern European Group and
the United States of America.

Administrative and technical matters

18. On the basis of a recommendation by the Council, the Assembly decided to
authorize the Secretary-General to apply on behalf of the Authority for
membership of the United Nations Joint Staff Pension Fund (ISBA/A/L.11).

19. The Assembly decided to seek observer status for the Authority at the
General Assembly of the United Nations (ISBA/A/L.12).

20. On the basis of the report submitted by the working group on the draft
protocol on the privileges and immunities of the Authority, the Assembly decided
to request the Secretariat to undertake further work on the draft protocol and
present the results of such work at an early stage during the next session of
the Authority.

<u>Future meetings</u>

21. The meetings of the International Seabed Authority in 1997 will take place from 17 to 28 March and 18 to 29 August at Kingston, Jamaica. The first item of business for the Assembly at its next meeting will be the election of its President.

-----

46. OBSERVER STATUS FOR THE ISBA - LETTER DATED 16 SEPTEMBER 1996 FROM THE REPRESENTATIVES OF AUSTRALIA, BRAZIL, CAMEROON, FIJI, FINLAND, GERMANY, ICELAND, INDIA, INDONESIA, ITALY, JAMAICA, JAPAN, NEW ZEALAND, PORTUGAL, SAMOA, SWEDEN, TRINIDAD AND TOBAGO AND THE UNITED KINGDOM TO THE UNITED NATIONS ADDRESSED TO THE SECRETARY-GENERAL

Doc. no.: A/51/231   18 September 1996

In accordance with rule 15 of the rules of procedure of the General Assembly, we have the honour to request the inclusion in the agenda of the fifty-first session of the General Assembly of an additional item of an urgent and important nature, entitled "Observer status for the International Seabed Authority".

The International Seabed Authority has been entrusted with responsibilities under the United Nations Convention on the Law of the Sea for certain matters pertaining to the law of the sea and ocean affairs that the Assembly should consider in its annual review of the implementation of the Convention and other developments relating to the law of the sea and ocean affairs.

In accordance with rule 20 of the rules of procedure of the General Assembly, an explanatory memorandum is attached to the present letter (see annex).

(Signed) Richard BUTLER, AM
  Permanent Representative of Australia
  to the United Nations

(Signed) Gunnar PÁLSSON
  Permanent Representative of Iceland
  to the United Nations

(Signed) Celso Luiz Nunes AMORIM
  Permanent Representative of Brazil
  to the United Nations

(Signed) Prakash SHAH
  Permanent Representative of India
  to the United Nations

(Signed) Paul BAMELA ENGO
  Permanent Representative of Cameroon
  to the United Nations

(Signed) Nugroho WISNUMURTI
  Permanent Representative of Indonesia
  to the United Nations

(Signed) Poseci W. BUNE
  Permanent Representative of Fiji
  to the United Nations

(Signed) Lorenzo FERRARIN
  Chargé d'affaires, Permanent Mission
  of Italy to the United Nations

(Signed) Fredrik Wilhelm BREITENSTEIN
  Permanent Representative of Finland
  to the United Nations

(Signed) M. Patricia DURRANT
  Permanent Representative of Jamaica
  to the United Nations

(Signed) Tono EITEL
  Permanent Representative of Germany
  to the United Nations

(Signed) Hisashi OWADA
  Permanent Representative of Japan
  to the United Nations

(Signed) Michael POWLES
  Permanent Representative of New
  Zealand to the United Nations

(Signed) Peter OSVALD
  Permanent Representative of Sweden
  to the United Nations

(Signed) Pedro CATARINO
  Permanent Representative of Portugal
  to the United Nations

(Signed) Annette des ILES
  Permanent Representative of Trinidad
  and Tobago to the United Nations

(Signed) Tuiloma Neroni SLADE
  Permanent Representative of Samoa
  to the United Nations

(Signed) John WESTON, KCMG
  Permanent Representative of the
  United Kingdom of Great Britain
  and Northern Ireland to the United
  Nations

ANNEX

Explanatory memorandum

The International Seabed Authority (hereinafter referred to as "the Authority") is an autonomous intergovernmental organization established under article 156 of the 1982 United Nations Convention on the Law of the Sea (hereinafter referred to as "the Convention"). The Authority has a legal personality and its seat is in Jamaica.

Under article 157 of the Convention and paragraph I of section I of the annex to the Agreement relating to the Implementation of part XI of the Convention (hereinafter referred to as "the Implementing Agreement"), the Authority is the organization through which States parties, in accordance with the regime for the international seabed area established in part XI of the Convention and the Implementing Agreement, organize and control activities in the international seabed area ("the Area"), in particular with a view to administering the resources of the Area. The powers and functions of the Authority are those expressly conferred upon it by the Convention.

The Authority has three principal organs, the Assembly, the Council and the Secretariat. The Authority is based on the sovereign equality of all its members. All States parties to the Convention are, ipso facto, members of the Authority. The Convention, together with the Implementing Agreement, is a universal instrument and has 106 States parties as at 20 August 1996.

Following the adoption of the Implementing Agreement on 29 July 1994 and the entry into force of the Convention on 16 November 1994, the first meeting of the International Seabed Authority took place at its headquarters at Kingston from 16 to 18 November 1994. In accordance with its provisions, the Implementing Agreement entered into force on 28 July 1996.

According to the Implementing Agreement, between the entry into force of the Convention and the approval of the first plan of work for exploitation, the initial functions of the Authority shall include:

(a) Processing of applications for approval of plans of work for exploration in accordance with part XI of the Convention and the Implementing Agreement;

(b) Implementation of decisions of the Preparatory Commission for the International Seabed Authority and for the International Tribunal for the Law of the Sea relating to the registered pioneer investors and their certifying States, including their rights and obligations, in accordance with article 308, paragraph 5, of the Convention and resolution II, paragraph 13;

(c) Monitoring of compliance with plans of work for exploration approved in the form of contracts;

(d) Monitoring and review of trends and developments relating to deep seabed mining activities, including regular analysis of world metal market conditions and metal prices, trends and prospects;

(e) Study of the potential impact of mineral production from the Area on the economics of developing land-based producers of those minerals which are likely to be most seriously affected, with a view to minimizing their difficulties and assisting them in their economic adjustment, taking into account the work done in this regard by the Preparatory Commission;

(f) Adoption of rules, regulations and procedures necessary for the conduct of activities in the Area as they progress;

(g) Adoption of rules, regulations and procedures incorporating applicable standards for the protection and preservation of the marine environment;

(h) Promotion and encouragement of the conduct of marine scientific research with respect to activities in the Area and the collection and dissemination of the results of such research and analysis, when available, with particular emphasis on research related to the environmental impact of activities in the Area;

(i) Acquisition of scientific knowledge and monitoring of the development of marine technology relevant to activities in the Area, in particular technology relating to the protection and preservation of the marine environment;

(j) Assessment of available data relating to prospecting and exploration;

(k) Timely elaboration of rules, regulations and procedures for exploitation, including those relating to the protection and preservation of the marine environment,

At its second session, held at Kingston from 5 to 16 August 1996, the Assembly of the Authority, recognizing that the Authority, owing to its responsibilities under the Convention, has an interest in the law of the sea and ocean affairs and other related matters considered by the General Assembly, decided that the Authority should seek to obtain observer status at the United Nations to enable it to participate in the deliberations of the Assembly and requested the Secretary-General of the Authority to take the necessary measures to seek such observer status.

Accordingly, the Authority requests that it be granted observer status at the United Nations.

-----

47. OBSERVER STATUS FOR THE ISBA IN THE GENERAL ASSEMBLY - UNGA RESOLUTION

Doc. no.: A/Res.51/6   24 October 1996

The General Assembly,

Aware of the importance of the effective implementation of the United Nations Convention on the Law of the Sea 6/ and of the Agreement relating to the implementation of Part XI of the United Nations Convention on the Law of the Sea of 10 December 1982, 7/ and their uniform consistent application, as well as of the growing need to promote and facilitate international cooperation on the law of the sea and ocean affairs at the global, regional and subregional levels,

Noting the decision of the Assembly of the International Seabed Authority at its resumed second session to seek observer status for the Authority at the United Nations in order to enable it to participate in the deliberations of the General Assembly,

1. Decides to invite the International Seabed Authority to participate in the deliberations of the General Assembly in the capacity of observer;

2. Requests the Secretary-General to take the necessary action to implement the present resolution.

6/   Official Records of the Third United Nations Conference on the Law of the Sea, vol. XII (United Nations publication, Sales No. E.84.V.3), document A/CONF.62/122.

7/   Resolution 48/263, annex.

48. ITLOS PRESS RELEASE (ISSUED BY THE REGISTRY)

Doc. no.: ITLOS/Press/1   5 October 1996

HAMBURG, 19 October.   The Judges of the International Tribunal for the Law of the Sea today elected Judge Thomas A. Mensah to serve as the first President of the Tribunal.   Judge Rüdiger Wolfrum was elected Vice-President.

The Judges held their first meeting on 1 October in Hamburg, the seat of the newly established International Tribunal for the Law of the Sea. This was the start of their first session devoted to organisational matters.   Mr. Hans Corell, the Legal Counsel of the United Nations, represented the Secretary-General of the United Nations on this occasion.   At the request of the Judges, Mr. Corell chaired the meetings of the Judges until the President of the Tribunal was elected.

The President and Vice-President are both elected for a period of 3 years.   The President will preside over the meetings of the Judges and over hearings in international disputes submitted to the Tribunal.   He has a casting vote in case of an equality of votes, and has an important supervisory function.   The President will reside permanently in Hamburg, Germany, and will direct the work of the Tribunal.   The Vice-President will take over the President's functions when the President is unable to act.

On 18 October 1996 there will be an inaugural session of the Judges in the City Hall of Hamburg.   The same day, Dr. Boutros Boutros-Ghali, the Secretary-General of the United Nations, will lay the foundation stone of the future Tribunal building at Elbchaussee 380.

President Mensah is a national of Ghana and has for more than 20 years been at the International Maritime Organization (IMO); first as its Director of Legal Affairs and later as the Assistant Secretary-General.   He was actively involved in the negotiations of the Law of the Sea Convention.   After retiring from the IMO, he was appointed Professor of Law and Director of the Law of the Sea Institute at the University of Hawaii and to the Cleveringa

Chair at the University of Leiden in the Netherlands. Since 1995 he has been the High Commissioner of Ghana to the Republic of South Africa.

Vice-President Wolfrum is of German nationality and has a long-standing career as a Professor of International Law at the Universities of Mainz, Kiel and Heidelberg. He was a member of the German delegation to the negotiations leading up to the Law of the Sea Convention. Vice-President Wolfrum was also a judge at the Court of Appeal for Administrative matters. Since 1993 he has been the director of the Max Planck Institute for Comparative Public Law and International Law.

The International Tribunal for the Law of the Sea

The International Tribunal for the Law of the Sea has been established by the United Nations Convention on the Law of the Sea. This Convention is one of the most comprehensive international treaties ever completed. It provides for the outer limits to which coastal States can claim jurisdiction in the waters surrounding them, and regulates prominent issues such as fisheries, navigation and the prevention of pollution of the marine environment. The Convention also pronounces the Deep Seabed as the common heritage of mankind and sets up the International Seabed Authority to regulate the exploitation of the Deep Seabed.

The Convention on the Law of the Sea is unique in that the mechanism for the settlement of disputes is incorporated into the document, making it obligatory for parties to the Convention to go through the settlement procedure in case of a dispute with another party. The Tribunal is the central forum for the settlement of disputes arising from the Convention.

The City of Hamburg with its rich maritime history as part of the League of Hanseatic Cities, obtained the seat of the Tribunal during the negotiation of the Convention which was signed in 1982. The temporary building, situated at Wexstrasse in the centre of Hamburg, opened on 1 October 1996.

On the bench are 21 Judges of different nationalities from all over the world. The Judges were elected among experts in the law of the sea, many of whom have been involved in negotiating the Convention. They were elected on 1 August 1996 by the hundred States that were parties to the Law of the Sea Convention on that day. One hundred and six States are at present party to the Convention, indicating the world wide approval which the Convention has obtained.

* * *

49. ITLOS PRESS RELEASE (ISSUED BY THE REGISTRY)

Doc. no.: ITLOS/Press/2   18 October 1996

HAMBURG, 18 October. At 10 a.m. this morning, the Judges of the International Tribunal for the Law of the Sea took their oath of office and signed solemn declarations in the presence of high dignitaries including, Dr. Boutros Boutros-Ghali, the Secretary-General of the United Nations, Dr. Klaus Kinkel, the German Federal Minister of Foreign Affairs, and Dr. Henning Voscherau, the First Lord Mayor of the Free and Hanseatic City of Hamburg. In attendance were also representatives of the International Seabed Authority, Mr. Satya Nandan, the Secretary-General of the Authority, Dr. Hasjim Djalal, the President of its Assembly, and Mr. Lennox Ballah, the President of its Council. The International Court of Justice was represented by the German judge on its bench, Dr. Carl August Fleischhauer and its Registrar, Mr. Valencia-Ospina. In addition, representatives from over 67 countries and an audience of 500 to 600 others witnessed the event.

The 21 Judges made their solemn declarations at a special inaugural session of the Tribunal in the stately Great Hall of the City Hall of Hamburg. After the more than 500 guests enjoyed Brahms, performed by the University of Music and Theatre, the Judges pledged that they will perform their duties and exercise their powers as judges honourably, faithfully, impartially and conscientiously. Officiating at the inauguration were Mr. Hans Corell, the Legal Counsel of the United Nations and Mr. Gritakumar Chitty, Director-in-Charge of the Registry. The session of the Tribunal was organized by the United Nations and the Registry of the Tribunal. Dr. Boutros-Ghali, Dr. Kinkel, Dr. Voscherau and Dr. Thomas A. Mensah, the President of the Tribunal, addressed the session. On behalf of the President of the Tribunal, Mr. Corell conducted the events. After the Judges had taken the solemn declaration, President Mensah closed the first public session of the Tribunal.

Dr. Boutros-Ghali said the session marked a "truly historic event" and pointed out that "Because maritime disputes can be a source of confrontation and conflict between States, the Tribunal has an important role to play in the building of an international society governed by the Rule of Law. The Law of the Sea Tribunal will be part of the system for the peaceful settlement of disputes as laid down by the founders of the United Nations. Though not an Organ of the United Nations the Tribunal finds its origin in efforts sponsored by the United Nations. As a sign of this excellent linkage a relationship agreement should soon be signed between the Tribunal and the United Nations."

From the City Hall the company went by the steamer "Schaarhörn" to the site on the Elbchaussee where, at a ceremony hosted by the Hamburg authorities, Dr. Boutros-Ghali laid the foundation stone for the future Tribunal. On this occasion, Dr. Boutros-Ghali, Dr. Kinkel, Prof. Edzard Schmidt-Jörtzig, the German Federal Minister of Justice, and Dr. Voscherau addressed the invitees.

Subsequently, at 7.45 p.m. Mr. Hedi M'Henni, the Tunisian Minister of Health, presented on behalf of the Tunisian Government a magnificent mosaic to the new International Tribunal for the Law of the Sea. The generous gift representing the sea-god Neptune, at present on display in the City Hall of Hamburg, will find its place in the future edifice of the Tribunal.

The International Tribunal for the Law of the Sea

The Judges were first convened and held their first meeting on 1 October in Hamburg, the seat of the newly established International Tribunal for the Law of the Sea. This was the start of their first session devoted to organizational matters. Mr. Corell represented the Secretary-General of the United Nations on this occasion. At the request of the Judges, Mr. Corell chaired the meetings of the Judges until the President of the Tribunal was elected.

On 5 October the Judges elected Judge Thomas A. Mensah from Ghana to serve as the first President of the Tribunal. The German national Judge Rüdiger Wolfrum was elected Vice-President.

The International Tribunal for the Law of the Sea has been established pursuant to the United Nations Convention on the Law of the Sea. This Convention is one of the most comprehensive international treaties ever completed. It provides for the outer limits to which coastal States can claim jurisdiction in their adjacent waters, and regulates prominent issues such as fisheries, navigation and the prevention of pollution of the marine environment. The Convention also pronounces the deep seabed as the common heritage of mankind and sets up the International Seabed Authority to regulate the exploitation of the deep seabed.

The Convention on the Law of the Sea is unique in that the mechanism for the settlement of disputes is incorporated into the document, making it obligatory for parties to the Convention to go through the settlement procedure in case of a dispute with another party. The Tribunal is the central forum for the settlement of disputes arising from the Convention. At present, one hundred and seven States are party to the Convention, indicating the world wide approval which the Convention has obtained. The Convention gives the Tribunal jurisdiction to resolve a variety of international disputes. Disputes that can be referred to the Tribunal may involve *inter alia* the delimitation of maritime zones, fisheries, navigation and ocean pollution. States parties to the Convention can bring their disputes for resolution to the Tribunal. In addition, the Tribunal can resolve disputes amongst States, the International Seabed Authority, companies and private individuals, arising out of the exploitation of the deep seabed. The Tribunal also has compulsory jurisdiction over the prompt release, upon the deposit of a bond, of arrested vessels and their crews. Furthermore, the International Seabed Authority may request legal opinions, advisory opinions, from the Tribunal.

The City of Hamburg, with its rich maritime history as part of the League of Hanseatic Cities, obtained the seat of the Tribunal during the negotiation of the Convention which was signed in 1982. The temporary building, situated at Wexstrasse in the centre of Hamburg, opened on 1 October 1996.

The Judges

On the bench are 21 Judges from all over the world. The Judges were elected among experts in the law of the sea, many of whom were involved in negotiating the Convention. They were elected on 1 August 1996 by the hundred States that were parties to the Law of the Sea Convention on that day. The composition of the International Tribunal for the Law of the Sea is as follows:

Order of precedence	*Country*
President	
Thomas A. Mensah	Ghana
Vice-President	
Rüdiger Wolfrum	Germany
Judges	
Lihai Zhao	China
Hugo Caminos	Argentina
Vicente Marotta Rangel	Brazil
Alexander Yankov	Bulgaria
Soji Yamamoto	Japan
Anatoly Lazarevich Kolodkin	Russian Federation
Choon-Ho Park	Republic of Korea
Paul Bamela Engo	Cameroon
L. Dolliver M. Nelson	Grenada
P. Chandrasekhara Rao	India
Joseph Akl	Lebanon
David Anderson	United Kingdom of Great Britain and Northern Ireland
Budislav Vukas	Croatia
Joseph Sinde Warioba	United Republic of Tanzania
Edward Arthur Laing	Belize
Tullio Treves	Italy
Mohamed Mouldi Marsit	Tunisia
Gudmundur Eiriksson	Iceland
Tafsir Malick Ndiaye	Senegal

(The *curricula vitae* of the Members of the International Tribunal for the Law of the Sea are to be found in United Nations Document SPLOS/11. A summary of the relevant part of the Document will be released in due course.)

* * *

50.   ITLOS PRESS RELEASE (ISSUED BY THE REGISTRY)

Doc. no.: ITLOS/Press/3   23 October 1996

HAMBURG, 21 October. Today, the Judges of the International Tribunal for the Law of the Sea elected Mr. Gritakumar E. Chitty, of Sri Lankan nationality, as the first Registrar of the International Tribunal for the Law of the Sea.

Mr. Chitty, who has over 20 years of experience in the United Nations Secretariat, has been involved in the establishment of the International Tribunal for the Law of the Sea from the very beginning. Mr. Chitty, in his function as Director-in-Charge, was responsible for setting up the Registry of the Tribunal.   The Registry and the United Nations Secretariat organized the ceremonial inauguration of the Judges of the Law of the Sea Tribunal last Friday, 18 October. On this occasion high dignitaries from all over the world were present in Hamburg, the seat of the Tribunal, to witness the swearing in of the Judges.

Mr. Chitty began his legal career in private national law practice and joined the United Nations in 1975 when he became the Special Assistant of the Under-Secretary-General for the Law of the Sea, Mr. Bernardo Zuleta. In his long-standing career with the United Nations, Mr. Chitty was the officer responsible for the subject of the settlement of disputes under the law of the sea continuously from 1975, the first time the topic was taken up by the Third United Nations Conference on the Law of the Sea. In May 1995, Mr. Chitty was appointed by the Secretary-General of the United Nations as the Officer responsible for making preparations for the establishment of the International Tribunal for the Law of the Sea which was followed by his appointment as Director-in-Charge of the Registry of the Tribunal in August 1996.

The Registrar of the Tribunal is elected for a term of seven years among candidates proposed by the Members of the Tribunal. For the duration of that period he is in charge of the Registry, which is the administrative organ of the Tribunal. The Registrar is responsible for all departments of the Registry. The Staff is under his control and he directs the work of the Registry, of which he is the Head. The Registrar's post is at the level of Assistant Secretary-General.

Mr. Chitty thanked the President and the Judges for their confidence in him and assured the Tribunal of his continued devotion to the institution and its members. He stated that it had been his goal to help establish the Tribunal and that he was grateful he could continue to serve it. Mr. Chitty also said he hoped to soon welcome the Tribunal's first cases.

The International Tribunal for the Law of the Sea

The Judges were first convened and held their first meeting on 1 October. This was the start of their work devoted to organizational matters. The Judges elected Judge Thomas A. Mensah from Ghana to serve as the first President of the Tribunal. Judge Rüdiger Wolfrum, a German national, was elected Vice-President.

The International Tribunal for the Law of the Sea has been established pursuant to the United Nations Convention on the Law of the Sea. This Convention is one of the most comprehensive international treaties ever completed. It provides for the outer limits to which coastal States can claim jurisdiction in their adjacent waters, and regulates prominent issues such as fisheries, navigation and the prevention of pollution of the marine environment. The Convention also pronounces the deep seabed as the common heritage of mankind and sets up the International Seabed Authority to regulate the exploitation of the deep seabed.

The Convention on the Law of the Sea is unique in that the mechanism for the settlement of disputes is incorporated into the document, making it obligatory for parties to the Convention to go through the settlement procedure in case of a dispute with another party. The Tribunal is the central forum for the settlement of disputes arising from the Convention. At present, one hundred and seven States are party to the Convention, indicating the world wide approval which the Convention has obtained. The Convention gives the Tribunal jurisdiction to resolve a variety of international disputes. Disputes that can be referred to the Tribunal may involve *inter alia* the delimitation of maritime zones, fisheries, navigation and ocean pollution. States parties to the Convention can bring their disputes for resolution to the Tribunal. In addition, the Tribunal can resolve disputes amongst States, the International Seabed Authority, companies and private individuals, arising out of the exploitation of the deep seabed. The Tribunal also has compulsory jurisdiction over the prompt release, upon the deposit of a bond, of arrested vessels and their crews. Furthermore, the International Seabed Authority may request legal opinions, advisory opinions, from the Tribunal.

The City of Hamburg, with its rich maritime history as part of the League of Hanseatic Cities, obtained the seat of the Tribunal during the negotiation of the Convention which was signed in 1982. The temporary building, situated at Wexstrasse in the centre of Hamburg, opened on 1 October 1996.

The Judges

On the bench are 21 Judges from all over the world. The Judges were elected among experts in the law of the sea, many of whom were involved in negotiating the Convention. They were elected on 1 August 1996 by the States that were parties to the Law of the Sea Convention on that day.

* * *

51. ITLOS PRESS RELEASE (ISSUED BY THE REGISTRY)

Doc. no.: ITLOS/Press/4   1 November 1996

HAMBURG, 1 November. The President of the International Tribunal for the Law of the Sea declared the first session of the Tribunal closed.

The Judges of the International Tribunal for the Law of the Sea have been meeting over the past four weeks in Hamburg, the seat of the newly established Tribunal to settle organizational matters. The first session of the International Tribunal for the Law of the Sea has been a great success. The Tribunal has taken up and resolved a plethora of issues, ranging from the election of officials to the examination and the adoption of certain rules of procedure.

21 Judges and the Registrar of the Intenational Tribunal of the Law of the Sea

The President of the Tribunal, Thomas A. Mensah, in his closing speech thanked all the Judges for their dedication and hard work. The President of the Tribunal expressed his conviction that the achievements of the present session are a solid basis for the future work of the Tribunal. The Tribunal has taken the necessary decisions to enable it to deal with a case or application that may be submitted to it.

Future Meetings of the Tribunal.

The Judges of the Tribunal are permanently at the disposal of the Tribunal and will be ready to meet at short notice in the event that a case is received by the Tribunal. Apart from the situation that the Tribunal would meet to review a case, the Judges decided to meet for two and possibly three sessions in 1997. The Judges set the calendar for a session during the whole month of February and a further session during the month of April. A third session was agreed on provisionally for the month of October. It will depend on funds being made available to the Tribunal by the State Parties to the Law of the Sea Convention. The Judges considered it important to have an additional session to ensure the swift resolution of urgent organizational matters and to ensure the continuity of the work of the Tribunal.

Establishment of the Chamber of Summary Procedure.

Beyond doubt one of the most important decisions by the Tribunal during its first session was to establish its Chamber of Summary Procedure. The Chamber is established with a view to the speedy dispatch of business. The Chamber can hear and determine cases on the request of States that are parties to a dispute. The disputes that can be referred to the Chamber are the same that can be submitted to the full Tribunal and range from the prompt release of vessels and crews to fisheries disputes or maritime delimitations.

Under its Statute, the Tribunal is directed to form the Chamber annually from five of its elected members. It was concluded in the rules approved by the Tribunal that by definition the President and the Vice-President are members of this Chamber. The three other members of the Tribunal selected for the Chamber of Summary Procedure, are Judges Hugo Caminos, Choon-Ho Park and Mohamed Mouldi Marsit. Judges Anatoly Lazarevich Kolodkin and L. Dolliver M. Nelson were selected as alternate Members of the Chamber.

Rules of Procedure and Evidence.

During the session, certain rules of procedure were provisionally adopted to facilitate the sessional work of the Tribunal. A formidable project is under way to scrutinize the rules drafted by the Preparatory Commission for the International Seabed Authority and for the International Tribunal for the Law of the Sea, which were recommended by the meeting of States Parties to the Tribunal. This undertaking will be executed with a view to making the rules user-friendly, cost-effective and efficient. An informal consultative mechanism has been set up among the Judges to undertake this work.

Privileges and Immunities.

The Tribunal discussed the Draft Agreement on the Privileges and Immunities of the International Tribunal for the Law of the Sea, which specifies the privileges and immunities of the Tribunal on a global level. The Judges also examined the Final Draft of the Headquarters Agreement, which specifies the privileges and immunities of the Tribunal in the Host Country. The Headquarters Agreement was approved by the Preparatory Commission and recommended to the Tribunal by the Meeting of States Parties as an appropriate basis to negotiate the Agreement. The Judges authorized the President and the Registrar to negotiate the Headquarters Agreement with the German authorities on the basis of this preparatory work.

Relationship Agreement with the United Nations.

The Secretary-General of the United Nations, in his speech on the occasion of the inauguration of the Judges of the Tribunal, noted that: "Though not an Organ of the United Nations the Tribunal finds its origin in efforts sponsored by the United Nations. As a sign of this excellent linkage a relationship agreement should soon be signed between the Tribunal and the United Nations." The Judges discussed the terms of the future relationship Agreement and decided to adopt *mutatis mutandis* the United Nations Common System, to proceed with the application for Staff Members to be admitted to the United Nations Pension Fund, and to apply for observer status at sessions of the General Assembly of the United Nations.

Budget of the Tribunal.

The Judges also examined the future budgetary requirements of the Tribunal. The Judges reviewed the current budget and identified important needs for which provision should be made. These needs will be brought to the attention of the next meeting of the State Parties to the Convention. A working group has been established to consider proposals for the 1998 budget. The Tribunal took note of a report of its Registry indicating that there is a substantial delay in the receipt of the contributions to its budget from the States Parties to the Convention.

Election of the President, Vice-President and Registrar.

On 5 October, the Judges elected Judge Thomas A. Mensah to serve as the first President of the Tribunal. On the same day, Judge Rüdiger Wolfrum was elected Vice-President.

President Mensah, a national of Ghana, had been with the International Maritime Organization (IMO) for more than twenty years; first as its Director of Legal Affairs and later as its Assistant Secretary-General. He was involved in the negotiations of the Law of the Sea Convention. After retiring from the IMO, he was appointed Professor of Law and Director of the Law of the Sea Institute at the University of Hawaii and to the Cleveringa Chair at the University of Leiden in the Netherlands. Since 1995, he has been the High Commissioner of Ghana to the Republic of South Africa.

Vice-President Wolfrum, a German national, has a long-standing career as a Professor of International Law at the Universities of Mainz, Kiel and Heidelberg. He was a member of the German delegation to the negotiations leading up to the Law of the Sea Convention. Since 1993, he has been director of the Max Planck Institute for Comparative Public Law and International Law.

On 23 October, the Tribunal elected Mr. Gritakumar E. Chitty, of Sri Lankan nationality, as the first Registrar of the International Tribunal for the Law of the Sea. In May 1995, Mr. Chitty had been appointed by the Secretary-General of the United Nations as the Officer responsible fór making preparations for the establishment of the Tribunal, which was followed by his appointment as Director-in-Charge of the Registry of the Tribunal in August 1996. Mr. Chitty brings to the Tribunal over twenty years of experience with the United Nations Secretariat, during which time he was the officer responsible for the subject of the settlement of disputes under the law of the sea.

On 25 October, the Tribunal elected Mr. Philippe Gautier, of Belgian nationality, as its Deputy Registrar.

The Ceremonial Inauguration of the Judges.

On 18 October, the Judges of the International Tribunal for the Law of the Sea took their oath of office and signed solemn declarations in the presence of high dignitaries including: Dr. Boutros Boutros-Ghali, the Secretary-General of the United Nations, Dr. Klaus Kinkel, the German

Federal Minister of Foreign Affairs, and Dr. Henning Voscherau, the First Mayor of the Free and Hanseatic City of Hamburg. In addition, representatives from over sixty-seven countries, representatives of the International Court of Justice and the International Seabed Authority, and an audience of five to six-hundred others witnessed the event.

The 21 Judges made their solemn declarations at a special inaugural session of the Tribunal in the stately Great Hall of Hamburg's City Hall. The Judges pledged that they will perform their duties and exercise their powers as judges honourably, faithfully, impartially and conscientiously.

The International Tribunal for the Law of the Sea.

The International Tribunal for the Law of the Sea is an independent international organization which has been established pursuant to the United Nations Convention on the Law of the Sea. This Convention is one of the most comprehensive international treaties ever completed. It provides for the outer limits to which coastal States can claim jurisdiction in their adjacent waters and regulates prominent issues such as fisheries and navigation. A whole chapter of the Convention is devoted to the prevention of pollution of the marine environment. The Convention also pronounces the deep seabed as the common heritage of mankind and sets up the International Seabed Authority to regulate the exploitation of the deep seabed.

The Convention on the Law of the Sea is unique in that the mechanism for the settlement of disputes is incorporated into the document, making it obligatory for parties to the Convention to go through the settlement procedure in case of a dispute with another party. The Tribunal is the central forum for the settlement of disputes arising from the Convention. At present, one hundred and eight States are party to the Convention, indicating the world wide approval which the Convention has obtained.

The Convention gives the Tribunal jurisdiction to resolve a variety of international disputes. Disputes amongst States that can be referred to the Tribunal may involve *inter alia* the delimitation of maritime zones, fisheries, navigation and ocean pollution. The Tribunal also has compulsory jurisdiction over the prompt release, upon the deposit of a bond, of arrested vessels and their crews. In addition, the Tribunal is competent to resolve disputes amongst States, the International Seabed Authority, companies and private individuals, arising out of the exploitation of the deep seabed. Furthermore, the International Seabed Authority may request advisory opinions from the Tribunal's Seabed Disputes Chamber. The Seabed Disputes Chamber will be elected during the next session. The Chamber is composed of 11 Judges selected from the 21 Judges of the Tribunal. It serves as a separate court within the structure of the Tribunal.

The City of Hamburg, with its rich maritime history as part of the League of Hanseatic Cities, obtained the seat of the Tribunal during the negotiation of the Convention which was signed in 1982. The temporary Tribunal building is situated at Wexstrasse in the centre of Hamburg. On 18 October 1996, Dr. Boutros-Ghali laid the foundation stone for the future Tribunal premises at the site on the Elbchaussee at Nienstedten in Hamburg overlooking the river Elbe. The future facility is scheduled to be ready just before the new millennium.

The Judges.

On the bench are twenty-one Judges from all over the world. The Judges were elected among experts in the law of the sea, many of whom were involved in negotiating the Convention. They were elected on 1 August 1996 by the States that were parties to the Law of the Sea Convention on that day. The representatives of 100 States voted in that election. The names of the Judges are set out below in order of precedence.

President
  Thomas A. Mensah   Ghana

Vice-President
  Rüdiger Wolfrum   Germany

Judges
  Lihai Zhao   China
  Hugo Caminos   Argentina
  Vicente Marotta Rangel   Brazil
  Alexander Yankov   Bulgaria
  Soji Yamamoto   Japan
  Anatoly Lazarevich Kolodkin   Russian Federation
  Choon-Ho Park   Republic of Korea
  Paul Bamela Engo   Cameroon
  L. Dolliver M. Nelson   Grenada
  P. Chandrasekhara Rao   India
  Joseph Akl   Lebanon
  David Anderson   United Kingdom of Great
                                       Britain and Northern Ireland

  Budislav Vukas   Croatia
  Joseph Sinde Warioba   United Republic of Tanzania
  Edward Arthur Laing   Belize
  Tullio Treves   Italy
  Mohamed Mouldi Marsit   Tunisia
  Gudmundur Eiriksson   Iceland
  Tafsir Malick Ndiaye   Senegal

(The *curricula vitae* of the Members of the International Tribunal for the Law of the Sea are contained in United Nations Document SPLOS/11. A summary of the relevant part of the Document will be released in due course.)

Previous Press Releases of the Tribunal can be obtained from the Tribunal's Registry. Please contact the office of the Registry at Tel: (49) (40) 3560-70 / Fax: (49) (40) 3560-7245 / (49) (40) 3560-7275

* * *

52. CURRICULA VITAE OF CANDIDATES NOMINATED BY STATES PARTIES FOR ELECTION TO THE ITLOS - REPORT BY THE UN SECRETARY-GENERAL (THOMAS A. MENSAH - ITLOS PRESIDENT; RÜDIGER WOLFRUM - ITLOS VICE-PRESIDENT)

Doc. no.: SPLOS/11

25 June 1996

CONTENTS

CONTENTS (continued)

[...]

MENSAH, Thomas A.

(Ghana)

STATEMENT ON QUALIFICATIONS AND EXPERIENCE

Dr. Thomas A. Mensah has had a long and distinguished career in the field of public international law and the law of the sea. After graduate studies leading to the doctorate degree at the Yale Law School, he has been engaged in studies and related activities in international law, as a University lecturer and instructor at international seminars and workshops and also as adviser and consultant within the United Nations system of organizations.

As the Director of Legal Affairs and Assistant Secretary-General at the INTERNATIONAL MARITIME ORGANIZATION (IMO) for more than 20 years (1968 to 1990), he directed the work of the secretariat of IMO in the development of a large body of international conventions and other instruments dealing with a variety of topics in the public and private international law of the sea. As Legal Counsel he was the chief official responsible for dealing with or advising IMO and its member States on issues of treaty law and problems of international administrative law.

He was actively involved in the negotiations at the Third United Nations Conference on the Law of the Sea which led to the adoption of the 1982 Convention. After 1982, he was in charge of studies within the IMO on the implications of the 1982 Convention for the IMO and on problems in connection with the implementation of the provisions of the Convention relating to navigation and the prevention of pollution of the sea from ships and by dumping.

Since retiring from the IMO in 1990, Dr. Mensah has continued to work in the maritime field. He has acted as consultant to several United Nations bodies and Governments on maritime legislation and the international environmental law of the sea.

He has also maintained his interest and work in public international law. In 1993 he was appointed to the prestigious CLEVERINGA CHAIR at the University of Leiden in the Netherlands, where he conducted a course on the International Negotiation Process and a seminar on Legislative Drafting during the 1993-94 academic year.

Before his appointment as Ghana's High Commissioner to the Republic of South Africa Dr. Mensah was Professor of Law and Director of the Law of the Sea Institute at the William S. Richardson School of Law at the University of Hawaii in Honolulu. In addition to directing the research and conference programme of the Institute, he gave courses in the Law of the Sea and International Environmental Law.

Apart from numerous papers and studies prepared by him or under his supervision in his official and academic functions, Dr. Mensah is the author of a number of articles and published monograms on various topics in international law and the international law of the sea.

Dr. Mensah has been a member of the American Society of International Law. He is a Member of the British and United States Maritime Law Associations, and a Temporary (Individual) Member of the Comité Maritime International. Since 1990 he has been a member of the Standing Committee of the International Maritime Arbitration Organization in Paris.

In 1989 he was elected an Associate Member of the INSTITUT DE DROIT INTERNATIONAL.

* * *

PRESENT POSITION:	**HIGH COMMISSIONER OF GHANA TO THE REPUBLIC OF SOUTH AFRICA**
PREVIOUS POSITION:	**PROFESSOR OF LAW AND DIRECTOR THE LAW OF THE SEA INSTITUTE UNIVERSITY OF HAWAII HONOLULU, HAWAII, USA**

EDUCATION:

Achimota School, Ghana	Cambridge School Certificate (Grade 1) - December 1951
University of Ghana	B.A. (First Class) - Philosophy June 1956
University of London	LLB (Honours) - June 1959
Yale University School of Law:	LL.M. - June 1962 J.S.D. - January 1964

PROFESSIONAL ASSOCIATIONS

1. Associate Member, Institut de Droit International

2. Member, Standing Committee on Maritime Arbitration, International Maritime Arbitration Organization, International Chamber of Commerce, Paris

3. Member, American Society of International Law

4. Member, British Maritime Law Association

5. Member, Commission on Environmental Law, World Conservation Union (IUCN)

6. Member, Legal Committee, Advisory Committee on Pollution of the Sea (ACOPS)

ACADEMIC POSITIONS HELD

1. Lecturer in Law, University of Ghana: 1963-68
    Acting Dean of the Faculty: 1967-68

2. Co-Director, Dag Hammarskjöld Seminars on International Law, Uppsala University, Sweden: 1966-67

3. Co-Director UNITAR/UNESCO African Seminar on International Law, Dar-es-Salaam, Tanzania, Summer 1967

4. Visiting Professor, World Maritime University, Malmo, Sweden: 1985-91

5. Visiting Professor, William S. Richardson School of Law, University of Hawaii, Spring Semester 1992

6. CLEVERINGA Professor of Law, Leiden University, Netherlands: 1993-94

7. Professor of Law and Director of the Law of the Sea Institute, University of Hawaii: October 1993-June 1995

ADMINISTRATIVE POSITIONS

1. Administrative Officer, Ghana Civil Service: 1956-58

2. Assistant Registrar (Academic), University of Ghana: 1960-62

3. Executive Secretary to International Diplomatic Conferences on Maritime Law:

    (i) International Legal Conference on Marine Pollution Damage, Brussels, 1969

    (ii) International Legal Conference on the Establishment of an International Fund for Compensation for Oil Pollution Damage, Brussels, 1971

    (iii) Athens Conference on the Carriage of Passengers and their Luggage by Sea, Athens, 1974

    (iv) International Conference on Limitation of Liability for Maritime Claims, London, 1976

    (v) Diplomatic Conference on Liability and Compensation for Damage in connection with the Carriage of Certain Substances by Sea, London, 1984

    (vi) Diplomatic Conference on the Suppression of Unlawful Acts against the Safety of Maritime Navigation, Rome, 1988

(vii)   Diplomatic Conference on Salvage, London, 1989

(viii) Diplomatic Conference to Revise the 1974 Athens Convention on the
        Carriage of Passengers and their Luggage by Sea, London, 1990

PROFESSIONAL POSITIONS

1.   Legal Adviser, Ghana Atomic Energy Commission, 1966-67

2.   Associate Legal Officer, International Atomic Energy Agency (IAFA), Vienna:
     1965-66

3.   International Maritime Organization (IMO), London:

     (i)   Head, Legal Division - September 1968-December 1973

     (ii)   Director, Legal Affairs and External Relations: January 1974-
            December 1981

     (iii) Assistant Secretary-General: December 1981-September

4.   Special Adviser on Environmental Law and Institutions, United Nations
     Environment Programme (UNEP), Nairobi, 1991-92

5.   Consultant on International Maritime and Environmental Law, 1990-1993 to:

     (i)   UN Economic and Social Commission for Asia and the Pacific (ESCAP),
            Bangkok

     (ii)   The World Bank, Washington, D.C.

     (iii) The International Oil Pollution Compensation Fund, London

     (iv)   The United Nations Environment Programme (UNEP), Nairobi

OTHER POSITIONS HELD

1.   Member, University Council, University of Ghana, 1966-67

2.   Master, AKUAFO HALL, University of Ghana, 1966-68

3.   Member, National Advisory Council of Ghana, 1966-68

4.   Chairman, Constitutional Drafting Commission, Ghana, 1978

5.   Member, Board of Editors, MARINE POLICY - JOURNAL FOR ECONOMICS PLANNING
     AND POLITICS OF OCEAN EXPLORATION

6.   Member, International Advisory Committee and Senior Editorial Board, the
     John D. and Catherine T. MacArthur Foundation Project on Governing Rules of
     International Law (American Society of International Law), 1990-92

PUBLICATIONS

1.   "L'Activité Reglementaire de l'OMCI" (with Christopher H. Zimmerli) in
     L'ELABORATION DU DROIT INTERNATIONAL PUBLIQUE (Societe Francaise pour le
     Droit International, Colloque de Toulouse) Edition Pedone, Paris, 1974

2.   "Legal Problems Relating to Marine Pollution" in WATER POLLUTION BY OIL,
     Peter Hepple, ed., The Institute of Petroleum, London, 1971

3.   "The IMO Experience" in LAW, INSTITUTIONS AND THE GLOBAL ENVIRONMENT,
     John Lawrence Hargrove, ed., Carnegie Endowment for International Peace and

American Society of International Law, Oceana Publications, N.Y.,
A. W. Sijthoff, Leiden, 1972

4. "International Conventions Concerning Pollution of the Sea", CASE WESTERN
    RESERVE JOURNAL OF INTERNATIONAL LAW, vol. 8, No. 1 (1976)

5. "The Law Relating to Pollution of the Seas" in ENVIRONMENTAL POLLUTION
    CONTROL, Allan D. McKnight, Pauline Marstrand and T. Craig Sinclair, eds.,
    George Allen and Unwin, London (1974)

6. "The Practice of International Law in International Organizations" in
    INTERNATIONAL LAW - TEACHING AND PRACTICE, Bin Cheng, ed., Stevens and
    Sons, London (1982)

7. "Environmental Protection: International Approaches" in MARINE POLICY,
    Butterworth and Co., Ltd. (April 1984)

8. "Universalism and Regionalism in the Law of Carriage of Goods by Sea: The
    IMCO Experience" in INTERNATIONAL ECONOMIC AND TRADE LAW - UNIVERSAL AND
    REGIONAL INTEGRATION, Clive Schmitthoff and Kenneth Simmonds, eds.,
    A. W. Sijthoff, Leiden (1976)

9. "The International Regulation of Maritime Traffic" in THE UN CONVENTION ON
    THE LAW OF THE SEA: IMPACT AND IMPLEMENTATION, E. D. Brown and
    R. R. Churchill, eds., Law of the Sea Institute, Honolulu (1988)

10. "The Implications of the UN Convention on the Law of the Sea for IMO".
    Document issued by the Secretariat of the International Maritime
    Organization (IMO), 1988

11. "The Group System in International Negotiations - An Appraisal". Inaugural
    Lecture for the CLEVERINGA CHAIR, Leiden University - November 1993

[...]

WOLFRUM, Rüdiger

(Germany)

STATEMENT OF QUALIFICATIONS

Education

Mr. Rüdiger Wolfrum, born in Berlin 1941, after completion of his high
school education and his military service (German Navy), passed through all
stages of German legal training which he finished with the Second State-
Examination in 1973. In the same year he graduated Dr. jur. and became
assistant professor at the Institute of International Law, University of Bonn,
Faculty of Law and Economics. In 1977/78 he spent a year as a research fellow
at the Center for Oceans Law and Policy at the University of Virginia completing
his book on the Internationalization of Common Spaces Outside National
Jurisdiction: "The Development of an International Administration for
Antarctica, Outer Space, High Seas and Deep Sea-Bed".

Professional career

Mr. Wolfrum is professor for national public and international public law
and held chairs at the University of Mainz (1982) and the University of Kiel
(1982-1993); since 1993 he holds a chair at the University of Heidelberg. He
was Director of the Institute of International Law at the University of Kiel and

from 1990 to 1993 elected Vice-Rector of that University. From 1986 until 1993
he served as a judge at the Court of Appeal for Administrative Matters in
Lüneburg and Schleswig, his cases mostly dealing with environmental law. Since
1993 he has been director of the Max Planck Institute for Comparative Public Law
and International Law, the major research institute on that topic in Germany.

International activities

Mr. Wolfrum was and still is involved in various international activities.
From 1980 until 1982 he was a member of the German delegation to the Third
United Nations Conference on the Law of the Sea. In this capacity he was
involved in the negotiations on Part XI of the United Nations Convention on the
Law of the Sea, in particular on production policy issues. In 1982 he also
participated at the meetings of the Preparatory Commission for the International
Seabed Authority and the Tribunal for the Law of the Sea.

Since 1982 he has further been actively involved in deliberations
concerning Antarctica. He participated at the Fourth Special Consultative
Meeting concerning Antarctic mineral resource activities as a member of the
German delegation (1983-1988) and as chairman to the Legal Working Group
(1985-1988). He participated in several Antarctic treaty Consultative Meetings
and since 1993 serves as the chairman to the Group of legal experts preparing an
Annex to the Protocol on Environmental Protection to the Antarctic Treaty on
responsibility for environmental damages.

Finally, in 1990 he was elected by the States Parties to the Convention on
the Elimination of All Forms of Racial Discrimination as an independent expert
member to the United Nations Committee on the Elimination of Racial
Discrimination for which he was re-elected in 1994.

Publication activities

Mr. Rüdiger Wolfrum has published widely on various issues of international
public law. His main publication concerning law of the sea issues is on the
Internationalization of Common Spaces Outside National Jurisdiction (more than
700 pages) in which he identifies and assesses the common denominations of
international rules concerning the high seas, Antarctica, the deep seabed and
outer space. The publication focuses heavily on the common heritage principle,
an issue which has also been taken up in several of his articles. Other law of
the sea subjects dealt with in his writings, which have been published in German
or in English, are marine scientific research, fishing deep seabed mining,
delimitation of maritime areas under national jurisdiction, navigation, the
protection of the marine environment and the structure and functions of the
International Seabed Authority. More than 35 of his publications (out of about
100) are devoted to law of the sea issues.

Many of the publications concentrate on the United Nations. Mr. Wolfrum is
the editor of a two-volume reference book on "United Nations: Law, Policies and
Practice" (1994) and he has participated in the edition of a Commentary to the
United Nations Charter (1994) (both in English). His other publications on the
United Nations deal in particular with the United Nations functions concerning
peace-keeping, economic cooperation and organizational matters.

Other publications deal with the law concerning Antarctica, especially with
activities undertaken in the Antarctic Treaty area, protection of the Antarctic
environment and the status of Antarctica.

Finally, Mr. Wolfrum has published on human rights issues in particular
drawing from his experience as member to the Committee against Racial
Discrimination.

As a director to the Institute of International Law in Kiel and of the
Max Planck Institute in Heidelberg, Mr. Wolfrum has organized several symposia

dealing with the law of the sea, United Nations, international environmental law, human rights and Antarctica. All these symposia brought together diplomats, judges and researchers from different countries. They were meant to provide a dialogue between these groups and a better understanding amongst those representing different legal systems.

* * *

Birthplace/birthdate	Berlin, 13 December 1941
	Completion of high school education (Abitur, 1962) and then military service
1964-1969	Study of Law at the Universities of Bonn and Tübingen
18 January 1969	First State-Examination
1969-1973	Junior barrister
29 June 1973	Graduation, Dr. jur.
14 September 1973	Second State-Examination
From 1973	Assistant professorship, Institute of International Law, University of Bonn
1 August 1977-31 July 1978	Research fellow at the Center for Oceans Law and Policy of the University of Virginia; scholarship from the German Research Foundation
July/August 1980 March/April 1981 March/April 1982	Participation at the Third United Nations Law of the Sea Conference (alternate) Representative of the German delegation and adviser to the Ministry of Economics
28 November 1980	Habilitation, venia legendi for national public and international public law
6 May 1982-30 November 1982	Professor, Chair of national public and international law, University of Mainz, Faculty of Law and Economics
2 December 1982-30 April 1993	Professor, Chair of national public and international public law, University of Kiel, Law Faculty, Director of the Institute of International Law
June 1983-May 1988	Participation at the 4th Special Antarctic Treaty Consultative Meeting concerning Antarctic mineral resource activities, Member of the German delegation and Chairman of the Legal Working Group (beginning in 1985)
August/September 1983	Participation at the Preparatory Commission for the International Sea-Bed Authority and for the International Tribunal for the Law of the Sea (Delegation of the Federal Republic of Germany)
29 April 1986-30 April 1993	Judge at the Court of Appeals for Administrative Matters for the states of Niedersachsen and Schleswig Holstein; since 1991 judge at the Court of Appeals for Administrative Matters of the Land Schleswig Holstein

August/September 1987	Visiting professor at the University of Minnesota, Minneapolis, Law School
January 1990	Election as member of the United Nations Committee on the Elimination of Racial Discrimination; re-elected in 1994
1 June 1990-30 April 1993	Vice-rector of the Christian-Albrechts University at Kiel
August/September 1990	Visiting professor at the University of Minnesota, Minneapolis, Law School
since 1 October 1990	Faculty adviser to the graduate program in Business Administration and Innovation, Kiel
since 1 January 1992	Faculty adviser to the graduate program in National and International Environmental Law, Kiel
since 30 June 1992	Member of the Senate of the German Research Foundation; re-elected in 1995
since 1 May 1993	Director of the Max Planck Institute for Comparative Public Law and International Law, Heidelberg
September/October 1993	Visiting professor at the University of Minnesota, Minneapolis, Law School
since 1 January 1994	Executive head of the United Nations Association for Germany
since 1 March 1994	Member of the Council of the German ILA (International Law Association) - Section
since 1 September 1994	Member of the Executive Board of the Law of the Sea Institute at the University of Hawaii
since 15 November 1995	Member of the Executive Board of the "Stiftung für marine Geowissenschaften" (Foundation for Marine Geosciences) (GEOMAR)

Publications

I.   Books (author/editor)

Die innerparteiliche demokratische Ordnung nach dem Parteiengesetz (The Democratic Structure of Political Parties according to the Law on Political Parties), Berlin, 1974

Handbuch Vereinte Nationen (Handbook on the United Nations) (edited with Norbert J. Prill and Jens A. Brückner), Munich, 1977 (578 pages)

Deep Sea-bed Mining in the Law of the Sea Negotiation (II): Toward a Balanced Development System (edited with John Norton Moore, Philip Stopford, Jutta Stender), Charlottesville, Virginia, 1979

Die Internationalisierung staatsfreier Räume: internationale Verwaltung von Antarktis, Weltraum, Hohe See und Meeresboden (The Internationalization of Common Spaces Outside National Jurisdiction: The Development of an International Administration for Antarctica, Outer Space, High Seas and Deep Sea-Bed), Berlin, 1984

Antarctic Challenge, Proceedings of an Interdisciplinary Symposium (ed.), Berlin, 1984

Recht auf Information - Schutz vor Information, Menschen- und staatsrechtliche Aspekte (The Right of Access to Information - the Protection from Information and the States' Rights) (ed.), Berlin, 1986

Antarctic Challenge II, Proceedings of an Interdisciplinary Symposium (Hrsg.), Berlin, 1986

Staatsgebiete und staatsfreie Räume - Studienbrief, Deutsches Institut für Fernstudien der Universität Tübingen (State Territories and International Commons - A short introduction)

Antarctic Challenge III, Proceedings of an Interdisciplinary Symposium (ed.), Berlin, 1988

International Law and Municipal Law, Proceedings of the German-Soviet Colloquy on International Law (edited with Grigory Tunkin), Berlin, 1988

Völkerrecht Band I/1, begründet von Georg Dahm (International Law, vol. I/1, founded by Georg Dahm, newly revised, updated and edited with Jost Delbrück), Berlin, 1989

Die Reform der Vereinten Nationen: Möglichkeiten und Grenzen (The Reform of the United Nations: Possibilities and Limits) (ed.), Berlin, 1989

Des Menschen Recht zwischen Freiheit und Vrantwortung, Festschrift für Karl Josef Partsch (Human Rights between Freedom and Responsibility, Essays in Honor of Karl Josef Partsch) (edited with Jürgen Jekewitz, Karl Heinz Klein, Jörg-Detlev Kühne, Hans Petersmann), Berlin, 1989

Meereswirtschaft in Europa: Rechtliche und ökonomische Rahmenbedingungen (Marine Economy in Europe: Legal and Economic Framework) (together with Juergen B. Donges/Federico Foders/Enno Harders), Tübingen, 1989

Strengthening the World Order: Universalism v. Regionalism, Symposium held on the occasion of the 75th Anniversary of the Institute of International Law (ed.), Berlin, 1990

Handbuch Vereinte Nationen (Hrsg.), 2 Aufl., Munich, 1991
United Nations Handbook (ed.)

Law of the Sea at the Crossroads: The Continuing Search for a Universally Accepted Régime (ed.), Berlin, 1991

The Convention on the Regulation of Antarctic Mineral Resource Activities, Berlin, etc., 1991

Wirtschafts- und Gesellschaftsrecht Osteuropas im Zeichen des Übergangs zur Marktwirtschaft (Economic and Social Law in Eastern Europe in the Transition Period to Market Economy) (edited with F. J. Säcker and W. Seiffert), vol. 1, Schriftenreihe zum osteuropäischen Recht (Publication Series on Eastern European Law), Munich, 1992

Die Rechtslage ausländischer Investitionen in den Nachfolgestaaten der Sowjetunion (The Legal Status for Foreign Investments in the States of the Former Soviet Union) (edited with F. J. Säcker and W. Seiffert), vol. 2, Schriftenreihe zum osteuropäischen Recht (Publication Series on Eastern European Law), Munich, 1993

Marktzutrittsbarrieren in den USA und Kanada. Der Markt für
meerestechnische Güter und Dienstleistungen (Barriers to Market Access in
the USA and Canada. The Market for Goods and Services in Maritime
Technology) (together with F. Foders, P.-T. Stoll and I. Townsend-Gault),
Kieler Studien (ed. H. Siebert), vol. 257, Tübingen, 1993

Anerkennung und Vollstreckung ausländischer Entscheidungen in Osteuropa
(Acknowledgement and Enforcement of Foreign Judgements in Eastern Europe)
(edited with F. J. Säcker and W. Seiffert), vol. 3, Schriftenreihe zum
osteuropäischen Recht (Publication Series on Eastern European Law), Munich,
1994

Verfahren der Kandidatenaufstellung und der Wahlprüfung im europäischen
Vergleich (Nomination of Candidates and Electoral Examination in European
Countries - A Comparative Study) (edited together with G. Schuster), Baden-
Baden, 1994, 213 pp.

United Nations: Law, Policies and Practice (edited with C. Philipp),
Dordrecht, 1995

Economic and Legal Aspects of International Environmental Agreements - The
case of enforcing and stabilising an international CO_2 agreement, Kieler
Arbeitspapiere/Kiel Working Papers, No. 711 (together with J. Heister,
E. Mohr, W. Plesmann, F. Stähler and T. Stoll), Kiel, 1995

II. Articles

Die Bewertung innerparteilicher Vorgänge bei der Zulassung von
Parteiwahlvorschlägen zu Landtags- und Bundestagswahlen (The Relevance of
Inner-Party Decisions for Candidature to the German Bundestag and the State
Parliaments), Zeitschrift für Parlamentsfragen, 1975, pp. 323-340

Die Beschränkungen für die Freiheit der Schiffahrt durch das Kanadische
"Arctic Waters Pollution Prevention Act" sowie die internationalen
Übereinkommen zum Schutze der Meeresumwelt (Restrictions Imposed upon the
Freedom of Navigation by the Canadian Arctic Waters Pollution Prevention
Act and International Agreements for the Protection of the Marine
Environment), Berichte der Deutschen Gesellschaft für Völkerrecht, vol. 15,
1975, pp. 143-162

Der Umweltschutz auf Hoher See - Internationale wie nationale Maßnahmen und
Bestrebungen (The Environmental Protection of the High Seas, International
and National Measures as well as Attempts), Verfassung und Recht in
Übersee, 1975, pp. 201-219

Der Schutz der Familie durch Art. 8 MRK sowie Art. 16 und 19 Ziff. 6 der
Europäischen Sozialcharta (The Protection of the Family through Art. 8
European Human Rights Convention as well as Art. 16 and 19 (para. 6) of the
European Social Charter), Die Friedenswarte, Bd. 58, 1975, pp. 264-278

Der Schutz der Meeresforschung im Völkerrecht (The Protection of Marine
Scientific Research in International Law), German Yearbook of International
Law, vol. 19, 1976, pp. 99-127

Bearbeitung folgender Stichworte in dem o.g. Handbuch Vereinte Nationen
(Text on the following Key Words in The Handbook on the United Nations),
Munich, 1977: Beitragssystem, Haushalt (Contributions, Budget)
(pp. 40-48), IMCO (pp. 204-207), Seerecht (Law of the Sea) (pp. 382-391),
Streitschlichtung (Settlement of Disputes) (pp. 430-437), Weltraumrecht
(Outer Space Law) (pp. 520-523)

Die Fischerei auf Hoher See (Fisheries on the High Seas), Zeitschrift für
ausländisches öffentliches Recht und Völkerrecht (ZaöRV), Bd. 38, 1978,
pp. 659-709

Transfer of Technology: Some Critical Remarks and Suggestions for Change, in: Alternatives in Deep-Sea-Mining, Proceedings of the Law of the Sea Institute, University of Hawaii, 1979, pp. 35-45

Reports of Member States before the United Nations Human Rights Committee on the International Covenant on Political and Civil Rights, in: World in Transition: Challenges to Human Rights, Development and World Order, edited by H. H. Han, Washington, 1979, pp. 55-63

The Common Heritage Principle: State Equality Versus Equity, in: World in Transition: Challenges to Human Rights, Development and World Order, edited by H. H. Han, Washington, 1979, pp. 297-304

Der Ausschluß von Einwendungen im Anhörungsverfahren und sein Einfluß auf den Verwaltungsrechtsschutz (The Exclusion of Objections in Hearings Procedure and its Impact upon the Protection of the Individual), DÖV, 1979, pp. 497-502

Der Mondvertrag von 1979 - Weiterentwicklung des Weltraumrechts (The Moon Treaty of 1979 - Further Development in Space Law), Europa-Archiv, 1980, pp. 665-672

Neue Elemente im Willensbildungsprozeß internationaler Wirtschaftsorganisationen (New Elements in the Decision-making Procedure of International Economic Organizations), Zeitschrift Vereinte Nationen, 1981, pp. 50-56

Durchsetzung von Umweltbelangen im Verwaltungsverfahren am Beispiel der Bauleitplanung (Enforcement of Environmental Standards in Administrative Procedures in Urban Development), DÖV, 1981, pp. 606-614

Renationalisierung des Fischereiregimes (Re-nationalization of Fisheries), Die Plünderung der Meere (ed. Wolfgang Graf Vitzthum), Frankfurt, 1981, pp. 231-246

Restricting the Use of the Sea to Peaceful Purposes: Demilitarization in Being? German Yearbook of International Law 24, 1981, pp. 200-241

German National Legislation on Deep Sea-bed Mining, in: Marine Mining: A New Beginning, Hilo, Hawaii, 1982, pp. 236-252

Indemnität im Kompetenzkonflikt zwischen Bund und Ländern (Regulating Indemnity in Conflict of Competence between the Federation and the States), Die Öffentliche Verwaltung, 1982, pp. 674-680

Entwicklungen neuer Weltordnungen (Development of New World Orders), Das Parlament v. 10.09.1983, p. 6

Die Bundesrepublik Deutschland und die Seerechtskonvention (The Federal Republic of Germany and the Law of the Sea Convention), Europa-Archiv, 1983, pp. 83-92

Die Seerechtskonvention - Ein Markstein auf dem Weg zur Staatengemeinschaft? (The Law of the Sea Convention - A first Step on the Way to a Community of States), VN, 1983, pp. 69-78

The Principle of the Common Heritage of Mankind, ZaöRV, 1983, pp. 311-337

Die Auflösung des 9. Deutschen Bundestages vor dem BVerfG - BVerfGE 62, 1 (The Dissolution of the 9th German Federal Parliament before the BVerfG - BVerfGE 62, 1), Juristische Schulung, 1983, pp. 758-764 (together with Jost Delbrück)

International Administrative Unions (pp. 42-49); International
Organizations, Financing and Budgeting (pp. 115-119); Pluri-national
Administrative Institutions (pp. 235-238), R. Bernhardt (ed.), Encyclopedia
of Public International Law/Instalment 5, 1983

The Use of Antarctic Non-Living Resources: The Search for a Trustee?,
Antarctic Challenge, Berlin, 1984, pp. 143-163

Die UN-Seerechtskonvention in der Perspektive der Neuen
Weltwirtschaftsordnung (The United Nations Convention on the Law of the Sea
in the Perspective of the New World Economic Order), Das neue Seerecht,
Berlin, 1984, pp. 143-163

Die grenzüberschreitende Luftverschmutzung im Schnittpunkt von nationalem
Recht und Völkerrecht (Transborder Air Pollution in the Centerpoint of
National and International Law), Deutsches Verwaltungsblatt, 1984,
pp. 493-501

Die Kunstfreiheitsgarantie des Grundgesetzes (The Freedom of Art according
to the German Constitution), Schleswig-Holsteinische Anzeigen, 1984,
pp. 2-8

Entwicklungen neuer Weltordnungen (Development of New World Orders),
Vereinte Nationen, Themenheft 5 (ed. Bundeszentrale für politische
Bildung), Bonn, 1984, pp. 32-36

Die amerikanische Seerechtspolitik (American Politics concerning the Law of
the Sea), Europa-Archiv, 1984, pp. 317-325

The Problems of Limitation and Prohibition of Military Use of Outer Space,
ZaöRV, 1984, pp. 784-805

Der Schutz des Kindes im Völkerrecht (The Protection of the Child in
International Law), Schriften der Hermann-Ehlers-Akademie, H. 16, 1984,
pp. 24-34

Internationale Organisationen (International Organizations), Ergänzbares
Lexikon des Rechts, edited by Ignaz Seidl-Hohenveldern, Neuwied und
Darmstadt, 1982, Gruppe 4/490, 10 pages; Luftraum, ebd., 1986,
Gruppe 4/650, 2 pp.

The Legal Status of Sinti and Roma in Europe: A Case Study Concerning the
Shortcomings of the Protection of Minorities, in: European Yearbook,
vol. XXXIII (1985), Dordrecht/Boston/Lancaster, 1986, pp. ART 75-91

Antarctica, in: Conflicts, Options, Strategies in a Threatened World,
edited by W. Kaltefleiter/U. Schumacher, Kiel, 1986, pp. 213-232

Das moderne Seerecht - eine angemessene Antwort auf neue technologische
Entwicklungen? (The Modern Law of the Sea: An Appropriate Answer to New
Technological Developments), Technologischer Fortschritt als Rechtsproblem,
edited by Universität Heidelberg, 1986, pp. 92-100

Konsens im Völkerrecht (Consensus in International Law), Mehrheitsprinzip,
Konsens und Verfassung, edited by H. Hattenhauer/W. Kaltefleiter,
Heidelberg, 1986, pp. 79-91

Verfassungsrechtliche Fragen der Zweitanmeldung von Arzneimitteln,
Pflanzenbehandlungsmitteln und Chemikalien - Zugleich ein Beitrag zum
Schutz technischer Innovationen (Constitutional Questions in Second
Applications regarding Pharmaceuticals, Plant Treatments and Chemicals -
The Protection of Technical Innovations), GRUR, 1986, pp. 512-518

Die Küstenmeergrenzen der Bundesrepublik Deutschland in Nord- und Ostsee (The Limits of the Territorial Sea of the Federal Republic of Germany in the North and Baltic Seas), AVR, 1986, pp. 247-276

Means of Ensuring Compliance with an Antarctic Mineral Resources Regime, in: Antarctic Challenge II, Berlin, 1986, pp. 177-190

International Law of Cooperation, pp. 193-198, in: Bernhardt (ed.), Encyclopedia of Public International Law/Instalment 9 (1986)

Rechtliche Ordnung des Weltraums (The Legal Order of Outer Space), Weltraum und internationale Politik, edited by Kaiser/Frhr. v. Welck, Munich, 1987, pp. 241-252

Weltraumpolitik der Vereinten Nationen (Outer Space Politics of the United Nations), Weltraum und international Politik, edited by Kaiser/Frhr. v. Welck, Munich, 1987, pp. 451-462

The Emerging Customary Law of Marine Zones: State Practice and the Convention on the Law of the Sea, in: Netherlands Yearbook of International Law, vol. XVIII, 1987, pp. 121-144

Internationalization, pp. 268-271, Internationally Wrongful Acts, pp. 271-277, Reparation for Internationally Wrongful Acts, pp. 352-353, in: R. Bernhardt (ed.), Encyclopedia of Public International Law/Instalment 10, 1987

Anmerkung zur C-Waffen-Entscheidung des Bundesverfassungsgerichts (A Note on the Chemical Weapons' Decision of the Supreme Federal Constitutional Court), Decision of 29.10.1987, EuGRZ, 1988, pp. 295-297

Internationale Rahmenbedingungen für eine Förderung der Meereswirtschaft (The International Framework of Maritime Economic Activity Endorsement) Christiana Albertina, Heft 26, neue Folge, April 1988, pp. 13-17

Im Bonner Kommentar: Zweitbearbeitung von Art. 27, 61, 124, 125 (In Bonn's Commentary: Commentaries on Arts. 27, 61, 124, 125, second revision), 55. Lieferung, 1988

Ursprüngliche Aufgabenzuweisung und jetzige Aktivitäten der Vereinten Nationen: Faktischer Wandel und normative Bewertung (The Original Assignment of Functions and the Current Activities of the United Nations: Factual Variation and Standard Assessment: The Reform of the United Nations - Possibilities and Limits), in: Die Reform der Vereinten Nationen; Möglichkeiten und Grenzen, Berlin, 1989, pp. 129-156

Coastal Fisheries, pp. 61-63, Common Heritage of Mankind, pp. 65-69, Fisheries, International Regulation, pp. 109-113, Fishery Commissions, pp. 117-121, in: R. Bernhardt (ed.), Encyclopedia of Public International Law/Instalment 11 (1989)

Reflagging and Escort Operations in the Persian Gulf: International Law Perspective, Virginia Journal of International Law, vol. 29 (1989), pp. 387-399

The Progressive Development of Human Rights: A Critical Appraisal of Recent United Nations Efforts, Festschrift für Karl Josef Partsch (Essays in Honour of Karl Josef Partsch), Berlin, 1989, pp. 67-95

Vorbeugung und Bewältigung von Krisen im Völkerrecht (Preventive Measures and Solutions of Crises in International Law), Krise und Krisenmanagement in den internationalen Beziehungen, edited by Hanspeter Neuhold und Hans-Joachim Heinemann, Stuttgart, 1989, pp. 13-30

Die Einrichtung der Verwaltungsgerichtsbarkeit und der
Verwaltungsrechtsprechung in Schleswig-Holstein bis 1945 (The Establishment
of Administrative Courts and Administrative Jurisdiction), in: 100 Jahre
Verwaltungsge-richtsbarkeit in Schleswig-Holstein, Schleswig-Holsteinische
Anzeigen, 1989, pp. 17-21

The Polar Regions: Legal Aspects, in: The Polar Regions and their
Strategic Significance, ed. by Lucius Caflisch/Fred Tanner, Programme for
Strategic and International Security Studies, PSIS Special Studies
Number 2/1989, pp. 3-18

Die Umsetzung des Seerechtsübereinkommens in nationales Recht, Vereinte
Nationen (Implementation of the Law of the Sea Convention in National Law),
1990, pp. 20-23

Tiefflüge vor den Verwaltungsgerichten (Low Altitude Flights before
Administrative Courts), NVwZ 1990, S. 237-240

Die UN-Konvention über die Rechte des Kindes: Entwicklung, Inhalt und
Einbettung in den internationalen Menschenrechtsschutz (The United Nations
Convention on the Rights of the Child: Development, Contents and Embedding
in International Human Rights Protection), in: Dokumentation
"UN-Konvention über die Rechte des Kindes", 1990, pp. 7-19

Das Verbot der Rassendiskriminierung im Spannungsfeld zwischen dem Schutz
individueller Freiheitsrechte und der Verpflichtung des einzelnen im
Allgemeininteresse (The Prohibition of Racial Discrimination: Tension
between the Protection of Individual Freedoms and the Obligation of the
Individual in the Public Interest), in Kritik und Vertrauen, Festschrift
für Peter Schneider, Frankfurt am Main, 1990, pp. 515-525

Recht der Flagge und "Billige Flaggen": Neuere Entwicklungen im
Völkerrecht (The Law of Flagging and Flags of Convenience: New
Developments in International Law), Berichte der Deutschen Gesellschaft für
Völkerrecht, Issue 31 (1990), pp. 121-147

Ziele und Grundsätze des Internationalen Umweltschutzrechts (Purposes and
Principles of International Environmental Law), Antrittsrede zur Übernahme
des Prorektorats am 31.Mai 1990, 20 pp.

Antarctica After 1991: A Possible Scenario, Presentation to the Chilean
Council on Foreign Relations, Lectures Series 1990, 20 pp.

Antarctica, in: Bernhardt (ed.), Encyclopedia of Public International Law,
Instalment 12 (1990), 10 pp. (together with Klemm)

Purposes and Principles of International Environmental Law, GYIL 33 (1990),
pp. 308-330

Kommentierung der Präambel und von Art. 1, 18, 55 (a) und (b), 56
(Commentary on the Preamble and Articles 1, 18, 55 (a)-(b), and 56), in:
Charta der Vereinten Nationen, Kommentar (Ed. Simma in Gemeinschaft mit
Mosler, Randelzhofer, Tomuschat, Wolfrum), Munich, 1991, 45 pp.

Einzelne Formen der Nutzung des Weltraums (Geostationäre Umlaufbahn,
Telekommunikation, Direct-Broadcasting-Satellites, Navigations - und
Notfunksatelliten, Wetterbeobachtungssatelliten) (Individual Forms of Uses
of Outer Space (Geostationary Orbit, Telecommunications, Direct
Meteorological Observation Satellites)), in: Handbuch des Weltraumrechts,
Böckstiegel (Hrsg.), Köln, 1991, S. 351-424

The Unfinished Task: CRAMRA and the Question of Liability, in: Jorgensen-
Dahl/Ostreng eds., The Antarctic Treaty System in World Politics, 1991,
pp. 120-132

Bearbeitung folgender Stichworte in dem Handbuch Vereinte Nationen (Treatment of the following topics in the United Nations Handbook) 2 Aufl. 1991 (ed. Wolfrum): Haushalt (Budget) (pp. 268-275); Konsens (Consensus) (pp. 529-534); Meeresbodenbehörde (Deep Sea Bed Authority) (pp. 538-544); Rohstoffabkommen/Rohstoffonds (Commodity Agreement/Commodity Fund) (pp. 707-714); Seerecht (Law of the Sea) (pp. 728-738); Stimmrecht und Abstimmungsverfahren (Voting Rights and Procedures) (pp. 806-812); Streitschlichtung, friedliche (Peaceful Settlement of Disputes) (pp. 812-820)

Die Aufgaben der Vereinten Nationen im Wandel: Aus Politik und Zeitgeschichte (The Functions of the United Nations in Transition), Beilage zur Wochenzeitung Das Parlament, B 36/91, 30 August 1991, pp. 3-13

Zweiter Golfkrieg: Anwendungsfall von Kapitel VII der UN Charta (The Second Gulf War, A Case of Applying Chapter VII of the United Nations Charter), Zeitschrift Vereinte Nationen, 1991, Heft 4 (zusammen mit Ursula Heinz und Christiane Philipp), pp. 121-128

Decision-making in the Council: An Assessment and Comparison, in: Law of the Sea at the Crossroads: The Continuing Search for a Universally Accepted Régime, Berlin, 1991, pp. 59-74

Japan and the European Community in the United Nations: Prospects for Collaboration, in: Publications of the Japanese-German Center Berlin, Series 3, vol. 4 (1991), pp. 188-194

The Decision-making Process of the Council Reconsidered: A Suggestion to Make the Deep Seabed Regime More Responsive to Vested Interests, in: M. H. Nordquist (ed.), Fifteenth Annual Seminar: Issues in Amending Part XI of the LOS Convention. Center for Oceans Law and Policy, University of Virginia, School of Law, 1991, pp. 110-124

The Legal Status of Minorities in South-Eastern Europe, in: The Changing Political Structure of Europe (hrsg. von R. Lefeber/M. Fitzmaurice/ E. W. Vierdag), 1991, pp. 131-148

Minderheitenschutz in Europa - Die staatsrechtliche Situation am Beispiel einzelner ausgewählter Staaten-Gutachten erstellt im Auftrag des Schleswig-Holsteinischen Landtages, in: Minderheiten in Europa, Landtagsforum am 7. Juni 1991 (hrsg. von der Präsidentin des Schleswig-Holsteinischen Landtages), S. 121-160 (Protection of Minorities in Europe - The Public Law Situation as seen in selected State Reports commissioned by the Schleswig-Holstein Parliament), edited by the President of the Schleswig-Holstein Parliament

Wem gehört die Antarktis? Nationale Gebietsansprüche aus völkerrechtlicher Sicht (Who owns Antarctica? National Territorial Claims from the Perspective of International Law), in: Geographische Rundschau, 1992, Jg. 44, Heft 4, pp. 196-200

The Exploitation of Antarctic Mineral Resources: Risks and Stakes, in: The Antarctic Environment and International Law (eds. J. Verhoeven/ P. Sands/M. Bruce), 1992, pp. 27-31

Mitarbeit am Endbericht "Hemmnisse in den USA und Kanada für den Zugang ausländischer Unternehmen zu Offshore-Aktivitäten und die Lieferung meerestechnischer Anlagen und Geräte" (Collaboration at the Final Report "Barriers in the USA and Canada for the Access of Foreign Enterprises to Offshore Activity and the Provision of Technical Marine Installations and Equipment"). Forschungsauftrag des Bundesministers für Wirtschaft, Institut für Weltwirtschaft 1992, Volumes I bis III

Aufgaben der UN nach Art. 55 der Charta - weitreichende Ansätze und
eingeschränkter Handlungsspielraum, in: Strukturreform der UN?
Notwendigkeit, Ansätze und Handlungsspielraum einer Reform der Vereinten
Nationen im Bereich der wirtschaftlichen Zusammenarbeit (Functions of the
United Nations under Article 55 of the Charter - Far-reaching Tasks with
Limited Ability to Act) (Reihe Dokumentationen, Informationen, Meinungen
Nr. 42, März 1992, ed. Deutsche Gesellschaft für die Vereinten Nationen),
pp. 11-16

Völker- und europarechtliche Bestimmungen zum Schutz von Ausländern.
Bürger unterschiedlichen Rechts - aber nicht rechtlos (International and
European Law Provisions for the Protection of Foreigners, Citizens with
Different Rights, but not Rightless), in: Das Parlament, 43. Jg./Nr. 2-3,
8./15. January 1993, p. 7

The Impact of Federalism on the Implementation of International Trade
Obligations (together with Professor Fred L. Morrison), in: National
Constitutions and International Economic Law (eds. M. Hilf/
E.-U. Petersmann), vol. 8, 1993, pp. 519-535

The Emergence of "New Minorities" as a Result of Migration, in: Peoples
and Minorities in International Law (eds. C. Brölmann et al.), 1993,
pp. 153-166

Die Bundesrepublik Deutschland im Verteidigungsbündnis (§ 176: The Federal
Republic of Germany in Self-Defence Organizations), in: Handbuch des
Staatsrechts, Bd. VII: Normativität und Schutz der Verfassung -
Internationale Beziehungen (eds. J. Isensee and P. Kirchhof), 1993,
pp. 647-667

Der Beitrag regionaler Abmachungen zur Friedenssicherung: Möglichkeiten
und Grenzen (The Contribution of Regional Arrangements and Agencies to the
Maintenance of International Peace and Security: Possibilities and
Limitations), in: Zeitschrift für ausländisches öffentliches Recht und
Völkerrecht, vol. 53, No. 3, 1993, pp. 567-602

Antarktis (Antarctica), in: Staatslexikon (edited by the Görres Society),
7th edition, vol. 7: Die Staaten der Welt II (The States of the World II),
1993, pp. 863-866

The Protection of the Environment of the Baltic Sea. The Legal Framework,
in: Report of the Third Conference of Baltic University Rectors,
16-19 September 1992 at Kiel (ed. M. Müller-Wille/Rector of the Christian-
Albrechts University, Kiel), 1993, pp. 71-76

Die Weltmenschenrechtskonferenz - Perspektiven für die Entwicklung des
internationalen Menschenrechtsschutzes (The World Conference on Human
Rights - Prospects of the Developing of International Human Rights
Protection), in: Europa-Archiv, vol. 48, No. 23, 1993, pp. 681-690

The Reform of the Human Rights Institutions of the European Communities,
in: Reform of International Institutions for the Protection of Human
Rights, First International Colloquium on Human Rights, La Laguna,
Tenerife, 1-4 November 1992 (ed. La Laguna University), 1993, pp. 251-278

Bridges over Straits, in: The Law of the Sea: New Worlds, New Discoveries
(eds. E. L. Miles/T. Treves), Proceedings of the Law of the Sea Institute
26th Annual Conference, 1993, pp. 38-56

Zur Durchsetzung des humanitären Völkerrechts (Kapitel 12) (The Compliance
with International Humanitarian Law (chap. 12)), in: Handbuch des
humanitären Völkerrechts in bewaffneten Konflikten (ed. D. Fleck), 1994,
pp. 413-440

Vereinte Nationen: Agenda für die Weiterentwicklung des Völkerrechts
(United Nations: Agenda for Peace as a Means for the Further Development
of International Law), in: Völkerrecht und Sicherheit (Bundesakademie für
Sicherheitspolitik - Schriftenreihe zur neuen Sicherheitspolitik, 5)
(ed. L. Souchon), 1994, pp. 59-75

Die Schranken des Rechts: Das Wachstum der rechtlichen Bindungen der
Forschung, Referat auf dem Ringberg-Symposium: "Der schrumpfende Freiraum
der Forschung" (Limitations by Law: The Increasing of Legal Restrictions
for Research, presentation given at the Ringberg-Symposium "The Shrinking
Freedom of Research"), in: MPG-Spiegel, 4/1994, pp. 53-62

Die Europäische Gemeinschaft als Partei seerechtlicher Verträge (The
European Communities as a Party to Maritime Treaties), in: Archiv des
Völkerrechts, vol. 32, No. 3/4, 1994, pp. 317-335

Commenting of the Preamble and of Articles 1, 18, 55 (a) and (b) as well as
56, in: The Charter of the United Nations: A Commentary (ed. B. Simma, in
collaboration with H. Mosler, A. Randelzhofer, C. Tomuschat and
R. Wolfrum), Oxford 1994, pp. 45-56, 317-326, 759-795

The Decentralized Prosecution of International Offences through National
Courts, in: Israel Yearbook on Human Rights, vol. 24, 1994, pp. 183-199

The Protection of the Marine Environment after the Rio Conference:
Progress or Stalemate?, in: Recht zwischen Umbruch und Bewahrung -
Festschrift für Rudolf Bernhardt (Law between Change and Preservation -
Essays in Honour of Rudolf Bernhardt), Beiträge zum ausländischen
öffentlichen Recht und Völkerrecht, vol. 120 (ed. U. Beyerlin/M. Bothe/
R. Hofmann/E.-U. Petersmann), 1995, pp. 1003-1017

Author of the following keyword texts in "United Nations: Law, Policies
and Practice", Dordrecht, 1995 (edited with C. Philipp): Budget
(pp. 78-86), Commodity Agreements/Common Fund (pp. 138-148), Conflicts,
Iraq/Kuwait (pp. 261-277), Consensus (pp. 350-355), International Sea-Bed
Authority (pp. 789-796), Law of the Sea (pp. 834-847), Peaceful Settlement
of Disputes (pp. 982-993), Voting and Decision-Making (pp. 1400-1407)

Die Schranken des Rechts: Das Wachstum der rechtlichen Bindungen der
Forschung (Limitations by Law: The Increasing of Legal Restrictions for
Research), in: Max-Planck-Gesellschaft - Berichte und Mitteilungen, MPG-
Symposium "Der schrumpfende Freiraum der Forschung" ("The Shrinking Freedom
of Research"), 1/95, pp. 43-66

Section Five: The Constituent Power and the Birth of the New Laender, in:
Studies in German Constitutionalism, Studien und Materialien zur
Verfassungsgerichtsbarkeit, vol. 64 (ed. C. Starck), 1995, pp. 125-139

Deutschlands Mitgliedschaft in NATO, WEU und KSZE (Germany's membership in
NATO, WEU and CSCE), in: Handbuch des Staatsrechts, vol. VIII (Die Einheit
Deutschlands - Entwicklung und Grundlagen (The unification of Germany -
development and principles)) (ed. J. Isensee/P. Kirchhof, 1995, pp. 282-319

The Decision-Making Process According to Section 3 of the Annex to the
Implementation Agreement: A Model to be Followed for Other International
Economic Organisations?, in: Zeitschrift für ausländisches öffentliches
Recht und Völkerrecht, vol. 55/2 (Symposium "The Entry into Force of the
Convention on the Law of the Sea: A Redistribution of Competences Between
States and International Organisations in Relation to the Management of the
International Commons?"), 1995, pp. 310-328

Law of the Sea: An Example of the Progressive Development of International
Law, in: The United Nations at Age Fifty - A Legal Perspective
(ed. C. Tomuschat), 1995, pp. 309-327

The Legal Order for the Seas and Oceans, in: 1994 Rhodes Papers - The
Entry into Force of the Law of the Sea Convention (ed. M. H. Nordquist/
J. Norton Moore), 1995, pp. 161-185

Enforcement of International Humanitarian Law (chapter 12), in: The
Handbook of Humanitarian Law in Armed Conflicts (ed. D. Fleck), 1995,
pp. 517-550

Neue völkerrechtliche Entwicklungen im Verhältnis von Bergbau und
Umweltschutz beim Tiefseebergbau und in der Antarktis (New Developments in
International Law with Regard to the Relations between Mining and
Environmental Protection in Deep Seabed Mining and in Antarctica), in:
Recht der Energiewirtschaft (RdE), No. 1, 1996, pp. 9-15

Das internationale Recht für den Austausch von Waren und Dienstleistungen
(International Law on the Exchange of Goods and Services), in:
Enzyklopädie der Rechts- und Staatswissenschaft, Öffentliches
Wirtschaftsrecht, Besonderer Teil 2 (ed. R. Schmidt), 1996, pp. 535-656

[...]

53.   OBSERVER STATUS FOR THE ITLOS - LETTER DATED 26 NOVEMBER 1996 FROM THE PERMANENT REPRESENTATIVE OF GERMANY TO THE UNITED NATIONS ADDRESSED TO THE SECRETARY-GENERAL

Doc. no.: A/51/234 & Add.1   27 & 29 November 1996

After consultations with other delegations and upon instructions from my Government, I have the honour to request, in accordance with rule 15 of the rules of procedure of the General Assembly, the inclusion in the agenda of the fifty-first session of the General Assembly of an additional item of an urgent and important nature entitled "Observer status for the International Tribunal for the Law of the Sea".

In accordance with rule 20 of the rules of procedure of the General Assembly, an explanatory memorandum concerning the request is attached as an annex to the present letter.

I further have the honour to request that the present letter be circulated as a document of the General Assembly.

(Signed)   Tono EITEL

ANNEX

Explanatory memorandum

The International Tribunal for the Law of the Sea (hereinafter referred to as "the Tribunal") is an intergovernmental institution established by the United Nations Convention on the Law of the Sea of 10 December 1992 (hereinafter referred to as "the Convention").   The seat of the Tribunal is in the Free and Hanseatic City of Hamburg in the Federal Republic of Germany.

The Tribunal is an institution established for the settlement of disputes by peaceful means consistent with Article 2, paragraph 3, of the Charter of the United Nations, and in accordance with Part XV of the Convention.   It is a forum for judicial settlement, being one of the means for the peaceful settlement of disputes referred to in Article 33 of the Charter.

The Tribunal serves to encourage States parties, in conjunction with their obligations under Article 2, paragraph 2, of the Charter, to fulfil in good faith the obligations assumed under the Convention and other international agreements.

The Tribunal has competence over all matters governed by the Convention relating to the seas and oceans, which constitute nearly three fourths of the Earth's surface. Under article 21 of annex VI of the Convention, the jurisdiction of the Tribunal comprises all disputes concerning the interpretation or application of the Convention in accordance with article 288 and of other international agreements related to the purposes of the Convention that confer jurisdiction on the Tribunal. The jurisdiction includes prescribing, modifying or revoking provisional measures to preserve the respective rights of the parties or to prevent serious harm to the marine environment, in disputes before the Tribunal, submitted in accordance with article 290 of the Convention.

Its Seabed Disputes Chamber has exclusive jurisdiction over all disputes involving activities in the exploitation of the resources of the seabed and ocean floor and subsoil thereof beyond the limits of national jurisdiction. The jurisdiction extends to disputes to which the parties could include the International Seabed Authority and other entities other than States parties, including natural and juridical persons. The Seabed Disputes Chamber, at the request of the Assembly or the Council of the International Seabed Authority, will provide advisory opinions on legal questions arising within the scope of their activities and referred to it under article 191 of the Convention. Disputes arising out of the Agreement relating to the implementation of Part XI of the Convention can also be submitted to the Tribunal, to its Seabed Disputes Chamber.

Other agreements conferring jurisdiction in the Tribunal include the Agreement for the implementation of the provisions of the Convention relating to the conservation of straddling fish stocks and highly migratory fish stocks (hereinafter referred to as "the Agreement"). Article 30 of the Agreement confers jurisdiction on the Tribunal with respect to any dispute between States parties to the Agreement concerning the interpretation or application of the Agreement or concerning the interpretation or application of a subregional, regional or global fisheries agreement relating to straddling fish stocks or highly migratory fish stocks to which they are parties.

The jurisdiction of the Tribunal includes exclusive jurisdiction in urgent cases of applications for the prompt release of arrested vessels and their crews submitted to the Tribunal in accordance with article 292 of the Convention.

The problems of ocean space are closely interrelated and need to be considered as a whole. The activities of the Tribunal are complementary to those of the United Nations in many fields, in particular the field of the law of the sea and ocean affairs, for which the Secretary-General serves as the secretariat of the Convention, and as an agency of cooperation, collation and some coordination. Furthermore, the Tribunal, being the central institution created under the Convention for the peaceful settlement of disputes, needs to be aware of all developments relating to the oceans and general principles and developments relating to peaceful settlements, in accordance with the Charter. The establishment and functioning of the Tribunal constitute important components of the developments relating to the Convention. These would also be included in the review by the General Assembly in its consideration of the item on the law of the sea.

At the fifth Meeting of States Parties, held in New York from 24 July to 2 August 1996, various matters relating to the establishment of the Tribunal were discussed. The Meeting decided, <u>inter alia</u>, that since the proceedings of the General Assembly were of interest to it, the Tribunal should be appropriately represented at the meetings of the General Assembly and should apply for observer status.'

The adoption of such a resolution is a matter of importance and urgency, since, without it, or if there be a delay, the Tribunal would, during its important organizational phase, be the only institution established by the Convention that would lack this essential link to the United Nations and its activities, a situation that would be inconsistent with the essentially interrelated nature of the problems of ocean space.

The Tribunal, at its first session, held at Hamburg from 1 to 31 October 1996, considered, <u>inter alia</u>, the report of the fifth Meeting of States Parties and took note of the decisions taken by it. Having an interest in the law of the sea and ocean affairs, including fisheries and navigation, the global environment, sustainable development, questions relating to administration and other related matters considered by the General Assembly, it decided that the Tribunal should seek to obtain observer status at the United Nations to enable it to participate as an observer in the deliberations of the Assembly with respect to topics of interest to the Tribunal. To this end, the Tribunal requested the Registrar to take the necessary measures in order to seek such observer status.

The Tribunal considers that the granting of observer status at the United Nations would assist in establishing and consolidating links between the Tribunal and the United Nations that would be of mutual benefit.

The Tribunal requests that it be granted observer status at the United Nations.

Notes

* **Report of the Fifth Meeting of States Parties, para. 36 (SPLOS/14, 20 September 1996).**

Addendum

Add the following names to the list of signatories:

(Signed) Fernando PETRELLA
  Permanent Representative of Argentina
  to the United Nations

(Signed) Wilhelm BREITENSTEIN
  Permanent Representative of Finland
  to the United Nations

(Signed) Samir MOUBARAK
  Permanent Representative of Lebanon
  to the United Nations

(Signed) Ibra DEGUÈNE
  Chargé d'affaires a.i. of the
  Permanent Mission of Senegal
  to the United Nations

(Signed) James O. C. JONAH
  Permanent Representative of Sierra Leone
  to the United Nations

-----

54. OBSERVER STATUS FOR THE ITLOS IN THE GENERAL ASSEMBLY - UNGA RESOLUTION

Doc. no.: A/Res.51/204   17 December 1996

The General Assembly,

Stressing the importance of the uniform interpretation or application of the provisions of the United Nations Convention on the Law of the Sea, 167/ the agreements related thereto and any other agreement which confers jurisdiction on the International Tribunal for the Law of the Sea,

Aware of the need for States to settle any disputes concerning the interpretation or application of the United Nations Convention on the Law of the Sea by peaceful means,

Welcoming the establishment of the Tribunal in the Free and Hanseatic City of Hamburg, Federal Republic of Germany,

Noting the decision of the meeting of States Parties at its fifth session to seek observer status for the International Tribunal for the Law of the Sea in order to enable it to participate in the sessions and the work of the General Assembly 168/ and the decision of the Tribunal at its first session to seek such observer status,

1.   Decides to invite the International Tribunal for the Law of the Sea to participate in the sessions and the work of the General Assembly in the capacity of observer;

2.   Requests the Secretary-General to take the necessary action to implement the present resolution.

167/ Official Records of the Third United Nations Conference on the Law of the Sea, vol. XVII (United Nations publication, Sales No. E.84.V.3), document A/CONF.62/122.

168/ See SPLOS/14, para. 36.

55. LAW OF THE SEA: AGREEMENT FOR THE IMPLEMENTATION OF THE PROVISIONS OF THE UNITED NATIONS CONVENTION ON THE LAW OF THE SEA OF 10 DECEMBER 1982 RELATING TO THE CONSERVATION AND MANAGEMENT OF STRADDLING FISH STOCKS AND HIGHLY MIGRATORY FISH STOCKS - REPORT OF THE UN SECRETARY-GENERAL

Doc. no.: A/51/383

4 October 1996

CONTENTS

I.   INTRODUCTION

1.   At its fiftieth session, in its resolution 50/24 of 5 December 1995, the General Assembly expressed its appreciation to the United Nations Conference on Straddling Fish Stocks and Highly Migratory Fish Stocks for discharging its mandate under Assembly resolution 47/192 of 22 December 1992 with the adoption of the Agreement for the Implementation of the Provisions of the United Nations Convention on the Law of the Sea of 10 December 1982 relating to the Conservation and Management of Straddling Fish Stocks and Highly Migratory Fish Stocks (hereafter referred to as "the 1995 Agreement"), and emphasized the importance of its early entry into force and effective implementation. 1/

2.   The General Assembly also called upon all States and other entities entitled to do so pursuant to the relevant provisions of the 1995 Agreement to sign and ratify or accede to it and to consider applying it provisionally. It further requested the Secretary-General to report to it at its fifty-first

session and biennially thereafter on developments relating to the conservation
and management of straddling fish stocks and highly migratory fish stocks,
taking into account information provided by States, relevant specialized
agencies, in particular the Food and Agriculture Organization of the United
Nations (FAO), and other appropriate organs, organizations and programmes of the
United Nations system, regional and subregional organizations and arrangements
for the conservation and management of straddling fish stocks and highly
migratory fish stocks, as well as other relevant intergovernmental bodies and
non-governmental organizations. 2/

3.   Accordingly, the Secretary-General sent a note verbale to all members of
the international community, drawing their attention to resolution 50/24.
Letters were also addressed to relevant intergovernmental organizations, and
organizations and bodies of the United Nations system, as well as regional and
subregional fisheries organizations and arrangements and relevant
non-governmental organizations. In response, the Secretary-General has received
a number of submissions and comments. He wishes to express his appreciation for
all the contributions, and in particular to FAO for its detailed report.

4.   The present report, which takes into account those contributions, is
submitted to the General Assembly in response to the request contained in
resolution 50/24.

II.   INFORMATION PROVIDED BY STATES

5.   In its response to the Secretary-General dated 10 June 1996, Colombia
informed him that, as a party to the 1992 La Jolla Agreement, 3/ it actively
participated in the International Review Panel through which specific studies on
straddling fish stocks and highly migratory fish stocks were being carried out.
In an additional communication dated 9 July 1996, it stated that the Colombian
Ministry of Agriculture and the National Institute for Fishing and Aquaculture
(INPA) continued to participate in the meetings of the Interamerican Committee
on Tropical Tuna, the mandate of which encompassed tuna fisheries and the
conservation of dolphins in the eastern Pacific. INPA had enacted mandatory
rules for the sound exploitation of tuna fisheries and the conservation of
dolphin, applicable to fishing vessels working for Colombian companies, and had
addressed the issue at several regional meetings of the Permanent Commission of
the Southern Pacific and the Fishery Commission of the Central Western Atlantic.

6.   In its submission of 10 June 1996 to the Secretary-General, Qatar indicated
that data and information on the conservation and management of straddling fish
stocks and highly migratory fish stocks were being exchanged on a cooperative
basis through its participation in the Technical Committee on Fisheries of the
Gulf Cooperation Council and in the Committee for the Development and Management
of the Fisheries Resources of the Gulf of the Indian Ocean Fishery Commission of
FAO.

7.   In its reply to the Secretary-General dated 18 June 1996, Maldives stated
that it would sign the 1995 Agreement in the very near future.

8.   In its response to the Secretary-General of 21 June 1996, Saudi Arabia
indicated that it had been cooperating with neighbouring States, particularly
States members of the Gulf Cooperation Council. One of the most salient results
of such cooperation had been the prohibition of the use of trawl nets for
demersal fish during mating seasons in the Arabian Gulf and for a three-month
period each year. Agreement was also reached on the establishment of a closed
season for shrimp fishing in the Arabian Gulf for a period of not less than six
months between January and September each year, as well as on coordination
between member States sharing fish stocks concerning fixed dates for the
beginning of fishing seasons and a global survey of the waters of the Arabian
Gulf.

9. In its reply of 28 June 1996 to the Secretary-General, Italy informed him that, with its signature of the 1995 Agreement on 26 June 1996, the procedure for ratification had already been initiated.

10. In its response to the Secretary-General dated 28 June 1996, Canada submitted the following information regarding developments relating to the conservation and management of straddling fish stocks and highly migratory fish stocks:

"(a) <u>Straddling stocks</u>

"Straddling stocks on the Atlantic coast are managed by the Northwest Atlantic Fisheries Organization (NAFO) in NAFO divisions 3LMNO. Canadian regulations and measures apply equally to Canadian vessels fishing inside and outside Canada's 200-mile limit. Management measures for these straddling stocks are put in place by NAFO. Canada complies with all NAFO rules and in several cases Canada's management measures are even more stringent.

"For instance, the NAFO mesh size for trawl nets is 130 millimetres. For Canadian vessels the minimum size is 145 mm for some of these stocks. Under NAFO, if the quantity of undersize fish in any one haul is 10 per cent by number, the vessel must move at least 5 nautical miles and all undersized fish must be discarded. For Canadian vessels, discarding is not permitted and, should the number of undersized fish in the catch exceed 15 per cent by number, the fishery is closed for the entire fleet for at least 10 days.

"(b) <u>Highly migratory stocks</u>

"Highly migratory stocks on Canada's east coast are large pelagics, managed by the International Commission on the Conservation of Atlantic Tunas (ICCAT). Each year, Canada implements all ICCAT measures for bluefin, albacore, yellowfin, bigeye tuna and swordfish.

"Sharks, although migratory, are not yet being managed multilaterally in the Atlantic. However, Canada has put in place a number of management measures to limit fishing effort on these species and to assist in gaining further scientific information."

11. In its submission of 2 July 1996, Norway informed the Secretary-General that the Norwegian Parliament had on 11 June 1996 unanimously given its consent to the ratification of the 1995 Agreement; the Norwegian Government, therefore, intended to ratify it shortly. Norway also indicated that a four-party Agreement on the 1996 Norwegian spring spawning herring stocks concluded among the coastal States, i.e., Norway, the Russian Federation, Iceland and the Faroe Islands, had been signed and had entered into force on 6 May 1996. The Agreement, which limited the fishery both in the fishery zones of the four parties and in the high seas areas of the north-east Atlantic, represented a major step forward in a policy designed to extend sustainable management to the herring stock throughout its range of distribution. In addition, Norway had in March 1996 become a party to a North-east Atlantic Fisheries Commission (NEAFC) Agreement relating to the fishery for the straddling stocks of redfish in the Irminger Sea in the north-west Atlantic. It had also expressed grave concern over the unregulated north-east Arctic cod fisheries in the high seas areas of the Barents Sea and indicated its intention to renew efforts towards finding a viable solution to the problem.

12. In its reply to the Secretary-General dated 3 July 1996, Finland indicated that, as a member of the European Union (EU), it had accepted the decision of the EU Council to sign the 1995 Agreement, which had been held up by the issue of jurisdiction between the European Community and member countries. A compromise had however been reached on the matter at the EU Fisheries Council on 10 June 1996. <u>4</u>/

13.   In its response of 10 July 1996 to the Secretary-General, Morocco reported that it had recently established a national institute for research on living marine resources (Institut National de Recherche Halieutique) which would deal with assessment of straddling fish stocks and highly migratory fish stocks at the regional level as well as through bilateral and multilateral scientific cooperation.

14.   In its submission of 10 July 1996 to the Secretary-General, Spain referred to two important developments relating to the conservation and management of straddling fish stocks and highly migratory fish stocks. The first concerned the opening for signature of the 1995 Agreement, which had been signed by the European Community along with some States members. The remaining members, including Spain, would sign it shortly. The second concerned the management of Atlantic redfish (<u>Sebastes mentella</u>) by NEAFC. Total allowable catch (TAC) for these straddling fish stocks had been established; quotas had been allocated to contracting parties; and quota reserves had been determined for future NEAFC members. The Agreement was an example of cooperation between coastal States and States fishing on the high seas, and the measures taken by NEAFC would apply within and beyond zones under national jurisdiction on the basis of the best available scientific evidence.

15.   In its reply to the Secretary-General dated 22 July 1996, Kuwait informed him that, although very little had been done so far at the subregional level to discuss measures that needed to be adopted for the management of particular highly migratory fish stocks or those in shared zones, steps had been taken towards protecting those stocks. States members of the Gulf Cooperation Council had undertaken a joint research project to study shrimp nets in shared zones, with Kuwait taking a leading role in the work, which was considered to be among the most innovative in its field. Another project was under way to prevent the migration of seerfish, a species of economic value. Every Gulf State had agreed to gather all available data on the species, including its biological characteristics, length and weight and other useful information, with Bahrain playing the leading role in the project. In addition, a group of Gulf States was coordinating efforts to survey particular aspects of fishing grounds through the compilation of statistical data on species of fish in order to establish a statistical database, and through the assessment of certain aspects of environmental damage to fish stocks, particularly where stocks were becoming depleted, in order to counter the contributory source of pollution.

16.   Finally, Kuwait indicated that, at the regional level, it had followed the general principles for the conservation of fish stocks laid down in its national legislation, which guaranteed that those who infringed those principles would not profit from their illegal activities. Its national scientific institutions also played a major role in conducting surveys on fish stocks, including collection of data on fishing efforts according to fishing method, the biological study of target and non-target species, research on environmental factors affecting the growth and survival of fish stocks, and stock enhancement or restoration in zones under its national jurisdiction.

17.   In its response to the Secretary-General dated 25 July 1996, Tunisia indicated that its signature of the 1995 Agreement would probably take place before the end of 1996, following assessment of the results of the Second Diplomatic Conference on the Management of Living Marine Resources in the Mediterranean, to be held from 27 to 29 November 1996.

18.   In its submission to the Secretary-General dated 29 July 1996, South Africa informed him that it was in the process of developing a new and integrated fisheries policy, to be completed by the end of 1996. It also indicated that it was committed to enhancing global fisheries resources by means of responsible fishing practices in cooperation with its regional partners in the Southern African Development Community (SADC) and reaffirmed its support for the cooperative international and regional marine resource management agreements aimed at protecting and conserving the marine environment, as embodied in the FAO Code of Conduct for Responsible Fisheries and the 1995 Agreement.

19. In its reply to the Secretary-General dated 7 August 1996, the United States of America stated that it considered the 1995 Agreement to be a major achievement in promoting better stewardship of living marine resources and was committed to bringing it into force as quickly as possible. In meeting that commitment the United States, in September 1995, had embarked on a campaign to promote, through diplomatic channels, the signing and ratification of the Agreement. Since then, the United States Department of State had presented démarches to more than 130 States Members of the United Nations. It had also made appeals to non-member States to adhere to the principles of the Agreement. The United States was currently a party to a number of regional and subregional fishery management organizations and arrangements to which the Agreement applied. The United States believed that the Agreement would strengthen the ability of regional organizations and arrangements to carry out their conservation and management responsibilities. It also believed that those organizations and arrangements that managed straddling fish stocks and highly migratory fish stocks should act immediately, prior to the entry into force of the Agreement, to implement its key provisions. Those key provisions included the precautionary approach to fisheries management, transparency, new members, compliance and enforcement, and non-member fishing activities. The United States would work diligently in the coming months and years to achieve this goal and was also prepared to work with other members of the international community to establish, in accordance with the provisions of the Agreement, organizations and arrangements in those regions where none currently existed.

20. The United States added that President Clinton had transmitted the Agreement to the Senate on 20 February 1996 for its advice and consent to ratification; on 28 June 1996, the Senate had provided its advice and consent. 5/

III. INFORMATION PROVIDED BY INTERNATIONAL ORGANIZATIONS

A. Specialized agencies of the United Nations

21. In its response to the Secretary-General dated 19 July 1996, FAO submitted the following report:

"Conservation and management of fisheries resources worldwide is generally in a poor state. There have been no major improvements in the situation since FAO reported in the early 1990s that approximately 70 per cent of the world's marine capture fisheries resources for which data were available were fully exploited, over-exploited or in a state of recovery. A more recent FAO study using catch statistics available since 1995 for the 200 main marine fisheries resources has come to similar conclusions.

"For straddling fish stocks and highly migratory fish stocks, many commercially important and valuable stocks have been subject to heavy and sparsely regulated fishing effort, and some stocks continue to be overfished.

"The 1993-1995 United Nations Conference on Straddling Fish Stocks and Highly Migratory Fish Stocks, which led to the conclusion of the 1995 Agreement for the Implementation of the Provisions of the United Nations Convention on the Law of the Sea of 10 December 1982 relating to the Conservation and Management of Straddling Fish Stocks and Highly Migratory Fish Stocks (United Nations Agreement) sought to address this matter in a substantive and comprehensive manner, within the framework of the 1982 United Nations Convention on the Law of the Sea (1982 Convention). Moreover, the 1993 Agreement to Promote Compliance with International Conservation and Management Measures by Fishing Vessels on the High Seas (Compliance Agreement) and the 1995 Code of Conduct for Responsible Fisheries (Code of Conduct) also substantively address the need for, and seek to facilitate, the rational and long-term sustainable utilization of high seas fisheries resources.

"Status of stocks and conservation and management

"The status of these stocks, summarized on an ocean-by-ocean basis, together with a brief description of the subregional and regional management organizations and arrangements that exist to facilitate conservation and management of these stocks, is provided below.

"Atlantic Ocean

"(i) Highly migratory fish stocks

"Many stocks of the principal market species appear to be heavily to fully exploited and some stocks are overfished or depleted.

"Albacore and bigeye tuna. The stock of albacore in the North Atlantic appears to be exploited at about the maximum sustainable yield (MSY) level. In the South Atlantic, since the mid-1980s exploitation has exceeded the MSY level. Bigeye tuna are fished substantially above the MSY level.

"Bluefin tuna. In the eastern Atlantic and the Mediterranean Sea, reductions in fishing effort, especially that directed at small fish, could increase the yield in the long term. In the western Atlantic, the stock is being fished substantially below the MSY level. Southern bluefin tuna are over-exploited.

"Skipjack tuna. In the Atlantic, skipjack are likely to be moderately exploited.

"Yellowfin tuna. In the eastern Atlantic, the stock of yellowfin tuna is exploited at about the MSY level.

"Billfish and swordfish. Blue and white marlin in the Atlantic could be over-exploited. There is some concern about the status of sailfish in the Western Atlantic and even greater concern about the status of swordfish in the Atlantic.

"(ii) Straddling fish stocks

"North-west Atlantic Ocean. Straddling species occurring in this area include the Grand Bank cod, American plaice, redfish, witch flounder, Atlantic and Greenland halibut, yellowtail flounder, grenadiers, mackerel and neritic squids. It appears that all straddling stocks of groundfish in this zone are fished at or beyond the MSY level and that the groundfish stocks are now generally in the worst condition they have ever been in.

"North-east Atlantic Ocean. Blue whiting is one of the main straddling resources. It was heavily overfished in the 1980s but since 1986 fishing mortality has decreased and is now close to natural mortality. The stock is increasing and is considered within safe biological limits. The oceanic redfish reached its peak landings in 1986 (105,000 tonnes) and has since dropped substantially to just over 20,000 tonnes in recent years. The reason for the decrease has not been ascertained and there is no scientific assessment of the present status of the stock. Catches of cod, haddock, Greenland halibut and redfish in the Barents Sea are believed by scientists to be insignificant. Pelagic straddling stocks of the Norwegian spring spawning herring are recovering from a historical collapse and are increasing progressively owing to good replenishment.

"Mediterranean Sea. The Mediterranean coastal countries have not extended their exclusive economic zones to 200 miles; most still have a 12-mile limit. For this reason most of the waters of the Mediterranean remain high seas. Hake and deep sea shrimps are the main straddling stocks in the Gulf of Lions and the Gulf of Gabes. Small pelagics such as sardines and horse mackerel most probably straddle everywhere beyond the 12-mile limit.

"East-central Atlantic Ocean. The oceanic horse mackerel is the only known straddling stock in this region and nothing is known of its potential and status.

"West-central Atlantic Ocean. Flying fish, dolphins, Atlantic sailfish, king mackerel and oceanic sharks are the main straddling fish stocks in this region. With a number of distant-water fishing nations fishing for these species and tunas in the area, the problem of overall management and resource allocation remains. The status of straddling stocks has not yet been investigated.

"South-west Atlantic Ocean. Many important demersal fish stocks are found in this area, including short-fin and common squids, both of which are considered to be fully to over-exploited. The stocks are mostly exploited by distant-water fishing nations. The hake stocks are fully exploited. Both the southern blue whiting and the grenadier are considered to be under- to moderately exploited. Other demersal fish stocks are the pink cusk eel, the Patagonian toothfish, the tadpole mora, the Antarctic cod, rockcods, and common squids, all of which are considered to be moderately exploited.

"South-east Atlantic Ocean. Straddling stocks in this area include the horse mackerel, the pomfret and myctophids. Most catches are carried out within exclusive economic zones. No straddling stock conflict is reported.

"(iii)   Subregional and regional organizations and arrangements

"Tuna and tuna-like species are covered by the International Commission for the Conservation of Atlantic Tunas (ICCAT). The Commission has the mandate to manage these stocks in all waters of the Atlantic Ocean and its adjacent seas. It has adopted a number of regulatory measures concerning the size limits for yellowfin, bigeye, bluefin and swordfish.

"In the Mediterranean Sea the General Fisheries Council for the Mediterranean (GFCM) is responsible for the conservation and management of all fisheries resources in the area. The Council is an FAO funded and administered body whose structure and functions in relation to highly migratory species and straddling stocks need to be modified in order to implement the provisions of the United Nations Agreement.

"The regional fishery organizations with regulatory powers to deal with the conservation and management of straddling fish stocks in the Atlantic Ocean and its adjacent seas are the Northwest Atlantic Fisheries Organization (NAFO), the Northeast Atlantic Fisheries Commission (NEAFC), the International Baltic Sea Fishery Commission (IBSFC) and GFCM.

"For straddling stocks, NAFO has been facing a crisis situation in recent years with the recommendations of its Scientific Commission being jeopardized by the uncontrolled fishing activities of both members and non-members within its regulatory area. Delays in catch reports by members have also resulted in assessments with incomplete data.

"The International Council for the Exploration of the Sea (ICES) is a purely scientific body providing scientific advice to a number of organizations and countries in the north-east Atlantic region.

"Other regional bodies, including the Fishery Committee for the Eastern Central Atlantic (CECAF) and the Western Central Atlantic Fishery Commission (WECAFC), are advisory bodies funded and administered by FAO.

"Two other regional bodies, the International Commission for the Southeast Atlantic and the Regional Fisheries Advisory Commission for the Southwest Atlantic, have been inactive for some time. There is an urgent need for some form of fishery management arrangements for these two areas.

"There are also a number of subregional fisheries organizations with some regulatory powers, e.g., the Subregional Commission on Fisheries, the Regional Fisheries Committee for the Gulf of Guinea, and the Regional Convention on Fisheries Cooperation among African States Bordering the Atlantic Ocean. All three operate in the east-central Atlantic.

"Indian Ocean

"(i) Highly migratory fish stocks

"Albacore and bigeye tuna. In the Indian Ocean, the stock of albacore may be heavily exploited, but its assessment is highly uncertain. With the termination of drift-net fishing, the albacore stocks should be under less pressure. Bigeye are heavily fished, but the stock may be in a healthy condition, though this is uncertain.

"Bluefin tuna. Southern bluefin are over-exploited.

"Skipjack tuna. The stock of skipjack looks to be in a healthy condition, regardless of recent declines of average sizes in its catch off the Maldives, which are a matter of concern.

"Yellowfin tuna. In the Indian Ocean, yellowfin tuna do not appear to be threatened by over-exploitation, if there is only one stock, despite the tremendous increase in catch during the last 10 years. If there is a separate stock in the western Indian Ocean, the intensity of fishing there may be moderate to above the MSY level. However, more research is needed before the status of the stocks can be precisely determined.

"Billfish and swordfish. Fishery statistics for billfish and swordfish in the Indian Ocean are incomplete and even basic biological information is limited. Consequently, the knowledge of the status of the stocks is generally poor. Swordfish, however, seem to be under-exploited.

"(ii) Straddling fish stocks

"There is no information available to FAO on the status of straddling fish stocks in the Indian Ocean.

"(iii) Subregional and regional organizations and arrangements

"Two fishery bodies have recently been established to deal with the conservation and management of tunas in the Indian Ocean. The Convention on the Western Indian Ocean Tuna Organization (WIOTO) entered into force in 1994 but is not yet operational. The Agreement for the establishment of the Indian Ocean Tuna Commission (IOTC) entered into force in March 1996, and the first session of the Commission is to be held in Rome in September 1996. Both bodies have regulatory power although certain amendments to their establishing agreements may be necessary to enable them to implement the provisions of the 1995 United Nations Agreement. The Indian Ocean Fishery Commission (IOFC), funded and administered by FAO, has only advisory functions and is the only region-wide body in the region.

"Pacific Ocean

"(i) Highly migratory fish stocks

"Albacore and bigeye tunas. In the North Pacific, the albacore stock seems to be fully exploited but is in a stable condition. In the South

Pacific, fishing effort has been reduced after the close of the large-scale pelagic drift-net fishery, in 1991, but even at the present intensity of fishing, there is a risk of overfishing. The stock of bigeye in the Pacific is exploited at a level close to MSY. The potential impact of surface catches of small bigeye on bigeye longline catches is a concern.

"Bluefin tuna. The status of northern bluefin tuna in the North Pacific is uncertain but may be overfished. The southern bluefin tuna is over-exploited.

"Skipjack tuna. Catches of skipjack can probably be further increased, especially in the eastern, central and western Pacific.

"Yellowfin tuna. In the western and central Pacific, recent analyses suggest that a significant increase of the present catch would be sustainable. In the eastern Pacific the stock appears to be slightly under-exploited.

"Billfish and swordfish. Fishery statistics for billfish and swordfish stocks in the Pacific are incomplete and even basic biological information is limited.

"(ii) Straddling fish stocks

"North-west Pacific Ocean. The Alaska pollack is widely distributed in the North Pacific (Bering Sea, Sea of Okhotsk). Total catches increased steadily in the North Pacific from 300,000 tonnes in the 1950s to 6.7 million tonnes in the late 1980s. About 25 per cent to 30 per cent of landings from the Bering Sea in the late 1980s came from the Donut Hole. Catches in the Donut Hole have decreased from 1 million tonnes in the late 1980s to 22,000 tonnes in 1992. The management of this resource in the international waters of the Bering Sea (Donut Hole and Peanut Hole) is a source of controversy. In August 1992, the United States, Japan, Poland, the Republic of Korea and China agreed to a harvest moratorium after it became apparent that most of the biomass had disappeared. The flying squid is another straddling stock considered to have been fully fished since 1987. Other straddling fish stocks on the North Pacific shelf and slope are the cephalopods, the Pacific Ocean perch (already overfished in the 1960s), the pelagic armourhead and the alfonsin.

"North-east Pacific Ocean. The condition of the North-east Pacific stock of the Alaska pollack is considered good. The jack mackerel is another straddling stock with a spawning biomass estimated at least 1.5 million tonnes but its potential is not known with precision.

"South-west Pacific Ocean. Direct fisheries for the orange roughy have developed in Australia and New Zealand. Japan, the Russian Federation, the Republic of Korea and Norway also fish this stock. The species may reach 100 years of age and matures at an age of 20 to 25 years. Thus maximum sustainable harvest rates are estimated at 1 to 5 per cent of the virgin biomass. Present harvest rates are higher than this in most areas, leading to unsustainable fisheries. Other straddling stocks include oceanic squids and sharks, flying fish and dolphin.

"South-east Pacific Ocean. The jumbo flying squid is found from California to the southern tip of Latin America. The stock is largely under-exploited. The Chilean jack mackerel has in the last two decades provided one of the largest increases in world fish catch, from about 110,000 to 150,000 tonnes in 1970-1973 to 4.3 million tonnes in 1994. There are some indications that the stock may have been heavily exploited (at least locally) but the data did not cover the whole resource. Thus the status of the full stock of the South Pacific is not known.

"(iii)   Subregional and regional organizations and arrangements

"Two fishery conservation and management organizations with regulatory powers deal with the tunas in the Pacific Ocean: the Inter-American Tropical Tuna Commission (I-ATTC) and the South Pacific Forum Fisheries Agency (FFA).

"FFA covers the South Pacific (central and west) and has the mandate to harmonize the fishery management policies of its members. The Agency is not a conservation management body but controls foreign tuna fishing in the exclusive economic zones of its members through a licensing system and cooperative monitoring, control and surveillance.

"The Eastern Pacific Ocean Tuna Fishing Agreement and its Protocol, signed by the United States of America, Costa Rica and Panama on 15 March 1983, has not yet entered into force. Similarly, the Agreement creating the Eastern Pacific Tuna Fishing Organization signed by Ecuador, El Salvador, Mexico, Nicaragua and Peru on 21 July 1989, has not yet entered into force.

"Other regional fishery bodies in the region with some regulatory powers to deal with the straddling stocks are the South Pacific Permanent Commission (CPPS) and the Asia-Pacific Fishery Commission (APFIC). The latter is an FAO funded and administered body with limited management power. It has a Committee on Marine Fisheries whose activities are concentrated on the South China Sea.

"Southern Ocean

"There are no straddling stocks in the Southern Ocean. The area is covered by the Commission for the Conservation of Antarctic Marine Living Resources (CCAMLR)."

B.   Organs, organizations and programmes of the
United Nations system

22. In its response of 20 June 1996 to the Secretary-General, the Economic Commission for Latin America and the Caribbean (ECLAC) provided the following information:

"1. Countries in the Latin America and the Caribbean region are undertaking analysis of the 1995 Agreement at different levels and through various approaches.

"2. A strong initiative to study the implications of the Agreement is being promoted by the private fishing industry.

"3. Some concern has been perceived in several countries as regards article 7 on "Compatibility of conservation and management measures", since it is felt that this provision could, in the end, undermine the focus on the high seas, introducing some disturbance to the proper implementation of Part V of the United Nations Convention on the Law of the Sea vis-a-vis sovereign rights of coastal States over the living resources of their exclusive economic zone.

"4. Similarly, there is a common feeling that an effort to emphasize the prevalence of the Convention's provisions will be needed in the future, especially in relation to its article 297 (3) on settlement of disputes referring to fisheries in the exclusive economic zone, and in view of the absence of consensus to have included in article 31 of the [1995] Agreement the possibility of application of provisional measures based on coastal State fishing regulations.

"5. Many countries in the region are also trying to consider the Agreement in the context of the discussion on environment and trade, since the role played by fisheries in the world economy will certainly necessitate consistency with the negotiations in the framework of the World Trade Organization (WTO), and the Uruguay Round. With regard to article 23 of the Agreement on "Measures taken by a port State" the controversies held by some Latin American countries and the European Union in the process of adopting free trade agreements are an indication of the need for further developments on the subject.

"6. A different type of assistance is required by countries of the region concerning implementation of article 24 of the Agreement on "Recognition of the special requirements of developing States", particularly in connection with social and environmental impacts.

"7. In the discussion on the formulation and application of national and regional strategies for implementation of the Convention on Biological Diversity in the marine environment, particular attention is being given to subparagraph (g) of article 5 of the Agreement on the protection of biodiversity in the marine environment.

"8. The need to develop further guidelines on the incorporation of the precautionary approach to the long-term sustainability of fisheries and on the environmental and economic factors affecting MSY fishery evaluation models are the issues on which regional discussions will be focused in the near future."

C. Other intergovernmental organizations

23. In its response to the Secretary-General dated 28 June 1996, the Commonwealth made the following submission:

"The Commonwealth's members have a vital interest in the conservation and sustainable management of fisheries and the control of harmful fishing practices. This issue was the main item on the agenda of the third meeting of the Commonwealth Consultative Group on Environment, which met in the wings of the high-level segment of the Commission on Sustainable Development on 30 April in New York. The Group agreed, *inter alia*, that it was vital for all countries to ratify and implement the 1995 United Nations Agreement on the conservation and management of straddling fish stocks and highly migratory stocks, in conjunction with the relevant provisions of the United Nations Convention on the Law of the Sea, with a sense of urgency. The Group made several suggestions for strengthening Commonwealth assistance and cooperation on fisheries. These included:

- The gathering, sharing and dissemination of scientific information on fisheries and other marine resources;

- Improving capacities for effective coastal zone management (including the use of environmental impact assessments) through technical assistance and training;

- Sharing information and expertise on effective methods for the sustainable management of fisheries and the reduction of marine pollution from land-based sources;

- Policy development, including the use of economic incentives to promote the sustainable management of fisheries;

- Promoting technical cooperation and exchange of information on fisheries management in small island developing States through mechanisms such as the Small Island Developing States Information

Network (SIDSNET) and the Small Island Developing States
Technical Assistance Programme (SIDSTAP);

-    Improving capacities for surveillance and monitoring of exclusive
     economic zones, especially in small island developing States, and
     exchange of information on the activities of distant water
     fishing fleets judged to be harmful to fisheries;

-    Mapping coastal zone resources and assessing fish stocks,
     particularly migratory species (with an emphasis on large
     pelagics);

-    Assistance for the upgrading and mechanization of fishing fleets
     and the development of fish processing industries, especially in
     small island developing States;

-    Legal assistance for the delimitation of maritime boundaries and
     the negotiation of agreements on fisheries;

-    Environmental education to increase awareness of the importance
     of conserving and harvesting fisheries in a sustainable manner."

D.   Regional and subregional fisheries organizations
      and arrangements

24.   It has been reported that the Fishery Committee for the Eastern Central
Atlantic (CECAF), at its thirteenth session (Dakar, 18-20 December 1995), had
discussions on the relevance of the 1995 Agreement to eastern Atlantic fisheries
in the light of the fact that few straddling stocks occurred in the region and
highly migratory species were already covered by the International Commission
for the Conservation of Atlantic Tuna (ICCAT), with which the Committee had
decided to strengthen cooperation. It was, however, recognized that many
principles contained in the Agreement, such as the precautionary approach, the
compatibility of conservation measures taken by the countries across the whole
range of species distribution, the need to strengthen subregional and regional
mechanisms and arrangements and to set up transparent operating procedures,
cooperation in enforcement, and peaceful settlement of disputes, were applicable
to all fisheries, with particular reference to those based on shared stocks,
which occurred throughout the CECAF region. The Committee therefore urged all
its members to consider becoming party to the 1995 Agreement; to ensure that the
provisions regarding highly migratory species were implemented by ICCAT; and to
implement the relevant provisions for the management of shared resources. 6/

25.   In its submission to the Secretary-General dated 16 April 1996, the Inter-
American Tropical Tuna Commission (I-ATTC) informed him that certain exploited
species, such as yellowfin tuna, were managed on a single stock basis within
I-ATTC's area of competence, while others, such as northern bluefin tuna and
swordfish, had stocks which ranged outside the eastern Pacific. It further
indicated that I-ATTC, which is the regional fisheries management organization
concerned with fisheries for tuna and other species taken by tuna fishing
vessels in the eastern Pacific Ocean, cooperated with other regional management
organizations and arrangements, and in respect of reporting on fisheries for
species whose encompassed areas lay outside its area of competence, it had
endeavoured to coordinate and eliminate duplication with States and other
fisheries management organizations and arrangements.

26.   In its reply of 24 April 1996 to the Secretary-General, ICCAT indicated
that the Commission, at its 14th regular meeting (Madrid, 10-17 November 1995),
had discussions on the United Nations Conference on Straddling Fish Stocks and
Highly Migratory Fish Stocks, including its relevance to the work of ICCAT in
the conservation and management of the highly migratory species under its
mandate. 7/ A proposal was made by one delegation regarding the implementation
by ICCAT of the 1995 Agreement, including steps that might be taken to create a

structure to ensure that ICCAT activities were aligned with the Agreement. 8/ Although several delegations stated that the proposal was premature, 9/ it was agreed that member countries would submit their views to the ICCAT secretariat during the course of the year and that the matter would be included in the agenda of the next Commission meeting, which could be preceded by informal discussions. 10/

27. In its response of 20 May 1996 to the Secretary-General, the South Pacific Commission (SPC) stated that, largely in response to the 1995 Agreement, Pacific Island nations had, over the past year, been considering ways in which they could better meet their obligations as coastal States under the United Nations Convention on the Law of the Sea and improve their cooperation with fishing nations in the conservation and management of tuna in the western and central Pacific. The SPC Oceanic Fisheries Programme (OFP), as the principal tuna research programme in the region, had played an important role in those discussions. While discussions were ongoing, Pacific Island nations had consistently expressed the view that the essential scientific support for any future international conservation and management arrangement for tuna and related species in the western and central Pacific region should be provided by OFP, supported by the research agencies of participating countries in the arrangement. It was expected that substantial progress towards establishing a scientific cooperation agreement among coastal States and fishing nations of the region would be made at a Technical Consultation on Arrangements for Data Collection and Exchange, Tuna Research and Stock Assessment, to be held at Commission headquarters in Nouméa, New Caledonia, from 15 to 19 July 1996.

28. In its reply to the Secretary-General dated 11 June 1996, the North-East Atlantic Fisheries Commission (NEAFC) reported that, at an extraordinary meeting in March 1996, the Commission had adopted by qualified majority a recommendation for the management within the NEAFC Convention Area of an entire stock of oceanic redfish, both inside and beyond waters under the national jurisdiction of coastal States, whereby a total allowable catch was established and allocated to contracting parties and an allocation was also set aside for non-contracting parties known to be fishing in the Convention Area. The catch reporting scheme introduced for 1995 had been continued, and the ongoing cooperation of non-contracting parties was sought in supplying catch data. One contracting party (Russian Federation) had since formally objected to the recommendation. NEAFC had also attempted to introduce management measures in respect of another straddling stock within the NEAFC Convention Area, the Norwegian spring spawning (Atlanto-Scandian) herring, but contracting parties had thus far been unable to reach agreement on measures within the Commission, other than a catch reporting system. Discussions in respect of those two stocks had tended to act as a focus for considering the role of NEAFC as a regional management organization in the light of the additional responsibilities placed on such bodies by the 1995 Agreement. It was the view of a number of contracting parties that the text of the NEAFC Convention should be reviewed to make any necessary clarifications and adaptations of the Convention as appropriate in the light of the 1995 Agreement. The capacity of the Commission to advance that work would depend to some extent on decisions taken by its contracting parties, not least with regard to their ratification of the Agreement. It was likely that there would be further discussion of how NEAFC should be responding to the Agreement and advancing this work at the annual meeting, to be held from 20 to 22 November 1996.

29. In its response of 18 June 1996 to the Secretary-General, the Northwest Atlantic Fisheries Organization (NAFO) provided the following information:

"6. Challenges to conservation in the NAFO Regulatory Area

"NAFO has faced many challenges to the conservation and optimum utilization of the fishery resources under its management. One particular concern has been the undermining of NAFO management decisions by unregulated fisheries of non-contracting parties, including 'flags-of-convenience'. Most of the NAFO-managed stocks have been severely depleted and continue to be under moratoriums.

"To address the problem of non-contracting party fishing, the General Council adopted several resolutions calling for compliance with the NAFO management framework and established a Standing Committee on Fishing Activities by non-Contracting Parties in the Regulatory Area in September 1990. The President of NAFO has sent letters annually to all non-contracting parties whose vessels had been fishing in the NAFO Regulatory Area during 1990-1995.

"All flag-of-convenience vessels left the Nose and Tail of the Grand Bank in mid-1994; a small number moved to the Flemish Cap (NAFO Division 3M) in the NAFO Regulatory Area. While vessels registered in Panama, the Cayman Islands, Saint Vincent and the Grenadines, and Venezuela left the NAFO Regulatory Area during 1995, some vessels registered in Honduras, Belize, Sierra Leone and New Zealand fished on the Flemish Cap. Catches by non-contracting party vessels in 1995 were estimated at 10,959 tons, comprising 7,700t 3M redfish, 2,250t 3M cod and 1,000t 3M American plaice. Currently there is only one non-contracting party vessel fishing in the NAFO Regulatory Area, the Honduran-registered Danica.

"At the annual meeting in September 1995, the Standing Committee decided to meet in May 1996 for an in-depth discussion of the non-contracting parties issue and, in particular, the consequences of the failure to cooperate in the conservation of the fish stocks concerned, in the light of the new United Nations Agreement on straddling fish stocks and highly migratory fish stocks and the FAO Code of Conduct for Responsible Fisheries.

"7. Effective conservation through enhanced cooperation

"In 1995, the European Union (EU) lodged an objection to a NAFO decision on the distribution of Greenland halibut quotas. A dispute arose between Canada and EU over the sharing of Greenland halibut. In order to resolve this dispute, Canada and the Union reached an agreement on 20 April 1995 which provided a new sharing arrangement for Greenland halibut and applied new stringent control and enforcement measures on all EU and Canadian vessels fishing in the NAFO Regulatory Area. NAFO subsequently adopted these conservation and control measures in September 1995 and they took effect for all NAFO members from 1 January 1996. They include the obligation to implement during the period from 1 January 1996 to 31 December 1997 a pilot project for observers and satellite tracking and for this purpose to place independent, full-time observers on board NAFO-member vessels at all times, and in cases of infractions, quick reporting and follow-up. This is the toughest set of control and enforcement measures of any fisheries management organization in the world. There is also an undertaking to deploy satellite tracking devices on 35 per cent of the NAFO-member vessels beginning in 1996.

"The new United Nations Agreement on straddling fish stocks and highly migratory fish stocks will have implications for NAFO and other regional fisheries management organizations. NAFO will begin to consider these implications at its 1996 annual meeting."

30. In its submission to the Secretary-General dated 24 June 1996, the Asia-Pacific Fishery Commission (APFIC) reported that 12 countries in the region had signed the 1995 Agreement. APFIC also reported that it would further discuss the implications of the Agreement at its forthcoming twenty-fifth session, to be held at Seoul from 15 to 24 October 1996. Many countries, e.g. Thailand, planned to conduct national workshops to discuss the implications of the implementation of the Agreement. The Commission also indicated that preliminary work on transboundary fish stocks in the South China Sea had been initiated by FAO and the South-east Asian Fisheries Development Centre (SEAFDEC) and a regional workshop was to be held in Malaysia in late 1996 to discuss shared stocks issues in the region. A regional proposal for fisheries management had

also been formulated by FAO and had been submitted to countries of the Association of South-East Asian Nations (ASEAN) for comments and endorsement to donors in order to strengthen regional management capacity.

31. In its reply of 22 July 1996 to the Secretary-General, the North Atlantic Salmon Conservation Organization (NASCO) welcomed the adoption by consensus and the opening for signature of the 1995 Agreement and indicated that, although it did not apply to salmon, the Agreement nevertheless contained provisions that could contribute to the international conservation and management of North Atlantic salmon.

IV. INFORMATION PROVIDED BY NON-GOVERNMENTAL ORGANIZATIONS

32. In a resolution adopted without a vote on 19 April 1996, the 95th Conference of the Inter-Parliamentary Union (Istanbul, 12-20 April 1996) urged States to sign and ratify the 1995 Agreement and emphasized in particular its importance "as a practical and enforceable means to end high-seas overfishing". 11/

33. In its response to the Secretary-General dated 28 June 1996, the Federation of Japan Tuna Fisheries Cooperative Associations stated that the 1995 Agreement had marked a great step towards the ultimate goal of the United Nations of achieving the lasting prosperity of mankind, and therefore it supported its basic ideas and principles. The Federation was certain that the Agreement would not only benefit the world community through the establishment of a global legal framework but would also contribute to the creation of greater job opportunities in the industrial sectors of the world.

34. The Federation, however, expressed some concerns with regard to General Assembly resolution 50/24 and the 1995 Agreement, as follows:

"1. The Agreement should be applied in a manner which would not hinder the sound development of commercial fishing industries, upon which are bestowed the indispensable role of supplying food to the peoples of the world. Such a viewpoint should have been incorporated into the resolution;

"2. The Agreement establishes the mechanism for the peaceful settlement of disputes concerning the interpretation or application of its provisions. We would like to welcome such a move. However, what is most important of all is that this mechanism should work effectively. Accordingly, we feel that the resolution should have reminded all the parties concerned of the importance of the mechanism and called for a cooperative attitude toward this framework;"

35. The Federation further indicated that, in spite of those concerns, it was convinced that the United Nations, when appropriate, would "reorient its course of action through a democratic process of debate among related nations".

36. In its reply of 5 July 1996 to the Secretary-General, the World Wide Fund for Nature (WWF) welcomed the adoption of the 1995 Agreement and attached extreme importance to the review of the Agreement by the General Assembly. WWF believed that the Assembly should focus on building common ground for achieving effective implementation of the Agreement, but it should also include a frank assessment of any shortcomings in the progress towards full implementation of the Agreement. The state of the world's fish stocks demanded such an assessment.

37. Two paramount concerns of the Fund which the General Assembly should address as priorities at its fifty-first session were adherence to the Agreement and a mechanism to ensure its implementation by regional fisheries organizations and arrangements. At the time of writing, several of the States which had participated in the negotiations on the Agreement had failed to signal clearly their intention to ratify it; this was a matter of great concern. The text of

the Agreement had been adopted by the United Nations Conference on Straddling Fish Stocks and Highly Migratory Fish Stocks after long negotiations in which all States had been provided with the opportunity to present their views. WWF proposes that when the General Assembly considers the Agreement, it should have before it an up-to-date list of signatures and ratifications, including a list which would identify States which had participated in the Conference but which had not made clear their intention to become bound by the Agreement. Those States might then wish to take the opportunity to clarify their respective situations, after which the Assembly should take appropriate action. What those courses of action might be could be considered closer to the time, but if the situation had not improved by then, the grave nature of the threats to the world's fish stocks would require action by the General Assembly.

38. Another area of great concern for WWF was the lack of a mechanism or mechanisms for ensuring that regional fisheries organizations and arrangements implemented the Agreement. The primary responsibility lay with States which were parties to the Agreement and participated in regional fisheries organizations and arrangements; they were the ones who must ensure that the required coordination took place at the national level. This also applied to other treaties, such as the Convention on Biological Diversity, the provisions of which were relevant to the conservation and management of fish stocks. While coordination at the national level was of critical importance, other modalities might need to be put in place to ensure implementation of the Agreement. The experience of WWF at the regional level since the adoption of the 1995 Agreement revealed an enormous lack of information concerning the Agreement, let alone understanding of its implications for regional fisheries organizations and arrangements. States which had participated in the Conference seemed to have made little or no effort to convey the results of the Conference to regional organizations or arrangements in which they participated. Full and rapid implementation of the Agreement at the regional level was a key criterion for the success of the Agreement and WWF believed that the General Assembly ought to consider how to remedy the situation. The actions of Governments did not inspire confidence. WWF participated in the annual meetings of several regional fisheries management bodies, which provided some examples. In WWF's experience, there seemed to be an unwillingness to move towards implementation of the Agreement. CCAMLR had indicated that the Agreement did not apply to it. In November 1995, ICCAT rejected as "premature" a proposal that would have directed a working group to develop a series of recommendations and prepare a report regarding the implementation of relevant provisions of the Agreement; this was a remarkable and discouraging decision. The Convention for the Conservation of Southern Bluefin Tuna had had such great difficulty agreeing on catch quotas for the severely depleted southern bluefin tuna that it raised serious questions about its ability even to begin to implement the 1995 Agreement.

39. WWF further indicated that the incorporation of the precautionary approach in the 1995 Agreement was one of its key features, stressing that it would become increasingly important as new threats to fisheries conservation and management emerged. Such threats included the impacts of climate change on marine ecosystems and growing evidence that certain chemicals, so-called "endocrine disruptors", were having far-reaching effects on species and ecosystems, both terrestrial and marine. Some of these synthetic chemicals, which mimicked human and animal hormones, had been shown to be present in fish, raising questions about the health of the stocks and about human consumption of fish from such stocks. The Agreement did not deal in any detail with questions such as excess fleet capacity or subsidies, but WWF believed these were priority issues. In particular, the Fund believed it was important to move beyond the oversimplified debate centred around "too many boats chasing too few fish" to the consideration of the structure of fleet overcapacity and the driving forces behind it. The situation of developing countries ought to be taken into account in any discussion about excess fleet capacity and related issues, as required by the Agreement. WWF recognized that current methods for controlling the world's overcapacity problem had failed to ensure the long-term sustainability of world fisheries. There was a need to create economic incentives which would drive the fishing industry towards this goal. WWF was currently working with industry partners to establish the Marine Stewardship Council, an independent, non-profit

organization which would establish a set of broad principles for sustainable fishing and set standards for individual fisheries. Fisheries meeting those standards would be marked with an on-pack logo, thus allowing consumers to select products which they are certain come from well-managed, sustainable sources. The standards and principles would build on those of the 1995 Agreement and the FAO Code of Conduct.

Notes

1/ General Assembly resolution 50/24, paras. 1 and 3.

2/ Ibid., paras. 4 and 5.

3/ Agreement to Reduce Dolphin Mortality in the Eastern Tropical Pacific Tuna Fishery, done at La Jolla, California, on 23 April 1992.

4/ Subsequently, on 27 June 1996, the European Community, together with several of its members, including Finland, signed the Agreement.

5/ Subsequently, on 20 August 1996, the United States deposited its instrument of ratification with the Secretary-General.

6/ Report of the Thirteenth Session of the Fishery Committee for the Eastern Central Atlantic, Dakar, 18-20 December 1995, FAO Fisheries Report No. 534 (FIPL/R534 (bi)), para. 50.

7/ Proceedings of the Fourteenth Regular Meeting of ICCAT, Madrid, 10-17 November 1996, item 10 (United Nations Conference on Straddling Fish Stocks and Highly Migratory Fish Stocks and the FAO Code of Conduct for Responsible Fishing), para. 10.1.

8/ Ibid., para. 10.7.

9/ Ibid., paras. 10.9, 10.10, 10.13, 10.15, 10.16 and 10.22.

10/ Ibid., para. 10.25

11/ For the text of the resolution see A/51/210, annex, p. 37.

-----

56. AGREEMENT FOR THE IMPLEMENTATION OF THE PROVISIONS OF THE UNITED NATIONS CONVENTION ON THE LAW OF THE SEA OF 10 DECEMBER 1982 RELATING TO THE CONSERVATION AND MANAGEMENT OF STRADDLING FISH STOCKS AND HIGHLY MIGRATORY FISH STOCKS - UNGA RESOLUTION

Doc. no.: A/Res.51/35

9 December 1996

The General Assembly,

Recalling its resolutions 47/192 of 22 December 1992, concerning the United Nations Conference on Straddling Fish Stocks and Highly Migratory Fish Stocks, and 50/24 of 5 December 1995, concerning the Agreement for the Implementation of the Provisions of the United Nations Convention on the Law of the Sea of 10 December 1982 relating to the Conservation and Management of Straddling Fish Stocks and Highly Migratory Fish Stocks,

Recalling also resolutions I and II adopted by the Conference, 94/

Noting the opening for signature of the Agreement on 4 December 1995,

Recognizing the importance of the Agreement for the conservation and management of straddling fish stocks and highly migratory fish stocks and the need for the regular consideration and review of developments relating thereto,

Recognizing also the importance of artisanal and subsistence fishers,

Noting with appreciation the information provided by States, relevant specialized agencies, international organizations, intergovernmental bodies and non-governmental organizations in accordance with resolution 50/24,

Taking note of the report of the Secretary-General, 95/

1.   Recognizes the significance of the Agreement for the Implementation of the Provisions of the United Nations Convention on the Law of the Sea of 10 December 1982 relating to the Conservation and Management of Straddling Fish Stocks and Highly Migratory Fish Stocks as an important contribution to ensuring the conservation and management of straddling fish stocks and highly migratory fish stock;

2.   Emphasizes the importance of the early entry into force and effective implementation of the Agreement;

3.   Calls upon all States and other entities referred to in article 1, paragraph 2 (b), of the Agreement that have not done so to ratify or accede to it and to consider applying it provisionally;

94/   A/50/550, annex II; see also A/CONF.164/38, annex.
95/   A/51/383.

4. Takes note with concern that many commercially important straddling fish stocks and highly migratory fish stocks have been subject to heavy and little-regulated fishing efforts, and that some stocks continue to be overfished;

5. Welcomes the fact that a growing number of States and other entities, as well as regional and subregional fishery management organizations and arrangements, have adopted legislation, established regulations or taken other measures to implement the provisions in the Agreement, and urges them to enforce those measures fully;

6. Calls upon States and other entities and regional and subregional fishery management organizations and arrangements that have not done so to consider taking measures to implement the provisions of the Agreement;

7. Urges States, relevant specialized agencies, international organizations, intergovernmental bodies and non-governmental organizations that have not yet done so to provide information to the Secretary-General to ensure as comprehensive a report as possible;

8. Requests the Secretary-General to report to the General Assembly at its fifty-second session and biennially thereafter on further developments relating to the conservation and management of straddling fish stocks and highly migratory fish stocks, including the status and implementation of the Agreement, taking into account information provided by States, relevant specialized agencies, in particular the Food and Agriculture Organization of the United Nations, and other appropriate organs, organizations and programmes of the United Nations system, regional and subregional organizations and arrangements for the conservation and management of straddling fish stocks and highly migratory fish stocks, as well as other relevant intergovernmental bodies and non-governmental organizations;

9. Also requests the Secretary-General to ensure that reporting on all major fishery-related activities and instruments is effectively coordinated and duplication of activities and reporting minimized, and that relevant scientific and technical studies are disseminated to the international community, and invites the relevant specialized agencies, including the Food and Agriculture Organization of the United Nations, as well as regional and subregional fishery organizations and arrangements, to cooperate with the Secretary-General to that end;

10. Decides to include in the provisional agenda of its fifty-second session, under an item entitled "Oceans and law of the sea", the sub-item entitled "Agreement for the Implementation of the Provisions of the United Nations Convention on the Law of the Sea of 10 December 1982 relating to the Conservation and Management of Straddling Fish Stocks and Highly Migratory Fish Stocks".

57. IMPLEMENTATION OF THE OUTCOME OF THE GLOBAL CONFERENCE ON THE SUSTAINABLE DEVELOPMENT OF SMALL ISLAND DEVELOPING STATES - UNGA RESOLUTION

Doc. no.:A/Res.51/183   16 December 1996

The General Assembly,

Recalling its resolutions 49/100 and 49/122 of 19 December 1994 and 50/116 of 20 December 1995, on or related to the implementation of the outcome of the Global Conference on the Sustainable Development of Small Island Developing States, and reaffirming Commission on Sustainable Development decision 4/16 69/ on the review of the implementation of the Programme of Action for the Sustainable Development of Small Island Developing States, 70/

Reaffirming that, because the development options of small island developing States are limited, there are special challenges to devising and implementing sustainable development plans, and that small island developing States will be constrained in meeting such challenges and overcoming obstacles to sustainable development without the active support and cooperation of the international community,

Stressing the need for greater attention to priority areas of the Programme of Action, particularly climate change and sea-level rise, energy resources, tourism resources, biodiversity resources, transport and communications and science and technology,

1. Takes note of the report of the Secretary-General 71/ on action taken at the international, regional and national levels, inter alia, by the organs, organizations and bodies of the United Nations system to implement the Programme of Action for the Sustainable Development of Small Island Developing States, 72/ and welcomes in particular the action that has been taken by the Department for Policy Coordination and Sustainable Development of the United Nations Secretariat to support the system-wide implementation of the Programme of Action;

2. Stresses the importance of maintaining the Small Island Developing States Unit within the above-mentioned Department, and requests the Secretary-General to maintain the Unit at an appropriate level of staff and improve the structure and organization of the Unit, in accordance with General Assembly resolution 49/122;

69/   See Official Records of the Economic and Social Council, 1996, Supplement No. 8 (E/1996/28), chap. I, sect. C.

70/   Report of the Global Conference on the Sustainable Development of Small Island Developing States, Bridgetown, Barbados, 25 April-6 May 1994 (United Nations publication, Sales No. E.94.I.18 and corrigenda), chap. I, resolution 1, annex II.

71/   A/51/354.

72/   Report of the Global Conference on the Sustainable Development of Small Island Developing States, Bridgetown Barbados, 25 April-6 May 1994 (United Nations publication, Sales No. E.94.I.18 and corrigenda), chap. I, resolution 1, annex II.

3. _Welcomes_ the work being done by the regional commissions to support activities to coordinate the outcome of the Global Conference on the Sustainable Development of Small Island Developing States;

4. _Takes note_ of the decisions of the United Nations Conference on Trade and Development, at its ninth session, related to programme support for small island developing countries,73/ within the framework of the Programme of Action, and requests the Secretary-General to implement fully the relevant provisions of General Assembly resolution 49/122;

5. _Calls upon_ Governments, as well as the organs, organizations and bodies of the United Nations system, other intergovernmental organizations and non-governmental organizations, to continue to implement fully all the commitments and recommendations that were made at the Global Conference, and to continue to take the necessary actions for effective follow-up to the Programme of Action, including action to ensure the provision of the means of implementation under chapter XV thereof;

6. _Recognizes_ the importance of the technical assistance programme (SIDSTAP) and the information network for small island developing States (SIDSNET) in the overall implementation of the Programme of Action, takes note of the progress made by the United Nations Development Programme in implementing General Assembly resolution 49/122, and requests the Programme, in cooperation with Governments, to continue its actions to implement fully all provisions in order to operationalize the two mechanisms;

7. _Takes note_ of the support that has been provided by the Commission on Sustainable Development to following up the implementation of the Programme of Action in accordance with General Assembly resolution 49/122 and the Programme of Action itself, and invites the Commission at its fifth session to continue its support for and attention to the Programme of Action, as an integral part of the preparations for the special session of the General Assembly to be held in June 1997;

8. _Requests_ that, in the context of the special session of the General Assembly, specific modalities will be recommended to examine all outstanding chapters of the Programme of Action, and for undertaking the full review of the Programme of Action in 1999;

9. _Welcomes_ the inclusion of the development of a vulnerability index for small island developing States as part of the work programme of the Department for Policy Coordination and Sustainable Development for 1996-1997, and in this regard requests the Secretary-General, in collaboration with the United Nations Conference on Trade and Development, the United Nations Environment Programme, other relevant United Nations organizations and non-United Nations organizations, to prepare a report based on the views of relevant experts on the vulnerability index, in 1997;

10. _Requests_ the Committee for Development Planning, at its thirty-second session, to formulate its views and recommendations on the above-mentioned report, with a view to submitting those views to the General Assembly at its fifty-third session, through the Economic and Social Council, and to make this information available to the Commission on Sustainable Development;

11. _Requests_ the Department for Policy Coordination and Sustainable Development, in its coordinating role, to look into appropriate modalities for mobilizing resources for effective implementation of the Programme of Action and provide information thereon;

12. _Requests_ closer collaboration and greater transparency between the Department for Policy Coordination and Sustainable Development and the United Nations Development Programme for effective implementation of the technical assistance programme (SIDSTAP), and requests detailed information to be made available to Governments on actions taken to this effect;

13. _Welcomes_ the report of the High-level Panel Meeting on Island Developing Countries 74/ on the challenges faced by island developing countries, particularly in the area of external trade, considered by the Commission on Sustainable Development at its fourth session;

14. _Requests_ the Secretary-General to seek the views of Governments on an informal open-ended working group within the existing Framework of Action for the International Decade for Natural Disaster Reduction, 75/ with the membership of all concerned States, including all relevant sectors in disaster

---

73/   TD/378.

74/   E/CN.17/1996/IDC/3-UNCTAD/LLDC/IDC.3.

75/   See resolution 44/236, annex.

reduction, with a view to ensuring full integration and participation of small island developing States in the mapping of a concerted strategy for disaster reduction into the twenty-first century and in improving access to disaster and warning information in order to enhance the capability of small island developing States with respect to disaster management;

15. Stresses that small island developing States are particularly vulnerable to global climate change and sea-level rise, and that the potential effects of global climate change and sea-level rise are increased strength and frequency of tropical storms and inundation of some islands, with loss of exclusive economic zones, economic infrastructure, human settlements and culture, and urges the international community to support small island developing States in their efforts to adapt to the sea-level rise that will be experienced as a result of the impact of greenhouse gases that have already been emitted into the atmosphere;

16. Calls upon the international community, including the Global Environment Facility, within the framework of its operational strategy, to support commercial energy development in small island developing States based on those environmentally sound renewable sources with demonstrated viability, to support improvement of the efficiency of existing technologies and end-use equipment based on conventional energy sources, and to assist with the financing of investments necessary to expand energy supplies beyond urban areas;

17. Further calls upon the international community, where appropriate, to support the efforts of and to provide assistance to small island developing States with respect to improving and acquiring, through appropriate investment incentives and innovative measures, the means of maritime transport and development of infrastructure in small island developing States, such as airports, harbours, roads and telecommunications;

18. Welcomes actions at the national and regional levels by small island developing States, and invites all Governments, with the assistance of international and regional organizations, to provide information on all of their major activities under the Programme of Action so as to enable an adequate review of the actions taken at the national and regional levels;

19. Requests the Secretary-General to submit to the General Assembly at its fifty-third session a report on the plans, programmes and projects for the sustainable development of small island developing States that have been implemented in response to the Programme of Action, as well as those that are under implementation and those that are envisaged for implementation within five years of the date of the report;

20. Decides to include in the provisional agenda of its fifty-second session, under the item entitled "Environment and sustainable development", the sub-item entitled "Implementation of the outcome of the Global Conference on the Sustainable Development of Small Island Developing States";

21. Further requests the Secretary-General to submit to the General Assembly at its fifty-second session a progress report on the particular actions taken to implement the present resolution.

58. UNIVERSAL CONGRESS ON THE PANAMA CANAL - UNGA RESOLUTION

Doc. no.: A/Res.51/5   24 October 1996

The General Assembly,

Recalling its resolution 50/12 of 7 November 1995 supporting the convening of the Universal Congress on the Panama Canal, which is to be held at Panama City from 7 to 10 September 1997,

Having examined the report of the Secretary-General on the implementation of resolution 50/12, 2/

Taking into account resolution 1376 (XXVI-0/96) of the General Assembly of the Organization of American States entitled "The Panama Canal in the Twenty-first Century" and resolution 1379 (XXVI-0/96) on the Universal Congress on the Panama Canal, both adopted on 6 June 1996, in which, inter alia, the General Assembly of the Organization of American States noted with satisfaction the harmonious transition process in which the Governments of Panama and the United States of America are participating, through their diplomatic missions, the Panama Canal Commission, the Interoceanic Region Authority and the Transition Commission,

Having also examined the letter dated 27 September 1996 from the Permanent Representative of Panama to the United Nations addressed to the Secretary-General, 3/ outlining the work being done by the Government of Panama in connection with the holding of the Universal Congress on the Panama Canal and indicating the progress made by the Organizing Commission for that Congress, under the direction of the Ministry of Foreign Affairs,

Bearing in mind that on 7 September 1977 the Panama Canal Treaty and the Treaty concerning the Permanent Neutrality and Operation of the Panama Canal, known as the Torrijos-Carter Treaties, were signed in Washington, D.C., which stipulate that, at noon on 31 December 1999, the Canal, including all improvements, is to come under the control of the Republic of Panama,

Acknowledging the importance that the international community attaches to the Treaty for the Prohibition of Nuclear Weapons in Latin America and the Caribbean (Treaty of Tlatelolco) and the positive implications that the strengthening of the nuclear-weapon-free regime established by that Treaty has for the permanent neutrality of the Panama Canal,

Welcoming the fact that, in anticipation of the holding of the Congress, Panama has ratified the United Nations Convention on the Law of the Sea, 4/ universally recognized as the framework for the adoption of

---

2/   A/51/281.

3/   A/51/477.

4/   Official Records of the Third United Nations Conference on the Law of the Sea, vol. XVII (United Nations publication, Sales No. E.84.V.3), document A/CONF.62/122.

national, regional and global measures in maritime matters, in harmony with chapter 17 of Agenda 21 *5/* adopted at the United Nations Conference on Environment and Development,

Reaffirming the utility of the Panama Canal for international maritime transport and the growth of the world economy, and the need to tackle the problems of interoceanic communication in the twenty-first century,

Noting with appreciation the activities being undertaken in various spheres by Governments, organizations and programmes of the United Nations system and other intergovernmental and non-governmental organizations in support of the holding of the Universal Congress,

Recognizing that the next stages of preparation and organization of the Congress require increased efforts and the availability of greater resources,

1. Notes with satisfaction the report of the Secretary-General on the implementation of resolution 50/12;

2. Reiterates its firm support for the initiative of the Government of Panama, and urges it to continue to intensify its efforts to organize the Universal Congress on the Panama Canal at Panama City from 7 to 10 September 1997;

3. Renews its appeal to Member States generously to assist the Government of Panama, and calls upon intergovernmental and non-governmental organizations to do likewise;

4. Again urges the competent organs, programmes and specialized agencies of the United Nations system, in particular the United Nations Development Programme, the United Nations Environment Programme and the International Maritime Organization, to make every effort to provide assistance from within existing resources for the holding of the Universal Congress on the Panama Canal;

5. Requests the Secretary-General to submit to the General Assembly at its fifty-second session a report on the implementation of the present resolution;

6. Decides to include in the provisional agenda of its fifty-second session the item entitled "Universal Congress on the Panama Canal".

5/ Report of the United Nations Conference on Environment and Development, Rio de Janeiro, 3-14 June 1992 (A/CONF.151/26/Rev.1 (Vol. I and Vol. I/Corr.1, Vol. II, Vol. III and Vol. III/Corr.1)) (United Nations publication, Sales No. E.93.I.8 and corrigenda), vol. I: Resolutions Adopted by the Conference, resolution 1, annex II.

59. PROTECTION OF THE OCEANS, ALL KINDS OF SEAS, INCLUDING ENCLOSED AND SEMI-ENCLOSED SEAS, AND COASTAL AREAS AND THE PROTECTION, RATIONAL USE AND DEVELOPMENT OF THEIR LIVING RESOURCES - REPORT OF THE UN SECRETARY-GENERAL

Doc. no.: E/CN.17/1996/3

12 February 1996

CONTENTS

INTRODUCTION

1. This report reviews progress in the implementation of the objectives set out in chapter 17 of Agenda 21 1/ (Protection of the oceans, all kinds of seas, including enclosed and semi-enclosed seas, and coastal areas and the protection, rational use and development of their living resources) since the United Nations Conference on Environment and Development (UNCED) in June 1992 and presents a set of recommendations for action. The report and its addendum were prepared by the Subcommittee on Oceans and Coastal Areas of the Administrative Committee on Coordination (ACC) as task manager for chapter 17 of Agenda 21, in consultation with the United Nations Secretariat, in accordance with arrangements agreed on by the ACC Inter-Agency Committee on Sustainable Development. The Subcommittee, which has held three sessions since April 1994, is composed of the following 14 organizations: Division for Ocean Affairs and the Law of the Sea of the Office of Legal Affairs of the United Nations Secretariat, United Nations Conference on Trade and Development (UNCTAD), United Nations Development Programme (UNDP), United Nations Environment Programme (UNEP), United Nations Centre for Human

Settlements (Habitat) (UNCHS), Food and Agriculture Organization of the United
Nations (FAO), Intergovernmental Oceanographic Commission (IOC) of the United
Nations Educational, Scientific and Cultural Organization (UNESCO), World Health
Organization (WHO), World Bank, International Telecommunication Union (ITU),
World Meteorological Organization (WMO), International Maritime Organization
(IMO), United Nations Industrial Development Organization (UNIDO), International
Atomic Energy Agency (IAEA).

I.   CURRENT STATE AND MAIN TRENDS

2.   UNCED recognized that "The marine environment - including the oceans and
all seas and adjacent coastal areas - forms an integrated whole that is an
essential component of the global life-support system and a positive asset that
presents opportunities for sustainable development". 2/   Coastal areas are home
to 60 per cent of the world's population. Oceans, which cover 71 per cent of
the Earth's surface, contain a vast proportion of the world's biodiversity.
They are a major sink for atmospheric carbon and for the toxins and chemical
substances (whether natural or man-made) carried by continental effluents and
through the atmosphere, as well as a powerful regulator of the world's climate.
The importance attached to oceans is further related to four significant
factors:

     (a) The high density of human population in the coastal zone, often within
a narrow band of about 60 km, which creates pressure on a potentially fragile
environment and its ecosystems and resources, both coastal and marine;

     (b) The progressive degradation of marine and coastal natural resources
under the combined effect of excessive rates of use and pollution;

     (c) An ever-increasing awareness that the ocean is a basic governing force
for life on this planet, particularly for small island countries, and that
better understanding of its physical and biological mechanisms, including their
interaction with atmospheric processes, is essential to decision-making aiming
at sustainable development;

     (d) The recognition that a precautionary approach to ocean development and
management is necessary to take into account current uncertainties regarding
ocean (and related atmospheric) processes and to protect the options for
development available to future generations.

3.   Over the past decade there have been rapid and revolutionary changes in
political boundaries, in the realignment and refinement of States' rights and
duties and in the creation of new legal regimes. The main decision points in
this process are represented by the adoption in 1982 of the United Nations
Convention on the Law of the Sea (1982 Convention) 3/ and its entry into force
in 1994; as of 1 January 1996 the Convention had been ratified by 83 States
parties. 4/ The Convention establishes the rights and duties of nations for
marine environmental protection and sustainable use and the development of
marine resources and provides for dispute resolution.

4.   In addition, very important complementary international law and policy were
laid down in 1995: the Agreement for the Implementation of the Provisions of
the United Nations Convention on the Law of the Sea of 10 December 1982 relating
to the Conservation and Management of Straddling Fish Stocks and Highly
Migratory Fish Stocks (United Nations, August 1995); the Code of Conduct for
Responsible Fisheries (FAO, October 1995); the Global Programme of Action for
the Protection of the Marine Environment from Land-based Activities (UNEP,
November 1995); and the Jakarta Mandate on Coastal and Marine Biodiversity
adopted at the second session of the Conference of Parties to the Convention on
Biological Diversity (UNEP, November 1995). Each international agreement and
instrument duly recognizes that it has a role in strengthening the
implementation of the 1982 Convention and in furthering the objectives of
Agenda 21.

5. The full consequences of these changes, in terms of both benefits and problems, have yet to be adequately recognized, however. The expectations associated with the extension of national jurisdiction have only partially been met: concrete knowledge of ocean processes and resources is still incomplete and sparse; short-term economic interests often work against the kind of long-term planning and investment required to extract real benefits.

6. While some relatively new resources, such as most deep-sea mineral resources, ocean energy and some non-conventional fishery resources, may offer opportunities, the sustainability of their development is questionable. The most important traditional ocean resources, including coastal environments and conventional fishery resources, are over-used and require improved management. In many cases, the unrestricted use of technology, the growing demand for goods and services from the ocean, uncontrolled population growth and continuous migration to coastal areas have led to the depletion of living resources and the degradation of the coastal and marine environment as well as of the economic conditions of some of the major sectors exploiting the ocean.

A. Constraints to implementation

7. Chapter 17 of Agenda 21 called for governmental action, with the assistance of the specialized agencies of the United Nations system when required and with the active participation of the people and sectors involved and that of the non-governmental organizations, in order to: (a) improve the use and conservation of coastal resources through integrated management and sustainable development of coastal areas, including exclusive economic zones (programme area A); (b) increase marine environmental protection from land-based and sea-based sources of pollution (programme area B); (c) promote sustainable use and conservation of marine living resources in the high seas (programme area C); promote sustainable use and conservation of marine living resources under national jurisdiction (programme area D); (e) address critical uncertainties for the management of the marine environment and climate change (programme area E); (f) strengthen international and regional cooperation and coordination (programme area F); and (g) promote sustainable development of small islands (programme area G).

8. Without appropriate action by Governments and the relevant economic sectors to improve information systems, research support and programmes, institutions and legal frameworks, the present situation can only worsen. Constraints to progress can be found in the fact that:

(a) Oceans and coastal areas are a finite economic asset yet to be fully understood by Governments, as is also the consequent need for their prudent and rational exploitation, and given commensurable priority in national development plans;

(b) Concerns of Member States, while often based upon similar scientific and socio-economic premises, are voiced by different governmental representatives in different intergovernmental forums and in different ways, depending upon the constituencies, with the result that there is a lack of coherent policy within the United Nations system (at global, regional and national levels);

(c) Most countries have not established national coordination mechanisms that could enhance implementation of chapter 17 of Agenda 21;

(d) The concerns of the private sector and many poor communities are driven by short-term economic priorities that tend to give low priority to resource conservation and the needs of future generations;

(e) Resource constraints, particularly but not only in developing countries, often limit the amount of attention and financial support Governments can devote to scientific research and its application to national policy options;

(f) There has been insufficient awareness of the need to identify and reduce "uncertainties" in human knowledge and their potential consequences, including the consequences for the health of exposed human populations, and thus of the need for a precautionary approach to management and development decisions;

(g) United Nations system efforts with respect to chapter 17 of Agenda 21 need to be based on a coordinated approach embracing scientific, technological and socio-economic factors.

B. Selected achievements 5/

9. Despite these difficulties, significant progress has been made since UNCED in the following areas:

(a) In relation to programme area A of chapter 17, guidelines for integrated coastal area management (ICAM) have been developed for various levels of governance and implementation and are being applied by countries and financing institutions in a growing number of technical assistance projects. As part and in support of these initiatives, the relevant United Nations organizations and mechanisms have developed a cooperative programme framework for ICAM. In addition, in 1995 the Consultative Group for International Agricultural Research (CGIAR) adopted "coastal environment" as the central theme of a system-wide initiative, with the International Centre for Living Aquatic Resources Management (ICLARM) as a lead centre;

(b) In relation to programme area B, the Global Programme of Action for the Protection of the Marine Environment from Land-based Activities was adopted in November 1995 in Washington, D.C. It will provide the basis for national and international action to reduce pollution of the oceans from land-based activities, contributing, inter alia, to: (i) improvement of coastal habitats and productivity; (ii) reduction of threats to food security and safety; (iii) reduction of hazards to human health; and (iv) increased control over coastal activities to stop and reverse the process of alteration of the coastal zone. A number of other actions can be noted, such as the 1993-1994 ban on the dumping of radioactive waste, sewage sludge and industrial waste and on incineration of toxic wastes at sea, as agreed in the 1972 Convention on the Prevention of Marine Pollution by Dumping of Wastes and Other Matter (London Convention);

(c) In relation to programme areas C and D, the legal framework for sustainable use and conservation of living aquatic resources in the oceans has been substantially improved since UNCED. First of all, the entry into force of the United Nations Convention on the Law of the Sea establishes the rights and duties of States with respect to marine environmental protection and conservation and management of resources. It also provides the basis for dispute resolution and the conclusion of further international agreements, inter alia, on high seas fisheries and those in exclusive economic zones (EEZs). Second, the legally binding Agreement to Promote Compliance with International Conservation and Management Measures by Fishing Vessels on the High Seas (the Compliance Agreement) was approved by the FAO Conference in November 1993 and has so far been signed by seven States. Third, the Agreement for the Implementation of the Provisions of the United Nations Convention on the Law of the Sea of 10 December 1982 relating to the Conservation and Management of Straddling Fish Stocks and Highly Migratory Fish Stocks (A/50/550, annex I), which usefully complements the 1982 Convention, was adopted in August 1995 in New York and opened for signature on 4 December 1995. Fourth, the Code of Conduct for Responsible Fisheries, which, together with the guidelines that support it, provides the guidance necessary for management and conservation of fishery resources as well as associated or dependent species and their environment, was developed by the members of FAO and approved by the FAO Conference in October 1995. The establishment of the Southern Ocean Whale Sanctuary by the International Whaling Commission (IWC) in 1994 also deserves special mention;

(d) In relation to programme area E, agreement has been reached on a development approach, strategy and time-frame for the Global Ocean Observing System (GOOS), involving many national institutions and the effective cooperation of a number of United Nations organizations (UNESCO-IOC, WMO, UNEP, FAO) and other international organizations. Several regional GOOS programmes have been initiated and there has been an increase in efforts to collect and share some critical types of data. In addition, significant progress has been made in numerous scientific domains critical to the understanding of the oceans: (i) the ability to forecast changing environmental, ocean-related conditions (flooding, cyclones, tsunamis), and the capacity to apply such forecasts through warning and protective measures has been considerably improved; (ii) the assessment of the role of oceans in the regulation of greenhouse gas concentrations, especially CO_2, has been updated; (iii) the number of case studies on the vulnerability of low-lying coastal areas and small islands to the potential impacts of climate change and sealevel rise have been completed; (iv) the impact of changing ultraviolet radiation on primary productivity of the marine environment has been assessed; and (v) the first field phase of the International Mussel Watch programme has been completed and several later phases have been initiated;

(e) In relation to programme area F, the issue of international cooperation and coordination for sustainable use of the oceans has been actively addressed in many international and regional initiatives, some of which have been reported above. The creation of the ACC Subcommittee on Oceans and Coastal Areas as a subsidiary body of the Inter-Agency Committee on Sustainable Development has facilitated and improved cooperation among bodies of the United Nations system and, apart from joint integrated reporting on progress achieved in the implementation of Agenda 21, has the potential to become a forum for joint programming. As a first step, a cooperative programme framework for integrated coastal area management is being developed. The Intergovernmental Conference to Adopt a Programme of Action for the Protection of the Marine Environment from Land-based Activities (Washington, D.C., 1995) recommended giving the United Nations Environment Programme a prominent role as the secretariat for institutional follow-up, a clearing-house mechanism and an intergovernmental forum for protection of the seas from land-based sources of pollution. GESAMP, the IMO/FAO/UNESCO-IOC/WMO/WHO/IAEA/UN/UNEP Joint Group of Experts on the Scientific Aspects of Marine Environmental Protection, originally founded to advise solely on marine pollution issues, has broadened its terms of reference so that it can fully respond to the needs of its sponsoring agencies for scientific advice on all aspects of marine environmental protection and management, including ICAM. Its relevance was confirmed by the 1995 London Workshop on Environmental Science, Comprehensiveness and Consistency in Global Decisions on Ocean Issues. The Aquatic Sciences and Fisheries Information System (ASFIS), co-sponsored by the United Nations (Division for Ocean Affairs and the Law of the Sea), UNESCO-IOC, FAO and UNEP, is responsible for the production of the Aquatic Sciences and Fisheries database (ASFA), the largest and most widely used database on fisheries and aquatic science. It is published in print as well as on CD-ROM. Also, the Conference of the Parties to the Convention on Biological Diversity, at its second session (Jakarta, November 1995), agreed on new initiatives for the conservation of marine and coastal biological diversity. At the regional level, the five United Nations regional commissions, the FAO regional fishery bodies, the UNEP regional seas coordination units and the regional groups of IOC and other organizations address sectoral and cross-sectoral issues related to oceans and marine resources. The UNEP Regional Seas Programme in particular is an important basis for action and cooperation among various institutions, although funding for this activity has been problematic;

(f) In relation to programme area G, the reports of the Secretary-General to the General Assembly at its forty-ninth and fiftieth sessions included detailed information on action taken by the United Nations system to implement the Programme of Action for the Sustainable Development of Small Island Developing States, adopted in Barbados in 1994. The concerns of these States, as related to oceans and coastal areas, are reflected in the main policy recommendations and required actions listed in sections III and IV of this report. These sections are generally relevant and even more critical for small island developing States than for States with larger continental masses.

10. In relation to all programme areas, non-governmental organizations (NGOs) have operated as partners in promoting the concepts of sustainable development and responsible fisheries and defending the views of the public or of minority groups as appropriate. Their actions have been complementary to the actions undertaken by the United Nations system. They have undertaken to raise awareness of the major issues affecting the marine environment and fisheries today, such as protection of marine mammals and endangered species; conservation of resources and the environment; training and education; by-catch and discards in fisheries; a precautionary approach to development and management; overcapitalization and governmental subsidies; consistency and compatibility between management schemes for shared resources; monitoring, control and surveillance; marine environmental protection; biodiversity; the rights and interests of small-scale entrepreneurs; international trade; and transparency and participation of people in management and resource allocation.

11. A number of non-United Nations activities have contributed to the implementation of chapter 17 of Agenda 21, e.g. the recent International Coral Reef Initiative and the 1995 London Workshop on Environmental Science, Comprehensiveness and Consistency in Global Decisions on Ocean Issues.

12. In the critical cross-sectoral area of financing, it should be noted that the Global Environment Facility (GEF), which was originally established as a pilot programme in 1991, was restructured in March 1994 into a permanent funding mechanism to provide grant and concessional funds to developing countries and countries with economies in transition. Over US$ 2 billion will be committed by participating Governments over the 1995-1998 period. While about 14 per cent of its current total resources are devoted to international water projects, this component has seen a sharp fall from US$ 127 million in the pilot phase (1991-1994) to US$ 4 million in the post-pilot phase (1995-1998) projects. About 44 per cent of GEF resources, accounting for approximately US$ 400 million, are spent on biodiversity projects. Both components in part support the objectives of chapter 17. In addition, UNDP has developed a portfolio of over US$ 70 million for ocean and coastal management. Finally, the World Bank developed a portfolio of more than US$ 100 million in coastal management between 1989 and 1994.

C. Areas for further progress

13. Areas where progress is not as satisfactory include, *inter alia*: (a) the continuing decline in the abundance of many fishery resources and in the economic health of fisheries in both the developed and developing world; (b) the gap between total financial resource needs estimated at UNCED and those being mobilized; (c) the insufficient development, in many countries, of the national capacity to implement sustainable development strategies; (d) the insufficient level of implementation by Governments of existing rules, regulations, international standards and conventions as reflected in the insufficient adaptation and harmonization of national legislation and procedures and in the inefficiency of enforcement; (e) the different implementation rates between developed and developing countries; and (f) the insufficient gender perspective in all policies and programmes, in line with the Beijing Declaration and Platform for Action. 6/ These and other issues will be addressed in sections III and IV of this report.

II. LINKAGES WITH OTHER MAIN PROGRAMME AREAS OF AGENDA 21

14. Given the nature of the ocean and coastal regions and their impact on the whole of the environment, most of the issues raised in Agenda 21 can be linked in one way or another to chapter 17. Those of most obvious relevance are:

(a) Chapter 2. International cooperation to accelerate sustainable development in developing countries and related domestic policies, particularly on issues related to international trade and the environment;

(b) Chapter 3. Combating poverty, enabling coastal communities and, in particular, poor small-scale fishermen to achieve acceptable and sustainable livelihoods;

(c) Chapter 4. Changing production and consumption patterns, in particular in relation to improving fisheries management and promoting the use of fish for food (including the improved use of by-catch), but also in relation to the more general use of the coastal areas;

(d) Chapter 6. Protecting and promoting human health by reducing risks from polluted coastal waters;

(e) Chapter 7. Promoting sustainable human settlement development, in particular the integrated provision of environmental infrastructure to reduce land-based causes of coastal and ocean pollution;

(f) Chapter 9. Protection of the atmosphere, in regard to: (i) absorption of greenhouse gases; (ii) climate change and its potentially drastic effects on marine living resources; (iii) energy optimization programmes and reduction of dangerous substances in exhaust gas emissions; and (iv) reduction in the use of chlorofluorocarbons (CFCs) in at-sea and coastal ocean industries;

(g) Chapter 10. Integrated approach to the planning and management of land resources, including scientific and technological means;

(h) Chapter 15. Conservation of biological diversity because the living marine resources are an important subset of the world's biodiversity and are affected by fishing activities, aquaculture development and environmental pressures resulting from tourism and other coastal and inland developments. Fishing pressure may influence species and stock composition, as well as the population structure and life history characteristics of target species. The expansion and augmentation of fisheries through such practices as the introduction and transfer of aquatic organisms and hatchery enhancement programmes poses special threats to the maintenance of the naturally well-adapted complex of resident fish. In regard to farmed and domesticated fishery resources, there is a need to develop means to further control, conserve and manage their genetic resources for sustainable food production;

(i) Chapter 18. Protection of the quality and supply of freshwater resources because freshwater inputs through rivers into the ocean and their seasonal patterns are a determining factor of the quality and productivity of related coastal areas (estuaries, mangroves, nurseries) and maintenance of critical habitats (e.g. sea-grass beds, coral reefs). They provide essential signals for ocean species reproduction. In addition, pollution of freshwater by industry, agriculture and mining or as a consequence of urban development has strongly negative effects on the potential for tourism or aquaculture development in coastal areas.

15. Chapter 17, in particular programme areas A and E on integrated coastal area management and on critical uncertainties, respectively, are also of great relevance to small island developing States, for which the ocean represents a significant opportunity for development, a formidable challenge and a persistent threat from the perspective of global climate change and sealevel rise.

III. MAIN POLICY RECOMMENDATIONS

16. The steps to be taken that will have the necessary impact within the required time-frame are often politically difficult, potentially unpopular and require resources not always available. Nevertheless, as stated as an

underlying theme of UNCED, the responsibilities that are avoided today will fall
upon future generations in an order of magnitude that even the most forward-
looking individuals may not be able to forecast. In many instances, today's
lack of responsibility will have far-reaching effects even on present
generations.

17. Having considered the significant achievements of Member States, the need
for even more significant efforts in the immediate future and the constraints to
proper conservation, rational use and development of ocean and coastal area
resources, it is suggested that the Commission on Sustainable Development:

     (a) Calling the attention of the international community to the role of
oceans and coastal areas as a major governing force of the planetary ecosystem,
as well as a determining factor of human life, recommend that greater priority
be accorded at national, regional and international levels to the action set out
in chapter 17 of Agenda 21;

     (b) Recognizing that the intersectoral nature of ocean and coastal areas
requires them to be dealt with in a coherent manner, recommend that Governments
adjust, as necessary, their administrative and policy structures in support of
integrated planning and management, addressing cross-sectoral issues and
promoting transparency and participation, including more effective participation
of non-governmental organizations;

     (c) Stressing the importance of the agreed international legislative and
guiding frameworks for harmonious and sustainable development of the oceans,
urge Governments to (i) ratify, as soon as possible, the United Nations
Convention on the Law of the Sea; (ii) sign and ratify the Agreement for the
Implementation of the Provisions of the United Nations Convention on the Law of
the Sea of 10 December 1982 relating to the Conservation and Management of
Straddling Fish Stocks and Highly Migratory Fish Stocks and, in the meantime,
apply the Agreement provisionally; (iii) apply the Code of Conduct for
Responsible Fisheries adopted by the FAO Conference in October 1995; (iv) accede
to the FAO Agreement to Promote Compliance with International Conservation and
Management Measures by Fishing Vessels on the High Seas; (v) ratify the 1992
Convention on Biological Diversity and apply the Jakarta Mandate on Coastal and
Marine Biodiversity, adopted at the second session of the Conference of the
Parties to the Convention on Biological Diversity in November 1995; and
(vi) demonstrate greater commitment to implementing these instruments;

     (d) Recognizing further the progress made during the post-UNCED process in
developing international and regional standards and action plans relevant to the
protection and management of coastal and marine environments and to the
sustainable use and conservation of its resources, recommend that Governments:
(i) continue to use existing mechanisms and forums to foster further progress;
(ii) actively participate in regional action plans, programmes and other
cooperative arrangements; and (iii) take advantage of international
collaboration, particularly in the area of financing;

     (e) Conscious of the importance of United Nations organizations and
programmes in the process of implementation and in the spirit of the outcome of
the Intergovernmental Conference to Adopt a Global Programme of Action for the
Protection of the Marine Environment from Land-based Activities
(Washington, D.C., 1995), recommend the further improvement and strengthening of
the ongoing cooperation and coordination among the organizations and bodies of
the United Nations system, in particular with the aim of:

          (i)   Promoting the implementation of a system-wide initiative on oceans
                using existing coordination mechanisms and the lead-agency concept
                widely accepted during the UNCED process;

          (ii) Encouraging the development of system-wide, cooperative programme
                frameworks for activities requiring interdisciplinary and
                cross-sectoral planning and/or implementation (with priority to the

development of such a programme framework for integrated coastal area management) and for education and training programmes in support of capacity-building;

(iii)   Pursuing a system-wide approach to mobilizing funding and other resources for common issues, pooling resources where appropriate, particularly at the regional level.

IV. ACTION REQUIRED

18.   It is suggested that the Commission on Sustainable Development agree on and call the attention of Governments, the United Nations system and major organizations and groups to the following actions to be taken at the national, regional and international levels to pursue further the implementation of chapter 17 of Agenda 21 towards the sustainable development of oceans and coastal areas.

Programme area A.   Integrated coastal area management

19.   In connection with programme area A:

(a)   Governments are encouraged to develop plans for integrated coastal area management and, by extension, for management of EEZs, within national development plans, and to that end, among other means, to promote and facilitate human resources development through appropriate education and training, drawing upon the experience of such programmes as the TRAIN-SEA-COAST Programme of the United Nations/UNDP;

(b)   Governments are asked to develop regional, national and/or local coral reef initiatives, using an ecosystem-based, integrated approach that encourages participation and includes programmes for community-based management or co-management of reef resources;

(c)   States are asked to consider the development of appropriate administrative and legislative arrangements that would assign rights and duties (responsibilities) to coastal dwellers and users in order to regulate activities undertaken in the coastal zone, thus promoting the sustainable development of those areas;

(d)   The respective governing bodies of the United Nations system should maximize the use of recently developed databases covering such areas as ICAM programmes, projects, courses, scientific data and information in order to improve coastal area planning and management in their respective areas;

(e)   External support agencies are asked to encourage increased cooperation and coordination between agencies dealing with water resource issues and development organizations, arrangements or mechanisms, drawing on the successful recent experience of the Black Sea and the Red Sea programmes and using other available mechanisms such as the UNDP-World Bank local donor groups.

Programme area B.   Marine pollution

20.   In connection with programme area B:

(a)   Governments should promote the establishment of self-sustaining financial mechanisms in support of, _inter alia_: (i) training of personnel; (ii) navigational safety and antipollution measures in international straits; (iii) waste reception facilities in ports; and (iv) salvage and emergency response facilities and capacity-building in hydrographic surveying and nautical charting.   No officially sanctioned multilateral schemes along these lines have been adopted so far, although they have been under consideration in IMO and elsewhere for some time.   Where appropriate, existing cooperation arrangements should be used (e.g. the UNCTAD/IMO/ILO Working Group on Coordination of Activities on Ports);

(b)   Governments should address the need to develop, at the global level, a regulatory framework for offshore oil and gas extraction activities, using IMO as the most appropriate lead organization to undertake this task;

(c)   Member States are urged to move towards early ratification of the newly adopted convention pertaining to standards of training, certification and watchkeeping for personnel on fishing vessels and amendments revising the 1978 International Convention on Standards of Training, Certification and Watchkeeping for Seafarers;

(d)   Member States are advised that priority should be accorded to developing and implementing adequate measures to protect the marine environment from land-based sources and activities through: (i) effective participation in and implementation of the Global Programme of Action for the Protection of the Marine Environment from Land-based Activities; and (ii) strengthening existing arrangements and infrastructure within the United Nations system for quality control of marine pollution data and the relevant training and capacity-building at the national and regional levels - for example, the recently developed trilateral cooperation arrangement between UNEP, IAEA and IOC.

Programme areas C and D.   Living marine resources

21.   In connection with programme areas C and D:

(a)   Governments and FAO are urged to establish and/or strengthen, as appropriate, subregional or regional fishery management organizations or arrangements to adopt and carry out conservation and management measures, particularly for transboundary and shared fishery resources;

(b)   Governments should undertake to develop or strengthen national fishery management authorities, with the active participation of the fishing communities, in the context of integrated coastal fisheries management (ICFM);

(c)   Governments are urged to reduce subsidies to the fishing industry and abolish incentives leading to over-fishing;

(d)   Funding organizations, investment banks and donors should provide developing countries with the financial assistance required to support their efforts to make sustainable use of their resources (e.g. to start the process of effort-reduction, which should lead to improved biological and economic viability of fisheries);

(e)   Governments are encouraged to draw from the potential offered by the enhancement of aquatic living resources in general, and by coastal aquaculture and ranching in particular, adopting a precautionary approach to development and sustainable practices;

(f)   Governments are urged to respect agreed international management measures such as the Southern Ocean Whale Sanctuary established by IWC and the General Assembly resolutions on large-scale pelagic drift-net fishing.

Programme area E.   Critical uncertainties

22.   In connection with programme area E:

(a)   Member States are encouraged to continue to strengthen the relevant national institutions and their infrastructures and to include, in particular, trained interdisciplinary expertise, promoting the development of the interface between research and the decision-making process and introducing ocean environmental subjects in school curricula at all levels;

(b)   States are reminded of the need to ensure, through the provision of sufficient resources to national institutions, that ongoing and planned cooperative research on the oceans can be completed for the benefit of all;

(c) Member States are urged to make commitments to and to support, through their national institutions, the continued gradual establishment of the Global Ocean Observing System (GOOS), building on the existing systems so as to form a globally coordinated strategy to secure sufficient information for adequate management, forecasting and periodic scientific assessments of the state of the marine environment; the information produced should be comparable (i.e. quality controlled);

(d) Member States, United Nations organizations, and bilateral assistance and financing institutions should cooperate in strengthening the capability of national institutions to manage and use data and products derived from the systematic monitoring, especially through GOOS, of marine environmental changes and should commit themselves to high-level intergovernmental cooperation in the exchange of data and information;

(e) Member States are urged to take early action to strengthen their data and information management capabilities, including telecommunication aspects, so as to better contribute to and benefit from global observation and data exchange systems;

(f) Member States and their institutions are encouraged to contribute to global efforts to improve the assessment, monitoring and control of the impact of marine and coastal pollution on human health.

Programme area F: International cooperation and coordination

Regional level

23. In connection with programme area F, recalling that regional cooperation has been endorsed by UNCED as a priority vehicle for the implementation of Agenda 21, especially in regard to intersectoral domains, of which the oceans and coastal areas are prime examples:

(a) Regional bodies and organizations with mandates in areas relevant to the oceans and coastal areas are urged to reflect the provisions and priorities of chapter 17 of Agenda 21 in their respective programmes and work plans and to strengthen cooperation among their organizations, thus contributing to harmonizing their work on ocean and coastal-related matters;

(b) Donors are encouraged to give priority to proposals that facilitate regional cooperation, *inter alia*, through the United Nations regional commissions or through regional banks, especially those that support technical and institutional collaboration, with associated assistance to human and infrastructure development;

(c) The ACC Subcommittee on Oceans and Coastal Areas is invited to pay specific attention to monitoring and advising on the implementation of Agenda 21 (chap. 17) at the regional level. It should, *inter alia*: (i) identify gaps and opportunities for joint programmes as an impetus for regional cooperation, using chapter 17 as a joint framework; (ii) continue to use the lead-agency and associated-agency concepts, which have led to a rational division of responsibilities and the use of the competencies available in the United Nations system. In this connection, more active participation of the regional commissions in the work of the Subcommittee is envisaged. Moreover, the work of the Subcommittee could also benefit from more interaction with non-governmental organizations.

Global level

24. In connection with programme area F, the Commission may wish to:

(a) Urge Governments that have not yet established appropriate national policy mechanisms on oceans and coastal areas to do so in order that positions taken at the United Nations and its specialized agencies are harmonized;

(b) Suggest appropriate use by the Global Environment Facility (especially for its international waters and biodiversity components) of the competence available in the specialized agencies of the United Nations system to support priority-setting, formulation of proposals and project execution, for fuller implementation of chapter 17;

(c) Encourage an intensified use of existing mechanisms for inter-agency cooperation that are viewed as being particularly effective - coordination mechanisms such as the Intersecretariat Committee on Scientific Programmes Relating to Oceanography (ICSPRO) and the ACC Subcommittee on Oceans and Coastal Areas; joint advisory groups such as GESAMP (the IMO/FAO/UNESCO-IOC/WMO/WHO/IAEA/UN/UNEP Joint Group of Experts on the Scientific Aspects of Marine Environmental Protection); joint programmes such as GIPME (Global Investigation of Pollution in the Marine Environment); and agreements through memorandums of understanding as a framework for issue-oriented action at all levels;

(d) Encourage the private sector and Governments to explore jointly opportunities for mutually beneficial partnerships with regional organizations and United Nations organizations in connection with the implementation of chapter 17 of Agenda 21;

(e) Encourage Governments, in closer cooperation with non-governmental organizations and major groups, to participate in activities to increase awareness of the impact of the oceans and coastal areas on the life of our planet, including those to be organized within the context of the International Year of the Ocean in 1998.

Financial implications of action required

25. Bearing in mind that (a) the implementation of chapter 17 of Agenda 21 will require a substantial increase in funding for the oceans and coastal regions, about 90 per cent of which will have to come from national sources (public and private); (b) the costs of not taking appropriate action, as reflected, for example, in the cost of over-fishing (over US$ 50,000 million per year) or in the recent outbreaks of diseases in Asian shrimp culture (hundreds of millions of dollars), have become unsustainable; and (c) the catalytic effect of initiatives undertaken through the United Nations system, which has already shifted resources towards the implementation of Agenda 21, with effective results:

(a) Governments of both developed and developing countries are urged to renew and increase their commitment to chapter 17 of Agenda 21 and to commit local resources for its implementation (particularly using user charges, taxes, etc.) in order to cover the immediate costs of the conservation and management of natural resources and foster development sustainability;

(b) Donor Governments should consider increasing their financial support to the initiatives undertaken by developing countries and countries with economies in transition, through bilateral and multilateral channels, for national, regional (including support to regional organizations) and global programmes. In particular, they are urged to enhance their contribution to the Global Environment Facility (GEF), which has become a critical funding source, especially in regard to the ocean-related activities under the international waters and biodiversity components, as reflected in the 1995 operational strategy for GEF.

Notes

1/ United Nations Conference on Environment and Development, Rio de Janeiro, 3-14 June 1992, vol. I, Resolutions Adopted by the Conference (United Nations publication, Sales No. E.93.I.8 and corrigendum), resolution 1, annex II.

2/ Ibid., para. 17.1.

3/ <u>Official Records of the Third United Nations Conference on the Law of the Sea</u>, vol. XVII (United Nations publication, Sales No. E.84.V.3), document A/CONF.62/122.

4/ See the report of the Secretary-General on the law of the sea (A/50/713 of 1 November 1995) and the January 1996 update (internal).

5/ A more extensive listing of achievements is given in the addendum to this report. It should be noted that detailed information on achievements at the national level has not yet become available through the process of national reporting and could not be included in this report or the addendum.

6/ <u>Report of the Fourth World Conference on Women, Beijing,</u> 4-15 September 1995 (A/CONF.177/20), chap. I, resolution 1, annexes I and II.

UNITED NATIONS ENVIRONMENT PROGRAMME
(UNEP)

DOCUMENTS REPRODUCED IN WHOLE OR IN PART:

INTERGOVERNMENTAL CONFERENCE TO ADOPT A GLOBAL PROGRAMME OF ACTION FOR THE PROTECTION OF THE MARINE ENVIRONMENT FROM LAND-BASED ACTIVITIES, WASHINGTON D.C., 23 OCTOBER-3 NOVEMBER 1995

UN General Assembly

UNEP CONVENTION ON BIOLOGICAL DIVERSITY

UN General Assembly

DOCUMENTS NOT REPRODUCED:

1. LAW OF THE SEA - NOTE VERBALE DATED 5 MARCH 1996 FROM THE UNITED STATES MISSION TO THE UNITED NATIONS ADDRESSED TO THE SECRETARY-GENERAL (REPORT OF THE INTERGOVERNMENTAL CONFERENCE TO ADOPT A GLOBAL PROGRAMME OF ACTION FOR THE PROTECTION OF THE MARINE ENVIRONMENT FROM LAND-BASED ACTIVITIES, WASHINGTON D.C., 23 OCTOBER-3 NOVEMBER 1995)*

Doc. no.: A/51/116

Date: 16 April 1996

The United States Mission to the United Nations has the honour to bring to the attention of the Secretary-General of the United Nations the Intergovernmental Conference to Adopt a Global Programme of Action for the Protection of the Marine Environment from Land-based Activities, held in Washington, D.C., from 23 October to 3 November 1995, the Washington Declaration on the Protection of the Marine Environment from Land-based Activities as well as the Programme of Action of the Conference. The United States was pleased to host this important intergovernmental conference which was attended by representatives from 109 countries. The United States considers the Global Programme of Action for the Protection of the Marine Environment from Land-based Activities a major contribution to international efforts to implement the recommendations of the United Nations Conference on Environment and Development (UNCED), in particular on oceans-related matters. In the light of the broad consensus reached at the meeting, the United States Mission to the United Nations respectfully requests the Secretary-General to circulated the text of the present letter together with the report of the Conference (annex I) and the Global Programme of Action (annex II) as an official document of the General Assembly, under item 24 of the preliminary list.

---

*   A/51/50.

ANNEX I*

REPORT OF THE INTERGOVERNMENTAL CONFERENCE TO ADOPT
A GLOBAL PROGRAMME OF ACTION FOR THE PROTECTION
OF THE MARINE ENVIRONMENT FROM
LAND-BASED ACTIVITIES

INTRODUCTION

1.   The Intergovernmental Conference to Adopt a Global Programme of
Action for the Protection of the Marine Environment from Land-based
Activities was convened by the Executive Director of the United Nations
Environment Programme (UNEP) pursuant to Governing Council decision 17/20
of 21 May 1993, in which the Council authorized the Executive Director to
organize a structured and sequenced preparatory process leading to a two-
week intergovernmental meeting in late 1995 for the purpose of adopting a
programme of action for the protection of the marine environment from
land-based activities. The Conference, which was the final meeting in the
process, was held in Washington, D.C., from 23 October to 3 November 1995.

I.   OPENING OF THE MEETING

2.   The Conference was opened by Ms. Elizabeth Dowdeswell, Executive
Director of the United Nations Environment Programme (UNEP) at 10.35 a.m.
on Monday, 23 October 1995.

3.   The Conference was attended by representatives of the following 109
countries: Antigua and Barbuda, Argentina, Australia, Austria, Bahrain,
Bangladesh, Belarus, Belgium, Belize, Benin, Bhutan, Botswana, Brazil,
Bulgaria, Burkina Faso, Burundi, Cambodia, Cameroon, Canada, Chad, Chile,
China, Colombia, Comoros, Congo, Costa Rica, Cote d'Ivoire, Croatia, Cuba,
Denmark, Dominica, Ecuador, Egypt, Estonia, Ethiopia, Finland, France,
Gambia, Georgia, Germany, Ghana, Greece, Honduras, Iceland, India,
Indonesia, Israel, Italy, Jamaica, Japan, Jordan, Kazakstan, Kenya,
Kiribati, Kuwait, Malawi, Malaysia, Maldives, Malta, Marshall Islands,
Mauritius, Mexico, Micronesia (Federated States of), Monaco, Mozambique,
Nauru, Netherlands, New Zealand, Nicaragua, Niger, Nigeria, Norway,
Pakistan, Peru, Philippines, Poland, Republic of Korea, Romania, Russian
Federation, Rwanda, Saint Lucia, Samoa, Sao Tome and Principe, Saudi
Arabia, Senegal, Seychelles, Sierra Leone, Slovenia, South Africa, Spain,
Sri Lanka, Sweden, Switzerland, Thailand, Togo, Tunisia, Turkey,
Turkmenistan, Uganda, United Kingdom of Great Britain and Northern Ireland,
United Republic of Tanzania, United States of America, Uruguay, Vanuatu,
Venezuela, Yemen, Zaire, Zambia and Zimbabwe.

4.   The Conference was also attended by representatives of the following
two United Nations bodies and Secretariat units: United Nations
Environment Programme (UNEP) and United Nations Development Programme
(UNDP).

---

*   Previously issued under the symbol UNEP(OCA)/LBA/IG.2/6.

5.   In addition, representatives of the following nine specialized agencies and other organizations of the United Nations system also attended: Food and Agriculture Organization (FAO), Global Environment Facility (GEF), International Atomic Energy Agency (IAEA), International Maritime Organization (IMO), United Nations Educational, Scientific and Cultural Organization (UNESCO/IOC), United Nations Industrial Development Organization (UNIDO), World Health Organization (WHO), World Bank and World Meteorological Organization (WMO).

6.   Also represented were the following seven intergovernmental organizations: Asia-Pacific Network for Global Change Research, Baltic Marine Environment Protection Commission (Helsinki Commission), Comision Permanente del Pacifico Sur (CPPS), European Commission (EC), International Council for the Exploration of the Sea (ICES), Regional Organization for the Protection of the Marine Environment (ROPME) and South Pacific Regional Environment Programme (SPREP).

7.   Observers from the following 29 non-governmental organizations were also present: Advisory Committee on Protection of the Sea (ACOPS), American Crop Protection Association (ACPA), Center for International Environmental Law (CIEL), Chemical Manufacturers Association (CMA), Chlorine Chemistry Council (CCC), Chlorine Institute (CI), Earth Action (EA), European Chemical Industry Council (CEFIC), Department of Planet Earth (DPE), Environmental Defense Fund (EDF), Environmental and Energy Study Institute (EESI), European Crop Protection Association, Foundation Hernandiana (FH), Foundation for International Environmental Law and Development (FIELD), Friends of the Earth, Greenpeace International, International Association of Ports and Harbors (IAPH), International Coastal and Ocean Organization (ICOA), International Council of Chemical Associations (ICCA), International Council of Environmental Law (ICEL), International Fertilizer Industry Association (IFA), The Cousteau Society (TCS), National Academy of Science (NAS), Rio Systems (RS), Société pour Vaincre la Pollution, Woods Hole Oceanographic Institution (WHOI), World Conservation Union (IUCN), World Resources Institute (WRI) and World Wide Fund for Nature (WWF).

8.   The full list of participants is attached as annex III to the present report.

9.   Opening statements were made by the Executive Director of UNEP and by Ms. Eileen Claussen on behalf of the Government of the United States of America.

10.   In her statement, the Executive Director welcomed participants, thanked the Government of the United States of America for its hospitality and said that the oceans, which covered 71 per cent of the earth's surface, provided a habitat for plants and animals, constituted a major source of human food and, through their interactions with the atmosphere, lithosphere and biosphere, were indispensable for maintaining the conditions making life possible. Human activities had, however, endangered the necessary balance, and almost 80 per cent of the pollution involved emanated from or related to land-based activities. Protection of the marine environment was a very complex issue which encompassed many diverse human activities and thus required a mix of measures of various kinds. It was necessary to bear in mind the indivisibility of the marine environment, the fact that virtually every substance released into the biosphere was carried seaward, the close connection of the marine environment and the freshwater drainage

basins and the fact that the world's coastlines were being increasingly overwhelmed by human settlement. The draft Global Programme of Action that was before the Conference (UNEP(OCA)/LBA/IG.2/3) contained a comprehensive, sequential and coordinated approach to the situation that built on the principles of the United Nations Conference on Environment and Development namely, sustainable development, the precautionary principle, holistic considerations and international cooperation. She thus recommended it to the serious consideration of the participants.

11. Ms. Eileen Claussen, Special Assistant to the President of the United States and Senior Director for Global Environmental Affairs of the United States National Security Council, welcomed the participants to the United States of America and said that land-based sources were undoubtedly the main cause of the ocean pollution and loss of marine habitat that threatened the health and economic well-being of the majority of the world's population living in coastal areas. It was evident from the statistics that the marine environment was of crucial importance to human survival and that it was by no means in a healthy condition. Its protection was thus a major challenge. Significant progress had been made in recent months in addressing fisheries issues, and the current Conference provided the opportunity to achieve comparable progress in controlling pollution from land-based activities. That meant not only completing the task of drafting the Global Programme of Action but also demonstrating political will by making a companion High-Level Declaration outlining in a succinct fashion steps to implement the Programme and reaffirming the commitment to do so.

12. The representative of Iceland, speaking as Chairman of the final preparatory meeting for the Conference, said that failure to act in the near future to halt the degradation of the oceans would be a blow to the people of the world and a betrayal of future generations. He stressed the importance of the effective implementation of the Global Programme of Action, reminding participants that the carefully drafted Montreal Guidelines for the Prevention of Marine Pollution from Land-based Sources, which contained no compliance requirements, had not had the effects that had been expected. He further stressed, in particular, the enormous threat to the environment posed by persistent organic pollutants (POPs), on which immediate international action was needed. Having given an account of the work done on the draft Global Programme of Action at the preparatory meeting in Reykjavik, he said that the work of the current Conference would be a major input to the forthcoming session of the Commission on Sustainable Development, in its consideration of chapter 17, relating to the oceans, of Agenda 21.

II. ORGANIZATION OF THE MEETING

A. Rules of procedure

13. The Conference decided to apply the rules of procedure of the Governing Council of UNEP *mutatis mutandis* to its proceedings.

B. Election of officers

14. The Conference elected by acclamation the following officers:

Chairperson: Ms. Eileen Claussen (United States of America)

<u>Vice-Chairpersons</u>:   Ms. Paula Caballero (Colombia)
                          Mr. Sakkie van der Westhuizen (South Africa)
                          Mr. Dariusz Stanislawski (Poland)

<u>Rapporteur</u>:   Mr. Laavasa Malua (Western Samoa)

<u>Chairpersons of the
Working Groups</u>

<u>Working Group A</u>:   Mr. Magnus Johannesson (Iceland)

<u>Working Group B</u>:   Mr. Salif Diop (Senegal)
     <u>assisted by</u>:   Mr. Mahmoud Abdulraheem (Kuwait)

C. <u>Organization of work</u>

15.   The Conference decided that it would work in plenary sessions
assisted by two substantive working groups. It further decided that
Working Group A would consider chapter IV of the draft Global Programme of
Action, and that Working Group B would consider chapters II and III as well
as chapters I and V, as deemed necessary.

16.   The Conference also adopted its programme of work on the basis of a
proposal submitted by the Secretariat (UNEP(OCA)/LBA/IG.2/INF.3).

III.   ADOPTION OF THE AGENDA

17.   At the suggestion of the Chairperson, the Conference adopted the
following agenda on the basis of the provisional agenda
(UNEP(OCA)/LBA/IG.2/1), which had been prepared by the Secretariat on the
basis of the draft provisional agenda approved by the Meeting of
Government-Designated Experts to Review and Revise a Global Programme of
Action for the Protection of the Marine Environment from Land-based
Activities, held at Reykjavik, from 6 to 10 March 1995:

1.   Opening of the meeting.

2.   Organization of the meeting:

      (a)   Rules of procedure;

      (b)   Election of officers;

      (c)   Organization of work.

3.   Adoption of the agenda.

4.   Review of the draft Global Programme of Action for the
      Protection of the Marine Environment from Land-based
      Activities.

5.   Future activities.

6.   Institutional arrangements.

7.   Other matters.

8.   Adoption of the Conference proceedings:

   (a)   Report of the Conference;

   (b)   Global Programme of Action.

9.   Closure of the meeting.

   IV.   REVIEW OF THE DRAFT PROGRAMME OF ACTION FOR THE PROTECTION
         OF THE MARINE ENVIRONMENT FROM LAND-BASED ACTIVITIES

18.   In considering agenda item 4, the Conference had before it the draft
Global Programme of Action (UNEP(OCA)/LBA/IG.2/3 and Add. 1-7 containing
the comments on the Global Programme of Action received by the secretariat
prior to the Conference). The Conference was also provided with a working
paper on "Financial and capacity-building aspects of the Global Programme
of Action for the Protection of the Marine Environment from Land-based
Activities" (UNEP(OCA)/LBA/IG.2/4) and other information documents. The
full list of documents before the Conference is contained in annex I below.

Work of the Working Groups

19.   As agreed by the Conference at its 1st plenary meeting, the draft
Global Programme of Action was considered by the Working Groups established
for that purpose, as per paragraph 15 above.

20.   Under the chairmanship of Mr. Magnus Johannesson (Iceland), Working
Group A held 10 meetings, from 23 to 30 October 1995, to consider
chapter IV of the draft Programme of Action. At its 1st meeting, the
Working Group elected Mr. Alan Simcock (United Kingdom) as Rapporteur by
acclamation.

21.   Under the chairmanship of Mr. Salif Diop (Senegal), Working Group B
held 13 meetings, from 23 October to 1 November, to consider chapters I,
II, III and V of the draft Programme of Action. At its 1st meeting, the
Working Group elected Mr. M. Abdulraheem (Kuwait) as Vice-Chairman and Mr.
J. Karau (Canada) as Rapporteur by acclamation.

22.   At its 2nd plenary meeting, on 26 October, the Conference heard a
progress report from the Chairmen of the Working Groups.

23.   Working Group A presented its final report to plenary
on 2 November 1995, together with a revised text of chapter IV of the draft
Programme of Action (UNEP(OCA)/LBA/IG.2/L.2 and annex).

24.   Working Group B presented its final report to plenary on
2 November 1995, together with a revised text of chapters I, II, III and V
of the draft Programme of Action (UNEP(OCA)/LBA/IG.2/L.3 and Add. 1-3). In
reviewing section D of chapter II of the revised text the representative of
Chile indicated that the term "best available techniques" should be
replaced by "best applicable technology". However, the Conference
subsequently agreed that throughout the Global Programme of Action, the
term "best available techniques" is understood to include socio-economic
factors.

High-level Segment

25.   As decided by the Conference at its 1st plenary meeting, the High-
Level Segment of the Conference was held on 31 October and 1 November 1995.
At the 1st session of the High-Level Segment of the Conference, statements
were made by Mr. Strobe Talbott, Deputy Secretary of State of the United
States; Mr. Wang Yuquing, Deputy Administrator of the National
Environmental Protection Agency of China; Mr. Ulrich Klinkert,
Parliamentary State Secretary, Ministry of the Environment, Nature
Conservation and Nuclear Safety, of Germany; Mr. Gudmundur Bjǝrnason,
Minister of the Environment of Iceland; Ms. Phyllis Mitchell,
Parliamentary Secretary, Ministry of Environment and Housing, of Jamaica;
Mr. Bernard Blaszczyk, Deputy Minister for Environmental Protection,
Natural Resources and Forestry, of Poland; Mr. Joaquin Perez Villanueva,
Minister-Counsellor, European Union Presidency, of Spain, on behalf of the
European Union; Mr. Lee Ki Choo, Ambassador for Economic and Trade
Affairs, Ministry of Foreign Affairs of the Republic of Korea; and Mr.
Antonio Dayrell de Lima, Minister, Ministry of Foreign Affairs of Brazil.
Ms. Christina Amoako-Nuama, Minister of Environment, Science and
Technology, of Ghana submitted a statement in writing to the secretariat.

26.   After the statements, the Conference heard a presentation by the Earl
of Lindsay (United Kingdom), Parliamentary Under-Secretary of State,
Scottish Office, on institutional follow-up and preparations for
consideration of oceans issues by the Commission on Sustainable
Development.

27.   Subsequent sessions of the High-Level Segment were devoted to: the
mobilization of resources/finance, with presentations by Mr. Anders Wijkman
(United Nations Development Programme), Mr. Stephen Lintner (World Bank),
Mr. Ian Johnson (Global Environment Facility), Mr. Lopez Ocana (Inter-
American Development Bank) and Mr. Curley (FINEX); persistent organic
pollutants (POPs), with presentations by Mr. Huggett, Assistant
Administrator for Research and Development, Environmental Protection Agency
of the United States of America, Mr. Paje, Assistant Secretary, Department
of the Environment and Natural Resources of the Philippines and Mr. Ritter
of the University of Guelph, Ontario, Canada, and the Canadian Network of
Toxicology Centres; and sewage and waste water, with presentations by
Dr. Herbert L. Windom, Acting Director of the Skidaway Institute of
Oceanography and Mr. Henry Salas, Advisor in Water Pollution Control at the
Pan American Center for Sanitary Engineering and Environmental Sciences.
At each of the sessions, the presentations were followed by a general
discussion on the topics concerned.

28.   At the 3rd session of the High-Level Segment, the Conference had the
privilege of hearing an address by United States Vice-President Albert
Gore, who stressed the importance of the oceans and the marine environment,
which were indispensable for life on Earth, and the serious degradation
afflicting them, stating that Homer's "wine-dark sea" was taking on more
ominous colours. Protection of the marine environment from land-based
activities was a major element of the remedial action required, and the
work of the Conference was thus both important and timely. He gave
examples of successful actions that have been carried out, in the United
States of America and elsewhere, based on partnership between the sectors,
local involvement, a comprehensive approach and innovative financing,
mentioning that, in many cases, they had produced very beneficial economic
effects. He ended by wishing the participants well in their deliberations

which, he hoped, would result in an effective, affordable and sustainable Global Programme of Action.

29.   At the closing session of the High-Level Segment, the Washington Declaration on Protection of the Marine Environment from Land-based Activities was adopted on the basis of a proposal introduced by the United Kingdom on behalf of a number of delegations.   The final text of the Declaration is contained in annex II to the present report.

V.   FUTURE ACTIVITIES

30.   At its 3rd plenary meeting, on 30 October, the Conference heard a statement from Mr. Jorge Illueca, Assistant Executive Director, Division of Environmental Management Support, on UNEP plans for the implementation of the Programme of Action in the period 1996-1997.

31.   The Assistant Executive Director said that, during the first two months of 1996, the secretariat would review the status of activities dealing with the protection of the marine environment from land-based activities in all 13 regions of the UNEP Regional Seas Programme and other regional seas and activities.   Based on that review, a series of regional workshops would be organized to identify the particular activities and projects that individual nations and regions would both have to carry out to develop and begin implementation of regional strategic programmes.   The workshops would agree on timetables and work programmes, considering the following steps identified in the Global Programme of Action for developing systematically action programmes dealing with land-based activities:

     (a)   Identification and ranking of public health, ecosystem health, and socio-economic/cultural problems;

     (b)   Identification of contaminants of concern;

     (c)   Identification of forms of physical alteration;

     (d)   Identification of areas (units) of special concern;

     (e)   Identification of public health and ecosystem health and biodiversity management objectives;

     (f)   Identification of relative contributions from land-based sources;

     (g)   Identification, evaluation and selection of strategies for the management of land-based sources; and

     (h)   Management strategy evaluation criteria.

32.   The Assistant Executive Director further indicated that the implementation plan that UNEP would be requested to prepare under the adopted Programme of Action would cover the secretariat's structure, modalities of operation, and three basic functions: coordination; clearing-house role;   and mobilization of resources.   A first draft would be prepared by the end of 1995 for submission to an inter-agency consultation in January 1996.   The paper would be finalized in January 1996, taking into consideration the outcome of that consultation, and would be available for the inter-sessional meeting of the Commission on Sustainable Development in February.

VI.   INSTITUTIONAL ARRANGEMENTS

33.   Agenda item 6 was not taken up separately in plenary, since the Conference considered that the subject-matter was adequately covered by the discussion on chapter IV in Working Group A, which focused on:

(a)   The need for a series of interlinked steps to develop the international institutional framework for the implementation of the Global Programme of Action, wl ich should be based upon concerted action by States within the relevant organizations and institutions to accord attention and priority to impacts on the marine environment from land-based activities and concerted action by States to ensure effective coordination and collaboration among such organizations and institutions;

(b)   The functions of UNEP, as the coordinator and catalyst of environmental activities within the United Nations system, in the implementation of the Programme of Action;

(c)   The need for UNEP to fulfil its role, including the secretariat function, in an efficient and cost-effective manner, supported largely by the existing resources, expertise and infrastructure available in all components of UNEP's programmes, and the need for UNEP to be flexible and responsive to the evolving needs of the Programme and the availability of resources, e.g. from trust funds;

(d)   The need for UNEP, in facilitating the implementation of the Programme of Action, to maintain a close partnership with other organizations and bodies, and the importance of an appropriate division of tasks for the efficient and cost-effective implementation of the Programme;

(e)   The terms of reference of periodic intergovernmental review meetings to be convened by UNEP, in close collaboration with the relevant organizations and institutions;

(f)   Reporting on the implementation of the Programme of Action;

(g)   The steps required to establish the clearing-house mechanism;

(h)   The steps for developing the institutional arrangements, including the preparation by UNEP of an implementation plan for submission to the Commission on Sustainable Development, and the preparation of a draft resolution setting forth the provisions of the Programme of Action for consideration and adoption by the General Assembly at its fifty-first session.

34.   The text of the agreed international institutional framework is included in section C of chapter IV of the Global Programme of Action as adopted (UNEP(OCA)/LBA/IG.2/7).

VII.   OTHER MATTERS

Statement by Australia on behalf of the Federated States of Micronesia, Kiribati, the Marshall Islands, Nauru, New Zealand, Samoa and Vanuatu

35.   The representative of Australia indicated that South Pacific environment ministers had met in Brisbane, Australia, in August 1995 and had called for an immediate end to all nuclear testing in all environments.

Consistent with the outcome of that meeting, Australia wished to make the following statement on behalf of the South Pacific Forum countries participating in the Conference:

> "Forum countries reiterate their profound concern and dismay over the continuation of French nuclear testing in the South Pacific, against the unambiguous and concerted opposition of the countries of the region.
>
> "Such testing is environmentally irresponsible and encourages scepticism about the Nuclear Non-Proliferation Treaty.
>
> "We call for the immediate cessation of nuclear testing and for all States, particularly nuclear weapon States, to commit themselves to concluding a zero-threshold comprehensive test-ban treaty no later than the end of 1996."

36.   Many other representatives expressed their support for the statement by Australia.

37.   The representative of India expressed her Government's belief that the Comprehensive Test Ban Treaty (CTBT), in order to be meaningful as a disarmament treaty, must be considered as part of a step-by-step process leading towards the complete elimination of all nuclear weapons within a specified timeframe.

VIII.   ADOPTION OF THE CONFERENCE PROCEEDINGS

A.   Report of the Conference

38.   At the final plenary meeting, on 3 November 1995, the Conference adopted its report on the basis of its draft report contained in document UNEP(OCA)/LBA/IG.2/L.1/Rev.1.

B.   Global Programme of Action

39.   The Conference adopted the Global Programme of Action, on the basis of the draft Global Programme of Action, as amended by the Working Groups (documents UNEP(OCA)/LBA/IG.2/L.2 and L.3 and Add.1-3).   It decided that the annex to the draft Global Programme of Action (UNEP(OCA)/LBA/IG.2/3, pp. 50-59) should not be attached to the adopted Programme but should be used for further elaboration by the UNEP secretariat in its future work of developing the Programme.

40.   The Global Programme of Action as adopted is contained in document UNEP(OCA)/LBA/IG.2/7.

41.   The Conference decided that the footnote to paragraph 26 (a) (i) a of the Global Programme of Action should also be deemed to apply to paragraph 16 of the Washington Declaration.

42.   The representative of Australia made a statement supporting the Conference decision on persistent organic pollutants.

43.   The representative of the Netherlands, supported by many other representatives, indicated that paragraph 88 of the Global Programme of

Action did not reflect the urgent need to develop an international legally-binding instrument on persistent organic pollutants. However, UNEP Governing Council decisions 18/31 and 18/32 would enable work to start on the elaboration of elements for inclusion in such an instrument.

44.   The representative of Greenpeace, also speaking on behalf of the Advisory Committee on Protection of the Sea (ACOPS), Friends of the Earth, and the World Wide Fund for Nature (WWF), said that those organizations supported the statement by the Netherlands.

45.   The representative of the United States indicated that paragraph 6 of the Global Programme of Action should be interpreted in a manner consistent with the language of the United Nations Convention on the Law of the Sea (UNCLOS).

46.   The representative of India indicated that the current approach of her Government, which had always been in the forefront of efforts and negotiations to achieve nuclear disarmament, was in line with that adopted by the non-aligned countries at their recent Cartagena meeting, namely that the process must be a step-by-step and time-specific one resulting in complete nuclear disarmament.

47.   The representative of Ecuador expressed the hope that the new and additional resources proposed in the Programme of Action would assist in addressing the serious problems of river pollution in his country as a result of the use of pesticides in agricultural areas. He also reaffirmed his Government's willingness to collaborate with all countries at the regional and international levels to reduce pollution of the marine environment, including its support for the policy of ending nuclear tests such as those being conducted in the Pacific Ocean.

48.   The representative of France stated that his delegation had joined in the consensus for the adoption of section C of chapter V of the Global Programme of Action. However, it regarded paragraph 107 of the Global Programme of Action, citing nuclear testing as among the potential sources of pollution of the marine environment, as referring exclusively to atmospheric tests.

49.   The representative of Greenpeace stated that three reports published under the auspices of the French Government outlined the existence of significant long-term risks in connection with underground testing at Mururoa and Fangataufa. It was the view of Greenpeace that the only responsible course of action consistent with the precautionary principle was an immediate end to underground nuclear testing.

50.   The representative of Peru expressed the hope that the developing countries would receive support from the developed world in their efforts to combat pollution of the marine environment.

51.   The representative of Colombia said that issue of marine pollution from land-based activities was a global one. The Programme of Action would be helpful for both developing and developed countries and represented a positive step for the future.

52.   The representative of Sri Lanka expressed the hope that all countries would take the necessary action for the implementation of the Programme of Action.

53. The representative of Brazil said that there could be no turning back from the agreements reached at the Conference. The Programme of Action would be a very important part of the coordination work on oceans by the Commission on Sustainable Development.

54. The representative of Poland stressed the importance his Government attached to the Programme of Action.

IX. CLOSURE OF THE MEETING

55. The Conference expressed its sincere gratitude to UNEP for organizing the Conference and to the Government of the United States of America for having acted as host. Several participants also thanked the Chairperson for the gracious and expeditious way in which she had guided the Conference.

56. The Deputy Executive Director of UNEP, Professor Reuben Olembo, speaking on behalf of the Executive Director, made a closing statement in which he expressed UNEP's satisfaction with the outcome of the Conference, and thanked the host Government, the Chairperson and all those involved in the organization and conduct of the Conference.

57. The Chairperson, in her turn, thanked all delegations for their active participation and cooperation and UNEP secretariat for its efficient organization of the Conference which, in her opinion, had been a great success. She then declared the Conference closed at 11 a.m. on 3 November 1995.

Appendix I

LIST OF DOCUMENTS.

A. Working documents

UNEP(OCA)/LBA/IG.2/1	Provisional agenda
UNEP(OCA)/LBA/IG.2/2	Annotated provisional agenda
UNEP(OCA)/LBA/IG.2/3	Draft Global Programme of Action for the Protection of the Marine Environment from Land-based Sources of Pollution
UNEP(OCA)/LBA/IG.2/3/Add.1	Comments on the draft Global Programme of Action: comments of the Netherlands
UNEP(OCA)/LBA/IG.2/3/Add.2	Comments on the draft Global Programme of Action: comments of Australia

UNEP(OCA)/LBA/IG.2/3/Add.3   Comments on the draft Global
                                    Programme of Action: comments of
                                    the Oslo and Paris Commissions
                                    (OSPAR)

UNEP(OCA)/LBA/IG.2/3/Add.4   United States of America:
                                    proposal for the revision of
                                    chapters I, II and III of the
                                    draft Global Programme of Action

UNEP(OCA)/LBA/IG.2/3/Add.5   Amendment proposals to the draft
                                    Programme of Action for the
                                    Protection of the Marine
                                    Environment from Land-based
                                    Sources of Pollution: proposals
                                    prepared by the Meeting of Experts
                                    to Prepare Regional Position to
                                    the Washington Intergovernmental
                                    Conference on the Global Programme
                                    of Action to Protect the Marine
                                    Environment from Land-based
                                    Activities

UNEP(OCA)/LBA/IG.2/3/Add.6   Comments on the draft Programme of
                                    Action: comments of Iceland

UNEP(OCA)/LBA/IG.2/3/Add.7   Comments on the draft Programme of
                                    Action: preliminary comments of
                                    Japan

UNEP(OCA)/LBA/IG.2/4   Financial and capacity-building
                                    aspects of the Global Programme of
                                    Action for the Protection of the
                                    Marine Environment from Land-based
                                    Activities: report of the
                                    secretariat (prepared on the basis
                                    of the discussion at the
                                    Consultation on Financial and
                                    Capacity-building Issues related
                                    to the Global Programme of Action
                                    for the Protection of the Marine
                                    Environment from Land-based
                                    Activities, held in Washington
                                    D.C. from 16 to 18 August 1995)

UNEP(OCA)/LBA/IG.2/5   Contribution of the United Nations
                                    Environment Programme to the
                                    Implementation of the Global
                                    Programme of Action for the
                                    Protection of the Marine
                                    Environment from Land-based
                                    Activities: note by the
                                    secretariat

B. **Information documents**

UNEP(OCA)/LBA/IG.2/INF.1   Provisional list of documents

UNEP(OCA)/LBA/IG.2/INF.2   Provisional list of participants

UNEP(OCA)/LBA/IG.2/INF.3   Conference programme and timetable

UNEP(OCA)/LBA/IG.2/INF.4   Report of the Meeting of Government-designated Experts to Review and Revise a Global Programme of Action to Protect the Marine Environment from Land-based Activities, Reykjavik, 6-10 March 1995

UNEP(OCA)/LBA/IG.2/INF.5   Report of the Preliminary Meeting of Experts to Assess the Effectiveness of Regional Seas Agreements

UNEP(OCA)/LBA/IG.2/INF.6   Report of the Meeting of Government-designated Experts Focusing on the 1985 Montreal Guidelines for the Protection of the Marine Environment from Land-based Sources of Pollution

UNEP(OCA)/LBA/IG.2/INF.7   Recommendations of the ACOPS Conference on Funding and Institutional Issues for the Washington Action Programme on Protection of the Marine Environment from Land-based Activities

UNEP(OCA)/LBA/IG.2/INF.8   Comments on annex, section G, "Litter", of the draft Global Programme of Action: submission of the Workshop on Legal and Policy Aspects of Land-based Sources of Marine Debris - Austin, Texas, USA, 22-24 June 1995

UNEP(OCA)/LBA/IG.2/INF.9   Persistent organic pollutants - an assessment report on: DDT-aldrin-dieldrin-endrin-chlorane, heptachlor-hexachlorobenzene-mirex-toxaphene, polychlorinated biphenyls, dioxins and furans: draft interim report prepared by the Inter-Organization Programme for the Sound Management of Chemicals: note by the secretariat

UNEP(OCA)/LBA/IG.2/INF.10/Rev.1   Arrangements for the High-level
and Corr.1   Segment of the Conference:
                                                 information paper submitted by the
                                                 United States of America

Appendix II

WASHINGTON DECLARATION ON PROTECTION OF 'THE MARINE ENVIRONMENT
FROM LAND-BASED ACTIVITIES

The representatives of Governments and the European Commission
participating in the Conference held in Washington from 23 October
to 3 November 1995,

Affirming the need and will to protect and preserve the marine
environment for present and future generations,

Reaffirming the relevant provisions of chapters 17, 33 and 34 of
Agenda 21 and the Rio Declaration on Environment and Development,

Recognizing the interdependence of human populations and the coastal
and marine environment, and the growing and serious threat from land-based
activities, to both human health and well-being and the integrity of
coastal and marine ecosystems and biodiversity,

Further recognizing the importance of integrated coastal area
management and the catchment-area-based approach as means of coordinating
programmes aimed at preventing marine degradation from land-based
activities with economic and social development programmes,

Also recognizing that the alleviation of poverty is an essential
factor in addressing the impacts of land-based activities on coastal and
marine areas,

Noting that there are major differences among the different regions
of the world, and the States which they comprise, in terms of
environmental, economic and social conditions and level of development
which will lead to different judgments on priorities in addressing problems
related to the degradation of the marine environment by land-based
activities,

Acknowledging the need to involve major groups in national, regional
and international activities to address degradation of the marine
environment by land-based activities,

Strongly supporting the processes set forth in decisions 18/31 and
18/32 of 25 May 1995 of the Governing Council of the United Nations
Environment Programme for addressing at the global level the priority
issues of persistent organic pollutants and adequate treatment of waste
water,

Having therefore adopted the Global Programme of Action for the
Protection of the Marine Environment from Land-based Activities,

Hereby declare their commitment to protect and preserve the marine
environment from the impacts of land-based activities, and

<u>Declare their intention to do so by</u>:

1. Setting as their common goal sustained and effective action to deal with all land-based impacts upon the marine environment, specifically those resulting from sewage, persistent organic pollutants, radioactive substances, heavy metals, oils (hydrocarbons), nutrients, sediment mobilization, litter, and physical alteration and destruction of habitat;

2. Developing or reviewing national action programmes within a few years on the basis of national priorities and strategies;

3. Taking forward action to implement these programmes in accordance with national capacities and priorities;

4. Cooperating to build capacities and mobilize resources for the development and implementation of such programmes, in particular for developing countries, especially the least developed countries, countries with economies in transition and small island developing States (hereinafter referred to as "countries in need of assistance");

5. Taking immediate preventive and remedial action, wherever possible, using existing knowledge, resources, plans and processes;

6. Promoting access to cleaner technologies, knowledge and expertise to address land-based activities that degrade the marine environment, in particular for countries in need of assistance;

7. Cooperating on a regional basis to coordinate efforts for maximum efficiency and to facilitate action at the national level, including, where appropriate, becoming parties to and strengthening regional cooperative agreements and creating new agreements where necessary;

8. Encouraging cooperative and collaborative action and partnerships, among governmental institutions and organizations, communities, the private sector and non-governmental organizations which have relevant responsibilities and/or experience;

9. Encouraging and/or making available external financing, given that funding from domestic sources and mechanisms for the implementation of the Global Programme of Action by countries in need of assistance may be insufficient;

10. Promoting the full range of available management tools and financing options in implementing national or regional programmes of action, including innovative managerial and financial techniques, while recognizing the differences between countries in need of assistance and developed States;

11. Urging national and international institutions and the private sector, bilateral donors and multilateral funding agencies to accord priority to projects within national and regional programmes to implement the Global Programme of Action and encouraging the Global Environment Facility to support these projects;

12. Calling upon the United Nations Environment Programme, the United Nations Development Programme, the World Bank, the regional development

banks, as well as the agencies within the United Nations system to ensure that their programmes support (through, <u>inter alia</u>, financial cooperation, capacity-building and institutional-strengthening mechanisms) the regional structures in place for the protection of the marine environment;

13.   According priority to implementation of the Global Programme of Action within the United Nations system, as well as in other global and regional institutions and organizations with responsibilities and capabilities for addressing marine degradation from land-based activities, and specifically:

(a)   Securing, formal endorsement of those parts of the Global Programme of Action that are relevant to such institutions and organizations and incorporating the relevant provisions into their work programmes;

(b)   Establishing a clearing-house mechanism to provide decision makers in all States with direct access to relevant sources of information, practical experience and scientific and technical expertise and to facilitate effective scientific, technical and financial cooperation as well as capacity-building; and

(c)   Providing for periodic intergovernmental review of the Global Programme of Action, taking into account regular assessments of the state of the marine environment;

14.   Promoting action to deal with the consequences of sea-based activities, such as shipping, offshore activities and ocean dumping, which require national and/or regional actions on land, including establishing adequate reception and recycling facilities;

15.   Giving priority to the treatment and management of waste water and industrial effluents, as part of the overall management of water resources, especially through the installation of environmentally and economically appropriate sewage systems, including studying mechanisms to channel additional resources for this purpose expeditiously to countries in need of assistance;

16.   Requesting the Executive Director of the United Nations Environment Programme, in close partnership with the World Health Organization, the United Nations Centre for Human Settlements (Habitat), the United Nations Development Programme and other relevant organizations, to prepare proposals for a plan to address the global nature of the problem of inadequate management and treatment of waste water and its consequences for human health and the environment, and to promote the transfer of appropriate and affordable technology drawn from the best available techniques;

17.   Acting to develop, in accordance with the provisions of the Global Programme of Action, a global, legally binding instrument for the reduction and/or elimination of emissions, discharges and, where appropriate, the elimination of the manufacture and use of the persistent organic pollutants identified in decision 18/32 of the Governing Council of the United Nations Environment Programme. The nature of the obligations undertaken must be developed recognizing the special circumstances of countries in need of assistance. Particular attention should be devoted to the potential need

for the continued use of certain persistent organic pollutants to safeguard human health, sustain food production and to alleviate poverty in the absence of alternatives and the difficulty of acquiring substitutes and transferring of technology for the development and/or production of those substitutes; and

18. Elaborating the steps relating to institutional follow-up, including the clearing-house mechanism, in a resolution of the United Nations General Assembly at its fifty-first session, and in that regard, States should coordinate with the United Nations Environment Programme, as secretariat of the Global Programme of Action, and other relevant agencies within the United Nations system in the development of the resolution and include it on the agenda of the Commission on Sustainable Development at its inter-sessional meeting in February 1996 and its session in April 1996.

<u>Washington, D.C., 1 November 1995</u>

ANNEX II*

GLOBAL PROGRAMME OF ACTION FOR THE PROTECTION OF THE
MARINE ENVIRONMENT FROM LAND-BASED ACTIVITIES

<u>Note by the secretariat</u>

The secretariat has the honour to circulate herewith the Global Programme of Action for the Protection of the Marine Environment from Land-based Activities, as adopted on 3 November 1995 by the Intergovernmental Conference which met for that purpose in Washington, D.C., from 23 October to 3 November 1995.

CONTENTS

---

* Previously issued under the symbol **UNEP(OCA)/LBA/IG.2/7.**

I.   INTRODUCTION

A.   The need for action

1.   The major threats to the health and productivity and biodiversity of the marine environment result from human activities on land - in coastal areas and further inland. Most of the pollution load of the oceans, including municipal, industrial and agricultural wastes and run-off, as well as atmospheric deposition, emanates from such land-based activities and affects the most productive areas of the marine environment, including estuaries and near-shore coastal waters. These areas are likewise threatened by physical alteration of the coastal environment, including destruction of habitats of vital importance for ecosystem health. Moreover, contaminants which pose risks to human health and living resources are transported long distances by watercourses, ocean currents and atmospheric processes.

2.   The bulk of the world's population lives in coastal areas, and there is a continuing trend towards its concentration in these regions. The health, well-being and, in some cases, the very survival of coastal populations depend upon the health and well-being of coastal systems - estuaries and wetlands - as well as their associated watersheds and drainage basins and near-shore coastal waters. Ultimately, sustainable patterns of human activity in coastal areas depend upon a healthy marine environment, and vice versa.

B.   Aims of the Global Programme of Action

3.   The Global Programme of Action aims at preventing the degradation of the marine environment from land-based activities by facilitating the realization of the duty of States to preserve and protect the marine environment. It is designed to assist States in taking actions individually or jointly within their respective policies, priorities and resources, which will lead to the prevention, reduction, control and/or elimination of the degradation of the marine environment, as well as to its recovery from the impacts of land-based activities. Achievement of the

aims of the Programme of Action will contribute to maintaining and, where appropriate, restoring the productive capacity and biodiversity of the marine environment, ensuring the protection of human health, as well as promoting the conservation and sustainable use of marine living resources.

C.   Legal and institutional framework

4.   International law, as reflected in the provisions of the United Nations Convention on the Law of the Sea (UNCLOS) and elsewhere, sets forth rights and obligations of States and provides the international basis upon which to pursue the protection and sustainable development of the marine and coastal environment and its resources.

5.   In accordance with general international law, while States have the sovereign right to exploit their natural resources pursuant to their environmental policies, the enjoyment of such right shall be in accordance with the duty to protect and preserve the marine environment. This fundamental duty is to protect and preserve the marine environment from all sources of pollution, including land-based activities. Of particular significance for the Global Programme of Action are the provisions contained in articles 207 and 213 of UNCLOS.

6.   Also of particular importance for the Programme of Action is the emphasis, in parts XII, XIII and XIV of the Convention, dealing, respectively, with protection and preservation of the marine environment, marine scientific research and the development and transfer of marine technology, on the obligation of States to cooperate in the development of the marine scientific and technological capacity of developing States and to provide them with scientific and technical assistance.

7.   The duty of States to preserve and protect the marine environment has been reflected and elaborated upon in numerous global conventions and regional instruments (e.g. the Convention on the Prevention of Marine Pollution by Dumping of Wastes and Other Matter; Basel Convention on the Control of Transboundary Movements of Hazardous Wastes and their Disposal; Convention on Biological Diversity; United Nations Framework Convention on Climate Change; Regional Seas Conventions; International Convention for the Prevention of Pollution from Ships (MARPOL 73/78), etc.). Innovative new principles and approaches applicable to the prevention of the degradation of the marine environment from land-based activities have been included in a number of such agreements.

8.   In 1982, the United Nations Environment Programme (UNEP) took the initiative to develop advice to Governments on addressing impacts on the marine environment from land-based activities. This initiative resulted in the preparation of the Montreal Guidelines for the Protection of the Marine Environment Against Pollution from Land-based Sources in 1985.

9.   The duty to protect the marine environment from land-based activities was placed squarely in the context of sustainable development by the United Nations Conference on Environment and Development in 1992. Therein, States agreed it is necessary:

   (a)   To apply preventive, precautionary, and anticipatory approaches so as to avoid degradation of the marine environment, as well as to reduce the risk of long-term or irreversible adverse effects upon it;

   (b)   To ensure prior assessment of activities that may have significant adverse impacts upon the marine environment;

(c) To integrate protection of the marine environment into relevant general environmental, social and economic development policies;

(d) To develop economic incentives, where appropriate, to apply clean technologies and other means consistent with the internalization of environmental costs, such as the "polluter pays" principle, so as to avoid degradation of the marine environment;

(e) To improve the living standards of coastal populations, particularly in developing countries, so as to contribute to reducing the degradation of the coastal and marine environment.

10. As set out in paragaph 17.23 of Agenda 21, States agree that provision of additional financial resources, through appropriate international mechanisms, as well as access to cleaner technologies and relevant research, would be necessary to support action by developing countries to implement this commitment.

11. Agenda 21 linked the implementation of those duties with action to implement commitments to integrated management and sustainable development of the marine environment, including coastal areas under national jurisdiction. In this regard, States agreed to implement the provisions of the programme of action adopted at the World Coast Conference in Noordwijk in 1993 and to further develop tnose provisions in order to make them more operational.

12. Agenda 21 also linked action to combat marine degradation caused by land-based activities to action to address the specific problems of small island developing States. In this regard, States agreed to implement the provisions of the priority areas of the Programme of Action for the Sustainable Development of Small Island Developing States, adopted in Barbados in 1994.

13. In order to promote, facilitate and finance implementation of Agenda 21 by developing countries, an objective of Agenda 21 is to provide additional financial resources that are both adequate and predictable. Another objective in this context is to promote, facilitate and finance, as appropriate, the access to and the transfer of environmentally sound technologies and corresponding know-how, in particular to developing countries, on favourable terms, including concessional and preferential terms, as mutually agreed, taking into account the need to protect intellectual property rights as well as the special needs of developing countries for the implementation of Agenda 21.

D. The Global Programme of Action

14.   The Programme of Action, therefore, is designed to be a source of conceptual and practical guidance to be drawn upon by national and/or regional authorities in devising and implementing sustained action to prevent, reduce, control and/or eliminate marine degradation from land-based activities. Effective implementation of this Programme of Action is a crucial and essential step forward in the protection of the marine environment and will promote the objectives and goals of sustainable development.

15. The Global Programme of Action reflects the fact that States face a growing number of commitments flowing from Agenda 21 and related conventions. Its implementation will require new approaches by, and new forms of collaboration among, Governments, organizations and institutions

with responsibilities and expertise relevant to marine and coastal areas,at all levels - national, regional and global. These include the promotion of innovative financial mechanisms to generate needed resources.

II. ACTIONS AT THE NATIONAL LEVEL

Basis for action

16. Sustainable use of the oceans depends on the maintenance of ecosystem health, public health, food security, and economic and social benefits including cultural values. Many countries depend on sources of income from activities that would be directly threatened by degradation of the marine environment: industries such as fishing and tourism are obvious examples. The subsistence economy of large coastal populations, in particular in the developing countries, is based on marine living resources that would also be threatened by such degradation. Also to be considered are the impacts of such degradation on maritime culture and traditional lifestyles.

17. Food security is threatened, in particular in developing countries, by the loss of marine living resources that are vital for the adequate provision of food and for combating poverty. Public health considerations from a degraded marine environment manifest themselves through the contamination of seafood, direct contact, such as through bathing, and the use of sea water in desalination and food-processing plants.

Objectives

18. To develop comprehensive, continuing and adaptive programmes of action within the framework of integrated coastal area management which should include provisions for:

    (a)   Identification and assessment of problems;

    (b)   Establishment of priorities;

    (c)   Setting management objectives for priority problems;

    (d)   Identification, evaluation and selection of strategies and measures, including management approaches;

    (e)   Criteria for evaluating the effectiveness of strategies and programmes;

    (f)   Programme support elements.

Actions

19. States should, in accordance with their policies, priorities and resources, develop or review national programmes of action within a few years and take forward action to implement these programmes with the assistance of the international cooperation identified in chapter IV, in particular to developing countries, especially the least developed countries, countries with economies in transition and small island developing States (hereinafter referred to as "countries in need of assistance"). The effective development and implementation of national programmes of action should focus on sustainable, pragmatic and integrated environmental management approaches and processes, such as integrated coastal area management, harmonized, as appropriate, with river basin management and land-use plans.

20. Recommended actions to give effect to the objectives in the development of national programmes of action by States are summarized in sections A, B, C, D, E and F below. They are illustrated in more detail in the actions and targets identified in chapter V below.

A. Identification and assessment of problems

21. The identification and assessment of problems is a process of combining five elements:

(a) Identification of the nature and severity of problems in relation to:

    (i) Food security and poverty alleviation;

    (ii) Public health;

    (iii) Coastal and marine resources and ecosystem health, including biological diversity;

    (iv) Economic and social benefits and uses, including cultural values;

(b) Contaminants:

    (not listed in order of priority)

    (i) Sewage;

    (ii) Persistent organic pollutants;

    (iii) Radioactive substances;

    (iv) Heavy metals;

    (v) Oils (hydrocarbons);

    (vi) Nutrients;

    (vii) Sediment mobilization;

    (viii) Litter;

(c) Physical alteration, including habitat modification and destruction in areas of concern;

(d) Sources of degradation:

    (i) Point sources (coastal and upstream), such as:

        (not listed in order of priority)

        a. Waste-water treatment facilities;

        b. Industrial facilities;

        c. Power plants;

        d. Military installations;

e. Recreational/tourism facilities;

f. Construction works (e.g., dams, coastal structures, harbour works and urban expansion);

g. Coastal mining (e.g., sand and gravel);

h. Research centres;

i. Aquaculture;

j. Habitat modification (e.g., dredging, filling of wetlands or clearing of mangrove areas);

k. Introduction of invasive species;

(ii) Non-point (diffuse) sources (coastal and upstream), such as:

(not listed in order of priority)

a. Urban run-off;

b. Agricultural and horticultural run-off;

c. Forestry run-off;

d. Mining waste run-off;

e. Construction run-off;

f. Landfills and hazardous waste sites;

g. Erosion as a result of physical modification of coastal features;

(iii) Atmospheric deposition caused by:

a. Transportation (e.g., vehicle emissions);

b. Power plants and industrial facilities;

c. Incinerators;

d. Agricultural operations;

(e) **Areas of concern (what areas are affected or vulnerable):**

(not listed in order of priority)

(i) Critical habitats, including coral reefs, wetlands, seagrass beds, coastal lagoons and mangrove forests;

(ii) Habitats of endangered species;

(iii) Ecosystem components, including spawning areas, nursery areas, feeding grounds and adult areas;

(iv) Shorelines;

(v) Coastal watersheds;

(vi)   Estuaries and their drainage basins;

(vii)   Specially protected marine and coastal areas;   and

(viii)   Small islands.

B.   Establishment of priorities

22. Priorities for action should be established by assessing the five factors described above and should specifically reflect:

(a)   The relative importance of impacts upon food security, public health, coastal and marine resources, ecosystem health, and socio-economic benefits, including cultural values, in relation to:

(i)   Source-categories (contaminants, physical alteration, and other forms of degradation and the source or practice from which they emanate);

(ii)   The area affected (including its uses and the importance of its ecological characteristics);

(b)   The costs, benefits and feasibility of options for action, including the long-term cost of no action.

23. In the process of establishing priorities for action and throughout all stages of developing and implementing national programmes of action, States should:

(a)   Apply integrated coastal area management approaches, including provision to involve stakeholders, in particular local authorities and communities and relevant social and economic sectors, including non-governmental organizations, women, indigenous people and other major groups;

(b)   Recognize the basic linkages between the freshwater and marine environments through, <u>inter alia</u>, application of watershed management approaches;

(c)   Recognize the basic linkages between sustainable management of coastal and marine resources, poverty alleviation and protection of the marine environment;

(d)   Apply environmental impact assessment procedures in assessing options;

(e)   Take into account the need to view such programmes as an integrated part of existing or future comprehensive environmental programmes;

(f)   Take steps to protect: (i) critical habitats, using community-based participatory approaches that are consistent with current approaches to conservation and uses compatible with sustainable development;   and (ii) endangered species;

(g)   Integrate national action with any relevant regional and global priorities, programmes and strategies;

(h)   Establish focal points to facilitate regional and international cooperation;

   (i)   Apply the precautionary approach and the principle of
intergenerational equity.

24. The precautionary approach should be applied through preventive and
corrective measures based on existing knowledge, impact assessments,
resources and capacities at national level, drawing on pertinent
information and analyses at the subregional, regional and global levels.
Where there are threats of serious or irreversible damage, lack of full
scientific certainty should not be used as a reason for postponing cost-
effective measures to prevent the degradation of the marine environment.

C. Setting management objectives for priority problems

25. On the basis of the priorities established, States should define
specific management objectives, both with respect to source categories and
areas affected. Such objectives should be set forth in terms of overall
goals, targets and timetables, as well as specific targets and timetables
for areas affected and for individual industrial, agricultural, urban and
other sectors. Wherever possible, States should take immediate preventive
and remedial action using existing knowledge, resources, plans and
processes.

D. Identification, evaluation and selection of strategies and measures

26. Strategies and programmes to achieve these management objectives
should include a combination of:

   (a)   Specific measures, including, as appropriate:

   (i)   Measures to promote sustainable use of coastal and marine
         resources and to prevent/reduce degradation of the marine
         environment, such as:

         a.   Best available techniques* and best environmental
              practices, including substitution of substances or
              processes entailing significant adverse effects;

         b.   Introduction of clean production practices, including
              efficient use of energy and water in all economic and
              social sectors;

         c.   Application of best management practices;

         d.   Use of appropriate, environmentally sound and efficient
              technologies;

         e.   Product substitution;

   (ii) Measures to modify contaminants or other forms of degradation
         after generation, such as:

         a.   Waste recovery;

         b.   Recycling, including effluent reuse;

---

   * For the purposes of this Programme, "best available techniques" is
understood to include socio-economic factors.

      c. Waste treatment;

(iii) Measures to prevent, reduce or ameliorate degradation of affected areas, such as:

      a. Environmental quality criteria, with biological, physical and/or chemical criteria for measuring progress;

      b. Land-use planning requirements, including criteria for ·iting of major facilities;

      c. Rehabilitation of degraded habitats;

(b) Requirements and incentives to induce action to comply with measures, such as:

(i) Economic instruments and incentives, taking into account the "polluter pays" principle and the internalization of environmental costs;

(ii) Regulatory measures;

(iii) Technical assistance/cooperation, including training of personnel;

(iv) Education and public awareness;

(c) Identification/designation of the institutional arrangement with the authority and resources to carry out management tasks associated with the strategies and programmes, including implementation of compliance provisions;

(d) Identification of short-term and long-term data-collection and research needs;

(e) Development of a monitoring and environmental-quality reporting system to review and, if necessary, help adapt the strategies and programmes;

(f) Identification of sources of finance and mechanisms available to cover the costs of administering and managing the strategies and programmes.

E. Criteria for evaluating the effectiveness of strategies and measures

27. A key element in successful strategies and programmes is to develop ongoing means of determining whether they are meeting their management objectives. States should develop specific criteria to evaluate the effectiveness of such strategies and programmes. While such criteria must be tailored to the particular mix of elements (illustrated in section C above) in each strategy or programme, they should address:

(a) Environmental effectiveness;

(b) Economic costs and benefits;

(c) Equity (costs and benefits of the strategy or programme are being shared fairly);

(d)   Flexibility in administration (the strategy or programme can adapt to changes in circumstances);

(e)   Effectiveness in administration (management of the strategy or programme is cost-effective and accountable);

(f)   Timing (the timetable needed to put the strategy or programme in place and to begin producing results);

(g)   Inter-media effects (the achievement of the objectives of the strategy or programme creates a net environmental benefit).

F.   Programme support elements

28. The long-term objective of national programmes of action should be to develop integrated strategies and programmes to address all action priorities in relation to impacts upon the marine environment from land-based activities. In addition, the programmes of action must themselves be integrated with overall national objectives and other relevant programmes in relation to sustainable development. States therefore should seek to ensure that there are administrative and management structures necessary to support the national programmes of action. These include, as appropriate:

(a)   Organizational arrangements to coordinate among sectors and sectoral institutions;

(b)   Legal and enforcement mechanisms (e.g., need for new legislation);

(c)   Financial mechanisms (including innovative approaches to provide continuing and predictable programme funding);

(d)   Means of identifying and pursuing research and monitoring requirements in support of the programme;

(e)   Contingency planning;

(f)   Human resources development and education;

(g)   Public participation and awareness (e.g., based on integrated coastal area management principles).

III.   REGIONAL COOPERATION

Basis for action

29. Regional and subregional cooperation and arrangements are crucial for successful actions to protect the marine environment from land-based activities. This is particularly so where a number of countries have coasts in the same marine and coastal area, most notably in enclosed or semi-enclosed seas. Such cooperation allows for more accurate identification and assessment of the problems in particular geographic areas and more appropriate establishment of priorities for action in these areas. Such cooperation also strengthens regional and national capacity-building and offers an important avenue for harmonizing and adjusting measures to fit the particular environmental and socio-economic circumstances. It, moreover, supports a more efficient and cost-effective implementation of the programmes of action.

Objectives

30. To strengthen and, where necessary, create new regional cooperative arrangements and joint actions to support effective action, strategies and programmes for:

(a) Identification and assessment of problems;

(b) Establishment of targets and priorities for action;

(c) Development and implementation of pragmatic and comprehensive management approaches and processes;

(d) Development and implementation of strategies to mitigate and remediate land-based sources of harm to the coastal and marine environment.

Activities

A. Participation in regional and subregional arrangements

31. States should:

(a) Pursue more active participation, including accession or ratification, as appropriate, in regional seas and other international marine and freshwater agreements, conventions and related arrangements;

(b) Strengthen existing regional conventions and programmes, and their institutional arrangements;

(c) Negotiate as, appropriate, new regional conventions and programmes.

B. Effective functioning of regional and subregional arrangements

32. With respect to the institutional aspects of regional and subregional arrangements, States should:

(a) Invite multilateral financing agencies, including regional development banks, and national institutions for bilateral development cooperation to cooperate in programming and in national implementation of regional agreements in the developing country regions;

(b) National action strategies and programmes can sometimes be best developed in a regional and subregional context. In developing such programmes of action, due consideration should be given to the suggested approaches and targets identified in chapter V of the present Programme of Action, and to the methodology specified in chapter II above. The programmes of action should be developed and implemented on a timetable appropriate to regional or subregional circumstances and decided upon by the governing bodies of the regional or subregional agreements, conventions or arrangements as appropriate;

(c) Establish or strengthen regional information networks and linkages for communicating with clearing-houses and other sources of information;

(d) Ensure close collaboration between the national and regional focal points and regional economic groupings, other relevant regional and international organizations, development banks and regional rivers authorities/commissions, in the development and implementation of regional programmes of action;

(e)   Encourage and facilitate cooperation between and among regional organizations/conventions to promote the exchange of information, experience and expertise;

(f)   Ensure that there is adequate secretariat support for regional and subregional arrangements (legal agreements and programmes of action), including:

(i)   Clear definition of secretariat functions and responsibilities;

(ii)   Consolidation of secretariats, including reliance on existing institutional arrangements, where cost-effective;

(iii) Cooperation between secretariats;

(iv)   Close integration of regional and subregional programmes of action and the relevant legal agreements that apply to the region and subregion.

33.   In the development and implementation of the regional programmes of action, consideration should also be given to the following:

(a)   Steps towards harmonization of environmental and control standards for emissions and discharges of pollutants, and agreement on data-quality assurance standards, data validation, comparative analyses, reference methods and training that are required for reliable monitoring and assessment carried out for the protection of the marine environment from land-based activities;

(b)   Steps to protect critical habitats and endangered species;

(c)   Exploring the use of innovative financing mechanisms that will assist the implementation of national and regional programmes of action;

(d)   Building capacity and, where appropriate, identifying regional centres of excellence for research, management tools and concepts, training and capacity-building as well as contingency-planning, monitoring and assessment, including environmentally sound technology assessment;

(e)   Arrangements to ensure that decision-making at the regional level is based on an integrated planning and management approach adopted at the national level;

(f)   Establishment of linkages with regional or subregional fisheries arrangements, as well as other mechanisms dealing with conservation of marine species, to promote collaboration in the exchange of data and information and mutual reinforcement in the achievement of respective objectives.

34.   Land-locked States whose river systems and drainage basins are linked to a particular marine region or subregion should be encouraged to participate in the relevant regional and subregional arrangements for:

(a)   Identification and characterization of drainage basins that are closely linked to degradation of the coastal areas and the marine environment;

(b) Assessment of scale and monitoring of national activities and practices that are associated with degradation of the marine environment;

(c) Establishment or strengthening of national environmental management and surveillance mechanisms and networks that are consistent with regional seas agreements or other arrangements.

35. States should encourage, where appropriate, regions to enter into interregional cooperation in order to exchange experiences and to help implement policies. Interregional cooperation may also be necessary to promote coordination of efforts for the protection and preservation of marine ecosystems and habitats.

IV. INTERNATIONAL COOPERATION

Basis for action

36. Effective international cooperation is important for the successful and cost-effective implementation of the Programme of Action. International cooperation serves a central role in enhancing capacity-building, technology transfer and cooperation, and financial support. Moreover, effective implementation of the Programme of Action requires efficient support from appropriate international agencies. Furthermore, international cooperation is required to ensure regular review of the implementation of the Programme and its further development and adjustment.

37. At the global level, there is a need for regular reviews of the state of the world marine environment, as well as dialogues, based on reports from relevant regional organizations, on implementation of regional action programmes, including exchange of experiences, the flow of financial resources in support of the implementation, in particular by countries in need of assistance, of national action to prevent and reduce marine degradation caused by land-based activities as well as scientific and technological cooperation and transfer of cleaner technology, in particular, to countries in need of assistance.

Objective

38. To strengthen existing international cooperation and institutional mechanisms and, where appropriate, to establish new arrangements, in order to support States and regional groups to undertake sustained action to address impacts upon the marine environment from land-based activities. Such actions should be based on the commitments with respect to financial resources contained in chapter 33 of Agenda 21, including paragraph 33.11, and those with respect to transfer of environmentally sound technology, cooperation and capacity-building contained in chapter 34 of Agenda 21, including paragraphs 34.4 and 34.14, as well as the commitments contained in paragraphs 17.23 and 17.48.

Activities

39. Recommended actions to give effect to these objectives in support of national and regional action to prevent and reduce marine degradation caused by land-based activities fall into four general categories:

(a) Capacity-building;

(b) The mobilization of financial resources;

(c)   The international institutional framework;

(d)   Additional areas of international cooperation.

A.   Capacity-building

40.   The mechanisms and cooperative actions should include:

(a)   The mobilization of experience in support of national and regional action to prevent and reduce marine degradation caused by land-based activities;

(b)   A clearing-house mechanism.

These mechanisms and cooperative actions should take into account the special needs of countries in need of assistance, including support for the establishment of infrastructures and the development of action programmes, as well as the alternatives and solutions that such countries are able to offer.

1.   Mobilization of experience and expertise

41.   States should cooperate to ensure that the most up-to-date information, experience and technical expertise with respect to each source-category of impacts upon the marine environment from land-based activities are made available and brought to bear upon national and regional actions to address such impacts. The steps to this end should include:

(a)   Establishment of linkages with international and regional organizations, including specialized agencies, with relevant expertise and responsibilities with respect to particular sources and sectors;

(b)   Promotion of cooperative interaction with private-sector groups and non-governmental organizations to introduce cost-effective and environmentally sound practices;

(c)   Facilitation and promotion of access, in particular for countries in need of assistance, to new and innovative technologies relevant to each source-category of impacts upon the marine environment from land-based activities, including those causing physical degradation and destruction of habitats;

(d)   Promotion of cleaner production techniques, *inter alia*, through training of industry personnel;

(e)   Promotion of new information technologies that facilitate knowledge transfer within countries and between States, including, in particular, from developed countries to countries in need of assistance;

(f)   Facilitation of access to sources (public or private, national or multilateral) of technical advice and assistance with respect to particular source-categories and sectors;

(g)   Facilitation of identification of opportunities for projects contributing to sustainable development for the private sector, including by industry and banks;

(h)   Establishment of linkages with the activities of ongoing international programmes monitoring and assessing the state of marine environment and relevant river systems, for example, the Joint Group of Experts on the Scientific Aspects of Marine Environmental Protection (GESAMP), the Global Ocean Observing System (GOOS), the Global Investigation of Pollution in the Marine Environment (GIPME), the Global Environment Monitoring System/Water, and the World Hydrological Cycle Observing System; and

(i) Establishment of linkages with international organizations, including specialized agencies and other organizations of the United Nations system, for dealing with environmental emergencies.

2. Clearing-house

42. As a means of mobilizing experience and expertise, including facilitation of effective scientific, technical and financial cooperation, as well as capacity-building, States should cooperate in the development of a clearing-house mechanism, i.e., a referral system through which decision makers at the national and regional level are provided with access to current sources of information, practical experience and scientific and technical expertise relevant to developing and implementing strategies to deal with the impacts of land-based activities. The referral system would be designed to allow decision makers to establish rapid and direct contact with the organizations, institutions, firms and/or individuals most able to provide relevant advice and assistance. It would therefore be a mechanism for responding to requests from national Governments on a timely basis. The clearing-house would consist of three basic elements:

(a) A data directory, with components organized by source-category, cross-referenced to economic sectors, containing information on current sources of information, practical experience and technical expertise;

(b) Information-delivery mechanisms to allow decision makers to have ready access to the data directory and obtain direct contact with the sources of information, practical experience and technical expertise identified therein (including the organizations, institutions, firms and/or individuals most able to provide relevant advice and assistance);

(c) Infrastructure — the institutional process for developing, organizing and maintaining the directory and delivery mechanisms.

43. Data directory. The data directory would include a component for each source-category delineated in this Programme of Action. Each such component would contain descriptions and contact information for each existing database and source of practical information and technical expertise. The descriptions and contact information would allow decision makers to determine which sources of information, experience and expertise are most relevant in a given situation and to contact these sources quickly. A key prerequisite for maintaining the directory is regular review of the descriptions and contact information to ensure that it is up-to-date. For each source-category, the relevant databases and sources of information, experience and expertise are likely to be dispersed among a large number of institutions and repositories, including global and regional organizations and national Governments, the private sector and non-governmental organizations. These institutions and repositories should be fully involved in the development of the data directory component for that source-category. In this way, the directory and its components should be built upon, not replicate, the work of organizations such as the World Bank, the United Nations Development Programme (UNDP), UNEP, including the UNEP International Cleaner Production Information Clearing-house (UNEP/ICPIC), the International Atomic Energy Agency (IAEA), the

International Maritime Organization (IMO), the Food and Agriculture
Organization of the United Nations (FAO), the United Nations Centre for
Human Settlements (UNCHS) (Habitat), the United Nations Industrial
Development Organization (UNIDO), the World Health Organization (WHO) and
the Arctic Monitoring and Assessment Programme (AMAP) It should in
addition make full use of the Small Island Developing States Network (SIDS-
NET). Where appropriate, it should also draw upon the work of other
intergovernmental and non-governmental organizations and the private
sector.

44. Each data-directory component should be organized so as to identify:

(a) Sources of current information, practical experience and
technical expertise on:

(i)   The nature, pathways, fate and effects of the contaminants or
other forms of degradation, including data-quality assurance
techniques;

(ii) Standards and reference methods for monitoring contamination, as
well as its concentrations, or other forms of degradation,
including biological-effects monitoring and data-quality
assurance techniques;

(iii) Policies, measures and strategies for action, including
mobilization and generation of resources, that have been
successfully applied (and those that have been unsuccessful) in
addressing activities generating the source-category
contaminants or other forms of degradation (what works and what
does not); and

(iv) Economically rational, environmentally sound and cleaner
practices, techniques and technologies to preven⁻. mitigate
and/or control adverse impacts on the marine environment of
land-based activities;

(b) Sources of relevant information:

(i)   In international and regional organizations (including non-
governmental organizations) with relevant expertise and
experience; and

(ii) Concerning intergovernmental and private sources of assistance,
scientific, technical and financial, including such matters as
the terms and conditions for the provision of such assistance.

45. Information-delivery mechanisms. The clearing-house mechanism must
include simple and widely available means of gaining entry to the directory
and retrieving information from its components, including directing
inquiries to the organizations, institutions, firms and/or individuals most
able to provide relevant advice and assistance. In other words, the data
directory must be easily accessible to decision makers on a real-time
basis. The objective would be user-friendly access to the data directory
and its components through electronic means. The World Wide Web on the
Internet offers such a basic access mechanism. It is recognized, however,
that the Internet is not universally available. It is important,
therefore, to also use and build upon existing information-delivery
systems, including the UNDP network of resident representatives, INFOTERRA,
and linked regional systems, including the secretariats of regional seas
and other regional conventions.

46. Infrastructure. The development, organization and maintenance of the data directory and its components and the delivery mechanisms have both specific (source-category) and general dimensions. At the general level, an inter-organizational group should be established by the relevant international organizations to coordinate the basic design and structure of the data directory as well as its linkages to information-delivery mechanisms. This group would be responsible for establishing a common format for the individual source-category components and for cross-referencing among components. It would include representatives of each lead organization responsible for coordinating development of individual data-directory components, those responsible for information-delivery mechanisms, and experts on information technology and other relevant fields.

47. For each source-category component of the data directory, a lead organization should be designated to convene or designate a group of experts to develop the content of specific entries for that component. Issues such as ensuring that entries meet quality and relevance criteria and keywords or search items relevant to the source-category would also be the responsibility of each group of experts. There would be provision to reconvene each such group periodically to update the source-category component, including ensuring that the sources of information, practical experience and technical expertise are relevant and do represent the best sources.

48. Recognizing that many developing States may not have the necessary capacity to benefit from the clearing-house mechanism, this process of implementation should provide for capacity-building, including technical training and infrastructure development.

49. The clearing-house mechanism should be designed to include feedback functions to provide for its refinement and evolution to meet the needs of its users. These feedback functions include:

(a) Identification of data and information gaps and recommendations as to how to address such gaps;

(b) Identification of training and infrastructure requirements for those using the clearing-house mechanism;

(c) Provision for establishment of links between the clearing-house mechanism and regional agreements, institutions and centres holding information, experience and technical expertise of specific relevance to the region concerned.

B. Mobilizing financial resources

50. Alongside the mobilization of experience and expertise, the mobilization of financial resources is the other indispensable foundation for the development and implementation of national and regional programmes for the protection of the marine environment from land-based activities. It is recognized that the development of national and regional action programmes are of primary international importance.

51. While States recognize that, in general, the financing for the implementation of the national and regional programmes of action that will embody this Global Programme of Action should come from each country's own public and private sectors, they reaffirm:

(a)   Their conclusion that international cooperation for sustainable development should be strengthened in order to support and complement the efforts of countries in need of assistance;

(b)   Their acknowledgement that, for countries in need of assistance, substantial new and additional funding will be required for the actions flowing from Agenda 21;

(c)   Their commitment that such funding should be provided in a way that maximizes the availability of new and additional resources and uses all available funding sources and mechanisms,

as set out in paragraph 17.23 and, more generally, in chapter 33 of Agenda 21.

52.   There is increasing realization worldwide of the need for action to protect the world's marine environment, described in the opening paragraphs of this Programme. Equally, it is increasingly realized that land-based activities are the predominant source of adverse impacts on the marine environment. This realization should lead to a correspondingly greater political emphasis, at national, regional and global levels, on the need to ensure the mobilization of the necessary funding for the action needed within the framework of integrated management of coastal zones and, where appropriate, associated watersheds. This in turn should be translated into an increased willingness by partners for international development cooperation to provide financing, including on concessionary and preferential terms, for projects aimed at fulfilling the objectives of this Programme of Action.

1.   Scale of funding required

53.   There are major differences among the different regions of the world, and the States which they comprise, in terms of geography, physiography, and ecology and, above all, in economic and social conditions, level of development and regional cooperation. In many cases, as well, the impacts on the marine environment of various contaminants and forms of physical disturbance will have different degrees of importance. All these variations will lead to different judgments on the appropriate priorities to be given to tackling the different problems mentioned in chapters II and III above. Each State will therefore develop its own appropriate set of priorities for the tasks that it decides to undertake to protect the marine environment, and these priorities will be reflected in the composition and scale of its national programme of action and any regional programme in which it participates.

54.   The amount of funding required for implementation of the present Programme, and the mix of sources and mechanisms that is appropriate, will therefore flow from these national decisions on priorities. The differing national priorities, the range of actions which may need to be undertaken and the variety of sources and mechanisms which may be used, separately or in combination, to finance them mean that there will be significant variations between States in the approach to mobilizing financial resources, in particular between developed and developing States.

2.   Range of financing possibilities

55.   The funding of action to address the priorities at the national and regional levels, consistent with chapters II, III and V of this Programme, requires, in the first place, the identification of all the various potential domestic funding sources and mechanisms, in order to determine

which are appropriate for the priority concerned, and to find ways of linking them in an innovative fashion. An illustrative list of domestic sources and mechanisms is set out in the annex to the present Programme of Action. There will be differences between States, particularly between developed countries and countries in need of assistance, in he extent to which use of these various options is possible. As part of the preparation of their national plans, States should evaluate the potential of these options.

56. For many States, whether developed, developing or in economic transition, it will also be appropriate to look more widely for appropriate sources of financial resources and mechanisms to mobilize them effectively. Funding from domestic sources and mechanisms may be insufficient, particularly for countries in need of assistance. An illustrative list of external sources and mechanisms is also included in the annex to the present Programme of Action. Where appropriate, in the preparation of their national programmes, States should investigate the potential roles of such sources and mechanisms.

57. For countries in need of assistance, there is a limited level of domestic resources available and a wide range of demanding challenges to be faced in many fields. Where the lack of domestic financial resources means that projects in such countries will not be able to proceed, there will be recourse to external financing, particularly funding through grants and concessionary loans. In other cases, external financing, through various innovative schemes (such as co-financing and joint ventures, underwriting of country risks, and venture capital funds) can also act as a catalyst for the mobilization of domestic financial resources and provide leverage to attract additional external financial resources in order to mobilize more efficiently new financial flows.

3. Funding the programmes

58. National and regional programmes should ensure that there is a balance between the projects to be undertaken to implement national and regional priorities and the sources of funding available.

59. Where recourse to external sources and mechanisms for financial resources is necessary, the mix of the various possibilities that will be appropriate will vary from country to country. The pattern of funding will have to be determined in accordance with the decisions on individual projects.

60. Further, countries in need of assistance may need help in capacity-building for:

    (a)   Development of national programmes of action;

    (b)   Preparation of national assessments on each source-category;

    (c)   Identification of ways and means of funding the implementation of the national plans.

61. National and international financial institutions, bilateral donors and other competent regional and international organizations should assist in this capacity-building task.

62. As part of the process of ensuring that intergovernmental agencies and other international bodies take due account of this Programme of Action, and in view of the particular significance of external finance for

countries in need of assistance, it will be necessary for those international agencies concerned with the provision of finance, particularly in the form of grants and concessionary loans, to ensure that their policies give appropriate priority to assistance for projects aimed at the implementation of the Programme. A similar approach is also needed for bilateral assistance. International financial institutions should provide information on the amounts and terms of the financial resources that they might provide, in particular to countries in need of assistance.

63. Improved cooperation and coordination is essential among national institutions, international organizations, including financial institutions, and the private sector and non-governmental organizations, to enhance the effectiveness of the delivery of financial and other support.

64. Mobilizing financial resources is not a one-off task. As part of the follow-up process to this Programme, periodical reviews should be undertaken by the intergovernmental meetings referred to in paragraph 77 below as to whether it has been possible to achieve an appropriate balance between the scale and type of funding required and that which has been available in practice. In the light of such reviews, a conclusion will have to be reached on any problems encountered over access to new and additional funding sources and mechanisms, in accordance with the commitments in Agenda 21.

4. Recommended approaches for projects to be funded

65. The recommendations set out below are intended to highlight features which are important for partners in international development cooperation in the design and evaluation of, and for decisions on, projects for the protection of the marine environment for which external financing is to be sought. With appropriate modifications, they will also apply where a national or regional programme contains a series of related projects.

66. Projects need to be prepared in the context of the overall national or regional strategies, policies and programmes related to the protection of the marine environment, on the basis of its sustainable use and development. Accordingly:

(a) Projects should be derived from the priorities established nationally for the prevention, control and reduction of marine and coastal degradation within the framework of integrated management of coastal zones and, where appropriate, their associated watersheds, and consistent with the national sustainable development strategy;

(b) Chapters II, III and V of this Programme should provide the policy framework for the identification of priorities;

(c) Projects should be consistent with the principles and duty set out in chapter I above.

67. The goals for projects responding to the impact of land-based activities upon the marine environment include:

(a) Protection of the health and public amenities of coastal populations, in particular those suffering from poverty and food insecurity, including addressing sewage and industrial effluents;

(b) Conservation of marine living resources, including maintenance or increase of future options for their sustainable use;

(c) Conservation and sustainable use, including restoration, of coastal and marine biological diversity;

(d) Protection, including restoration, of habitats of marine living resources, including critical spawning and feeding areas, as well as areas used or suitable for mariculture;

(e) Alleviation of poverty as a means of reducing pressure on coastal and marine environments;

(f) Addressing, where appropriate, management of associated watersheds.

68. Other features which will make projects more likely to be effective or which will enhance their value generally include:

(a) The involvement of user and local communities that are interested, particularly the economic and social sectors affected;

(b) Consultation with organized civil society and non-governmental organizations, and the private sector;

(c) Provision for capacity-building and the development of institutions, including relevant technology and management training, human-resources development and public outreach and education;

(d) Coordination between those providing external support when several international development partners are involved;

(e) Partnerships and co-financing with the private sector;

(f) Promotion of knowledge and understanding of the marine environment;

(g) Innovation and replicability.

5. The Global Environment Facility

69. The Global Environment Facility (GEF) provides new and additional grants and concessionary loans to eligible countries to meet the agreed environmental costs of measures to achieve agreed global incremental benefits in four focal areas: climate change, biological diversity, international waters and ozone-layer depletion. The agreed incremental costs of activities concerning land degradation, primarily desertification and deforestation, as they relate to the four focal areas, are also eligible for funding. The international waters and biodiversity focal areas are most directly related to the goals of this Programme of Action, although links between land-based activities and other focal areas should be recognized. Where consistent with its operational strategies, GEF assistance can play an important role in catalysing the necessary national and regional action to address those international concerns identified in this Programme which ultimately have global linkages and global policy implications. GEF funding cannot, however, be a substitute for ordinary development aid.

70. GEF is invited to build upon the work that will be undertaken to implement this Programme of Action and fund the agreed incremental costs of activities consistent with the GEF operational strategy. It is also invited to consider:

(a)   Reflecting the unity of the marine environment and its linkages to freshwater systems;

(b)   Recognizing that, while the focal area of international waters is to be distinct from other areas of GEF funding, land-based activities may have links both with it and with biological diversity and climate change;

(c)   Recognizing the international significance of transboundary pollution which may have its origin in a local area;

(d)   Recognizing that, even where pollution or its root cause is confined to a local area, some types of pollution may affect the waters of more than one State, and thus be of international significance;

(e)   Including, where appropriate, clearly defined and targeted research and monitoring within projects.

71.   States welcome the priority to be given by the GEF operational strategy for international waters to impacts upon the marine environment from land-based activities.

C.   International institutional framework

72.   A number of international organizations and institutions, including non-governmental organizations, regional and global, have responsibilities and experience with respect to prevention, reduction and control of impacts upon the marine environment from one or more of the source-categories of land-based activities.   The international institutional framework for implementation of this Programme of Action, therefore, should be based upon concerted action by States within the relevant organizations and institutions to accord attention and priority to impacts on the marine environment from land-based activities and. concerted action by States to ensure effective coordination and collaboration among such organizations and institutions.   In addition, the framework should make provision for regular review of the Programme of Action, including its implementation and necessary adjustments.

73.   The process of developing this institutional framework will require a series of interlinked steps.   States should commit themselves to taking action within the international organizations and institutions with responsibilitie and experience regarding impacts upon the marine environment from land-based activities:

(a)   To secure formal endorsement of those parts of the Programme of Action that are of relevance to such organizations and institutions;

(b)   To accord priority to the prevention, reduction and control of impacts upon the marine environment from land-based activities through the economic, social and environmental mandates of such organizations and institutions; and

(c)   To review regularly the state of knowledge and the state of the art with respect to the prevention, reduction and control of impacts upon the marine environment from land-based activities through the economic, social and environmental mandates of such organizations and institutions.

74.   Recognizing that States have the primary role in the implementation of this Programme of Action, UNEP, as the coordinator and catalyst of

environmental activities within the United Nations system and beyond, should, through its programmes and secretariat role:

(a) Promote and facilitate implementation of the Programme of Action at the national level;

(b) Promote and facilitate implementation at the regional, including subregional, level through, in particular, a revitalization of the Regional Seas Programme; and

(c) Play a catalytic role in the implementation at the international level with other organizations and institutions.

75. It is important that in fulfilling this role, including the secretariat function, UNEP should undertake it in an efficient and cost-effective manner, supported largely by the existing resources, expertise and infrastructure available in all components of UNEP's programmes. UNEP should be flexible and responsive to the evolving needs of the Programme and the availability of resources, e.g. from trust funds.

76. In facilitating the effective implementation of the Programme of Action, UNEP should maintain a close partnership with other organizations and bodies, such as IMO, WHO, FAO, the World Meteorological Organization (WMO), UNDP, UNIDO, the Intergovernmental Oceanographic Commission of the United Nations Educational, Scientific and Cultural Organization (UNESCO/IOC), IAEA, the World Bank and regional development banks, GEF and UNCHS (Habitat), as well as regional bodies supporting the implementation of regional seas and relevant freshwater programmes. An appropriate division of tasks is of essential importance to ensure the efficient and cost-effective implementation of the Programme of Action.

77. UNEP should, in close collaboration with the relevant organizations and institutions, convene periodic intergovernmental meetings to:

(a) Review progress on implementation of the Programme of Action;

(b) Review the results of scientific assessments regarding land-based impacts upon the marine environment provided by relevant scientific organizations and institutions, including GESAMP;

(c) Consider reports provided on national plans to implement the Programme of Action;

(d) Review coordination and collaboration among organizations and institutions, regional and global, that have responsibilities and experience with respect to prevention, reduction and control of impacts upon the marine environment from land-based activities;

(e) Promote exchange of experience between regions;

(f) Review progress on capacity-building (section A of this chapter) and on mobilization of resources (section B of this chapter) to support the implementation of the Programme of Action, in particular by countries in need of assistance and, where appropriate, provide guidance;

(g) Consider the need for international rules, as well as recommended practices and procedures, to further the objectives of the Programme of Action.

78. In preparation for these meetings, States should be encouraged to
provide reports, directly or through relevant regional organizations, on
the implementation of the Programme of Action. Non-governmental
organizations would also be invited to report on relevant activities.

79. A component of the institutional framework for implementation of the
Programme of Action is establishment of the clearing-house mechanism called
for in section A of this chapter. This will require collaboration between
UNEP and a variety of international organizations and institutions,
including the United Nations system and international financial
institutions. Specific steps include:

     (a) Determination of the composition and providing for the
establishment of the inter-organizational steering group;

     (b) Designation of lead organization(s) for the development and
updating of each source-category component in the data directory;

     (c) Identification of the appropriate mix of information-delivery
systems.

Steps for developing institutional arrangements

80. The process of articulating the institutional framework to support and
implement this Programme of Action cuts across existing institutional
mandates and will require action within relevant international
organizations and institutions, including those of the United Nations
system and international financial institutions. It is recommended,
therefore, that pertinent provisions outlined in this Programme of Action
be set forth in a resolution to be adopted by the United Nations General
Assembly at its fifty-first session.

81. The resolution would set forth commitment to the institutional
framework outlined in the Programme of Action and agree on specific steps
towards its establishment, including the clearing-house. Such steps would
include identification of the international organizations and institutions,
regional and global, with responsibilities and experience regarding impacts
upon the marine environment from land-based activities.

82. It is recommended that the issue of the General Assembly resolution be
specifically included on the agenda of the Commission on Sustainable
Development for consideration in the context of its review of chapter 17 of
Agenda 21, on oceans.

83. The Executive Director of UNEP is called upon to prepare a proposal
setting forth a specific plan for implementing the institutional
arrangements contained in this Programme of Action, including, in
collaboration with other organizations, the preparation of a draft
implementation plan and pilot project for the clearing-house. This
proposal should be submitted to the inter-sessional meeting for the
Commission on Sustainable Development, to be held in February 1996. This
plan should include a clear indication of how UNEP intends to carry out its
functions in this regard, including secretariat functions, its
contributions to the clearing-house mechanism, proposals and action taken
on coordination among relevant United Nations and other organizations and
how the relevant UNEP programmes, including the Regional Seas Programme,
could be strengthened to carry out an effective role in the implementation
of this Programme of Action.

D. Additional areas of international cooperation

1. Waste-water treatment and management

84. In accordance with Agenda 21, especially its chapters 17 and 18, States should address the serious public health problems and the degradation of coastal ecosystems that result from the disposal in coastal areas of inadequately treated waste waters. This situation still affects many countries, particularly countries in need of assistance.

85. States agree that planning for pollution prevention, including cleaner-production approaches and best-practice urban design, and the treatment and management of urban waste water, including urban storm-water and separation of industrial effluent, are priorities in the fulfilment of the objectives of this Programme of Action and of Agenda 21. Mechanisms should be studied to expeditiously channel additional resources for this purpose to countries in need of assistance.

86. The Executive Director of UNEP, in close partnership with WHO, UNDP, UNCHS (Habitat) and other relevant organizations, is called upon to prepare a proposal setting forth a specific plan for addressing the global nature of the problems related to the inadequate management and treatment of waste water. This should take account of work already in progress in WHO and other competent international organizations, including the Noordwijk Action Programme. This plan will enable the issue to be addressed in an expeditious and efficient manner in the follow-up to the Global Programme of Action at the international level.

2. Persistent organic pollutants (POPs)

87. Consistent with decision 18/32 adopted by the UNEP Governing Council in May 1995, States should participate actively in the assessment and development of recommendations concerning the list of twelve substances identified in the UNEP decision.

88. There is agreement that:

(a) International action is needed to develop a global, legally binding instrument, amongst other international and regional actions, for the reduction and/or elimination of emissions and discharges, whether intentional or not, and, where appropriate, the elimination of the manufacture and the use of, and illegal traffic in, the persistent organic pollutants identified in UNEP Governing Council decision 18/32, for which the scientific and technical basis for action is already demonstrated, consistent with the principles of the Rio Declaration, in particular Principle 15;

(b) In developing the instrument called for above, the nature of the obligations undertaken must be developed recognizing the special circumstances of countries in need of assistance. Particular attention should be devoted to the potential need for the continued use of certain POPs and the difficulty of acquiring substitutes and of the transfer of technology for the development of those substitutes. This will require special consideration to be given to economically feasible and environmentally sound ways of ceasing to use, discharge or emit POPs selected for priority action. The reduction and/or elimination of use, emissions and discharges of POPs should, if necessary, be taken on a step-by-step basis;

(c)   The range of substances iden' .fied in UNEP Governing Council
decision 18/32 require differentiated actions depending on their source,
nature and use. For example, polychlorinated biphenyls (PCBs) require
international cooperation for their proper management and disposal;
unintended by-products, such as dioxins and furans, warrant investigation
of best available technologies and alternative technologies; while
pesticides require approaches addressing use and production;

(d)   Furthermore, States should commit themselves to an open and
transparent process to facilitate t:e work of the International Programme
on Chemical Safety (IPCS), the Inter-Organization Programme for the Sound
Management of Chemicals (IOMC) and the Intergovernmental Forum on Chemical
Safety (IFCS), to assess and evaluate the environmental and socio-economic
impact of other persistent organic pollutants consistent with the purpose,
functions and priorities for action identified by IFCS with a view to their
inclusion as appropriate in the global, 'legally binding instrument
mentioned above.

89. To implement Governing Council decision 18/32, UNEP is undertaking a
transparent process under the auspices of IOMC, involving Governments,
industry, public-interest groups and relevant international organizations.
This process is critical to ensuring a balanced consideration of the
principal technical matters and central policy issues relevant to global
action in this area.

90. States are encouraged to participate actively in the development of a
legal instrument for the application of the prior informed consent (PIC)
procedure for certain hazardous chemicals in international trade,
consistent with UNEP Governing Council decision 18/12, adopted in May 1995.

V.   RECOMMENDED APPROACHES BY SOURCE CATEGORY

91. This chapter provides guidance as to the actions that States should
consider at national, regional and global levels, in accordance with their
national capacities, priorities and available resources, and with the
cooperation of the United Nations and other relevant organizations, as
appropriate, and with the international cooperation for building capacities
and mobilizing resources identified in chapter IV.

92. In the light of the differences between regions and States and the
national priorities referred to in paragraphs 53 and 54 above, each State
and each regional grouping should develop its own programme of action.
This may or may not be a separate document but it should include specific
targets and a clear timetable showing the dates by which the State or
States involved commit themselves at a political level to achieve these
targets.

93. In addition, action will be needed on certain matters at the global
level, either to address global effects or to facilitate action at the
national or regional levels. Specific targets for these matters are set
out in this chapter.

A.   Sewage '

1.   Basis for action

94. Recognizing variation in local conditions, domestic waste water
improperly discharged to freshwater and coastal environments may present a
variety of concerns. These are associated with: (a) pathogens that may
result in human health problems through exposure via bathing waters or

through contaminated shellfish, (b) suspended solids, (c) significant nutrient inputs, (d) biochemical oxygen demand (BOD), (e) cultural issues such as taboos in some areas, (f) plastics and other marine debris, (g) ecosystem population effects, and (h) heavy metals and other toxic substances, e.g. hydrocarbons, in those cases where industrial sources may have discharged effluent to municipal collection systems.

95. Environmental effects associated with domestic waste-water discharges are generally local with transboundary implications in certain geographic areas. The commonality of sewage-related problems throughout coastal areas of the world is significant. Consequently, domestic waste-water discharges are considered one of the most significant threats to coastal environments worldwide.

2. <u>Objective/proposed target</u>

96. With regard to objectives and targets, paragraph 21.29 of Agenda 21 states:

> "Governments, according to their capacities and available resources and with the cooperation of the United Nations and other relevant organizations, as appropriate, should:
>
> "(a) By the year 2000, establish waste treatment and disposal quality criteria, objectives and standards based on the nature and assimilative capacity of the receiving environment;
>
> "(b) By the year 2000, establish sufficient capacity to undertake waste-related pollution impact monitoring and conduct regular surveillance, including epidemiological surveillance, where appropriate;
>
> "(c) By the year 1995, in industrialized countries, and by the year 2005, in developing countries, ensure that at least 50 per cent of all sewage, waste waters and solid wastes are treated or disposed of in conformity with national or international environmental and health quality guidelines;
>
> "(d) By the year 2025, dispose of all sewage, waste waters and solid wastes in conformity with national or international environmental quality guidelines."

3. <u>Activities</u>

(a) <u>National actions, policies and measures</u>

97. Actions, policies and measures of States within their national capacities should include:

    (a) Identification of major sewage sources and areas where sewage poses major environmental and health-related hazards;

    (b) Development of national programmes of action for the installation of appropriate and environmentally sound sewage facilities, and to this end ensure:

        (i) Incorporation of sewage concerns when formulating or reviewing coastal-development and land-use plans, including human-settlements plans;

(ii)   Building and maintenance of sewer systems and sewage-treatment facilities or other appropriate systems, in accordance with national policies and capacities and international cooperation available;

(iii) Location of coastal outfalls so as to obtain or maintain agreed environmental quality criteria and to avoid exposing shell fisheries, water intakes, and bathing areas to pathogens and to avoid the exposure of sensitive environments (such as lagoons, coral reefs, seagrass beds, mangroves, etc.) to excess nutrient loads;

(iv)   Promotion of the reuse of treated effluents for the conservation of water resources. To this end, infrastructural measures, treatment at source and segregation of industrial effluents, shall be encouraged, as well as:

   a.   Encouragement of the beneficial reuses of sewage effluents and sludges by the appropriate design of treatment plants and processes and controls of the quality of influent waste waters;

   b.   Ensuring the environmentally sound treatment when domestic and compatible industrial effluents are treated together;

(v)   Promotion of primary, secondary and, where appropriate and feasible, tertiary treatment of municipal sewage discharged to rivers, estuaries and the sea;

(vi)   Reduction and beneficial use of sewage or other solutions appropriate to specific sites such as no-water and low-water solutions;

(vii) Establishment and improvement of local and national regulatory and monitoring programmes to control and assess effluent discharge, using minimum sewage effluent guidelines and water quality criteria and giving due consideration to the characteristics of receiving bodies and the volume and type of pollutants;

(viii) Identification of the availability and sustainability of productive uses of sewage sludge, such as land-spreading, composting, etc.;

(ix)   Establishment of research programmes to identify, validate and develop waste-water treatment technologies;

(c)   Provision of sufficient training and education for local administrations to plan, build and run adequate sewage treatment facilities;

(d)   Formulation and implementation of awareness campaigns for the general public to gain general recognition for the need for the installation of appropriate and environmentally sound sewage facilities.

(b)   Regional actions

98.   Regional actions should include:

   (a)   Promotion and implementation of regional cooperation for the establishment and implementation of programmes and priority measures for sewage, particularly in case of transboundary effects;

   (b)   Development of regional programmes for sharing and exchanging technical information and advice regarding environmentally sound sewage treatment and facilities.

(c)   International actions

99.   International actions should include:

   (a)   Participation in a clearing-house on environmentally sound sewage technology and practices;

   (b)   Facilitation of transfer of environmentally sound sewage technology;

   (c)   Scientific, technical and financial cooperation with countries in need of assistance, in developing, installing, operating and monitoring appropriate and environmentally sound sewage facilities.

B.   Persistent organic pollutants (POPs)

1.   Basis for action

100.   Persistent organic pollutants (POPs) are a set of organic compounds that: (i) possess toxic characteristics; (ii) are persistent; (iii) are liable to bioaccumulate; (iv) are prone to long-range transport and deposition; and (v) can result in adverse environmental and human health effects at locations near and far from their source. POPs are typically characterized as having low water solubility and high fat solubility. Most POPs are anthropogenic in origin. Anthropogenic emissions, both point and diffuse, are associated with industrial processes, product use and applications, waste disposal, leaks and spills, and combustion of fuels and waste materials. Once dispersed, clean-up is rarely possible. Because many POPs are relatively volatile, their remobilization and long-distance redistribution through atmospheric pathways often complicates the identification of specific sources.

101.   POPs have long environmental half-lives. Accordingly, successive releases over time result in continued accumulation and the ubiquitous presence of POPs in the global environment.

102.   The primary transport routes into the marine and coastal environment include atmospheric deposition and surface run-off. Regional and global transport is predominately mediated by atmospheric circulation, but also occurs through sediment transport and oceanic circulation. Movement may also occur through a successive migration of short-range movements that result from a sequence of volatilization, deposition, and revolatilization. Due to these transport patterns and chemical characteristics, there is a growing body of evidence demonstrating the systematic migration of these substances to cooler latitudes.

2. Objective/proposed target

103. The objective/proposed target is:

(a) To reduce and/or eliminate emissions and discharges of POPs that threaten to accumulate to dangerous levels in the marine and coastal environment;

(b) To give immediate attention to finding and introducing preferable substitutes for chemicals that pose unreasonable and otherwise unmanageable risks to human health and the environment;

(c) To use cleaner production processes, including best available techniques, to reduce and/or eliminate hazardous by-products associated with production, incineration and combustion (e.g. dioxins, furans, hexaclorobenzene, poycyclic aromatic hydrocarbons (PAHs));

(d) To promote best environmental practice for pest control in agriculture and aquaculture.

3. Activitiés

(a) National actions, policies and measures

104. Actions, policies and measures of States within their national capacities should include:

(a) Development, compilation and maintenance of inventories of point-source releases of POPs, identification and assessment of diffuse sources and sinks from which POPs may remobilize, and assessment of ir. its from these sources as a basis for pollution control and prevention measures;

(b) Development of comprehensive national programmes of action for the reduction and/or elimination of emissions and discharges, and where applicable, remobilization from all significant sources of POPs, including targets and timetables and sector-specific measures for industry and agriculture:

(i)   Adoption of appropriate policy instruments - which could include regulation, economic instruments and voluntary agreements - on POPs applying the precautionary principle and the "polluter pays" principle. Priority should be given to phasing out or banning of chemicals that pose unreasonable and otherwise unmanageable risks to human health and the environment and whose use can not be adequately controlled. This can be achieved through substitution by environmentally sound substances, use of best available techniques (BAT), application of best environmental practice (BEP) and implementation of integrated pollution prevention and control (IPPC);

(ii)   Development of appropriate regulatory measures and establishment of facilities for environmentally sound collection and disposal of wastes containing POPs;

(iii) Establishment of an environmental monitoring programme for POPs including the development of assessment criteria and the adoption of internationally accepted quality control and quality assurance procedures;

(iv) Development of programmes to promote the informed use of substances which can result in discharges and emissions of POPs from diffuse sources, including the promotion of good agricultural practice to limit the use of pesticides to the application rates essential for crop protection, and restraint in the non-agricultural use of pesticides, especially on roads and railways;

(v)   Establishment of information services for industry and agriculture on least environmentally hazardous handling and use of POPs, and on substitutes, technology and ways and means to prevent, reduce and eliminate pollution by POPs, including best environmental practice (BEP), best available techniques (BAT) and integrated pollution prevention and control (IPPC);

(vi) Ratification and implementation of relevant international and regional conventions and agreements;

(vii) Ensuring the effective implementation of relevant bilateral, regional and international decisions and recommendations, *inter alia*, b :

   a. Assessing regularly whether the national goals and measures to reduce and eliminate pollution by POPs are being accomplished;

   b. Compliance monitoring, assessing and reporting the effects of these measures;   and

   c. Establishing or strengthening, as appropriate, institutions to deal effectively with the problems of POPs.

(b)   Regional actions

105. Regional actions should include:

   (a) Encouraging existing regional agreements and programmes of action on the prevention and elimination of pollution of the marine and coastal environment from land-based activities, to set up and implement programmes and priority measures to prevent, reduce and/or eliminate emissions and discharges of POPs and materials containing POPs from all sources. To this end, they should, *inter alia*:

   (i)   Adopt targets and timetables for reduction and/or elimination of POPs releases through their substitution, and on best available techniques (BAT), best environmental practice (BEP), and integrated pollution prevention and control (IPPC);

   (ii) Adopt decisions and recommendations on the development of harmonized assessment criteria and monitoring programmes based on regionally or internationally agreed quality control and quality assurance procedures;

   (iii) Provide member States with technical information and advice regarding handling, use and disposal of POPs and their substitutes and ways and means to minimize and eliminate their release to the environment;

(iv)   Ensure transparency of the implementation of decisions and
       recommendations by adopting regular reporting on implementation
       and monitoring of measures regarding POPs; and

(v)   Assess compliance with, and the éffects of, the agreed measures;

(b)   Encouraging States that are not already parties to regional
agreements and action plans on the prevention and eliminaticn of pollution
of the marine and coastal environment from land-based activities to join
such cooperation and to cooperate on a bilateral and/or a multilateral
basis in the regulation of POPs;

(c)   Encouraging the strengthening of or, as appropriate,
establishing regional institutions to deal effectively with the problems of
POPs.

(c)   International actions

106.   International actions should include:

(a)   Urging international, regional and subregional funding sources
and mechanisms and donor countries, to ensure that the objectives,
principles and measures laid down in this chapter be taken into account
when supporting projects that directly or indirectly relate to emissions,
discharges and, where appropriate, the manufacture and use of POPs, as well
as the clean-up and restoration of areas polluted with POPs;

(b)   Encouraging international, regional and subregional funding
sources and mechanisms to ensure that available financial resources are
made available for supporting measures to reduce or eliminate releases of
POPs to the environment;

(c)   Inviting appropriate international agencies and bodies to
strengthen necessary information exchange, transfer of environmentally
sound technology and capacity-building for the implementation of the
objectives, principles and measures laid down in this chapter for the
reduction and/or elimination of POPs releases to the environment;

(d)   Strengthening and extending existing international quality
assurance, standardization and classification mechanisms for POPs to ensure
that inventories and assessments are both reliable and intercomparable.
Such existing mechanisms include those co-sponsored by IOC, UNEP and IAEA
under the GIPME programme, and the associated activities of the Marine
Environmental Studies Laboratory in Monaco;

(e)   Cooperation with countries in need of assistance, through
financial, technical and scientific support, in order to reduce and/or
eliminate emissions and discharges of POPs that threaten to accumulate to
dangerous levels in the marine and coastal environment;

(f)   Priority attention should be given to finding and introducing
preferable substitutes for POPs that pose unreasonable and c herwise
unmanageable risks to human health and the environment.

C. Radioactive substances

1. Basis for action

107. Radioactive substances (i.e., materials containing radionuclides) have entered and/or are entering the marine and coastal environment, directly or indirectly, as a result of a variety of human activities and practices. These activities include production of energy, reprocessing of spent fuel, military operations, nuclear testing, medical applications and other operations associated with the management and disposal of radioactive wastes and the processing of natural materials by industrial processes. Other activities, such as the transport of radioactive material, pose risks of such releases.

108. Radioactive materials can present hazards to human health and to the environment. Suspected radioactive contamination of foodstuffs can also have negative effects on marketing of such foodstuffs.

2. Objective/proposed target

109. The objective/proposed target is to reduce and/or eliminate emissions and discharges of radioactive substances in order to prevent, reduce and eliminate pollution of the marine and coastal environment by human-enhanced levels of radioactive substances.

3. Activities

(a) National actions, policies and measures

110. Actions, policies and measures of States within their national capacities should include:

(a) Promotion of policies and practical measures including setting targets and timetables to minimize and limit the generation of radioactive wastes and provide for their safe processing, storage, conditioning, transportation and disposal;

(b) Ensuring the safe storage, transportation and disposal of radioactive wastes, as well as spent radiation sources and spent fuel from nuclear reactors destined for final disposal, in accordance with international regulations or guidelines;

(c) Ensuring proper planning, including environmental impact assessment, of safe and environmentally sound management of radioactive waste, including emergency procedures, storage, transportation and disposal, prior to and after activities that generate such waste;

(d) Adoption of measures, including best available techniques and best environmental practice, for the reduction and/or elimination of inputs of radioactive substances to the marine and coastal environment for the purpose of preventing and eliminating pollution of the marine and coastal environment;

(e) Ratification and/or implementation of relevant international and regional conventions, decisions and resolutions.

111. States should:

(a) Not promote or allow the storage or disposal of high-level, intermediate-level and low-level radioactive wastes near the marine and coastal environment unless they determine that scientific evidence, consistent with the applicable internationally agreed principles and guidelines, shows that such storage or disposal poses no unacceptable risk to people and the marine and coastal environment or does not interfere with other legitimate uses of the sea, making, in the process of consideration, appropriate use of the concept of the precautionary approach;

(b)   Respect, in accordance with international law, the decisions, as far as applicable to them, under other relevant regional and other international environmental conventions dealing with other aspects of safe and environmentally sound management of radioactive wastes;

(c)   Conclude and sign the Comprehensive Test Ban Treaty by no later than 1996;*

(d)   Make available information on the characteristics of terrestrial dump sites in coastal areas through, and consistent with, agreed regional and international reporting procedures. The information should include the magnitude, types of materials, characteristics of storage and status of the dump sites.

(b)   Regional actions

112.   Relevant regional organizations, in accordance with regional needs and capacities, should ensure:

(a)   Monitoring of radioactivity in their regions and identification of any problem areas;

(b)   The establishment of criteria for assessing and/or reporting on the use in their region of best available techniques to prevent and eliminate pollution by inputs of radioactive substances;

(c)   The preparation of comprehensive environmental assessments of the effect on the marine and coastal environment of historical discharges and current discharges of radioactive substances.

(c)   International actions

113.   International actions should include:

(a)   Support for efforts under the auspices of IAEA to develop and promulgate radioactive waste management safety standards, guidelines or codes of practice, including work being undertaken towards an international convention on the safety of radioactive waste management, in order to provide an internationally accepted basis for the safe and environmentally sound management and disposal of radioactive wastes. This work should take account of the application of best available techniques and best environmental practice for all nuclear applications not currently covered by internationally binding agreements making such provisions;

(b)   Cooperation with developing countries and economies in transition, through financial, technical and scientific support, in ensuring environmentally sound management and storage of radioactive materials as well as supporting environmental restoration efforts;

---

*   Note. This subparagraph has to read in conjunction with the report of the Intergovernmental Conference (UNEP(OCA)/LBA/IG.2/6).

(c) Maintenance of existing international quality assurance and standardization mechanisms supporting the reliable measurement and assessment of radionuclides in the environment. Such existing mechanisms include the Analytical Quality Control Services provided by the Marine Environmental Studies Laboratory of IAEA;

(d) Consideration by all Governments and international organizations that have expertise in the field of clean-up and disposal of radioactive contaminants to give appropriate assistance as may be requested for remedial purposes in adversely affected areas.

D. Heavy metals

1. Basis for action

114. Heavy metals are natural constituents of the Earth's crust. Human activities have drastically altered the biochemical and geochemical cycles and balance of some heavy metals. Heavy metals are stable and persistent environmental contaminants since they cannot be degraded or destroyed. Therefore, they tend to accumulate in the soils and sediments. Excessive levels of metals in the marine environment can affect marine biota and pose risk to human consumers of sea food.

115. Metals and their compounds, both inorganic and organic, are released to the environment as a result of a variety of human activities. A wide range of metals and metallic compounds found in the marine environment pose risks to human health through the consumption of seafood where contaminant content and exposure are significant. Many metals are essential to life and only become toxic when exposures to biota become excessive (i.e., exceed some threshold for the introduction of adverse effects). While certain non-essential metals do not have explicit exposure thresholds for the introduction of effects, the nature of biological responses to metal exposure are a direct consequence of exposure and are defined through dose-effect relationships. This differs from the dose-response relationship associated with many synthetic organic contaminants and radionuclides where risk of adverse effects is assumed to be proportional to exposure. Accordingly, it is desirable to minimize such exposures. In contrast, the predominant challenge in the case of heavy metals is one of limiting exposure to levels that do not cause adverse effects.

116. The main anthropogenic sources of heavy metals are various industrial point sources, including present and former mining activities, foundries and smelters, and diffuse sources such as piping, constituents of products, combustion by-products, traffic, etc. Relatively volatile heavy metals and those that become attached to air-borne particles can be widely dispersed on very large scales. Heavy metals conveyed in aqueous and sedimentary transport (e.g., river run-off) enter the normal coastal biogeochemical cycle and are largely retained within near-shore and shelf regions.

2. Objective/proposed target

117. The objective/proposed target is to reduce and/or eliminate anthropogenic emissions and discharges in order to prevent, reduce and eliminate pollution caused by heavy metals.

3. Activities

(a) National actions, policies and measures

118. Actions, policies and measures of States within their national capacities should include:

(a)   Development, compilation and maintenance of inventories on significant sources, including natural sources, of priority heavy metals and their compounds and subsequent assessment of inputs and establishment of priority (geographic or subject) areas for action. They should also, where appropriate, take into account input from long-range transport of these pollutants;

(b)   Development of comprehensive national programmes of action for reduction and/or elimination of emissions and discharges of heavy metals from anthropogenic sources could include:

(i)   Targets, timetables and sector-specific measures, respecting the precautionary principle, best available techniques (BAT), best environmental practice (BEP) and integrated pollution prevention and control (IPPC);

(ii)   Fiscal and economic incentives and measures, including voluntary agreements to encourage reduction and/or elimination of emissions and discharges of heavy metals;

(iii) Appropriate regulatory measures and establishment of facilities for environmentally sound collection and disposal of hazardous wastes containing heavy metals taking into account the technical document on landfill agreed upon within the framework of the Basel Convention on the Control of Transboundary Movements of Hazardous Wastes and their Disposal;

(iv)   Promotion of technical solutions, such as the use of unleaded petrol and filter systems for smelters;

(v)   Means to ensure effective implementation of the programme of action;

(vi)   The establishment of cleaner production programmes in cooperation with industry;

(c)   Establishment of an environmental monitoring programme for heavy metals including the development of assessment criteria and the adoption of internationally accepted quality control and quality assurance procedures;

(d)   Formulation and implementation of awareness and education campaigns for the public and industry, to gain general recognition of the need to reduce and eliminate pollution by heavy metals and in particular to further reduce diffuse inputs through waste systems, including sewerage systems;

(e)   Establishment of information services for industry on technology and ways and means to prevent, reduce and eliminate pollution by heavy metals, including best environmental practice (BEP), best available techniques (BAT) and integrated pollution prevention and control (IPPC);

(f)   Promotion of private initiatives for the establishment and implementation of systems of internal environmental management within industry.

(b)   Regional actions

119. Regional actions should include:

(a) Encouraging existing regional agreements and programmes of action dealing with the prevention and elimination of pollution of the marine and coastal environment from land-based activities, to develop or continue to develop and implement programmes and measures to reduce and/or eliminate emissions and discharges of heavy metals and material containing these substances from the appropriate industrial sectors, products and groups of products;

(b) Development and implementation of monitoring programmes and regular assessments of levels, inputs and effects based on regionally agreed quality control and quality assurance procedures and harmonized assessment criteria;

(c) Encouraging States, including land-locked States, that are not already parties to regional seas arrangements regarding the protection of the marine and coastal environment from land-based activities to join such cooperation and to cooperate on bilateral and multilateral basis in the control of pollution from heavy metals;

(d) Promotion of cooperation in the development of cleaner production programmes.

(c) International actions

120. International actions should include:

(a) Strengthening and extending existing international quality assurance, standardization and classification mechanisms for heavy metals and their compounds to ensure that inventories and assessments are both reliable and intercomparable. Such existing mechanisms include those co-sponsored by IOC, UNEP and IAEA under the GIPME programme and the associated activities of the Marine Environmental Studies Laboratory in Monaco;

(b) Participation in a clearing-house for information on best available techniques (BAT), best environmental practice (BEP) and integrated pollution prevention and control (IPPC) to reduce and/or eliminate emissions and discharges of heavy metals;

(c) Cooperation with countries in need of assistance, through financial, scientific and technical support to maximize the best practicable control and reduction of anthropogenic emissions and discharges of heavy metals.

E. Oils (Hydrocarbons)

1. Basis for action

121. Many oils are liquid and gaseous hydrocarbons of geological origin. While some oils are naturally occurring, a significant proportion of those in the marine and coastal environment have been derived from anthropogenic sources. Most oils from land-based sources are refined petroleum products or their derivatives. Some oils are volatile or easily degraded and disappear rapidly from aquatic systems, but some may persist in the water column or in sediments. Oils may be toxic to aquatic life when ingested or absorbed through skin or gills, interfere with respiratory, can foul fur and feathers, smother aquatic communities, habitats, and bathing beaches, taint seafood and contaminate water supplies.

122. Land-based sources of oils include operational and accidental
discharges and emissions from oil exploration, exploitation, refining and
storage facilities; urban, industrial and agricultural run-off; transport;
and the inappropriate disposal of used lubricating oils. The main pathways
to the marine environment include atmospheric dispersion of volatile
fractions; storm sewers and sewage treatment works; and rivers. Impacts
from land-derived oils will be regional for the more volatile fractions,
and local (occasionally regional) for more refractory components.

2. Objective/proposed target

123. The objective is to prevent, reduce and/or eliminate anthropogenic
emissions and discharges in order to prevent, reduce and eliminate
pollution caused by oil.

3. Activities

(a) National actions, policies and measures

124. Actions, policies and measures of States within their national
capacities should include:

(a) Development, compilation and maintenance of inventories of
significant sources of oils, and subsequent assessment and establishment of
areas (geographic or substance) for action. They should also, where
appropriate, take into account inputs from long-range transport of these
pollutants;

(b) Development of comprehensive national programmes of action for
the reduction and/or elimination of priority emissions and discharges from
anthropogenic sources could include:

(i)   Targets, timetables, and sector-specific measures respecting the
      precautionary principle and applying best available techniques
      (BAT), best environmental practice (BEP), and integrated
      pollution prevention and control (IPPC);

(ii) Fiscal and economic incentives and measures, including voluntary
      agreements, to encourage reductions in emissions and discharges
      of oils, to encourage the recycling of used lubricating oils,
      and to encourage fuel-use efficiencies;

(iii) The provision of reception and recycling facilities for oily
      wastes;

(iv) Development of plans and measures to prevent accidental releases
      of oils, particularly from coastal refineries, storage
      facilities and waste reception facilities and of capacities to
      respond to such accidents;

(v)   Establishment of cleaner production programmes in cooperation
      with industry;

(vi) Means to ensure the effective implementation of the programme of
      action;

(c) Establishment of environmental monitoring programmes for oil,
including the development of assessment criteria and the adoption of
internationally accepted quality control and quality assurance procedures;

(d)   Formulation and implementation of awareness and education campaigns for the public and industry to gain general recognition of the need and ways to reduce emissions and discharges of oil, and, in particular, to further reduce diffuse inputs through waste systems, including sewerage systems;

(e)   Establishment of information services for industry on technology and ways and means to prevent, reduce and eliminate pollution by oil, including best environmental practice (BEP), best available techniques (BAT), and integrated pollution prevention and control (IPPC);

(f)   Promotion of private initiatives for the establishment and implementation of systems of internal environmental management within industry.

(b)   Regional actions

125.   Regional actions should include:

(a)   Encouraging existing regional agreements and programmes of action on the prevention and elimination of pollution of the marine and coastal environment from land-based activities, to develop or continue to develop and implement programmes and measures to reduce and/or eliminate emissions and discharges of oils from the appropriate industrial sectors, products and groups of products;

(b)   Adoption of programmes and measures on the development of harmonized assessment criteria and monitoring programmes based on regionally or internationally agreed quality control and quality assurance procedures;

(c)   Encouraging States, including land-locked States, that are not already parties to regional seas arrangements regarding the protection of the marine and coastal environment from land-based activities, to join such cooperation and to cooperate on bilateral and multilateral basis in the control of pollution from oil;

(d)   Promoting cooperation on the development of cleaner- production programmes, best available techniques, and best environmental practice;

(e)   Development of regional plans and measures to prevent accidental releases of oils, and development of regional capacities to respond to such accidents;

(f)   Where appropriate, the provision of regional reception and recycling facilities for oily wastes.

(c)   International actions

126.   International actions should include:

(a)   Strengthening and extending existing international quality assurance, standardization and classification mechanisms for oil, oil products and their constituents to ensure that inventories and assessments are both reliable and intercomparable. Such existing mechanisms include those co-sponsored by IOC, UNEP, and IAEA under the GIPME programme, and the associated activities of the Marine Environmental Studies Laboratory in Monaco;

(b)   Participation in a clearing-house for information on best available techniques (BAT), best environmental practice (BEP), and integrated pollution prevention and control (IPPC) to reduce and/or eliminate emissions and discharges of oil;

(c)   Cooperation with countries in need of assistance through financial, technical, and scientific support, to maximize the best practicable control and reduction in emissions and discharges of oil.

F.   Nutrients

1.   Basis for action

127.   Eutrophication can result from augmentation of nutrient inputs to coastal and marine areas as a consequence of human activities. In general, such eutrophication is usually confined to the vicinity of coastal discharges but, because of both the multiplicity of such discharges and regional atmospheric transport of nutrients, such affected coastal areas can be extensive.

128.   The effects of the enhanced mobilization of nutrients are enhanced productivity but these can also result in changes in species diversity, excessive algal growth, dissolved oxygen reductions and associated fish kills and, it is suspected, the increased prevalence or frequency of toxic algal blooms.

2.   Objective/proposed target

129.   The objective/proposed target is:

(a)   To identify, in broad terms, marine areas where nutrient inputs are causing or are likely to cause pollution, directly or indirectly;

(b)   To reduce nutrient inputs into the areas identified;

(c)   To reduce the number of marine areas where eutrophication is evident;

(d)   To protect and, where appropriate, to restore areas of natural denitrification.

3.   Activities

(a)   National actions, policies and measures

130.   Actions, policies and measures of States within their capacities should include:

(a)   Identification of-areas where nutrient inputs are likely to cause pollution, directly or indirectly;

(b)   Identification of point sources and diffuse sources of nutrient inputs into these areas;

(c)   Identification of areas where changes in anthropogenic nutrient inputs are causing or are likely to cause pollution, either directly or indirectly, and prioritization of these areas for action;

(d)   Adoption of appropriate cost-effective policy instruments, including regulatory measures, economic instruments and voluntary agreements, to control anthropogenic sources of nutrients affecting these areas, including:

(i)   Activities related to sewage treatment and management mentioned in paragraph 97 (b) above;

(ii)   Minimization of the release of nutrients by the use of best environmental practice (BEP) in agriculture and aquaculture operations;

(iii) Minimization of the release of nutrients by the use of best environmental practice (BEP), best available techniques (BAT) and integrated pollution prevention and control (IPPC) in industrial operations;

(iv)   Formulation and implementation of awareness and information campaigns for the adoption of appropriate agricultural techniques, including balanced fertilization and ecological agriculture, to minimize nutrient losses from agricultural activities;

(v)   Introduction of measures to reduce inputs of nutrients via atmospheric deposition from transportation, industrial plants and agriculture;

(e)   Strengthening the capacities of local authorities to take account of likely impacts of inputs of nutrients from agriculture and urban development in carrying out their functions of planning and controlling land-use and development;

(f)   Establishment or improvement, as appropriate, of monitoring of all aspects of eutrophication;

(g)   Promotion of scientific research on the suspected linkages between eutrophication and toxic algal blooms;

(h)   Development and adoption of programmes to protect and, where appropriate, restore habitats acting as natural sinks for nutrients such as wetlands.

(b)   Regional actions

131.   Regional actions should include:

(a)   Establishment of common criteria for the identification of existing and potential problem areas including possible solutions with regard to eutrophication;

(b)   Identification of marine areas in the region where nutrient inputs are causing or are likely to cause pollution, directly or indirectly;

(c)   Identification of areas for priority actions;

(d)   Establishment of uniform approaches to the calculation of anthropogenic nutrient inputs to the aquatic environment from agriculture and other sources, as appropriate, with the aim of improving the estimation of these inputs;

(e)   Development and implementation of programmes and measures for
reducing nutrient inputs from anthropogenic activities to areas where these
inputs are causing or are likely to cause pollution directly or indirectly
and, where the agricultural sector is a predominant source, to pay
particular attention to that sector and the implementation of measures
identified for it;

(f)   Establishment of mechanisms for assessing the effectiveness of
the measures taken to reduce nutrient inputs to the aquatic environment
from both point and diffuse sources;

(g)   Development of strategies for reducing eutrophication in areas
already affected and those susceptible to being affected.

(c)   International actions

132.   International actions should include:

(a)   Participation in a clearing-house for providing information
about best environmental practice and access to best available techniques
to reduce and/or eliminate causes of anthropogenic eutrophication;

(b)   Strengthening of international programmes for enhancing capacity
for:

(i)   Identification of areas where inputs of nutrients are causing or
      are likely to cause pollution, directly or indirectly;

(ii)   Nutrient control and removal techniques;

(iii)   Application of best environmental practice in aquaculture and
        agriculture;

(c)   Cooperation with countries in need of assistance, through
financial, technological and scientific support, in developing and
implementing practices which minimize releases of nutrients to the
environment, including environmentally sound land-use techniques, planning
and practices;

(d)   Provision of forums for establishing criteria for determining
the circumstances in which nutrients are likely to cause pollution,
directly or indirectly;

(e)   Maintaining existing international quality assurance and quality
control procedures relevant to eutrophication.

G.   Sediment mobilization

1.   Basis for action

133.   Natural sedimentation and siltation are important in the development
and maintenance of numerous coastal habitats.   Habitats requiring sediment
input include coastal wetlands, lagoons, estuaries and mangroves.
Reduction in natural rates of sedimentation can compromise the integrity of
these habitats, as can excessive sediment loads, which may bury benthic
communities and threaten sensitive habitats such as coral reefs, mangroves,
seagrass beds, and rocky substrates.

134.   Contaminated sediments, whether they are fresh inputs or dredged, may
also lead to pollution, the latter through resuspension or improper
disposal.

135. Anthropogenic modifications to sediment mobilization and sedimentation are made by, _inter alia_, construction activities, forestry operations, agricultural practices, mining practices, hydrological modifications, dredging activities, and coastal erosion. Effects are generally local in nature, but transboundary implications may occur in some areas where major river systems form a common border and where littoral currents carry inputs across international boundaries.

2. Objective/proposed target

136. The objective/proposed target is to reduce, control and prevent the degradation of the marine environment due to changes in coastal erosion and siltation caused by human activities.

3. Activities

(a) **National actions, policies and measures**

137. Actions, policies and measures of States within their capacities should include:

(a) Development and implementation of environmentally sound land-use practices to control sediment discharges to watercourses and estuaries which cause degradation of the marine environment;

(b) Establishment of measures to control, reduce and prevent coastal erosion and siltation due to anthropogenic factors such as land-use, including coastal mining and construction practices, while ensuring that natural erosion supplying sedimentary habitats is not impeded;

(c) Introduction of watershed management and land-use practices to prevent, control and reduce degradation of the marine environment due to anthropogenic changes in sediment loads and contamination of sediments;

(d) Application of practices developed under existing international regulations to prevent marine pollution/degradation from dumping of dredged material and associated dredging operations;

(e) Establishment or improvement of monitoring of sediment transport to the marine environment and associated sedimentation patterns and rates;

(f) Application of environmentally sound management and storage practices for polluted dredged material;

(g) Adoption of measures to minimize changes to natural erosion, sediment transport and sedimentation resulting from the construction of barriers and barrages.

(b) **Regional actions**

138. Regional actions should include:

(a) Promotion of regional cooperation, where appropriate, for the establishment of programmes and priority measures to control anthropogenic modifications to sedimentation/siltation;

(b) Development or enhancement, as appropriate, of regional programmes for the exchange of information on technology and techniques and experience regarding sedimentation/siltation.

(c)   International actions

139.   International actions should include:

(a)   Development of methodologies to reduce, control and prevent
adverse effects of sedimentation/siltation, including the formulation of
mechanisms for determining changes in sediment mobilization and transport,
incorporating relevant quality assurance and standardization procedures;

(b)   Participation in a clearing-house for providing information on
technologies, measures and experiences regarding sedimentation/siltation;

(c)   Cooperation with countries in need of assistance, through
financial, scientific and technical support, in the development and
implementation of environmentally sound land-use techniques, planning and
practices to reduce, control and prevent the negative effects of changes in
erosion and siltation rates.

H.   Litter

1.   Basis for action

140.   Litter threatens marine life through entanglement, suffocation and
ingestion and is widely recognized to degrade the visual amenities of
marine and coastal areas with negative effects on tourism and general
aesthetics.   Litter is any persistent manufactured or processed solid
material which is discarded, disposed of, or abandoned in the marine and
coastal environment, sometimes called marine debris.   Litter in the marine
environment can also destroy coastal habitats and in some situations
interfere with biological production in coastal areas.

141.   Litter entering the marine and coastal environment has multiple
sources.   Sources include poorly managed or illegal waste dumps adjacent to
rivers and coastal areas, windblown litter from coastal communities, resin
pellets used as industrial feedstocks, and litter that is channelled to the
marine and coastal environment through municipal stormwater systems and
rivers.   Marine litter is also caused by dumping of garbage into the marine
and coastal environment by municipal authorities as well as recreational
and commercial vessels.

142.   While international action has been taken to prevent the discharge of
plastics and other persistent wastes from vessels, it has been estimated
that approximately 80 per cent of persistent wastes originate from land.
Floatable litter is known to travel considerable distances with regional
and sometimes broader implications.   Resin pellets used as industrial
feedstock circulate and deposit on oceanic scales.

143.   Uncontrolled burning of litter containing plastics may generate
significant quantities of POPs, metals and hydrocarbons which can reach the
marine and coastal environment.

2.   Objective/proposed target

144.   The objective/proposed target is:

(a)   To establish controlled and environmentally sound facilities for
receiving, collecting, handling and disposing of litter from coastal area
communities;

(b)   To reduce significantly the amount of litter reaching the marine
and coastal environment by the prevention or reduction of the generation of

solid waste and improvements in its management, including collection and recycling of litter.

145. In this context, paragraph 21.39 of Agenda 21 states:

"The overall objective of this programme is to provide health-protecting environmentally safe waste collection and disposal services to all people. Governments, according to their capacities and available resources and with the cooperation of the United Nations and other relevant organizations, as appropriate, should:

"(a)   By the year 2000, have the necessary technical, financial and human resource capacity to provide waste collection services commensurate with needs;

"(b)   By the year 2025, provide all urban populations with adequate waste services;

"(c)   By the year 2025, ensure that full urban waste service coverage is maintained and sanitation coverage achieved in all rural areas."

3. **Activities**

(a) **National actions, policies and measures**

146. Actions, policies and measures of States within their capacities should include:

(a) Introduction of appropriate measures - which could include regulatory measures and/or economic instruments and voluntary agreements - to encourage reduction in the generation of solid wastes;

(b) Installation of garbage containers for citizens in public areas for the purposes of appropriate collection and/or recycling;

(c) Establishment and ensuring the proper operation of solid-waste-management facilities on shore for wastes from all sources, including shipping and harbour wastes;

(d) Formulation and implementation of awareness and education campaigns for the general public, industry, and municipal authorities, as well as recreational and commercial vessels, on the need to reduce waste generation and the need for environmentally sound disposal and reuse;

(e) Increasing local planning and management capacity to avoid location of waste-dump sites near coastlines or waterways or to avoid litter escape to the marine and coastal environment;

(f) Formulation and implementation of improved management programmes in small rural communities to prevent litter escape into rivers and the marine and coastal environment;

(g) Establishment of campaigns and/or permanent services for collecting solid wastes that pollute coastal and marine areas.

(b) **Regional actions**

147. Regional actions should include the promotion of regional cooperation for the exchange of information on practices and experiences regarding waste management, recycling and reuse, and cleaner production, as well as regional arrangements for solid waste management.

(c)   International actions

148. International actions should include:

(a)   Participation in a clearing-house on waste management, recycling and reuse, and waste-minimization technologies;

(b)   Cooperation with countries in need of assistance, through financial, scientific and technological support, in developing and establishing environmentally sound waste-disposal methods and alternatives to disposal.

I. Physical alterations and destruction of habitats

1. Basis for action

149. The increase of populations and economic activities in coastal areas is leading to an expansion of construction and alterations to coastal areas and waters. Excavation, oil and gas exploration and exploitation, mining, such as sand and aggregate extraction, the building of ports and marinas and building of coastal defences and other activities linked to urban expansion are giving rise to alterations of coral reefs, shorelands, beachfronts and the seafloor. Important habitats are being destroyed. Wetlands are being transformed into agricultural lands and through coastal development. Tourism, unrestricted and uncontrolled aquaculture, clearance of mangroves and destructive fishing practices, such as the use of dynamite and chemicals, are also causing the physical destruction of important habitats. The introduction of alien species can also have serious effects upon marine ecosystem integrity. Spawning grounds, nurseries and feeding grounds of major living marine resources of crucial importance to world food security are being destroyed. This destruction of habitat exacerbates overharvesting of these living marine resources leading to a growing risk that they are being depleted. This is an increasing threat to the food security of coastal populations, in particular in developing countries.

150. The damming of river systems can result in upstream sedimentation, possible changes in estuarine conditions and interference with fish migration. These adversely affect biological diversity and biological productivity. The practice of saltwinning from saltpan construction in coastal areas can also affect salt concentration levels and biological diversity.

2. Objective/proposed target

151. The objective/proposed target is to:

(a)   Safeguard the ecosystem function, maintain the integrity and biological diversity of habitats which are of major socio-economic and ecological interest through integrated management of coastal areas;

(b)   Where practicable, restore marine and coastal habitats that have been adversely affected by anthropogenic activities.

3. Activities

(a)   National actions, policies and measures

152. Actions, policies and measures of States within their capacities should include the formulation, adoption and implementation of programmes for integrated coastal area management, in accordance with Agenda 21, chapter 17, programme area A. These programmes should include, where appropriate:

(a)   The identification of habitats of major socio-economic and ecological significance such as spawning grounds, breeding grounds and nurseries of marine living resources which guarantee food security of large coastal populations;

(b)   Conducting assessments that involve the use of community-based participatory approaches, to identify land-based activities that threaten physical degradation or destruction of key habitats;

(c)   Encouraging economic and social sectors whose activities may lead to physical degradation or destruction of such habitats to adjust those activities so as to reduce or avoid such effects;

(d)   The establishment of marine protected areas in coastal areas to maintain the integrity and biological diversity of their habitats;

(e)   Restoration of coastal habitats that have suffered decline or loss as a result of human activities.

(b)   <u>Regional actions</u>

153.   Regional actions should include formulation and adoption of regional-scale approaches to safeguarding critical habitats such as:

(a)   Regional systems of marine and coastal protected areas;

(b)   Regional programmes of action and protocols on important species and habitats;

(c)   Regional approaches to management of important living marine resources, in particular where the spatial scales of their life-stages transcend national boundaries;

(d)   Cooperation between regional marine environment programmes and regional fisheries organizations.

(c)   <u>International actions</u>

154.   International actions include:

(a)   The coordination and formulation of guidelines for the preservation of habitat and normal ecosystem functions in coastal areas, particularly in the context of integrated coastal area management.   Such activities should take advantage of and be consistent with existing international mechanisms and agreements;

(b)   Participation in a clearing-house for providing information on technologies and experiences regarding coastal-zone-management methodology;

(c)   Cooperation with countries in need of assistance, through financial, scientific and technical support, in the development and implementation of environmentally sound land-use techniques, planning and practices to prevent and control the negative effects of physical alterations.

Appendix

ILLUSTRATIVE LIST OF FUNDING SOURCES AND MECHANISMS

The possible funding sources and mechanisms that may be appropriate and which will need to be considered include:

A. <u>Financing sources internal to the State concerned</u>

1. <u>User charges</u>: User charges ensure that those who benefit immediately and directly from the provision of a service contribute towards the costs of that service;

2. <u>Charging the polluter</u>: Those who impose burdens on the aquatic environment (for example, by discharging waste water) can be required to contribute to the external costs of their actions;

3. <u>Local taxes</u>: A municipality, or other organized community, that benefits from improvements in water management, can contribute to the costs of those improvements from local taxes, either by a specific tax for that purpose or by a contribution from general tax revenues;

4. <u>National taxes</u>: Where the costs of some local improvement in water management would bear unreasonably on the local community concerned, or where the improvement benefits the public at large, the national budget can contribute part or all of the cost;

5. <u>Private-sector borrowing</u>: Where a project requires substantial initial investments, the public authority responsible can borrow the capital cost from national private-sector financial institutions, with the resulting loan-charges being serviced from any of the foregoing sources;

6. <u>National revolving funds</u>: A fund can be set up, financed from either any of the foregoing sources, from external financing sources or mechanisms or from a mix of any of these, from which advances can be made to finance project costs. Subsequent repayments from the projects are then used to refill the fund to permit new advances;

7. <u>Private-sector participation</u>: Private-sector firms can take responsibility for all, or parts, of the operation of a project instead of simply providing funds; this may involve:

    (a) Improving and/or operating the assets necessary for a service ("the service assets"), which remain in public ownership;

    (b) Providing and operating the service assets on their own account for a specific period, after which the assets revert to public ownership;

    (c) Taking over ownership of the service assets and then improving and operating them on their own account, either for a specific period or permanently;

B. <u>External financing sources and mechanisms</u>

8. <u>International private-sector institutions</u>: Loans may be taken out from international private-sector financial institutions in

the same way as from equivalent national institutions; in the same way, private-sector participation can equally be organized through international companies;

9. Export credit agencies: These are a source of shorter-term project financing, especially for specialized equipment;

10. Grant and concessionary assistance: Part of the costs of creating service assets or the necessary management infrastructure may be met by grants or loans, including loans of concessionary terms, from donor States or multilateral aid agencies, associations and programmes. Separate arrangements often exist to finance the acquisition of the "know-how" needed to plan and organize projects. In particular, GEF supports, by means of limited grant assistance up to the amount of the agreed incremental cost of global environmental benefits, actions consistent with its operational strategy in four focal areas: climate change, biological diversity, international waters and ozone-layer depletion;

11. Multilateral loans: The World Bank and regional development banks can provide loan finance for larger projects and technical assistance directly, and for smaller projects through financial intermediaries in the borrowing country, normally at rates lower than those obtainable on the commercial market;

12. Multilateral equity funds: Certain projects are more appropriately supported by means of equity capital than by interest-bearing loans. Where equity participation from the private-sector market is not available or not appropriate, certain public-sector financing agencies can provide support of this kind;

13. Debt-for-equity swaps and eco-conversion programmes: Creditors agree to convert the debts owed to them into local funds to be applied for environmentally beneficial expenditure;

14. Foundation grants: Many privately or publicly endowed foundations may use their resources to support innovative approaches to environmental management or the development of human resources;

15. Twinning arrangements: Arrangements between authorities, either central or local, in one country and their counterparts in another, or analogous arrangements between regional seas organizations, have proved to be an important mechanism for the effective and sustained transfer of experience between parties with similar interests and concerns.

- - - - - -

2. INSTITUTIONAL ARRANGEMENTS FOR THE IMPLEMENTATION OF THE GLOBAL PROGRAMME OF ACTION FOR THE PROTECTION OF THE MARINE ENVIRONMENT FROM LAND-BASED ACTIVITIES - UNGA RESOLUTION

Doc. no.: A/Res.51/189   Date: 16 December 1996

Recalling the relevant provisions of Agenda 21, 100/ in particular chapters 17, 33, 34, 38 and other related chapters, and the Rio Declaration on Environment and Development, 101/

Recalling also its resolution 50/110 of 20 December 1995 on the report of the Governing Council of the United Nations Environment Programme, in which it endorsed, inter alia, Governing Council decision 18/31 on the protection of the marine environment from land-based activities,

Noting the successful conclusion of the Intergovernmental Conference to Adopt a Global Programme of Action for the Protection of the Marine Environment from Land-based Activities, which was held in Washington, D.C., from 23 October to 3 November 1995,

Having considered the Washington Declaration on Protection of the Marine Environment from Land-based Activities 102/ and the Global Programme of Action for the Protection of the Marine Environment from Land-based Activities, 103/ as well as the proposal of the United Nations Environment Programme on institutional arrangements and implementation of the Global Programme of Action and relevant recommendations of the Commission on Sustainable Development,

1. Endorses the Washington Declaration on Protection of the Marine Environment from Land-based Activities and the Global Programme of Action for the Protection of the Marine Environment from Land-based Activities;

2. Stresses the need for States to take the necessary measures for the implementation of the Global Programme of Action at the national and, as appropriate, the regional and international levels;

3. Also stresses the need for States to take action for the formal endorsement by each competent international organization of those parts of the Global Programme of Action that are relevant to their mandates and to accord appropriate priority to the implementation of the Global Programme of Action in the work programme of each organization;

100/   Report of the United Nations Conference on Environment and Development, Rio de Janeiro, 3-14 June 1992, vol. I, Resolutions Adopted by the Conference (United Nations publication, Sales No. E.93.I.8 and corrigendum), resolution 1, annex II.

101/   Ibid., annex I.

102/   A/51/116, annex I, appendix II.

103/   Ibid., annex II.

4. <u>Further stresses</u> the need for States to take such action at the next meetings of the governing bodies of the United Nations Environment Programme, the United Nations Development Programme, the United Nations Centre for Human Settlements (Habitat), the Food and Agriculture Organization of the United Nations, the World Health Organization, the International Maritime Organization, the International Atomic Energy Agency, the International Labour Organization and the United Nations Industrial Development Organization and in the Intergovernmental Oceanographic Commission of the United Nations Educational, Scientific and Cultural Organization and the relevant bodies of the International Monetary Fund and the World Bank, as well as in other competent international and regional organizations within and outside the United Nations system;

5. <u>Further stresses</u> the need for international cooperation, as outlined in sections IV.A and B of the Global Programme of Action, in capacity-building, technology transfer and cooperation, and the mobilization of financial resources, including support, in particular for developing countries, especially the least developed countries, countries with economies in transition and small island developing States, and to this end calls upon bilateral donors and international, regional and subregional financial institutions and mechanisms, including the Global Environment Facility, and other competent development and financial institutions:

(a) To ensure that their programmes give appropriate priority for country-driven projects aimed at the implementation of the Global Programme of Action;

(b) To assist with capacity-building in the preparation and implementation of national programmes and in identifying ways and means of funding them;

(c) To improve their coordination so as to enhance the delivery of financial and other support;

6. <u>Invites</u> non-governmental organizations and major groups to initiate and strengthen their actions to facilitate and support the effective implementation of the Global Programme of Action;

7. <u>Requests</u> the Executive Director of the United Nations Environment Programme to prepare, for the consideration of the Governing Council at its nineteenth session, specific proposals on:

(a) The role of the United Nations Environment Programme in the implementation of the Global Programme of Action, including the relevant role of its Regional Seas Programme and Freshwater Unit;

(b) Arrangements for secretariat support to the Global Programme of Action;

(c) Modalities for periodic intergovernmental review of progress in implementing the Global Programme of Action;

8. <u>Calls upon</u> the United Nations Environment Programme, within its available resources, and with the aid of voluntary contributions from States for this purpose, to take expeditious action to provide for the establishment and implementation of the clearing-house mechanism referred to in the Global Programme of Action, and requests the Executive Director of the United Nations Environment Programme to prepare and submit to the Governing Council at its nineteenth session specific proposals on, <u>inter alia</u>:

(a) The establishment of an inter-organizational group to develop the basic design and structure of the clearing-house data directory and its linkages to information delivery mechanisms;

(b) The means of linking the inter-organizational group to ongoing work within the United Nations system on the identification of and access to relevant databases and the comparability of data;

(c) The outline of a pilot project on the development of the clearing-house's source category component on sewage, to be implemented in partnership with the World Health Organization;

9. <u>Calls upon</u> States, in relation to the clearing-house mechanism, to take action in the governing bodies of relevant intergovernmental organizations and programmes so as to ensure that those organizations and programmes take the lead in coordinating the development of the clearing-house mechanism with respect to the following source categories, which are listed in conjunction with the relevant organization(s) and/or programme(s) but not in order of priority:

(a) Sewage - the World Health Organization;

(b) Persistent organic pollutants - the Inter-Organization Programme for the Sound Management of Chemicals, the International Programme on Chemical Safety and the Intergovernmental Forum on Chemical Safety;

(c) Heavy metals - the United Nations Environment Programme in cooperation with the Inter-Organization Programme for the Sound Management of Chemicals;

(d) Radioactive substances - the International Atomic Energy Agency;

(e) Nutrients and sediment mobilization - the Food and Agriculture Organization of the United Nations;

(f) Oils (hydrocarbons) and litter - the International Maritime Organization;

(g) Physical alterations, including habitat modification and destruction of areas of concern - the United Nations Environment Programme;

10. Decides to determine, at its special session to be held in June 1997 in accordance with its resolution 50/113 of 20 December 1995, specific arrangements for integrating the outcomes of periodic intergovernmental reviews, as envisaged in paragraph 7 (c) above, in the future work of the Commission on Sustainable Development related to the monitoring of the implementation of and follow-up to Agenda 21, in particular chapter 17.

3. CONVENTION ON BIOLOGICAL DIVERSITY - UNGA RESOLUTION

Doc. no.: A/Res.51/182   Date: 16 December 1996

The General Assembly,

Reaffirming its resolutions 49/117 of 19 December 1994 and 50/111 of 20 December 1995 on the Convention on Biological Diversity, and resolution 49/119 of 19 December 1994 on the International Day for Biological Diversity,

Recalling the provisions of the Convention on Biological Diversity, 64/

Also recalling Agenda 21, 65/ particularly its chapter 15, on the conservation of biological diversity, and related chapters,

Further recalling the recommendations made at the third session of the Commission on Sustainable Development on the review of chapter 15 of Agenda 21 on the conservation of biological diversity, 66/

Deeply concerned by the continued loss of the world's biological diversity and, on the basis of the provisions of the Convention, reaffirming the commitment to the conservation of biological diversity, the sustainable use of its components, and the fair and equitable sharing of benefits arising out of the utilization of genetic resources,

Emphasizing that the Convention on Biological Diversity is an important instrument for achieving sustainable development, taking into account its three objectives,

Notes with satisfaction that most States and one regional economic integration organization have ratified or acceded to the Convention,

Taking note with appreciation of the generous offer of the Government of Argentina to host the third session of the Conference of the Parties to the Convention at Buenos Aires from 4 to 15 November 1996,

Encouraged by the work carried out to date under the Convention,

---

64/   See United Nations Environment Programme, Convention on Biological Diversity (Environmental Law and Institution Programme Activity Centre), June 1992.

65/   Report of the United Nations Conference on Environment and Development, Rio de Janeiro, 3-14 June 1992 (United Nations publication, Sales No. E.93.I.8 and corrigendum), vol. I: Resolutions Adopted by the Conference, resolution 1, annex II.

66/   See Official Records of the Economic and Social Council, 1995, Supplement No. 12 (E/1995/32), chap. I, para. 230 (i)).

1. Welcomes the results of the second meeting of the Conference of the Parties to the Convention on Biological Diversity, held in Jakarta, Indonesia from 6 to 17 November 1995, as reflected in the report of the meetings, 67/ submitted in accordance with General Assembly resolution 50/111, and in that context reaffirms the need to take concrete action to fulfil the three objectives of the Convention, and takes note of the Jakarta Mandate on Marine and Coastal Biological Diversity, which proposes a framework for global action; 68/

2. Takes note of the results of the second meeting of the Convention's Subsidiary Body on Scientific, Technical and Technological Advice, held at the seat of the secretariat of the Convention in Montreal from 2 to 6 September 1996, and of the work carried out at the first meeting of the Open-ended Ad Hoc Working Group on Biosafety, held in Aarhus, Denmark from 22 to 26 July 1996;

3. Encourages those States that have not yet ratified the Convention to do so;

4. Recognizes that States Parties have agreed to provide financial resources for the implementation of the Convention in accordance with article 20, paragraphs 1 and 2, of the Convention;

5. Invites the Executive Secretary of the Convention to provide to the General Assembly at its special session in 1997, inter alia, information on experience gained under the Convention to date, and information on effective arrangements for the coordination of activities related to the objectives of the Convention;

6. Welcomes the work being carried out under the Convention to enhance cooperation with the Commission on Sustainable Development and biodiversity-related conventions, and invites the Conference of the Parties to the Convention to take into account the outcome of the 1997 special session at its fourth meeting, when considering ways of promoting greater cooperation with the United Nations system and the international community in relation to activities relevant to the objectives of the Convention;

7. Invites the Executive Secretary of the Convention on Biological Diversity to report to the General Assembly at its fifty-second session, and pending the outcome of the 1997 special session, to report to the Assembly on the results of future meetings of the Conference of the Parties to the Convention;

8. Decides to include in the provisional agenda of its fifty-second session the item entitled "Convention on Biological Diversity".

67/   A/51/312, annex.

68/   Ibid., appendix.

UNITED NATIONS CONFERENCE ON TRADE
AND DEVELOPMENT
(UNCTAD)

DOCUMENTS REPRODUCED IN WHOLE OR IN PART:

UNCTAD SECRETARIAT

JOINT UNCTAD/IMO INTERGOVERNMENTAL GROUP OF EXPERTS ON MARITIME LIENS AND MORTGAGES AND RELATED SUBJECTS, 9TH SESSION, GENEVA, 2 DECEMBER 1996

DOCUMENTS NOT REPRODUCED:

STANDING COMMITTEE ON DEVELOPING SERVICES SECTORS: FOSTERING COMPETITIVE SERVICES SECTORS IN DEVELOPING COUNTRIES - SHIPPING INTERGOVERNMENTAL GROUP OF EXPERTS ON PORTS, 2ND SESSION, GENEVA, 18-22 MARCH 1996

1. COOPERATION AMONG DEVELOPING COUNTRIES IN THE FIELD OF SHIPPING, PORTS AND MULTIMODAL TRANSPORT: ADDENDUM - NOTE BY THE UNCTAD SECRETARIAT

Doc. no.: UNCTAD/SDD/SHIP/1/Add.1   Date: 15 March 1996

CONTENTS

INTRODUCTION

(i)   Paragraph C.4 of the work programme of the Standing Committee on
       Developing Services Sectors: Fostering Competitive Services Sectors in
       Developing Countries (Shipping) provides for the Standing Committee to
       "identify and examine possible activities and policies aimed at enhancing
       cooperation in the field of shipping, ports and multimodal transport, as
       a means of stimulating the development of the maritime transport sector
       in developing countries and countries in transition;".

(ii)   In response to this request, the UNCTAD secretariat had prepared document
       UNCTAD/SDD/SHIP/1, issued on 24 January 1994, reporting on the experience
       of a number of intergovernmental organizations in cooperative problem-
       solving in the field of shipping, ports and multimodal transport. The
       resulting document was available to the Standing Committee for discussion
       at its second session.

(iii) The present addendum to UNCTAD/SDD/SHIP/1 contains additional replies
       received by the secretariat to a follow-up letter addressed to
       intergovernmental organizations of developing countries in all regions,

dealing with maritime and related transport either exclusively or in the context of more embracing integration programmes. The secretariat, in its request, particularly referred to the need for information on the experience in implementing cooperative solutions to shipping problems, which could possibly also serve as a guide to other organizations in their search for enhanced effectiveness.

(iv) The document contains the replies received from the Common Market for Eastern and Southern Africa (COMESA) and the Southern Africa Transport and Communications Commission (SATCC) in Africa, as well as the Caribbean Community (CARICOM) and the Cartagena Agreement (Andean Group) in Latin America.

Part One

COOPERATIVE ARRANGEMENTS IN AFRICA

A. Common Market for Eastern and Southern Africa (COMESA)

1. Short history of COMESA

1.   The Common Market for Eastern and Southern Africa (COMESA) was launched on 8 December 1994 in Lilongwe, Malawi. The establishment of the COMESA was a transformation of the Preferential Trade Area for Eastern and Southern African States (PTA). The transformation of the PTA into COMESA is a step-by-step approach which will lead our region to an economic community.

2.   The Treaty establishing the PTA was signed on 21 December 1981 as the first step towards higher forms of regional economic cooperation and integration. To that end, it was provided in the Treaty that 10 years after the entry into force of the PTA Treaty, measures should be taken to transform PTA into a Common Market and eventually an economic community for Eastern and Southern Africa. The PTA Treaty came into force in September 1982.

3.   The following 20 countries comprise the COMESA membership: Angola, Burundi, Comoros, Eritrea, Ethiopia, Kenya, Lesotho, Madagascar, Malawi, Mauritius, Mozambique, Namibia, Rwanda, Swaziland, Sudan, United Republic of Tanzania, Uganda, Zaire, Zambia, Zimbabwe. Botswana, Djibouti, Seychelles, Somalia and South Africa are eligible for COMESA membership.

4.   One of the objectives of the COMESA is to promote joint development in all fields of economic activity (Trade and Customs cooperation; Transport and Communications; Industry and Energy; Monetary Affairs and Finance, Agriculture, Economic and Social Development) and the joint adoption of macro-economic policies and programmes to raise the standard of living of its peoples and to fasten closer relations among its member States.

5.   With regard to shipping, the objective of the COMESA is to establish a common maritime policy and create/strengthen economically and financially viable shipping companies through regional cooperation.

2. Administrative arrangements

6.   The policy and operational issues are discussed and approved through the following main established organs of the COMESA:

(a) The Authority

7.   The Authority is the supreme policy organ responsible for the general policy and direction and control of the performance of the executive functions of the COMESA and the achievement of its aims and objectives. The Authority is composed of Heads of States and Government of all member States.

(b) The Council of Ministers

8.   The Council of Ministers of the COMESA is the second highest organ of the organization. This organ consists of such Ministers as may be designated by each member State. The role of the Council is to take decisions on operational policy and technical matters of the organization. The Council has to advise or make recommendations to the Authority on policy matters aimed at the efficient and harmonious functioning and development of the COMESA.

(c)   The Intergovernmental Committee of Experts

9.   The Intergovernmental Committee of Experts consists of such Permanent or Principal Secretaries as may be designated by each member State. The Committee is responsible for the development of programmes and action plans in all the sectors of cooperation and submits from time to time either on its own initiative or upon the request of the Council reports and recommendations to the Council.

(d)   The Technical Committees

10.   The Technical Committees are 12 and the Committee on Transport and Communication is one of them. These Technical Committees are responsible for the implementation of the Treaty. To this end the Technical Committee are responsible for the setting up of the implementation Action Plan and monitoring the status of its execution.

(e)   The secretariat

11.   The secretariat which is headed by the Secretary-General is responsible for advising, servicing and assisting the organs of the COMESA in the performance of their functions.

3.   Areas covered by COMESA in the field of shipping, ports and multimodal transport

(a)   Shipping

12.   The COMESA Treaty provides for promotion of the coordination and harmonization of maritime transport policies and the eventual establishment of a common maritime transport policy in the COMESA region. The Treaty urges the member States to take measures to ratify or accede to international conventions on maritime transport and to establish a harmonious traffic organization system for the optional ease of maritime transport services. Countries are requested to coordinate measures with respect to, and cooperate in the maintenance of the safety of maritime transport services. The member States are requested to encourage their respective national shipping lines to form subregional associations. They are also requested to review their national maritime legislations in accordance with the existing international maritime conventions.

13.   In the COMESA region, only five countries (Burundi, Lesotho, Malawi, Rwanda and Zimbabwe) are not participating actively in the shipping industry. The other member countries are coastal countries or have national shipping companies or both. But the shipping market share by COMESA countries is insignificant. It is therefore not surprising that the region is a net importer of shipping services and this is graphically illustrated by the deficit on current accounts on services.

(b)   Ports

14.   The COMESA Treaty provides for promotion of the development of efficient and profitable sea port services and for promotion of cooperation among port authorities in the management and operations of ports and maritime transport so as to facilitate the efficient movement of traffic between the member States. The Treaty urges the member States to install and maintain efficient cargo handling equipment, cargo storage facilities and general operations and train related manpower.

15.   Some COMESA member States have been able to mobilize external financing from donor countries for port rehabilitation and development. Essentially, this work has entailed reconverting existing berths into dry cargo container and break bulk berths. Additionally modern port handling equipment has been installed.

16.   To sustain this ongoing investment and improvements in port productivity, COMESA has undertaken to assist port authorities:

-      to develop management policies for the maintenance and procurement of cargo handling equipment and other machinery;

-      to commercialize their services and to be run as any private enterprises;

-      to embark on a continuous human resource development because of rapid changes in maritime technology and practices;

(c)   Multimodal transport

17.   The COMESA Treaty provides for harmonization and simplification of regulations, goods classification, procedures and documentation required for multimodal inter-States transport. The member States are requested to take measures to ratify or accede to international conventions on multimodal transport and containerization and take such steps as necessary to implement them.

18.   In the COMESA region, the past 15 years has seen a tremendous growth in containerized traffic which is the basis for multimodal transport. Containerization has resulted in rapid technological changes in the transport industry which is reflected through massive investments in port infrastructure and equipment and land-based transportation systems. Port investment has entailed the conversion of general cargo berths into container berths, installation of ship to short cranes with increased outreach. The investment in landward transportation includes the introduction of container trains, vehicle container trailers, fixed and mobile cranes at intermodal exchange points and the construction of inland container depots.

19.   In order for the multimodal transport operations to succeed in our region, COMESA has undertaken to assist member countries to:

-     Ratify the United Nations Convention on Multimodal Transport. This will create a legal and economic environment for the establishment of multimodal transport operations;

-     Effect behavioural and administrative reforms which would result in better utilization of existing human, material and financial resources;

-     Promote investment that facilitates and enhances multimodal transport operations;

-     Introduce EDI (Electronic Data Interchange) which facilitates and speeds up border controls and other official intervention, such as customs clearance of goods and means of transport.

4.   Major resolutions and regulations passed

20.   At its 3rd Meeting held in Bujumbura, Burundi, the Authority decided that a Multinational Coastal Shipping Company be established.

21.   The Authority also decided at its 10th Meeting held in Lusaka, Zambia in January 1992, that the Intergovernmental Standing Committee on Shipping (ISCOS) be reorganized and transformed into a COMESA specialized agency on maritime matters.

22.   At its 13th Meeting in 1988, the Council decided that:

-     COMESA member States should establish national shippers' councils or equivalent mechanisms in order to bring shippers together so as to enable them to have the negotiating power to obtain adequate and efficient services at the least cost.

-     COMESA member States should separate the management of stevedoring (cargo handling) and port administration in order to enhance efficiency.

-     COMESA member States should review their national maritime legislations and harmonize them with relevant international conventions.

23.   At its 16th Meeting in 1990, the Council decided that a Ministerial Committee for Maritime Transport should be established to coordinate and develop maritime policies and programmes in the COMESA region. The Ministerial Committee for Maritime Transport would among its other functions, be responsible for the rationalization of the activities of all intergovernmental organizations that deal with maritime transport within the COMESA region.

5.   Implementation mechanisms

24.   All the resolutions, regulations and decisions made by COMESA policy organs have to be implemented by the member States or such other governmental agencies responsible in the respective member countries. The mechanisms of implementation vary from one member State to another and also with the nature of each resolution.

6.   Major experiences of success and failure and reasons thereof

(a)   Success

-      COMESA has strengthened the political will of the member States to defend their maritime interests through unity and solidarity,

-      Notwithstanding financial constraints, it has been possible to mobilize external financing from donor countries for port rehabilitation and development. Port development has either been completed or about to be completed at the port of Assab, Beira, Dar es Salaam, Maputo, Mombasa, Nacala and Port Louis.

-      There are several regional governmental and non-governmental organizations dealing with maritime matters in the region. There has been rationalization of activities of these regional organizations and duplication has been avoided.

(b)   Weaknesses

25.   The widespread economic crisis has had serious repercussions on the public finances of the member States and consequently on their projects for the development of the shipping services in the region.

26.   The delay by member States in implementing the Council's decisions has made it difficult to achieve the objectives set in COMESA's shipping programme of action.

27.   This situation is aggravated by the scale and persistence of numerous factors, including the threats of deregulation from the World Bank, the International Monetary Fund and GATT through the liberalization of shipping services, leading to limited access to cargo for the region's merchant fleets, which are still too fragile to face free competition.

28.   The merchant fleet in the region has remained static due to lack of resources. Efforts made to develop merchant fleets have often been hampered by uncompetitive financing from external sources of COMESA countries. The conditions which are generally proposed are characterized by payment of considerable advance deposits, short grace periods, short repayment deadlines and relatively high interest rates.

29.   Bearing in mind the technological and organizational changes in the world's merchant shipping, it is evident that lack of adaptation to new structures will have considerable repercussions on present and future competitiveness of the fleet of COMESA countries.

7.   Future perspectives

30.   Within this overall framework, the challenges facing COMESA countries will be formidable. There is therefore an urgent need to consider possible global regional strategies which may assist our countries in surmounting the obstacles.

31.   With regard to coastal shipping services, COMESA will improve them in establishing a multinational coastal shipping company which will ensure the availability of cargo movements to any destination in the COMESA region. This will increase the intra-COMESA maritime trade. COMESA will also introduce a shipping magazine dedicated to increasing trade in the region by publishing specific trade opportunities, providing lists of shipping schedules and being generally informative on all matters related to maritime trade in the COMESA region.

32.   Concerning international shipping of goods originating from or bound for the COMESA region, in the short and medium term what is required for COMESA, rather than ownership of vessels, is commercial control over the services offered. This is particularly relevant for COMESA countries as the financial requirements for the acquisition of large, sophisticated vessels employed in long distance sea trade cause such tonnage to be beyond the reach of most of the COMESA countries.

B.   Southern Africa Transport and Communications Commission (SATCC)

1.   History

33.   The Southern Africa Transport and Communications Commission (SATCC) is a Commission of the Southern African Development Community (SADC). Presently, SADC

has 12 members: Angola, Botswana, Lesotho, Malawi, Mauritius, Mozambique, Namibia, South Africa, Swaziland, United Republic of Tanzania, Zambia and Zimbabwe. SATCC was established in July 1981.

34. According to the Convention that established SATCC, the Commission's responsibilities are:

- to provide coordination in overcoming transport and communications problems in the region;

- to provide economic and efficient means of transport and communications in the region;

- to achieve self-sufficiency in technical manpower, training and development;

- to encourage the efficient utilization of available resources for the improvement of transport and communications in the region.

35. The Protocol that established the Commission was signed by all nine SADC founding member countries, viz. Angola, Botswana, Lesotho, Malawi, Mozambique, Swaziland, United Republic of Tanzania, Zambia and Zimbabwe. Namibia joined SADC in 1990, followed by South Africa in August 1994. Mauritius, the twelfth member joined SADC in August 1995.

36. SATCC's supreme body is the Committee of Ministers which comprises of one member from each SADC member State, generally the Minister responsible for transport and communications. The Committee of Ministers is advised by the Coordinating Committee, which is a committee of Permanent/Principal Secretaries or other senior government officials from the same ministries of Transport and Communications. Both the Committee of Ministers and the Coordinating Committee are chaired by Mozambique which is the coordinator of transport and communications issues within SADC. The SATCC Technical Unit (SATCC-TU) is based in Maputo, Mozambique.

2. Ports and shipping

37. SATCC operates through subsectoral working groups. These are made up of principal actors in each subsector: operators, relevant policy makers and experts who meet at least once a year to deliberate on regional cooperation/integration issues. There is a working group for each of the seven subsectors of transport and communications that SATCC is coordinating.

38. The Working Group for ports and shipping brings together port administrations, national shipping companies, representatives of freight forwarders' associations and government officials responsible for maritime transport issues. The Working Group meets once a year in different venues within the region. Recommendations of the Working Group are presented first to SATCC's Coordinating Committee for scrutiny and later (upon acceptance) to the Committee of Ministers.

39. During the first 10 years of its existence, SATCC's programmes laid emphasis on infrastructure development in order to provide adequate transport capacity in the region. As part of this programme, several port projects were undertaken mainly in Mozambique and Tanzania.

40. While further development of port infrastructure and other physical facilities is continuing, emphasis is now being placed on efficiency improvements: this includes operational coordination and integration of the region's transport systems, restructuring and operational management improvement, also development of the human resource.

41. Consequently, major issues currently being discussed by the Working Group of Port Administration, Shipping, Clearing and Forwarding including the following:

- development of a shipping policy for the SADC region
- maritime safety
- improvement of transport corridor operations including multimodal transport operations
- development of protocols in the area of ports and shipping. (When signed these protocols will form part of the 1992 SADC Treaty).

In this regard a preliminary phase of a maritime safety study for the region has just been completed. It covered five coastal member States: Angola, Namibia, Mozambique, South Africa and the United Republic of Tanzania; and also one land-locked member State, Malawi. Further, a shipping policy study covering the whole region is due to commence shortly.

3.   Programme implementation

42.   According to established practice within SADC, implementation of agreed regional programmes is usually undertaken by individual member countries. Follow up on such programmes is however, done through the subsectoral working groups meetings.

43.   Although many regional programmes have been implemented by member States, under existing arrangements there are no penalties for non-compliance of decisions taken by the various SADC organs. It is expected that this shortcoming will be addressed during the development of protocols for the transport and communications sectors currently underway.

44.   The new SADC protocol(s) for the transport and communications sectors is(are) expected to be signed in 1996. It is expected that the new protocol will spell out in detail areas of cooperation for each subsector of the transport and communications sectors being coordinated by SATCC: it will also spell out, among other things, the obligations and/or responsibilities of the parties that will be party to the protocol.

4.   Future perspective

45.   The development of SADC's protocol for the transport and communications sectors has been a consultative process. Consultations with stakeholders in ports and shipping, rail transport, roads and road transport among others, were undertaken between February 1995 and July 1995. The identified protocol areas for each subsector are now being elaborated ready for negotiations and final endorsement. The signed protocol will be annexed to the 1992 SADC Treaty.

46.   For the ports and shipping subsector, the following, among other things, have been identified as protocol issues:

-        a regional maritime policy
-        a regional maritime body
-        establishment of corridor groups (to monitor the movement of goods along
         the various transport corridors)
-        setting up a regional bond guarantee scheme
-        restructuring and commercialization of State-owned enterprises
-        environmental protection, pollution control and maritime safety
-        search and rescue
-        treatment of international conventions.

The above issues will form SATCC's future activities in the area of ports and shipping.

                                    Part Two

                COOPERATIVE ARRANGEMENTS IN LATIN AMERICA

A.   The Caribbean Community (CARICOM)

1.   Brief history - Institutional and administrative arrangements

47.   The Caribbean Community and Common Market - CARICOM - was established by the Treaty of Chaguaramas on 4 July 1973, by Barbados, Guyana, Jamaica and Trinidad and Tobago. Subsequently, eight other Caribbean countries, namely, Antigua and Barbuda, Belize, Dominica, Grenada, Montserrat, St. Kitts and Nevis, Saint Lucia, and St. Vincent and the Grenadines (the LDCs) joined CARICOM. The Bahamas became the thirteenth member State of the Community on 4 July 1983 and Suriname became the fourteenth member State on 29 June 1985.

48.   In July 1991, the British Virgin Islands and the Turks and Caicos Islands were accorded Associated Membership of CARICOM. Twelve other States from Latin America and the Caribbean enjoy Observer status in various Institutions of the Community and CARICOM Ministerial bodies.

49.   During its 21 years of operation, the Community has concentrated on the promotion of the integration of the economies of the member States, in coordinating the foreign policies of the independent member States and in functional cooperation, especially in relation to various areas of social and human endeavour.

50.   The Caribbean Community has three objectives:

(a)   economic cooperation through the Caribbean Common Market;

(b)   coordination of foreign policy among the independent member States; and

(c)   common services and cooperation in functional matters such as health, education, transportation and culture, communications and industrial relations.

Institutions of the Community

51.   The principal organs of the Community are:

(a)   the Conference of Heads of Government, commonly referred to as The Conference;

(b)   the Common Market Council, commonly referred to as The Council.

52.   The Conference consists of Heads of Government of all member States of the Caribbean Community. Guyana is represented by its Executive President and in the case of Montserrat, its Chief Minister. Its primary responsibility is to determine the policy of the Community and is the final authority of the conclusion of treaties on behalf of the Community and for entering into relationships between the Community and international organizations and third States. The Conference is also responsible for making the financial arrangements to meet the expense of the Community but has delegated this function to the Common Market Council.   Decisions of the Conference are generally taken unanimously.

53.   The Council consists of one Minister of Government designated by each member State. It is responsible for the efficient operation and development of the Common Market including the settlement of problems arising out of its functions.

54.   The decision to restructure the Organs and Institutions of the Community was made at the Special Meeting of CARICOM Heads of Government in October 1992. The proposed new institutional structure will comprise:

(a)   the Conference of Heads of Government;

(b)   the Bureau of the Conference;

(c)   the Community Council of Ministers - which will replace the Common Market Council.

The responsibility of the Bureau is to initiate proposals, update consensus, mobilize and secure implementation of CARICOM decisions in an expeditious and informed manner. The Bureau commenced operations in December 1992.

55.   There are several Institutions of the Caribbean Community responsible for formulating policies and performing functions in relation to cooperation in services such as education, health, labour matters and foreign policy.   Each member State is represented on each Institution by a member of Government of the member State.   The Institutions are designated the Conference of Ministers responsible for Health; Standing Committee of Ministers responsible for the other 12 functional cooperation areas of Education; Science and Technology; Foreign Affairs;   Agriculture;   Energy,   Mines   and   Natural   Resources;   Industry; Transportation; Finance; Labour; Tourism; Legal Affairs; and Information.

56.   Under the Treaty, the following bodies are Associate Institutions of the Community: Caribbean Development Bank; Caribbean Examinations Council; Caribbean Meteorological Organisation; Council of Legal Education; University of Guyana; and the University of the West Indies.

57.   The CARICOM Secretariat is the main administrative organ of the Community. It is organized into three offices comprising the Office of the Secretary-General, the Deputy Secretary-General and the General Counsel and has

three Directorates each headed by an Assistant Secretary-General with responsibility for the areas of Foreign and Community Relations; Regional Trade and Economic Integration; and Human and Social Development.

58.   The principal functions of the secretariat are:

(a)   to service meetings of the Community and of its Institutions or Committees as may from time to time be determined by the Conference;

(b)   to take appropriate follow-up action on decisions made at such meetings;

(c)   to initiate, arrange and carry out studies on questions of economic and functional cooperation relating to the Region as a whole;

(d)   to provide services to member States at their request in respect of matters relating to the achievement of the objectives of the Community;

(e)   to undertake any other duties which may be assigned to it by the Conference or any of the Institutions of the Community.

The decision-making process

59.   The role of the secretariat is to allow for the greatest possible accommodations of national interests in policy formulation and provide forward movement in the regional development process in the specific areas targeted by the Governments or proposed by the secretariat.

60.   The long-term objectives of the Community are defined by the Treaty of Chaguaramas. Heads of Government periodically sharpen their focus or define in more concrete terms the objectives to be pursued. The Conference of Heads of Government which makes the decisions relative to the direction of the Community and its efforts, is supported in this decision-making process by the Institutions of the Community represented by the Common Market Council and the various Ministerial Standing Committees (Transport, Energy, Labour, Industry, Education, Health, Science and Technology and the Environment).

61.   Back-stopping the Ministerial negotiations are the regional officials of the member State who prior to each meeting, examine issues, help identify policy options and seek to identify common ground among member States. The secretariat is responsible for facilitating this process by organizing the preparation of the technical work.

2.   Areas covered in shipping, ports and multimodal transport

62.   A regional shipping council had been established as early as 1967 after the dissolution of the West Indies Federation, and entrusted with the function and provisions formerly exercised by the Federal Government, in relation to the West Indies Shipping Corporation (WISCO). Apart from its original powers and functions, as the overall authority in the matter of the administration and operation of WISCO, the Regional Shipping Council (RSC) gradually gave increasing attention to other ocean shipping problems, regional and intra-regional, of the members of the CARIFTA and its successes the Caribbean Community.

63.   The RSC was replaced as an institution of the Community by the Standing Committee of Ministers responsible for Transportation (SCMT) following a decision of the Conference of Heads of Government in 1974.

64.   The SCMT has overall responsibility for all matters in regional transport policy, and for the establishment and supervision of other regional agencies, entrusted with the operation, control or development of regional air and sea transport.

65.   Decisions taken by the SCMT are referred to the Head of Government for ratification. These then become the mandates of the secretariat.

Shipping

66.   The paucity of contiguous borders renders CARICOM States heavily dependent on maritime transport for the conduct of intra- and extra-regional trade. It is estimated that 90 per cent of goods traded intra-regionally are moved by sea. As a means of securing trade as well as developing the maritime sector, States had sought, individually and collectively, to establish shipping lines.

67.   National lines (such as Jamaican Merchant Marine, the Shipping Corporation of Trinidad and Tobago and GUYBULK of Guyana) were public sector enterprises owned by the larger States to service their extra-regional trades.   The regionally-owned line, WISCO, provided that vital intra-regional link as well as connections to Miami, which is the major US port as far as CARICOM trade is concerned.   The operation of these enterprises proved to be unsuccessful, both financially and in terms of the quality of service needed by the trade of the region.

68.   In this scenario, foreign shipping lines continued to dominate trade particularly with extra-regional partners. This situation resulted in inadequate services to all States, as some routes were over supplied and experienced low freight rates as the lines competed for cargoes in both directions. Simultaneously, the smaller States experienced a paucity of shipping services, except for those of the small vessels fleet, and high freight rates.

69.   The ability of national lines to provide services at viable levels was affected by fluctuation in freight rates. The relatively low cargo volume of the smaller States also militated against the provision of viable shipping services.

70.   WISCO, the regionally-owned shipping line was Government-subsidized and mandated to serve all CARICOM ports despite the financial viability of such calls, in order to afford some measure of security to the trade of the region. This impacted negatively on the financial performance of the Corporation.

71.   Against the background of the above inadequacies, the SCMT in 1987, decided to establish a Committee of Maritime Technicians to investigate viable options to satisfy the demands of the Region for shipping services. This resulted in the execution of several studies aimed at developing a Caribbean Shipping Service, central to which would have been a restructured and later privatized WISCO, as well as the upgrading of the small vessels which service intra-regional trade, in the Southern Caribbean.

72.   In the face of its continued losses and the inability of member States to finance these, particularly at that junction, the SCMT decided in 1992 to wind up the Corporation.

Small vessel fleet

73.   There exists a small fleet of small vessels which are privately owned and operated by nationals of the member States of the Community. These vessels provide intra-regional services to CARICOM States as well as the French and Dutch Antilles. The fleet also provides the transhipment link to those smaller States which are unable to access regular shipping services to extra-regional destinations. The services provided by these vessels are however inadequate due to the age and physical profile of the vessels relative to trade needs as well as scheduling and cargo handling practices among others.

74.   With the closure of WISCO the importance of these vessels to the trade security of the region has increased. This prompted the SCMT in 1992, following its decision to wind up WISCO, to mandate the secretariat to develop a project for the upgrading of the Small Vessel Fleet to meet the needs of intra-regional trade.   This area is now actively being pursued by the secretariat.   It is anticipated that funding will be secured in 1996 to conduct a feasibility study to design an intra-regional shipping network, detailing vessel size, technology and itinerary and a strategy for the establishment of the network.

Ports

75.   The majority of ports are Government-owned but are operated autonomously by port authority. Most ports are equipped to receive container vessels. Ro-ro facilities are more dominant among the smaller States.

76.   Historically, CARICOM ports have been regarded as high-cost low-efficiency entities. This is partly a result of the low cargo volumes handled by the ports relative to the overhead costs of investments in modern port facilities much of which had been undertaken in the last decade or so.   Some degree of over-investment in port facilities exists in the region, as a result of competition among States to vie for transhipment traffic. There also exist ports which are underdeveloped.

77.   Recognising the problems of efficiency and cost affecting the provision of shipping services to States, active cooperation has been fostered between the port authorities of member States which has resulted in training exchanges and

attachment between ports, active involvement in TRAINMAR and the formation of a Port Management Association in the Eastern Caribbean (PMAEC). These efforts are aimed at providing training to all levels of port staff (Operational Management) in order to improve efficiency.

78.   More recently, as a further step to improve efficiency and reduce port costs, ports have, while maintaining the Government ownership of facilities, sought to privatize various aspects of their operations. At the regional level the SCMT has also targeted the training of port personnel, and the rationalization of port development as vital areas in improving the ability of the region to secure adequate shipping services at competitive freight rates. These areas are currently a part of the Work Programme of the Secretariat in Transportation.

Other areas of activity

79.   Efforts to develop a Regional Maritime Transport system, in addition to focusing on shipping services and improved port facilities and operation, have been extensive with regards to the development of modern maritime regulatory framework to ensure safe and efficient shipping and trade, and the prevention of marine pollution.

80.   At the regional level, projects have been implemented to increase the awareness of member States to the need to have in place effective maritime administrations supported by the necessary modern legislation, supporting regulatory administrative and technical capabilities to develop and regulate their maritime sectors.

81.   As a result, an increased number of States are now parties to the major International Maritime Conventions on Maritime Safety and Pollution Prevention, have enacted or are in the process of enacting modern merchant shipping regulations and are actively engaged in the training of maritime administrative and safety personnel to effect enforcement activities.

82.   Essential to the progress achieved above, has been the development of a Regional Maritime Code - Draft Shipping Legislation - through the assistance of IMO, for use by member States as a basis in the drafting of their national legislation; and the provision of a Regional Maritime Safety Advisor to work with individual States as well as coordinate regional efforts. In 1993, CARICOM States along with other Island States of the Caribbean (approximately 23 countries) agreed to cooperate to establish a system of Port State Control (PSC) in the Caribbean. A Memorandum of Agreement has been finalized following two preparatory meetings and is to signed at the Third Preparatory Meeting in Barbados in February 1996.

83.   Draft Cargo Shipping Regulations have also been developed for application to the Small Vessel Fleet, the majority of which, by virtue of size (less than 500 grt) are not regulated under the International Maritime Conventions. The training of the first batch of ship inspectors to enforce these regulations concluded in November 1995.

3.   Future perspectives

84.   To facilitate the goal of economic and social integration of the Community and in the absence of direct ownership of shipping services, efforts of the region are now focussed at putting in place the various mechanisms to ensure the availability of appropriate and competitively priced shipping services.

85.   The Regional Agenda for the future has been developed to address the following:

(a)   the development of incentives to encourage the provision of shipping services by regional private sector interests as well as other providers;

(b)   assist shippers in attracting shipping services through cargo consolidation efforts. The feasibility of establishing a Caribbean Non-Vessel Owning Common Carrier (NVOCC) has been recommended by a recent study and is to be further developed and promoted;

(c)   improvement of the negotiating capacity of the region relative to shipping lines in order to secure advantageous freight rates. One element seen as vital to this process and that of the NVOCC is the establishment of a transportation database to provide the necessary data for analysis and decision-making. A project in this regard has been initiated and should commence in 1996;

(d)   upgrading of port facilities among the smaller States particularly with respect to cargo-handling and temperature-controlled facilities necessary for the export of non-traditional agricultural cargo;

(e)   improvement of the intra-regional shipping services provided by the small vessels including the training of owners and crew in the commercial, cargo handling and safety areas;

(f)   continued training of port sea-going and maritime administrative personnel.   The region has two maritime training institutions.   The Jamaica Maritime Institute (JMI) and the Caribbean Fisheries Development Training Institute (CFTDI) which cater for the training of seafarers, the former up to the Officer level. The Regional TRAINMAR Centre and its sub-centres are utilized for the provision of commercial and operational training in the shipping and port fields. A regional training committee has been formed out of the PSC activities comprising the two regional institutions to develop an overall training strategy to meet the future needs of the region.   The high level of collaboration which exists between TRAINMAR and JMI is expected to provide for an integrated and cost-effective strategy;

(g)   improving the capacity of member States to enforce PSC measures. This will include:

(i)   the development of model shipping regulations to support the primary legislation. Activities in this regard commenced in 1995;

(ii)   the provision of maritime safety advisor to the region to support the States PSC activities and coordinate other regional maritime activities.   The region lost this service in 1994 due to funding difficulties;   and

(iii)   the expansion of the corp of PSC Inspectors through the delivery of the necessary training.

86.   With the increased dependence of Caribbean States on tourism as a major economic activity and the designation of the Caribbean as a "Special Area" under MARPOL Annex V, the areas of ports and allied facilities including waste disposal arrangements for cruise and cargo vessels has become important. In this context, CARICOM States are participating in the current IMO/World Bank Wider Caribbean Initiative on Ship-generated Waste (WCISW) project which is geared at devising the necessary legislative and operational framework to enable States to activate the Special Area status.

B.   Cartagena Agreement (Andean Group)

1.   Institutional features

87.   The Cartagena Agreement, better known as the Andean Group, was established in 1969.   It is a cluster of developing countries in South America, comprising Bolivia, Colombia, Ecuador, Peru and Venezuela.   Its various activities are managed by a communal institutional structure, the principal bodies being the following:

(a)   The Commission, which is the guiding body for the process of subregional integration, comprising ministers of industry and/or foreign trade; its actions take the form of Decisions binding on member countries. Commission members are plenipotentiary representatives accountable at the national level for the supranational nature of the guidelines they set.

(b)   The Board, which is the technical body responsible for coordinating the process of subregional integration and overseeing compliance with the Cartagena Agreement and with Decisions. It also has the authority to submit draft decisions to the Commission for consideration and to issue Resolutions, which are also binding.   The Board is divided into departments and technical units.   Dealing with transport- and maritime transport-related matters is the responsibility of the Department of Physical Integration (DIF).

(c)   The Andean Court of Justice, which is the legal body responsible for maintaining transparency in the application of the communal standards governing intrasubregional trade. Its rulings are binding on the national courts of member countries.

88.   The Andean Presidential Council, which lays down policy guidelines for the process of subregional integration, and the Andean Council (of foreign ministers) which is responsible for overseeing and evaluating implementation of the

arrangements agreed on at presidential meetings, were also established in 1989. The political side of the Andean Group is concentrated in the activities of the Andean Parliament which is made up of delegations from the five national congresses.

89.   There are two further communal institutions which have a significant impact on the strengthening of subregional integration: the Andean Development Corporation (CAF) and the Latin American Reserve Fund.   Both financial bodies have since 1990 been channelling an increasing percentage of their resources towards national initiatives and/or initiatives of common interest designed to encourage and facilitate production in and foreign trade by member countries. Principal areas of investment include the construction, improvement and consolidation of physical infrastructure (roads, airports and ports).

2.   Specific areas of concern

90.   In the late 1980s the Andean Presidents adopted a Strategic Plan. This, a technically and politically consistent document, established a doctrinal basis and guidelines that pointed the Andean Group towards consolidation of the subregional economic space and improvement of its links with the world beyond. Each of these broad objectives was accompanied by a set of specific targets. One of the most important was the definition and execution of projects to improve, expand and modernize the capacity of physical transport and communications infrastructure and the services provided, in order to permit swift and secure links between producers and consumers both within the subregion and elsewhere around the world.

91.   In 1990, the Fourth Andean Presidential Council decided to improve member countries' competitiveness in international trade. It called for a review of the situation in maritime transport in order to do away as quickly as possible with legal and economic obstacles to commercial competition. At that time, national shipping companies enjoyed the protectionist benefits of "reserved cargo", which prevented foreign firms from offering or providing services.

92.   As a result of that review, a number of provisions were adopted which profoundly altered the way maritime transport operated in the Andean Group.

Maritime transport

93.   In 1990, the Board fostered the establishment of the Andean Water Transport Authorities Committee (CAATA). It was considered necessary to have a sectoral advisory body where national maritime transport officials could discuss common problems and define the lines of action best suited to meeting requirements in this complex area. With the creation of the Committee, water transport ceased to be a matter of strictly national interest and became one of communal concern. One of its first agreements, and the most far-reaching, was to propose the abolition of reserved cargo.   The public sector realized that, in order to advance towards its strategic objectives, it had to escape from the prevailing restrictive situation and make room for commercial competition in shipping.

94.   It is appropriate to mention that the Committee has so far held 15 meetings, basing its proposals on the recommendations of an ad hoc working group comprising national experts and advisers from regional and international bodies concerned with the subject, including representatives of the subregional shipowners' and users' (importers and exporters) associations. It operates in a climate of growing cooperation between the public and private sectors.

95.   Responding to a presidential directive and on the recommendation of the Committee, the Commission, acting on a proposal by the Board, in 1991 passed decision 288, "Freedom of access to cargoes originating in and bound, by sea, for the subregion", which ordered a progressive liberalization of maritime transport services, abolishing reserved cargo in no more than two years.   Thus goods originating in and/or bound for the subregion can now be freely transported by sea within the subregion by vessels owned, chartered or operated by shipping companies of member countries or third countries. Only Ecuador has reserved for itself the right to transport its hydrocarbons.

96.   This common policy, approved as member countries opened up commercially, had an immediate impact in two different senses. First, operators offering efficient, competitive services came onto the market; the diversification of supply in turn permitted an increase in the number of trade routes; fleets were reduced substantially; the use of containers rose; foreign traders' operations became more fluid and reliable; and merchants with ties to shipping companies began to speak of the need to promote multimodal transport. Maritime and port

authorities underwent a substantial alternation in status *vis-à-vis* the economics of shipping, changing from bulwarks of protection into market regulators.

97.   Second, shipping companies in the subregion, including Bolivia, suffered severe economic effects as shipping, vital to external trade, was opened up to competition. The sudden disappearance of their cargo oligopoly spotlighted their financial, managerial, operative and technological limitations and difficulties in competing on an equal footing with the foreign shipping companies that were beginning to make successful inroads into their former captive markets. With few exceptions, national shipping companies had survived for years with little effort and had not troubled to look ahead. They were businesses suffering from structural obsolescence (disinvestment, high operating costs, shallow-draught vessels designed for bulk cargoes, overstaffing etc.). The competitive costs and efficiency shown by outside operators ended up forcing a large number of Andean shipping companies off the market, and they had to concentrate on the proportion of freight reserved for national cabotage.

98.   The economic impact suffered by Andean shipping companies made necessary a communal standard constructed around three criteria: the abolition of cargo reservation, with the exception of national cabotage, which remained reserved; regulation of access to freight and application of the principle of reciprocity; and a definition of broad policy guidelines for the strengthening and development of the Andean Group's merchant fleets.

99.   The authorities realized that they must respond to the situation that had arisen since the market in maritime transport services in the subregion was liberalized.   They affirmed their commitment to open trading but argued that movements in the market must be regulated more effectively. They indicated that they had soon encountered difficulties with foreign companies using unfair trading practices; some countries and communities of countries were not offering reciprocal conditions to their shipowners, restricting their access to cargoes; and some of the largest companies in member countries, to reduce their financial, tax and labour costs, were abandoning national registries and registering their ships under flags of convenience (chiefly in Panama), which had begun to reduce the Andean Group's tonnage markedly by 1995, it was less than 20 per cent of what it had been in 1991.

100.   In order to deal with these problems, the Commission, early in 1992, passed Decision 314, "Free access to cargo shipped by sea and policies for the development of the merchant marine in the Andean Group", which embodied suggestions put forward by CAATA.   This was a communal standard intended to address a situation that was affecting both the maritime transport market and national shipping companies; it sought to better the national companies' economic position and prevent their flight to other, more flexible, less burdensome registries. To attain these objectives, it required the passage of a regulation on application of the principle of reciprocity and the shaping of a policy to promote shipping.

101.   Over the past three years the Board and the Committee - and more recently, since its establishment in 1994, Andean Shipowners' Association   - have been exploring a variety of ways to comply efficiently with the undertakings given in decision 314.   Their efforts have given rise to several documents:

(1)   Draft Decision "Regulations on the common application of the principle of reciprocity".

    This draft has been approved by CAATA and the Andean Shipowners' Association, and the Board will shortly bring it before the Commission for adoption as a Decision. Its central aim is that, when third countries or communities of countries impose any kind of limit or apply restrictions, exclusions or discriminatory treatment to national shipping companies as regards access to cargo, member countries should reciprocate with total or partial restrictions on shipping companies belonging to those countries or communities, even if they have links to national shipping companies. The principle of reciprocity will be applied throughout the community.

(2)   Draft Decision "Establishment of the Andean Ship Registry".

    This draft has been approved by CAATA and the Andean Shipowners' Association. Besides dealing with shipping, however, it also contains regulatory provisions on preferential fiscal and tax treatment and less stringent requirements governing the composition of ships' crews. These have not been endorsed by other national authorities, since member countries have eliminated exemptions and direct subsidies for economic activities, particularly in services, from their economic policies. This difficulty is keeping the possibility of establishing an Andean shipping registry in abeyance, in the short term. Nevertheless, the necessary institutional steps are continuing to be taken.

(3)   Draft Decision "Use of financial leasing to encourage Andean merchant shipping companies".

This draft is being evaluated by the CAATA Ad Hoc Working Group, advised on this occasion by experts on maritime finance. The Committee is awaiting word from the advisers before embarking on a thorough discussion of the proposal, which has important implications for the subregional financial system.

(4)   Draft Decision "Regulations on tariff registration".

CAATA believes there is a need for a communal standard enabling it to regulate changes in the tariffs charged by shipping companies offering and providing services within the Andean Group more effectively. The principal aim of this project is that any non-conference general cargo shipping company, national or foreign, engaged in traffic that includes national ports in member countries must register with the competent authorities its schedule of tariffs, charges and other components that might affect the end cost of its services. The object is to avoid unfair competition. Consideration is also being given to a set of conditions that would give operators sufficient flexibility to change their tariffs within periods that will not affect their provision of services.

(5)   Draft Decision "Adoption of the agreement on control of shipping by the State with jurisdiction over a port".

The Andean Group authorities recognize the need for effective action to prevent operations by ships flying any flag which do not comply with maritime safety standards, including standards designed to prevent marine pollution. They have therefore seen fit to adopt the Latin American Agreement on control of shipping by the State with jurisdiction over a port, better known as the Viña del Mar Agreement (Chile, 1992). This regional agreement is in turn based on the agreements on the subject reached at the International Maritime Organization (IMO).

102.   This list of draft communal standards (Decisions) shows the various aspects on which work is being done at the subregional level. The Board, in conjunction with CAATA and the Andean Shipowners' Association and with support from recognized subregional and Latin American experts, has produced these drafts in response to the problems affecting shipping companies in the subregion. The authorities are aware of the vital need to recover member countries' cargo capacity and ensure commercial transparency. Businessmen are taking steps to update their management, operations and technology so as to compete on better terms in the demanding market for maritime transport services. These efforts will produce results quickly since they are motivated by the desire to strengthen and improve maritime transport in the Andean Group, this being essential to the future of its external trade which is growing apace.

Port system

103.   The geography of the subregion gives it direct access to the Atlantic and Pacific oceans. On the Caribbean, Colombia and Venezuela have eight ports of significance. On the Pacific, Colombia, Ecuador and Peru have nine ports used for international trade. Bolivia, being land-locked, has no maritime ports.

104.   Since the late 1980s a debate has grown up in the subregion over the restructuring and privatization of ports. Almost simultaneously, member countries began taking steps nationally and internationally to launch studies that would show them how to move swiftly to deal with the organizational, administrative and operative inefficiency afflicting almost all the Andean Group's main ports. The maritime and port authorities were convinced that port management and operations should be handed over to the private sector in order to make them work efficiently, and that that would benefit external trade.

105.   So far, progress in this direction has been rather unsatisfactory. The Andean States have begun once again to question whether it is appropriate to privatize their ports, since their few experiments with putting administration into private hands have not produced the qualitative changes hoped for. Member countries therefore have a motive for arriving as quickly as possible at a common

policy on port modernization that will take up and articulate, within an overall framework, the positive aspects of the various national-level initiatives that have been put into effect with favourable results.

106. Accordingly, the Board has organized several "port colloquia" (October 1993 and March 1994) attended by maritime and port authorities from the Andean Group, representatives of the Latin American Integration Association (ALADI), the United Nations Economic Commission for Latin America and the Caribbean, the Organization of American States and the UNCTAD Maritime Management Training Project (TRAINMAR), and experts from the European Union. These have gone deeply into the port situation in the subregion and identified a series of economic and technological options that are being used as the basis for the common port policy now being drafted, and have been used as a reference for activities of each member country. There is an interesting variety of modernization projections in progress.

107. Communal treatment of ports is one of the Andean Group's basic priorities over the next few years. The New Strategic Plan, adopted by the Seventh Andean Presidential Council in August 1995, gives specific guidelines on the strengthening of maritime transport and the modernization of ports in the subregion. The two topics will be worked on together and in coordination, since they are vital pieces of the distribution chain and basic components of multimodal transport.

Multimodal transport

108. The Andean Group is perhaps the first subregional integration scheme in Latin American to have a communal standard referring specifically to multimodal transport. In early 1993, the Commission adopted Decision 331. It was considered that new transport procedures implied the intensive use of containers and were progressively taking over from the old, single-mode goods distribution systems. It was therefore appropriate to add to the community's framework of standards on transport by adopting a Decision on the matter.

109. Later, in the light of developments in international standards, these standards were revised to bring them in line with new regulatory provisions (INCOTERMS 90, the Hamburg Rules, the UNCTAD-ICC rules etc.). With advice from UNCTAD and ECLAC, several draft decisions were prepared to make the necessary amendments to Decision 331, extending its scope and making it more precise. One was "Regulations on the registration of international multimodal transport operators" (MTO), registration to be the responsibility of the competent national body in each member country; member countries were to take such steps as were necessary to enable a registry to be set up and to operate. Swift approval of the proposal would provide the authorities with the criteria they needed to register businesses in the subregion which had shown an interest in engaging in multimodal transport. Over the past few years there has been a significant rise in the numbers of national operators seeking to break into this new field, which is still just developing in the Andean Group.

110. None the less, growing attention is being paid to the advantages of multimodal transport. Associations of shipping companies and user (importers and exporters) associations in member countries are holding more and more specialized meetings with the objective of studying more closely the subregional regulatory framework, economic opportunities, operating requirements and international conditions governing their activities. This shows that steps are being taken within the Andean Group to put multimodal transport progressively into practice.

111. One important detail to note is that Decision 331 has served as a template for similar initiatives now being taken in other economic integration schemes on the continent, particularly in Central America (MERCOCENTRO) and the Caribbean islands (CARICOM). An effort has also been made at the South American level to ensure that the common standards applicable in the Andean Group and in Mercosur are compatible so that there can shortly be a standard of regional scope. The countries of ASEAN (south-east Asia) have been observing with interest developments in regulatory standards on multimodal transport within the subregion.

3.   Prospects

112. The foregoing indicates that the Andean Group is making systematic efforts to help strengthen, diversify and develop transport services, in particular maritime transport, the port system and multimodal transport. For this purpose, communal bodies, in particular the Commission and the Board, are tending to pursue the following objectives:

- Establishment of communal guidelines to bring about substantial improvements in institutional arrangements and in the management and regulatory capacity of the national authorities concerned;

- Support for the activities of the Andean Water Transport Authorities Committee (CAATA), the subregional body where economic and legal options for responding effectively to problems in maritime transport and ports are systematically dealt with;

- Collaboration with the Andean Shipowners' Association (AAA) and promotion of the establishment of an Andean Port Authorities Association (AAAP), with a view to their active involvement in the process of identifying and formulating communal projects to overcome their difficulties;

- Adoption of Decisions to supplement the regulatory framework so that the market for maritime transport in the subregion can be more efficiently regulated, and the growth of shipping companies in member countries can be encouraged and promoted;

- Studies to ascertain the organizational, administrative and operational conditions obtaining at the principal ports in the subregion;

- Application to specialized international bodies (UNCTAD-TRAINMAR), for advisory services so that the staff responsible for port management can be given technical and managerial training;

- Procurement from subregional, regional and international financial bodies of funds to be used in modernizing port infrastructure and establishing conditions conductive to efficient multimodal transport; and

- Participation, as a subregional bloc, in all international bodies discussing maritime transport problems and defining economic and political options for overcoming them.

Assessment of the work done by CAATA since April 1994 and suggested priority topics for the subregion in the maritime transport sector

113. In assessing the work done by the Andean Water Transport Authorities Committee (CAATA) since April 1994, in particular during the period while the Committee met under the Chairmanship of the authority which I have the honour to represent, it is appropriate to begin by refreshing our memory with a little of the Committee's history.

114. It was established at the fourth meeting of Ministers of Transport Communications and Public Works of States parties to the Cartagena Agreement, in the city of Quito in November 1988, to facilitate the development of water transport among countries in the sub-region.

115. Later, as a result of the policy of reactivating the Cartagena Agreement and a presidential directive in the form of the act of La Paz, the Andean countries undertook to adopt a policy of abolishing reserved cargo in intrasubregional maritime transport and *vis-à-vis* third parties in a drive to make the subregion's external trade more competitive. This made it necessary to extend CAATA's terms of reference, which was done in Decision 314, chapter III, of the Commission of the Cartagena agreement: more specifically in articles 18 and 19, which gave the Committee clear functions and powers that have kept it effective to this day.

116. To summarize after this review, the Andean Water Transport Authorities Committee has worked intensively, at 5 regular meetings and 10 extraordinary meetings, producing 59 resolutions putting forward recommendations to the Board of the Cartagena Agreement and to maritime authorities themselves, and draft regulations and decisions.

117. Of all this hard work, Decisions 288, 314 and 331, the last drafted in collaboration with affiliated committees, are the most relevant, they have been adopted and published in the Official Gazette of the Cartagena Agreement, thereby establishing new regulations to improve water transport, including multimodal transport, in the subregion.

118. Given CAATA's excellent output and the few final results specified in the Decisions mentioned above, it is clearly not good follow-up to administrative

action in the higher levels of the organization that is lacking. Thus it is procedures that need to be revised.

119. As is well known, over the past three years, thanks to easier access to freight originating in and bound for the subregion by sea called for in Decision 314, the following benefits have been secured within the subregion:

(a) More frequent dockings and a better choice of services on offer in subregional ports;

(b) A reduction in the level of charters to transport commodities to and from Andean Group countries, leading to better access to consumer markets for our countries' traditional export.

120. At the same time, national shipping companies have been weakened virtually to the point of disappearance because the compensatory measures set forth in Chapter II, article 9, of Decision 314 were not applied at the same time.

121. Given this fact, the maritime authorities in CAATA have duly supported all efforts before their respective Governments to secure the promulgation of such measures - so far without success.

122. The urgent need to promote the subregion's shipping companies has made necessary a new strategy which consists in taking up all the resolutions dealing with such promotion in common standards or Decisions by the Commission of the Cartagena Agreement, which are binding on States under supranational law.

123. The following draft Decisions were adopted as priority topics at the fifth ordinary meeting in Guayaquil and the eighth and ninth extraordinary meetings, in Bogota and Caraballeda respectively, : the Andean Ship Registry; the Regulations on the application of the principle of reciprocity; and the Regulations on leasing, with an option to buy, vessels to be used by shipping companies in the subregion. These draft decisions have since been revised by the Committee's Working Group, resulting, at the latest CAATA meeting on 15 August 1995, in a Resolution which distinguishes between two broad areas of action within what is referred to as "access to cargo": the first, concerned with the common application of the principle of reciprocity, which already exists as a draft Decision, and the second, governing trade competition in maritime transport, under which heading the following must also be considered:

(a) Regulations on the registration of tariffs by national shipping companies and the shipping countries of third countries or communities of countries offering international shipping services;

(b) The imposition of restrictions on commercial shipowners' organizations when they impose similar measures on national shipping companies;

(c) Regulations on access to cargo for ships that do not comply with international rules on maritime safety and protection of the marine environment;

(d) Consideration of international transport of goods by sea as an export service.

124. Further meetings will have to be held shortly to consider and finalize such draft decisions as prove necessary.

125. But CAATA also has a duty to help attain the ultimate objectives set at the highest level, integrating the subregion with other economic blocs in Latin America and the world as a whole; these have been defined as follows:

(a) Consolidating the Andean economic space in a climate of competition which will allow sufficient resources to be allocated to entrepreneurial development and increasing the productive capacity of subregional economic agents;

(b) Adapting the communal policy of the Andean Group to its international setting and increasing the Group's contribution to Latin American unity through joint action as a subregional bloc to establish a competitive and consistent international presence.

126. To help reach these objectives the external trade of the subregion as a bloc must be boosted; as maritime transport is a decisive factor in exchanges of goods and services, its major components - shipping companies and ports - have been given special attention in the definition of an overall Andean policy on water transport.

127.   The situation prevailing since March 1992 has without question brought about a wider range of choice in subregional maritime transport, but it is also clear that national shipping companies are being displaced by foreign ones with better infrastructure, more advanced technology, subsidies and legislative advantages.

128.   To counter this, we believe it is necessary to lay down the following guidelines before embarking on the appropriate policies as regards shipping and ports:

(a)   Strengthen shipping companies so that they can meet the demands of present-day maritime transport in the face of extensive competition from international shipping companies;

(b)   Modernize ports handling foreign trade for countries in the subregion, making them efficient, safe and competitive.

129.   We in the Andean Water Transport Authorities Committee thus have a historic responsibility to give effect to the policies on shipping and ports that have already been laid down, and to do so within two years.   But, before that, after six years of institutional existence, thought must be given to certain organizational changes within the Committee to make it more dynamic and adaptable and ensure better follow-up on the administrative action taken within the Committee; we have therefore decided that the "Bases for agreement and Rules of Procedure of CAATA" adopted in CAATA Resolution No. II-12, which governs our activities, must be revised.

130.   In the strengthening of shipping companies, action will be taken to convert the draft decision on community application of the principle of reciprocity into a proper Decision as soon as possible: this in the belief that adoption of this principle will not hinder member countries' foreign trade, affect the fluidity of bilateral and multilateral relations between each member country and third countries or communities of countries, or restrict the supply and demand of maritime transport services, but will help to reactivate and strengthen commercial activity by national shipping companies and provide national authorities with communal resources with which to apply the principle of reciprocity called for in Decision 314 vigorously, efficiently and community-wide.

131.   As another urgent matter, a decision regulating commercial competition in maritime transport, as called for in CAATA Resolution X-EX-58, must be discussed and drafted in the Working Group.

132.   This must be without prejudice to the consideration by the Working Group, as soon as possible, of the draft decisions on the leasing, with an option to buy, of vessels for use by subregional shipping companies and the Andean Shipping Register.

133.   These drafts are at the moment regarded as the only possible means of achieving the expansion and strengthening of shipping companies in subregional countries.   They must therefore be pushed through all the bodies required to get them adopted, including the Andean Presidential Council.

134.   As regards port policy, there must be a move to hasten implementation of Decision 314, article 13, so as to optimize port services and, thus, reduce current tariffs, making for a more flexible supply of services and competitive operations.

135.   We also consider it necessary to adopt a communal standard governing the consolidation and break-up of cargoes, given the impact that these operations have on member countries' foreign trade; this has been adopted as a Resolution (CAATA Resolution V-51) but no effective response has yet been received.

136.   As regards multimodal transport, the Board of the Cartagena Agreement and the water transport authorities must put Decision 331 into effect and promote the establishment of appropriate legislation and the necessary infrastructure in their respective countries.

137.   To obtain maximum benefit from these activities, we shall be keen to promote lasting contacts between the water transport authorities in the subregion and our counterparts in Latin America and the rest of the world.   We must not forget that by the end of the century we shall have to be thinking about internationalizing relations: while the internal, subregional aspect is important, we cannot then escape being influenced by the potential of the Pacific

rim and its impact on countries on this side of the continent; we will therefore also seek to orient our activities towards expanding relations between regional groups, i.e. towards globalization.

138. To conclude, considering that the external trade of a country or group of countries is affected by different and varying factors, we think it is difficult to formulate rigid or deterministic policies to help water transport adapt in a timely and effective manner to the present-day demands of highly dynamic foreign trade. Such formulation must be regarded as a cyclic or recurrent process, dependent for planning, execution and supervision on the efforts of all involved, and as a preponderant factor in the process of subregional integration. There is a risk that our efforts will come to nought if we do not also receive determined backing from the Board of the Cartagena Agreement, and we take this opportunity to voice our gratitude for the support we have so far had and to ask for this support to be strengthened.

139. Hence we must all continue to seek new ways of strengthening the shipping and port sector in our countries and successfully taking up the challenge of the future.

2. CONSIDERATION OF THE REVIEW OF THE INTERNATIONAL CONVENTION FOR THE UNIFICATION OF CERTAIN RULES RELATING TO THE ARREST OF SEA-GOING SHIPS, 1952 - NOTE BY THE SECRETARIAT OF UNCTAD AND IMO

Doc. no.: TD/B/IGE.1/2

Date: 6 June 1996

The attached document */ has been prepared for the ninth session of the Joint Intergovernmental Group of Experts.

Introduction

The Joint Intergovernmental Group of Experts at its eighth session agreed to use the text of draft articles for a convention on arrest of ships contained in document JIGE(VIII)/2, TD/B/CN.4/GE.2/5, LEG/MLM/32 as a basis for discussion at its ninth session. To facilitate the work of the Joint Group, a comparison between the text of the provisions of the 1952 Convention on Arrest of Ships and the draft articles as contained in JIGE(VIII)/2 is provided in this document.

Draft articles for a convention on arrest of ships and the 1952 Arrest Convention compared

DRAFT ARTICLES	1952 CONVENTION
Article 1 - Definitions	**Article 1** ,
Article 1(1)	**Article 1(1)**
	In this Convention the following words shall have the meanings hereby assigned to them:
(1) "Maritime claim" means any claim concerning or arising out of the ownership, construction, possession, management, operation or trading of any ship, or out of a mortgage or an "hypothèque" or a registrable charge of the same nature on any ship, or out of salvage operations relating to any ship, such as any claim in respect of:	(1) "Maritime claim" means a claim arising out of one or more of the following:

---

*/ Also circulated by IMO under the symbol LEG/MLM/39.

DRAFT ARTICLES	1952 CONVENTION

Article 1(1), continued

(a) physical loss or damage caused by the operation of the ship other than loss of or damage to cargo, containers and passengers' effects carried on the ship;

(b) loss of life or personal injury occurring, whether on land or on water, in direct connection with the operation of the ship;

(c) salvage operations or any salvage agreement;

(d) liability to pay compensation or other remuneration in respect of the removal or attempted removal of a threat of damage, or of preventive measures or similar operations, whether or not arising under any international convention, or any enactment or agreement;

(e) costs or expenses relating to the raising, removal, recovery or destruction of the wreck of the ship or its cargo;

(f) any agreement relating to the use or hire of the ship, whether contained in a charter party or otherwise;

(g) any agreement relating to the carriage of goods or passengers in the ship, whether contained in a charter party or otherwise;

(h) loss of or damage to or in connection with goods (including luggage) carried in the ship;

(i) general average;

- - - - - - - - - - - - - - - -

(j) towage;

(k) pilotage;

(l) goods, materials, provisions, bunkers, equipment (including containers) or services supplied to the ship for its operation or maintenance;

(m) construction, repair, converting or equipping of the ship;

(n) port, canal, and other waterway dues and pilotage dues;

Article 1(1), continued

(a) damage caused by any ship either in collision or otherwise;

(b) loss of life or personal injury caused by any ship or occuring in connection with the operation of any ship;

(c) salvage;

- - - - - - - - - - - - - - - -

- - - - - - - - - - - - - - - -

(d) agreement relating to the use or hire of any ship whether by charter party or otherwise;

(e) agreement relating to the carriage of goods in any ship whether by charter party or otherwise;

(f) loss of or damage to goods including baggage carried in any ship;

(g) general average;

(h) bottomry;

(i) towage;

(j) pilotage;

(k) goods or materials wherever supplied to a ship for her operation or maintenance;

(l) construction, repair or equipment of any ship or dock charges and dues;

- - - - - - - - - - - - - - - -

DRAFT ARTICLES	1952 CONVENTION
Article 1(1), continued	**Article 1(1), continued**
(o) wages and other sums due to the master, officers and other members of the ship's complement in respect of their employment on the ship, including costs of repatriation and social insurance contributions payable on their behalf;	(m) wages of masters, officers, or crew;
(p) disbursements made in respect of the ship, by or on behalf of the master, owner, demise or other charterer or agent;	(n) master's disbursements, including disbursements made by shippers, charterers or agents on behalf of a ship or her owner;
(q) insurance premiums (including mutual insurance calls) in respect of the ship, payable by or on behalf of the shipowner or demise charterer;	- - - - - - - - - - - - - - - -
(r) any commissions, brokerages or agency fees payable in respect of the ship by or on behalf of the shipowner or demise charterer;	- - - - - - - - - - - - - - - -
(s) any dispute as to ownership or possession of the ship;	(o) disputes as to the title to or ownership of any ship;
(t) any dispute between co-owners of the ship as to the employment or earnings of the ship;	(p) disputes between co-owners of any ship as to the ownership, possession, employment or earnings of that ship;
(u) a mortgage or an "hypothèque" or a registrable charge of the same nature on the ship;	(q) the mortgage or hypothecation of any ship;
(v) any dispute arising out of a contract for the sale of the ship.	- - - - - - - - - - - - - - - -

Comment

The draft articles for a convention on arrest of ships contained in document *JIGE(VIII)/2, TD/B/CN.4/GE.2/5, LEG/MLM/32*, are based on the CMI Draft Revision of the International Convention for the Unification of Certain Rules Relating to the Arrest of Seagoing Ships 1952 prepared at the CMI Lisbon Conference in 1985, together with the amendments made necessary as a result of the adoption of the 1993 International Convention on Maritime Liens and Mortgages and observations/proposals made by delegations during the seventh session of the JIGE.

Article 1(1) of the draft articles corresponds to article 1(1) of the 1952 Convention. While the 1952 Convention contains an exhaustive list of maritime claims, the draft articles adopt a mixed approach of providing for a definition of the term "maritime claim" together with the general words "such as", so that while allowing some flexibility, it introduces an element of ejusdem generis with the list of maritime claims which follow. The list of maritime claims is expanded so as to cover all claims which have been granted maritime lien status under the 1993 MLM Convention and to include further claims of maritime nature. Sub-paragraphs (a), (b), (n) and (o) are based on article 4(1) of the 1993 MLM Convention. Sub-paragraphs (d), (e), (p), (q), (r) and (v) are new and they were added at the CMI Lisbon Conference so as to include other claims of maritime character. The outdated concept of "bottomry" has been deleted, and further modifications are made to ensure clarity.

During the eighth session of the JIGE an informal group was set up with the task of ensuring that all claims with maritime lien status under the 1993 MLM Convention are included in the list of maritime claims without creating duplication or conflict between sub-paragraphs of article 1(1). The Working Group did not complete its work and will continue consideration of the matter at the next session of the JIGE. The report of the Chairman of the Working Group is annexed to the report of JIGE.1/

DRAFT ARTICLES	1952 CONVENTION
Article 1(2)	**Article 1(2)**
(2) "Arrest" means any detention, or restriction on removal, of a ship by order of a Court to secure a maritime claim when at the time of such detention or restriction that ship is physically within the jurisdiction of the State where the order has been made.	(2) "Arrest means the detention of a ship by judicial process to secure a maritime claim, but does not include the seizure of a ship in execution or satisfaction of a judgement.
"Arrest" includes "attachment" or other conservatory measures, but does not include measures taken in execution or satisfaction of an enforceable judgement or arbitral award.	

Comment

Article 1(2) corresponds to the same paragraph of article 1 of the 1952 Convention. The text of this paragraph, which was adopted at the CMI Lisbon Conference, clearly limits the application of the Convention to cases where the ship is physically within the jurisdiction of the State of arrest. It therefore excludes the so-called documentary arrest by entering an order on the file of the ship in the ship's register.2/ This sub-paragraph was the subject of exensive discussion by the JIGE at its eighth session, where the definition of arrest contained in article 1(2) of the 1952 Convention was preferred by the majority of delegations.3/

1/. See the Report of the JIGE on its eighth session, document JIGE(VIII)/7, TD/B/CN.4/GE.2/10, LEG/MLM/37, annex II, and for discussions on article 1(1), see annex 1, paras 11-20.

2/. See the proceedings of the Lisbon Conference, CMI, 1985, Lisboa 11, p. 130.

3/. For discussion of the JIGE see the Report of the JIGE on its eighth session, JIGE(V111), TD/B/CN.4/GE.2/10, LEG/MLM/37, Annex, paras. 21-27.

DRAFT ARTICLES	1952 CONVENTION
Article 1(3)	**Article 1(3)**
(3) "Person" includes individuals, partnerships, unincorporated associations and bodies corporate, governments, their departments and public authorities.	(3) "Person" includes individuals, partnerships and bodies corporate, Governments, their Departments, and Public Authorities.

Comment

Article 1(3) of the draft articles corresponds to article 1(3) of the 1952 Convention.4/

Article 1(4)	**Article 1(4)**
(4) "Claimant" means any person asserting a maritime claim.	(4) "Claimant" means a person who alleges that a maritime claim exists in his favour.

Comment

Article 1(4) of the draft articles corresponds to article 1(4) of the 1952 Convention, with some drafting amendments.

Article 1(5)	- - - - - - - - - - - - - - - - - -
(5) "Court" means any competent judicial authority of a State.	

Comment

Article 1(5) is new and is considered as having only drafting significance.5/

Article 2 · Powers of arrest

Article 2(1)	**Article 4**
(1) A ship may be arrested or released from arrest only by or under the authority of a Court of the State in which the arrest is demanded or has been effected.	A ship may only be arrested under the authority of a Court or of the appropriate judicial authority of the Contracting State in which the arrest is made.

4/. For discussion on article 1(3), see the Report of the JIGE on its eighth session, *ibid.*, para. 28.

5/. See the proceedings of the CMI Lisbon Conference, 1985, Lisboa II (hereinafter referred to as Lisboa II), p. 132.

DRAFT ARTICLES   1952 CONVENTION

Comment

Article 2(1) of the draft articles corresponds to article 4 of the 1952 Convention.

Article 2(2)

(2) A ship may be arrested in respect of a maritime claim but in respect of no other claim.

Article 2

A ship flying the flag of one of the Contracting States may be arrested in the jurisdiction of any of the Contracting States in respect of any maritime claim, *but in respect of no other claim*; but nothing in this Convention shall be deemed to extend or restrict any right or powers vested in any Governments or their Departments, Public Authorities, or Dock or Harbour Authorities under their existing domestic laws or regulations to arrest, detain or otherwise prevent the sailing of vessels within their jurisdiction.

Comment

Article 2(2) of the draft articles reflects the concept contained in the first sentence of article 2 of the 1952 Convention.

Article 2(3)

(3) A ship may be arrested even though it is ready to sail or is sailing.

Article 3(1)

(1) Subject to the provisions of paragraph (4) of this article and of article 10, a claimant may arrest either the particular ship in respect of which the maritime claim arose, or any other ship which is owned by the person who was, at the time when the maritime claim arose, the owner of the particular ship, *even though the ship arrested be ready to sail*; but no ship, other than the particular ship in respect of which the claim arose, may be arrested in respect of any of the maritime claims enumerated in article 1(1)(o), (p) or (q).

Comment

Article 2(3) of the draft article is based on the provision contained in article 3(1) of the 1952 Convention.*6/*

6/. See Lisboa II, p. 132.

DRAFT ARTICLES

1952 CONVENTION

- - - - - - - - - - - - - - - - - - -

Article 2(4)

(4)   A ship may be arrested for the purpose of obtaining security notwithstanding that by virtue of a jurisdiction clause, arbitration clause or choice of law clause in any relevant contract the maritime claim in respect of which the arrest is effected is to be adjudicated in a State other than the State where the arrest is effected, or is to be arbitrated, or is to be adjudicated subject to the law of another State.

Comment

Article 2(4) of the draft articles is new.   It was adopted at the CMI Lisbon Conference.

Article 2(5)

(5)   Subject to the provisions of this Convention, the procedure relating to the arrest of a ship or its release shall be governed by the law of the State in which the arrest is demanded or has been effected.

Article 6(2)

The rules of procedure relating to the arrest of a ship, to the application for obtaining the authority referred to in article 4, and to all matters of procedure which the arrest may entail, shall be governed by the law of the Contracting State in which the arrest was made or applied for.

Comment

Article 2(5) of the draft articles corresponds to the second paragraph of article 6 of the 1952 Convention.7/

Article 3 - Exercise of right of arrest

(1)   Arrest is permissible of any ship in respect of which a maritime claim is asserted if:

Alternative 1:

[(a) the claim is secured by a maritime lien and is within any of the following categories;

(i) wages and other sums due to the master, officers and other members of the ship's

Article 3 (1), (2), (4)

(1)   Subject to the provisions of paragraph (4) of this article and of article 10, a claimant may arrest either the particular ship in respect of which the maritime claim arose, or any other ship which is owned by the person who was, at the time when the maritime claim arose, the owner of the particular ship, even though the ship arrested be ready to sail; but no ship, other than the particular ship in respect of which the claim arose, may be arrested in respect of

---

7/. For discussions held by the Joint Group on article 2 see the report of the JIGE on its eighth session, document JIGE(VIII)/7, annex 1, paragraphs 31-43.

DRAFT ARTICLES	1952 CONVENTION

Article 3, continued

complement in respect of their employment on the ship, including costs of repatriation and social insurance contributions payable on their behalf,

(ii) loss of life or personal injury occurring, whether on land of on water, in direct connection with the operation of the ship,

(iii) reward for the salvage of the ship,

(iv) port, canal, and other waterway dues and pilotage dues,

(v) physical loss or damage caused by the operation of the ship other than loss of or damage to cargo, containers and passengers' effects carried on the ship;] or

Alternative 2:

[(a) the claim is secured by a maritime lien;]

Alternative 3:

This alternative requires keeping the text of the paragraph 1(a) of alternative 1 together with a new sub-paragraph (b) which would read as follows:

[(b) the claim is secured by a maritime lien granted by the law of the State where the arrest is requested pursuant to the provisions of article 6 of the International Convention on Maritime Liens and Mortgages, 1993;]

(b) the claim is based upon a registered mortgage or a registered "hypothèque" or a registered charge of the same nature; or

(c) the claim is related to ownership or possession of the ship; or

(d) the claim is not covered by (a), (b) or (c) above and if:

(i) the person who owned the ship at the time when the maritime claim arose is personally liable for the claim and is owner of the ship when the arrest is effected, or

Article 3 (1), (2), (4), continued

any of the maritime claims enumerated in article 1(1)(o), (p) or (q).

(2) Ships shall be deemed to be in the same ownership when all the shares therein are owned by the same person or persons.

(4) When in the case of a charter by demise of a ship the charterer and not the registered owner is liable in respect of a maritime claim relating to that ship, the claimant may arrest such ship or any other ship in the ownership of the charterer by demise, subject to the provisions of this Convention, but no other ship in the ownership of the registered owner shall be liable to arrest in respect of such maritime claims.

The provisions of this paragraph shall apply to any case in which a person other than the registered owner of a ship is liable in respect of a maritime claim relating to that ship.

DRAFT ARTICLES   1952 CONVENTION

Article 3, continued

(ii) the demise charterer of
the ship is personally liable
for the claim and is demise
charterer or owner of the ship
when the arrest is effected.

(2)   Arrest is also permissible of
any other ship or ships which, when
the arrest is effected, is or are
owned by the person who is personally
liable for the maritime claim and who
was, when the claim arose:

(a)   owner of the ship in respect
of which the maritime claim arose;
or

(b)   demise   charterer,   time
charterer or voyage charterer of
that ship.

This provision does not apply to
claims in respect of ownership or
possession of a ship.

(3)   Notwithstanding the provisions
of paragraphs (1) and (2) of this
article, the arrest of a ship which
is not owned by the person allegedly
liable   for   the   claim   shall   be
permissible only if, under the law of
the   State   where   the   arrest   is
demanded, a judgement in respect of
that claim can be enforced against
that ship by judicial or forced sale
of that ship.

Comment

*Article 3 of the draft articles reflects the provisions of paragraphs (1),
(2) and (4) of the 1952 Convention.8/   Article 3(1)(a) includes three
alternative texts.   Alternative 1 is based on the Lisbon draft using the
terminology of article 4(1) of the 1993 MLM Convention.   Alternative 2 had been
proposed by the delegation of the United States of America during the seventh
session of the JIGE, and alternative 3 had been proposed by the Chairman of the
Informal Group on consideration of national maritime liens set out during the
same session.   If alternative 3 is adopted, sub-paragraphs (b), (c) and (d) which
follow will accordingly be reordered as (c), (d) and (e).9/*

8/. See Lisboa II, pp. 134-143.

9/. For discussion on the three alternatives see the Report of the JIGE on
its seventh session, document JIGE(VII)/3, TD/B/CN.4/GE.2/3, LEG/MLM/30, annex
1, para. 42.   See also the Report of the JIGE on its eighth session, document
JIGE(VIII)/7, TD/B/CN.4/GE.2/10, LEG/MLM/37, annex 1, paras. 44-53, for a
further alternative proposed by the delegation of the United States of
America.

DRAFT ARTICLES | 1952 CONVENTION

Article 4 - Release from arrest

(1) A ship which has been arrested shall be released when sufficient security has been furnished in a satisfactory form.

(2) In the absence of agreement between the parties as to the sufficiency and form of the security, the Court shall determine its nature and the amount thereof, not exceeding the value of the ship.

(3) Any request for the ship to be released upon security being provided shall not be construed as an acknowledgement of liability nor as a waiver of any defence or any right to limit liability.

(4) (a) If a ship has been arrested in a non-party State and is not released although security has been given in a State Party, that security shall be ordered released on application to the Court in the State Party save in exceptional cases where it would be unjust to do so.

(b) If in a non-party State the ship is released upon satisfactory security being provided, any security given in a State Party shall be ordered released to the extent that the total amount of security given in the two States exceeds:

(i) the claim for which the ship has been arrested, or

(ii) the value of the ship,

whichever is the lower.

Such release shall, however, not be ordered unless the security given in the non-party State will actually be available to the claimant and will be freely transferable.

(5) Where pursuant to paragraph (1) of this article security has been provided, the person providing such security may at any time apply to the Court to have that security reduced, modified, or cancelled.

Article 5

The Court or other appropriate judicial authority within whose jurisdiction the ship has been arrested shall permit the release of the ship upon sufficient bail or other security being furnished, save in cases in which a ship has been arrested in respect of any of the maritime claims enumerated in article 1(1)(o) and (p). In such cases, the Court or other appropriate judicial authority may permit the person in possession of the ship to continue trading the ship, upon such person furnishing sufficient bail or other security, or may otherwise deal with the operation of the ship during the period of the arrest.

In default of agreement between the parties as to the sufficiency of the bail or other security, the Court or other appropriate judicial authority shall determine the nature and amount thereof.

The request to release the ship against such security shall not be construed as an acknowledgement of liability or as a waiver of the benefit of the legal limitation of liability of the owner of the ship.

Comment

Article 4 of the draft articles corresponds to article 5 of the 1952 Convention.10/

10/. See Lisboa II, 1985, p. 144. For the discussion on article 4 by the Joint Group see the Report of the JIGE on its eighth session, document JIGE(VIII)/7, ibid. paras. 54-65.

DRAFT ARTICLES   **1952 CONVENTION**

Article 5 - Right of rearrest and multiple arrest

<u>Alternative 1</u>:

(1)   Where in any State a ship has already been arrested and released or security in respect of that ship has already been given to secure a maritime claim, that ship shall not thereafter be rearrested or arrested in respect of the same maritime claim unless:

    (a) the nature or amount of the security already obtained in respect of the same claim is inadequate, provided that the aggregate amount of security may not exceed the value of the ship; or

    (b) the person who has already given the security is not, or is unlikely to be, able to fulfil some or all of his obligatiions[; or

    (c) the ship arrested or the security previously given was released either:

        (i) upon the application or with the consent of the claimant acting on reasonable grounds, or

        (ii) because the claimant could not by taking reasonable steps prevent the release].

(2)   Any other ship which would otherwise be subject to arrest in respect of the same maritime claim shall not be arrested unless:

    (a) the nature or amount of the security already obtained in respect of the same claim is inadequate; or

    (b) the provisions of paragraph (1)(b) or (c) of this article are applicable.

(3)   "Release" for the purpose of this article shall not include any unlawful release or escape from arrest.

<u>Alternative 2</u>:

[(1) Where in any State a ship has already been arrested and released or security in respect of that ship has already been given to secure a maritime claim, that ship shall not thereafter be rearrested or arrested in respect of the same maritime claim, unless there has been fraud or

Article 3(3)

(3)   A ship shall not be arrested, nor shall bail or other security be given more than once in any one or more of the jurisdictions of any of the Contracting States in respect of the same maritime claim by the same claimant; and, if a ship has been arrested in any one of such jurisdictions, or bail or other security has been given in such jurisdiction either to release the ship or to avoid a threatened arrest, any subsequent arrest of the ship or of any ship in the same ownership by the same claimant for the same maritime claim shall be set aside, and the ship released by the Court or other appropriate judicial authority of that State, unless the claimant can satisfy the Court or other appropriate judicial authority that the bail or other security had been finally released before the subsequent arrest or that there is other good cause for maintaining that arrest.

DRAFT ARTICLES	1952 CONVENTION

Article 5, continued

material misrepresentation in connection with the release or the posting of the security.

(2) Any other ship which would otherwise be subject to arrest in respect of the same maritime claim shall not be arrested unless the nature or the amount of the security already obtained in respect of the same claim is inadequate.

(3) "Release" for the purpose of this article shall not include any unlawful release or escape from arrest.]

Comment

Article 5 of the draft articles corresponds to article 3(3) of the 1952 Convention. It includes two alternatives. Alternative 1 is based on the Lisbon draft and paragraph (c) is placed in brackets during the seventh session of the JIGE. Alternative 2 had been proposed by the delegations of the United States of America, Liberia and the Republic of Korea at the seventh session of the JIGE.11/

Article 6 - Protection of owners and demise charterers of arrested ships

(1) The court may as a condition of the arrest of a ship, or of permitting an arrest already effected to be maintained, impose upon the claimant who seeks to arrest or who has procured the arrest of the ship the obligation to provide security of a kind and for an amount, and upon such terms, as may be determined by that Court for any loss which may be incurred by the defendant as a result of the arrest, and for which the claimant may be found liable, including but not restricted to such loss or damage as may be incurred by that defendant in consequence of:

(a) the arrest having been wrongful or unjustified; or

(b) excessive security having been demanded and obtained.

(2) The Courts of the State in which an arrest has been effected shall have jurisdiction to determine

Article 6 (1)

All questions whether in any case the claimant is liable in damages for the arrest of a ship or for the costs of the bail or other security furnished to release or prevent the arrest of a ship, shall be determined by the law of the Contracting State in whose jurisdiction the arrest was made or applied for.

11/. For discussion on article 5 see the Report of the JIGE on its seventh session, document JIGE(VII)/3, TD/B/CN.4/GE.2/3, LEG/MLM/30, annex I, paras. 46-51.

Article 6, continued

the extent of the liability, if any, of the claimant for loss or damage caused by the arrest of a ship, including but not restricted to such loss or damage as may be caused in consequence of:

(a) the arrest having been wrongful or unjustified, or

(b) excessive security having been demanded and obtained.

(3) The liability, if any, of the claimant in accordance with paragraph (2) of this article shall be determined by application of the law of the State where the arrest was effected.

(4) If a Court in another State or an arbitral tribunal is to determine the merits of the case in accordance with the provisions of article 7, then proceedings relating to the liability of the claimant in accordance with paragraph (2) of this article may be stayed pending that decision.

(5) Where pursuant to paragraph (1) of this article security has been provided, the person providing such security may at any time apply to the Court to have that security reduced, modified or cancelled.

Comment

Article 6 of the draft articles corresponds to the first paragraph of article 6 of the 1952 Convention.

Article 7 - Jurisdiction on the merits of the case

(1) The Courts of the State in which an arrest has been effected or security given to prevent arrest or obtain the release of the ship shall have jurisdiction to determine the case upon its merits, unless the Parties validly agree or have agreed to submit the dispute to a Court of another State which accepts jurisdiction, or to arbitration.

(2) Notwithstanding the provisions of paragraph (1) of this article, the Courts of the State in which an arrest has been effected, or security given to prevent arrest or obtain the release of the ship, may refuse to exercise that jurisdiction where that

Article 7

(1) The Courts of the country in which the arrest was made shall have jurisdiction to determine the case upon its merits if the domestic law of the country in which the arrest is made gives jurisdiction to such Courts; or in any of the following cases namely:

(a) if the claimant has his habitual residence or principal place of business in the country in which the arrest was made;

(b) if the claim arose in the country in which the arrest was made;

DRAFT ARTICLES	1952 CONVENTION

Article 7, continued

refusal is permitted by the law of that State and a Court of another State accepts jurisdiction.

(3) In cases where a Court of the State where an arrest has been effected or security given to prevent arrest or obtain the release of the ship:

    (a) does not have jurisdiction to determine the case upon its merits; or

    (b) has refused to exercise jurisdiction in accordance with the provisions of paragraph (2) of this article,

such Court may, and upon request shall, order a period of time within which the claimant shall being proceedings before a competent Court or arbitral tribunal.

(4) If proceedings are not brought within the period of time ordered in accordance with paragraph (3) of this article then the ship arrested or the security given shall, upon request, be ordered released.

(5) If proceedings are brought within the period of time ordered in accordance with paragraph (3) of this article, or if proceedings before a competent Court in another State are brought in the absence of any such order, then unless such proceedings do not satisfy general requirements in respect of due process of law, any final decision resulting therefrom shall be recognized and given effect with respect to the arrested ship or to the security given in order to prevent its arrest or obtain its release.

(6) Nothing contained in the provisions of paragraph (5) of this article shall restrict any further effect given to a foreign judgement or arbitral award under the law of the State where the arrest of the ship was made or security given to prevent its arrest or obtain its release.

Article 7, continued

    (c) if the claim concerns the voyage of the ship during which the arrest was made;

    (d) if the claim arose out of a collision or in circumstances covered by article 13 of the International Convention for the Unification of Certain Rules of Law with respect to Collisions between Vessels, signed at Brussels on 23 September 1910;

    (e) if the claim is for salvage;

    (f) if the claim is upon a mortgage or hypothecation of the ship arrested.

(2) If the Court within whose jurisdiction the ship was arrested has no jurisdiction to decide upon the merits, the bail or other security given in accordance with article 5 to procure the release of the ship shall specifically provide that it is given as security for the satisfaction of any judgement which may eventually be pronounced by a Court having jurisdiction so to decide; and the Court or other appropriate judicial authority of the country in which the arrest is made shall fix the time within which the claimant shall bring an action before a Court having such jurisdiction.

(3) If the parties have agreed to submit the dispute to the jurisdiction of a particular Court other than that within whose jurisdiction the arrest was made or to arbitration, the Court or other appropriate judicial authority within whose jurisdiction the arrest was made may fix the time within which the claimant shall bring proceedings.

(4) If, in any of the cases mentioned in the two preceding paragraphs, the action or proceedings are not brought within the time so fixed, the defendant may apply for the release of the ship or of the bail or other security.

(5) This article shall not apply in cases covered by the provisions of the revised Rhine Navigation Convention of 17 October 1868.

Comment

    Article 7 of the draft articles corresponds to article 7 of the 1952 Convention.

DRAFT ARTICLES	1952 CONVENTION

Article 8 · Application

(1) This Convention shall apply to any seagoing ship, whether or not that ship is flying the flag of a State Party.

Article 8

(1) The provisions of this Convention shall apply to any vessel flying the flag of a Contracting State in the jurisdiction of any Contracting State.

(2) A ship flying the flag of a non-Contracting State may be arrested in the jurisdiction of any Contracting State in respect of any of the maritime claims enumerated in article 1 or of any other claim for which the law of the Contracting State permits arrest.

(3) Nevertheless any Contracting State shall be entitled wholly or partly to exclude from the benefits of this Convention any Government of a non-Contracting State or any person who has not, at the time of the arrest, his habitual residence or principal place of business in one of the Contracting States.

(2) The Convention shall not apply to ships owned or operated by a State and used only on Government non-commercial service.

- - - - - - - - - - - - - - - - -

Article 9

(3) Nothing in this Convention shall be construed as creating a maritime lien.

Nothing in this Convention shall be construed as creating a right of action, which, apart from the provisions of this Convention, would not arise under the law applied by the Court which had seisin of the case, nor as creating any maritime liens which do not exist under such law or under the Convention on Maritime Mortgages and Liens, if the latter is applicable.

Article 2

(4) This Convention does not affect any rights or powers vested in any Government or its departments, or in any public authority, or in any dock or harbour authority, under any international convention or under any domestic law or regulation, to detain or otherwise prevent from sailing any ship within their jurisdiction.

A ship flying the flag of one of the Contracting States may be arrested in the jurisdiction of any of the Contracting States in respect of any maritime claim, but in respect of no other claim; but nothing in this Convention shall be deemed to extend or restrict any right or powers vested in any Governments on their Departments, Public Authorities, or Dock or Harbour Authorities under their existing domestic laws or regulations to arrest, detain or otherwise prevent the sailing of vessels within their jurisdiction.

(5) This Convention shall not affect the power of any State or Court to make orders affecting the totality of a debtor's assets.

- - - - - - - - - - - - - - - - -

DRAFT ARTICLES	1952 CONVENTION

Article 8, continued

(6) Nothing in this Convention shall affect the application of international conventions providing for limitation of liability, or domestic law giving effect thereto, in the State where an arrest is effected.

- - - - - - - - - - - - - - - - - - - -

Article 8 - paragraphs 4 and 5

(7) Nothing in this Convention shall modify or affect the rules of law in force in the States Parties relating to the arrest of any ship physically within the jurisdiction of the State of its flag procured by a person who has his habitual residence or principal place of business in that State, or by any other person who has acquired a claim from such person by subrogation, assignment or otherwise.

(4) Nothing in this Convention shall modify or affect the rules of law in force in the respective Contracting States relating to the arrest of any ship within the jurisdiction of the State of her flag by a person who has his habitual residence or principal place of business in that State.

(5) When a maritime claim is asserted by a third party other than the original claimant, whether by subrogation, assignment or otherwise, such third party shall, for the purpose of this Convention, be deemed to have the same habitual residence or principal residence or principal place of business as the original claimant.

Comment

Article 8 of the draft articles corresponds to articles 2, 8 and 9 of the 1952 Convention. Article 8(1) is based on paragraphs (1) to (3) of article 8 of the 1952 Convention. Unlike the provisions of the 1952 Convention, and following the trends in modern maritime conventions, it provides for general application of the draft convention. Paragraph (2) is new and excludes the application of the draft convention to State-owned ships, provided they are used for non-commercial services. The terminology is based on that of article 3(2) of the 1993 MLM Convention. Paragraph (3) is based on article 9 of the 1952 Convention. The placement of this paragraph in article 8 which deals with application of the draft convention may be questioned. Paragraph (4) is based on article 2 of the 1952 Convention. Paragraphs (5) and (6) are new. The latter is to avoid conflict between conventions. Paragraph (7) is based on article 8 paragraphs (4) and (5) of the 1952 Convention.

Article 9 - Reservations

A State may, when signing, ratifying, accepting or acceding to this Convention, reserve the right to refrain from applying the Convention to ships not flying the flag of a State Party.

Article 8(1)

(1) The provisions of this Convention shall apply to any vessel flying the flag of a Contracting State in the jurisdiction of any Contracting State.

Comment

Article 9 of the draft articles corresponds to paragraph (1) of article 8 of the 1952 Convention.

3. CONSIDERATION OF THE REVIEW OF THE INTERNATIONAL CONVENTION FOR THE UNIFICATION OF CERTAIN RULES RELATING TO THE ARREST OF SEA-GOING SHIPS, 1952 - NOTE BY THE SECRETARIAT OF UNCTAD AND IMO (COMMENTS AND PROPOSALS BY JAPAN AND THE UNITED KINGDOM)

Doc. no.: TD/B/IGE.1/3   Date: 23 October 1996

Compilation of comments and proposals by Governments,
on the draft articles for a convention on arrest of ships */

CONTENTS

INTRODUCTION

1.   This document sets out the comments and proposals of Governments on the draft articles for a convention on arrest of ships that were received as of Thursday, 22 August 1996. Up to that date comments had been received from the following:

    Governments: Japan; United Kingdom of Great Britain and Northern Ireland.

─────────────────

*/ Also circulated under the symbol LEG/MLM/40

COMPILATION OF COMMENTS AND PROPOSALS

JAPAN

Article 1, para 2:

2.   Add the following phrase at the end of paragraph 2: "or other documents
which are enforceable under the law of the State where such measures have
been taken".

3.   So, para 2, amended by the above addition, will read as follows:

> *"Arrest" means the detention of a ship by judicial process to
> secure maritime claim, but does not include the seizure of a ship in
> execution or satisfaction of a judgement or other documents which are
> enforceable under the law of the State where such measures have been
> taken.*

3.   Reason for the above amendment: We believe that this Convention aims at
restriction of the detention of a ship as provisional measures prior to
obtaining enforceable judgement. Its article 4, which regulates release from
arrest by sufficient security, and the article 7, which sets forth a tribunal
to determine the merits of the case, can be understood only in that context.
Therefore, the seizure of a ship based on the documents which are enforceable
in the same way as judgements under the law of the State should be excluded
from the definition of "Arrest". In Japan, such documents include:

-       conciliation protocol;

-       officially authenticated instruments which are agreements of the
        parties, written before a judge or a notary public;

-       copy of register that certifies the right of hypothecation, and so
        forth.

Article 3:

4.   According to the Law of Civil Provisional Remedies of Japan, provisional
detention measures against a ship can be granted if the ship, regardless of
whether the claim arose in respect of that ship or not, is owned by the
debtor at the time when the detention measure is effected. From this
standpoint, with respect to paragraph 1(d)(i) and paragraph 2, it is not
necessary to require that the debtor who owns the ship at the time of arrest
also possess or charter the ship when the claim arose.

Article 4:

5.   Article 4, which concerns mandatory release from arrest by security,
should not apply to the arrest relating to the disputes as to ownership or
possession of the ship, because such disputes can not be always solved by
pecuniary compensation. In this connection, paragraph 1 of article 5 of 1952
Arrest Convention clearly excludes the arrests in respect of such disputes
from the application of release by security. Therefore, we propose that
paragraph 1 of Article 4 of the revised draft should be reverted to the text
of 1952 Arrest Convention.

UNITED KINGDOM OF GREAT BRITAIN AND NORTHERN IRELAND

Introduction

6.   At the close of the eighth session of the Joint Intergovernmental Group
of Experts (JIGE) the Chairman urged delegations wishing to propose
amendments to the draft articles to submit written proposals, in order that

these might be considered at the group's ninth session (document JIGE(VIII)/7, Annex I, paragraph 67). This submission sets out the UK delegation's comments on, and proposals for amendments to, the draft articles contained in document JIGE(VIII)/2 (the "JIGE text").

Article 1(2)

7.   Following the discussion on this provision at the eighth session of the JIGE, it was concluded that the definition of "arrest" in the JIGE text should be identical to that in the 1952 Convention (document JIGE(VIII)/7, Annex I, paragraph 27).

8.   The United Kingdom delegation entirely agrees that the JIGE definition should be modelled more closely on that of the 1952 Convention and, in particular, that the phrase "when at the time of such detention or restriction the ship is physically within the jurisdiction of the State where the order has been made" in the first sentence of the JIGE text should be deleted. There is no equivalent of this phrase in the 1952 Convention. Its inclusion would add unnecessary ambiguity to the definition. Article 2(1) of the JIGE text contains rules on which courts are able to order the arrest of a ship. Article 7 contains rules on which courts have jurisdiction to consider the case upon its merits.

9.   Discussions are under-way in the United Kingdom on whether it would be desirable for the Mareva injunction to be covered by the definition of "arrest".

Article 1(3)

10.   There is a clear definition of "person" in Article I(2) of the 1969 Civil Liability Convention. The 1992 Protocol did not change the definition.The same definition has now also been adopted in Article 1(2) of the 1996 HNS Convention. The United Kingdom delegation therefore proposes that the JIGE should not adopt a revised wording for the sake of it but should adopt this tried and tested definition:

> *"Person" means any individual or partnership or any public or private body, whether corporate or not, including a State or any of its constituent subdivisions.*

11.   The United Kingdom delegation submits that the intended meaning of the definition contained in Article 1(3) of the JIGE text is the same as that of the CLC precedent. However, while the meaning of the JIGE text has been queried, that of the text used in CLC is well understood.

Article 2(1)

12.   The United Kingdom delegation believes that the reference, in Article 2(1) of the JIGE text, to the State in which the arrest is _demanded_ is unnecessary and misleading. The provision should, as in Article 4 of the 1952 Convention, refer only to the State in which the arrest is made:

> *A ship may be arrested or released from arrest only by ur under the authority of a Court of the State in which the arrest is _made_.*

Article 2(4)

13.   The United Kingdom delegation agrees that it is helpful to clarify that a ship may be arrested for the purpose of obtaining security under the authority of a court other than that with jurisdiction to examine the case on its merits. As currently drafted, however, Article 2(4) of the JIGE text suggests that an arrest in such circumstances is only possible in two

specific cases: namely, where there is a jurisdiction clause or arbitration clause in any relevant contract.

14.   There are other circumstances which could result in the merits of the case being considered by a court or arbitrator in a State other than that in which the arrest was made. For example, the Brussels Convention on Jurisdiction and the Enforcement of Judgements may prevent the court under the authority of which the ship has been arrested from assuming jurisdiction over the merits (*The Tatry*); the application of the doctrine of *forum non conveniens* or rules on *lis alibi pendens* may also prevent the court under the authority of which the ship has been arrested from exercising jurisdiction over the merits. It is therefore necessary to amend Article 2(4) so as to separate more clearly the ability of a court: (a) to hear a claim on the merits, and (b) to award provisional security by way of arrest.

15.   The UK delegation proposes that clarification be added to Article 2(4) of the JIGE text by amending the provision as follows:

> *A ship may be arrested for the purpose of obtaining security notwithstanding that, by virtue of a jurisdiction clause or arbitration clause in any relevant contract, or otherwise, the maritime claim in respect of which the arrest is made is to be adjudicated in a State other than the State where the arrest is made, or is to be arbitrated, or is to be adjudicated subject to the law of another State.*

Article 2(5)

16.   As in Article 2(1) (see paragraph 12), the United Kingdom delegation believes that the reference to the State in which the arrest is *demanded* is unnecessary and misleading. The provision should instead, as in Article 6 of the 1952 Convention, refer to the State in which the arrest is made:

> *Subject to the provisions of this Convention, the procedure relating to the arrest of a ship or its release shall be governed by the law of the State in which the arrest is made.*

Article 3(1)

17.   While there are differing interpretations of Article 3(1) of the 1952 Convention, it can be argued that that Convention provides an unfettered right for a claimant to arrest the particular ship in respect of which a maritime claim arose, irrespective of whether the claim is secured by a maritime lien or whether the shipowner is personally liable for the claim. It is generally agreed, however, that - even if the 1952 Convention does not provide such an unfettered right - there is nothing in the Convention to prevent a State from providing such a right under national law.

18.   The United Kingdom delegation is not convinced that there is any need to depart from the general approach of the 1952 Convention, particularly if it is agreed that the list of maritime claims in Article 1(1) should be exhaustive. However, if there is to be a link between the right to arrest a ship and the existence of a maritime lien, the drafting of Article 3(1) could be made considerably simpler by referring only to maritime liens recognized by the law of the State in which the arrest was made.

19.   The United Kingdom delegation also proposes that the reference to mortgages, "hypothèques" and registrable charges of a similar nature in Article 3(1)(b) should follow the wording used in the chapeau, and subparagraph (u), of Article 1(1).

20.   In order to implement the two changes proposed above, Article 3(1) of the JIGE text should be amended as follows:

> *Arrest is permissible of any ship in respect of which a maritime
> claim is asserted if:*
>
> *(a)   the claim is secured by a maritime lien recognized under the law
>   of the State where the arrest is made;*
>
> *(b)   the claim is based upon a mortgage, an "hypothèque" or registrable
>   charge of a similar nature;*
>
> *(c)   [...]; or*
>
> *(d)   [...].*

Article 4(2)

21.   Unlike Article 5 of the 1952 Convention, Article 4(2) of the JIGE text
provides that the amount of security should not exceed the value of the ship.
Article 8(6) of the JIGE text, however, provides that international
conventions on limitation of liability would take precedence over the new
Arrest Convention.

22.   The reference to the value of the ship in Article 4(2) is confusing,
therefore, since the applicable limitation amount will very often exceed the
value of the ship.   The recent entry into force of the 1992 Protocol to the
1969 Civil Liability Convention and the adoption of the HNS Convention and
the 1996 Protocol to the Convention on the Limitation of Liability for
Maritime Claims 1976 make this even more likely than in the past.

23.   The United Kingdom delegation believes that it is poor drafting to
suggest, in Article 4(2), that the amount of security is restricted to the
value of the ship when, by virtue of Article 8(6), the relevant restriction
in most cases will be the applicable limit on the shipowner's liability,
which will generally be a greater amount.   Article 4(2) should therefore
provide, as Article 5 of the 1952 Convention does, that:

> *In the absence of agreement between the parties as to the
> sufficiency and form of the security, the Court shall determine its
> nature and the amount thereof.*

24.   Consequential amendments will be needed to Articles 4(4)(b) and 5(1)(a).

Article 6

25.   The United Kingdom delegation is not convinced that there is any valid
reason to change the simple provision contained in Article 6 of the 1952
Convention.   If, however, the majority view is that the additional detail
contained in Article 6 of the JIGE text *is* desirable, the United Kingdom
delegation would suggest that the references to "unjustified" arrest should
be deleted from paragraphs 1(a) and 2(a).

26.   Without the deletion of the references to "unjustified" arrest, the
provision might conflict with United Kingdom law, which is based on the
premise that, with the exception of wrongful arrest, a claimant should not be
penalised for having arrested a ship, even if the action fails on the merits.
The concept of an "unjustified" arrest is also ambiguous: an arrest might be
perfectly justified based on the facts available to the claimant at the time
the arrest is demanded, but could turn out not to be justified when the true
facts of the case become clear.   Paragraphs 1(a) and 2(b) should therefore be
amended to refer only to:

> *the arrest having been wrongful.*

FOOD AND AGRICULTURE ORGANIZATION
(FAO)

DOCUMENT REPRODUCED IN WHOLE OR IN PART:

10.	Doc. no.:	FAO Fisheries Circular No. 913
	Date:	1996
	Title:	Process for the Establishment of the Indian Ocean Tuna Commission

11.	Doc. no.:	FAO Fisheries Circular No. 917
	Date:	1996
	Title:	A Checklist for Fisheries Resource Management Issues Seen from the Perspective of the FAO Code of Conduct for Responsible Fisheries

12.	Doc. no.:	FAO Fisheries Circular No. 919
	Date:	1996
	Title:	Fisheries and Aquaculture in the Near East and North Africa: Situation and Outlook in 1996

13.	Doc. no.:	FAO Fisheries Circular No. 921
	Date:	1996
	Title:	Fisheries and Aquaculture in Latin America and the Caribbean: Situation and Outlook in 1996

14.	Doc. no.:	FAO Fisheries Circular No. 922
	Date:	1996
	Title:	Fisheries and Aquaculture in Sub-Saharan Africa: Situation and Outlook in 1996

FAO FISHERIES REPORTS

15.	Doc. no.:	FAO Fisheries Report No. 533
	Date:	1996
	Title:	General Fisheries Council for the Mediterranean. Report of the Third Technical Consultation on Stock Assessment in the Central Mediterranean

16.	Doc. no.:	FAO Fisheries Report No. 534
	Date:	1996
	Title:	Report of the Thirteenth Session of the Fishery Committee for the Eastern Central Atlantic

17.	Doc. no.:	FAO Fisheries Report No. 536
	Date:	1996
	Title:	Indian Ocean Fishery Commission. Report of the Eighth Session of the Committee for the Development and Management of Fishery Resources in the Gulfs

18.	Doc. no.:	FAO Fisheries Report No. 543
	Date:	1996
	Title:	Report of the Eighth Session of the Western Central Atlantic Fishery Commission

FAO FISHERIES TECHNICAL PAPERS

19.	Doc. no.:	FAO Fisheries Technical Paper No. 357
	Date:	1996
	Title:	Fisheries and Research for Tunas and Tuna-Like-Species in the Western Central Atlantic: Implications of the Agreement for the Implementation of the Provisions of the United Nations Convention on the Law of the Sea of 10 December 1982 relating to the Conservation and Management of Straddling Fish Stocks and Highly Migratory Fish Stocks

FAO TECHNICAL GUIDELINES FOR RESPONSIBLE FISHERIES

20.   Doc. no.:   1
       Date: 1996
       Title: Fishing Operations

21.   Doc. no.:   2
       Date: 1996
       Title: Precautionary Approach to Capture Fisheries and Species
                    Introduction

22.   Doc. no.:   3
       Date: 1996
       Title: Integration of Fisheries into Coastal Area Management

FAO YEARBOOK OF FISHERY STATISTICS

23.   Doc. no.:   78
       Date: 1996
       Title: Fishery Statistics. Catches and Landings [1994]

24.   Doc. no.:   79
       Date: 1996
       Title: Fishery Statistics. Commodities [1994]

1. ISSUES OF INTERNATIONAL TRADE, ENVIRONMENT AND SUSTAINABLE FISHERIES DEVELOPMENT*

Doc. no.:COFI:FT/V/96/5   March 1996

CONTENTS

INTRODUCTION

1.   There are several roots why matters of international trade, environment and sustainable fisheries development continue to appear on the agenda of this Sub-Committee on Fish Trade:

———————
*   Only paras 1-19 and Appendix I are reproduced here.

a) the discussion of the Sub-Committee at its Third Session in 1990 regarding trade sanctions related to a resource conservation and catch technology issue[1] which was one of the forerunners of the COFI debate in 1991 resulting in the proposal to elaborate a Code of Conduct for Responsible Fisheries[2]

b) the requirement embedded in Chapter 2 of the UNCED Agenda 21 that "environment and trade policies should be mutually supportive[3]

c) at its Fourth Session the Sub-Committee stressed the importance of immediately addressing environmental issues[4]

d) the request of COFI at its Twenty-first Session that FAO take a stronger role in the discussion on fish trade and environment issues in other international bodies, e.g. in the World Trade Organization (WTO)[5].

2.   Paragraph 55 of the Sub-Committee's Fourth Session had suggested that the Regional Fish Marketing Information and Technical Advisory Services (INFOFISH, INFOPECHE, INFOPESCA and INFOSAMAK) should obtain opinions and comments from government and industry in this regard. The Services/Centres will report on the outcome of their enquiries at the Fifth Session.

FAO STUDIES

3.   In line with the recommendations of the Sub-Committee referred to in paragraph 1. c) above, the Secretariat has prepared an internal working paper on the dimensions of the environmental impact of trade in fishery products. The Executive Summary of this study is attached as Appendix I. The main purpose of this working paper is to identify the principal relationships between fishery trade and the environment and to elaborate a checklist of factors to be covered in country case studies which should be prepared by national experts in a second phase of the exercise. Once these are available, an attempt will be made to quantify in order of magnitude - initially accepting a likely wide margin of error - the impacts of fishery trade on the environment. This analysis will give due attention to the forward and backward links of export production and possible repercussions on output which does not enter international trade.

4.   A second study compiling information on quantitative effects of pollution of the environment from filleting, canning and reduction operations has been prepared. However, it may be of interest to note that precise quantitative information is scarce and some of it rather aged, but hopefully not outdated. A recent FAO publication on economics of engineering in fisheries[6] may be helpful in broadening the quantitative knowledge in the future. At present, there seems to be a clear need for the systematic collection of pertinent data and it is hoped that with the collaboration of academic and research institutions a useful body of knowledge can be accumulated within a few years.

5.   Within FAO's general programme on trade, environment and sustainable agricultural development, a study has been commissioned to specifically investigate the environmental impact of one of the main international fishery commodities, shrimp. Preliminary results of the study will be presented to the Sub-Committee at this session by the observer from INFOFISH, the organization coordinating this work.

PERTINENT ACTIVITIES IN OTHER INTERNATIONAL ORGANIZATIONS

6.   The attention of the Sub-Committee is drawn to the entries from the Convention on International Trade in Endangered Species of Wild Fauna and Flora (CITES) and the Organisation for Economic Co-operation and Development (OECD) in Appendix I of document COFI:FT/V/96/2 which contain references to pertinent activities in the organizations. As Task Manager for

---

[1]   Paragraphs 10 and 11 of FAO Fisheries Report No. 440 (Report of Third Session of COFI Sub-Committee on Fish Trade)
[2]   Paragraph 82 of FAO Fisheries Report No. 459 (Report of Nineteenth Session of COFI)
[3]   Paragraph 2.19 of Chapter 2
[4]   Paragraph 52 of FAO Fisheries Report No. 492 (Report of Fourth Session of COFI Sub-Committee on Fish Trade)
[5]   Paragraph 23 of FAO Council document CL 108/7 (Report of Twenty-first Session of COFI)
[6]   FAO Fisheries Technical Paper No. 351 (Economic Engineering applied to the Fishery Industry)

Chapter 2 of Agenda 21 (International policies to accelerate sustainable development in developing countries and related domestic policies), United Nations Conference on Trade and Development (UNCTAD) prepared a comprehensive paper "Trade, Environment and Sustainable Development" in April 1996. The document is not product specific and there are hardly any references to ongoing work in FAO, i.e., fishery product trade is not dealt with by UNCTAD as was also reflected in their negative reply to the survey on which Appendix I of COFI:FT/V/96/2 is based. Therefore, there is no danger of duplicating effort.

7.   In a document prepared in 1993 as background information for the UN Conference on Straddling Fish Stocks and Highly Migratory Fish Stocks, FAO[7] expressed concern about the status of shark stocks since the potential and state of most of them are unknown. Most oceanic sharks have low fecundity, slow growth and a long lifespan, and consequently a low resilience to fishing. Very careful management is required in order to achieve the appropriate, relatively low, levels of sustainable production. At the time of writing, the CITES/FAO cooperation in collating biological and trade data on sharks[8] reached the final stage of preparation following a rather long waiting period until funding could be confirmed. With funds becoming available in the immediate future, the opportunity of reporting on progress will be used at this session of the Sub-Committee. For the information of the Sub-Committee, the currently valid listing of species in the appendices of CITES is attached as Appendix II to this document. In this connection, it should be kept in mind that according to the CITES Secretariat "most of these species have been in the appendices for many years and were included because of general concern at the time that exploitation of these resources was not sustainable".

8.   In WTO, the Committee on Trade and Environment has begun its work and the WTO Dispute Settlement Body (DSB) has been established. With requests regarding the trade description of scallops and measures affecting the importation of salmon, two items related to international trade in fishery products reached the agenda of the DSB in 1995. FAO has observer status with WTO and care is being taken to avoid any duplication of effort but to contribute, when appropriate, to transparency in technical aspects and in doing so to comply with COFI's instruction mentioned in paragraph 1. d) of this document. The priority accorded to WTO in matters related to international trade in fishery products is reflected in the Code of Conduct for Responsible Fisheries, e.g., Articles 6.14, 11.2.1, 11.2.4, 11.2.5, 11.2.13, 11.2.14 and 11.3.8 where specific mention is made to this effect.

9.   Also for the information of the Sub-Committee, a list of international environmental instruments which are relevant for fisheries is provided in Appendix III. It is taken with minor changes from the final report of a research project carried out by the University of Wollongong and the Australian Maritime College[9].

10.   The trade/environment debate is not going away and the sometimes conflicting issues of trade and environment will have to be reconciled in order to ensure that the benefits of trade liberalization are realized while the disbenefits are countered[10]. There are a number of recent examples of disagreement and conflicts between trade and the environment related to international trade in fishery products on which the Sub-Committee may wish to exchange experience with a view to providing guidance as to how FAO's contribution to transparency on technical matters and to problem solving procedures in other fora or at different levels should preferably be organized and which subjects might be attributed priority in these considerations.

---

[7]   Chapter 2.2 of FAO Fisheries Technical Paper No. 337 (World Review of Highly Migratory Species and Straddling Stocks)

[8]   Paragraph 22 of FAO Council document CL 108/7 (Report of Twenty-first Session of COFI)

[9]   Tsamenyi, M. and A. McIlgorm, International Environmental Instruments - Their Effect on the Fishing Industry. Canberra, University of Wollongong and Australian Maritime College, September 1995

[10]   The words are Duncan Brack's, Balancing trade and the environment in "International Affairs" 71,3 (1995) pp.497-514; quoted from pp.513-4

11.   Analysis[11] shows that the structure of interests and power on trade-environment issues lead to different expectations with regard to the extent of environment friendly convergence in a given trade institution. Increased integration creates increased demand for environment-friendly trade-environment rules. Only few environment-friendly rules are expected at the least integrated level, the WTO, more at North American Free Trade Agreement (NAFTA) and most at the European Community (EC). So that the overall extent of convergence moves from low (WTO) through moderate (NAFTA) to highest (EC). Steinberg's model "helps to explain the process of regionalization of environment-friendly convergence on trade issues. Interest in environment-friendly convergence is associated with deepening integration. Institutions within trade organizations that facilitate environment-friendly outcomes have developed more extensively on a regional than a multilateral basis." Therefore, the conclusions are:

a)   the Americas and Europe are separately enhancing environmental protection in their respective regions, meaning that there is western convergence towards a higher level of protection, but

b)   trade-environment rules are only converging regionally, with each region likely to adopt its own particular product standards, process and production methods (PPM), associated industrial behaviour, and institutions for environmental cooperation, and

c)   multilateral trade-environment rule-building and institution-building is proceeding slowly relative to regional efforts.

12.   The author further states that international trade organizations can be an important source of environment-friendly convergence of national environmental standards. In this case, international trade could be an important source of protection for the global environment contrasting with the assertions of some environmentalists that such trade is generally detrimental to the environment.

13.   These considerations are not specifically related to international trade in fishery products but it is believed that they bear very significant relevance since they show that regional cooperation in such difficult subjects can be highly rewarding and efficient as compared to soloist performance in a multilateral arena and that there are ways of realizing one of the demands of Chapter 2 of the UNCED Agenda 21, namely that trade and environment should be mutually supportive.

14.   At the time of writing several International Non-Governmental Organizations have identified initiatives which would aim at increasing the awareness of traders and consumers with regard to sustainable resource use and environment protection, and to make these considerations important or even decisive parts of purchasing decisions. It is expected that these organizations will provide more information at the Sub-Committee's session.

SUGGESTED ACTION BY THE SUB-COMMITTEE

15.   The Sub-Committee is requested to review the work programme outlined and to advise on its future direction and contents with due regard to the complexity of the issues and the appropriate priorities in the light of the roles of other international, governmental and non-governmental organizations.

16.   Specifically, advice is sought on aspects which may be relevant for the implementation of the Code of Conduct for Responsible Fisheries and activities following up the Kyoto Declaration and Plan of Action on the Sustainable Contribution of Fisheries to Food Security, and to identify issues which are related to international trade in fishery products, the environment and sustainable development.

17.   Suggestions are invited as to specific action which may be prepared, assisted or implemented by the Regional Centres (INFOFISH, INFOPECHE, INFOPESCA and INFOSAMAK) and which

---

[11]   See for example the working paper "Trade-Environment Negotiations in the EU, NAFTA and GATT/WTO: State Power, Interests and the Structure of Regime Solutions" by Richard H. Steinberg (BRIE Working Paper No. 75, 1995)

their governing bodies may wish to take into account when deliberating on the programmes of work of these Centres.

18.   This Sub-Committee is also asked to advise on work required for the development of methodologies of economic evaluation of environmental impacts on selected fishery commodities and on methodologies for assessing the trade effects of environmental measures.

19.   Advice is sought from the Sub-Committee on whether and, if yes, under which form FAO should be associated with initiatives such as those referred to in paragraph 14.

APPENDIX I
EXECUTIVE SUMMARY OF DIMENSIONS OF THE ENVIRONMENTAL IMPACT OF TRADE IN FISHERY PRODUCTS

The focus of the report is an attempt to create a conceptual framework based on the identification and analysis of the possible interactions between international trade in fishery products and the environment. The prime instrument for ensuring that trade and environment policies are mutually supportive is an open multilateral trading system which, through an efficient allocation and use of resources, production and incomes increases while lessening the impact on the environment. The environmental costs would be duly incorporated into resource pricing. Heightened environmental awareness has resulted in the application of the concepts of life-cycle management and the processes and production method (PPM) so as to promote recyclability and reduce waste. Manufacturers being held more accountable toward "environmental well-being" can expect greater incentives to better utilize such secondary resources. Competitiveness in the global market place may be defined by the ability that imported fishery products comply with environmental mandates built around domestic regulations in the importing country. Greater international demand for fishery products is a specific potential source for post-harvest environmental stress.

The post-harvest impact begins with the handling and storage of the fresh seafood, involving unloading, washing and separating ice, sorting, grading, and re-icing before shipping. Quality deterioration both in refrigerated and frozen fish can often be attributed to lipid oxidation. Moreover, almost half of all fish filleted or dressed for human consumption usually ends up as by-products in the form of bones, shell, skin and viscera; the proportion discarded during processing amounting to an average of 30 percent by weight of the original raw material. In a surimi plant, waste from the repeated leaching of fish mince invites microbial growth, and loss of the original raw material weight may be substantial. Fishmeal and shrimp, due to the high volume entering international trade, present particularly serious impacts. For example, waste in fishmeal plants can total up to 25 percent of the original raw material. In particular, health issues concerning the bacterium *Listeria monocytogenes* in processed shrimp and other seafood products may act as potential non-tariff barriers should the importing country apply more stringent regulations to imports.

Furthermore, in the case of aquaculture, intensive systems are generally dependent on high feed inputs and therefore can generate eutrophication. Also the interbreeding of cultured and wild stocks and disease transfer risk could be problematic. Equally severe impacts, namely nutrient loading, sedimentation and Biochemical Oxygen Demand (BOD), can arise from cage and pen-culture in open waters and shellfish-culture in coastal areas. Furthermore, in nutrient-enriched estuaries there may be a risk of toxic phytoplankton blooms causing fish mortality.

As a representative example of intensive finfish aquaculture, land-based salmonid farms are particularly prone to a variety of infectious diseases. The worldwide transfer and introduction of both salmon and shrimp for culture carry the risk of spread of viral pathogens to wild, native species, stressing the need for disease management as an integral component of a yield maximization strategy.

As for shellfish, both the inter-tidal culture of molluscs and the rack culture of oysters can produce heavy sedimentation obstructing coastal flow. Pest and predator control chemicals in mollusc farms present a potential problem of leaching. Brackishwater culture of shrimp can result in the destruction of wetlands, mangroves and coastal lagoons. Solid organic waste decomposing on the pond bed emits methane and hydrogen sulphide, jeopardizing both fish and human health as well as farm viability.

Having identified the environmental impacts, it may be pertinent to consider whether these can be monetarily quantified to ensure greater accountability in decision-making and optimization strategy. Three valuation methodologies that may be considered are replacement cost, hedonic price and willingness to pay.

The next question would be how to minimize or mitigate the impact if prevention is not possible, both centring on process design modification. In this regard, the merits and methodology of performing a Cleaner Production Assessment (CPA) or Environmental Improvement Cycle, based on the concepts of Life Cycle Design, Total Cost Assessment and Multi-Objective Decision-making are outlined. The three main steps in a CPA, namely identification of the source and cause of environmental burden, evaluation of possible improvement options and incorporation of improvements into the production process are described.

In the evaluation of improvement options, maximum utilization of processing by-products has to figure prominently with due regard to their market potential. Examples are composting both solid and liquid waste to derive a soil additive as a substitute for costly inorganic fertilizer and the potential use of "high organic load" residue through composting or ensilage and use for livestock feed. Another example of converting a waste into a value-added product is chitosan from shrimp peeling waste.

The profit motive being the ultimate driving force behind adoption of Cleaner Production technologies underlines the need for efficient policy instruments as an integral component of a legislative package. The use of eco-labelling programmes is discussed and the possible trade-distorting implications of such programmes are mentioned. It is concluded that the success of impact mitigation in a liberalized trade environment rests on due incorporation of the concerns of both importer and exporter, and that consumer demand for "nature friendly" products would drive the market of fishery products including those using by-products as a resource.

[...]

2. SUMMARY INFORMATION ON THE ROLE OF INTERNATIONAL FISHERY AND OTHER BODIES WITH REGARD TO THE CONSERVATION AND MANAGEMENT OF THE LIVING RESOURCES OF THE HIGH SEAS

Doc. no.:FAO Fisheries Circular No. 908   1996

CORRIGENDUM

p. 35	CORÉP	Membership: delete Equatorial Guinea and Guinea
p. 52	first line:	Article XIV instead of Article XV
p. 97	IOTC	Establishment: delete "Resolution FAO Council to be followed by"
p. 98	CCAMLR	Membership: include Ukraine
p. 102	CCSBT	Footnote: replace Commission by Secretariat.

[...]

PREPARATION OF THIS CIRCULAR

This Circular was prepared within the framework of the Regular Programme as part of on-going activities of the FAO International Institutions and Liaison Service (FIPL) aimed at providing information on regional fishery bodies.

Marashi, S.H.
Summary Information on the Role of International Fishery and Other Bodies with Regard to the Conservation and Management of Living Resources of the High Seas.
FAO Fisheries Circular. No. 908, Rome, FAO. 1996. 104p.

ABSTRACT

The present Circular provides summary information on the role of the international fishery bodies with regard to the conservation and management of living resources of the high seas. It describes 35 fisheries organizations throughout the world. For each body, information on the establishment, area of competence, species covered, membership and objectives and activities is given. Whenever possible, maps showing their area of competence are provided. In part one, a comprehensive account of the recent developments in high seas fisheries is included since these developments will have profound influence on the future role of these bodies. In addition, a brief review of the fisheries in each region, based on FAO Statistical Areas, is given to show the relation between the fisheries of various regions and the work of each regional fishery body.

FOREWORD

A number of recent developments in the world of fisheries namely the United Nations Conference on Environment and Development (UNCED) held in Rio de Janeiro, Brazil in June 1992, the Rome Consensus on World Fisheries adopted by the FAO Ministerial Conference on Fisheries held in Rome in March 1995 and the Agreement for the Implementation of the Provisions of the United Nations Convention on the Law of the Sea of 10 December 1982 Relating to the Conservation and Management of Straddling Fish Stocks and Highly Migratory Fish Stocks adopted in New York in December 1995 stressed the importance of cooperation for conservation and management of fish stocks through sub-regional and regional fisheries organizations and arrangements.

The present document provides a comprehensive amount of information on the recent developments concerning the high seas fisheries as well as on fisheries organizations, their role and general activities. This document has its origin in FAO Fisheries Circular No. 835 Rev.1 "Summary Information on the Role of International Fishery Bodies with Regard to the Conservation and Management of Living Resources of the High Seas" prepared by Mr M.J. Savini in 1991. Detailed description of the activities of fisheries organizations are periodically updated and published in FAO Fisheries Circular No. 807.

Dr Y. Kato
Director
Fishery Policy and Planning Division

CONTENTS

Page

I. RECENT DEVELOPMENTS CONCERNING THE CONSERVATION AND MANAGEMENT OF HIGH SEAS FISHERIES

I.1   1982 UNITED NATIONS CONVENTION ON THE LAW OF THE SEA (UNCLOS): PROVISIONS ON CONSERVATION AND MANAGEMENT OF THE LIVING RESOURCES OF THE HIGH SEAS[1]

(a)   Freedom of the High Seas

1. Article 87 of UNCLOS while referring generally to the freedoms of the high seas including the freedom of fishing, qualifies this by stating that "these freedoms shall be exercised by all States with due regard for the interests of other States in their exercise of the freedom of the high seas."

(b)   Conservation and Management

2. Articles 116 to 120 of UNCLOS deal with the conservation and management of the living resources of the high seas. Under the provisions of these articles all States have the right to engage in fishing on the high seas subject to their treaty obligations (Article 116), their duty to adopt measures for the conservation of the living resources of the high seas (Article 117), and their obligation to cooperate with other States in conservation and management of living resources in the areas of the high seas (Article 118). In all these cases it is generally the responsibility of States whose nationals are engaged in fishing on the high seas to negotiate with other States fishing in the same area or fishing the same stocks to enter into negotiations with a view to taking the necessary measures for the conservation of the living resources concerned. They should, as appropriate, cooperate to establish sub-regional or regional fisheries organizations to achieve these objectives.

(c)   Straddling Stocks and Highly Migratory Species.

3. Article 63(2) refers to stocks that straddle the outer limit of the EEZs and the high seas while Article 64 deals with the highly migratory species. In these cases it is the responsibility of States whose nationals are engaged in the fishing of these resources in the high seas and the coastal States involved to negotiate directly or through sub-regional or regional fisheries organizations to agree upon the measures necessary for the conservation of these resources.

---

[1] The Convention entered into force on 16 November 1994.

I.2 FAO WORLD CONFERENCE ON FISHERIES MANAGEMENT AND DEVELOPMENT

4. The FAO World Conference on Fisheries Management and Development was held in Rome from 27 June to 6 July 1984. The Strategy endorsed by the 1984 World Fisheries Conference placed primary emphasis upon the need for better use and management of the world's fishery resources. It drew attention to the fact that the successful exercise of national authority to extract greater benefit from fish resources depends in large measure upon the ability of coastal States to manage their resources more effectively. It underlined that rational management is the essential basis for sound, sustainable development of fisheries.

5. The fundamental issue that must be tackled if expectations and needs in this respect are to be fulfilled is that of controlling open access to fisheries. The extension of national jurisdiction was a necessary but insufficient step towards this objective, and open access continues to exist within exclusive zones of most coastal States as well as on the high seas. The consequences of continued open access are extremely damaging. They include the further depletion of marine stocks, the dissipation of economic rents and increased conflicts among users. When no price or value is placed on the resource, capital and labour continue to enter the fishery as long as revenues exceed costs, leading to wasteful misallocations of inputs. There is thus an increasingly urgent need to address the problems associated with free and open access and to review and install alternative management concepts and mechanisms, in particular property allocation systems including exclusive use rights.

6. Such a move towards more efficient and effective management, through the creation of property rights in the resources, will require fundamental institutional changes involving licensing programmes, the allocation of individual quotas of total allowable catch or territorial use rights. It will also necessitate a shift away from the traditional concept of fishery resources as free goods towards their treatment as economic resources with specific values or prices. International collaboration in fisheries research and management has to take full account of the sovereignty of the participating States. Furthermore, the framework of international cooperation must have flexibility to take into account the particular circumstances of individual countries.

Text of the Strategy Endorsed by the 1984 FAO Conference

7. The following principles and guidelines should be taken into account when examining the changing needs for international collaboration in fisheries development and management and reviewing the present and prospective roles of existing mechanisms for such collaboration, including FAO regional fishery bodies, should include inter alia the following principles:

(i)   Objectives of international cooperation should include contributions from all the parties involved on the basis of their experience and capacity, leading to enhancement of national capabilities and transfer of technology.

(ii)   Cooperative research efforts and technical cooperation programmes should have clearly identified objectives, responsibilities and deadlines, be given carefully evaluated priorities and be fully integrated with overall national fisheries management and development plans. The research should be practical, make fullest possible use of existing facilities and encourage the development of appropriate technology.

(iii)   Scientific and technical advice provided by international bodies should be objective and made available to all concerned. Such advice has proved especially valuable to countries negotiating fishing agreements or formulating joint management measures.

(iv)   Planning of effective management and development requires adequate data and information upon the socio-economic aspects of fisheries. Collaboration at the regional level in the analysis of such data collected by national institutions should be encouraged, particularly through regional or sub-regional technical assistance projects.

(v)   Central collection and analysis of data from all fleets fishing a common resource, with the participation of all interested States, are essential and should be encouraged to allow for proper management of that resource. These data could be provided through data centres associated with regional fishery bodies. Data should be collected and analysed under the same conditions for all countries, taking every step to avoid an excessive burden on fishermen to provide such information.

(vi)   Adequate financial and other resources, administrative servicing and technical backstopping should be provided to support regional fishery bodies and their associated technical assistance projects. There is thus an urgent need to mobilize greater funds for regional collaboration. As soon as possible, developing countries themselves should increase their participation and commitment to the technical support of such bodies, as well as take full responsibility for their management.

(vii)   Where appropriate, closer collaboration should be established between FAO regional fishery bodies and projects on the one hand and regional economic groupings and organizations concerned with fisheries on the other, and

(viii) More effective steps should be taken to facilitate the coordination of activities in fishery, oceanography and related environmental research, as well as in integrated marine affairs policy-making and management.

I.3   CANCÚN DECLARATION ON RESPONSIBLE FISHING

8.   The concept of responsible fishing was first raised at the FAO Committee on Fisheries (COFI) in April 1991. In May 1992, the Government of Mexico in close consultation with FAO, organized the International Conference on Responsible Fishing that led to the adoption of the Declaration of Cancún. The Conference requested FAO to draft, in consultation with relevant international organizations, an International Code of Conduct for Responsible Fishing, taking into account the provisions set out in the Declaration. The Declaration also called on the United Nations to declare the next ten years the "Decade of Responsible Fishing" to ensure concerted efforts towards sustainable fisheries practices.

9.   The principles embodied in the Declaration reflect the recent problems concerning the conservation and management of the fisheries resources both within the EEZs and on the high seas as well as those related to the environment. The following principles are relevant to the conservation and management of high seas resources:

(i)   States should cooperate on bilateral, regional and multilateral levels to establish, reinforce and implement effective means and mechanisms to ensure responsible fishing on the high seas, in accordance with relevant provisions of UNCLOS;

(ii)   The freedom of States to fish on the high seas must be balanced with the obligation to cooperate with other States to ensure conservation and rational management of the living resources, in accordance with relevant provisions of UNCLOS;

(iii)   States should take effective action, consistent with international law, to deter reflagging of vessels as a means of avoiding compliance with applicable conservation and management rules for fishing activities on the high seas;

(iv)   States should enhance international cooperation to prevent illicit fishing that constitutes an obstacle to achieving responsible fishing objectives.

I.4   UN CONFERENCE ON ENVIRONMENT AND DEVELOPMENT (UNCED)

10.   The United Nations Conference on Environment and Development (UNCED) was held in Rio de Janeiro, Brazil, from 3 to 14 June 1992. FAO cooperated with the UNCED Secretariat in the preparation of the draft Agenda 21 for the sustainable development of the oceans, particularly in the high seas[2]. Section C entitled "Sustainable Use and Conservation of Marine Living Resources of the High Seas" points out that management of high seas fisheries, including the adoption, monitoring and enforcement of effective conservation measures, is inadequate in many areas and some resources are overutilized. It further notes that "There are problems of unregulated fishing, overcapitalization, excessive fleet size, vessel reflagging to escape controls, insufficiently selective gear, unreliable databases and lack of sufficient cooperation between States. Actions by States whose nationals and vessels fish on the high seas, as well as cooperation at the bilateral, sub-regional, regional and global levels, is essential particularly for highly migratory species and straddling stocks".

11.   Under paragraph 17.52(e) it was recommended that "States should convene, as soon as possible, an intergovernmental conference under the United Nations auspices, taking into account relevant activities at the sub-regional, regional and global levels, with a view to promoting effective implementation of the provisions of the United Nations Convention on the Law of the Sea on straddling fish stocks and highly migratory fish stocks." The Conference should identify and assess existing problems related to the conservation and management of such fish stocks, and consider means of improving cooperation on fisheries among States, and formulate appropriate recommendations. UNCED also called on States to take effective action to deter reflagging of vessels by their nationals as a means of avoiding compliance with applicable conservation and management rules for fishing activities on the high seas.

I.5   FAO TECHNICAL CONSULTATION ON HIGH SEAS FISHING

12.   The FAO Technical Consultation on High Seas Fishing was held in Rome from 7 to 15 September 1992. The Consultation was held in close cooperation with the UN Division of Ocean Affairs and Law of the Sea and was attended by 66 FAO Members, three non-member States and 15 international and regional organizations[3]. The prime objective of the Consultation was to obtain scientific and technical information that might be used for the proper management of high seas fisheries without prejudice to the deliberations of the UN Conference on Straddling Fish Stocks and Highly Migratory Fish Stocks scheduled for July 1993. The Consultation addressed the issues of statistics, research, management (responsible fishing practices and new concepts and techniques), institutions, participation of developing countries in high seas fishing, and legal framework. The conclusions arrived at by the Consultation included:

-       management of high seas fisheries was necessary;

-       the provisions of the 1982 UN Convention on the Law of the Sea constituted the principal legal framework for the development of a regime for high seas fishing,

---

[2]   United Nations Conference on Environment and Development, Rio de Janeiro, 3-14 June 1992
[3]   Technical Consultation on High Seas Fishing, Rome 7-15 September 1992, FAO Fisheries Report No. 484.

supplemented by provisions agreed at UNCED and those contained in the Declaration of Cancún;

- FAO should prepare an International Code of Conduct for Responsible Fishing in consultation with other organizations;

- reflagging of fishing vessels to "flags of convenience" was considered a matter of critical concern and one which should be addressed urgently;

- high seas fisheries management should be, wherever possible, undertaken on a regional basis through regional and sub-regional organizations;

- effective monitoring, control and surveillance was identified as an essential requirement for high seas fisheries management; and

- consideration should be given to reviving the COFI Sub-Committee on the Development of cooperation with International Organizations to assist regional fisheries organizations in this task.

I.6   AGREEMENT TO PROMOTE COMPLIANCE WITH INTERNATIONAL CONSERVATION AND MANAGEMENT MEASURES BY FISHING VESSELS ON THE HIGH SEAS

13.   The need for an agreement to promote compliance with international conservation and management measures by fishing vessels on the high seas was first underlined at the Cancún Conference on Responsible Fishing in May 1992. The call for an agreement was reiterated by UNCED in June 1992 and supported by the FAO Technical Consultation on High Seas Fishing in September 1992. At its One hundred and second Session held in November 1992, the FAO Council agreed that the Organization should draw up an international agreement with a view to its formal approval at the Twenty-seventh Session of the FAO Conference in November 1993. The Draft Agreement to Promote Compliance with International Conservation and Management Measures by Fishing Vessels on the High Seas was approved unanimously by the FAO Conference at its Twenty-seventh Session in November 1993[4].

14.   The Preamble to the Agreement outlines three important aspects of high seas fishing. First, it refers to the duties of every State to exercise effectively its jurisdiction and control over vessels' trans-shipment of fish. Secondly, it points out that the practice of flagging or reflagging fishing vessels as a means of avoiding compliance with international conservation and management measures for living marine resources is among the factors that seriously undermines the effectiveness of such measures. Thirdly, it sets out the main objectives of the Agreement including Flag States' responsibility in respect of fishing vessels entitled to fly their flags and operating on the high seas.

15.   The general and specific provisions on Flag States' responsibilities laid down in Article III of the Agreement include (a) an obligation on the part of Flag States to take measures to ensure that vessels flying their flags do not undermine the effectiveness of international conservation and management measures, (b) States are required to authorize vessels wishing to fish on the high seas only if there are sufficient links between them and the vessels in order to allow them to exercise adequate control over the vessels and fulfil their obligations under the Agreement, (c) vessels are not allowed to act under double authorization, (d) authorization may not be issued to a vessel which had been registered in another State and had its authorization revoked or suspended for breach of international

---

4   FAO Conference, Twenty-seventh Session, rome, 6-25 November 1993, C93/REP/11 Revision of C93/III/REP/2, 23 November 1993.

conservation and management measures, (e) all vessels authorized to fish must bear standard markings and Flag States commit themselves to take enforcement action against vessels flying their flags that act in contravention of the provisions of the Agreement, and (f) sanctions are to be of sufficient gravity to secure compliance with the requirements of the Agreement and include suspension or withdrawal of the authorization.

16.   Flag States are required to maintain detailed records on all their vessels authorized to fish on the high seas (Art. IV) and make all such information available to FAO (Art. VI) which will then circulate the information to all Contracting Parties. Any infringements by vessels flying their flags which undermine the effectiveness of the conservation and management measures are to be promptly communicated by Flag States to FAO, which will then pass the information to all contracting parties (Art. VI). Vessels under 24 metres are exempted from the application of the Agreement unless such an exemption would undermine the object and purposes of the Agreement (Art. III.1(b).

17.   Finally, coastal States in areas where exclusive economic zones or equivalent zones of national jurisdiction over fisheries have not yet been declared, may set their own limits collectively for their own flag vessels operating exclusively in those regions (Art.II.3). The agreement will form an integral part of the Code of Conduct for Responsible Fisheries (Preamble). The Agreement has, so far, been ratified by Canada, Saint Kitts and Nevis, Georgia, Myanmar, Sweden, Madagascar, Norway and USA.

I.7   ROME CONSENSUS ON WORLD FISHERIES

18.   On 14 and 15 March 1995 a Ministerial Meeting on Fisheries was held in Rome at the invitation of the Director-General of FAO to review the state of world fisheries and the FAO follow-up to the United Nations Conference on Environment and Development (UNCED). The meeting adopted the Rome Consensus on World Fisheries[5]. In the discussion, the Ministerial Meeting noted the FAO analysis which indicated that the problems of overfishing in general, and overcapacity of industrial fishing fleets in particular, threaten the sustainability of the world's fisheries resources for present and future generations. It recognized the need for continuing international cooperation and coordination toward reestablishing sustainability of world fisheries. It stated that improved fisheries conservation and management, along with better protection of fisheries from harmful sea- and land-based activities, are crucial to maintaining world fish resources and aquatic ecosystems. The particular importance of the fisheries sector for small island developing States was noted.

---

[5]   The meeting was attended by 63 Ministers from Albania, Angola, Australia, Bahamas, Bangladesh, Brazil, Burkina Faso, Cambodia, Cameroon, Canada, Cape Verde, Central African Republic, Chile, China, Congo, Côte d'Ivoire, Croatia, Cuba, Czech Republic, Estonia, Fiji, Gabon, Gambia, Ghana, Guinea, India, Islamic Republic of Iran, Israel, Italy, Jamaica, Japan, Lebanon, Lesotho, Malawi, Malaysia, Maldives, Mali, Malta, Mauritius, Mexico, Morocco, Niger, Pakistan, Peru, Philippines, Poland, Saint Lucia, Samoa, Sao Tomé and Principe, Seychelles, Spain, Sri Lanka, Swaziland, Sweden, Thailand, The Former Yugoslav Republic of Macedonia, Trinidad and Tobago, Tunisia, Uganda, United Arab Emirates, United States of America, Yemen and the Russian Federation.

Senior Officials also participated from Algeria, Argentina, Austria, Bahrain, Belgium, Bolivia, Burundi, Chad, Colombia, Comoros, Cook Islands, Costa Rica, Cyprus, Democratic People's Republic of Korea, Denmark, Dominican Republic, Ecuador, Egypt, El Salvador, Equatorial Guinea, Ethiopia, European Community (Member Organization), Finland, France, Germany, Greece, Guinea Bissau, Haiti, Honduras, Hungary, Iceland, Indonesia, Iraq, Ireland, Kenya, Republic of Korea, Kuwait, Latvia, Liberia, Libya, Lithuania, Madagascar, Mauritania, Myanmar, Namibia, Netherlands, New Zealand, Nigeria, Norway, Oman, Panama, Portugal, Qatar, Romania, Saudi Arabia, Senegal, Sierra Leone, Slovakia, Somalia, South Africa, Sudan, Syria, Tanzania, Tonga, Turkey, United Kingdom, Uruguay, Vanuatu, Venezuela and Zimbabwe.

19.   Recognizing the socio-economic, environmental, and nutritional importance of fisheries, and the growing demand for fish products, the Ministerial Meeting concluded that additional actions are urgently required to:

-    eliminate overfishing,
-    rebuild and enhance fish stocks,
-    minimize wasteful fisheries practices,
-    develop sustainable aquaculture,
-    rehabilitate fish habitats, and
-    develop fisheries for new and alternate species based on principles of scientific sustainability and responsible management.

20.   To respond effectively to the current fisheries situation and the difficulties that can be foreseen in satisfying growing demand for fish and in conserving aquatic ecosystems, the Rome Ministerial Meeting urged that governments and international organizations take prompt action to:

-    reduce fishing to sustainable levels in areas and on stocks currently heavily exploited or overfished;

-    review the capacity of fishing fleets in relation to sustainable yields of fishery resources and where necessary reduce these fleets;

-    strengthen and support regional, sub-regional, and national fisheries organizations and arrangements for implementing conservation and management measures;

-    keep under review the effectiveness of conservation and management measures for ensuring the long-term sustainability of fisheries and aquatic ecosystems;

-    continue and, when possible, increase technical, financial, and other assistance to developing countries, in particular to least developed countries, to support their efforts in fisheries conservation and management, and in aquaculture development;

-    encourage States to further develop ecologically sound aquaculture as an important contributor to overall food security;

-    strengthen fisheries research and increase cooperation among research institutions;

-    increase consultation on fisheries with the private sector and non-governmental organizations;

-    effectively implement the relevant rules of international law on fisheries and related matters which are reflected in the provisions of the UN Convention on the Law of the Sea;

-    consider ratifying the Agreement to Promote Compliance with International Conservation and Management Measures by Fishing Vessels on the High Seas.

I.8   AGREEMENT FOR THE IMPLEMENTATION OF THE PROVISIONS OF THE UNITED NATIONS CONVENTION ON THE LAW OF THE SEA OF 10 DECEMBER 1982 RELATING TO THE CONSERVATION AND MANAGEMENT OF STRADDLING FISH STOCKS AND HIGHLY MIGRATORY FISH STOCKS

21.   The Agreement for the Implementation of the Provisions of the United Nations Convention on the Law of the Sea of 10 December 1982 Relating to the Conservation and Management of Straddling Fish Stocks and Highly Migratory Fish Stocks was adopted by the United Nations Conference on Straddling Fish Stocks and Highly Migratory Fish Stocks in

New York on 4 August 1995. The Final Act of the Conference and the Agreement opened for signature on 4 December 1995. The Agreement will enter into force 30 days after the date of deposit of the thirtieth instrument of ratification or accession. The objective of the Agreement is "to ensure the long-term conservation and sustainable use of straddling fish stocks and highly migratory fish stocks through effective implementation of the relevant provisions of the (LOS) Convention". It is, by far, the most detailed and comprehensive international legal instrument on the subject of conservation and management of straddling and highly migratory fish stocks.

22.   Part III of the Agreement is entitled "Mechanisms for International Cooperation Concerning Straddling Fish Stocks and Highly Migratory Fish Stocks". In general, coastal States and States fishing on the high seas shall cooperate in relation to straddling fish stocks and highly migratory fish stocks either directly or through appropriate subregional or regional fisheries management organizations or arrangements. The purpose of such cooperation is to agree on conservation and management measures with respect to particular fish stock(s) where there is evidence that such stock(s) may be under threat of over-exploitation or where a new fishery is being developed for such stock(s). Where a regional or sub-regional fisheries body exists and has the competence to establish conservation and management measures for straddling and highly migratory fish stocks, States fishing for the stock(s)on the high seas and coastal States with an interest in the stock(s) are to give effect to their duty to cooperate by participating in the work of that body. States with an interest in the stock(s) which are not parties to an existing fishery organization or arrangements are encouraged to participate in the work of the organization. Only those States which are members of such an organization or participants in such an arrangement, or which agree to apply the conservation and management measures established by such organization or arrangement, are to have access to the fishery resources to which those measures apply.

23.   Article 9 of the Agreement "subregional and regional fisheries management organizations and arrangements" states that:

> 1.   In establishing subregional or regional fisheries management organizations or in entering into subregional or regional fisheries management arrangements for straddling fish stocks and highly migratory fish stocks, States shall agree, inter alia, on:

> (a)   the stocks to which conservation and management measures apply, taking into account the biological characteristics of the stocks directly concerned and the nature of all the fisheries involved;

> (b)   the area of application, taking into account the characteristics of the subregion or region, including socio-economic, geographical and environmental factors;

> (c)   the relationship between the work of the new organization or arrangement and the role, objectives and operations of any relevant existing fisheries management organizations or arrangements; and

> (d)   the mechanisms by which the organization or arrangement will obtain scientific advice and review the status of the stocks, including, where appropriate, the establishment of a scientific advisory body.

24.   States cooperating in the formation of a subregional or regional fisheries management organization or arrangement shall inform other States which they are aware have a real interest in the work of the proposed organization or arrangement of such cooperation.

25.   The Provisions embodied in Article 10 of the Agreement "Functions of subregional and regional fisheries management organizations and arrangements" are of particular relevance to the future role of the regional fishery bodies:

In fulfilling their obligation to cooperate through subregional or regional fisheries management organizations or arrangements, States shall:

(a)   agree on and comply with conservation and management measures to ensure the long-term sustainability of straddling fish stocks and highly migratory fish stocks;

(b)   agree, as appropriate, on participatory rights such as allocations of allowable catch or levels of fishing effort;

(c)   adopt and apply any generally recommended international minimum standards for the responsible conduct of fishing operations;

(d)   obtain and evaluate scientific advice, review the status of the stocks and assess the impact of fishing on non-target and associated or dependent species;

(e)   agree on standards for collection, reporting, verification and exchange of data on fisheries for the stocks;

(f)   compile and disseminate accurate and complete statistical data to ensure that the best scientific evidence is available, while maintaining confidentiality where appropriate;

(g)   promote and conduct scientific assessments of the stocks and relevant research and disseminate the results thereof;

(h)   establish appropriate cooperative mechanisms for effective monitoring, control, surveillance and enforcement;

(i)   agree on means by which the fishing interests of new members of, or participants in, the organization or arrangement will be accommodated;

(j)   agree on decision-making procedures which facilitate the adoption of conservation and management measures in a timely and effective manner;

(k)   promote the peaceful settlement of disputes in accordance with Part VIII;

(l)   ensure the full cooperation of their relevant national agencies and industries in implementing the recommendations and decisions of the subregional or regional fisheries management organization or arrangement; and

(m)   give due publicity to the conservation and management measures established by the organization or arrangement.

26.   Under Article 13, States are required to cooperate to strengthen existing subregional and regional fisheries management organizations and arrangements in order to improve their effectiveness in establishing and implementing conservation and management measures for straddling fish stocks and highly migratory fish stocks. The Agreement also provides detailed provisions on Compliance and Enforcement (Part IV) and Peaceful Settlement of Disputes (Part VIII). In general, States parties to a subregional or regional fishery management organization or arrangement are obliged to enforce the conservation and management measures adopted by that body and the disputes arising from the adoption of such measures are to be settled by compulsory means should it become necessary. These provisions go beyond the present commitment by States in the work of existing fishery management organizations.

I.9   FAO CODE OF CONDUCT FOR RESPONSIBLE FISHERIES

27.   The Declaration of Cancún called on FAO to draft an International Code of Conduct for Responsible Fishing in consultation with relevant international organizations taking into account the provisions of the Declaration.   This call was endorsed by the Technical Consultation on High Seas Fishing and in November 1992 the FAO Council formally approved the commencement of the preparation of the Code, taking into account the Declaration of Cancún, the provisions of Agenda 21 of UNCED and the conclusions and recommendations of the Technical Consultation on High Seas Fishing. Proposals regarding the content of the Code and a time-frame for its adoption and implementation were submitted to and discussed by FAO Committee on Fisheries (COFI) in March 1993[6]. The Committee recommended that the Code should have an encompassing umbrella of general principles which would provide the framework for the detailed guidelines on the issues to be covered.

28.   Paragraph 1 of the Declaration of Cancún calls on States to adopt effective fisheries planning and management standards within the context of sustainable development.   The concept of sustainable development was first defined in 1988 by the FAO Ad hoc Working Group on Sustainable Development as "the management and conservation of the natural resource base, and the orientation of technological and institutional change in such a manner as to ensure the attainment and continued satisfaction of human needs for present and future generations. Such sustainable development (in the agriculture, forestry and fisheries sector) conserves land, water, plant and animal genetic resources, is environmentally non-degrading, technically appropriate, economically viable and socially acceptable"[7]. Thus the preamble of the declaration of Cancún uses the above definition in defining responsible fishing by stating that "this concept encompasses the sustainable utilization of fisheries resources in harmony with the environment, the use of capture and aquaculture practices which are not harmful to ecosystems, resources or their quality; the incorporation of added value to such products through transformation processes meeting the required sanitary standards; the conduct of commercial practices so as to provide consumers access to good quality products". In this context the essential element of sustainable utilization or development is the cornerstone of the Code.

29.   The FAO Code of Conduct for Responsible Fisheries was adopted by the FAO Conference at its Twenty-eighth Session, Rome, 20 October to 2 November 1995. The Code sets out principles and international standards of behaviour for responsible practices with a view to ensuring the effective conservation, management and development of living aquatic resources, with due respect for the ecosystem and biodiversity. The application of the Code is voluntary and it contains provisions that have already given binding effect by means of other obligatory legal instruments. The Agreement to Promote Compliance with International Conservation and Management Measures by Fishing Vessels on the High Seas forms an integral part of the Code. The Code consists of twelve Articles. The first five deal with nature and scope, objectives, relationship with other international instruments, implementation, monitoring and updating, and special requirements of developing countries. Article 6 deals with general principles while the remaining Articles cover specific subjects. These are: Fisheries management, fishing operations, aquaculture developments, integration of fisheries into coastal area management, post-harvest practice and trade, and fisheries research. The Code places a great emphasis on the regional and sub-regional fisheries organizations for its implementation.

---

6   Report of the Twentieth Session of the Committee on Fisheries, Rome, 15-19 March 1993, FAO Fisheries Report No. 488, paras 65-76.

7   FAO Council, Ninety-fourth Session, Rome, 15-25 November 1988, CL/94/6, September 1988, para. 5.

Map 1

FAO Statistical Areas

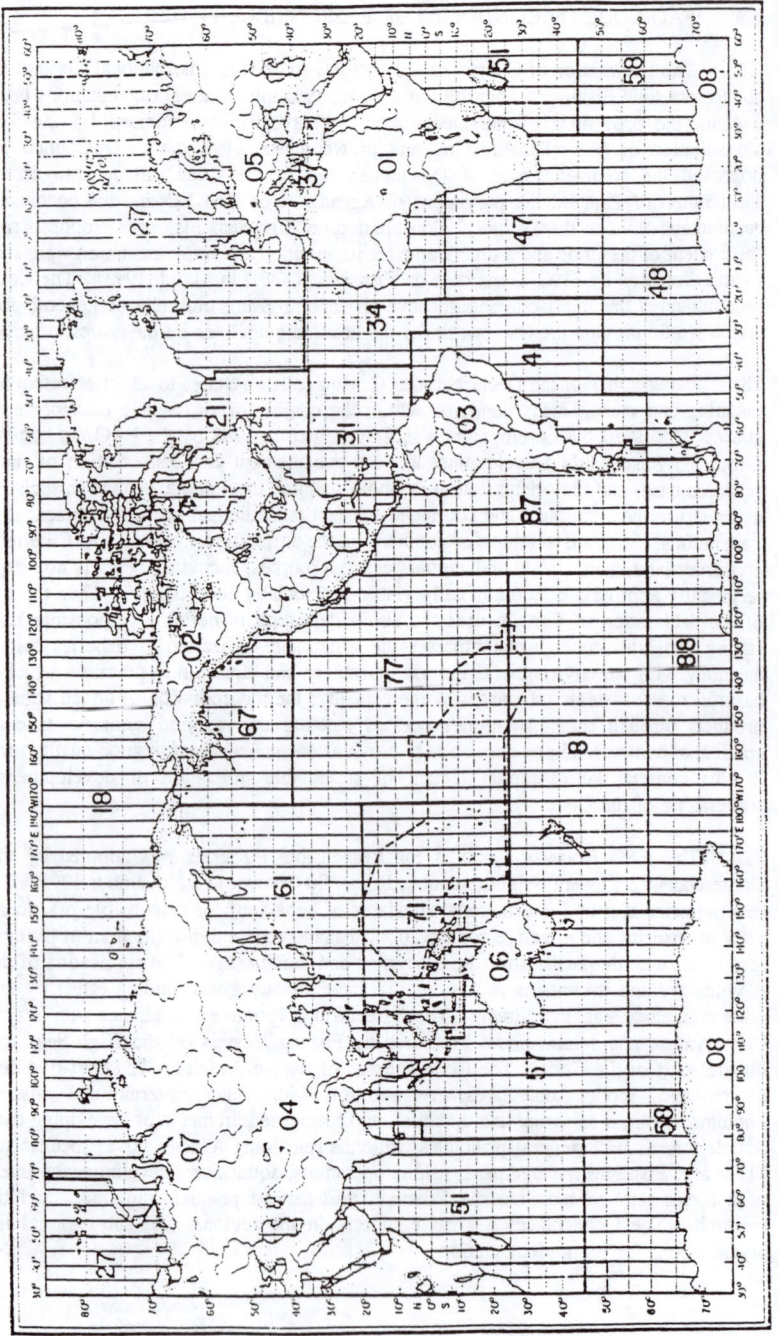

II.   ATLANTIC OCEAN AND ADJACENT SEAS

II.1   A BRIEF REVIEW OF MAJOR FISHING AREAS IN THE ATLANTIC OCEAN
AND ADJACENT SEAS[8]

II.1.1 Northwest Atlantic (Area 21)

Total landings of finfish and invertebrates in 1993 were 2.4 million metric tons (t),
a reduction of 19.5% compared to 1990 and below the average level of landings seen during
the 1970s and 1980s. The main fisheries within Area 21 are: Atlantic cod, pollock, hake,
Atlantic red fishes, Atlantic herring, Atlantic menhadin, Atlantic mackerel, plaice, halibut,
haddock, crabs, lobsters, northern prawn, pink shrimps, American sea scallop, ocean
quahog, clams and squids. The downward trend in landings from 1990 to 1992 can be
attributed to the decline in catches of demersal fish, with nearly 50% of the drop being due
to the reduced catch of Northern Atlantic cod. However, landings for all major species
groups declined. The shift by demersal fisheries toward landing formerly low value species
following the gadoid collapse continues, although the absolute quantities being landed have
decreased markedly between 1990 and 1992, particularly for silver hake, Atlantic redfish,
and pollack. Total landings of capelin declined significantly (from 183 792 t in 1990 to 30
978 t in 1992).

The problems encountered in managing stocks which extend beyond the 200 miles
zone of coastal States continues. A key feature is the continuing fishing activities of non-
Contracting Parties in the Northwest Atlantic Fisheries Organization (NAFO) Regulatory
Area. Of particular note is the problem caused by flag of convenience vessels. Despite
declines in the size of stocks of several species in traditional areas, fishing effort has
expanded at an alarming rate outside the 200-mile limit, in the Davis Strait and on the deep
continental slope. Another management problem in Area 21 is getting timely data for stock
assessments which has now been explicitly recognized in the management of Atlantic
Canada's fisheries. Due to unavoidable delays in collecting and processing data, the most
"recent" data that can be used in annual stock assessments is often two years old. It has been
observed that incidences of misreporting by species and areas correspond with periods when
quotas should have been limiting landings from specific stocks.

II.1.2 Northeast Atlantic (Area 27)

Total reported catches in 1993 were 10.7 million t, down slightly from 11.1 million
t in 1992. The main fisheries in Area 27 are for cod, haddock, whiting, sole, mackerel,
capelin, herring, hake, blue whiting, and plaice. Most of the demersal stocks continued to
exhibit long-term downward trends due to excessive fishing pressure, undesirable fishing
patterns (i.e., too much fishing on young fish and discarding) and poor recruitment, probably
related to reduced spawning stock biomass and unfavourable environmental changes.

The level of exploitation of the North Sea cod, haddock, and whiting stocks is very
high. Most of the catch consists of fish which are one or two years old, and fewer than one
third of the fish alive at the start of the year survive to the end of the year. The fisheries
are therefore very dependent upon newly-recruited young fish. The industrial fishery in the
North Sea is targeted on small species like sandeel, Norway pout, and sprat for fish meal and
oil production. Landings were around 1.8 million t in the mid-1970s and have fluctuated

---

[8]   All regional reviews of major fishing areas are based on the information provided in: Review of the
State of World Fishery Resources: Marine Fisheries, FAO Fisheries Circular No. 884, FAO, Rome,
Italy, 1995; Review of the State of World Marine Fishery Resources, FAO Fisheries Technical Paper
No. 335, FAO, Rome, 1994, and FAO Yearbook, Fishery Statistics, Catches and Landings, Vol. 76,
1993.

between 1.0 and 1.5 million t since then. Sandeel is the most important species and makes up more than 60% of the total in all years.

The Total Allowable Catch system has been used as the standard tool in managing the stocks in Area 27. As a general rule, agreed TACs throughout Area 27 have exceeded the TACs recommended by ICES and actual catches have exceeded the agreed TACs. Enforcement of management measures has not been adequate in all areas and problems arise from the fact that many of the regulated stocks are harvested in mixed fisheries. The reliability of reported landings statistics has deteriorated for some stocks as a result of management/enforcement problems which, in turn, has reduced the reliability of the scientific advice on those stocks. Discarding of undersized fish or due to low prices for specific sizes appears to be an increasing problem. Besides this obvious waste of resources this phenomenon makes the assessment of the stocks more difficult as data on the amount discarded are difficult to obtain.

ICES has in some cases in recent years departed from the practice of giving advice based on a TAC. For cod in the North Sea misreporting undermined the TAC system and ICES recommended an effort reduction with restrictions on the number of days each fishing vessel is allowed to fish in addition to TACs.

II.1.3 Western Central Atlantic (Area 31)

After increasing over 15 years to a high of 2.6 million t in 1984, landings in the area have decreased steadily to 1.7 million t in 1992 and then rose to 1.9 million t in 1993. Most of the decline was due to three US fisheries: Gulf menhaden, American oyster and calico scallop, which constituted 60% of landings from Area 31 in 1984, but only 35% of landings in 1992. Total landings from the remaining finfish fisheries of the region (i.e. excluding menhaden) were relatively stable at an average of about 620,000 t from 1982-1989 but increased to an average of about 715,000 t for 1990 through 1992. Over this period landings of sharks and rays, other pelagics, snappers, king and Spanish mackerel, and unidentified fishes have increased while other finfishes have remained stable or decreased slightly.

The main fisheries within Area 31 are for small pelagics (menhadens, flyingfish, mackerels), large pelagics (tunas, billfishes and sharks), reef fish (snappers and groupers), coastal demersal fish (drums, weakfish, croaker), crustaceans (shrimps, lobsters and crabs) and molluscs (oysters, scallops and conch). The landings of bony fishes not identified were 299,677 t in 1993. There are some under-utilized resources like cephalopods (squid and octopus), small pelagics, deep water shrimps and deep water snappers which may lead to increases in landings, but it is unlikely, excepting cephalopods, that these increases will be significant in the near future.

II.1.4 Eastern Central Atlantic (Area 34)

The total of reported landings for Area 34 for 1993 were 2.9 million t a significant decrease from the 1990 peak of 4.1 million t. Apart from the higher than average landings reported between 1988 and 1991, annual totals varied between 2.5 million t and 3.3 million t throughout the 1970s and 1980s. The main fisheries in Area 34 are European pilchard, sardinellas, bonga, horse mackerels, mackerels, hakes, sea breams, shrimps, cephalopods (octopus, cuttlefish, squids) and tunas. The landings of bony fishes not identified were 233,266 t in 1993.

Catches were recorded by 21 coastal countries and more than 18 non-coastal countries, giving a markedly international character to many of the region's fisheries and the share of landings by non-African long-range fleets remains high. It has decreased from 67% of the catch during the period 1970-74 to 43% in 1975-79, and was 58% in 1980-84. This share remained at 58% in 1989 and 1990, partly reflecting policy decision by coastal states, but also the current difficulty of some African countries in fully exploiting the resources themselves, especially given the large fluctuations of pelagic offshore resources which are of principal interest to foreign fleets.

II.1.5 Mediterranean and Black Sea (Area 37)

The total landings in the Mediterranean and Black Sea were 1.7 million t in 1993. A substantial decrease from around 2 million t between 1982 to 1988 was mainly due to the collapse of Black Sea stocks of small pelagics, whose landings dropped from   833,000 t in 1988 to 428,000 t in 1990, and continued to decline in 1991 to 257,000 t. The main fisheries in Area 37 are: anchovy, pilchard, sprat, horse mackerel, hake, whitings, mullets, sardinella, tunas cephalopods, crustaceans and molluscs. The landings of bony fishes not identified were 92,025 t in 1993.

The Compliance Agreement (see above paras. 13-17), requires that vessels above a certain size be registered and fly a national flag while operating on the high seas, and this question is currently being addressed by the General Fisheries Council of the Mediterranean (GFCM). In the case of the Mediterranean, the provisions of the Compliance Agreement apply to fisheries beyond territorial seas, and its application is complicated by the small dimensions of many fishing vessels. At least a quarter of the total fishing pressure is exerted by vessels of less than 7-9 t GRT; and more than 70% of the registered catch is taken by vessels at or below 15 t GRT. These figures are probably a significant under-estimate of the importance of small fishing vessels, whose catch and existence are seriously under-estimated in FAO databases.

II.1.6 Southwest Atlantic (Area 41)

Total landings in Southwest Atlantic remains fairly stable. Since mid 1980s the total annual landings have been around 2,000,000 t. The total landings in Area 41 were 2.2 million t in 1993. The main fisheries in Area 41 are Argentine hake, southern blue whiting, grenadiers, sardinella, mackerel, squid, tunas and shrimps. The landings of bony fishes not identified were 212,417 t in 1993.

The fluctuations in the total catches of certain species or groups of species can be considered to be within the normal limits prevalent since 1987. Total landings of Argentinian hake (*Merluccius hubbsi*) increased from 421,000 t in 1990 to 521,000 t in 1991, and then decreased to 455,000 t in 1992. This increase with respect to previous years, has been primarily due to an increase in catches by Argentinean and Uruguayan fleets, mostly as a result of an increase, more particularly in the availability, of the stock in the traditional fishing grounds. These are mostly located in the Common Argentinian-Uruguayan Fishing Zone, but some active fishing also goes on further south.

Landings of sardinella (*Sardinella brasiliensis*) increased slightly to a total of 65,000 t in 1991-92, but are still far below the figure of more than 100,000 t per year reached in the 1970s and early 1980s. Although this might be a sign of recovery with respect to 1990, when total catches dropped to only 32,000 t, the stocks continue to be in poor condition.

Catches of squids increased consistently with respect to 1990, but are of the same order of magnitude at 700,000 t per year, as in the mid 1980s. Some improvements have been made with respect to the management of these squid stocks, particularly in the Falklands (Malvinas) area, where joint efforts are made to regulate the active offshore international fisheries that have developed in this area over the years.

II.1.7 Southeast Atlantic (Area 47)

Following the effective cessation of distant water fishing in 1990 in the EEZs of the then newly independent Namibia, and with increasing awareness of fisheries development in

Angola, total reported landings between 1990 and 1993 in this highly productive area remained relatively constant (1,409,468 t, 1,429.055 t) at approximately 50% below the average 2.7 million t per year taken in the 1970s and 1980s. The main fisheries in Area 47 are: Cape horse mackerel, cunene horse mackerel, hakes, sardinellas, pilchard, round herring, Southern African anchovy, snoek, kingklip, sole, rock lobster, dentext, and squid.

While the relatively few species that accounted for both the major share of biomass and catches in the area continue to dominate, there have been some changes of note between 1990 and 1992, notably, the increase in landings of Southern African anchovy (up 186,000 t, or 92%) and the decline in catches of Cape hake (down 88,000 t, or 88%). Total landings of the two species of hakes from all of Area 47 dropped by 60,000 t (22%). All the hake stocks have been over-exploited, although the most southerly stocks seem to show some sign of recovery. Landings in 1991 and 1992 were 183,000 t and 208,000 t, respectively.

The Cape horse mackerel stock is currently considered in a healthy state and the policy is to maintain fishing at a high level. The anchovy stock is less valuable than pilchard and used mainly for fish meal production. Exploited almost entirely by coastal South African fleets, the anchovy stock yielded almost 373,000 t in 1989 and was considered to be fully exploited. Landings totalling 386,000 t were reported for 1992. Landings from the heavily exploited cunene horse mackerel, chub mackerel and Southern African pilchard stocks continued to decline. The high biomass of round herring (*Etrumeus whiteheadi*) reported towards the end of 1989 failed to translate into significantly increased landings.

II.2   REGIONAL FISHERY BODIES IN THE ATLANTIC OCEAN AND ADJACENT SEAS

II.2.1 International Council for the Exploration of the Sea (ICES)

Established by the Convention for the International Council for the Exploration of the Sea, signed in Copenhagen, Denmark, on 12 September 1964. The Council had been established in 1902 and the new Convention aimed to facilitate the implementation of its Programme. The Convention entered into force on 22 July 1968.

Area of Competence

The area of competence of the Council as described in Article 2 of the Convention is the Atlantic Ocean and its adjacent seas with emphasis on the North Atlantic. There is no precise delimitation of this area by lines of longitude and latitude. In practice ICES is primarily, but not exclusively, concerned with FAO Statistical Area 27 (Map 2).

Species Covered

The Council covers all living marine resources in its area of competence.

Membership

Membership of the Council is subject to the approval of three quarters of the Member States. The present members of the Council are: Belgium, Canada, Denmark, Estonia, Finland, France, Germany, Iceland, Ireland, Latvia, Netherlands, Norway, Poland, Portugal, Russia, Spain, Sweden, UK, and USA.

Map 2

FAO Statistical Area 27 in which ICES concentrates its activities.
The dotted line is the northern area of NEAFC.

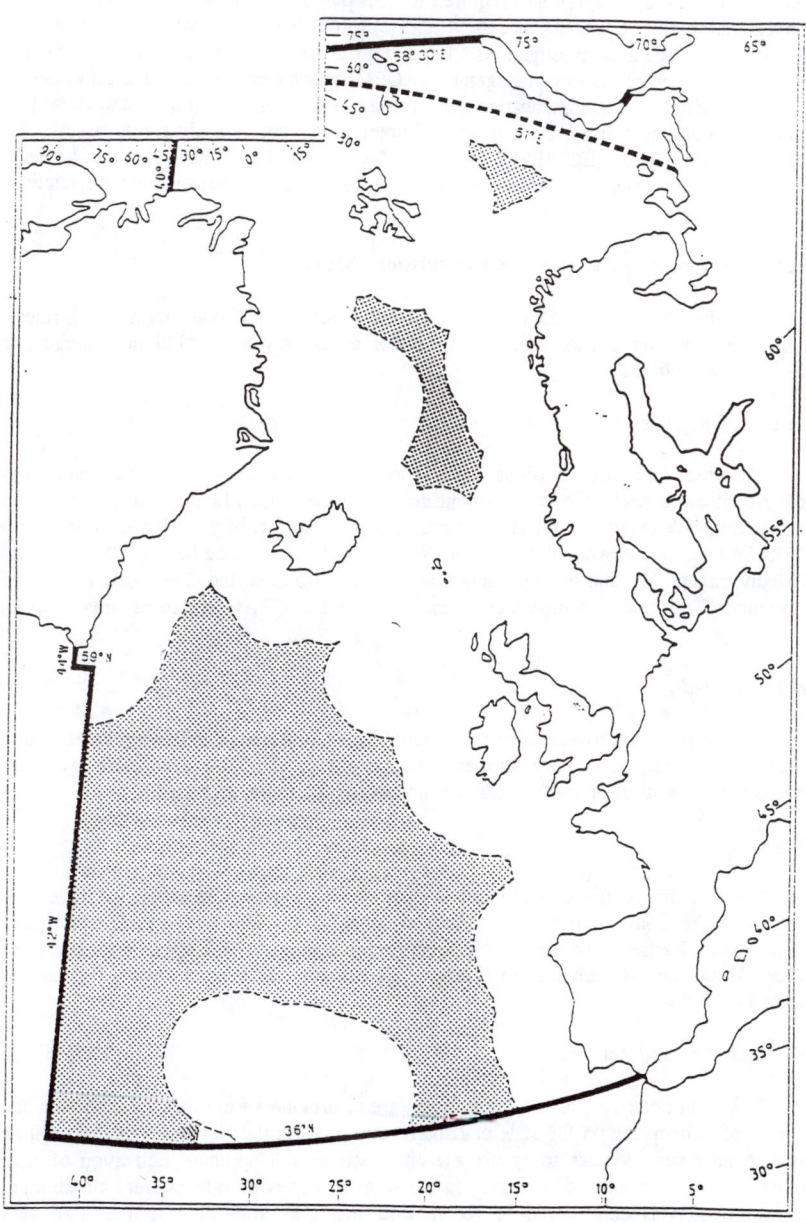

Main Objectives and Activities

The main objectives of the Council are (a) to promote and encourage research and investigations for the study of the sea particularly those related to the living resources thereof; (b) to draw up programmes required for this purpose and to organize such research and investigation as may appear necessary; and (c) to publish or otherwise disseminate the results of its research and investigations. ICES itself is not a management body. It has an Advisory Committee on Fishery Management (ACFM) which provides scientific information and advice, including recommendations for management measures (e.g. total allowable catches, minimum mesh sizes, etc.), to several international bodies dealing with fisheries in the North Atlantic Ocean (EC, IBSFC, NASCO, NEAFC) and to its Member States. Such information and advice concern fishery resources both within areas under national jurisdiction and on high seas.

II.2.2 Northeast Atlantic Fisheries Commission (NEAFC)

Established by the Convention on Future Multilateral Cooperation in Northeast Atlantic Fisheries, opened for signature in London on 18 November 1980 and entered into force on 17 March 1982.

Area of Competence

The area of competence of the Commission is defined as the waters within those parts of the Atlantic and Arctic Oceans and their dependent seas which lie north of 36°N latitude and between 42°W longitude and 51°E longitude; within that part of the Atlantic Ocean north of 59°N latitude and between 44°W and 42°W longitude. The Baltic Sea and the belts and the Mediterranean Sea and its dependent seas are excluded from the Commission's area of competence. This area of competence coincides with most of FAO Statistical Area 27 (Map 3).

Species Covered

The Commission covers fishery resources of the Northeast Atlantic with the exception of marine mammals, sedentary species and, insofar as they are dealt with by other international agreements, highly migratory species and anadromous stocks.

Membership

Membership of the Commission is open to the founding members (Article 20). Accession to the Convention by other States is subject to the approval of three quarters of the Contracting Parties. The present Members of the Commission are: Denmark (in respect of Faroe Island and Greenland, the European Community, Iceland, Norway, Poland and Russian Federation.

Main Objectives and Activities

The main objectives of the Commission are to provide a forum for Consultation and exchange of information on the state of fisheries resources in the Northeast Atlantic and on related management policies to ensure the conservation and optimum utilization of such resources, and to recommend conservation measures in waters outside national jurisdiction. The Commission is empowered to recommend measures applicable to the high seas concerning (i) the conduct of fisheries (ii) the control of fisheries and (iii) the collection of statistical information. In recent years, NEAFC has agreed on measures such as setting total allowable catches for certain species and establishing minimum fish sizes and mesh sizes. The recommendations formulated by NEAFC are subject to the objection procedure.

Map 3

Area of competence of NEAFC. The dotted lines delimit the
FAO Statistical Area 27. The stripped areas are parts of
Statistical Area 27 not covered by NEAFC.

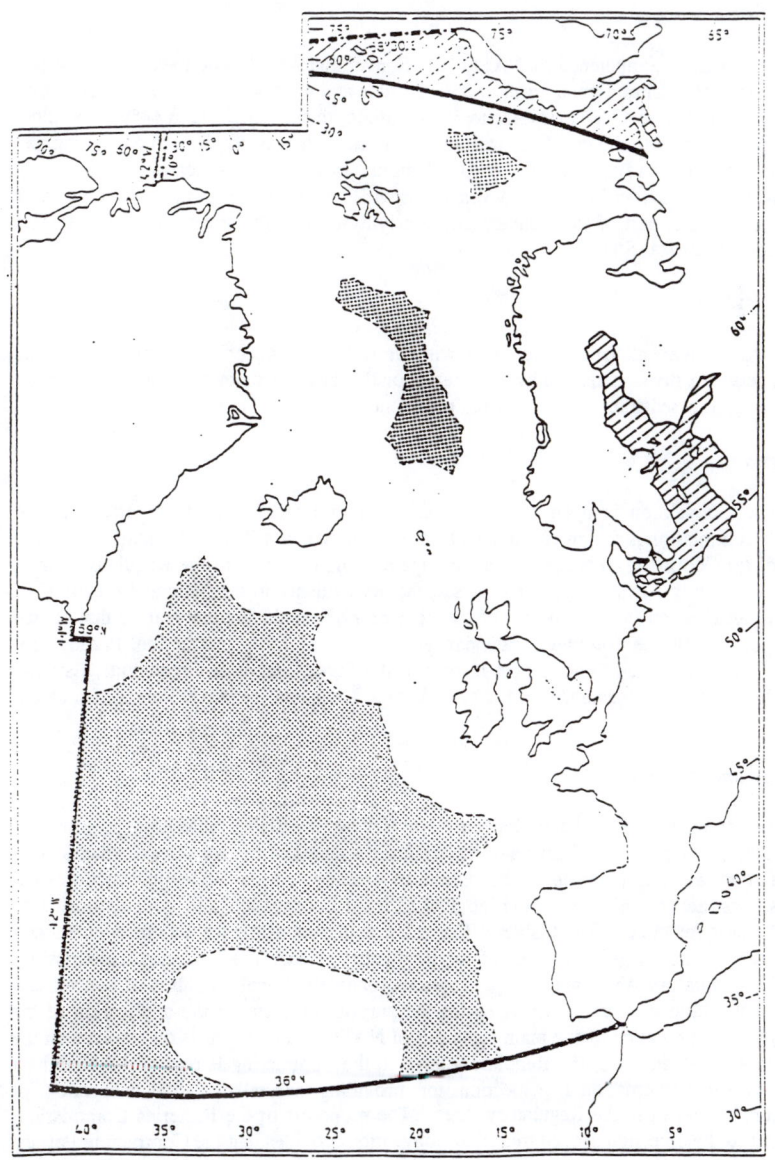

II.2.3 Northwest Atlantic Fisheries Organization (NAFO)

Established by the Convention on Future Multilateral Cooperation in the Northwest Atlantic Fisheries, concluded at Ottawa, Canada, on 24 October 1978 and entered into force on 1 January 1979.

Area of Competence

The area of competence of NAFO "the Convention Area" is defined as "the waters of the Northwest Atlantic Ocean north of 35°N latitude and west of a line extending due north from 35°N latitude and 42°W longitude to 59°N latitude, thence due west to 44°W longitude, and thence due north to the coast of Greenland, and the waters of the Gulf of St. Lawrence, Davis Strait and Baffin Bay south of 78°10'N latitude" (Map 4). This area coincides exactly with FAO Statistical Area 21. The Convention provides for the establishment of "Regulatory Area" which is that part of the Convention Area lying beyond the areas under the fisheries jurisdiction of Coastal States.

Species Covered

NAFO covers all fishery resources with the following exceptions: salmon, tunas and marlins, cetacean stocks managed by the International Whaling Commission or any successor organization, and sedentary species of the continental shelf.

Membership

The Convention is open for accession by other States. The membership of the Fisheries Commission is reviewed annually by the Organization's General Council and should consist of (a) Contracting Parties which participate in the Fisheries of the Regulatory Area, and (b) Contracting Parties which provide satisfactory evidence to the General Council of its expected participation in the fisheries of the Regulatory Area during the year of that annual meeting or during the following calendar year. The present Contracting Parties are: Bulgaria, Canada, Cuba, Denmark (in respect of the Faroe Islands & Greenland), Estonia, European Community, Iceland, Japan, Korea, Latvia, Lithuania, Norway, Poland, Romania, Russia, and the USA.

Objectives and Activities

The main objective of the Convention as set out in its Preamble is to promote the conservation and optimum utilization of the fishery resources of the Northwest Atlantic area within a framework appropriate to the regime of extended coastal States jurisdiction over fisheries, and accordingly to encourage international cooperation and consultation with respect to these resources. The Fisheries Commission is responsible for the management and conservation of the fishery resources of the Regulatory Area. The Fisheries Commission, within the Regulatory Area, may adopt proposals for international measures of control and enforcement within the Regulatory Area for the purpose of ensuring the application of the Convention and execution of the main functions of NAFO. The Commission resolves on the allocations of the catches in the Regulatory Area to the Contracting Parties and maintains a scheme of joint international inspection for providing surveillance and inspection of international fisheries in the Regulatory Area. The proposals of the Fisheries Commission are subject to the objection procedure. The Convention provides that the Contracting Parties may invite the attention of any State not a Party to this Convention to any matter relating to the fishing activities in the Regulatory Area of the nationals or vessels of that State which appear to affect adversely the attainment of the objectives of this Convention.

Map 4

The area of competence of NAFO

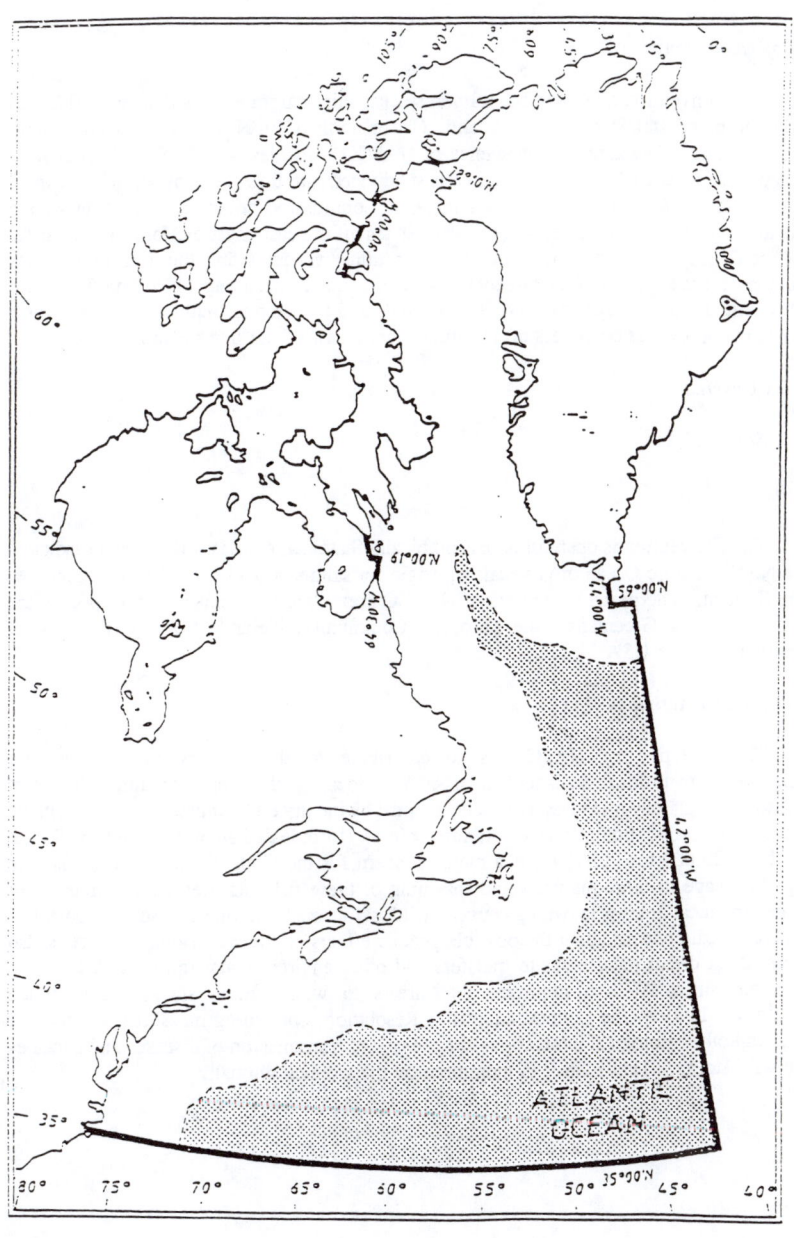

II.2.4 North Atlantic Salmon Conservation Organization (NASCO)

Established by the Convention for the Conservation of Salmon in the North Atlantic Ocean, signed in Reykjavik, Iceland, on 2 March 1982 and entered into force on 1 October 1983.

Area of Competence

The Convention applies to the salmon stocks which migrate beyond areas of fisheries jurisdiction of coastal States of the Atlantic Ocean north of 36°N latitude throughout their migratory range. The area of competence of NASCO coincides with FAO Statistical Area 27 and part of Area 21 (Map 5). This area is subdivided into three regions serviced by three different commissions: (1) The North American Commission covers all maritime waters within areas of fisheries jurisdiction of coastal States off the east coast of North America; (2) the West Greenland Commission covers all maritime waters within the area of fisheries jurisdiction off the coast of West Greenland west of a line drawn along 44°W longitude south to 59°N latitude, thence due east to 42°W longitude and thence due south; and (3) the North East Atlantic Commission covers all maritime waters east of the line mentioned above.

Species Covered

Salmon.

Membership

The Convention is open for accession by any State that exercises fisheries jurisdiction in the North Atlantic Ocean or is a State of origin for salmon stocks provided, it is approved by the Council. The present members of NASCO are: Canada, Denmark (in respect of the Faroe Islands and Greenland), the European Community, Iceland, Norway, the Russian Federation, and the USA.

Objectives and Activities

The objective of NASCO is to contribute to the conservation, restoration, enhancement and rational management of salmon stocks in the North Atlantic. In recent years, some regulatory measures have been adopted by the three Commissions. The dramatic increase in the production of farmed Atlantic salmon (from less than 30,000 tons in 1984 to more than 320,000 tons in 1994) is a major concern for the Council since farmed fish are known to escape in large numbers and spawning of these fish has been demonstrated over wide geographical areas. Spawning between wild and farmed salmon has also been observed and there is real concern about the possible genetic effects on the wild stocks. There is also concern about disease and parasite transfers and other environmental impacts. Steps have been taken since 1991 to minimize the threats to wild salmon stocks from salmon aquaculture. In 1994 the Council adopted a Resolution, containing measures to minimize genetic and other biological interactions and the risk of transmission of diseases and parasites to the wild stocks. This subject is monitored by the Council annually.

Map 5

The area of competence of NASCO. The dotted lines delimit
FAO Statistical Areas 21 (on the left) and 27 (on the right)

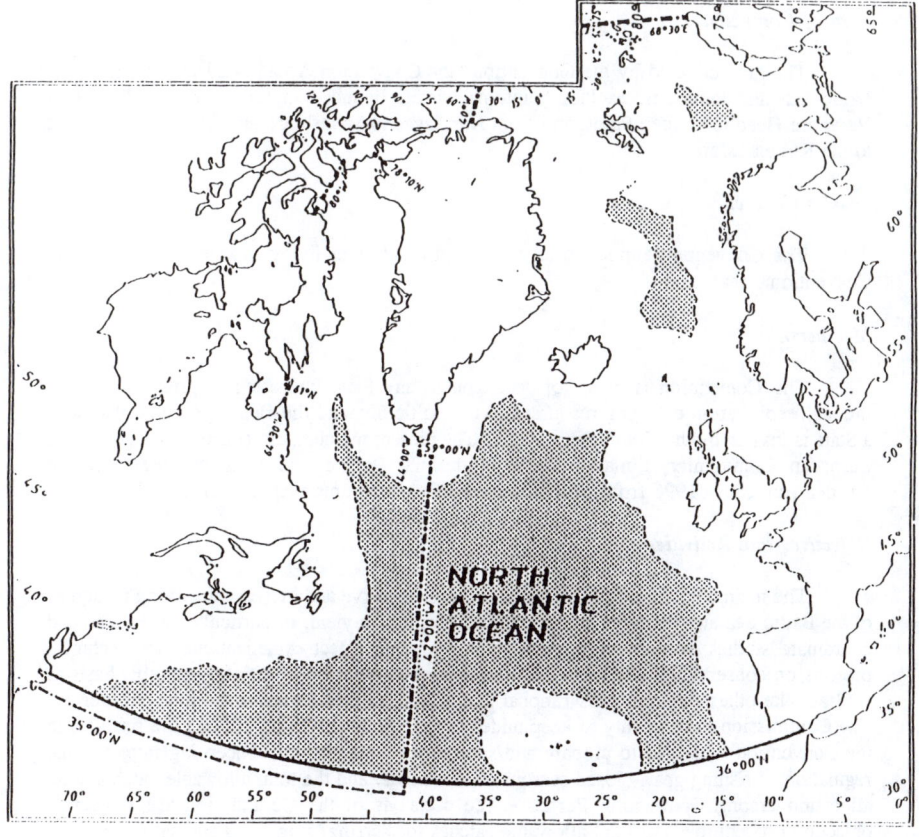

II.2.5 International Baltic Sea Fishery Commission (IBSFC)

Established by the Convention on Fishing and Conservation of the Living Resources in the Baltic Sea and Belt, signed at Gdansk on 13 September 1973 and entered into force on 28 July 1974.

Area of Competence

The area covered by the Convention "the Convention Area" is all the waters of the Baltic Sea and the Belts, excluding internal waters bounded in the west by a line from Hasenore Head to Gniben Point, and from Korshagae to Spodsbierg and from Gilbierg Head to the Kullen (Map 6).

Species Covered

The Convention applies to all fish species and other living marine resources in the Convention Area.

Membership

The Convention is open for accession to any State interested in preservation and rational exploitation of living resources in the Baltic Sea and the Belts, provided that such a State is invited by the Contracting States. The present membership consists of Estonia, the European Community, Finland, Latvia, Lithuania, Poland, the Russian Federation and Sweden (until July 1996 from which date the EC will assume responsibility).

Objectives and Activities

The main objectives of the Convention is to preserve and increase the living resources of the Baltic Sea and the Belts and to obtain the optimum yield, in particular, to expand and coordinate studies towards these ends and to put into effect organizational and technical projects on conservation and growth of the living resources on a just and equitable basis as well as take other steps towards rational and effective exploitation of the living resources. The Commission has the duty to keep under review the living resources and the fisheries in the Convention Area and to prepare and submit recommendations concerning inter alia the regulation of fishing gear, closed seasons, closed areas, and the total allowable catch and its allocation among Contracting Parties. The decisions of the Commission are subject to objection procedure. The total allowable catches for herring, sprat, cod and salmon as well as their allocations among member States are annually set by the Commission.

Map 6

The area of competence of IBSFC and Baltic subdivisions for reporting purposes

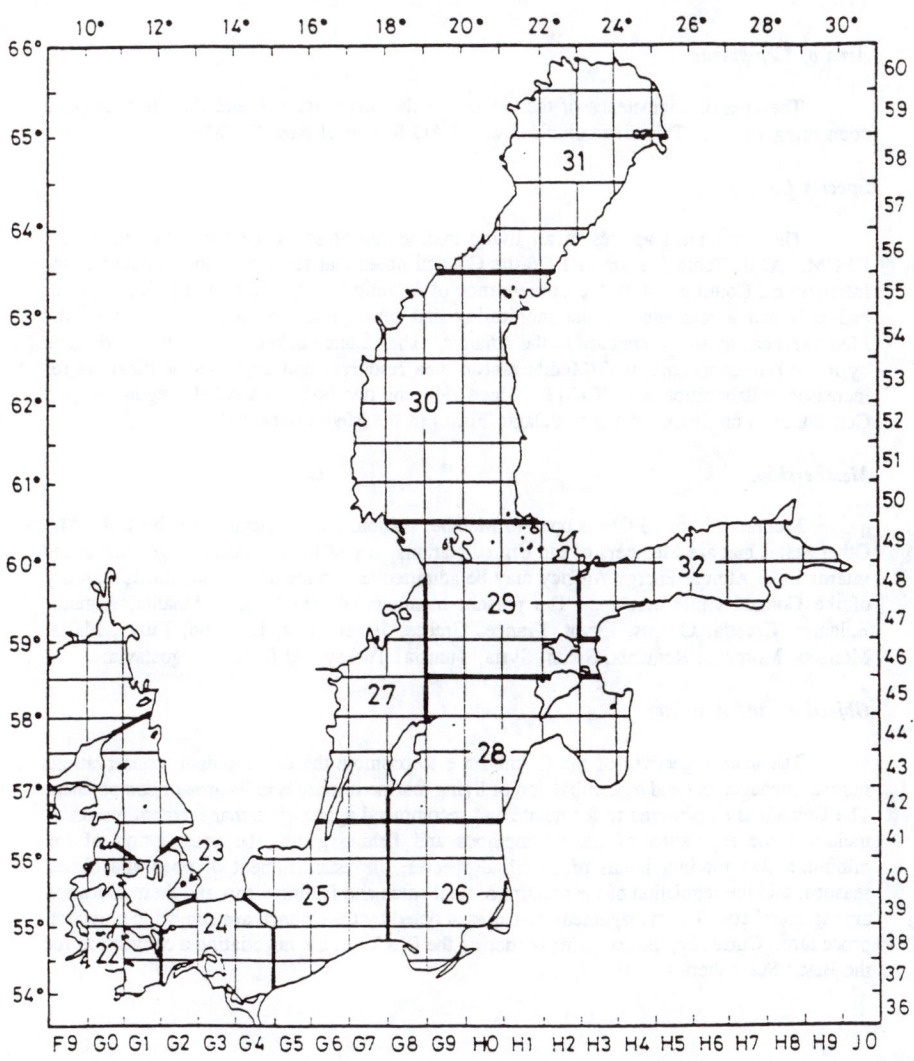

II.2.6 General Fisheries Council for the Mediterranean (GFCM)

Established by an Agreement drawn up in Rome on 24 September 1949 under Article XIV of the FAO Constitution and approved by the FAO Conference at its Fifth Session in 1949. The Agreement entered into force on 20 February 1952. It was amended in 1963 and 1976.

Area of Competence

The area of competence of the Council is the Mediterranean and the Black Sea and connecting waters. This area coincides with FAO Statistical Area 37 (Map 7).

Species Covered

The Agreement applies to all living marine resources in the area covered by the GFCM. At its Tenth Session in 1976 the Council noted that since the establishment of the International Commission for the Conservation of Atlantic Tunas (ICCAT) in 1966, this body had also had a mandate for the monitoring and management of tuna resources of the Mediterranean as an adjacent sea to the Atlantic. The Council acknowledged the work done by ICCAT in connection with Mediterranean tuna resources and expressed willingness for increased collaboration with ICCAT. Since 1990 the two bodies have held regular Expert Consultations on Stocks of Large Pelagic Fishes in the Mediterranean.

Membership

Membership of GFCM is open to Member Nations and Associate Members of FAO. Other States that are Members of the United Nations, any of its Specialized Agencies or the International Atomic Energy Agency may be admitted as members by a two-thirds majority of the Council's membership. The present members of GFCM are: Albania, Algeria, Bulgaria, Croatia, Cyprus, Egypt, France, Greece, Israel, Italy, Lebanon, Libya, Malta, Monaco, Morocco, Romania, Spain, Syria, Tunisia, Turkey and former Yugoslavia.

Objectives and Activities

The main objectives of the Council are to promote the development, conservation, rational management and best utilization of living marine resources in its area of competence. The Council is empowered to formulate and recommend appropriate management measures including the regulation of fishing methods and fishing gears, the prescription of the minimum size for individuals of specified species, the establishment of open and closed seasons, and the regulation of the amount of total catch and fishing effort and their allocation among members. The management measures adopted by the Council are subject to objection procedure. Currently, the countries bordering the Black Sea are negotiating a convention for the Black Sea fisheries.

Map 7

Area of competence of GFCM

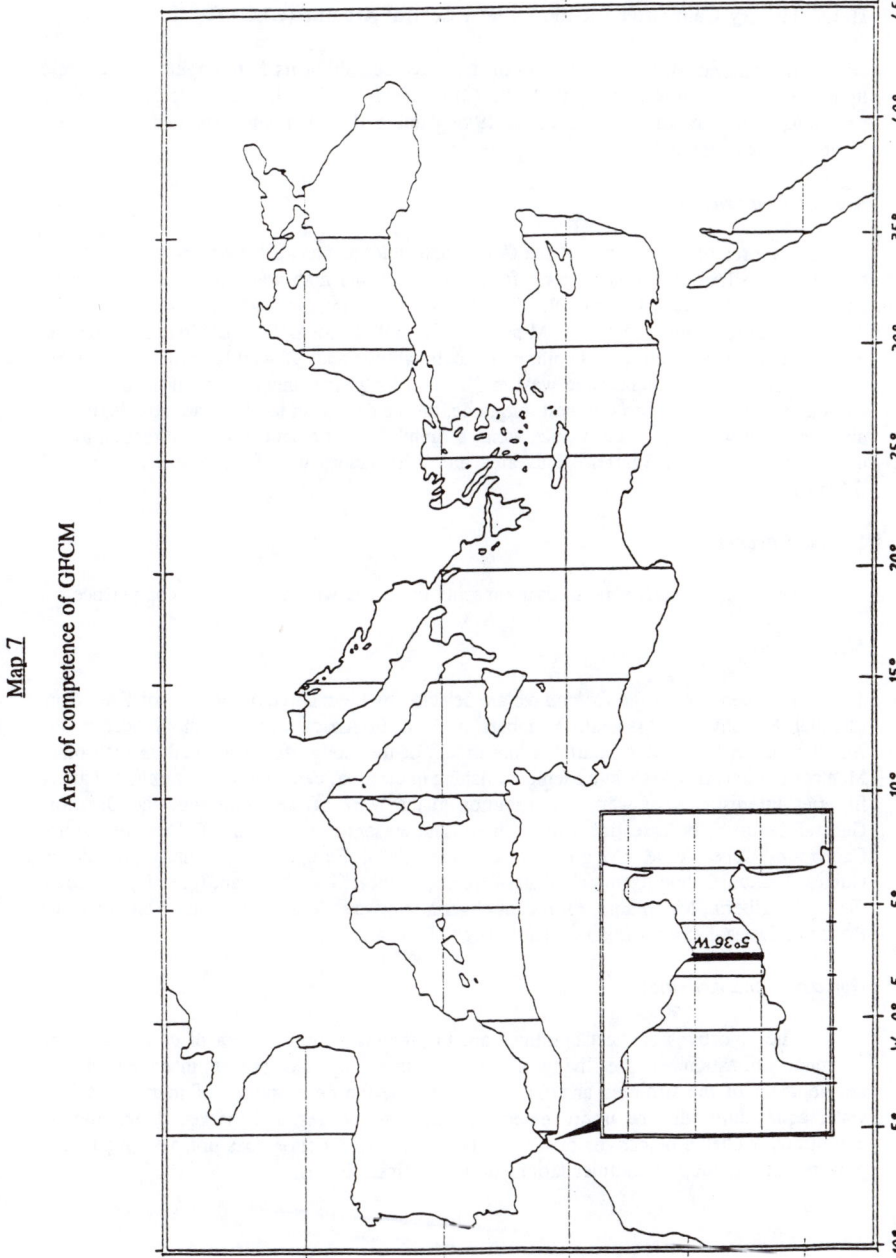

II.2.7 Fishery Committee for the Eastern Central Atlantic (CECAF)

Established by Resolution 1/48 of the FAO Council at its Forty-eighth Session held in Rome in June 1967 under Article VI (2) of the FAO Constitution. Its Statutes were promulgated by the Director-General on 19 September 1967 and were amended by the FAO Council in November 1992.

Area of Competence

The area of competence of the Committee is defined as all the waters of the Atlantic bounded by a line drawn as follows: from a point on the high water mark on the African coast at Cape Spartel (lat. 35°47'N, long.5°55'W) following the high water mark along the African coast to a point at Ponta da Moita Seca (lat.6°07'S, long.12°16'E) along a rhumb line in a northwesterly direction to a point on 6° south latitude and 12° west longitude, thence due north to the Equator, thence due west to 30° west longitude, thence due north to 5° north latitude, thence due west to 40° west longitude, thence due north to 36° north latitude, thence due east to 6° west longitude, thence along a rhumb line in a southeasterly direction to the original point at Cape Spartel. This area mostly coincides with FAO Statistical Area 34 (Map 8).

Species Covered

The Committee covers all living marine resources within its area of competence.

Membership

The members of the Committee are selected by their Director-General of FAO from Member Nations and Associate Members of FAO in Africa whose territory borders the Atlantic Ocean from Cape Spartel to the mouth of the Congo River as well as such other Member Nations and Associate Members fishing in the area, carrying out research, or having fisheries interest thereof whose contribution to the work of the Committee the Director-General deems to be essential or desirable. The present members of CECAF are: Benin, Cameroon, Cape Verde, Congo, Côte d'Ivoire, Cuba, European Community, Equatorial Guinea, France, Gabon, Gambia, Ghana, Greece, Guinea, Guinea-Bissau, Italy, Japan, Korea (Rep. of), Liberia, Mauritania, Morocco, Nigeria, Norway, Poland, Romania, Sao Tome and Principe, Senegal, Sierra Leone, Spain, Togo, USA and Zaire.

Objectives and Activities

The objectives of the Committee are to promote within its area of competence the optimum utilization of the living aquatic resources by the proper management and development of the fisheries and fishing operations, the development of marine brackish water aquaculture and the improvement of related processing and marketing activities in conformity with the objectives of its members. The Committee does not have regulatory powers but can adopt recommendations on management issues.

Map 8

Area of competence of CECAF

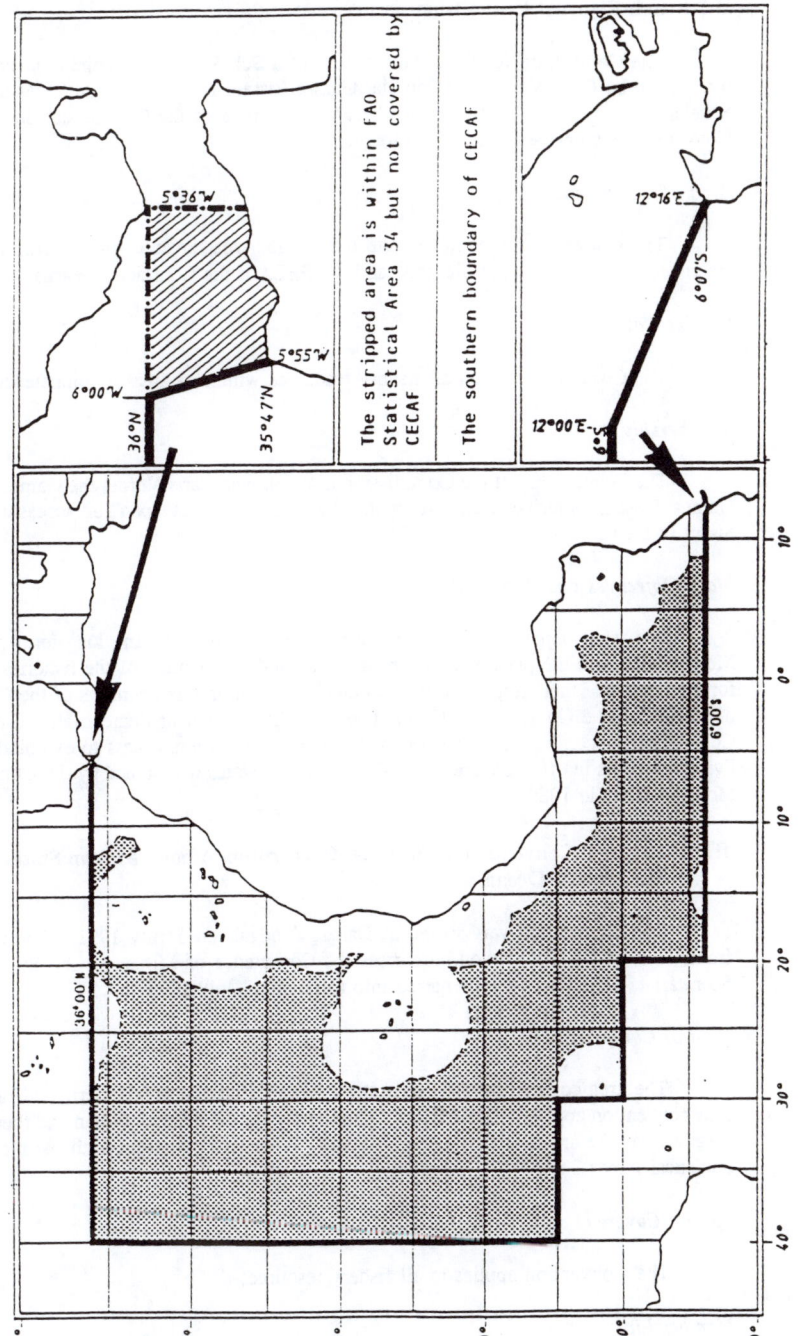

The stripped area is within FAO Statistical Area 34 but not covered by CECAF

The southern boundary of CECAF

II.2.8 Sub-Regional Commission on Fisheries (SRCF)

The Convention for the Establishment of a Sub-Regional Commission on Fisheries was signed by Cape-Verde, the Gambia, Guinea Bissau, Mauritania, and Senegal in Dakar, Senegal, on 29 March 1985. Guinea became a member of the Commission in 1987. The Convention has not yet entered into force.

Area of Competence

The Convention does not define the precise area covered by the Commission but references are made to "Sub-Region" and the EEZs of the Contracting Parties.

Species Covered

The Convention covers all fishery resources within its area of competence.

Membership

The Membership of the Commission is as follows: Cape-Verde, the Gambia, Guinea, Guinea Bissau, Mauritania and Senegal. The Convention is open for accession to other States in the sub-region.

Main Objectives and Activities

The main objective of the Commission is to harmonize the long-term policies of Member States in the preservation, conservation and exploitation of the fisheries resources for the benefit of their respective populations. The Commission consists of the Conference of Ministers, the Coordinating Committee, and the Permanent Secretariat. The Conakry Convention concerning determination of conditions for foreign access to exploitation of the living resources in off-shore areas of SRCF Member States was signed by the Commission's Member States in 1989.

II.2.9 Regional Convention on Fisheries Cooperation Among African States Bordering the Atlantic Ocean

The Convention was signed at Dakar, Senegal, on 5 July 1991. The institutional framework of the Convention comprises the Conference of Ministers, the Bureau and the Secretariat. The Convention entered into force on 12 July 1995.

Area of Competence

The area covered by the Convention is not defined in precise terms. Under Article I the convention applies to the African States bordering the Atlantic Ocean and then it defines "regions" as the area comprising those States. This area coincides with parts of the FAO Statistical Areas 34 and 47.

Species Covered

The Convention applies to all fishery resources.

Membership

The Convention is open for ratification, approval or acceptance only by the following States: Angola, Benin, Cameroon, Cape-Verde, Congo, Côte-d'Ivoire, Gabon, Gambia, Guinea, Guinea Bissau, Equatorial Guinea, Liberia, Morocco, Mauritania, Namibia, Nigeria, Sao Tome and Principe, Senegal, Sierra Leone, Togo and Zaire.

Main Objectives and Activities

The main objectives of the Convention are to enable the Parties inter alia to (i) promote an active and organized cooperation in the area of fisheries management and development in the region, and (ii) take up the challenge of food self-sufficiency through the rational utilization of fishery resources, within the context of an integrated approach that would embrace all the components of the fishing sector. Under Article 3, Parties should combine their efforts to ensure the conservation and rational management of their fishery resources and take concerted action for the assessment of fish stocks occurring within the waters under the sovereignty or jurisdiction of more than one Party. In addition, contracting Parties should endeavour to adopt harmonized policies concerning the conservation, management and exploitation of fishery resources, in particular with regard to the determination of catch quotas and, as appropriate, the adoption of joint regulation of fishing seasons.

II.2.10 Regional Fisheries Committee for the Gulf of Guinea (Comité Régional des Pêches du Golfe de Guinée (CORÉP)

Established by the Convention Concerning the Regional Development of Fisheries in the Gulf of Guinea, signed at Libreville, Gabon, on 21 June 1984. The Convention has not yet entered into force.

Area of Competence

The area of competence of the Committee is defined as the Central and Southern Gulf of Guinea.

Species Covered

The species covered by the Committee are all living resources within its area of competence.

Membership

The Convention is open for signature and accession to States bordering the Gulf of Guinea. The present members of the Committee are as follows: Congo, Gabon, Equatorial Guinea, Guinea, Sao Tome and Principe, and Zaire.

Main Objectives and Activities

The main objectives of the Convention inter alia are (i) to determine a concerted attitude towards the activities of foreign fishing vessels and give priority to the needs of fishing vessels originating from member countries; (ii) to harmonize the national regulations with a view to having a unified regulation fixing the conditions of fishing and the control of fishing operations in the area covered by the Convention, and (iii) to collect the maximum scientific, technical and economic data on fishing operations.

II.2.11 Western Central Atlantic Fishery Commission (WECAFC)

Established by Resolution 4/61 of the FAO Council at its Sixty-first Session held in Rome in November 1973 under Article VI (1) of the FAO Constitution. The Statutes of the Commission were amended by the FAO Council at its Seventy-fourth Session in December 1978.

Area of Competence

The Commission's area of competence is defined as all marine waters of the Western Central Atlantic bounded by a line drawn as follows: from a point on the coast of South America at 10°S latitude in a northerly direction along this coast past the Atlantic entry to the Panama canal; thence continue along the coasts of central and north America to a point on this coast at 35°N latitude; thence due east along this parallel to 42°W longitude; thence due north along this meridian to 36°N latitude; thence due east along this parallel to 40°W longitude; thence due south along this meridian to 5°N latitude; thence due east along this parallel to 30°W longitude; thence due south along this meridian to the Equator; thence due east along the Equator to 20°W longitude; thence due south along this meridian to 10°S latitude; thence due west along this parallel to the original point at 10°S latitude on the coast of South America. This area coincides with FAO Statistical Area 31 and part of Area 41 (Map 9).

Species Covered

The Commission has competence to deal with all living marine resources.

Membership

The membership of the WECAFC is open to all Member Nations and Associate Members of FAO which notify the Director-General of their desire to be considered as members. The present members of the Commission are: Antigua and Burbuda, Bahamas, Barbados, Belize, Brazil, Colombia, Costa Rica, Cuba, Dominica, France, Grenada, Guatemala, Guinea, Guyana, Haiti, Honduras, Jamaica, Japan, Korea (Rep. of), Mexico, Netherlands, Nicaragua, Panama, Saint Christopher and Nevis, Saint Lucia, Saint Vincent and the Grenadines, Spain, Suriname, Trinidad and Tobago, UK, USA, Venezuela.

Main Objectives and Activities

The main objectives of the Commission are to facilitate the coordination of research, to encourage education and training, to assist Member Governments in establishing rational policies and to promote the rational management of resources that are of interest for two or more countries. The Commission does not have any regulatory powers and can only perform advisory functions on management.

Map 9

Area of competence of WECAFC. The dotted line delimits FAO Statistical Area 31 (in the north) from FAO Statistical Area 41 (in the south)

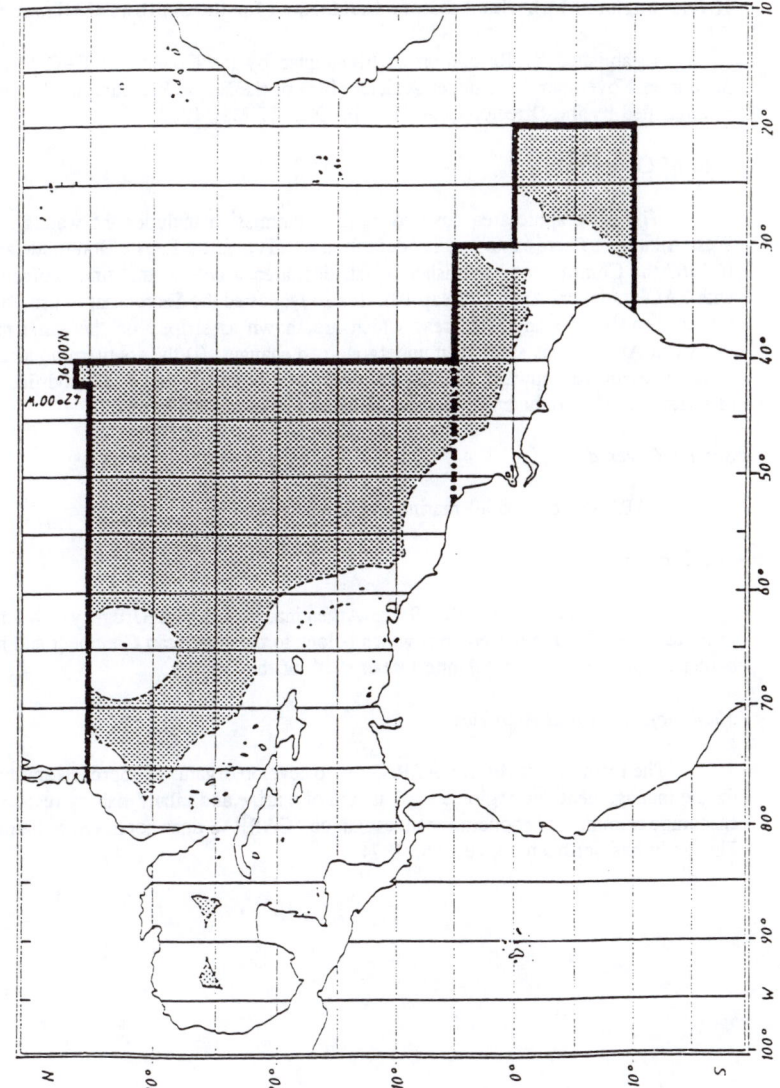

II.2.12 Regional Fisheries Advisory Commission for the Southwest Atlantic (CARPAS)

Established by Resolution 25/61 adopted by the Council of FAO at its Eleventh Session in November 1961 under Article VI (1) of the FAO Constitution. Its Statutes were promulgated by the Director-General of FAO on 17 May 1962.

Area of Competence

The geographic area covered by the Commission includes the waters of the South West Atlantic. There is no precise definition of this area by lines of longitude and latitude. In 1968 the Commission established a statistical area which, at that time, coincided exactly with FAO Statistical Area 41 (Map 10). It also requested the Secretariat to provide statistical information on two adjacent areas which are shown as striped on the same map. FAO Statistical Area 41 has since then undergone two changes: (i) the southern boundary of Area 41 has been moved upward, and (ii) the south west boundary has been modified since 1982 as a result of the boundary agreement between Chile and Argentina.

Species Covered

CARPAS covered all marine living resources.

Membership

The members of CARPAS are Argentina, Brazil and Uruguay. Membership is restricted to FAO Member Nations which belong to the American Continent and have coasts bordering on the Western Atlantic Ocean south of the Equator.

Main Objectives and Activities

The main objectives of CARPAS are to develop organized approach among members for the management and regional exploitation of marine and inland fishery resources, and to encourage training and cooperative investigation. CARPAS does not have regulatory powers. This body has not been active since 1974.

Map 10

CARPAS Statistical Area. The two adjacent areas are shown as stripped.

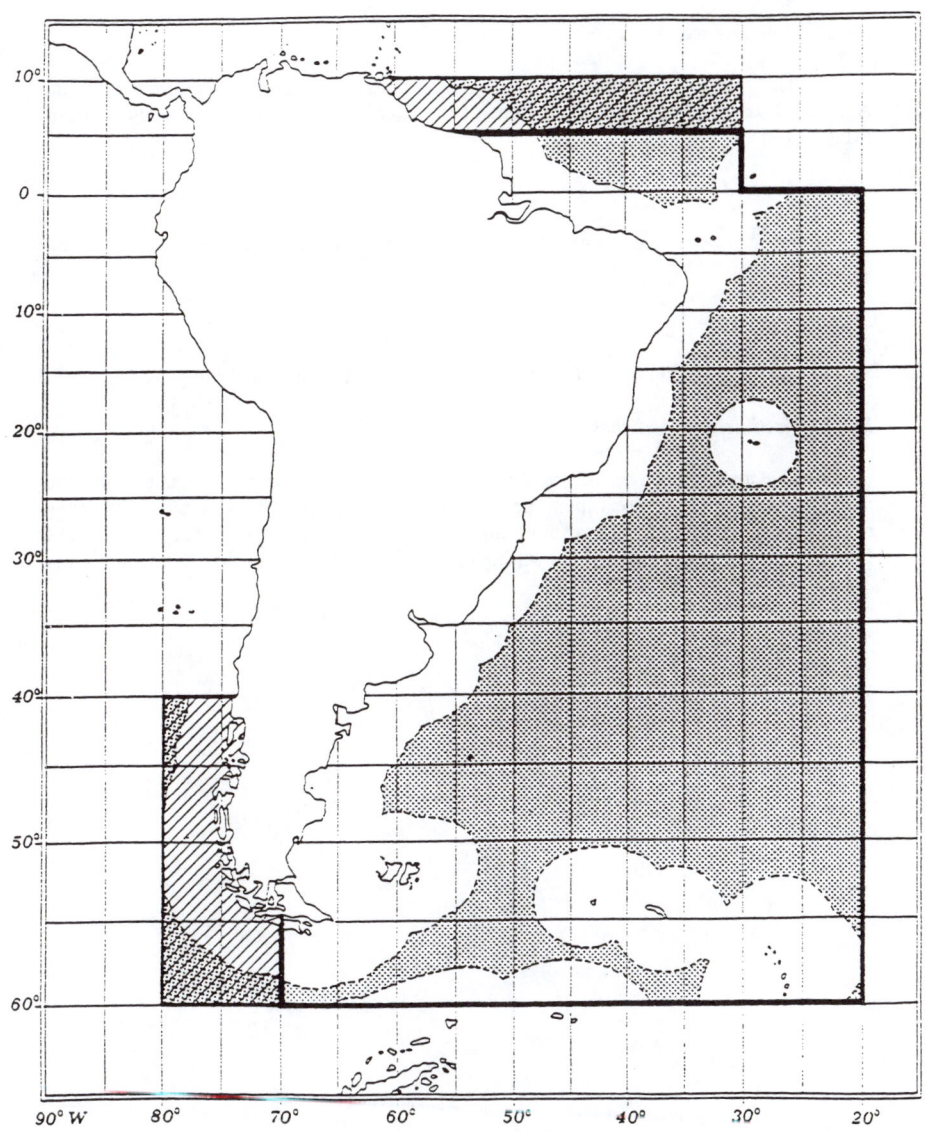

II.2.13 Joint Technical Commission for the Argentina/Uruguay Maritime Front (CTMFM)

Established by the Agreement "Tratado del Río de la Plata y sus Frente Maritimo", signed by Argentina and Uruguay in 1973.

Area of Competence

The area of competence of the Joint Technical Commission is referred to in the Agreement as the Common Fishing Zone of the Contracting Parties in the South Atlantic (Map 11).

Species Covered

All marine living resources of the Common Fishing Zone are covered by the Commission.

Membership

The membership of the Commission consists of Argentina and Uruguay.

Main Objectives and Activities

The main objectives of the Commission are to adopt and coordinate plans and measures relevant to conservation, preservation and the rational exploitation of living resources and to protect the maritime environment in the Common Fishing Zone. The Commission has regulatory powers setting quotas for each Party in the Common Fishery Zone.

Map 11*

Area of competence of CTMFM

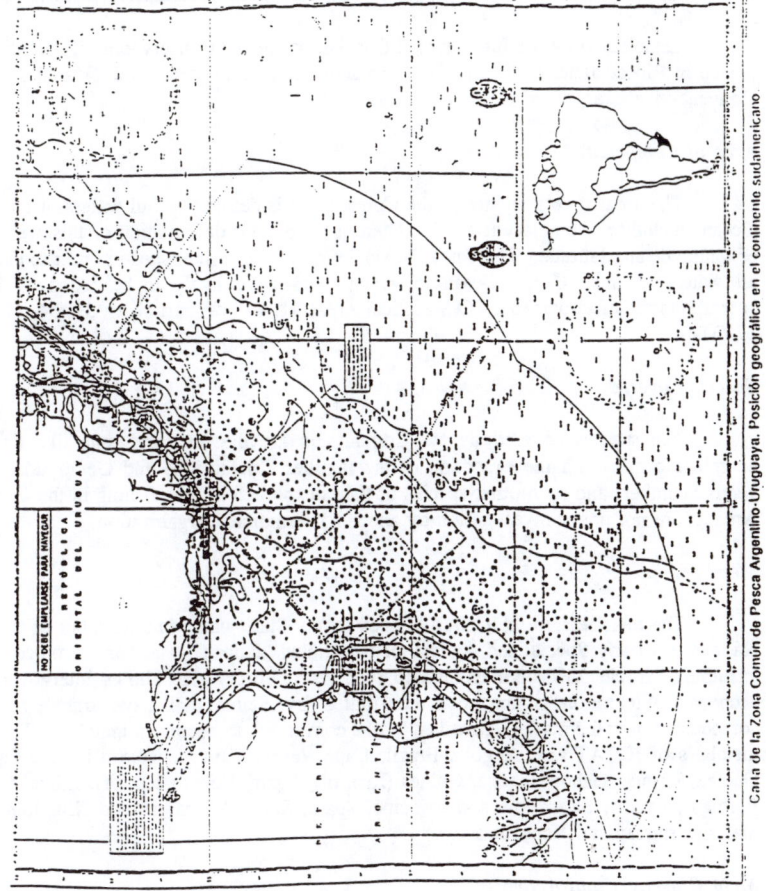

Carta de la Zona Común de Pesca Argentino-Uruguaya. Posición geográfica en el continente sudamericano

*This map is a reproduction of the map printed in the official publication of CTMFM, 'Frente Marítimo' in June 1994.

II.2.14 International Commission for the Conservation of Atlantic Tunas (ICCAT)

Established by the International Convention for the Conservation of Atlantic Tunas, signed in Rio de Janeiro, on 14 May 1966 and entered into force on 21 March 1969. The Convention was amended in 1984 and 1992[9].

Area of Competence

The area of competence of the Commission is defined as "all waters of the Atlantic Ocean, including the adjacent seas". There is no precise delimitation of this area by lines of longitude and latitude. This rather broad definition was established in order to encompass all waters of the Atlantic Ocean in which tunas were likely to be found. This area corresponds in most part to FAO Statistical Areas 41, 47, 48 (part of it), 31, 34, 37, 21 and 27 (Map 12).

Species Covered

The species covered by the Commission are the tuna and tuna like fishes (the Scombrioformes with the exception of the families Trichiuridae and Gempylidae and the genus Scomber) and such other species of fishes exploited in tuna fishing in the Convention Area as are not under investigation by another international organization.

Membership

The membership of ICCAT is open to any State which is a Member of the United Nations or of any Specialized Agency of the United Nations. The Paris Protocol of 1984 amending Article XIV on membership (not yet in force) also allows intergovernmental economic integration organization constituted by States that have transferred to its competence over the matters governed by the convention to become a member. The present members of ICCAT are: Angola, Brazil, Cape Verde, Canada, Côte d'Ivoire, Equatorial Guinea, France, Gabon, Ghana, Guinea (Rep. of), Japan, Korea (Rep. of), Libya, Morocco, Portugal, Russia, Sao Tomé and Principe, Spain, South Africa, United Kingdom, United States, Uruguay and Venezuela.

Main Objectives and Activities

The main objective of the Convention is to maintain the populations of tuna and tuna-like species found in the Atlantic at levels which permit the maximum sustainable catch for food and other purposes. The Commission's functions inter alia include: (i) to study the populations of tuna and tuna-like fishes, (ii) to collect and analyse statistical information relating to the current conditions and trends of the tuna fishery resources of the Convention Area, and (iii) recommend studies and investigations to the Contracting Parties. The Commission has regulatory powers and so far has recommended a number of measures on catch quotas, minimum weight of fish and limitation of incidental catches. It has a scheme for Port Inspection as well as an Infraction Committee. The regulatory measures adopted by ICCAT are subject to objection procedure.

---

[9]   The 1984 Protocol concerned Article XIV of the Convention allowing the membership of the Commission by intergovernmental economic integration organization constituted by States that have transferred to its competence over the matters governed by the Convention. The 1992 Protocol concerned Article X of the Convention on financial contributions of Members.

Map 12

FAO Statistical Areas 21, 27, 31, 34, 37, 41, 47 and 48 covered by ICCAT

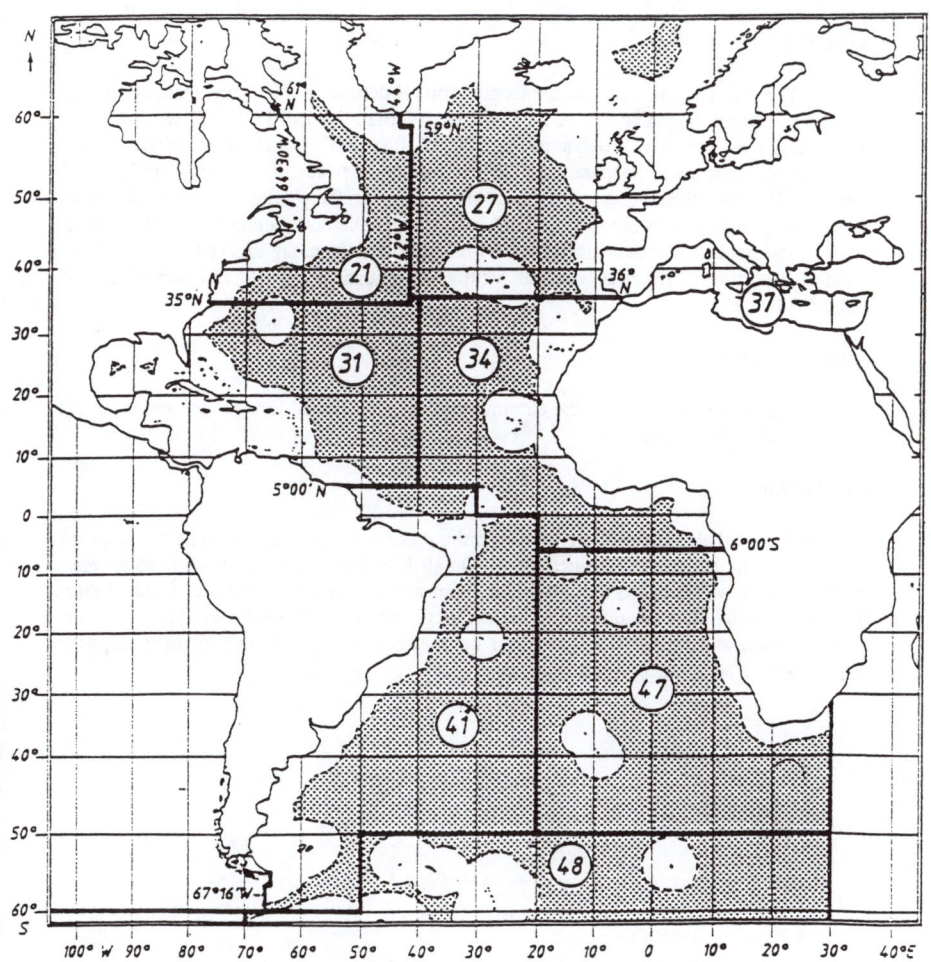

II.2.15 International Commission for the Southeast Atlantic Fisheries (ICSEAF)

Established by the Convention on the Conservation of the Living Resources of the South Atlantic, drawn up in Rome on 23 October 1969, and entered into force on 24 October 1971. On 19 July 1990, a Conference of Plenipotentiaries adopted a Protocol for the Termination of the Convention. In accordance with the Protocol, the Convention shall terminate when all Contracting Parties have deposited an instrument of acceptance of the Protocol with the Director-General of FAO. The Convention has not yet been terminated.

Area of Competence

The area of competence of the Commission is defined as all waters bounded by a line drawn as follows: beginning at a point 6°04'36" south latitude and 12°19-48" east longitude, thence in a northwesterly direction along a rhumb line to a point at the intersection of the meridian 12° east with the parallel 6° south, thence due west along this parallel to the meridian 20° west, thence due south along this meridian to the parallel 50° south, thence due east along this parallel to the meridian 40° east, thence due north along this meridian to the coast of the African continent, thence in a westerly direction along this coast to the original point of departure. This area coincides with FAO Statistical Area 47 and part of areas 51 and 58 (Map 13).

Species Covered

The species covered by the Commission are all fish and living resources subject to arrangement with other bodies.

Membership

As noted above the Convention is in the process of being terminated. No session of the Commission has been held since 1990. On 19 July 1990 when the Protocol to terminate the Convention was adopted the membership consisted of Angola, Bulgaria, Cuba, France, Germany, Israel, Italy, Iraq, Japan, Korea (Rep. of), Poland, Portugal, Romania, South Africa, Spain, and former USSR. So far only Angola and Cuba have formally deposited instruments of acceptance of the Protocol.

Map 13

The ICSEAF area of competence. The dotted lines delimit FAO Statistical Areas 51
(on the east) and 58 (on south east)

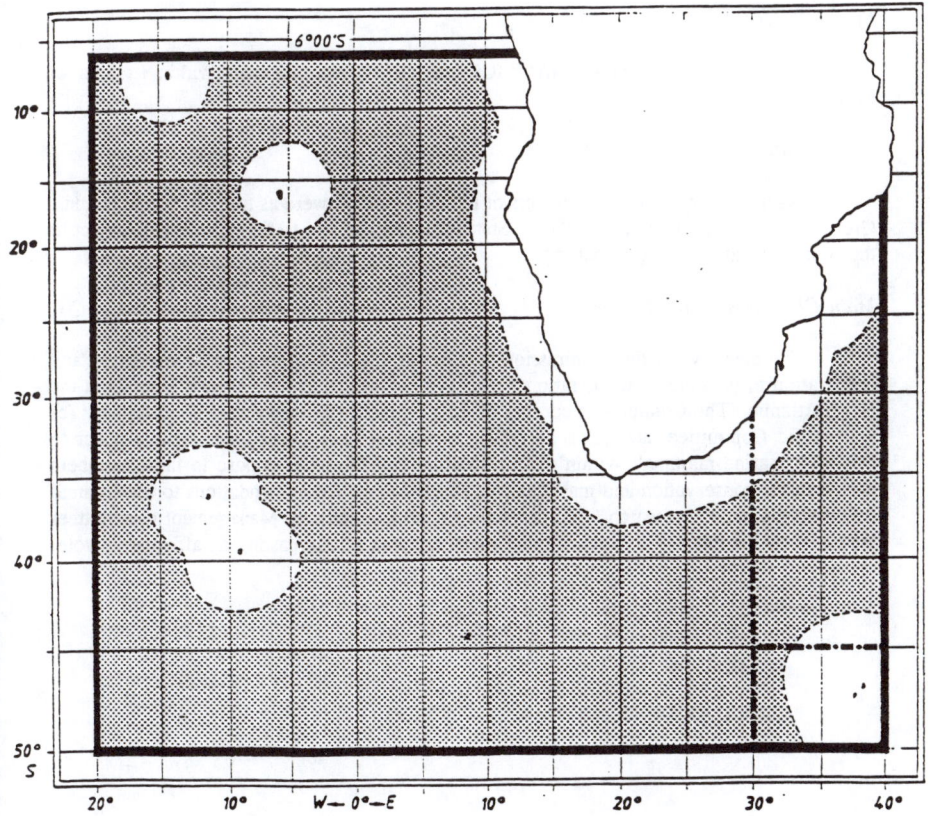

II.2.16 North Atlantic Marine Mammal Commission (NAMMCO)

Established by the Agreement on Cooperation in Research, Conservation and Management of Marine Mammals in the North Atlantic, signed at Nuuk, Greenland on 9 April 1992. It entered into force on 7 July 1992.

Area of Competence

The area of competence of the Commission is the North Atlantic. There is no precise delimitation of this area by lines of longitude and latitude. In practice, this area coincides with FAO Statistical Area 27 (Map 14).

Species Covered

The species covered by NAMMCO are all marine mammals within its area of competence.

Membership

As of January 1994 the members of the Commission were as follows: Faroe Islands, Greenland, Iceland and Norway. Other States may also adhere to the Agreement subject to the consent of the existing signatories.

Main Objectives and Activities

The objective of the Commission is to contribute through regional consultation and cooperation to the conservation, rational management and study of marine mammals in the North Atlantic. The Commission consists of (a) a Council; (b) management Committees; (c) a scientific Committee; and (d) a Secretariat. Management Committees, with respect to stocks of marine mammals within their respective mandates (i) propose to their members measures for conservation and management, and (ii) make recommendations to the Council concerning scientific research. All decisions of the Council and Management Committees are taken by the unanimous vote of those members present and casting an affirmative vote.

Map 14

FAO Statistical Area 27 where NAMMCO concentrates its activities

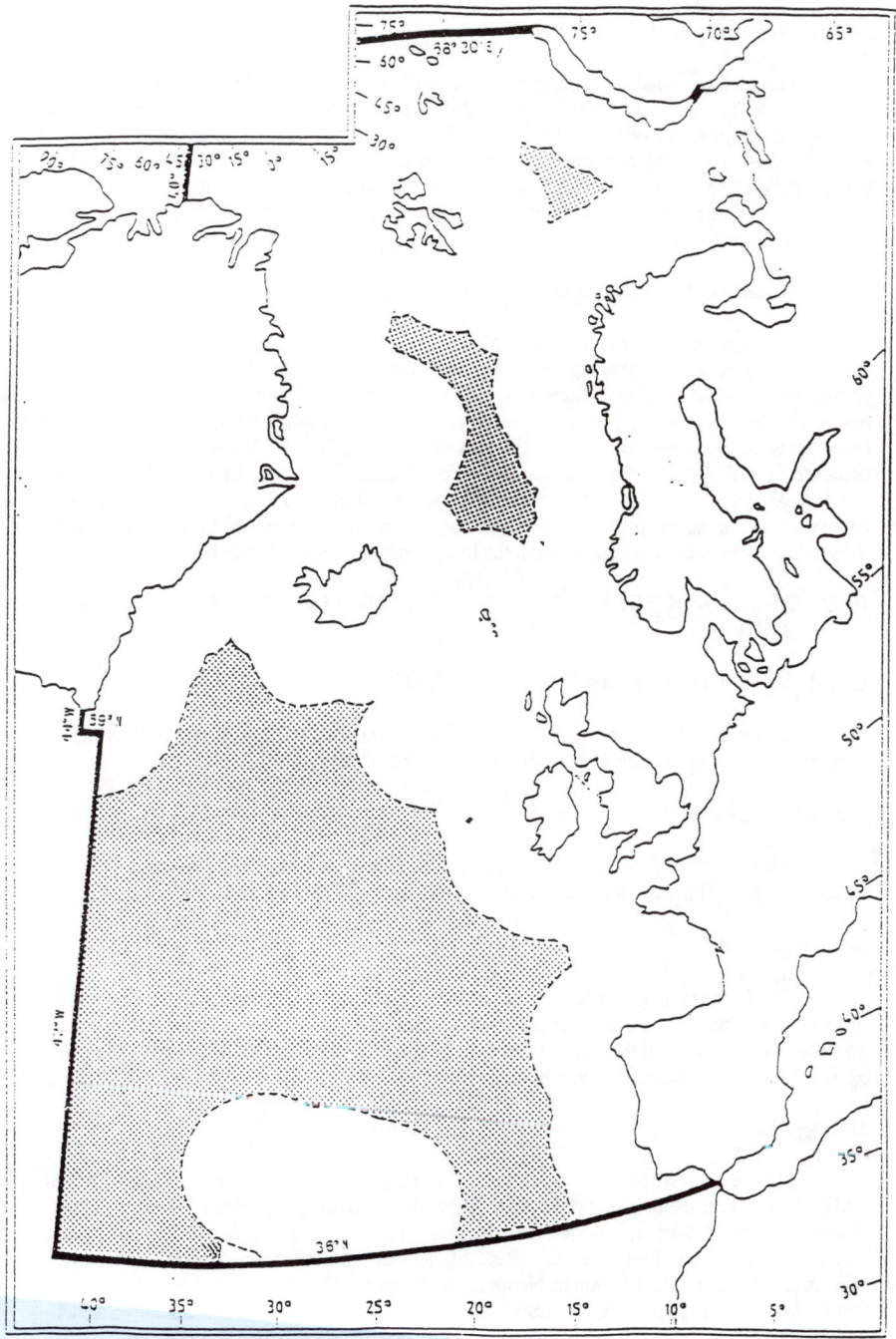

III.   INDIAN OCEAN AND INDO-PACIFIC AREA

III.1   A BRIEF REVIEW OF MAJOR FISHING AREAS IN THE INDIAN OCEAN AND INDO-PACIFIC AREA

III.1.1 Western Indian Ocean (Area 51)

The total recorded landings for the area in 1993 were up 14.5% compared to 1990; reaching 3.8 million t. Of this increase, 25% can be attributed to the rise in reported landings of skipjack and yellowfin tuna by predominantly distant-water fishing nations. The main fisheries in Area 51 are: Bombay duck, catfish, croakers, emperos, jacks, pompanos, carangids, sardine, anchovies, clupeoids, tuna and tuna-like species, mackerel (chub and Indian), sharks, shrimps, and cephalopods. The landings of bony fishes not identified were 661,551 tons in 1993.

III.1.2 Eastern Indian Ocean (Area 57)

The reported landings for Area 57 in 1993 totalled 3.4 million t, an increase of 22.5% compared to the 1990 figure. The main fisheries in Area 57 are: shads, catfish, ponyfishes, croakers, mullets, carangids, sardines, anchovies, tuna and tuna-like species, mackerel, sharks, prawns, shrimps, lobsters, cockles, and cephalopods. The landings of bony fishes not identified were 1,461,219 tons in 1993. A 32% rise in invertebrate landings accounted for 27% of the total increase between 1990 and 1992, while reported landings of fish increased by about 14%. The 56% rise in penaeid shrimp landings (due to both a good fishing season for banana prawn and increased aquaculture production, primarily by India and Bangladesh) accounted for half of the total improvement in invertebrate landings.

III.2   REGIONAL FISHERY BODIES IN THE INDIAN OCEAN AND INDO-PACIFIC AREA

III.2.1 Indian Ocean Fishery Commission (IOFC)

Established by Resolution 2/48 adopted by the FAO Council at its Forty-eighth Session in June 1967 under Article VI(1) of the FAO Constitution.

Area of Competence

IOFC's area of competence is the Indian Ocean and adjacent seas excluding the Antarctic area. This area coincides with FAO Statistical Areas 51 and 57 (Map 15).

Species Covered

The Commission covers all living marine resources. With the establishment of the Indian Ocean Tuna Commission, the future activities of IOFC will be substantially reduced. Species other than tuna in the Indian Ocean are geographically localized and may be managed by smaller fishery bodies at sub-regional levels.

Membership

Membership of IOFC is open to all Member Nations and Associate Members of FAO. The present members of IOFC are: Australia, Bahrain, Bangladesh, Comoros, Cuba, Djibouti, Egypt, Ethiopia, France, Greece, India, Indonesia, Iran (Islamic Rep. of), Iraq, Israel, Japan, Jordan, Kenya, Korea (Rep. of) Kuwait, Madagascar, Malaysia, Maldives, Mauritius, Mozambique, Myanmar, Netherlands, Norway, Oman, Pakistan, Portugal, Qatar, Saudi Arabia (Kingdom of), Seychelles, Somalia, Spain, Sri Lanka, Sudan, Sweden, Tanzania, Thailand, United Arab Emirates, UK, USA and Viet Nam.

Main Objectives and Activities

The objectives of IOFC are to promote, assist and coordinate national programmes over the entire field of fishery development and conservation; to promote research and development activities in the area through international sources, in particular through international aid programmes; and to examine management problems, with special emphasis on the management of offshore resources. IOFC does not have regulatory powers. With the establishment of IOTC, the future role of IOFC will have to be considered by its members. The three remaining subsidiary bodies of the Commission, i.e., Committee for the Development and Management of the Fisheries Resources of the Gulfs, Committee for the Development and Management of Fisheries in the Southwest Indian Ocean, and Committee for the Development and Management of Fisheries in the Bay of Bengal, are well placed to manage other fishery resources of the Indian Ocean at sub-regional levels. They would need a proper mandate to do so while some minor adjustments to their geographical coverage would ensure that major fishing areas of the Indian Ocean are covered by them.

Map 15

FAO Statistical Areas 51 (left) and 57 (right)

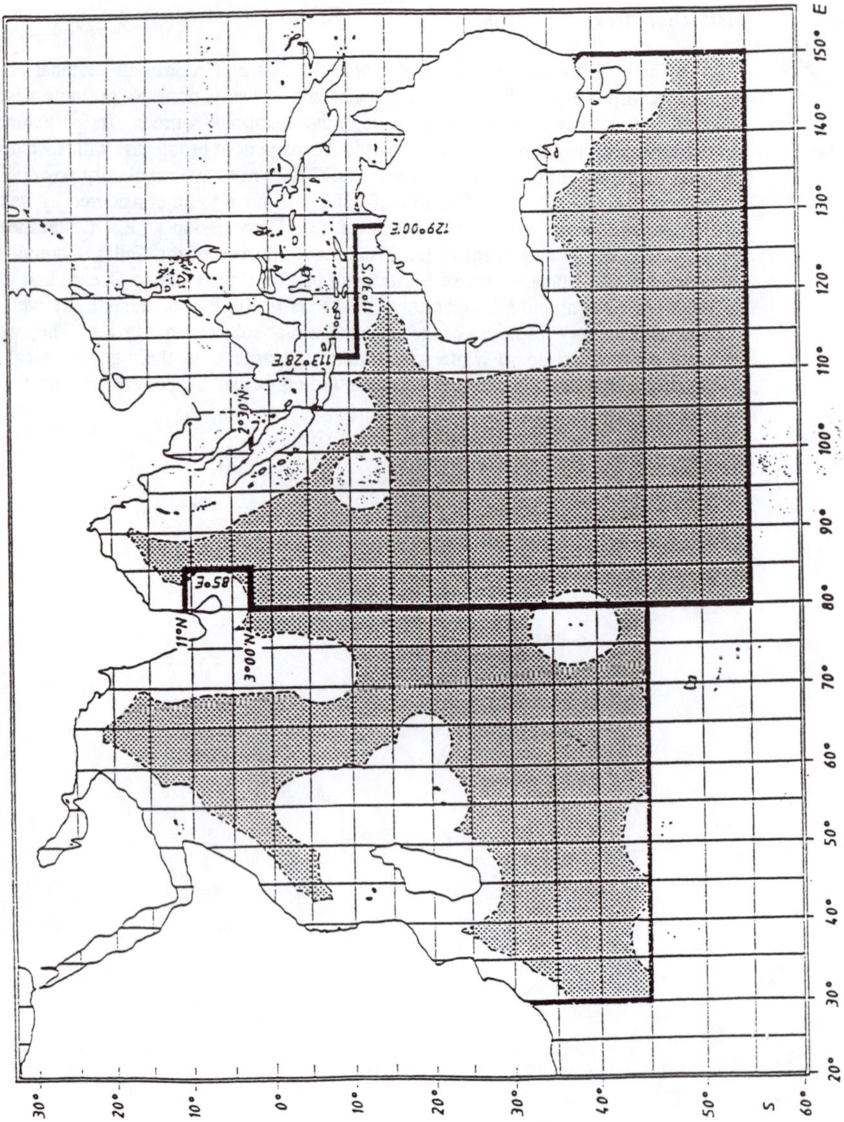

III.2.2 Indian Ocean Tuna Commission (IOTC)

Established by an Agreement drawn up at Rome under Article XV of the FAO Constitution and was approved by the FAO Conference at its Twenty-seventh Session and adopted by the Council at its Hundred and Fifth Session in November 1993. The Agreement entered into force upon the receipt of the tenth instrument of acceptance by the Director-General of the FAO, from Republic of Korea on 27 March 1996.

Area of Competence

The area of competence of the Commission is defined as the Indian Ocean and adjacent seas, north of the Antarctic convergence, in so far as it is necessary to cover such seas for the purpose of conserving and managing stocks that migrate into or out of the Indian Ocean. This area coincides exactly with the FAO Statistical Areas 51 and 57 (Map 16).

Species Covered

The species covered by the Convention are as follows: yellowfin tuna, skipjack tuna, bigeye tuna, albacore, Southern bluefin tuna, longtail tuna, kawakawa, frigate tuna, bullet tuna, narrow-barred Spanish mackerel, Indo-Pacific king mackerel, Indo-Pacific blue marlin, black marlin, striped marlin, Indo-Pacific sailfish, and swordfish.

Membership

The Convention is open for acceptance by Members and Associate Members of FAO that are (i) coastal States or Associate Members situated wholly or partly within the area; (ii) States responsible for the international relations of territories situated wholly or partly within the area covered by the Agreement; (iii) States or Associate Members whose vessels engage in fishing in the area of stocks covered by the Agreement; and (iv) regional economic integration organizations of which any State has transferred competence over matters covered by the Agreement. The Commission may, by a two-third majority of its members, admit other States which are Members of the United Nations or of any of its Specialized Agencies or the International Atomic Energy Agency provided that they are coastal States situated wholly or partly within the area or States whose vessels engage in fishing in the area for stocks covered by the Agreement.

Main Objectives and Activities

The main objectives of the Agreement are to promote cooperation among members with a view to ensuring through appropriate management, the conservation and optimum utilization of stocks as well as to encourage sustainable development of fisheries based on them. The Commission may be a two-third majority of the Members present and voting adopt conservation and management measures binding on its Members. Such regulatory measures are subject to objection procedure.

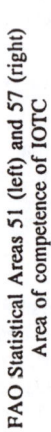

Map 16

FAO Statistical Areas 51 (left) and 57 (right)
Area of competence of IOTC

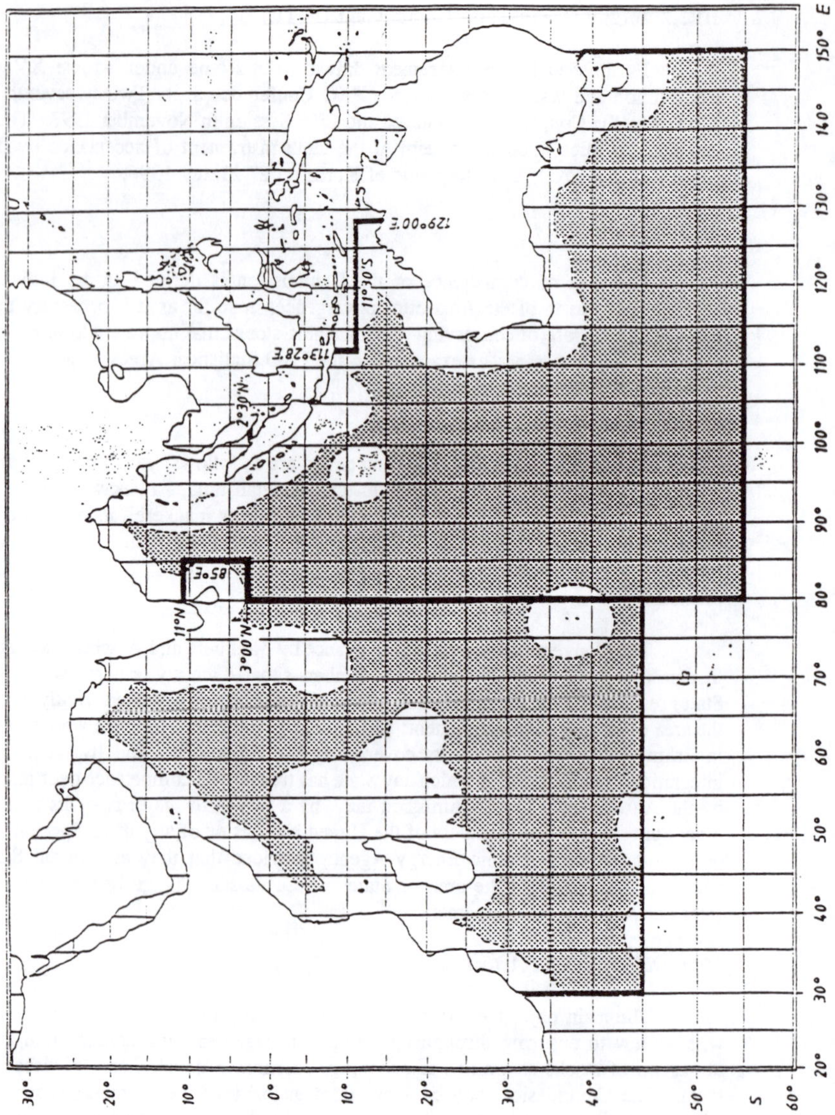

III.2.3 Western Indian Ocean Tuna Organization (WIOTO)

Established by the Western Indian Ocean Tuna Organization Convention, signed at Mahé, Seychelles, on 19 June 1991 and entered into force in 1994.

Area of Competence

The area of competence of the Organization as described in Annex II of the Convention starts along 11°N latitude from the Eastern coast of India and through the following coordinates: 11°N latitude to 85°E longitude and 3°N latitude to 85°E longitude and 3°N latitude to 80°E longitude and 45°S latitude to 80°E longitude and 45°S latitude to 30°E longitude and then proceed along meridian 30°E to the coast of Africa. This area coincides with the FAO Statistical Area 51.

Species Covered

The species covered by the Convention are as follows: yellowfin tuna, skipjack tuna, bigeye tuna, albacore tuna, southern bluefin tuna, longtail tuna, frigate tuna, bullet tuna, kawakawa, narrow-barred Spanish mackerel, Indo-Pacific king mackerel, Indo-Pacific blue marlin, black marlin, striped marlin, Indo-Pacific sailfish, and swordfish.

Membership

The membership of the Organization is open to the funding States (Comoros, India, Kenya, Madagascar, Maldives, Mauritius, Mozambique, Seychelles, Sri Lanka, and Tanzania). Any independent coastal State bordering the Western Indian Ocean whose territory is situated principally in the Western Indian Ocean region may also be admitted by unanimous approval of the parties to the Convention. The present members of WIOTO are Seychelles, Mauritius, Comoros and India.

Main Objectives and Activities

The Organization's objectives are (a) harmonization of policies with respect to fisheries; (b) relations with distant water fishing nations; (c) fisheries surveillance and enforcement; (d) fisheries development; and (e) access to exclusive economic zones of members. There are no provisions in the Convention for establishing regulatory measures in the area covered by the Organization. The First Ministerial Meeting of WIOTO was held in August 1994.

III.2.4 Asia-Pacific Fishery Commission (APFIC)

Established (as Indo-Pacific Fisheries Council) by an Agreement adopted at Baguio, Philippines, on 26 February 1948 under Article XIV of the FAO Constitution. The Agreement entered into force on 9 November 1948 and has been amended in 1952, 1955, 1958, 1961, 1977 and 1993. The 1976 amendment changed the title from Indo-Pacific Fisheries Council to Indo-Pacific Fishery Commission (IPFC). The 1993 amendments included the change of the title to Asia-Pacific Fishery Commission.

Area of Competence

The area of competence of the Commission is referred to as Asia-Pacific area. There is no precise definition of this area by lines of longitude and latitude. The APFIC Committee on Marine Fisheries (COMAF) is responsible for the management of Asia-Pacific area with priority on marine fishery resources in the South China Sea and adjacent waters (Map 17).

Species Covered

The Commission covers all living marine resources as well as living inland aquatic resources. APFIC Aquaculture and Inland Fisheries Committee established in 1993 is responsible for the management and development of aquaculture and inland fisheries of Asia-Pacific area.

Membership

Membership of the Commission is open to Member Nations and Associate Members of FAO. Non-member States of FAO which are Members of the United Nations, or any of its Specialized Agencies or the International Atomic Energy Agency may be admitted as members by a two-thirds majority of the Commission's membership. The present members of APFIC are: Australia, Bangladesh, Cambodia, China (People's Republic of), France, India, Indonesia, Japan, Korea (Republic of), Malaysia, Myanmar (Union of), Nepal, New Zealand, Pakistan, Philippines, Sri Lanka, Thailand, United Kingdom, United States of America, and Viet Nam.

Main Objectives and Activities

The main objectives of APFIC are to promote the full and proper utilization of living aquatic resources by the development and management of fishing and culture operations and by the development of related processing and marketing activities in conformity with the objectives of its members. The Commission has a broad mandate (Article IV) to formulate and recommend measures in respect of conservation and management of the resources in the Asia-Pacific area. It does not have regulatory powers.

Map 17

FAO Statistical Area 71 where APFIC concentrates its marine activities

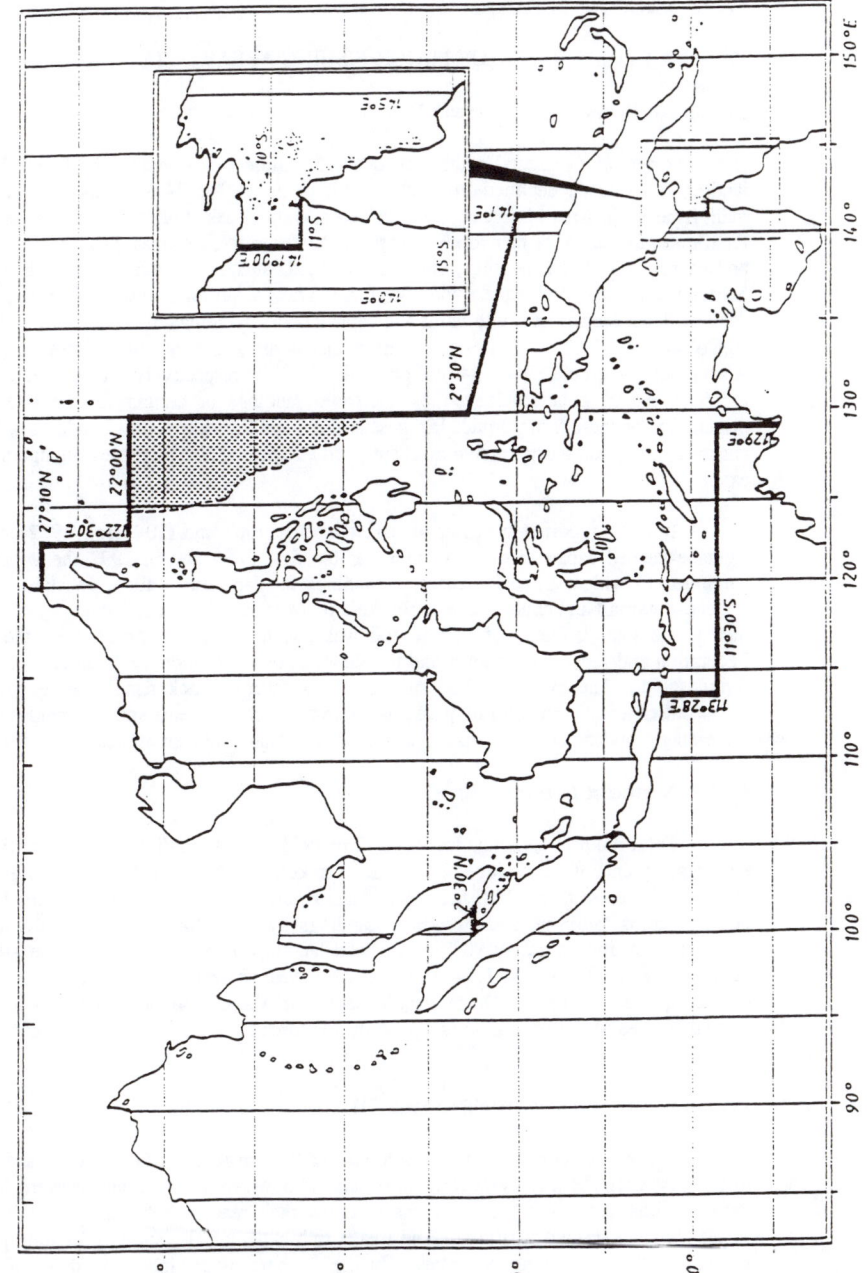

IV.   PACIFIC OCEAN

IV.1   A BRIEF REVIEW OF MAJOR FISHING AREAS IN THE PACIFIC OCEAN

IV.1.1 Northwest Pacific (Area 61)

After the peak total catches of over 26 million t observed in the late 1980s, total landings in Area 61 declined from 25.7 million t in 1990 to 24.8 million t in 1993. The main fisheries in Area 61 are: salmon, flatfishes, cods, Alaska pollock, croakers, seabreams, Pacific sandlance, Atka mackerel, filefishes, Pacific saury, Japanese jack mackerel, scads, amberjacks, pomfrets, herrings, Japanese pilchard, anchovies, tuna and tuna-like species, hairtails, chub mackerel, sharks and rays, crabs, prawns, shrimps, oysters, mussels, scallops, cockles, Japanese carpet shell, clams and cephalopods. Landings of bony fishes not included above was 5,362,532 t in 1993.   During that period, landings of Japanese sardine and Alaska pollock dropped by 2.24 million t and 678,000 t respectively. These declines were, to some extent, counterbalanced by increased landings of certain invertebrate species, principally Japanese flying squid, Japanese scallop, and Japanese clam. Landings of Japanese anchovy, largehead hairtail, chub mackerel, and Pacific cod also increased, though to a lesser extent.

In 1991, reported increases in marine landings (up some 150% from 1982) meant that China exceeded Japan in catch volume for the first time, and in 1992 the apparent gap continued to widen.   The increases in landings for Japanese scallop, Japanese anchovy, largehead hairtail and chub mackerel for Area 61 were due to increased catch by China. The increase in total landings of Pacific cod was due to increased landings by the Russian Federation and Japan while Japan and the Republic of Korea increased landings of Japanese flying squid.   The over-exploited state of the Alaskan pollack fishery, especially in the Okhotsk Sea and Nemuro Strait areas, has become more apparent, and the trend towards an increasing proportion of landings consisting of low value, undifferentiated fish has continued.

IV.1.2 Northeast Pacific (Area 67)

Total reported landings for Area 67 in 1993, at 3.38 million t, remain within a few percentage points of the average 3.24 million t reported in the late 1980s. The main fisheries in Area 67 are: salmon, flatfishes, cod, Alaska pollock, hake, lingcod, mackerel, Pacific herring, crabs, shrimps and oysters.   Landings by the USA continue to dominate the statistics, constituting nearly 90% of the total landings by all countries for the area.   The relatively low 1991 total of 2.97 million t, the lowest on record since 1985, was primarily due to reduced catches of North Pacific hake and Alaskan pollack, although lower than normal catches of flatfish due to early closures enforced by halibut by-catch restrictions also contributed.

IV.1.3 Western Central Pacific (Area 71)

The Western Central Pacific is dominated by a large area of continental shelf, which to the west stretches from Viet Nam and Thailand down to Malaysia and western Indonesia before ending at the Java Sea. To the east, the shelf reaches between eastern Indonesia, Papua New Guinea and Australia. The area is rich in demersal resources, including penaeid shrimp, and small pelagic resources.   In the offshore areas, including those adjacent to oceanic islands of the Pacific, there are rich tuna resources.

Total fisheries landings in this area in 1993 was 8.3 million t, representing a slight increase on the 1992 figure. The main fisheries in Area 71 are: catfishes, snappers, breams, ponyfishes, croakers, barracudas, mullets, scads, carangids, sardinellas, anchovies, tuna and tuna-like species, mackerels, sharks and rays, crabs, prawns, shrimps, cockles, clams and squids. Landings of bony fishes not included above were: 1,678,340 t in 1993. The main landings are still contributed by Thailand, the Philippines and Indonesia with the bulk of the landings in Indonesia and the Philippines coming from the small-scale fisheries sector, whereas in Thailand the fisheries sector is on a larger, more commercial scale. Shrimp catches continued to increase due to increases in coastal aquaculture production throughout Southeast Asia, and landings of banana prawn in the Australian northern prawn fishery.

IV.1.4 Eastern Central Pacific (Area 77)

The total catches in this area continued to decrease. This has mainly been due to the impact of a medium intensity "El Niño" that affected the area in 1991 and 1992. Total catches decreased from 1.7 million t per year in the late 1980s, to 1.5 million t in 1991 and 1.3 million t in 1992 and 1.2 million t in 1993 (1.247.063). The main fisheries in Area 77 are: pilchard, mackerel, herring, anchoveta, tuna and tuna-like species, sharks and rays, shrimps and squids. Landings of bony fishes not included above were 232,109 t in 1993.

The most noticeable change has been in the landings of the North Pacific anchovy (*Engraulis mordax*) whose catches dropped sharply from 111,000 t in 1989 to only 6,000 t in 1990, 21,000 t in 1991, and 10,000 t in 1992 and 4,700 t in 1993. This is a sharp loss compared to catches well above 100,000 t per year obtained in the early 1970s and 1980s, and is due to a sharp decrease in stock size, which has mainly affected Mexican fish stocks and fisheries.

Some decrease has also been noticed in the total catches of the Californian sardine (*Sardinops sagax caeruleus*), chub mackerel (*Scomber japonicus*), Central Pacific anchoveta (*Cetengraulis mysticetus*), Eastern Pacific bonito (*Sarda chiliensis*) and several species of large pelagic fish, including the yellowfin tuna (*Thunnus albacares*).
Catches of other species have remained more or less unchanged in recent years. Squids (mostly *Dosidiscus gigas*) seem to be abundant in the area and still remains underexploited.

IV.1.5 Southwest Pacific (Area 81)

The reported landings for 1993 totalled 777,157 t; down by 16% on the 1992 figure. Landings of southern blue whiting which had showed a clear trend; increasing from 34,050 t in 1990 to 92,167 t in 1992, fell to 32,443 t in 1993. The Foveaux Strait oyster fishery (for *Ostrea spp.*), once the largest dredge fishery for oysters in the world, continues to be in an extremely depressed state because of severe mortalities caused by disease. Vessels are permitted a catch of two sacks, where at one time catches of 115,000 sacks/vessel/season were permitted. Thus, in reality, the fishery has been closed.

IV.1.6 Southeast Pacific (Area 87)

Total reported catches in Area 87 were 14,979,981 t in 1993. Total landings in this area seem to be levelling off at around 14 million t per year since 1990, after an increasing trend that started in 1983-84 and brought the total catches from around 10 million t per year to the current 14 million t per year. Major changes seem to be occurring in this area, with respect to the pelagic fish stocks such as anchoveta, sardine, mackerel and horse mackerel.

The Peruvian anchoveta (*Engraulis ringens*) has replaced sardine (*Sardinops sagax*) as the main fish stock in the area. Catches of anchovy continue in an increasing trend, which seems to be associated with a recovery of this stock after the 1972 collapse and the low stock levels observed since then. Catches of Chilean horse mackerel (*Trachurus symmetricus murphy*) continued to increase, reaching almost 4 million t in 1991, to decrease to 3.3 million t in 1993. To some extent, the reduced landings in this species are due to the reduced catches of the long-range fleets (mostly from the Russian Federation) that were exploiting this stock in the high seas. Total catches of the sardine (*Sardinops sagax*) continued in their decreasing trend which started in 1985. From a maximum catch of 6.5 million t in 1985, total catches have dropped almost continuously to 3.1 million t in 1992 and again to 1.6 million t in 1993. The decrease in the total landings of this species is related to reduction in the stock-size and total area of distribution of the species.

Changes in the abundance and total landings of anchovy, sardine and other small pelagic fishes in the area seem to be associated with similar "regime changes" in other areas of the world. Inside the Gulf of California in the Eastern-Central Pacific, the stocks of California sardine (*Sardinops caeruleus*) are decreasing consistently, while the stocks of anchovies in the same area seem to be increasing, as is the case for the Japanese sardine (*Sardinops melanostictus*) in the Northwest Pacific.

Catches of hake in area 87 decreased slightly in the last couple of years. Another major change occurring in this area has been the increase in abundance of catches of the squid (*Dosidiscus gigas*). Catches of this species increased from around 10,000 t per year during the 1980s to more than 200,000 t in 1993. Catches of other species are relatively stable or showing light year-to-year fluctuations.

IV.1.7 South Pacific Islands (Areas 71 and 77)

Stretching across the eastern half of FAO Statistical Area 71 and the southern parts of FAO Statistical Area 77, there is a distinctive fisheries region encompassing Micronesia, Polynesia and Melanesia. The following review concentrates predominantly on this region, but certain parts may also be relevant to fisheries off adjacent Asian countries, northern and eastern Australia and Hawaii, USA. The small island countries support 5.25 million residents (67% in Papua New Guinea), who rely heavily on living marine resources as a source of food and foreign currencies from licence fees as well as exports. The average consumption of fish is about 50 kg per person per year, but reaches 250 kg in some atolls. This can be compared with 8 kg per person each year in a continental country such as Australia. Tuna (especially skipjack, yellowfin and, to a lesser extent, bigeye and albacore) are the primary living resources of the region. Landings from the capture fisheries in the coastal waters of the islands are relatively modest amounting to about 104,000 t per year.

IV.2   REGIONAL FISHERY BODIES IN THE PACIFIC OCEAN

IV.2.1 North Pacific Marine Science Organization (PICES)

Established by the Convention for a North Pacific Marine Science by Canada, China, Japan, the United States and the Soviet Union Organization, signed in Ottawa, Canada on 12 December 1990 and entered into force on 24 March 1992.

Area of Competence

The area covered by the Convention is the temperate and Sub-Arctic region of the North Pacific Ocean and adjacent seas, especially northward from 30°N latitude. The activities of the Organization may, for scientific reasons, extend farther southward in the North Pacific Ocean. This area coincides with FAO Statistical Area 67 as well as part of FAO Statistical Areas 61 and 77 (Map 18).

Species Covered

The species covered by the Organization are all living marine resources within its area of competence.

Membership

The membership of the Organization is open to the five signatory States. After entry into force, the Convention is open for accession by non-signatory States subject to a unanimous approval by the Contracting Parties. The present members of PICES are: Canada, Japan, China (People's Republic of), Korea (Republic of), Russian Federation and the United States.

Objectives and Activities

The objectives of the Organization are (a) to promote and coordinate marine scientific research in order to advance scientific knowledge of the area concerned and of its living resources, including but not necessarily limited to research with respect to the ocean environment and its interactions with land and atmosphere, its role in and response to global weather and climate change, its flora, fauna and ecosystems, its uses and resources, and impacts upon it from human activities; and (b) to promote the collection and exchange of information and data related to marine scientific research in the area concerned.

The Organization consists of (a) a Governing Council, (b) Finance and Administration Committee, (c) Science Board, and (d) a Secretariat. The activities of the Organization is purely scientific and will cover both areas under national jurisdiction and the high seas under its competence. The Organization is not empowered to recommend regulatory measures.

Map 18

Area to be especially covered by PICES

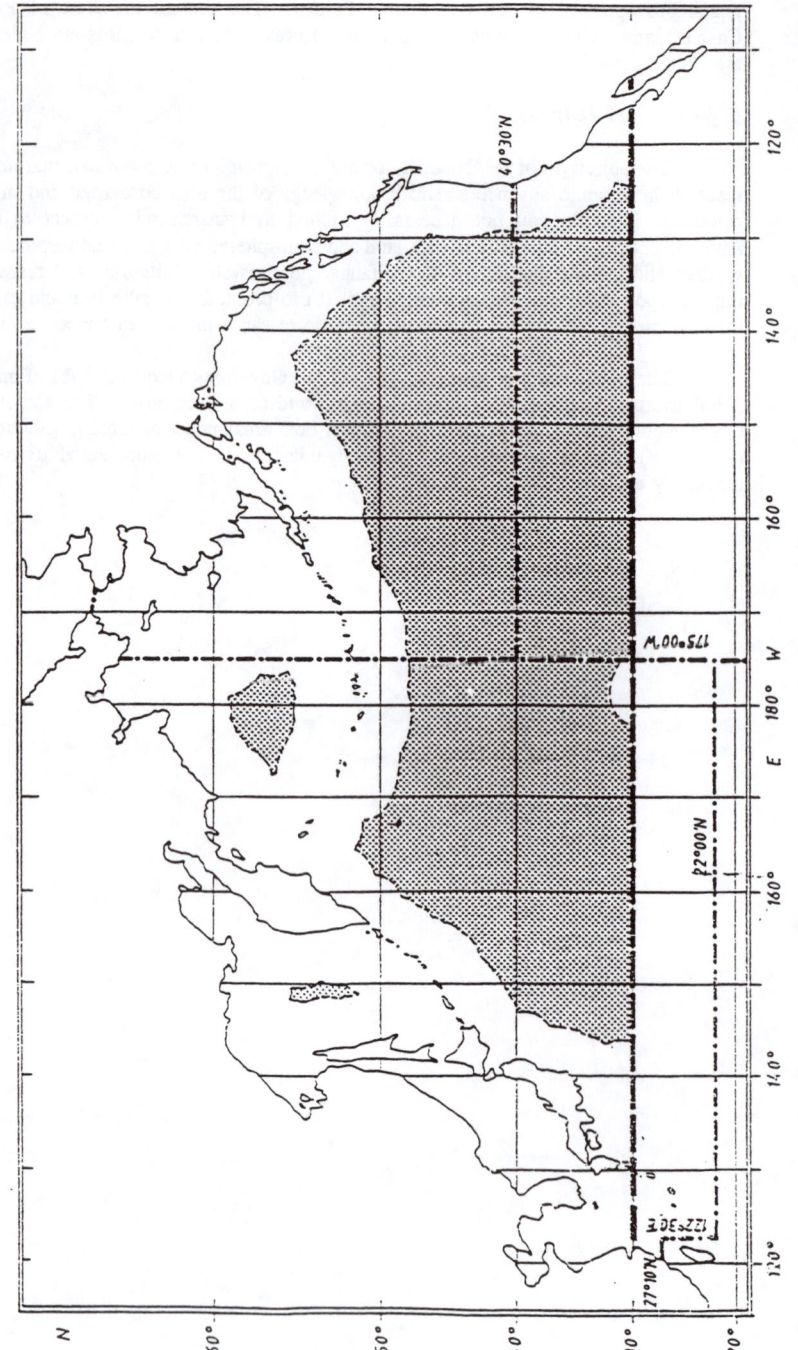

IV.2.2 North Pacific Anadromous Fish Commission (NPAFC)

Established by the Convention for the Conservation of Anadromous Stocks in the North Pacific Ocean, signed at Moscow, Russia, on 11 February 1992 and entered into force on 16 February 1993. It replaced the International Convention for the High Seas Fisheries of the North Pacific which had been in force since 1952.

Area of Competence

The area of competence of the Commission, referred to as the "Convention Area" is defined as the waters of the North Pacific Ocean and its adjacent seas, north of 33°N latitude beyond 200 nautical miles from the baselines from which the breadth of the territorial sea is measured. It is understood that activities under the Convention, for scientific purposes, may extend further southward in the North Pacific Ocean and its adjacent seas. "The Convention Area" coincides mainly with the FAO Statistical Areas 61 and 67 and part of 77.

Species Covered

The species covered by the Commission are as follows: chum salmon, coho salmon, pink salmon, sockeye salmon, chinook salmon, cherry salmon, and steelhead trout.

Membership

The members of the Commission are: the Untied States, Canada, Japan, and the Russian Federation. The Convention is not open to other States but at the invitation of the original Parties by unanimous agreement, other States may accede to it.

Main Objectives and Activities

The main objectives of the Convention are to prohibit directed high seas fishing for North Pacific salmon and to strictly limit the incidental taking of Pacific salmon. The Commission inter alia has the authority (i) to recommend to the parties measures for the conservation of anadromous stocks and ecologically related species in the Convention Area; (ii) to promote the exchange of information of any activities contrary to the provisions of the Convention; (iii) to consider and make proposals to the Parties for the enactment of schedules of equivalent penalties for activities contrary to the provisions of the Convention; and (i) to review and evaluate enforcement actions taken by the Parties. The Parties may take action individually or collectively to prevent unauthorized fishing activities by others and prevent trafficking in illegally harvested Pacific salmon. Decisions of the Commission on all important matters are taken by consensus among all Parties that are States of origin of anadromous stocks which migrate into the Convention Area.

IV.2.3 Inter-American Tropical Tuna Commission (I-ATTC)

Created by the Convention for the Establishment of an Inter-American Tropical Tuna Commission signed by the Governments of the United States and Costa Rica, in Washington on 31 May 1949 and entered into force on 3 March 1950.

Area of Competence

The area of competence of the Commission is defined was the "Eastern Pacific Ocean". There is no precise definition of this area by lines of longitudes and latitudes. In 1962, a Commission's Yellowfin Regulatory Area (CYRA) was created. This "Regulatory area" was defined as follows: All waters of the Eastern Pacific Ocean bounded by the mainland of the Americas and the following lines: beginning at a point on the mainland where the parallel of 40 degrees north latitude intersects the coast; thence due west to the meridian of 125 degrees west longitude; thence due south to the parallel of 20 degrees north latitude; thence due east to the meridian of 120 degrees west longitude; thence due south to the parallel of 5 degrees north latitude; thence due east to the meridian of 110 degrees west longitude; thence due south to the parallel of 30 degrees south latitude; thence due east to a point on the mainland where the parallel of 30 degrees south latitude intersects the coast. This area which includes substantive areas of high seas, coincides with part of FAO Statistical Areas 77 and 87 (Map 19).

Species Covered

The species covered by I-ATTC are as follows: yellowfin and skipjack tuna, fish used as bait for tuna and other fish taken by tuna vessels. The I-ATTC staff has also studied other species of tuna (bigeye, black skipjack, bluefin tuna, albacore) and billfishes.

Membership

Membership of the Committee is open to any States whose nationals participate in fisheries in the I-ATTC Convention Area, provided that the Contracting Parties given their unanimous consent. The present members of I-ATTC are: Costa Rica, France, Japan, Nicaragua, Panama, the United States of America, Vanuatu and Venezuela.

Main Objectives and Activities

The main objectives of the Convention are to maintain the populations of yellowfin and skipjack tuna and other kind of fish taken by tuna fishing vessels in the eastern Pacific and to cooperate in the gathering and interpretation of factual information to facilitate maintaining the populations of these fishes at a level which permits maximum sustainable catches year after year. The functions of the Commission include inter alia (a) to gather and interpret information on tuna, (b) to conduct scientific investigation concerning the abundance, biology, biometry, and ecology of yellowfin and skipjack tuna in the Convention Area, and to recommend proposals for joint action for conservation. The Commission has regulatory powers and catch quotas for yellowfin tuna have been set by the Commission since 1962. Since 1976, the Commission has implemented a programme on tuna dolphin relationship and since 1992 it has developed an International Dolphin Conservation Programme aiming at progressively reducing dolphin mortality in tuna fishing. In 1995 the 30th Intergovernmental Meeting of members and observer nations of I-ATTC, held in Panama, made two declarations. The first, the Declaration of Panama, called for strengthening the Agreement for the Conservation of Dolphins. The second, the Declaration on Strengthening the Objectives and Operation of the Convention establishing I-ATTC, called for amending the Convention to conform with the 1982 United Nations Convention on the Law of the Sea, including giving effect to the provisions of the 1995 Agreement for the Implementation of the Provisions of the United Nations Convention on the Law of the Sea of 10 December 1982 Relating to the Conservation and Management of Straddling Fish Stocks and Highly Migratory Fish Stocks.

Map 19

The I-ATTC Yellowfin Regulatory Area

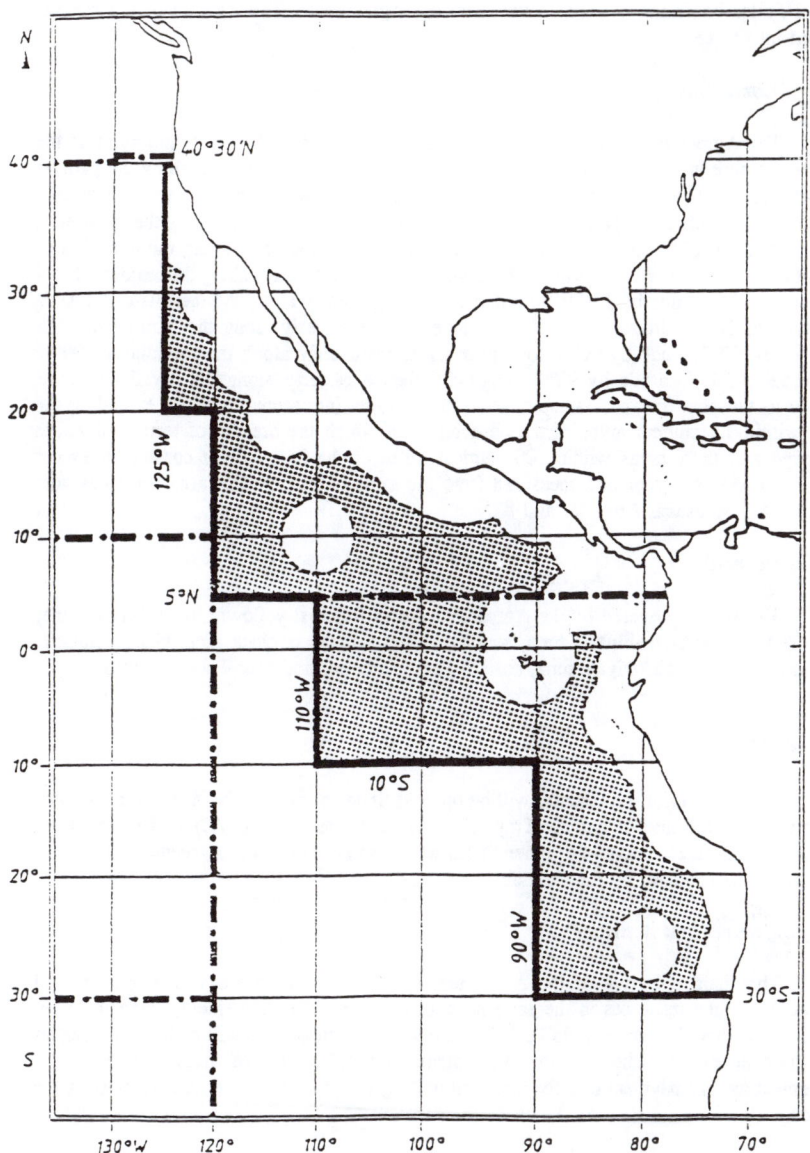

IV.2.4 Council of the Eastern Pacific Tuna Fishing Agreement (CEPTFA)

The Eastern Pacific Ocean Tuna Fishing Agreement and its Protocol was signed in San José, Costa Rica, by the United States of America, Costa Rica and Panama on 15 March 1983. The Agreement will enter into force after it has been ratified or adhered to by five coastal States bordering the area covered by the Agreement. The Agreement has not yet entered into force.

Area of Competence

The Agreement Area is defined as the area bounded by a line from the point on the mainland where the parallel of 40°N latitude intersects the coast westward along the parallel of 40°N latitude to 40°N latitude by 125°W longitude, thence southerly along the meridian of 125°W longitude to 20°N latitude by 125°W longitude, then easterly along the parallel of 20°N latitude to 20°N latitude by 120°W longitude, thence southerly along the meridian of 120°W longitude to 5°N latitude by 120°W longitude, thence easterly along the parallel of 5°N latitude to 5°N latitude by 110°W longitude, thence southerly along the meridian of 110°W longitude to 10°S latitude by 110°W longitude, thence easterly along the parallel of 10°S latitude to 10°S latitude by 90°W longitude, thence southerly along the meridian of 90°W longitude to 30°S latitude by 90°W longitude, thence easterly along the parallel of 30°S latitude to the point on the mainland where the parallel intersects the coast, excluding the areas within 12 nautical miles of the baseline from which the breadth of territorial sea is measured and those areas within 200 nautical miles of the baselines of coastal States not signatories to this Agreement, measured from the same baseline. This area coincides with part of FAO Statistical Areas 77 and 87.

Species Covered

The species covered by the Agreement are as follows: yellowfin tuna, bigeye tuna, albacore tuna, northern bluefin tuna, southern bluefin tuna, skipjack tuna, black skipjack, kawakawa, bullet tuna, frigate tuna, eastern Pacific bonito, and Indo-Pacific bonito.

Membership

Membership of the Council will be open to States bordering the Agreement Area or to members of the Inter-American Tropical Tuna Commission (I-ATTC) at the time when the Agreement enters into force, other States may also adhere to the Agreement subject to the unanimous approval by the Council.

Main Objectives and Activities

The main objective of the Agreement is to ensure the conservation and rational utilization of tuna resources in the eastern Pacific Ocean. The Agreement, when in force, would establish an Eastern Pacific Tuna Council whose main activity will be to issue licences permitting access to fishing in the Agreement Area to vessels of States parties to the Agreement against payment of a fee based on net registered tons of the vessel requesting the licence.

IV.2.5 International Pacific Halibut Commission (IPHC)

Established by the Convention for the Preservation of the Halibut Fishery, signed at Washington on March 2, 1923. The Convention was amended in 1930 and 1937. A new Convention between the United States of America and Canada for the Preservation of the Halibut Fishery of the Northern Pacific Ocean and Berring Sea was signed in Ottawa, Canada on 2 March 1953 and entered into force on 28 October 1953. When the two countries extended their fishery jurisdictions a Protocol Amending the Convention was signed in Washington on 29 March 1979 and entered into force on 15 October 1980.

Area of Competence

The Convention covers the "Convention Area" defined as the waters off the west coasts of the United States and Canada, including the southern as well as the western coasts of Alaska, within the respective maritime areas in which either partly exercises exclusive fisheries jurisdiction. Maritime area includes without distinction areas within and seaward of the territorial sea or internal waters of the Parties. This area coincides with FAO Statistical Area 67.

Species Covered

The species covered by the Convention is halibut (*Hippoglossus*) found in the Convention Area.

Membership

The Convention is not open to other States. Membership is limited to Canada and the United States.

Objectives and Activities

The objective of the Convention are the preservation of the halibut fishery of the Northern Pacific Ocean and Bering Sea. The main functions of the Commission are to coordinate scientific studies relating to the halibut fishery and to formulate regulations designed to develop the stocks of halibut to those levels which permit optimum utilization. The Commission has regulatory powers and sets the total allowable catch of halibut in the Convention Area.

IV.2.6 Eastern Pacific Tuna Fishing Organization (OAPO)

An Agreement Creating the Eastern Pacific Tuna Fishing Organization was signed by Ecuador, El Salvador, Mexico, Nicaragua and Peru in Lima on 21 July 1989. The Agreement has not yet entered into force.

Area of Competence

The area covered is defined as the Eastern Pacific Ocean through which the species covered by the Agreement roam. This area includes, not only the 200 miles zones adjacent to island and continental territories of the States parties, but also high seas areas adjacent to these zones, up to the meridian 145°W longitude (Map 20). This area coincides with part of FAO Statistical Areas 77, 81, 87 and 71.

Species Covered

The species covered by the Agreement are: yellowfin tuna, skipjack, northern bluefin tuna, southern bluefin tuna, albacore, and bigeye tuna.

Membership

The membership of the Organization will be open to Eastern Pacific Coastal Nations and other States whose vessels have fished the species covered by the Agreement within its area of competence. The admission of non-coastal States will be subject to the approval of the Governing Body of the Organization.

Objectives and Activities

The main objectives of the Organization are (i) to achieve the conservation, protection and optimum utilization of the highly migratory species, (ii) to provide training, transfer of technology and to assist with development of fishing capacity and infrastructure of disadvantaged Latin American Eastern Pacific Coastal States who are Parties to the Agreement. The structure of the Organization will consist of the Governing Board, the Scientific Committee and the Secretariat. The Organization will have regulatory powers and its decisions are made by consensus or by a two-third majority.

Map 20

Area covered by the OAPO Convention

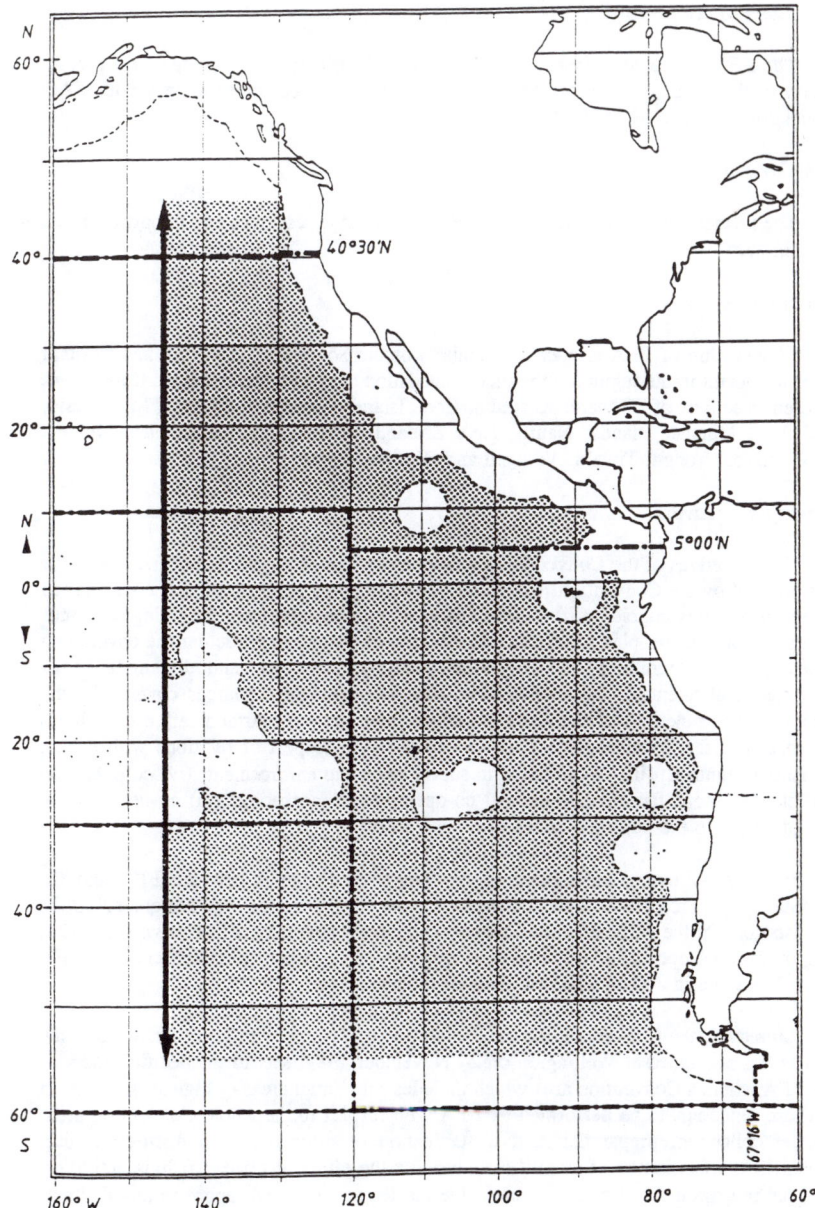

IV.2.7 South Pacific Forum Fisheries Agency (FFA)

Established by South Pacific Forum Fisheries Agency Convention, signed in Honiara, Solomon Islands on 10 July 1979. The Convention entered into force on 9 August 1979.

Area of Competence

The FFA's area of competence is the South Pacific region. There is no precise definition of this area by lines of longitude and latitude. It coincides mainly with FAO Statistical Areas 71 and 81 (Map 21).

Species Covered

The species covered by the FFA are all living marine resources and in particular the highly migratory species.

Membership

Membership of FFA is open to members of the South Pacific Forum and to other States or territories in the region on the recommendation of the Forum Fisheries Committee. The present members of FFA are: Australia, Cook Islands, Federated States of Micronesia, Fiji, Kiribati, Marshal Islands, Nauru, New Zealand, Niue, Palau, Papua New Guinea, Solomon Islands, Tonga, Tuvalu, Vanuatu and Western Samoa.

Objectives and Activities

The objectives of the Convention are (i) conservation and optimum utilization of the species covered by the Convention, (ii) promotion of regional cooperation and coordination in respect of fisheries policies, (iii) securing of maximum benefits from the living resources of the region for their peoples and for the region as a whole and in particular the developing countries, and (iv) facilitating the collection, analysis, evaluation and dissemination of relevant statistical scientific and economic information about the resources covered by the Convention. The functions of the Agency include inter alia: (i) harmonization of policies with respect to fisheries management; (ii) co-operation in respect of relations with distant water fishing countries; (iii) co-operation in surveillance and enforcement; (iv) co-operation in respect of onshore fish processing; (v) co-operation in marketing; (vi) co-operation in respect of access to the 200 mile zones of other Parties.

In 1987, following the signing of the Treaty on Fisheries between FFA and the United States (the Treaty was amended in 1992), the FFA Director was designated as the "Administrator" for the purpose of the Treaty. This Treaty covers tuna fishing vessels flying the flag of the USA operating both in certain areas under the fishery jurisdiction of the FFA Member States and in certain adjacent areas of high seas (see Map 21).

Moreover, the Convention for the Prohibition of Fishing with Long Driftnets in the South Pacific, concluded at Wellington on 24 November 1989, sets forth specific functions for the FFA within a Convention area which includes substantial areas of high seas (see Map 22). These functions, to be performed by FFA with respect to the whole Convention area, are (i) the collection, preparation and dissemination of information on driftnet fishing activities, (ii) the facilitation of scientific analysis on the effect of driftnet fishing activities and (iii) the preparation and transmission to the Parties of an annual report on any driftnet fishing activities and the measures taken to implement the Convention. In July 1992 the FFA members signed the Niue Treaty which entered into force in May 1993 under which they cooperate in the coordination of their surveillance and enforcement activities.

Map 21

Areas under fisheries jurisdiction of FFA Island Member Countries

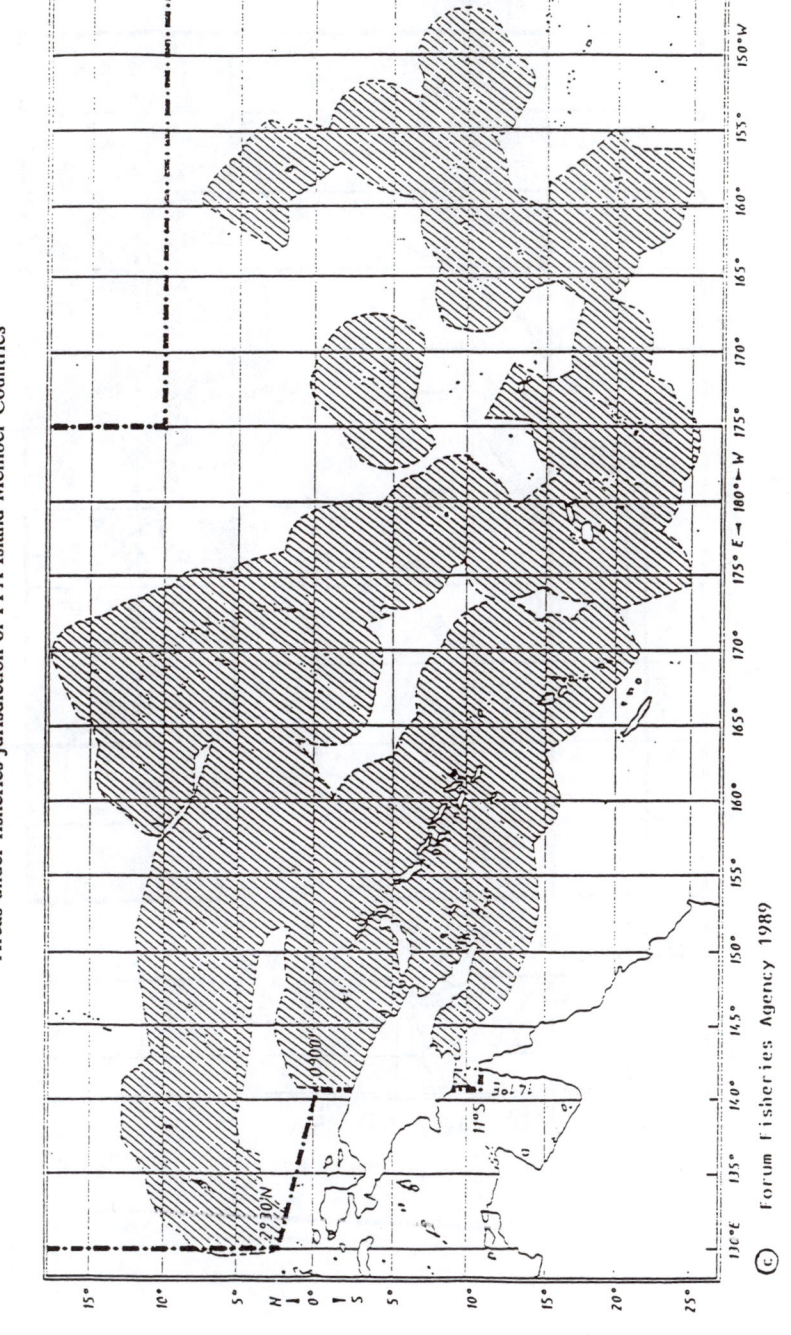

© Forum Fisheries Agency 1989

N.B.: This map, prepared by the FFA, was published in "Marine Policy" in July 1990 together with an article by the Deputy Director of FFA.

Map 22

Area covered by the Wellington Convention

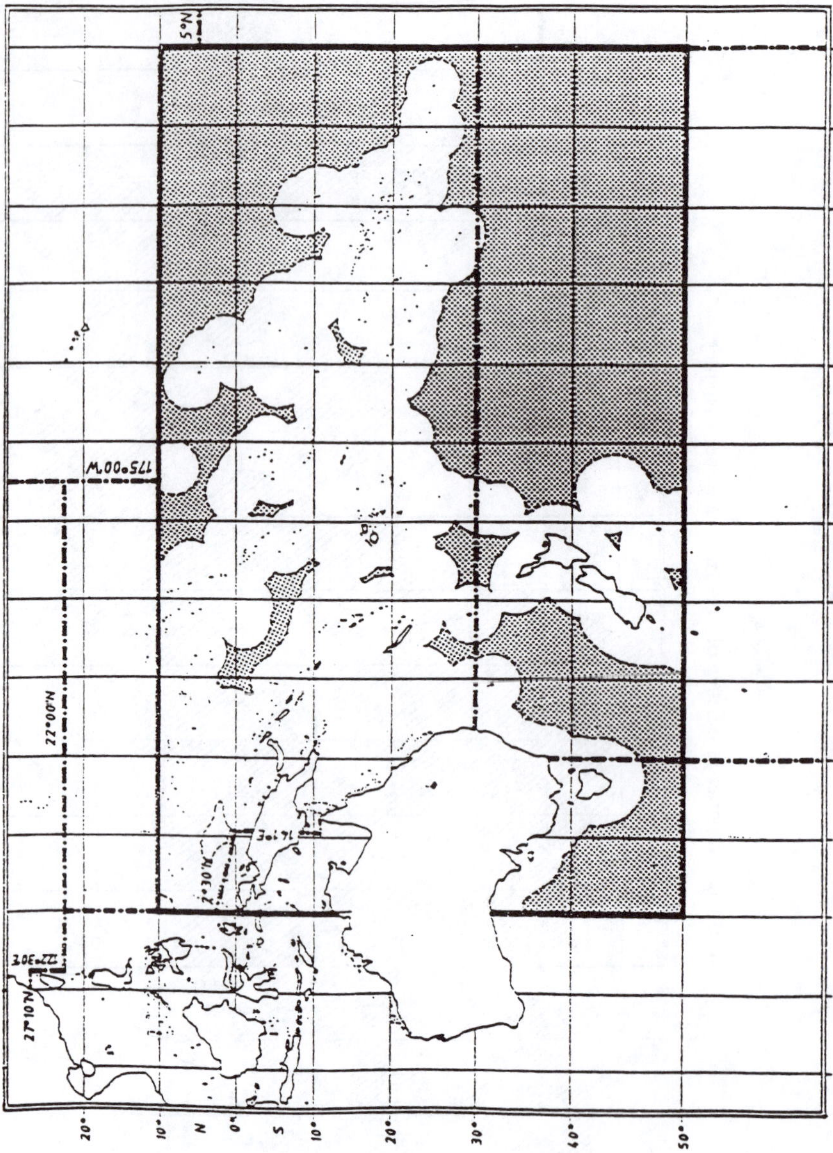

IV.2.8 Permanent South Pacific Commission/Commission permanente du Pacific Sud (CPPS)

Established by the Agreement on the Organization of the Permanent Commission of the Conference on the Use and Conservation of the Maritime Resources of the South Pacific, signed by Chile, Ecuador and Peru at the First Conference on the Use and Conservation of the Marine Resources of the South Pacific, held in Santiago, Chile, in August 1952.

Area of Competence

The Agreement does not define the precise area to be served by the Commission by lines of longitude and latitude. It merely provides that the Permanent Commission is established in order to achieve the objectives set forth in the Declaration on the Maritime Zone. This Declaration states that the three Governments proclaim as a principle of their international maritime policy that each of them possesses sole sovereignty and jurisdiction over the area of the sea, the sea floor and sub-soil thereof adjacent to the coast of its own country and extending not less than 200 nautical miles from the said coast. This area is part of FAO Statistical Area 87 (Map 23). In 1984, the Ministers for Foreign Affairs of CPPS member countries referred to the "legitimate interests of the Coastal States in the conservation and optimum utilization of the marine resources beyond their 200 mile zones, when these resources are part of the same populations of species existing in their 200 mile zones, or populations of species associated with them". They instructed the CPPS Secretariat to take action with a view to considering the possibility of establishing adequate mechanisms for the conservation and optimum utilization of these resources.

Species Covered

The species covered by the Agreement are all living marine resources.

Membership

Neither the Agreement establishing the Commission nor any of the Declarations, resolutions or recommendations of the Commission mention conditions regarding eligibility for membership. The present members of the Commission are: Chile, Colombia, Ecuador and Peru.

Objectives and Activities

The objectives of the Agreement are those set out in the Declaration on Maritime Zone. The objectives of the Declaration were, inter alia, the necessity to provide for the peoples of the three governments food supplies and to furnish them with the means of developing their economy. To do so it is essential to ensure the conservation and protection of their natural resources in the areas of the sea adjacent to their coasts and to regulate the use thereof. The functions of the Commission, are inter alia, (i) to determine protected species; open and closed seasons and areas of sea; fishing and hunting times, methods and equipment; prohibited gear and methods; and to lay down general regulations for hunting and fishing, (ii) to study and propose to the Parties such measures as it considers suitable for the protection, defence, conservation and use of marine resources, (iii) to encourage scientific and technical study of and research into biological phenomena in the South Pacific, and (iv) to prepare general statistics of the industrial use of marine resources by the Parties, and to suggest protective measures based on the study thereof.

The Commission collaborates closely with FAO and OLDEPESCA. CPPS, in collaboration with FAO has published a number of Bulletins on Fisheries Statistics of the Southeast Pacific. A monthly Bulletin on Climatic Alert, providing information on El Niño Phenomenon is also published by the Commission.

Map 23

FAO Statistical Area 87

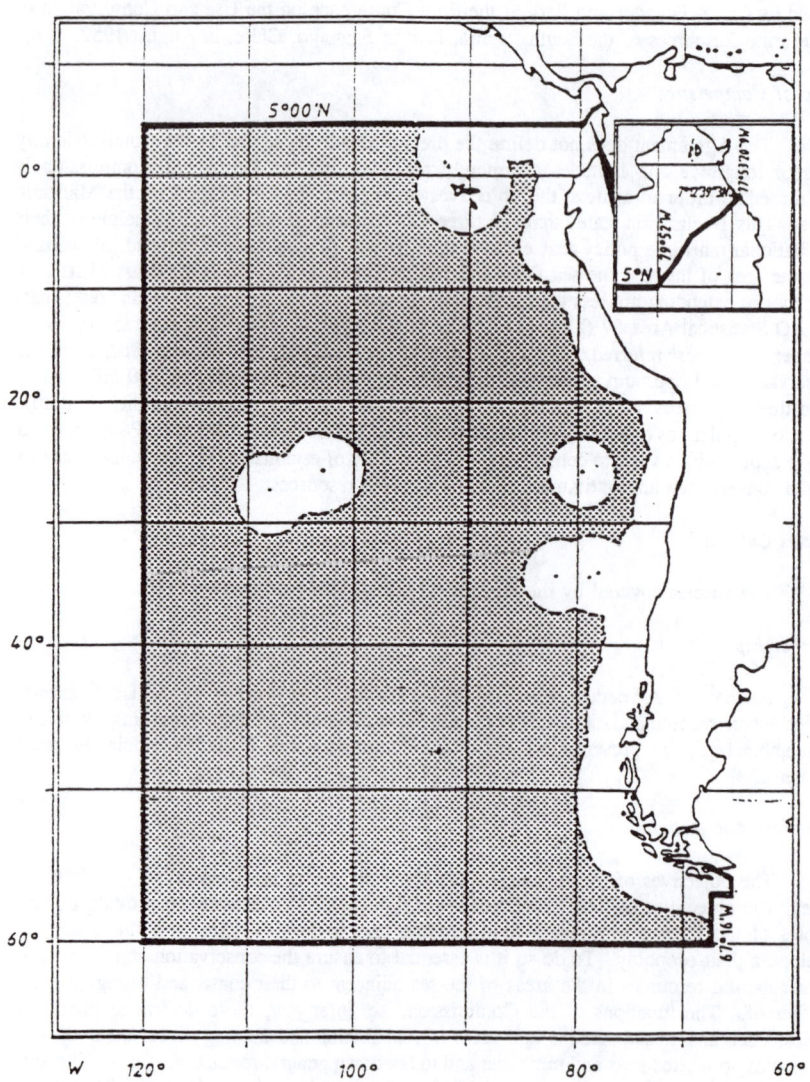

IV.2.9 South Pacific Commission (SPC)

Established by an Agreement signed by Australia, France, the Netherlands, New Zealand, the United Kingdom and the United States at Canberra on 6 February 1947, entered into force on 29 July 1948, amended in 1952, 1954, 1964 and supplemented by Protocols of understanding in 1974 and 1976. The Commission activities are not restricted to fisheries and also cover agriculture and plant protection, rural development, education, health information and cultural exchanges.

Area of Competence

The territorial scope of the Commission was defined by the Canberra Agreement as all those territories in the Pacific Ocean which are administered by the participating Governments and which lie wholly or in part south of the Equator and east from and including the Australian Territory of Papua and the Trust Territory of New Guinea, and Guam and the Trust Territory of the Pacific Islands. There is no precise definition of this area by lines of longitude and latitude in the Agreement. During many years the Commission published a map showing its area of competence (Map 24). This area coincides with part of FAO Statistical Areas 71 and 77.

Species Covered

The Commission operates a number of coastal fisheries projects covering all living marine resources and an oceanic programme, which deals exclusively with tunas and billfishes and consists of two projects (statistics, research).

Membership

The membership of the South Pacific Commission is as follows: American Samoa, Australia, Cook Islands, Federated States of Micronesia, Fiji, France, French Polynesia, Guam, Kiribati, Marshall Islands, Nauru, New Caledonia, New Zealand, Niue, Northern Mariana Islands, Palau, Papua New Guinea, Pitcairn Islands, Solomon Islands, Samoa, Tokelau, Tonga, Tuvalu, U.K., U.S.A., Vanuatu, Wallis and Futuna.

Main Objectives and Activities

The main objective of the Agreement is to encourage and strengthen international cooperation in promoting the economic and social welfare and advancement of the peoples of the South Pacific region. SPC does not recommend any management measures to its Member Countries but does provide scientific advice on the status of exploited stocks. With regard to high seas fishing, its works includes (i) the collection and analysis of catch statistics and related data, and (ii) scientific research on tuna and billfish.

Map 24

The SPC Area

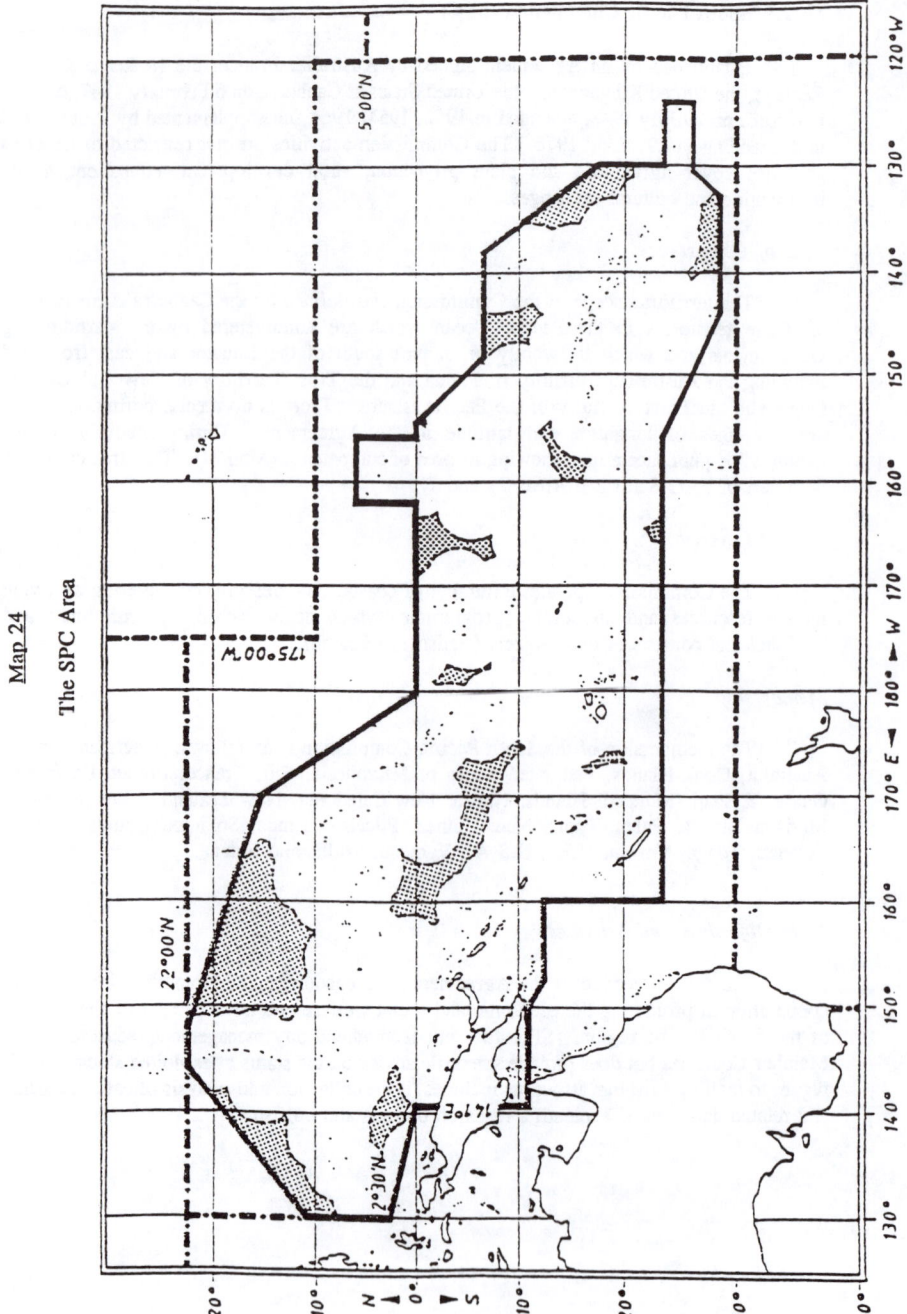

IV.2.10 Pacific Salmon Commission (PSC)

Established by Treaty Between the Government of the United States of America and the Government of Canada concerning Pacific salmon, signed in Ottawa, Canada on 28 January 1985 and entered into force on 18 March 1985.

Area of Competence

The Treaty applies to "Pacific salmon stocks". There is no precise definition of the area covered by the Treaty although the area covered by the Fraser River Panel for Fraser River sockeye and pink salmon is defined in Annex 23 of the Treaty as follows:

1.   The territorial waters and the high seas westward from the western coast of Canada and the United States of America and from a direct line drawn from Bonilla Point, Vancouver Island, to the lighthouse on Tatoosh Island, Washington--which line marks the entrance to Juan de Fuca Strait, --and embraced between 48 and 49 degrees north latitude, excepting therefrom, however, all the waters of Barkley Sound, eastward of a straight line drawn from Amphitrite Point to Cape Beale and all the waters of Nitinat Lake and the entrance thereto.

2.   The waters included within the following boundaries:

Beginning at Bonilla Point, Vancouver Island, thence along the aforesaid direct line drawn from Bonilla Point to Tatoosh Lighthouse, Washington, described in paragraph numbered 1 of this Article thence to the nearest point of Cape Flattery, thence following the southerly shore of Juan de Fuca Strait to Point Wilson, on Quimper Peninsula, thence in a straight line to Point Partridge on Whidbey Island thence following the western shore of the said Whidbey Island, to the entrance to Deception Pass, thence across said entrance to the southern side of Reservation Bay, on Fidalgo Island, thence following the western and northern shore line of the said Fidalgo Island to Swinomish Slough, crossing the said Swinomish Slough, in line with the track of the Great Northern Railway, thence northerly following the shore line of the mainland to Atkinson Point at the northerly entrance to Burrard Inlet, British Columbia, thence in a straight line to the southern end of Bowen Island, thence westerly following the southern shore of Bowen Island to Cape Roger Curtis, thence in a straight line to Gower Point, thence westerly following the shore line to Welcome Point on Sechelt Peninsula, thence in a straight line to Point Young on Lasqueti Island, thence in a straight line to Dorcas Point on Vancouver Island, thence following the eastern and southern shores of the said Vancouver Island, to the starting point at Bonilla Point, as shown on the British Admiralty Chart Number 579, and on the United States Coast and Geodetic Survey Chart Number 6300, as corrected to March 14, 1930, copies of which are annexed to the 1930 Convention and made a part thereof.

3.   The Fraser River and the streams and lakes tributary thereto.

Species Covered

The Treaty covers all Pacific salmon stocks.

Membership

Membership of PSC is not open to other States. The membership consists of Canada and the United States of America.

Main Objectives and Activities

The main objectives of the Treaty are the conservation and rational management of Pacific salmon stocks and the promotion of optimum production of such stocks and the cooperation in the management, research and enhancement of Pacific salmon stocks. The Commission has established three panels: Southern Panel, Fraser River Panel, and Northern Panel. These Panels provide information and make recommendations to the Commission which the latter reviews and then recommends fishery regimes to the Parties.

V.   OTHERS

V.1   A BRIEF REVIEW OF MAJOR FISHING IN OTHER AREAS

V.1.1   Southern Oceans (Areas 48, 58 and 88)

An important development in the Southern Oceans has been the reduction in krill harvests. While the catch has been about 300,000 t in recent years, in the 1992/93 season it fell to about 87,000 t because of a reduction in Russian and Ukrainian fishing effort for this species. Surveys indicated an abundance of 30.8 million t of krill in Area 48. A resource issue of particular concern was that "significant" numbers of juvenile icefish, *Champsocephalus gunnari*, and other species were being taken as by-catch in the krill fishery.

No catches of icefish were reported for 1992/3. The Commission for the Conservation of Antarctic Marine Living Resources (CCAMLR), set low quotas for icefish following stock assessments, but the decline in catches has been predominantly due to a couple of large declines in biomass detected by UK trawl surveys. The cause(s) of these major declines is unknown but is believed to be related to the recent poor years for krill. The only reported catches of finfish species in the CCAMLR Convention area during the 1992/3 season were of Patagonian toothfish, *Dissostichus eleginoides*, of which 5,771 t were taken in subareas 48.3 and 58.5.1 combined. Concern is arising within the Commission regarding the control of this straddling stock in areas that lie immediately outside the CCAMLR Convention Area.

V.2   OTHER BODIES CONCERNED WITH THE CONSERVATION, MANAGEMENT OR OTHER ACTIVITIES RELATED TO THE LIVING RESOURCES

V.2.1   International Whaling Commission (IWC)

Established by the International Convention for the Regulation of Whaling, signed in Washington D.C. on 2 December 1946 and entered into force on 10 November 1948. The Convention was amended in 1956 and the Schedule to the Convention is amended annually.

Area of Competence

The Convention applies to factory ships, land stations, and whale catchers under the jurisdiction of the Contracting Governments, and to all waters in which whaling is prosecuted by such factory ships, land stations, and whale catchers.

Species Covered

The 1946 Convention refers to the proper conservation of "whale stocks" and does not define the species covered by the term "whale". Contracting Governments are not of one view on such a definition. When formulating the Convention, the 1946 International Whaling

Conference adopted a recommendation that a chart of Nomenclature of whales, annexed to the Final Act of the Conference, be accepted as a guide by the governments represented at the Conference. This list included in toto the baleen, sperm and bottlenose whales. Several Contracting Governments are of the view that the Commission is not empowered to recommend management measures for those species of small cetaceans which are not included in the list.

In 1972, a Sub-Committee of the Scientific Committee was set up to improve data collection on all world catches of small cetaceans and to review species and stock identification. At its Twenty-Seventh Session in 1976, the Commission noted the Scientific Committee's view that there was a need for an international body to manage stocks of all cetaceans not covered by the IWC Schedule. In 1990, IWC requested the Scientific Committee to commence a process of drawing together all available relevant information on the present status of the stocks of small cetaceans which are subjected to significant directed and incidental takes, on the impact of those takes on the stocks, and providing an assessment of the present threats to the stocks concerned.

Membership

The membership of the Commission is open to all States who wish to ratify or adhere to the Convention. The present members of the Commission are: Antigua and Barbuda, Argentina, Australia, Austria, Brazil, Chile, People's Republic of China, Costa Rica, Denmark, Dominica, Finland, France, Germany, Grenada, India, Ireland, Japan, Kenya, Republic of Korea, Mexico, Monaco, Netherlands, New Zealand, Norway, Oman, Peru, Russian Federation, Saint Kitts and Nevis, Saint Lucia, Saint Vincent and the Grenadines, Senegal, Solomon Islands, South Africa, Spain, Sweden, Switzerland, UK, USA and Venezuela.

Objectives and Activities

The purpose of the Convention is to provide for the proper conservation of whale stocks and thus make possible the orderly development of the whaling industry. The main duty of the Commission is to keep under review and revise as necessary the measures laid down in the Schedule to the Convention which govern the conduct of whaling throughout the world. These measures, among other things, provide for the complete protection of certain species; designate specified areas as whale sanctuaries; set limits on the numbers and size of whales which may be taken; prescribe open and closed seasons and areas of whaling; and prohibit the capture of suckling calves and female whales accompanied by calves. In 1975 a new management policy for whales was adopted by the IWC. This was designed to bring all stocks to the levels providing the greatest long-term harvests, by setting catch limits for individual stocks below their sustainable yields. Because of uncertainties in the scientific analyses and therefore the precise status of the various whale stocks, the IWC decided at its meeting in 1982 that there should be a pause in commercial whaling on all stocks from 1985/1986. A revised management procedure has been developed subsequently, which the Commission accepted and endorsed in 1994. This balances the somewhat conflicting requirements to ensure that the risk to individual stocks is not seriously increased, while maintaining the highest continuing yield. The regulatory measures adopted by the Commission are subject to an objection procedure.

V.2.2 Commission for the Conservation of Antarctic Marine Living Resources (CCAMLR)

Established by the Convention on the Conservation of Antarctic Marine Living Resources drawn up at Canberra on 20 May 1980 and entered into force on 7 April 1982.

Area of Competence

The area of competence of the CCAMLR is the area south of the line joining the following points along parallels of latitude and meridians of longitude:

50°S, 0°, 50°S, 30°E, 45°S, 30°E, 45°S, 80°E, 55°S, 150°E, 60°S, 150°E, 60°S, 50°S, 50°W, 50°S, 0°.

This area coincides exactly with FAO statistical areas 48, 58 and 88 (Map 25).

Species Covered

The Convention applies to the Antarctic marine living resources defined by the Convention as: "the populations of finfish, molluscs, crustaceans, and all other species of living organisms, including birds, found south of the Antarctic Convergence".

Membership

The Convention is open for accession by any State interested in research or harvesting activities in relation to the marine living resources to which the Convention applies. In addition, the Convention is also open for accession by regional economic integration organizations constituted by sovereign States which include among their members one or more States Members of the Commission and to which the States members of the organization have transferred, in whole or in part, competence with regard to the matters covered by this Convention. The accession of such regional economic integration organizations is the subject of consultations among Members of the Commission. The membership of the Commission consists of (a) Contracting Parties
which participated in the meeting at which the Convention was adopted, (b) each State Party acceded to the Convention becomes a member of the Commission during the period when the acceding Party is engaged in research or harvesting activities in relation to the marine living resources to which the Convention applies, and (c) each regional economic integration organization which has acceded to the Convention is entitled to become a member of the Commission during such time as its States members are so entitled. The members of the Commission are: Argentina, Australia, Belgium, Brazil, Chile, European Union, France, Germany, India, Italy, Japan, Korea (Republic of), New Zealand, Norway, Poland, Russian Federation, South Africa, Spain, Sweden, Ukraine, UK and USA. States which have acceded to the Convention but are not Members of the Commission are: Bulgaria, Canada, Finland, Greece, Netherlands, Peru and Uruguay.

Objectives and Activities

The main objective of the Convention is the conservation of Antarctic marine living resources. The main functions of the Commission are (i) to ensure that all harvesting and research activities are conducted in accordance with the objectives of the Convention, (ii) to formulate, adopt and revise conservation measures, (iii) to compile, analyze and disseminate information on the status of resources, and (iv) to facilitate research activities. The Commission has regulatory powers and its regulatory measures are subject to an objection procedure. The Commission has a scientific Committee which itself is advised by specialist working groups. The Commission also has a Standing Committee on Observation and Inspection whose primary functions are to report on inspections of fishing vessels and to ensure compliance with conservation measures in force.

Map 25

Area of competence of CCAMLR. The dotted lines indicated the limits of
FAO Statistical Areas 58, 48 and 88

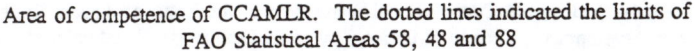

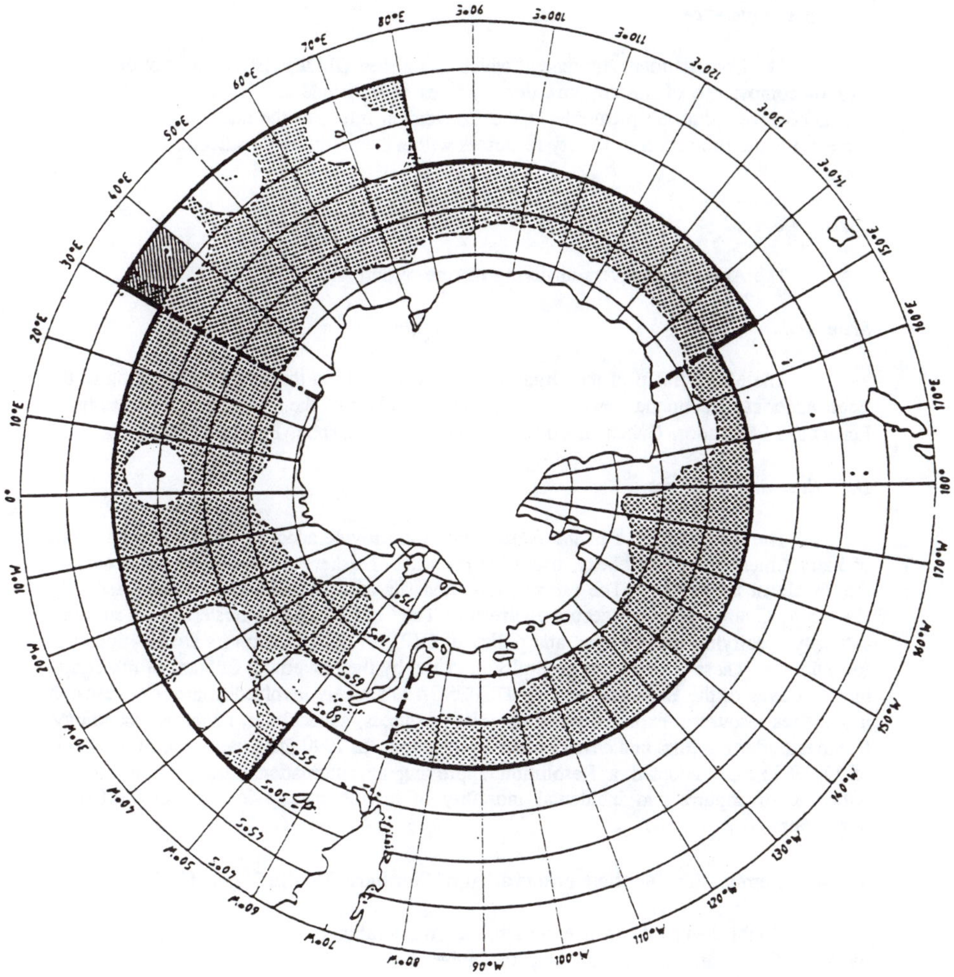

V.2.3   Latin American Organization for Development of Fisheries (OLDEPESCA)

Established by the Constitutional Agreement of the Latin American Organization for Fishery Development, signed in Mexico City on 29 October 1982 and entered into force on 2 November 1984. The Agreement was amended twice in 1984.

Area of Competence

The Constitutional Agreement which established OLDEPESCA does not define the area of competence of the Organization by lines of longitude and latitude. It should be noted, however, that the preamble to the Convention refers to the need to encourage the correct use and protection of fishery resources within the maritime jurisdiction zones of each State.

Species Covered

The Agreement covers all living marine resources.

Membership

The Membership of the Organization is open only to those States belonging to the Latin American Economic System. The present members of the Organization are: Bolivia, Ecuador, El Salvador, Guatemala, Mexico, Nicaragua, Panama, Peru and Venezuela.

Objectives and Activities

The main objective of the Agreement is to provide adequately for the food needs of Latin America and Caribbean, using the potential of fishery resources for the benefit of the people in the region. The Organization consists of the Conference of Ministers, the Governing Council and the Executive Director. The Conference of Ministers is the supreme authority specifying the direction and policy of OLDEPESCA through its Declarations and Resolutions. These policies are generally prepared by the Governing Council in relation to the objectives of the Organization. OLDEPESCA is actively involved in areas of research in fisheries resources, exploitation of fisheries resources, aquaculture, fisheries technology, fisheries trade, training, and environmental protection. In 1990 the Conference of Ministers of OLDEPESCA adopted a Resolution approving an International Programme for the reduction of capture and incidental mortality of marine species in commercial fishing operations.

V.2.4   Commission for the Conservation of Southern Bluefin Tuna (CCSBT)

Established by the Convention for the Conservation of Southern Bluefin Tuna signed by Australia, Japan and New Zealand in Canberra on 10 May 1993 and entered into force on 20 May 1994.

Area of Competence

The Convention does not mention any specific geographical area or areas to be covered by its provisions. Southern bluefin tuna (*Thunnus maccoyii*) constitute a stock fished in the Indian Ocean, the Southern Atlantic and the South Pacific. The species spawns south off Java, Indonesia, from where juveniles migrate east through the southern part of the Australian Fishing Zone towards New Zealand. Some other juveniles from the same spawning ground migrate west through the Indian Ocean towards South Africa. It is therefore assumed that the Commission is responsible for the whole area mentioned above.

Species Covered

Species covered by the Convention is Southern Bluefin Tuna. The Commission is also responsible for collecting information on "ecologically related species" defined in the Convention as living marine species which are associated with southern bluefin tuna, including but not restricted to both predators and prey of southern bluefin tuna.

Membership

The Convention is open for accession to (a) any State whose vessels engage in fishing for southern bluefin tuna and (b) any coastal State through whose exclusive economic or fishery zone southern bluefin tuna migrates. The present members of CCSBT are Australia, Japan and New Zealand.

Objectives and Activities

The objective of the Convention is to ensure, through appropriate management, the conservation and optimum utilization of southern bluefin tuna. The functions of the Commission include: (i) collecting, analysing and interpreting scientific and other relevant information on SBT, and (ii) to adopt conservation and management measures including the total allowable catch and its allocation among the Members. Other additional measures may be adopted by the CCSBT. The decisions of the Commission are taken by unanimous vote.

It must be noted that the exploitation of SBT began with an Australian surface fishery and a Japanese longline fishery in the early 1950s, while New Zealand started handline fishing in the early 1980s. The catch of SBT increased rapidly to a peak of 82 thousand metric tonnes (MT) in 1961. Since then, it has gradually decreased to 45 thousand MT in 1980 and 14 thousand MT in 1990. Since 1982 a scientific meeting and a subsequent management meeting have been held annually by the three countries. Total allowable catch and its allocation had been set by these meetings since 1985. In order to assist the scientific assessment, Australia, Japan and New Zealand cooperate in a Real Time Monitoring Programme which collects information in areas on catch rates and size composition of SBT.

V.2.5   Coordinating Working Party on Fishery Statistics (CWP)

Established by Resolution 23/59 of the FAO Conference under Article VI-2 of the Organization's Constitution at its Tenth Session in 1959. It was called "Continuing Working Party on Fishery Statistics in the North Atlantic Area". The establishment of this Working Party was the outcome of the recommendations of an Expert Meeting on Fishery Statistics in the North Atlantic Area held in Edinburgh in September 1959. The Statutes of CWP were amended and approved by the FAO Council at its Hundred and Eighth Session in June 1995.

Area of Competence

Although the area of competence of the Coordinating Working Party on Fishery Statistics has been the Atlantic Ocean since 1995 its area of competence has no geographical limitations. It covers the requirements for fishery statistics of all fisheries including aquaculture.

Species Covered

All species are covered by CWP.

Membership

The Working Party is composed of experts nominated by intergovernmental organizations which have competence in fishery statistics. The following are the participating organizations initially:

Commission for the Conservation of Antarctic Marine Living Resources (CCAMLR)
Food and Agriculture Organization of the United Nations (FAO)
International Commission for the Conservation of Atlantic Tunas (ICCAT)
International Council for the Exploration of the Sea (ICES)
North Atlantic Salmon Conservation Organization (NASCO)
Northwest Atlantic Fisheries Organization (NAFO)
Organization for Economic Cooperation and Development (OECD)
Statistical Office of the European Communities (EU/Eurostat)

Participating organizations may admit other intergovernmental organizations having competence in fishery statistics. Participating organizations may withdraw from the Working Party. In 1995, International Whaling Commission (IWC) made a formal request to become a participating organization in CWP.

Objectives and Activities

The objectives of the CWP are to: (a) keep under continuous review the requirements for fishery statistics (including aquaculture) for the purposes of research, policy-making and management, taking into account *inter alia* their purpose, usefulness, cost, burden in collection and collation, timeliness, quality, confidentiality needs and regional differences; (b) agree standard concepts, definitions, classifications and methodologies for the collection and collation of fishery statistics; and (c) make proposals and recommendations for action in relation to the collection, collation and dissemination of fishery statistics, recognizing the need to coordinate activities so as to avoid duplication.

The CWP supported by the participating organizations has served since 1960 as the premier international and inter-organization forum for agreeing common definitions, classifications and standards for the collection of fishery statistics. It has developed common procedures for statistics collation which have streamlined the collation process and reduced the burden on national fisheries statistical offices. It has provided technical advice on fishery statistical matters to participating organizations and has facilitated the publication of methodological and reference documents. In the process it has shaped the statistical programmes of all participating organizations to some extent, and those of FAO in particular, while leaving organizations with complete autonomy in their area of responsibility.

The new statutes for the CWP were designed to provide a sound basis for the Working Party to meet the challenges resulting from the enhanced role of regional fishery organizations in relation to statistics following the UN Conference on Straddling Fish Stocks and Highly Migratory Fish Stocks, and to facilitate the participation of other agencies with a remit for fisheries statistics outside the Atlantic.

SUMMARY INFORMATION ON FISHERY BODIES

ANNEX I

Atlantic Ocean and Adjacent Seas

Body	Establishment	Headquarters	Membership	Area of competence	Main functions
CARPAS Regional Fisheries Advisory Commission for the Southwest Atlantic	1961 Resolution of FAO Conference (under Article VI-1 of FAO Constitution)	Rome (Italy)	Argentina, Brazil, Uruguay	Southwest Atlantic and inland waters of member countries	To develop organized approach among members for the management and regional exploitation of marine and inland fishery resources; to encourage training and cooperative investigations
CECAF Fishery Committee for the Eastern Central Atlantic	1967 Resolution of FAO Council (under Article VI-2 of FAO Constitution)	Rome (Italy)	Benin, Cameroon, Cape Verde, Congo, Côte d'Ivoire, Cuba, EC, Equatorial Guinea, France, Gabon, Gambia, Ghana, Greece, Guinea, Guinea-Bissau, Italy, Japan, Korea (Rep. of), Liberia, Mauritania, Morocco, Nigeria, Norway, Poland, Romania, Sao Tome and Principe, Senegal, Sierra Leone, Spain, Togo, USA, Zaire.	Eastern Central Atlantic between Cape Spartel and the Congo River	To promote programmes of development for the rational utilization of fishery resources; to assist in establishing basis for regulatory measures; to encourage training.
COREP Comité régional des pêches cu Golfe de Guinée	1984 International Convention	Libreville, Gabon	Congo, Gabon, Sao Tomé et Principe, Zaire.	Central and southern Gulf of Guinea	Coordination, harmonization of policies on development and exploitation of shared stocks found within EEZ of Member States.
CSRP Commission Sous-régionale des pêches	1985 International Convention	Dakar, Senegal	Cape Verde, The Gambia, Guinea, Guinea-Bissau, Mauritania, Senegal.	N.W. Africa (Mauritania to Guinea including Cape Verde)	To facilitate harmonization of policies concerning the preservation, conservation and exploitation of fisheries resources, cooperation among the countries with a view to deriving maximum benefit from the resources for their populations.

ANNEX I
Cont'd

SUMMARY INFORMATION ON FISHERY BODIES

Atlantic Ocean and Adjacent Seas

Body	Establishment	Headquarters	Membership	Area of competence	Main functions
CTMFM Joint Technical Commission for the Argentina/Uruguay Maritime Front	1974 International Agreement	Montevideo (Uruguay)	Argentina, Uruguay	South Atlantic	To adopt and coordinate plans and measures relevent to conservation, preservation and the rational exploitation of living resources and the protection of the maritime environment in the common fishing zone.
GFCM General Fisheries Council for the Mediterranean	1949 International Agreement under aegis of FAO (Article XIV of FAO Constitution)	Rome (Italy)	Albania, Algeria, Bulgaria, Croatia, Cyprus, Egypt, France, Greece, Israel, Italy, Lebanon, Libya, Malta, Monaco, Morocco, Romania, Spain, Syria, Tunisia, Turkey.	Mediterranean, Black Sea and connecting waters	To promote the development, conservation and management of living marine resources; to formulate and recommend conservation measures; to encourage training cooperative projects
IBSFC International Baltic Sea Fishery Commission	1973 International Convention	Warsaw (Poland)	Estonia, EC, Finland, Latvia, Lithuania Poland, Russian Federation, Sweden	Baltic Sea and the Belts	To keep the fisheries under review; to coordinate scientific research; to recommend regulatory measures including catch quotas and enforcement schemes
ICCAT International Commission for the Conservation of Atlantic Tunas	1966 International Convention	Madrid (Spain)	Angola, Brazil, Cape Verde, Canada, Côte d'Ivoire, Equatorial Guinea, Guinea (Rep. of), France, Gabon, Ghana, Japan, Korea (Rep. of), Libya, Morocco, Portugal, Russian Federation, Sao Tome and Principe, South Africa, Spain, UK, USA, Uruguay, Venezuela	Atlantic Ocean including the adjacent seas	To study the population of tuna and tuna-like fishes; to make recommendations designed to maintain these populations at levels permitting maximum sustainable catch.

SUMMARY INFORMATION ON FISHERY BODIES

Atlantic Ocean and Adjacent Seas

Body	Establishment	Headquarters	Membership	Area of competence	Main functions
ICES International Council for the Exploration of the Sea	1902 International Convention	Copenhagen (Denmark)	Belgium, Canada, Denmark, Estonia, Finland, France, Germany, Iceland, Ireland, Latvia, Netherlands, Norway, Poland, Portugal, Russian Federation, Spain, Sweden, UK, USA	Atlantic Ocean and adjacent seas with particular reference to the North Atlantic	To promote and encourage research and investigation on the seas, particularly those related to the living resources thereof; to draw up programmes required for this purpose; to publish or otherwise disseminate the result of research and investigation.
ICSEAF[1] International Commission for the Southeast Atlantic Fisheries	1969 International Convention	Madrid (Spain)	Angola, Bulgaria, Cuba, France, Germany, Iraq, Israel, Italy, Japan, Korea (Rep. of), Poland, Portugal, Romania, Russian Federation, South Africa, Spain	Southeast Atlantic south of the Congo River and north of parallel 50°S	To carry out studies and research; to make recommendations for joint action through closed areas and seasons, size limitations, gear control, total catch limit and other measures.
NAFO Northwest Atlantic Fisheries Organization	1978 International Convention	Dartmouth, Nova Scotia (Canada)	Bulgaria, Canada, Cuba, Denmark, (for Faroe Islands and Greenland), EC, Estonia, Iceland, Japan, Korea (Rep. of), Latvia, Lithuania, Norway, Poland, Romania, Russian Federation, USA.	Northwest Atlantic Ocean	To contribute to the optimum utilization and rational management and conservation of the fishery resources.

---

[1] This Commission is in the process of being disbanded.

SUMMARY INFORMATION ON FISHERY BODIES

Atlantic Ocean and Adjacent Seas

Body	Establishment	Headquarters	Membership	Area of competence	Main functions
NAMMCO North Atlantic Marine Mammal Commission	1992 International Convention	Tromso, Norway	Faroe Islands, Greenland, Iceland, Norway	North Atlantic	To provide a forum for the study, analysis and exchange of information among the Parties on matters concerning marine mammals in the North Atlantic; to establish appropriate Management Committees and coordinate their activities; to establish guidelines and objectives for the work of the Management Committees; to establish working arrangements with the International Council for the Exploration of the Sea and other appropriate organizations; and to coordinate requests for scientific advice.
NASCO North Atlantic Salmon Conservation Organization	1982 International Convention	Edinburgh (UK)	Canada, Denmark (for Faroe Islands and Greenland), EC, Iceland, Norway, Russian Federation, USA	Atlantic Ocean north of 36°N latitude	To promote the acquisition analysis and dissemination of scientific information pertaining to salmon stocks in the North Atlantic Ocean; to promote the conservation, restoration, enhancement and rational management of salmon stocks in the North Atlantic Ocean through international cooperation.
NEAFC North-East Atlantic Fisheries Commission	1980 International Convention	London (UK)	Bulgaria, Denmark (for Faroe Islands and Greenland), EC, Iceland, Norway, Poland, Russian Federation.	Northeast Atlantic Ocean	To provide a forum for consultation and exchange of information on the state of fisheries resources in the Northeast Atlantic, and on related management policies to ensure the conservation and optimum utilization of such resources; and to recommend conservation measures in waters outside national jurisdiction.
WECAFC Western Central Atlantic Fishery Commission	1973 Resolution of FAO Council (under Article VI-1 of FAO Constitution)	Rome (Italy)	Antigua and Barbuda, Bahamas, Barbados, Belize, Brazil, Colombia, Costa Rica, Cuba, Dominica, France, Grenada, Guatemala, Guinea, Guyana, Haiti, Honduras, Jamaica, Japan, Korea (Rep. of), Mexico, Netherlands, Nicaragua, Panama, Saint Christopher and Nevis, Saint Lucia, Saint Vincent and the Grenadines, Spain, Suriname, Trinidad and Tobago, UK, USA, Venezuela.	Western Central Atlantic Ocean	To facilitate the coordination of research; to encourage education and training; to assist Member Governments in establishing rational policies, to promote the rational management of resources that are of interest for two or more countries.

ANNEX I
Cont'd

SUMMARY INFORMATION ON FISHERY BODIES

Pacific Ocean

Body	Establishment	Headquarters	Membership	Area of competence	Main functions
I-ATTC Inter-American Tropical Tuna Commission	1949 International Convention	La Jolla, California (USA)	Costa Rica, France, Japan, Nicaragua, Panama, USA, Vanuatu, Venezuela	Eastern Pacific Ocean	To gather and interpret information on tuna; to conduct scientific investigation; to recommend proposals for joint action for conservation.
IPHC International Pacific Halibut Commission	1953 International Convention	Seattle, Washington (USA)	Canada, USA	North Pacific Ocean and Bering Sea	To coordinate scientific studies relating to the halibut fishery; to formulate regulations designed to develop the stocks of halibut to those levels which will permit optimum yield.
NPAFC North Pacific Anadromous Fish Commission	1993 International Convention	Vancouver, Canada	Canada, Japan, Russian Federation, USA	North Pacific Ocean and its adjacent seas north of 33°N	To recommend to the Parties measures for the Conservation of Anadromous Stocks and ecologically related species in the Convention area; to promote the exchange of information on any activities contrary to the provisions of the Convention; to consider and make proposals to the Parties for the enactment of schedules of equivalent penalties for activities contrary to the provisions of the Convention; and to review and evaluate enforcement actions taken by Parties.
PICES North Pacific Marine Science Organization	1992	Sydney, B.C., Canada	Canada, Japon, China (People's Rep. of), Korea (Rep. of), Russian Federation, USA	North Pacific and adjacent Seas	To promote and coordinate marine scientific research in order to advance scientific knowledge of the area concerned and of its living resources and to promote the collection and echange of information and data related to marine scientific research in its area of competence.
PSC Pacific Salmon Commission	1985 International Convention	Vancouver, British Columbia (Canada)	Canada, USA	Northwest Pacific	To prevent overfishing and provide for optimum production and to provide for each country to receive benefits equivalent to the production of salmon originating in its waters.

SUMMARY INFORMATION ON FISHERY BODIES

Pacific Ocean

Body	Establishment	Headquarters	Membership	Area of competence	Main functions
SPFFA South Pacific Forum Fisheries Agency	1979 International	Honiara (Solomon Islands)	Australia, Cook Islands, Federated States of Micronesia, Fiji, Kiribati, Marshall Islands, Nauru, New Zealand, Niue, Palau, Papua New Guinea, Solomon Islands, Tonga, Tuvalu, Vanuatu, Western Samoa.	South Pacific (Central and West)	To harmonize fishery management policies; to facilitate cooperation in surveillance and enforcement, processing, marketing and relations with third countries; to arrange for reciprocal access by member countries to their respective 200-mile zones.
SPPC (CPPS) South Pacific Permanent Commission	1952 International Convention	Santiago, Chile	Chile, Colombia, Ecuador, Peru.	South Pacific (East)	To carry out studies and adopt resolutions with a view to the conservation and improved use of resources; to standardize the regulations governing fishing.
SPC South Pacific Commission	1948	Noumea, New Caledonia	American Samoa, Australia, Cook Islands, Federated States of Micronesia, Fiji, France, French Polynesia, Guam, Kiribati, Marshall Islands, Nauru, New Caledonia, New Zealand, Niue, Northern Mariana Islands, Palau, Papua New Guinea, Pitcairn Islands, Solomon Islands, Samoa, Tokelau, Tonga, Tuvalu, UK, USA, Vanuatu, Wallis and Futuna	South Pacific South of the Equator.	To encourage and strengthen international cooperation in promoting the economic and social welfare and advancement of the peoples of the South Pacific region, to collect and analyse catch statistics and related data, and to conduct scientific research on tuna and billfish.

SUMMARY INFORMATION ON FISHERY BODIES

Indian Ocean and Indo-Pacific Area

Body	Establishment	Headquarters	Membership	Area of competence	Main functions
APFIC Asia-Pacific Fishery Commission	1948 International Agreement under aegis of FAO (Article XIV of FAO Constitution)	Bangkok (Thailand)	Australia, Bangladesh, China (People's Republic of), Democratic Kampuchea, France, India, Indonesia, Japan, Korea (Rep. of), Malaysia, Myanmar, Nepal, New Zealand, Pakistan, Philippines, Sri Lanka, Thailand, UK, USA, Viet Nam.	Indo-Pacific area (including inland waters)	To keep fishery resources under review; to formulate and recommend conservation and management measures; to keep under review the economic and social aspects of fishing; to encourage training and research.
IOFC Indian Ocean Fishery Commission	1967 Resolution of FAO Council (under Article VI-1 of FAO Constitution)	Rome (Italy)	Australia, Bahrain, Bangladesh, Comoros, Cuba, Djibouti, Egypt, Ethiopia, France, Greece, India, Indonesia, Iran (Islamic Rep. of), Iraq, Israel, Japan, Jordan, Kenya, Korea (Rep. of) Kuwait, Madagascar, Malaysia, Maldives, Mauritius, Mozambique, Myanmar, Netherlands, Norway, Oman, Pakistan, Portugal, Qatar, Saudi Arabia (Kingdom of), Seychelles, Somalia, Spain, Sri Lanka, Sudan, Sweden, Tanzania, Thailand, United Arab Emirates, UK, USA, Viet Nam.	Indian Ocean and adjacent seas (excluding the Antarctic area)	To promote programmes for fishery development and conservation; to promote research and development activities; to examine management problems with particular reference to offshore resources.
IOTC Indian Ocean Tuna Commission	1993 Resolution FAO Council to be followed by International Agreement under aegis of FAO (Article XIV of FAO Constitution)	To be determined	Sri Lanka, Eritrea, Mauritius, India, UK, Pakistan, Seychelles, EC, Madagascar, Republic of Korea.	Indian Ocean and adjacent seas north of the Antarctic Convergence	To promote cooperation in the conservation of tuna and tuna like species and also promote their optimum utilization, and the sustainable development of the fisheries.
WIOTO Western Indian Ocean Tuna Organization	1991 International Convention	Mahé, Seychelles	Seychelles, Mauritius, Comoros, India	Western Indian Ocean	To harmonize policies with respect to fisheries; to determine relations with distant water fishing nations; to establish mechanism for fisheries surveillance and enforcement; to cooperate for fisheries development; and to coordinate access to EEZs of the members.

ANNEX I
Cont'd

SUMMARY INFORMATION ON FISHERY BODIES

Others

Body	Establishment	Headquarters	Membership	Area of competence	Main functions
CCAMLR Commission for the Conservation of Antarctic Marine Living Resources	1980 International Convention	Hobart (Australia)	Argentina, Australia, Belgium, Brazil, Chile, EU, France, Germany, India, Italy, Japan, Korea (Rep. of), New Zealand, Norway, Poland, Russian Federation, South Africa, Spain, Sweden, UK, USA.	Antarctic Ocean	To ensure that all harvesting and research activities are conducted in accordance with the objectives of the Convention; to formulate, adopt and revise conservation measures; to compile, analyze and disseminate information on the status of resources and to facilitate research activities.
OLDEPESCA Latin American Organization for the Development of Fisheries	1984 International Convention	Lima (Peru)	Bolivia, Ecuador, El Salvador, Guatemala, Mexico, Nicaragua, Panama, Peru, Venezuela.	Oceans bordering Latin America	To provide adequately for the food needs of Latin America and Caribbean, using the potential of fishery resources for the benefit of the people in the region.
IWC International Whaling Commission	1946 International Convention	Cambridge (UK)	Antigua and Barbuda, Argentina, Australia, Brazil, Chile, China, Costa Rica, Denmark, Dominica, Ecuador, Finland, France, Germany, India, Ireland, Japan, Kenya, Korea (Rep. of), Mexico, Monaco, Netherlands, New Zealand, Norway, Oman, Peru, Russian Federation, Saint Kitts and Nevis, Saint Lucia, Saint Vincent and the Grenadines, Senegal, Seychelles, South Africa, Spain, Sweden, Switzerland, UK, USA, Venezuela	All waters in which whaling is carried out and land stations	To encourage or organize studies relating to whales; to collect and analyze information; to adopt regulations with respect to the conservation and utilization of whale resources.
CCSBT Commission for the Conservation of Southern Bluefin Tuna	1994 International Convention	Canberra, Australia	Australia, Japon, New Zealand	Atlantic, Pacific and Indian Oceans where SBT are found	To collect, analyse, and interpret scientific and other relevant information on SBT, to adopt conservation and management measures including the total allowable catch and its allocation among the Members.
CWP Coordinating Working Party on Fishery Statistics	1959 Resolution of FAO Conference (under Article VI-2 of FAO Constitution)	Rome, Italy	Consists of International Organizations: CCAMLR, FAO, ICCAT, ICES, NASCO, NAFO, OECD, EC (EUROSTAT)	All oceans	To keep under continuous review the requirements for fishery statistics for the purposes of research, policy-making and management, aqua standard concepts, definitions, classifications and methodologies for the collection and collation of fishery statistics.

ANNEX II

Address, Telephone and Fax Numbers of Fisheries Organizations

ICES

Palaegade 2-4,
DK-1261 Copenhagen K,
Denmark
Tel: (33) 154225
Fax: (33) 934215

NEAFC

425 Noble House
17 Smith Square
London SW1P 3JR,
United Kingdom
Tel: (0171) 238 5923
Fax: (0171) 238 5721

NAFO

P.O. Box 638,
Dartmouth,
Nova Scotia,
B2Y 3Y9,
Canada
Tel: (902) 469 9105
Fax: (902) 469 5729

NASCO

11 Rutland Square,
Edinburgh EH1 2AS,
Scotland
United Kingdom
Tel: (0131) 228 2551
Fax: (0131) 228 4384

WECAFC

FAO
Room NF-408
Viale delle Terme di Caracalla
00100 Rome,
Italy
Tel: (6) 5225 5802
Fax: (6) 5225 6500

IBSFC

Hoza 20,
00-528 Warszawa,
Poland
Tel: (2) 628 8647
Fax: (2) 625 3372

GFCM

FAO
Room NF411
Viale delle Terme di Caracalla
00100 Rome,
Italy
Tel: (6) 5225 6435
Fax: (6) 5225 6500

CECAF

P.O. Box 1628
Accra,
Ghana
Tel: 666 851-4
Fax: 00233-21 668 427; 233999

CSRP

Km.11, Route de Rufisque
B.P. 20505
Dakar,
Senegal
Tel: 345580

CORÉP

B.P. 161
Libreville,
Gabon
Tel: 73 7149
Fax:
Telex: 5265 GO

CARPAS

Not operational
Adva. Santa Maria 6700/or
Casilla 10095,
Santiago,
Chile
Tel: 22 88056
Fax: (562) 484 312

CTMFM

JUNCAL 1355,
P.6 ESC. 604,
11000 Montevideo,
Uruguay
Tel: 962047
Fax: (5982) 961578

ICCAT

Principe de Vergara, 17-7°,
28001 Madrid,
Spain
Tel: 431 0329
Fax: (34) 1 576 1968

ICSEAF

Not applicable

NAMMCO

University of Tromso,
9037 Tromso,
Norway
Tel: (77) 645 908
Fax: (77) 645 905

IOFC

FAO
Room NF-412
Viale delle Terme di Caracalla
00100 Rome,
Italy
Tel: (6) 5225 3637
Fax: (6) 5225 6500

IOTC

Until a Headquarters is chosen:
FAO
Room NF-412
Viale delle Terme di Caracalla
00100 Rome,
Italy
Tel: (6) 5225 3637
Fax: (6) 5225 6500

WIOTO

Not yet operational, temporary address:
Seychelles Fishing Authority
P.O. Box 449,
Fishing Port,
Mahé,
Seychelles
Tel: 224 597
Fax: 224 508

APFIC

Maliwan Mansion
Phra Atit Road,
Bangkok,
Thailand
Tel: 281 7844
Fax: 280 0445

PICES

Institute of Ocean Sciences,
P.O. Box 6000,
Sidney, B.C.,
Canada V8L 4B2
Tel: (604) 363 6366
Fax: (604) 363 6827

NPAFC

6640 Northwest Marine Drive
Vancouver, B.C., V6T 1X2,
Canada
Tel: (604) 228 1128
Fax: (604) 228 1135

I-ATTC

Scripps Institution of Oceanography
8604 La Jolla Shores Drive
La Jolla,
CA 92037,
U.S.A.
Tel: (619) 546 7100
Fax: (619) 546 7133

CEPTFA

Not applicable

IPHC

P.O. Box 95009
Seattle,
Washington 98145-2009,
U.S.A.
Tel:
Fax:

OAPO

Not applicable

SPFFA

P.O. Box 629,
Honiara,
Solomon Islands
Tel: (6777) 21124
Fax: (677) 23995

CPPS

Casilla 16638,
Agencia 6400-9,
Santiago 9,
Chile
Tel: 726652
Fax: 6951100

PSC

1155 Robson Street,
Sixth Floor,
Vancouver,
British Columbia V6E 189,
Canada
Tel:
Fax:

SPC

P.O. Box D5,
98848 Nouméa Cedex,
New Caledonia
Tel: (687) 262000
Fax: (687) 263818

IWC

The Red House
Station Road Histon,
Cambridge CB$ 4NP,
U.K.
Tel: (01223) 233 971
Fax: (01223) 232 876

CCAMLR

25 Old Wharf
Hobart,
Tasmania,
Australia 7000
Tel: (002) 310 366
Fax: (002) 232714

OLDEPESCA

Calle las Palomas No. 422,
Urbanización Limatambo,
Lima 34, Apartado 10168,
Lima,
Peru
Tel: 413858
Fax: 51-1442 9925

*CCSBT

GPO Box 856
Canberra ACT 2601
Australia
Tel: (06) 2716396
Fax: (06) 272 4215

CWP

FAO
Room NF-217
Viale delle Terme di Caracalla
00100 Rome,
Italy
Tel: (6) 5225 4828
Fax: (6) 5225 3605

*The Commission has not been established yet. This is a temporary address.

ANNEX III

List of Abbreviations

APEC	Asia Pacific Economic Cooperation
APFIC	Asia-Pacific Fishery Commission
ASEAN	Association of Southeast Asian Nations
CARPAS	Regional Fisheries Advisory Commission for the Southwest Atlantic
CCAMLR	Commission for the Conservation of Antarctic Marine Living Resources
CCSBT	Commission for the Conservation of Southern Bluefin Tuna
CECAF	Fishery Commission for the Eastern Central Atlantic
CEPTFA	Council of the Eastern Pacific Tuna Fishing Agreement
CORÉP	Regional Fisheries Committee for the Gulf of Guinea (Comité régional des pêches du Golfe de Guinée)
CPPS	South Pacific Permanent Commission
CSRP	Sub-Regional Commission on Fisheries (Commission sous-régionale des pêches)
CTMFM	Joint Technical Commission for the Argentina/Uruguay Maritime Front
CWP	Coordinating Working Party on Fishery Statistics
FAO	Food and Agriculture Organization of the United Nations
FFA	South Pacific Forum Fisheries Agency
GFCM	General Fisheries Council for the Mediterranean
I-ATTC	Inter-American Tropical Tuna Commission
IBSFC	International Baltic Sea Fishery Commission
ICCAT	International Commission for the Conservation of Atlantic Tunas
ICES	International Council for the Exploration of the Sea
ICSEAF	International Commission for the Southeast Atlantic Fisheries
INFOFISH	Marketing Information and Advisory Services for Fish Products in the Asia/Pacific Region
IOFC	Indian Ocean Fishery Commission
IOTC	Indian Ocean Tuna Commission
IPHC	International Pacific Halibut Commission
IWC	International Whaling Commission
NAFO	Northwest Atlantic Fisheries Organization
NAMMCO	North Atlantic Marine Mammal Commission
NASCO	North Atlantic Salmon Conservation Organization
NEAFC	North-East Atlantic Fisheries Commission
NPAFC	North Pacific Anadromous Fish Commission
OAPO	Eastern Pacific Tuna Fishing Organization
OECD	Organization for Economic Cooperation and Development
OECS	Organization of Eastern Caribbean States
OLDEPESCA	Latin American Organization for the Development of Fisheries
PICES	North Pacific Marine Science Organization
PSC	Pacific Salmon Commission
SEAFDEC	Southeast Asian Fisheries Development Center
SPC	South Pacific Commission
UNCED	United Nations Conference on Environment and Development
UNCLOS	United Nations Convention on the Law of the Sea
WECAFC	Western Central Atlantic Fishery Commission
WIOTO	Western Indian Ocean Tuna Organization

3. THE ROLE OF FAO REGIONAL FISHERY BODIES IN THE CONSERVATION AND MANAGEMENT OF FISHERIES*

Doc. no.:FAO Fisheries Circular No. 916   1996

[...]

CONTENTS

---

*   Only pp. iii-iv, 10-39 and 49-52 are reproduced here.

[...]

II.   REGIONAL APPROACH TO FISHERIES MANAGEMENT

22.   The important role of regional and subregional fisheries organizations in the conservation and management of the high seas fisheries has long been recognized[6]. The provisions of UNCLOS concerning the role of regional and subregional fisheries organizations are reiterated, emphasized and expanded by the UN Agreement on Straddling Fish Stocks and Highly Migratory Fish Stocks. The core of the UN Agreement is that high seas fisheries must by managed effectively on a regional or subregional basis through existing fisheries organizations or arrangements or by establishing new ones. The Rome Consensus on World Fisheries adopted by the FAO Ministerial Conference on Fisheries (Rome, 14-15 March 1995) urged the governments and international organizations to take prompt action, inter alia, to:

"reduce fishing to sustainable levels in areas and on stocks currently heavily exploited or overfished; to strengthen and support regional, sub-regional, and

---

[6]   See Articles 116 to 120 of UNCLOS. "Specialized intergovernmental fishery bodies have an important part to play in furthering the conservation and ensuring the management of the living resources of the sea. This was recognized both by the International Technical Conference on the Conservation of the Living Resources of the Sea, held in Rome in April/May 1955 and by the First United Nations Conference on the Law of the Sea, held in Geneva in February/April 1958". See International Fishery Bodies, COFI, First Session, Rome, 13-18 June 1966, COFI/66/6, 20 May 1966.

national fisheries organizations and arrangements for implementing conservation and management measures."

23.   Regional and subregional fisheries organizations must first and foremost identify with the region or the subregion they are representing. They must manage and be seen to manage the resources of the region in the interest of the coastal States of the region and DWFNs with legitimate interest in the conservation and management of the resources of that region. To be able to respond quickly and efficiently to the conservation and management needs of a region or a subregion it is imperative that the relationship between the fisheries organizations and their members become more of a partnership bridging the gap between the advisory and decision-making functions.

(i)   Present Fisheries Organizations

24.   There are more than twenty regional and subregional fishery bodies whose mandates include the conservation and management of high seas fisheries. some have full regulatory powers while others have an advisory role related to management issues. The functions of these bodies vary from dealing with a single species or a group of closely related species such as the North Atlantic Salmon Conservation Organization (NASCO), the Inter-American Tropical Tuna Commission (I-ATTC) and the Indian Ocean Tuna Commission (IOTC), to those based more on a region and covering a whole range of species within their areas of competence such as the North-West Atlantic Fisheries Organization (NAFO), the North-East Atlantic Fisheries Commission (NEAFC), and the Commission for the Conservation of Antarctic Marine Living Resources (CCAMLR).

25.   There are other fishery organizations which do not have conservation and management functions but provide scientific advice relating to conservation and management such as the International Council for the Exploration of the Sea (ICES) and the North Pacific Marine Science Organization (PICES). In addition, there are a number of regional economic and other organizations that have intensified their activities in the field of fisheries such as the Asia Pacific Economic Cooperation (APEC), the Association of South-East Asian Nations (ASEAN), the European Community (EC), the Cooperation Council for the Arab States of the Gulf (GCC), the Organization of Eastern Caribbean States (OECS), the Pacific Economic Cooperation Conference (PECC), the Common Market for Eastern and Southern Africa (COMESA), and the Southern Africa Development Community (SADC). Although regional economic groupings are, in most cases, based upon linguistic, economic interests or political affinities which might not always coincide with fisheries natural conservation and management areas, they represent, however, strong links among their members. Regional fishery bodies should be encouraged to increase further their cooperation with these groupings since they could provide the necessary political will for implementing conservation and management measures[7]

(ii)   Measures Required to Make Fishery Organizations More Effective

26.   The FAO Technical Consultation on High Seas Fishing, held in Rome in September 1992, discussed the role of regional fisheries organizations and outlined a number of

---

[7]   Annex I provides detailed information on the FAO regional fishery bodies.

measures required to make regional fisheries organizations more effective[8]. These requirements should form an integral part of any fishery management organization whose main objective is the effective conservation and management of the fisheries resources of the high seas.

1) Membership and Participation

27. It is of paramount importance that the membership of a regional or subregional fisheries organization or arrangement include all the countries in the region as well as those which have a legitimate interest in the conservation and management of the resources covered by that body. Membership should entail active participation in the work of the fishery organization as well as a clear commitment towards achieving its objectives.

2) Mandate to Adopt Management Measures

28. To be effective in the conservation and management of the resources, regional and subregional fisheries organizations must have a clear mandate to discharge their management duties. In addition, they should have mechanisms through which they receive scientific advice related to management issues. Whether such advice is provided by internal sources or external organizations, they should be conceived by the organizations' members as fair and neutral and free from national interests, politics and economics.

3) Implementation of Management Measures

29. The effectiveness of fisheries management organizations depend on the commitment of their members to implement the regulatory measures adopted by them. Annual reports of many fisheries management organizations bear witness to the number of regulatory measures adopted by them and which have not been implemented by their members. One of the existing problems for many fisheries organizations with management powers is the inclusion of the objection procedure in the conventions or agreements establishing them. Many contracting parties have used this to avoid the implementation of management measures. Members States of a fisheries management organization should promptly and without delay give effect to the management measures adopted by that organization. Any objection should be settled in accordance with provisions of disputes settlement incorporated in the conventions or agreements.

4) Role of Flag States

30. A major problem faced by many fisheries management organizations is the undermining of their regulatory and other conservation measures by countries not parties to the conventions or agreements who allow their flag vessels to be used for fishing on the high seas. The Provisions of the UN Agreement on Straddling Fish Stocks and Highly Migratory Fish Stocks and the Agreement to Promote Compliance with International Conservation and Management Measures by Fishing Vessels on the High Seas are designed to tackle this problem. The FAO Code of Conduct on Responsible Fisheries also addresses this problem.

---

[8] Technical Consultation on High Seas Fishing, Rome, 7-15 September 1992, FAO Fisheries Report N°484. See also Articles 8,9,10 and 30 of the UN Agreement on Straddling Fish Stocks and Highly Migratory Fish Stocks.

5)   Control, Surveillance and Enforcement

31.   Regional and subregional fisheries organizations or arrangements must have a mechanism through which their conservation and management measures are enforced. Thus, control, surveillance and enforcement must be part of the activities of any fisheries organization whose mandate includes the conservation and management of fisheries resources.

6)   Accountability of Fisheries Organizations

32.   Accountability of the regional or subregional fisheries organizations concerning their functions is a new concept. The FAO Technical Consultation on the High Seas Fishing acknowledged that fisheries organizations were accountable to their members. The UN Agreement on Straddling Fish Stocks and Highly Migratory Fish Stocks provides (Article 36) for a review conference, to be held four years after entry into force of the Agreement, to assess the adequacy of the Agreement and, if necessary, to propose means of strengthening the substance and methods of implementation of those provisions in order better to address any continuing problems in the conservation and management of straddling fish stocks and highly migratory fish stocks.

7)   Compulsory Settlement of Disputes

33.   Most conventions and Agreements establishing fisheries organizations do not include any provision concerning the settlement of disputes. Articles 27 to 32 of the UN Agreement on Straddling Fish Stocks and Highly Migratory Fish Stocks require that regional and subregional fisheries management organizations or arrangements dealing with straddling and highly migratory fish stocks adopt procedures for compulsory settlement of disputes to ensure the expeditious resolution of disputes relating to the conservation and management of these stocks. The adoption of settlement disputes procedures is indispensable if the decisions of the fisheries management organizations or arrangements concerning the conservation and management measures are to be applied without delay.

8)   Financing

34.   A regional or subregional fisheries organization needs adequate funding to be able to function properly. Many requirements by the UN Agreement on Straddling Fish Stocks and Highly Migratory Fish Stocks mean that most existing bodies will need a budget which could meet those requirements. To have a mandate for conservation and management without the financial means to execute them will not improve the effectiveness of the fisheries organizations. Member States of a regional or subregional fisheries organization or arrangement should agree among themselves as to how the financial needs of their organization should be secured.

9)   Effective Cooperation between Fisheries Organizations

35.   Cooperation between fisheries organizations operating in the same area or overlapping areas as well as those dealing with highly migratory and straddling fish stocks, is essential. At the FAO Technical Consultation on High Seas Fishing (Rome, 1992), I-ATTC reported that "there is a high degree of overlap among the extant tuna organizations and this will increase as more regional bodies are created". Greater efficiency could be

achieved if the regional bodies worked together more closely through for example, an "umbrella mechanism". The management issues related to straddling stocks depend on their biological characteristics and, in particular, on the degree of mixing between the EEZ and high Seas compartments of stocks. In many instances where mixing is considerable because of random dispersion, ontogenic or seasonal migrations, the stock should be managed as one single unit and management measures must be harmonized over the entire range of distribution of the stock. In this context, cooperation is seen as an essential part of conservation and management functions of fisheries organizations.

III. THE FUTURE ROLE OF FAO FISHERY BODIES IN THE CONSERVATION AND MANAGEMENT OF THE HIGH SEAS RESOURCES

36.   With the entry into force of the UNCLOS in November 1994, the Convention will have a marked impact on the practice of States, particularly those which are parties to it as well as on the activities of international organizations competent in the fields of fisheries. The Convention places a great emphasis (Articles 116 to 120) on the need and desirability of cooperation concerning the conservation and management of fisheries resources of the high seas.   Together with the Provisions of the Agreement to Promote Compliance with International Conservation and Management Measures by Fishing Vessels in the High Seas and those of the UN Agreement on Straddling Fish Stocks and Highly Migratory Fish Stocks, subregional and regional fisheries organizations are expected to play a more comprehensive, constructive, effective role in the conservation and management of the high seas resources.

37.   With the exception of the Indian Ocean Tuna Commission which covers the tuna stocks of the Indian Ocean, all other FAO fishery bodies were set up before the new fisheries regime was incorporated in the 1982 Law of the Sea Convention. Each body was set up by FAO to address a wide range of fisheries needs of a region and its members and covered all marine living resources within its area of competence.   The terms of reference of these bodies have been periodically reviewed and changed in order to make them more responsive to the needs of the regions for which they had been set up.   The recent developments concerning the conservation and management of the high seas resources have underlined the shortcomings of the existing fisheries organizations, including those of the FAO fishery bodies, and require fundamental changes in the functions of these organizations.

38.   The role of fisheries organizations on conservation and management issues is now expected to include effective implementation of the management measures they adopt through a series of mechanisms including monitoring, control, surveillance and enforcement as well as the compulsory settlement of disputes. FAO regional fishery bodies have always had an advisory role. Any management measures proposed by these bodies were recommendations which could not, if rejected, be imposed on member States.   It is in this context that the future role of these bodies will have to be examined. As bodies established within the framework of FAO, their powers and functions are all subject to the Organization's Constitution.

(i)   The Constitutional Position of FAO

39.   Within the UN system, FAO has the mandate to collect, analyse, interpret and disseminate information relating to nutrition, food and agriculture (including fisheries and marine products). The Organization is entrusted to promote and where appropriate,

recommend national and international action with respect to scientific, technological, social and economic research as well as the improvement of education and administration relating to nutrition, food and agriculture. It is also the function of the Organization to promote and, where appropriate, recommend national and international action with respect to inter alia the conservation of natural resources[9].

40.   The role of FAO in relation to the natural resources is to recommend national and international action for their conservation.   The degree of FAO involvement in the management of fishery resources was extensively discussed at the Sixth Session of COFI in 1971.   The concept of management was recognized as being wider than concern with the stocks alone and included at least concern with fishery development.   While the importance of COFI as a world body, responsible for reviewing the general progress in management, was emphasized, the Committee "pointed out that neither FAO nor its regional fishery bodies have powers to enforce regulations.   For this reason, some delegations felt that effective management would in every instance require a treaty-based commission or other body"[10]. At its Ninth Session held in Rome in October 1974, the Committee on Fisheries emphasized the growing importance of regional fisheries bodies, and the need for increased support to them, and strongly urged FAO to give greater support to its regional bodies, and other regional activities.   The Committee re-emphasized the role that it could play in discussing problems of management and development that were of common interest to many regions. It stressed the importance of having appropriate national or international machinery to ensure that management measures agreed upon were properly implemented and enforced.[11]   The 1984 FAO World Conference on Fisheries Management and Development acknowledged the political nature of the management of fisheries by outlining the role of the governments[12]. Recognizing this fact, the FAO Technical Consultation on High Seas fishing, held in Rome in September 1992, emphasized that the effectiveness of regional fishery bodies and hence their ability to manage high seas fisheries on a sustainable basis was dependent upon inter alia the political will of the States concerned.

41.   Under Article VI-1 of the FAO Constitution, the Conference may establish commissions or regional commissions "to advise on the formulation and implementation of policy and to coordinate the implementation of policy"[13].   The Indian Ocean Fishery Commission (IOFC), the Western Central Atlantic Fishery Commission (WECAFC) and the Regional Fishery Advisory Commission for the Southwest Atlantic (CARPAS), were all established under Article VI-1 of the FAO Constitution. None of these bodies can, under the FAO Constitution, perform direct management functions, but must rely on addressing recommendations on management measures to their members.

---

[9]   Article I of the Basic Text of the FAO, Volumes I and II, 1994 edition.

[10]   Report of the Sixth Session of the Committee on Fisheries, Rome, 15-21 April 1971, FAO Fisheries Reports, N° 103, para. 47-56.

[11]   Report of the Ninth Session of the Committee on Fisheries, Rome, 15-22 October 1974, paragraphs 14 and 21.

[12]   Report of the FAO World Conference on Fisheries Management and Development, Rome, 27 June - 6 July 1984, Section 14.

[13]   Article VI-I of the Basic Text of the FAO, Volumes I and II, 1994 edition.

42.   Article VI-2 of the FAO Constitution provides that the Conference, the Council, or the Director-General on the authority of the Conference or Council may establish committees and working parties to "Study and report on matters pertaining to the purpose of the Organization[14]". The Fishery Committee for the Eastern Central Atlantic (CECAF) was established under Article VI-2 of the Constitution.

43.   The FAO regional bodies established under Article VI of the Constitution are all dependent on the Organization for financial and secretariat support. None has an autonomous budget and their expenses are met by the Organization's Regular Programme and ad hoc voluntary contributions by member States. The terms of reference and reporting procedures of these bodies are determined by the Conference, the Council, or the Director-General on the authority of the Conference or Council. Within the specific mandates provided in Article VI of the Constitution, the commissions or committees established under this Article can only perform advisory functions.

44.   According to Article XIV of the FAO Constitution, the Council, under rules to be adopted by the Conference, may, by a vote concurred in by at least two thirds of the membership of the Council, approve and submit to Member Nations agreements concerning questions relating to food and agriculture which are of particular interest to Member Nations of geographical areas specified in such agreements and are designed to apply only to such areas. Article XIV agreements, though adopted within the framework of the FAO Constitution, have a legal life of their own. They can therefore provide for different and greater contractual obligations among the parties thereto that extend beyond the obligations already assumed under the FAO Constitution.

45.   The Conference pointed out that:

"The procedure of multilateral agreements has been used on several occasions to establish commissions and committees entrusted with specific tasks which fall within the general terms of reference of the Organization.

Indeed the Conference has already pointed out that agreements concluded under Article XIV of the Constitution should only be used when the purpose is to provide for "financial or other obligations going beyond those already assumed under the Constitution of the Organization"[15].

46.   Bodies established under Article XIV of the Constitution fall into one of the three following categories:

(a) bodies entirely financed by the Organization;
(b) bodies that, in addition to being financed by the Organization, may undertake cooperative projects financed by members of the body;
(c) bodies that, in addition to being financed by the Organization, have autonomous budgets[16].

---

[14]   Ibid.

[15]   Basic Texts of FAO, Volumes I and II, 1994 edition, Part R, pp. 185/186.

[16]   Ibid, at p. 197.

47.   During the Twenty-six Session of the FAO Conference in November 1991, amendments were adopted to Part R of the Basic Texts of the FAO, which were intended to devolve more independence and autonomy on Commissions established by agreements concluded under Article XIV of the Constitution, and in particular, those with autonomous budgets[17]. The amendments were intended to allow for more independent decision-making by such bodies in such matters as the adoption of management measures, the approval of autonomous budgets, amendments to the constitutive agreements, adoption of financial regulations and rules of procedure, and the selection and appointment of the secretary of the Commission concerned.

(ii)   The Present Mandates of FAO Fishery Bodies in Relation to High Seas Fisheries

(a)   Fishery Bodies Established under Article VI

48.   The fishery bodies established under Article VI of the Constitution have limited power in management of the resources of the high seas. They were set up as advisory bodies and in some cases have acquired a competent status as technical bodies capable of providing scientific advice necessary for conservation and management decisions. The Indian Ocean Fishery Commission (IOFC), the Western Central Atlantic Fishery Commission (WECAFC), the Fishery Committee for the Eastern Central Atlantic (CECAF), and the Regional Fisheries Advisory commission for the Southwest Atlantic (CARPAS) were all established under Article VI of the FAO Constitution. CECAF has undertaken some management initiatives but its role under the Organization's Constitution remains an advisory one. With the establishment of the Indian Ocean Tuna Commission (IOTC), the IOFC will need a more appropriate structure in order to address other fisheries problems of the region on a sub-regional basis. CARPAS has not been active since 1974.

(b)   Fishery Bodies Established under Article XIV

49.   The Asia-Pacific Fishery Commission (APFIC)[18] and the General Fisheries Council for the Mediterranean (GFCM) were established by agreements concluded under Article XIV of the FAO Constitution. The Agreement for the Establishment of the Indian Ocean Tuna Commission (IOTC) adopted by the FAO Council in 1993, entered into force in March 1996.

50.   Article IV of the Agreement establishing APFIC provides a broad mandate for the Commission in respect of the management of the fisheries. The purpose of the Commission includes the promotion and the full and proper utilization of living aquatic resources by the development and management of fishing and culture operations. Its functions in respect of management is to formulate and recommend measures and to initiate and carry out programmes or projects to conserve and manage resources.

51.   Article III of the Agreement establishing GFCM defines the purpose of the Council as to promote the development, conservation, rational management and best utilization of

---

[17]   Ibid, pp. 189-199.

[18]   Former Indo-Pacific Fishery Commission (IPFC).

living marine resources. The Council has the mandate to formulate and recommend measures for the conservation and management of living marine resources which could include regulating fishing methods and fishing gear, prescribing the minimum size for individuals of specified species, establishing open and closed fishing seasons and areas, regulating the amount of total catch and fishing effort and their allocation among Members. Such Recommendations should be adopted by a two-thirds majority of Members of the Council present and voting. The recommendations of the Council are subject to objection procedure and if objections are made by more than one-third of members of the Council, the recommendation does not become binding on any Member.

52.   The Agreement establishing IOTC gives the Commission the power to adopt, by a two-third majority of the Members present and voting, regulatory measures. Subject to objection procedure, Members of the Commission must take action, under their national legislation, to make effective the provisions of the Agreement and to implement conservation and management measures which have become binding.

(iii)   **The Implementation of the Provisions of the UN Agreement on Straddling Fish Stocks and Highly Migratory Fish Stocks by FAO**

(a)   **Justification for Regional Management Fishery Bodies**

53.   It is imperative that prior to any changes to the existing institutional arrangements of the FAO regional fishery bodies their members are convinced that such changes are necessary, justified and beneficial to them and the regions or the sub-regions. The implementation of the UN Agreement on Straddling Fish Stocks and Highly Migratory Fish Stocks should be considered when the management of such stocks is concerned. Thus there is no justification in restructuring the existing FAO regional fishery bodies in accordance with the provisions of the UN Agreement if such stocks are not present in the areas covered by these bodies or for which there are already independent fisheries management organizations dealing with them.

54.   While it may thus not be appropriate to restructure all of FAO regional fishery bodies in order to bring them into line with UN Agreement it is, however, necessary that the role of FAO fishery bodies in relation to the conservation and management of the resources of the high seas is clearly determined and defined by their members and the Organization. Whether they are required to function as technical/scientific bodies or technical/scientific bodies with advisory roles on management issues or function as management bodies they must be given a clear mandate and support to discharge their duties. In this respect, the restructuring of these bodies should take note of the measures discussed (paras. 26-35) with a view of strengthening these bodies and making them more effective.

(b)   **Constitutional Implications**

55.   FAO regional fishery bodies and in particular those established under Article VI of the Constitution, are essentially non-political entities which operate within the framework of the Organization and its overall objectives[19]. This characteristic has ensured the

---

[19]   See paras. 39-40.

impartiality of these bodies in respect of their objectives, functions and activities. The establishment of the IPFC (now APFIC) in 1948 and the GFCM in 1949 preceded even the first codification of the law of the sea by the UN in 1958. Other FAO fishery bodies with a mandate for high seas fisheries were established long before the adoption of UNCLOS in 1982. The main activities of these bodies have been helping their members in educational, technological, scientific, and research programmes related to fisheries.

56.   The management of the resources, especially when it involves the allocations of allowable catch, levels of fishing effort and monitoring, control, surveillance and enforcement are highly political. Such functions can only be undertaken properly by bodies established by separate agreements under Article XIV of the Constitution or alternatively outside the framework of FAO entirely.

(c)   Financial Implications

57.   The FAO regional fishery bodies are for the most part dependent on the Organization for financial and secretariat support, and their expenses are met by the Organization's Regular Programme and ad hoc contributions by member States. In this context, the implementation of the recommendations of the regional fishery bodies and their subsidiaries concerning their work and even their regular sessions may be and indeed have been delayed or cancelled due to the financial constraints on the Organization. In addition, many projects which were funded by external budgets have been instrumental in the progress and achievements of these bodies. Support from donors has been declining in recent years and many projects have been phased out or terminated. Only the newly established Indian Ocean Tuna Commission has an autonomous budget.

58.   At its Twenty-eighth Session (Rome, 20 October - 2 November 1995), the FAO Conference adopted the Code of Conduct for Responsible Fisheries. In doing so, the Conference urged FAO to strengthen Regional Fisheries Bodies in order to deal more effectively with fisheries conservation and management issues in support of subregional, regional and global cooperation and coordination in fisheries.

59.   The future role of FAO Regional Fishery Bodies in the Conservation and management of the high seas fisheries, as well as their role in providing advice to developing countries on the implementation of the Code, can only be effected if necessary funds to meet these obligations are made available.

60.   The financial implications of strengthening FAO Regional Fishery Bodies, as urged by the Conference, are very significant. The non-FAO fisheries organizations operate on annual budgets ranging from US$ 500,000 to over US$ 1,000,000 paid by members' contributions[20]. The restructuring of these bodies, with a view to strengthening them, provide an excellent opportunity for the FAO and the members of these bodies to agree on viable solutions for their future. There are three ways by which the existing FAO regional fishery bodies can be strengthened in order to perform management functions.

---

[20]   See Annex III.

i) Independent Bodies

61.   Members of the existing FAO fishery bodies may wish to establish independent fishery bodies under international agreements to replace the existing ones. In this case, the agreements will provide provisions relating to the budgets and funding of the new bodies (e.g., ICCAT). Like all independent fishery organizations, the expenses of the new bodies will be met by members' contributions. These bodies can be given full powers to adopt regulatory measures (total allowable catch and allocations) , as well as implementing all the measures relating to monitoring, control and surveillance, and enforcement and settlement of all disputes.

ii) Bodies Within the Framework of FAO

62.   Some of the existing FAO regional fishery bodies could become independent bodies operating under Article XIV of the FAO Constitution. As bodies operating within the framework of FAO, they can have autonomous budgets and administrative independence. Financial commitment towards their budgets by their members is an integral part of this process. These bodies can have management powers to adopt regulatory measures, although it may not be thought appropriate for them, as they operate within the framework of the Organization, to get involved in matters relating, for example, to enforcement.

iii) Bilateral or Multilateral Agreements

63.   In restructuring the existing FAO regional fishery bodies, the fisheries resources of some smaller areas currently covered by IOFC, WECAFC and APFIC can be more effectively managed through bilateral, trilateral or multilateral agreements or arrangements. Member States can agree among themselves to establish the most suitable institutional arrangements for the management of the resources concerned.

(d)   Other Arrangements

64.   Under Article 117 of UNCLOS "All States have the duty to take, or to cooperate with other States in taking, such measures for their respective national as may be necessary for the conservation of the living resources of the high seas". The need for cooperation between States on conservation and management of the living resources of the high seas is further emphasized in Article 118 of the Convention.

65.   The UN Agreement on Straddling Fish Stocks and Highly Migratory Fish Stocks requires States to cooperate through sub-regional or regional fisheries management organizations or arrangements for the conservation and management of such stocks. Article 1 of the Agreement defines the term "arrangement" as "a cooperative mechanism established in accordance with the Convention and this Agreement by two or more States for the purpose, inter alia, of establishing conservation and management measures in a subregion or region...".

66.   The conservation and management of some fisheries resources and in some areas, particularly at sub-regional levels, may be carried out more effectively by cooperation between two or more States through agreements without having to formally establish fishery management organizations. In addition, many fisheries management organizations don not have the power to implement the regulatory measures (monitoring, control surveillance and

enforcement as well as settlement of disputes). It may be both necessary and desirable that members of these organizations use the term "arrangement" for establishing a mechanism through which the regulatory measures adopted by their Commissions are effectively implemented.

IV.   SOME POSSIBLE OPTIONS ON STRENGTHENING THE FUTURE ROLE OF FAO REGIONAL FISHERY BODIES

67.   Excluding the constitutional and financial implications associated with giving the FAO Regional Fishery Bodies a comprehensive and clear mandate for the conservation and management of the fisheries of the high seas or strengthening them, there are other considerations which will have to be taken into account while deciding the future role of these bodies.

68.   The first consideration is that the main objective of the Organization should be to help these bodies to reach an independent status, i.e., to give the overall responsibility of these bodies to their members. The member States of these bodies should, therefore, be responsible for the activities of these bodies and the bodies should be accountable to their members. An independent regional or sub-regional fishery body with its secretariat and technical support unit located in the region or sub-region has the advantage of accessing the political will of its members as well as being able to identify and react quickly to the general and particular fisheries needs of the region or sub-region and its members.

69.   The second consideration is to maintain the impartiality of the FAO Fishery Bodies as long as they remain within the framework of the Organization. The non-political nature of these bodies has been instrumental in providing a platform for dialogue and cooperation among their members. In some areas, notably parts of the Indian Ocean, the South China Sea and the Western Central Atlantic, fisheries cooperation may not continue among some members if FAO were to withdraw its direct involvement in the fisheries of these areas.

70.   The third consideration is that FAO Regional Fishery Bodies have had different mandates and have performed different functions according to the needs of the regions and the extent of support they have received form their members. Consequently, any restructuring of these bodies should reflect on the realistic objectives and functions to be assigned to these bodies in the future.

71.   The final consideration is that even without a mandate to manage fisheries of the high Seas, any FAO body which continues to have an advisory role must be financed adequately and receive active support from its members in order to perform its functions and achieve its objectives. They should be able to hold their regular sessions and carry out their intersessional activities. Of the present FAO regional fishery bodies, some are potentially management bodies and are ready to undertake management functions either as independent fisheries management organizations or as management bodies operating under Article XIV of the FAO Constitution (IOTC model). These are GFCM, CECAF, the Gulfs Committee of IOFC and APFIC Committee on Marine Fisheries.

72.   The following suggested options for each FAO Regional Fishery Body have been drawn up taking into account of relevant factors discussed so far in this document. In addition, a more detailed analysis of the possible fishery management scenario and a model

institutional arrangements for future fisheries management of the CECAF area is presented. This will serve as a model for similar studies to be undertaken on other FAO regional fishery bodies. The options proposed in this document are not by any means exhaustive but they indicate the practical directions these bodies may be expected to take in the very near future.

(1)   General Fisheries Council for the Mediterranean (GFCM)

I)   Present Structure

73.   GFCM was established by an Agreement concluded under Article XIV of the FAO Constitution in 1949. The Agreement establishing the Council entered into force in 1952. The area of competence of the Council is the Mediterranean and the Black Sea and connecting waters (FAO Statistical Area 37). Membership of the Council is open to all Member Nations and Associate Members of FAO. Members of the United Nations, any of its Specialized Agencies or the International Atomic Energy Agency may be admitted by a two-thirds majority of the Council's members. GFCM is financed and administered by the Organization. Under Article III of the Agreement establishing GFCM, the purpose of the Council is to promote the development, conservation, rational management and best utilization of living marine resources in its area of competence. It has the mandate to formulate and recommend measures for the conservation and management which includes regulating fishing methods and fishing gear, presenting the minimum size for individuals of specified species, establishing open and closed fishing seasons and areas, and regulating the amount of total catch and fishing effort and their allocation among its members. The recommendations are adopted by a two-thirds majority of members present and voting and are subject to objecting procedure.

The Council has the following subsidiary bodies:

(i)   GFCM Executive Committee
(ii)   GFCM Committee on Fisheries Management
(iii) Working Party on Fisheries Economics and Statistics
(iv)   GFCM Committee on Aquaculture

II)   Considerations

74.   Coastal States in the Mediterranean have not declared extended fisheries jurisdiction and therefore the Mediterranean for the most part remains a high seas area. With the exception of Greece (6 miles), Syria (35 miles) and Algeria (32-52 miles)[21], all other States bordering the Mediterranean Sea have 12 miles territorial sea. In some areas of the Mediterranean Sea, the continental shelf extends far beyond 12 miles and stocks occurring on the shelf are therefore accessible to fishermen form outside the region. Demersal straddling stocks are found in the Gulf of Lions and the Gulf of Gabes and pelagic straddling stocks exist probably in most parts of the Mediterranean Sea. There is also the question of tuna which is currently managed by the Council and is also within the mandate of the International Commission for the Conservation of Atlantic Tunas (ICCAT). Thus the unique

---

[21]   In May 1994, Algeria extended its Fishing Zone to 32 miles between western maritime boundary and Ras Ténés, and 52 miles from Ras Ténés to eastern maritime boundary.

fisheries aspects in the Mediterranean makes it a prime candidate for adopting the Provisions of the 1995 UN Agreement on Straddling Fish Stocks and Highly Migratory Fish Stocks. This cannot be done easily by a body which is financially and administratively dependent on FAO and is ultimately responsible to the Organization.

75.   The countries bordering the Black Sea (Bulgaria, Georgia, Romania, Turkey, Ukraine, and the Russian Federation) are currently negotiating to establish a Commission for the conservation and management of the living resources of the Black Sea. With the establishment of a new fishery body for the Black Sea, the Council will have a reduced area of competence as well as a possible reduction in its membership.

76.   The membership of the Council consists of a number of very important fishing nations which could meet all scientific and technical requirements of the Council. At its Twenty-First Session (Alicante, Spain, May 1995), the Council called for strengthening of GFCM and proposed voluntary contributions from members to supplement the regular budget provided by FAO. It must be pointed out that in the light of serious financial cuts in the budget of the Fisheries Department, the present level of support for the Council through the Regular Programme of FAO may not be possible to maintain. For a body to function properly and effectively a firm financial commitment by its members is of paramount importance. In addition, other FAO regional fishery bodies such as WECAFC, CECAF, and IOFC serving less developed areas, are in greater needs of the Organization's financial, technical and scientific support.

77.   As a result of the decentralization policy, all of FAO regional fishery bodies are, or shortly will be, located on Regional Offices of the Organization or located in a member country. Possibilities of the GFCM Secretariat being located in a member country to host the Secretariat outside the Organization need to be investigated. This could reduce the Organization's expenditure for hosting GFCM as well as demonstrate the rationale regarding its policy on decentralization.

III)   Proposed Options

a)   Amendments of the Present Agreement

78.   FAO, in consultation with member countries of GFCM, could amend the present Agreement. The amendments could include provisions for strengthening GFCM, providing for an autonomous budget and greater administrative independence. The changes could re-establish GFCM on the same footing as IOTC. The new GFCM might still fall short of being able to meet all the requirements of the UN Agreement on Straddling Fish Stocks and Highly Migratory Fish Stocks.

b)   To Establish an Independent Commission

79.   Under this option, members of the Council could terminate the Agreement establishing GFCM in accordance with the Provision of Article XIV of the Agreement. Under the aegis of FAO or other arrangements, GFCM members could agree on a new treaty for the establishment of a new intergovernmental fishery organization for the conservation and management of the fisheries resources of the Mediterranean Sea. GFCM could remain operational until the new body is in place. Cooperation between FAO and the new fishery body could, thereafter, be determined in accordance with the Provisions of Article XIII of

the Organization's Constitution. The new independent body could be in a position to fully implement the Provisions of the UN Agreement on Straddling Fish Stocks and Highly Migratory Fish Stocks.

(2) Asia-Pacific Fishery Commission (APFIC)[22]

I) Present Structure

80. APFIC was established by an Agreement concluded under Article XIV of the FAO Constitution in 1948. The area of competence of the Commission is broadly defined as the "Indo-Pacific area" although in 1990 the Commission agreed that in practice it would give priority to marine fishery resources in the FAO Statistical Area 71. Membership of the Commission is open to all Member Nations and Associate Members of FAO. Other States that are Members of the Untied Nations, any of its Specialized Agencies or the International Atomic Energy Agency may be admitted as members by a two-thirds majority of the Commission's membership. APFIC is financed and administered by the Organization. Article IV of the Agreement establishing APFIC provides a broad mandate for the Commission in respect of the management of the fisheries. The purpose of the Commission includes the promotion and the full and proper utilization of living aquatic resources by the development and management of fishing and culture operations. Its function in respect of management is to formulate and recommend measures and to initiate and carry out programmes or projects to conserve and manage resources. The Commission has the following subsidiary bodies:

(i) Executive Committee

(ii) APFIC Committee on Marine Fisheries

(iii) APFIC Aquaculture and Inland Fisheries Committee

(iv) Joint Working Party on Fish Technology and Marketing

(v) Joint Working Party on Fishery Statistics and Economics

(vi) Working Party on Aquaculture and Inland Fisheries

(vii) Working Party on Marine Fisheries

II) Considerations

81. Following the recommendation of the Eighteenth Session of COFI (Rome, April 1989), the Commission established an Ad hoc Committee (Twenty-third Session, May 1990) to draw up a report reviewing the structure, functions and responsibilities of IPFC and its subsidiary bodies. The report of the Ad hoc Committee was considered by the IPFC Committee for the Development and Management of Fisheries in the South China Sea (CDMSCS) at its Seventh Session held in Kowloon, Hong Kong, in July 1991. The

---

[22] Former Indo-Pacific Fishery Commission (IPFC).

Committee also had the report of its own Working Group on the Structure, Functions and Responsibilities of CDMSCS. It decided that (i) the Commission should not be disbanded but be restructured, (ii) the membership of the Commission should be enlarged, (iii) IPFC should have an autonomous budget, and (iv) the work of CDMSCS should be strengthened.

82.   At its Twenty-fourth Session (Bangkok, Thailand, 23 November - 4 December 1993), the Commission, taking into account the report of the Ad hoc Committee, the views of the CDMSCS and the report of the IPFC Executive Committee, decided to adopt a number of changes concerning its structure, functions and responsibilities. These included (i) changing the name of the Commission to Asia-Pacific Fishery Commission (APFIC), (ii) establishing an Inland Fishery and Aquaculture Committee, (iii) disbanding the Special Committee on Management of Indo-Pacific Tuna and the Standing Committee on Resource Research and Development (SCORRAD), and (iv) concentrating on the development and management of the marine fisheries in the South China Sea. The Commission did not address some of the fundamental issues concerning its own future. The functions and responsibilities of the two Committees are very distinct from one another. They are geographically separated and the functions envisaged for the Marine Fisheries Committee have no bearing on the functions of the Committee for Inland Fishery and Aquaculture. These bodies can exist and function independently pursuing their own separate mandates. This means that there is little justification for the existence of the Commission itself as well as that of its Executive Committee since there will be practically nothing for either of them to do.

83.   At present, there are nine fishery bodies in the Pacific Ocean. These are Inter-American Tropical Tuna Commission (I-ATTC), International Pacific Halibut Commission (IPHC), North Pacific Anadromous Fish Commission (NPAFC), Council of the Eastern Pacific Tuna Fishing Agreement (CEPTFA), Eastern Pacific Tuna Fishing Organization (OAPO), South Pacific Permanent Commission (SPPC), South Pacific Forum Fisheries Agency (SPFFA), Pacific Salmon Commission (PSC), and North Pacific Marine Science Organization (PICES). In addition, there are a number of regional organizations which also deal with fisheries including Association of Southeast Asian Nations (ASEAN), Southeast Asian Fisheries Development Centre (SEAFDEC), Marketing Information and Advisory Services for Fish Products in the Asia/Pacific Region (INFOFISH), Asia/Pacific Economic Cooperation (APEC), and Pacific Economic Cooperation (PECC). The region as a whole is well covered by these bodies except for the management of the resources of the South China Sea which is the responsibility of APFIC.

III)   Proposed Options

a)   Amendments to the Agreements Establishing APFIC

84.   Under this option, APFIC will remain as an Article XIV body with an autonomous budget, more management powers and greater flexibility. It could have the following subsidiary bodies:

> (i)   The IOFC Committee for the Development and Management of Fisheries in the Bay of Bengal could become a subsidiary body of APFIC. This would provide greater conservation and management powers enjoyed by bodies operating under Article XIV.

(ii) The Committee on Marine Fisheries would remain as a subsidiary body of APFIC with greater management and administrative powers.

b) **Terminating the Agreement Establishing APFIC and Promoting the Committee on Marine Fisheries to a Commission under Article XIV of the FAO Constitution**

85.   The Commission and the Executive Committee of APFIC do not appear to serve a useful purpose. Consideration could therefore be given to terminate the Agreement. FAO, in consultation with the countries concerned could consider the establishment of a new Commission for the Conservation and management of the main resources of the South China Sea and the Eastern Indian Ocean (Area 51) under Article XIV of the FAO Constitution. The new commission could have autonomous budget and management powers similar to those provided in the Agreement establishing IOTC could be given to the new commission.

c) **Establishing an Independent Commission to Replace the Committee on Marine Fisheries**

86.   Under the aegis of FAO or other arrangements a new international treaty could be negotiated by the Countries of the South China Sea. The treaty could establish an independent commission to deal effectively with the conservation and management of the fisheries resources in the South China Sea.

d) **The Future Arrangements for the Aquaculture and Inland Fisheries Committee**

87.   In 1994, the total fish supply from inland resources in Asia reached 15,279,042 tons (77.5% of total inland production). Thus the importance of inland fisheries in the region is obvious. Like other FAO inland fishery bodies, this Committee could be restructured and strengthened to perform effective advisory functions. This could be done by establishing this Committee as a commission under Article VI of the FAO Constitution.

(3) **Indian Ocean Fishery Commission (IOFC)**

I) **The Present Structure of IOFC**

88.   IOFC was established by the Council in 1967 under Article VI-1 of the FAO Constitution. The area of competence of the Commission is the Indian Ocean and its adjacent seas (FAO Statistical Areas 51 and 57), excluding the Antarctic area. Membership in the commission is open to all Member Nations and Associate Members of FAO. The commission and its subsidiary bodies are financed and administered by FAO. The Commission's terms of reference as set out in paragraph 2 of its Statutes are:

(i) To promote, assist and coordinate national programmes over the entire field of fishery development and conservation;

(ii) to promote research and development activities in the area through international sources, and in particular international aid programmes, and

(iii) to examine management problems with particular reference, because of the need to take action, to those relating to the management of offshore resources.

The Commission has four subsidiary bodies:

(i)   Committee for the Indian Ocean Tunas;

(ii) Committee for the Development and Management of the Fishery Resources of the Gulfs (the Gulfs Committee);

(iii) Committee for the Development and Management of Fisheries in the Southwest Indian Ocean (SWIO); and

(iv) Committee for the Development and Management of Fisheries in the Bay of Bengal (BOB).

II)   Considerations

89.   The recent developments concerning high seas fisheries have made it clear that regional and subregional fishery organizations should play a more active and effective role in the conservation and management of the resources of the high seas. These bodies should have proper mandate and firm commitments by their members in order to function effectively. The IOFC and its subsidiaries have an advisory role which is not appropriate for dealing with management issues. If there is a need for conservation and management of the high seas fisheries in the Indian Ocean, the present institutional arrangements will have to be fundamentally changed.

90.   FAO has responded positively to the need of the region by establishing the Indian Ocean Tuna Commission (IOTC) which will deal with the tuna and tuna like species on a regional basis which is necessary for the conservation and management of the tuna stocks. This has two implications on the functions of IOFC. First, the IOFC Committee for the Indian Ocean Tuna will be abolished. Secondly, the membership of the Commission will be substantially affected since many present members joined the Commission for its involvement with tuna fishing. With the abolition of the Committee for the Indian Ocean Tunas the remaining three Committees are, subject to minor adjustments to their geographical coverage, well placed to serve the countries bordering the Indian Ocean on a subregional basis. The adjustments could provide for proper conservation and management of the resources of the Red Sea, the Gulf of Aden and the Arabian Sea which so far have been only nominally covered by the Commission.

91.   The IOFC, like other FAO regional fishery bodies, has not been able to hold its sessions regularly. The financial constraints on the Organization in recent years have caused the delay or even cancelation of regular sessions and the implementation of its recommendations. The Commission has held three sessions in the past ten years (1985,1989,1994). For a body to be effective, it needs to hold it sessions regularly and be able to carry out its programmes of work.

92.   The participation of the members at regular sessions of the Commission has been very poor. At its last session (Mombasa, Kenya, November 1994) only fourteen out of forty five members attended; not enough to provide a quorum necessary for making decisions. Non-FAO fishery organizations whose budgets are met by members' contributions and have more specific functions enjoy a better participation and support by their members. It is, therefore, imperative that any restructuring of the Commission should include proper support and commitments, including financial commitment, by the members.

III)   Proposed Options

93.   With the establishment of the Indian Ocean Tuna Commission to manage tuna and tuna-like species throughout the Indian Ocean, one of the main region-wide tasks of the IOFC, operating through its Committee on the Management of Indian Ocean Tuna, would be removed.   There are a few other highly migratory or transboundary fish stocks but the range of migration of such stocks is too poorly known at present to allow for the establishment of a Commission.   Other fish stocks in the Indian Ocean are more localized, with fisheries based on those stocks demonstrating diverse conditions in the various localities. It would appear more logical to look more to the strengthening of fisheries management at the sub-region level.   The IOFC Committees (Committee for the Development and Management of the Fishery Resources of the Gulfs, Committee for the Development and Management of Fisheries in the Southwest Indian Ocean, and Committee for the Development and Management of Fisheries in the Bay of Bengal), subject to minor adjustments to their geographical coverage, are well placed to serve the countries bordering the Indian Ocean on a subregional basis.   The adjustments could provide for proper conservation and management of the resources of the Red Sea, the Gulf of Aden and the Arabian Sea which so far have been only nominally covered by IOFC.

a)   Transforming the Existing Three Committees of IOFC into New Commissions under Article XIV with New Management Mandates, Autonomous Budgets and New Areas of Competence

94.   Agreements could be concluded under Article XIV to establish fishery commissions to replace the three subsidiary committees. The structure of constructive agreements under Article XIV is preferred because of the possibility of enhanced powers and flexibility that go with it.

(i) Fishery Commission for the Eastern Indian Ocean

95.   This commission could replace the Committee for the Development and Management of Fisheries in the Bay of Bengal. Its area of competence could be extended but would correspond mainly to that of the FAO Statistical Area 57. In order to be effective, it could be endowed with management power and an autonomous budget. Full participation and support by the countries in the sub-region would be essential if conservation and management measures are to be adopted and implemented at the sub-regional level. It would appear that the region is homogeneous enough to provide such support. Another alternative is to set up a new BOB committee as a subsidiary body of APFIC.[23]

(ii) Fishery Commission for the North West Indian Ocean

96.   At present, the Arabian Sea, the Gulf of Aden and the Red Sea fall under the area of competence of IOFC. With the exception of the Persian Gulf and the Gulf of Oman whose fisheries are covered by the Gulfs Committee, there is no sub-regional mechanism in place to deal with the other areas. In addition, the biological characteristics of the fisheries of the Persian Gulf have little in common with those of the Gulf of Oman or Arabian Sea.

---

[23]   See above paragraph 85.

Similarly, the Red Sea has its own distinct biological characteristics. The fisheries of the Gulf of Oman and the Gulf of Aden however have much in common with those of the Arabian Sea.

97.   A commission for the North West Indian Ocean could thus be established to deal with the Persian Gulf, the Gulf of Oman, the Arabian Sea and the Gulf of Aden and the Red Sea. The commission could have three geographical subsidiary bodies dealing with the fisheries of the three specific areas - the Persian Gulf, the Gulfs of Oman and Aden and the Arabian Sea and lastly the Red Sea. The management decisions of the three Sub-commissions would be taken by their members and not by the commission. The area of competence would correspond to the northern part of FAO Statistical Area 51.

(iii) Fishery Commission for the South West Indian Ocean

98.   The present SWIO Committee appears to be well placed to become a commission under Article XIV with management power and an autonomous budget. Its area of competence would correspond to the southern part of the FAO Statistical Area 51. The region comprises countries which have many similar problems and aspirations. There are, at present, a number of other organizations promoting collaboration in this area, e.g. Organization for Indian Ocean Marine Affairs Cooperation (IOMAC) and the Western Indian Ocean Tuna Organization (WIOTO). Most countries are also members of economic groupings e.g. the Common Market for Eastern and Southern Africa (COMESA) while a few belong to the Southern Africa Development Community (SADC). Such economic groupings could in the future provide the nucleus for injecting the political will required for management decisions.

b)   Independent Commissions

99.   The Director-General of FAO in consultation with the member countries of the IOFC three Committees, convenes conferences of plenipotentiaries with a view to establishing independent fishery Commissions for the three sub-regions. Cooperation between FAO and the new bodies will be agreed according to the provisions of Article XIII of the FAO Constitution.

c)   Future Role of IOFC

100.   Even if the fisheries management function is devolved to new and strengthened commissions at the sub-regional levels, there may still be a role for the IOFC to play at a region-wide level in the area of research and data collection and dissemination. The Indian Ocean Marine Affairs Cooperation (IOMAC) is another ocean-wide body but its mandate and activities extend beyond fisheries. Thus, in the interest of the region as a whole consideration should therefore be given to redefining the mandate of the IOFC. It may be feasible to reconstitute the Commission as an Indian Ocean Marine Fisheries Research Committee under Article VI.2 of the FAO Constitution as an organization whose functions would be of purely scientific and technical nature. The purpose of such a body would be to promote and coordinate marine scientific research in order to advance scientific knowledge of the region and its living resources, to promote the collection and exchange of information related to marine scientific research in the area concerned, and to cooperate closely with fisheries and fisheries related organizations in the region. Its membership could consist of Coastal States and distant water fishing nations. In view of the lack of adequate information on the

resources and their interaction in the Indian Ocean, the existence of such a body seems to be desirable to supplement the information that would be acquired by the regional bodies.

IV) Financial Implications to the Organization

101.   In transforming the existing three IOFC Committees into commissions under Article XIV of the FAO Constitution, the Organization would not have any financial responsibility towards these bodies since the new commissions would have their own autonomous budgets. However, if a region-wide body is established by FAO to promote and coordinate marine scientific research in order to advance scientific knowledge of the region, the cost will not be substantial.

(4)   Fishery Committee for the Eastern Central Atlantic (CECAF)

I)   Geographical Coverage and Membership

102.   The Fishery Committee for the Eastern Central Atlantic (CECAF) was established under Article VI-2 of the FAO Constitution in 1967 to replace the Regional Fisheries Commission for Western Africa (RFCWA). The Statutes of CECAF define its area of competence as the Eastern-Central Atlantic between Cape Spartel and the Congo River. This area mostly coincides with FAO Statistical Area 34. The membership of CECAF consists of Members whose territories border the Atlantic Ocean from Cape Spartel to the mouth of the Congo River and those Member Nations and Associate Members fishing or conducting research in the area. At present, all the coastal countries of the area covered by CECAF are members of the Committee. Other members of CECAF are Cuba, France, Greece, Italy, Japan, Korea, (Rep. of), Norway, Poland, Romania, Spain, and the USA.

II)   Marine Resources

103.   The continental shelf off this area is fairly narrow and most catches are taken inside 200 miles. The highly migratory species in the area are tune and tuna-like species and possibly oceanic sharks. Only oceanic horse mackerel (*Trachurus picturatus*) is known to migrate between the coast of Sahara and the offshore seamounts possibly reaching the Cape Verde Islands. This pelagic straddling stock is exploited by Eastern Europe fleets and by coastal countries. The main shared stocks in CECAF region are *Sardinella aurita*, *Trachurus trachurus*, *Scomber japonicus*, Cephalopods/Cuttlefish, small pelagics, demersal resources, *Sardinella maderensis*, and *Trachurus trecae*. Of these, *Scomber japonicus*, *Trachurus trachurus* and *Trachurus trecae* do straddle between the EEZs and the high Seas.

III)   Structure and Mandate

104.   The Committee has four subsidiary bodies:

(i)   Sub-Committee on Management of Resources within the Limits of National Jurisdiction
(ii)   Sub-Committee on Fishery Development
(iii)   Working Party on Resources Evaluation
(iv)   Working Party on Fishery Statistics

The Terms of Reference of CECAF, as amended in 1992, include:

(a) to keep under review the state of these resources and of the industries based on them;

(b) to promote the collection, interchange, dissemination and analysis or study of statistical socio-economic, biological and environmental data and other marine fishery information;

(c) to establish the scientific basis for regulatory measures leading to the conservation and management of marine fishery resources, to formulate such measures through subsidiary bodies, as required, and to make appropriate recommendations for the adoption and implementation of these measures;

(d) to encourage, recommend and coordinate training and extension activities in all aspects of marine fisheries; and

(e) to assist Member Governments in formulating programmes to be implemented through international aid sources to achieve the objectives described in (a), (b), (c), (d) above.

IV)   CECAF Activities

105.   CECAF has been very successful in achieving the objectives for which it had been set up by FAO in 1967. With the help of "CECAF Projects", funded by UNDP from 1973 to 1985 and other donors since then, the Committee has carried out many activities in the fields of collecting statistics, assessing resources, management principles, training and regional cooperation. It has played an important role in coordinating the management of fisheries in West Africa and has created an awareness on the part of senior officials as to the economic importance of fisheries. These activities and the promotion of the development of international collaboration have been instrumental to the development of management structures as well as the establishment of some research centres in the region.

106.   CECAF, through extensive activities related to its advisory functions, has become the only organization capable of providing scientific advice and technical support to its members and other fishery organizations in the region. Its important role in the coordination of the fishery activities of its members and those of the fishery bodies in the region is well acknowledged by its members and those organizations. In 1992, the terms of reference of CECAF were amended in order to give the Committee more power in respect of the Conservation and management of the resources of the region. The function of the Committee concerning the conservation and management of the high Seas resources is still of an advisory nature. In the past, CECAF has recommended a number of management measures which have been implemented by its members.

107.   At its Twelfth Session (Accra, Ghana, 27 April-1 May 1992), the Committee's members recognized unanimously that CECAF had played in the past and should continue to play in the future, an invaluable role as the main technical body for cooperation in fisheries management and development in the region. They also expressed their concern at the infrequency of meetings which could undermine the overall efficiency and that quality

of the Committee's technical work. It was recognized by the Committee that the general activities of CECAF, as well as any additional activities would have to remain within the Organization's overall budget and programme. CECAF members were also informed that traditional donors were now reluctant to support institutions on a long-term basis and therefore it was imperative for the Committee to consider appropriate arrangements to have adequate support on a more regular basis.

108.   At its Thirteenth Session (Dakar, Senegal, 18-20 December 1995), the Committee discussed the decision of COFI (Twenty-first Session, March 1995) concerning the future role of the FAO fishery bodies. It decided that a thorough analysis of the future role of CECAF should be prepared by the Secretariat. This document should be then circulated to all CECAF members by June 1996 in order to enable them to discuss it at the Tenth Session of CECAF Sub-Committee on Management of Resources within the Limits of National Jurisdiction provisionally scheduled for December 1996.

V)   Other Fishery Organizations in the Region

(i)   International Commission for the Conservation of Atlantic Tunas (ICCAT)

109.   ICCAT was established by the International Convention for the Conservation of Atlantic Tunas, signed in Madrid, Spain on 14 May 1966 and entered into force on 21 March 1969. The area covered by the Convention is defined as "all waters of the Atlantic Ocean, including the adjacent seas". the species covered by the Commission are the tuna and tuna like fishes (The Scombriformes with the exception of the families *Trichiuridae* and *Gempylidae* and the *genus Scomber*) and such other species exploited in tuna fishing in the Convention area which are not covered by other international organizations. ICCAT has regulatory powers and its conservation and management measures are subject to the objection procedure.

(ii)   Sub-Regional Commission on Fisheries (Commission sous-régionale des pêches) (CSRP)

110.   The Convention establishing a Sub-Regional Fisheries Commission was signed at the First Extraordinary Conference of Ministers in charge of fisheries from Cape Verde, the Gambia, Guinea Bissau, Mauritania and Senegal in Dakar, Senegal, on 29 March 1985. Guinea became a member of the Commission in 1987. The Convention does not define the precise area covered by the Commission but references are made to "Sub-Region" and the EEZs of the Contracting parties. The membership of CSRP consists of Cape Verde, the Gambia, Guinea, Guinea Bissau, Mauritania and Senegal. The Convention covers all fishery resources within its area of competence. The main objective of the Commission is to harmonize the long-term policies of member States in the preservation, conservation and exploitation of the fisheries resources for the benefit of their respective populations. The Commission consists of the Conference of Ministers, the Coordinating Committee, and the Permanent Secretariat. The Conakry Convention concerning determination of conditions for foreign access to exploitation of the living resources in off-shore areas of CSRP Member States was signed by the Commission's member States in 1989.

(iii) **Regional Fisheries Committee for the Gulf of Guinea (Comité régional des pêches du Golfe de Guinée)(COREP)**

111.   The Regional Fisheries Committee for the Gulf of Guinea was established by the Convention Concerning the Regional Development of Fisheries in the Gulf of Guinea, signed at Libreville, Gabon on 21 June 1984. The area of competence of the Committee is defined as the Central and Southern Gulf of Guinea. The species covered by the Committee are all living resources within its area of competence. The Convention is open for signature and accession to States bordering the Gulf of Guinea. the present members are Congo, Gabon, Sao Tome and Principe, and Zaire.

112.   The main objectives of the Convention *inter alia* are (i) determine a concerted attitude towards the activities of foreign fishing vessels and give priority to the needs of fishing vessels originating from member countries; (ii) harmonize the national regulations with a view to having a unified regulation fixing the conditions of fishing and the control of fishing operations in the area covered by the Convention, and (iii) collect the maximum scientific, technical and economic data on fishing operations. The organs of the Committee are the Council of Ministers and the Secretariat. The Secretariat is based in Libreville, Gabon. To support the Committee, the EC is funding specific projects established in each of the member countries as well as some sub-regional activities.

(iv) **Ministerial Conference on Fisheries Cooperation Among African States Bordering the Atlantic**

113.   A Ministerial Conference on Fisheries Cooperating Among African States Bordering the Atlantic Ocean was held form 30 March to 1 April 1989 in Rabat, Morocco. The Conference unanimously adopted the Rabat Declaration which referred to the common will of all the States of the region to strengthen and develop their fisheries cooperation namely in the fields of assessment and conservation of fisheries resources as well as the promotion of marine scientific research; development of fisheries production and land infrastructure; marketing of fishing products; enhancement of vocational and technical training; solidarity with land locked and other geographically disadvantaged African States; and all other actions likely to contribute to the development of the fisheries sector in the region. The Regional Convention on Fisheries Cooperation Among African States Bordering the Atlantic Ocean was adopted at the Second Session of the Ministerial Conference in Dakar, Senegal on 5 July 1991.

114.   The objectives of this Convention are: (a) to promote an active and organized cooperation in the area of fisheries management and development in the Region; (b) to take up the challenge of food self-sufficiency through the rational utilization of fishery resources within the context of an integrated approach that would embrace all the components of the fishing sector; (c) to stimulate the national economic sectors through the direct and secondary effects resulting from fishery resources exploitation, bearing in mind the importance of the fisheries sector in the economic, social and nutritional development process of the people of the Region; (d) to enhance, coordinate and harmonize their efforts and capabilities for the purpose of conserving, exploiting, upgrading and marketing fishery resources, considering in particular fish stocks occurring within the waters under the sovereignty or jurisdiction of more than one Party; and (e) to reinforce solidarity with African land-locked States and geographically disadvantaged States of the Region. The institutional framework of the Convention comprises the Conference of Ministers, the Bureau and the Secretariat. The

Conference of Ministers is the governing and decision-making body with respect to fisheries cooperation among the Parties. The Bureau is the coordinating organ of the Conference of Ministers and the Secretariat is the executive organ.

VI) Management Measures and their Implementation

115.   There are highly migratory species, a few straddling stocks and a number of shared stocks in the CECAF region. While the management of tuna and tuna-like species is the responsibility of ICCAT, there is no fishery body in the region with management advisory mechanism in relation to straddling and shared stocks. The two sub-regional bodies are well placed to execute management measures at sub-regional level. The Western Gulf of Guinea remains without a sub-regional body. The Ministerial Conference has the political power to execute management measures at regional level. The future restructuring of CECAF should take account of the existing bodies in the region. A mechanism by which management issues are properly addressed and management measures are adopted is needed in the region.

VII) Proposed Options

a) Transforming the Existing Committee into a Scientific Commission by an Agreement concluded under Article XIV of the FAO Constitution with an Autonomous Budget

116.   Under this option, FAO in consultation with the members of the Committee and other fishery organizations in the region, could conclude an agreement under Article XIV of the Organization's Constitution to establish a commission which could be financed entirely by members' contributions. The new body could become purely a scientific and technical commission providing conservation and management advice to its members as well as to the fishery organizations in the region. The functions and activities of the new commission would be very similar to those of ICES in the North Atlantic.

b) Transforming CECAF into a Management Body under Article XIV of the FAO Constitution with an Autonomous Budget

117.   An Agreement could be concluded under Article XIV of the FAO Constitution to establish a fishery commission to replace the present Committee. The new commission would be financed by the members and could have management powers similar to those of IOTC.

c) Establishing an Independent Commission to Replace CECAF

118.   It would also be possible, if CECAF members so wished, to replace CECAF with an independent fishery commission. In this case, a Conference of Plenipotentiaries would establish a new body under an international agreement. Serious considerations should, however, be given to the existing management bodies in the region and the possible future management functions of the new body. The agreement would provide detail provisions concerning the functions, activities and powers of the new commission.

(5)   Western Central Atlantic Fishery Commission (WECAFC)

I)   Present Structure of WECAFC

119.   WECAFC was established by the Council under Article VI.1 of the FAO constitution. The area covered by the Commission is all marine waters of the Western Central Atlantic Ocean (FAO Statistical Areas 31 and part of 41). Membership of WECAFC is open to all Member Nations and Associate Members of FAO. The Commission and its subsidiary bodies are financed and administered by the Organization. The purpose of the Commission is to promote the optimum utilization of the living aquatic resources of the Western Central Atlantic by the proper management and development of the fisheries and fishing operations. The terms of reference of the Commission include:

(a) to keep under review the state of these resources and of the industries based on them;

(b) to promote the collection, interchange, dissemination and analysis or study of statistical socio-economic, biological and environmental data and other marine fishery information;

(c) to establish the scientific basis for regulatory measures leading to the conservation and management of marine fishery resources, to formulate such measures through subsidiary bodies, as required, and to make appropriate recommendations for the adoption and implementation of these measures;

(d) to encourage, recommend and coordinate training and extension activities in all aspects of marine fisheries; and

(e) to assist Member Governments in formulating programmes to be implemented through international aid sources to achieve the objectives described in (a), (b), (c), (d), above.

The Commission's subsidiary bodies are:

(i) Committee for the Development and Management of Fisheries in the Lesser Antilles

(ii) Working Party on Assessment of Marine Fishery Resources

(iii) Working Party on Fishery Economics and Planning

II)   Considerations

120.   The area covered by WECAFC is one of the most diverse area in terms of cultural, economical and political structures and backgrounds regarding its members. This diversity is, inevitably, reflected in their policies and approach to fisheries matters. According to FAO, the total amount of fish landed from the Western Central Atlantic (FAO Statistical Area 31) in 1994 was 2,241,379 mt, including the catches by DWFNs. In 1993, the island nations in the region (with the exception of Cuba) had limited landings while the United States, the Central and Latin American members of WECAFC and the DWFNs with well developed fisheries sector, were the main beneficiaries of the resources of the high seas.[24]

---

[24]   FAO Yearbook, Fishery Statistics, Catches and Landings, Vol. 76, 1993, pp. 95-97.

121.   Flying fish, dolphin fish, the Atlantic sailfish, the white marlin, the blue marlin and the king mackerel occur as straddling stocks in the Western Central Atlantic. Stock assessment, data collection and other information in the EEZs of many WECAFC members are patchy and incomplete. There is an urgent need for such studies as well as closer collaboration among the Commission's members on these subjects. At present, there is no mechanism through which the requirements of 1995 UN Agreement on Straddling Fish Stocks and Highly Migratory Fish Stocks can be implemented in that region. Only in the Lesser Antilles an attempt was made (1986) to examine and identify the shared fishery resources. Further studies to update that work and to assess the shared stocks in other areas covered by WECAFC are badly needed.

122.   There is a lack of coordination concerning fisheries activities of the existing organizations in the region. Extensive collaboration between WECAFC and ICCAT, CARICOM, OECS and OLDEPESCA is necessary to focus on common interests in the fisheries of the region in order to identify and promote better conservation and management of the fisheries resources in the region. At its last session (Caracas, Venezuela, November 1995), the Commission's Members discussed the role of WECAFC and requested the Secretariat of the Commission to prepare a comprehensive report on this subject.

123.   At the last session of COFI (Rome, March 1995), some delegations requested FAO to consider the reactivation of WECAFC in the interest of more adequately meeting the fishery needs of the member countries, especially those of small island States and developing countries. At its last session (Caracas, Venezuela, November 1995), WECAFC extensively discussed its role and delegates agreed that the decision on the future of WECAFC would have to be made by members at the political level because of the obligations and commitments that might be involved. The Commission recommended that FAO conduct a comprehensive assessment of the situation of fisheries in the region in respect of the future role of the Commission and the prospects for enhancing regional cooperation in the region. Based on a thorough review of the regional and subregional fishery sector, the study should:

- identify the main obstacles to and opportunities for fisheries development, and present the strategic regional and subregional management option;

- identify the main areas for possible cooperation among the countries of the WECAFC region;

- identify organizations, arrangements and mechanisms available to address adequately the cooperation issues identified;

- elaborate possible proposals for the future structure and mandate of WECAFC based on analysis of the identified regional cooperation issues and mechanisms;

- present cost estimates of the functioning of WECAFC for each of the proposals.

III)   **Proposed Options**

a)   **Restructuring WECAFC under Article VI.1**

124.   FAO, in consultation with WECAFC members, could revise the terms of reference of the Commission. More emphasis could be placed on stock assessments, data collections

and research programmes, particularly in relation to shared stocks, straddling stocks and highly migratory fish stocks. A regional project on shared stocks in the WECAFC region could be prepared by FAO for submission to donor agencies. The Commission could intensify its role to promote cooperation and collaboration on fisheries matters among its members and the existing regional organizations. The work of the Commission could become of a purely scientific and technical nature. Active support by its members is essential while FAO should increase its technical support for the Commission, so it can hold its sessions regularly and carry out its intersessional activities in accordance with its terms of reference.

125.   In restructuring WECAFC, the Committee for the Development and Management of Fisheries in the Lesser Antilles, could be promoted to an Article XIV commission. This commission could have management powers and financed by its members.

b)   **Transforming WECAFC to a Management Body under Article XIV of the FAO Constitution**

126.   The second option could be to promote WECAFC to a management body under Article XIV of the FAO Constitution. The new commission could have management powers and be financed by its members. In this case, the Committee for the Lesser Antilles could become a commission under Article XIV as proposed in the preceding paragraph, or remain as a subsidiary body of the new commission.

c)   **To Establish an Independent Body to Replace WECAFC**

127.   It would also be possible to replace WECAFC with a new independent fishery commission. FAO should consult the WECAFC members on the possibilities of establishing an independent commission under an international agreement.

IV)   **Financial Implications to the Organization**

128.   If WECAFC is to function properly and effectively as an FAO body, the Organization will have to increase its technical and if possible financial support. Thus the technical/scientific support by the Organization will have to be increased in order to enable WECAFC to function properly. Members of WECAFC should also undertake to actively support the Commission and participate in its work.

(6)   **Regional Fisheries Advisory Commission for the Southwest Atlantic (CARPAS)**

I)   **Present Structure**

129.   CARPAS was established by a Resolution of the FAO Conference in 1961. The area covered by the Commission is the Southwest Atlantic and inland waters of member States (Part of FAO Statistical Area 41). Membership is restricted to FAO Member Nations which belong to the American Continent and have coasts bordering on the Western Atlantic Ocean South of the Equator. The Commission is financed and administered by FAO. Its terms of reference are to promote fuller use of the marine resources in the Western South Atlantic in accordance with Sound economic and scientific principles; to coordinate studies, research and techniques; and to determine common needs.

The Commission has the following subsidiary bodies:

(i) Working Party on Fisheries Statistics

(ii) Ad Hoc Working Party on Fishery Economic Development in the Southern Atlantic

(iii) Working Party on Biological Research and Evaluation of Fishery Resources

II)   Considerations

130.   CARPAS has not been active since 1974.

III)   Proposed Options

a)   Reviving the Commission under Article VI.1

131.   FAO could consult CARPAS members (Argentina, Brazil and Uruguay) with a view of reviving this body with new terms of reference and structure under Article VI.1 of the FAO Constitution.

b)   Transforming the Commission to an Article XIV Body

132.   FAO, in consultation with CARPAS members, could prepare an agreement under Article XIV of the Organization's Constitution for the establishment of a commission for the conservation and management of the region to replace CARPAS. The new body, with autonomous budget, could have management powers similar to those of IOTC.

c)   Establishing an Independent Body

133.   FAO could initiate consultation with CARPAS members with a view of exploring the possibilities of establishing a new independent fisheries commission to replace CARPAS.

[...]

ANNEX II: SHARED STOCKS IN THE AREAS COVERED BY FAO REGIONAL FISHERY BODIES

1.   **IOFC**

- ▶ **Red Sea:** All large scombrids; probably most small clupeoids and carangids but this will depend on the location of the stocks as those most affected will be those near maritime boundaries. But nothing is known (or at least documented) about stocks structure of small pelagics in the Red Sea. Areas of special concern are most likely to be handled on a bilateral or multilateral basis, eg, head of gulf of Eilat/Aqaba; head of Gulf migration could e handled by a series of bilateral treaties.

- ▶ **North West Arabian Sea:** Myctophids: Iran (Islamic Rep. of) and Oman and possibly UAE; also maybe Pakistan, Yemen and India but not essential. Tunas, Tunalike species already covered by IOTC. Scomberoids covered by Tuna Commission ? If not then Iran (Islamic Rep. of), Oman, UAE and Pakistan. Possibly Yemen and India.

- ▶ **Gulf of Aden:** Small pelagics: Yemen, Somalia, possibly Djibouti.

- ▶ **Persian Gulf:** Some shrimp, most large demersals (eg, serranids, breams, etc.) some small pelagics, large pelagics.

2.   **CECAF**

For CECAF, the following shared stocks (for which evaluation exists) and countries concerned are listed.

▶	Sardinella aurita:	Morocco, Mauritania, Senegal, The Gambia
▶	Trachurus trachurus:	Morocco, Mauritania, Senegal, The Gambia
▶	Scomber japonicus:	Morocco, Mauritania
▶	Cephalopods/cuttlefish:	Guinea, Guinea Bissau, Sierra Leone
▶	Small pelagics:	Western and Central Gulf of Guinea
▶	Scomber japonicus:	Western and Central Gulf of Guinea
▶	Demersal resources:	Western and Central Gulf of Guinea
▶	Sardinella aurita and S. maderensis:	Congo and Gabon
▶	Trachurus trecae:	Congo and Gabon

3.   **WECAFC**

1) Bilateral

Shrimp for Venezuela and Trinidad. There are also moves towards spiny lobster between Cuba and Bahamas. The penaid shrimp of the Gulf of Mexico (US/Mexico).

There are probably several groundfish stocks, such as the snappers and groupers, which are shared between two or a small number of states in the region. There is not much information, at this stage, on stock identity of such species in the region.

2) Subregional

The shrimp resources of the Guyanas-Brazil continental shelf are the topic of a WECAFC ad hoc Working Group and are an obvious example of a sub-regionally shared stock, along with many of the groundfish species that occur in the same area. The flying fish resource of the Lesser Antilles is supporting a growing fishery in the southeastern Caribbean. Other less abundant small pelagics may also justify consideration.

Again, several of the groundfish species may justify sub-regional management.

Caribbean spiny lobster is an important and widely distributed species in the region. Major producers include Cuba, USA, Nicaragua and Honduras. Again, the stock structure is not well understood. Adult distribution would certainly suggest shared stocks, but widespread distribution and movement of larvae could result in sub-regional or even regional distribution of a single stock.

3) Regional and extra-regional

The group referred to within WECAFC as "coastal pelagics" require regional approaches to management. These include Atlantic Spanish mackerel and king mackerel, blackfin tuna and dolphinfish.

4.   GFCM

1) Bilateral arrangements

Sardine stocks of the Sea of Alboran between Morocco and Spain are already covered by EC agreements. Internally to the EC, similar arrangements apply to internal seas, such as the Gulf of Lions for groundfish.

2) Subregional arrangements

Special management regime for groundfish. Notable here are the Gulf of Gabes and Straits of Sicily (Tunisia, Libya, Malta and Italy), the Adriatic and Northern Ionian Seas (Italy, Albania, Craotia, Greece, Slovenia and possibly Montenegro ?), and the Black Sea.

3) Regional and extra-regional

Bluefin tuna is the most noteworthy resource that spawns in the Mediterranean and extends into the Atlantic. ICCAT has data and maps on this species. Swordfish can probably be regarded as a regional resource, as can Bonito and minor pelagics such as Dolphin fish.

5.   **APFIC**

Eastern Indian Ocean (Area 57)

(1)   tuna and tuna-like fishes. This area falls within the coverage of the proposed IOTC, therefore, those resources (including small tunas) may well be covered by IOTC.

(2)   round scads (Decapterus spp.): some shared stocks have been identified include:
          ▶ Sri Lanka - Southern part of India
          ▶ Malaka Strait (Thailand-Malaysia-Indonesia)

(3)   chub mackerel (Rastrelliger spp.):
          ▶ Malaka Strait (Thailand, Malaysia, Indonesia)
          ▶ Andaman Sea (Myanmare, Thailand)
          ▶ Bay of Bengal (Sri Lanka, India, Bangladesh, Myanmare)

(4)   Hilsa toli
          ▶ India-Bangladesh, Myanmar

Western Central Pacific (Area 71):

(1)   tuna and tuna-like fishes: Philippines and Indonesia. SEAFDEC may facilitate for such an initiative with a close cooperation with SPC/FFA.

(2)   chub mackerel (Rastrelliger spp.):
          ▶ Southern Gulf of Thailand (Thialand, Cambodia, Vietnam)
          ▶ Eastern Gulf of Thailand (Thailand, Cambodia, Vietnam)
          ▶ Gulf of Tonkin (Vietnam and southern China)
          ▶ Southern part of South China Sea (Indonesia, East Malaysia)
          ▶ Sulu Sea (Indonesia, Philippines)

(3)   round scads (Decapterus spp.)
          ▶ Gulf of Thailand (Malaysia, Thailand, Cambodia, Vietnam)
          ▶ Gulf of Tonkin (Vietnam and China)
          ▶ Southern part of SCS (Indonesia, Malaysia)
          ▶ Sulu Sea (Indonesia, Philippines)

(4)   no study has yet been made on the potential shared resources between Indonesia and Australia in the Arafura Sea. However, potential shared resources include: sharks, roundscads, jacks, etc. Good cooperation between the two countries in fisheries in recent years may lead to such joint management in the future.

[...]

INTERNATIONAL ATOMIC ENERGY AGENCY
(IAEA)

DOCUMENTS REPRODUCED IN WHOLE OR IN PART:

IAEA GENERAL CONFERENCE

IAEA PRESS RELEASES

DOCUMENTS NOT REPRODUCED:

See List of Publications in 1996 contained in No.1 *supra*.

1. IAEA ANNUAL REPORT FOR 1996*

Doc. no.: GC(41)/8

Date: July 1997

MEMBER STATES OF THE INTERNATIONAL ATOMIC ENERGY AGENCY

AFGHANISTAN
ALBANIA
ALGERIA
ARGENTINA
ARMENIA
AUSTRALIA
AUSTRIA
BANGLADESH
BELARUS
BELGIUM
BOLIVIA
BOSNIA AND
 HERZEGOVINA
BRAZIL
BULGARIA
CAMBODIA
CAMEROON
CANADA
CHILE
CHINA
COLOMBIA
COSTA RICA
COTE D'IVOIRE
CROATIA
CUBA
CYPRUS
CZECH REPUBLIC
DEMOCRATIC REPUBLIC
 OF CONGO
DENMARK
DOMINICAN REPUBLIC
ECUADOR

EGYPT
EL SALVADOR
ESTONIA
ETHIOPIA
FINLAND
FRANCE
GABON
GEORGIA
GERMANY
GHANA
GREECE
GUATEMALA
HAITI
HOLY SEE
HUNGARY
ICELAND
INDIA
INDONESIA
IRAN, ISLAMIC REPUBLIC OF
IRAQ
IRELAND
ISRAEL
ITALY
JAMAICA
JAPAN
JORDAN
KAZAKSTAN
KENYA
KOREA, REPUBLIC OF
KUWAIT
LATVIA
LEBANON

LIBERIA
LIBYAN ARAB JAMAHIRIYA
LIECHTENSTEIN
LITHUANIA
LUXEMBOURG
MADAGASCAR
MALAYSIA
MALI
MARSHALL ISLANDS
MAURITIUS
MEXICO
MONACO
MONGOLIA
MOROCCO
MYANMAR
NAMIBIA
NETHERLANDS
NEW ZEALAND
NICARAGUA
NIGER
NIGERIA
NORWAY
PAKISTAN
PANAMA
PARAGUAY
PERU
PHILIPPINES
POLAND
PORTUGAL
QATAR
ROMANIA
RUSSIAN FEDERATION

* Only Contents, pages 1-6, 13-16 and 107-117 are reproduced here.

SAUDI ARABIA	SYRIAN ARAB REPUBLIC	UNITED REPUBLIC
SENEGAL	THAILAND	OF TANZANIA
SIERRA LEONE	THE FORMER YUGOSLAV	UNITED STATES
SINGAPORE	REPUBLIC OF MACEDONIA	OF AMERICA
SLOVAKIA	TUNISIA	URUGUAY
SLOVENIA	TURKEY	UZBEKISTAN
SOUTH AFRICA	UGANDA	VENEZUELA
SPAIN	UKRAINE	VIET NAM
SRI LANKA	UNITED ARAB EMIRATES	YEMEN
SUDAN	UNITED KINGDOM OF	YUGOSLAVIA
SWEDEN	GREAT BRITAIN AND	ZAMBIA
SWITZERLAND	NORTHERN IRELAND	ZIMBABWE

The Agency's Statute was approved on 23 October 1956 by the Conference on the Statute of the IAEA held at United Nations Headquarters, New York; it entered into force on 29 July 1957. The Headquarters of the Agency are situated in Vienna. Its principal objective is "to accelerate and enlarge the contribution of atomic energy to peace, health and prosperity throughout the world".

Note

1. All sums of money are expressed in United States dollars.

2. The designations employed and the presentation of material in this document do not imply the expression of any opinion whatsoever on the part of the Secretariat concerning the legal status of any country or territory or of its authorities, or concerning the delimitation of its frontiers.

3. The mention of names of specific companies or products (whether or not indicated as registered) does not imply any intention to infringe proprietary rights, nor should it be construed as an endorsement or recommendation on the part of the Agency.

4. The term "non-nuclear-weapon State" is used as in the Final Document of the 1968 Conference of Non-Nuclear-Weapon States (United Nations document A/7277) and in the Treaty on the Non-Proliferation of Nuclear Weapons.

5. Further information on the Agency's activities can be obtained from the Division of Public Information and from the Agency's Internet home page (http://www.iaea.or.at) on the World Wide Web.

CONTENTS

PREFACE

The Agency's approved 1996 programme was implemented for the most part as planned. Additionally, with the assistance of extrabudgetary funding, the Agency responded to unanticipated requirements such as the radiological assessments of nuclear test sites and the provision of advice on physical protection.

Progress was made in important areas including extension of the model project concept in technical co-operation, the introduction of measures for the strengthening of safeguards and the implementation of new procedures for the preparation and review of safety standards. Advances took place in the negotiation of new legal instruments relating to nuclear safety, the safety of spent fuel and waste management, liability and safeguards.

An Integrated Approach to Technical Co-operation

Recent initiatives such as model projects, country programme frameworks (CPFs) and thematic/sectoral planning became increasingly central to technical co-operation activities in 1996. An additional 36 model projects were approved, many of them based on CPFs. The financial implementation of the technical co-operation programme remained at a high level, with a satisfactory balance of resources at the end of the year (equivalent to about two months of new obligations).

One of the largest ever technical co-operation projects, covering radiation and waste safety, progressed significantly during the year. This project will eventually

---

Box 1

MODEL PROJECT ON UPGRADING RADIATION AND WASTE SAFETY INFRASTRUCTURES

The use of nuclear energy and the applications of radiation and radioactive substances have become a widespread and integral part of such diverse sectors as power generation, health care, industrial diagnostics and quality control, and research in the physical, chemical and agricultural sciences. The production, use, storage and disposal of radiation sources must be carried out in such a way that the risks to people and the environment are minimized and the appropriate national infrastructures need to be at an adequate level.

An interregional model project has adopted a new approach to upgrading radiation safety infrastructures in Member States. Action plans tailored to each Member State have been prepared, as have standardized draft texts which can serve as a basis for the formulation of national laws and regulations which are in accordance with the *International Basic Safety Standards for Protection against Ionizing Radiation and for the Safety of Radiation Sources* (BSS). The plans include both generic and specific activities. Generic activities apply to all countries and as a first priority cover a system of notification, authorization and subsequent control of all radioactive sources, whatever their use, within the country. By the end of 1996, more than 90% of the participating countries had officially endorsed their action plans. The target is for most, if not all, participating countries to comply with the BSS by the year 2000.

---

cover some 50 developing countries and will help develop national legislation and practices in this area to an acceptable level by the year 2000 (*see Box 1*).

Nuclear Techniques and Water Resources Development

Isotope hydrology techniques, with unique capabilities for tracing and mapping water resources essential for sustainable development, were used in a recently completed project in the Moyale region in southern Ethiopia. Covering 45 000 km^2, this region, which has three million inhabitants and one of the largest cattle herds on the continent, depends entirely on scarce groundwater resources. Isotope data were used to distinguish between renewable and non-renewable water resources, leading to better estimates of the total sustainable capacity for meeting water needs.

Eradication of the Tsetse Fly

Under a model project in Zanzibar, United Republic of Tanzania, to eradicate the tsetse fly, the last wild fly was captured in September with no detections since then. Improved techniques for the rearing of flies were passed on during the year to the tsetse production facility in Tanga, United Republic of Tanzania.

Therapeutic Applications of Radiopharmaceuticals

Priority continued to be given to the use of nuclear techniques and materials in treatment strategies against cancer. The Agency carried out a unique therapeutic clinical study to compare the use of phosphorus-32 and

strontium-89 in the palliation treatment of bone pain from cancer metastases (*see Box 2*).

Moscow Summit

A Summit on Nuclear Safety and Security was held in Moscow in April. The participants — the G7 countries and the Russian Federation — stressed the importance of nuclear power as an energy source consistent with the goal of sustainable development, commitment to an international nuclear safety culture, strengthening of the Agency's safeguards system, and the need to combat trafficking in nuclear materials. The Agency provided background material for the meeting.

Nuclear Safety

The Agency's nuclear safety efforts are focused on establishing an international infrastructure with three main elements — basic binding conventions, recommended standards and advisory services, and technical assistance. Within the Secretariat, these activities became the charge of a separate Department. In addition, the various advisory groups in which Member State experts consider draft international safety standards and guides were strengthened and reorganized.

Nuclear Liability Convention

The Standing Committee on Liability for Nuclear Damage reached the final stage of preparatory work on a draft protocol to amend the 1963 Vienna Convention and a draft convention on supplementary funding. At its

---

Box 2

PALLIATION OF CANCER BONE PAIN AT REDUCED COST

The primary aim of cancer treatment is to cure. This is not always achievable, especially when the disease is advanced. In such situations, the goal of treatment is to provide a certain measure of physical and mental comfort, promote self-reliance to the extent possible and preserve the dignity of the individual during the remaining period of life. Relieving pain therefore has an important place in the care of cancer patients, since pain is one of the most common symptoms in patients with advanced cancer.

Bone pain is the most usual form of pain in patients with cancer of the breast, prostate, lung, thyroid and colon which has invaded the bone. The cause is expanding lesions in the bone. Of the available treatments designed to shrink the cancer deposits in bones and relieve pain, such as chemotherapy, X ray irradiation and radio-pharmaceutical administration, the last alternative is the one widely accepted as being the most effective and least toxic, especially in cases where the pain sites are numerous and widespread.

There are only a few radiopharmaceuticals which are suitable and available for clinical applications. Phosphorus-32 has been in use for some time, but strontium-89, a recent arrival on the clinical practice scene, has received wide publicity. However, it is also four to six times more expensive than phosphorus-32. This is significant, since cost is a serious obstacle to the widespread use of radiopharmaceuticals for alleviating bone pain in cancer patients, especially in developing countries.

Following an Advisory Group meeting, the Agency initiated a CRP with the specific aim of comparing the efficacy and toxicity of phosphorus-32 with that of strontium-89 in the treatment of cancer induced bone pain. This CRP, designed as a multicentre, randomized and controlled investigation, was the first therapeutic clinical study co-ordinated by the Agency and is the only one of its kind known in the world. Five countries — Austria, India, Indonesia, Slovenia and Peru — participated in this project, which involved 110 patients. The study was completed in 1996 and the results will be known in April 1997 when the final Research Co-ordination meeting is held.

---

session in October, the full texts of the two instruments were prepared and the Committee agreed to refer the texts to governments for detailed scrutiny.

Conventions on Safety

The Convention on Nuclear Safety entered into force on 24 October. While recognizing that national authorities have responsibility for the safety of nuclear power plants, the Convention lays down a number of fundamental safety principles. It also establishes a procedure under which the parties are obliged to submit reports on the safety of nuclear power plants on their territory and accept review of these reports at meetings of the Contracting Parties.

Negotiations on a convention covering the safety of spent fuel and waste management continued to make progress. The sixth session of the open ended group of legal and technical experts was held in November in Pilansberg at the invitation of the South African Government.

Operational Safety Services

The deterioration of spent fuel from research reactors is a new area of concern. In this context, a team consisting

of technical experts from the Agency, France, the Russian Federation and the USA visited the Vinča reactor near Belgrade. Two specific problems were identified that warranted prompt remedial action; a report was trans-mitted to the authorities concerned.

Consequences of the Chernobyl Accident

On the tenth anniversary of the Chernobyl accident the Agency, the European Commission and WHO co-sponsored an international conference to consolidate the various technical and scientific assessments that have been made over the years (*see Box 3*).

Radiological Assessments of Nuclear Test Sites

An assessment of the Semipalatinsk nuclear test site in Kazakstan provided assurance that radiation levels in villages around the site are very low. However, it was also concluded that lengthy human occupation of the test site itself would lead to unacceptably high radiation doses and the authorities of Kazakstan have been advised to take steps to clean up the site or prevent access to it. A report will be published in 1997.

Box 3

**INTERNATIONAL CONFERENCE ON THE CONSEQUENCES OF
THE CHERNOBYL ACCIDENT**

On the tenth anniversary of the Chernobyl accident the Agency, the European Commission and WHO co-sponsored an international conference chaired by Minister Angela Merkel of Germany to 'sum up' the results of the various assessments made and the specialized meetings held on the consequences of the accident. It attracted the participation of over 800 experts from some 70 countries. There was a consensus on the early health effects clinically attributable to radiation exposure as a result of the accident. It was also confirmed that:

• There was a significant increase in the incidence of thyroid cancer among children;

• There was no increase in the incidence of any other malignancies or hereditary effects that could be attributed to the accident;

• In the population affected by the accident there was a high incidence of psychological disorders which could not, however, be related to radiation exposure and were difficult to distinguish from effects associated with the economic and social hardship being experienced in the regions;

• No sustained severe impacts on ecosystems had so far been observed.

Officials from the affected countries reported to the conference on the severe economic, social and institutional consequences of the accident. At the technical level it was agreed that renewed attention must be paid to the 'sarcophagus' around the destroyed reactor.

An assessment was carried out of the radiological situation on Bikini Atoll in the Marshall Islands. A final report is being prepared. Another study of conditions at the Mururoa and Fangataufa Atolls in French Polynesia was initiated. Specifically, a sampling expedition was carried out to study the spatial distribution of radionuclides; the water, biota and sediment samples taken are currently being analysed. The radioactive materials remaining in the deep geological structure and their possible transfer to the biosphere are also being studied.

Nuclear Power and Fuel Cycle

Experts from Member States and international nuclear organizations commenced preparation of key issue papers for the symposium on Nuclear Fuel Cycle and Reactor Strategy: Adjusting to New Realities, to be held in June 1997. The papers will provide background for discussions on the different options for development of the fuel cycle, the management of spent fuel and plutonium and the disposal of radioactive wastes.

Producing Potable Water Economically

The availability of potable water is an emerging issue in many Member States. A two year programme, with the aim of selecting a set of practical options for demonstration projects in seawater desalination using nuclear energy, was completed (*see Box 4*).

Demonstration of Predisposal Waste Management

Agreements were finalized for the establishment of a reference centre for demonstration of predisposal waste management methods and procedures at the Çekmece Nuclear Research and Training Centre in Turkey, and a first demonstration took place in early 1996. Participants from Albania, Greece, the Syrian Arab Republic and Turkey attended this exercise, which dealt with the collection, segregation and treatment of liquid waste, the conditioning of solid low level waste and spent sealed sources, and interim storage. A reference centre for Latin America was also established at a nuclear research establishment in Chile.

Co-operation in Radioactive Waste Management

A Contact Expert Group was formally established in 1996 under Agency auspices to harmonize and follow up on co-operative activities between the Russian Federation and other States in the field of radioactive waste management. The Group currently numbers 11 full members and 3 observers. A list of co-operative projects being implemented or planned was prepared.

Nuclear-Weapon-Free Zones

Two new treaties were signed in 1996 with a view to establishing nuclear-weapon-free zones (NWFZs) in Africa and South East Asia. Both treaties entrust the Agency with the

---

Box 4

NUCLEAR SEAWATER DESALINATION

In the 'Options Identification Programme', which was requested by a resolution of the 38th session of the General Conference and was completed in 1996, the list of available reactors was reviewed in order to identify practical options for the demonstration of seawater desalination using nuclear energy. Consideration was also given to the desalination technologies suitable for coupling to a nuclear reactor. The scheduling, infrastructure and investment requirements were taken into account.

As a result of the screening process, three options were identified as practical candidates that could be recommended for demonstration. (The details were published in IAEA-TECDOC-898, *Options Identification Programme for Demonstration of Nuclear Desalination*.) These options use well proven water cooled reactors and desalination technologies.

Option 1: Reverse osmosis (RO) desalination in combination with a medium size nuclear power reactor of a type now being constructed or at the advanced design stage.

Option 2: Reverse osmosis desalination in combination with a currently operating (preferably medium size) reactor (some minor design modifications may be required to the periphery of the existing nuclear system).

Option 3: Multi-effect distillation (MED) desalination in combination with a small reactor for capacities of up to 80 000 m^3/d.

It was concluded that these demonstration options could be implemented if there is interest from investors. The investment required would be in the order of $25–50 million for the RO options and $200–300 million for the MED option, the latter including the cost of the reactor.

---

task of verifying compliance with the peaceful use undertakings of the signatories. The Pelindaba Treaty, signed in Cairo in April, goes further than earlier NWFZ accords and the Treaty on the Non-Proliferation of Nuclear Weapons (NPT) in that it addresses issues such as prohibition of armed attack on nuclear installations and the possibility of hitherto undeclared nuclear explosive devices. In meeting the specific interests of the region, the South East Asian NWFZ treaty, signed in Bangkok in December, requires the Parties to comply not only with their non-proliferation obligations, but also with commitments in such areas as nuclear trade, nuclear safety and radioactive waste management.

Verification and Disarmament

In the USA, the Agency has been engaged since 1994 in the verification of nuclear material removed from weapon programmes. This material includes separated plutonium and high enriched uranium. At a trilateral meeting of the Russian Minister of Atomic Energy, the US Secretary of Energy and the Director General in September, it was agreed to explore the technical, legal and financial issues connected with the verification of such material in both the USA and the Russian Federation.

Comprehensive Test Ban Treaty

In September, the Comprehensive Test Ban Treaty (CTBT) was adopted by the General Assembly of the United Nations. The Preparatory Commission of the CTBT Organization (CTBTO), responsible for the verification of compliance by States Parties to the Treaty, held its first session in November in New York. Preliminary discussions took place about possible future co-operation between the Agency and the Provisional Secretariat for the CTBTO.

Strengthening of Safeguards

Progress was made in the introduction of measures to strengthen the effectiveness and increase the efficiency of Agency safeguards (programme '93+2', Part 1). In February, the 'Clean Laboratory' at the Agency's Safeguards Analytical Laboratory in Seibersdorf was commissioned and work on introducing environmental sampling as a standard safeguards measure was started. Baseline environmental samples from enrichment plants and hot cells were collected in a large number of States.

Additional information required for the measures relating to States' systems of accounting for and control of

---

Box 5

REMOTE MONITORING FOR SAFEGUARDS

One element of the Agency's continuing efforts to strengthen and improve the efficiency of the safeguards system is the introduction of new procedures and technologies to reduce the frequency of on-site inspections. In this regard, the use of remote monitoring technologies is expected to provide a significant opportunity for Agency safeguards to provide the required level of assurance with less intrusion on facility operators.

A variety of advanced unattended systems for remote monitoring and transmission are being examined. These include digital surveillance cameras, electronic seals and radiation detectors which can transmit their information directly by satellite and telephone lines to the Agency. To expedite the early implementation of these technologies, a systematic evaluation of commercially available systems was initiated in 1996 in collaboration with a number of Member States. Other related activities include:

- A field trial of a remote monitoring system installed in a mixed oxide fuel storage vault in Switzerland, which showed that the system was effective in monitoring events of safeguards relevance in near real time. The system is competitive from a cost standpoint with current methods and is suitable for use at other facilities under safeguards.

- Installation and testing of remote monitoring system components at an HEU storage vault in the USA.

- Preparatory work on establishing a remote monitoring system at an HEU storage vault in South Africa.

---

nuclear material, decommissioned and closed down facilities, and fuel cycles was received and analysed. In a related area, a plan for the introduction of remote monitoring was developed (*see Box 5*).

Further strengthening measures, requiring supplementary legal authority (93+2, 'Part 2'), were considered by a committee of the Board of Governors in July and October. Following discussions, the Chairman prepared a "Rolling Text of the Draft Protocol" to provide the necessary legal authority. The text will be considered by the Board in 1997.

The nearly 180 non-nuclear-weapon States now party to the NPT have committed themselves to concluding comprehensive safeguards agreements with the Agency. Nevertheless, over 60 of these States — most of which have no nuclear activities — have yet to do so.

Iraq

The Agency's ongoing monitoring and verification system, which has been in place since August 1994, remained the principal means to deter any effort by Iraq to reconstitute a nuclear weapon oriented programme, and to provide early warning in the event that the nuclear knowledge and know-how still existing in Iraq were to be used for proscribed activities. In parallel with its field work, the Agency's UNSC 687 Action Team continued the analysis

of the vast number of Iraqi documents which were obtained in August 1995 and the assessment of the so-called 'Full, Final and Complete Declaration' — a detailed description of Iraq's past covert nuclear programme — provided by the Iraqi authorities in September.

Democratic People's Republic of Korea

The Agency remained unable to verify the initial declaration of nuclear material made by the Democratic People's Republic of Korea (DPRK). The DPRK was still not in compliance with its safeguards agreement.

The sixth round of technical discussions with the DPRK took place in Vienna in September. No progress was made on important issues, including the preservation of information to enable the Agency to verify in the future the correctness and completeness of the DPRK's initial declaration under its safeguards agreement. The Agency informed the Security Council of the United Nations and the Board of Governors that it cannot provide any assurance that the information required is actually being preserved.

The canning of spent fuel from the 5 MW Experimental Reactor, which began in April, was discontinued at the beginning of November, when about 50% of the fuel rods had been canned.

Trafficking in Nuclear Materials

The database on illicit trafficking incidents, established to provide accurate and timely information to three audiences — Member States, the public and the Agency — became fully functioning and recognized as an authoritative list of incidents verified by Member States. The International Physical Protection Advisory Service (IPPAS) was established to give advice to Member States on improving national nuclear security systems. IPPAS missions were conducted to Bulgaria and Slovenia.

Staffing

In 1981, when the first resolution on the 'Staffing of the Secretariat' was under discussion, a number of Member States proposed that a target of 33% be set for the representation of developing countries among Professional staff. At the end of 1996, 32.9% of the Agency's staff came from developing countries. However, the number of women in the Professional category, even though it had doubled since 1981, stood at only 17.3%.

Efficiency and Management

Despite the limitations on resources, the Agency's programme has expanded over the years to take on new activities. The resources for these new activities have become available both through the phasing out of some programmes and through gains in efficiency. This process continued in 1996 and included systematic, routine evaluations of programme performance to increase efficiency.

[...]

RADIOACTIVE WASTE MANAGEMENT

Regular Budget expenditure: $7 505 404

Expenditure by subprogramme

Handling, treatment, conditioning and storage of radioactive wastes	$854 637
Radioactive waste disposal	$542 571
Decontamination and decommissioning of nuclear installations	$716 536
Radiological and environmental aspects of waste management	$728 910 + $2 606 536 (IAEA-MEL): 3 335 446
Waste management planning and infrastructure	$2 056 214

Extrabudgetary programme resources utilized (not included in chart): $245 078

The Agency's 1996 programme on radioactive waste management focused on: the establishment of international principles and standards for the safe management of wastes; preparations for the convention on the safe management of radioactive waste; development of infrastructures and tools for strengthening and solving waste management problems in developing Member States; and assessing waste management situations and needs as a consequence of past practices. New advisory committees were established to advise the Agency on its activities related to waste technology and safety. The International Radioactive Waste Technology Advisory Committee (WATAC) met for the first time in October to review the 1995–1998 Agency programme in these areas and to facilitate the exchange of information and experience between Member States represented on WATAC. The Waste Safety Standards Advisory Committee (WASSAC) was established to review waste safety documents intended for publication in the Safety Standards series.

Handling, Treatment, Conditioning and Storage of Radioactive Wastes

Progress was made in the preparation of guidance on waste minimization methods applicable at different nuclear facilities. A report completed in 1996 provides a number of different options and technologies for the treatment of boric acid containing waste. These are aimed at the recovery of boric acid from waste streams and its possible reuse.

In co-operation with national authorities, the Agency implemented a training programme with the aim of providing technical expertise to developing Member States in various aspects of radioactive waste management. Incorporating the results of over 20 regional and interregional training courses held between 1991 and 1995, guidance material was prepared for use by Member States in conducting training courses on the management of low and intermediate level waste (LILW). The report covers the requirements for organizing courses, an annotated outline of such courses and a selection of practical exercises and demonstrations.

Two CRPs on fostering research in developing Member States in the field of waste processing technologies for LILW from nuclear applications were concluded in 1996. One CRP on treatment technologies for LILW was designed to help develop reliable, simple and low cost processes for specific institutional waste to be made compatible with long lived radioactive waste forms. A number of new treatment technologies were developed and tested, and are in use in some of the countries that participated in the project. The other CRP dealt with inorganic sorbents that in many cases have been proved to be advantageous in the treatment and immobilization of liquid radioactive waste. Specific properties of synthetic and composite sorbents can be designed and controlled during their synthesis. This facilitates the preparation of a range of sorbents suitable for the treatment of specific waste streams. However, the variety of inorganic sorbents, both natural and synthetic, that are in use worldwide requires the setting up of standardized procedures for comparative evaluation. Several standard testing procedures and sets of reference waste streams were thus developed in the CRP.

Difficulties encountered in the short term in many Member States in the development of disposal facilities

have led to more effort being devoted to the storage of radioactive wastes. A report was prepared to provide guidance on various technological aspects of radioactive waste package storage, and to place storage in the context of the entire waste management process. The report reviews current practices and experience in waste storage, summarizes the various actions required before, during and after interim storage and links various activities involving the storage of radioactive waste.

Radioactive Waste Disposal

At a symposium entitled 'Experience in the Planning and Operation of Low Level Waste Disposal Facilities', held in Vienna in July, it was demonstrated that the majority of the Agency's Member States, while not employing nuclear power, were utilizing nuclear technology in such areas as medicine, industry and research. These applications as a rule produce low level waste (LLW) which has to be managed and disposed of. The symposium showed that LLW disposal is based on proven technologies and the safety of disposal can be satisfactorily ensured over the time periods currently envisaged. It was also pointed out that while developing Member States are looking for adequate, affordable and safe solutions, in developed Member States there is a trend towards increasing technical sophistication.

Radiological and Environmental Aspects of Waste Management

For several years the Agency has organized an annual group forum for the discussion and resolution of outstanding issues related to the disposal of radioactive wastes, mainly the problem of assuring and demonstrating the long term safety of waste repositories. The second report of this group was issued in 1996 and contains discussions on interface issues between nuclear safeguards and radioactive waste management, aspects of the post-closure phase of a repository and the application of the concept of 'radiological optimization' to radioactive waste disposal.

A three year assessment study of the radiological impact of high level radioactive waste dumping in the Arctic seas (the International Arctic Seas Assessment Project (IASAP)) was completed. An executive summary of the study report was presented to the Contracting Parties to the Convention on the Prevention of Marine Pollution by Dumping Of Wastes and Other Matter (the London Convention, 1972). The study examined various aspects of radiological assessment, making use of the results obtained from several exploratory cruises to the affected area. In addition, three-dimensional hydrodynamic and compartmental modelling of dispersal from possible releases of radionuclides from dumped wastes to the open Kara Sea and the Arctic Ocean was carried out by IAEA-MEL. One of the study's conclusions was that the current radiological risks presented by the dumped wastes are negligible and that the future risks to population groups most likely to be exposed are also small. No justification was found on radiological grounds for instituting a programme of remedial action in relation to the wastes. However, a reassessment of the situation was recommended if the current military restrictions over the fjords of Novaya Zemlya, where much of the waste was dumped, are removed.

As a contribution to IASAP, IAEA-MEL verified laboratory experimental approaches to estimating radionuclide coefficients (K_ds) for Kara Sea sediments. Comparisons of field derived and radiotracer derived K_ds values showed that radiotracer techniques used with natural sediments can, under carefully controlled conditions in the laboratory, accurately predict K_ds coefficients that have been measured in far more costly field tests.

Closely related radioecological experiments have determined the potential usefulness of starfish, a common bottom species in the Arctic seas, as bioindicators of americium-241, caesium-137 and cobalt-60 contamination in these waters. Laboratory radiotracer food chain studies demonstrated that starfish can accumulate from 75 to 100% of the radionuclides ingested with their food and can retain them in their tissues for several months.

The analysis of sediment and seawater samples collected during the 1994 and 1995 Japan–Republic of Korea–Russian Federation expeditions to the Far Eastern seas has been completed and a final report issued. The analytical results did not show any effects from the dump sites. Dispersion modelling of possible releases of radionuclides from dumped wastes in the Far Eastern seas was also completed. The results have shown that the turnover time of water in the Far Eastern seas may be about 25 years, which is shorter than expected by a factor of 4. However, the simulated surface water concentrations of caesium-137 released from wastes may reach values an order of magnitude lower than the present environmental levels.

A sampling expedition to the Mururoa and Fangataufa Atolls in French Polynesia was carried out. A new progressive technique based on in situ gamma spectrometry of seabed sediments was used to study the spatial distribution of radionuclides in sediment and to optimize sediment sampling. Hundreds of water, biota and sedi-

ment samples were collected in both lagoons and are being analysed in seven Member State laboratories and at IAEA-MEL.

A Global Marine Radioactivity Database (GLOMARD) was established to provide Member States with information on radioactivity baselines and records for radiological assessments and international and national monitoring programmes. All available data on radionuclide concentrations in the Arctic seas have been included in GLOMARD to study the temporal and spatial distributions of radionuclides. The data show that in recent years the concentrations of strontium-90 and caesium-137 in the Kara and Barents Seas have been decreasing, the dominant contribution being from reprocessing plants and global fallout.

A CRP on the applications of tracer techniques in studies of processes and pollution in the Black Sea was completed. The project resulted in: a comprehensive and up to date assessment of radionuclide distributions, trends, inventories and sources in the Black Sea environment; an evaluation of doses delivered through marine exposure pathways to humans and biota; and the development of applications of radioactive and stable isotope tracers to understand the fate of pollutants in this particularly complex and stressed environment.

Bioassay tests have been designed to examine the possible enhancement of natural radioactivity in marine organisms living in the vicinity of non-nuclear industries. Initial experimental results indicate that polonium-210 in gypsum and other phosphatic wastes from the phosphoric acid industry is bioavailable to marine molluscs exposed to sea water containing such wastes.

Progress was made in 1996 to broaden the funding base for Agency projects focused on the application of nuclear techniques to understand oceanic processes. A subcontract was established under the European Union sponsored Aegean Sea Hydrothermal Fluxes project through which the Agency will use nuclear techniques to examine the potential environmental enhancement of natural radionuclides and trace elements emanating from shallow water hydrothermal vents off Milos Island. Such background data on geochemical sources are important in order to gauge the relative importance of industrial inputs of the same elements to enclosed seas such as the Mediterranean.

Waste Management Planning and Infrastructure

At the request of the French authorities, the Agency convened an international team of experts to review the short lived waste management programme and activities, both planned and implemented, at the Centre de l'Aube. On the basis of source material and a report provided by Andra (Agence nationale pour la gestion des déchets radioactifs, France), the team evaluated the programme and formulated recommendations in several areas such as verification, control and testing, and safety assessment.

A Contact Expert Group (CEG) was established by a number of countries interested in having an international forum for harmonizing and following up co-operation in the area of radioactive waste management in the Russian Federation. The first CEG meeting was held in March 1996 in Moscow. CEG Secretariat services are being provided by the Agency.

The first demonstration of predisposal waste management methods and procedures was held at the Çekmece Nuclear Research and Training Centre in Turkey.

Participants from Albania, Greece, the Syrian Arab Republic and the host country attended this hands-on training session. A regional centre for Latin America has also been established at the Lo Aguierre nuclear research centre in Chile.

Proper assessment of the waste management situation in Member States is necessary in order to prepare adequate work plans for technical co-operation activities. To support these activities, a waste management part in the Country Profile Database was established. This section will complement the corresponding database on radiation protection. Information on more than 20 countries has so far been included.

A team of specialists from Brazil completed the conditioning of the national inventory of old radium sources in Uruguay. The conditioning, which was carried out with Agency staff in attendance, will ensure that these radium sources can be safely stored until deep geological repositories are available for disposal. This operation was the first in a series that will eventually remove spent radium sources from the list of highly dangerous radiation sources in Member States.

[...]

Conventions negotiated and adopted under the auspices of the Agency and for which the Director General is the Depositary (status and relevant developments)

Agreement on the Privileges and Immunities of the IAEA (reproduced in INFCIRC/9/Rev.1): During 1996, there was no change in the number of Parties to the Agreement. The number of Member States who have accepted the Agreement remains at 65.

Vienna Convention on Civil Liability for Nuclear Damage (reproduced in INFCIRC/500): Entered into force on 12 November 1977. Now has 27 Parties as a result of accession by 1 State, and 12 signatories as a result of signature by 1 State.

Convention on the Physical Protection of Nuclear Material (reproduced in INFCIRC/274/Rev.1): Entered into force on 8 February 1987. In 1996, 4 States became Party to the convention. By the end of the year there were 57 Parties.

Convention on Early Notification of a Nuclear Accident (reproduced in INFCIRC/335): Entered into force on 27 October 1986. In 1996, succession by 1 State brought the total number of Parties at the end of the year to 76.

Convention on Assistance in the Case of a Nuclear Accident or Radiological Emergency (reproduced in INFCIRC/336): Entered into force on 26 February 1987. There were a total of 72 Parties by the end of 1995 as a result of succession by 1 State.

Joint Protocol Relating to the Application of the Vienna Convention and the Paris Convention (reproduced in INFCIRC/402): Entered into force on 27 April 1992. Its status remained unchanged during 1996, with 20 Parties.

Extension of the African Regional Co-operative Agreement for Research, Development and Training Related to Nuclear Energy (AFRA) (reproduced in INFCIRC/377/Add.6): Entered into force on 4 April 1995. Now has 20 Parties as a result of acceptance by 2 States during 1996.

Agreement to Extend the Regional Co-operative Agreement for Research, Development and Training Related to Nuclear Science and Technology, 1987 (RCA) (reproduced in INFCIRC/167/Add.15): Entered into force on 11 June 1992. There was no change in its status during the year, leaving at 17 the total number of acceptances.

Convention on Nuclear Safety (reproduced in INFCIRC/449): Entered into force on 24 October 1996. By the end of 1996, there were 65 signatories and 32 States had consented to be bound. Pursuant to Article 28 of the Convention, the Agency will convene the preparatory meeting of the Contracting Parties provided by Article 21 for 21–25 April 1997.

[...]

Publications issued in 1996
(with series and number)

Nuclear Power

Energy, electricity and nuclear power estimates for the period up to 2015	Reference Data Series No. 1
Nuclear power reactors in the world	Reference Data Series No. 2
Quality assurance for safety in nuclear power plants and other nuclear installations	Safety Series No. 50-C/SG-Q
Policy issues for nuclear power programmes	Special publication
Operating experience with nuclear power stations in Member States	Annual publication
Nuclear power plant personnel training and its evaluation: A guidebook. Executive summary	Technical Reports Series No. 380/ES
Nuclear power, nuclear fuel cycle and waste management: Status and trends 1996	Part C of the IAEA Yearbook 1996
Recent experience in the use of IAEA planning methodologies for energy, electricity and nuclear power planning among Member States of Europe, the Middle East and North Africa	IAEA-TECDOC-863
Design and development status of small and medium reactor systems 1995	IAEA-TECDOC-881
Technical feasibility and reliability of passive safety systems for nuclear power plants	IAEA-TECDOC-920
Review of design approaches of advanced pressurized LWRs	IAEA-TECDOC-861
Progress in design, research and development and testing of safety systems for advanced water cooled reactors	IAEA-TECDOC-872
Fast reactor database	IAEA-TECDOC-866
Progress in liquid metal fast reactor technology	IAEA-TECDOC-876
Comparison of observed effects with computer simulated effects on reactor cores from seismic disturbances	IAEA-TECDOC-882
Absorber materials, control rods and designs of shutdown systems for advanced liquid metal fast reactors	IAEA-TECDOC-884
Conceptual design of advanced fast reactors	IAEA-TECDOC-907
Fast reactor fuel failures and steam generator leaks: Transient and accident analysis approaches	IAEA-TECDOC-908

ANNEX

Publications issued in 1996 (cont.)

Design and development of gas cooled reactors with closed cycle gas turbines	IAEA-TECDOC-899
Graphite moderator life cycle behaviour	IAEA-TECDOC-901
Safe core management with burnable absorbers in WWERs	IAEA-TECDOC-858
Options identification programme for demonstration of nuclear desalination	IAEA-TECDOC-898
Potential for nuclear desalination as a source of low cost potable water in North Africa	IAEA-TECDOC-917
Advanced fuels with reduced actinide generation	IAEA-TECDOC-916
Designing nuclear power plants for improved operation and maintenance	IAEA-TECDOC-906
Good practices for cost effective maintenance of nuclear power plants	IAEA-TECDOC-928
Performance analysis of WWER-440/230 reactors	IAEA-TECDOC-922
Computerized support systems in nuclear power plants	IAEA-TECDOC-912
Management of procurement activities in a nuclear installation	IAEA-TECDOC-919
Processing of nuclear power plant waste streams containing boric acid	IAEA-TECDOC-911
In-core fuel management benchmarks for PHWRs	IAEA-TECDOC-887
Technical basis for the ITER interim design report, cost review and safety analysis	IAEA/ITER EDA/DS/07
ITER Council proceedings: 1995	IAEA/ITER EDA/DS/08
ITER interim design report package and relevant documents	IAEA/ITER EDA/DS/09
ITER interim design report package documents	IAEA/ITER EDA/DS/10
ITER monthly newsletter	
Nuclear Fusion	Monthly journal

Nuclear Fuel Cycle

Guidebook to accompany the IAEA map: World distribution of uranium deposits	Special publication
The Nuclear Fuel Cycle Information System. A directory of nuclear fuel cycle facilities: 1996 edition	Special publication
Design and performance of WWER fuel	Technical Reports Series No. 379
Management and storage of spent nuclear fuel at research and test reactors	IAEA-TECDOC-900
Spent fuel management: Current status and prospects 1995	IAEA-TECDOC-894
Significant incidents in nuclear fuel cycle facilities	IAEA-TECDOC-867
Fuel technology and performance of non-water cooled reactors	IAEA-TECDOC-850
Behaviour of LWR core materials under accident conditions	IAEA-TECDOC-921
Guidebook on the development of regulations for uranium deposit development and production	IAEA-TECDOC-862
Uranium Production Safety Assessment Team — UPSAT — An international peer review service for uranium production facilities	IAEA-UPSAT-96
Innovations in uranium exploration, mining and processing techniques, and new exploration target areas	IAEA-TECDOC-868
Steps for preparing uranium production feasibility studies: A guidebook	IAEA-TECDOC-885
UPSAT guidelines: 1996 edition	IAEA-TECDOC-878

Publications issued in 1996 (cont.)

Radioactive Waste Management

Environmental impact of radioactive releases	Proceedings Series
Clearance levels for radionuclides in solid materials. Application of exemption principles. Interim report for comment	IAEA-TECDOC-855
Modelling of radionuclide interception and loss processes in vegetation and of transfer in semi-natural ecosystems. Second report of the VAMP Terrestrial Working Group	IAEA-TECDOC-857
Planning for environmental restoration of radioactively contaminated sites in central and eastern Europe	IAEA-TECDOC-865
Application of quality assurance to radioactive waste disposal facilities	IAEA-TECDOC-895
Validation of models using Chernobyl fallout data from southern Finland — Scenario S. Second report of the VAMP Multiple Pathways Assessment Working Group	IAEA-TECDOC-904
Issues in radioactive waste disposal	IAEA-TECDOC-909
Requirements and methods for low and intermediate level waste package acceptability	IAEA-TECDOC-864
Conditioning and interim storage of spent radium sources	IAEA-TECDOC-886

Comparative Assessment of Nuclear Power and Other Energy Sources

Electricity, health and the environment: Comparative assessment in support of decision making	Proceedings Series
Comparison of energy sources in terms of their full-energy-chain emission factors of greenhouse gases	IAEA-TECDOC-892
Health and environmental aspects of nuclear fuel cycle facilities	IAEA-TECDOC-918

Food and Agriculture

Food irradiation with emphasis on process control and acceptance in Asia	IAEA-TECDOC-871
Nuclear methods for plant nutrients and water balance studies	IAEA-TECDOC-875
Nuclear techniques to assess irrigation schedules for field crops	IAEA-TECDOC-888
Isotope studies on plant productivity	IAEA-TECDOC-889
Use of mutation techniques for improvement of cereals in Latin America	IAEA-TECDOC-859
Development of feed supplementation strategies for improving ruminant productivity on smallholder farms in Latin America through the use of radioimmunoassay techniques	IAEA-TECDOC-877
Standardization of medfly trapping for use in sterile insect technique programmes	IAEA-TECDOC-883
Application of an immunoassay method to improve the diagnosis and control of African trypanosomosis	IAEA-TECDOC-925
Irradiation of "red" meat	IAEA-TECDOC-902
Insect and pest control newsletter	
Agrochemicals and residues newsletter	
Soils newsletter	

ANNEX

Publications issued in 1996 (cont.)

Mutation breeding newsletter

Animal production and health newsletter

Food irradiation newsletter

Human Health

Radiation dose in radiotherapy from prescription to delivery	IAEA-TECDOC-896
Review of data and methods recommended in the international code of practice IAEA Technical Reports Series No. 277, absorbed dose determination in photon and electron beams	IAEA-TECDOC-897
Survey of reference materials, Vol. 2: Environmentally related reference materials for trace elements, nuclides and microcontaminants	IAEA-TECDOC-880
SSDL Newsletter	

Industry and Earth Sciences

Residence time distribution software analysis. User's manual	Computer Manual Series No. 11
Nuclear techniques in the coal industry	IAEA-TECDOC-845
Isotope field applications for groundwater studies in the Middle East	IAEA-TECDOC-890
Manual on mathematical models in isotope hydrogeology	IAEA-TECDOC-910
Thin layer activation method and its applications in industry	IAEA-TECDOC-924

Physical and Chemical Sciences

Plasma physics and controlled nuclear fusion research 1994	Proceedings Series
Nuclear research reactors in the world	Reference Data Series No. 3
CINDA 96: Index to literature and computer files of microscopic neutron data	Annual publication
Microanalysis data acquisition and control program: User's manual	Computer Manual Series No. 9
SPEDAC Pro for DOS. Format conversion of spectral data from nuclear experiments. User's manual	Computer Manual Series No. 10
Manual for troubleshooting and upgrading of neutron generators	IAEA-TECDOC-913
Antibodies immobilized on magnetic particles for radioimmunoassay and immunoradiometric assay of hormones	IAEA-TECDOC-914
International Centre for Theoretical Physics, Trieste, Scientific activities in 1995	IAEA-TECDOC-915
Accelerator Newsletter	
International bulletin on atomic and molecular data for fusion, Nos 50, 51	IBAMD/50–51
Nuclear Data Newsletter	
Index of nuclear data libraries (revision 96)	IAEA-NDS-7
On-line nuclear data services: A user's manual (revision 96)	IAEA-NDS-150
Selection of evaluations for the FENDL/A-2 activation cross-section library	INDC(NDS)-341
Activation cross-sections for the generation of long lived radionuclides of importance in fusion reactor technology	INDC(NDS)-342

Publications issued in 1996 (cont.)

First Research Co-ordination meeting on tritium retention in fusion reactor plasma facing components	INDC(NDS)-345
Final Research Co-ordination meeting on plasma-interaction induced erosion of fusion reactor materials	INDC(NDS)-346
Neutron Metrology File NMF-9: An integrated database for performing neutron spectrum adjustment calculations	INDC(NDS)-347
Electron impact excitation cross-section data for helium	INDC(NDS)-348
First Research Co-ordination meeting on reference charged particle cross-section database for medical radioisotope production	INDC(NDS)-349
Second Research Co-ordination meeting on development of reference input parameter library for nuclear model calculations of nuclear data	INDC(NDS)-350
Benchmark validation of FENDL-1	INDC(NDS)-351
Advisory Group meeting on completion of FENDL-1 and start of FENDL-2	INDC(NDS)-352
Improvement of measurements: Theoretical computations and evaluations of neutron induced helium production cross-sections	INDC(NDS)-353
Second Research Co-ordination meeting on collection and evaluation of reference data for thermomechanical properties of fusion reactor plasma facing materials	INDC(NDS)-354
International benchmark calculations of radioactive inventory for fission reactor decommissioning	INDC(NDS)-355
Selection of basic evaluations for the FENDL-2 library	INDC(NDS)-356
Nuclear Reaction Data Centres Network	INDC(NDS)-359
Advisory Group meeting on co-ordination of the Nuclear Reaction Data Centres report	INDC(NDS)-360

Radiation Safety

Direct methods for measuring radionuclides in the human body	Safety Series No. 114
International basic safety standards for protection against ionizing radiation and for the safety of radiation sources	Safety Series No. 115
Emergency planning and preparedness for re-entry of a nuclear powered satellite	Safety Series No. 119
Radiation protection and the safety of radiation sources	Safety Series No. 120
Radiation and society: Comprehending radiation risk, vol. 2	Proceedings Series
One decade after Chernobyl: Summing up the consequences of the accident	Proceedings Series
The International Chernobyl Project. An Overview	Miscellaneous publication
An electron accelerator accident in Hanoi, Viet Nam	Miscellaneous publication
The radiological accident at the irradiation facility in Nesvizh	Miscellaneous publication
Lessons learned from accidents in industrial irradiation facilities	Miscellaneous publication
Radiological conditions at Bikini Atoll: Prospects for resettlement	Special publication
Manual for the classification and prioritization of risks due to major accidents in process and related industries	IAEA-TECDOC-727 (Rev. 1)
Assessment and treatment of external and internal radionuclide contamination	IAEA-TECDOC-869
Methods for estimating the probability of cancer from occupational radiation exposure	IAEA-TECDOC-870

Publications issued in 1996 (cont.)

Establishment and use of national registries for actinide elements in humans	IAEA-TECDOC-879
Radiodosimetry and preventive measures in the event of a nuclear accident	IAEA-TECDOC-893
Directory of national competent authorities' approval certificates for package design, special form material and shipment of radioactive material, 1996 edition	IAEA-TECDOC-903
Supplement to safe transport of radioactive material — Second edition	Training Courses Series No. 1
The safe use of radiation sources	Training Courses Series No. 6
Manual on gamma radiography	IAEA-PRSM-1 (Rev. 1)
Manual on shielded enclosures	IAEA-PRSM-2 (Rev. 1)
Manual on nuclear gauges	IAEA-PRSM-3 (Rev. 1)
Manual on high energy teletherapy	IAEA-PRSM-4 (Rev. 1)
Manual on brachytherapy	IAEA-PRSM-5 (Rev. 1)
Manual on therapeutic uses of iodine-131	IAEA-PRSM-6 (Rev. 1)
Manual on self-contained gamma irradiators (categories I and III)	IAEA-PRSM-7 (Rev. 1)
Manual on panoramic gamma irradiators (categories II and IV)	IAEA-PRSM-8 (Rev. 1)
National competent authorities responsible for approvals and authorizations in respect of the transport of radioactive material — List No. 27 (1996 edition)	IAEA-NCAL-27

Safety of Nuclear Installations

Human reliability analysis in probabilistic safety assessment for nuclear power plants	Safety Series No. 50-P-10
Assessment of the overall fire safety arrangements at nuclear power plants	Safety Series No. 50-P-11
Procedures for conducting probabilistic safety assessments of nuclear power plants (level 3)	Safety Series No. 50-P-12
External man-induced events in relation to nuclear power plant design	Safety Series No. 50-SG-D5 (Rev.1)
Inspection and enforcement by the regulatory body for nuclear power plants	Safety Series No. 50-SG-G4 (Rev.1)
Defence in depth in nuclear safety	INSAG Series No. 10
Nuclear Safety Review 1996	Part D of the IAEA Yearbook 1996
Advances in the operational safety of nuclear power plants	Proceedings Series
Selected safety aspects of WWER-440 model 213 nuclear power plants	Miscellaneous publication
Simulation of a loss of coolant accident without high pressure injection but with secondary side bleed and feed	IAEA-TECDOC-848
Development of safety related expert systems	IAEA-TECDOC-856
ASCOT guidelines — revised 1996 edition	IAEA-TECDOC-860
Application and development of probabilistic safety assessment for nuclear power plant operations	IAEA-TECDOC-873
OSART programme highlights 1993–1994. Operational safety practices in nuclear power plants	IAEA-TECDOC-874
Operational safety experience feedback by means of unusual event reports	IAEA-TECDOC-891

Publications issued in 1996 (cont.)

Approaches to the safety of future nuclear power plants	IAEA-TECDOC-905
RBMK nuclear power plants. Generic safety issues	IAEA-EBP-RBMK-04
Guidelines for accident analysis of WWER nuclear power plants	IAEA-EBP-WWER-01
Technical basis for instrumentation and control design improvements in WWER-440/230 nuclear power plants	IAEA-EBP-WWER-02
Safety issues and their ranking for WWER-440 model 213 nuclear power plants	IAEA-EBP-WWER-03
Databases on safety issues for WWER and RBMK reactors: User's manual	IAEA-EBP-WWER-04
Safety issues and their ranking for WWER-1000 model 320 nuclear power plants	IAEA-EBP-WWER-05
WWER-440/230 reactor pressure vessel integrity	IAEA-EBP-WWER-06
Development of measures to assess the safety of existing nuclear power plants and the effectiveness of regulations and regulatory actions (including 'prescriptive' and 'performance based' approaches)	PDRP-1

Direction and Support

IAEA Yearbook 1996	Annual publication
INIS Periodic Report 1995	IAEA-INIS-PER95

[...]

ABBREVIATIONS

ABACC	Brazilian–Argentine Agency for Accounting and Control of Nuclear Materials
ARCAL	Regional Co-operative Arrangements for the Promotion of Nuclear Science and Technology in Latin America
BWR	Boiling water reactor
CRP	Co-ordinated research programme
EURATOM	European Atomic Energy Community
FAO	Food and Agriculture Organization of the United Nations
FORATOM	Forum atomique européen
HWR	Heavy water reactor
IAEA-MEL	IAEA Marine Environment Laboratory
ICTP	International Centre for Theoretical Physics
ILO	International Labour Organisation
INDC	International Nuclear Data Committee
IOC	Intergovernmental Oceanographic Commission (UNESCO)
ISO	International Organization for Standardization
LWR	Light water reactor
NEA	Nuclear Energy Agency of the OECD
OECD	Organisation for Economic Co-operation and Development
OLADE	Organización Latinoamericana de Energía
OPANAL	Organismo para la Proscripción de las Armas Nucleares en América Latina y el Caribe
PAHO	Pan American Health Organization/WHO
PHWR	Pressurized heavy water reactor
PWR	Pressurized water reactor
RBMK	Light boiling water cooled graphite moderated pressure tube reactor (former USSR)
RCA	Regional Co-operative Agreement for Research, Development and Training Related to Nuclear Science and Technology
SQ	Significant quantity
UNDP	United Nations Development Programme
UNEP	United Nations Environment Programme
UNESCO	United Nations Educational, Scientific and Cultural Organization
UNIDO	United Nations Industrial Development Organization
UNSCEAR	United Nations Scientific Committee on the Effects of Atomic Radiation
WHO	World Health Organization
WMO	World Meteorological Organization
WWER	Water cooled and moderated energy reactor (former USSR)

ORGANIZATIONAL CHART

(as of 31 December 1996)

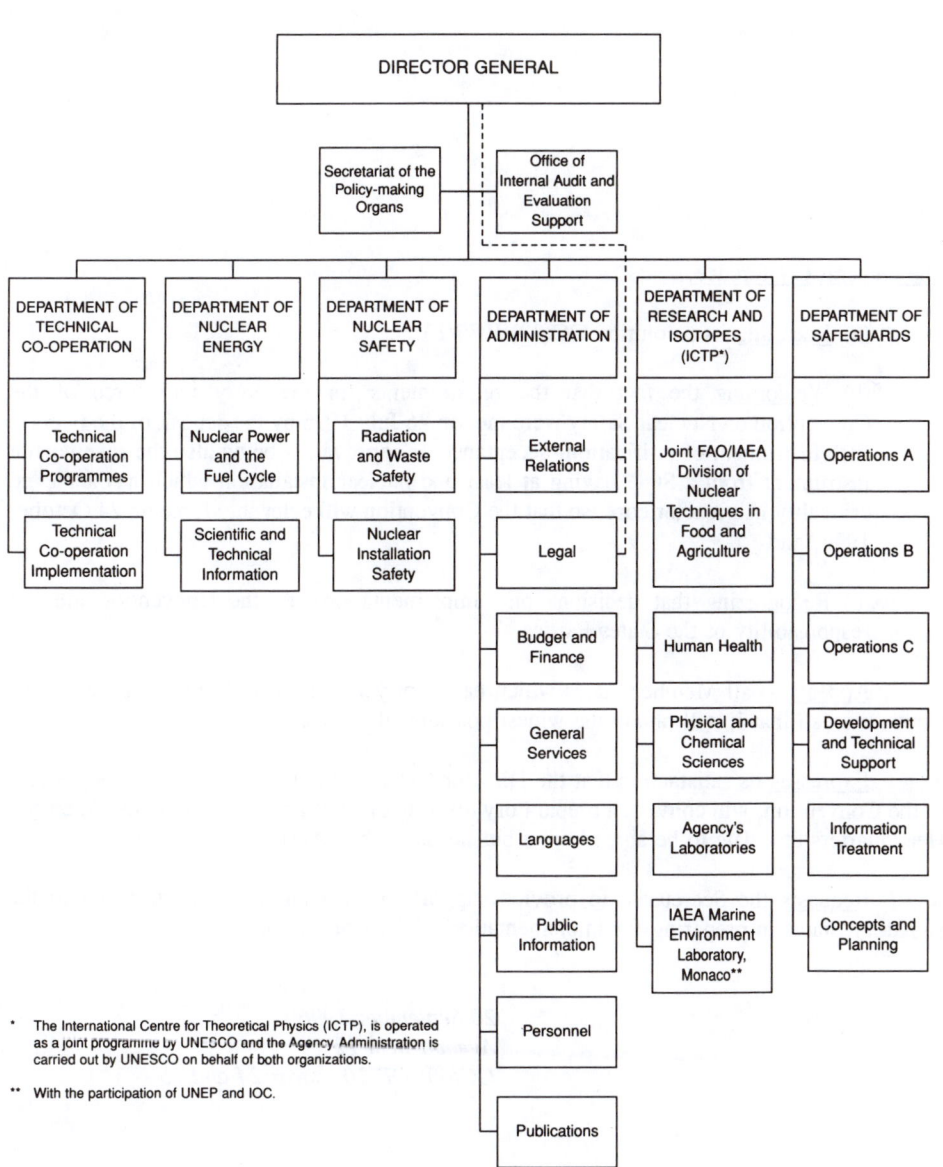

DIRECTOR GENERAL

Secretariat of the Policy-making Organs

Office of Internal Audit and Evaluation Support

DEPARTMENT OF TECHNICAL CO-OPERATION
- Technical Co-operation Programmes
- Technical Co-operation Implementation

DEPARTMENT OF NUCLEAR ENERGY
- Nuclear Power and the Fuel Cycle
- Scientific and Technical Information

DEPARTMENT OF NUCLEAR SAFETY
- Radiation and Waste Safety
- Nuclear Installation Safety

DEPARTMENT OF ADMINISTRATION
- External Relations
- Legal
- Budget and Finance
- General Services
- Languages
- Public Information
- Personnel
- Publications

DEPARTMENT OF RESEARCH AND ISOTOPES (ICTP*)
- Joint FAO/IAEA Division of Nuclear Techniques in Food and Agriculture
- Human Health
- Physical and Chemical Sciences
- Agency's Laboratories
- IAEA Marine Environment Laboratory, Monaco**

DEPARTMENT OF SAFEGUARDS
- Operations A
- Operations B
- Operations C
- Development and Technical Support
- Information Treatment
- Concepts and Planning

* The International Centre for Theoretical Physics (ICTP), is operated as a joint programme by UNESCO and the Agency. Administration is carried out by UNESCO on behalf of both organizations.

** With the participation of UNEP and IOC.

2. THE CONVENTION ON NUCLEAR SAFETY - RESOLUTION OF THE IAEA GENERAL CONFERENCE

Doc. no.: GC(40)/RES/10   Date: 20 September 1996

The General Conference,

    (a) Recalling its resolution GC(39)/RES/13,

    (b) Welcoming the fact that the requirements for the entry into force of the Convention on Nuclear Safety were met on 26 July 1996 by the deposit of the twenty-fifth instrument of ratification, acceptance or approval, it being also the seventeenth instrument from a State having at least one nuclear installation which has achieved criticality in a reactor core, so that the Convention will enter into force on 24 October 1996, and

    (c) Recognizing that decisions on implementation of the Convention are the responsibility of the States Parties,

1.   Appeals to all Member States which have not yet done so to become Parties to the Convention so that it will obtain the widest possible adherence;

2.   Expresses its satisfaction that the Director General, in his capacity as the Depositary of the Convention, will convene a preparatory meeting of Contracting Parties at the Agency's Headquarters at a date to be agreed upon but not later than April 1997; and

3.   Requests the Secretariat to provide support to the Contracting Parties and to the signatory States in preparing for implementation of the Convention.

20 September 1996
Agenda item 12
GC(40)/OR.10, paras 24 and 25

3. A CONVENTION ON THE SAFETY OF RADIOACTIVE WASTE MANAGEMENT - RESOLUTION OF THE IAEA GENERAL CONFERENCE

Doc. no.: GC(40)RES/11   Date: 20 September 1996

The General Conference,

(a) Recalling resolution GC(XXXVIII)/RES/6, by which the General Conference invited the Board and the Director General inter alia "to commence preparations for a convention on the safety and waste management",

(b) Welcoming the Convention on Nuclear Safety, which will enter into force on 24 October 1996, and recalling that its preambular paragraph (ix) affirms "the need to begin promptly the development of an international convention on the safety of radioactive waste management as soon as the ongoing process to develop waste management safety fundamentals has resulted in broad international agreement",

(c) Recalling also resolution GC(XXXIV)/RES/530, by which the General Conference adopted the IAEA Code of Practice on the International Transboundary Movement of Radioactive Waste and expressed, inter alia, "the desirability of concluding a legally binding instrument under the auspices of the IAEA", and

(d) Mindful of the needs of Member States, particularly the developing countries, to upgrade, with the co-operation and assistance of the Agency, their institutional and technical capabilities to safely manage radioactive waste,

1.   Expresses its appreciation to the Open-ended Group of Legal and Technical Experts on a Convention on the Safety of Radioactive Waste Management for the progress achieved so far;

2.   Welcomes the invitation of the Government of South Africa to host the forthcoming fifth meeting of the Group in Pilansberg, South Africa, and expresses the hope that substantial progress will be made in resolving the outstanding issues in a spirit of compromise so as to allow timely completion of the preparatory work and adoption of a convention in the near future; and

3.   <u>Requests</u> the Board and the Director General to report on the implementation of this resolution to the Conference at its forty-first regular session.

20 September 1996
Agenda item 12
GC(40)/OR.10, paras 24 and 25

4. MEASURES TO RESOLVE INTERNATIONAL RADIOACTIVE WASTE MANAGEMENT ISSUES: ESTABLISHING PREDISPOSAL WASTE DEMONSTRATION CENTRES - RESOLUTION OF THE IAEA GENERAL CONFERENCE

Doc. no.: GC(40)RES/12   Date: 20 September 1996

The General Conference,

(a) Appreciating the work undertaken by the Agency regarding measures to resolve international radioactive waste management issues in response to resolution GC(XXXVIII)/RES/6,

(b) Welcoming the efforts made as part of this work by the Agency in establishing, as a "pilot programme", a regional training centre suitable for demonstrating techniques for the processing and storage of radioactive waste arising from the application of nuclear techniques in medicine, research and industry,

(c) Reaffirming the importance to the international community of ensuring that sound practices are planned and implemented for the management and disposal of radioactive waste from nuclear application technologies and nuclear power generation,

(d) Reaffirming that the ultimate responsibility for ensuring the safe management of radioactive waste rests with the respective State,

(e) Affirming the importance of international co-operation in enhancing the safe management of radioactive waste through bilateral and multilateral mechanisms, and

(f) Convinced that radioactive waste should, as far as is compatible with the safe management of such material, be disposed of in the State in which it was generated whilst recognizing that, in certain circumstances, safe management of radioactive waste might be fostered through voluntary agreements among Member States to use facilities in one of them for the benefit of the other States,

1.   Stresses the importance of continuing to facilitate the transfer of theoretical knowledge and practical skills for the management of radioactive waste from the application of nuclear techniques;

2.   <u>Invites</u> the Director General to assist Member States upon request in expanding the utilization of suitable existing regional training centres for practical training and demonstration of techniques for the processing and storage of radioactive waste from the application of nuclear techniques in medicine, research and industry, so that a demonstration and training facility would be available in respective regions by strengthening co-operation and by seeking to co-ordinate resources, including those existing in developing countries; and

3.   <u>Requests</u> the Board of Governors and the Director General to report on the implementation of this resolution to the General Conference.

20 September 1996
Agenda item 12
GC(40)/OR.10, paras 24 and 25

5. PLAN FOR PRODUCING POTABLE WATER ECONOMICALLY - RESOLUTION OF THE IAEA GENERAL CONFERENCE

Doc. no.: GC(40)RES/14   Date: 20 September 1996

The General Conference,

(a) Recalling resolutions GC(XXXIII)/RES/515, GC(XXXIV)/RES/540, GC(XXXV)/RES/563, GC(XXXVI)/RES/592, GC(XXXVII)/RES/617, GC(XXXVIII)/RES/7 and GC(39)/RES/15,

(b) Noting the study on the "Technical and economic evaluation of potable water production through the desalination of sea water by using nuclear energy or other means" attached to document GC(XXXVI)/1013, which concludes that the use of nuclear energy as an alternative option to the use of fossil fuelled plants for supplying energy for sea water desalination is technically feasible and in general economically competitive, and document GOV/INF/708,

(c) Noting the main conclusion of the Advisory Group on Demonstration Facilities, attached to document GC(XXXVIII)/8, which includes the conclusion that there is a need to establish a programme for identifying a practical set of options from which one or more demonstration facilities with well-defined objectives might be chosen,

(d) Noting also the interest of a number of Member States in activities relating to sea water desalination using nuclear energy as reflected in document GC(XXXVII)/INF/323,

(e) Aware that the acute shortage of potable water in some Member States remains a major problem,

(f) Underlining the vital importance of sufficient potable water supplies for mankind and of regional and international co-operation in solving the problem of potable water shortages in Member States and the interest of potential beneficiaries and technology holders in the provision of low-cost potable water,

(g) Welcoming the holding of an international symposium on sea water desalination in the Republic of Korea next year and inviting Member States to promote international co-operation and collaboration in this area,

(h) Taking note with interest of the World Bank President's call to hold in 1997 a world conference on water in order that a strategy and partnership be established by governments, the private and the public sector, and international organizations, and

(i) Taking note with appreciation of the report of the Director General contained in document GC(40)/4,

1.   Welcomes the progress made in this regard, and especially the completion of the two-phase Options Identification Programme described in document GC(39)/12, which aims at evaluating data relevant to a demonstration and analysing the most practical options for demonstration;

2.   Requests the Director General to continue consultations with interested States, the competent organizations of the United Nations system and other relevant intergovernmental organizations concerning the main conclusions of the "Technical and economic evaluation of potable water production through the desalination of sea water by using nuclear energy or other means";

3.   Stresses the vital importance of producing potable water and further requests the Director General to assign appropriate priority to the nuclear desalination of sea water in the process of preparing the Agency's programme and budget;

4.   Invites the Director General to establish an advisory body on the Agency's activities relating to nuclear desalination with the participation of interested Member States and to take appropriate measures to assist Member States concerned in the process of preparatory actions for demonstration projects; and

5.   Requests the Director General to report on the progress made in the implementation of this resolution to the Board of Governors and to the General Conference at its forty-first session under an appropriate agenda item.

20 September 1996
Agenda item 14
GC(40)/OR.10, para. 27

6. MEASURES AGAINST ILLICIT TRAFFICKING IN NUCLEAR MATERIALS AND OTHER RADIOACTIVE SOURCES - RESOLUTION OF THE IAEA GENERAL CONFERENCE

Doc. no.: GC(40)RES/17

Date: 20 September 1996

The General Conference,

(a) Recalling its resolutions GC(XXXVIII)/RES/15 and GC(39)/RES/18 regarding measures against illicit trafficking in nuclear materials and other radioactive sources, and

(b) Noting the programme for preventing and combatting illicit trafficking in nuclear material agreed upon by the participants in the Moscow Nuclear Summit of April 1996 contained in document INFCIRC/509,

1.   Takes note of the progress report submitted by the Secretariat in document GC(40)/15;

2.   Welcomes the activities in the fields of prevention, response, training and information exchange undertaken by the Secretariat in support of efforts against illicit trafficking;

3.   Invites the Director General to continue working during the coming year in accordance with the relevant conclusions of the Board of Governors; and

4.   Requests the Director General to submit a report to the General Conference at its next regular session on activities undertaken by the Agency in the intervening period.

20 September 1996
Agenda item 17
GC(40)/OR.10, para. 30

7. NUCLEAR POWER STATUS IN 1995

Doc. no.: PR 96/8   Date: 19 April 1996

A total of 476 nuclear power plants were operating or being built around the world in 1995, based on data reported to the International Atomic Energy Agency (IAEA) Power Reactor Information System (PRIS). During 1995, four nuclear power plants with altogether 3290 MW(e) were newly connnected to electricity grids in India, Republic of Korea, UK and Ukraine, bringing the world's total number of operating reactors to 437 in 30 countries and Taiwan, China. Additionally, a total of 39 reactors were reported as being constructed in 14 countries.

Nuclear power's share of electricity production remained high in 1995, in seven countries - Lithuania, 85.59; France, 76.14; Belgium, 55.52; Sweden, 46.61; Bulgaria, 46.43; Slovak Republic, 44.14; Hungary, 42.30; - representing close to half or more of their total electricity use. All in all, 17 countries (including Taiwan, China) relied upon nuclear power plants to supply at least a quarter of their total electricity needs.

Worldwide in 1995, total nuclear power generation grew to 2227.94 terawatt-hours of electricity. This is more than the world's total electricity generation - 1912 terawatt-hours - from all sources in 1958. Overall nuclear power plants provided approximately 17 percent of the world's electricity production in 1995. Cumulative worldwide operating experience from civil nuclear reactors at the end of 1995 was over 7696 years.

A table showing the electricity supplied by nuclear power reactors in 1995 and the respective percentages of electricity produced by nuclear energy is attached.

Nuclear Power Reactors in operation and under construction at the end of 1995

Country Name	Reactors in operation		Reactors under construction		Electricity supplied by nuclear power reactors in 1995		Total operating Experience to end 1995	
	No. of units	Total MW(e)	No. of Units	Total MW(e)	TW(e).h	% of total	Years	Months
Argentina	2	935	1	692	7.07	11.79	34	7
Armenia	1	376					28	4
Belgium	7	5631			39.20	55.52	135	7
Brazil	1	626	1	1245	2.50	0.97	13	9
Bulgaria	6	3538			17.26	46.43	83	1
Canada	21	14907			92.31	17.26	348	9
China	3	2167			12.38	1.24	8	5
Czech R.	4	1648	2	1824	12.23	20.10	38	8
Finland	4	2310			18.13	29.91	67	4
France	56	58493	4	5810	358.60	76.14	878	10
Germany	20	22017			154.14	29.09	510	7
Hungary	4	1729			13.20	42.30	42	2
India	10	1695	4	808	6.46	1.89	129	1
Iran			2	2146			0	0
Japan	51	39893	3	3757	286.9	33.40	704	5
Kazakh.	1	70			0.08	0.13	22	6
Korea RP	11	9120	5	3870	63.68	36.10	100	10
Lithuania	2	2370			10.64	85.59	20	6
Mexico	2	1308			8.44	6.00	7	11
Nethlnds	2	504			3.70	4.86	49	9
Pakistan	1	125	1	300	0.46	0.88	24	3
Romania			2	1300			0	0
Russia	29	19843	4	3375	99.38	11.79	526	6
S. Africa	2	1842			11.28	6.48	22	3
Slovak R.	4	1632	4	1552	11.44	44.14	61	5
Slovenia	1	632			4.56	39.46	14	3
Spain	9	7124			53.10	34.06	147	2
Sweden	12	10002			66.70	46.61	219	2
Switzrld	5	3050			23.49	39.92	103	10
UK	35	12908			77.64	24.99	1063	4
Ukraine	16	13629	5	4750	65.64	37.83	174	2
USA	109	98784	1	1165	673.40	22.49	2028	8
Total	**437**	**343792**	**39**	**32594**	**2227.94**		**7696**	**2**

Note: The total includes the following data in Taiwan, China:

6 unit(s), 4884 MW(e) in operation;

33.93 TW(e).h of nuclear electricity generation, representing 28.79% of the total electricity generated there;

86 year(s) 1 month(s) of total operating experience.

2 Shutdowns in 1995: Bruce 2 in Canada but it can re-start in future, Wuergassen in Germany.

Connection to the grid during 1995

India	IN-10, Kakrapar-2	PHWR
Korea RP	KR-12, Yonggwang-4	PWR
UK	GB-24, Sizewell-B	PWR
Ukraine	UA-127, Zaporozhe-6	WWER

Note: Japan reported that Onagawa 2 and Monju NPP were connected to the grid in 1994

Armenia 2 was re-connected to grid in 1995.

8. INTERNATIONAL RADIOLOGICAL SURVEY OF MURUROA AND FANGATAUFA ATOLLS GETS UNDERWAY

Doc. no.: PR 96/12   Date: 25 June 1996

International teams of scientists will be collecting terrestrial and marine samples at the Pacific atolls of Mururoa and Fangataufa for about one month starting in early July in the context of the radiological study requested from the International Atomic Energy Agency (IAEA) by the Government of France. Teams will visit the atolls in relays, to collect samples including plankton, fish, seawater, lagoon sediment, coral, soil, coconuts and vegetation.

The samples will be shared subsequently for analysis with a grid of laboratories worldwide, including the Pacific region. Results will be forwarded to the International Atomic Energy (IAEA) in Vienna, whose own laboratories in Seibersdorf, Austria and in Monaco will also be participating both in the sample-taking and the analytical work. Data from French studies already undertaken will be available for comparative purposes in the scientific work to determine the radiological situation at the atolls. This part of the overall study is expected to take up to six months to complete.

Separately, geological specialists will be examining the situation regarding possible future scenarios, including the very long-term, using modelling techniques taking as their starting point inter alia the geological characteristics of the atolls, experience gained at other nuclear test sites, and information provided by the French authorities regarding their own series of tests. The results of this work will then be consolidated with the other part of the study and be made publicly available. The estimated date of publication of the complete, final report is early 1998.

The study is being conducted under the guidance and direction of an International Advisory Committee of distinguished scientists from ten countries , chaired by Dr. E. Gail de Planque of the United States, and including ex officio representatives of the South Pacific Forum, the UN Scientific Committee on the Effects of Atomic Radiation, the World Health Organization and the European Commission. The

Committee itself intends to visit French Polynesia at a later date, at which time a press conference is foreseen.

Note: For practical reasons it will not be possible for print or electronic media to cover the scientific field work. However, an IAEA film crew will be present to shoot footage which can be obtained, with descriptive material, on request from the IAEA as of the end of July (tel. in Vienna 43-1-206021276 or fax 43-1-206029616).

9. INTERNATIONAL SCIENTIFIC TEAMS COMPLETE SAMPLE-TAKING AT MURUROA AND FANGATAUFA ATOLLS

Doc. no.: PR 96/16   Date: 6 August 1996

Teams of scientists from around the world, working in the framework of a radiological study requested from the International Atomic Energy Agency (IAEA) by the Government of France, have just completed the collection of marine and terrestrial samples at the atolls of Mururoa and Fangataufa in the South Pacific, where French nuclear testing took place until earlier this year.

The samples -- including soil, vegetation, coconuts, coral, seawater, fish, lagoon sediment and plankton -- will now be shared among a network of laboratories for analysis. The laboratories include scientific establishments in the Pacific region. Results will subsequently be collated by the IAEA in Vienna, and comparisons will be made with data provided by France based on its own earlier national studies.
A total of 11 scientists from 5 countries, as well as staff members of the IAEA's own laboratories in Seibersdorf (Austria) and Monaco, participated during a five week period in the collection of samples on-site, with full logistic support and cooperation from the French authorities.

Results of this part of the study -- which will provide an overview of the current radiological situation at the atolls -- are expected by the end of the year. The second part of the study, in which geologists will examine possible future scenarios including the medium and longer terms, using modelling techniques, will be performed by the end of next year. A full report will be published in early 1998.

Guidance and direction for the study are being given by an International Advisory Committee of distinguished scientists from ten countries, chaired by Dr. E. Gail de Planque of the United States, with ex officio representatives of the South Pacific Forum, the UN Scientific Committee on the Effects of Atomic Radiation, the World Health Organization and the European Commission. The Advisory Committee itself plans to meet in French Polynesia in the coming months.

Note: A short spot for TV stations and still photography of the sample-taking can be obtained from the IAEA Division of Public Information in Vienna upon request.

10. IAEA DIRECTOR GENERAL HANS BLIX ADDRESSES UNITED NATIONS GENERAL ASSEMBLY

Doc. no.: PR 96/23   Date: 28 October 1996

Speaking before the United Nations General Assembly today in New York, IAEA Director General Hans Blix underlined the Agency's growing role to help prevent the spread of nuclear weapons and to verify nuclear arms control and disarmament agreements. Dr. Blix also reviewed the changing agenda in other areas of nuclear energy's safe development worldwide.

"With the nuclear arms race over, a number of arms control or disarmament treaties have been concluded or are in the making that may require additional verification tasks from the IAEA," he said. In this context, he noted that the United States and Russian Federation are exploring with the IAEA technical and other issues connected to the further verification of certain nuclear material from dismantled nuclear weapons. Verification in nuclear-weapon States, he said, can provide "assurance that fissionable material from dismantled weapons does not go into new weapons". Additionally, he noted, it could assure that a possible future cut-off agreement prohibiting the production of plutonium or highly enriched uranium for weapons is respected.

In reviewing the IAEA's verification role, Dr. Blix also pointed to the increasing number of regional nuclear-weapon-free zone treaties and to the longstanding multilateral Treaty on the Non-Proliferation of Nuclear Weapons (NPT) which all require and rely upon IAEA safeguards. Though the recently adopted Comprehensive Test Ban Treaty will have its own verification organization, Dr. Blix emphasized the IAEA's existing role under the NPT, which obliges non-nuclear-weapon States to refrain from nuclear weapons tests and entrusts the verification of these obligations to the IAEA.

Dr. Blix underlined the IAEA's ongoing efforts to strengthen its safeguards system, noting that many measures already have been introduced under the Agency's existing legal authority. Other measures that go beyond this authority remain under discussion by the IAEA's Board of Governors. Most of these measures have been tried out in several States without great problems for the Agency or the State concerned, Dr. Blix said. While a few other countries have raised objections about the burden they may impose, Dr. Blix said the measures were needed for improving the IAEA's verification capabilities. "Regrettably, as we all know from our experience of controls at airports, security against possible violations by a few requires some inconveniencing of many," he said.

Following are other highlights of the Director General's address. *(Editor's advisory: The full text of the statement is accessible on line through the IAEA's World Atom Internet services on the World Wide Web at http://www.iaea.org/worldatom)*

Programmes and resources. The changing global agenda continues to significantly influence the IAEA's programmes and resources: "There is no lack of challenges in the nuclear sphere," he said "Over time the work of the Agency has both expanded and changed considerably....Suffice it to mention the names Three Mile Island and Chernobyl, Iraq and the DPRK, Semipalatinsk and Mururoa to evoke the growing engagement of the IAEA in the fields of nuclear safety, safeguards verification, and assessment of the radiological situation at nuclear weapons test sites." He emphasized, however, that the IAEA's budget frequently "limits what can be tackled." Many new tasks, he said, such as measures countering illicit trafficking in nuclear materials or projects concerning nuclear safety and waste are, in fact, handled in large measure on the basis of extrabudgetary voluntary contributions from countries. "This is not satisfactory," he said, "but far better than inaction."

Energy and the environment. Dr. Blix emphasized concerns over issues of global warming and climate change, and the need for full assessments of all energy options. "At the IAEA, the goal of sustainable development is fully accepted and it has been considered important that all energy sources be impartially and scientifically analysed for their impact upon life, health and the environment, including climate," he said. Although governments are aware that greater use of nuclear power and renewable sources can help to restrain greenhouse gas emissions, he pointed out that most countries continue to expand their use of fossil fuels and are falling short of carbon emission targets. "There is a regrettable gap between the rhetoric of restraint and the reality of growing greenhouse gas emissions," he said.

Nuclear and radiation safety. Dr. Blix focused on elements of an "international nuclear safety culture" to which countries are committing themselves. Elements include the Convention on Nuclear Safety, which entered into force 24 October and commits States to a process of expert safety reviews for nuclear power plants. He noted that three new legal instruments relevant to safety are expected to be finalized over the coming year. They include a convention on the safe management, including disposal, of radioactive waste; revision of the Vienna Convention on Civil Liability for Nuclear Damage; and an arrangement for nuclear liability supplementary funding.

Technical cooperation for development. He placed particular emphasis on IAEA-supported projects in Africa that are helping countries to develop and manage their water resources, and to eradicate some insect pests that affect food production and health. Within a major regional project in Africa, for example, scarce groundwater resources in Ethiopia are being more fully assessed using nuclear-related techniques. On the island of Zanzibar in Tanzania, a radiation-based technology is being applied effectively to eradicate the health-threatening tsetse fly over the next twelve months. Similar projects are foreseen in other parts of Africa.

Inspections in Iraq. As part of its on going monitoring and verification in Iraq under terms of UN Security Council resolutions, the IAEA now is assessing Iraq's re-issued "full, final and complete declaration" of its former nuclear weapons programme, Dr. Blix said. Since August 1994, he noted, more than 600 inspections have been carried out in Iraq, most of them without prior notice, by the IAEA Action Team itself or jointly with UNSCOM.

Safeguards in the Democratic People's Republic of Korea (DPRK). Existing verification arrangements give confidence that nuclear installations subjected to a freeze under the US-DPRK Agreed Framework are actually frozen, he said. Yet questions remain about the completeness of the DPRK's initial declaration of nuclear activities because the IAEA's access to information and sites remains insufficient for a comprehensive picture. Greater confidence about the DPRK's compliance with its non-proliferation commitments under the NPT can only come about through more information and full implementation of the DPRK's safeguards agreement with the Agency, he said.

INTERNATIONAL MARITIME ORGANIZATION
(IMO)

DOCUMENTS REPRODUCED IN WHOLE OR IN PART:

MARINE ENVIRONMENT PROTECTION COMMITTEE

MARITIME SAFETY COMMITTEE

LEGAL COMMITTEE

SUB-COMMITTEE ON SAFETY OF NAVIGATION

DOCUMENTS NOT REPRODUCED:

COUNCIL 76th Session 17-21 June 1996; 77th Session 18-22 November 1996

LEGAL COMMITTEE 74th Session 14-18 October 1996

10.	Doc. no.:	LEG 74/4/1
	Date:	9 August 1996
	Title:	Compensation for Pollution from Ships' Bunkers. Submitted by Australia, Finland, the Netherlands, Norway, Ireland, South Africa and the United Kingdom
11.	Doc. no.:	LEG 74/5
	Date:	17 June 1996
	Title:	Draft Convention on Wreck Removal. Note by the Secretariat
12.	Doc. no.:	LEG 74/5/2
	Date:	20 August 1996
	Title:	Draft Convention on Wreck Removal. Submitted by CMI
13.	Doc. no.:	LEG 74/5/2/Add. 1
	Date:	5 September 1996
	Title:	Draft Convention on Wreck Removal. Submitted by the CMI
14.	Doc. no.:	LEG 74/6/1
	Date:	13 September 1996
	Title:	Compulsory Insurance. Submitted by the United Kingdom
15.	Doc. no.:	LEG 74/6/2
	Date:	13 September 1996
	Title:	Compulsory Insurance. Note by the International Chamber of Shipping
16.	Doc. no.:	LEG 74/12/1 + Corr. 1
	Date:	9 August 1996
	Title:	Any Other Business. Adequate Regulation of Ships Carrying Materials Covered by the INF Code. Submitted by Argentina
17.	Doc. no.:	LEG 74/12/2
	Date:	15 August 1996
	Title:	Any Other Business. Code for the Safe Carriage of Irradiated Nuclear Fuel, Plutonium and High-Level Radioactive Wastes in Flasks on Board Ships (INF Code) and Cargoes Associated Therewith. Submitted by Ireland
18.	Doc. no.:	LEG 74/12/4
	Date:	12 September 1996
	Title:	Any Other Business. Relationship between the International Convention on Liability and Compensation for Damage in Connection with the Carriage of Hazardous and Noxious Substances by Sea, 1996 (HNS Convention) and a Prospective Regime on Liability for Damage in Connection with the Transboundary Movements of Hazardous Wastes. Note by the Secretariat

MARINE ENVIRONMENT PROTECTION COMMITTEE 38th Session 1-10 July 1996

19.	Doc. no.:	MEPC 38/7/1
	Date:	2 May 1996
	Title:	Follow-Up Action to UNCED. Protection of Particularly Sensitive Sea Areas. Implementation of Paragraph 17.31(a)(iv) of Agenda 21. Submitted by WWF and IUCN
20.	Doc. no.:	MEPC 38/7/2
	Date:	2 May 1996
	Title:	Follow-Up Action to UNCED. Ensuring Respect for Areas Designated by Coastal States in their Exclusive Economic Zones: Implementation of Paragraph 17.31(v) of Agenda 21. Submitted by WWF and IUCN

21.	Doc. no.:	MEPC 38/8/3
	Date:	4 April 1996
	Title:	Interpretation and Amendments of MARPOL 73/78 and Related Codes. Consideration of the North Sea as a Special Area under Annex I of MARPOL 73/78. Submitted by Germany

22.	Doc. no.:	MEPC 38/9 + Corr. 1
	Date:	6 November 1995
	Title:	Prevention of Air Pollution from Ships. Draft Protocol of 1997 to Amend the International Convention for the Prevention of Pollution from Ships, 1973, as Modified by the Protocol of 1978 Relating Thereto. Submitted by the Secretariat

23.	Doc. no.:	MEPC 38/9/6
	Date:	4 April 1996
	Title:	Prevention of Air Pollution from Ships. An Effective Regime for Sulphur Emissions from Ships. Submitted by FOEI

24.	Doc. no.:	MEPC 38/9/9
	Date:	4 April 1996
	Title:	Prevention of Air Pollution from Ships. Draft Protocol of 1997 to Amend the International Convention for the Prevention of Pollution from Ships, 1973, as Modified by the Protocol of 1978 Relating Thereto. Entry into Force: Scope of Application: Enforcement. Submitted by the United States

25.	Doc. no.:	MEPC 38/9/11
	Date:	30 April 1996
	Title:	Prevention of Air Pollution from Ships. Draft Protocol of 1997 to Amend MARPOL 73/78. Regulation 15(1) - Sulphur Oxides (Sox) Global Capping of Sulphur. Submitted by Antigua, Barbados, Bahrain, Bahamas, Barbuda, Brazil, Ecuador, Ethiopia, Hungary, Liberia, Maldives, Mexico, Peru, Romania, Singapore, Tunisia, Turkey, Vanuatu and Venezuela

26.	Doc. no.:	MEPC 38/9/13
	Date:	3 May 1996
	Title:	Prevention of Air Pollution from Ships. Application of the Precautionary Approach to Sulphur Content of Fuel Oil. Submitted by WWF

27.	Doc. no.:	MEPC 38/13
	Date:	18 October 1995
	Title:	Unwanted Aquatic Organisms in Ballast Water. Report of the Ballast Water Working Group convened during MEPC 37

28.	Doc. no.:	MEPC 38/13/1
	Date:	3 April 1996
	Title:	Unwanted Aquatic Organisms in Ballast Waters. Guidelines for the Implementation of Annex VI of MARPOL 73/78 to Minimize the Introduction of Unwanted Aquatic Organisms and Pathogens from Ships' Ballast Water and Sediment Discharges. Note by the Secretariat

29.	Doc. no.:	MEPC 38/15/3
	Date:	14 March 1996
	Title:	Implementation of the OPRC Convention and the OPPR Conference Resolutions. Guidelines for the Development of Emergency Plans for Vessels Carrying Material Subject to the INF Code. Note by the Secretariat

30.	Doc. no.:	MEPC 38/15/3/1
	Date:	3 May 1996
	Title:	Implementation of the OPRC Convention and the OPPR Conference Resolutions. Emergency Preparedness/Response Aspects of the Carriage of Nuclear Material under the INF Code. Comments on the Review of the Code for the Safe Carriage of Irradiated Nuclear Fuel, Plutonium and High Level Radioactive Wastes in Flasks on Board Ships (INF Code). Submitted by Greenpeace International

31.	Doc. no.:	MEPC 38/15/3/2
	Date:	3 May 1996
	Title:	Implementation of the OPRC Convention and the OPPR Conference Resolutions. Emergency Preparedness/Response Aspects of the Carriage of Nuclear Material under the INF Code. Development of Measures Complementary to the INF Code and the Augmentation and Upgrading of the INF Code. Submitted by Solomon Islands

32.	Doc. no.:	MEPC 38/19
	Date:	31 January 1996
	Title:	Any Other Business. (Determination of Particularly Sensitive Areas). Designation of the Sabana-Camaguey Archipelago as a Particularly Sensitive Sea Area. Submitted by Cuba

MARITIME SAFETY COMMITTEE 66th Session 28 May - 6 June 1996; 67th Session 2-6 December 1996

33.	Doc. no.:	MSC 66/2/3/Add. 3
	Date:	27 March 1996
	Title:	Decision of Other IMO Bodies. Outcome of Meetings in Stockholm, Sweden, concerning Regional Specific Stability Requirements for Ro-ro Passenger Ships. Submitted by Sweden

34.	Doc. no.:	MSC 66/13/12
	Date:	29 March 1996
	Title:	Role of the Human Element in Maritime Casualties. Implementation of the International Safety Management (ISM) Code. Note by ICS and INTERTANKO

35.	Doc. no.:	MSC 66/16/Add. 1
	Date:	1 March 1996
	Title:	Piracy and Armed Robbery against Ships. Note by the Secretariat

36.	Doc. no.:	MSC 67/7/2
	Date:	30 August 1996
	Title:	Safety of Navigation. Designation of Certain Sea Lanes and Air Routes Thereabove Through Indonesian Archipelagic Waters. Note by Indonesia

37.	Doc. no.:	MSC 67/7/8
	Date:	26 September 1996
	Title:	Safety of Navigation. Implementation of Resolution A.827(19) of the IMO Assembly. "Ships' routeing". Submitted by the Russian Federation

38.	Doc. no.:	MSC 67/7/9
	Date:	2 October 1996
	Title:	Safety of Navigation. Navigation Aids and Related Equipment. Automatic Ship Identification Transponder/ receiver Systems. Submitted by INTERTANKO

39.	Doc. no.:	MSC 67/7/12
	Date:	4 October 1996
	Title:	Safety of Navigation. Safety of Navigation in the Straits of Istanbul and Canakkale. Submitted by OCIMF

40.	Doc. no.:	MSC 67/21/9
	Date:	4 October 1996
	Title:	Any Other Business. Violations of the SOLAS Convention. Submitted by France

SUB-COMMITTEE ON BULK LIQUIDS AND GASES 1st Session 4-8 March 1996

41.	Doc. no.:	BLG 1/20 + Corr. 1, Add. 1(+ Corr. 1), 2(+ Corr. 2)
	Date:	22 March 1996
	Title:	Report of the First Session

SUB-COMMITTEE ON DANGEROUS GOODS, CARGOES AND CONTAINERS 1st Session 5-9 February 1996

42.	Doc. no.:	DSC 1/27
	Date:	11 March 1996
	Title:	Report to the Maritime Safety Committee

SUB-COMMITTEE ON FLAG STATE IMPLEMENTATION 4th Session 18-22 March 1996

43.	Doc. no.:	FSI 4/3/1
	Date:	18 January 1996
	Title:	Implementation of IMO Instruments. Responsibilities of Governments under Safety and Pollution Prevention Conventions. Flag State Responsibility. Submitted by Canada

44.	Doc. no.:	FSI 4/3/3
	Date:	19 January 1996
	Title:	Implementation of IMO Instruments. Responsibilities of Governments under Safety and Pollution Prevention Conventions. Flag State Responsibility. Submitted by the United Kingdom and Australia

45.	Doc. no.:	FSI 4/7/2
	Date:	19 January 1996
	Title:	Port State Control. Regional Co-operation. Progress Report on Regional Port State Control Agreements. Note by the Secretariat

46.	Doc. no.:	FSI 4/7/4
	Date:	17 January 1996
	Title:	Port State Control. Avoiding Undue Detention of Ships during Port State Control. Note by Norway

47.	Doc. no.:	FSI 4/8
	Date:	22 December 1995
	Title:	Guidelines for Flag States. Report of the Correspondence Group on the Review of Resolution A.740(18). Submitted by the United States

48.	Doc. no.:	FSI 4/18
	Date:	12 April 1996
	Title:	Report to the Maritime Safety Committee and the Marine Environment Protection Committee

SUB-COMMITTEE ON RADIOCOMMUNICATIONS AND SEARCH AND RESCUE 1st Session 19-23 February 1996

49.	Doc. no.:	COMSAR 1/30
	Date:	18 March 1996
	Title:	Report to the Maritime Safety Committee

SUB-COMMITTEE ON SAFETY OF NAVIGATION 42nd Session 15-19 July 1996

50.
Doc. no.: NAV 42/6
Date: 10 May 1996
Title: Development of Measures Complementary to the Code for the Safe Carriage of Irradiated Nuclear Fuel (INF). Review of the Code for the Safe Carriage of INF, Plutonium and High Level Radioactive Wastes in Flasks on Board Ships. Submitted by the Solomon Islands

SUB-COMMITTEE ON STANDARDS OF TRAINING AND WATCHKEEPING 28th Session 16-20 September 1996

51.
Doc. no.: STW 28/20
Date: 10 October 1996
Title: Report to the Maritime Safety Committee

TECHNICAL CO-OPERATION COMMITTEE 42nd Session 20 June 1996; 43rd Session 21 November 1996

52.
Doc. no.: TC 42/12
Date: 2 July 1996
Title: Report of the Technical Co-operation Committee on its Forty-Second Session

53.
Doc. no.: TC 43/12
Date: 28 November 1996
Title: Report of the Technical Co-operation Committee on its Forty-Third Session

LONDON CONVENTION 1972 JURISTS AND LINGUISTS GROUP, held from 12-16 February 1996

54.
Doc. no.: LC/JL 1/6
Date: 1 March 1996
Title: Report of the London Convention 1972 Jurists and Linguists Group

SCIENTIFIC GROUP ON DUMPING 19th Meeting 13-17 May 1996, Rio de Janeiro

55.
Doc. no.: LC/SG 19/3/1
Date: 20 March 1996
Title: Review of the Status of Disposal at Sea of Offshore Installations. Submitted by Greenpeace International

56.
Doc. no.: LC/SG 19/3/3
Date: 26 March 1996
Title: Review of the Status of Disposal at Sea of Offshore Installations. Decommissioning of Oil and Gas Installations. Submitted by the United Kingdom

57.
Doc. no.: LC/SG 19/11
Date: 14 June 1996
Title: Report of the Nineteenth Meeting of the Scientific Group

INTERNATIONAL OIL POLLUTION COMPENSATION FUND 1971, ASSEMBLY 2nd Extraordinary Session 24-28 June 1996; 19th Session 22-25 October 1996

58.
Doc. no.: 71FUND/A/ES.2/22
Date: 28 June 1996
Title: Record of Decisions of the Second Extraordinary Session of the Assembly

59.   Doc. no.:   71FUND/A.19/30
             Date: 25 October 1996
             Title: Record of Decisions of the Nineteenth Session of the Assembly

INTERNATIONAL OIL POLLUTION COMPENSATION FUND 1992, ASSEMBLY
1st Session 24-28 June 1996; 1st Extraordinary Session 23-25 October

60.   Doc. no.:   92FUND/A.1/34
             Date: 28 June 1996
             Title: Record of Decisions of the 1st Session of the Assembly

61.   Doc. no.:   92FUND/A/ES.1/22
             Date: 25 October 1996
             Title: Record of Decisions of the 1st Extraordinary Session of the Assembly

SPECIAL CONSULTATIVE MEETING OF ENTITIES INVOLVED IN THE MARITIME TRANSPORT OF MATERIALS COVERED BY THE INF CODE held, from 4-6 March 1996

No regular documents have been issued on this Meeting. Nevertheless, IMO intends to publish the proceedings of the Meeting in an official publication.

INTERNATIONAL CONFERENCE ON HAZARDOUS AND NOXIOUS SUBSTANCES AND LIMITATION OF LIABILITY, 1996 held from 15 April - 3 May 1996

62.   Doc. no.:   LEG/CONF.10/8
             Date: 9 May 1996
             Title: Adoption of the Final Act and Any Instruments, Recommendations and Resolutions Resulting from the Work of the Conference. Protocol of 1996 to Amend the Convention on Limitation of Liability for Maritime Claims, 1976. Text Approved by the Conference

63.   Doc. no.:   LEG/CONF.10/8/1 + Corr. 1
             Date: 9 May 1996
             Title: Adoption of the Final Act and Any Instruments, Recommendations and Resolutions Resulting from the Work of the Conference. Conference Resolutions. Text Approved by the Conference.

64.   Doc. no.:   LEG/CONF.10/8/2
             Date: 9 May 1996
             Title: Adoption of the Final Act and Any Instruments, Recommendations and Resolutions Resulting from the Work of the Conference. International Convention on Liability and Compensation for Damage in Connection with the Carriage of Hazardous and Noxious Substances by Sea, 1996. Text Approved by the Conference

65.   Doc. no.:   LEG/CONF.10/8/3
             Date: 9 May 1996
             Title: Adoption of the Final Act and Any Instruments, Recommendations and Resolutions Resulting from the Work of the Conference. Final Act of the International Conference on Hazardous and Noxious Substances and Limitation of Liability, 1996. Text Approved by the Conference

SPECIAL MEETING OF CONTRACTING PARTIES TO CONSIDER AND ADOPT THE 1996 PROTOCOL TO THE LONDON CONVENTION 1972 held from 28 October - 8 November 1996

66.	Doc. no.:	LC/S 1/5
	Date:	7 November 1996
	Title:	Adoption of the Final Act, Recommendations and Resolutions. Final Act of the Special Meeting of Contracting Parties to Consider and Adopt the 1996 Protocol to the London Convention 1972. Text Adopted by the Special Meeting

67.	Doc. no.:	LC/S 1/6
	Date:	14 November 1996
	Title:	1996 Protocol to the Convention on the Prevention of Marine Pollution by Dumping of Wastes and Other Matter, 1972 and Resolutions Adopted by the Special Meeting. As Adopted by the Special Meeting of Contracting Parties to the London Convention 1972 on 7 November 1996

1. REPORT OF THE MARINE ENVIRONMENT PROTECTION COMMITTEE ON ITS THIRTY-EIGHT SESSION*

Doc. no.: MEPC 38/20 + Corr. 1

Date: 16 August 1996

---

* Only paras 9.1-9.62 and 13.1-13.10 are reproduced.

ANNEXES

Corrigenda

It should be noted that the resolutions of MEPC 38 have been incorrectly numbered from resolution MEPC.67(38). Since MEPC.67(37) exists already, resolutions from the thirty-eighth session should be renumbered. The following are the annexes of the MEPC 38 report with the correct resolution numbers:

ANNEX 2   RESOLUTION MEPC.68(38) - AMENDMENTS TO THE ANNEX OF THE PROTOCOL OF 1978 RELATING TO THE INTERNATIONAL CONVENTION FOR THE PREVENTION OF POLLUTION FROM SHIPS, 1973 (AMENDMENTS TO PROTOCOL I)

ANNEX 3   RESOLUTION MEPC.69(38) - AMENDMENTS TO THE INTERNATIONAL CODE FOR THE CONSTRUCTION AND EQUIPMENT OF SHIPS CARRYING DANGEROUS CHEMICALS IN BULK (IBC CODE)

ANNEX 4   RESOLUTION MEPC.70(38) - AMENDMENTS TO THE CODE FOR THE CONSTRUCTION AND EQUIPMENT OF SHIPS CARRYING DANGEROUS CHEMICALS IN BULK (BCH CODE)

ANNEX 6   RESOLUTION MEPC.71(38) - GUIDELINES FOR THE DEVELOPMENT OF GARBAGE MANAGEMENT PLANS

ANNEX 8   RESOLUTION MEPC.72(38) - REVISION OF THE LIST OF SUBSTANCES TO BE ANNEXED TO THE PROTOCOL RELATING TO THE INTERVENTION ON THE HIGH SEAS IN CASES OF MARINE POLLUTION BY SUBSTANCES OTHER THAN OIL

[...]

9   PREVENTION OF AIR POLLUTION FROM SHIPS

9.1   In order to finalize the draft Protocol for the Prevention of Air Pollution from Ships, which will form Annex VI of MARPOL 73/78, the Committee requested and was granted three extra working days for this session, which were devoted to the in-depth discussion on articles and regulations of the draft Protocol. In addition to the basic document prepared by the Secretariat (MEPC 38/9 and MEPC 38/9/Corr.1), the Committee had before it the following documents: MEPC 38/9/1 (Secretariat); MEPC 38/9/2 (Norway); MEPC 38/9/3 (Russian Federation); MEPC 38/9/4, MEPC 38/9/5 and MEPC 38/INF.3 (Russian Federation); MEPC 38/9/6 (FOEI); MEPC 38/9/7 (United Kingdom); MEPC 38/9/8 (OCIMF); MEPC 38/9/9 (United States); MEPC 38/9/10 (Co-ordinator of the Correspondence Group (Germany)); MEPC 38/9/11 (Antigua and Barbuda, Bahamas, Barbados, Bahrain, Brazil, Ecuador, Ethiopia, Hungary, Liberia, Maldives, Mexico, Peru, Romania, Singapore, Tunisia, Vanuatu, Venezuela); MEPC 38/9/12 (Japan); MEPC 38/9/13 (WWF); MEPC 38/9/14 (INTERTANKO); MEPC 38/9/15 (Germany); MEPC 38/9/16 (Belgium, Denmark, EC, France, Germany, Netherlands, Norway, Sweden and United Kingdom); MEPC 38/9/17 (United States); MEPC 38/INF.12 (Liberia); and MEPC 38/WP. 1 (Chairman).

9.2   In addition, the Committee considered the following submissions received at its last session: MEPC 37/13/3 (Bahamas, Liberia and Panama); MEPC 37/13/4 and MEPC 37/13/5 (OCIMF); MEPC 37/13/6 and MEPC 37/13/6/Add.1 (Norway); MEPC 37/13/7 (Denmark, Estonia, Finland, Germany, Latvia, Lithuania, Poland, Russian Federation and Sweden); MEPC 37/13/8 (INTERTANKO); MEPC 37/13/9 and MEPC 37/13/10 (United Kingdom); MEPC 37/13/11 (Netherlands); MEPC 37/13/14 (ICS); MEPC 37/13/16 and MEPC 37/13/17 (IAPH); MEPC 37/13/19 (Denmark); MEPC 37/13/20 (Greece); MEPC 37/13/21 (Australia, Bahrain, India, Mexico, Singapore, Solomon Islands, Vanuatu and Venezuela); MEPC 37/13/22 (Netherlands); MEPC 37/13/23 (Japan); MEPC 37/13/26 (Germany).

9.3   The Committee reconvened the Drafting Group under the chairmanship of Mr. Bryan Wood-Thomas (United States). The Committee instructed the Drafting Group to prepare a "clean" version of the draft Protocol 1997 taking into consideration the outcome of the deliberations of the Committee and suggestions for amendments submitted by Member States where agreement was reached on the desired policy outcome. The Drafting Group was also directed to review the draft Protocol text, concentrating on editorial and drafting issues that do not require further discussion in plenary. In this connection, some delegations suggested that the NO_x Technical Code might follow the format of the STCW Code, i.e., the Code should be divided into two parts - mandatory provisions contained in Part A and recommendatory provisions in Part B.

Legal framework

9.4   Under this issue, the Committee noted the two written submissions from the United States and Germany (MEPC 38/9/9 and MEPC 38/9/15) offering comments on, and amendments to, the draft Protocol and decided to consider the draft Protocol article by article.

9.5   The Committee agreed with the draft articles 1 to 3 without debate.

9.6   With regard to article 4, the Committee agreed with a proposal of Germany to add in the first line after "to Annex VI" the words "and its appendices" since the appendices constitute part of the Annex.

9.7   The conditions for entry into force stipulated in article 6 remain a contentious issue. The majority of delegations were in favour of "twelve months", "fifteen States" and "50 per cent" of the gross tonnage of the world's merchant shipping, the main reason being that the entry into force conditions for this Annex should be in accordance with article 16 of the Convention.

9.8   A number of delegations preferred "six months" although they agreed with "fifteen States" and "50 per cent". An indicative vote showed that a large number of delegations favoured "twelve months".

9.9   A number of other delegations argued that Annex VI should enter into force within a reasonable period of time, therefore, the conditions for entry into force, especially the percentage of tonnage, should be lowered. In the opinion of those delegations, under the "50 per cent" provision, it would take a long time to bring the Annex to enter into force or, in a worse-case scenario, it may never enter into force. Examples noted in this regard were Annex IV of MARPOL and the 1977 Torremolinos Convention on Fishing Vessels Safety. The statement made by the Netherlands delegation on behalf of several other delegations, which gives a specific proposal containing the number of States as 20 and percentage tonnage 25, is set out at annex 5 to this report.

9.10   After numerous interventions, it became clear that the majority of delegations preferred "twelve months", "fifteen States" and "50 per cent". Therefore, the Committee decided to reflect these three conditions for entry into force in the draft Protocol. While some delegations suggested removal of the square brackets, others noted that until the Committee has basically agreed with the technical regulations, it would be inappropriate to make final decisions on the conditions for entry into force. Since this view was shared by many delegations, the Committee decided to keep the three conditions in square brackets.

9.11   Following the suggestion of a number of delegations, the Committee decided to remove the footnote to article 6 which provided an alternative to the entry into force conditions in the main text of the draft Protocol. This decision was based on an understanding that alternative views or proposals can be submitted directly to the Diplomatic Conference.

9.12   The Committee, without discussion, agreed with articles 7 to 9 which deal with denunciation, depositary and languages.

9.13   With regard to the United States proposal (MEPC 38/9/9) on vessels entitled to sovereign immunity, the Committee agreed that such vessels are to be excluded from Annex VI since MARPOL article 3(3) excludes vessels entitled to sovereign immunity from Annexes I to V.

Global sulphur cap (regulations 15(1) and 15(3))

9.14   In the general discussion concerning a global sulphur cap, which remains as one of the main outstanding issues, it became apparent that numerous countries were maintaining their previous positions, i.e., those preferring a higher global cap and those preferring a lower global cap.

9.15   The Chairman of the Executive Body to the Convention on Long Range Transboundary Air Pollution (LRTAP), Mr. Ian Thompson, addressed the Committee and stressed that it is of the utmost importance that the new Air Pollution Annex to MARPOL 73/78 will result in a true reduction of the pollution problems caused by the air emissions from ships. With no control measures, the relative contribution from ships to the acidification problems in the LRTAP area will increase significantly in the years ahead.

9.16   In order to break this impasse, two proposals were tabled (MEPC 38/WP.4 by an informal drafting group and MEPC 38/WP.5 by the Netherlands delegation). However, the Committee could not agree on these alternative proposals. After an indicative vote of those who prefer a 5% sulphur global cap and those who prefer a figure lower than 5%, the Committee found that these two groups are evenly divided and, therefore, the Committee agreed that the 5% figure in regulation 15(1) should remain in square brackets. The alternative proposals in MEPC 38/WP.4 and WP.5 were later merged by a group of experts and presented to the Committee as MEPC 38/WP.11. The Committee decided not to discuss the content of WP.11, but to annex it to the basic document for MEPC 39 for further discussion.

9.17   The delegation of Japan observed that, in MEPC 38/WP.11, guidelines to be developed by the Organization are mentioned and that the draft of such guidelines should be submitted to MEPC 39 in order to facilitate a meaningful discussion on the proposed paragraphs to regulation 15.

9.18   The Committee accepted with appreciation an offer from the delegations of the Netherlands, and the United Kingdom to provide a draft of the guidelines for monitoring the worldwide average sulphur content in residual fuel oils supplied for use on board ships, for consideration during MEPC 39.

9.19   The Committee was informed by the Chairman of BCH 24 that, in the discussion of this subject by the Sub-Committee, agreement was almost reached on the figure of 4.5%. Various proposals have now been suggested and agreement on a common value at the Conference appears to be a realistic expectation.

Delineation of Special Areas

9.20   The Committee recalled that, due to time constraints at the last session, the Committee was unable to discuss the requirements within Special Areas as well as the criteria and procedures for designation of such areas, as outlined in Appendix II of the draft Annex VI. After general discussion, it became apparent that the scientific evidence as to how far the sulphur emitted from ships may travel had led to different interpretations among the Parties. Some Members reiterated their view that the width of a Special Area should not extend beyond twelve miles from the baseline, whilst other delegations proposed that large, clearly defined areas should be designated as special areas. It was pointed out that delineation of Special Areas should also take into account the competitive position of ports, cargo flow, trade patterns, etc.

9.21   Some delegations questioned the need for the criteria and procedures for the designation of Special Areas for SO_x emission control areas outlined in Appendix II of draft Annex VI since, in their opinion, the Guidelines for designation of Special Areas established for particularly sensitive sea areas (resolution A.720(17)) could be used for the designation of Special Areas for SO_x emission control purposes. Other delegations noted that the resolution A.720 guidelines are created for the purpose of protecting unique marine environments, while the purpose of Appendix II is to designate areas of the marine environment where SO_x emissions from ships harm terrestrial and aquatic systems.

9.22   The Committee requested a group of experts to review Appendix II of draft Annex VI to explore if solutions could be identified and to produce a clean version of Appendix II that would serve the interests of all Parties.

9.23   The product of the group of experts' deliberation was presented to the Committee in MEPC 38/WP.12 on Tuesday, 9 July 1996. The Committee agreed to replace the existing Appendix II with the text as presented in MEPC 38/WP.12 and refer to such areas as "SOx Emission Control Areas".

Baltic Sea as Special Area (SOx emission control area)

9.24   The Committee noted the views of a number of delegations that the determination of a Special area (SOx Emission Control Area) under the draft new Annex VI can only be done after the criteria and procedure for designation of such areas have been agreed, and until such time as the Organization has completed the evaluation of the information provided by the States desirous of having certain area(s) designated as a Special Area (SOx Emission Control Area) under the draft new Annex VI.

9.25   In this regard, it was pointed out that the information provided thus far by the Baltic Sea States addresses most of the criteria, but does not fully substantiate the extent to which ships' SOx emission contributes to the acidification of the marine and land-based ecosystems in the Baltic Sea Area. It was suggested that a supplemental submission may resolve this issue.

9.26   The Committee agreed to discuss the designation of the Baltic Sea as a SOx emission control area, together with the proposal to designate the North Sea as such an area, on the basis of the revised Appendix II at MEPC 39.

Bunker delivery note and fuel oil quality

9.27   With regard to the bunker delivery note required in regulation 19, some delegations preferred a simple form as outlined in Appendix III, while other delegations preferred a standard form of bunker delivery note appearing in Appendix IV of draft Annex VI. The Committee was also informed that ISO is developing a formal bunker delivery note. In the discussion that followed, the Committee agreed to incorporate certain elements found in Appendix IV within the list of data items found in Appendix III and instructed the Drafting Group to delete Appendix IV and to work out the appropriate text of revised Appendix III.

9.28   INTERTANKO, in its submission (MEPC 38/9/14), proposed that regulation 19(5) should be amended in order to attribute the responsibility for the quality of the fuel delivered to the supplier, which would require, *inter alia*, sampling of fuel when delivered to the vessels. The Committee agreed that it is not the responsibility of the Master to ensure that the correct fuel is delivered, since requiring samples to be taken at the time of delivery was considered by some to be too expensive and time consuming in light of the time required for laboratory analysis. With regard to the phrase "port authorities or other appropriate authorities", found in regulation 19(5), the Committee agreed to delete "port authorities or other".

9.29   The Committee discussed a proposal by Japan to exclude smaller vessels from the requirements to retain bunker delivery notes on ships where the installed engines are designed to operate only on gas oil, kerosene or gasoline and on ships engaged exclusively in voyages outside of the Special Areas and which are not equipped with engines of power output of 750 kW or above. The Committee agreed with the need to exempt smaller vessels from this requirement as well as vessels engaged in domestic trade only and instructed the Drafting Group to determine what mechanism best served this purpose.

9.30   The Committee agreed to include a proposal from the Russian Federation (MEPC 38/9/4) to require licensing of local suppliers of bunker fuel oils and certification of the fuel oil quality. Many delegations objected to the administrative burden associated with the proposal. A group of experts later reviewed the proposal and developed an alterative proposal which was presented to the Committee as MEPC 38/WP.10.

9.31   After a brief review of MEPC 38/WP.10, the Committee decided not to discuss the content of this paper but to annex it to the basic document for consideration of MEPC 39 for further consideration.

9.32   On suggestion from the Secretary-General, the Committee decided to attach MEPC 38/WP.10 to the text of the draft Protocol of 1997 as amended by the Drafting Group, to facilitate the work of the Committee during its next session.

9.33   The delegation of Japan, reiterating its proposal made at MEPC 37 (MEPC 37/13/23) for the exemption from the supply of bunker delivery note for small ships and pleasure craft. Japan was of the opinion that since the sulphur content of bunker fuel available in the market worldwide is likely to be less than the global capping value specified in regulation 14 (no bunker fuel with sulphur content exceeding 3.5% is supplied in Japan), careful consideration should be given to the need to introduce complex measures for the control of sulphur contents for ships not engaged in trades within SO_x Emission Control Areas. The delegation of Japan expressed its intention to submit a proposal for exemption from the requirements for the mandatory carriage of bunker delivery note.

9.34   Finland, referring to resolution A.719(17), expressed the view that regulation 19(1) in its present form would allow incineration of chemical waste through the ships' engine, and reserved its position.

Ozone depleting substances

9.35   The Committee agreed to the proposal by the United Kingdom to merge regulations 12 and 13 into one regulation (MEPC 38/9/7) and asked the Drafting Group to work out the appropriate language. The Committee instructed the FP Sub-Committee to review the draft regulation on ozone depleting substances with a view to ensuring consistency of the proposed regulation under MARPOL with corresponding regulations in SOLAS chapter II-2.

9.36   The United States proposed that perfluorocarbons (PFCs) be prohibited for use on ships through regulation 12 and invited the Committee to consider this issue (document MEPC 38/9/17). PFCs are greenhouse gases with extremely long atmospheric lives which are increasing in use as substitutes for halons in fire extinguishing systems. Some delegations expressed doubts about addressing PFCs without input from the FP Sub-Committee. The purpose of the United States' proposal is to avoid replacing one environmental problem (ozone depletion) with another (global warming) through the expanded use of PFCs on board ships. Consequently, the Committee decided, before taking any action, to instruct the FP Sub-Committee to examine whether the use of PFCs on board ships is regulated under the current SOLAS Convention and to recommend what action may be appropriate through SOLAS or through the proposed Annex on air pollution.

9.37   The Committee discussed whether new installations of fire-extinguishing equipment should include portable or hand-held type fire extinguishers or not, and agreed that existing equipment (including portable units) may be recharged. The Committee also decided, however, that the prohibition on new installations should include new portable units.

9.38   The Committee further instructed the Drafting Group to clarify the meaning of deliberate emissions and new installations, as used in the regulation on ozone-depleting substances.

NO_x Technical Code/Guidelines

9.39   The Committee considered the report of the Correspondence Group on the Technical Guidelines for NO_x requirements under the new Annex for Prevention of Air Pollution from Ships (MEPC 38/9/10). The Correspondence Group proposed that the existing Guidelines should become mandatory as a Technical Code. The co-ordinator of the Group reported that a number of technical issues remain unresolved and that further work would be necessary during this session.

9.40   A considerable number of delegations supported the idea of making the NO_x Technical Code mandatory. However, some delegations felt that more work is needed. The present proposed Code needs redrafting and format changes to conform with other mandatory IMO Codes. In addition, a thorough review of the revised text will be necessary before formal adoption is possible.

9.41   Japan noted its interest in addressing test cycles within the nitrogen oxide regulation, while others noted that various issues remain outstanding in the test cycles that require further resolution. The Committee agreed to refer discussion of the Japanese proposal (MEPC 38/9/12) concerning the transfer of certain provisions found in the draft Code into regulation 13 of the draft Annex. For consideration by the NO_x Technical Code Group of Experts, chaired by Mr. K. Hadler (Germany), Japan further proposed new regulations 14-1 and 14-2 which require a Technical File and Record Book of Engine Parameters to be carried on board (MEPC 38/9/12).

9.42   The Committee requested the group of NO_x experts to identify technical issues to be solved and to estimate how much time would be required to resolve these issues. The Chairman of the Expert Group reported that the Group identified 17 different issues and stated that it would take some three days to resolve them. He stated that the Group had offered to meet during the remainder of this session and solve as many of the issues as possible.

9.43   The NO_x experts met from 5 to 10 July and considered the following outstanding issues:

.1	test cycles,		.10	test fuels,
.2	allowances,		.11	ready means of verification,
.3	mutual recognition,		.12	monitoring and recording,
.4	table b,		.13	operating parameters,
.5	fa-factor,		.14	guidelines for exhaust gas cleaning,
.6	definitions,		.15	off-shore units,
.7	recreational vessels,		.16	130 kW power output threshold, and
.8	dual fuel engines,		.17	regulation on technical file and record book of engine parameters.
.9	responsibility of manufacturers,			

9.44   Of the issues listed in paragraph 9.43, the Group was able, through drafting only, to resolve all of the issues except three, i.e., .15, .16 and .17. The Group recommended to change 100 kW to 130 kW as a new threshold for diesel engines, but the Group referred to the Committee all decisions on how to handle, within the regulations of the new Annex, the mutual recognition issue for off-shore units and whether to accept 130 kW. Also, due to time constraints, the Group was unable to resolve the issue on a regulation covering the technical file and record book of engine parameters. The Committee decided, due to time constraints, that it was unable to resolve these three issues. The Committee invited the Members to consider the revised NO_x Technical Code, to be circulated by the Secretariat, which would contain the texts of technical issues resolved by the Group of experts (see paragraphs 9.43.1-9.43.14) and, in particular, the three issues mentioned above and submit comments for consideration at MEPC 39.

9.45   Based on a proposal by Japan to improve the link between Annex VI and the NO_x Technical Code, the Committee agreed to include information on test cycles as an appendix to new regulation 13, Nitrogen Oxides (NO_x), and amendments to regulation 13 to make reference to that Appendix. The draft text of the Appendix to new regulation 13 is included in the basic document on this subject for MEPC 39.

9.46   In the light of the priority given to completing the draft NO_x Technical Code at MEPC 39, the Committee agreed to the following:

.1   the draft NO$_x$ Technical Code must be finalized as a mandatory instrument;

.2   the format of the draft NO$_x$ Technical Code shall be retained per MEPC 38/9/10;

.3   MEPC 38/9/10, including the technical revisions proposed by the informal NO$_x$ group, shall be used as the base document for the future work on the draft Code;

.4   the Secretariat is instructed to prepare a document reflecting only the editorial changes to the draft NO$_x$ Technical Code necessary for the text to become mandatory; and

.5   the Secretariat is instructed to submit the NO$_x$ Technical Code as a final, mandatory Code for consideration and approval by MEPC 39.

Shipboard incinerators

9.47   A number of delegations expressed concern that the regulation, as currently constructed, presents a number of substantive questions requiring further consideration. Issues noted included: difficulties associated with the proposed prohibition of incineration in Antarctica in ports, harbours and estuaries; the need to specify what products and substances should be prohibited from incineration as well as a need to establish a workable threshold for "trace" levels. It was also pointed out that there is a need to establish appropriate practice in implementing the requirements on board a ship; whether the prohibition concerning halogenated substances and heavy metals should also apply to the main propulsion unit, and the need to clarify that shipboard incinerators are limited to the incineration of materials generated on board since the incineration at sea of industrial wastes is prohibited under the 1972 London Convention for the Prevention of Marine Pollution by Dumping of Wastes and Other Matter at Sea.

9.48   Due to time constraints, the Committee decided to postpone the discussion of these issues to its next session.

Other regulations

9.49   Regulation 5. The Committee agreed with regulation 5, and instructed the Drafting Group to review the regulation.

9.50   Regulation 11. The United States delegation expressed the view that there is a need for regulation 11, which states that article 6 of the 1973 Convention applies to Annex IV *mutatis mutandis*; this is placed in square brackets. He also proposed that the regulation should refer as well to the 1982 United Nations Convention on the Law of the Sea (MEPC 38/9/9, paragraphs 13-15). Several delegations supported the proposal of the United States in principle whilst other delegations wished to further consider the implications of the proposal at their capitals. The Committee agreed to discuss this issue at MEPC 39.

Information papers

9.51   The Committee took note of the following information papers:

MEPC 38/INF.3	Russian Federation	Marine Exhaust Emission Research
MEPC 38/INF.12	Liberia	Investigation on position of ships at sea

Outcome of the Drafting Group

9.52   The report of the work of the Drafting Group, including a revised text of the Protocol of 1997 and the draft Annex VI, was presented to the Committee as MEPC 38/WP.17. Due to time constraints, the report was not considered.

9.53   The Committee instructed the Secretariat to issue as soon as possible after the session a consolidated text of the draft Protocol of 1997, including articles and regulations as reviewed and revised by the Drafting Group as the basic paper for consideration of this subject at MEPC 39.

Outstanding issues

9.54   As a result of discussions within the Air Pollution Drafting Group as well as discussions in plenary, a number of outstanding main issues have been identified that require decisions by the Committee. The issues identified range from major policy questions raised in the Committee with respect to the proposed regulation on shipboard incinerators to more minor, but still substantative questions raised with respect to various regulations in the draft Annex. A brief and not exhaustive summary of the outstanding issues noted during discussion at MEPC 38, in addition to those identified above, are recorded in the paragraphs below.

9.55   Regulation 12 - Ozone Depleting Substances

In reviewing Section 2 of the Supplement to the IAPPC, a question arose whether the certificate, and regulation 12, should cover those ships already prohibited by SOLAS from allowing new installations of halogenated hydrocarbon systems?

Many refrigerated cargo containers use CFCs. The Committee agreed to decide whether it is appropriate to prohibit "installation" or new construction of refrigerated units using CFCs following entry into force of this Annex.

9.56   Regulation 13 - Nitrogen Oxides

Installed Power: While there is agreement that "installed power" is clearly different from "propulsion power," some delegations have suggested that a definition of "installed power" should be developed to clarify what engines are included under this term.

Other Definitions relating to NO_x: The NO_x Technical Group developed a number of definitions clarifying the meaning of various terms used throughout the NO_x Technical Code and Regulation 13 (e.g., continuous means of verification, maximum continuous rating, major modification, etc.). While each of these definitions will be included in the NO_x Technical Code, the Committee agreed to consider which definitions, if any, are appropriate for inclusion in regulation 2 of the proposed Annex.

9.57   Regulation 14 - Sulphur Oxides (SOx) (Special Areas)

The Baltic Sea Areas as defined in Annex I of MARPOL 73/78 and the North Sea, as defined in Annex V of MARPOL 73/78, have been suggested as "Special Areas" or "SOx Emission Control Areas" under the new Annex VI (see paragraphs 9.24-9.26).

9.58   Regulation 15 - Volatile Organic Compounds

"In ports or terminals" vs "shoreside terminals": The Committee agreed to decide which term is most appropriate for use in regulation 15 considering the availability of vapour recovery systems for VOC recovery at offshore terminals or during lightering operations.

"Tanker": Should the term "tanker", as used in regulation 15, include gas tankers as well as oil tankers with respect to the capture of VOCs?

9.59   Regulation 16 - Shipboard Incinerators

Numerous policy questions were raised in plenary regarding the requirements currently proposed concerning shipboard incinerators. Questions and other observations raised in plenary include:

-       Is a prohibition of incineration within Antarctica appropriate?

-       Is a prohibition of incineration within ports, harbours, and estuaries practical?

-       The need for practical guidance with respect to what heavy metals and halogenated compounds shall be prohibited from incineration and the need to develop a practical measure of "trace levels" for purposes of the requirement found in (2)(c) of the regulation.

-       Whether certain requirements set forward for shipboard incinerators should also apply to the ship's main propulsion plant? and

-       Recognition that shipboard incinerators are restricted to the incineration of wastes generated on board the ship due to the prohibition of "incineration at sea" effective under the 1972 London Convention on the Prevention of Marine Pollution from the Dumping of Wastes and Other Matter at Sea.

In addition, the Committee is invited to make a decision with respect to the alternative texts presented under paragraph (1) of regulation 16: "comply with" or "approved by the Administration". A decision needs to be made regarding which term is most appropriate in the light of earlier discussions within the Committee concerning "standards developed outside the Organization".

9.60   Regulation 17 - Reception Facilities

Two issues require attention with respect to regulation 17. First, the Committee is invited to decide how practical it may be to require all ports to possess appropriate facilities and equipment for the reception of CFCs and for the "banking" of halons. In addition, the Committee is invited to decide whether a positive notification of available reception facilities, as called for by OCIMF in MEPC 38/9/8, is warranted.

9.61   Offshore Platforms - Application of Annex VI

The Committee agreed to consider how the various regulations proposed in the draft Annex will apply to offshore platforms and MODUs. Various questions have been raised in this regard and are briefly summarized below:

-       Special survey requirements for drilling rigs and floating platforms with regard to coastal State/Flag State administration have been suggested by IADC in MEPC 37/13/13 (page 4, item 5).

-       Incinerators are often used on board platforms for the disposal of garbage, drilling muds, and other wastes. Whilst the design of some incinerators installed on platforms may differ from units typically used on board ships, should regulation 16 of the proposed Annex apply?

-       It is common practice on off-shore platforms to use containers with mobile power plants. The power output from such mobile power plants is frequently higher than the lower limits for installations addressed under regulation 13. Should such mobile units be covered by the proposed Annex?

9.62   Before concluding the discussion of air pollution issues, the Chairman invited delegations to submit comments and proposals on the outstanding issues, working paper proposals, revised draft text, and other matters relating to air pollution from ships well in advance of the 13 December 1996 deadline for submissions to MEPC 39.

[...]

13   UNWANTED AQUATIC ORGANISMS IN BALLAST WATER

13.1   The Committee approved the report of its Working Group on Ballast Water (MEPC 38/13), which had met during MEPC 37 and re-convened the Working Group to continue work as set out in the Working Group's Programme (MEPC 38/13, annex), taking into account documents submitted under this agenda item (MEPC 38/13/1 (Secretariat), MEPC 38/13/2 (Brazil), MEPC 38/INF.23 (United Kingdom), and MEPC 38/INF.26 (Germany)).

13.2   Noting that the Chairman of the Working Group on Ballast Water, Mr. R. Gaudiosi (United States) was unable to attend this session, the Committee accepted with appreciation the offer of Mr. M. Alexander (New Zealand) to act as Chairman for this meeting of the Working Group.

13.3   The Committee was informed by the Secretariat of intersessional activities on ballast water research, control and management carried out in co-operation with other organizations.   In this connection, the Secretariat drew attention to discussions held with members of the Secretariats of ICES and IOC with a view to developing arrangements and terms of reference for a joint ICES/IMO/IOC Study Group on Ballast Water and Sediments that had been proposed by the IOC Assembly.

13.4   The Committee requested the Working Group on Ballast Water to consider the proposal concerning co-operation with ICES and IOC and to advise the Committee on this matter. The Working Group was also requested to consider questions raised by the DE Sub-Committee concerning the relationship between the currently developed draft Regulations for the Control and Management of Ships' Ballast Water and the guidance considered by the DE Sub-Committee on ballast water management plans.

13.5   The Working Group met from 1 to 9 July 1996. The progress of work achieved by the Working Group during this meeting was introduced orally by the Chairman of the Working Group on Ballast Water (MEPC 38/WP.16). The Chairman reported on several observations made by the Working Group and summarized these as follows:

.1   the level of international concern in relation to consequences of uncontrolled releases of ballast water is increasing, resulting in a higher level of representation in this meeting of the Working Group than ever before. The Working Group considered it essential that the Committee realizes that firm action should be taken at this stage;

.2   the Working Group completed a first review of the draft "Regulations for the Control and Management of Ships' Ballast Water to Minimize the Transfer of Harmful Aquatic Organisms and Pathogens" (MEPC 38/WP.16, annex 1). The Committee was requested to comment on the draft regulations and to advise the Working Group at MEPC 39 on additional requirements or provisions for inclusion, as appropriate;

.3   the Working Group did not develop "safety requirements" but agreed that these be left open until such time as the outcome of work on safety issues that is under consideration by both the DE and SLF Sub-Committees becomes available. Recalling that these Sub-Committees had been requested to consider draft guidance on the preparation of ballast water management plans in respect of the structural integrity of ships, e.g., when exchanging ballast water in deep sea areas, the Working Group expressed keen interest in the results of respective considerations. The Working Group also expressed the view that guidance on safety aspects, even in the form of preliminary advice, was urgently needed in the light of the fact that many ships are requested to conduct ballast water exchange at sea in water depths of 2,000 m or more;

.4   the Working Group reviewed the draft Guidelines for the Implementation of the Regulations mentioned in sub-paragraph .2 above. These had been prepared during the intersessional period and the Working Group was able to prepare a first revision. The Working Group requested the Secretariat to distribute the revised draft guidelines as part of its report for further and more detailed consideration at the next meeting of the Working Group during MEPC 39;

.5 plans have been developed pursuant to recommendations of the IOC Assembly in 1995, to establish an ICES/IMO/IOC Joint Study Group on Ballast Water and Sediments which should operate under the ICES Working Group on Introductions and Transfers of Marine Organisms. The operational procedures and terms of reference for the Joint Group were reviewed by the Working Group (MEPC 38/WP.16, annex 2); and

.6 during its review of the above-mentioned Implementation Guidelines, the Working Group took into account two recommendations made by the United States National Research Council's Committee on Ships' Ballast Operations, addressing IMO Member States as follows:

.6.1 "future international considerations should include establishing guidelines for performing baseline sampling of ports for specific organisms. Such efforts should incorporate the testing of samples to agreed-upon international standards to facilitate comparison of the water of each ballast uptake port with the water of receiving ports;" and

.6.2 "in future discussions and updates of the existing voluntary guidelines (IMO Assembly resolution A.774(18), 1993), further consideration should be given to the maintenance of appropriate ships' logs, records of ballast water movements, and any management practices used. These data could be valuable when used in conjunction with basic water-quality parameter measurements to verify that approaches to managing ballast water have been effective."

13.6 The Committee took note of the report of the Working Group presented by its Chairman. Members of the Committee undertook to consider the draft regulations with a view to providing their comments and advice during MEPC 39, at which time the Committee decided also to discuss the appropriate legal framework through which the regulations could be introduced and implemented. In this connection the Committee agreed that the development of a legal framework was a matter to be considered in the first instance by the Working Group on Ballast Water.

13.7 The delegation of the Netherlands noted that in its view there was an interrelationship between the issues related to ballast water control and management and those related to the use and application of anti-fouling paints. That delegation invited other Members of the Committee to consider at some future stage the need to incorporate these issues within one legal framework under the MARPOL Convention.

13.8 The Committee endorsed the recommendations provided by ICES and IOC and supported by the Working Group in regard to future co-operation between ICES, IMO and IOC within a joint study group as outlined in MEPC 38/WP.16, annex 2.

13.9 The consideration of future activities of the Working Group on Ballast Water, in particular its continued review of the draft guidelines at MEPC 39, is reflected under item 17: Future work programme of this report. In this connection it was noted that the development of draft regulations, and of draft implementation guidelines thereto, should be undertaken at the same time. In this regard the Working Programme presented by the Group (MEPC 38/WP.16, annex 3) needs to be adjusted. The Committee agreed that this should be included in the report of the Working Group, which the Secretariat was requested to distribute well in advance of MEPC 39.

13.10 The Committee noted the advice of the Working Group on the questions raised by the DE Sub-Committee that:

.1   the terms of reference for both the Sub-Committees on Ship Design and Equipment (DE) and on Stability and Load Lines and Fishing Vessels (SLF) from the viewpoint of MEPC seem appropriate to continue their work;

.2   under the draft regulations prepared for ballast water management, safety requirements will be included, with reference either directly to the guidance prepared by the DE and SLF Sub-Committees, or to the Guidelines which are in preparation. The latter could incorporate the safety guidance provided by the two Sub-Committees, or refer to it. This would depend on the type and content of the final product, as well as on the result of joint considerations within the two Sub-Committees. However, recognizing that many ships at this stage are required to conduct ballast water exchange at sea, guidance on safety aspects is urgently needed, even in the form of preliminary advice.

[...]

2. REPORT OF THE MARITIME SAFETY COMMITTEE ON ITS SIXTY-SIXTH SESSION*

Doc. no.: MSC 66/24

Date: 18 June 1996

---

* Only paras 16.1-16.13, 21.16-21.23, and 23.16-23.20 are reproduced.

LIST OF ANNEXES

[...]

16   PIRACY AND ARMED ROBBERY AGAINST SHIPS

16.1   The Committee noted MSC/Circ.700 issued by the Secretary-General in July 1995 expressing concern at the sharp rise in the number of piracy attacks reported to the Organization during the second quarter of 1995.

16.2   The Committee also noted, along with this development, the changing pattern in both the likely location and the severity of the attacks with the areas most affected being the South China Sea, the coast of Somalia, the Arabian Peninsula and the north eastern coast of South America.

16.3   The Committee shared the Secretary-General's concern that most of the attacks reported in the above areas involved the use of firearms by the pirates and robbers, which had resulted in a number of fatalities and that the pirates in the South China Sea and the coast of Somalia at times used craft disguised as Government boats and posed as Government officials while approaching innocent ships and before launching their attacks.

16.4   The Committee recalled that, at its sixty-fifth session (MSC 65/25, paragraph 16.10), it instructed the Secretariat to issue, as from 31 July 1995, monthly reports of all incidents of piracy and armed robbery against ships reported to the Organization and, in addition, on a quarterly basis, composite reports accompanied by an analysis, on a regional basis, of the situation and an indication whether the frequency of incidents was increasing or decreasing and advising any new feature or pattern of significance.

16.5   In this regard, the Committee noted (MSC 66/16) that, in accordance with the above instructions, the Secretariat had compiled monthly reports of incidents reported to it (issued as MSC/Circs.701, 703, 708, 711, 712, 713, 716, 717, 719 and 722) and quarterly reports (issued as MSC/Circs. 698, 709, 714 and 720).

16.6   The Committee also noted a composite report (MSC 66/16/Add.1) covering all acts of piracy and armed robbery against ships, which had been reported to the Organization in 1995 based on their actual date and time of occurrence and agreed that such a yearly summary would be useful in analysing and understanding the trend. The Committee instructed the Secretariat to prepare such a yearly summary after March of every year to cover the whole of the previous year.

16.7   The Committee, noting with concern that the graph in annex 5 to document MSC 66/16/Add.1 showed an upward trend in 1995 after a lull at the beginning of that year, particularly in the South China Sea, reiterated its invitation to all Governments concerned and the industry to intensify their efforts to prevent and eliminate all unlawful activities in all areas of their concern.

16.8   The Committee noted information (MSC 66/16/1) provided by the Governments of Brazil, Colombia, Sierra Leone, Thailand and Hong Kong, on acts of piracy and armed robbery reported to have occurred in their waters.

16.9   The delegation of Brazil referred to initiatives of their national authorities by setting up a National Safety Committee in Brazilian ports that will co-ordinate efforts of all governmental sectors involved in improving the safety of ships in their waters and preventing piracy attacks. The National Safety Committee, besides co-operating with other international agencies, will promote the provision of police patrol services in national waters and the dissemination of safety instructions as part of national prevention of piracy actions. The Brazilian delegation appealed to Member Governments to urge ships under their flag and shipping companies to co-operate with their national authorities to improve safety and prevent piracy by registering the event with the local police authority enabling the relevant report of occurrence to be filed, so that the National Safety Committee can follow up on the occurrence.

16.10   The French delegation informed the Committee of initiatives taken in early 1996 to improve the security of ships and to prevent pirate attacks. A destroyer and a commando section were on patrol from Djibouti in the Red Sea and surrounding waters. This action could be repeated, if necessary.

The m.v. Anna Sierra incident

16.11   The Committee noted (MSC 66/16/2) information provided by the IMB (ICC) on the m.v. **Anna Sierra**, which had been attacked and hijacked by pirates on a voyage from Thailand to the Philippines and its crew had been forced overboard onto a small raft in rough seas without food, water or navigation equipment. The ship was later found in Southern China with the pirates and cargo on board. IMB (ICC) reported that the ship was still in the port of Beihai, pointing to the length of time it has taken to resolve the situation where indisputable evidence existed as to the true identity of the ship and ownership of the cargo. The IMB (ICC) observer, in introducing document MSC 66/16/2 questioned whether the International Convention on the Suppression of Unlawful Acts against the Safety of Navigation, 1988 was sufficient to deal with an incident similar to the hijacking of the m.v. **Anna Sierra**.

16.12   The delegation of Cyprus thanked the International Maritime Bureau and the People's Republic of China for their assistance in the case of the m.v. **Anna Sierra** hijacking and informed the Committee about another piracy attack on the m.v. **San Marino** in South America on 3 May 1996.

16.13   The delegation of China informed the Committee of its Government's strong opposition to piracy attacks, such as those reported above and stated that their Government was making every possible endeavour to prevent and suppress them.

[...]

21   WORK PROGRAMME

Review of the INF Code

21.16   The Committee, recalling that A 18 in adopting the INF Code by resolution A.748(18), requested, *inter alia*, its augmentation and a progress report to its nineteenth session, noted (MSC 66/2/3, paragraph 5 and MSC 66/2/3/Add.1) that A 19, in considering the progress report prepared by the Committee and the MEPC, approved a new resolution A.790(19) on the review of the INF Code and endorsed the Secretary-General's proposal for a Special Consultative Meeting (SCM) of entities involved in the maritime transport of nuclear materials covered by the INF Code. The Committee further noted that the SCM took place from 4 to 6 March 1996 (see document MSC 66/2/3/Add.1 and paragraph 2.15 above) and its proceedings have been issued under the symbol SCM 5, which, *inter alia*, contained a statement of thirteen countries on the need for the mandatory application of the INF Code made available to the Committee in document MSC 66/WP.9.

21.17   Following some discussion of the matter, the Committee, taking into account the operative paragraphs of resolution A.790(19) and the concerns aired at the SCM, agreed that, bearing in mind relevant international conventions, treaties, standards and regulations in force, the following specific issues should be considered:

.1   specific hazards associated with maritime transport of flasks, and consequences of severe accident scenarios - by the DSC Sub-Committee, the MEPC and also IAEA;

.2   ship structural design requirements for securing flasks to avoid separation from the ship in the event of an accident - by the DE Sub-Committee;

.3   adequacy of existing requirements for marking, labelling and placarding of the flasks - by the DSC Sub-Committee;

.4   route planning, notification to coastal States and availability of information on the type of cargo being carried, including its hazards - by the NAV Sub-Committee;

.5   restriction or exclusion of INF-carrying ships from particularly sensitive sea areas - by the MEPC which may request the NAV Sub-Committee to consider the matter from a safety of navigation point of view;

.6   adequacy of existing emergency response arrangements - by the MEPC;

.7   measures to locate, identify and salvage a sunken ship or flasks lost - by both the MSC and MEPC;

.8   tracking of ships carrying INF materials throughout the voyage by a shore-based authority - by the NAV Sub-Committee;

.9   adequacy of existing liability regimes covering accidents with INF materials (a matter considered by the 1996 HNS Conference, which resolved that no radioactive materials should be covered by the HNS Convention) - also by IAEA;

.10   environmental impact of accidents involving INF materials - by the MEPC, the GESAMP EHS Working Group and UNEP;

.11   materials being transported under the INF Code (plutonium - liquid (nitrate), INF - Ceramic) - by the DSC Sub-Committee;

.12   mandatory application of the INF Code - by both the MSC and the MEPC and possibly the Legal Committee; and

.13   adequacy of flask design and tests - by IAEA.

21.18   The Committee noted that the notification of coastal States in the event of an accident was regulated by existing reporting requirements under both the SOLAS and MARPOL Conventions and, therefore, no further action was required in this regard at present.

21.19   With regard to paragraphs 21.17.7 and 21.17.12 above, the Committee agreed to invite Member Governments to submit substantive proposals to its sixty-seventh session when these issues would be considered.   Concerning the suggestions made by some delegations to refer the question of mandatory application of the INF Code to the Legal Committee, the Committee requested these delegations to submit proposals indicating the specific issues to be adressed to the Legal Committee for consideration. Meanwhile, the Committee would take a definitive action on the referral of this matter to the Legal Committee at its next session.

21.20   Noting that the mandatory application of the INF Code might have its problems and that there was a difference of opinions as to what a mandatory INF Code should contain, the Committee agreed that submissions on this matter should address which items might be clarified as mandatory in the Code.

21.21   The Committee further agreed to include in the work programme of the DE Sub-Committee and retain in the work programmes of the DSC and NAV Sub-Committees an item "Development of measures complementary to the INF Code" with a target completion date of 1997, and instructed the Sub-Committees to deal with the respective issues indicated in paragraph 21.17 above.

21.22   The Committee instructed the Secretariat, following agreement by MEPC 38, to convey, to the organizations referred to in the above allocation of work, the outcome of the SCM and the consideration of the matter by the two Committees for consideration and action as appropriate.   The Committee further instructed the Secretariat to bring the relevant outcome of the above consideration to the attention of the MEPC and the Legal Committee.

21.23   Noting that, in accordance with resolution A.790(19), the outcome of the consideration of the aforementioned issues should be reported to the Assembly at its twentieth session, the Committee instructed the Secretariat to prepare, in due course, a relevant progress report, including MEPC's input, for consideration by MSC 68, for submission to the twentieth session of the Assembly.

[...]

23   ANY OTHER BUSINESS

[...]

Statement by the delegation of Lebanon

23.16   The Committee took note of a statement by the delegation of Lebanon that, since April 1996, the Israeli Navy had violated Lebanese territorial waters and committed acts of aggression and forcibly prevented commercial vessels from entering the port of Beirut and other commercial ports on the coast of southern Lebanon by imposing a maritime blockade on these ports from Lebanese territorial waters. (The full statement of the delegation of Lebanon is reproduced in annex 29).

23.17   The Committee also noted a statement by the delegation of Israel in reply to the statement by the delegation of Lebanon. The Israeli delegation expressed the view that the Committee was not a suitable forum for the consideration of security issues. (The full statement of the delegation of Israel is reproduced in annex 30).

23.18   The delegations of the United Arab Emirates, Egypt, League of Arab States, Iran, Saudi Arabia, Tunisia and the Syrian Arab Republic expressed their full support for the statement of the delegation of Lebanon, considering the Israeli actions in the incidents described to be contrary to international law, the freedom of navigation and a threat to maritime safety. (The full statement of the delegation of the Syrian Arab Republic is reproduced in annex 31).

23.19   The delegation of Italy, referring to IMO circular letter No.1898 of 25 April 1996, page 2, paragraph 3 informed the Committee that the ro-ro vessel **Pelander**, referred therein as Italian was not, according to the Register of Ships 1995/96, registered under the Italian flag.

23.20   The delegations of France and the United States expressed the view that the Committee should only address the technical aspects of maritime issues. Both delegations recalled their previous position and statements at MSC 65 and strongly supported the principles of freedom of navigation in accordance with international law for now and for the future. The United States also strongly supported the right of self-defence in accordance with international law and believed in the demonstrated effectiveness of diplomatic efforts to restore calm in the area.

[...]

3. SAFETY OF NAVIGATION. SEA LANES IN ARCHIPELAGIC WATERS. IMO PROCEDURES FOR ADOPTING ARCHIPELAGIC SEA LANES UNDER ARTICLE 53(9) OF THE UNITED NATIONS CONVENTION ON THE LAW OF THE SEA (UNCLOS). SUBMITTED BY AUSTRALIA

Doc. no.: MSC 67/7/3   Date: 5 September 1996

Introduction

1   The purpose of this paper is to assist the Organization to determine the procedures for addressing the complex issues associated with its role as the "competent international organization" in implementing those provisions of the United Nations Convention on the Law of the Sea (UNCLOS) concerning adoption of archipelagic sea lanes.

2   Indonesia foreshadowed at MSC 66 that it will be submitting a proposal for designation of archipelagic sea lanes for consideration at MSC 67 in December 1996 (MSC 67/7/2). This will be the first occasion IMO will consider such a proposal and Australia considers it essential that IMO agrees on and establishes appropriate procedures.

3   While there are possible precedents in IMO's adoption of routeing measures, there are as yet no established procedures for the adoption of archipelagic sea lanes which, it is suggested, must take into account the legitimate rights and concerns of the archipelagic State and those of the States whose ships and aircraft transit archipelagic waters.

4   Australia suggests that the adoption of archipelagic sea lanes involves navigational, safety and legal issues associated with the number and location of proposed sea lanes. This paper explores a number of procedural issues that should be addressed in considering the adoption of archipelagic sea lanes proposals.

Issues

5   Article 53(9) of UNCLOS requires an archipelagic State to refer its sea lane designation proposals to the competent international organization with a view to their adoption. This requirement raises a number of issues for consideration:

- is IMO the only "competent international organization"?

- what does "adoption" involve?;

- what procedures are required to give effect to "adoption"?; and

- what are the roles of the Assembly, Council and other IMO committees in the adoption process?

The "competent international organization"

6 UNCLOS Article 53(1) states that "An archipelagic State may designate *sea lanes* and *air routes* thereabove, suitable for continuous and expeditious passage of *foreign ships* and *aircraft* through or over its archipelagic waters and the adjacent territorial sea"[1]. The remaining clauses under Article 53 expand on technical aspects of designation, with clear distinctions being made between the requirements for routeing measures and traffic separation schemes and the requirements for aircraft overflight.

7 The distinction between sea lanes and air routes has its origins in the earlier negotiating drafts of UNCLOS which referred only to sea lanes and ships, and not to aircraft, which were first included in 1977. As Article 53(9) refers only to sea lanes and traffic separation schemes, it could be argued that only sea lanes designation proposals need to be referred to the competent international organization, and that would be the competent *maritime* international organization, IMO.

8 This conclusion seems consistent with findings of the United Nations Division for Ocean Affairs and Law of the Sea in the Office of Legal Affairs. The Office issued a table in November 1994 listing which organizations it considers to be the competent international organization for particular subject areas. It nominated the International Maritime Organization (IMO), a specialized agency of the United Nations dealing with maritime affairs, to be the competent international organization for the purposes of adopting proposals concerning sea lanes and traffic separation schemes under Article 53(9) of UNCLOS.

9 What is not clear from either UNCLOS or the UN Office of Legal Affairs note is the extent of ICAO involvement in the adoption process in relation to air routes. As both IMO and ICAO have a clearly defined role in relation to safety and environment issues, it is now necessary for these organizations to examine their role in relation to UNCLOS.

10 In order for the adoption process to proceed smoothly, it is suggested that legal advice be sought on whether there are any circumstances under Article 53(9) where ICAO could also be considered to have a complementary or independent role in relation to air routes over proposed designated sea lanes.

Meaning of "adoption"

11 UNCLOS provides little guidance as to what is envisaged by "adoption" of sea lanes proposals and how it should be achieved.

12 The Organization adopts or endorses a number of safety and navigation measures, such as ships routeing and traffic separation schemes. Adoption in these instances normally takes the form of a recommended practice. However, SOLAS chapter V makes provision for mandatory routeing measures. This form of adoption, resulting in a mandatory routeing measure, does not seem to be what was envisaged under Article 53 of UNCLOS. An archipelagic sea lanes proposal by comparison contains both mandatory and advisory elements. For example, compliance with the archipelagic sea lanes management regime may be mandatory, but the use of the archipelagic sea lanes themselves is not compulsory. The right of innocent passage continues to exist in undesignated waters and there is no requirement to use a

---

[1] Emphasis added.

right of innocent passage continues to exist in undesignated waters and there is no requirement to use a designated archipelagic sea lane (unless the ship or aircraft[1] wishes to enjoy rights of archipelagic sea lane passage).

13   IMO will need to ensure that there is a clear understanding of what "adoption" means in the context of the relevant requirements of UNCLOS. It is suggested that adoption by IMO is a process by which the international community, with the archipelagic State, agree that the proposal is consistent with UNCLOS and that the users and the archipelagic State accordingly accept their legal rights and duties under UNCLOS.

14   IMO adoption of an archipelagic sea lanes proposal must therefore ensure that the proposal is consistent with UNCLOS.

15   To facilitate consideration of the process of adoption of archipelagic sea lanes proposals, the Organization may also feel it necessary to consult appropriate sources of legal expertise on the meaning of "adoption" and associated issues.

Are new procedures required for adoption?

16   In the case of a standard ship routeing measure, the adoption process commences when a State submits a routeing proposal to IMO for consideration. In the first instance, the technical aspects will be considered by the Working Group on ships routeing within the Sub-Committee on Safety of Navigation.

17   Subject to its meeting the necessary technical and safety criteria and endorsement by the Sub-Committee, the proposal would be recommended to the Maritime Safety Committee for adoption. Once adopted, the routeing measure would come into effect after a period of not less than six months. Under certain circumstances, aspects of the routeing proposal may be referred to other IMO committees for consideration.

18   In the case of archipelagic sea lanes, additional processes may need to be established to take into account the specific requirements of Article 53 of UNCLOS, in particular, the requirement that sea lanes proposals provide for:

- continuous, expeditious and unobstructed passage in the normal mode;

- designation of all normal passage routes;

- designation of all normal navigation channels[2]; and

- a requirement that ships and aircraft shall not deviate more than 25 miles to either side of axis lines and shall not navigate closer to the coast than 10% of the distance between the nearest points on islands bordering the sea lane.

19   In addition to consideration by the MSC of the safety aspects of a sea lanes proposal, which would utilize existing ships routeing procedures, there may be a specific role for:

- the Legal Committee in considering whether any archipelagic sea lanes proposal meets the requirements of UNCLOS as outlined in paragraph 18; and

---

[1]Aircraft do not have a right of innocent passage.

[2]Duplication of routes of similar convenience between the same entry/exit points is not necessary.

- the Marine Environment Protection Committee (MEPC) in considering environmental issues arising from any proposal.

20   The complexity of the issues require involvement of several IMO bodies in considering aspects of an archipelagic sea lanes proposal. This suggests that the Assembly may see itself as the appropriate final forum for consideration of the Committees' recommendations and adoption of the sea lanes proposal itself.

Conclusion

21   Australia considers that the adoption process for archipelagic sea lanes proposals needs to take into account other issues in addition to the safety of navigation, such as the number and location of sea lanes. Legal and environmental issues also need to be considered. This may entail discussions in the appropriate IMO committees such as the Maritime Safety Committee, the Legal Committee and the Marine Environment Protection Committee. In order for IMO to arrive at an outcome which is consistent with the provisions of Article 53 of UNCLOS, Australia also suggests that it may be necessary for the proposal to be put to the Assembly for adoption after resolution of the issues by the various IMO committees.

22   IMO has been identified by the United Nations Office of Legal Affairs as the competent international organization to consider the adoption of archipelagic sea lanes proposals. Indonesia's archipelagic sea lanes proposal is the precedent case for IMO and UNCLOS. As UNCLOS provides little guidance on the adoption process *per se* Australia considers it critical that IMO assesses the proposal in such a way that the needs and interests of all Member States are accommodated within a reasonable time-frame.

Action requested of the Committee

23   The Committee is invited to take the above views into account when considering procedures for the adoption of archipelagic sea lanes.

4. REPORT OF THE MARITIME SAFETY COMMITTEE ON ITS SIXTY-SEVENTH SESSION*

Doc. no.: MSC 67/22 + Add. 1, 2   Date: 19 December 1996

---

*   Only paras 7.30-7.56 are reproduced.

Section		Page No.

LIST OF ANNEXES

[...]

7   SAFETY OF NAVIGATION

[...]

Sea lanes in archipelagic waters

7.30   The Committee, having recalled Indonesia's intention expressed at MSC 66 (MSC 66/24, paragraph 7.29), to accelerate the implementation of the United Nations Convention on the Law of the Sea (UNCLOS), 1982, and submit a proposal to IMO for the purpose of designating sea lanes for the use and passage of foreign ships and aircraft through or over its archipelagic waters, considered submissions by Indonesia (MSC 67/7/2) and Australia (MSC 67/7/3) outlining specific proposals relating to this issue.

7.31   In introducing document MSC 67/7/2, the delegation of Indonesia recognized IMO as the "competent international organization" under article 53 of UNCLOS and therefore, proposed that IMO should consider the matter of designation of archipelagic sea lanes from the point of view of safety of navigation and on the basis of relevant proposals submitted; and that discussion on such proposals should be limited to this Committee rather than other IMO Committees. Indonesia, in preparing their proposals, after discussions with other concerned States, had taken into account their main concerns, including:

    .1   the location of the proposed sea lanes;

    .2   the nature of future proposals for archipelagic sea lane passages in other parts of their archipelago (MSC 67/7/2, paragraph 11);

    .3   the nature of navigation outside the sea lanes in relevant waters (MSC 67/7/2, paragraph 10);

    .4   navigation in general through Indonesian archipelagic waters under the regime of innocent passage (MSC 67/7/2, paragraph 12); and

    .5   the need for ships navigating through archipelagic sea lanes to follow rules and regulations to be enacted by Indonesia (MSC 67/7/2, paragraph 9).

Indonesia had also consulted with IHO concerning the location of the sea lanes and had studied and surveyed the areas concerned. Further work in this regard was required in other parts of the archipelagic waters, specifically with regard to the possible east-west route, before proposals to designate sea lanes in other parts could be made. The Indonesian delegation considered the procedure for adoption of the proposals should be simple and enable adoption of the proposed archipelagic sea lanes before the end of 1997.

7.32   The Australian delegation also recognized IMO as the competent international organization for the adoption of archipelagic sea lanes proposals. UNCLOS provides little guidance on adoption and, while IMO's General Provisions on Ships' Routeing may form a useful starting point on the technical aspects, much broader considerations, including questions of international law and decisions on the number of normal passage routes under UNCLOS, should be addressed. The outcome should reflect the balance between user States (including the international shipping industry) and archipelagic States, which is reflected in UNCLOS. The Committee should carry out the adoption process and seek advice from the NAV Sub-Committee and other relevant IMO bodies. In view of the precedent that will be set in the first archipelagic sea lanes adoption process, the Committee might wish to consider whether final adoption should be left to the Assembly.

7.33   The delegation of the United States stated that the UNCLOS Convention had assigned to IMO a very specific role but did not describe how IMO should deal with a proposal to designate archipelagic sea lanes, and IMO had not previously decided how to deal with such proposals. Nevertheless, archipelagic sea lanes are conceptually akin to other routeing measures for which this Organization has well established and smoothly working procedures. The United States delegation therefore proposed referring the Indonesian proposal, and that of Australia, to NAV 43 and ask it to report to MSC 69. The delegation noted that an east-west lane and associated lanes and connections were not proposed for adoption. In this regard, in connection with further review of this proposal, the United States delegation believed that:

.1   IMO should be advised by Indonesia of its plans for conducting further surveys and studies that will result in the submission to IMO of proposals for the designation of additional sea lanes, along with the general location of these sea lanes and time frame for this effort, and an undertaking to provide IMO with periodic reports of progress made;

.2   that any necessary conforming changes be made so that the proposed sea lanes do not extend beyond the limit of Indonesia's territorial sea;

.3   that this submission be viewed as a proposal for partial designation only, and that IMO continue to have responsibility (i.e. jurisdiction) over the archipelagic sea lanes designation process until a complete plan is adopted by IMO;

.4   that, pending identification of all other normal passage routes used as routes for international navigation and overflight, the right of archipelagic sea lanes passage may be exercised by all ships and aircraft in such normal routes in accordance with the UNCLOS Convention; and

.5   that designation of archipelagic sea lanes does not affect the exercise of the right of innocent passage by all ships throughout the archipelago, in accordance with international law.

7.34   The delegation of France stressed the need to proceed carefully in this matter and was of the opinion that the proposals submitted to the current session of the Committee should be referred to NAV 43 for consideration.

7.35   The delegation of the Russian Federation shared some of the concerns expressed by the delegations of Australia, the United States, France and other countries. They were of the opinion that, questions such as to whether the archipelagic sea lanes to be designated by Indonesia, cover all the traditional routes of navigation or whether the rules for archipelagic sea lane passages to be adopted by Indonesia conform with UNCLOS, should be a matter for consultations with other countries, both bilaterally and within IMO. At the same time, the delegation noted the correct procedure followed by Indonesia in the matter of designating archipelagic sea lanes.

7.36   The delegation of the United Kingdom welcomed the Indonesian proposals and their referral to IMO for adoption, thus recognizing the Organization as the competent international organization in this respect. However, there was a need to ensure that an appropriate balance is struck between the interests of the archipelagic State and the interests of foreign States whose ships use the archipelagic State's waters on passage between parts of the high sea. UNCLOS provides the necessary framework to strike such a balance and the end result of IMO's work should comply with all the relevant provisions of UNCLOS. The United Kingdom supported the referral of the proposals to NAV 43 and considered referral of the matter to any other Committee premature until the NAV Sub-Committee has considered the matter and established any issues which could not be resolved.

7.37   The delegations of China, Germany, Ghana, Greece, Jamaica, Japan, Mexico, New Zealand, Norway, the Philippines, Poland, the Republic of Korea, Singapore, South Africa, Thailand and the observers of IHO, FOEI and IFSMA welcomed the Indonesian initiative; they recognized the competence of IMO to deal with the issue, which, because it would be considered for the first time, emphasized the significance and importance which should be attached to the proposals. The aforementioned delegations and observers shared the concerns expressed by the delegations of Australia, France, the Russian

Federation, the United Kingdom and the United States, as summarized above and expressed the view that the matter should be forwarded to the NAV Sub-Committee for consideration and action as appropriate.

7.38   Referring to overflight issues mentioned in the Indonesian submission, the ICAO representative explained the role ICAO should play as far as the designation of air routes through archipelagic waters was concerned. He mentioned that, while paragraph 9 of Article 53 of UNCLOS explicitly refers to sea lanes, without specifically mentioning the air routes there above, Article 53 on the Right of archipelagic sea lanes passage establishes a right which is declared applicable to both sea lanes and air routes. The Rules of the Air established by ICAO will be applicable to archipelagic passage, by virtue of combination of Articles 54 and 39.3 which expressly recognize the competence of ICAO on the matter. Air route networks constitute the basis for establishing in detail the facilities, services and procedures required for international air navigation within a specified area, as set forth by ICAO Regional Air Navigation plans. Those Plans are approved by the Council of ICAO, further to agreements reached among the States concerned, generally in the framework of Regional Air Navigation Meetings. If the airspace organization in an area is no longer considered by a Contracting State as consistent with the current and foreseen requirements on international civil aviation, it may propose an amendment to the Plan concerned, in accordance with the Procedure established by the Council of ICAO on 7 March 1975. Therefore, in case of designation of new air routes, suitable for the right of archipelagic sea lanes passage, the well-established amendment procedure applicable to ICAO Regional Air Navigation Plans should be resorted to. Indeed, for the sake of safety of international air navigation, which is a primary concern to ICAO according to its constitutive instrument, ICAO is, so far as air routes to be used by civil aircraft are concerned, the competent organization in the matter covered by Article 53 of UNCLOS.

7.39   In his summing up, the Chairman stressed that, since this was the first time the Organization would consider the issue, it should proceed with due caution. From the various interventions made, it had become evident that the issue as a whole, together with the proposals of Indonesia, should be conveyed to NAV 43, which should be instructed to develop a mechanism for the consideration of archipelagic sea lane proposals on the basis of which recommendations would be put to the Committee for adoption in accordance with paragraph 9 of Article 53 of the UNCLOS Convention.

7.40   The Committee endorsed the Chairman's proposals and instructed NAV 43 to consider the above matters, on the basis of the terms of reference given in annex 16, and submit its recommendations to MSC 69 to enable the Committee to give further consideration to archipelagic sea lanes and decide on the Indonesian proposals.

7.41   The Committee invited the twentieth session of the Assembly to confirm that the delegation of responsibility to the MSC for the adoption of routeing measures, in accordance with resolution A.826(19), should also apply to routeing measures related to archipelagic sea lanes.

Rules and Recommendations on navigation through the Strait of Istanbul, the Strait of Çanakkale and the Marmara Sea

7.42   The Committee recalled that paragraph 5 of resolution A.827(19) had requested the Committee to review, on the basis of submissions from Governments, the operation of the Rules and Recommendations on navigation set out in Annex 2 to the resolution and the conditions in the Strait of Istanbul, the Strait of Çanakkale and the Marmara Sea; to consider, as appropriate, any suggestions for changes in the said Rules and Recommendations; and to report on these matters to the twentieth session of the Assembly.

7.43   The Committee noted that, under this subitem, there were two documents for consideration, namely MSC 67/7/8 (Russian Federation) and MSC 67/7/12 (OCIMF). Before they were introduced, the delegation of Turkey reiterated the statement they made under item 1 (see paragraph 1.7) and strongly objected to their introduction and consideration by the Committee. The Turkish delegation stated that the paper of the Russian Federation, in particular, was of a purely political nature and stressed that IMO is a technical organization which provides a forum for the discussion of technical issues only and, therefore, consideration of the said documents, which they considered political, was not acceptable. The delegation added that, if the documents were considered, they would not attend their presentation and would not take part in any related discussions. (The statement made by the Turkish delegation is reproduced in annex 29.)

7.44   The Chairman responded by stating his decision to allow the introduction of the two documents and their consideration, recalling the Committee's obligation under resolution A.827(19), operative paragraph 5 to "review, on the basis of submissions from Governments, the operation of the Rules and Recommendations set out in Annex 2 and the conditions in the Strait of Istanbul, the Strait of Çanakkale and the Marmara Sea, to consider, as appropriate, any suggestions for changes in the said Rules and Recommendations and to report on these matters to the next session of the Assembly".

7.45   A number of delegations supported the introduction and consideration of the two documents; however, this was opposed by two delegations.

7.46   In a short intervention, the Secretary-General, having stated that he did not consider that it was appropriate nor did he intend to comment on the substance of the matter, appealed to the Committee to maintain the technical character of IMO which had always been considered its great strength and avoid the discussion of political issues; he asked the Committee not to lose sight of the objectives of the Organization but to continue with the usual spirit of co-operation within the MSC to assure that those objectives were achieved.

7.47   In his intervention, the Chairman:

- thanked the Secretary-General for his statement and invited the Committee to respond positively to the Secretary-General's appeal,

- concurred with the Secretary-General's request that the Committee should maintain the technical character of the Organization;

- in this context, associated himself with the Turkish statement to that effect;

- appealed to the Committee to focus on the technical aspect of the issue in hand;

- appealed particularly to the parties which had submitted documents MSC 67/7/8 and MSC 67/7/12 to focus on the technical aspects of the issue only;

- asked the Committee to act within the remit of resolution A.827(19); and

- appealed to the delegation of Turkey to co-operate within the scope of resolution A.827(19).

Following this, he invited the authors of the two documents to introduce them.

7.48   The delegation of Turkey, noting that the Chairman intended to proceed with the presentation of documents MSC 67/7/8 and MSC 67/7/12, reiterated their statement that they would neither take part in the discussion of these documents nor would they be present in the meeting room and acted accordingly.

7.49   The delegation of the Russian Federation, introducing MSC 67/7/8, first of all, stated that they would respond to the Secretary-General's and Chairman's appeals. They then referred to operative paragraph 5 of resolution A.827(19) and invited the Committee to send to the Straits area a mission composed of Black Sea and Mediterranean coastal States and of other main users of the Straits to assess the operation of the aforementioned Rules and Recommendations and the overall navigation and hydrographic situation in the Straits and submit a report and recommendations to MSC 68 to form the basis of the Committee's report to the twentieth session of the Assembly.

7.50 The OCIMF observer likewise pledged his positive response to the Secretary-General's and Chairman's appeals and, introducing document MSC 67/7/12, referred to the IMO Rules and Recommendations, which, in their view, needed a review for the purpose of enhancing the safety of navigation through and environmental protection in the areas they cover.

7.51 The Russian Federation (MSC 67/7/8) and OCIMF (MSC 67/7/12) proposals were generally supported by several delegations; however, some other delegations voiced concern over the political character of the proposals as they might imply an infringement of the sovereignty of Turkey. Many delegations expressed the desirability for a continued dialogue between IMO and Turkey to consider the technical aspects of the issue in hand.

7.52 Some delegations expressed the opinion that a common approach to ensure safety and prevention of pollution in the Straits should be arrived at by all the interested parties. This could possibly be achieved with the assistance of senior representatives of the IMO Secretariat so that a balanced report could be submitted to the twentieth session of the Assembly.

7.53 The statements made by the various delegations on this matter are given in annex 29.

7.54 After an extensive discussion, the Chairman stated that he would welcome any informal consultations relating to the proposal by the Russian Federation that could take place and, therefore, he suggested that time be allowed for such consultations to take place, in which case the Committee should receive a report by the end of the week.

In the meantime, he suggested that the Committee concentrate strictly on the technical nature of the issue and, therefore, taking into account the limited time available for the consideration of important technical topics on the Committee's agenda, he further suggested that the Committee request the NAV Sub-Committee, at its forty-third session in July 1997, to consider those proposals contained in the OCIMF document which aim at improving the IMO Rules and Recommendations adopted by the Committee in 1994 and confirmed by the Assembly in 1995.

Furthermore, he suggested that the Committee instruct the NAV Sub-Committee to bring the outcome of its consideration of the matter to the attention of IMO Member Governments and the Turkish Government for information and action as appropriate so that there is no contradiction between the international and national rules and recommendations concerned, as stated by the Turkish delegation at MSC 63 (MSC 63/23, paragraph 7.22).

As the Committee was under obligation, under resolution A.827(19), to review, on the basis of submissions from Governments, the operation of the Rules and Recommendations and the conditions in the Strait of Istanbul, the Strait of Çanakkale and the Marmara Sea, to consider, as appropriate, any suggestions for changes in the said Rules and Recommendations and to report on these matters to the twentieth session of the Assembly, the Chairman, therefore, recommended, because the forty-third session of the NAV Sub-Committee is scheduled to take place after MSC 68, that the Committee authorizes the NAV Sub-Committee to submit its report on the consideration of the OCIMF and other proposals, as may be submitted, directly to the twentieth session of the Assembly. He would welcome Turkey's co-operation in the process.

7.55 The Committee endorsed, in general, the course of action proposed by the Chairman and authorized NAV 43 accordingly.

7.56 The Committee, being subsequently informed of consultations among interested parties and the Secretary-General's intention to hold consultations with a group of countries as early as possible in 1997 for the purpose of facilitating the process of the review requested of the Committee by resolution A.827(19), agreed that no further action should be taken in this respect at the present session.

[...]

5. REPORT OF THE LEGAL COMMITTEE ON THE WORK OF ITS SEVENTY-FOURTH SESSION*

Doc. no.: LEG 74/13   Date: 22 October 1996

Table of Contents

---

* Only paras 12-62 and 86-103 are reproduced.

[...]

D   COMPENSATION FOR POLLUTION FROM SHIPS' BUNKERS (agenda item 4)

12   The Committee considered submissions by Governments and observer delegations and discussed the need for the adoption of an international regime for liability and compensation for damage caused by oil from ships' bunkers. It also expressed preliminary views on the main issues to be discussed in connection with the possible adoption of international regulations in this regard. The Committee noted that Sweden should be included among the delegations which submitted document LEG 74/4/1.

13   In introducing document LEG 74/4/1 on behalf of all sponsoring delegations, the delegation of Australia referred to the advantages of a free-standing convention regulating strict liability channelled to the shipowner and backed up by compulsory insurance. In this regard, the delegation highlighted several aspects of the draft convention included in the document, namely, the extension of the scope to cover not only pollution but also other types of damage, and the inclusion of all ships other than tankers. The draft was restricted to discharges from ships associated with the carriage of bunker oil, thus excluding bunkering operations. Other issues requiring further analysis were:

    -    the possibility of attaching liability not only to the shipowner but to parties responsible
for the day to day operation of the ship;

- the alternative of introducing detailed regulations on compulsory insurance similar to those contained in the CLC and the HNS Conventions;

- the definition of "oil", which had no precedent in either the CLC or the HNS Convention;

- the jurisdiction of the court of the State of the ship's registry even if this State was not party to the prospective treaty.

14   The observer delegation of the International Maritime Committee (CMI) indicated that following the creation of a working group in that organization, it had sent its national associations a questionnaire on aspects of national law and practice which might affect the operation of an international convention on this subject. In connection with its document LEG 74/4/2, the delegation highlighted the importance of relating strict liability to specific amounts of limitation in order to avoid the legal uncertainty which would result if limits were to vary in accordance with different national legal systems. In the opinion of this delegation the introduction of fixed limits was also an important factor to enable the operation of compulsory insurance. Mention was also made of the difficulties that might arise from the inclusion of pollution damage caused by bunker oil within the scope of the LLMC, on account of the wording used to define the claims under this Convention. This wording did not make reference to claims for pollution or environmental damage. The observer delegation re-stated the willingness of the CMI to assist further deliberations of the Committee in connection with this agenda item.

15   The observer delegation of Greenpeace International introduced document LEG 74/4/3 by highlighting the need to ensure that an international regime of compensation for damage caused by bunker oil fulfilled the objectives of full compensation as well as those of repair, restoration and rehabilitation or replacement of damaged or destroyed natural resources, or acquisition of equivalent resources in cases where full restoration was impossible. In the opinion of this delegation these objectives could only be achieved, among other things, by a system of absolute and unlimited liability, channelled to the shipowner.

16   Document LEG 74/4/4 was introduced by the observer delegation of the International Chamber of Shipping (ICS), which cast doubt on the need for the adoption of a free-standing treaty. The delegation noted that liability and compensation for pollution damage caused by bunker spills from both laden and unladen tankers was covered by the 1992 CLC and Fund Conventions. Ninety per cent of the world fleet was insured against such incidents by P&I Clubs. Only incidents caused by uninsured fish factory ships had not been compensated. If international regulations were considered to be necessary, they could be introduced in the form of a protocol amending the CLC. The delegation further noted that the draft referred to limits of liability established by national law, which in most cases would be based on the LLMC. The high limits which were agreed in the 1996 LLMC Protocol would ensure that adequate compensation is available for claims arising from bunker incidents into the future.

Need

17   The Committee initially discussed whether there was a need to establish an international regime regulating liability and compensation for damage from bunker fuel oil.

18   In the opinion of many delegations this need did not exist at present. There was no evidence demonstrating that a substantial number of incidents causing damage had not been properly compensated. In most cases, compensation was provided for in national legislation which introduced strict liability also for oil pollution damage caused by any type of ships and also by the availability of P&I insurance cover. In this regard, it was recalled that in accordance with resolution A.777(18) of the IMO Assembly, proposals for new conventions and amendments to existing ones should be entertained only on the basis of clear and well-documented compelling need and having regard to the costs to the maritime industry and the burden of the legislative and administrative resources of Member States. Only

upon availability of the information necessary to support these requirements should the Committee further consider adoption of treaty provisions on liability and compensation for damage caused by bunker oil.

19   Many other delegations stated, however, that the need had already been acknowledged by the Marine Environment Protection Committee (MEPC) of IMO. Reference was also made to the highly hazardous character of some types of bunker oil and to several incidents which had caused damage which could not be fully compensated. It was, however, pointed out that claims were uncompensated largely because of the operation of the 1976 LLMC whose limits had now been substantially increased. It was further suggested that it should not be necessary to wait for a major disaster for the need to be established. An international regime would be preferable to national legislation in connection with issues such as the recognition of certificates and the availability of direct action against the insurer.

Form of instrument

20   Many delegations did not support the proposal for a free-standing convention since this would lead to further fragmentation of treaties in the field of third party liability. However, they indicated that, if necessary, they would be prepared to consider a protocol to CLC regulating liability and compensation for damage caused by bunker fuel oil from non-tankers.

21   Delegations in favour of a free-standing convention recalled that in the past suggestions either to amend the CLC or include bunkers in the HNS Convention had been discussed extensively but rejected. The re-opening of these discussions could therefore not be expected to produce any fruitful result and therefore the only option seemed to be a free-standing instrument.

22   Leaving aside the form of the instrument, some preliminary views were expressed on the main issues which would have to be addressed if the Committee decided to go forward with this subject. These preliminary views are summarized in the following paragraphs.

Application to vessels

23   In principle, an international liability and compensation regime should apply to all vessels and their bunkers, except those covered by CLC and the Fund Convention. However, distinctions regarding the extent of this application should be made in order not to impose excessive burdens on certain sectors of the world fleet, such as fishing vessels. Consideration should also be given to the possibility of exempting small ships from certain requirements, such as compulsory insurance, bearing in mind that the regime of strict liability would still apply to them. The establishment of thresholds for small ships would have to take into account the size of ships and bunkers and the potential damage a spill could cause. Another factor to be considered was the need not to burden excessively Administrations with the performance of tasks of control in respect of ships which were not likely to cause a significant degree of damage on account of the size of their bunkers and type of bunker oil carried. Since not all kinds of bunker oil had the same risk factor, technical advice would have to be requested in order to relate properly the quantity of oil to the damage it could cause.

Period of application

24   Some delegations were of the view that the instrument should not cover bunkering operations. Other delegations suggested that consideration should be given to the possibility of including such operations, bearing in mind however that such an extension should not be allowed to alter the distinction between liability provisions related to the operation of ships and liability regimes established by national law in respect of potential land-based sources of pollution. The need to preserve this distinction should not prevent the consideration of the possibility for a maritime law convention to deal with incidents in respect of which liability can be clearly attributed to a deficiency in the operation of the ship (such as fault in the ship's equipment) during the process of bunkering.

Risks to be covered

25   In the opinion of some delegations the instrument should only cover pollution damage in order
to maintain consistency between the prospective liability provisions in respect of damage caused by
bunker spills of non-tankers with the risks covered by CLC and the FUND Convention in respect of
bunker spills from tankers. Other delegations favoured the extension of the concept of damage to cover
also fire and explosion as in the case of the HNS Convention. It was noted that this question had to be
seen in the light of the consideration of issues such as applicable limits in cases of incidents causing both
pollution and other damage. This was particularly important especially if, as it was suggested in the
draft, limits should be established, not in treaty provisions, but in accordance with the national law.

Channelling of liability

26   A significant number of interventions suggested that consideration be given to attaching liability
to the person responsible for the operation of the ship. There was, however, a predominance of views
in favour of channelling the liability to the shipowner. In this connection it was stated that channelling
of liability ensured legal certainty in favour of the victim claiming compensation, as well as the
possibility of avoiding double insurance. At the same time it was suggested that channelling was not
really necessary if there was a requirement for compulsory insurance.

Compulsory insurance

27   It was noted that consideration on how to introduce compulsory insurance within the framework
of an international liability and compensation regime for damage caused by bunker fuel oil depended
on the conclusions of the correspondence group established to deal with the broader issue of compulsory
insurance in general (agenda item 6). Nevertheless, preliminary views were expressed on whether
provisions on compulsory insurance should be internationally regulated, as in the case of CLC and the
HNS Convention, or simply refer to applicable national law. The first option would ensure legal
certainty on subjects of decisive importance such as the recognition of certificates, recourse to direct
action, and defences available to ensure payment of compensation. The advantages of the second option
were its simplicity and the greater flexibility which allowed States to establish their own system of
control.

28   The concept of compulsory insurance should be a flexible one and contemplate different options
such as bank guarantees, self insurance, etc. However, it was important to note that in order to establish
the availability of international insurance capacity, the compulsory insurance should be related to
international regulations establishing concrete amounts of limitation and a specification of the claims
to be covered. The definition of compulsory insurance by simple reference to national law would create
difficult problems for P&I Clubs on account of the disparity of figures of limitation, and the existence
of national legislation providing for unlimited liability.

29   While port State control of CLC certificates was a relatively simple task on account of the small
size of the world tanker fleet, the administrative burden would be considerable if this control had to be
exercised in respect of all non-tankers carrying bunker oil. An obligation on flag States to check the
existence of an appropriate insurance cover or financial guarantee and to issue the corresponding
certificates would create similar problems.

30   Although the Committee did not reach agreement as to the need for an international instrument
regulating this matter it decided to continue with its deliberations on this agenda item at its next session.

E   DRAFT CONVENTION ON WRECK REMOVAL (agenda item 5)

31   The Committee recalled that at its seventy-third session, it had taken note of a draft international
convention on wreck removal prepared by the delegations of Germany, the Netherlands and the

United Kingdom. However, time constraint did not allow detailed discussions on the various provisions in the proposal to take place at that session. The Committee noted that the draft convention, as originally submitted by the above-mentioned delegations in document LEG 73/11, had been reproduced in the annex to document LEG 74/5.

32   The observer delegation of the CMI introduced document LEG 74/5/2 relating to the work so far carried out by the CMI international sub-committee on wreck removal, and a CMI study on the status of current international law concerning removal of wrecks contained in document LEG 74/5/2/Add.1. It informed the Committee that the CMI is also undertaking a study on whether or not the proposed draft convention on wreck removal should be made applicable to territorial waters. Obviously the application of the convention also in territorial waters would lead to wider unification. In this connection it indicated that existing national rules do not differ very much, in which case it was likely that an extension of the draft convention to territorial waters should not cause any difficulties for many States. In the view of the CMI this was an important project which merits to be finalised as soon as possible.

33   The delegation of France introduced its submission contained in document LEG 74/5/1. While endorsing the aspects of the draft convention concerning safety of navigation, the delegation expressed the concern that the provisions of the draft were not as comprehensive as the provisions of some existing international instruments on environmental protection. This, in its opinion, could lead to a conflict between conventions and subsequent difficulties for coastal states.

34   The observer delegation of the International Chamber of Shipping (ICS) introduced document LEG 74/5/3. It questioned the need for an international convention, not from a legal point of view, but from the practical aspect. The number of cases of wrecks in areas outside the territorial sea was rather restricted and national regulations regarding wreck removal within their territorial waters had been capable of resolving most cases of removal of wrecks. It suggested that, should a new convention be deemed necessary, its scope should be confined to eliminating impediments to safety of navigation by the shipwreck and/or its cargo. Should cargo create a hazard to navigation that necessitates removal of the ship, then cargo should be required to contribute to the cost of removal. A new convention should also create a right and duty for shipowners to remove ships and wrecks by their own means or by the assistance of any available salvor irrespective of flag.

35   The delegation of the Netherlands recalled that the Committee has had wreck removal on its agenda since its twelfth session and at its last session had decided to include the subject as a priority item for the current biennium. It stated that the aim of the draft was to enhance the uniformity and clarity of international law. In principle, the convention would apply to wrecks and ships reasonably expected to result in wrecks, which are located beyond the territorial sea of States Parties. The convention would complement existing international law relating to maritime casualties. Since wrecked aircraft can also constitute a hazard, consideration should therefore be given to including such wrecks within the scope of application of the convention. Having highlighted the key provisions of the draft convention, It stated that the requirements for compulsory insurance in the draft should be further considered by the Committee in the light of the work on that subject. It informed the Committee that in the years between 1987 and 1994, the Netherlands authorities had been obliged to remove at least 12 wrecks located just outside their territorial waters for which there is at present no legal regime available. The adoption of a new treaty instrument was, therefore, an urgent matter to be dealt with in the short term.

36   The Chairman invited the Committee to address some preliminary issues regarding wreck removal and in particular the need for a convention on the subject and to identify the key items which would require further, detailed consideration.

Need

37   A number of delegations were of the view that there is a need for an international convention on wreck removal. Reference was made in this connection to the number of wrecks which remained in both territorial waters and beyond without any action being taken for their removal. It was suggested that this was a particular concern for developing countries who often lack the technical know-how and the financial capability for taking such measures.

38   The delegation of Germany, in addition to the statement made by the Netherlands, stressed that in the light of recent experiences in Germany there is an urgent need for an international instrument, especially applying to wrecks beyond the territorial sea of States. It underlined that it was not the intention of the sponsoring delegations to put additional financial burdens on shipowners and that the draft convention provides for limitation of liability in accordance with the applicable international convention or the applicable national law. Furthermore the draft aims to concur completely with international law, namely the United Nations Convention on the Law of the Sea, 1982.

39   Some delegations, however, indicated that they had not experienced any major problems in respect of wreck removal in their territorial waters or waters adjacent thereto, neither from a legal nor from a practical point of view. From their perspective they did not, therefore, see any particular need for the proposed international regulation. They would not object, however, to the matter being brought forward. Several delegations suggested that higher priority should be given to the other two priority items, namely compensation for pollution from ships' bunkers and compulsory insurance.

Geographic scope of application

40   Regarding the scope of the convention, a variety of views were expressed. Some delegations were of the opinion that it should apply only beyond the territorial sea. Others stated that most problems were caused by wrecks within territorial waters and that it was therefore imperative that this area be included.

Relationship with other conventions

41   With regard to the relationship between the draft convention and other conventions, particularly the aspect of the mixture of public and private international law in the draft and the question of its overlap with the 1969 Intervention Convention, the Committee agreed that these issues needed further study. In this connection, special attention had to be given to the question of delimitation between preventive measures undertaken under the CLC or the HNS Conventions on the one hand and wreck removal on the other. Reference was also made to the possible complications related to the civil liability aspects involved and the need to avoid a discussion on linkage between the proposed convention and existing regimes on liability and limitation of liability, similar to that which had arisen during the work on the HNS Convention.

The right to remove wrecks

42   Some delegations were of the view that the draft should also contain rules stating the shipowner's right to remove ships and wrecks by his own means or by salvors chosen by him.

Conclusion

43   The Committee preliminary concluded that, even if there were no objections to continuing the discussion on this subject, there was at the same time general agreement that the bulk of the Committee's time during the next session should be devoted to the other two priority items. From the discussion it was obvious that the number of important points which had been identified would have to be further considered with a view to introducing necessary changes to the present draft.

Correspondence group

44   Following consultations, the delegation of the United Kingdom, speaking on behalf also of the delegations of Germany and the Netherlands, suggested that in order to advance this important subject and to assist the Committee in its future deliberations, a correspondence group should be established. The delegation of the Netherlands was prepared to assume the "lead country" role.*

45   The Committee agreed to this proposal and established a correspondence group in accordance with the applicable rules and guidelines and with the following terms of reference:

"Identify and, where appropriate, develop options for dealing with the following issues:

1   scope of application: (a) geographical
                             (b) safety/environmental
                             (c) wrecks/ships

2   relationship between public international law and private law provisions

3   avoiding overlapping with the 1969 Intervention Convention

4   relationship with other conventions."

46   The correspondence group is to report to the seventy-fifth session of the Legal Committee.

F   COMPULSORY INSURANCE (agenda item 6)

47   The delegation of the United Kingdom introduced its submission contained in document LEG 74/6/1. Its overriding concern was to establish a uniform regime to ensure that shipowners will meet their liabilities. Even if 90% of the world's shipping tonnage was insured through P & I Clubs, and a further 5% had other forms of security, there was a need to close that gap in order to avoid unfair competition from uninsured shipowners. The need for a uniform international regime was documented by instances in the United Kingdom where the Government had experienced difficulties in recovering costs for actions associated with pollution response. The object was to ensure the shipowner's ability to pay compensation. This would require evidence of third party liability insurance, financial guarantee or security.

48   In introducing document LEG 74/6/2 the observer delegation of the ICS pointed out that it was not clear what percentage of uninsured shipowners were unable to meet their liabilities. The question arises whether there is need for an international convention which concerns only a problem in relation to 5% of the world fleet. It was also necessary to consider matters such as coverage, damage related deductibles and direct action. To some extent public concern has already been addressed in the CLC and FUND Conventions, the HNS Convention and the nuclear liability regimes. If transport of passengers was an issue, then a protocol to the 1974 Athens Convention could be developed.

49   The observer delegation of the P & I Clubs emphasized that the meaning of the term "compulsory insurance" must be addressed with particular reference to whether this would be a system of independent guarantee as in the CLC with provision for direct action, or would require that an insurance certificate be carried on board - with or without specifying the risks covered. It was suggested that requiring production of a document confirming P & I cover would merely formalize existing

---

*Contact point: Mr. Jan de Boer, Legal Department, Directorate General of Shipping and Maritime Affairs, P.O. Box 5817, 2280 HV Rijswijk, The Netherlands
Telephone: 31-70-3955720, Telefax: 31-70-3996274

practice, which could be accomplished through port State control or domestic legislation. The Committee was urged to give detailed consideration to the need for and purpose of such a convention as it could involve a heavy cost for Administrations without providing further protection for claimants or affecting substandard shipping.

50   The Committee noted with interest a proposal by the delegation of Norway that, while the instrument may be an international convention, it may also take the form of a code or a recommendation.

51   Many delegations were of the view that further consideration of an international compulsory insurance regime by the Committee was justified and indicated that the rationale for such a regime was to achieve harmonization and uniformity. Some delegations felt that there was a need to address matters such as standard insurance clauses, defenses, passenger claims, certificates, direct action, and uniform rules for recognition and control of certificates. They pointed out that the objective was not to develop a comprehensive liability convention or limitation convention, but to ensure the shipowners' capacity to pay liabilities.

52   Other delegations, while supporting the need for further review of the matter felt that the rules on compulsory insurance must be linked to rules on liability. Examples of strict liability such as the CLC and HNS regimes were cited in this context. It was further noted that the issue of linkage with limitation of liability might need consideration.

53   Many delegations opposed an international compulsory insurance regime on the grounds that no compelling need had been demonstrated. It was pointed out that the shipping industry was self regulated to a high degree, and the problem raised was capable of settlement through the normal process of international shipping business. Furthermore, the introduction of a new convention could create problems with existing practice. It was questioned whether the general public was exposed to exceptional risks which require a special regime.

54   In summing up the discussion on this topic the Chairman noted that the discussions were in the very preliminary stages at this session and no specific proposals for draft articles of an international instrument were before the Committee. Delegations had expressed strong opinions on both sides of the question. While there was quite a strong call to continue consideration of the question of compulsory insurance, problems had been identified regarding the compelling need for an international regime. Notwithstanding the lack of hard facts and figures on the issue, sufficient interest was demonstrated to warrant further consideration in the Committee.

55   It was noted that several delegations had referred to domestic pressures to address the matter of compulsory insurance at the international level and that such calls could not be ignored. It was emphasized that the proposed instrument need not take the form of an international convention but could be in the form of a code or regulation, and need not be limited to insurance but could cover any form of financial security.

56   It was agreed to establish a correspondence group in accordance with applicable rules and guidelines and with the following terms of reference on the understanding that the group should have the flexibility to discuss any subject relevant to its work:

"A   To consider suitable means for introducing rules on evidence of financial security for vessels, in particular in respect of:

(1)   coverage for a number of different claims attracting public interest that occur frequently;

(2)   defenses that a provider of financial security could be allowed to invoke;

(3)   direct action against the providers of financial security;

(4)   documentation of the financial security and criteria for determining the acceptability of the financial security;

(5)   recognition of certificates containing evidence of the financial security; and

(6)   control of certificates containing evidence of the financial security.

B   Evaluate whether a convention, a code or a recommendation would be the more appropriate type of instrument in respect of international rules on evidence of financial security.

C   The group shall consider both third party security and other evidence of the ability to pay."

57   The correspondence group is to report to the seventy-fifth session of the Legal Committee. The lead country shall be Norway.*

G   REPORT ON THE INTERNATIONAL CONFERENCE ON HAZARDOUS AND NOXIOUS SUBSTANCES AND LIMITATION OF LIABILITY, 1996 (agenda item 7)

58   The Committee took note of the contents of document LEG 74/7 which reports on the outcome of the Conference.

59   It was equally noted that, due to a material error, some words in article 12, paragraph 5 of the HNS Convention had been omitted from the final text of this Convention contained in document LEG/CONF.10/8/2. The Committee agreed that the words omitted should be read as part of the text of the Convention. It also requested the Secretariat to consider the appropriate procedure for rectification. Accordingly, the first sentence of article 12, paragraph 5, should read as follows (words originally omitted in bold): "An insurance or other financial security shall not satisfy the requirements of this article if it can cease, for reasons other than the expiry of the period of validity of the insurance or security specified in the certificate under paragraph 2, before three months have elapsed from the date on which notice of its termination is given to the authorities referred to in paragraph 4, unless the compulsory insurance certificate has been **surrendered to these authorities or a new certificate has been** issued within the said period."

60   The delegation of Japan noted that reference to preventive measures in article 3, subparagraph (d) of the HNS Convention should, in its opinion, have included explicit reference to the cases of damage mentioned in subparagraphs (a), (b) and (c) of the same article by including the words "to prevent or minimize such damage." In the view of this delegation, it would be useful to supplement this omission by means of a common understanding by the Committee that the Convention only applies to preventive measures undertaken to prevent or minimize damage falling under the geographic scope of application regulated in subparagraphs (a), (b) and (c).

61   The delegation of Japan noted that the expression "to prevent or minimize such damage" had been excluded from the reference of "preventive measures" contained in article 2 of the proposed draft convention on liability for damage caused by ships' bunkers contained in document LEG 74/4/1. This

*Contact point: Dr. Erik Røsæg, Legal Adviser, dr.juris, Ministry of Justice, Akersgaten 42, Box 8005 Dep, N-0030 OSLO - Norway
Tel. 47-22-245381, Telefax 47-22-242725, E.mail: erik.rosag @ jus.uio.no

delegation expressed the view that this expression, which is used in the CLC and reflected a more precise wording, should be included in that draft text, or other draft texts in future similar provisions.

62   The Committee agreed with the proposed interpretation of the HNS Convention.

[...]

L   ANY OTHER BUSINESS (agenda item 12)

(a)   Carriage by sea of radioactive material

86   The Committee considered several submissions in connection with the carriage by sea of nuclear material.

87   In introducing document LEG 74/12 the delegation of Solomon Islands *inter alia* suggested that IMO should address the question of liability in connection with carriage of nuclear material by sea as an interim measure, pending the progress of work undertaken at present at IAEA to update and expand the liability regime established by the 1963 Vienna Convention. The present liability system had many gaps and interim consideration by IMO was advisable not only on account of the delays experienced at IAEA to find an appropriate solution to this problem, but also the total exclusion of the carriage of all types of radioactive material from the scope of the HNS Convention. A liability regime in respect of the carriage of nuclear materials covered by the INF Code should be based upon the principles of strict liability and unlimited (or adequate) guarantee to meet the liabilities for damage, clean-up and/or damage prevention.

88   In introducing document LEG 74/12/1, the delegation of Argentina noted that the proposal contained therein in respect of routeing of ships carrying INF material did not contravene the basic principle of freedom of navigation or innocent passage. The implementation of this principle would have to balance the interests of the flag States whose ships were engaged in the transport of this material with the obligation of the coastal States to protect the marine environment in areas under their jurisdiction. The regulations proposed did not seek to prohibit the carriage of INF material within jurisdictional waters of coastal States, but to regulate it by means of providing the adequate legal framework on the basis of the understanding that ships carrying INF material should follow high seas routes unless otherwise agreed by the coastal and the flag State. These agreements operated within the legal framework established by the United Nations Convention on the Law of the Sea (the LOS Convention). The regulations proposed would adequately complement rule V/8 of the SOLAS Convention in connection with the specific case of transport of INF material. After consideration of technical factors regarding routeing by the NAV Sub-Committee, confirmation was sought from the Legal Committee that the proposed regulation is in conformity with international law.

89   In introducing document LEG 74/12/5, the delegation expressed its view that, after the exclusion of nuclear material from the HNS Convention, the Committee, in co-operation with IAEA, should take the initiative to ensure the avoidance of gaps in the field of liability and compensation for damage in connection with the carriage by sea of INF material. The proposal for the establishment of an IAEA/IMO joint working group followed the recommendation included in the resolution adopted by the 1996 International Conference on Hazardous and Noxious Substances and Limitation of Liability, that IAEA and IMO work together in defining and considering issues of liability and compensation for damage occurring during the transport by sea of radioactive material.

90   The delegation of Ireland introduced document LEG 74/12/2 which called for the adoption of an adequate liability and compensation regime for carriage by sea of radioactive material and proposed that the INF Code be made mandatory. The Paris and Vienna Conventions did not provide adequate liability regimes in that they did not apply to non parties, and the notion of damage is not adequate when

it comes to damage to the environment and losses to fishing and tourism interests. In the opinion of this delegation the present process of review of the Paris and Vienna Conventions could not be expected to solve those concerns. With respect to the need for a mandatory INF Code the delegation noted that there had been cases off the coast of Ireland, and presumably elsewhere, where ship operators had not complied with the provisions of the INF Code.

91   For the purpose of their discussion by the Committee, the subject matter referred to in the submissions was divided into three main items, namely, liability and compensation, routeing and prior notification and mandatory character of the INF Code.

Liability and compensation

92   The Chairman, quoting from a letter from IAEA, drew attention to modifications under consideration in that Organization which would address some of the issues raised in these submissions.

93   Some delegations, however, expressed the view that IMO, as the UN agency competent for matters relating to liability for damage caused by the maritime transport of dangerous substances, should take the initiative to establish an adequate regime for liability and compensation in connection with the carriage of INF nuclear material by sea. Prompt action in this regard should help to ensure that innocent bystanders enjoy adequate protection as an interim measure, since the process leading to the amendment of the Vienna Convention could still take a very long time. Reference was also made to the fact that, in general, the concept of nuclear damage under the Vienna Convention was much more restricted than the concept of environmental damage regulated in IMO instruments. It was not clear whether all radioactive substances referred to in the INF Code would in the end be included within the framework of amendments at present under consideration at the IAEA. A joint working group would assist in establishing to what extent the amendments under consideration would include INF material. As an alternative, close contacts should be entertained between the IMO and the IAEA Secretariats to ensure that the Committee is kept informed regarding the progress of the discussions in IAEA.

94   Several delegations strongly opposed any action by IMO, even on an interim basis, since this could hamper on-going work by IAEA. Furthermore, IMO should not take steps which could result in duplicating or overlapping the work in IAEA.

95   The Committee noted the discussion of the subject at the HNS Conference. Furthermore, it took note of the amendments being considered in IAEA. It was considered that IAEA should be given the time to complete its work and that it would not be a useful employment of the Committee's time to work on the same issues. The Secretariat was requested to contact the Secretariat of IAEA in order to obtain a report on the progress and extent of the work and to encourage that Organization to make such information available in a form that it could be submitted to the Committee. Finally, the observation was noted that the Vienna Convention was open to non nuclear States and that, where this was possible, delegations should contact their national delegations participating in IAEA negotiations to supplement the information.

96   The delegation of Ireland expressed the view that it was the role of the International Maritime Organization to address the subject of liability and compensation in connection with the carriage by sea of INF substances. The delegation expressed its deep disappointment that this subject had not been acknowledged as falling under the mandate of IMO, bearing in mind the objective of this Organization to protect the marine environment in connection with the operation of ships. The delegation of Solomon Islands expressed support for these views.

Routeing and prior notification

97   Several delegations strongly opposed the adoption of regulations aiming at preventing or restricting the rights of navigation of ships carrying INF in the territorial sea, archipelagic waters,

international straits and Exclusive Economic Zone (EEZ). The implementation of such regulations would, in their view, result in the violation of fundamental principles of customary international law and basic rights and freedoms explicitly regulated in the LOS Convention. These rights and freedoms were found to be ignored by the proposed draft regulations submitted for the consideration of the Committee in that they placed restrictions on the transit of ships carrying INF material to the high seas, thus limiting the right of these ships to navigate the EEZ, or engage in innocent passage in the territorial sea. In this regard note should be taken of specific provisions of the LOS Convention, notably those relating to innocent passage and high seas freedom of navigation in the EEZ for ships carrying nuclear or other inherently dangerous nuclear substances. Reference was made to articles 22 and 23 regarding existing authority to regulate ships carrying nuclear cargoes in the territorial sea. Reference was also made to article 211 of the LOS Convention, which allowed for the delimitation by international agreement of certain areas on account of their particular environmental sensitivity. These agreements could relate specific restrictions to navigation to the concrete needs for environmental protection in areas with clearly defined limits.

98   The requirements for prior notification were also opposed by several delegations on the grounds that such requirements would not only restrict freedom of navigation or the right of innocent passage, but could also endanger the physical security of INF material by increasing the threat of terrorist incidents as a result of the disclosure of routeing information.

99   The delegations opposed to the adoption of the proposed routeing restrictions recalled that States could always move for the adoption of appropriate routeing measures in the NAV Sub-Committee. They expressed, however, their opposition to forwarding these particular regulations to the NAV Sub Committee.

100   Several other delegations expressed their support for the proposal for routeing restrictions for ships carrying INF material, as well as the requirement for previous notification. In the light of what they saw as the exceptionally hazardous nature of INF material such routeing restrictions were, in their view, justified on the basis of rights of coastal States acknowledged in the LOS Convention to adopt special measures to protect vital coastal interests and the marine environment under their jurisdiction. The provisions of the LOS Convention should not be interpreted as obstacles for the adoption of preventive measures of a general kind. Instead they should be considered as providing a framework for flag and coastal States to reconcile potentially conflicting interests. In this regard, the principle of freedom of navigation could not be upheld at the expense of equally legitimate rights of coastal States to protect their interests and resources. The changing circumstances which had occurred since the adoption of the LOS Convention in 1982, in particular the potential hazard for coastal States involved in the transport of INF material, provided sufficient reason for States to continuously reassess the way in which freedom of navigation and the right of innocent passage should be exerted, bearing in mind the increasing threat posed to coastal States and the marine environment generally, by the transport of such material. While the role of the NAV Sub-Committee and the MSC to discuss technical aspects of routeing measures was uncontested, the role of the Legal Committee to discuss the legal issues involved in the adoption of such measures should also be acknowledged. A proper co-ordination between IMO organs was necessary to avoid the progress of proposals presented for the consideration of one of these organs being neutralized with the excuse that either technical or legal components had not been properly addressed.

101   The Committee noted the divergent views expressed and encouraged delegations to engage in informal discussions on this subject. Any such discussions should include representatives from both sides of the argument.

102   Taking particular account of the suggestion by the Chairman of the Committee the delegation of Argentina stated that it would pursue the matter on that basis.

Mandatory character of the INF Code

103   There was general consensus that the decision on whether the INF Code should be mandatory was exclusively a policy matter, not a legal matter, to be addressed by the technical bodies concerned. It was noted, however, that many delegations who spoke favoured the notion of making the Code mandatory.

[...]

6.   REPORT TO THE MARITIME SAFETY COMMITTEE*

Doc. no.: NAV 42/23 + Add. 1(+ Corr. 1), 2   Date: 12 August 1996

Table of contents

*   Only paras 6.1-6.17 are reproduced.

LIST OF ANNEXES

[...]

6   DEVELOPMENT OF MEASURES COMPLEMENTARY TO THE CODE FOR THE SAFE CARRIAGE OF IRRADIATED NUCLEAR FUEL (INF CODE)

6.1   As instructed by the Committee, the Sub-Committee considered:

.1   route planning, notification to coastal States and availability of information on the type of cargo being carried, including its hazards;

.2   restriction or exclusion of ships carrying materials subject to the INF Code from particularly sensitive sea areas; and

.3   tracking of ships carrying INF Code materials throughout the voyage by a shore-based authority.

6.2   The delegation of the Solomon Islands in presenting NAV 42/6, saw the need for a binding comprehensive and consolidated code of conduct to address the issues of voyage planning, notification of coastal states and tracking of ships throughout the voyage by a shore-based authority. Its view was supported by some delegations.

6.3   The Sub-Committee noted the information provided by Greenpeace International (NAV 42/INF.12) recommending inclusion in the INF Code of new provisions relating to voyage planning, notification and consultation including development of guidelines detailing the minimum information to be provided and recommending appropriate procedures for notification and consultation.

6.4   Some other delegations were of the opinion that the existing provisions concerning routeing, reporting and voyage planning were adequate to ensure safe navigation of ships carrying INF materials.

6.5   Another delegation expressed the opinion that deficiencies in existing provisions concerning routeing and reporting should be identified; noted that voyage planning and secure tracking of such ships is currently being undertaken by shipowners and/or States engaged in the transport of INF Code materials; and pointed out that any measures adopted must be consistent with the Law of the Sea

Convention and IMO and IAEA instruments, and in particular preserve the navigational rights and freedoms in the Law of the Sea Convention.

Route planning

6.6   The Sub-Committee noted that a general requirement for voyage planning is presently contained in the STCW Convention. However, the Sub-Committee was of the opinion that provisions for voyage planning on all ships engaged in international voyages should be further developed to include principles, criteria and guidelines.

6.7   The Sub-Committee invited Member Governments to submit proposals for the development of provisions for voyage planning for all ships engaged in international voyages to NAV 43.

6.8   Solomon Islands was of the opinion that voyage planning should include, *inter alia*:

    .1   a safe route, taking into account the risk presented by the cargo; and

    .2   diversion ports offering assistance in case of an emergency involving the cargo.

Prior notification and consultation

6.9   Solomon Islands supported by some other delegations were of the opinion that provisions for prior notification and consultation should be established for the following purposes only:

    .1   indicate facilities or lack of facilities to offer assistance;

    .2   discuss shore support; and

    .3   agree on routes, areas to be avoided and particularly sensitive sea areas.

The notification could be limited to the coastal States' sector.

6.10   A majority of delegates opposed prior notification to coastal States for voyages of ships carrying materials subject to the INF Code. The reasons stated included that prior notification could endanger the physical protection of INF Code materials; it may lead to States trying to veto or prevent the passage of such ships through their territorial sea or Exclusive Economic Zone (EEZ); and it could establish a precedent so that prior notification could be required for the passage of all classes of vessels. Some delegations noted that if a requirement for such notification is imposed, it should be for all vessels carrying hazardous or polluting cargoes and not just INF Code materials.

Restriction or exclusion of ships carrying INF Code materials from particularly sensitive sea areas

6.11   The Sub-Committee noted that the MEPC at its thirty-eighth session had considered this matter and suggested that this item could normally be addressed if proposals from individual Member States were submitted for consideration by the Committee and other appropriate bodies on the basis of the criteria developed by the Organization.

Tracking of ships carrying INF Code materials throughout the voyage by a shore-based authority

6.12   The Sub-Committee noted that ships carrying INF Code materials are in general tracked throughout the voyage, either by the shipowner or a shore-based authority of one of the countries involved in the transport activity.

6.13   The Sub-Committee also noted that the COMSAR Sub-Committee is giving consideration to this matter.

6.14   The majority of delegations had no objection to the development of provisions for the tracking of ships carrying INF Code materials, based on the present practice.

6.15   The delegations of the United Kingdom, France, Japan and the Russian Federation could not support the establishment of provisions for tracking solely aimed at ships carrying INF Code materials and were of the opinion that if tracking would be required, it should apply to all ships carrying hazardous cargoes.

6.16   With regard to paragraphs 6.6 to 6.8 on route planning and paragraphs 6.12 to 6.15 on tracking of ships carrying INF Code materials, the Sub-Committee invited the Committee to consider expanding its terms of reference for voyage planning to include all ships and, if appropriate, to review SN/Circ.92 - Guide to the planning and conduct of passages.

6.17   The Sub-Committee, noting resolution A.790(19) regarding preparation of a progress report to the twentieth session of the IMO Assembly, invited the Committee to authorize NAV 43 to submit relevant parts of the report prepared at the session directly to the Assembly.

[...]

UNITED NATIONS EDUCATIONAL,
SCIENTIFIC AND CULTURAL ORGANIZATION
(UNESCO)

DOCUMENTS REPRODUCED IN WHOLE OR IN PART:

INTERGOVERNMENTAL OCEANOGRAPHIC COMMISSION

REPORTS OF GOVERNING AND MAJOR SUBSIDIARY BODIES

DOCUMENTS NOT REPRODUCED:

INTERGOVERNMENTAL OCEANOGRAPHIC COMMISSION

REPORTS OF GOVERNING AND MAJOR SUBSIDIARY BODIES

9. Doc. no.: UNESCO SC-96/WS/48; IOC/SOC-VI/3
    Date: 26 November 1996
    Title: Report No. 71: Sixth Session for the IOC Regional Committee for
               the Southern Ocean and the First Southern Ocean Forum,
               Bremerhaven, Germany, 9-13 September 1996.

1. REPORT NO. 70: TWENTY-NINTH SESSION OF THE IOC EXECUTIVE COUNCIL, PARIS, 24 SEPTEMBER-2 OCTOBER 1996

Doc. no.: UNESCO SC-96/CONF.211/CLD.28; IOC/EC-XXIX/3   Date: 7 October 1996

TABLE OF CONTENTS

C.   Statement by Dr Gunnar Kullenberg, Executive Secretary IOC, on his Intersessional Report

IV.   **List of Working Documents**

V.   **List of Participants**

VI.   **Statement by the Brazilian Delegation on item 5.4**

VII.   **List of Acronyms**

1.   OPENING

1   The Chairman, Mr G. Holland, opened the Twenty-ninth Session of the IOC Executive Council at 10.00 on 24 September 1996.

2   **The Executive Council received with interest and appreciation** the statements given by the Chairman and Director-General of UNESCO (see Annex III - A and B).

2.   ADMINISTRATIVE ARRANGEMENTS

2.1   ADOPTION OF THE AGENDA

3   **The Executive Council adopted** the Agenda as given in Annex I.

2.2   DESIGNATION OF THE RAPPORTEUR

4   **The Executive Council accepted** the proposal by the USA to designate Prof. M. Fortes (Philippines) as Rapporteur for the Session.

2.3   CONDUCT OF THE SESSION, TIMETABLE AND DOCUMENTATION

5   The Executive Secretary reviewed the arrangements of the Session and introduced a Provisional Timetable (Document IOC/EC-XXIX/1 Add. prov.) and the Provisional List of Documents (Document IOC/EC-XXIX/4 prov.).

6   Some delegations pointed out that they had only received documents very late or not at all. This was regretted by the Executive Secretary who recalled that statutory despatch time had been followed. He also suggested more use of electronic mail to speed up communications. **The Executive Council suggested** that in future the Executive Secretary also should check that documents were received.

7   The Executive Secretary informed the Executive Council that, unfortunately, the scientist invited to give the Roger Revelle Memorial Lecture at the last minute was unable to attend and the lecture was cancelled.

8   In accordance with the decisions of the Fifteenth Session of the Assembly, **the Executive Council established** a Technical Review Committee for the Resolutions under the Chairmanship of Dr E. Okemwa (Kenya), comprising the Delegates of Argentina, Brazil, China, Cuba, Egypt, France, Russian Federation and USA.

9   The Resolutions adopted by the Executive Council are given in Annex II. The List of Working Documents, the List of Participants and the List of Acronyms are given in Annexes IV, V and VII, respectively.

3.   DEVELOPMENTS SINCE THE EIGHTEENTH SESSION OF THE IOC ASSEMBLY

3.1   REPORT ON INTERSESSIONAL ACTIVITIES AND BUDGETARY MATTERS

10   The Executive Secretary IOC presented the Annual Report 1995. He highlighted major policy issues related to IOC flagship programmes, in particular: the development of GOOS; the capacity building programme and TEMA; follow-up to UNCED in science programmes, and UN system-wide co-operation; public awareness creation as regards the role of the ocean and marine science and ocean observations including, in particular, the preparation for the 1998 International Year of the Ocean. He recalled the grave resource situation of the IOC. He stressed the follow-up to DOSS, the report on DOSS-II, the report on UNCLOS and the support received from the UNESCO General Conference for the resolutions of the Assembly, and reiterated the strong support of the Director-General to IOC. His Statement is given in Annex III-C.

11   Most Council Members made statements in response to the presentation of the 1995 Annual Report, expressing their strong support of IOC actions and programmes and informing the Council about relevant national and international actions. They all found the 1995 Annual Report very good. They stressed the importance of the 1998 International Year of the Ocean for IOC and concurred that the IOC should aim for a progressive, quality-ensured development for 1998 and with a quantum jump in resources in this conjunction. A commitment to such a step should be obtained from governments and Member States of IOC in 1998. The Executive Council reiterated the commitment of their governments to work through the IOC e.g., in matters related to the development of GOOS, and other important ocean affairs within the evolving mandate of the IOC.

12   The Executive Council stressed that we are going through challenging times and that we need to take up the challenge, very much in the way the IOC is doing it. The IOC should now exercise proper and adequate leadership and focus its programmes. Member States of the IOC now realize more than before the importance of the oceans and this should naturally imply a willingness also to strengthen the IOC. The breadth of the activities of the IOC demonstrates the interest Member States have in IOC. The imbalance with respect to resources needs to be addressed and the connection to governments and national institutions must be strengthened so as to help solve this question of imbalance. Governments and Member States must be made more aware of the IOC and its potential and the important tool they have in IOC, and hence the need to address the adequacy of the Secretariat for the task.

13   The Executive Council emphasized the importance of the IOC regional subsidiary bodies. The Executive Council also stressed the role of the IOC in the follow-up to UNCED and in conjunction with Member States' efforts to implement UNCLOS. The co-operation with other intergovernmental bodies and in particular the ICSPRO Agencies was strongly endorsed, and the role of the IOC in this connection was stressed.

14   The importance of IOC's contribution to coastal zone research and observations was re-emphasized, and the strong involvement with the interdisciplinary project on Coastal Zones and Small Islands was likewise strongly endorsed. In this connection the proper use of resources, including the IMS was again reiterated by several members of the Council. The continuation and increasing association of IOC with IMS was stressed.

15   The Executive Council reiterated in particular the importance of:

(i)   GOOS and its orderly development, under the leadership of the IOC, and with the support of most other IOC programmes;

(ii)   contributions from IOC to coastal zone development and management with emphasis on an appropriate scientifically based approach to the overall problem of ICAM;

(iii)   Training, Education and Mutual Assistance (TEMA), centered on the training activities of all IOC programmes, with a strong linkage between science and education, as well as awareness creation of the importance of the oceans;

(iv)   the need to find the most appropriate internal structure and organization within UNESCO of the IOC Secretariat and the need to address the perception of IOC in the UN system;

(v)   the need to obtain real commitments on the part of IOC Member States.

16   Several members of the Council referred to the important statement made by the Director-General in his address and stressed the importance of his support and guidance (Annex III-B). The Executive Council expressed its appreciation to the Director-General and UNESCO for the support provided to IOC.

17   Several members of the Council specifically informed about support provided from their governments to the IOC, including: Brazil - with the co-operation of Argentina and Uruguay, publication of the atlas entitled "Morphology and Sedimentology of the Southwest Atlantic Coastal Zone and Continental Shelf from Cabo Frio (Brazil) to Peninsula Valdez (Argentina)" and intention to provide, through its Ministry of Science and Technology, financial support to the IOC Trust Fund in 1997; the Russian Federation provided financial support to the IOC Trust Fund in 1996 for the Tsunami Warning System Programme; the Republic of Korea seconded a specialist to the IOC Secretariat through a fund-in-trust contribution from August 1995; it likewise wishes the IOC to be associated with their regional training programme in the WESTPAC area; Greece announced the establishment of an IOC regional project office for the Eastern Mediterranean; the Chilean Delegation informed about its Government's intention to set-up a bill on ocean research which will also lead to increased direct support to the IOC; Portugal's intention to pursue and support IOC's association with EXPO 98, and readiness to respond to the spirit of decentralization within UNESCO through sharing in due course some of their resources with IOC.

18   In conclusion, members of **the Executive Council reiterated** the strong commitment to the IOC of their governments and the need to consolidate this, while evolving and reshaping the IOC in a strategic fashion so that it can respond to the rapidly changing conditions in the world, and the related changes in the oceans.

19   **The Executive Council endorsed** the 1995 Annual Report and **expressed** its great appreciation to the Executive Secretary and the IOC Secretariat for work well done.

3.2   DEVELOPMENTS RELEVANT TO IOC WITHIN UNESCO: 28ᵀᴴ GENERAL CONFERENCE AND EXECUTIVE BOARD

20   The Chairman introduced this item referring to the Annual Report 1995, Document IOC/EC-XXIX/2 and its Annex 1 and noting that most of the relevant developments had already been covered in the Director-General's address, by the Executive Secretary in his report on intersessional activities (Item 3.1), and by the ensuing plenary discussion of that item. The Chairman also noted that the paragraphs for item 3.2 in the Provisional Annotated Agenda provide a clear and concise background of developments since the statutes of the Intergovernmental Oceanographic Commission were amended in 1987.

21   There was, however, an outstanding issue on which the advice of the Executive Council is required. This is on mechanisms to facilitate the provision of dependable resources to the IOC Special Account from those Member States of IOC which are not members of UNESCO. The Chairman drew attention to Document IOC/EC-XXIX/2 Annex 1 which gives the background to this matter; the 150ᵗʰ Session of the UNESCO Executive Board will be considering the matter, and it will be valuable if the views of the Executive Council can be conveyed to the Director-General before the Executive Board meets.

22   The Chairman emphasized that this is a long-standing issue of some sensitivity and suggested that an effective way to proceed would be for him to chair a small *ad hoc* group to discuss this issue, and prepare a draft statement from the Executive Council to be brought back to the Plenary under item 5.1 (DOSS). He suggested membership of the *ad hoc* group be his vice-chairs together with the UK, USA, France and Japan.

23   **The Executive Council accepted** the Chairman's suggestion, noting that there is the broader question of Member States providing support to the Commission. This is part of the task given to DOSS-II, and the context and timing of this comprehensive exercise should be taken into consideration by the drafting group.

4.   **PROGRAMME MATTERS REQUIRING DECISIONS BY THE EXECUTIVE COUNCIL**

4.1   OCEANS AND CLIMATE (JSC; OOPC, FCCC; IPCC-RELATED MATTERS)

24   The Executive Secretary made an overall introduction referring to the Annual Report 1995 and Document IOC/EC-XXIX/2. He recalled Resolution XVIII-6 and the in-depth discussion of the Assembly of this issue on the basis of the review presented to the Assembly in Document IOC-XVIII/2, Annex 5. He stressed the responsibilities given to IOC by UNCED through Agenda 21, Chapter 17, as regards oceans and CO_2, sea-level change and development of GOOS, together with proper capacity building. Some of these matters may also be discussed under Agenda Item 8. He drew the attention of the Executive Council to paragraph 35 in Document IOC/EC-XXIX/2, where the actions decided by the Assembly have been followed-up, and to the proposed actions for the remainder of the 1996-1997 biennium given in paragraph 38 of the same document. Some of these points may also be considered relevant to Agenda Item 9.

25   Mr Arthur Alexiou continued with the introduction of this item covering the activities of the IOC jointly with SCOR/JGOFS, the OOPC, and JSC for the WCRP. He noted the long productive IOC partnership with SCOR/JGOFS in co-operation with WOCE in the quest for quantifying the role of the ocean in mitigating increases in atmospheric greenhouse gas concentrations. He cited the IOC-JGOFS Panel members' contributions to the work of the IPCC and to their part in organizing the first International Symposium on Ocean CO_2, the proceedings of which have been published in a special issue of the Caribbean Journal of Science. He brought the Council's attention to other greenhouse gases which are influenced by ocean processes such as methane and nitrous oxide and informed the delegates that consideration was being given to broadening the Panel's scope and membership to address the ocean processes, sources and sinks of these gases as well. The IPCC is considering a workshop on non-CO_2 greenhouse gases in its work plan for 1997-1999 and an ocean component would be welcomed should this proposed workshop survive the IPCC budget cuts.

26   Mr Alexiou then presented progress by the OOPC of GOOS, which is jointly sponsored by the WCRP and GCOS. At its first meeting in March 1996, the OOPC recognized a need to bring the scientific plan developed by the OOSDP to the users and implementors via a more user friendly strategy. The favored strategy was to select key observation-to-product lines and produce illustrative documents demonstrating the value of these lines. These end-to-end demonstrations would be faithful to the OOSDP design, but would be in a form that would enable "selling" the design by explaining exactly what agencies being asked to make observations can be expected to gain. The aim is to encourage participation and to provide agencies with easy to understand descriptions of where their contributions will lead and the benefits that will ensue. The upper ocean TOGA network in support of operational climate prediction was chosen as the first case. The lines from observations from the Ship of Opportunity Program and the TOGA TAO array, to operational climate prediction, to agricultural crop planning, water resource management, etc., are now real and of some substance. Sea-level monitoring was the second case selected.

27   The OOPC is organizing a workshop in March 1997 on the vexing problem of establishing new and maintaining existing time-series observations. Vital as they are to understanding climate change, long-range funding for time-series programmes has always been problematical. The workshop will examine priorities, needs and new technologies with more attractive cost/benefit ratios with the aim of establishing the basis for formulating a realistically implementable time-series observation program for GOOS.

28   Mr Alexiou then summarized actions by the JSC for the WCRP that had bearing on the work of the IOC. The JSC met in March 1996 in Toulouse. Of particular interest to the Executive Council was the JSC decision to include climate monitoring as a specific agenda item in future JSC sessions in order to review, in conjunction with GCOS and GOOS progress in developing operational monitoring and climate data products. It was believed this would assure a reinforcement of co-ordination with and development of WCRP contributions to GOOS and GCOS. This item will include reports on GOOS, GCOS, GTOS, activities of the OOPC, etc. The JSC also intends to assist with the evolution of WCRP research data projects and observing systems to operational status under GOOS and GCOS. The JSC recognized the need for more involvement of developing countries through capacity building and reaffirmed its intention to reinforce liaison between the WCRP, IGBP, and IHDP in guiding the development of appropriate START activities. The CLIVAR Implementation Plan was scheduled to be produced by the end of 1996 and made available to the Member States shortly thereafter. The JSC also planned to write a letter to the Member States stressing the need for resources for developing and using global ocean models for both prognostic studies and assimilation, in particular for analysis of the WOCE global data sets, and requesting national commitments to support these efforts. The JSC plans to hold a "mid-term" scientific conference in Geneva in August of 1997. Conference participation will be aimed at senior scientists, policy makers, senior government administrators, etc. This will be done via special invitations. Finally, it was decided that a bi-annual newsletter will be produced for the WCRP. The next JSC meeting will be held in March 1997 in Toronto.

29   Several delegates and the Representative from SCOR made interventions. Japan brought the attention of the Council to the importance of the ocean processes in the WESTPAC region such as the Indonesian through-flow that affect El Niño and the southeast Asian monsoon. He noted the large commitment Japan is making in instrumented moored buoys, satellite observations including ocean colour, and oceanographic ship surveys.

30   Brazil described briefly its participation in a tripartite pilot-project involving also France and the USA as co-partners to the establishment and implementation of a moored-buoy array in the Tropical Atlantic. Those activities will generate an operational programme whose data would represent a substantive contribution to the climate module of GOOS in that region. Kenya expressed interest in making a greater contribution to the studies in the east African region and asked for assistance in interpreting data from WCRP observations in terms of regional impacts.

31   The Philippines reported its focus on sea-level rise and has socio-economic studies in process aimed at establishing a long range management plan to adapt to climate change.

32   The Russian Federation underscored the importance of ocean climate research and expects to resume its large scale ocean climate field studies as the economy improves. The establishment of a global ocean CO_2 data bank is under consideration. A strong model development component in Russia is expected to continue.

33   The Indian Delegate expressed the view that the growing profusion in the IOC's work of a large number of working groups, panels, sub-panels, etc., tended to give a perhaps unwarranted impression of lack of focus. He further believed that this complexity made it very difficult for the Executive Council to address and advise on the work of so many science panels with all the issues involved, and encouraged a reexamination of the structure. He noted that the JGOFS process study in the Arabian Sea had just been completed and looked forward to obtaining the complete data set from JGOFS. He further expressed strong support to the programmes of IOC on climate change.

34   The Delegate of the United States expressed that:

(i)   The United States encourage the Executive Secretary to prepare a consolidated plan for IOC participation in the IPCC Work and Plenary Session;

(ii)   The United States support the continued role of IOC in sponsoring meetings of scientific and technical experts on ocean-related climate issues, and

(iii)   IOC should continue to use IODE and IGOSS to produce timely and policy-relevant data products for utilization by scientific bodies and the FCCC.

35   The Delegate of the United States furthermore stressed that the IOC should formally endorse the results of both the 2nd Conference of the Parties to the UNFCCC and the 2nd Assessment Report of the IPCC, since the IOC has been present at and contributed to the work of each body and should get the recognition for having done so.

36   The Delegate of the United States suggested that, with regard to the reports of panels and committees, there is a continued need for the Ocean CO_2 Advisory Panel. Further, the Delegate suggested that the IOC may wish to keep this panel informed of developments in the work being done by GESAMP under IOC sponsorship on the oceanic storage of CO_2.

37   The Delegate of the United States stated that the United States feel that the key issue for the climate programme is the need for an early transition of those ocean-observing systems implemented

under WOCE/TOGA into similar continuing systems to be a part of CLIVAR and the Climate Module of GOOS.

38   The Australian Delegate recognized the danger of overstretching the IOC Secretariat in attempting to be represented by IOC staff at all the important ocean fora and encouraged the IOC Secretariat to make greater use of individuals who are members of its subsidiary bodies to represent the IOC at important functions. Australia endorsed the OOPC strategy for developing specific end-to-end illustrations that clearly showed the benefits to result from ocean monitoring.

39   Mexico reported it has groups working on sea-level looking at specific impact possibilities resulting from climate change. Mexico is also installing instrumented buoys off its shores. The Delegate from China voiced strong support for the IOC efforts in climate change. He maintained that current climate models do not adequately represent the ocean and that IPCC documents do not give sufficient consideration to ocean processes.

40   The Delegate from Portugal noted that the very complexity of existing mechanisms for dealing with climate change makes participation by small countries difficult. He recognized the need for a large apparatus for such a multi-dimensional problem but nevertheless made a plea for some streamlining of the machinery. He supported the regional approach to problems through IOC regional bodies whenever possible.

41   The Representative of SCOR noted that the JGOFS programme is moving towards the completion of its field phase in 1998 and to an intensive 3 to 4 year period of data analysis, synthesis and modelling. These activities will ensure that the efforts and funds spent on cruises, time-series stations, etc, will result in a truly global view of the oceanic carbon cycle and its role in climate change.

42   She noted the continuing co-operation between SCOR and IOC in their joint support of the Carbon Dioxide Advisory Panel and requested that discussions between the panel's sponsors precede any expansion of its mandate to consideration of other greenhouse gases.

43   The Representative of SCOR drew attention to two particular JGOFS activities. The recently completed Arabian Sea Process Study involved 6 countries and resulted in numerous publications and the production of data sets on CD-ROMs. More than 2.5 million dollars was spent by participating nations and international organizations to provide training courses, shipboard fellowships and equipment to countries in the Arabian Sea region.

44   A JGOFS continental margins study of fluxes of materials from the land to the open ocean is being developed in co-operation with IGBP-LOICZ (Core Project on Land-Ocean Interactions in the Coastal Zone). A scientific Workshop on this topic will take place in Lagos, Nigeria in October 1996. It will be co-sponsored by IOC.

45   SCOR extended its thanks to Norway for its generous support for the newly-established JGOFS International Core Project Office at the University of Bergen.

46   Turning to OOPC, the Representative of SCOR noted that SCOR is providing funding and staff support for a workshop on time-series stations which will take place at the SCOR Secretariat in March 1997.

47   **The Executive Council strongly endorsed** continued actions of IOC in climate research, observation and change issues.

48   **The Executive Council expressed its endorsement** of IPCC and COP-II results.

4.2   OCEAN SCIENCE IN RELATION TO LIVING RESOURCES (OSLR), IPHAB, GLOBEC, LME, CONVENTION ON BIOLOGICAL DIVERSITY

(i)   **OSLR, IPHAB; GLOBEC; LME**

49   The Executive Secretary made an overall introduction referring to the IOC Annual Report 1995 and Document IOC/EC-XXIX/2. He recalled Resolution XVIII-8 on the Intergovernmental Panel on

Harmful Algal Blooms (IPHAB), and stressed the very strong development and implementation of the HAB Programme, with support of major donors, in particular DANIDA, SIDA, Japan and CIDA. He informed about the significance of the agreement with Spain, in the spring of 1996, on the establishment of a science and communication centre on harmful algae at the Instituto Español de Oceanografía in Vigo, Spain, complementary to the Centre already established at the University of Copenhagen, Denmark.

50   He recalled the decision by the Assembly that a special group be established to review the problem of transfer of non-indigenous species through ballast of ships and informed that a joint ICES-IOC-IMO Working Group is proposed with draft Terms of Reference provided in Document IOC/EC-XXIX/2, Appendix 1. These have been considered by the GIPME Programme.

51   He referred to the IOC association with GLOBEC as a co-sponsor and with several regional LME programmes. The possibility of developing an MOU with the LME programmes was brought up. He finally recalled that the IOC is supporting the CPR Programme and the gradual expansion of this Programme to cover other sea areas than the Atlantic Ocean. He draw attention to the serious problem of lack of senior professional staff in the IOC Secretariat to lead the further development and implementation of the OSLR Programme.

52   On behalf of the Chair of the IPHAB, the Secretariat supplemented with highlights of achievements of the HAB Programme in the intersessional period. Emphasis was given to presentation of the 500-page IOC Manual on Harmful Marine Microalgae, an IOC Technical Series (No. 44) on design and implementation of some HAB monitoring systems (prepared jointly with ICES), training and capacity building achievements, developments of the IOC Science and Communication Centre in Copenhagen (see IOC Training Course Report No. 40), and the successful scientific workshop, planned and organized jointly with SCOR, on the physiological ecology of harmful algal blooms, where the proceedings will constitute an important state-of-the-art reference book on research methods.

53   Several Members of the Council provided information on ongoing national activities of relevance to OSLR. The Delegate of Spain informed that the Science and Communication Centre in Vigo will start its activities before the end of the year, and that Spain will host the 8th International Conference on Harmful Algae, June 1997. The Delegate of Chile informed that it will host the next meeting of the IOC Regional Working Group on HAB (COI-FANSA), and reported on positive experience with involvement of the private salmon industry in funding of HAB research, as an example of new ways of identifying resources nationally. The Delegations of the Republic of Korea and China are currently negotiating with GEF for a joint study on marine resources, productivity and ecosystem health of the Yellow Sea.

54   The Representative of SCOR provided additional information on the successful SCOR-IOC Workshop on the Physiological Ecology of Harmful Algal Blooms, Bermuda Biological Station, May 1996. A set of recommendations on future research priorities was made by the Workshop, and the Chair of the now disbanded SCOR-IOC WG 97 has been invited to propose two or three of these as priorities for new SCOR working groups. SCOR expressed the hope that IOC would be interested in continuing its joint activities with SCOR on HAB. In relation to GLOBEC, negotiations towards the establishment of an international Core Project Office for GLOBEC are well advanced and SCOR hopes that IOC and its Member States may contribute resources in support of the GLOBEC planning process, in consultation with the other international sponsors of GLOBEC, namely SCOR and IGBP.

55   The Executive Council expressed its great appreciation of the results achieved by the HAB Programme in the intersessional period, **and emphasized** its continued strong support for the HAB Programme.

56   The Executive Council **took note of and approved** the draft Terms of Reference for the proposed ICES-IOC-IMO Working Group on the Transfer of Marine Organisms by Ballast Water.

57   The Secretariat also informed about the most recent developments of the Global Ecosystems Dynamics Programme (GLOBEC), specifically that the GLOBEC Programme has become an IGBP Core Project. Dr Roger Harris of the Plymouth Marine Laboratory has been elected as new Chair of GLOBEC-International. The GLOBEC Scientific Steering Committee will have its first meeting in November 1996 in Baltimore, USA. The GLOBEC Committee held the International Symposium "Development of New Techniques and Models for the Study of Marine Ecosystems", in co-operation with PICES (Hemuro City, 27-28 June 1996). In 1997, six GLOBEC cruises will be undertaken in the North Pacific Bering Sea using training ships from universities and the Japan Fisheries Agency.

58   It was noted that negotiations leading to the establishment of an International Core Project Office for GLOBEC are underway. The IOC as one of the international sponsors of GLOBEC should consider its role in relation to this implementation programme. The Executive Council was in this respect invited to consider the way that IOC can contribute to the provision of the support for the development of the SPACC Programme.

59   It was also noted that the connection of GOOS-LMR to the GLOBEC Programme is suggested to be relatively strong in the Report from the GOOS-LMR Meeting in Dartmouth, Massachusetts, March 1996. The principle is that the development of GOOS should use the scientific results of the GLOBEC as being one programme scientifically addressing some of the same parts of the marine environment as the GOOS-LMR aims to monitor and predict.

60   Several Members of the Council recognized the importance of the Small Pelagic Fish and Climate Change Programme (SPACC) being a sub-programme of GLOBEC. It was furthermore expressed that an extended co-operation with the IOC Secretariat and Regional bodies was sought with respect to the implementation of SPACC in Africa and Latin America, as recommended at implementation and planning meetings in Namibia and Mexico.

61   **The Executive Council expressed** strong support for the activities of the Small Pelagic Fish and Climate Change Programme, SPACC, being a sub-programme of GLOBEC important to Member States who depend on coastal fisheries.

62   **The Executive Council noted** that the activities of the Sir Alister Hardy Foundation of Ocean Sciences (SAHFOS) on the Continuous Plankton Recorder Survey (CPR) were most important for the development of the Large Marine Ecosystems (LME). Several Members of the Council informed on the activities of CPR with respect to new routes and regional co-operation.

63   **The Executive Council welcomed** the developments of new routes of CPR worldwide and noted the importance of these developments with respect to research on Large Marine Ecosystems (LME) and furthermore its association and co-operation with other programmes like GLOBEC and GOOS.

64   **The Executive Council expressed** support for developments of the Large Marine Ecosystem (LME) concept and its association and co-operation with other IOC or IOC-related programmes and activities including CPR and GLOBEC.

65   The Representative of the Philippines referred to the importance of the IOC International Directory of Seagrass Bed Institutions currently being prepared. He also referred to the Second International Seagrass Biology Workshop (Australia, January 1996), co-sponsored by IOC, and invited IOC to consider to co-sponsor the Third Workshop, to be held in the Philippines in 1998.

66   The United States offered to provide, jointly with United Kingdom, funding for a Technical Secretary for OSLR. The Representative of the United States underlined that funds at this stage are only available for one year and thus encouraged other Member States to provide additional funding for the post.

67   **The Executive Council welcomed** the offer of the United States and the United Kingdom.

(ii)   **Convention on Biological Diversity**

68   The IOC Secretariat introduced the section of Agenda item 4.2 dealing with marine biodiversity. Reference was made to the Provisional Annotated Agenda (Document IOC/EC-XXIX/2), Document IOC/EC-XXIX/Inf.2, Resolution XVIII-9 on Marine Biodiversity and the Decision of the Conference of the Parties (COP) to the Convention on Biological Diversity on Conservation and Sustainable Use of Marine and Coastal Biodiversity ("The Jakarta Mandate"), as adopted by COP at its Second Session held in Jakarta, Indonesia, November 1995.

69   The IOC was represented at the Second Session of the Subsidiary Body on Scientific, Technical and Technological Advice to the Convention (SBSTTA-2), which met in Montreal, Canada (2-6 September 1996); SBSTTA-2 recommended to COP-3 (to be held in Argentina, November 1996) that the Convention Secretariat convene a Meeting of Experts in early 1997 and IOC will be invited to attend the Meeting.

70   The Executive Council was furthermore informed that the IOC Secretariat was asked by the CBD Secretariat for assistance in identifying criteria for the selection of marine and coastal biodiversity experts, which was delivered. The Executive Council was also informed that the two Secretariats are considering elements for a possible Memorandum of Understanding on co-operation, with a view towards the harmonization of programmes and the development of joint activities in the field of coastal and marine biodiversity.

71   The Delegate of Norway congratulated the efforts of the Secretariat concerning the issue of marine biodiversity and stressed that the document prepared by the Secretariat had to be seen as a continuation of the 'IOC Marine Biodiversity Strategy', as developed by the IOC-NOAA *Ad Hoc* Consultation on Marine Biodiversity (Paris, 3-5 May 1995). It was pointed out that new issues have arisen as a consequence of the continuous interaction between IOC, CBD and other biodiversity-related bodies, including the research issues identified by SBSTTA-1, to which IOC is in a position to contribute. However, in view of the very broad definition of biological diversity within the Convention, IOC must ensure that its role with respect to marine biodiversity does not stretch beyond the limited funds which are available for this activity area. The Delegate of Norway stressed the importance to continue linking up marine biodiversity activities with the relevant existing activities and programmes of IOC, which can contribute to the biodiversity programme. He strongly encouraged, in particular, the implementation of training activities within the IOC Marine Biodiversity Strategy and the related Work Plan 1996-97.

72   Several Members of the Council supported Norway in stressing the importance of bearing in mind the limited resources of IOC, which might lead to the need to limit responsibilities in this field.

73   The Representative of Italy made reference to the joint statement circulated by the President of the National Academy of Science of Italy and the President of the National Academy of Agricultural Sciences of India on the importance to take action towards providing the general public with information on the biodiversity concept and related issues. He suggested that the same kind of practical presentation be made in the context of documents prepared by the IOC Secretariat dealing with the issue of marine biodiversity.

74   The Observer from Pakistan stressed the need for studies aimed at assessing the economic value of biodiversity.

75   Canada stated that the GESAMP document on biodiversity, which was adopted at the last GESAMP Session in Paris in March 1996, could be considered by IOC in its efforts devoted to marine biodiversity, IOC being a co-sponsor of GESAMP.

76   The Executive Secretary IOC stated that the IOC-NOAA *Ad hoc* Consultation on Marine Biodiversity, which the IOC Assembly at its Eighteenth Session decided to retain, will be used as an advisory mechanism to ensure that the involvement of IOC in the field of marine biodiversity do not overcome present capabilities, both in terms of secretarial manpower and financial resources, and that existing activities and programmes be used for biodiversity study purposes. He said that the Consultation mechanism can work by correspondence, also in accordance with its Terms of Reference. Furthermore, he pointed out that the actions taken covered the instructions contained in Resolution XVIII-9.

4.3   INTERNATIONAL OCEANOGRAPHIC DATA AND INFORMATION EXCHANGE (IODE)

77   Mr B. Searle, Chairman of the Committee on IODE, introduced this agenda item and informed the Executive Council on the achievements of the Committee and briefly presented some views on the future direction. He informed the Executive Council of the great success of the Fifteenth Session of the Committee held in Athens in January 1996. This success was due to the considerable efforts of the Greek Government, Hellenic NODC and the local organizing committee and with the assistance of the European Union MAST programme. The importance of marine data and information exchange was reflected by the attendance of almost 100 participants from 38 Member States and 17 partner organizations. He emphasized that the discussions held at IODE-XV raised a new wave of interest in IODE among the IOC Member States resulting in the subsequent creation of NODCs in Kenya, Ukraine, Croatia and the nomination of contact points in Georgia and Bulgaria.

78   The Chairman IODE focused on some of the achievements of IODE. He mentioned the Global Ocean Data Archeology and Rescue (GODAR) project which had made significant contribution to the global database of ocean profiles with, in excess of 2 million profiles of T, $S^o/_{oo}$, O_2, nitrates being added. Four regional workshops have been held with two further planned in Colombia (October 1996) and Nigeria (March 1997). An international conference to sum up the progress and identify future directions, is planned for 1997. The Global Temperature and Salinity Pilot Project (GTSPP) was highlighted as an example of IODE's success in working with other data collection programmes, such as IGOSS and with the scientific community through WOCE. GTSPP demonstrates an ideal model of a fully integrated 'end-to-end' data management system of the type needed to support GOOS. GTSPP's success was demonstrated through the recommendation of both IGOSS and IODE committees to make GTSPP an operational programme. In support of GOOS, IODE and IGOSS developed a joint data and information management strategy which was approved by the Second Planning meeting of I-GOOS in Washington, May 1996, and will create the framework for the comprehensive GOOS data management plan. The contribution of Canada to GTSPP, Australia to the development of the Strategy Plan and the USA to the GODAR project were specially acknowledged.

79   IODE confirmed its continuing commitment to training and capacity building with an emphasis on improving the effectiveness of training through techniques such as "train the trainer" (the OceanPC training course jointly with ICES was especially mentioned) and through the use of electronic training technologies such as computer-aided training. IODE recognized the success of the regional approach to IODE-TEMA activities and has introduced IODE Regional Co-ordinators to support this. The Chairman specifically acknowledged the efforts of Japan in running marine data management training courses for the WESTPAC region over the past 10 years. The continuing success of OceanPC was highlighted with over 300 users worldwide and the increasing importance of marine information management was stressed. The use of technology to support the management and dissemination of data and information was given considerable emphasis, and the value of the IOC's WWW Homepage was demonstrated by more than 40,000 visitors to the site in the past year.

80   Recalling the Director-General's opening remarks concerning the need for the delivery of products and solutions to support the decision-making process, the Chairman IODE informed the Council of the steps taken by IODE to respond to these demands. He stated that the delivery of products and services is one of IODE's strengths with a range of products developed and made freely and widely available, including the CD-ROMs on GTSPP, GEBCO, GLOSS, the World Ocean Atlas '94 and the Global Directory of Marine Scientists.

81   Looking towards the future, it was recognized that IODE needed to expand the types of data managed and exchanged, provide more user-oriented products and address the needs of the wider user community, in addition to supporting the traditional scientific community, including a focus on priority areas such as the coastal zone and the health of the ocean issues. To achieve this, IODE will improve the skills and capabilities of IODE centres through the continuation of training and capacity building, introduction of advanced data and information management technologies and through the strengthening and building of partnership with other programmes in all regions.

82   IODE's continuing emphasis on information was demonstrated by a wide range of activities and projects undertaken by the Group of Experts on Marine Information Management (GEMIM). The production of the MIM publication series, IOC WWW Server, a pilot project for the dissemination of information across developed and developing countries via Internet and a further pilot project to enhance the Marine Environmental Data Inventory (MEDI) is a clear demonstration of IODE's initiative in marine information management.

83   IODE-XV recommended the creation of an IODE strategy sub-committee which was aimed at reducing the duplication of efforts between programmes, seeking additional resources for the programme implementation, and improving the awareness of IODE's capabilities and skills.

84   The Chairman IODE closed his presentation by stressing his concern relating to the amount of resources allocated to IODE which was not keeping pace with the growth of IODE activities. He called upon the Executive Council to continue its strong commitment to IODE and to examine ways to provide the resources necessary to continue the momentum of IODE.

85   **The Executive Council expressed satisfaction** with the efforts of IODE and identified the programme as a flagship of the IOC, because of its considerable successes. Many delegates supported the IODE's four-year programme and stressed the fundamental role of data and information management in many of the IOC's programmes and in support of many other programmes. **The Executive Council approved** the Summary Report of the Fifteenth Session of IODE and endorsed the recommendations.

86   Many delegates commended the progress of IODE and informed the Executive Council of specific activities in their countries. The Delegate of India described the success of the GODAR Meeting held in Goa in 1995 and offered to host a joint IODE-IGOSS Officers Meeting in 1997. The Delegate reiterated India's willingness to making marine data and information available to the international community through the newly established RNODC for the Indian Ocean.

87   The Delegate of Kenya referred to the success of IODE in Africa, particularly with the introduction of new technologies such as the use of E-mail and CD-ROMs, and he requested IOC to continue and reinforce support of IODE activities in developing countries. He recalled that IOCINCWIO-III selected RECOSCIX-WIO network as an appropriate mechanism for TOGA and WOCE data delivery. He identified the need to further increase IOCINCWIO's participation in the IODE programme through the strengthening of national capabilities and by assisting in the development of NODCs in the region. He reported that the use of the RECOSCIX-WIO network for the exchange of data in addition to information has been initiated. The Council joined the Delegate in thanking Belgium for its continued support of RECOSCIX-WIO through the launching of Phase 2 (1996-1999) of the project. The Delegate concluded by welcoming the development of the RECOSCIX-CEA network for the IOCEA region, but called on the IOC to avail more resources to this project.

88   The Delegate from the United Kingdom highlighted national initiatives including the support of a pilot international data and information directory system. He stressed the importance of the national data archaeology and rescue activities following the results of the survey made in the country.

89   **The Executive Council stressed the importance** of using new technology to further the capabilities of IODE. In particular, the use of the IOC Home Page as a method of disseminating information about IODE and IOC activities such as meeting documentation and schedules was identified as a key area for development.

90   **The Executive Council expressed** its appreciation to the many Member States including Japan, Australia, USA, Canada and the UK who have used new technologies to make data and information products more easily available through such mechanisms as on-line access through Internet. This decision supported and strengthened the IODE's policy of free and open exchange of data and information, and should be extended.

91   The Delegate of France acknowledged the importance of IODE's activities and encouraged to continue efforts in establishing end-to-end data management schemes and implementing regional projects such as MEDAR/MEDATLAS.

92   The Delegates of Cuba, Pakistan and Thailand identified the need to develop data management in their countries, requesting support in strengthening existing capabilities, particularly as regards coastal waters through arranging training courses and assisting in the data and information management infrastructure development. **The Executive Council expressed satisfaction** with those members of the Executive Council who stated their countries' readiness to provide facilities for training, in this instance France, Russian Federation and USA.

93   **The Executive Council identified** some specific areas for IODE to focus its efforts including strengthening training and co-operation activities, the use and promotion of new technological tools, increase the range of data types managed within IODE with emphasis on biological and chemical data.

94   **The Executive Council noted** a request from the Islamic Republic of Iran for establishing a RNODC-MARPOLMON for the Persian Gulf area and recommended the Committee on IODE to give consideration to this request in accordance with existing IODE procedures. **The Executive Council noted** the willingness of the Islamic Republic of Iran to host the regional training course on oceanographic data and information management in 1997, and invited the Executive Secretary to implement the course jointly with other international bodies operating in the region.

95   The Executive Council welcomed the decision to establish the IODE strategy sub-committee and recommended that links with IODE and other organizations and programmes such as EU/MAST, WMO, ICSU, ICES, should be continued and strengthened. The Executive Council reiterated the importance of IODE and called on Member States to continue their excellent efforts and continue with their support of the Secretariat in IODE activities.

96   The Executive Council adopted Resolution EC-XXIX.1.

4.4   INTERNATIONAL TSUNAMI WARNING SYSTEM IN THE PACIFIC (ITSU) and IDNDR-RELATED MATTERS

97   The Chairman of the ICG/ITSU, Capt. H. Gorziglia, introduced the progress report on the international activities of the Group and called on Members of the Executive Council to approve the Summary Report of ITSU-XV and adopt recommendations contained in the Report. In his presentation he emphasized that the intersessional period marked an increasing interest of the Member States in the tsunami programme, not only in the Pacific but in the IOCARIBE and Mediterranean regions as well. The Tsunami Warning System in the Pacific continues to be a unique operational warning system which comprises hazard assessment, warning and educated response.

98   The Fifteenth Session of the International Co-ordination Group for the Tsunami Warning System in the Pacific took place in Papetee, Tahiti from 24-28 July 1995. The Session focused on the further development of the network of seismic and sea-level measurement stations; improvement of communications links for real-time exchange of telemetry, seismic and tsunami data and dissemination of tsunami notices and warnings; implementation of the Tsunami Inundation Modelling Exchange (TIME) project; development of the expert Tsunami Data Base (ETDB) for the Pacific; on training and education activities, and on actions targeted to increase the awareness of the population about earthquake and tsunami dangers. Special attention was given to the discussion of ways and means of improving the quality of the system components and expanding the knowledge and experience in tsunami mitigation gained in the Pacific to other geographic areas such as IOCARIBE and the Mediterranean.

99   Two comprehensive projects which have been embarked upon bore their first fruit: under the TIME Project, due to generous contributions from Japan and the USA, the Manual of Numerical Simulation of Tsunamis was finalized and is now being published by IOC. A few numerical models have been transferred free of charge to leading institutions involved in the tsunami mitigation and research, and the description of the characteristics of a work station and peripherals necessary for the tsunami simulation and computer graphics animation have been drafted and distributed. Training components constituted an important part of the project, and facilities for training have been provided by Japan, Chile and Mexico through the training course held in Valparaiso, Chile in March-April 1996; under the ETDB project the first set of floppy disks containing software and the full dataset of the tsunami-related data for the Kuril-Kamchatka region have been issued; the work is proceeding to have Pacific-wide coverage with the support of Russia and IOC.

100   The Chairman emphasized that the warning system cannot be successful without efforts and contribution of Member States in improving the effectiveness of their national system components.

101   The Chairman pointed out that the International Tsunami Information Centre (ITIC) continued its activities successfully in providing training, services and increasing awareness to the Pacific population of the tsunami danger. Special acknowledgement was given to Mexico for providing the services of Mr S. Ferreras from April 1995 for a one-year posting in the position of the ITIC Associate Director. This position was partly supported financially by IOC.

102   The Chairman informed the Council of ITSU-XV decision to invite Member States to explore the possibility of proposing candidates for the post of the ITIC Associate Director who will perform his duties in his regular line of work, using the capabilities of electronic communication and assisting the ITIC Director in implementing his duties.

103   Co-operation among Member States and other international agencies in seeking support for the development and maintenance of the system is the key to the ICG/ITSU operation. Science was always considered as the basis for wise decision-making. Jointly with the IUGG Tsunami Commission, the

Tsunami Measurements Workshop took place in Estes Park, Colorado, USA, 28-30 June 1995; a second joint workshop took place in Petropavlovsk-Kamchatskiv, Russia, from 19-23 August 1996. The workshop formulated scientifically-proven recommendations targeted to improve the effectiveness of the warning system.

104   At the awareness building level, the ICG/ITSU launched initiatives along two directions: one through facilitating the publication of new materials related to the tsunami danger and placing information on the IOC tsunami programme and ICG/ITSU activities on Internet; and two, through implementing training. The goal is to make all levels of society and different communities aware of the dangers of this natural phenomenon and to bring the programme objectives to schools.

105   An updated version of the ITIC Brochure was published in English, French and Spanish, as well as "Tsunami-the Great Waves", a colour booklet describing tsunami and tsunami safety guidelines. The text of the booklet is also available in digital format. The publication of a set of textbooks and teacher's guides on earthquakes and tsunamis, which was available in Spanish only, is now being published by UNESCO in English. Publication in other languages is under consideration. Indonesia and Russia expressed interest in translating them.

106   The electronic Tsunami Bulletin Board system was developed by the USA NOAA/PMEL as an experimental e-mail notification system for the international tsunami community. A World Wide Web home page with access to a broad range of tsunami information was developed at the University of Washington (USA) and at the IOC Secretariat.

107   The International Tsunami Information Centre (ITIC), sponsored by IOC, implemented the visiting experts' programme in October-November 1995 - a regular annual training exercise for 2-3 experts from the Pacific and another one is planned for October-November 1996.

108   Finally, the Chairman noted a few shortcomings of the programme. In spite of all the efforts there was no progress in the development of a regional tsunami warning system in the Southwestern Pacific. Tsunami survey teams, though they have been established, could not be used effectively due to the lack of special funds and established procedures for sending the teams to the disaster area. He invited the Council to provide guidance to the Group in solving these problems and requested Member States to increase support in funds and through active participation in the Tsunami Programme.

109   **The Executive Council complimented** the progress achieved by ITIC under the Directorship of Mr D. Sigrist and acknowledged with thanks his, and the Associate Director's accomplishments during the intersessional period. **The Executive Council noted** with interest an option proposed by ITSU-XV on the condition of the Associate Director's nomination and working conditions and **urged** Member States to take the necessary measures for supporting ITIC activities, in general, particularly filling the post of the Associate Director.

110   **The Executive Council expressed** full support to the ITSU-XV decision to formulate a project proposal for ITSU-XVI based on a concept of the wide utilization of tsunami inundation and detection technologies and requested the ICG/ITSU Chairman and the Executive Secretary IOC to take all necessary action for the development of the project proposal.

111   **The Executive Council was pleased** to note the progress made by Chile, France, Mexico and the USA in the wide utilization of modern reliable TREMOR and NGWLM systems, by Australia in developing a project for improving and upgrading the national and tsunami warning system, by Russia in rebuilding national systems destroyed by the 1994 earthquake and tsunamis. Progress in Canada, Costa Rica, Ecuador, Nicaragua, Singapore and the Republic of Korea were also especially noted.

112   **The Executive Council requested** to increase efforts in providing technical advice and training to developing countries in the usage of new technologies. The requests of Peru and Indonesia have been specially noted.

113   The experience gained by Japan and Indonesia in the transfer of know-how and technology on a bilateral basis was noted with interest and **the Executive Council recommended** to explore the continuation and widening of this type of arrangement. It also comments the effort of Japan to establish the headquarters for promoting the activities of IDNDR headed by the Prime Ministry himself.

114   The Executive Council expressed satisfaction with the progress achieved by the ICG/ITSU during the intersessional period and thanked the Chairman of the Group for his devotion, energy and guidance in the programme implementation. The Executive Council approved the ITSU-XV Summary Report and all Recommendations contained therein. The Executive Council adopted Resolution EC-XXIX.2.

115   The Delegate of Peru confirmed his Government's invitation to host ITSU-XVI in 1997 in Lima. The Executive Council noted this with appreciation.

116   The Executive Council noted the proposal for expansion of the International Tsunami Warning System in the Pacific into other regions, such as the Caribbean and considered that the necessary resources to support this expansion should be identified prior to accepting these additional responsibilities.

117   The Executive Council expressed satisfaction with the action taken by the Executive Secretary IOC, Russia and USA in rebuilding the tsunami warning system in the Kuril-Kamchatka region and expressed hope that the installation of new equipment will be completed, necessary training provided during 1997, in order to bring the system into full operation.

118   Dr Oliounine, IOC Senior Assistant Secretary, informed the Council of the progress achieved in the implementation of the decision of the Assembly taken at its Eighteenth Session by which it was recommended to start the development of a storm surges project, particularly for the Bay of Bengal and the northern part of the Indian Ocean. In response to this decision a regional storm surge workshop will be organized in India from 5-7 December 1996 in conjunction with the IOCINDIO Meeting and the International Conference on Natural and Technological Coastal Hazards. This will provide an opportunity for consultations with other international organizations which may have potential interest to co-operate in the development of the project. The representative of India expressed wholehearted support to the IOC initiatives and conveyed to the Council the readiness of his country to provide all necessary facilities for these meetings.

119   The Executive Council noted with pleasure the December 1996 workshop being planned in India for intercomparison of storm surge models in the Bay of Bengal. It is recommended that the validation of the storm surge prediction models should constitute an important item for the workshop discussions.

4.5   GLOBAL OCEAN OBSERVING SYSTEM DEVELOPMENT AND RELATED MATTERS

(i)   **Global Ocean Observing System (GOOS)**

120   This item was introduced by Dr A. McEwan on behalf of the Chairman of I-GOOS, Prof. M. Glass. Dr McEwan conveyed Prof. Glass' apologies for being unable to present the report personally. He reported on the progress in GOOS design and planning since the Eighteenth Session of the IOC Assembly. Particular attention was brought to the outcome and recommendations of the Second Planning Session of I-GOOS which was preceded by a Workshop on Socio-economic Aspects of GOOS (Washington, USA, May 1996), the Second Session of the Strategy Sub-Committee of I-GOOS (Paris, March 1996) and the Third Session of J-GOOS (April 1996). In his presentation, Dr McEwan highlighted the following points:

(a)   The regional approach to GOOS planning and implementation has been strongly encouraged. Examples of successful developments are EuroGOOS and NEARGOOS. However, regional GOOS development requires harmonization between regional, national and global activities so a set of guidelines for inclusion as parts of GOOS was needed;

(b)   among the five GOOS modules, the greatest progress has been achieved in planning the Climate and Health of the Ocean Modules. Although the GOOS Coastal module has received high priority among countries, it still requires a good definition and special efforts to initiate its planning;

(c)   the LMR and operational marine meteorological and oceanographic modules are under consideration for closer definition by J-GOOS and I-GOOS;

(d)   the document "Approach to GOOS" has been revised and entitled "Towards Operational Oceanography". The SSC has prepared a draft GOOS Strategic Plan and actions have been taken by J-GOOS to prepare a GOOS Scientific Plan. A recent meeting of GOOS sponsors has decided to ensure co-ordination of the activities in order to have a unique GOOS Plan by 1998;

(e)   a GOOS Data Management Strategy has been developed jointly with IODE and IGOSS. The concept of a common GOOS-GCOS-GTOS Data Management Panel has been agreed upon; and

(f)   capacity building activities will be developed through regional workshops.

121   Dr McEwan stated that although some progress has been achieved in GOOS planning, special attention should be given to obtaining the resources needed to implement the identified activities. Therefore, the proposed Priority Agreement meeting in 1997 should receive particular attention by IOC and other sponsoring agencies. He noted that support had been given at I-GOOS-PS-II for the concept of a "two tier" agreement meetings, the first tier being a high-level meeting to gain agreement on the principles of GOOS involvement and the second tier focusing upon "pragmatic" commitment to elements of GOOS that could be implemented immediately from existing systems and observations.

122   Dr T. Spence, Director of the Joint Planning Office for GCOS, noted the role of GCOS in integrating the climate elements including atmosphere, ocean and land surface. He stressed the close co-operation among these elements via GOOS, GTOS, and existing programmes of their sponsoring organizations. He indicated the key role of the joint GCOS-GOOS-WCRP OOPC in advancing the climate module of GOOS, and the significance of newly-reconstituted GCOS-GOOS-GTOS panels in co-ordinating activities of the three observing systems.

123   Regarding implementation, he complimented the responsiveness of programmes-bodies such as IODE, IGOSS, DBCP, and the TOGA TAO Implementation Panel, especially in so far as they are striving to improve and enhance their services.

124   He noted the need for national participation in the development of the GCOS and GOOS, and informed the Executive Council that the JSTC for GCOS will give consideration to an appropriate strategy to support national involvement in establishing principles, priorities, and enhanced participation.

125   Many delegates reported on national activities related to GOOS and reaffirmed their strong, continued support for GOOS development.

126   The Delegate of Peru stressed the need, so as to permit the South Pacific region to participate effectively in GOOS, for the installation of oceanic-meteorological floating platforms in that region. He called for IOC assistance to that effect.

127   The Delegation of Brazil expressed some concern with respect to the Marine Living Resources Module of GOOS, that seems to lack a precise definition of its profile and end-users. It has also been mentioned that Capacity Building, as a major building block of GOOS, has still to fulfil its most important role, that relates to the generation of a community of operational oceanographers within member countries interested in GOOS. Finally, the representative of Brazil reaffirmed the intention of his government in seconding an expert to the GOOS Support Office in 1997, now pending approval by the highest decision-making level of the Brazilian Government.

128   The Delegation of France stressed the importance of GOOS and its country's interest in the GOOS Programme, and recalled that France has put at the disposal of the GOOS Support Office the services of an expert who has been its Acting Director since 1995.

129   The Republic of Korea informed that KORDI organized a regional Workshop of Operational Oil Spill Modelling jointly with IMO and IOC/WESTPAC, in Pusan, Korea, April 1996.

130   The Delegate of Japan informed that Japan has sent an associate expert to the GOOS Support Office of IOC.

131   The Executive Council acknowledged these statements with great appreciation.

132   The Representative of WMO reaffirmed WMO's strong support for GOOS development, especially its climate and services modules. He invited IOC to continue to support the implementation of the CMM SEACAMP (South-East Asian Center for Atmospheric and Marine Prediction) Project as a possible contribution to GOOS in the ASEAN region.

133   **The Executive Council noted** with satisfaction the progress of NEARGOOS, and, in particular, the implementation of a real-time exchange system for physical oceanographic data. **The Executive Council also noted** with satisfaction progress in the development of EuroGOOS, as well as initiatives to develop GOOS activities in the Black Sea and the Mediterranean. **The Executive Council also noted** the initiative to set up a Mediterranean Forecasting System (MFS) for the prediction of ocean weather in the basin, and **further noted with interest** the potential of MFS in enhancing the regional scientific co-operation in the Mediterranean.

134   **The Executive Council strongly endorsed** the concept of regional development of GOOS and related regional co-operation.

135   **The Executive Council encouraged** the integration of GOOS activities with GCOS and GTOS in relation to data management and space observations.

136   Some participants expressed their views on the use of existing systems. This could be seen to include the continuing involvement of IGOSS and IODE in the data management strategy development.

137   The need to accelerate progress on the coastal module was emphasized and concern was expressed about the slow progress in its development.

138   Some support was given to the themes proposed by the US Coastal GOOS as an approach to defining an international coastal GOOS.

139   A common theme of many interventions was the need to minimize the number of subsidiary panels and bodies involved in GOOS planning to streamline the GOOS structure. Concerns were expressed about possible divergence of the SSC Strategic Plan and the proposed J-GOOS Scientific Plan for GOOS. **The Executive Council requested** I-GOOS and J-GOOS to work together on this matter as recommended by the recent meeting of GOOS sponsors and incorporate a "phased approach" into the SSC Strategic Plan to allow the implementation of GOOS elements as they become feasible.

140   **The Executive Council supported** the holding of a "two-tier Priority Agreement" meeting in 1997, the second tier being to accelerate the immediate implementation of GOOS elements that are ready.

141   The involvement of private agencies at an Agreement Meeting in was discussed. It was clarified that GOOS, though it can become permanent only if the governments are involved, should not exclude private agencies who may be able to contribute to GOOS observations. **The Executive Council felt** that the "Priority Agreement" meeting should assist in defining the principles of GOOS and in integrating the needs for implementation.

142   **The Executive Council endorsed** the recommendations of the Second Planning Session of I-GOOS. **The Executive Council agreed** that a two-day meeting of I-GOOS should be organized in conjunction with the Nineteenth Session of the IOC Assembly in July 1997, in accordance with the decision of the Assembly in 1995. The question of whether the Priorities Agreement meeting could be held in conjunction with the I-GOOS meeting would be addressed intersessionally.

(ii)   **Integrated Global Ocean Services System (IGOSS)**

143   The Chairman of the Joint IOC-WMO Committee for IGOSS, Prof. Dr D. Kohnke, introduced the topic in highlighting that IGOSS, though considered under this agenda item, was not a subsidiary GOOS group, but rather a building block of GOOS. He recalled the IGOSS objectives and the variables presently taken into account within the system, among which the salinity data were still quite inadequate, as was in general the geographic coverage of the data. He then summarized the main issues dealt with by the Seventh Session of the Joint Committee (Paris, 20-28 November 1995) and focused primarily on measures taken to ensure the continuation of a viable ship-of-opportunity programme (SOOP), after the completion of TOGA and with the field programme of WOCE due to be completed by the end of 1997. These included the establishment of a new organizational structure, made up of the IGOSS SOOP Implementation Panel (SOOPIP) which would monitor and co-ordinate the observations to maintain an adequate sampling strategy (as defined by the Ocean Observation Systems Development Panel and refined by the Ocean Observations Panel for Climate, *inter alia*), under the overall guidance of the newly formed SOOP Management Committee (SMC). The latter body had held its First Session from 21-23 May 1996 in Toulouse, France, whereas the former should probably meet in 1997 in South Africa.

144   Prof. Kohnke further underlined that one of the IGOSS strengths resided in its Plans and Implementation Programmes (PIPs) and that IGOSS-VII had adopted a new PIP to cover at least the period 1996-2003. As far as co-operation with IODE was concerned, he referred to agenda item 4.3 (IODE) where this topic had been fully taken into account. Finally, he referred to the relationship between IGOSS on the one hand and GCOS, GOOS and WCRP on the other. He expressed the view that, for the foreseeable future, the IGOSS support to those programmes would most likely concentrate on climate and services issues, but that there were in principle no objections to IGOSS embarking on exchanging other real- or near real-time kinds of data, if requested to do so.

145   The Executive Council recalled: (a) it had to consider only aspects of IGOSS relevant to the period 1996-1997, since the forthcoming session of the Assembly would review the overall programme proposed by the system; and (b) the relevant decisions taken by the WMO Executive Council at its Forty-eighth Session, through *inter alia* Resolution 2 (EC-XLVIII). It therefore recorded its decisions regarding IGOSS-VII conclusions in Resolution EC-XXIX.3. In so doing, the Executive Council recalled that, however critical the ship-of-opportunity programme is to IGOSS and other major programmes of IOC and WMO, other means of obtaining relevant data did exist, in the form of *inter alia* declassified naval XBT measurements, and CTD measurements from scientific or fishing vessels, as well as from profiling ALACE floats. It finally noted with regret the termination of operations of one of the last existing weather ship, commissioned in the United Kingdom, which had, as other weather ships in the past, provided for invaluable time series of ocean measurements for decades.

(iii)   **Remote Sensing and Relation to CEOS**

146   This item was introduced by Mr J. Withrow who noted that IOC remote sensing activities were focused in two areas. The first was the traditional relationship with World Meteorological Organization (WMO) and the second the relationship with the Committee on Earth Observation Satellites (CEOS). He described the effort by the IOC/GOOS in co-operation with the other affiliates of CEOS to generate a data base of user requirements. This effort was realized through the implementation of the CEOS affiliates database which is accessible through the IOC home page.

147   The IOC strategy to work with CEOS in the international development of ocean colour was described along with the need for, and timeliness of, the ocean colour activity. The current international mechanisms for realizing the value and benefit of ocean colour data were set forth. The origin of the International Ocean Colour Co-ordination Group was described along with its objectives in the context of the promotion of ocean colour.

148   Other activities related to the development of a coastal high resolution AVHRR product for coastal studies, training, including the CSI distance learning modules, and the development of a remote sensing project in North-western Africa were also described.

149   The Director of the GCOS Joint Planning Office provided a brief report on the recent *"In situ* Observations for the Global Observing System" meeting hosted by GCOS, 10-13 September in Geneva. He reviewed several recommendations from the meeting which encouraged close partnerships among the three global observing systems. Results from the meeting will be communicated to the CEOS plenary, and may lead to further consideration of an Integrated Global Observation Strategy.

150   The Executive Council welcomed the report on the remote sensing and CEOS and strongly supported the increased development of remote sensing activities in IOC programmes and maintenance of close ties with CEOS. It endorsed the formation of the International Ocean Colour Co-ordination Group and, noting the extra-budgetary support, directed the Secretariat to provide staff support as necessary to continue its work. The Executive Council also noted with appreciation the information provided by Dr Spence, Director of the GCOS Joint Planning Office, regarding the CEOS efforts in pursuing an Integrated Global Observing Strategy and instructed the Director of the GOOS Support Office to continue to monitor these activities. **The Executive Council expressed its appreciation** to India for its offer to host training activities either in ocean colour or in other areas of ocean remote sensing. **The Executive Council noted** with interest the publication of the first status report on ocean remote sensing by the Joint CMM-IGOSS-IODE Sub-group on Ocean Satellites and Remote Sensing (OSRS) **and endorsed** further support for the activities of the sub-group in the context of IGOSS.

4.6　　　TEMA AND CAPACITY BUILDING

151　　　　　　Lic. G. Garcia-Montero, First Vice-Chairman, introduced this agenda item referring to the Summary Report of the First Meeting of the TEMA Group of Experts for Capacity Building (Document IOC/TEMA-CB-I/3), which he chaired. He elaborated in particular on the recommendations and interpretations of the Group as regards the mandate provided through Resolution XVIII-15. The terms of reference and the tasks provided through this resolution, basically derived from the Draft TEMA Strategy in Response to UNCLOS and UNCED (Document IOC-XVIII/2 Annex 6) and the TEMA Strategy *ad hoc* Meeting 1995 (Document IOC/INF-999). The work of the Group is an evolving process with a number of issues to be further considered during the intersessional period.

152　　　　　　The introduction was supplemented by Dr F. Robles, Senior Assistant Secretary, up-dating recent developments on regional capacity building networking, with particular reference to the Workshop on Management of Oceanographic Systems of the Eastern Pacific, held at Concepcion, Chile, April this year (Document IOC/INF-1042). A similar effort is organized for the Atlantic South American countries, in Porto Alegre, Brazil, May 1997, and for the IOCARIBE region. The latter will focus on integrated coastal area management. Some preliminary steps have also been taken for the Mediterranean, in conjunction with the insular coastal dynamics (ICOD) programme of the Council of Europe, based in Malta; and, relevant activities may evolve for IOCEA, from a recent agreement established between the Commission and the University of Las Palmas, Canary Islands, Spain.

153　　　　　　Most Members of the Executive Council participated in the following discussion. All Member States expressed their strong support for the TEMA-Capacity Building programme and agreed it should remain as a continuing high priority for the Commission. The Brazilian Delegation stressed the necessity of Member States to support and facilitate access to information related to the work of the group.

154　　　　　　There was general support for the findings of the Group of Experts although some specific suggestions were made as to the direction and the tasks assigned by the Assembly.

155　　　　　　Various delegations pointed out that the small resources allocated to IOC should be focussed on TEMA activities related to major programmes and services of the Commission, and the overall strategy, co-ordination and evaluation should be reviewed and established to this end. Several delegations indicated willingness to provide further support to TEMA.

　　　　　　The Delegate of France expressed the wish that the TEMA Committee be replaced by a "Steering Committee", comprising officers responsible for the programme as well the regional representatives concerned, in charge of aligning training activities within the IOC programmes.

156　　　　　　**The Executive Council concurred** with the suggestion for an extended debate on the TEMA strategy to be organized in conjunction with the next Session of the Assembly, based upon additional elements developed by the Group of Experts during the intersessional period and its second meeting, in May 1997.

157　　　　　　**The Executive Council recognized** that many opportunities exist at the national, regional and global levels, for extrabudgetary funding of TEMA-Capacity Building efforts and these could and should be supported through concerted actions of Member States. The IOC regional programmes, in particular, can provide a focus for relevant Member States to co-ordinate their requirements for development and funding to multilateral and bilateral agencies. **The Executive Council emphasized** that it is mainly at the regional level that large programmes are most capable of providing infrastructure facilities and educational support, necessary to underpin marine programmes and services of IOC.

158   **The Executive Council supported** the idea that a survey conducted by Member States to identify their own national contributions to and requirements for TEMA activities related to the IOC programmes and services be prepared, possibly for the discussion during the next Assembly. This may also be a very useful activity to be considered in conjunction with the 1998 International Year of the Ocean.

159   **The Executive Council** endorsed the Summary Report of the First Meeting of the TEMA Group of Experts for Capacity Building.

5.   **OTHER MATTERS ARISING FROM THE EIGHTEENTH SESSION OF THE ASSEMBLY**

5.1   PROGRESS REPORT OF THE *AD HOC* STUDY GROUP ON IOC DEVELOPMENT, OPERATIONS, STRUCTURE AND STATUTES (DOSS-II)

160   The Chairman of DOSS-II, Dr Manuel Murillo, introduced the item, noting that DOSS-II was working to the schedule and terms of reference given in Resolution XVIII-1 of the Eighteenth Session of the Assembly and the Annex to that Resolution. He referred to Document IOC/EC-XXIX/6 and to paras 102 to 108 in the Annotated Provisional Agenda (Document IOC/EC-XXIX/2). He also drew attention to IOC/EC-XXIX/2 Annex 1 and the related IOC/EC-XXIX/Inf.5 which had just been circulated; it was the draft text prepared by the Chairman's *ad hoc* advisory group considering mechanisms to facilitate the provision of dependable resources to the IOC Special Account from Member States of the IOC, non-members of UNESCO, for consideration by the Executive Council.

161   Dr Murillo informed the Executive Council on working arrangements for the Group, noting that the Interim Report to the Nineteenth Session of the Assembly is expected to be ready by April 1997. Using Document IOC/EC-XXIX/6 as the reference, he reported on progress, drawing attention to a number of specific issues on which the advice of the Executive Council would guide the Group's future work.

162   In particular, he reported on the work of the sub-group on Statutes, Rules of Procedures and Pledging System which had met in Lisbon on 26-29 August 1996. It had considered various options for mobilization of support for the IOC: a voluntary pledging system based on a binding legal instrument, as described in *"Quo Vadis* IOC" (Document IOC/DOSS-III/3); establishing an annual or biannual membership fee structure; and a voluntary pledging system using a soft law measure adopted by the IOC Assembly in the form of a recommendation to be addressed to the governments of Member States. The sub-group had also considered the merits of focussing pledging arrangements to support regional activities or specific programmes, on the basis that such a focussing might be more attractive to Member States. The report of the sub-group will be discussed at the next DOSS-II meeting.

163   Finally, Dr Murillo drew attention to Document IOC/EC-XXIX/6 Add., which asked the Executive Council to consider a change in Article I para 2 of the Statutes, and to provide advice and instructions to the Executive Secretary with respect to its possible transmission to the Nineteenth Session of the Assembly.

164   The Chairman IOC thanked Dr Murillo for his lucid and comprehensive presentation and noted that the Executive Council should provide advice generally on the work of the Group, and also provide its view on two specific actions: advice to the Director-General on mechanisms to facilitate the provision of dependable resources from Member States of IOC non-members of UNESCO, for discussion of this matter at the 150th Session of the Executive Board; and on the proposed Amendment to Article I of the Statutes. In response to comments and questions from delegations, he asked all delegations to ensure that advice on these three matters was clearly differentiated.

165   In regard to the proposed Amendment to Article I of the Statutes, **the Executive Council determined** that it should not transmit it to the next Assembly. The Chair accordingly withdrew Document IOC/EC-XXIX/6 Add. Decisions resulting from the work of DOSS-II will almost certainly result in other changes to the Statutes and it is preferable if these be handled in totality. A careful and orderly approach would help to ensure that the revised Statutes fully reflect the expanded role and responsibilities of the IOC. Furthermore, this process provides an opportunity also to raise the profile of the IOC with governments and other organizations.

166   **The Executive Council agreed** that, when next the Statutes and Rules of Procedure are addressed, consideration should be given to two additional clauses to Rule 55:

(i)   Voluntary contributions made by Member States of the Commission that are not Member States of UNESCO can be calculated on a basis of a known incompressible appropriation to IOC by the General Conference of UNESCO, using the current assessment scales for Member States contributions to the United Nations.

(ii)   Additional voluntary contributions may be obtained from Member States of the Commission, from other Organizations of the United Nations system, as well as other sources.

167   **The Executive Council recognized** that two Member States of IOC, non-members of UNESCO, contribute to and participate in activities of the Commission at a level currently which comfortably satisfies the first of the above clauses. This is not always immediately obvious, however, as the contributions are often received in a variety of ways from a variety of sources, which makes it difficult to identify the totality. This is true generally, but is a particular problem for in-kind contributions.

168   **The Executive Council welcomed** the efforts of the USA to identify the support they provide to the Commission through contributions to the IOC Trust Fund and in-kind support for IOC programmes and secretariat. It also welcomes the announcement by the UK that it will undertake a similar exercise. Indeed, the Executive Council considers that this would be a useful exercise for all IOC Member States, and would provide a more realistic picture of IOC's activities and influence than is presently available.

169   The contributions made to the IOC Trust Fund can be readily identified, and a listing of those contributions is already prepared on a regular basis. In-kind contributions can in general only be identified and evaluated by the Member States making the contribution. **The Executive Council invites** all Member States to undertake this exercise on an annual basis, guided by the Modalities of Support document approved by the Sixteenth Session of the Assembly in 1991 (Document SC/MD/97 Annex VIII).

170   **The Executive Council recommended** that the Officers of the Commission meet annually, in the course of the Governing Bodies meetings, to consider this listing of contributions; to ensure that all contributions are consistent with the Commission's programmes and priorities as determined by the Assembly; and to evaluate the in-kind contributions. The Officers could ask for assistance and clarifications from Member States as necessary. The Chairman would report to the Governing Bodies in Plenary Session on the Officers deliberations and conclusions.

171   Such a process would make clear both the level and relevance of Member States' contributions, and would also help to identify those programme areas in which more support is needed, either in cash or in kind, to achieve the agreed programme objectives.

172   As this matter is to be discussed at the 150th Session of the Executive Board, **the Executive Council requests** the Chairman to ensure these views are brought to the attention of the Director-General prior to the Session.

173   **The Executive Council endorsed** the general thrust of DOSS-II's work. Many delegations provided advice to the *ad hoc* Study Group on content and direction, summarized as follows:

(i)   prioritizing and focussing IOC activities needed to be examined thoroughly, recognizing that there is likely to be a need to reduce the number of programmes in order to meet budget constraints; the regular process of evaluation should be used as an instrument for this purpose;

(ii)   the content and length of governing body meetings should be considered; the Executive Council still resembles a mini-assembly despite decisions taken on the first DOSS' recommendations, and further and stronger steps may be necessary;

(iii)   while supporting an increase in the number of vice-chairpersons, more detailed consideration of the role and responsibilities was needed;

(iv)   in seeking to increase financial resources there was a need to examine ways to raise IOC's profile and image, both with Member States and with other institutions; this was particularly pertinent given the opportunities presented by the 1998 International Year of the Ocean and the turn of the Century;

(v)   linkages to Member States through National Commissions and other arrangements needed to be strengthened; delegates to the IOC should be expected to carry a large part of the responsibility for this;

(vi)   the open session, which DOSS-II introduced to inform Permanent Delegates and Observer Missions of its deliberations and to benefit from their comments and advice, was welcomed; it would be more effective if earlier notification of such sessions could be given;

(vii)   the IOC needs to ensure that processes do not take precedence over purpose; DOSS is an effective way to do this, and it must continue to focus on main issues;

(viii)   all the work of the DOSS-II group should bear in mind that IOC is a body with functional autonomy within the UNESCO, and that the options for mobilization of support for the IOC or the adequacy of financial contributions shall consider this aspect.

174   Several delegations spoke on the options for mobilization of support for the IOC, but no clear conclusion emerged. Other delegations noted that they would provide comments when a document describing the options was available to them.

175   The Chairman of DOSS-II thanked the Executive Council for its valuable advice and guidance, and assured the Executive Council that careful note would be taken. He assured the Executive Council that DOSS-II was addressing the need to focus and cut back on activities, an important requirement in the dynamic field in which the IOC operates.

5.2   FINANCIAL RULES APPLICABLE TO THE SPECIAL ACCOUNT OF THE IOC

176   The Executive Secretary IOC introduced this item, referring to Document IOC/EC-XXIX/2 Annex 2, responding to IOC Resolution XVIII-2 requiring detailed financial rules applicable to the IOC Special Account to be prepared for initial consideration by the Twenty-ninth Session of the IOC Executive Council. The draft Financial Rules, included as the appendix to the above document, were based on the current Financial Rules for UNESCO. The intention was that, after discussion and possible amendment by the Executive Council, the draft Financial Rules would be referred to the UNESCO Comptroller's Office, then brought for consideration to the next Assembly after necessary revisions and modifications.

177   Several delegations indicated that they had a number of concerns regarding the draft Financial Rules as currently formulated. **The Executive Council agreed** with the Chairman's suggestion to form a small *Ad hoc* sessional group to consider these concerns and report back to Plenary.

178   The *Ad hoc* sessional group identified a number of questions in the current draft which will need to be referred to the appropriate experts in UNESCO for resolution. **The Executive Council instructed** the Executive Secretary IOC to undertake the necessary consultations and prepare a revised set of draft Financial Rules for consideration at the Nineteenth Session of the IOC Assembly.

179   The Chairman IOC also informed the Executive Council that the Financial Regulations provided in Document IOC/EC-XXIX/2 Annex 2 Add. were not those finally approved by the UNESCO Executive Board. The approved Financial Regulations would be circulated to all Member States of the IOC as soon as they are available in all working languages.

5.3   1998 INTERNATIONAL YEAR OF THE OCEAN: PROPOSALS AND PROGRESS REPORT

180   In introducing this agenda item, the Chair recalled that the UN General Assembly had declared 1998 as the UN International Year of the Ocean following a proposal of the UNESCO General Conference that had been based upon Resolution XVII-17 as adopted by the Seventeenth Session of the IOC Assembly. As referred to in the Expanded Annotated Agenda (Document IOC/EC-XXIX/2, para 113-

118), the Eighteenth Session of the Assembly had requested the Executive Secretary to report to both the Executive Council and the Assembly on progress being made in formulating proposals for celebration of the international year by the IOC. These are found in Document IOC/EC-XXIX/2 Annex 3 and its Addendum.

181   The Chair also recalled that, throughout the process leading up to declaration of the international year, there had been wide support from Member States at the governing bodies of the IOC, UNESCO and the UN. In his view, the initiative is considered as a unique opportunity to increase awareness of the importance of the ocean and coastal environment and to raise greater political visibility for ocean-related issues, including their socio-economic dimensions. To reach this goal, however, concrete steps need to be taken in the near future towards developing an overall management plan for the event.

182   As guidance to the Executive Council, the Chair suggested that the deliberations focus on: (i) a review of the proposals with a view to approving the type of activities that IOC should assist in mobilizing; and (ii) instructions to the Executive Secretary regarding further steps to be taken in developing a plan for implementation, including staff and resource implications.

183   The Executive Secretary provided complementary information regarding action that had been taken to foster inter-agency collaboration through the ACC Sub-Committee on Oceans and Coastal Areas as well as through the Inter-secretariat Committee on Scientific Programmes Relating to Oceanography (ICSPRO). Likewise, within UNESCO, the Director-General had requested him to lead an intersectoral task team so that UNESCO activities for the year could benefit from the whole spectrum of the Organization's competence.

184   During the ensuing discussion, a large number of Member States reiterated their commitment to this endeavour and referred to planning that had already begun at the national level, both in regard to the international year as well as to participation at EXPO-98 in Lisbon. Examples include dedicated research cruises, special scientific publications, travelling exhibits, educational materials for schools and the general public, national scientific conferences, etc. In many member states, events such as that of the proposed launching of ocean satellite by India, are being planned to take place in 1998, to fittingly commemorate the celebration of the International Year of the Ocean. Japan will host the Fourth WESTPAC Scientific Symposium in early 1998 in connection with the celebration.

185   In agreeing with the views of the Chair regarding the need for development of a management plan, numerous Member States expressed interest in providing support and facilities. The Delegates of Argentina and France reminded the Executive Council that, in accordance with UN rules, no costs should be borne through the regular programme budget for celebration of the international year.

186   The Delegate of France recalled that, due to budgetary constraints, the transfer of IOC activities - especially its Executive Council and the TEMA Group of experts - should not be done on the occasion of EXPO 98.

187   Recalling the invitation of the Director-General of UNESCO in his opening address that the IOC programme should include activities that will sensitize governments, the general public and society as a whole to the significance of the ocean to our common future, the Canadian Delegation authorized the Executive Secretary to expend the $Cdn 15,000 IOC Trust Fund contribution, together with any other remaining voluntary contributions made by Canada during the last two years, on such activities that he deems a priority to support the Year of the Ocean initiatives by IOC.

188   He hoped that this action, and similar actions and donations from other IOC Member States would provide the Executive Secretary with the necessary flexibility to undertake activities on this important topic.

189   Noting the value of sharing information in stimulating further action at the national level by all IOC Member States, **the Executive Council instructed** the Executive Secretary to solicit reports from national contacts for compilation and dissemination to all interested parties. Such information should also be included within the progress report that will be presented to the Nineteenth Session of the Assembly.

190   In endorsing the scope of the proposals presented in Document IOC/EC-XXIX/2 Annex 3 and its Addendum, **the Executive Council emphasized** that activities should be based upon the on-going programmes of the Commission, as had been suggested by the Officers. **The Executive Council noted** the plans to develop a logo and basic theme for the international year and **encouraged** that this be done as soon as possible.

5.4   IOC AND UNCLOS: PROGRESS REPORT OF INTERSESSIONAL WORKING GROUP

191   Mr Haiqing Li, Assistant Secretary IOC, introduced the agenda item, referring to the Annotated Provisional Agenda (IOC/EC-XXIX/2) and the Progress Report on the Intersessional Working Group on IOC's Possible Role in Relation to the United Nations Convention on the Law of the Sea (Document IOC/EC-XXIX/2 Annex 4).

192   Mr Li first referred to some important events that took place over the past year in the field of the Law of the Sea. He informed the meeting that the Agreement Relating to the Implementation of Part XI of the Convention entered into force on 28 July 1996, and with the election of the 36 members of the Council of the International Seabed Authority and of the Secretary-General, Mr Satya Nandan, the Authority's Secretariat has been established and the International Sea-Bed Authority has come into full operation. In the programmes identified by the Authority, the study and assessment of the impact of the activities in the international sea-bed area on the marine environment, the reduction and control of pollution of the marine environment from the activities in the area, as well as the related marine scientific research and monitoring are encouraged. These programmes promise broad aspects for co-operation between IOC and the Authority.

193   Mr Li also informed the meeting of the latest results on the election of the 21 members of the International Tribunal for the Law of the Sea and congratulated Profs. Yankov, Kolodkin and Treves, well-known to IOC, on their being elected as the members of the Tribunal.

194   He recalled the preparatory activities for the establishment of the Commission on the Limits of the Continental Shelf (CLCS) initiated by the United Nations Division for Ocean Affairs and the Law of the Sea (UN-DOALOS) serving as the Secretariat of CLCS, including the invitation to the IOC and the International Hydrographic Organization (IHO), to prepare a review on science and technology associated with the continental shelf definition under UNCLOS.

195   He also informed about other actions related to the Law of the Sea, taken by the international community, including as regards the issue of straddling fish stocks and highly migratory species, the large-scale pelagic drift-net fishing and its impact on marine living resources, as well as the activities of the non-governmental organizations, notably the Independent World Commission on the Oceans. He drew attention to the various resolutions on the Law of the Sea adopted by the United Nations General Assembly at its Fifteenth Session, December 1995, calling upon the competent international organizations, including IOC, to adopt a consistent and co-ordinated approach to the implementation of provisions of the Law of the Sea Convention, and particularly to assist and support developing countries in their efforts aimed at co-operation in the effective implementation of the Convention.

196   Turning to IOC activities in relation to the provision of support toward efforts to Member States in the implementation of the Law of the Sea Convention, he drew the attention of the meeting, particularly to the activities that took place in 1996. He urged the Member States who are parties to the Convention, but have not nominated their experts to do so, so that the list of experts in the field of marine scientific research for use by the Special Arbitral Tribunal would be further updated.

197   He informed the Executive Council of the establishment of the joint IOC-IHO Editorial Board on the preparation of a synthesis on science and technology associated with the definition of the continental shelf upon the invitation of UN-DOALOS as the Secretariat of CLCS. He informed the Executive Council about the invitation from IHO to IOC to possibly co-sponsor the Advisory Board on the Law of the Sea (ABLOS) presently co-sponsored by IHO and the International Association on Geodesy (IAG).

198   He finally stressed the work of the Intersessional Working Group on IOC's Possible Role in Relation to UNCLOS, established through Resolution XVIII-4 adopted by the Eighteenth Session of the

IOC Assembly. He presented the Progress Report (Document IOC/EC-XXIX/2 Annex 4) summarizing the results of the first meeting of the Working Group, Paris, May 1996. He invited the Executive Council to provide guidance on the report and related IOC actions, particularly the actions to be taken during 1996-1997.

199   **The Executive Council expressed** its satisfaction with the work of the Intersessional Working Group on IOC's Possible Role in Relation to UNCLOS, and **endorsed** the Progress Report of the Intersessional Working Group, together with the table identifying IOC's role in relation to UNCLOS, as well as relevant recommendations therein, for submission to the Nineteenth Session of the IOC Assembly for approval.

200   Recalling that the IOC is not the main body for the application of the Convention, the Delegate of France requested that the IOC remain within the two explicit references of the Convention with which it is concerned. He has also asked for extreme prudence concerning the political depositions arising from the sovereignty of States or of the last resort of the United Nations authorities. Lastly, he added that the IOC, through its programmes, already played a role in the UNCLOS implementation.

201   **The Executive Council considered** it necessary to plan the short-term and medium-term priority actions to be taken by the IOC, based on the recommendations of the Intersessional Working Group on IOC's Possible Role in Relation to UNCLOS. **The Executive Council recognized** particularly, the IOC's role within the framework of Part XIV of the Convention on Development and Transfer of Technology, and considered it useful that guidelines be formulated with regard to the transfer of marine technology within the IOC fields of competence, and emphasized that TEMA work should be further strengthened in the context of UNCLOS.

202   Other matters discussed by the Executive Council include, as proposed by the delegations of China, Russia and the USA, the establishment of an open-ended intersessional working Group to analyze the procedures mentioned in Article 247, taking into account Document IOC/EC-XXIX/2 Annex 4; further consideration of existing guidelines on the identification, markings and warning signals of oceanographic equipment and facilities, and the system of publicizing the development of oceanographic equipment and facilities in EEZ, on the Continental Shelf and in the High Seas, which might hamper international navigation, including an update of present ODAS draft proposals in co-operation with the International Maritime Organization; updating of the list of experts in marine scientific research for use in Special Arbitration.

203   **The Executive Council expressed** its general support for IOC to co-ordinate and co-operate with other international bodies, particularly UN-DOALOS, IHO and CLCS in the implementation of the provisions of the UN Convention on the Law of the Sea, particularly with due regard to avoiding duplication.

204   The IHO invitation for IOC to join the Advisory Board on the Law of the Sea (ABLOS), presently co-sponsored by the International Hydrographic Organization and the International Association on Geodesy, was provided to the Council.

205   Many delegations informed the Executive Council of their actions taken in terms of the ratification of the Law of the Sea Convention, as well as their national legislation within the context of the Law of the Sea, and encouraged IOC to play a positive and leading role as a competent international organization in marine scientific research, especially by providing scientific and technical assistance to the Member States, particularly the developing countries, in their efforts to implement the Law of the Sea Convention.

206   The Delegation of Greece expressed its support for the UN Convention on the Law of the Sea of 1982 and invited IOC to apply guidelines regarding the conduct of marine research, the relevant provisions of this Convention which constitute rules of international customary law binding all states, without any exception. Concerning the draft agreement on ODAS the delegation of Greece has requested its finalization in order to avoid implications from the use of these oceanographic instruments in marine areas.

207   With regard to the actions taken by the IOC in relation to the preparation of a review and synthesis on science and technology associated with the definition of the continental shelf, at the

recommendation of the UN Group of Experts on Preparation for CLCS and at the invitation of the UN-DOALOS, the Delegate of Brazil made a statement recorded in Annex VI.

208   The Delegate for the UK, Chairman of OSNLR, explained the background to the make up of the Editorial Board and advised that it did now include a member from Brazil. It was also re-emphasized that the volume was concerned with science and technology, not with law, and as such it would make a particularly useful contribution to TEMA.

209   The Executive Council acknowledged that the review proposed by the Joint IOC-IHO Editorial Board addresses the scientific and technical issues within the purview of the IOC, but considered that actions in this connection should be handled with special care, and that the policy should be considered by the IOC Assembly at its Nineteenth Session in 1997.

6.   GUIDELINES FOR CONSULTATIONS WITH THE DIRECTOR-GENERAL ON THE APPOINTMENT OF THE SECRETARY IOC

210   The Chairman IOC introduced this item, referring to Document IOC/EC-XXIX/2 Annex 5 which provided the background and suggested a procedure to be followed by the Executive Council when it is consulted by the Director-General. The suggested procedure reflected what had transpired on previous occasions, but which had never been documented.

211   Some delegations considered the proposed procedure did not comply with UNESCO Rules; other delegations considered that it did. Noting that there was no intention to contravene UNESCO Rules, the Chairman proposed that the UNESCO Legal Adviser should be consulted to ensure that any process adopted by the Executive Council was in accord with UNESCO Rules; **the Executive Council accepted the proposal of the Chair.**

212   Recognizing that the advice of the UNESCO Legal Adviser can influence the final outcome, the Executive Council already had asked for a number of changes to the current text now and henceforth. These related mainly to the view that the current incumbent should have no direct role in the appointment of his successor. These will be taken into account in the revision which will be sent to the Legal Adviser.

213   Some delegations considered it would be useful if the Executive Council was consulted on the job description and on the advertisement for the position. Some delegations also stressed that they do not wish the IOC office to take charge of drawing up "the short list". Some other delegations considered that the names of all applicants should be provided to Member States on the Executive Council.

214   The Executive Council will only make a definitive statement on the text after having received the conclusions of the Legal Adviser.

7.   REGIONAL SUBSIDIARY BODIES

7.1   IOCARIBE-V

215   The IOC Acting Secretary for IOCARIBE, Mr Rafael Steer-Ruiz, introduced this agenda item referring to the Annotated Agenda (Document IOC/EC-XXIX/2, pages 20 and 21) where the Executive Council is requested to review the report of the Fifth Session of the Sub-Commission with a view to endorsing the decisions and recommendations of policy-oriented and financial nature, relevant for the present biennium.

216   In addition, document IOC/INF-1043 "Report on IOCARIBE Evaluation" and document IOC/INF-1027 "IOCARIBE Medium Term Strategy, 1996-2000 (revised version)" were presented. The Executive Council was invited to endorse these documents as well, as far as the present biennium is concerned.

217   Mr Steer explained the evolution and sequence of these documents by referring to the decision taken by the 27th General Conference of UNESCO, as well as the request from the Seventeenth

Session of the IOC Assembly, (Paris, 25 February - 11 March 1993) to carry out an Evaluation of the IOC Sub-Commission for the Caribbean and Adjacent Regions.

218   Based on the evaluation document, the Medium Term Strategy as well as the IOCARIBE Action Plan 1996-1998 were amended and approved by the Fifth Session of IOCARIBE.

219   The positive trend of an increased participation of Member States in the last Session of the Sub-Commission was highlighted.

220   Mr Steer also informed the Council of the Seminar on Integrated Coastal Zone Management in Small Island Developing States, which took place just before the IOCARIBE Session. Its report is included as Annex VI to the SC-IOCARIBE-V Report.

221   The Executive Secretary of IOC informed the Executive Council on the actions taken following Resolutions of the Seventeenth and Eighteenth Sessions of the IOC Assembly, with regard to obtaining a permanent professional post in the IOCARIBE Secretariat. It has not so far been possible to obtain neither a new post, nor the return of the previous professional position to the region. He stressed the need for Member States to provide funds and advice on this matter in order to solve what has become a problematic situation for the Sub-Commission.

222   Mr Stefan Andersson informed the Executive Council about the decision taken by the Swedish International Development Co-operation Agency (SIDA) to provide financial support for programme implementation for a period of three years. The support is based on the Recommendations of SC-IOCARIBE-V.

223   Several delegations expressed their strong support to the three documents submitted to the Executive Council for endorsement and approval.

224   The Delegate of Colombia informed that, besides the current in-kind contribution of US$25,000 for the Regional Secretariat, his Government is prepared to increase the current office space in Cartagena as required by the expanding activities of IOCARIBE, and to appoint one young professional as seconded expert, once UNESCO/IOC provide the post for the regional Secretary for IOCARIBE.

225   The Delegate of Costa Rica also expressed the concern of her country because of the difficulties in contracting the regional Secretary. She informed the Executive Council that her Government is willing to provide one expert, located in Costa Rica, to collaborate with the IOCARIBE Secretariat.

226   The Delegate of the USA reaffirmed the concerns expressed regarding the absence of a post for the IOCARIBE Secretary, particularly in consideration that the Director-General of UNESCO expressed his desire to increase the regional staff. He also urged Member States to provide experts, not necessarily based in Cartagena, as is the case for Mr Fred Berry, provided by USA and working out of SEFC-NOAA in Miami.

227   The Delegate of Cuba pointed out the total support of his Government to the IOCARIBE Symposium planned for 1998 as a contribution to the International Year of the Ocean. He also informed that his government will have a Seminar on the Sea for Children in 1998, and invited UNESCO/IOC to participate. The Delegate of Cuba also informed the disposition of Cuban institutions to identify experts, as mentioned by other delegations.

228   The Delegate of Brazil informed the Executive Council that her Government will conduct a workshop on OSNLR in Recife, December 1996, in which experts from the IOCARIBE region are invited to participate. The IOC is supporting the participation of these experts. She expressed her concern for GOOS not having been mentioned in the Medium Term Strategy, and also encouraged the offers made by other delegations to strengthen the Regional Secretariat.

229   The Delegate of Mexico also underlined the importance of the post of regional Secretary and the need for an "incompressible" budget for the Sub-Commission. He particularly drew attention on the redefinition of the region as recommended in the report of the Fifth Session of the Sub-Commission.

230   **The Executive Council adopted Resolution EC-XXIX.4.**

7.2   WESTPAC-III

231   The Chairman of WESTPAC, Prof. Keisuke Taira, introduced this agenda item. He informed the Executive Council that the most important event since the last IOC Assembly for the WESTPAC Sub-Commission was the Third Session of the IOC Sub-Commission for WESTPAC, which was held in Tokyo, Japan, 26 February - 1 March 1996. Thirteen countries and six international and regional co-operating agencies were represented at the meeting. Emphasis was given to the need for science in providing pertinent advice as an input towards solving both global and regional problems. In this context, the Session adopted a new project called the "Co-operative Study on the Gulf of Thailand".

232   The regional component of GOOS was discussed in the meeting and the Co-ordinating Committee for NEAR-GOOS was established to further develop the NEAR-GOOS Implementation Plan and to prepare the Operational Manual for NEAR-GOOS.

233   There were six recommendations submitted to the Executive Council, including as regards the International WESTPAC Symposium, Work Programme and Budget for the Sub-Commission, Asian-Australia Monsoon Oceanography, NEAR-GOOS Co-ordinating Committee, International Coral Reef Initiative and the dates and place of next Session.

234   Prof. Taira informed the Executive Council that as a follow-up of the decision made by the Session, the NEAR-GOOS Co-ordinating Committee had its First Meeting in the IOC Regional Secretariat in Bangkok, Thailand, 4-6 September 1996. Thanks to the efforts made by all participating countries, the Implementation Plan and the Operational Manual were finalized during the meeting. To operate the NEAR-GOOS system, the Real-Time and Delayed Mode databases have been established, as well as the Associate Databases in the participating countries. The draft meeting report, together with the Implementation Plan and the Operational Manual, has been prepared by the WESTPAC Secretariat and will be published soon. The experimental operation of the NEAR-GOOS has started. He encouraged those who are interested in accessing oceanographic data in the NEAR-GOOS region or those who want to know the detailed information about NEAR-GOOS to access the Home Pages of the NEAR-GOOS databases. Relevant technical information is available in the WESTPAC Secretariat. He emphasized that the data available in the system is free of charge and open to everyone.

235   The project on the Co-operative Study in the Gulf of Thailand is being initiated. A questionnaire has been sent to all coastal countries and others who are interested in the project and more than 20 responses have been received, with identification of available oceanographic observations and existing data. A draft scientific plan for the project is being prepared based on contributions from participating institutions.

236   Thanks to the continued support from the National Research Council of Thailand and the Government of the United States, the IOC Regional Secretariat is fully operational in Bangkok, with increasing tasks and responsibilities. The staff situation needs to be improved with additional support and contribution from Member States.

237   Co-operation with other regional and international organizations such as CCOP, ESCAP, APEC, SOPAC, WMO and UNEP, has been or is being undertaken by the WESTPAC Secretariat, to ensure wide co-operation at the regional level.

238   Information was provided to the Executive Council on the Fourth IOC/WESTPAC International Scientific Symposium, which will be held in Okinawa, Japan, 2-7 February 1998, as a contribution to the 1998 Year of Ocean. The Chair WESTPAC encouraged, on behalf of the organizing committee, the Executive Council and Member States to take all possible actions ensuring widest possible participation of scientists in the Symposium, especially young scientists from developing countries.

239   **The Executive Council expressed** appreciation to the Government of Japan for hosting the Third Session of the IOC Sub-Commission for WESTPAC in Tokyo, Japan, 26 February - 1 March 1996. Appreciation was also extended to the Government of Thailand for the continued support provided to the WESTPAC Secretariat.

240   The Delegate of the Republic of Korea confirmed his Government's offer to host the Fourth Session of WESTPAC in Seoul in March 1999, the exact dates to be confirmed. **The Executive Council noted** this with great appreciation.

241   With regard to the implementation of the North-East Asian Regional-Global Ocean Observing System (NEAR-GOOS), **the Executive Council noted** with great interest and satisfaction the progress achieved. For the implementation and further improvement of the system, it was suggested that:

(i)   due consideration should be given to extend its activities from data exchange to other aspects, such as the provision of necessary services to various user communities;

(ii)   while implementing the initial phase of NEAR-GOOS, focusing on the physical parameters, additional measurements need to be added; this concerns, in particular, the chemical parameters, so as to develop a GOOS-HOTO Pilot Project in the region in the near future;

(iii)   training activities should be an important aspect of NEAR-GOOS, not only for the participating countries, but also for scientists from other WESTPAC countries so as to further the possible extension of NEAR-GOOS to the entire WESTPAC region;

(iv)   co-ordination and co-operation with other regional and national components of GOOS should be ensured, e.g., SEACAMP, SEAWATCH.

242   To further implement the WESTPAC Programme and to ensure the effective operation of the Secretariat, it will be necessary to increase the number of staff in the WESTPAC Secretariat. **The Executive Council instructed** the Executive Secretary IOC to make the best possible efforts to complete the P-4 post in the WESTPAC Secretariat rapidly, with a person with experience and knowledge about the IOC and the region.

243   The Executive Council was informed and acknowledged that the Government of Sweden through SIDA (SAREC) will provide an Associate Expert to the IOC Regional Secretariat for WESTPAC in Bangkok, and financial support for the implementation of the WESTPAC projects. The support of Canadian CIDA to the WESTPAC programme implementation and the Third Session of WESTPAC was also noted and acknowledged.

244   The Delegation of China informed the Executive Council that their Government will provide financial support to the amount of US$ 20,000 for the implementation of the WESTPAC programmes, including in particular training activities.

245   The Delegations of Germany and the Republic of Korea informed the Executive Council about training activities provided from their countries for supporting the WESTPAC activities.

246   **The Executive Council expressed** its appreciation to these Governments for their generous support to the WESTPAC activities.

247   **The Executive Council adopted** Resolution EC-XXIX.5.

7.3   SOUTHERN OCEAN FORUM AND REGIONAL COMMITTEE FOR THE SOUTHERN OCEAN

248   The German Delegate, Dr Giermann, speaking on behalf of the newly elected Chairman of IOCSOC, Prof Dr Max Tilzer, introduced this item referring to Document IOC/SOC-VI/3S "Executive Summary of the Sixth Session of the IOC Regional Committee for SOC and the First Southern Ocean Forum".

249   He reminded the Executive Council that the Sixth Session of the Regional Committee held in Bremerhaven, 12-13 September 1996, was preceded by a three-day Southern Ocean Forum in which 26 scientists, science administrators and representatives of international organizations and programmes discussed items of great concern such as Climate and Climate Change, Southern Ocean Ecosystems and their Living Resources, Marine Pollution and Monitoring, GOOS and Data Management, laying particular emphasis on the implementation of the regional components of global programmes such as WCRP, GOOS, IGBP/GLOBEC/JGOFS. They stressed that co-operation with other international organizations and the Antarctic Treaty System has to be pursued and if possible increased.

250   The Forum formulated several recommendations, which were taken up and discussed by the Regional Committee and condensed into five recommendations herewith submitted to the Executive Council for approval.

251   In the Regional Committee, 10 Member States were present, including Argentina, Australia, Brazil, Chile, France, Germany, Russia, South Africa, UK and the USA, as well as representatives of WMO, WCRP, IWC, COMNAP and ICSU/SCOR. It was regretted that SCAR, despite repeated invitations, did not attend. In support of the new Chairman, an advisory group was set up to work by correspondence, with members from Argentina, Australia, Russia, UK and the USA. The Regional Committee also adopted new Terms of Reference available as Annex to Recommendation IOCSOC-VI.1, and reproduced here in the Annex to Resolution EC-XXIX.6.

252   The German Delegate recommended to the Executive Council to give high priority to the Southern Ocean and to adopt the proposed resolution.

253   Many delegates expressed their support for the activities proposed by the IOC Regional Committee and **the Executive Council endorsed** the Executive Summary and Recommendations of the Sixth Session of the Regional Committee for the Southern Ocean.

254   The Delegate of Argentina emphasized that existing rights of coastal states in the region, as the rights and obligations emanating from the Antarctic Treaty and related instruments, shall be taken into account, as laid down in the proposed resolution.

255   The Delegate of Brazil, referring to the Recommendation IOCSOC-VI.5 on GOOS, expressed concern regarding the use of the CCAMLR Ecosystem monitoring as a specific model for further planning and possible implementation of the LMR module of GOOS, as the LMR module still requires more precise definition.

256   **The Executive Council invited** the Chairman of IOCSOC and the Advisory Group to prepare a more specific plan of activities and present it to the next Session of the Assembly.

257   The Representative of SCOR expressed the willingness of SCOR to co-operate with the Regional Committee and referred particularly, to the activities of Working Group 86 - Sea-Ice Ecology and the recently established programme (iAnZone) - International Antarctic Zone Programme, and invited the IOC to be associated with these activities and to continue its collaboration with SCOR and IGBP in the Southern Ocean Components of JGOFS and GLOBEC.

258   **The Executive Council adopted Resolution EC-XXIX.6.**

7.4   BLACK SEA REGIONAL COMMITTEE

259   The Executive Secretary IOC introduced the item referring to Document IOC/EC-XXIX/2, the Annual Report 1995, and the Summary Report of the First Session of the Black Sea Regional Committee and Related Draft Resolution (Document IOC/BS-RC-I/3), as well as the relevant parts of the report of the Eighteenth Session of the Assembly.

260   The First Session of the Committee was held in Varna, Bulgaria, 10-13 September 1996. The Executive Secretary IOC expressed appreciation to the host country, Bulgaria, its UNESCO National Commission and the Bulgarian National Committee for Oceanography for hosting the session and for the excellent arrangements for the meeting.

261   He recalled Resolution XVIII-17 and its Annexes establishing the Regional Committee, giving its Terms of Reference and initial tasks. He stressed that the First Session had addressed the structure and working method of the Committee.

262   The Committee had reviewed and further developed its two pilot projects and had agreed on a work programme for 1996-1998. The Committee had also reviewed and initiated several of the initial tasks, in addition to the pilot projects, specified in Resolution XVIII-17, Annex 2.

263   The Executive Secretary IOC who is also Chairman of the Black Sea Regional Committee, presented in particular some aspects of the report of the First Session drawing attention to the recommendations of the Session, particularly regarding the initiation of two regional pilot projects "The Black Sea-GOOS" and "the Assessment of the Sediment Flux in the Black Sea". He pointed out that the implementation of these projects would require active participation and support from all Black Sea countries and also some financial support from other international organizations and programmes active in the region.

264   The working plan for the next two years of the Black Sea Regional Committee and scientific programmes for two pilot projects are attached in the annex of the report of the First Session.

265   The Delegates of Germany, Ukraine, Turkey, Russian Federation and Bulgaria expressed full support for the programme and stressed the following points:

(i)   all Member States, not only from the region, interested in the Black Sea studies should be invited to participate in the next meeting and activities of the regional committee;

(ii)   the need for close co-operation and co-ordination with other on-going Black Sea programmes such as GEF, NATO, ComsBLACK, EROS;

(iii)   close interaction with other relevant IOC programmes, as well as international oceanographic programmes, particularly GOOS, GCOS, JGOFS, IODE, TEMA and GIPME;

(iv)   the importance of the initiation of some specific joint activities in conjunction with the Year of the Ocean 1998.

266   **The Executive Council endorsed** the report of the First Session of the Black Sea Regional Committee (Document IOC/BS-RC-I/3) and **urged** all countries interested in the Black Sea to participate in the work towards the implementation of the adopted pilot projects and seek extra-budgetary funds from different sources, as well as the Regional Committee and the Executive Secretary IOC to do the same.

267   **The Executive Council requested** the Executive Secretary IOC to inform Member States of the region and their National Commissions for UNESCO, as well as regional Black Sea programmes GEF, NATO, EROS, etc., on the establishment of the regional committee and the outcome of its first session, as well as the decisions of the Executive Council, and **urged** The Executive Secretary IOC to take actions to implement them and support the projects proposed by the first session of the Regional Committee.

268   **The Executive Council invited** the Regional Committee to report to the Nineteenth Session of the IOC Assembly on the progress and further actions to be taken to strengthen co-operation in the region.

269   **The Executive Council adopted** Resolution EC-XXIX.7.

7.5   OTHER REGIONAL SUBSIDIARY BODIES

270   The Delegate of India informed the Executive Council of the forthcoming Session of IOCINDIO, to take place in Goa, India, from 20 to 22 November 1996. In conjunction with this event, a regional workshop on capacity building related to GOOS will be held from 18 to 19 November 1996.

271   Several delegations stressed the enormous importance of the Indian Ocean, e.g. vis-à-vis its role in climate regulation and the related need for further co-operation at the intergovernmental level. In this respect, it was stated that representatives of WESTPAC and IOCINCWIO could also be requested to attend the meeting of IOCINDIO. The Delegate of the Islamic Republic of Iran reiterated the importance of holding the IOCINDIO meeting as planned, and to reinforce actions in the region from the IOC.

272   The Delegate of Argentina referred to on-going co-operation between Argentina, Brazil and Uruguay in the framework of the "Sub-regional Programme for the Upper Southwest Atlantic Ocean" (ASOS in Spanish), started in 1993. The Fourth Session of ASOS will take place in Brasilia, Brazil, October 1996, where further developments of IOC-UNEP co-operation in the region will also be dealt

with. He informed the Executive Council of two TEMA-related activities within this co-operation framework: (i) training on-board a research vessel provided by Argentina for experts coming from the three countries to start in October 1996 and (ii) the organization of a GLOSS Training Course, to be held in Argentina at the end of November this year, with participation of around twenty specialists from Latin American countries.

273   The Delegate of Greece pointed out the importance of research activities such as POEM and recalled the debate at IOC-XVIII as regards the need to involve Member States from the Southern Mediterranean in such activities. He also stated that this was consistent with the establishment of an IOC Project Office for the Eastern Mediterranean in Greece.

274   The Delegate of Guinea informed about actions in the IOCEA region and the need to provide more support for these.

275   The Executive Secretary referred to IOC actions in other regional subsidiary bodies (such as IOCEA) where, despite the number of activities developed recently, intergovernmental communication and co-operation still needs to be strengthened. He invited all Member States to join the different efforts that are going on regionally.

276   The Executive Council stressed the enormous potential of regional bodies as essential tools and instruments to link Member States as well as for the implementation of major programmes and services of the Commission. Careful selection of issue-oriented activities of importance to the specific regions should be taken into account.

277   The Executive Council concurred with the suggestion made by the Delegate of Portugal that a dedicated debate be held on a strategic approach on how to strengthen the capacities of and interaction between the IOC Regional Subsidiary Bodies, including relevant TEMA capacity building, and technical assistance activities in general in this respect. This will be first addressed within the special session on TEMA planned for the Nineteenth Session of the IOC Assembly.

8.   FOLLOW-UP TO UNCED

(i)   **Agenda 21 and the ACC Sub-Committee on Oceans and Coastal Areas**

278   The Senior Assistant Secretary IOC for Information and Co-ordination, also in her capacity as Secretary of the ACC Sub-Committee for Oceans and Coastal Areas, introduced this agenda item, referring to the Annotated Provisional Agenda (Document IOC/EC-XXIX/2: paras 156-160).

279   Recalling relevant statements made under previous agenda items in regard to the need for close inter-agency co-operation within Agenda 21, and especially Chapter 17, Ms Philippon-Tulloch emphasized the importance of linkages between the work of IOC and that being undertaken by other bodies of the UN system. Given that Agenda 21 is the established framework for collaborative efforts at the national, regional and international levels, she reiterated the key role to be assumed by IOC national contacts in ensuring that decisions taken by the IOC Governing Bodies are properly reflected in national positions.

280   **The Executive Council agreed** that the post-UNCED process in regard to implementation of Chapter 17 at the national level would be facilitated by the establishment and strengthening of national co-ordination mechanisms for ocean and coastal areas together with an appropriate interface amongst and between the various UN structures, in particular the Commission for Sustainable Development.

281   In regard to the recognized need for better communication between all levels of action that lead towards better implementation of Agenda 21, she stressed the need for rapid exchange of information with established points of contact.

282   Within this perspective, **the Executive Council recalled** that the work of FURES had led to agreement by the Sixteenth Assembly (Paris, 1991) of the IOC that an essential modality of support which Member States could provide to the IOC (Document SC/MD/97: Annex VIII) is:

"Improving and establishing, when required, proper liaison mechanisms and adequate national co-ordinating structures and counterpart arrangements for marine science activities, in general, and for the purposes of IOC co-ordination, in particular. In this context, the importance of rapid communication .... is underlined. "

283   In concluding the information statement on this agenda item, Ms Philippon-Tulloch reminded the Executive Council that the Fifth Session of the Commission on Sustainable Development would provide guidance to the Special Session of the UN General Assembly in 1997. The Chair, referring to his own experiences in representing IOC at UN bodies, encouraged Members of the Executive Council to ensure adequate briefings to their focal points within the UN system.

284   **The Executive Council took note** of the information and **strongly endorsed** the role of the IOC in the ACC Sub-Committee and the related follow-up to UNCED, particularly the Global Programme of Action for Protection of the Marine Environment from Land-Based Activities.

(ii)   **ICSPRO, GESAMP and Co-operation not otherwise covered**

285   The Executive Secretary IOC introduced this sub-item by referring to Document IOC/EC-XXIX/2, the Annual Report 1995 and the report of the Eighteenth Session of the IOC Assembly (Document SC/MD/106). He recalled the significance of ICSPRO and several joint programmes associated with ICSPRO Agencies in which IOC is a partner, e.g., GIPME, WCRP, GOOS. He referred to the close co-operation with UNEP and brought attention to the UNEP statement which had been circulated. He recalled that ICSPRO consultations had agreed to use ICSPRO as the inter-agency co-ordination mechanism for the 1998 International Year of the Ocean. He informed about the involvement of UNESCO-IOC in GESAMP as a co-sponsor, and in several associated GESAMP Working Groups; in particular the Review of the State of the Marine Environment, and the possible implications of potential deep ocean storage of CO_2.

286   He referred to the decision of CSD-IV and the related United Nations General Assembly Resolution on the institutional arrangements for the implementation of the Global Programme of Action for the Protection of the Marine Environment from Land-based Activities and the reference to the IOC of UNESCO therein, as one of the relevant competent international bodies. He informed the Executive Council that a recent meeting called by UNEP on the associated clearing house mechanism has expressed strong interest on the part of UNEP for IOC involvement in this. He concurred that the IOC stands ready to provide scientific and technical advice through its relevant subject area and regional programmes.

287   He referred to the decision of CSD-IV on the Protection of the Oceans, all kinds of seas, including enclosed and semi-enclosed seas, and coastal areas and the protection, rational use and development of their living resources, within which the CSD expresses its support for GOOS, established by UNESCO/IOC.

288   Finally, the Executive Secretary IOC recalled the growing co-operation in-house UNESCO, the interdisciplinary project referred to as CSI and the joint statement by the chairpersons of the IOC, MAB, IHP, IGCP and MOST Programme resulting from their meeting on 3 November 1995 in conjunction with the 28th General Conference. This joint statement is printed in Volume 2 of the Records of the General Conference, Reports, Programme Commissions, Administrative Commission, and Legal Committee.

289   The Chair then invited Dr G. Glaser, Co-ordinator of Environmental Programmes, to present a report on the subsequent developments.

290   The Executive Council heard with interest presentations made by the UNESCO Environment Co-ordinator and the Representative for the UNESCO CSI project. It was pointed out that UNESCO was in a unique position to ensure useful cross-disciplinary work in bringing together IOC, MAB, IHP, IGCP and MOST within the context of their specified areas of responsibility. The CSI programme, in particular, represented a specific action towards focusing input from the above-mentioned UNESCO programmes on problems relating to coastal zone management.

291   Many delegates welcomed the exercise and some pointed out that programme planning with IHP in particular, had already taken place during the period in which the current Executive Council

has been in session. It was also noted that an intricate web of programmes and activities relating to the marine environment existed and the Executive Council welcomed UNESCO's work in co-ordinating such actions. It was proposed that the IOC Secretariat produce a tabulation summarizing IOC interactions with agencies and joint programmes with which it shares activities or commitments. This tabulation was envisaged as being in a regularly and easily updated form using modern word-processing software suitable for electronic distribution or access and which would form part of the basic documentation of future IOC Assembly and Council sessions.

292   Member States generally expressed support for the UNESCO-CSI initiative with some indicating that caution should, nonetheless, be exercised in maintaining an appropriate focus for activities and urged that every opportunity should be grasped to make sure that existing regional IOC machinery is fully utilized in carrying the project forward.

293   It was noted that particular attention should be focused by highlighting the oceans as a medium through which peace might be promoted and that both IOC and CSI should strive towards this end.

294   Some Member States also emphasized the valuable co-operation with GESAMP, IMO, HOTO, GOOS, IODE and GIPME. Many reported favourably on particular efforts by CSI that had been undertaken in their regions and others noted specific problems that might yet be addressed (e.g. Persian Gulf). In connection with the IOC co-operation with IMO it was emphasized that problems that might arise during the shipment of hazardous wastes, in particular of radio-active materials, should be given particular attention in the appropriate context by IOC.

295   The Islamic Republic of Iran stated that the Persian Gulf, because of its enormous hydrocarbon reserve and related interventions from industrialized countries, is a highly disturbed area in different ways. Economic development in the region is very difficult, and the marine environment is in danger. The Islamic Republic of Iran emphasized the need for IOC, UNESCO, and ·ÜN to take the necessary measures and find specific and acceptable solutions to the problems of the Persian Gulf.

296   The Delegate of Canada drew attention to the Rimouski Declaration from the International Conference Coastal Zone Canada'96 calling for the sustainable and wise use of coastal and ocean resources world-wide.

297   The Executive Secretary IOC responded that an IOC homepage covering interactions with UN bodies would be set-up and maintained by the Secretariat. He agreed that work with the Interagency Committee on Sustainable Development deserved continued attention, particularly with regard to interagency co-ordination regarding the upcoming "Year of the Ocean". He noted the problems of ballast water discharges and transport of dangerous goods as areas of particular concern. He also mentioned that co-operation would be maintained in relation to GESAMP, the operational elements of GIPME and he identified specific instances of CSI co-operation through IOCARIBE and IOCINCWIO. The Executive Secretary IOC noted that IOC would continue to co-sponsor coastal zone meetings and would take a closer look at economic and social linkages in relation to the marine environment.

298   The proposal by WMO to investigate concrete co-operative relationships in the form of IOC-WMO co-sponsorship of the CMM was viewed by the Executive Council in a cautious but positive light and it was decided to field a joint IOC-WMO effort to assess the implications. This would involve two consultants, respectively appointed by IOC and WMO, to jointly prepare an assessment which could be properly reviewed by experts associated with the various relevant programmes. The resulting information and preliminary analysis should be presented to the Governing Bodies; in the case of IOC the Assembly, for further consideration.

299   The Chairman of IODE brought to the attention of the Executive Council information on a new legal regime proposed in the World Intellectual Property Organization (WIPO). One of the basic proposals under consideration in WIPO is a Treaty on Intellectual Property in Respect to Databases which may have potential implications for the data exchange programmes of the IOC and the World Data Centers system, and for ocean sciences and services programmes in general. He pointed out that unfortunately the information available on this issue is very limited and that the issue has some urgency given the timeframe for proposed action on the treaty. It will be considered for adoption at a Diplomatic Conference to be held in Geneva, 2-20 December 1996. He emphasized that certain provisions of the proposed treaty might be contrary to the IOC policy on Data Management for Global Ocean Programmes adopted by the IOC

Assembly at its Seventeenth Session (Paris, 25 February - 11 March 1993). The main principle of this policy is a full and open access to quality ocean data.

300   **The Executive Council was fully aware** that without adequate information and special consultations it would be premature and inappropriate to take direct actions. At the same time **the Executive Council was in agreement** that all necessary measures should be taken in order to discourage any decisions being taken by WIPO that might be detrimental to ocean science and operational programmes in general and in particular to the IOC programmes and IOC policy on full and open data exchange.

301   **The Executive Council instructed** the Executive Secretary IOC to undertake urgently the following actions:

(a)   contact WIPO as soon as possible and obtain documents and other information regarding the proposed database treaty;

(b)   distribute this information without delay to the Member States;

(c)   seek advice within UNESCO on the interpretation of the treaty and its implications for IOC and UNESCO and inform Member States of this interpretation;

(d)   employ as far as possible expertise within UNESCO in dealing with this issue;

(e)   consult with the WIPO Secretariat on possible implications the treaty may have on the IOC's data exchange policy and on the exchange of marine environmental data generally between and within national agencies and data centers worldwide, convey the results of consultations to the Member States;

(f)   consult with ICSPRO agencies and relevant non-governmental scientific and academic organizations in order to provide a consistent view on the WIPO proposal.

302   **The Executive Council stressed** that, since the new legal regime proposed by the World Intellectual Property Organization (WIPO) could have repercussion on the activities of other scientific programmes, as well as other sectors in UNESCO, it should be borne in mind that any action of the Organization towards WIPO should be taken as a whole and it would be advisable that the question be submitted to the next session of the UNESCO Executive Board.

303   **The Executive Council urged** Member States to bring to the attention of their national authorities and academic institutions, as well as their representatives to WIPO regarding the possible implications of the proposed treaty for science, education and capacity building in order to help in developing a balanced approach at the national level.

304   **The Executive Council**, having considered the invitation and terms of reference which had been received from the IHO to the IOC, to co-sponsor with IHO and the International Association of Geodesy, the joint Advisory Board on the Law of the Sea, **instructed** the Executive Secretary to accept the invitation.

9.   THE ROLE OF IOC IN INTEGRATED ASSESSMENT OF AVAILABLE SCIENTIFIC UNDERSTANDING, OBSERVATIONS AND DATA FOR SUSTAINABLE DEVELOPMENT AND OCEAN MANAGEMENT

305   The Executive Secretary IOC gave an overall introduction to this agenda item, referring to Document IOC/EC-XXIX/2. He also drew attention to discussions under Agenda Items 3.2, 5.1, 5.3 and 8 which are relevant to this agenda item.

306   He recalled the discussions of the Eighteenth Session of the Assembly under the Assembly Agenda Items 6 and 7. These brought out, *inter alia*, the need for reinforcement of ocean partnership for integrated management and an increasing dialogue with management, economic and socio-economic sectors, with an associated strengthening of links to user-communities, as well as evaluation and assessment.

307 He informed the Executive Council about the activities of assessment under the GESAMP within the review of the state of the marine environment; the CSD review of implementation of UNCED after 5 years in 1997; a proposal to prepare an "integrated assessment of environmental problems of the oceans" by SCOPE, the Scientific Committee on Problems of the Environment of ICSU. He referred to the Independent World Commission on Oceans and its aim to obtain an overview of ocean-related issues of primary interest to society. He informed the Executive Council about a consultation arranged by Executive Secretary IOC held at IMO, London, 30 May 1996, after the fourth session of the ACC Sub-Committee on Oceans and Coastal Areas. This consultation had involved: UNEP, GESAMP, ICSU-SCOPE, IWCO, IOC, SCOR, IMO, GEF-STAP. At this meeting, a need identified by GEF-STAP to prepare an International Assessment of the International Waters Problems was also presented and discussed. There is clearly a need for co-operation/co-ordination, and IOC can help in this respect. There is also a need, it appears, for IOC to actively associate itself with these assessment efforts. It is certainly one factor relevant to previous discussions on the evolving role of IOC.

308 The Chairman IOC also emphasized that there is an increasing debate about the oceans, their importance and their interaction with many aspects of our life and society. This debate would be helped by a scientific assessment of where we stand with regard to our ability to handle present and future ocean issues.

309 This scientific assessment would not discuss the political situation, jurisdictions, the legal regime, demographic changes and societal pressures, such considerations will, of course, dictate many, if not all, of the problems to be addressed. The assessment would evaluate the ocean knowledge that we have, or need to have, to solve present and future problems, including the capacity of countries, at all levels, to deal with these problems.

310 The Chairman IOC expressed belief that IOC is well placed to provide such an assessment and it would be timely.

311 The IOC is intergovernmental, it is a body in the UN system and, as we have been reminded frequently, a body whose programmes are founded in ocean science and services. Its Member States contain most of the coastal states of the world and certainly all of these with major ocean science capability. The Commission works through the concerted efforts of its Member States and therefore has the potential power of the combined resources of all these Member States should they so desire. Although the Commission has a modest voice in the world community at large and is not seen by many as the focus of the world effort in marine science, it has programmes that influence this effort in many ways: data formats, standards, manuals, global and regional co-ordination, training and capacity building. This network of IOC programmes and the links that have been forged with other intergovernmental and international bodies and organizations could be used in putting together the scientific assessment that is needed.

312 If such an assessment was carried out, it would need to address specific ocean issues and discuss the scientific and technical ability available, and needed to resolve them. The assessment would need to look ahead at least 25 years in addition to building on past experience and the present status.

313 The Chairman IOC felt that a scientific assessment of this sort would complement those considered or already underway and contribute to them. It could also form the basis for a strategic outlook at the ocean science programmes of the future, set priorities for scientific capacity building and evaluate the impact of technological development.

314 Several delegations provided their views on the proposed action. There was a general trend in favour of proceeding with the proposed action, although with great care so as to avoid any duplication. The IOC should continue to co-operate with, or seek co-operation with other ongoing or planned related activities. In particular the IOC should continue to work with and support the related work within GESAMP. Co-operation should be sought with the SCOPE-SCOR-ICSU proposed assessment.

315 Specific points made in the debate include:

(i) aim for a review of modern ocean research and related capacities;

(ii) base the review on the IOC programme structure;

(iii)   the IOC Member States should provide input and feel an ownership of the assessment;

(iv)   the relation to and co-operation with IWCO was emphasized and clarifications were sought which were provided by the Delegate of Portugal;

(v)   an assessment should be made of marine science and its role in relation to sustainable ocean and coastal area development, management and socio-economics;

(vi)   an exercise like the one proposed would fill a gap in the IOC vision and help ensure that scientific results and options for solutions to problems are transmitted in understandable form useful for user-sectors and managers;

(vii)   various mechanisms of the IOC, including Bruun Memorial Lectures could be used to contribute to the assessment work;

(viii)   we know about the issues, the problems and we have solutions, but nevertheless the marine environment continues to degrade - why?;

(ix)   why scientific results and solutions are not applied?;

(x)   the assessment product should fill a gap in addressing users and needs at national and regional level;

(xi)   the assessment action of the IOC should be focused and specifically address scientific capacity and understanding, and such a product would also be useful for the GOOS establishment;

(xii)   we should aim to provide an interim product for 1998, and the related work should also serve as an input to the programme for 1998;

(xiii)   the assessment work of the IOC could also support and give inputs to the implementation of GPA-LBA, the GESAMP review of the state of the marine environment and the SCOPE-SCOR-ICSU work.

316   The Executive Secretary proposed that an assessment undertaken by the IOC as specified by the IOC Assembly would imply an ownership and a commitment on the part of IOC Member States, so that the assessment product would be appropriately used at national and other levels.

317   The Chair concluded that the Executive Council basically endorsed the proposal with the provision that there is no duplication, that co-operation is maintained with others and that the assessment work is well focused.

318   The Executive Council established a small *ad hoc* sessional group to further elaborate the proposal and scope and to give guidance to the Executive Secretary. This should be used by the Executive Secretary to prepare, with the help of experts involved in IOC programmes, a substantial document to be presented to the Nineteenth Session of the Assembly, for its consideration and decision on possible further work of IOC on this matter. The Chair of the *ad hoc* sessional group reported briefly on the results of the deliberations, and provided advice to the Chair and the Executive Secretary IOC.

10.   ADJUSTMENTS TO THE IOC PROGRAMME AND BUDGET FOR 1996-97 AS REQUIRED AND WORKPLANS

319   In introducing this subject, the Chair first recalled the suggestion made by the Executive Secretary at the opening session that the scope of this agenda item be enlarged to include preliminary considerations of future workplans. The Executive Council would thus consider matters dealing with the present budgetary period and also provide initial guidance to the Executive Secretary that he may use in developing proposals in regard to the IOC component of the UNESCO Draft 29 C/5 for 1998-99. He noted that relevant information is provided in the Budgetary Status Report (Document IOC/EC-XXIX/2 Annex 6) and in the Expanded Annotated Agenda (Document IOC/EC-XXIX/2: paras 177-184).

320   The Chair also reminded the Executive Council that previous discussion on this matter by IOC Governing Bodies had indicated the desire of Member States to have before them a more transparent and clear presentation of the programme and budget. The present report had been developed within that perspective. He requested the Executive Council to provide its views as to any further improvements that could be made.

321   Note was also taken that the primary role of the Executive Council as a management body is indeed to provide guidance and instruction regarding the use of IOC resources in support of its programmes during the intersessional period between the Assemblies. Such considerations are based upon two complementary elements.

322   One element, as reflected under previous agenda items, concerns the reports of subsidiary bodies and related draft resolutions. The Assembly has requested IOC Subsidiary Bodies to submit financial implications within their reporting functions.

323   Discussion under this Agenda Item indicated strong support for the proposals made, including the new budgetary reporting methodology. A number of suggestions were made to improve the presentation, including:

(i)   to the extent possible, prepare budgetary documents in such a way that they show precisely by objective and, within each objective, by programme, the desired objectives, the actions planned and budgetary forecasts and receipts (with an operational timetable, personnel assigned, etc). The documents should allow the Secretariat and IOC Member States to follow periodically the execution of the programme;

(ii)   greater detail to link the four objectives to IOC programmes, including regional and capacity building components;

(iii)   more explanatory information regarding the linkages between reporting by object-of-expenditure (with selected case studies), the four IOC objectives and their overall impact in regard to required, forecast and real expenditure;

(iv)   the need to ensure that relevant documentation is prepared in the four working languages of the IOC and distributed in advance of IOC Governing Body sessions, eventually with an addendum to update tabular material.

324   For budgetary implications to the present biennial period, **the Executive Council instructed** the Executive Secretary, based upon the present forecast of available funding, to give priority to ensuring that the IOC Programme of Work and Budget for 1996-97 is respected, as approved by the Eighteenth Session of the Assembly as a basis for planning.

325   Depending upon the receipt and timing during the remainder of the present biennial period of general and special purpose voluntary contributions to the IOC Trust Fund, **the Executive Council charged** the Executive Secretary, in consultation with the Chair as required, to ensure that the forecast distribution of funding between the four basic objectives of the IOC programme are respected. In this regard the necessity of ensuring implementation of activities throughout the IOC programmes for capacity building and TEMA was highlighted.

326   The Chair then turned to the second element under agenda item 10 in regard to preliminary considerations of the IOC Programme and Budget for the next biennium (1998-99). He encouraged the Executive Council to exercise its managerial role to guide the Executive Secretary and the Officers in further development of the IOC Programmes, as found in section 2 of Document IOC/EC-XXIX/2 Annex 6.

327   For budgetary implications of draft resolutions to the next biennial period, **the Executive Council instructed** the Executive Secretary to include requested provisions within the draft workplans for the 1998-99 biennium and alert the Assembly to any activities that cannot be accommodated within the anticipated funding.

328   The Executive Council instructed the Executive Secretary IOC to prepare detailed budgetary forecasts by programme with a view to their inclusion in Document 29 C/5.

329   The Executive Council endorsed the preliminary framework for the 1998-99 budgetary period within which the four objective structure is maintained and a proposal is made for increase in support both from UNESCO and from Member States to the IOC Trust Fund, given the unique opportunity offered by the 1998 UN International Year of the Ocean as a focus for greater impetus.

330   In regard to the present resources from UNESCO, the Executive Council expressed appreciation to its parent body for the steps taken to ensure an "incompressible" budget.

331   In expressing its appreciation to the Executive Secretary for the considerable progress made in presenting programme and budget matters for its consideration, the Executive Council instructed the Executive Secretary to take into account specific suggestions proposed for further improvement.

11.   ARRANGEMENTS FOR THE THIRTIETH SESSION OF THE EXECUTIVE COUNCIL AND THE NINETEENTH SESSION OF THE ASSEMBLY

332   The Executive Secretary IOC introduced this item referring to Document IOC/EC-XXIX/2. He recalled that the presently proposed dates for the Executive Council, 1 July 1997, and the Assembly, 2-17 July 1997, were different from those identified at the Eighteenth Session of the IOC Assembly, due to the need to adjust these dates in light of the meeting of the Executive Board of UNESCO.

333   He recalled that the Executive Council, under this agenda item, also normally gave consideration to the theme for the Bruun Memorial Lecture, and recalled that as a possible theme "Aspects of Coastal Area Management, including Socio-economic Ones" had been proposed at the Assembly. He gave further elaboration on this theme. He also recalled that other current issues could well be the address of the Bruun Memorial Lecture.

334   The Executive Secretary IOC finally recalled the decision of the Assembly to establish the Dr Panikhar lecture on TEMA-related matters, and that the TEMA Group of Experts has addressed this and identified the first one for the Nineteenth Session of the Assembly. This would be given during the one-day extended debate on TEMA and would consist of 2 parts given by separate lecturers. In view of this extended debate, it may also be required to extend the session of the Assembly for one day, so as to be 2-18 July 1997.

335   The Chair then referred to the discussions in relation to the 1998 International Year of the Ocean and suggested that the Executive Council give preliminary consideration to convene its regular session in 1998 in Lisbon during EXPO 98, should an invitation to this effect be forthcoming from the Government of Portugal. He stressed that no such invitation had, as yet, been received.

336   The Chair also suggested that an advance action as regards the election of the rapporteur might be useful and invited delegations to indicate their willingness to provide a rapporteur for the forthcoming session(s).

337   The Executive Council endorsed the dates of its next session as well as the Nineteenth Session of the Assembly.

338   The Executive Council endorsed the general theme for the Bruun Memorial Lecture of the role of coastal and open sea oceanography and observations for integrated coastal zone management, possibly focusing on some specific examples. The Great Barrier Reef was referred to.

339   The Executive Council expressed considerable caution about locating the ordinary Executive Council in 1998 outside UNESCO headquarters. Delegates emphasized that it should not imply any additional cost to the IOC, nor any confusion between the Independent World Commission on the Oceans and the IOC which would not be favourable to the full and entire acknowledgement by the public of the latter. Moreover, one Delegation was worried about the eventual lack of logistics due to the distance between the delegations participating in the IOC Executive Council and their delegations at UNESCO Headquarters.

340   **The Executive Council requested** the Executive Secretary IOC to informally investigate the implications and possibilities, so as to provide the Nineteenth Session of the Assembly with the required information for its decision.

341   The Delegate of the USA volunteered to offer a rapporteur for the Nineteenth Session of the Assembly.

12.   ADOPTION OF RESOLUTIONS, SUMMARY REPORT AND CLOSURE

342   The Delegate of Italy had raised a point of order earlier in the session with respect to the use of working languages, referring to the IOC Rules of Procedure No. 33 and 34. He demanded strict adherence to existing rules, and requested a clarification from the Chair. The Delegate of the Netherlands seconded this statement. After consultations the Chair informed the Council that Rules of Procedure No. 33 and 34 are being respected. This was taken note of by the Delegates of Italy and the Netherlands.

343   **The Executive Council reviewed** the draft resolutions and the draft report. **The Executive Council adopted** the resolutions and the report as herein presented.

344   The Chair expressed his thanks to all delegations for their constructive participation in the debates, to the interpreters, the translators, the Secretariat, and in particular thanked Mme J. Dombret for her long-term excellent and distinguished service as Documentalist of IOC and Conference Officer for the IOC Governing Body meetings. He also welcomed her successor, Mr J. Banaag. He closed the Session at 17h50 on 2 October 1996.

ANNEX I

AGENDA

1.   OPENING

2.   ADMINISTRATIVE ARRANGEMENTS

2.1   ADOPTION OF THE AGENDA
2.2   DESIGNATION OF RAPPORTEUR
2.3   CONDUCT OF THE SESSION, TIMETABLE AND DOCUMENTATION

3.   DEVELOPMENTS SINCE THE EIGHTEENTH SESSION OF THE IOC ASSEMBLY

3.1   REPORT ON INTERSESSIONAL ACTIVITIES AND BUDGETARY MATTERS
3.2   DEVELOPMENTS RELEVANT TO IOC WITHIN UNESCO: 28TH GENERAL CONFERENCE AND EXECUTIVE BOARD

4.   PROGRAMME MATTERS REQUIRING DECISIONS BY THE EXECUTIVE COUNCIL

4.1   OCEAN AND CLIMATE (JSC; OOPC; FCC; IPCC-RELATED MATTERS)
4.2   OCEAN SCIENCE IN RELATION TO LIVING RESOURCES (OSLR), IPHAB, GLOBEC, LME, CONVENTION ON BIOLOGICAL DIVERSITY
4.3   INTERNATIONAL OCEANOGRAPHIC DATA AND INFORMATION EXCHANGE (IODE)
4.4   INTERNATIONAL TSUNAMI WARNING SYSTEM IN THE PACIFIC (ITSU) AND IDNDR-RELATED MATTERS
4.5   GLOBAL OCEAN OBSERVING SYSTEM DEVELOPMENT AND RELATED MATTERS
4.6   TEMA AND CAPACITY BUILDING

ANNEX II

RESOLUTIONS

No.	Agenda Item	Title
1	4.3	International Oceanographic Data and Information Exchange (IODE)
2	4.4	International tsunami Warning System in the Pacific (ITSU) and IDNDR-related Matters
3	4.5	Seventh Session of the Joint IOC-WMO Committee for the Integrated Global Ocean Services System (IGOSS)
4	7.1	IOC Sub-Commission for the Caribbean and Adjacent Regions
5	7.2	Third Session of the IOC Sub-Commission for the Western Pacific (WESTPAC)
6	7.3	Southern Ocean Forum and Regional Committee for the Southern Ocean
7	7.4	Black Sea Regional Committee (IOC-BSRC)

Resolution EC-XXIX.1

INTERNATIONAL OCEANOGRAPHIC DATA AND INFORMATION EXCHANGE (IODE)

The Executive Council,

Recognizing the high level of interest in marine data and information management due to increasing public and government awareness of sea-level rise and global warming issues and as a tool for decision making, as well as the valuable contributions made by many Member States to the implementation of the programme and especially its IODE/TEMA component,

Noting with satisfaction the significant advances made by IODE in increasing the size of, and access to, the global databases and improving the flow of data through such activities as GODAR, GTSPP and OceanPC,

Being concerned with the lack of sufficient secretariat resources allocated to IODE activities, while acknowledging the efforts of the IOC Executive Secretary in creating a professional post in the Secretariat for the IODE programme,

Acknowledging the recommendations of the IODE Think Tank meeting to improve the skill base of IODE centres and to increase the linkages with other marine related programmes, and the efforts made by IODE and IGOSS in responding to the GOOS objectives in data management by the preparation of the joint IGOSS/IODE Data and Information Management Strategy Paper,

Accepts the Summary Report of IODE-XV and **approves** the Recommendations contained therein, particularly to:

(i)   continue the support provided by IODE to the GOOS and GCOS data and information management activities through mechanisms such as the Joint IGOSS/IODE Data and Information Management Strategy Paper and the Joint GCOS/GOOS/GTOS Data and Information Panel,

(ii)   establish the IODE Strategic Sub-Committee to promote IODE and encourage co-operation and collaboration with other marine related programmes both within and outside the UN system, with the Terms of Reference shown in Annex 1 to the Resolution,

(iii)   continue and expand a comprehensive TEMA programme to improve the skill base of IODE centres through the IODE regional co-ordinators, through training courses and fellowships and by developing appropriate electronic training tools,

(iv)   further develop OceanPC and seek extrabudgetary funding for a re-engineering of the system,

(v)   increase the use of technology such as Internet, World Wide Web (WWW) and CD-ROM as methods of data and information exchange and dissemination,

(vi)   support and continue the development of the IOC WWW Home Page as well as its related services and products,

(vii)   continue support for the GODAR project;

Urges Member States to increase their involvement with IODE through facilitating data and information exchanges, improving national data and information management infrastructures and by providing extrabudgetary funding and secondment of experts to the IOC Secretariat to further improve the IODE system;

Instructs the Executive Secretary IOC to assist in seeking extrabudgetary funding for the further development of the IODE programme.

Annex 1 to Resolution EC-XXIX.1

Terms of Reference for IODE Strategic Sub-Committee

(i)   Create additional collaborative and co-operative linkages with other Global and Regional Programmes in the field of marine data and information management and exchange;

(ii)   Undertake these tasks through expert consultations with appropriate data managers and other senior managers from programmes and funding agencies;

(iii)   Work at a senior level to maintain the linkages as they are developed and assist the IODE Committee with planning and implementation of the joint projects that may arise between IODE and other programmes.

Annex 2 to Resolution EC-XXIX.1

IODE Work Plan and Provisional Budgetary Implications

Note: *   Figures are given as (extra-budgetary)/(UNESCO regular funds) all in thousand US dollars;
         *   An average of 2-2.5 thousand dollars per person is assumed for travel and per diem for meetings;
         *   Secretariat support other than travel is not included.

Activity	1996	1997
Fifteenth Session of IOC Committee on IODE, GEMIM Meeting (Athens, Jan.'96)	> 150/30	
GTSPP (Apr.'96, Washington; 1998, place to be identified)	10/15	
GODAR-V, for Central & South America (Colombia, Sept.'96)	35/20	
GODAR-VI for Western Africa (Lagos, Nigeria, Feb.'97)		40/10
GODAR Global Conference (Washington DC, 2nd half '97)		100/30
OceanPC Meeting of Experts		10/10
IODE Officers Meetings		15
Seminar of IODE Regional Co-ordinators (co-joint with IODE Officers Meeting)		10
GETADE Meetings (1997, co-joint with Workshop on New Technology; 1999, co-joint with IODE Officers Meeting)		5/10
Strategy Sub-Committee Meeting (up to 8 participants, 2nd half '96)	10/15	
Data Managers Consultation on Co-operation & Sharing Responsibilities		20/10
Workshop on Biological & Chemical Data Management (Hamburg, May '96, up to 50 participants)	60/10	
Workshop on New Technology for Ocean Data Management, Ireland, Mar.'97		40/25
Development & Maintenance of the IOC WWW Home Page (equipment, software)		10
Production, Distribution & Updating of IOC CD-ROM		10
IOC ASFA input	2	2
Support to IAMSLIC Conference participants	6	10
Support to EURASLIC Conference participants	15/10	
MEDI Pilot Project Technical Workshop		30/10
NOPs & MEDI WWW Server & System Development	6	
Marine-related Document Delivery over Internet - Pilot Project	10/5	10/5
Participation of IODE Officers, Experts & Staff in Data Management-related Meetings: of other International Organizations (Bremerhaven Conference on Southern Oceans); IGBP & WCRP; GOOS & GCOS; Remote-sensed Data (CEOS & IGOSS/IODE/CMM)	10 3	10 10 5 3

Activity	1996	1997
TEMA		
Training Courses		
WESTPAC (Japanese NODC)	15/	15/
ROPME/PERSGA & Caspian Sea area (Iranian NODC)		20/10
Black & Caspian Sea Member States (WDC-B, MGG, On Marine Geological & Geophysical Data)		20/20
RECOSCIX-CEA		20/20
IOCINCWIO (MIM/ASFA)		
Eastern Africa (on OceanPC)	20/10	
Western Africa (Mauritania, on OceanPC)		
Central & South America (Argentinean NODC, for spanish & portuguese-speaking countries)		
On Development of National WWW Servers		20/10
IOCINCWIO/IOCINDIO (RNODC-INDO, Goa)	20/5	
Western & Eastern Europe (LOICZ/ICES, Copenhagen)		
Eastern Mediterranean & North African Countries (Hellenic NODC)	40/10	
Missions (Feasibility Study & Assistance)		
Western Africa		10/5
Cuba (Sept, co-joint with GODAR-V)	1/1	
Ecuador (WDC-A, Oceanography offer)	3/	
Colombia (Sept, co-joint with GODAR-V)	1/2	
ROPME/PERSGA (Nov/Dec)	3/1.5	
Study Grants & Fellowships		
Not more than 2 per year		15
Regions		
RECOSCIX-CEA Development (staff travel & contract)		
RECOSCIX-CAR Feasibility Study & Implementation	13	20
Black Sea Pilot Project Data Meeting		
ROPME/PERSGA Data Workshops		5/
MEDATLAS Implementation		5/5
ODINA Project		10/5
		10
	15/10	20/10
Publications		
Global Directory of Scientists & Marine Institutions		
IGOSS/IODE Brochure	1/2	
Manuals & Guides N° 5 (consultant contract)	5/5	
Revised version of IOC-CEC QC Manual		
	3	
		5/2.5
Awareness		
IODE participation in the Year of the Oceans, 1998 (development of demonstration material, travel)		
Development & Publication of IODE Posters & Logo		5
		5
IODE Programme Implementation		
Communication costs, Office supplies, Word processing equipment, etc.	10	10
Total	>400/204.5	>400/357.5

Resolution EC-XXIX.2

INTERNATIONAL TSUNAMI WARNING SYSTEM IN THE PACIFIC (ITSU) AND IDNDR-RELATED MATTERS

The Executive Council,

Noting the Summary Report and the Recommendations of the Fifteenth Session of the International Co-ordination Group for the Tsunami Warning System in the Pacific (ICG/ITSU), Papeete, Tahiti, French Polynesia, 24-28 July 1995,

Recognizing the progress achieved by the Group in the implementation of the IOC Tsunami programme,

Concurring with the view of the ICG/ITSU of the need to facilitate the ITIC activities through increased financial support and nominating candidates for the position of the ITIC Associate Director,

Acknowledging the importance of the IOC Tsunami Programme in saving lives and diminishing the socio-economic impact of natural disasters and the contribution made by the programme in meeting IDNDR objectives,

Being aware that the establishment of Tsunami Warning Systems for the Caribbean and Adjacent Regions (IOCARIBE) and the Mediterranean Sea is now being considered,

Accepts the Summary Report of ITSU-XV and **approves** the Recommendations of the ICG/ITSU Fifteenth Session;

Invites Member States to support the programme through contributions to the IOC Trust Fund and in-kind, through national and regional efforts, to make national authorities aware of the programme and of the potential benefits of tsunami disaster reduction and preparedness by making commitments and allocating resources;

Urges all Member States to share the burden of operational costs of the Tsunami Warning System and of the resources required for the implementation of the programme;

Expresses concern that extending the programme to other geographical regions may hamper the effectiveness of the Tsunami Warning System in the Pacific, unless additional funding is provided;

Urges the Member States of IOCARIBE and the Mediterranean Sea region to spare no efforts in ensuring that additional funds are made available for the establishment of tsunami warning systems in these regions and **instructs** the Executive Secretary IOC to assist in this effort.

Financial implications:
Required funds based on the ITSU programme of work for 1997: US$ 100,000; IOC Budget for 1997: US$ 50,000.

Resolution EC-XXIX.3

SEVENTH SESSION OF THE JOINT IOC-WMO COMMITTEE FOR THE INTEGRATED GLOBAL OCEAN SERVICES SYSTEM (IGOSS)

The Executive Council,

Having considered the Summary Report of the seventh session of the Joint IOC-WMO Committee for IGOSS, together with the 5 Resolutions and the 7 Recommendations adopted at the session,

Noting Resolution 2 (EC-XLVIII) adopted by the WMO Executive Council on the same topic,

Takes note of the report and **endorses** the Resolutions,

Decides to take the following action on the Recommendations:

Recommendation 1 (JC-IGOSS-VII) - IGOSS Ship-of-Opportunity Programme Plan

(i)   **Approves** the Recommendation;

(ii)   **Invites** WCRP, GOOS and GCOS to co-sponsor the SOOP Management Committee (SMC) with the terms of reference and membership as given in the annex to the Recommendation;

(iii)   **Urges** Member States to support continued SOO XBT operations through the long-term maintenance of SOO lines;

(iv)   **Requests** I-GOOS to support the implementation of the Plan, in particular through identifying and generating resources at the national level for use by operational agencies;

Recommendation 2 (JC-IGOSS-VII) -·IGOSS GTS Data Flow Monitoring

(i)   **Approves** the Recommendation;

(ii)   **Urges** Member States to designate focal points for the exchange of oceanographic bulletins over the GTS, within both GTS and oceanographic centres;

Recommendation 3 (JC-IGOSS-VII) - Global Temperature Salinity Programme

(i)   **Approves** the Recommendation;

(ii)   **Urges** Member States to expand their participation in the Programme, and especially Canada and the USA to maintain and support the Programme;

(iii)   **Agrees** to retain the former recognized acronym GTSPP and hence call the Programme Global Temperature Salinity Profile Programme;

Recommendation 4 (JC-IGOSS-VII) - IGOSS Products in support of GOOS and GCOS

(i)   **Approves** the Recommendation;

(ii)   **Invites** the Joint IOC-WMO-ICSU Scientific and Technical Committee for GOOS (J-GOOS) to call upon IGOSS experts to participate in the work of its panels, as appropriate;

Recommendation 5 (JC-IGOSS-VII) - Draft IGOSS-IODE Data Management Strategy

Acknowledges with satisfaction that the Recommendation has already been implemented.

Recommendation 6 (JC-IGOSS-VII) - IGOSS Plan and Implementation Programme 1996-2003

(i)   **Approves** the Recommendation;

(ii)   **Urges** Member States to participate actively in IGOSS through the implementation of the various components of the System as detailed in the Plan;

Recommendation 7 (JC-IGOSS-VII) - Review of Previous Resolutions of the IOC and WMO governing bodies relevant to the field of activity of the Joint IOC-WMO Committee for IGOSS

Approves the Recommendation.

Annex to Resolution EC-XXIX.3

Estimate of Financial and Staff Requirements
for the Bienniums 1996-1997 and 1998-1999 (in US$)

Activities	1996-1997		1998-1999		Total
IGOSS Bureau - 2nd session (end 97)	participants travel: staff travel:	12 500 2 500 ———— 15 000	-		15 000
Group of Experts on Communications and Products - 1st session (mid 98)	-		participants travel: staff travel:	12 500 2 500 ———— 15 000	15 000
SOOP Management Committee (SMC) - 2 sessions (96 & 97)	participants travel: staff travel:	2x8 500 2x2 500 ———— 22 000	-		22 000
SOOP Implementation Panel (SOOPIP) - 2 sessions (97 & 99)	participants travel: staff travel:	12 500 2 500 ———— 15 000	participants travel: staff travel:	12 500 2 500 ———— 15 000	30 000
SOOPIP *ad hoc* task team - 2 sessions (96 & 98)	participants travel: staff travel:	12 500 2 500 ———— 15 000	participants travel: staff travel:	12 500 2 500 ———— 15 000	30 000
Joint CMM-IGOSS-IODE Sub-Group on Ocean Satellites and Remote Sensing (OSRS) - 2 sessions (97 & 98)	participants travel: staff travel:	7 500 2 500 ———— 10 000	participants travel: staff travel:	7 500 2 500 ———— 10 000	20 000
IGOSS-VIII (1999)	-		participants travel: 2 staff travel:	10 000 5 000 ———— 15 000	15 000
Expert/Staff participation in various meetings (4 per year)	travel:	8x2000 ———— 16 000	travel:	8x2000 ———— 16 000	32 000
Training courses on use of remote sensing (97 & 99)	30 000		30 000		60 000
Communications	6 000		6 000		12 000
TOTAL (not including staff)	**129 000**		**122 000**		**251 000**

Activities	1996-1997	1998-1999	Total
STAFF REQUIREMENTS (IOC)			
IGOSS Operations Co-ordinator (full time) (seconded)	-	-	-
Assistant Secretary IOC (½ time) (seconded)	-	-	-
Consultant (¼ time) (fund in trust)	55 000	58 000	113 000
TOTAL (staff)	**55 000**	**58 000**	**113 000**

Resolution EC-XXIX.4

IOC SUB-COMMISSION FOR THE CARIBBEAN AND ADJACENT REGIONS

The Executive Council,

Noting the Report on IOCARIBE Evaluation (Document IOC/INF-1043), the Report of the Fifth Session of IOCARIBE (Barbados, December 1995) and the IOCARIBE Medium-Term Strategy 1996-2000 (Document IOC/INF-1027),

Expressing its appreciation to the Government of Barbados for hosting the Fifth Session of the Sub-Commission,

Also expressing its appreciation to the Government of Colombia for hosting the Secretariat of IOCARIBE in Cartagena and for its continuous interest and support provided to this UNESCO field office,

Noting with satisfaction the unanimous endorsement of IOCARIBE Member States of the continuation and reinforcement of the Sub-Commission,

Accepts the Report on IOCARIBE Evaluation, which is considered a valuable instrument to determine the future course of the Sub-Commission;

Also accepts the Report of the Fifth Session of the IOC Sub-Commission for the Caribbean and Adjacent Regions, **approves** the Recommendations **and notes** the IOCARIBE Action Plan 1996-1998, as shown in Annex II and Annex V of the Report of the Fifth Session of IOCARIBE, respectively;

Instructs the Executive Secretary IOC to take all possible measures to obtain financial support for the implementation of the IOCARIBE Action Plan;

Endorses the IOCARIBE Medium-Term Strategy 1996-2000;

Takes note of the offers made by several delegations for seconding experts, who would be based in their respective home countries, **and instructs** the Executive Secretary IOC to set up proper mechanisms to implement this offer, establishing clear terms of reference;

Recognizes that the IOCARIBE Symposium and the IOCARIBE Award are important contributions from the Sub-Commission to the 1998 International Year of the Ocean; **thanks** Cuba for its offer to host the IOCARIBE Symposium in La Havana, in early 1998, **and instructs** the Executive Secretary IOC to establish the necessary co-ordinating mechanisms to implement both activities;

Notes with concern the difficulties reported by the Executive Secretary IOC for implementing previous Resolutions of the IOC Assembly regarding provision of UNESCO/IOC staff in the regional Secretariat, **and instructs** him to continue searching for ways and means to provide staffing for the IOCARIBE Secretariat;

Urges Member States to support the Sub-Commission for IOCARIBE and make contributions to the IOC Trust Fund for implementing IOCARIBE programmes and activities, including the operation of the regional Secretariat in Cartagena; **and instructs** the Executive Secretary IOC to take appropriate measures to ensure its implementation with respect to the present biennium.

Financial implications: US$ 145,000 - Action Plan 96/97, of which for IOC US$ 40,000
US$ 40,000 - Operational Costs (1997)
US$ 60,000 - Secretary IOCARIBE (1997)
Total **$245,000**

Resolution EC-XXIX.5

THIRD SESSION OF THE IOC-SUB-COMMISSION FOR THE WESTERN PACIFIC (WESTPAC)

The Executive Council,

Noting the Summary Report of the Third Session of the IOC Sub-Commission for the Western Pacific together with six Recommendations adopted by the Session,

Expressing its appreciation to the Government of Japan for hosting the Third Session of the Sub-Commission, 26 February-1 March 1996,

Noting with appreciation the offer of the Republic of Korea for hosting the Fourth Session of the Sub-Commission in Seoul, March 1999,

Decides to take the following actions on the Recommendations:

Recommendation SC-WESTPAC-III.1 - International IOC/WESTPAC Scientific Symposium

(i) **Approves** the Recommendation, including the establishment of a Scientific Organizing Committee charged to organize the Symposium in Okinawa, Japan, 2-7 February 1998;

(ii) **Instructs** the Executive Secretary IOC to provide, within available financial resources, support for the Symposium and to take appropriate actions to invite other regional and international organizations to support and co-sponsor the Symposium.

Recommendation SC-WESTPAC-III.2 - Work Programme and Budget Estimate of the Sub-Commission for 1996-1998

(i) **Approves** the Recommendation;

(ii) **Instructs** the Executive Secretary IOC to provide support from the IOC Regular Budget and Trust Fund for the implementation of the 1996-1997 regional activities, as well as the operation of the IOC Regional Secretariat for WESTPAC, taking into account the overall requirements of the IOC programmes;

(iii) **Urges** Member States of the IOC and of the Sub-Commission in particular, to provide further financial support through the IOC Trust Fund dedicated to the Sub-Commission's programme implementation.

Recommendation SC-WESTPAC-III.3 - Asian-Australian Monsoon Oceanography

(i) **Approves** the Recommendation;

(ii) **Instructs** the Executive Secretary IOC to find all possible ways to ensure the co-ordination of this activity with other relevant programmes sponsored by the IOC and/or other national, regional and international organizations;

(iii)   **Calls** upon the Member States to provide further support in terms of financial and human resources to implement the project activity.

Recommendation SC-WESTPAC-III.4 - Near-GOOS Co-ordinating Committee

(i)   **Approves** the Recommendation;

(ii)   **Agrees** to initiate the Near-GOOS operational phase as soon as possible, accompanied by relevant training activities;

(iii)   **Instructs** the Executive Secretary IOC to provide necessary resources to ensure the effective implementation of the Near-GOOS project;

(iv)   **Urges** all participating countries to make further efforts in supporting the implementation of the system, including provision of oceanographic data and facilities necessary for the on-line data exchange required by the Near-GOOS operation.

Recommendation SC-WESTPAC-III.5 - International Coral Reef Initiative

(i)   **Approves** the Recommendation;

(ii)   **Instructs** the Executive Secretary IOC to use all possible means to encourage the widest participation of Member States in the implementation of the Global Coral Reef Monitoring Network at the regional level;

(iii)   **Urges** Member States to mobilize financial and human resources towards the implementation of the project.

Recommendation SC-WESTPAC-III.6 - Dates and Place of the Next Session

(i)   **Approves** the Recommendation;

(ii)   **Instructs** the Executive Secretary IOC to take appropriate actions, to confirm the dates and place of the next session, in consultation with the Officers of the Sub-Commission and the governments concerned, and to ensure the widest possible participation in the Fourth Session of the WESTPAC Sub-Commission by the Member States.

Financial implications: US$ 503,700 - Action Plan (96-98; US$ 30,000 - Operational costs (1997); US$ 202,000 - two staff in WESTPAC (1997).

Resolution EC-XXIX.6

SOUTHERN OCEAN FORUM AND REGIONAL COMMITTEE FOR THE SOUTHERN OCEAN

The Executive Council,

Having considered the Executive Summary of the First Southern Ocean Forum and the Sixth Session of the IOC Regional Committee for the Southern Ocean (Document IOC/SOC-VI/3S), held in Bremerhaven, Germany, 9-13 September 1996,

Noting with satisfaction that the Forum has reviewed the present knowledge, gaps and needs for future ocean research and related services in the Southern Ocean, as well as the international framework for co-operation,

Having reviewed the recommendations of the Sixth Session of the Regional Committee (Document IOC/SOC-VI/3S) prepared on the basis of the Forum's conclusions and proposals, covering the following broad themes: International cooperation in the Southern Ocean; Climate Change; Southern Ocean Ecosystems and their living resources; Pollution and monitoring; GOOS and data management,

Noting also that many important events have taken place since the establishment of the IOC Regional Committee for the Southern Ocean in 1967, in particular, UNCED and its Agenda 21, the entering into force of UNCLOS, UN Framework Convention on Climate Change (FCCC), UN Convention on Biological Diversity (CBD), the initiatives of the Antarctic Treaty Consultative Meeting (ATCM), the Protocol on Environmental Protection to the Antarctic Treaty, the development of global research and observational programmes such as WCRP, IGBP, GOOS and GCOS as joint efforts of intergovernmental and non-governmental international organizations,

Emphasizing that the Southern Ocean is unique in its physical and biological characteristics; that its study is of great importance for the understanding of the world's climate and climate change, as well as for the global cycling of carbon and other elements; and that it is a potential source of marine living resources,

Recognizing that the study of the Southern Ocean and its resources, as well as the development of observing systems, require close co-operation with other international governmental and non-governmental organizations, particularly WMO, UNEP, FAO, IHO, CCAMLR, IWC, COMNAP, ATCM, ICSU/SCAR/SCOR,

Expressing its strong intention to continue close collaboration with WMO, UNEP and ICSU in the planning and implementation of the Southern Ocean components of WCRP, particularly CLIVAR, IGBP and its projects JGOFS and GLOBEC, GOOS and GCOS,

Approves the recommendations of the Sixth Session of the IOC Regional Committee for the Southern Ocean (Document IOCSOC-VI/3S);

Decides to revise the terms of reference of the IOC Regional Committee for the Southern Ocean as shown in the Annex to this Resolution;

Invites SCAR, SCOR, CCAMLR, COMNAP and IWC to consider adequate ways and means to strengthen co-operation with the IOC Regional Committee for the Southern Ocean, particularly within the framework of GOOS, as well as the exchange of environmental data and information on Southern Ocean ecology and marine living resources;

Invites the JSC for WCRP, SC for IGBP, I-GOOS, DBCP, GE/GLOSS to bear in mind the recommendations of the Regional Committee with a view to establishing close interaction with its activities;

Urges Member States of IOC to participate in the activities of the Regional Committee and designate official national contacts for SOC;

Instructs the Executive Secretary to establish and maintain the information network on the Southern Ocean national and international activities through World Wide Web and to arrange for publication of the proceedings of the First Southern Ocean Forum.

Annex to Resolution EC-XXIX.6

Terms of Reference of the IOC Regional Committee for the Southern Ocean (IOCSOC)

The IOC Regional Committee for the Southern Ocean (IOCSOC) shall:

(i)   promote plans for a comprehensive study of the Southern Ocean, within the context of global scientific issues and programmes;

(ii)   promote the development and coordination of joint ocean research and systematic ocean observations in the Southern Ocean, the latter in particular within the framework of WCRP and IGBP, GOOS and the GCOS;

(iii)   promote co-operation, training, education and mutual assistance among Member States and relevant international organizations in the study of the role of the Southern Ocean in global environmental and climate change; and in the investigation of marine pollution, living marine resources and ocean ecosystem dynamics; particularly within the frameworks of WCRP, IGBP, GIPME, OSLR and TEMA;

(iv)   closely co-operate and encourage exchange of relevant information with relevant international governmental and non-governmental organizations (e.g. ATCM, CCAMLR, WMO, FAO, UNEP, IWC, ICSU, SCAR, SCOR);

(v)   encourage timely exchange and evaluation of various types of oceanographic data and information in this region among Member States and relevant international organizations;

(vi)   in performing its activities, the Committee will take into account the need to not affect the respective sovereignties and jurisdictions of the coastal states of the region, nor to affect the rights and obligations emanating from the Antarctic Treaty and related instruments.

Estimate of financial requirements (in US$) for 1996-1997 only:

Activity	1996	1997
Participation of the Chairman in the Antarctic Treaty Consultative Meeting, May, New-Zealand	--	3,500
Preparation, scientific editing and publication of proceedings of the Forum	--	4,000
Total:		7,500

Resolution EC-XXIX.7

BLACK SEA REGIONAL COMMITTEE (IOC-BSRC)

The Executive Council,

Noting the Summary Report of the First Session of the IOC Black Sea Regional Committee (Document IOC/BS-RC-I/3) held in Varna, Bulgaria, 9-13 September 1996,

Noting with satisfaction that the IOC Black Sea Regional Committee has reviewed the present knowledge, gaps and needs for future Black Sea research and related services in this region, as well as the international framework for co-operation with GEF, WMO, IAEA, UNEP, EU, NATO and other international governmental and non-governmental organizations,

Emphasizing that the Black Sea is unique in its physical and biochemical characteristics, and that its state plays an important role in the socio-economic aspects of the region,

Accepts the Summary Report, **approves** the Recommendations of the First Session of the IOC Black Sea Regional Committee and **notes** the workplan for 1996-1997 (Annex II of Document IOC/BS-RC-I/3);

Invites GEF, WMO, IAEA, UNEP, EU and NATO to consider ways and means to strengthen co-operation with the IOC Black Sea Regional Committee (BSRC), particularly within the framework of GOOS, JGOFS, GIPME, including the exchange of environmental data and information on Black Sea ecology and marine living resources;

Urges Member States of IOC to participate in the activities of the Regional Committee and designate official national contacts for the BSRC;

Requests the Executive Secretary IOC, *inter alia* in his capacity as Chairman of the Black Sea Regional Committee, to investigate the possibilities of financial and technical support for this programme from UNESCO and other international organizations, as well as interested institutes of countries not only from the Black Sea region.

Financial implications: US$ 357,500 ; for the IOC: US$ 60,000.

ANNEX III

ADDRESSES

A. Opening Address by Mr. Geoffrey L. Holland,
Chairman, Intergovernmental Oceanographic Commission (IOC)

Mr. Executive Secretary,
Vice-Chairman,
Members of Delegations,
Representatives of governmental organizations and of non-governmental
 bodies and organizations,
Ladies and Gentlemen,

It is a pleasure to welcome you to the Twenty-ninth Session of the Executive Council of the Intergovernmental Oceanographic Commission.

This is the first governing body meeting over which I have had the honour to preside. I feel particularly privileged, because I regard this Session as a most important one. We are in a time of opportunity, time when the decisions that we make and the actions that we take can and will influence global ocean programmes well into the next century.

It is easy to appreciate the relevance of this particular period. This decade has already seen many important events that have generated global issues and actions of direct concern to the oceans.

Over the last ten years we have seen the launching of many intergovernmental and international research programmes of global significance, most with direct or indirect ocean interests, the World Ocean Circulation Experiment (WOCE), the Joint Global Ocean Flux Study (JGOFS) and others, such as CLIVAR, GEWEX, GLOBEC, ACSYS and LOICZ.

Four years ago, the widely acclaimed UN Conference on Environment and Development made its recommendations regarding the future of the planet and its resources, resulting in many global programmes, activities and agreements involving the oceans and the work of our Commission. Notable among these are the Framework Convention on Climate Change, the Biodiversity Convention and our own Global Ocean Observing System which the IOC Assembly established in 1993.

Less than two years ago, the long-awaited UN Convention on the Law of the Sea came into force. The IOC has specific responsibilities within that convention, the role of which we will be addressing later in our agenda.

Only a year ago, an intergovernmental agreement was reached in Washington on the protection of the marine environment from land-based activities - an agreement with obvious implications for the Commission.

In May of this year, with the IOC assistance, the UN Commission on Sustainable Development reviewed the follow-up to the ocean activities in Chapter 17 of the UNCED Agenda 21, and in just over a year from now, the 1998 UN Year of the Ocean will commence with all its potential for focusing attention on ocean issues and emphasizing the need for collective national action.

This Session of the Executive Council will provide a springboard for the IOC programmes and initiatives leading up to, and beyond 1998. On the one hand, we are faced with an unparalleled opportunity for progress; on the other hand, if we fail to deliver, the future of the Commission as a global intergovernmental organization for the oceans will be jeopardized.

At this Session, as usual, you will hear from the Executive Secretary how the IOC programmes have fared over the past intersessional period, of the successes and of the weaknesses of our activities. We will be dealing with the development of the Commission within UNESCO, the programmes of that development and the need to evaluate our role and the need to strengthen our influence in Global Ocean Affairs. The DOSS-II *ad hoc* Study Group will be reporting on the results of its deliberations in the past intersessional period. We will need to supply guidance to the Executive Secretary on many matters relating to the capability of the Secretariat to manage our programmes over the next few critical years.

In May of this year, a meeting took place to further review the role of the Commission in the UN Convention on the Law of the Sea. You will be receiving the report of that meeting and be able to advise on future actions to complete these deliberations. In this respect, although the present emphasis is on the response to the existing articles, an equally important, but yet to be debated issue, is the future role of the Commission in revisions to the UNCLOS. Although in itself a landmark of international law, the UNCLOS is already dated and must surely be revised in the next ten years. Accurate data and dependable scientific advice will be needed to identify issues and to guide the subsequent debate and implementation. It is my personal opinion that the Commission must assume some responsibility in this regard.

This Session will need to consider actions and give guidance on many aspects' of ocean observation and science. The Global Ocean Observing System is a necessary part of our future, but progress to-date has been disappointing. During the intersessional period, there have been several meetings related to GOOS and guidance as to the direction of this programme and how to obtain further commitments by Member States will be required. Related service programmes of the Commission such as IGOSS, IODE and ITSU, must also be considered in the future development of our ocean service related programmes.

Ocean measurements must be guided by science and the promotion and co-ordination of research programmes must remain an essential element of our activities. The Commission is a full partner in the continuing quest to reduce the scientific uncertainty of climate prediction, in the provision of seasonal forecasts of ocean and atmospheric environments, in the understandings of ocean ecology and productivity, in the health of the ocean and in the exploration of its living and non-living resources. Some of these issues are well in hand, others need to be examined and implemented.

Data and scientific advice relating to ocean issues are two important contributions that the IOC can make to the solution of national, regional and global problems. The Commission should also consider its role as a contributor to intergovernmental ocean management and policy development.

As a global organization, the Commission needs the full involvement of all of its Member States. This Session will hear the Summary Report from the First Meeting of the TEMA Group of Experts, and must advise on actions to be taken to improve our Training, Education and Assistance programme.

The IOC Statutes proclaim that the Commission will carry out ocean programmes through the collective efforts of its Member States. Unfortunately, we often make decisions and take actions at our governing body meetings that we then leave in the hands of the Secretariat to accomplish. If the Commission is to fulfil its role and function, we as Member States must take charge of the intersessional programme. The Secretariat has neither the capacity nor the responsibility to carry out programmes. The role of the Secretariat is to facilitate and co-ordinate the programmes and efforts of the Member States, to provide information, organize necessary meetings and to generally monitor the work of the Commission. It is up to ourselves, as Member States, to implement the actual programmes and to supply the political will to make things happen.

I hope that during this meeting, we will not only take the necessary steps to generate action but to make commitments to follow-up these actions through our national efforts.

B. Opening Address by Mr. Federico Mayor,
Director-General of the United Nations Educational, Scientific and Cultural Organization (UNESCO)

Mr Chairperson,
Distinguished Delegates and Observers,
Ladies and Gentlemen,

I am very pleased to welcome you all to the Twenty-ninth Session of the IOC Executive Council, which is of course the first meeting of the new Council. The issues on your agenda are of importance for IOC, for UNESCO and for the world at large and I wish you a successful and constructive meeting.

In my address to the IOC Assembly in June 1995, I referred to the status and development of the Commission within UNESCO, in particular the implications for the IOC of the relevant proposals in the draft Medium-Term Strategy. I am pleased that these proposals to the 28th General Conference were in principle endorsed. The IOC was given an incompressible budget with respect to both programme and staffing components. The Executive Board had debated these matters in detail at its 147th session before the General Conference, as well as the experimental elements of administrative and operational flexibility which I gave to the IOC by delegating certain of my responsibilities to the Executive Secretary IOC. All these measures were taken in response to the general endorsement given by the General Conference at its 27th session to the proposals made by the IOC Assembly at its Seventeenth Session in 1993.

Since the General Conference in 1987 when the present Statutes of the IOC were adopted, there has been continuous and carefully monitored progress toward the functional autonomy of the IOC within UNESCO. Dialogue with the Executive Board on this question has benefitted from close reporting of developments concerning IOC.

At its 149th Session the Executive Board requested me "to submit to it for decision at its next session a detailed report, specifying the scope of the measures aimed at conferring operational flexibility on the Intergovernmental Oceanographic Commission (IOC) at the administrative and financial level, and reviewing the work of the *ad hoc* Group on the Development, Operations, Structure and Statutes (DOSS II) of IOC." This has been done in document 150EX/9. I would like to emphasize that I have specifically referred in this report to the wishes and proposals expressed by the IOC Assembly and Executive Council. Allow me to re-emphasize in this context your responsibility to ensure that proper briefing and information is provided at the national level so that the views and positions adopted in the IOC bodies are properly reflected in the debates and decisions of the Executive Board. It is your responsibility to inform your relevant national bodies about the importance of the IOC and your wishes concerning its development within UNESCO.

At its 147th session, the Executive Board had recommended in 147 EX/Decision 5.1 that: "a report be presented to the Executive Board at its 150th session on the possibility of establishing a financial allocation for the functioning of IOC, to which the Member States of IOC, non-members of UNESCO, will be invited, through an appropriate mechanism, to make a regular contribution". The response to this recommendation is also to be found in document 150 EX/9. I should like to underline the special importance of this matter, which I know the Executive Secretary is presenting to you in one of your agenda items.

I am very pleased that the Executive Secretary now has the rank of Assistant Director-General. I am also very pleased to confirm that three senior professional posts are under recruitment for the IOC, including that of Deputy Secretary. You should be aware that IOC is privileged in this respect within UNESCO, as we are generally not able to recruit staff given our present resource situation. As regards further staff evolution, I consider that the proper way forward for UNESCO at the present juncture is further decentralization to Field Offices. The possibility exists of a UNESCO Office being established for the IOC in Lisbon. I consider this an attractive option, and I understand that the Executive Secretary is waiting for a firm offer from Portugal.

Do not hesitate to request new modalities of action, new procedures, etc. We must adapt, we must anticipate... we must respond to the pace of life... to the pace of the oceans. It is not an excuse to say that institutional obstacles prevented us succeeding. I am ready to dare.

With respect to the future evolution of IOC, I would encourage you to reflect on the importance of the United Nations 1998 International Year of the Ocean and related initiatives. One such initiative is the Independent World Commission on Oceans started in 1995, to which I attach great significance. I would like the IOC to co-operate with that Commission to the extent possible. With respect to the 1998 Year of the Ocean, it is important to me that you define the overall aim of the undertaking and that you spell out the means to achieve them.

I agree that the overall aim of our joint efforts should be to focus attention on the importance of the oceans and the marine environment as a resource for sustainable development in its own right. To achieve this goal, it is necessary for IOC to ensure that its Member States give to ocean issues the level of priority they deserve. This is most important in view of the finite resource the oceans represent and increasing pollution threats, population pressures and overfishing. We now understand that without healthy oceans the life-support systems of the Earth would be seriously endangered. The goal of the IOC must be to underscore this point strongly. To this end, the IOC should project itself as a body which can deliver both the scientific rationale and the elements of a global management system based on the sustainable use of oceans. Co-operation with the Independent World Commission on Oceans will be important in this connection.

I also propose that a major objective of IOC in 1998 should be to obtain a commitment from governments to further strengthen the IOC within UNESCO. This means: (i) increasing the operational budget from contributions and extrabudgetary resources; (ii) expanding the staff through secondment from governments and organizations to boost intellectual and working capacity; (iii) ensuring the availability of international leadership for the development and expansion of GOOS. In order to achieve all this, it is first necessary to demonstrate the importance of the oceans for life and sustainable development, and the consequent need for a mechanism such as the IOC. Thus the programme should include actions which sensitize governments, the public and society at large to the significance of oceans for our common future.

In your discussions on these matters, I hope you will bear the following aspect in mind. I consider that science and systematic observations can provide solutions to many of our problems, but that we should offer not only diagnoses but also prognoses and remedies. It is therefore important that the IOC should provide users and decision-makers with a clear assessment of the problems and summaries of the results of its efforts. I suspect that the IOC - like UNESCO as a whole - can improve substantially in this regard. It is also of utmost importance that GOOS receive all possible support and that IOC maintain its leadership in this programme. The follow-up to UNCED and response to UNCLOS is of great relevance for IOC and must be continued and strengthened. These are important matters for you to evaluate in order to ensure a more effective IOC for the 21st Century.

I wish you every success in your work and I take this opportunity to underline my strong commitment to the Oceans and my support to the IOC of UNESCO.

C. Statement by Dr. Gunnar Kullenberg, Executive Secretary IOC, on his Intersessional Report

Mr. Chairman,
Distinguished Delegates and Observers,
Colleagues,
Ladies and Gentlemen,

It is an honor for me to briefly present again the intersessional report on activates since the Assembly, June 1995. My presentation is essentially based on the Annual Report 1995 which you should have received. I will only highlight certain matters which I consider the Council needs to address, and inform you about some programmes which do not appear on this EC agenda. I address both items 3.1 and 3.2. Refer to Annual Report 95, Annotated Agenda and Annexes.

The structure of the Annual Report follows the suggestions and instructions brought out by the Assembly and EC in 1993 and 1994. First the implementation of the Resolutions is reviewed. I wish to draw attention to Resolution XVIII-7 on Coastal Regions and Small Islands. The instructions have been implemented. After the 28th Session of the General Conference, the Director-General issued instructions on the establishment of the CSI unit, the joint management committee for the Project, and the role of the Executive Secretary IOC as Vice-Chairman of that committee. The co-operation between the intergovernmental programmes, including the social programme on Management of Social Transformations (MOST) follows the Joint Statement of the Chairs of these programmes and the IOC. The implementation of the Joint Statement has a high priority in UNESCO. The expert meeting on the Coastal Zones and Small Islands project is now scheduled for 25-28 November 1996 here at UNESCO. The Chairman IOC will attend ex-officio, and the Fourth Vice Chairman, Dr Okemwa, has also been invited. Mr Chairman, discussion about the project and related matters can also be made under EC Agenda item 8, point (II).

I would like to bring to your attention the developments regarding Resolutions XVIII-10, 11 and 12, in particular as regards the staffing situation within IOC Secretariat. The post of Director of the GOOS Support Office is expected to be filled by the end of this year. A short list of the preferred candidates has been presented to the Director-General of UNESCO, following consultations with WMO, UNEP and ICSU, co-sponsors of GOOS. The Director-General will make the final selection and appointment, (possibly after consultation with the UNESCO Executive Board). Two other senior posts are in the process of being filled. The P-5 in charge of GIPME is expected to be recruited by the end of the year, and the P-4 stationed at the WESTPAC Secretariat in Bangkok fairly early in 1997. I wish to point out that the so-called lapse factor maintaining vacant posts vacant for a period of time in order to save money, is also being applied to the IOC despite our so-called functional autonomy and incompressible budget! Although we are allowed to use the money from vacant posts, this situations has caused considerable problems in relation to the recruitment of the post of documentalist, chief clerk. In the case of one secretary, the delay is until end March 1997, despite the fact that this secretary has been duly selected, nominated, appointed, and is working in the IOC Secretariat. With respect to the Coral Reef Co-ordinator (Resolution XVIII-12), it must be noted that we do not have funds beyond 12-18 months. I hope other Member States will contribute dedicated funds in addition to the USA. I would also like to inform you about the support of the UK-ODA through the secondment of an expert to the IOC to be out stationed in the Indian Ocean Region to prepare a consolidated project for that region. This is a very positive development.

The section on Resolutions is followed by a brief General Overview in which the Executive Secretary brings to the attention of Member States certain important points. This policy-oriented statement responds to wishes expressed at the Assembly in 1993 and EC 27 in 1994.

First, I wish of course to refer to the very considerable positive developments regarding the IOC within UNESCO, on the basis of decisions of the Executive Board and the 28th General Conference. The Financial Regulations for the Special Account were adopted. Following your instructions, draft financial rules are presented to you in Annex 2 to the Annotated Agenda for preliminary consideration and advice. The General Conference approved an incompressible budget for the IOC, including a total staff allocation of 22 UNESCO staff. We have 7 filled UNESCO professional posts and 2 vacant, and 13 General Service. In addition, 1 P-4 for WESTPAC, Bangkok and 1 P-4 and 1 GS from WMO, IMO and FAO. This should be compared with the statement in 1993 by the DDG in his address to the Assembly. It was stated that there were 39 posts in all under supervision of the Secretary IOC. So, we have been cut in half! Mind you, I have many dedicated staff who work hard for the IOC and I wish to express my appreciation and thanks to all of them.

An overview of reasonable staff requirements was presented to DOSS-II at its first meeting. We need to at least double professional posts to cover the programme demands. The project on coastal zones and small islands reduced the IOC-MRI office to only IOC, in that the MRI part was transferred to the CSI Unit, including the financial resources. This was, in all, 4 professional posts. At the same time, the IOC Secretariat has been requested to take over fully or partly some of the former MRI programmes, in particular, the floating university and part of the remote sensing modules, both as regards finances and services of these actions. At the same time we have lost the publication unit which we shared: this is now listed as CSI.

The CSI project itself and the Joint Statement of the Chairs also put additional demands on the staff. Several joint activities involving IOC and IHP, MAB, IGCP are underway. Of course, these and other programmes also contribute to ocean activities. We have additionally made a drive for intersectoral co-operation and we are leading a task team for UNESCO preparations for 1998. I wish to emphasize that 1998 preparations will demand special attention from now on and that I will have to dedicate one professional for that purpose alone. The question is who? We need a co-ordinator for that purpose, and we can only obtain one by secondment. Who is willing and able to provide this quickly?

However, it is not only this positive result. It is also the implications as regards the changing role of the IOC and the IOC evolving role as an on-going process, highlighted in Lisbon in 1994. In UNESCO, the IOC is not viewed as having a larger role in relation to interpretation or research results than before, as regards the implications for policy and sustainable management, as regards preparing synthesis and assessments and options for solutions and decisions. Science can produce and suggest solutions to problems of society, and the IOC has now a confirmed role to play in this process. The IOC must now follow-up these implications of the positive development in UNESCO - and take on our role in sustainable development, ocean management and coastal area development, as real follow-up to UNCED, as well as to support Member States' efforts in UNCLOS, in global and regional change. We have been given the task of protecting/safeguarding humanity with respect to physical changes resulting from changes of the oceans. This is the most important implication for IOC and we must live up to it - we must now take this on.

The IOC can no longer be a specialized club of government marine scientists and the various research projects - we are now viewed as much more. This follows not only from the decision of the Executive Board and General Conference, but is fully in line with the Assembly's adoption of the IOC Medium-Term Strategy last year, and of GOOS, etc. This is also why the Agenda item 9 on assessment is on the Agenda; as well as UNCED follow-up.

The IOC Secretariat is hard pressed to deliver. Following your concurrence, the Director of the GOOS Support Office post is the former Deputy Secretary. The Assembly in its Resolution XVIII-11 instructed me to arrange so - and this was the only way of doing it at the level we have agreed. This means that the Executive Secretary will have continuous work with all details in the Office. It will have to fall on the professional staff to ensure delivery of programme actions. There are many new developments which IOC should follow closely. The Independent World Commission on Oceans is one; preparations of assessments and synthesis of results for presentation to users, governments, Member States are becoming increasingly important, and IOC needs to produce these materials; information and public awareness material likewise. This is required not only for 1998 but also for the CSD 1997 session, the special session of the UNGA with the review of UNGA of follow-up to UNCED, etc.

I am very well aware that we are not achieving what we want to achieve in this regard. Unfortunately, I have not been able to dedicate sufficient resources for this very important part. Neither have I been able to obtain support for additional dedicated staff for OSLR and OSNLR and Ocean Mapping. This cannot be achieved without more help from the Member States. I would like in this context to refer to evaluation - this is being much discussed - I would welcome evaluation - please refer to Statutes of IOC.

The credibility of the IOC is strongly dependent upon our ability to deliver results and to meet our commitments as regards joint programmes, e.g., GOOS, GCOS, GIPME, where we have signed agreements. I have to admit some difficulties in this context. We have difficulties in providing the financial support required for our co-sponsorship of the WCRP, GCOS and even GIPME. We can anticipate further similar problems in relation to UNCLOS and possibly ICAM. Furthermore, the 1998 programme will require large commitments which must be met by the IOC. Several of these points should be discussed under other Agenda items of this EC.

With respect to programme implementation which is presented in Section B. of the Report, I wish to emphasize: the climate programme, in which IOC is playing an important role, including in relation to the UNFCCC. At COP II we delivered a CD ROM with all sea level data and presented it to the Secretariat for delivery to small island states.

OSLR: there is a strong need for a professional post in the Secretariat, especially for the successful HAB, but also to cover biodiversity, and regional OSLR projects. OSNLR and OSLR are important for our coastal zone activities; OSNLR is concentrating on these matters. Ocean Mapping also needs a post. The GIPME programme is going well, but we have problems with our co-operation with IAEA-MESL and UNEP with respect to resources. The IOC is not in a position to provide sufficient financial support to MESL under the present conditions. This was never intended , but is now increasingly demanded by our partners. My inclination is to provide financial support for specific joint actions only, and clarify that the IOC support to GIPME is the main base for GIPME.

However, we are presently endeavoring to match the contribution of UNEP so as to maintain the base for this very important and unique activity. Consultations with UNEP have agreed that we for the time being maintain the GIPME Panel and aim at convening a meeting in Nairobi at the General Conference in 1997.

The Ocean Services programmes require and deserve more attention. It is clear that there is a shift in interests and that IOC must ensure adequate delivery. The IODE is developing very well but GOOS could do better . Specific elements which are related to GOOS, like GLOSS, IGOSS, Ocean PC are developing very well. Many of the IOC programmes are contributing towards the development of GOOS. In several regions regional GOOS are emerging - e.g. NEAR-GOOS, Black Sea GOOS,

IOCARIBE-GOOS. These are all related to IOC efforts. However, GOOS needs much more attention from Governments, and they have to decide on using IOC as the intergovernmental mechanism for GOOS. Commitments and clear signals and some leaderships from the Member States are necessary now.

The TEMA activities cover all programmes of IOC, and at least 50% of our resources in different ways are allocated to, and used for, capacity building. Special attention is given to TEMA in a separate agenda item.

The regional activities and associated bodies are becoming increasingly important. We must maintain these, and at the same time obtain increasing support for them from the regions themselves. You must help in this process. Most of them are relevant for coastal zones and for follow-up to UNCED and UNCLOS. We have brought these regional mechanisms to the attention of national donor agencies, such as SIDA (SAREC), CIDA, DANIDA, Flanders, and have achieved some response and success. However the Governments must also come out and stand behind IOC.

The co-operation with other bodies and joint programming has obtained additional importance after UNCED. It is now mandatory - but is also putting an increasing pressure on us. It is most difficult for IOC to achieve proper acknowledgment; since we are a part of UNESCO we are not noted in our own right except in cases where we have penetrated sufficiently. I would have thought we had achieved this in UNEP, but it does not appear so. There are in increasing number of UNEP documents in which there is no reference to IOC even when we have joint programmes relevant to the subject, e.g., GIPME, GOOS, WCP. I have referred to the increasing interaction with UNESCO.

Follow-up to UNCED and UNCLOS is of course essential for IOC. However, it is not enough for the IOC Secretariat to try as well as it can. Member States must help at the national level. The CSD delegation must know about the existence of IOC - most of them do not. You must help there. Likewise as regards UNCLOS - you must inform your national delegations about IOC. We are well known in WMO, and now in COP of FCCC and biodiversity, thanks to dedicated efforts on the part of the IOC Secretariat. We do not have enough resources to achieve this for other important bodies only through the Secretariat. You need to work nationally to obtain a high-level champion for IOC! Or you have to decide that you do not want IOC - so serious people like myself can go somewhere else to work.

With respect to 1998, some ideas and plans are given in the report, and more in Annex 3 to the Annotated Agenda. I wish to call this to your particular attention, especially with reference to the Section headed "Overall Aim and the Means to Achieve It". You must provide your advice on these matters and give instructions. And you must get yourself engaged in this process for 1998. Additional information and ideas are given in the Appendix to Annex 3 - by the Chair IOC. However, now we need action - not only ideas.

A special section of the Annual Report is devoted to the Developments of IOC within UNESCO. This is given in order to provide a record of developments since about 1990. I think it is important that such a record exists, and this account was reviewed by the IOC Officers earlier this year.

You will recall that the Assembly instructed me to present a model of a programme and budget presentation for 1998-1999 for your comments and advice. This is being done in conjunction with the item on programme and budget, i.e. item 10 of the Agenda; in Annex 6, the model relates to the structure used for the IOC TF in the Special Account and to the structure of the IOC Secretariat.

You will recall that the Assembly endorsed a structure based on three major pillars: sciences, services, TEMA and regional activities (IOC-XVIII, para 74). This is essentially the model now being used, and gradually strengthened. Ultimately, the expected contributions to the IOC TF are related to the financial model.

Allow me also to draw to your special attention my own situation. I have informed the Director-General that I consider it best for the IOC that I retire end of 1997 or early 1998 and I prepared a post description earlier this year. The Chairman IOC has reviewed it, and I was hoping it would appear and that the post would be announced soon. The EC meeting during the next Assembly will have to express its views as regards the candidates to the Director-General in accordance with the Statutes, Article 9(2). This is why the agenda item on clarification or guidance for the EC procedure is on the Agenda.

Let me conclude with some personal remarks. The credibility of the IOC and ability to deliver is of paramount importance in relation to all our efforts and especially the follow-up to UNCED, development of GOOS, the related conventions as well as with respect to UNCLOS. It is the actions which now count - not talk. It appears to me that one most important positive action which can be obtained is that Member States positively acknowledge and support the IOC as an instrument and existing body which should be used, which can deliver, and which is made to work and function.

It is time for Member States to make up their minds with the respect to the IOC. I have recently visited Member States which represent the majority of the population of the Earth - and their strong support of the IOC is at least very clearly communicated to me. However, I told them that they should also inform other important Member States about their views. The IOC is established within UNESCO and much support is provided from the mother organization. I hope that you will seriously consider what the IOC wants or should get out of 1998. I have indicated in Annex 3 of the Annotated Agenda what I consider we should aim for.

Thank you for your attention.

ANNEX IV

LIST OF WORKING DOCUMENTS [1]

IOC/EC-XXIX/1	Agenda
IOC/EC-XXIX/1 Add.prov.	Provisional Timetable
IOC/EC-XXIX/2	Annotated Provisional Agenda (Expanded)
IOC/EC-XXIX/2 Annex 1	Mechanisms to Facilitate the Provision of Dependable Resources to the IOC Special Account also from Member States of IOC not Member States of UNESCO
IOC/EC-XXIX/2 Annex 2	Draft Financial Rules for the Special Account of the IOC
IOC/EC-XXIX/2 Annex 2 Add.	Financial Regulations applicable to the Special Account of the IOC
IOC/EC-XXIX/2 Annex 3	Programme proposal for the IOC Contribution to 1998 International Year of the Ocean
IOC/EC-XXIX/2 Annex 3 Add.	1998 International Year of the Ocean: A Prospectus for Development
IOC/EC-XXIX/2 Annex 4	Progress report of the Intersessional Working Group on IOC's Possible Role in Relation to UNCLOS
IOC/EC-XXIX/2 Annex 5	Proposed Clarifications for Consultations with the Director-General on the Appointment of the Secretary IOC
IOC/EC-XXIX/2 Annex 6	Budgetary Status Report
IOC/EC-XXIX/2 Appendix 1	Draft Terms of Reference for the Working Group on the Transfer of Organisms by Ballast Water
IOC/EC-XXIX/3	Summary Report
IOC/EC-XXIX/4	List of Documents

---

[1]   This list is for reference only. No stocks of these documents are maintained, except for the Summary Report.

[...]

ANNEX VI

STATEMENT BY THE BRAZILIAN DELEGATION ON ITEM 5.4

My Delegation wishes to recognize, for the records, the excellent work done by the intersessional working group on IOC's role in relation to the UNCLOS, whose report the Brazilian Delegation wishes to see approved by this Executive Council.

I believe, Mr Chairman, that this document is highly satisfactory to all Member States that do not wish to see a duplication of efforts nor a conflict of tasks of international organizations who deal with matters related to the sea.

My Delegation proposes that the document IOC/EC-XXIX/2 Annex 4 is approved and recommends that it is also approved by the Nineteenth Session of the IOC Assembly to be held in 1997.

The Brazilian Delegation also wishes to make a statement on another topic, mentioned by the Technical Secretary, related to the edition of a technical and scientific publication on the definition of the continental shelf of coastal states.

I could not abstain from stating that my Delegation was surprised as it took notice of document IOC/INF-1040 yesterday, containing the report of the meeting of the IOC-IHO Editorial Board about the preparation of the said publication.

I noticed that the report of the First Session of the Editorial Board states that it will focus on technical and scientific aspects of the definition of the continental shelf of coastal states. But, Mr Chairman, even though it is so intended, the matter involves political and legal implications, which means a due evaluation must be taken by the governments of the Member States of IOC and UNCLOS.

In the light of these comments, I must say that my Delegation has many objections to formulate. If not objections, at least some serious doubts which undermine my country's support to the mentioned initiative of IOC-IHO.

First of all, my Delegation was puzzled by the fact that there were neither official consultations with the Brazilian Government, nor with other Governments about the elaboration of a manual on the definition of the continental shelf. We were also surprised that many steps were taken regarding the subject without any information being circulated among Member States of IOC.

I should also add that my Government was not officially notified about the existence of a formal request of DOALOS to elaborate the manual. It seems most probable that some parallel understandings took place, either between experts or IOC and DOALOS Secretariats.

Finally, Mr Chairman, considering the implications I have just referred to, bearing in mind the inevitable legal and political aspects that concern the matter and considering the co-operation between DOALOS, IOC and IHO, my Delegation believes that this initiative of publishing the manual should be submitted beforehand, to the forthcoming IOC Assembly.

I also wish to state that my Government recognizes the efforts carried out by the IOC Secretariat. In this case, however, there are reservations that lead me to express my Delegation's disapproval of the manner in which the subject was carried on.

I have to state, as well, that it seems impossible that Brazil participate in the efforts to elaborate the manual or that it endorse the initiative if the manner in which the subject is carried out persists.

Thank you, Mr Chairman.

ANNEX VII

LIST OF ACRONYMS

ABLOS	Advisory Board on the Law of the Sea
ACC	Administrative Committee on Co-ordination (UN)
ACSYS	Arctic Climate System Study
ALACE	Autonomous Lagrangian Circulation Explorer
AODC	Australian Oceanographic Data Centre
APEC	Asia-Pacific Economic Co-operation Council
ASEAN	Association of South-East Asian Nations
ASFA	Aquatic Sciences and Fisheries Abstracts
ASOS	Automated Seismological Observation System
ASOS	Programa Subregional del Atlántico Sud-Occidental Superior/Sub-regional Programme for the Upper Southwest Atlantic Ocean (Argentina, Brazil, Uruguay)
ATCM	Antarctic Treaty Consultative Meeting
AVHRR	Advanced Very High Resolution Radiometer
BRGM	Bureau de recherches géologiques et minières (France)
BSRC	Black Sea Regional Committee
CBD	Convention on Biological Diversity
CCAMLR	Commission for the Conservation of Antarctic Marine Living Resources
CCOP	Committee for Co-ordination of Joint Prospecting for Mineral Resources in Asian Offshore Areas
CEA	Commissariat à l'énergie atomique (France)
CEC	Commission of the European Communities
CEOS	Committee on Earth Observation Satellites

CERESCOR	Centre de recherche scientifique de Conakry (Guinea)
CICESE	Centro de Investigación Científica y de Educación Superior de Ensenanda (México)
CIDA	Canadian International Development Agency
CIRM	Comisión Interministerial para los Recursos del Mar (Brazil)
CLCS	Commission on the Limits of the Continental Shelf
CLIVAR	Climate Variability and Predictability
CMM	Commission for Marine Meteorology
COMNAP	Council of Managers of National Antarctic Programmes
COMSBLACK	Co-operative Marine Science Programme for the Black Sea
CPR	Continuous Plankton Recorder
CSD	Commission on Sustainable Development
CSI	Project on Environment and Development in Coastal and Small Island Regions (UNESCO)
CSIRO	Commonwealth Scientific and Industrial Research Organization
CTD	Conductivity-Temperature-Depth Probe
DANIDA	Danish Agency for International Development
DBCP	Data Buoy Co-operation Panel
DOALOS	Division for Ocean Affairs and the Law of the Sea (UN)
DOSS	Ad hoc Study Group on IOC Development, Operations, Structure and Statutes
EC	European Community
EEZ	Exclusive Economic Zone
ESCAP	Economic and Social Commission for Asia and the Pacific
ETDB	Expert Tsunami Database for the Pacific
EU	European Union
EURASLIC	European Aquatic Sciences and Libraries and Information Centres
EuroGOOS	European Programme for the Global Ocean Observing System
FANSA	Floraciones Algales Nocivas en Sudamérica (Harmful Algal Blooms in South America)
FAO	Food and Agriculture Organization of the United Nations
FCCC	Framework Convention on Climate Change
FURES	Ad hoc Study Group on Measures to Ensure Adequate and Dependable Resources for the Commission's Programme of Work
GCOS	Global Climate Observing System
GEBCO	General Bathymetric Chart of the Oceans
GEF	Global Environment Facility
GEMIM	Group of Experts on Marine Information Management
GESAMP	Group of Experts on the Scientific Aspects of Marine Environmental Protection
GETADE	Group of Experts on Technical Aspects of Data Exchange
GEWEX	Global Energy and Water Cycle Experiment
GIPME	Global Investigation of Pollution in the Marine Environment

GLOBEC	Global Ocean Ecosystems Dynamics
GLOSS	Global Sea-Level Observing System
GODAR	Global Oceanographic Data Archaeology and Rescue Project
GOOS	Global Ocean Observing System
GPA	Global Programme Action
GTOS	Global Terrestrial Observing System
GTS	Global Telecommunication System
GTSPP	Global Temperature-Salinity Pilot Project
HAB	Harmful Algal Blooms
HOTO	Health of the Oceans (Module of GOOS)
IAEA	International Atomic Energy Agency
IAMSLIC	International Association of Aquatic and Marine Science Libraries and Information Centres
ICAM	Integrated Coastal Areas Management (IOG/GIPME)
ICES	International Council for the Exploration of the Sea
ICG	International Co-ordination Group
ICOD	International Centre for Ocean Development (Canada)
ICSPRO	Inter-secretariat Committee on Scientific Programmes Relating to Oceanography
ICSU	International Council of Scientific Unions
IDNDR	International Decade for Natural Disaster Reduction (1990-1999)
IFREMER	Institut français de recherche pour l'exploitation de la mer
IGBP	International Geosphere-Biosphere Programme (UNESCO)
IGCP	International Geological Correlation Progamme (UNESCO)
IGOSS	Integrated Global Ocean Services System
IHDP	International Human Dimensions Programme
IHO	International Hydrographic Organization
IHP	International Hydrological Programme (UNESCO)
IMO	International Maritime Organization
IMS	International Marine Science Newsletter
IOC	Intergovernmental Oceanographic Commission
IOCARIBE	IOC Sub-Commission for the Caribbean & Adjacent Regions
IOCEA	IOC Regional Committee for the Central Eastern Atlantic
IOCINCWIO	IOC Regional Committee for the Co-operative Investigation in the North and Central Western Indian Ocean
IOCINDIO	IOC Regional Committee for the Central Indian Ocean
IOCSOC	IOC Regional Committee for the Southern Ocean
IODE	International Oceanographic Data and Information Exchange
IPCC	Intergovernmental Panel on Climate Change
IPHAB	Intergovernmental Panel on Harmful Algal Blooms
ITIC	International Tsunami Information Centre

ITSU	International Co-ordination Group for the Tsunami Warning System in the Pacific
IUGG	International Union of Geodesy and Geophysics
IWC	International Whaling Commission
IWCO	Independent World Commission on Oceans
JGOFS	Joint Global Ocean Flux Study
JSC	Joint Steering Committee (for WCRP)
JSTC	Joint Scientific and Technical Committee (for GCOS)
KMFRI	Kenya Marine and Fisheries Research Institute
KORDI	Korean Ocean Research and Development Institute
LIPI	Indonesian Institute of Sciences
LME	Large Marine Ecosystems
LMR	Living Marine Resources
LOICZ	Land-Ocean Interaction in the Coastal Zone
MAB	Programme on Man and the Biosphere (UNESCO)
MARPOLMON	Marine Pollution Monitoring System
MAST	Specific Research and Technological Development Programme in the field of Marine and Science Technology
MEDAR	Mediterannean Data Archaeology
MEDATLAS	Mediterrranean Atlas
MEDI	Marine Environmental Data Information Referral System
MESL	Marine Environment Studies Laboratory
METU	Middle East Technical University (Turkey)
MFS	Minor Field Study
MGG	Marine Geology and Geophysics
MIM	Marine Information Management
MOU	Memorandum of Understanding
MRI	Meteorological Research Institute
NATO	North Atlantic Treaty Organization
NEAR-GOOS	North-East Asian Regional-Global Ocean Observing System
NGWLMS	Next Generation Water-Level Measurement System
NOAA	National Oceanic and Atmospheric Administration (USA)
NODC	National Oceanographic Data Centre
NOP	National Oceanographic Programme
OCEAN-PC	Ocean Personal Computer Project
ODAS	Ocean Data Acquisition Systems, Aids and Devices
ODINEA	Ocean Data and Information Network for Eastern Africa
OOPC	Ocean Observations Panel for Climate
OOSDP	Ocean Observing System Development Panel
OSLR	Ocean Sciences and Living Resources
OSNLR	Ocean Sciences in Relation to Non-Living Resources

OSRS	Ocean Satellites and Remote Sensing
PERSGA	Red Sea and Gulf of Aden Environment Programme
PICES	North Pacific Marine Science Organization
PIP	Plans and Implementation Programme
PMEL	Pacific Marine Environmental Laboratory
POEM	Physical Oceanography of the Eastern Mediterranean
QC	Quality Control (of Data)
RECOSCIX	Regional Co-operation in Scientific Information and Exchange
RNODC	Responsible National Oceanographic Data Centre
ROPME	Regional Organization for the Protection of the Marine Environment
SAHFOS	Sir Alister Hardy Foundation for Ocean Science (UK)
SAREC	Swedish Agency for Research Co-operation with Developing Countries
SBSTTA	Subsidiary Body on Scientific, Technical and Technological Advice
SCOPE	Scientific Committee on Problems of the Environment
SCOR	Scientific Committee on Oceanic Research
SEACAMP	South-East Asian Center for Atmospheric and Marine Prediction
SEFC	Southeast Fisheries Centre
SIDA	Swedish International Development Authority
SOA	State Oceanic Administration (China)
SOC	Specialized Oceanographic Centre
SOO	Ship-of-Opportunity
SOOP	Ship-of-Opportunity Programme
SOOPIP	Ship-of-Opportunity Implementation Panel
SOPAC	South Pacific Applied Geoscience Commission
SPACC	Small Pelagic Fish and Climate Change Programme
SSC	Scientific Steering Committee
STAP	Scientific and Technical Advisory Panel
START	Global Change System for Analysis, Research and Training
TAO	Tropical Atmosphere Ocean Array
TOGA	Tropical Ocean and Global Atmosphere
TIME	Tsunami Inundation Modelling Exchange Project
TREMORS	Tsunami Risk Evaluation through Seismic Movement from Real-time System
TEMA	Training, Education and Mutual Assistance in Marine Sciences
UATI	Union internationale des associations et organismes techniques
UNCED	United Nations Conference on Environment and Development
UNCLOS	United Nations Convention on the Law of the Sea
UNEP	United Nations Environment Programme
UNESCO	United Nations Educational, Scientific and Cultural Organization
UNFCCC	United Nations Framework Convention on Climate Change
UNGA	United Nations General Assembly

WCP	World Climate Programme
WCRP	World Climate Research Programme
WCS	World Conservation Strategy
WDC	World Data Centre
WESTPAC	IOC Sub-Commission for the Western Pacific
WIO	Western Indian Ocean
WIPO	World Intellectual Property Organization
WMO	World Meteorological Organization
WOCE	World Ocean Circulation Experiment
WWW	World Weather Watch
WWW	World Wide Web
XBT	Expendable Bathythermograph

2. SUMMARY REPORT OF THE FIRST SESSION OF THE OPEN-ENDED INTERSESSIONAL WORKING GROUP ON IOC'S POSSIBLE ROLE IN RELATION TO THE UNITED NATIONS CONVENTION ON THE LAW OF THE SEA (IOC-LOS), PARIS, 13-15 MAY 1996

Doc. no.: IOC/INF-1035

Date: 10 June 1996

TABLE OF CONTENTS

SUMMARY REPORT

ANNEXES

I   **AGENDA**

II   **LIST OF PARTICIPANTS**

1.   **OPENING**

The First Session of the Open-ended Intersessional Working Group on IOC's Possible Role in Relation to the United Nations Convention on the Law of the Sea (IOC-LOS) was opened in UNESCO, Paris, at 9:30 on 13 May 1996, by Dr. Gunnar Kullenberg, the Executive Secretary of IOC. He welcomed all the participants on behalf of the Organization and himself. He emphasized the impact of UNCLOS on the work of the international organizations and the importance to respond to the needs of the Convention. He recalled the decision of the Eighteenth Session of the IOC Assembly to establish an open-ended intersessional working group to study the explicit and implicit role of IOC in relation to the UN Convention on the Law of the Sea and hoped that the Working Group would come up with some specific recommendations which will be presented to the forthcoming sessions of the IOC Executive Council and Assembly.

Dr. Kullenberg then proposed Prof. A.H.A. Soons to be the Chair of the meeting following a consultation with the Chairman of IOC, Mr. Geoffrey Holland. The Working Group welcomed the proposal and confirmed Prof. Soons as the Chair.

2.   **ADMINISTRATIVE ARRANGEMENTS**

2.1   DESIGNATION OF THE RAPPORTEUR

Consultations suggested that the Group did not consider it necessary to identify and designate a Rapporteur.

2.2   ADOPTION OF AGENDA

Mr. Haiqing LI, the Technical Secretary for the meeting, introduced this Agenda Item, referring to document IOC/WG-LOS-I/1 prov. The Group adopted the proposed Agenda for the meeting without any change, which is attached as Annex I.

2.3   DOCUMENTATION

The Technical Secretary introduced this Agenda Item, referring particularly to documents IOC/WG-LOS-I/4 prov. and IOC/WG-LOS-I/5 prov. He informed the meeting that a new document IOC/WG-LOS-I/6 Add. 1 was added to the list of documents. He also thanked Mrs. de Marffy from the United Nations Division for Ocean Affairs and the Law of the Sea for her efforts to bring the finalized version of the table on the role of the competent international organizations under UNCLOS, as well as other useful background documents to the meeting. The List of Participants is attached as Annex II.

2.4   CONDUCT OF THE SESSION

The Chairman made a proposal on the conduct of the session. The basis for the discussion would be document IOC/WG-LOS-I/6: A Synthesis on IOC Possible Role and Responsibilities under UN Convention on the Law of the Sea. The Group agreed on this proposal as well as the time table for the session.

The Delegate of Turkey made a statement that the participation of Turkey in this meeting can in no way be interpreted as acceptance of the UNCLOS by the Turkish Government. The Delegates of Chile and Peru also provided statements on their Governments' positions with regard to IOC's role in relation to UNCLOS, which were distributed during the meeting.

3.   EXAMINATION OF UNCLOS PROVISIONS THAT MAY HAVE EXPLICIT RELEVANCE TO IOC

The result of the deliberations under Agenda Items 3 and 4 is reflected in Table 1: IOC's Role in Relation to UNCLOS, which forms an integral part of this Report.

The Group examined the document IOC/WG-LOS-I/6, and concurred with the IOC's role and responsibilities explicitly mentioned under UNCLOS, as presented in Part 1 of Table 1: Provisions Which Explicitly Mention IOC.

4.   EXAMINATION OF UNCLOS PROVISIONS THAT MAY HAVE IMPLICIT RELEVANCE TO IOC

The Group carefully examined the UNCLOS provisions that may have implicit relevance to IOC based on the document IOC/WG-LOS-I/6, and agreed on the IOC's role in this respect as a competent international organization in marine scientific research, as presented in Part 2 of Table 1: Provisions Which Provide a Basis for An IOC Role.

5.   RECOMMENDATIONS ON POSSIBLE IOC'S ROLE AND RESPONSIBILITIES IN RELATION TO UNCLOS

The Group examined the following important issues as a result of discussion under Agenda Items 3 and 4, with conclusions and recommendations.

a.   IOC present activities relevant to the Law of the Sea but not based on UNCLOS Provisions

The Working Group recommended that several programme activities of the IOC in relation to research, observation, and capacity building can inherently provide input to the efforts of Member States who are also States parties to UNCLOS to exercise their rights and fulfill their obligations under UNCLOS. These programmes are evolving as main elements of the IOC mandate and provide scientific inputs, information, data and capacity to Member States and other competent international organizations cooperating with IOC. Thus, in this respect the IOC can act as a body for consultation and provision of information also in context of UNCLOS if Member States so wish. Several of these activities are also part of joint global programmes like the WCRP, IGBP, (GLOBEC, LOICZ, JGOFS) GOOS and GCOS. The GIPME programme is also jointly sponsored by IOC, UNEP, IMO and partly IAEA. The OSLR programme deals with research on marine living resources, harmful algal blooms and supports the LMR module of GOOS. The OSNLR deals with non-living resources. The IODE is an operational programme addressing major needs with respect to data exchange, retrieval and management.

The capacity building actions are part of all the IOC programmes and also constitute a separate programme in order to ensure that national and regional needs can be properly addressed.

The regional perspective is covered through the IOC regional subsidiary bodies, two Sub-commissions (IOCARIBE and WESTPAC), with regional secretariat support, and 5 regional sub-committees. In addition cooperative programme arrangements have been established in regions not covered by these subsidiary bodies, e.g. the south-western part of the Atlantic and the south-east Pacific.

Through the IOC participation in UN system-wide mechanisms like GESAMP, ACC Sub-Committee on Oceans and Coastal Areas and ICSPRO, coordination is achieved and duplications avoided. As a specific example of cooperation in this context, the IOC could assist the Scientific Group of the London Convention 1972 in the development and updating of scientific guidelines on dumping, particularly in the light of the probable adoption of a 1996 Protocol to the Convention. This work could be done within GESAMP. Another example is the cooperation as has been requested by IMO and UNEP in studying the dynamics and impact of the foreign species to ecosystem and biodiversity and provide scientific information for management.

The IOC Medium Term Strategy (Annex VI of Report of Eighteenth Session of the IOC Assembly, June 1995) endeavours to relate the IOC programmes to major issues. The relevance of the IOC programmes for several international agreements, e.g. resulting from UNCED as well as UNCLOS is also referred to.

The Working Group in reviewing the working document (IOC/WG-LOS-I/6) noted several articles of UNCLOS in the context of which the on-going IOC programmes can provide support to efforts of Member States and other organizations. However, the Working Group also recognized that UNCLOS may imply the need to strengthen some of the programmes of IOC.

The Working Group also noted that it would not be appropriate to present this situation as if these programmes are driven by UNCLOS provisions. On the other hand the Working Group stressed that the considerable experiences and results obtained through the IOC programmes should be properly used in support of UNCLOS implementations and related actions of Member States. The Working Group suggested that the Executive Council give consideration to how IOC can best achieve this goal. This should help ensure that the relevant IOC programmes and actions are not overlooked in relation to the UNCLOS-related work. Any duplication of work by international organisations should of course be prevented. This can to a degree be ensured through the existing cooperation and coordination mechanisms referred to above, but can also be pursued through direct inter-secretariat contacts and consultations. The Working Group suggested that the cooperation between UN-DOALOS and IOC should be reported specifically to the Assembly under the relevant agenda item.

The Working Group also emphasized that Training, Education and Mutual Assistance (TEMA) as an inherent part of capacity development is a priority of the IOC. It can as such contribute considerably towards helping States parties to the Convention to fulfil their obligations and exercise their rights in the context of the Convention. One aim of this action is to help ensure that scientific information, understanding, observations and data can be shared by all for the benefit of all States and peaceful uses and sustainable development of the ocean. As a competent international organization the IOC should be conceived by Member States as a mechanism which can help produce the required information and capacity basis for overall implementation of UNCLOS. The Working Group recalled the UNESCO-IOC Comprehensive Plan for a Major Assistance Programme to Enhance the Marine Science Capabilities of Developing Countries prepared by the IOC. The Working Group suggested that the constituted Group of Experts on TEMA should also address issues of UNCLOS within the mandate of IOC.

The Working Group stressed the importance of GOOS for IOC as a whole, and suggested that the relevant UNCLOS aspects and issues should also be considered in the context of the GOOS development. Explicit reference was made to the GOOS Health of the Ocean module as an important future monitoring activity to evaluate biological effects of pollution, as a particular example.

Specific examples of on-going or planned activities include:

(i)   capacity development of coastal area studies, e.g. in Western Indian Ocean;

(ii)   development of regional GOOS-components in WESTPAC (NEAR-GOOS), and IOCARIBE;

(iii)   training courses and workshops on international oceanographic data retrieval, archiving, management and exchange;

(iv)   regional GOOS capacity building workshops;

(v)   studies of oceans and climate, and ocean role in CO_2 balance;

(vi)   establishment of observations and monitoring of oceans and coastal areas as part of GOOS, in GLOSS, DBCP, IGOSS.

b.   Issues of liability/responsibility of competent international organizations actually conducting MSR and settlement of disputes to which an international organization conducting MSR is a party

It was concluded by the Working Group that these are new issues derived from the entry into force of the UN Convention on the Law of the Sea, which raise complex legal questions. However, IOC, as a marine scientific body, is not the appropriate forum to address these issues and there is not an urgent need to address them at present. Nonetheless, IOC may wish to clarify these issues in the future, together with other international organizations, when the need arises.

c.   **Establishment of criteria and guidelines for ascertaining the nature and implications of MSR**

It was concluded by the Working Group that IOC, as a competent international organization in marine scientific research, has a role to play in assisting the Member States to establish general criteria and guidelines as provided for in Article 251 in ascertaining the nature and implications of marine scientific research, including the marine scientific research in the exclusive economic zone and on the continental shelf.

For this purpose it is essential to obtain information on State practice regarding these criteria; this issue is addressed in the next item.

d.   **IOC acting as a depository of national legislation/rules/ administrative practices and making such information available to Member States**

Though it was recognized that IOC has a role to play in this respect, it was noted that UN-DOALOS has already been collecting and publishing national legislation with regard to marine scientific research, and to some extent, is also doing analysis of State practice, in light of the mandate entrusted to it by the UN General Assembly, and IOC should avoid duplication of efforts.   However, IOC could, through the ICSPRO mechanism, help UN-DOALOS reach the marine scientific community for the collection of necessary information, and help the scientific community get access to the information published by the former.

The importance of this function was stressed in connection with the previous item.

e.   **IOC regional bodies to promote projects on national legislation/rule/administrative practices**

The Working Group took note of a Report on the Implementation of the Marine Scientific Research Regime in the South Pacific, prepared under the auspices of the South Pacific Forum Fisheries Agency and SOPAC (Report no. FFA Report 95/14) as a positive example as to how international organizations may help coastal States in formulating national legislation, rules and administrative practices. The Working Group took note of this Report and concluded that the IOC regional subsidiary bodies may make similar efforts if they so decide through the appropriate mechanism.

f.   **ODAS: a study on the actual need of drafting an international instrument**

The Working Group noted that the status of ODAS is an issue which has been addressed over a long time. The preparatory work for an international instrument was suspended during UNCLOS-III. Taking into consideration that the use of ODAS has substantially increased and is expected to continue to increase there may now be a need for a legal instrument. IOC has an important role to play in this connection which is not necessarily derived from UNCLOS. At present, the draft agreement on ODAS has been transmitted, through IOC, to ICSPRO. The Working Group concluded that this is a policy decision and it is up to IOC and IMO to decide whether this issue should be revisited taking into consideration the actual needs of the marine scientific community.

g.   **Article 247: lay down procedures to be followed within international organizations to invoke Article 247 in future cases**

The Working Group recognized that the general procedure for obtaining consent for conducting marine scientific projects undertaken by or under the auspices of international organizations for States parties to UNCLOS is already in place in Article 247 of the Convention. However, if IOC and its regional subsidiary bodies are to properly put it into practice, IOC should define specific rules and procedures to be followed.

Given the sensitiveness of the issue, it was felt by the Working Group that this issue should be handled with special care with due regard to the rights of the coastal States, and in this context, attention was drawn to the implications of the approval of IOC with regard to a project for an IOC Member State who is not a party to UNCLOS.

6. FUTURE WORK OF THE WORKING GROUP

The Working Group felt that, by the adoption of this Summary Report of the meeting, it had completed its work under its terms of reference given by the Eighteenth Session of the IOC Assembly.

7. ADOPTION OF THE SUMMARY REPORT

The Working Group adopted the Summary Report of the meeting, which will be distributed by the Executive Secretary IOC to the Member States at least three months prior to the Twenty-ninth Session of the IOC Executive Council.

8. CLOSURE

The First Session of the Open-ended Intersessional Working Group on IOC's Possible Role in Relation to UNCLOS was closed by the Chair at 13:30 hours on 15 May 1996.

TABLE 1

IOC'S ROLE IN RELATION TO UNCLOS

1. **PROVISIONS WHICH EXPLICITY MENTION IOC**

Article(s)	Subject	IOC Role/Responsibilities
3 (2) of Annex II	Commission on Limits of Continental Shelf (established under Article 76 (8) of UNCLOS	upon express request from CLCS IOC should assist the Commission through exchange of scientific and technical information. IOC may cooperate with IHO and other competent international organizations in this respect.
2 (2) of Annex VIII	Special Arbitral Tribunal (Article 287 1 (d) and Annex VIII of UNCLOS) Experts in compulsory procedures entailing binding decisions (Article 289 of UNCLOS)	draw up and maintain a list of experts in the field of marine scientific research who can serve as arbitrators. The list is circulated to the members of the UN by UN Secretariat.

2. PROVISIONS WHICH PROVIDE A BASIS FOR AN IOC ROLE

2.1 PROVISIONS ON MARINE SCIENTIFIC RESEARCH

IOC as a competent international organization in marine scientific research under UNCLOS.

Article(s)	Subject	IOC Role/Responsiblities
238	Right to conduct marine scientific research	IOC enjoys the general right to conduct marine scientific research, subject to the rights and duties of States as provided for in UNCLOS.
239	Promotion of marine scientific research	IOC has a general responsibility to promote and facilitate the development and conduct of marine scientific research.
242 (1)	Promotion of international cooperation	IOC should promote international cooperation in marine scientific research for peaceful purposes.
243	Creation of favourable condictions	IOC should, through conclusion of bilateral and multilateral agreements, cooperate with States and other competent international organizations to create favourable conditions for marine scientific research.

Article(s)	Subject	IOC Role/Responsibilities
244	Publication and dissemination of information and knowledge	IOC should actively promote the dissemination and flow of marine scientific information and knowledge.
247	MSR projects undertaken by or/ under the auspices of international organizations	IOC could help establish clearl procedures in order to avoid misunderstandings with due regard to the rights of coastal States. It would be advisable to specify expressly in the text of the decision by the organization as regards the undertaking of the project that it is approved under this article. (ref. to para 5 g of the Summary Report).
251	General criteria and guidelines	IOC could assist States in establishing general criteria and guidelines for ascertaining the nature and implications of MSR (ref.to para 5 c of the Summary Report).
262	Scientific research installations or equipment in the marine environment	IOC, in cooperation with IMO, could take actions related to the identification of markings and warning signals in the light of these provisions and the decisions of IMO (IMO resolution A.50 (III) and its Annex).

2.2   PROVISIONS DEVELOPMENT OF MARINE SCIENCE AND TECHNOLOGY

Article(s)	Subject	IOC Role/Responsibilities
266 and 268	Promotion of the development and transfer of marine technology	IOC has statutory responsibility to promote cooperation among Member States in the development and transfer of marine science and marine technology through further strengthening its TEMA and capacity building programme.
269 and 270	Measures to achieve the basic objectives and ways and means of international cooperation	IOC should support States, and respond to the request of States, in taking specific actions in developing a programme on promotion of marine technology within the fields of IOC competence. This may be achieved through expansion of the existing TEMA programme, technical assistance in particular, both at the global and regional levels, taking advantage of IOC's regional subsidiary bodies and other regional oceanographic cooperative arrangements.
271	Guidelines, criteria and standards	IOC at the request of Member States could strengthen its technical assistance through establishing generally accepted guidelines, criteria and standards for transfer of marine technology.
272 and 278	Coordination and cooperation among international programmes and organizations	IOC should cooperate and coordinate with other international organizations and programmes in promoting transfer of marine technology.
273	Cooperation with international organizations and Authority	IOC, at the request of Member States, shall encourage and facilitate the transfer of skills and marine technology with regard to activities in the Area.

Article(s)	Subject	IOC Role/Responsibilities
275	Establishment of national centres	IOC could assist the developing Member States in establishing and strengthening marine scientific and technological research centres.
276 and 277	Establishment of regional centres	IOC could strengthen its regional cooperation through its regional subsidiary bodies, through establishing regional marine scientific and technological research centres, and the establishment and strengthening of networks of national centres under IOC's various programmes as part of capacity building.

2.3 PROVISIONS ON MSR AND OCEAN SERVICES FOR THE MANAGEMENT AND RATIONAL USE OF MARINE LIVING AND NON-LIVING RESOURCES

Article(s)	Subject	IOC Role/Responsibilities
61 (2), last sentence	Conservation of living resources in EEZ	IOC could, if need be, at the request of coastal States, cooperate with other competent international organisations (e.g. through its OSLR programme), to help identify the best scientific evidence, for the conservation and management of marine living resources.
123 (d)	Cooperation of States bordering enclosed or semi-enclosed seas	When invited by the coastal States, IOC, through its regional subsidiary bodies, could coordinate with other regional organizations' efforts in management, conservation, exploration of the living resources of the sea.
143 (3) (b) and (c) and Section 1, paragraph 5 (h) of the Annex to Agreement Relating to the Implementation of Part XI of UNCLOS	MSR in the international seabed area	IOC could, at the request of the International Sea-Bed Authority, assist it in developing its marine scientific research and provide scientific advice to the Authority. IOC could also cooperate with the Authority in disseminating results of research and analysis.
163 (13) and 169 (4), of the Annex to the Agreement Relating to the Implementation of Part XI of UNCLOS	Consultation and cooperation with international and non-governmental organizations	IOC could, on request, consult with the Legal and Technical Commission (when performing the functions of the Economic Planning Commission) of the Authority in the fields where IOC has competence.

2.4   PROVISIONS ON MSR AND OCEAN SERVICES IN THE PROTECTION SAND PRESERVATION OF THE MARINE
       ENVIRONMENT

Article(s)	Subject	IOC Role/Responsibilities
200	Studies, research programmes and exchange of information and data	IOC, e.g. through GIPME mechanism, could strengthen its efforts in promoting studies, undertaking scientific research and encourage the exchange of scientific, technical information and data acquired both at the global and regional levels.
201	Scientific criteria for regulations	IOC could, e.g. through its GIPME programme, assist coastal States and other competent international organisations in establishing appropriate scientific criteria for the purpose of formulating rules, standards and recommended practices and procedures. (cf. also Art. 197, 207 (4), 208 (5), 210 (4), 211 (1) and 212 (3)).
202 and 203	Scientific and technical assistance to developing countries	IOC could, e.g. through its GIPME and TEMA programmes, continue to provide scientific and technical assistance to developing countries and strengthen capacity building in these countries. Measures should be taken to ensure preferential treatment to be given to the developing countries.
204 (1)	Monitoring of the risk or effects of pollution	IOC, through its GIPME/MARPOLMON programme, as well as its GOOS initiative, could continue its efforts in marine pollution monitoring and the establishment of pollution monitoring networks both on a global and regional levels, partly as inherent elements of GOOS.
205	Publication of reports	IOC should continue to publish and make available scientific and technical reports on the monitoring of risks or effects of pollution.

ANNEX I

AGENDA

1. **OPENING**

2. **ADMINSITRATIVE ARRANGEMENTS**

    2.1   DESIGNATION OF THE RAPPORTEUR

    2.2   ADOPTION OF AGENDA

    2.3   DOCUMENTATION

    2.4   CONDUCT OF THE SESSION

3. **EXAMINATION OF UNCLOS PROVISIONS THAT MAY HAVE EXPLICIT RELEVANCE TO IOC**

4. **EXAMINATION OF UNCLOS PROVISIONS THAT MAY HAVE IMPLICIT RELEVANCE TO IOC**

5. **RECOMMENDATIONS ON POSSIBLE IOC'S ROLE AND RESPONSIBILITIES IN RELATION TO UNCLOS**

6. **FUTURE WORK OF THE WORKING GROUP**

7. **ADOPTION OF THE SUMMARY REPORT**

8. **CLOSURE**

ANNEX II
LIST OF PARTICIPANTS

Mr. Tomur BAYER
Head of
Maritime Affairs Department
Ministry of Foreign Affairs
Disisceri Bakanligi (DHGY-II)
Balgat - Ankara
TURKEY

Tel: (90 312) 287 1876
Fax: (90 312) 285 3698

Dr. J.Peter A. BERNHARDT
Room 5801
Bureau of Oceans and International
Environmental and Scientific Affairs
Department of State
Washington, D.C. 20520
USA
Tel: (1 202) 647 9616, 9098
Fax: (1 202) 647 1106

Mrs. Annick DE MARFFY
Senior Law of the sea officer
DOALOS/OLA UN
United Nations
DCII 0434
New York
USA

Tel: (1 212) 963 3962
Fax: (1 212) 963 5847
Email: marffy@un.org

Mr. Luiz A. FIGUEIREDO MACHADO
Head of the Sea, Antarctic and Outer Space
Affairs Division
Ministry of External Relations
Esplanada Dos Ministerios, Bloco H
Anexo 1 Sala
BRAZIL

Tel: (5561) 211 6730
Fax: (5561) 224 1079

Sr. Felix GARCIA VARGAS
Asesor Juridico (Legal Adviser)
Sericio Hidrografico y Oceanografico de la
Armada de Chile
Errazuriz No. 232, Playa Ancha
Valparaiso
CHILE

Tel: 56-32-282697
Fax: 56-32-283537

Mr. Monsieur Bernard GERARD
Director at the French Geological
Survey - BRGM
Avenue de Concyr
La Source
BP 6009 ORLEANS Cedex 2
FRANCE

Tel: (33) (16) 3864 3621
Fax: (33) (16) 3864 3990
Email: b.gerard@brgm.fr

Prof. Maria Eduarda GONCALVES
iscte
Av. das Forcas Armadas
Edificio ISCTE
1600 Lisbon
PORTUGAL

Tel: 351-1-7935000   est.52102   or
            7903068
Fax: 351-1-7903008

Dr. Ariel Walter GONZALES
Legal Advisor Office, Ministry of Foreign Affairs
Reconquista 1088 - 12th floor
Buenos Aires
ARGENTINA

Tel: (00541) 315 4821
and fax as well
Email: awg@atina.mrec.ar

Mr. Hiroshi YOSHIMOTO
First Secretary
Permanent Delegation of
Japan to UNESCO
1, rue Miollis
75015, Paris
FRANCE

Tel: (33 1) 4568 3541
Fax: (33 1) 4734 4670

Mr. Elie JARMACHE
IFREMER
155, rue Jean-Jacques Rousseau -92138
ISSY-LES-MOULINEAUX
FRANCE

Tel: 46482284
Fax: 46482188

Prof. Anataly KOLODKIN
Professor, Deputy Director
President International Maritime Law Association
Staste Scientific Research Institute
of Marine Fleet of Russian Federation
3.B. Koptevsky pr.
Moscow 125319
RUSSIA

Tel: 7-095 151 7588
Fax: 7-095 152 0916
        7-095 152 3651
        7-502 224 1701
Email:

Mr. MAO Bin
Deputy Director-General
Department of International Cooperation
State Oceanic Administration
1, Fuxingmenwei Ave.
Beijing 100860
CHINA

Tel: (86-10) 6851 9791
Fax: (86-10) 6853 3515
Email: XUYUKUN@sun.ihep.ac.cn

Prof. Carlo MORELLI
CNR
University of Trieste - DINMA
ITALY

Tel: (40) 676 7158
Fax: (40) 676 3497

Ms. Aelin PEREZ
Primera Secretaria
Delegacion del Peru
ante la UNESCO
1, rue Miollis, 75015
FRANCE

Tel: (33 1) 4568 2931

Ms. Srinoi POVATONG
Deputy Permanent Delegate
of Thailand to UNESCO
Permanent Delegation of
Thailand to UNESCO
1, rue Miollis
75015 Paris
FRANCE

Tel: (33 1) 4568 2566/67
Fax: (33 1) 4449 0146

Dr. David PUGH
Marine and Atmospheric Sciences Directorate
Institute of Oceanographic Sciences
Deacon Laboratory, Brook Road
Wormley, Godalming
Surrey, GU8 5UB
UNITED KINGDOM

Tel: 44-1428-684141
Fax: 44-1428-683066
Email: D.PUGH (Omnet)

**Ms. Ravaomalala
RASOANAIVO-RANDRIAMOMONJY**
Adviser
Permanent Delegation of Madagascar
to UNESCO
4 Av Raphael
75016 Paris
FRANCE

Tel: (33 1) 4504 6216

Mr. Boris SMIRNOV
Deputy Secretary-General
Commission of the Russian Federation
for UNESCO - 9 Vozdvizhenka - Moscow
121019
RUSSIA

Tel: 7-095-290 0853
Fax: 7-095-202 1083

Prof. A.H.A. SOONS (Chairman)
Netherlands Institute for the Law of the Sea
Utrecht University
Janskerkhof 3
3512 BK Utrecht
THE NETHERLANDS

Tel: 31-30 253 7056
Fax: 31-30 253 7073
Email: A.soons@RGL.RUU.NL

Prof. Tullio TREVES
l'Universite de Milano
Ministry of Foreign Affairs
via Lusardi No.2
20122 Milano
ITALY

        Tel: (02) 5830 3398
        Fax: (02) 5830 6826

Ms Janice Romaguera TROTTE
Directoria de Hidrografia e Navegacao
Assesoria pars Asuntos Internacionais
Rua Barao de Jaceguai, s/no
CEP - 24.048-900 - Ponta de Armacao
Niterioi - Rio de Janeiro
BRASIL

        Tel: (005521) 620 0073 ext. 32
             (005521) 620 2626 ext. 192 or
             (005521) 717·7675
        Fax: (005521) 620 7921
             (005521) 719 4989

Sr. Javier VALLADARES
Capitan de Fragata
Jefe Departamento de Oceanografia
Servicio de Hidrografia Naval - Representante
Alterno argentino ante la COI
Montes de Oca 2124 Bs. As. -
Buenos Aires - ARGENTINA
        Tel: (54-1) 301 3091
        Fax: (54-1) 301 2918
        Email: SHN@OCEANAR.MIL.AR/
        POSTMASTER@SERHI.MIL.AR

SECRETARIAT

Dr. Gunnar KULLENBERG
Executive Secretary IOC
1, rue Miollis ·
75732 Paris cedex 15
FRANCE

        Tel: (33 1) 4568 3983
        Fax: (33 1) 4056 9316
        Email: g.kullenberg@unesco.org

Mr. Haiqing LI (Technical Secretary)
1, rue Miollis
75732 Paris cedex 15
FRANCE

        Tel: (33 1) 4568 3994
        Fax: (33 1) 4056 9316
        Email: h.li@unesco.org

IOFC (see Indian Ocean)

IOTC (see Indian Ocean)

Iran IMO-2 (para.23.18); UNESCO-1 (para.295)
        1993 Act on the Marine Areas UN-2 (IV.C), UN-19/27
        /UAE (Abu Musa) UN-2 (VIII), UN-11/12
        /USA UN-2 (VIII)

Iraq UN-16/18; IAEA-1, 10

Ireland IMO-5 (para.90), 10, 17

ISBA (International Sea-Bed Authority) (see deep sea-bed)

Islands (see also UN Global Programme of Action for Small Island States; individual islands) UN-2 (VIII)

Israel
        /Jordan UN-2 (VIII)
        /Lebanon UN-2 (VIII); IMO-2 (paras.23.16/23.20)

Italy UN-3 (para.33); IMO-2 (para.23.19); UNESCO-1 (para.73)

ITLOS (International Tribunal for the Law of the Sea) UN-2 (VI), UN-28, UN-35, UN-41, UN-43, UN-48/54
        Election of the President and the Vice-President UN-48, UN-52
        Election of the Registrar UN-50

IUCN (International Union for Conservation of Nature and Natural Resources) IMO-19/20

IWC (International Whaling Commission) UN-2 (VII.F), UN-59; FAO-2 (para.V.2.1)

J

Jamaica UN-2 (IV.C)

Japan (see also China) UNEP-1 (App.I); UNCTAD-3 (paras.2/5); IAEA-1; IMO-1 (paras.9.29, 9.33, 9.41,9.45), 5 (paras.60/61); UNESCO-1 (para.29)
        fisheries (see fisheries - drift nets/gill nets)
        /Republic of Korea (Takeshima) UN-2 (VIII)

Jordan (see Israel)

K

Kara Sea IAEA-1

Kazakhstan UN-14

Kenya UNESCO-1 (paras.30, 87)

Kerch Strait UN-2 (VIII)